Citizens for Public Justice
#337, 10765-98 St.
Edmonton, Alta T5H 2P2
429-3540
454-2691

Report of the Royal Commission on the Economic Union and Development Prospects for Canada

Report

Royal Commission on the Economic Union and Development Prospects for Canada

VOLUME TWO

Minister of Supply and Services Canada

COVER DESIGN: Will Rueter
INTERIOR DESIGN: Brant Cowie

Available in Canada through authorized bookstore agents and other bookstores or by mail from
Canadian Government Publishing Centre
Supply and Services Canada
Ottawa, Canada K1A 0S9

Also available in French

Printed in Canada

Catalogue No. Z1-1983/1-2E

ISBN 0-660-11852-1 (Vol. 2)

ISBN 0-660-11850-5 (Set)

Canada: $45.00
Other countries: $54.00
Price subject to change without notice.

CONTENTS

Detailed Contents lists appear at the beginning of each chapter.

Volume Two

VOLUME THREE

PART III

GROWTH AND EMPLOYMENT

PART III

Contents

PART III

Introduction

The broad issues of economic growth and employment are central to this Commission's mandate, and they were central concerns in the hearings we conducted across Canada. Key aspects of these issues, in particular trade, the development of our human resources, and the functioning of labour markets, are considered primarily in other parts of this Report. We are concerned in this part with the roles in economic growth of the capital stock, of technology, and of the organization of economic activity. We are also concerned with the role of policy and institutions in achieving high levels of employment and general economic stability.

Economic growth is fundamental to the maintenance of our standard of living. High employment is fundamental to the economic and social welfare of the great majority of families and individuals. Given that we Commissioners held our hearings at the outset of a rather shaky recovery from a very deep and traumatic recession, it is perhaps not surprising that many of the representations to this Commission expressed more worry about employment than they did about growth. One intervenor argued that:

> *If there were no improvement in GNP . . . it would still be immensely important to have full employment. I think I would go so far as to say that if the GNP fell and [we] had full employment, it would be well worth the price. [We] would have a better and different kind of society.*
>
> (John Weldon, Transcript, Montreal, May 30, 1984 [vol. 1], p. 44.)

A study[1] of public opinion surveys prepared for this Commission reveals that unemployment is a major concern to far more Canadians than the number actually unemployed at any point in time. But the current high levels of unemployment are at least partly a cyclical phenomenon, and our primary concern, under the terms of our mandate, is with the longer term. Thus we shall deal with the issue of economic growth – that is, the potential productivity of our economy – before we turn to the issue of stability and the full use of that potential. In the course of Part III of this Report, we shall also explicate our belief that there is no basic conflict between growth and high employment: that they are, in fact, complementary, rather than competing, goals.

By way of introduction to both of these broad areas, Chapter 7 reviews the economic experience of the last several decades in terms of growth, of structural adjustment in our economy, and of the major indicators of economic instability: unemployment and inflation. This chapter also discusses the growing role of government, since this growth has been one of the most important structural changes in the economy, and since the remainder of Part III will be concerned, to a substantial extent, with what government can do to promote growth and economic stability.

Chapter 8 looks first at the various factors that contribute to growth and at the question of whether growth and, in particular, growth that results from technological change is likely to be consistent with the achievement of high employment. We then consider in more detail the contributions to economic growth of capital formation, technology, and management. In the course of this discussion, we consider the desirability of relying upon more or different government action to promote capital formation and technological development.

Chapter 9 deals with industrial policy in a broad sense. We consider a wide range of factors in the organization of economic activity and ask whether there are changes that might improve Canada's economic performance. We survey Canadian views on the role of government in industrial policy, review the evolution of both federal and provincial activities to promote economic development, and present an analysis of other countries' experience with industrial policy. Finally, we suggest a framework for industrial policy in the future, a framework that emphasizes productivity and competitiveness.

Chapter 10 deals with short-term economic stability and high employment. After setting out a framework for the analysis of the macro-economic functioning of the economy, we look at the strengths and the limitations of monetary policy and fiscal policy as means of achieving stability and high employment. We then consider the contribution that adoption of an incomes policy and other changes in the wage-determination system might make to economic stability and to an improved employment performance.

Note

1. Richard Johnston, *Public Opinion and Public Policy in Canada*, vol. 35, prepared for the Royal Commission on the Economic Union and Development Prospects for Canada (Toronto: University of Toronto Press, 1985).

CHAPTER 7

Economic Performance and Prospects

CHAPTER 7

Economic Performance and Prospects

Main Structural Developments

Key Economic Indicators

Like the economies of most other developed countries, the Canadian economy, since the Second World War, has experienced both substantial growth in output and income and major structural change. In order to identify these major trends, it is useful to abstract from cyclical fluctuations. Since the war, there have been five major cycles. In order to avoid having reference years falling variously at the peak or bottom of these cycles, the average annual growth rates of selected demographic and economic indicators shown in Tables 7-1 and 7-2 are recorded between successive cyclical peak years. The post-1981 cyclical downturn is reviewed later. To provide a comparison with earlier trends, these tables also include average data for 1927–46. These averages, however, mask key features of the period, such as the high level of unemployment and the substantial decline in real output that occurred during the Great Depression.

As Table 7-1 shows, Canada's population increased at a relatively rapid rate over the first 20 years of the post-war period. Immigration contributed significantly to this growth, but natural increase was its predominant source. Immigration slowed after 1957, and the rate of natural increase dropped sharply as the birth rate fell after the early 1960s.

In retrospect, the period from the end of the Second World War to 1973 was something of a "golden age" of economic performance. Table 7-2 records that total output and output per person employed increased at rates higher than those that are generally thought to have prevailed before the Second World War, and at rates higher than those that have prevailed since 1973. This increase in output was reflected in a strong growth in the real income of Canadians as measured by real gross national expenditure (GNE) per capita.

TABLE 7-1 Canadian Demographic Trends

Population Growth	1927–46	1947–56	1957–66	1967–73	1974–81
	(average annual per cent rate of increase)				
Total	1.3	2.7[a]	2.2	1.4	1.2
Natural	1.2	1.9	1.8	1.0	0.8
Net immigration	0.1	0.6	0.4	0.4	0.4

Source: Statistics Canada, *Historical Statistical Compendium*, prepared for the Royal Commission on the Economic Union and Development Prospects for Canada (Ottawa: Statistics Canada, 1985), Table 1-6.

Note: Growth rates are average annual compound increases from the level in the year before the period specified to the level in the final year of the period specified.

a. The entry of Newfoundland into Confederation accounted for 0.3 percentage points of the average growth rate from 1947 to 1956.

TABLE 7-2 Key Canadian Economic Indicators

	1927–46	1947–56	1957–66	1967–73	1974–81
	(average annual per cent rate of increase)				
Employment[a]	1.4	1.8	2.5	3.0	2.9
Real output[b]	3.9	5.4	4.6	5.3	3.0
Real income[c] per capita	2.2	2.6	2.4	3.9	1.7
Productivity[d]	2.1	3.5	2.1	2.3	0.1
Inflation[e]	0.2	4.4	2.0	4.4	9.7
Unemployment rate[f]	8.1	3.2	5.5	5.2	7.3

Sources: Statistics Canada, *Historical Statistical Compendium*, prepared for the Royal Commission on the Economic Union and Development Prospects for Canada (Ottawa: Statistics Canada, 1985), Tables 2.6, 9.1 and 9.2; and Finance Canada, *Economic Review, April 1984* (Ottawa: Minister of Supply and Services Canada, 1984).

Note: Growth rates are average annual compound increases from the level in the year before the period specified to the level in the final year of the period specified.

a. Civilian employment: minor non-comparabilities in series occur in 1946 and 1966.
b. Real Gross National Expenditure (GNE).
c. Real GNE divided by population.
d. Real GNE per person employed.
e. As measured by Canada Price Index.
f. Minor non-comparabilities in series occur in 1946 and 1966.

Employment also grew rapidly between 1946 and 1973, and unemployment rates were generally lower than they had been before that period or than they have been since. In 1947, during the post-war adjustment period, inflation flared briefly into the double-digit range and made a similar rise at the outset of the Korean War. Generally, however, rates of price increase were low between 1946 and 1973. Even during this period of comparatively good performance, public discussion gave considerable emphasis to the current problems: an upward creep in inflation from the mid-1950s; slow growth and relatively high unemployment in the late 1950s and early 1960s, reoccurring about 1970. In the late 1950s and early 1960s, there was much concern, just as there is today, that Canada might be facing an extended period of structural unemployment.

The period since 1973 has seen a deterioration in most aspects of performance, though the falling off has been more severe in some respects than in others. A sharp break in productivity growth appears to have occurred after 1973, and the situation may have worsened in the late 1970s.

A full and satisfactory explanation of the slow-down of productivity growth still eludes analysts. No doubt the increased degree of slack in the economy after 1973 helped to slow productivity growth. A sharp break in that growth in the oil and gas industry, reflecting both increased dependence on less productive wells and increased investment in exploration, also contributed to the decline in overall productivity, as did the impact of higher energy prices on energy-using industries. According to most analyses, however, these factors do not fully account for the decline in productivity growth from an average annual rate of 2.3 per cent, between 1967 and 1973, to virtually zero during the period from 1974 to 1981. Furthermore, investment and the resulting growth in capital stock, the age-sex composition of the labour force, and the industrial composition of output did not change in ways that would have caused any significant slow-down in productivity growth after 1973. Most analysts believe that in addition to weaker cyclical conditions and the energy shock, there was some decline in the "underlying" rate of productivity growth. This rate is presumably determined largely by the development and application of new technology.[1]

The cessation of productivity growth between 1974 and 1981 contributed to a slow-down in the growth of real income per capita. Table 7-3 shows the relative significance of each of the factors that account for the growth of real income per capita. From 1947 to 1956, productivity growth was strong (3.5 per cent), but demographic and labour-force developments dampened the growth of real income per capita. The population of labour-force age (over 15 years) grew less rapidly than total population, and labour-force participation declined as many women left wartime employment. Between 1957 and 1966, rising participation rates made a small contribution to real income growth per capita, offsetting the effect of a decline in productivity growth. The 1967–73 period saw remarkably rapid growth of real income per capita: almost 4 per cent per year, on average. The proportion of the population of labour-force age increased, and participation rates continued to rise. Annual productivity growth averaged over 2 per cent. The growth of real income per capita slowed markedly from 1974 to 1981, when an increase in the population of labour-force age and higher labour-force participation rates were offset by the cessation of productivity growth.

Inflation increased sharply in Canada after 1973, although some upward trend in the inflation rate had been evident since the mid-1960s. The drastic oil-price increases of 1973 and 1979–80, imposed by the Organization of Petroleum Exporting Countries (OPEC) were, of course, the most dramatic

TABLE 7-3 Contribution of Various Factors to Real Income Growth per Capita in Canada

	1947–56	1957–66	1967–73	1974–81
	(average annual per cent growth)			
1. Changes in population of labour-force age relative to total population	−0.62	0.02	1.10	0.87
2. Changes in labour-force participation rates	−0.28	0.30	0.83	1.03
3. Changes in employment relative to labour force	−0.01	−0.03	−0.31	−0.28
4. Total changes in employment relative to population[a]	−0.91	0.29	1.62	1.62
5. Productivity	3.46	2.08	2.29	0.07
6. Real income per capita[b]	2.55	2.37	3.91	1.69

Sources: Statistics Canada, *Historical Statistical Compendium*, prepared for the Royal Commission on the Economic Union and Development Prospects for Canada (Ottawa: Statistics Canada, 1985), and calculations by the Commission.

a. Row 4 represents the combined impact of rows 1, 2, and 3.
b. Row 6 represents the combined impact of rows 1, 2, 3, and 5 (or of rows 4 and 5).

single factor in this upward trend. The rise in inflation also reflected the delayed impact of the strong demand conditions that developed in Canada and internationally in the late 1960s and early 1970s.

The average level of unemployment rose after 1973, even though employment continued to grow rapidly. However, the highest proportion of the initial increase in the unemployment rate in the 1967–73 period may be attributable to the effect of the 1971 changes in the Unemployment Insurance system on the behaviour of the unemployed and, to a lesser extent, to changes in the age-sex composition of the labour force. Inadequate growth in aggregate demand during the latter half of the 1970s and especially during the outset of the 1980s caused the cyclical component of unemployment to rise significantly.

Demographic and Labour-Force Trends

Table 7-4 presents demographic data for each of the census periods from 1921 to 1981.[2] The table shows a continuous decline of the death rate and a parallel increase in life expectancy for both men and women, over the entire 1921–81 period. On the other hand, both the birth rate and the fertility rate varied substantially over this period, declining throughout the 1930s and 1940s, increasing in the 1950s and 1960s, and then declining steeply to 1976. Both rates have since declined further, but at a much slower pace. Net immigration has exhibited no clear trend; Part V of our Report explores this area in some detail.

TABLE 7-4 **Historical Demographic Data**

	Total Population								0 to 14		15 to 24		25 to 64		65+	
Year	Pop. (000s)	Average Annual Growth Rate[a]	Average Birth Rate[a] (per 1 000 pop.)	Average Death Rate[a] (per 1 000 pop.)	Average Immig. Rate[a] (per 1 000 pop.)	Fertility Rate per Woman	Life Expectancy at Birth: Male	Life Expectancy at Birth: Female	Average Annual Growth Rate[a]	% of Pop.	Average Annual Growth Rate[a]	% of Pop.	Average Annual Growth Rate[a]	% of Pop.	Average Annual Growth Rate[a]	% of Pop.
1921	8 788	2.0	N.A.	N.A.	1.9	3.5	N.A	N.A	2.4	34.4	0.8	17.3	1.2	43.5	2.3	4.8
1931	10 377	1.7	25.2	11.1	2.8	3.2	60.0	62.1	0.8	31.6	2.6	18.8	1.8	44.0	3.2	5.6
1941	11 507	1.0	21.0	9.9	−0.8	2.8	63.0	66.3	−0.3	27.8	1.0	18.7	1.7	46.8	2.9	6.7
1951	14 009	2.0	26.1	9.5	1.3	3.5	66.3	70.8	2.9	30.3	0.0	15.3	1.9	46.6	3.5	7.8
1961	18 238	2.7	27.7	8.2	7.0	3.8	68.4	74.2	3.8	34.0	2.0	14.3	3.1	44.1	2.5	7.6
1971	21 568	1.7	20.2	7.5	3.6	2.2	69.3	76.4	0.3	29.6	4.4	18.6	1.6	43.8	2.3	8.1
1976	22 997	1.3	15.7	7.4	4.5	1.8	70.2	77.5	−1.6	25.6	2.3	19.5	2.4	46.1	2.8	8.7
1981	24 342	1.2	15.4	7.1	3.1	1.7	71.9	78.9	−1.5	22.5	0.8	19.1	2.2	48.6	3.4	9.7

Sources: Statistics Canada, *Historical Statistical Compendium*, prepared for the Royal Commission on the Economic Union and Development Prospects for Canada (Ottawa: Statistics Canada, 1985), Tables 1.6 and 1.7, and *Historical Statistics of Canada*, 2d ed. (Ottawa: Statistics Canada, 1983), pp. B1-14, B15-22, B59-74; and Finance Canada, *Economic Review, April 1984* (Ottawa: Minister of Supply and Services Canada, 1984), p. 121.

Note: N.A. = not available.

a. For preceding ten years with the exception of 1976 and 1981; these last are for the preceding five years.

TABLE 7-5 Sources of Labour-Force Growth

	1955–66	1966–73	1973–79	1979–83
	(average annual per cent rates of growth)			
Source Population				
(Both sexes, aged 15 years and over)	2.2	2.6	2.2	1.7
Net immigration	0.5	0.4	0.4	0.3
Natural increase	1.7	2.2	1.9	1.4
Participation rate	0.4	0.7	1.0	0.3
Total labour force	2.6	3.3	3.3	2.1
Employment	2.6	2.8	2.9	0.8

Sources: 1956–1979 data from Canada, Employment and Immigration Canada, Task Force on Labour Market Development, *Labour Market Development in the 1980s* (Ottawa: Minister of Supply and Services Canada, 1981), p. 58. Employment data from Statistics Canada, *Historical Labour Force Statistics*, Cat. No. 71-201 (Ottawa, various years). 1980–1983 data recalculated using actual net immigration and employment data from Statistics Canada, *Historical Statistical Compendium*, prepared for the Royal Commission on the Economic Union and Development Prospects for Canada (Ottawa: Statistics Canada, 1985), CANSIM data on source population (767284), labour force (both sexes, aged 15 years and over) (767285).

Note: All calculations of net immigration's contributions to the source population assume that 60% of immigrants are 15 years of age and over, a figure in the range of recent historical experience. (See T. Samuel and B. Woloski, "The Labour Market Experiences of Canadian Immigrants", mimeo, 1984.) The age distribution of emigrants is assumed to be the same.

Population growth reached a peak annual average rate of 2.7 per cent between 1951 and 1961, and by 1961 the population share of those aged 14 or under was almost as high as it had been in 1921. Between 1961 and 1971, population growth slowed to an average annual rate of 1.7 per cent. The proportion of the population represented by those 14 years old and younger declined significantly to 29.6 per cent. Meanwhile, the maturation of the "baby-boom" generation increased the proportion of those aged 15 to 24 from 14.3 per cent to 18.6 per cent.

The average annual population-growth rate continued to decline between 1971 and 1981, to approximately 1.2 per cent. This decline was associated with a further steep contraction of the share of the aged-14 and younger group to 22.5 per cent. The proportion of the population aged 15 to 24 rose until the mid-1970s and diminished thereafter, falling to 19.1 per cent by 1981. The aging of the baby-boom cohort led to a significant increase in the share of the population aged 25 to 64, while the share of the 65-years and older group continued its upward trend. During the 1970s, the share accounted for by the young was smaller than it had ever been before, and the share accounted for by the elderly was larger; more than two Canadians in three were of working age, and this proportion also represented a record high. Figure 7-1 illustrates the effect on population shares of the maturation of the baby-boom cohort.

FIGURE 7-1 Percentage Share of Selected Age Groups, 1921–1981

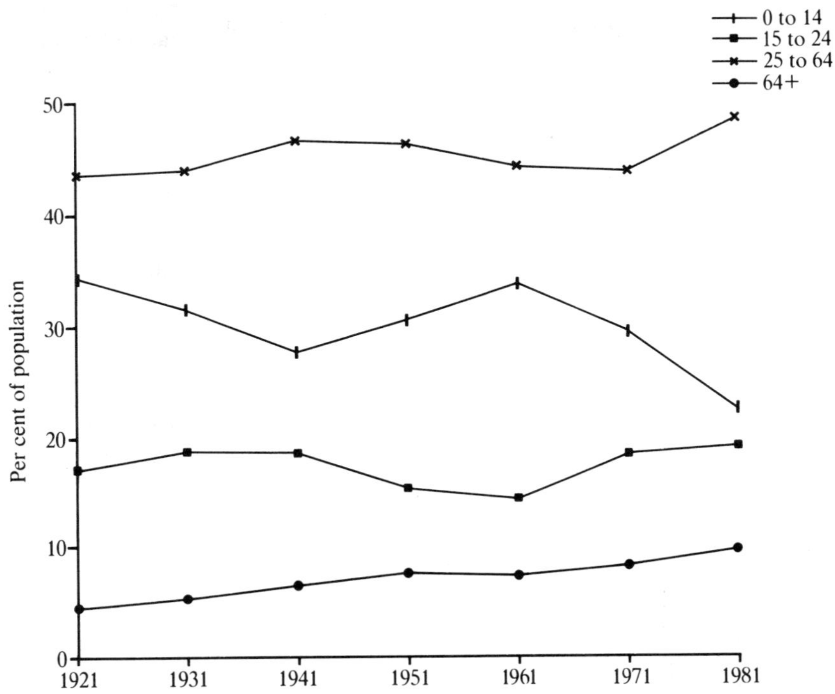

Source: Statistics Canada, *Historical Statistical Compendium,* prepared for the Royal Commission on the Economic Union and Development Prospects for Canada (Ottawa: Statistics Canada, 1985), Table 1-7.

As Table 7-5 shows, the Canadian labour force has grown rapidly over the past three decades. Growth was especially rapid in the late 1960s and the 1970s. It has now slowed and, according to most predictions, will slow even further. This rapid development has reflected both a very substantial increase in the source population[3] and a more modest increase in the percentage of the source population that has participated in the labour force.[4]

Table 7-6 disaggregates the growth rate for the source population by age and sex. Much of the growth in the source population (and even more of the growth in the labour force) during the 1960s resulted from the maturation of the baby-boom generation. The number of 15- to 24-year-olds in the source population reached a peak of nearly 4 600 000 in 1980 and is now declining. The labour force of the near future will be aging as well as growing less rapidly.

TABLE 7-6 **Source Population Growth Rates, by Age-Sex Group, Canada, 1966–83 (Actual) and 1984–85 (Projected)**

Age	15–24		25–44		45–64		65 and over		Total		
Sex	Men	Women	Men	Women	Men	Women	Men	Women	Men	Women	Both sexes
1966-67	5.3	4.8	1.6	1.2	2.3	3.1	1.4	3.1	2.7	2.8	2.7
1967–68	4.6	4.3	1.5	1.1	2.3	3.0	1.4	3.0	2.5	2.6	2.5
1968–69	3.9	3.6	1.5	1.2	2.3	3.0	1.8	3.2	2.4	2.5	2.5
1969–70	3.4	3.6	1.9	1.4	2.1	2.7	1.9	3.2	2.4	2.5	2.4
1970–71	2.8	3.2	2.0	1.7	1.8	2.2	2.3	3.3	2.2	2.4	2.3
1971–72	1.8	1.3	2.4	2.9	1.7	2.1	1.9	3.0	2.0	2.3	2.1
1972–73	2.0	2.0	2.5	2.6	1.7	2.0	2.1	3.0	2.1	2.3	2.2
1973–74	2.9	2.7	3.1	3.1	1.6	2.0	2.3	3.1	2.5	2.7	2.6
1974–75	2.6	2.7	2.9	3.0	1.7	2.0	2.4	3.2	2.5	2.7	2.6
1975–76	2.2	2.2	2.8	2.8	1.5	1.6	2.6	3.2	2.3	2.4	2.3
1976–77	1.5	1.5	2.6	2.8	1.4	1.4	2.8	3.4	2.0	2.2	2.1
1977–78	1.1	1.1	2.6	2.7	1.3	1.2	2.7	3.5	1.8	2.0	1.9
1978–79	0.7	0.6	2.8	3.0	1.0	0.9	3.0	3.7	1.8	1.9	1.9
1979–80	0.5	0.4	3.2	3.3	1.0	1.0	3.0	3.7	1.9	2.0	2.0
1980–81	−0.3	−0.4	3.1	3.3	1.3	1.1	2.6	3.5	1.7	1.8	1.8
1981–82	−1.0	−1.3	3.1	3.2	1.2	1.1	2.5	3.2	1.5	1.6	1.6
1982–83	−1.5	−1.8	2.8	3.0	1.2	1.2	2.3	2.8	1.3	1.4	1.4
1983–84	−2.2	−2.0	3.1	2.7	1.1	0.9	2.6	3.2	1.3	1.3	1.3
1984–85	−2.1	−2.1	2.4	2.6	0.5	0.8	2.5	3.1	0.9	1.2	1.0

Source: Economic Council of Canada, *In Short Supply: Jobs and Skills in the 1980s* (Ottawa: Minister of Supply and Services Canada, 1982), Table 4-8. (Re-estimated for 1975–83, using Statistics Canada, *Labour Force Annual Averages, 1975–1983*, Cat. No. 71-529 (Ottawa: Minister of Supply and Services Canada, 1984), pp. 9–17.

Note: The source population, as defined by the Labour Force Survey, includes the population, aged 15 years and over, residing in Canada, with the exception of residents of Yukon and the Northwest Territories, persons living on Indian reserves, inmates of institutions, and full-time members of Canada's armed forces.

As Figure 7-2 indicates, the modest overall increase in labour-force participation is the result of a dramatic rise in the participation rate for women aged 25 and over, a moderate decline in the rate for adult males, and a slight increase in the rate for youth. Figure 7-3 shows that the net result of these changes in demography and participation rates is that adult females' share of the labour force has become much larger since the mid-1960s, and adult males' share has become significantly smaller; youth's share has changed relatively little.

While more women of all ages have been joining Canada's work-force since 1956, the participation rate varies significantly from one female age group to another as Figure 7-4 illustrates. Participation rates by age group and the changes in such rates over time are conditioned by sociological, generational and attitudinal factors. The conditions of work and the availability of child care probably also influence female participation rates.

Not surprisingly, the dramatic nature of these major changes in the size and composition of the Canadian labour force has made them an important topic of national discussion. Other changes in the pattern of employment are scarcely less important. Employment in the service industries and, consequently, part-time and white-collar employment grew rapidly between 1956 and 1979, especially before 1973. (See Tables 7-7, 7-8, and 7-9.) The share of manufacturing in the labour market has declined since 1956, and so has the number of people employed in primary industries. While women continue to be employed principally in services, manufacturing and trade, the proportion of female employees, as Tables 7-10 and 7-11 show, has increased substantially in every industry group. Table 7-12 indicates that women and youths are far more likely than adult males to seek or to hold part-time jobs.

Another key labour-market trend is the rise in average unemployment rates, shown in Table 7-13. The increases in unemployment rates have been most pronounced for young people, particularly young men, but the unemployment rate has also increased substantially for both men and women over 25 years of age.

The dramatic increase in the unemployment rate from 7.5 per cent in 1980 to 11.9 per cent in 1983 is one measure of the intensity of the 1981–82 recession. Between 1980 and 1983, the total number of unemployed workers jumped by 69 per cent. The proportion of long-term unemployed, representing Canadians without work for six months or longer, almost doubled, as Table 7-14 records. While all age groups were hard hit by unemployment, men aged 25 to 44 were hardest hit because they tended to be concentrated in the industries, such as construction and manufacturing, that were most affected by the recession. (See Table 7-15.) High unemployment must be regarded as the most serious current economic problem. It will take a strong and sustained recovery to reduce the unemployment rate to its pre-recession level. Even if we achieve such a recovery, the problem of structural unemployment will still remain. The increase in unemployment in Canada over the two decades that preceded the recent recession can be attributed largely to structural factors such as changes in demography and social legislation. The demographic change that tended to raise the unemployment rate was the shift in the composition of the labour force towards young and female workers,

FIGURE 7-2 Participation Rates among Certain Demographic Groups, 1966-1983

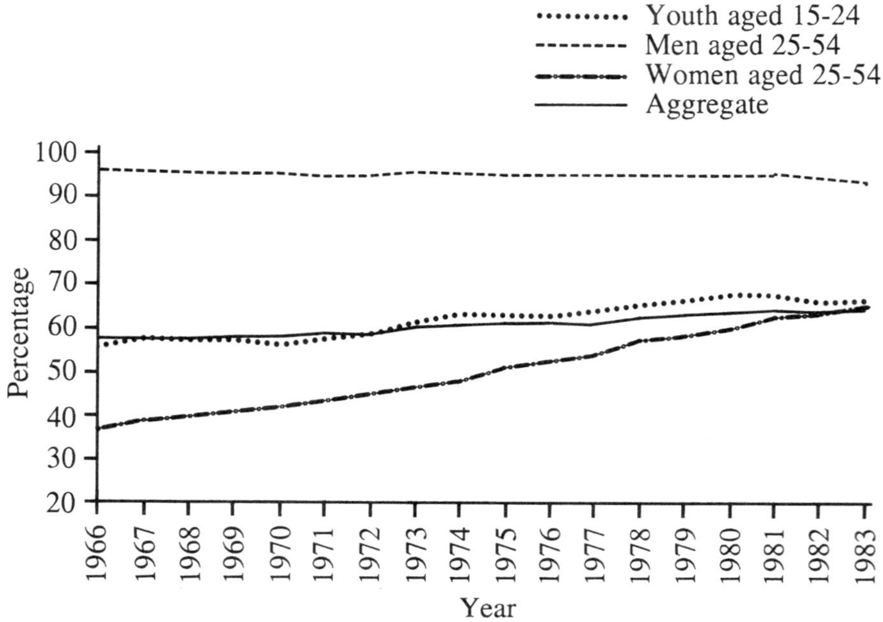

Source: Statistics Canada, *Historical Labour Force Statistics-Actual Data, Seasonal Factors, Seasonally Adjusted Data, 1983* (Ottawa: Minister of Supply and Services Canada, 1984).

FIGURE 7-3 Labour Force Composition by Demographic Groups, 1966-1983

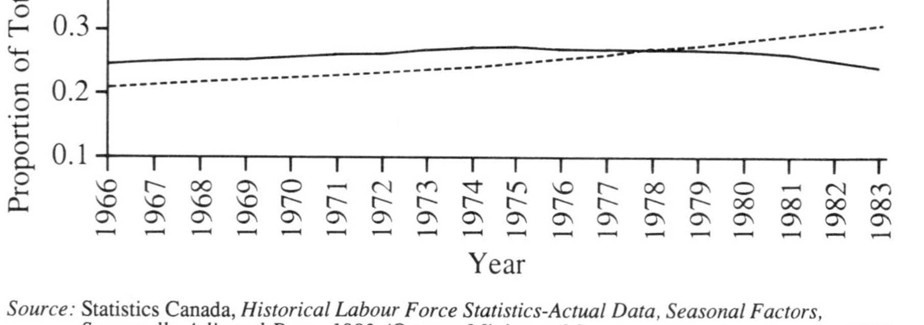

Source: Statistics Canada, *Historical Labour Force Statistics-Actual Data, Seasonal Factors, Seasonally Adjusted Data, 1983* (Ottawa: Minister of Supply and Services Canada, 1984).

FIGURE 7-4 Female Participation Rates by Age, Canada

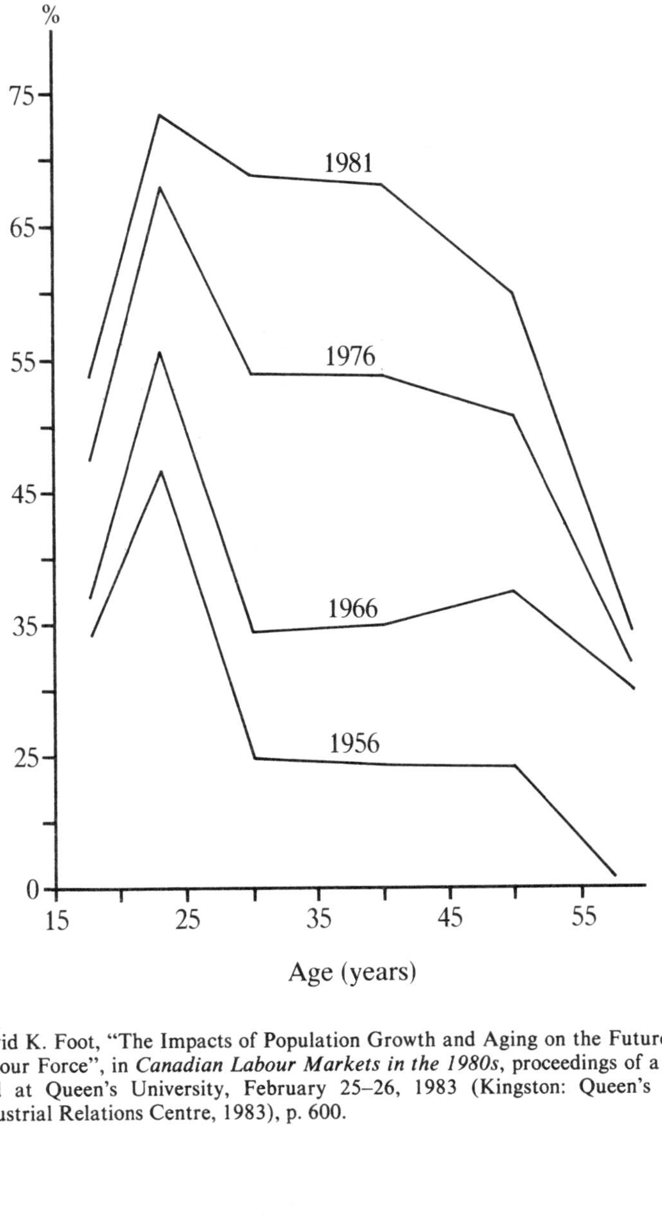

Source: David K. Foot, "The Impacts of Population Growth and Aging on the Future Canadian Labour Force", in *Canadian Labour Markets in the 1980s*, proceedings of a conference held at Queen's University, February 25–26, 1983 (Kingston: Queen's University, Industrial Relations Centre, 1983), p. 600.

who usually experience higher unemployment rates than adult males. The most relevant items of social legislation were the increases in the minimum wage in the early 1970s, and the 1971 revisions of the Unemployment Insurance Act, which increased the generosity of the scheme in several respects. We shall take a closer look, in Chapter 10, at factors that increase the structural unemployment rate.

TABLE 7-7 **Industrial Composition of Employment Growth**

	Average Annual Rates of Growth				Per Cent Contribution to Overall Employment Growth			
	1956–66	1966–73	1973–79	1979–83	1956–66	1966–73	1973–79	1979–83
Primary goods	–2.9	–1.7	1.2	0.0	–16.6	–5.4	2.9	–0.6
Mining	0.9	2.1	4.3	—	0.6	1.0	2.1	—
Other primary	–3.5	–2.4	0.4	—	–17.2	–6.4	0.7	—
Secondary goods	2.8	2.1	2.3	–2.5	32.5	20.4	19.4	–77.6
Manufacturing	2.6	2.1	1.8	–2.3	23.7	15.9	12.2	–54.6
Construction	3.5	2.2	3.8	–3.2	8.8	4.5	7.2	–23.0
Services	4.2	4.4	3.8	2.1	84.1	85.0	77.7	178.2
Total	2.6	3.1	3.2	0.8	100.0	100.0	100.0	100.0

Source: Based on Statistics Canada, *Labour Force Survey*.

TABLE 7-8 **Occupational Composition of Employment Growth**

	Average Annual Rates of Growth			Per Cent Contribution to Overall Employment Growth		
	1966–73	1973–79	1979–83	1966–73	1973–79	1979–83
White-collar occupations[a]	4.4	4.2	2.4	84.7	81.1	194.4
Blue-collar occupations[b]	1.0	1.6	–2.2	15.3	18.9	–94.9
Total economy	3.1	3.2	0.8	100.0	100.0	100.0

Sources: Based on Statistics Canada, *Labour Force Survey*, and *Labour Force Annual Averages, 1975–1983*, Cat. No. 71-529 (Ottawa: Minister of Supply and Services Canada, 1984), pp. 220–24, 239–42; and Employment and Immigration Canada, Task Force on Labour Market Development, *Labour Market Development in the 1980s* (Ottawa: Minister of Supply and Services Canada, 1981), Table 2-6.

a. Managerial, professional, clerical, sales and services occupations.

b. Primary occupations, processing, construction, transportation, materials handling and other crafts.

TABLE 7-9 **Part-Time/Full-Time Employment for Demographic Groups and Industries**

	Average Annual per Cent Rate of Growth			Percentage Contribution to Employment Growth		
	1966–73	**1973–79**	**1979–83**	**1966–73**	**1973–79**	**1979–83**
Total employment	2.7	3.4	0.8	100.0	100.0	100.0
Full-time	2.3	3.3	0.0	74.0	85.6	0.0
Part-time	6.9	4.0	6.1	26.0	14.4	100.0
Part-time employment	6.9	4.0	6.2	100.0	100.0	100.0
Youth	10.8	6.0	4.6	55.5	62.6	32.7
Adult women	4.8	3.6	6.5	35.9	43.5	48.9
Adult men	4.8	−2.6	12.3	8.6	−6.4	18.4
Goods-producing industries	3.7	0.2	6.2	10.2	1.0	7.7
Services-producing industries	7.6	4.7	6.4	89.8	99.0	92.3
Full-time employment	2.3	3.3	0.0	100.0	100.0	100.0
Youth	2.6	3.6	−5.2	26.2	23.9	—
Adult women	4.6	6.7	3.7	37.1	43.0	—
Adult men	1.4	2.0	0.2	36.7	33.0	—
Goods-producing industries	0.5	2.2	−2.2	10.0	25.1	—
Services-producing industries	3.5	4.0	1.1	90.0	74.9	—

Sources: Canada, Employment and Immigration Canada, Task Force on Labour Market Development, *Labour Market Development in the 1980s* (Ottawa: Minister of Supply and Services Canada, 1981), Table 2-7; and Statistics Canada, *Labour Force Annual Averages, 1975–1983*, Cat. No. 71-529 (Ottawa: Minister of Supply and Services Canada, 1984), pp. 301–5, 319–23.

TABLE 7-10 **Historical Composition of Employment of Men and Women by Industry**

Industry	1956		1966		1973			1979			1983			Industry share of total employment		
					(percentage of total industry employment)											
	Men	Women	Men	Women	Men	Women	Per cent of female employment	Men	Women	Per cent of female employment	Men	Women	Per cent of female employment	1973	1979	1983
Mining	96.6	3.4	95.6	4.1	94.3	5.7	0.2	89.8	10.2	0.4	77.8	22.2	3.7	1.4	1.6	7.0
Other primary	95.6	4.4	89.3	10.7	87.3	12.7	2.4	78.1	21.9	3.2				6.1	5.7	
Manufacturing	78.9	21.1	78.0	22.0	76.0	24.0	15.6	73.5	26.5	13.6	71.8	28.2	11.8	22.4	20.0	17.5
Construction	97.6	2.4	96.6	3.4	95.2	4.8	0.9	92.0	8.0	1.3	89.9	10.1	1.3	6.3	6.2	5.2
Transportation	86.1	13.9	85.5	14.5	83.2	16.8	4.3	79.3	20.7	4.6	76.0	24.0	4.6	8.9	8.7	8.1
Trade	70.9	29.1	67.2	32.8	62.4	37.6	18.7	57.9	42.1	18.9	56.7	43.3	17.8	17.1	17.4	17.2
Finance, insurance	54.9	45.1	52.3	47.7	45.3	54.7	7.5	40.7	59.3	8.2	41.2	58.8	7.9	4.7	5.3	5.6
Services	43.3	56.7	39.6	60.4	41.0	59.0	45.1	40.3	59.7	43.7	39.1	60.9	46.4	26.1	28.4	31.9
Public administration	77.2	22.8	77.3	22.7	72.7	27.3	5.3	65.3	34.7	6.1	63.0	37.0	6.4	6.7	6.7	7.3
Total	76.4	23.6	69.7	30.3	65.7	34.3	100.0	61.2	38.8	100.0	58.1	41.9	100.0	100.0	100.0	100.0

Source: Based on Statistics Canada, *Labour Force Survey*.

TABLE 7-11 Occupational Contribution to Female Employment Growth by Industry, 1975–79

	Agri-culture	Other Primary	Manufac-turing	Construc-tion	Transpor-tation, Communi-cations, Utilities	Trade	Finance, Insurance, Real Estate	Services	Public Adminis-tration	Total	
										Women	Men
						(per cent)					
Highly qualified occupations		55.3	23.5	39.7	28.4	14.5	32.5	29.0	74.1	28.0	42.9
Clerical	24.1	44.7	15.9	26.0	34.9	35.7	35.7	17.1	0.7	22.9	
Sales			5.9		11.0	42.4	21.2	3.3		12.5	−6.3
Service[a]			1.2		3.1	6.3	10.3	49.1	25.3	24.9	10.6
Primary occupations	75.9									1.6	5.4
Processing[b]			39.5			1.6		1.1		6.2	30.5
Construction				34.3						0.8	3.4
Transportation					22.6					1.3	7.9
Material handling			14.0					0.4		1.9	6.1
Total	100.0	100.0	100.0	100.0	100.0	100.0	100.0	100.0	100.0	100.0	100.0

Source: Canada, Employment and Immigration Canada, Task Force on Labour Market Development, *Labour Market Development in the 1980s* (Ottawa: Minister of Supply and Services Canada, 1981), p. 26, based on Statistics Canada, *Labour Force Survey*.

Note: This table shows the extent to which employment of women increased over 1975–79 in various occupational categories. For example, in manufacturing industries, 23.5% of the total increase in employment of women occurred in highly qualified occupations.

a. Includes occupations such as waiters, chambermaids, janitors, dry-cleaning occupations.

b. Includes occupations in the processing of metal, rubber, plastic, food and beverages, wood and textiles.

TABLE 7-12 **The Composition of Employment and Unemployment by Type of Work Sought, Canada, 1981**

Sex and Age Group (Years)	Employment		Unemployment		Labour Force	
	Full-Time	Part-Time	Full-Time	Part-Time	Full-Time	Part-Time
Male	64.6	28.0	58.0	37.0	64.1	28.7
15–19	3.3	16.2	10.7	27.7	3.8	17.1
20–24	8.7	4.0	15.6	4.2	9.2	4.0
25–44	32.9	2.8	22.0	2.5	32.1	2.8
45–64	18.6	2.5	9.7	2.5	18.0	2.5
65+	1.0	2.4	0.1	0.0	1.0	2.3
Female	35.4	72.0	42.0	63.0	35.9	71.3
15–19	2.5	17.1	8.4	23.5	2.9	17.5
20–24	6.9	6.8	10.3	6.7	7.1	6.8
25–44	17.6	29.9	18.4	22.7	17.7	29.4
45–64	8.0	16.7	4.9	9.2	7.8	16.1
65+	0.3	1.6	0.0	0.8	0.3	1.5
Total	100.0	100.0	100.0	100.0	100.0	100.0

Source: Statistics Canada, *The Labour Force*, Catalogue No. 71-001 (Canada: Minister of Supply and Services Canada, monthly), December 1981, p. 100, and unpublished data with estimates and calculations by the author.

Capital Formation

Capital formation has an important function in the growth process. As Table 7-16 shows, investment has been sufficient to cause our total capital stock and our capital stock per person employed to increase at a very rapid rate since the Second World War.

Capital stock grew slowly between 1926 and 1946, reflecting low investment during the Depression, as the result of low total demand, and throughout the Second World War, when investment in the private sector was "crowded out" by government borrowing. After 1946 and before the onset of the recent recession, capital investment in Canada increased at a relatively high rate. It grew somewhat more rapidly than employment, producing a substantial increase in real capital per person employed. While the growth rate of the latter measure decreased over time, there was no sharp step downward after 1973. This suggests that at least at the aggregate level, very little of the post-1973 slow-down in productivity can be attributed to insufficient investment.

TABLE 7-13 Unemployment Rates by Sex and Age Groups[a]

	Men			Women			Total		
Year	Total	14–24	25+	Total	14–24	25+	Total	14–24	25+
1953	3.4	6.0	2.8	1.6	2.4	1.2	3.0	4.6	2.5
1954	5.2	8.8	4.3	2.6	3.9	1.8	4.6	7.0	3.9
1955	5.0	8.6	4.2	2.6	3.7	1.9	4.4	6.8	3.7
1956	3.9	6.9	3.3	1.9	2.8	1.4	3.4	5.3	2.9
1957	5.4	9.7	4.4	2.3	3.6	1.6	4.7	7.4	3.9
1958	8.2	14.5	6.8	3.6	5.6	2.6	7.1	11.1	5.9
1959	7.0	12.3	5.8	3.0	5.2	2.0	6.0	9.6	5.0
1960	8.2	14.2	6.8	3.6	6.3	2.4	7.0	11.1	5.8
1961	8.4	14.1	7.2	3.8	6.4	2.5	7.2	11.0	6.2
1962	6.9	12.1	5.8	3.3	5.6	2.2	6.0	9.5	5.0
1963	6.4	11.7	5.2	3.3	5.9	2.1	5.6	9.4	4.5
1964	5.4	9.9	4.3	3.1	5.3	2.0	4.7	8.0	3.7
1965	4.5	7.7	3.6	2.7	4.8	1.7	4.0	6.5	3.1
1966	4.1	7.2	3.3	2.6	4.3	1.7	3.6	6.0	2.9
1967	4.6	8.2	3.7	3.0	5.1	1.9	4.1	6.9	3.2
1968	5.5	9.9	4.3	3.4	6.0	2.1	4.9	8.2	3.7
1969	5.2	9.5	4.0	3.6	5.9	2.4	4.7	8.0	3.6
1970	6.6	12.4	5.0	4.5	7.7	2.9	5.9	10.4	4.4
1966	3.3	6.3	2.6	3.4	4.8	2.7	3.4	5.6	2.6
1967	3.9	7.2	3.0	3.7	5.5	2.8	3.8	6.5	2.9
1968	4.6	8.7	3.5	4.4	6.5	3.3	4.5	7.7	3.4
1969	4.3	8.3	3.2	4.7	6.5	3.7	4.4	7.5	3.4
1970	5.6	11.2	4.1	5.8	8.6	4.4	5.7	10.0	4.2
1971	6.0	12.0	4.3	6.6	9.8	5.0	6.2	11.1	4.5
1972	5.8	11.9	4.1	7.0	9.6	5.7	6.2	10.9	4.6
1973	4.9	10.0	3.4	6.7	9.2	5.4	5.5	9.6	4.1
1974	4.8	9.6	3.3	6.4	8.9	5.1	5.3	9.3	3.9
1975	6.2	12.5	4.3	8.1	11.4	6.5	6.9	12.0	5.0
1976	6.3	13.2	4.2	8.4	12.1	6.6	7.1	12.7	5.1
1977	7.3	14.9	4.9	9.4	13.8	7.4	8.1	14.4	5.8
1978	7.5	15.0	5.2	9.6	13.8	7.7	8.3	14.5	6.1
1979	6.6	13.2	4.5	8.8	12.7	7.0	7.4	12.9	5.4
1980	6.9	13.7	4.8	8.4	12.6	6.5	7.5	13.2	5.4
1981	7.0	14.1	4.8	8.3	12.3	6.7	7.5	13.2	5.6
1982	11.1	21.1	8.2	10.9	16.1	8.8	11.0	18.8	8.4
1983	12.1	22.4	9.2	11.6	17.0	9.6	11.9	19.9	9.4

Source: Statistics Canada, *Historical Labour Force Statistics – Actual Data, Seasonal Factors, Seasonally Adjusted Data, 1973, 1983*, Cat. No. 71-201 (Ottawa: Minister of Supply and Services Canada, 1974, 1984).

a. The data up to 1970 reflect the concepts used in the "old" labour-force survey. The data from 1966 to 1983 are based on a "new" labour-force survey. The data for the years 1966 to 1970 provide for a period of overlap.

TABLE 7-14 Percentage Distribution of Unemployment, by Duration, Canada, 1980 and 1983

Duration of Spell of Unemployment	1980	1983
Less than 1 month	33.4	23.5
1 to 3 months	31.4	26.5
3 to 6 months	19.7	21.6
6 months or more	15.5	28.4
	100.0	100.0

Source: Economic Council of Canada, *Steering the Course*, Twenty-First Annual Review (Ottawa: Minister of Supply and Services Canada, 1984), p. 71.

TABLE 7-15 Percentage Distribution of Long-Term Unemployment among the Demographic Groups, Canada, 1980 and 1983

Age-Sex Group	1980	1983
Men		
15 to 24 years	19.2	20.5
25 to 44 years	23.1	30.0
45 years or older	13.8	13.9
Women		
15 to 24 years	16.2	11.4
25 to 44 years	18.5	17.1
45 years or older	9.2	7.4
	100.0	100.0

Source: Economic Council of Canada, *Steering the Course*, Twenty-First Annual Review (Ottawa: Minister of Supply and Services Canada, 1984), p. 71.

TABLE 7-16 Canadian Non-Residential Net Capital Stock[a]

Year	Level Billions 1971 $	Average Annual Growth Rate (%)	Level Per Unit of Real GNE	Average Annual Rate of Change in Capital Stock/GNE Ratio (%)	Level Per Person Employed ('000 71$)	Average Annual Growth Rate in Capital Stock/ Employment Ratio (%)
1926	32.8		2.33			
1946	43.2	1.4	1.53	−2.1	9.23	0.0
1956	78.6	6.2	1.65	0.8	14.1	4.3
1966	136.0	5.6	1.82	1.0	19.1	3.1
1973	192.7	5.1	1.73	−0.7	22.0	2.0
1981	278.4	4.7	2.05	2.2	25.3	1.8

Source: Statistics Canada, *Historical Statistical Compendium*, prepared for the Royal Commission on the Economic Union and Development Prospects for Canada (Ottawa: Statistics Canada, 1985), Tables 4-2, 2-5 and 9-1.

a. Private and public.

Investment and savings are key dynamic factors in the growth of the economy's potential. They are also important determinants of aggregate demand and of the economy's cyclical performance. As Tables 7-17A and 17B show, total investment, business investment, and residential (housing) investment were all higher, on average, in the years from 1974 to 1980 than they were in the period from 1967 to 1973. Only government investment decreased as a share of GNE from one period to the other.[5]

The composition of investment did not change substantially between 1967–73 and 1974–80; at first sight, the composition of the matching savings shows more change. The overall increase in savings between 1974 and 1980 appears to have resulted from significant increases in the savings rates of the personal sector and the non-resident sector.[6] These increases were only partially offset by a decrease in government savings (government investment less the government deficit). Recorded savings, however, are distorted by inflation, and the distortion has been greater in the more recent periods because of the increase in the average inflation rate. The distortion of gross savings rates reflects the fact that no allowance is made for the decline in the real value (as a result of inflation) of assets and liabilities, the dollar values of which are fixed. (Net savings rates are distorted by the failure of conventional business or national accounts to adjust depreciation provisions for inflation.)

When savings ratios are adjusted for inflation, the compositional shifts are reduced, although the directions of change remain. Inflation adjustment reduces the savings of those sectors that are net holders of fixed-dollar assets: that is, the personal and non-resident sectors. It increases the (gross) savings (or reduces the deficit) of sectors that are net debtors: that is, the corporate sector and the government sector. (The increase in corporate gross savings would not necessarily translate into an increase in corporate net savings, since depreciation allowances would also be adjusted upwards.) For the economy as a whole, the inflation adjustments are exactly offsetting; thus total domestic savings, which include savings provided to Canada by non-residents, are not affected.

TABLE 7-17A Average Ratios of Investment to GNP in Canada, 1967–1980

Gross Investment	1967–73 (%)	1974–80 (%)
Government gross fixed capital formation	3.9	3.2
Private gross fixed capital formation:	18.1	20.1
Residential construction	4.9	5.8
Business construction[a]	13.2	14.3
Inventory investment	0.8	0.8
Total investment[b]	22.8	24.0

Source: Statistics Canada, National Accounts data; and "Inflation-adjusted Gross and Net Sector and Subsector Savings" (Ottawa, 1985).

a. Non-residential construction plus machinery and equipment.

b. Includes energy investment equal, on average, to 3.0% of GDP (1967–73) and 3.8% of GNP (1974–80).

TABLE 7-17B Average Ratios of Savings to GNP in Canada, 1967–1980

			Inflation Adjusted	
Gross Savings Recorded	1967–73 (%)	1974–80 (%)	1967–73 (%)	1974–80 (%)
Private sector:	17.7	20.5	17.7	20.8
Personal sector	7.5	10.5	4.6	6.2
Corporate sector	10.2	10.0	13.0	14.6
Government sector[a]	4.7	1.5	5.6	2.8
Federal government	0.8	−2.1	1.2	−1.1
Non-residents	0.3	2.0	−0.5	0.5
Total national savings[b] (excludes non-residents)	22.4	22.0	23.2	23.6
Total domestic savings[c]	22.7	24.1	22.7	24.1

Sources: Statistics Canada, National Accounts data, and "Inflation-adjusted Gross and Net Sector and Subsector Savings" (Ottawa, 1985).

a. Government-sector savings equal the government surplus plus government gross fixed-capital formation.

b. Excludes non-residents.

c. Total investment equals total domestic savings except for residual error of estimate.

Overall, then, modestly larger shares of the total output of the Canadian economy were devoted to total investment and to business investment in the seven years before the 1981–82 recession than were so directed in the preceding seven years. The resources for this investment were provided by a small increase, given inflation-adjusted figures, in the ratio of personal savings to GNP, and larger increases in the ratios of corporate and non-resident savings to GNP, with a partially offsetting reduction in the savings provided by the government sector.

Industrial Structure

Table 7-18 shows the distribution of current dollar or nominal output by industry in 1947, 1963 and 1981. The sharp decline in the proportion of output in agriculture, from 11.7 per cent in 1947 to 3.3 per cent in 1981, is one striking feature of the post-war industrial landscape. An even more important feature is the relative decline of manufacturing and the rise of the service sector. The manufacturing sector's share of total output fell from 28.5 per cent in 1947 to 20.4 per cent in 1981; meanwhile the share of output of finance, insurance and real estate climbed from 8.5 per cent to 11.3 per cent, and the share of other services jumped from 10.4 per cent to 21.5 per cent. This shift corresponds to developments in other industrialized countries and is usually cited as a fundamental change in industrial structure with wide-ranging implications. In fact, however, the change in the composition of nominal industrial output is not a very satisfactory indicator of structural change, since it incorporates differential sectoral price trends as well as underlying real changes. The trends in real shares are portrayed in Table 7-19.

The largest changes in real gross domestic product (GDP) have occurred in the primary sectors. By 1981, their combined share of GDP had fallen by more than half of its 1947 level. This relative decline in the primary GDP share was offset by increases in all other sectors, except manufacturing and public administration. The manufacturing sector rose in relative importance in the 1960s, and then returned to approximately its 1947 share in 1981. This pattern contrasts with the steady decrease in manufacturing's share of nominal GDP, which is accounted for, in part, by the fact that prices for manufactured goods have increased less than average prices. The real share of public administration decreased after 1963 as the increase in the nominal share slowed down. The difference between the trends in the nominal and real shares of this sector reflects the assumed lack of productivity growth in the sector, in which output is measured primarily in terms of inputs.

Perhaps the most notable feature of Table 7-19 – one that contradicts popular belief – is the absence of a substantial gain in the shares of non-goods-producing sectors relative to the goods-producing sectors. In fact, in real terms, the GDP share of the goods-producing sector declined only slightly, from 38.8 per cent in 1947 to 37.2 per cent in 1981.

TABLE 7-18 Share Distribution of Canada's Nominal GDP

	1947	1963 (per cent of total)	1981
Agriculture	11.7	5.6	3.3
Forestry, fishing, and trapping	2.9	1.2	1.0
Mines[a]	3.6	4.0	5.9
Manufacturing	28.5	26.2	20.4
Construction	5.1	5.6	6.3
Utilities	2.2	2.8	3.5
Transportation, storage, and communications	10.2	9.2	8.2
Trade	12.0	12.4	10.9
Finance, insurance, and real estate[b]	8.5	11.4	11.3
Other services	10.4	14.7	21.5
Public administration	4.9	6.9	7.6

Source: Statistics Canada, *Historical Statistical Compendium*, prepared for the Royal Commission on the Economic Union and Development Prospects for Canada (Ottawa: Statistics Canada, 1985), Table 12.2.

a. The share of oil in GDP for mining was 56.4 per cent in 1981.

b. The share of imputed rent or owner-occupied housing in GDP in Finance, Insurance and Real Estate was 30 per cent in 1981.

Real Income and Productivity Growth

The conventional approach to analysing the sources of economic growth has been to focus on increases in the quantity and the quality of the inputs used to produce output. This approach, which is called "growth accounting",[7] also considers the degree to which the inputs are employed and the efficiency with which they are used. Economic studies devoted to growth accounting usually calculate indirectly changes in the efficiency of input use (including efficiency gains derived from technological change); that is, the efficiency gain is what remains after all other contributions to the growth process have been quantified. This section presents some elementary growth-accounting calculations for Canada.

Table 7-20 provides estimates of the relative contributions made by various factors to economic growth over the periods 1962 to 1973 and 1973 to 1981. The average annual growth of real gross national expenditure fell from 5.7 per cent in 1962–73 to 3.0 per cent in 1973–81. To gain an understanding of the causes of this slow-down in real growth, it is useful to refer to an output measure called "gross output of the non-energy sector at factor cost". This measure differs from real GNE in that it excludes the final output of the energy sector and includes all income generated in Canada, rather than all income accruing to Canadian residents from domestic and foreign sources.

TABLE 7-19 Share Distribution of Canada's Real GDP

	1947	1963 (per cent of total)	1981
Agriculture	6.4	4.7	2.5
Forestry, fishing, and trapping	1.8	1.2	0.8
Mines[a]	1.9	3.7	2.9
Manufacturing	21.8	22.2	21.6
Construction	5.8	7.3	6.2
Utilities	1.1	2.2	3.2
Transportation, storage, and communications	8.5	8.3	10.5
Trade	12.1	11.5	12.5
Finance, insurance, and real estate[b]	11.9	12.3	13.2
Other services	19.4	18.2	19.7
Public administration	8.9	8.9	6.7

Source: Michael Charette, Robert R. Henry, and Barry Kaufman, "The Evolution of the Canadian Industrial Structure: An International Perspective", in *Canadian Industry in Transition*, vol. 2, prepared for the Royal Commission on the Economic Union and Development Prospects for Canada (Toronto: University of Toronto Press, 1985).

a. The share of oil in GDP for mining was 36.4 per cent in 1981.
b. The share of imputed rent or owner-occupied housing in GDP in Finance, Insurance and Real Estate was 30 per cent in 1981.

We have chosen to examine the gross output of the non-energy sector because the energy sector itself experienced a decline in productivity growth over the 1973–81 period. Consequently, this approach also allows us to identify the effect of the changing level of use of energy inputs on productivity in the non-energy sector.

As Table 7-20 indicates, the gross output of the non-energy sector at factor cost grew more slowly than GNE in the 1962–73 period and more quickly than GNE in the 1973–81 period. The difference arises largely from the fact that the growth of energy output was relatively high in the first period and declined sharply in the second. This leaves to be explained by other factors a slow-down of 2.2 percentage points in the average annual growth of output. When allowance is made for a decrease in the average annual rate of growth of employment in the non-energy sector of 0.2 percentage points (from 3.1 per cent in the 1962–73 period to 2.9 per cent in the 1973–81 period), average annual labour productivity growth declines by 1.8 percentage points (from 2.4 per cent per year in the first period to 0.6 per cent in the second period).

A significant portion of the decline in output and productivity growth between the two periods considered is a result of the weaker cyclical conditions after 1973. If output and employment are adjusted to eliminate the effect of the business cycle, then the average annual slow-down in the rate of

TABLE 7-20 Components of Economic Growth in Canada, 1962–81

	1962–73	1973–81	Change from 1962–73 to 1973–81
	(average annual rates of change)		
Gross national expenditure	5.7	3.0	−2.7
Gross output of non-energy sector (at factor cost)	5.6	3.4	−2.2
Employment (non-energy sector)	3.1	2.9	−0.2
Labour productivity	2.4	0.6	−1.8
Cyclically adjusted gross output of non-energy sector (at factor cost)	5.1	4.2	−0.9
Employment (non-energy sector)	2.8	3.0	0.2
Labour productivity	2.2	1.1	−1.1
Labour productivity resulting from cyclical factors	0.3	−0.5	−0.8
Capital (non-energy sector)	4.5	4.3	−0.2
Capital/labour ratio	1.3	1.4	0.1
Capital/labour substitution[a]	0.4	0.4	0.0
Energy	7.0	2.7	−4.3
Energy/labour ratio	3.8	−0.2	−4.0
Energy/labour substitution[b]	0.3	0.0	−0.3
Total factor productivity	1.7	0.2	−1.5
Total factor productivity excluding impact of cyclical factors	1.5	0.7	−0.8
Changes to labour composition			
Sex-age mix	−0.2	−0.2	0.0
Education	0.5	0.8	0.3
Employment shifts	−0.1	−0.3	−0.2
Final residual	1.3	0.5	−0.8

Source: Estimates by Commission staff.

a. Capital/labour ratio weighted by the capital-income share.
b. Energy/labour ratio weighted by the energy-income share.

growth of output of the non-energy sector is only 0.9 percentage points; the change in annual average employment growth in the non-energy sector becomes a gain of 0.2 percentage points. The slow-down in average annual productivity growth on a cyclically adjusted basis of 1.1 percentage points is significantly less than the actual slow-down of 1.8 percentage points. This analysis indicates that cyclical factors raised the growth of labour productivity by 0.3 percentage points per year between 1962 and 1973, and lowered it by 0.5 percentage points between 1973 and 1981, thus accounting for 0.8 percentage points of the slowing in productivity growth.[8]

A change in the capital intensity of the economy is one factor that can affect the growth of labour productivity. Table 7-20 shows that the capital stock grew an average of 4.5 per cent per year, from 1962 to 1973, and 4.3 per cent per year from 1973 to 1981. This rate was faster than that of employment growth in both periods; the result was that the capital/labour ratio rose by 1.3 per cent per year, on average, from 1962 to 1973, and by 1.4 per cent per year from 1973 to 1981. Multiplying the change in the capital/labour ratio by the share of capital income in total output provides an estimate of the change in labour productivity that derives from the substitution of capital for labour. This change amounted to an increase of about 0.4 percentage points per year in both periods and therefore did not contribute to the slow-down in the growth of labour productivity.

Another factor that can affect the growth of labour productivity is change in the level of energy use. Energy input grew by a hefty 7 per cent per year, on average, from 1962 to 1973, a period when energy was relatively cheap; its growth rate fell to 2.7 per cent per year from 1973 to 1981, a period that included two rounds of major increases in world oil prices. Viewed in relation to employment, the shift is even more dramatic. The energy/labour ratio increased by an average of 3.8 per cent per year from 1962 to 1973, and fell by 0.2 per cent per year from 1973 to 1981. According to our rough estimates, the substitution of energy for labour added 0.3 percentage points per year to the growth of labour productivity from 1962 to 1973, and had an insignificant negative effect from 1973 to 1981. This shift accounts for roughly 0.3 percentage points per year of the slow-down in labour-productivity growth between 1973 and 1981.

If one takes into account the growth of the economy's capital stock and the growth in energy use, their total factor productivity rose by 1.7 per cent per year from 1962 to 1973, and by 0.2 per cent from 1973 to 1981. The decline in the growth of total factor productivity of 1.5 percentage points was only slightly less than the decline in labour-productivity growth of 1.8 percentage points.

Cyclically adjusted total factor productivity increased by 1.5 per cent per year between 1962 and 1973, and by 0.7 per cent per year from 1973 to 1981. Thus the decline in cyclically adjusted total factor-productivity growth was 0.8 percentage points per year.

Some observers argue that the increase in the number of women and young people as new entrants to the work-force has reduced productivity growth, since members of these groups are likely to be less productive than long-term workers. However, less experience in the work-force and greater emphasis on part-time work are explanations for this alleged lower productivity of new labour-force entrants. To test the contention that the reduced productivity growth stems, in part, from the changing sex-age mix of the labour force, Commission researchers broke the labour force down into six age groups by sex and used the relative wage of each age-sex group as a measure of differences in productivity. The results of this analysis suggest that the increase in the proportion of women and young people in the work-force has reduced the growth of productivity by about 0.2 percentage points per year between 1962 and 1973, and by the same amount between 1973 and 1981. Thus the changing sex-age mix of employment does not help to explain the post-1973 change in the rate of productivity growth.

Commissioners took a similar approach in estimating the effect of an increasingly better-educated work force on productivity growth. Again, we used relative earnings as a rough index of productivity differences. The analysis indicates that the improvement in the educational level of workers added 0.5 percentage points per year to productivity growth over the 1962–73 period and 0.8 percentage points from 1973 to 1981, thus raising productivity growth by 0.3 percentage points per year from one period to the next.

A final factor is the effect on productivity of employment shifts among industries. The sectors used for this analysis were agriculture, manufacturing, other commercial goods-producing industries, commercial service-producing industries, and non-commercial industries. The analysis shows that the shift, mainly out of relatively high-productivity manufacturing into lower-productivity commercial services, depressed the growth of productivity by 0.1 percentage points per year from 1962 to 1973, and by 0.3 percentage points per year from 1973 to 1981. Consequently, this factor explains 0.2 percentage points of the average annual slow-down in growth after 1973.

Even if allowance is made for all of the factors mentioned above, a significant proportion of the post-1973 productivity slow-down is left unexplained. If the effects of the business cycle are eliminated, the unexplained residual amounts to 1.3 percentage points per year in the 1962–73 period and 0.5 percentage points per year in the 1973–81 period, a decline of 0.8 percentage points per year.

This residual is sometimes taken to be an indicator of the contribution of technological change to growth, though it is hard to believe that the contribution of this factor diminished by the amount suggested by the change in the residual, especially at a time when casual empiricism suggests a quickening of the pace of change.

The slow-down in the growth of productivity is a matter of considerable concern, affecting, as it does, all Canadians' prospects for an improvement in living standards.

Government Expenditures and Employment

An important development in the post-war period has been the growth in the size of government. Spending at all levels of government has increased relative to the size of the economy, as has spending on almost all major government functions. A few aggregate statistics cannot provide an adequate view of the changes in size and role of government. Given the importance of these changes, it is necessary to examine in more detail the evolution of government expenditure over the post-war period.

The ratio of total government expenditure to gross national product (GNP) is frequently used as an indicator of the size of government. It is important, however, to be aware that the ratio does not actually measure the proportion of the economy's output that is absorbed or consumed by government. Total government expenditure includes a number of items, such as transfer payments to persons and public debt interest, that have no counterpart in GNP. Thus the ratio of government expenditure to GNP provides only a rough indication of growth in government spending in relation to growth of the economy.

Table 7-21 starts with this overall indicator of the size of government. Figures for the years shown, 1926 (a pre-Depression year and the first year for which National Accounts data are available), 1950, 1960, 1970, and 1980, allow identification of the general trends. They do not, however, mark certain interesting turning points, such as the virtual cessation in growth of the relative size of government from 1975 until 1981. A subsequent further increase in the relative size of government is mainly the result of the recent recession, which has led to an increase in Unemployment Insurance and welfare expenditure and reduced GNP growth.

Government expenditure as a percentage of GNP was somewhat higher in 1950, after the post-war adjustment period, than it had been immediately before the Depression. It grew rapidly between 1950 and 1975. This growth was not concentrated in any one of the major areas of expenditure. Table 7-21 also presents a number of indicators that are, in some respects, more

TABLE 7-21 Relative Size of Government

	(national accounts basis)				
	1926	**1950**	**1960**	**1970**	**1980**
Expenditures of total government sector as share of GNP[a]	15.7	22.1	29.7	36.4	41.8
Government current expenditure on goods and services as % of consumer plus government current expenditures on goods and services	10.0	13.4	17.2	24.8	25.9
Government fixed capital formation as % of total fixed capital formation	13.0	13.5	18.4	17.6	12.0
Government transfer payments to persons as % of total personal income	1.8	7.2	10.4	10.5	12.6
Government wages and salaries as % of total wages & salaries[b]	10.1	11.7	16.0	22.9	24.2

Sources: Statistics Canada, *Historical Statistical Compendium*, prepared for the Royal Commission on the Economic Union and Development Prospects for Canada (Ottawa: Statistics Canada, 1985), Tables 2.1, 2.16, 2.9 and 5.2; and *National Income and Expenditure Accounts*, vol. 1, Cat. No. 13-531 (Ottawa: Minister of Supply and Services Canada, 1984).

a. Net of intergovernmental transfers.

b. Wages, salaries and supplementary labour income (including military pay and allowances).

meaningful than the expenditure-to-GNP ratio. We shall review these indicators in conjunction with the information on government expenditure by type and function provided in Tables 7-22 and 7-23.

TABLE 7-22 Government Expenditures by Type and Budget Balances

National Accounts Categories (% of GNP)	(national accounts basis) 1926	1950	1960	1970	1980
Total government sector					
Current goods and services and capital formation	9.6	13.1	17.7	23.1	22.9
Transfers to persons	1.4	5.5	8.1	8.2	10.3
Subsidies and capital assistance	—	0.4	0.9	1.0	2.8
Transfers to non-residents	0.1	0.1	0.2	0.3	0.3
Interest on the public debt	4.5	2.9	2.8	3.8	5.6
Total	15.7	22.1	29.7	36.4	41.9
For reference: surplus or deficit	1.1	3.0	−1.7	0.9	−2.5
Federal government sector					
Current goods and services and capital formation	2.5	5.4	6.9	5.9	5.0
Transfers to persons	0.8	3.3	5.1	4.7	5.6
Subsidies and capital assistance	—	0.3	0.8	0.8	2.1
Transfers to non-residents	0.1	0.1	0.2	0.3	0.3
Interest on the public debt	2.5	2.3	2.0	2.2	3.3
Transfers to provincial/local governments	0.3	1.4	2.6	4.0	4.3
Total	6.2	12.8	17.6	17.8	20.6
For reference: surplus or deficit	1.3	3.5	−0.6	0.3	−3.3
Provincial, local and hospital sectors					
Current goods and services and capital formation	7.2	7.7	10.8	17.2	17.9
Transfers to persons	0.7	2.2	2.9	3.3	3.9
Subsidies and capital assistance	–	0.1	0.1	0.2	0.7
Interest on the public debt	2.0	0.6	0.9	1.6	2.3
Total	9.8	10.6	14.7	22.4	24.8
For reference: surplus or deficit	−0.2	−0.5	−1.2	−0.8	−0.1
CPP/QPP sector					
Transfers to persons	—	—	—	0.1	0.7
Total	—	—	—	0.2	0.7
For reference: surplus or deficit	—	—	—	1.4	1.0

Sources: Statistics Canada, *National Income and Expenditure Accounts 1926–1974*, vol. 1, Cat. No. 13-531 (Ottawa: Minister of Supply and Services Canada, 1976); and Finance Canada, *Economic Review, April 1984* (Ottawa: Minister of Supply and Services Canada, 1984).

Note: The inclusion of the hospital sector as part of the government sector after 1961 gives rise to some non-compatibility. In 1950 and 1960, provincial and local transfers to hospitals, equal respectively to 0.5 per cent and 1.3 per cent of GNP, were included in transfers to persons. From 1961 on, total operating expenditures by hospitals were included in government (provincial-local-hospital) expenditures on current goods and services.

TABLE 7-23 **Government Expenditures by Function**

Functional Categories	1937	1950	1960	1970	1980
	(based on financial management accounting system)				
	(as % of GNP)				
Consolidated government sector					
General government	n.a.	1.3	1.4	2.3	3.1
National Defence	0.6	3.3	4.0	2.0	1.7
Other protection of persons and property	n.a.	0.4	1.2	1.6	1.8
Health	0.8	1.3	2.2	5.0	5.0
Social Welfare	4.7	5.0	6.1	6.8	9.7
Education	2.2	2.4	4.1	7.0	6.2
Transportation & Communications	3.1	2.6	3.8	3.7	3.7
Foreign Affairs (including aid)	—	0.1	0.2	0.3	0.4
Debt charges	6.1	3.1	2.8	3.1	4.7
Other	n.a.	3.9	4.1	4.9	7.8
Total	22.7	23.3	29.9	36.7	44.0
Federal sector					
General government	0.7	1.1	0.7	1.2	1.2
National Defence	0.6	3.3	4.0	2.0	1.7
Other protection of persons and property	0.2	0.2	0.2	0.4	0.5
Health	—	0.2	0.7	1.5	1.5
Social Welfare	2.4	4.1	5.3	5.2	7.3
Education	0.1	0.1	0.2	1.0	0.8
Transportation & Communications	0.6	0.6	1.0	1.2	1.4
Foreign Affairs (including aid)	—	0.1	0.2	0.3	0.4
Debt charges	3.4	2.4	2.1	1.4	2.5
Unconditional transfers to other levels	0.4	0.7	1.5	1.5	1.5
Other	1.5	2.4	2.4	2.5	4.2
Total	10.1	15.1	18.3	18.4	22.9
Consolidated provincial-local sector					
General government	n.a.	n.a.	0.7	1.2	1.9
Other protection of persons and property	n.a.	n.a.	1.0	1.3	1.4
Health	0.8	1.2	2.1	4.8	4.9
Social Welfare	2.9	1.4	1.0	2.0	3.2
Education	2.2	2.3	3.8	6.8	6.1
Transportation & Communications	2.5	1.9	2.9	2.7	2.3
Debt charges	2.7	0.6	0.8	1.6	2.2
Other	n.a.	2.0	1.7	2.7	3.8
Total	13.8	9.5	14.0	23.0	25.7

Source: Statistics Canada data on Gross General Expenditures for 1970 and 1980, and on Net General Expenditures for 1937, 1950, and 1960. The latter figures have been adjusted by Commission staff to provide approximate historical comparability.

Note: Federal sector and consolidated provincial-local sector do not add to total, as federal transfers to provinces are included with federal, but not netted out of provincial-local. Consolidated total government-sector data are net of all intergovernmental transfers.

Total expenditures on the financial management-system basis are slightly higher than on the national accounts system basis used in most other tables. (Certain tax credits are counted as expenditures under the financial management system, but serve to reduce tax revenues under the national accounts system).

The ratio of government expenditures on current goods and services, termed "government-operating expenditures", to the sum of consumer expenditures, plus these government expenditures (total consumption in the economy) was slightly higher in 1950 than it had been in 1926, largely because defence expenditures were higher. The ratio rose substantially from 1950 to 1960, reflecting growth in most categories of government operations, but particularly in education. It increased again in the 1960s, in spite of a decline in defence expenditures relative to GNP, largely because of further growth in education expenditures and the government's adoption of major new roles in the hospital and Medicare areas. Government consumption showed only modest further growth relative to total consumption in the 1970s.

Government capital spending has actually been lower in the last few years, relative to total capital spending in the economy, than it was immediately before the Depression. From the mid-1950s to the mid-1970s, however, the period of major government investment in highways, schools and hospitals, it, too, stood at much higher levels.

The fraction of total personal income provided by government-transfer payments to persons, through programs such as the Old Age Security (OAS), Guaranteed Income Supplement (GIS), Unemployment Insurance (UI), Family Allowance, and welfare payments, has increased in each post-war decade, though it, too, levelled off between 1975 and 1981, before increasing again during the recent recession. The upward trend reflected the successive introduction of major new programs: Unemployment Insurance in 1942, Family Allowances in 1945, old-age pensions in 1952, the Canada/Quebec Pension Plans (CPP/QPP) in 1967, and the Guaranteed Income Supplement (GIS). It also reflected the enrichment of some programs in real terms, notably the changes in the UI system that took effect in 1972, the gradual growth in the proportion of retired persons eligible for full rates of CPP/QPP benefits, and the liberalization of provincial/municipal welfare systems, especially from the mid-1960s onward.

Finally, Table 7-21 shows that the proportion of total wages and salaries originating in the government sector was somewhat higher in 1950 than it had been in 1926. That proportion increased sharply between 1950 and 1960, reflecting the general growth in government operations, especially in education; it increased again, after 1961, when hospitals came to be treated as part of the government sector. By 1980, government employment provided about one-quarter of total wages in the economy. Government wages do not include wages in the post-secondary education sector or doctors' fees: these payments are treated respectively as transfers to non-profit institutions and purchases of services. The provincial, local and hospital sectors accounted for some 80 per cent of total wage payments by government in 1980.

Other categories of expenditures, which cannot be readily related to particular bases, have also increased relative to the size of the economy. (See Table 7-23.) Subsidies and capital assistance increased moderately relative to GNP until the 1970s, when expenditure in this category ballooned, especially with the introduction of the oil-import subsidy program. Growth in foreign aid is reflected in growth in transfers to non-residents.

The cost of interest on the public debt fell relative to the size of the economy from the end of the Second World War to the 1960s, reflecting the decline in debt relative to GNP during a period of stable interest rates. Debt interest then increased because of the rising trend of interest rates and, after 1975, the rising ratio of federal debt to GNP. The interpretation of debt costs is clouded, however, during an inflationary period. While inflation tends to cause high nominal interest rates and thus an escalation of interest charges, it also erodes the real value of the existing debt stock. The standard government and national accounts allow only for the first effect. "Inflation-adjusted" debt costs would show substantially less increase, relative to the size of the economy, over the last two decades.

Table 7-24 ranks the three orders of government by their shares of total government spending. If inter-governmental transfers are counted as part of the expenditure of the government making the transfer, the post-war growth of government expenditure, relative to the economy, has been most rapid for the provincial order and least rapid for the local order. If intergovernmental transfers are not included as part of the expenditures of the government providing the transfer, the provincial sector still shows the most growth, but it is now followed by the local sector, rather than by the federal government.

TABLE 7-24 Shares of Total Government Spending by Order of Government

	(national accounts basis)				
	1926	**1950**	**1960**	**1970**	**1980**
Before intergovernmental transfers[a]					
Federal	39.6	58.1	59.3	49.0	49.1
Provincial-hospital	20.5	23.8	22.4	34.8	37.8
Local	39.9	18.2	18.3	15.8	10.9
CPP/QPP	—	—	—	0.4	2.1
Total	100.0	100.0	100.0	100.0	100.0
After intergovernmental transfers[b]					
Federal	37.8	51.9	50.5	38.1	38.8
Provincial-hospital[c]	20.2	26.0	24.8	35.7	39.1
Local	42.0	22.1	24.7	25.8	20.0
CPP/QPP	—	—	—	0.4	2.1
Total	100.0	100.0	100.0	100.0	100.0

Source: Statistics Canada, National Income and Expenditure Accounts 1926–1974, Vol. 1 Cat. No. 13-531 (Ottawa: Minister of Supply and Services Canada, 1976); and Finance Canada, *Economic Review*, April 1984 (Ottawa: Minister of Supply and Services Canada, 1984).

a. Expenditures net of intergovernmental transfers received.
b. Expenditures net of intergovernmental transfers paid to other levels.
c. Includes the "hospital" sector, starting in 1961.

The changes in the shares of the various orders of government shown in Table 7-24 reflect the pattern of relative growth in the different functions of government. Health and education, two important functions that have experienced rapid growth over the post-war period as a whole, are carried out by the provincial or the provincial-local orders. While spending on one important federal function, that of defence, has declined quite substantially, on balance, since 1950, spending on most other federal functions has increased relative to the size of the economy. Federal transfers to the provinces have increased substantially since 1950. This generalization applies both to federal transfers that finance a portion of health, education and welfare expenditures in all provinces, and to transfers under the equalization program, which provides unconditional financial support to provinces with less-than-average fiscal capacity.

Tables 7-25 and 7-26 show expenditure and revenue-growth rates for the federal government and selected provincial governments during selected periods from 1962 to 1982. While there was a major increase in the provincial share of total government expenditures during the 1960s and the early 1970s, and a corresponding decline in the federal share, there was little further change after 1976. Indeed, since 1976, both orders of government have exercised a significant degree of restraint.

Table 7-27 looks at the growth of public sector employment, one direct indicator of the growth of "bureaucracy". Again growth was considerably greater at the provincial level until the mid-1970s. Federal employment as a percentage of the labour force declined over the entire two decades, and total government employment stayed relatively constant.

TABLE 7-25 Expenditure Growth Rates of Government for Selected Intervals, 1962–82: Constant Dollar Terms

	(average annual per cent increase[a])		
	1962–68	1969–75	1976–82
Federal	3.5	6.7	2.0
Alberta	8.5	9.0	8.3
British Columbia	5.8	11.5	3.3
Nova Scotia	8.1	7.4	3.9
Ontario	10.2	9.2	0.0
Quebec	13.0	8.5	3.4

Source: Allan M. Maslove, Michael J. Prince, and G. Bruce Doern, *Federal and Provincial Budgeting*, vol. 41, prepared for the Royal Commission on the Economic Union and Development Prospects for Canada (Toronto: University of Toronto Press, 1985). Calculated from Tables A-4, A-6, A-7, A-10, A-11, A-14, and A-24 in the Appendix.

a. Averages are calculated on the basis of the annual percentage change of gross general expenditure in constant dollars (1971) for each government in each of the interval periods.

TABLE 7-26 Revenue Growth Rates of Governments for Selected Intervals, 1969–82: Constant Dollar Terms

	1969–75	1976–82
	(average annual per cent increase[a])	
Federal	8.3	0.4
Alberta	16.8	7.3
British Columbia	11.0	3.3
Nova Scotia	8.1	1.2
Ontario	8.9	0.0
Quebec	10.3	2.1

Source: Allan M. Maslove, Michael J. Prince, and G. Bruce Doern, *Federal and Provincial Budgeting*, vol. 41, prepared for the Royal Commission on the Economic Union and Development Prospects for Canada (Toronto: University of Toronto Press, 1985). See Tables A-30, A-32, A-33, A-36, A-37 and A-40. We cannot include the 1962–68 interval, as in Table 7-27, because data on total provincial revenue from own sources is not available for years before 1967.

a. Averages are calculated on the basis of the annual percent change of total revenue from own sources in constant dollars for the provincial governments and the gross general revenue in constant dollars for the federal government.

TABLE 7-27 Total Government Employment

	1960	% LF	1965	% LF	1970	% LF	1975	% LF	1980	% LF	1982	% LF
Labour force (000s)	6 430	–	7 185	–	8 329	–	9 923	–	11 522	–	11 743	–
Federal												
General[a]	203 013	3.2	211 913	3.0	251 237	3.0	323 902	3.3	335 375	2.9	351 295	3.0
Enterprise	131 118	2.0	129 916	1.8	123 906	1.5	132 046	1.3	157 988	1.4	138 281	1.2
Total	334 131	5.2	341 829	4.8	375 143	4.5	455 948	4.6	493 363	4.3	489 576	4.2
Provincial												
General[b]	139 434	2.2	168 536	2.3	216 475	2.6	288 937	2.9	311 634	2.7	317 407	2.7
Enterprise	63 444	1.0	70 281	1.0	95 520	1.1	134 513	1.4	148 105	1.3	159 260	1.4
Total	202 878	3.2	238 817	3.3	311 995	3.7	423 450	4.3	459 739	4.0	476 667	4.1
Local[c]												
General	149 403	2.3	162 901	2.3	201 425	2.4	247 199	2.5	274 126	2.4	287 103	2.4
Enterprise	23 718	0.4	25 860	-0.4	31 976	0.4	39 242	0.4	43 517	0.4	45 577	0.4
Total	173 121	2.7	188 761	2.7	233 401	2.8	286 441	2.9	317 643	2.8	332 680	2.8
Total government												
General	491 850	7.6	543 350	7.6	669 137	8.0	860 038	8.7	921 135	8.0	955 805	8.1
Enterprise	218 280	3.4	226 057	3.2	251 402	3.0	305 801	3.1	349 610	3.0	343 118	2.9
Total	710 130	11.0	769 407	10.8	920 539	11.0	1 165 839	11.8	1 270 745	11.0	1 298 923	11.0

Education sector												
Teaching[d]	160 800	2.5	211 463	2.9	291 624	3.5	313 341	3.1	328 975	2.9	314 201	2.7
Non-teaching[e]	99 696	1.6	131 107	1.8	180 807	2.2	194 271	2.0	203 965	1.8	194 805	1.7
Total	260 496	4.1	342 570	4.7	472 431	5.7	507 612	5.1	532 940	4.7	509 006	4.4
Hospital sector[f]	183 189	2.8	251 511	3.5	319 826	3.8	339 517	3.4	299 388	2.6	297 195	2.5
Grand total	1 153 815	17.9	1 363 488	19.0	1 712 796	20.5	2 012 968	20.3	2 103 073	18.3	2 105 124	17.9

Source: Sharon L. Sutherland and G. Bruce Doern, *Bureaucracy in Canada: Control and Reform*, vol. 43, prepared for the Royal Commission on the Economic Union and Development Prospects for Canada (Toronto: University of Toronto Press, 1985), Table 3.26.

Note: LF = labour force.

a. Excludes federal hospital-care workers. They are included in the hospital-sector totals.
b. Excludes provincial hospital-care workers. They are included in the hospital-sector totals.
c. Local general employment totals for 1960 and 1965 are estimated. Local enterprise totals are estimated for 1960–82.
d. Figures for 1960 and 1965 do not include community-college teachers.
e. Non-teaching personnel are estimated for 1960–82.
f. The 1979–80 hospital statistics were used for 1980 total. The 1980–81 statistics were used as estimates for 1982 total.

Notes

1. A research study undertaken for this Commission by John Helliwell of the University of British Columbia provides an important exception to this view. See John Helliwell, Mary E. MacGregor, and Tim Padmore, "Economic Growth and Productivity in Canada: 1955 to 1990", in *Economic Growth: Prospects and Determinants*, vol. 22 (Toronto: University of Toronto Press, 1985). Helliwell's analysis, in the Commission study and elsewhere, suggests that the bulk of the post-1973 slow-down in productivity growth can be attributed to weaker cyclical conditions and the energy-price increase. Thus Helliwell sees little basis for the implication that the "underlying" rate of productivity growth decreased after 1973.
2. A fuller discussion of historical and projected demographic trends may be found in this Commission's research study by Douglas S. Green, Judith Gold, and John Sargent, "A Note on Demographic Projections for Canada: Review and Implications", in *Economic Growth: Prospects and Determinants*, vol. 22 (Toronto: University of Toronto Press, 1985).
3. Roughly speaking, the civilian, non-institutional population 15 years of age and over, excluding inhabitants of the Territories and of Indian Reserves, who are not covered by the Labour Force Survey.
4. Roughly speaking, those who work or seek to work.
5. The slight increase in the investment-to-GNE ratio during the latter period is not inconsistent with the slight decrease in the growth rate of the capital stock between these two periods shown in Table 7-16. The larger the initial level of the capital stock relative to GNE, the higher is the ratio of investment to GNE required just to offset depreciation, and the higher is the ratio of net investment to GNE required to maintain a constant growth rate of the capital stock.
6. The savings of the non-resident sector include all forms of investment in Canada, such as non-residents' purchases of bonds, as well as direct investment.
7. Edward F. Denison, *Accounting for Slower Economic Growth: The United States in the 1970s* (Washington, D.C.: Brookings Institution, 1979), and earlier studies.
8. Our analysis of the impact of cyclical factors on labour productivity and total factor productivity depends on our particular assumptions about the extent of the cyclical shortfall in output in 1981. The estimates we use are based on those made by the Department of Finance for purposes of its cyclically adjusted, budget-balance calculations. We believe that they are in the range which would be considered reasonable by a majority of analysts. However, some students of the productivity slow-down, notably John Helliwell of the University of British Columbia, argue that the cyclical shortfall of output in 1981 is much larger than we have assumed and, correspondingly, that the slow-down in cyclically adjusted productivity after 1973 is much less than that shown in our estimates. Hence, as we mentioned in note 1, Helliwell sees little or nothing puzzling about the post-1973 decline in productivity growth.

Business Cycles

Since the Second World War, there have been nine distinct economic growth cycles of varying duration and intensity, including the most recent recession and the ongoing recovery. A growth cycle differs from the classical cycle of ups and downs in the level of activity in that it represents deviations in real economic activity from longer-term trends. A "peak" is thus defined as the maximum deviation above the long-term/growth path and a "trough" as the maximum deviation below. Table 7-28 presents some key data on the post-war growth cycles.

The period from 1947 to early 1953, when the economy converted from a wartime to a peacetime footing, was one of strong and sustained expansion. It was followed by the sharp recession of 1953–54. The brief but vigorous expansion that began in the third quarter of 1954 and ended in the fourth quarter of 1956 was driven primarily by an investment boom. The subsequent recession, which lasted until the third quarter of 1958, was moderate.

TABLE 7-28 Summary of post-War Canadian Growth Cycles

			(change between turning points)		
			Real GNE		
Phase	Date	Duration in Quarters	Cumulative	Average Quarterly	Unemployment Rate
Expansion	1947Q4–53Q2	23	39.1	1.4	—
Contraction	1953Q2–54Q3	5	–1.2	–0.2	2.5
Expansion	1954Q3–56Q4	9	21.5	2.2	–2.1
Contraction	1956Q4–58Q3	7	2.6	0.4	4.3
Expansion	1958Q3–59Q3	4	4.1	1.0	–1.8
Contraction	1959Q3–61Q1	6	1.4	0.2	2.0
Expansion	1961Q1–66Q2	21	41.6	1.7	–4.5
Contraction	1966Q2–68Q1	7	6.0	0.8	1.3
Expansion	1968Q1–69Q1	4	7.9	1.9	–0.2
Contraction	1969Q1–70Q4	7	3.7	0.5	1.8
Expansion	1970Q1–74Q4	13	26.4	1.8	0.9
Contraction	1974Q1–75Q3	6	1.2	0.2	1.8
Expansion	1975Q3–76Q2	3	6.1	2.0	0.0
Contraction	1976Q2–77Q3	5	1.7	0.3	1.3
Expansion	1977Q3–79Q3	8	7.0	0.8	–1.1
Contraction	1979Q3–80Q3	4	0.1	0.0	0.3
Expansion	1980Q3–81Q2	3	4.9	1.6	–0.3
Contraction	1981Q2–82Q4	6	–6.6	–1.1	5.6
Average					
Expansion		9.8	17.6	1.6	–1.4
Contraction		5.9	1.0	0.1	2.3

Source: Calculations by the Commission from National Accounts data.

Note: The dating of growth cycles, except for the 1947Q4 to 1953Q2 expansion, follows the dating in *Royal Bank Trendicator Report* (December 1982).

However, it was not followed by a vigorous recovery, partly, at least, because of the relatively restrictive stance of Canadian monetary policy.

A long and buoyant expansion began in the first quarter of 1961 and continued through the 1960s, with a minor interruption in 1966 and 1967. A mild slow-down in 1969–70 yielded to a period of strong expansion that continued until the first quarter of 1974, when the sharp worldwide recession of 1974–75 took hold in response to the quadrupling of the international price of oil. The recovery from this recession was interrupted by a period of cyclical weakness in 1976 and 1977. Recovery resumed in 1977 and carried on into 1979.

While the brief recession of 1979–80 was relatively mild, the recession of 1981–82 was by far the deepest of the post-war period. Both recessions followed dramatic increases in interest rates. In the earlier of the two, the interest-rate run-up was quickly reversed. The increase in interest rates that triggered the latter recession persisted for an extended period.

Overall, the average expansion lasted about 10 quarters and the average downturn about six quarters. During expansions, the average cumulative increase in real gross national expenditure was 17.6 per cent, or 1.6 per cent per quarter. During contractions, the average cumulative increase fell to 1.0 per cent, or only just above zero per quarter.

The unemployment rate declined by an average of 1.4 percentage points during expansions and rose by 2.3 percentage points during contractions. A troubling feature of the cycles since 1966 has been the small decline in the unemployment rate during expansions and the much larger increases in the unemployment rate during contractions. While a certain proportion of this overall rise in the unemployment rate can be attributed to structural factors, such as the changing age-sex composition of the labour force and the adverse effects on the incentive to work of more generous Unemployment Insurance benefits, a significant share must be attributed to the unsatisfactory cyclical position of the Canadian economy.

The Recent Recession

In order to make a clearer identification of longer-term trends in the economy, our review to this point has excluded the impact of the severe economic downturn that started in the second half of 1981. However, the recent recession has also had an important influence on perceptions about the principal economic issues facing Canada. As we have noted, the 1981–82 downturn was by far the most severe recession Canadians have experienced since the Second World War. Real gross national expenditure (GNE) fell by 4.2 per cent between 1981 and 1982; the only other post-war instance of an absolute decline in output, on an annual basis, occurred in 1954, when real GNE fell by 1.2 per cent during the recession that followed the Korean War. The unemployment rate rose from an annual average of 7.5 per cent in 1981 to 11.9 per cent in 1983, an increase of 4.4 percentage points. This rise compares with an increase of 1.6 percentage points between 1953 and 1954, of 3.7 percentage points between 1969 and 1971, and of 3.1 percentage points between 1974 and 1978.

Furthermore, the recession was much more severe in Canada than it was in the United States, where real GNE fell by only about 2 per cent between 1981 and 1982, and the unemployment rate rose by 2 percentage points. Most of the earlier post-war recessions were milder in Canada than they were in the United States. While other member countries of the Organisation for Economic Co-operation and Development (OECD) also experienced a less-severe annual decline in real output over the 1979–83 period, taken as a whole, than did Canada, the cumulative decline in the United Kingdom over 1980 and 1981 approached the extent of the 1982 decline in Canada. Many Western European countries experienced as large, or larger, increases in unemployment over the 1979–83 period. In fact, some of the smaller European countries, notably Belgium and the Netherlands, now have unemployment rates well above Canadian levels, whereas their rates were, on average, well below Canadian levels throughout the 1960s and 1970s. During and after the recession, inflation fell sharply in the United States, the United Kingdom, and Canada, and declined somewhat from lower initial levels in Germany and Japan. France and Italy have made comparatively less progress to date in bringing down inflation.

While a full analysis of the reasons for the greater severity of the recession in Canada is beyond the scope of this review, a number of the more important reasons should be mentioned. There was a sharp tightening of monetary policy and some tightening of fiscal policy after 1979, in both Canada and the United States. Canada, however, appears to have experienced a stronger inflationary boom in late 1980 and early 1981 than did the United States; this boom became apparent in a speculative rise in housing prices in a number of Canadian cities, in a wave of business take-overs in Canada, and in a greater build-up of inventories in Canada than in the United States. Thus the Canadian economy had further to fall when monetary curbs finally took hold. The overextension of certain sectors added to the severity of the adjustment. Prices and wages did not respond as quickly in Canada as they did in the United States to the increased slack in the economy, with the result that the restraint did more initially to reduce real output. In part, the smaller initial decline in Canada's inflation reflected the unfortunate coincidence that the delayed rise in energy prices in Canada was concentrated in the recession and immediate pre-recession periods. The slower decline may also indicate that prices and wages are inherently less flexible in Canada than they are in the United States. In any event, rates of price and wage increase in Canada have now declined very sharply.

The severity of the recession, coupled with the projection by most analysts of only a gradual decline in unemployment from the current high levels, has made unemployment Canada's single most important, public economic concern. Canadians fear that employment in a number of industries will not return to pre-recession levels, and that the "shake-out" forced on these industries will result in future loss of jobs, thus further slowing any return to high employment. At this early stage, it is still very difficult to distinguish the effects of the recession from more fundamental changes. So far there is little hard evidence of any increase in the pace of technological change and job displacement for the economy as a whole. If anything, the slow-down in productivity growth over the past decade has tended to retard job displacement.

The International Economic Environment and International Comparisons

As we have noted in Chapter 2, most developed market economies have experienced the same broad trends during the post-war period as those we have outlined for Canada: relatively rapid real growth of output and productivity, on average, until 1973, followed by a slow-down; higher unemployment and inflation rates over the last decade; a decline in the relative importance of the agricultural sector and an increase in the importance of the service sector; and an increase in the openness of the economy, as measured by the ratio of international trade to gross national product (GNP).

Table 7-29 shows the ratios of trade to GNP for 19 OECD countries. Openness has increased less in Canada since the pre-war era than in most other countries because Canada's ratio of trade to GNP was already high before the war. Canada is one of the more open, larger economies, although the Federal Republic of Germany, Italy and the United Kingdom now have similar ratios of trade to GNP. The ratios of several of the smaller European countries, especially those that belong to the European Community, are substantially higher than Canada's. Nonetheless, Canada may be considerably more vulnerable to international developments than the countries mentioned above, since it is unique among Western industrialized nations (except for Australia) in not having secure access to a market of 100 million people or more.

The international trends are of interest both because they exert major influences on the Canadian economy, and because they provide an international perspective on Canadian performance. The relatively rapid growth in the economies of Canada's trading partners before 1973 was critical to our favourable economic performance over that period. The slower world growth served to lower Canada's growth possibilities. Although our flexible exchange rate precluded any direct link between Canadian inflation and foreign inflation, it is clear that an increasingly inflationary world environment and, particularly, the international oil-price shocks added to the inflationary pressures in Canada.

Table 7-30 shows changes in the main economic indicators for Canada, the other six largest Western industrialized countries, and the OECD as a whole over the periods 1960–68, 1968–73, and 1973–79; it also provides annual data for the years from 1980 to 1984. In the years preceding 1973, Canada's real growth was above both the average for the seven largest OECD countries and the average for the OECD as a whole. Our growth in employment was the highest of all OECD nations, and our productivity growth, while somewhat below the OECD average, compared favourably with that of the United States. Canadian unemployment rates were higher than those in most OECD countries, but similar, on average, to U.S. rates. Inflation tended to be lower

TABLE 7-29 International Comparisons of Foreign Trade in Goods and Services as a Percentage of GNP in 19 OECD Countries, 1929, 1938, and 1976–78[a]

	1929	1938	Avg. 1976-78
Australia[b]	19.3	18.3	17.1
Austria	N.A.	17.6[c]	35.6
Belgium	N.A.	28.2	56.3
Canada	29.0	24.3	26.4
Denmark	N.A.	26.2	33.5
France	N.A.	13.1	21.9
Germany	N.A.	16.5[d]	26.3
Greece	N.A.	17.8	21.2
Iceland	N.A.	46.8	42.1
Ireland	N.A.	25.5	57.7
Italy	N.A.	7.6	26.8
Japan	19.4	19.7	12.3
Netherlands	N.A.	28.1	49.0
Norway	33.6	29.2[e]	48.6
Portugal	N.A.	13.0	26.6
Sweden	N.A.	20.1[f]	30.2
Switzerland	N.A.	17.9	35.9
United Kingdom	N.A.	16.9	32.2
United States	6.3	4.3	10.1
All countries[g]	N.A.	20.6	32.1

Source: United States, Congress, Joint Economic Committee, *The Business Cycle and Public Policy, 1929–80* (Washington, D.C.: U.S. Government Printing Office, 1980) p. 83.

Note: N.A. = not available.

a. Percentages are based on data in current prices. Trade is defined as one-half of the sum of exports and imports of goods and services, including merchandise, non-monetary gold, freight, other transportation, travel, investment income in gross amounts received and paid, and other current public and private services.
b. Fiscal years ending June 30.
c. 1937.
d. 1936.
e. 1939.
f. Based on GNP for fiscal year.
g. Unweighted averages of percentages for all countries.

in Canada and the United States than in the other OECD countries. There was virtually universal increase in inflation between the 1960–68 and 1968–73 periods, and there was a notable decline in productivity growth in the United States between these two periods.

As we have remarked, economic performance throughout the world tended to deteriorate after 1973. While Canada maintained high employment growth in relative terms – a circumstance that reflected our high labour-force growth – our productivity performance declined slightly more than the average. If 1980 and 1981 are added to the 1973–79 period, productivity growth in Canada actually fell below the U.S. average.

TABLE 7-30 International Comparisons: Main Economic Indicators

	1960–1968	1968–1973	1973–1979	1980	1981	1982	1983	1984
		(annual average)						
Growth in real GNE/GDP								
United States	4.5	3.3	2.6	−0.2	2.5	−2.1	3.7	6.8
Japan	10.5	8.8	3.6	4.9	4.0	3.3	3.0	5.8
Germany	4.2	4.9	2.4	1.8	−0.2	−1.1	1.3	2.5
France	5.4	5.9	3.1	1.1	0.2	2.0	0.7	1.8
United Kingdom	3.1	3.1	1.4	−2.6	−1.5	2.5	3.2	2.0
Italy	5.7	4.6	2.6	3.9	0.1	−0.4	−1.2	3.0
Canada	5.6	5.6	3.4	1.0	3.3	−4.4	3.3	4.3
Total OECD	5.1	4.8	2.7	1.3	1.7	−0.3	2.6	4.8
Growth in productivity[a]								
United States	2.6	1.2	0.2	−0.7	1.4	−1.3	2.4	2.5
Japan	8.9	7.7	2.9	3.9	3.2	2.2	1.3	5.3
Germany	4.3	4.1	3.0	0.8	0.6	0.7	3.1	3.0
France	4.9	4.8	2.9	1.1	1.0	1.8	1.5	2.8
United Kingdom	2.7	3.0	1.2	−2.4	2.0	4.1	3.6	1.0
Italy	6.3	4.9	1.6	2.4	−0.3	0.0	−1.3	3.0
Canada	2.7	2.7	0.5	−1.9	0.5	−1.2	2.5	2.0
Total OECD	4.1	3.5	1.6	0.6	1.4	0.2	2.2	3.3
Employment growth								
United States	1.8	2.1	2.5	0.5	1.1	−0.9	1.3	4.3
Japan	1.5	0.9	0.7	1.0	0.8	1.0	1.7	0.5
Germany	−0.1	0.7	−0.6	1.0	−0.8	−1.8	−1.7	−0.3
France	0.4	1.0	0.2	—	−0.8	0.1	−0.8	−1.0
United Kingdom	0.3	0.2	0.2	−0.3	−3.4	−1.5	−0.4	1.0

Italy	−0.6	−0.2	1.0	1.5	0.5	−0.4	0.1	0.0
Canada	2.8	2.8	2.9	3.0	2.8	−3.3	0.8	2.3
Total OECD	1.0	1.2	1.1	0.7	0.4	−0.5	0.4	1.5
Standardized unemployment rates[b]								
United States	5.0	4.6	6.7	7.0	7.6	9.7	9.6	7.5
Japan	1.2	1.2	1.9	2.0	2.2	2.4	2.6	2.7
Germany	0.6	1.0	3.2	3.0	4.4	6.1	8.0	8.1
France	1.7	2.5	4.5	6.3	7.3	8.0	8.0	8.9
United Kingdom	2.5	3.5	5.3	6.9	10.6	12.3	13.1	13.2
Italy	5.1	5.7	6.5	7.4	8.3	8.9	9.7	10.6
Canada	4.8	5.4	7.2	7.5	7.5	11.1	11.9	11.5
Total OECD	2.7	3.2	4.9	5.8	6.7	8.2	8.7	8.3
Consumer price inflation								
United States	2.0	5.0	8.5	13.5	10.4	6.1	3.2	4.2
Japan	5.7	7.0	10.0	8.0	4.9	2.7	1.9	2.3
Germany	2.7	4.6	4.7	5.5	6.3	5.3	3.3	1.5
France	3.6	6.1	10.7	13.6	13.4	11.8	9.6	7.1
United Kingdom	3.6	7.5	15.6	18.0	11.9	8.6	4.6	4.7
Italy	4.0	5.8	16.1	21.2	17.8	16.6	14.6	9.9
Canada	2.4	4.6	9.2	10.2	12.5	10.8	5.9	3.8
Total OECD	2.9	5.6	10.0	12.9	10.5	7.8	5.3	5.0
Total government expenditures as a percentage of GNP/GDP[c]								
United States	28.8	31.7	33.7	35.0	35.3	37.6	—	—
Japan	19.0	20.4	28.5	32.4	34.5	34.5	—	—
Germany	35.8	39.8	47.5	48.3	49.3	49.4	—	—
France	37.4	39.0	43.7	46.4	49.2	50.7	—	—
United Kingdom	34.8	39.8	44.6	45.4	48.0	47.4	—	—
Italy	31.9	36.0	42.9	46.1	51.2	53.7	—	—
Canada	29.8	35.3	39.7	41.0	41.5	45.8	—	—
Total OECD	29.9	32.9	37.7	40.2	40.9	42.5	—	—

TABLE 7-30 (cont'd.)

	1960–1968	1968–1973	1973–1979	1980	1981	1982	1983	1984
		(annual average)						
Total government-budget balances as a percentage of GNP/GDP								
United States	—	—	—	–1.2	–0.9	–3.8	–4.1	–3.2
Japan	—	—	—	–4.5	–4.0	–3.4	–3.3	–2.2
Germany	—	—	—	–3.1	–3.8	–3.4	–2.7	–1.7
France	—	—	—	0.2	–1.8	–2.5	–3.4	–3.5
United Kingdom	—	—	—	–3.8	–3.1	–2.4	–3.3	–3.1
Italy	—	—	—	–8.0	–11.9	–12.7	–11.8	–13.5
Canada	—	—	—	–2.7	–1.6	–5.0	–6.2	–6.0
Total OECD	—	—	—	–2.4	–2.7	–4.1	–4.4	–3.8

Sources: Organisation for Economic Co-operation and Development, *Historical Statistics, 1960–81* (Paris: OECD, 1983), p. 41; *Historical Statistics, 1960–1982* (Paris: OECD, 1984), pp. 26, 39, 41, 44, 47, 64, 83; and *Economic Outlook, December 1984* (Paris: OECD, 1984), pp. 29, 43, 50, 51, 68, 173, 175, 177.

Note: Average growth rates are compound annual rates from level in year before first year of period specified to level in final year of period specified.

a. Productivity increased as real GNP/GDP per member of the civilian labour force.

b. Standardized unemployment rates for all but United States and Canada. United States and Canada are actual, which correspond closely to the OECD standardized concept. Figures for 1984 are estimates based on gap between actual and standardized unemployment rates in 1983. Average standardized unemployment rates are for 1960–67, rather than 1960–68.

c. Data are for 1960–67, rather than 1960–68.

The percentage rise in unemployment in Canada after 1973 was similar to that experienced elsewhere, as was the increase in the average rate of inflation. In both instances, however, there was some deterioration relative to the performance of the United States. The structural changes in our Canadian Unemployment Insurance system may explain most of the increase in our unemployment rate relative to that of the United States. Germany, Austria, the Netherlands and Switzerland managed to avoid much increase in the rate of inflation.

Comparisons with other OECD countries indicate that the economic problems experienced in Canada since 1973 have been widely shared. However, there is at least a hint of a tendency for Canadian performance to deteriorate relative to the OECD average, especially in the areas of productivity growth and inflation. This possible tendency is all the more disturbing because Canada's energy self-sufficiency meant that we were not as adversely affected by the energy shock as were most other OECD countries. On the other hand, our improvement in relative inflation performance in 1984 augurs well for the future.

Government expenditure as a proportion of GNP has risen somewhat more in Canada since 1973 than it has in the OECD countries considered as a group; the difference between the two ratios was especially great during the 1981–82 recession. The increase in Canada since 1973 has been much greater than the increase in the United States. The level of government spending in relation to GNP is higher in Canada than it is in the United States and Japan, but lower than it is in Germany, France, the United Kingdom and Italy.

Canada has experienced a marked increase in the total government deficit as a percentage of GNP. In 1984, our percentage was twice that of the United States. The only major industrialized country with a proportionately larger deficit in 1984 was Italy.

General Observations on Recent Performance

Over the post-Second World War period, Canada has adjusted to major structural changes in the economy. We have also enjoyed broadly distributed gains in economic welfare. One of the economy's most notable achievements has been its provision of a high rate of employment growth in the face of a high rate of growth in labour-force supply. While the economy has not created jobs for all new entrants to the labour force, until the recession struck in 1981, it had at least created jobs for the great majority. Few of the economic projections made in the late 1950s and early 1960s anticipated the extent to which employment (or the labour force) would grow in the 1960s and 1970s. Except for the "supply siders", who believe that supply creates its own demand, economists do not claim to have fully satisfactory empirical models of the process by which jobs are created and the relationship of that process to labour-force growth. We shall consider this issue further in Chapter 8.

Although economic progress during the post-war period has been impressive, and the economy has been successful in making major adjustments to changing conditions, a number of developments over the past decade have given rise to concern. If productivity growth were to stay at the low level of the past decade, Canadians could not look forward to any appreciable further gains in their standard of living. Inflation has proved to be very stubborn, confronting Canadians with the difficult choice between living with a relatively high rate of inflation, with all of its potential long-term social and economic dangers, and paying the heavy short- to medium-term costs of achieving lower inflation. Although the growth of employment in Canada during the post-war period has substantially exceeded that of most other industrial countries, our level of unemployment has generally been at the high end of the range of international experience. The introduction of restrictive monetary and fiscal policies in order to curtail inflation has driven unemployment even higher.

Recent developments have altered the emphasis that Canadians give to each of these concerns. Before the recession, most observers held that the most disturbing aspects of Canadian economic performance were the low rate of productivity growth and the stubbornness of inflation. Especially worrisome was the apparent deterioration in Canada's performance relative to the performances of the United States and many other countries. Nevertheless, productivity growth since 1981 has not been as low as might have been expected, given the severity of the recession, and a major reduction in inflation has occurred. On the other hand, unemployment has become an ever-more-pressing concern.

Overall Prospects for the Economy

Population Projections, 1981–2030

A good understanding of likely demographic developments is a necessary first step in forming a view about our Canadian economy's long-term prospects, though our demographic future is only somewhat less uncertain than our economic future. To provide an indication both of our demographic prospects and of the degree of uncertainty about these prospects, we shall consider four recent official Statistics Canada demographic projections for the period from 1981 to 2030. These projections differ in their assumptions about the fertility rate, the mortality rate, and net immigration. We shall also consider very long-run demographic projections to the year 2100, underlying the Statutory Actuarial Report No. 8 of the Canada Pension Plan.

The four Statistics Canada demographic projections are as follows:

- *A low-fertility,*[1] *low-immigration case.* It assumes that the fertility rate will decline to 1.4 by 1996, dropping from the 1981 level of 1.7, and that thereafter it will remain constant. Net immigration is set at 50 000 entrants per year throughout the projection period.
- *A medium-fertility, low-immigration case.* It assumes a fertility rate of 1.6 throughout the entire projection period and the same net immigration postulated in the first projection.
- *A medium-fertility, high-immigration case.* It uses the same fertility rate as the second projection and assumes that net immigration will increase

from 45 000 in 1983 to 100 000 in 1994 by increments of 5000; after 1994, immigration will remain constant.

- *A high-fertility, high-immigration case.* It assumes a fertility rate of 1.6 until 1985, increasing to 2.2 by 1996, and remaining constant thereafter; net immigration remains the same as it was in the third projection.

All the projections use the same mortality rate. They assume that the rate will decrease more slowly than it did between 1976 and 1981. They also assume that the difference between male and female life expectancy at birth will narrow slightly: life expectancy will rise by 1996 to 74.9 years for males (from 71.9 in 1981) and to 81.5 for females (from 78.9 in 1981).

The Canada Pension Plan (CPP) projection assumes that the fertility rate will increase to approximately 2.0 by 1999 and remain constant thereafter. It further assumes that net immigration throughout the entire projection period will equal 0.32 per cent of the total population, and that the mortality rate will decline moderately.

A cursory examination of the five projections, which are set out in Tables 7-31 to 7-35, reveals a number of similarities among them:

- The proportion of Canadians aged 65 and older rises continuously in all of the projections from 1981 to 2030, with particularly large increases from 2010 to 2030. This represents a continuation of the trend in the 1921–81 period. The share of the aged-65 and older group increases substantially over the 1980s. In the 1990s, the rate of increase in this group's share declines as a result of the births to the baby-boom generation and the advance to retirement age of the relatively small age cohort born in the 1930s. After 2010, as the baby-boom generation reaches the age of retirement, the proportion of those aged 65 and older within the total population again expands significantly.
- All projections indicate that the shares of the population represented by the two younger-age categories (0–14 years and 15–24 years) will decline continuously, or virtually continuously, until the year 2030.
- The share of the population aged 25–64 increases until the year 2010 and declines thereafter, except in the high-fertility, high-net/immigration case, where this share decreases slowly and steadily after 1990.
- In none of the projections is the proportion of the working-age population (15–64 years) smaller than it was in 1961; for three of the four Statistics Canada projections, this proportion falls below the 1971 proportion only in 2030.

Of course, the extent and the rapidity of these trends vary significantly with the assumptions that underlie each projection. In the low-fertility, low-immigration projection for 2030, for example, the share of those aged 14 and under is 12.2 per cent, while in the high-fertility, high-immigration projection, the corresponding figure is 20.7 per cent. The fertility-rate assumptions determine most, but not all, of this difference: the immigration assumptions also play a part, since the immigrant population is younger than the population as a whole. This point becomes clear when we compare the medium-fertility, high-immigration projection with the medium-fertility, low-immigration projection. In the first projection, the population share of

TABLE 7-31 Population Projections by Age Group Level, Rate of Growth and Percentage Share: Low Fertility, Low Immigration

	Total		0 to 14			15 to 24			25 to 64			65+		
Year	Pop. ('000)	Average Annual Growth Rate[a]	Pop. ('000)	Average Annual Growth Rate[a]	% of Pop.	Pop. ('000)	Average Annual Growth Rate[a]	% of Pop.	Pop. ('000)	Average Annual Growth Rate[a]	% of Pop.	Pop. ('000)	Average Annual Growth Rate[a]	% of Pop.
1981	24 343	1.2	5 481	−1.5	22.5	4 659	1.5	19.1	11 842	2.3	48.6	2 361	3.1	9.7
1990	26 428	0.9	5 404	0.1	20.4	3 842	−2.1	14.5	14 097	2.0	53.3	3 086	3.0	11.7
2000	27 741	0.5	4 730	−1.3	17.1	3 716	−0.8	13.4	15 462	0.9	55.7	3 830	2.2	13.8
2010	28 203	0.2	4 006	−1.6	14.2	3 435	−0.8	12.2	16 315	0.5	57.9	4 449	1.5	15.8
2020	28 004	−0.1	3 755	−0.6	13.4	2 797	−2.0	10.0	15 725	−0.4	56.2	5 733	2.6	20.5
2030	26 948	−0.4	3 285	−1.3	12.2	2 663	−0.5	9.9	13 950	−1.2	51.8	7 064	2.1	26.2

Sources: Statistics Canada, *Historical Statistical Compendium,* prepared for the Royal Commission on the Economic Union and Development Prospects for Canada (Ottawa: Statistics Canada, 1985), Table 1.7, and *Population Projections for Canada, Provinces and Territories 1984 to 2006* (Ottawa: Minister of Supply and Services Canada, forthcoming), Projection Series Number 1.

a. For the preceding 10 years, with the exception of 1990, which is for the preceding 9 years.

TABLE 7-32 Population Projections by Age Group Level, Rate of Growth and Percentage Share: Medium Fertility, Low Immigration

	Total		0 to 14			15 to 24			25 to 64			65+		
Year	Pop. ('000)	Average Annual Growth Rate[a]	Pop. ('000)	Average Annual Growth Rate[a]	% of Pop.	Pop. ('000)	Average Annual Growth Rate[a]	% of Pop.	Pop. ('000)	Average Annual Growth Rate[a]	% of Pop.	Pop. ('000)	Average Annual Growth Rate[a]	% of Pop.
1981	24 343	1.2	5 481	−1.5	22.5	4 659	1.5	19.1	11 842	2.3	48.6	2 361	3.1	9.7
1990	26 558	1.0	5 534	0.1	20.8	3 842	−2.1	14.5	14 097	2.0	53.1	3 086	3.0	11.6
2000	28 397	0.7	5 377	−0.3	18.9	3 727	−0.3	13.1	15 462	0.9	54.5	3 831	2.2	13.5
2010	29 447	0.4	4 884	−1.0	16.6	3 789	0.2	12.9	16 325	0.5	55.4	4 449	1.5	15.1
2020	30 005	0.2	4 817	−0.1	16.1	3 369	−1.2	11.2	16 086	−0.1	53.6	5 733	2.6	19.1
2030	29 839	−0.1	4 587	−0.5	15.4	3 315	−0.2	11.1	14 873	−0.8	49.8	7 064	2.1	23.7

Sources: Statistics Canada, *Historical Statistical Compendium*, prepared for the Royal Commission on the Economic Union and Development Prospects for Canada (Ottawa: Statistics Canada, 1985), Table 1.7, and *Population Projections for Canada, Provinces and Territories 1984 to 2006* (Ottawa: Minister of Supply and Services Canada, forthcoming), Projection Series Number 1.

a. For the preceding 10 years, with the exception of 1990, which is for the preceding 9 years.

TABLE 7-33 **Population Projections by Age Group Level, Rate of Growth and Percentage Share: Medium Fertility, High Immigration**

	Total		0 to 14			15 to 24			25 to 64			65+		
Year	Pop. ('000)	Average Annual Growth Rate[a]	Pop. ('000)	Average Annual Growth Rate[a]	% of Pop.	Pop. ('000)	Average Annual Growth Rate[a]	% of Pop.	Pop. ('000)	Average Annual Growth Rate[a]	% of Pop.	Pop. ('000)	Average Annual Growth Rate[a]	% of Pop.
1981	24 343	1.2	5 481	−1.5	22.5	4 659	1.5	19.1	11 842	2.3	48.6	2 361	3.1	9.7
1990	26 648	1.0	5 561	0.2	20.9	3 859	−2.1	14.5	14 144	2.0	53.1	3 084	3.0	11.6
2000	29 011	0.9	5 565	0.0	19.2	3 814	−0.1	13.1	15 822	1.1	54.5	3 811	2.1	13.1
2010	30 730	0.6	5 229	−0.6	17.0	3 988	0.4	13.0	17 108	0.8	55.7	4 404	1.5	14.3
2020	32 034	0.4	5 290	0.1	16.5	3 682	−0.8	11.5	17 365	0.1	54.2	5 696	2.6	17.8
2030	36 672	0.2	5 193	−0.2	15.9	3 711	0.1	11.4	16 647	−0.4	51.0	7 122	2.3	21.8

Sources: Statistics Canada, *Historical Statistical Compendium*, prepared for the Royal Commission on the Economic Union and Development Prospects for Canada (Ottawa: Statistics Canada, 1985), Table 1.7, and *Population Projections for Canada, Provinces and Territories 1984 to 2006* (Ottawa: Minister of Supply and Services Canada, forthcoming), Projection Series Number 1.

a. For the preceding 10 years, with the exception of 1990, which is for the preceding 9 years.

TABLE 7-34 **Population Projections by Age Group Level, Rate of Growth and Percentage Share: High Fertility, High Immigration**

Year	Total		0 to 14			15 to 24			25 to 64			65+		
	Pop. ('000)	Average Annual Growth Rate[a]	Pop. ('000)	Average Annual Growth Rate[a]	% of Pop.	Pop. ('000)	Average Annual Growth Rate[a]	% of Pop.	Pop. ('000)	Average Annual Growth Rate[a]	% of Pop.	Pop. ('000)	Average Annual Growth Rate[a]	% of Pop.
1981	24 343	1.2	5 481	−1.5	22.5	4 659	1.5	19.1	11 842	2.3	48.6	2 361	3.1	9.7
1990	26 749	1.1	5 662	0.4	21.2	3 859	−2.0	14.4	14 144	2.0	52.9	3 084	3.0	11.5
2000	29 967	1.1	6 519	1.4	21.8	3 814	−0.1	12.7	15 822	1.1	52.8	3 811	2.1	12.7
2010	32 690	0.9	6 736	0.3	20.6	4 440	1.5	13.6	17 109	0.8	52.3	4 406	1.5	13.5
2020	35 360	0.8	7 177	0.6	20.3	4 669	0.5	13.2	17 815	0.4	50.4	5 599	2.6	16.1
2030	37 846	0.7	7 818	0.9	20.7	4 830	0.3	12.8	18 071	0.1	47.8	7 127	2.3	18.8

Sources: Statistics Canada, *Historical Statistical Compendium*, prepared for the Royal Commission on the Economic Union and Development Prospects for Canada (Ottawa: Statistics Canada, 1985), Table 1.7, and *Population Projections for Canada, Provinces and Territories 1984 to 2006* (Ottawa: Minister of Supply and Services Canada, forthcoming), Projection Series Number 1.

a. For the preceding 10 years, with the exception of 1990, which is for the preceding 9 years.

TABLE 7-35 Population Projections by Age Group Level, Rate of Growth and Percentage Share: CPP 'Case' Projection

Year	Total		0 to 14			15 to 24			25 to 64			65+		
	Pop. ('000)	Average Annual Growth Rate[a]	Pop. ('000)	Average Annual Growth Rate[a]	% of Pop.	Pop. ('000)	Average Annual Growth Rate[a]	% of Pop.	Pop. ('000)	Average Annual Growth Rate[a]	% of Pop.	Pop. ('000)	Average Annual Growth Rate[a]	% of Pop.
1981	24 342	1.2	5 477	−1.5	22.5	4 649	1.5	19.1	11 830	2.3	48.6	2 361	3.1	9.7
1990	27 333	1.3	5 935	0.9	21.7	3 966	−1.7	14.5	14 463	2.3	52.9	2 969	2.6	10.9
2000	29 991	0.9	6 319	0.6	21.1	4 059	0.2	13.5	16 042	1.0	53.5	3 571	1.9	11.9
2010	32 352	0.8	6 345	0.0	19.6	4 477	1.0	13.8	17 349	0.8	53.6	4 181	1.6	12.9
2020	34 666	0.7	6 726	0.6	19.4	4 461	0.0	12.9	17 881	0.3	51.6	5 598	3.0	16.2
2030	36 688	0.6	7 043	0.5	19.2	4 694	0.5	12.8	17 762	−0.1	48.4	7 189	2.5	19.6
2040	38 424	0.5	7 277	0.3	18.9	4 977	0.6	13.0	18 615	0.5	48.4	7 555	0.5	19.7
2050	40 134	0.4	7 673	0.5	19.1	5 111	0.3	12.7	19 618	0.5	48.9	7 732	0.2	19.3
2060	41 895	0.4	8 006	0.4	19.1	5 387	0.5	12.9	20 352	0.4	48.6	8 150	0.5	19.5
2070	43 811	0.5	8 346	0.4	19.1	5 641	0.5	12.9	21 337	0.5	48.7	8 487	0.4	19.4
2080	45 827	0.5	8 754	0.5	19.1	5 862	0.4	12.8	22 335	0.5	48.7	8 876	0.4	19.4
2090	47 890	0.4	9 136	0.4	19.1	6 155	0.5	12.9	23 281	0.4	48.6	9 318	0.5	19.5
2100	50 069	0.4	9 548	0.4	19.1	6 429	0.4	12.8	24 381	0.5	48.7	9 711	0.4	19.4

Sources: Statistics Canada, *Historical Statistical Compendium*, prepared for the Royal Commission on the Economic Union and Development Prospects for Canada (Ottawa: Statistics Canada, 1985), Table 1.7, and *Population Projections for Canada, Provinces and Territories 1984 to 2006* (Ottawa: Minister of Supply and Services Canada, forthcoming), Projection Series Number 5.

a. For the preceding 10 years with the exception of 1990, which is for the preceding 9 years.

Canadians under 65 in 2030 is 78.3 per cent; in the second projection, their share is 76.3 per cent. Figure 7-5 illustrates the distribution of the age groups in 2030, under each of the Statistics Canada projections, and provides a comparison with the situation in 1981.

The projections also differ substantially in their conclusions about total population growth. In the low-fertility case, the total population starts to decline after 2010; the medium-fertility, low-immigration case shows a slight decline after 2020. The other cases project continuing, though modest, growth of total population.

Given constant age-specific rates of fertility, mortality and immigration, a population will eventually approach a "steady state" characterized by a roughly constant growth rate and constant age-group shares. Most of the projections assume something like constancy in fertility rates, mortality rates and net immigration rates after 2000; in the very long-term CPP projection shown in Table 7-35, a steady state appears to set in after about 2030, by which time there would be relatively few survivors of the baby-boom cohort of the 1940s to 1960s.

Whether such steady-state projections show continuing growth or decline in total population depends, subject to a qualification for immigration, on whether the fertility rate exceeds or falls short of the "replacement value" of

FIGURE 7-5 Percentage Share of Selected Age Groups, 1981 and Alternative Projections for 2030

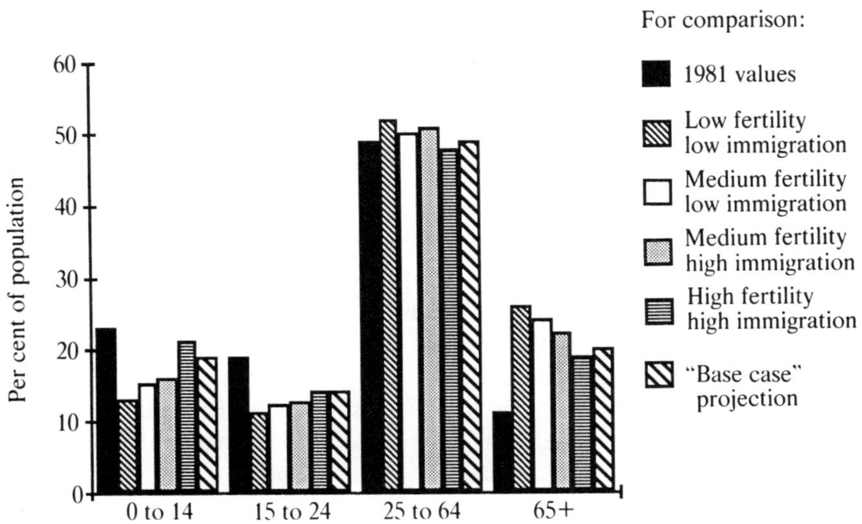

Source: Historical Compendium, 1.7, Statistics Canada; *Components of Population Growth, 1983-2006*, Statistics Canada, Demography Division; *Components of Population Growth, 1983-2031*, Statistics Canada, Demography Division (Unpublished); and Department of Insurance.

2.1 children per woman.[2] In the CPP projection illustrated in Table 7-35, the assumed fertility rate of 2.0 per cent is marginally below the replacement value, but this difference is more than offset by the assumption that net immigration will occur at an annual rate of 0.32 per cent.

Several general conclusions about Canada's population outlook can be drawn from the demographic projections we have just reviewed. The medium-fertility assumption of 1.6 children per woman is very close to the latest observed rate, but it is clearly possible that fertility will either drop below the rate of 1.4 per cent projected in the low-fertility case or rise above the assumed rate of 2.2 per cent in the high-fertility case. Even so, the following generalizations can be offered:

- A substantial increase over the next 50 years in the population share of those aged 65 and over is a virtual certainty; but the increase in this share by 2030 could range from a doubling to somewhat less than a tripling relative to the current ratio. The most dramatic increase in the share will occur between 2010 and 2030.
- A period of several decades of virtually continuous decline in the absolute numbers of the 0–14 and 15–24 age groups – and hence a more dramatic decline in their shares – is a very real possibility.
- If fertility and net immigration rates stabilize in the near future, the population will approach a "steady state" configuration by about 2030; that is, age-group shares will remain, thereafter, at approximately their 2030 levels.
- Canada's total population will almost certainly continue to grow, but at continuously declining rates, until at least 2010, when it will probably have reached a range of 28 million to 32 million. Given low fertility, the total population will then tend to decline slowly. Given medium fertility, which is still below the replacement rate, the total population will eventually start to decline if the net immigration rate (relative to total population) is lower than the average rate over the post-war period. Total population will stabilize or continue to grow very slowly if the net immigration rate continues at the average post-war rate.

Long-Term Economic Projections, 1984–2000

Many government agencies and private sector consulting firms regularly provide projections and analyses of the Canadian economy's short- and longer-term growth prospects. This Commission decided that it would be more efficient to draw on this available expertise and to make use of existing sources of information than to develop its own independent forecasting capability. In any event, the latter course would have required much more time and resources than were available for the task.

As part of our effort to gather information on the longer-term outlook, this Commission convoked a conference of forecasters. Three leading, private sector, forecasting groups were invited to present their current views of likely long-term/growth paths for the economy. These groups were Data Resources Incorporated, Informetrica Limited, and the Institute for Policy Analysis at the University of Toronto. A number of specialists in particular sectors of the economy were also asked to attend in order to comment on the prospects for their sectors. The material presented at this conference, as up-dated in late 1984 and augmented by a long-term projection prepared by Chase Econometrics Canada, provides a reasonable indication of the general nature of economic projections currently available from expert analysts.[3]

Before we discuss the prospects for the economy, it is useful to consider the nature of long-term projections. Experience with medium- and long-term projections prepared by the Royal Commission on Canada's Economic Prospects (the Gordon Commission), the Economic Council of Canada, and a number of other agencies in more recent years, as well as experience in other countries, suggests that while carefully prepared projections provide some basis for identifying likely future trends, such projections are subject to substantial margins of error.

There are some noteworthy examples of the failure of projections to anticipate major new developments. Both the post-war rise in birth rates and their decline in the late-1960s came as surprises to Canadians. Neither the dramatic rises in oil prices of 1973 and 1979–80, nor the significant decline in real oil prices from 1980–81 peak levels were built into short-term forecasts, to say nothing of long-term projections. Finally, it was the common practice in the early 1970s to project the continuation of experience approximating the average productivity growth of the 1950s and 1960s.

In spite of their shortcomings, however, long-term projections are useful. They represent considered and consistent views of future developments. Thus they are likely to be closer to the mark than less-sophisticated and less-systematic methods of anticipating future developments. The future is inherently unknowable, but it is necessary to have some forward view. In developing such a view, it is important to take advantage of the best information available. It is in this spirit that Commissioners consider long-term projections here. These projections assume a continuation of existing policies and programs. They also assume that there will be no major changes in the external environment facing the Canadian economy.

The average of the four long-term projections considered by this Commission is presented in Table 7-36. The annual growth rate of real gross national expenditure (GNE) is expected to decline from about 3 per cent, on average, over the late-1980s, to 2.6 per cent in the 1990s, as Figure 7-6 illustrates. This rate of decline is significantly slower than the annual growth of 4.25 per cent achieved, on average, over the 1956–81 period. Projected real growth for the late 1980s is roughly similar to the growth forecast for this period by the Minister of Finance, in November 1984, in *A New Direction for Canada: An Agenda for Economic Renewal.*

The growth of real GNE depends on the growth of employment and productivity, among other factors, as shown in Figure 7-7. Employment growth is expected to decline from an annual average of 2.8 per cent over the 1966–81 period to 2.1 per cent in the late 1980s, and to 1.4 per cent in the 1990s. Annual productivity growth is expected to average about 1 to 1.5 per cent for the balance of the century, a moderately higher rate than the average rate for the past decade. This means that declining employment growth alone will be more than sufficient to account for the projected decline in Canada's real output growth.

TABLE 7-36 Average of Four Long-Term Projections: Main Economic Indicators, 1984–2000

	1984–90	1990–2000
Real GNE	3.0	2.6
Employment	2.1	1.4
Unemployment rate (level)	9.7	7.5
Consumer price index	4.9	5.1

Sources: Peter Dungan, "Outlook for the Canadian Economy Through 2005" (Toronto: University of Toronto, Institute for Policy Analysis, 1983); T.W. McCormack, "The Next 25 Years", *Canadian Review* (Fall 1983); Informetrica, "Post II-83 Reference Forecast" (Ottawa: Informetrica, National Forecast Service, 1984); and Chase Econometrics Canada.

The anticipated sources of the decreased employment growth are present in Figure 7-8. One factor is an anticipated decline in population growth from an average of about 0.9 per cent per year in the late 1980s, to 0.7 per cent in the 1990s. Forecasters also expect a slight slowing of growth in the labour-force/participation rate as a consequence of less-rapid growth in the female participation rates and some long-term decline in the male participation rate.[4] Employment growth is expected to exceed labour-force growth by a small but significant margin for the balance of this century.

FIGURE 7-6 Real Gross National Product: Average of Four Projections

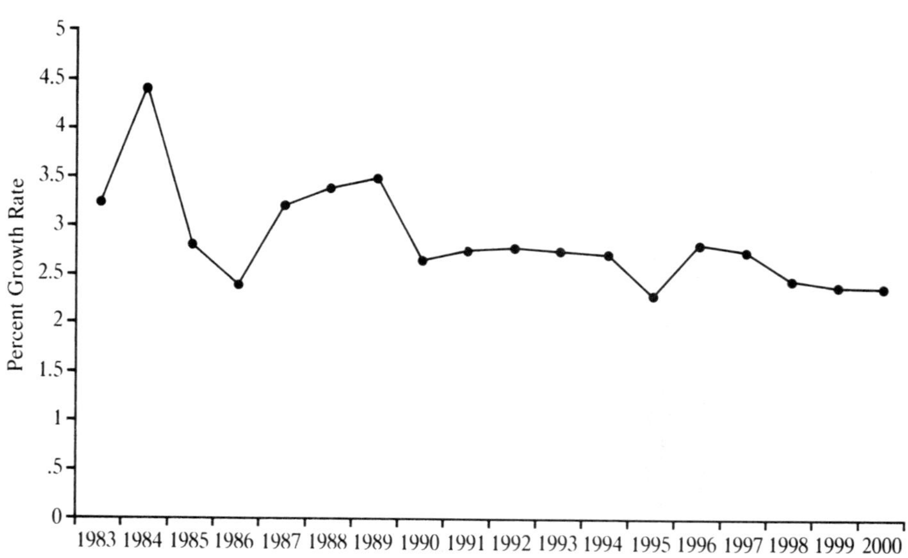

Sources: Chase Econometrics; Data Resources Inc.; Informetrica; and Institute for Policy Analysis, University of Toronto.

FIGURE 7-7 Sources of Growth of Real Gross National Expenditure

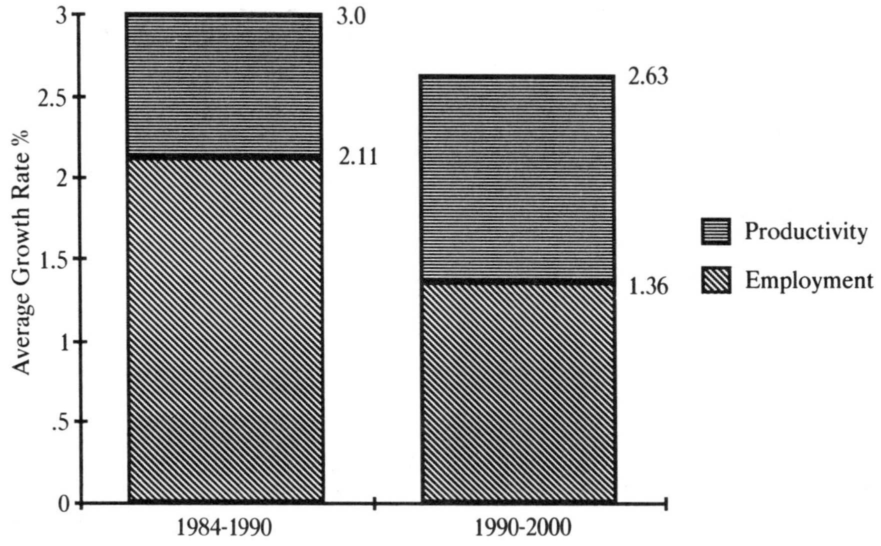

Sources: Chase Econometrics; Data Resources Inc.; Informetrica; and Institute for Policy Analysis, University of Toronto.

FIGURE 7-8 Sources of Growth of Employment

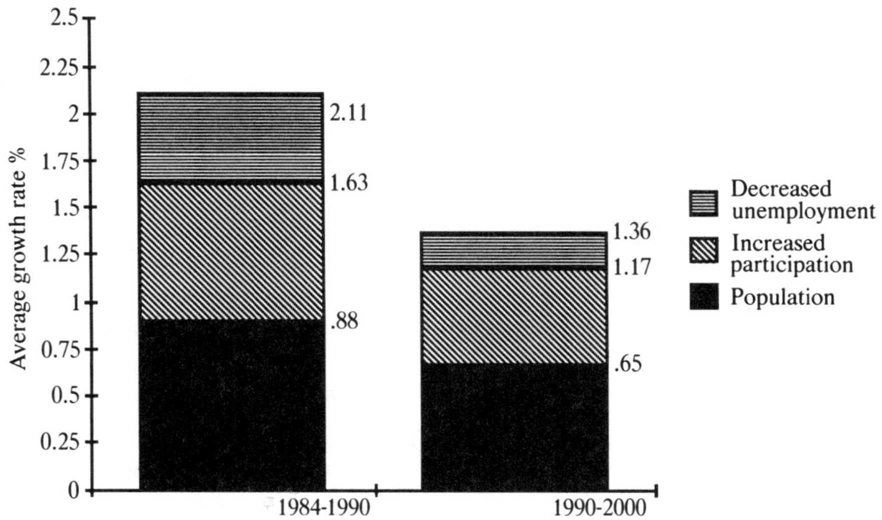

Sources: Chase Econometrics; Data Resources Inc.; Informetrica; and Institute for Policy Analysis, University of Toronto.

The unemployment rate is expected to decrease only very gradually from its current high level. It is projected to average 9.7 per cent in the late 1980s, and 7.5 per cent in the late 1990s. In November 1984, the Minister of Finance projected that the unemployment rate would average 9.25 per cent over the rest of the 1980s.

Inflation is expected to diminish only slightly, until 2000, from its current level of about 5 per cent. This figure is in line with average inflation over the 1956–81 period and well down from the double-digit levels of much of the 1970s and early 1980s. The Minister of Finance has predicted a lower rate of inflation, an average below 4 per cent, for the remainder of the decade.

Canadian prospects are critically dependent on developments in the United States. Figure 7-9 compares the average real growth rate for the Canadian economy projected by the four forecasting groups and the average real growth projected for the United States. During the late 1980s and 1990s, real growth is expected to be only marginally higher in Canada. This projection stands in contrast with the 1 per cent differential in real growth rates in Canada's favour that was characteristic of the 1956–81 period.

FIGURE 7-9 Projected Real Gross National Product in Canada and the United States

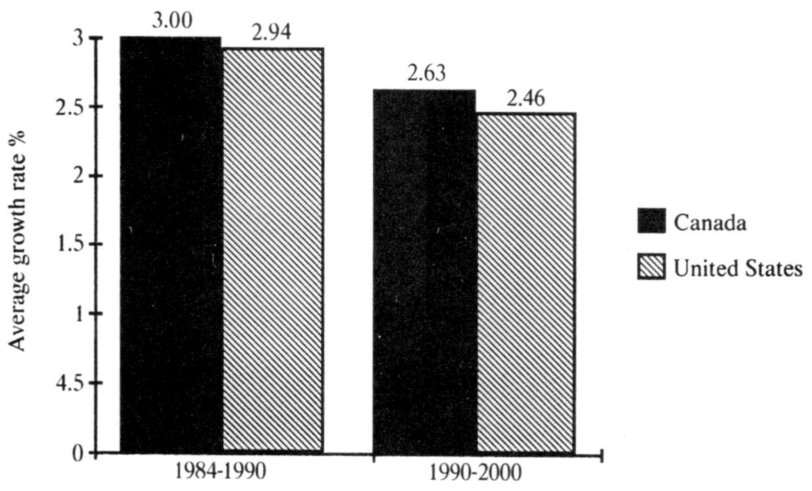

Sources: Chase Econometrics; Data Resources Inc.; Informetrica; and Institute for Policy Analysis, University of Toronto.

As Figure 7-10 indicates, inflation rates in Canada are also expected to be very similar to those in the United States. Inflation is expected to average about 5 per cent in both countries. With a floating Canadian dollar, it is possible, in theory, for inflation to differ widely between Canada and the United States. Experience has not borne out this theory because monetary policy in Canada has been similar to that practised in the United States.

FIGURE 7-10 Projected Consumer Price Index in Canada and the United States

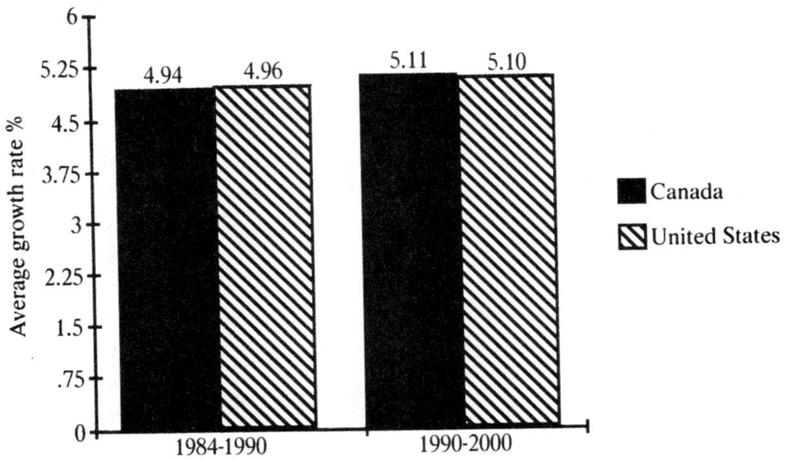

Sources: Chase Econometrics; Data Resources Inc.; Informetrica; and Institute for Policy Analysis, University of Toronto.

The projection considered so far represents an average of the four projections reviewed by this Commission. The extent to which the four forecasting groups differ in their views of the prospects for real growth is indicated in Figure 7-11. The projections for both the late 1980s and the 1990s vary within a range of only about 0.5 percentage points.

FIGURE 7-11 Real Gross National Product: Projections of Four Forecasting Groups

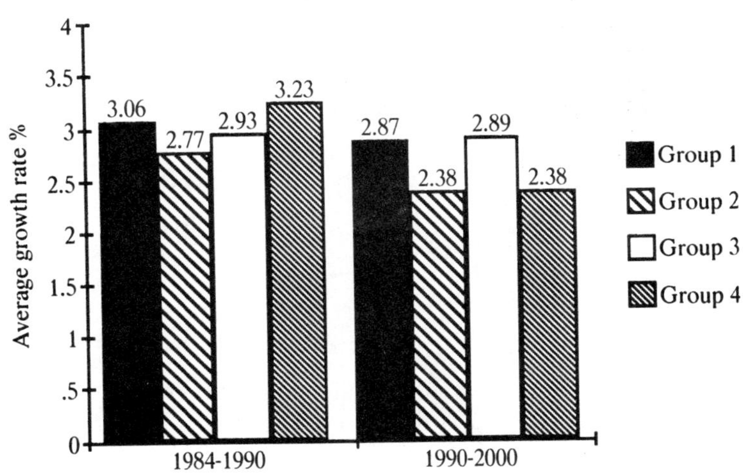

Sources: Chase Econometrics; Data Resources Inc.; Informetrica; and Institute for Policy Analysis, University of Toronto.

As Figure 7-12 shows, the range of views about the likely growth of Canada's labour force is even narrower. For the late 1980s, the average annual growth rates of the labour force, projected by the forecasting agencies, range from 1.4 per cent to 1.9 per cent; for the 1990s, the range is from 1.0 per cent to 1.3 per cent.

FIGURE 7-12 Labour Force: Projections of Four Forecasting Groups

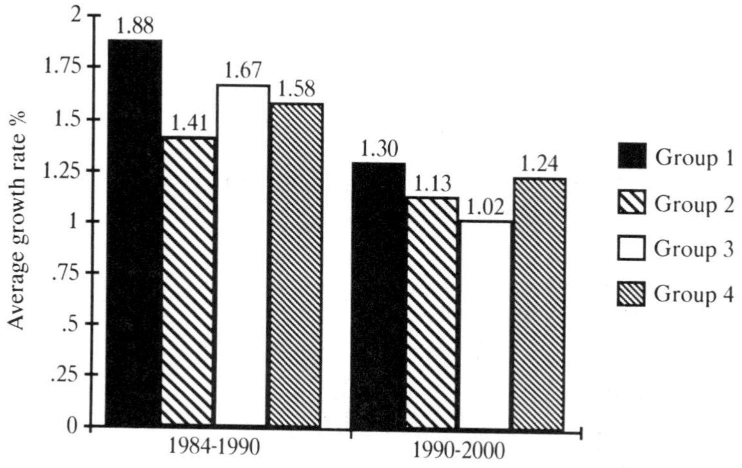

Sources: Chase Econometrics; Data Resources Inc.; Informetrica; and Institute for Policy Analysis, University of Toronto.

FIGURE 7-13 Unemployment Rate: Projections of Four Forecasting Groups

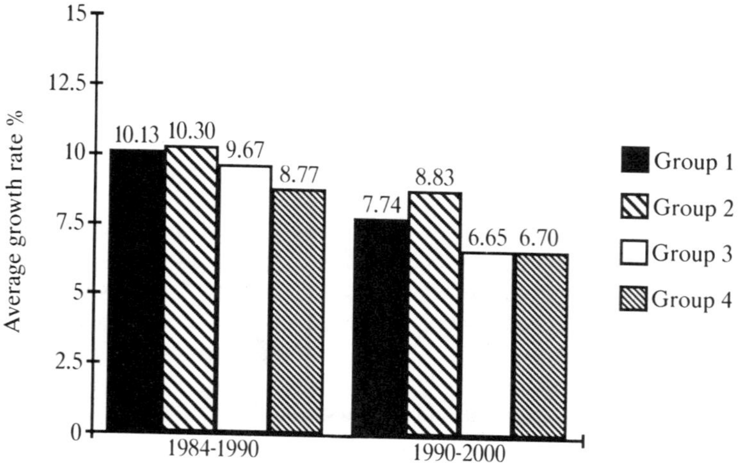

Sources: Chase Econometrics; Data Resources Inc.; Informetrica; and Institute for Policy Analysis, University of Toronto.

Views about the likely path of the unemployment rate differ more significantly, as Figure 7-13 shows. For the late 1980s, the low projection for the average unemployment rate is 8.8 per cent, the high projection is 10.3 per cent, and the mean of the four forecasts is 9.7 per cent. For the 1990s, the low forecast is 6.7 per cent, the high forecast is 8.8 per cent, and the mean of the four forecasts is 7.5 per cent.

Figure 7-14 shows the range of projections for employment growth. The low projection for average employment growth in the late-1980s is 1.7 per cent, the high projection is 2.3 per cent, and the mean forecast is 2.1 per cent. For the 1990s, the low projection is 1.2 per cent, the high projection is 1.5 per cent, and the mean projection is 1.4 per cent.

FIGURE 7-14 Employment: Projections of Four Forecasting Groups

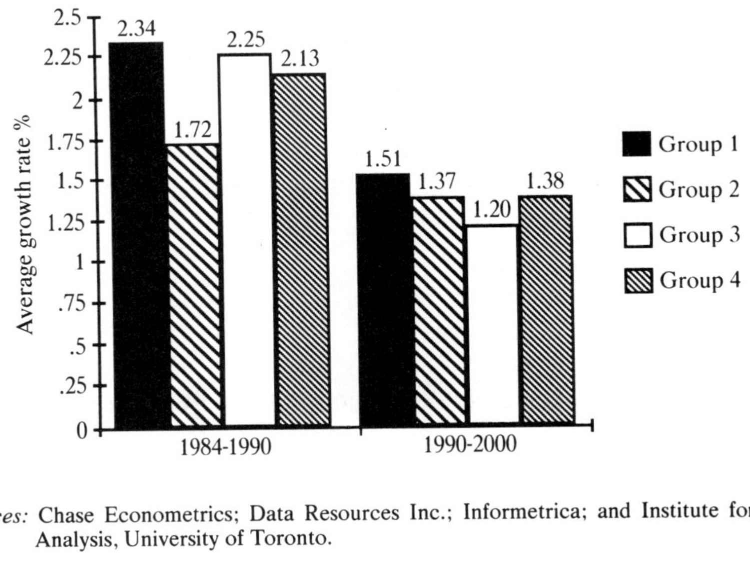

Sources: Chase Econometrics; Data Resources Inc.; Informetrica; and Institute for Policy Analysis, University of Toronto.

There is less agreement about productivity growth than there is about labour-force and employment growth. (See Figure 7-15.) The divergence in the projections stems, in part, from differences of opinion about the causes of the post-1973 slow-down in productivity, and about the extent to which the slow-down can be expected to continue. The mean projection for average annual productivity growth in the late 1980s is 1.1 per cent, while the low projection is 0.8 per cent, and the high projection is 1.6 per cent. For the 1990s, the mean forecast for average annual productivity growth is 1.5 per cent, the low forecast is 0.8 per cent, and the high forecast is 2.1 per cent.

FIGURE 7-15 Productivity: Projections of Four Forecasting Groups

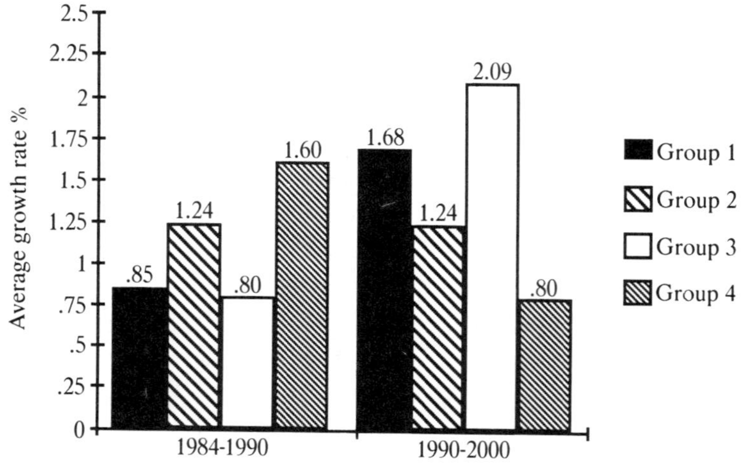

Sources: Chase Econometrics; Data Resources Inc.; Informetrica; and Institute for Policy Analysis, University of Toronto.

FIGURE 7-16 Consumer Price Index: Projections of Four Forecasting Groups

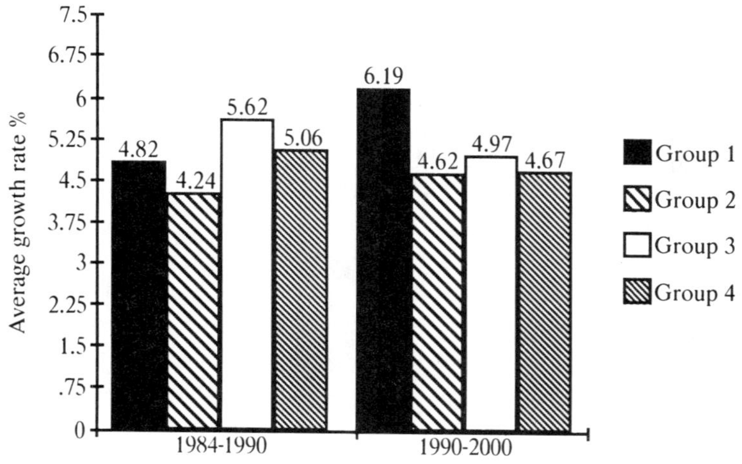

Sources: Chase Econometrics; Data Resources Inc.; Informetrica; and Institute for Policy Analysis, University of Toronto.

The forecasters express a fairly wide range of views about the prospects for inflation, although none of them expects a return to double-digit inflation. (See Figure 7-16.) Projections of average annual inflation in the late-1980s vary from 4.2 per cent to 5.6 per cent. Inflation projections for the 1990s range from 4.6 per cent to 6.2 per cent. This is a remarkably compact range for a monetary phenomenon such as inflation which, in the long run, could vary quite widely, depending on the rate of growth of the money supply. It reflects the judgements of the various forecasting groups about the likely profile of monetary policy in Canada and the United States.

The range defined by the projections of the four forecasting groups is indicative of our economy's probable performance if there are no major unanticipated events or changes in behaviour. However, it is not representative of the full range of possible outcomes. There are risks and uncertainties associated with any forecast. In order to take these into account, forecasters often prepare optimistic and pessimistic scenarios to accompany their "best-guess" projections. While Commissioners have not followed this practice here, in order to restrict to manageable proportions the number of forecasts we have considered, it is useful to mention at least a few of the most important risks.

One significant risk is the possibility of another run-up in interest rates. The future of interest rates depends on the stance of monetary policy in the United States and on the resolution of the U.S. deficit problem. Any severe tightening of U.S. monetary policy could have a disastrous impact on the global economy, given the debt overhang of many developing countries and the vulnerability of leading banks in the industrialized world. Nor can other disruptive international developments be ruled out. The memory of the energy shocks of 1973–74 and 1979–80 should serve to reinforce this point.

There are also domestic risks. While long-term projections tend to be driven, primarily, by expectations about supply, the forecasters voiced some concern that demand might not be strong enough to elicit the potential supply. A specific worry was that investment spending might not, in fact, be as strong as projected in the light of present and anticipated excess capacity and of the expected financial position of the corporate sector. There was also concern that consumers might not be willing to reduce their rate of savings, thereby causing consumer spending to be less than forecast.

In spite of recent experience, not all the uncertainties involve unfavourable outcomes. It is not outside the realm of possibility that inflation will continue to slow, leading to a new era of international price stability. Real interest rates could decline world wide, spurring a global surge in domestic consumer and investment spending, and in exports. This eventuality would have the felicitous effect of restoring the world's economy, including Canada's, to relatively full employment much more quickly than is now expected.

This review has focused on the broad outlines of the macro-economic prospects of Canada's economy. The projections prepared for this Commission also contained detail relating to industry. All of the projections anticipate relatively weak growth for natural-resource/based production, exports and relative prices, with the possible exception of energy and agricultural products. This weakness, which is especially pronounced in the areas of mining and forestry, reflects a number of factors, including slower average growth in overall world demand than in the pre-1974 period; increased dependence on higher-cost sources of supply in Canada; and increased international competition, particularly from developing countries that may still have the benefit of large, relatively untapped, and lower-cost sources of supply. The resources sector is considered in detail in Part IV of this Report, where a number of very fundamental sectoral policy reforms are recommended to ensure that any further relative decline cannot be attributed to mismanagement.

Notes

1. The fertility rate is the number of live births per woman over her child-bearing years.
2. The "replacement value" is slightly higher than 2 live births per woman over her child-bearing years because slightly more than half of live births are males, and because some females die before they reach child-bearing age.
3. John Sargent, *Long-term Economic Prospects for Canada: A Symposium*, vol. 23, prepared for the Royal Commission on the Economic Union and Development Prospects for Canada (Toronto: University of Toronto Press, 1985).
4. Chase Econometrics, one of the four forecasting groups, projects that the aggregate participation rate will rise from 64.7 per cent in 1984 to 66.9 per cent in 1990, and to 67.6 per cent in 2000. The basis of this projected increase is a forecast that the female participation rate will rise from 53.4 per cent in 1984, to 57.6 per cent in 1990, and to 61.2 per cent in 2000; and that the male participation rate will increase only marginally from 76.5 per cent in 1984, to 76.7 per cent in 1990, and then decrease to 74.4 per cent in 2000.

CHAPTER 8

Economic Growth, Investment, Technology, Management and Entrepreneurship

CHAPTER 8

Economic Growth, Investment, Technology, Management and Entrepreneurship

This is the first of two chapters devoted to considering means of achieving higher levels of real income over the longer term. In this chapter, Commissioners' primary concerns are the contributions made to economic growth by capital formation, technological progress, management and entrepreneurship. By way of introduction, we address first the concern that technological progress – or a more efficient allocation of the economy's resources across different activities – may produce not economic growth, but unemployment.

The Relation between Jobs, Productivity, Technological Change and Real Growth in the Longer Term

While improvements in productivity provide the foundation for increases in real incomes over time, many submissions to this Commission expressed concern that greater efficiency in production might result in job losses. Some see technological advances, such as the development of robots and other creations of the micro-electronic "revolution", as displacing workers or slowing the creation of new jobs. Furthermore, the increase of economic growth expected from freer trade could demand extensive rationalization of industry, again at the expense of jobs. The fundamental issue, therefore, is whether or not there is a trade-off between growth in employment and growth in output, productivity and incomes.

The view of most economists is that there is little or no trade-off of this type in the longer run of, say, a decade or more. Most economists believe that over the long run, growth of employment and increases in productivity evolve independently to a considerable degree. In other words, if technological change or industrial rationalization produced higher productivity, there would be little net effect on total employment; rather, there would be higher output and higher real incomes, but little, if any, change in the number of jobs, although the mix of jobs might well change.

Underlying this conviction is the belief that in the long run, factors relating to the supply of goods and services determine levels of employment and real income.[1] "Demand-side" factors, resulting from cyclical developments and policies of demand management, tend to average out or lose significance over time.[2] The range of variations in the economy over the course of the "business cycle" is normally much smaller than the cumulative impact on economic growth of supply-side changes if these extend over a period of ten or more years.

It is difficult, if not impossible, to prove that the concern about adverse effects of technological change on total employment is groundless. It is, however, possible to assess the strength of logical arguments and historical evidence in favour of the economists' view, advanced above, of the relation between productivity, real growth and employment.[3] Since many people feel deep concern about the possible connection between technological change and unemployment, the following sections explore both the theoretical and the empirical arguments that relate to this issue.

The Theoretical Arguments

In a "closed" (non-trading) economy, productivity growth secures not only an increase in the potential supply of output, but also an increase in real income and, consequently, in potential real purchasing power. The spending of that increased purchasing power will create an increased demand for goods and services that should approximately match the increased supply resulting from the increased productivity. If we consider, rather than a closed economy, a small open economy such as Canada's, the additional potential output made possible by improved productivity would generally sell on the world market at prices little lower than those current before the increase in productivity. In either case, demand growth will match the output growth made possible by greater productivity, at least over the long run. Nevertheless, there will be adjustment problems to consider.

Sometimes adjustment to the increase in productivity can take place with minimal disruption in employment patterns. This will tend to occur where the "new" production processes make use of workers with skills similar to those associated with old processes, and when the demand for the product is "price elastic" (that is, the volume of demand increases by more, in percentage terms, than the reduction in price). Then, as costs decline with the growth in productivity and prices fall, sales and, therefore, output increase more than proportionately. Given the resulting increase in output, employment in the industry need not fall and may rise. Examples of this possibility include the communications industry over much of its history and, more recently, the computer industry. In these cases, the relative price reductions resulting from labour-saving innovations – sometimes coupled with growth in demand as general levels of real income have risen – have led, as a rule, to sufficiently large growth in sales to ensure a substantial increase in employment.

Nevertheless, adjustment to an increase in productivity often involves both disruption and reduction in employment in particular industries. This can occur when either the skills demanded by the new production processes are different from those required for the old, and/or the demand for the product is relatively "price inelastic" (that is, percentage increase in volume demanded is less than the percentage reduction in price). The latter situation is typical of the demand conditions for many agricultural products. As a result, the major increase in agricultural productivity that began in the eighteenth century and accelerated rapidly after the Second World War led to a dramatic decline absolutely and relatively in employment in farming.[4] In this sector, productivity increases led to an increase in real income and real spending, but the objects of that expenditure and, hence, the new jobs created were not in agriculture but in other industries, some of them in agriculture-supporting industries such as the manufacture of farm machinery or fertilizer. As consumers spent a smaller fraction of their budgets on food, because of the drop in relative cost, they were able to spend more on consumer durables and services, which resulted in the creation of new jobs.

If one looks only at total employment (or unemployment) statistics for North America and Western Europe in the period after the Second World War, it is, in fact, hard to see much evidence of difficulty in adjusting to the huge decline in agricultural employment. This is not to deny that many people and communities had to make difficult and far-reaching adjustments. In Canada, hundreds of thousands of individuals left farming and generally had to relocate; hundreds of communities declined in size, and some of them became ghost towns; one province, Saskatchewan, experienced extended periods of population decline.[5] Despite all this, the massive adjustments imposed by the dramatic increases in agricultural productivity did not produce substantial unemployment in the regions concerned, nor did they initiate extended periods of unemployment for most of those dislocated.

The introduction of new technologies can result in a decline in demand for workers experienced in older production processes who find it difficult to re-establish themselves in expanding industries requiring different skills. Adjustment can be extremely difficult for such workers, particularly if the shift in demand takes place rapidly. If this happens, adjustment often requires learning new skills – frequently a time-consuming process – and possibly accepting a lower wage, temporarily or permanently. These problems tend to be especially acute for older workers.

This simplified outline of the varying effects on employment of improved productivity leads to several broad conclusions. First, to the extent that productivity increases result in employment losses in one area, there are powerful economic mechanisms at work to generate a comparable number of jobs elsewhere. Secondly, the effectiveness of these mechanisms depends, to a considerable extent, on the responsiveness of the price and wage system to market forces. Declines in price are needed to encourage the purchase of a larger volume of products where productivity has increased and, if the demand response is low, to permit declines in aggregate spending on those items so that purchasing power may be transferred elsewhere. In the same circumstances, increases in average real wages (which will tend automatically to accompany productivity growth if prices are flexible) are also needed to permit increased real spending. Increases in relative wages for certain occupational groups are required to draw workers to areas where new employment opportunities are available. Declines must occur in relative and, quite possibly, in absolute wages for occupational groups in declining industries in order to cushion the drop in demand for their services. A reduction in relative wages in geographic areas where the demand for labour has fallen can help to minimize unemployment. As a general rule, the effectiveness of these adjustment mechanisms will decline to the extent that impediments occur to the necessary adjustment of prices and/or wages in response to market forces. Such impediments will reduce the ability of an economy experiencing improved productivity to sustain employment. Thirdly, even though average real incomes will increase with improved productivity, some individuals will face difficult adjustments that may involve a change of jobs, the undertaking of a new occupation, a move to a new community, and/or a temporary or permanent decline in income.

Most economists would subscribe, in general terms, to the preceding description of the processes by which our economic system adjusts to the ongoing technological and other changes that contribute to productivity growth. Canadians looking back over the post-Second World War period would recognize that on the whole, our economy has adjusted extraordinarily well to dramatic changes in its structure. Some, however – particularly those who are or may soon become victims of change – may not find the case either convincing or comforting. These people might well ask whether the massive unemployment of the 1930s and even the high levels being experienced today, not only in Canada but also in Western Europe, are consistent with a "self-equilibrating system". What explanation – or solution – is there for the significant portion of unemployment that exists today in certain occupations and regions that seems to be the result of major structural changes in our economy? Are today's technological changes of a different order of magnitude than any experienced in the past? The answers to such questions are not easy, and they involve issues of widespread concern.

There is no significant evidence that the massive unemployment of the 1930s or of the present day resulted from technological change. Most of those examining both periods would agree that the sharp rise in unemployment resulted from the fact that total demand for goods and services in the economy fell considerably short of the economy's ability to produce them. One or more forces in the system may produce wide swings in real and nominal demand.[6] Substantial unemployment may occur if monetary or fiscal policy is not adjusted sufficiently to offset a decline in aggregate demand. A similar outcome may result if the general level of wages and prices does not adjust sufficiently to ensure that nominal demand produces sufficient real demand to match the economy's capacity to supply goods and services. If, for example, nominal demand increases as a result of a change in fiscal or monetary policy, there will be no increase in real demand if prices and wages increase by the same amount. The issues of short-run economic stability and demand-management policy are the subject of Chapter 10 of this Report.

Over the period for which we have reasonable data on the composition of unemployment, there is no evidence that structural unemployment caused by technological change has ever accounted for a major share of total unemployment over a large geographic area and during extended periods of time. Structural unemployment caused by technological change can be significant in smaller regions and for certain groups of workers (especially older workers), but it has not been a major contributor to the long-term pattern of national unemployment in Canada or in other comparably industrial countries.

These arguments may not have convinced the sceptical reader. Will the economic mechanisms described above and, particularly, the price/wage mechanisms that are nowadays widely thought to be subject to many inflexibilities and imperfections work smoothly enough to provide jobs for those displaced by technological change and for new entrants to the labour force? It is, after all, easier to see where Canadians have lost or are likely to lose jobs as a result of technological change than to recognize where the working of the economy has created or will create them.

Commissioners' assumption that these mechanisms do work and will continue to work rests, in part, on the reasoning outlined earlier. It rests, as well, on the historical evidence, to which we now turn, that such mechanisms have operated more or less satisfactorily in recent decades. The weight of evidence is, we believe, compelling.

Historical Evidence

Both in Canada and in a number of other countries, historical evidence strongly suggests that over the longer run, growth in the supply of labour (the labour force) primarily determines employment growth. Underlying productivity trends primarily determine real wage growth which, in turn, broadly determines real growth in per capita income. Growth in employment and growth in productivity are, to a considerable degree, independent of each other, although this statement requires some significant qualifications which we shall review below.

Let us consider first Canada's experience since 1926, the first year for which national accounts data are available as indicated in Table 8-1. Trends in growth of employment during the periods shown match within a few tenths of a percentage point the trends of growth of the labour force. The growth of the labour force stems primarily from such independent factors as population, age structure and social forces. Thus, it is the growth of the labour force that should be considered as the factor causing employment rather than the reverse. Table 8-1 also provides significant evidence that growth of employment and productivity are, to a considerable extent, independent of each other over time. Between 1926 and 1946, for instance, productivity grew moderately, but the labour force and employment experienced low levels of growth. Between 1946 and 1956, productivity increased substantially, but the labour force and employment grew little. Between 1956 and 1973, productivity increased moderately to quickly, while the labour force and employment

TABLE 8-1 **Longer-Term Trends in Employment and Productivity, Canada**

Time Period	Average Annual % Growth Rates		
	Labour Force	Employment	Productivity
1926–46	1.4	1.4	2.1
1946–56	1.8	1.8	3.5
1956–66	2.5	2.5	2.1
1966–73	3.1	2.8	2.5
1973–81	3.2	2.9	0.1
(1973–82)[a]	2.9	2.2	−0.1

Source: Statistics Canada, *National Income and Expenditure Accounts* (Ottawa: Minister of Supply and Services Canada, various years).

a. The 1973–82 period is not even roughly cyclically neutral, as 1973 was a very strong year and 1982 a very weak year. Over an interval as short as nine years, this can cause the average growth rate of employment to diverge appreciably from the average growth rate of labour force, thus causing unemployment to change substantially.

also grew substantially. After 1973, productivity remained virtually static, while the labour force and employment grew quickly.

Let us look next at the average record for the highly developed OECD economies over the period from 1960 to 1982.[7] Table 8-2 presents basic data relating to this record, as reflected in changes in the labour force, employment and productivity. Figure 8-1 further illustrates the relation between changes in the labour force and employment, and between changes in employment and productivity. The data support and reinforce the evidence noted for Canada: there is a very close long-term correlation between growth in the labour force and growth in employment. There is no marked relationship between growth of productivity and growth of employment; but such a relationship as there is probably stems from the tendency of high labour-force growth to result in lower growth of productivity, rather than vice versa.

International evidence, then, does not suggest that rapid growth in productivity causes employment to lag behind growth in the labour force for long periods of time. Demand for workers tends to keep up with growth in the labour force, whatever the rate of productivity growth. In other words, the demand for output of goods and services tends to keep up with the increase in potential supply brought about by an increase in productivity and/or the labour force.

Governments have helped to promote this growth in employment over the short to medium term through the exercise of macro-economic policies. Since the Second World War, growth in nominal aggregate demand has been significantly more stable than it was in earlier years; to a considerable measure, this was the result of a concerted exercise of fiscal and monetary policies. It cannot be claimed, however, that the demand-management

TABLE 8-2 Average Annual Per Cent Change in the Labour Force, Civilian Employment and Productivity, OECD, 1960–82

	Labour Force	Civilian Employment	Productivity[a]
United States	2.1	1.9	1.2
Japan	1.1	1.1	6.2
Germany	0.2	−0.2	3.4
France	0.7	0.6	3.8
United Kingdom	0.4	0.0	2.2
Italy	0.2	0.1	3.9
Canada	2.8	2.6	1.6
Austria	0.1	0.0	3.9
Belgium	0.7	0.3	3.4
Finland	0.6	0.3	3.6
Iceland	2.2	2.2	2.1
Ireland	0.6	0.4	3.6
Netherlands	1.3	0.8	2.7
Sweden	0.8	0.7	2.3
Switzerland	0.5	0.5	2.1
Australia	2.3	2.0	1.8
New Zealand	1.9	1.8	0.8
Total OECD	1.2	1.0	2.8

Source: Organisation for Economic Co-operation and Development, *Historical Statistics 1960-1982* (Paris: OECD, 1984), Tables 1.3, 1.7, 3.7.

a. Real GDP per person employed.

policies of individual countries have been very closely correlated to their particular patterns of productivity and employment growth. It is reasonable, therefore, to assign the primary role in achieving this rough match between employment and labour-force growth over the longer run, in the face of quite different productivity experiences, to the self-correcting adjustment mechanisms described earlier.

Qualifications

Commissioners have argued that labour-force growth tends to be the "independent" or "driving" factor in the creation of employment. We wish, however, to qualify this causal relationship and the related concept that employment growth is substantially independent of productivity:

- Independent growth in employment opportunities can occur – where a region or industry opens up, for example, as in the Alberta oil boom – and can increase the labour force, directly or indirectly, by drawing previous non-participants into the labour force and by encouraging immigration.
- Rapid growth in productivity is probably more difficult to achieve when the labour force and employment are growing quickly, since rapid growth demands high rates of investment just to keep constant the amount of

FIGURE 8-1 Average Annual Rates of Growth: Advanced OECD Countries, 1960–1981

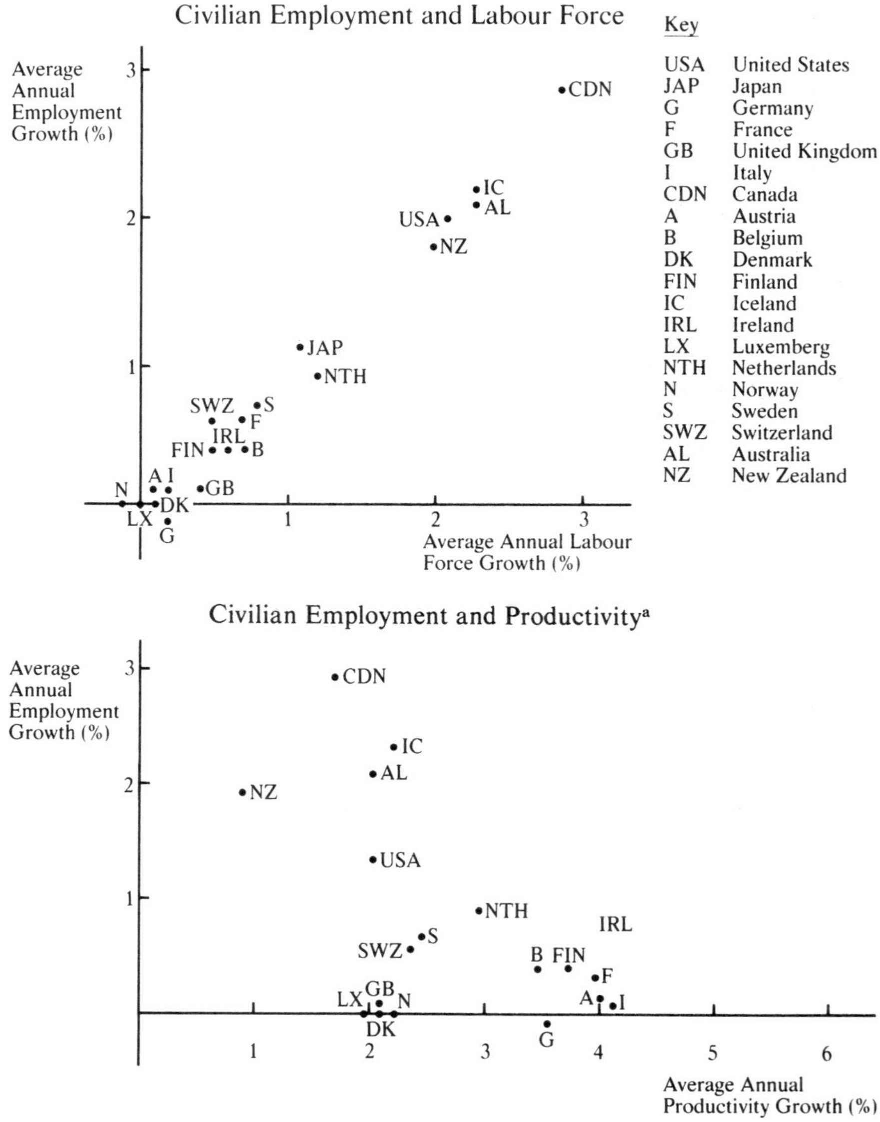

Source: Organisation for Economic Co-operation and Development, *Historical Statistics 1960-1982* (Paris: OECD, 1984).

a. Real GDP per person employed.

capital per employee (as compared with the capital investment required to increase productivity), and since a larger share of the labour force is inexperienced.[8] The evidence of some tendency toward an inverse relation between productivity and employment growth probably reflects this point.

- While rapid growth in productivity is unlikely, in the long run, to slow employment growth significantly, it will disrupt the economy more and necessitate more extensive readjustment. Somewhat greater "frictional unemployment", on average, might result from an increase in job changes brought about by improvement in productivity: employment might grow in line with the labour force, but the margin between them might be higher. This is the most important qualification to the general assertion that faster technological change is not expected to have much effect on employment.

In the short term, qualifications and interdependencies involving changes in the labour force, employment and productivity become still more important. The reasons are as follows:

- Aggregate demand can vary substantially, from the peak to the trough of the business cycle, in relation to change in the economy's potential productive capacity. The variations can be noticeable over several years and quite sharp in any given year. Thus, employment growth can depart quite sharply from labour-force growth over shorter periods, and substantial swings in unemployment can and do occur.
- In the short run, swings in employment opportunities often induce similar, though weaker, swings in labour-force participation. When employment opportunities decline during periods of recession or slow growth, so-called "discouraged workers" (unemployed persons not actively engaged in job search) withdraw from the labour force, thus reducing the level of recorded unemployment below the "real" figure. Conversely, the revival of economic growth will draw previous non-participants into the labour force, thus tempering, to some extent, the decline in recorded unemployment that would otherwise take place.
- Fluctuations in demand tend to cause both employment and productivity to move in the same direction as falling demand leads to a decline in employment and productivity, and vice versa. This tendency substantially qualifies, in the short run, the longer-term independence of employment and productivity.
- Under some circumstances, the relation between productivity and real wages can "get out of line". If, for example, real wages become too high in relation to underlying productivity, then a downward adjustment in real wages may help achieve higher employment. This would constitute short-run divergence between real wages/income and productivity, and an inverse relation between real income and employment. Acceptance of a downward adjustment in real wages, but not in the continuing rate of real wage growth, would lead to an increase in employment, but not in its continuing rate of growth.
- Over the short to medium term, the rate of technological change may affect the strength of demand. The famous economist and student of business cycles, Joseph Schumpeter[9] (1883–1950) suggested that the growth of technological innovations does not follow a perfectly even path; instead, periods of "bunching" of major innovations can occur. In general, application of innovations requires investment in new machinery and equipment; bunching of new innovations ready for implementation would stimulate demand for investment. The investment in new, more productive processes tends to increase productivity. Thus there may be extended

periods, lasting a decade or more, of above-average investment demand, and employment and productivity growth. Periods of weak investment, total demand, and employment and productivity growth might follow if the stimulus caused by one "bunching" of major technological innovations had tended to disappear, and if no equivalent new innovations had yet appeared. This view suggests that all other factors being equal, periods of above-average technological change and productivity growth will tend to produce above-average employment growth, rather than below-average employment growth, as many Canadians fear.

While Commissioners previously emphasized the view held by most economists that there is little or no relation, over the long run, between technological change and levels of employment, some connection may be formed over the medium term, as Schumpeter suggested; this relation may occur between the pace of technological change and the growth both of productivity and of employment. Indeed, such dynamic forces may override the qualification, noted above, that rapid growth of the labour force and employment make the rapid growth of productivity difficult to achieve at the same time. The kind of circumstance described by Schumpeter could offset the qualification that higher rates of technological change tend to cause higher levels of "frictional" unemployment, which result from the process of adjustment in the economy.

Faster Productivity Growth and Employment

As Commissioners have already stressed, there is no evidence from the post-Second World War period that quicker productivity growth has slowed growth of employment over any extended period. Technological change has not increased the level of structural unemployment as might be expected if a substantial percentage of those who lost jobs experienced prolonged difficulty in finding new jobs. Nevertheless, rapid productivity growth could raise the level of unemployment: if the "creative destruction" of existing jobs increases with faster productivity growth, the higher turnover of employment could cause more frictional unemployment.

In order to illustrate the working of this mechanism, let us assume that annual productivity increases involve a loss of jobs equal to 3 per cent of the labour force and the creation of an equal number of new jobs, the productivity of which exceeds that of the old jobs by 33.3 per cent. It follows from these assumptions that productivity will increase by 1 per cent each year. Assume further that each time a worker loses a job, it takes him or her an average of four months to find a new one.[10] These circumstances will produce additional frictional unemployment equal to 1 per cent of the labour force, representing 3 per cent of workers, each one unemployed, on average, for four months of a year.

Would slowing productivity growth reduce unemployment? We could, in principle, discourage implementation of productivity changes that involve job losses. This would seem undesirable, however, since to avoid an increase in unemployment of 1 percentage point would sacrifice a cumulative gain in real income of 1 per cent per year, which works out to a gain of 28 per cent over 25 years. Furthermore, this frictional unemployment might be reduced by other means, such as facilitating job searches by displaced workers.

Even if we discouraged job-displacing productivity changes, we might not alter employment levels. Measures to discourage companies from taking advantage of potential productivity gains could prove to be counter to the intent of maintaining employment. Employers could, for example, be required to make large severance payments to all laid-off workers; it would be difficult to distinguish between lay-offs resulting from productivity changes and lay-offs for other reasons. Employers might respond to such a measure in various ways. They might become more willing to retrain employees for new jobs and less eager to implement job-displacing productivity changes. To hire a new employee, however, would involve substantially more risks, including an inability to introduce productivity measures which would eliminate the need for that employee. The risks would also include the possibility of incurring larger losses if the demand for the new output fluctuated, or if the employee proved unsuitable for the job. Employers might become much more selective in their hiring, recruiting only employees who were likely to carry out well a particular job or a number of jobs. Such selective recruiting would tend to raise frictional unemployment; it would lengthen the time required to find a job, and it might make some higher-risk candidates virtually unemployable, especially if minimum wages were in effect. Thus such action might not lower unemployment, although it might well slow growth in productivity and real income.

Conclusions

Economic theory and history provide very little evidence that over the longer run, growth and employment are in conflict to any significant degree. This conclusion is essential to Commissioners' subsequent discussion in this Part of our Report and, indeed, throughout our Report. First, given reasonable confidence that improvements in productivity will not increase unemployment, we can consider on their own merits measures for achieving such improvements. However, measures to improve productivity and other sources of economic change can threaten particular jobs, and the job prospects and income of particular individuals. We shall keep this consideration very much in mind.

Secondly, the conclusion that improvements in productivity do not increase unemployment reinforces Commissioners' confidence in considering separately issues involving economic efficiency (including productivity) and maintenance, on a stable basis, of high levels of employment and low levels of inflation. The former issues are the subject of Chapters 8 and 9 of Part III, and of several other Parts of this Report. The latter issue is the subject of Chapter 10 of Part III.

Thirdly, while some observers have suggested that cumulative growth in structural unemployment caused by technological change would compel Canadians as a nation to develop "new types of work" in order to provide people with "something to do" and/or "ways of separating work and income",

Commissioners' conclusions about technology and unemployment indicate that these developments are not likely to be problems for Canada in the foreseeable future.

Notes

1. In referring to the economic effect of factors on the supply side, we Commissioners do not intend to associate our remarks with the views of "supply-side" advocates of the Laffer curve, who contend that a reduction in tax levels will generate sufficient increase in economic output and tax revenue to compensate for any initial loss of tax revenues. Rather, we suggest that factors influencing potential supply such as labour-force growth and productivity trends, and not "demand-side" factors, primarily determine longer-run trends in such economic variables as employment and real income levels.
2. The Depression of the 1930s represents an important exception and the 1981–82 recession may be a partial exception. Apart from fluctuations in demand, such as those caused by the factors cited in the text, real demand tends to grow at the same rate as real supply over the longer run.
3. See Robert C. Allen, "The Impact of Technical Change on Employment, Wages, and the Distribution of Skills: A Historical Perspective", in *Adapting to Change: Labour Market Adjustment in Canada*, vol. 18, prepared for the Royal Commission on the Economic Union and Development Prospects for Canada (Toronto: University of Toronto Press, 1985).
4. The fact that the demand for many agricultural products is also relatively "income inelastic" (that is, percentage increase in volume demanded is less than percentage increase in real income) helps to explain the relatively slow growth in real demand for agricultural products.
5. Saskatchewan experienced an absolute decline in population virtually continuously from 1936 to 1946 and from 1968 to 1974.
6. Nominal demand is total spending in current dollar terms at actual prices; real demand is total spending in real terms at constant prices.
7. 1960–81 is an approximately cyclically neutral period. The period 1960–82 would generally show wider divergences in rates of growth of labour force and employment because 1982 was a year of severe recession in practically all of the countries considered, whereas 1960 was generally a year of closer-to-average levels of economic activity.
8. Some analysts, however, have suggested that relatively high labour-force growth may increase productivity by making it easier, over time, to reallocate the labour force to sectors/regions of higher potential growth. Under these circumstances, to concentrate the flow of new entrants in areas of higher potential can produce substantial reallocation without requiring or inducing people to change from their current jobs.
9. See, for example, Joseph A. Schumpeter, *Theory of Economic Development: An Inquiry into Profits, Capital, Credit, Interest and Business Cycles* (New York: Oxford University Press, 1961), and *Business Cycles: A Theoretical, Historical and Statistical Analysis of the Capitalist Approach* (New York: McGraw-Hill, 1939).
10. Commissioners are not suggesting that the job losers necessarily find employment in the new, higher-productivity jobs. Associated with the 3 per cent assumed change in the composition of employment, there would probably be substantially larger flows between jobs, but many of the changes would not involve a spell of unemployment. See Part III, Chapter 10 for a fuller consideration of the nature of unemployment.

Capital Formation

While the pace of capital formation did not contribute significantly to the post-1973 slow-down in productivity growth,[1] it is not clear whether accelerated capital formation can help to restore productivity growth. The real capital stock increased on average about 5 per cent per year from 1962 to 1981.[2] The growth in capital stock reflects the amount of investment or, in the language of the national accounts, gross fixed capital formation.

Table 8-3 provides an international comparison of gross fixed capital formation as a percentage of gross domestic product (GDP). The share of total output devoted to investment in Canada has been higher than the comparable share in the United States or the United Kingdom, much lower than that share in Japan, and similar to the levels for the other major Western European countries. In Japan and the four largest Western European countries, the average investment/GDP ratios fell moderately after 1973. The ratio remained constant in the United States and rose in Canada. A higher ratio of energy investment to GDP after 1973 was the most important factor in the rise in Canada's overall investment ratio, but the ratio of non-energy investment to GDP also increased slightly.

Many people believe that Canada needs more capital per unit of output per employee than most other countries because of our colder climate, which requires higher investment in construction; our lower-density population, which requires higher investment in transportation infrastructure; the larger share of our output in such capital-intensive industries as agriculture, mining (including oil and gas), and hydro-electric/power generation; and our smaller-scale production runs in manufacturing, which may make less efficient use of plant and equipment. Furthermore, our rapid employment growth requires a higher ratio of investment just to provide the same growth in capital per

TABLE 8-3 Capital Investment, Major OECD Countries, 1960–1982

Gross Fixed Capital Formation as % of Gross Domestic Product	Averages				
	1960–67	1968–73	1974–79	1960–82	1980–82
United States	18.0	18.3	18.3	18.1	17.6
Japan	31.3	34.7	32.0	32.3	31.0
Germany	25.2	24.4	20.9	23.4	21.7
France	22.3	23.5	22.7	22.6	21.1
United Kingdom	17.5	18.6	18.7	18.0	16.2
Italy	21.7	20.6	20.0	20.7	19.7
Canada	22.1	21.6	22.9	22.3	22.5
Total: above	20.3	21.6	21.6	21.0	20.9
Total: OECD	20.7	21.9	21.8	21.4	21.0

Source: Organisation for Economic Co-operation and Development, *Historical Statistics 1960–1982* (Paris: OECD, 1984), Table 6.8.

worker as do other countries. Most experts consider growth in capital per worker a major factor in productivity growth.

Nevertheless, given that after 1973, investment was higher in Canada than in any of the other countries except Japan, our investment performance relative to other countries appears adequate, at least before the 1981–82 recession. However, there may at present be cause for concern. Real investment in Canada suffered a sharp decline during the recession and has not yet begun to recover significantly; investment in the United States, on the other hand, has since rebounded sharply.

Another recent source of anxiety has been the deteriorating financial position of corporations during the 1981–82 recession. Table 8-4 presents a few of the financial ratios most frequently used to describe the position of industrial corporations. The ratio of internal funds to capital outlays shows the extent to which corporations had fewer internal funds to draw on to finance investment during 1981 and 1982. The decline in the ratio of current assets and current assets less inventories to current liabilities provides a measure of the erosion of corporate liquidity after 1980. The increase in the debt/equity ratio made corporations more vulnerable to fluctuations in interest rates. There was a pronounced compression of profit margins in 1981 and 1982. The financial position of the corporate sector began to improve in 1983, and improvement continued in 1984. However, this process has necessarily entailed some retrenchment of investment. It is only after corporations have rebuilt their balance sheets that investment can be expected to strengthen. As long as the build-up does not take too long, however, it should not be a source of undue concern.

Some observers expressed misgivings about the effects of the tax system on incentives to invest. In particular, there is worry about the degree to which inflation might have raised and distorted effective corporate tax rates, thus creating a disincentive for investment. Calculations made by the Economic

TABLE 8-4 Selected Financial Ratios of Large Canadian Industrial Corporations, 1980–83

	1980	1981	1982	1983
		(ratio)		
Internal funds/capital outlays	0.76	0.46	0.41	0.84
Current assets/liabilities	1.60	1.52	1.41	1.43
Current assets less inventories/liabilities	0.89	0.83	0.76	0.81
Total debt/equity	1.26	1.38	1.53	1.42
		(per cent)		
Pre-tax profit margin on sales	9.8	8.1	4.5	6.3
Interest burden	27.4	40.2	65.1	49.6

Source: Canada, Finance Canada, *Economic Review, April 1984* (Ottawa: Minister of Supply and Services Canada, 1984), p. 27.

Council of Canada seem to suggest that this has occurred. According to these estimates, the real effective tax rate in the non-farm/non-financial sector rose from 37.2 per cent in 1963–65 to 44.3 per cent in 1978; in the manufacturing sector, it rose, during the same period, from 42.6 per cent to 47.2 per cent.[3] Other data show that the real tax rate rose considerably over the period 1966–78 and actually exceeded the statutory nominal rate in 1975–77.[4] Other economists, however, have raised questions about the interpretation of the data; if we exclude corporations that are in a loss position, no upward trend appears in the effective tax rate for the non-resource sector as a whole or for the manufacturing sector.

An important factor countering the effect of inflation on the effective tax rate or, at the very least, mitigating the extent of any increase has been the introduction of a number of Canadian corporate tax provisions. These include the 50 per cent rate of capital-consumption allowance and the lower corporate-tax rate for manufacturing and processing; the investment tax credit; and the 3 per cent inventory allowance. More generally, rates of capital-consumption allowance have been higher than required to offset depreciation.

Taking these various incentives into account, a recent study concluded:

> *Despite the lack of indexing of the tax system, inflation does not seem to have significantly affected the incentive to invest or the effective tax rate, except for investment in inventories. Similarly . . . the corporate tax structure itself does not much affect the marginal investment decision, with the exception of inventories.*[5]

The stock of capital kept growing strongly through the period 1973–81 and thus did not contribute to the apparent decline in productivity growth after 1973.

Would it be beneficial to encourage even higher rates of investment and capital formation than existed prior to 1981 (which might be possible after full cyclical recovery)? Conventional economic analysis does not suggest that additions to the capital stock would produce dramatic gains in output. One calculation that relates output to the quantity of labour and capital inputs estimates that an increase in investment equal to 3 per cent of GNP (an increase in investment which amounted to more than 20 per cent in 1983) would only raise the total capital stock of the nation by 1 per cent and would raise output by the relatively small amount of 0.3 per cent. More sophisticated calculations, which assume that technical change is embodied in the capital stock, also indicate that it would take a massive increase in investment spending to manage even a relatively moderate increase in output and productivity. We should harbour no illusions that modest increases in investment will result in huge increases in productivity in the short or medium run.

An increase in investment raises only the level of output and not its growth rate over time. Higher growth occurs only in the interim, between the time of investment and the point when the economy reaches the new increased level of output. Moreover, to maintain the new level of output, it is necessary to devote an increased proportion of output to investment; otherwise, the economy will eventually return to its original growth path.

However, the benefits from increased investment, while not dramatic, might still be worthwhile.[6] It might be possible to improve economic welfare and raise living standards by increasing investment as long as the pre-tax return on capital exceeds the after-tax rate of return on savings.

One policy prescription to stimulate investment is to reduce the taxation of capital. Another is for the government to increase savings available to finance investment by reducing its own deficit. Some of the discussion of policy alternatives, particularly in the United States, has focused on the desirability of fully funding social security pension plans; this action, of course, would increase the level of savings for this purpose and, in all likelihood, the total level of national savings.

While international comparisons of investment performance and a review of the treatment of investment in the existing Canadian tax system do not suggest a strong case for increasing the long-run level of investment, there are theoretical grounds for believing that such an increase might offer net benefits. Perhaps the main immediate concern, however, is whether investment will recover quickly and sufficiently from its present cyclically weak level. If it does not, governments may need to induce more investment.

Notes

1. See Chapter 7.
2. Canada, Finance Canada, *Economic Review, April 1984* (Ottawa: Minister of Supply and Services Canada, 1984), p. 125.
3. Abraham Tarasofsky and H. Bert Waslander, "Inflation-Adjusted Rates of Return and Effective Tax Rates, by Aggregate and Industry Groups", in *Peering under the Inflationary Veil*, edited by Patrick Grady, Proceedings of an Economic Council of Canada Conference on Inflation-Induced Distortions in Financial Reporting and Taxation, Toronto, October 15–16, 1981, pp. 26–27.
4. *Ibid.*, p. 28.
5. Robin Boadway, Neil Bruce, and Jack Mintz, "Taxation, Inflation, and the Effective Marginal Tax Rate on Capital in Canada", *Canadian Journal of Economics* 17 (February 1984), p. 78.
6. In the United States the leading proponent of this view has been Martin Feldstein of the National Bureau of Economic Research. This same case has been stated for Canada. Robin W. Boadway and W. Steven Clark, "The Government Budget, the Accumulation of Capital, and Long-run Welfare", in *Fiscal and Monetary Policy*, vol. 21, prepared for the Royal Commission on the Economic Union and Development Prospects for Canada (Toronto: University of Toronto Press, 1985).

Technological Progress

Technological Improvements in Perspective

The rate of growth of our income per capita – a measure of our wealth as a nation – ultimately depends on the rate of productivity growth of labour and capital. The rate of productivity growth depends, to a considerable extent, on the rate of technical advance or progress. While a number of authors[1] have attempted to quantify the various sources of technical progress, the term continues to describe a residual category of economic developments about which we know relatively little.

Fundamentally, technical progress embraces any innovation that improves the way we do things. Thus, innovations in the political decision-making process or improvements in the organizational design of corporations or non-profit organizations have no less potential to increase wealth than has the discovery of a better carburetor. We must keep in mind that technological change involves a broad process of improvement in products, methods of production, organizational design and management, and, indeed, in the organization of political institutions and the operation of the political process.

Most discussions of technological change concentrate on improvements in products and processes, and on formal research and development. This tendency can be seen in the frequently-voiced concern that Canada is devoting far too few resources to research and development. A few analysts have argued that we have mechanisms in place to develop new products and processes, but that as a society, we have neglected to encourage innovative activity in the field of managerial techniques and organizational design.

One observer contends that political innovation is necessary if technological innovation is to continue.[2] In his view, a society's ability to adopt new technologies depends on its ability to limit the political power of special-interest groups or to induce these groups to act in ways more conducive to the general good. Political innovation is not only productive in its own right, the argument goes, but it also increases the return on more conventional types of innovative activity.

The Nature, Sources and Rate of Technological Change

A discussion of the evolution of industrial structure would obviously be incomplete without some analysis of changes in the extent, nature and sources of improvement in technology. Unfortunately, the process of technological change does not yield easily to such analysis. One approach, however, is to measure rates of growth in total factor productivity within various industries and to accept the result as the rate of technical advance. While there has been considerable progress in making such measurements, this approach has yet to convey much insight into the causes and nature of technical change. A number of econometric studies have suggested that the rate of technical change in a number of industries in the late 1970s was negative. This does not seem likely; it suggests merely that we still do not define or measure technical change very well. Another approach is to attempt to draw conclusions from actual experience in particular cases. This involves identifying "major innovations" and, subsequently, drawing inferences from their characteristics of "areas of strength", or appropriate managerial or public policies. This approach, too, entails problems.

One analyst has argued that one-half, perhaps more, of observed increases in total factor productivity are the result of "prosaic, unremarkable improvements".[3] Technical change, according to this view, is generally a consequence, not of some great leap forward, but of continual small changes – learning by doing and by using.

During a meeting organized in 1984 by this Commission and the Conference Board of Canada, an executive of the Dominion Foundries and Steel Company (Dofasco) outlined examples of small, yet discernible, improvements resulting in technical change:

> *We have entered into a study with Nippon Steel which extended over about a six month period where they sent a team of fifteen people to our plant and examined all our operations and they went back home to Japan and analysed that work. We sent about fifteen people over there to work with them. They came back for about another month or so and then they went back.*
>
> *Anyway what they told us, there is no quick fix to management. It is something that you have to work on continuously, and they were all basic fundamental things they told us that we could improve. And we are a pretty efficient steel company, and they said: "Why are you taking a half inch side trim on that coil?" I don't know. Somebody started doing that and we continued to do it. "Well, you should only take a quarter inch and that would give you a certain percent yield improvement. Why are you moving that coil from here to here? . . . The forklift truck has to pick it up and you get a damaged edge. Do your workers know where you are going?"*
>
> (Ben Ciprietti, at Royal Commission and Conference Board of Canada, Meeting of Council of Corporate Planning Executives, Transcript, May 10, 1984, pp. 58–59.)

The changes described involved neither new technology nor formal research and development (R&D), yet they unquestionably enhanced productivity. Formal R&D is important, but we should not emphasize it to the exclusion of other productivity-enhancing policies, including the timely adoption or adaptation of technological advances initiated elsewhere.

The Rate and Pattern of Technical Change

Is the rate of technical change accelerating? In the opinion of many observers, it is. For example, the recent federal Task Force on Micro-Electronics and Employment concluded in a brief to this Commission:

> *It is worth repeating that this wave of new technologies differs radically from that of the past. Previous technological changes have typically come into public use in isolation and in series. Today the rate and breadth of technological change [are] so great that the interactions between old and new technologies have further-reaching, more complex implications than any time at least since World War II.*

Technology is now rapidly changing on a global scale. In fact, we are witnessing nothing less than a transformation of the whole manufacturing system of the world. The geopolitical map of the world is being rewritten in front of our eyes.

(Task Force on Micro-Electronics and Employment, Brief, November 28, 1983, p. 3.)

The Canadian Manufacturers' Association sees the matter in similar terms:

The challenge for Canada is not only to find ways of riding the current wave of technological innovation but, given that the rate of change is accelerating, we must also find ways of remaining *on the wave of technological innovation. To do so, our industrial system must be flexible and quickly self-adjusting.*

(Canadian Manufacturers' Association, Brief, September 6, 1983, p. 5.)

The Calgary Council for Advanced Technology voiced the same opinion:

Never has time been so critical as it has been with high technology. The product that is viable today is literally obsolete tomorrow.

(Calgary Council for Advanced Technology, Transcript, Calgary, November 9, 1983 [vol. 43], pp. 8833–34.)

During the 1984 meeting sponsored by this Commission and the Conference Board of Canada, participants asked members of the Conference Board's panel of corporate planners whether the rate of technical change is accelerating. Their responses were to the effect that technical change occurs in waves, affecting different industries at different times. Although change is rapid in some sectors, it is not necessarily taking place on a broad front. One participant concluded:

In terms of technical change, I would come back and say that you can look at some areas that are under a phenomenal rate of change now. The micro-electronic area: tremendously rapid rate of change. And the company I work for has one business venture, one in which we measure the life span of the technology in months. But if you look at the oil refining area, I would argue that the rate of change was far faster in 1950 for fundamental process changes . . .

So I think in the oil industry, the rate of process change is not particularly high; micro-electronics is very high; pharmaceuticals and the whole biochemical process [has] a very high rate of change; [for] the chemical and plastic business, in my mind, the rate of change was faster in the sixties than it is now.

(Peter Flynn, at Royal Commission and Conference Board of Canada, Meeting of Council of Corporate Planning Executives, Transcript, May 10, 1984, pp. 98–99.)

Attempts to measure the acceleration of the rate of technical change using various indices of inventive activity produced results that did not accord with the public perception. After surveying the econometric evidence, indices of patenting activity, and other measures of inventive activity, an American economist concluded that these measures provide "evidence that the rate of technological innovation may have slowed down in the 1970s and early 1980s."[4] He concedes that the available studies are somewhat out of date and notes recent significant increases in research and development (R&D)

spending in the United States and Canada. Thus, at least one index of technical change is on the rise.

International Diffusion of Technology

Which nations are the major contributors to the world-wide pool of technologies on which Canada and other nations draw heavily? The United States has been and remains the most important source of new technologies, but its relative contribution has declined in recent years. Two studies bear on this record. First, a National Science Foundation study on the sources of significant technological innovations showed that the U.S. share had declined from 80 per cent during the period 1953–58, to 57 per cent for the period 1965–73,[5] while the Japanese share had risen from zero to 10 per cent. Secondly, a U.S. survey confirmed that while the United States retains world leadership in most fields, the greatest improvements in technological expertise over the period 1968–83 occurred for the most part in Japan and occasionally in West Germany.[6]

Patent data graphically illustrate the decline in the U.S. share and the increase in the Japanese share of world-wide inventive activity. The U.S. share of patents granted to "own nationals" by seven leading industrial countries fell from 49 per cent in 1970 to 34 per cent in 1980, while the Japanese share increased from 22 per cent to 42 per cent. The West German share edged up slightly, while the Canadian share held constant. Changes in the world-wide distribution of R&D spending show that Japanese and German R&D spending have risen more quickly than that in the United States.

There have also been changes in the extent to which new technologies become adopted internationally and in the speed with which this development occurs. New technologies now find their way to more countries and travel more quickly in the process than they did 25 years ago. There is now little or no time lag between reception of a new technology in industrialized countries and its reception in less-developed or newly industrialized countries (NICs).

Researchers are in general agreement that new technologies are transferred abroad earlier in their "life cycle" and more frequently than was usual prior to 1970. One analyst concludes that the product cycle – during which a technology has a period of solely domestic exploitation, with exports serving foreign markets, before it is transferred abroad – has been compressed to the point of non-existence.[7]

Another analyst provides additional evidence on the extent to which new technologies are spreading around the world.[8] He calculated changes in shares of world market for industries of selected countries ranked by relative expenditures on R&D between 1967 and 1981. The results clearly showed that the NICs such as Hong Kong, Singapore, South Korea, Taiwan and, of course, Japan have increased their relative market shares in the more R&D-intensive product classes, while the reverse is generally true of Western Europe and the United States. The implication is that the NICs are moving toward specialization in export industries involving extensive R&D spending (and presumably new technology) and away from exports involving low R&D expenditure (and presumably older technology). To do this, they must also be acquiring the latest technologies in one way or another, and much sooner, comparatively speaking, than they ever did before.

Canada appears generally to have received new technologies as quickly as other industrialized countries, although the evidence is mixed. The Economic Council of Canada has interpreted the evidence as indicating that technology diffuses slowly into Canada.[9] Table 8-5 summarizes the evidence from three large sample surveys, including that of the Economic Council. As the table illustrates, transfers within multi-nationals generally involve newer technologies. One of the benefits of foreign investment is the access it brings to the most recent technological developments.

Diffusion of New Technologies within Canada

Do new technologies spread as rapidly through Canadian industry as they do through the industries of foreign countries? The leading investigators in the field have concluded that new technologies spread more slowly within Canadian manufacturing industries than in other countries.

> *The evidence from the various case studies cited is consistent in demonstrating slower adoption of capital-embodied innovations in Canada than in several other developed countries. In cases where the innovation was more capital intensive than existing techniques, thus requiring longer product lengths of run for efficient use, slower adoption reflected the impact of the domestic tariff on plant level production conditions. The experience of the carpet industry suggests that the anti-competitive effects of the tariff might retard the adoption of new techniques even when the innovations are less capital intensive than existing techniques.*[10]

Acquisition costs related to identification and evaluation may discourage Canadian firms, especially if they are small, from applying new technologies. Even though a new technology might require little capital to implement, significant acquisition costs might delay its adoption. Acquisition costs, however, tend to decline over time; hence delayed diffusion is more common than limited or zero diffusion, such as one would expect with capital indivisibilities.

Tariffs, quotas and other forms of trade protection seriously impede technological diffusion. Protection sustains small producers who find the new technologies uneconomic, and it reduces the "competitive pressure" to lower costs. Some economists have proposed the remedy of a decrease in trade protection. In their view, trade liberalization would lead to specialization and longer production runs, which would enable producers to spread the costs of new technologies over a larger output. This procedure would make it more feasible for them to adopt new technologies early and more costly to postpone such adoptions.[11]

The Economic Council of Canada has echoed these same concerns:

> *Our general finding is that new technology diffuses slowly into Canada from other countries. It also diffuses slowly from firm to firm and from region to*

TABLE 8-5 Three Estimates of the Mean Lag Years for Diffusion of New Technology, 1960–1979

Multinational Enterprise Database:

	Canada			Europe		
	Intra-corporate	Arm's Length	Both	Intra-corporate	Arm's Length	Both
Mean lag	6.93	10.0	7.11	10.27	10.86	10.42
No. cases surveyed	115	7	122	340	116	456

Economic Council of Canada:

	Canada		
	Intra-corporate	Arm's Length	Both
Mean lag	5.8	8.8	6.94
No. cases surveyed	37	19	56

Mansfield and Romeo (1960–1978):

	Overseas Developed Countries[a]		Less-Developed Countries
	Intra-corporate	Licensing/ Joint Venture	Intracorporate
Mean lag	5.8	13.1	9.8
No. cases surveyed	27	26	12

Sources: Multinational Enterprises Database, Economic Council Database and E. Mansfield and A. Romeo, "Technology Transfer to Overseas Subsidiaries by U.S.-Based Firms", *Quarterly Journal of Economics* (December 1980): 737–50.

a. Including Canada.

region within the country. By "new technology" we mean new and improved products, processes, and organizational structures. Although there are some exceptions, case studies show that often the process of diffusion of technical change into and throughout Canada occurs more slowly than in other Western developed nations, and not only in the manufacturing sector but in the service sector as well. Substantial benefits could be realized if the diffusion process into and throughout Canada were to be speeded up. We find that scope does exist for policies designed to achieve this.[12]

The Economic Council attributed the problem in the service industries to organization size, lack of technological receptiveness and, in public-sector service organizations such as hospitals and libraries, lack of managerial incentives.

Technology Diffusion and Public Policy

Public policy can affect the rate of adoption of new technologies in a number of ways. Government policies on trade and on foreign investment fundamentally affect the rate of adoption. Liberalization of trade would increase the rate at which Canadian firms adopt new technologies, as would lowering of barriers to direct foreign investment, at least in technology-oriented areas. Public policy on education and the gathering and dissemination of information also affects the diffusion of technology. The universities provide training in science and engineering for a technological society. Many Canadians believe that still further emphasis on science, engineering and business may be necessary. Northern Telecom, for instance, has recommended that:

> 1. *Canada's education system must emphasize the development of a literate population armed with the tools needed to communicate in a world increasingly dependent on the production and transfer of information.*
> 2. *A high priority must be the development of world class post-secondary centers of excellence in mathematics, computer science and the general sciences.* (Northern Telecom, Brief, November 2, 1983, p. 29.)

Universities can also assist the diffusion process. In Ontario, the University of Waterloo has been operating the highly successful Canadian Industrial Innovation Centre and Innovation Place, both of which assist in the commercialization of inventions and the incubation of fledgling high-technology firms.

A number of new initiatives have also taken place in the gathering and dissemination of information. In 1981, the National Research Council (NRC) combined its Industrial Research Assistance Program (IRAP) and its Technical Information Service and began an expansion of the combined programs. As of 1984, its field staff of industrial technology advisers totalled 121 persons, of whom 74 worked for provincial or other research institutes under contract to the NRC.[13] During fiscal 1983–84, the combined programs gave support to 2540 projects and dealt with over 37 000 queries from industry. At the same time, the federal government announced a series of technology centres, and the Ontario government set up six technology centres (with a total budget of over $100 million over five years) to provide information on currently available technologies to small companies.[14]

Representatives of the Canadian Manufacturers' Association testified before the Senate Committee on National Finance that both corporations and industry associations are disseminating the latest developments in manufacturing technology. Indeed, the Senate Committee commented:

> The Committee is concerned about the proliferation of technology centres in Canada *supported by federal or provincial governments that may not be meeting identified needs.* It recommends that the federal government, as a matter of urgency, examine its policies with respect to the support of technology centres, taking into account provincial government initiatives in this area, with a view to ensuring that the centre it supports clearly meets existing or potential needs of industry.[15]

Several quarters have suggested expansion of government activity in the area of international information gathering. The Senate Committee recommended that the government review the activities of Canada's science counsellors in six Canadian missions abroad in gathering technical intelligence.[16] In 1984, the Science Council of Canada recommended expansion of, and increased support for, this network of science counsellors.[17] According to another authority, technology brokers, contract-research organizations and long-term technology "think-tanks" have greatly helped other countries acquire technology. These resources are lacking in Canada, he notes, and governments should assist in establishing them.[18]

The Generation of New Technologies: R&D Spending

Any analysis of technology turns, sooner or later, to the adequacy of the various individual components of the national R&D effort. Commissioners have attempted to put this in perspective, noting that innovation includes political and social developments. Much technological innovation represents an accumulation of small changes resulting from ongoing improvement to product performance and production methods, based on experience rather than on formal R&D.

Nevertheless, R&D is important, and we must look at the adequacy and efficiency of Canadian R&D spending. The standard measure of the extent of the national R&D effort is the ratio of gross expenditures on research and development (GERD) to gross national product (GNP). Table 8-6 reports this ratio. As the table indicates, this ratio bottomed out at 0.96 per cent in 1976 and has since increased steadily. By 1985, it may reach 1.5 per cent, the revised target set by the federal government in 1981. Table 8-6 reports also the recent experience of the United States. The U.S. GERD/GNP ratio hit its low point in 1977–78 and has increased steadily since then. Thus, the two countries have had the same experience with the GERD/GNP ratio. However, most of the decline in the U.S. GERD/GNP ratio during the 1970s resulted from a decrease in space research, which fell from 0.6 per cent of GNP in 1965, to 0.2 per cent in 1977. As the table indicates, non-defence R&D in the United States declined only marginally during the early 1970s.

At present, the ratio of Canadian non-defence R&D to GNP is approximately 73 per cent of the U.S. ratio of non-defence and space R&D to GNP. How does the Canadian R&D effort compare with that of other countries? Table 8-7 reports the R&D intensities of selected OECD countries. There is considerable year-to-year variation in national R&D intensities. Except for the Japanese figures, which clearly move upward over the period 1971–81, the R&D intensities show no clear trend. Canada's R&D intensity is consistently the lowest of those of the countries listed. Other comparisons show that Canadian industrial R&D intensity is above that of Norway, Denmark and Italy; still other data rank Canada above Australia. The United States is not the only country to devote a significant proportion of its R&D effort to defence. France devotes approximately one-third of its R&D effort to defence and space, and Britain, one-quarter.

TABLE 8-6 Gross Expenditures on Research and Development as a Percentage of Gross National Product, U.S. and Canada, 1965–1983

Year	Canada	Canada non-Defence[a]	U.S. Total	U.S. non-Defence and non-Space
1965	1.20	1.06	2.9	1.3
1966	1.22	1.12	2.9	1.4
1967	1.29	1.19	2.9	1.5
1968	1.25	1.17	2.8	1.5
1969	1.26	1.18	2.7	1.5
1970	1.24	1.17	2.6	1.5
1971	1.22	1.16	2.5	1.5
1972	1.13	1.08	2.4	1.4
1973	1.04	0.99	2.3	1.4
1974	1.02	0.97	2.3	1.5
1975	1.02	0.98	2.3	1.5
1976	0.96	0.92	2.3	1.5
1977	0.98	0.94	2.2	1.5
1978	1.02	0.98	2.2	1.5
1979	1.03	0.99	2.3	1.6
1980	1.09	1.06	2.4	1.7
1981	1.17	1.13	2.5	1.7
1982[b]	1.34	1.31	2.6	1.8
1983[b]	1.36	1.32	2.7	1.8

Sources: Statistics Canada, *R&D Expenditures in Canada 1963–1983* (Ottawa: Statistics Canada, Science Statistics Centre, 1983), p. 6, and *Federal Government Expenditures on Activities in the Natural Sciences 1963–64 to 1983–84* (Ottawa: Statistics Canada, Science Statistics Centre, 1983), Table 17; and data from the U.S. National Science Foundation.

a. Calculated as total expenditures less expenditures by the Department of National Defence.

b. Preliminary data.

Those looking for hopeful signs for Canada from the GERD/GNP data would note that the Canadian ratio is rising, although it is not keeping pace with the growth in Japan, for example; that Canada ranks above a number of small, high-income countries in industrial R&D intensity; and that Canada's R&D intensity looks better relative to countries such as the United States, Britain and France when we exclude space and defence R&D from the comparison. The fact remains, however, that Canada is not as R&D intensive as countries

TABLE 8-7 Gross Expenditures on Research and Development (GERD) as a Percentage of Gross Domestic Product (GDP) of Selected OECD Countries

Country	1971	1973	1975	1977	1979	1981
			(%)			
Canada	1.35	1.12	1.11	1.07	1.12	1.25
France	1.91	1.78	1.80	1.76	1.81	1.97
Germany	2.19	2.09	2.22	2.14	2.40	—
Japan	1.83	1.87	2.94	1.91	2.10	2.40
Netherlands	2.17	2.01	2.12	1.99	1.88	1.90
Sweden	1.48	1.60	1.15	1.87	1.88	—
Switzerland	2.33	2.25	2.40	2.29	2.40	—
U.S.A	2.68	2.50	2.44	2.39	2.37	2.54

Source: Statistics Canada, *Historical Statistical Compendium*, prepared for the Royal Commission on the Economic Union and Development Prospects for Canada (Ottawa: Statistics Canada, 1985), Table 16.6.

such as Sweden, Switzerland and the Netherlands. What, if anything, should we do about this situation? Should we have a national target for R&D expenditures in relation to GNP? In 1978, the federal government set a GERD/GNP target for 1983 of 1.5 per cent. In 1981, it postponed the target year to 1985. As we have said, it appears that we shall reach this latter target.

Recent commentaries, including those of the Economic Council of Canada, the Task Force on Federal Policies and Programs for Technology Development (the Wright Task Force),[19] and the Doody Committee,[20] – have cautioned that the principal merit of a GERD/GNP target is to increase public awareness of the importance of R&D. It is a device to motivate and focus debate; it is not an end in itself, nor is it of much use as a planning tool. The three studies listed concluded that we should worry less about the quantity of R&D than about its quality and effectiveness. The Wright Task Force concluded about Canada's low GERD/GNP ratio:

> *This is not necessarily grounds for concern. The effectiveness with which our R&D funds are deployed, in the context of our particular circumstances, is more important than how much we spend. If we doubled R&D spending tomorrow, the economic impact of that increase would be quite marginal.* Spending more on R&D makes no sense unless it's spent in a culture that feels compelled to compete. *Such competitive environments create a need for innovation, which generates demands for still more research. This self-reinforcing pattern is the hallmark of all vigorously growing economies.*[21]

The Senate Committee noted that the "ideal" GERD/GNP ratio for any country depends on its industrial structure, the importance of defence-related research, its market size, and its ability to gain access to, and use the results of, R&D performed elsewhere:

> *Investment in advanced technology must continue to be an important area of government concern, not only in terms of the level of that investment but more important . . . in terms of the quality of that investment.*[22]

In the view of these observers (and of Commissioners as well), a willingness to compete and to face competition is essential. Canadians must do whatever is necessary to meet the competition. Some think that to meet this necessity requires much more R&D and more government support. Others think that more or more relevant R&D will be a consequence of a more direct orientation to trade. There is apparent agreement, however, that the willingness to face international competition is essential.

If we are not to set national expenditure targets, at least as a planning device, what are we to do? The alternative is to assess various types of R&D activity on their respective merits as investments. One analyst would focus on the quality and composition of R&D, rather than the amount:

> *What that suggests in turn is that the focus of the policy issue should shift from R&D levels to the portfolio of R&D projects an industry tends to generate. This entails turning our attention toward the incentive effects of policies and institutional structures and toward considerations of access, secrecy, and information flow. In practice, some kinds of R&D projects will tend to be "underfunded" and some to be "overfunded"; and a simple R&D subsidy is not the sort of policy such a situation demands.*[23]

To attempt to determine the merits of various types of R&D is difficult. It involves, where possible, an assessment of past social rates of return for industrial R&D; it requires a judgement of the discrepancy between the private and the social rates of return: that is, benefits from R&D to the nation as a whole rather than just to particular companies or industries.

Let us begin with research and development performed by the government. This support at present accounts for approximately 29 per cent of all R&D performed in Canada. This proportion is down markedly from the levels for the 1960s and early 1970s, when the government undertook or funded over one-third of all Canadian R&D. A comparison of the most recent Canadian figures with the 1977 figures for OECD countries indicates that government in Canada continues to undertake proportionately much more R&D than the governments of the United States, Germany, Switzerland, Japan and Belgium. Our government, however, performs a smaller proportion of R&D than the governments of Australia, Finland, Italy and France.

The decline in the proportion of Canadian R&D undertaken by government occurred largely because business R&D spending grew faster than that of government. Attempts to contract out government R&D have not altered the government share significantly. The federal Department of Agriculture accounts for some 20 per cent of the government R&D effort, and the National Research Council is responsible for another 20 per cent. Atomic Energy of Canada and the Departments of Environment, Fisheries and

Oceans, National Defence and Energy, Mines and Resources account for roughly 10 per cent each.[24]

The Professional Institute of the Public Service included the following government-research achievements in its 1983 survey:[25]

- *Rapeseed* (*canola*). R&D expenditures, $12 million; annual value of crop, $600 million.
- *Spring wheat*. R&D cost of rust resistant, hard, red spring wheat, $450 000; value of crop losses avoided, $200 million.
- *Hybrid corn*. R&D cost, $32 million; value of increased yield, $2.6 billion (over the 1959–78 period).
- *The development of styroblock containerized seedlings* for reforestation, resulting in wage savings of millions of dollars.
- *The development of forest fire information systems* that has resulted in the saving of millions of dollars per year in fire suppression and damage costs.
- *Fisheries research* that has resulted in an increase of 80 per cent in the value of British Columbia coho salmon catch and a new snow-crab fishery off New Brunswick with an annual value of $40 million.
- *Remote sensing technology*.
- *The development of an efficient hydro-cracking process for heavy oils*, to be used at Lloydminster and Cold Lake and in the Athabasca tar sands.
- *A retrofit oil burner kit* that achieves 20 per cent fuel savings.
- *The CRV-7 Rocket system*.
- *Advances in the treatment of pulp and paper effluent*.
- *Telidon*, an advanced video-technology system for facilitating multi-purpose access to diverse computer data-bank resources.

This partial list conveys the essence of the case made by the Professional Institute: government research has yielded significant returns, especially in the resource and environment sectors.

Instances of evidence of a more systematic nature also exist. U.S. studies show high rates of return on agricultural research. Two corresponding Canadian studies also show high rates of return. Researchers at the University of Saskatchewan[26] found that research leading to the improvement of canola from the original strains of rapeseed grown in Poland and Argentina has yielded an annual rate of return of 101 per cent.[27] The rates of return on successful projects will not, of course, represent the return on the entire research effort. Existing evidence, however, suggests that agricultural research has been a good investment for Canada. The Science Council of Canada[28] has suggested that a greater investment in forestry research would also bring relatively high returns.

A large portion of government research over the last 25 years has focused on nuclear power, specifically the CANDU reactor. A recent study put the R&D cost of the CANDU at approximately $7 billion.[29] Another study, which used an alternative costing method, concluded:

> *Evidently, to this point in time the CANDU project has been a commercial failure that has cost Canadians between $16 and $18 billion (1981) dollars. The benefit, largely to citizens of Ontario, totals about $2 billion (1981) dollars.*[30]

Other cost/benefit calculations on Canada's nuclear reactor expenditures are more favourable. While there is dispute over savings resulting from the use of CANDU (as compared with coal or the U.S. light-water/moderated reactors), calculations done for this Commission indicate that there is a range of reasonable assumptions regarding reactor and fuel costs and real discount rates, over which the net advantage of the CANDU may be sufficient to cover its R&D costs.

Whatever the past record, the Wright Task Force believes that as currently managed, government laboratories will not make the contribution their resources would suggest:

> *Canada's federal laboratories are justly proud of their long tradition of excellence and innovation* ... We believe, however, that these traditions of excellence are being undermined by a growing atmosphere of irrelevance and an excessively bureaucratic management style.[31]

The Task Force suggests the remedy of greater use of peer review and contracting out: government laboratories need better management, not more money.

R&D performed in Canadian universities totalled $1 billion in 1983, a sum amounting to approximately 20 per cent of all Canadian R&D. This represents a decline of some six percentage points from the level in the early 1970s: a consequence of the growth of industrial R&D. Canada performs more R&D in universities than does the United States, which devoted 8.6 per cent of its 1983 R&D spending to university projects, but Canadian activity is not out of line with that of other OECD countries.

The Wright Task Force has argued that the universities, representing a crucial link in the innovation chain, have a function beyond basic research. Some universities have seized the initiative in this area, most notably the University of Waterloo, which described some of its activities as follows:

> *The University formed the Waterloo Research Institute to coordinate the research activities and to assist industry in matching their research needs to the expertise resident within the Faculty. Industrial sponsored research at Waterloo now totals more than [that] of any other Canadian University. Contract research this year has experienced a 57% increase over last year.*
>
> *Waterloo pioneered the concept of "Open Computing" by creating the world-famous WARFOR fast fortran computer in the late 1960's and has moved along this innovative path continuously with the most recent endeavour in this area being the Waterloo-IBM accord to sell MICRONET, an educational computer networking system (Oct. 24, 1983). Waterloo developed software sales last year exceeded those of MIT [Massachusetts Institute of Technology] and Stanford [University] combined.*
>
> *Research activities have been highlighted this year by the recent award to the VLSI research group of the highest-ever NSERC* [National Science and Engineering Research Council] Strategic Grant Award ($1.6M/3 years).
>
> *Waterloo initiated the concept of what has now become the Canadian Industrial Innovation Centre/Waterloo. The aim of the centre is to turn innovative ideas into marketable new products or services.*
>
> (University of Waterloo, Brief, November 2, 1983, p. 3 of Introduction.)

The Task Force and participants in this Commission's seminar on emerging technologies judged that the National Science and Engineering Research Council (NSERC) and the Medical Research Council (MRC) are performing well. They recommended that R&D support be changed to cover not only direct costs of particular projects, but also all indirect costs associated with the establishment and maintenance of the relevant facilities and services: in other words, the establishment of "full-cost" funding. While this need not involve an increase in total support of university R&D, it would ultimately lead to specialized research-oriented universities, which many Canadians believe our country requires.

A number of observers have noted the lack of business support for university research in Canada. Some have suggested extension of R&D tax incentives to apply to contributions made by firms in support of university R&D. Given probable substantial national benefits from this type of research, it would seem a candidate for preferential tax treatment.

Canadian R&D expenditures by industry in 1984 amounted to about $2.7 billion: over 55 per cent of total R&D expenditures in the country. This represents an increase of more than 14 percentage points over the level in the 1960s: business R&D spending has grown faster than government R&D spending. Canada continues to perform less of its R&D in the business sector than do the United States, Switzerland, West Germany, Japan, France and Belgium, but more than do the Netherlands, Norway, Finland and Australia.

The essential features of the Canadian R&D effort by industry, as of 1982, were as follows.

- There were 1296 firms engaged in formal R&D activities, of which 379 were foreign controlled.
- Two hundred and thirty-one firms spent more than $1 million on R&D.
- Canadian-owned firms accounted for 57 per cent of industrial R&D expenditures; foreign-owned firms made up the balance.
- Seventy-one per cent of the funding for industrial R&D came from the performing firm, and some 13 per cent (excluding tax incentives) came from either the federal or provincial governments.
- The average ratio of R&D to sales was 1.2 per cent, a 50 per cent increase over 1975. Both foreign- and domestically-owned firms increased their R&D/sales ratios. As a group, Canadian-owned firms tend to spend a higher proportion on R&D in relation to sales than do foreign-owned firms operating in this country.
- R&D/sales ratios tended to be highest in the aircraft, communications equipment and engineering-services industries. Some 28 per cent of industrial R&D occurred in the communications-equipment industry, 12 per cent in wells and petroleum products, and 10 per cent in aircraft and parts.[32]

Direct government support for industrial R&D currently takes the form of subsidies, contracts and tax concessions. The largest subsidy programs are the Defence Industry Productivity Program (DIPP), of which expenditures totalled $169.2 million in 1983–84; the Industrial and Regional Development Program (IRDP), with expenditures of $102.7 million in 1983–84; and the

Industrial Research Assistance Program (IRAP), which spent $48 million in 1983–84. Government R&D contracts totalled $268 million in 1983. Tax concessions at present take the form of a 100 per cent write-off of current R&D expenses; a 100 per cent write-off of capital R&D expenditures; 20 per cent tax credit which reduces the cost base for capital consumption allowances; and a flow-through provision for unused deductions and credits, the Scientific Research Tax Credit (SRTC), which the government has substantially tightened.[33]

Table 8-8 outlines the support for R&D provided by the tax incentives in effect between 1978 and 1982. The incentives consisted of a 10 per cent (taxable) tax credit and an allowance equal to 50 per cent of the increase in current-period R&D expenditures over a three-year/average base. As indicated, these incentives had a value (tax cost) of approximately $178 million in 1981 and $203 million for 1982. Tables 8-9 and 8-10 present additional information concerning the degree of government support for R&D.

When we compare the various types of R&D support both over time and across countries, it is important to note that R&D contracts generally do not involve the same level of support to industry as a subsidy or a tax measure. The Canadian government retains the rights to *all* technology developed under federal contract; the contractor generally has the status of a non-exclusive licensee of any technology it wishes to use. Of course, technology developed with the assistance of a subsidy or a tax measure is the exclusive property of the firm involved.

The comparison of support levels internationally hinges on the weight that we assign to R&D work done under contract for governments. That is, if we view a contract as equivalent, dollar for dollar, with a subsidy or a tax credit,

TABLE 8-8 Tax Incentives for Research and Development and their Cost

			($ millions)			
Year	Credit Claimed	Effective[a] Credit Rate	After-Tax[b] Value	Allowance	Tax Saving Implied	Total Saving
1978	28	4.8	13.4	50	21.0	34.4
1979	58	7.5	27.8	128	53.8	81.6
1980	80	7.9	38.4	188	79.0	117.4
1981	125	8.5	60.0	282	118.4	178.4
1982	142.3[c]	8.5	68.2	322	135.2	203.4[c]

Source: Statistics Canada, *Industrial Research and Development Statistics, 1982*, Cat. No. 88-202 (Ottawa: Minister of Supply and Services Canada, 1984), Table 2.1, and Appendix III, Table 23.

a. Credit claimed ÷ R&D expenditures of claimants.

b. Assuming recipients are taxed at 42 per cent.

c. Estimated by Commission staff.

TABLE 8-9 Federal Payments to Canadian Industry for R&D[a]

Fiscal Year	Contracts	Contributions	Fellowships	Total
1977–78	85.9	100.4	1.2	187.6
1978–79	101.0	76.3	1.5	178.8
1979–80	99.1	103.4	1.5	204.0
1980–81	100.2	113.7	1.6	215.5
1981–82	126.8	153.5	1.9	282.2
1982–83	165.1	197.3	2.2	364.6
1983–84	190.2	268.2	3.1	461.5

Source: Statistics Canada, *Federal Government Expenditures on Activities in the Natural Sciences 1963–64 to 1983–84* (Ottawa: Statistics Canada, Science Statistics Centre, 1983), p. 33.

a. Natural Sciences R&D.

TABLE 8-10 R&D Support, Canada, 1978–1982

Year	Tax Saving	Grants and Contracts	Grants and Contracts after Tax[a]	Total Support	Support ÷ R&D Performed in Business Sector
1978	34.4	178.8	123.7	157.6	15.7
1979	81.6	204.0	150.2	231.8	18.2
1980	117.4	215.5	156.4	273.8	17.5
1981	178.4	282.2	202.4	380.8	19.0
1982	203.4[b]	364.4	322.0	525.4	20.4

Source: Statistics Canada, *Industrial Research and Development Statistics, 1982*, Cat. No. 88-202 (Ottawa: Minister of Supply and Services Canada, 1984).

a. Grants assumed taxed at 42%.

b. Estimated by Commission staff.

then R&D support in the United States, Britain, France, West Germany and Sweden is higher than it is in Canada. If we view an R&D contract as something less than a 100 per cent subsidy, Canadian support comes much closer to the level of those countries.

If we wish to evaluate industrial R&D on its merits, we should ask not only whether the Canadian support is comparable with those of other countries, but also what it should be ideally. The issue here turns on the so-called "externality considerations": the extent to which society's return on R&D exceeds the return earned by the firm that engages in it.

The Economic Council of Canada concluded that R&D spending in Canada was too low, and that more public and private R&D spending was necessary.[34] The Council did not indicate whether the additional government spending should be in support of industrial R&D or in other areas. The Senate Committee recommended against further tax incentives and did not suggest any change in subsidies or contracts. The Wright Task Force recommended reviewing all subsidy programs and gradually phasing out those that fail to win the endorsement of clients. It recommended more contracting-out of existing government R&D, but not more overall R&D by government. It concluded that the Canadian R&D tax incentives are "generous", and that any alterations should be in the direction of broadening the definition of R&D.

A study done for this Commission on industrial strategy[35] contends that the social return on R&D is much higher than most people realize, and it supports much more generous funding for R&D in Canada. Not only does R&D result in innovations that bestow benefits on society in excess of the compensation paid the innovator (the "spill-over" effect), but also the workers producing new products acquire skills on the job that enable them to command higher wages. These higher wages are, according to this study, an additional positive spill-over from R&D.

> *Estimates of the social return to industrial R&D based on a closed economy assumption are quite high – often in the 30 to 50 percent range. Yet these estimates do not include any of the returns to domestic labour which would be earned if R&D was the means by which a technology gap is maintained. In an open economy context if the basic idea of the technology gap theories is correct, the national social returns to R&D which allow the maintenance of a gap may be far in excess of the conventional estimates.*[36]

This study encourages "support" for R&D through any one of a variety of tax, subsidy, loan guarantee or procurement policies.[37] The level of support would be much higher than at present; the argument is made that Canada's target of R&D expenditures, equal to 1.5 per cent of GNP, is probably too low:

> *If Canada is to have its share of the technologically progressive industries, it will have to devote resources closer to the proportion spent in the major industrial countries. In 1977, these shares within the manufacturing sector were closer to 5 and 6 percent.*[38]

This conclusion indicates the possibility that greater support of some kind should be forthcoming.

Thus, insofar as federal funding of R&D is concerned, there is consensus that the federal government need not increase its R&D activities, but might, in some situations, usefully shift them to private contractors. University R&D should receive more support from the business sector, and tax incentives to achieve this end are desirable. A greater proportion of federal assistance to universities should take the form of grants in aid of R&D.

There is no such consensus regarding the support of industrial R&D. Had the Scientific Research Tax Credit remained in force as originally established, the Canadian system would be very generous by any standard. As it is, the system's relative generosity turns on the degree of support attributed to R&D work contracted out by government.

Relative support levels notwithstanding, the study on industrial strategy done for this Commission argues for *much more* generous support. Its arguments require attention, but not necessarily an immediate policy response. The federal government, however, should consider reformulating the Scientific Research Tax Credit. It might refund part of expenditures for R&D undertaken by firms lacking sufficient taxable income to benefit from the tax credit, that is, employ a form of negative income tax. Reliance on the tax system is preferable to a grants program, which tends to be cumbersome and might invalidate basic market indicators of those sectors where R&D expenditure would yield the best returns.

Notes

1. Edward Denison is the most prominent. See *The Sources of Economic Growth in the United States and the Alternatives Before Us* (New York: Committee for Economic Development, 1962).
2. Mancur Olson, *The Rise and Decline of Nations: Economic Growth, Stagflation, and Social Rigidities* (New Haven: Yale University Press, 1982).
3. Nathan Rosenberg, *Inside the Black Box: Technology and Economics* (London: Cambridge University Press, 1982), pp. 62–70.
4. Edwin Mansfield, "Technological Change and the International Diffusion of Technology: A Survey of Findings", in *Technological Change in Canadian Industry*, vol. 3, prepared for the Royal Commission on the Economic Union and Development Prospects for Canada (Toronto: University of Toronto Press, 1985).
5. National Science Foundation, *Science Indicators, 1974* (Washington, D.C.: U.S. Government Printing Office, 1975).
6. Edwin Mansfield, "International Technology Gaps and the Intelligence-Gathering Activities of Firms" (Pittsburgh: University of Pennsylvania, 1984).
7. Raymond Vernon, *Storm over the Multinationals: The Real Issues* (Cambridge, Mass: Harvard University Press, 1977).
8. Bruce R. Scott, "American Competitiveness: Concepts, Performance and Implications", paper presented to the Harvard Business School 75th Anniversary Colloquium on United States Competitiveness in the World Economy, 1984.
9. Economic Council of Canada, *The Bottom Line: Technology, Trade, and Income Growth* (Ottawa: Minister of Supply and Services Canada, 1983).
10. D.J. Daly and S. Globerman, *Tariff and Science Policies: Applications of a Model of Nationalism* (Toronto: University of Toronto Press for Ontario Economic Council, 1976), pp. 97–98.
11. *Ibid.*, p. 95.
12. Economic Council, *The Bottom Line*, p. 61.
13. National Research Council, *NRC Annual Report 1983–1984* (Ottawa: Minister of Supply and Services Canada, 1984), pp. 18–20.
14. Ontario maintains technology centres in Ottawa (micro-electronics), Peterborough (robotics), Cambridge (CAD/CAM), Sudbury (resource machinery), Chatham (farm machinery and food processing), and St. Catharines (automotive parts).
15. Canada, Senate, Standing Committee on National Finance, *Federal Government Support for Technological Advancement: An Overview* (Ottawa: Minister of Supply and Services Canada, 1984), p. 43 (emphasis in original).

16. *Ibid.*, p. 34.

17. Science Council of Canada, *The Canadian Science Counsellors*, Council Statement (Ottawa: Minister of Supply and Services Canada, 1984).

18. Z.P. Zeman, "Towards Technology Acquisition Policy: Six National Approaches", paper prepared for the Royal Commission on the Economic Union and Development Prospects for Canada (Toronto, 1984).

19. Canada, Ministry of State for Science and Technology, Task Force on Federal Policies and Programs for Technology Development, *Report* (Ottawa: Minister of Supply and Services Canada, 1984) (Douglas Wright, Chairman).

20. Canada, Senate, Standing Committee on National Finance (C. William Doody, Chairman).

21. Task Force on Federal Policies and Programs for Technology Development, *Report*, p. 3.

22. Standing Committee on National Finance, *Federal Government Support for Technological Advancement*, p. 13.

23. Richard R. Nelson and Richard N. Langlois, "Industrial Innovation Policy: Lessons from American History", *Science* 219 (February 18, 1983), p. 815.

24. Statistics Canada, *Canadian Science Indicators, 1983*, Cat. No. 88-201 (Ottawa: Minister of Supply and Services Canada, 1983), p. 23.

25. Professional Institute of the Public Service of Canada, *Intramural Research and Development: Problems and Remedies*, a discussion paper (Ottawa: The Institute, 1983), pp. 4–6.

26. J.G. Nagy and W.H. Furtan, "The Socio-economic Costs and Returns from Rapeseed Breeding in Canada" (Saskatoon: University of Saskatchewan, Department of Agricultural Economics, 1977).

27. Another widely quoted study is B.E. Prentice and G.L. Brinkman, *The Value of Agricultural Research in Ontario* (Guelph: University of Guelph, Ontario Agricultural College, 1982).

28. Science Council of Canada, *Canada's Threatened Forests* (Ottawa: The Council, 1983).

29. Kristian S. Palda, *Industrial Innovation: Its Place in the Public Policy Agenda* (Vancouver: Fraser Institute, 1984), p. 108.

30. George Lermer, "AECL – An Evaluation of a Crown Corporation as a Strategist in an Entrepreneurial, Global Scale Industry", paper presented to the Research Conference on Government Enterprise, sponsored by the Economic Council of Canada, held at the University of Toronto, November 21–22, 1984, p. 7.

31. Task Force on Federal Policies and Programs for Technology Development, *Report*, p. 25 (emphasis in original).

32. Statistics Canada, *Industrial Research and Development Statistics, 1982 (with 1984 forecasts)*, Cat. No. 88-202 (Ottawa: Minister of Supply and Services Canada, 1984), p. 26.

33. Canadian Tax Foundation, *The National Finances, 1983–84* (Toronto: The Foundation, 1984), p. 243.

34. Economic Council, *The Bottom Line*, p. 83.

35. Richard G. Harris, *Trade, Industrial Policy and International Competition*, vol. 13 (Toronto: University of Toronto Press, 1985).

36. *Ibid.*

37. *Ibid.*

38. *Ibid.*

The Role of Entrepreneurship and Management

The development and growth of Canada's economy depend on our human, capital and natural resources, together with the technology that uses those resources. But our economic well-being depends, also, on two other critically important factors: the bringing together of all these elements to form a productive enterprise, which is the essence of entrepreneurship, and the ongoing process of efficiently organizing and managing each of these facets.

Most people think of entrepreneurs as a few innovative individuals who dare to take risks in pursuit of profit, individuals most often associated with small and medium-sized firms, rather than with large corporations. While individual entrepreneurship continues to be most evident in smaller enterprises, entrepreneurship is also the critical element that has permitted many of today's corporations to develop and maintain large-scale operations. A sophisticated system of management is vital to the efficient operation of such large corporations and, in most instances, is provided by a professional management team concerned with every phase of the business, from production to advertising, marketing and distribution. However, if these larger enterprises are to survive and thrive, their professional managers must also provide an element of entrepreneurship, which may manifest itself in many forms, such as the development of new technologies or new products, the introduction of new marketing methods, or the take-over of another enterprise as a means of increasing the efficiency of operations.

While there are differences in concept, it is often difficult, in practice, to draw a clear distinction between entrepreneurship and management, particularly when the former is exemplified in the ongoing process of change and innovation of existing enterprises as contrasted with the launching of new ventures. Although Commissioners propose to focus initially on management and then look at entrepreneurship, some overlap is unavoidable.

Managerial Techniques, Quality and Organization

The Canadian Federation of Deans of Management and Administrative Studies has outlined the critical role played by management in the development of a nation's economy:

> *Management itself must be regarded as a national resource alongside technical, natural, financial, labour and other resources, as it is both the catalyst and the "glue" in assembling, organizing and mobilizing these resources.*
>
> *Increased international competition for markets at home and abroad clearly demands that we produce world-class management talent if we are to achieve economic success and support the attainment of our other social goals. Assuring the availability of such talent should rank high in the nation's priorities.*
>
> (Canadian Federation of Deans of Management and Administrative Studies, Brief, November 30, 1983, p. 1.)

With regard to managerial techniques, quality and organization in Canada, several questions arise: How does the overall quality of Canadian management rate by international standards? Does the Canadian managerial approach differ significantly from that of other countries? How does the quality of Canadian managers rate by international standards? Have our managers had as much formal education or an education of the same quality as their foreign counterparts? Have they had the same experience in critically important management functions as their foreign counterparts?

The United States developed most of the concepts and practices that made possible the efficient management of large-scale corporate organizations. Canadian management methods and practices parallel those of the United States, though ours may be less effective in some important respects. Recently there has been considerable discussion as to whether U.S. management, which once set the standard for the world, has fallen behind. This Commission examined the debate over U.S. managerial ideas and practice as part of its research;[1] it may be useful to note some of the issues that have emerged south of the border.

One of the foremost critics of U.S. economic organization contends that the American economy has been "slowly unravelling" since the late 1960s.[2] This process is a result of political disarray and of the failure of U.S. corporations to move out of mass production methods that they originally pioneered into other, more competitive forms of production and organization:

> *The rigid management-centered organization has become inappropriate to an America now linked to an integrated world economy. That pattern of organization can be duplicated anywhere on the globe, including areas with lower-wage labor and cheaper access to raw materials and emerging markets. Since 1970, therefore, the economies of America and every other industrialized nation have undergone a profound structural change, as the high-volume industries that underpinned these economies in the previous half-century — steel, textiles, automobiles, rubber, shipbuilding, and chemicals — have become less competitive in world markets. The only way industrialized nations can increase their citizens' standards of living in the future is to concentrate on the high-value niches within these industries and to seize and keep world leadership in new industries based on advanced and emerging technologies. This requires a different form of organization, one far more flexible and adaptable than the structures designed to support high-volume, standardized production.*[3]

In the view of this observer, managers of the U.S. corporate system have responded in a variety of ways to the new challenges confronting them, but not in ways likely to prove beneficial over the longer term:

> *The innovations have not been technological or institutional. Rather, they have been based on accounting, tax avoidance, financial management, mergers, acquisitions, and litigation. They have been innovations on paper. Gradually, over the past fifteen years, America's professional managers have become paper entrepreneurs.*[4]

Paper entrepreneurship, the critic contends, can be a ruthless game in which those who win do so at the expense of others: investors, taxpayers or consumers. While the game can be lucrative for those who play it well, "it does not create new wealth . . . It merely rearranges industrial assets. And it has hastened our collective decline."[5]

Paper entrepreneurship is an umbrella covering a number of the failures or imperfections of democratic societies with market economies. It appears to be another term for "rent seeking", a process which involves the use of real resources in an attempt to extract wealth from other members of society. Since the early 1970s, the problem of rent seeking has been central to discussion of the economic difficulties faced by Western industrial democracies.[6] Paper entrepreneurship is, in part, rent seeking in the corporate sector. An example is the large public- and government-relations staffs that corporations maintain to assist in rent seeking. Members of these staffs may lobby governments to protect existing benefits or secure new ones. In some industries, profitability may depend less on the quality of the technology and production techniques employed than on the manner in which the government manipulates the general and sectoral economic environment. As a member of the Conference Board of Canada's panel of corporate planners observed:

> *You have to look on an industry by industry basis, and say: What is the cutting edge? But in micro-electronics, if you spend all your time flying to Ottawa, you have missed the point.*
>
> *In the energy industry if you spend all your time flying to Ottawa you have exactly the point because that is where the money gets made.*
>
> (Peter Flynn, at Royal Commission and Conference Board of Canada, Meeting of Council of Corporate Planning Executives, Transcript, May 10, 1984, p. 100.)

Paper entrepreneurship attempts to influence government in order to alter or defend the existing distribution of income. It also seeks ends quite apart from government: these include mergers of companies, which some critics consider socially unproductive, particularly when they lead to creation of large conglomerates. As Commissioners see the situation, however, mergers may benefit one of three groups: society as a whole; the owners of one or both of the firms involved, at the expense of society; the managers of those firms; or a group of "insiders", at the expense of all or some owners and of society as a whole.

Mergers benefit society as a whole when they allow the firms involved to take advantage of economies of scale, which in turn, simply effect a better matching of talents and capabilities with opportunities. Mergers that facilitate increased specialization, larger-scale production, or better use of management or marketing capabilities may increase efficiency and lower costs. We would expect to see and, indeed, have seen, a flurry of acquisitions and divestitures in an economy that is in the process of rationalizing its production arrangements as a consequence of trade liberalization or of a broadly based change in technology.

A merger may benefit the owners of the firms involved at the expense of society if it confers on the new entity additional market power, such as an ability to earn monopoly profits. This result will be unlikely in industries characterized by relatively free trade or by an absence of regulatory or other impediments to the entry of new competitors.

Sometimes a merger will bring about both economies of resource use and increased market power. The consensus of those who have examined this possibility is that the beneficial effects of the economies will generally offset the harmful effects of the additional market power.

A merger, as well as many other arrangements, will benefit the owners, but not society, if it occurs simply to make use of otherwise unusable tax deductions and credits. This type of activity might be less common if the tax system provided for the transfer or refund of at least some unused deductions and credits. In addition, mergers may be undertaken in order to distort earnings results and to pump up stock prices for the benefit of insiders, promoters or management, at the expense of other investors and perhaps of society as a whole. This latter type of outcome is part of the essence of paper entrepreneurship.

A recent study of the extent, disposition and source of the gains from merger activity in the United States concluded:

> *Corporate takeovers generate positive gains, that target firm shareholders benefit, and that bidding firm shareholders do not lose. The gains created by corporate takeovers do not appear to come from the creation of market power.*[7]

Thus, at least in the United States, mergers may generate gains in wealth that are a consequence of economies of resource use, creation of more efficient management, or realization of tax benefits. The last element would not be wealth increasing from the standpoint of society as a whole.

Because the make-up of the Canadian economy differs from that of the United States, the conclusion about the possible contribution of mergers to the U.S. economy – even if the conclusions were accepted as valid – might not apply to the Canadian economy. In Canada, during the past decade or so, large conglomerate organizations have emerged. Do they represent counter-productive paper entrepreneurship? In its 1978 *Report*, the Royal Commission on Corporate Concentration found that conglomerates had facilitated the transfer of resources from old static industries to newer and more dynamic ones, and that they had also promoted increased Canadian ownership. Nevertheless, the Commission concluded:

> *On balance ... conglomerate diversification has probably decreased the efficiency of resource allocation in the Canadian economy, although not seriously. Firms that have followed a strategy of conglomerate diversification have, in general, given their shareholders and given their investors below-average returns in the market. Over a long period, therefore, the practice of unrelated diversification is likely to cease through the force of competition.*[8]

Continued conglomerate diversification since 1978 belies the conclusion that competition would discourage the practice. Most conglomerates have diversified out of unattractive base industries, a procedure which perhaps represents the best strategy available. Whether it would have been more efficient for the shareholders to diversify on their own behalf is open to debate.

Other criticisms of American, perhaps North American, managerial theory and practice also relate to the same factors that reputedly give rise to paper entrepreneurship. These include preoccupation with short-term earnings performance at the expense of long-term growth and development and neglect of the so-called "real side" of business operations. Modern-day business operations demand managerial concern for the advancement of production techniques and technologies, new product development, "zero-defect" quality control, "just-in-time" inventory management, and reduction in the hierarchical structure prevalent in most large North American corporations, which tends to be costly and to work against the motivation of employees.

Some observers contend that the limited period that individual managers tend to spend on any given job exacerbates short-term focus of many North American corporations. This creates an incentive for the manager to produce visible results quickly enough so that he or she, rather than a successor, can garner the credit. According to a number of observers, Japanese firms take a longer-term approach. They may have a lower cost of capital, with perhaps a longer period in which to pay back their investment. The lifetime employment provided by many Japanese firms and the absence of stock-market pressures and take-over threats may also permit Japanese managers to take a longer view.

A recent U.S. study[9] found that more successful American companies also take the long view. Similarly, a study of Canadian companies with a reputation for excellence reports that these, too, operate from a similar perspective:

> *Continuity in the CEO [chief executive officer] and management teams of these companies, together with their symbiotic relationships with their boards, help give them the confidence and experience to sacrifice short-term advantage for long-term benefits. While the pressure from financial analysts, the stock market, and shareholders for increases in quarterly earnings is a matter of considerable importance and concern, the excellent companies seem to be able to strike the appropriate balance . . .*
>
> *In achieving this careful balance between the company's short- and long-term interests, they seem to have avoided the malaise that media and academic commentators in North America cite as the cause of the decline of North American industry: an overemphasis on today's profitability by managers anxious to show quick impact before they move on to another job, and commensurate failure to invest in the future through commitments to developing new products, better technology and modern facilities.*[10]

Two studies[11] note that companies with a reputation for good management share a number of common characteristics. These include: a clear definition of the business they are in – and not in; an explicit commitment to leadership, which they seek to achieve through the provision of good value to their customers, and through the identification and exploitation of their competitive edge; and adoption of organizational structures and operational approaches that motivate employees to contribute to the achievement of company goals by instilling a sense of participation. According to a study undertaken for this Commission,[12] certain Canadian steel firms have become world leaders in productivity and productivity growth by confining their interests to a single industry and pursuing a business strategy strongly influenced by technological considerations.

A 1984 survey of 28 countries ranked Canada seventh in overall competitiveness.[13] Canada ranked eleventh in 1983 and sixth in 1982. In 1984, Canada ranked first in natural endowments, third in financial dynamism, fifth in human resources, and sixth in market dynamics. In other categories, however, it fared considerably less well. We ranked eleventh in economic dynamism, fourteenth in both industrial efficacy and socio-political consensus and stability, fifteenth in outward and innovative forward orientation, and sixteenth in terms of state interference in the economy. The countries that ranked ahead of Canada in overall competitiveness were the United States, which held the first position, Switzerland, Japan, Germany, Denmark and Sweden.

At the time of writing, detailed comparisons of production performance in 1984 were not yet available. In 1983, Canada fared poorly in product quality, design and styling, product safety, on-time delivery and after-sales service. Canadian performance was also poor in the categories of innovation in production techniques and product lines, readiness to exploit inventions, and industrial flexibility. Over the period 1977–82, Canadian employees ranked last in productivity growth; moreover, they compared unfavourably in their willingness to work efficiently and to accept labour-saving devices. Canadian management ranked poorly in managerial drive and entrepreneurship.

A number of other observers have commented on the lack of Canadian managerial entrepreneurship. One brief to this Commission noted:

> *I have found the average Canadian to be as entrepreneurial as any other national—within the limits of his resources. Canadians in general are not to blame. Rather the entrepreneurial spirit of a few hundred people in the management of our big companies must be questioned.*
>
> *In some cases the low quotient of entrepreneurship is because the company is simply a "branch plant" and lacks the skills and, more importantly, the mandate for diversification and further processing. In other cases the cause is not so obvious. A comfortable niche conferred on the company by ownership of a rich mine or of a rich forest licence or being shielded from the pressures of competition may be contributing factors.*
>
> (H.N. Halvorson Consultants Ltd., Brief, August 19, 1983, p. 3.)

Others have questioned the entrepreneurial capacities of many of Canada's smaller firms:

> *New product development in [threshold] firms is essentially an exercise in intra-corporate entrepreneurship, dependent more on marketing expertise than its technological capability.*
>
> *The ability to discover, design and develop products in the face of changing technology and markets is the essence of entrepreneurship. And it is precisely in doing so that Canada's firms have apparently failed.*[14]

There is no shortage of opinion to the effect that Canadian managers and managements are very good. A member of the Conference Board of Canada's panel of corporate planners said to this Commission:

I have worked with managements all over the world and I do not for a moment accept that Canadian management is not as good as anything I know of in the world, and I include in this the Japanese and German and all of the other rightfully praised managements.

(Arthur Earle, at Royal Commission and Conference Board of Canada, Meeting of Council of Corporate Planning Executives, Transcript, May 10, 1984, pp. 87–88.)

But a presentation to this Commission's symposium on small business gave a less optimistic opinion:

We are second to none in terms of technology, but we are second to a lot of people in management and marketing. Having managed a multinational company and having been exposed to the U.S. management, I am perhaps not as critical of our Canadian management. I sent five vice-presidents down to the parent company [during the] years that I ran Digital, so it speaks for something. I will admit that we lack the discipline that multinational companies will force upon themselves, particularly discipline relative to marketing.

(Denzil Doyle, at Royal Commission, Small Business Seminar, Transcript, October 15, 1984, p. 130.)

As a number of submissions to this Commission have suggested, the apparent lack of emphasis on managerial entrepreneurship may be a product of the relatively protected environment in which many Canadian firms have operated. As protection decreases, the inducement to adapt, to innovate and generally to perform the entrepreneurial function will increase, and experience will sharpen our entrepreneurial skills:

Management education had a role to play in [upgrading] the quality of management, but much less than one might suppose in terms of making it adaptable to change. Adaptation to change, I am quite convinced, derives from industrial experience rather than from a teachable scientific body of thought.

(Arthur Earle, at Royal Commission and Conference Board of Canada, Meeting of Council of Corporate Planning Executives, Transcript, May 10, 1984, pp. 62–63.)

In this view, then, the development of the appropriate skills will be a consequence of a greater exposure to competition. Governments can encourage this development by shunning protective policies and measures that perpetuate managements that are unable to meet the competitive challenge.

Another policy issue suggests reorientation of assistance programs for small business:

Entrepreneurship and marketing are the major weaknesses, not R&D support. Perhaps our greatest failing in attempting to manage the growth of Canada's technology-producing sector is in over-estimating the importance of technology and under-estimating the importance of entrepreneurship and marketing.[15]

As we saw above, the 1983 survey ranked Canada sixteenth out of the 22 OECD countries in product design and styling. Governments could well pay closer attention to the way in which the arts and cultural community contribute to Canadian economic performance. Canadian sculptor William McElcheran told this Commission:

What possible connection could there be between art and the economy? To answer this question properly, it is necessary to see the word "art" in a much larger sense than most people are used to.

If "art" means that precious activity indulged in by very special people for a limited audience of well to do culture seekers, the connection with the main stream of society is extremely tenuous. If, however, the word "art" means the use of human intelligence, imagination and creativity in the making of things generally, *I believe that a case can be made for the importance of art in the economic life of the nation.*

It is in seeing the relationship between people who make sculpture and painting, etc. and people who make more ordinary, useful things, that the importance of art can be appreciated in the economic sense. We need to see a return to quality and individuality *in the environment we create for ourselves and this cannot happen unless pride of workmanship is reborn. When workmen are proud of their work, they are artists of sorts.*

When price and quantity are the only criteria, it is natural that the cheapest, mass-produced products will have the advantage. In producing low-priced products of very advanced technology, Canada will always be at a disadvantage because of extremely high research and development costs, a small domestic market and a high wage scale relative to Asian countries. When low-priced Japanese goods are also of very high quality it becomes very difficult to compete, even for the U.S. The international race to produce super computers and robotized production systems reads like a life or death winner-take-all struggle which powerful western nations could lose.

There are a tremendous number of things which do not necessarily have to be produced in huge factories but which can generate a great deal of employment (and enjoyment). I know that this sounds like a return to the past, but I believe that it is actually a prediction of the future.

(William McElcheran, Brief, June 18, 1983, pp. 1–2.)

There is, then, another aspect to culture, namely good taste, good design and creative innovation, that should enable smaller industrial economies to compete effectively in the world market. As a country with an even better forest endowment than Sweden, why are we importing Swedish furniture? The answer, of course, is design, which has enabled the Swedes, and the Danes, to sell higher-quality products on world markets. Another example is Italian shoes, particularly for women. Shoemakers in Italy earn less than in North America, but shoemakers in the Far East earn less than those in Italy. It is creative design that has kept Italy a leader in the shoe market.

This Commission suggests that Canadians as consumers should demand high quality and creative innovation in goods produced in this country. They can thus help to create a more competitive Canadian manufacturing sector. In this endeavour, higher quality implies an organic relationship between business and engineering, on the one hand, and design and craftsmanship, on the other. This relationship is hard to establish. In countries that have achieved such success, it has resulted from artists, business persons and engineers working together. In some situations, this co-operation appears to have happened "naturally"; in other instances, public policies supported it.

To promote this process, this Commission endorses the following recommendations of the *Report* of the Federal Cultural Policy Review Committee:

> *33. The proposed Canadian Heritage Council should promote liaison among various federal departments and agencies involved in heritage, among all levels of government and between government and the private sector . . .*
>
> *37. The government should amend the National Design Council Act of 1960 to designate a Canadian Council for Design and the Applied Arts and fund the Council to a level that will enable it to fulfill its mandate. The Council should report to the Minister of Communications.*[16]

In addition, this Commission recommends particular attention to pages 161–66 of the Committee *Report*.

High-quality products, technologies, plants, homes, cities and locales require the presence of creative artists of all kinds. To increase the long-run supply of artists in all these areas of our national life, as well as their artistic and cultural expression, governments must support the artists and the arts. The long-term return to investment in artists and the arts is real and substantial. In the absence of strong public support of this sector, Canada will not reap these benefits. Governments at all levels should increase their contribution to their respective arts councils.

Business education is also worthy of examination. One analyst has characterized Canadian management as less well educated and less open than that in the United States:

> *There have been clear tendencies for managers in the United States to be drawn increasingly from those in the labour force who have had university training, especially those with training related to business, science and law. There is also a clear shift towards younger managers. Some of these tendencies are also appearing in Canada, but the shifts are occurring more slowly and have not gone as far. For example, the proportion of managers in Canada with some university in 1971 was only approaching the levels reached in the United States in the 1940's. To some extent, this reflects the continued smaller proportion . . . taking commerce and business at both the undergraduate and graduate levels. In addition, however, those who move into senior management levels in Canada move into positions of middle and senior management later in their working lives than in the United States. The proportion of the Canadian elite that come from the upper class was even higher in the early 1970's than two decades earlier, and this was more pronounced for younger than older managers. The low proportion of Canadian managers with relevant university training thus reflects company selection and promotion patterns and not just the composition and availability of persons with relevant education and experience.*[17]

Perhaps the wider social and educational background of more recent graduates will enable them to contribute more innovative qualities to Canadian management. However, another study[18] emphasizes the advantages of lengthy internal experience and longevity of tenure. Commissioners believe that public policy should foster the creation of a competitive environment that encourages experimentation with alternative approaches and efforts to identify and adopt those management practices that are superior.

In its submission to this Commission, the Canadian Federation of Deans of Management and Administrative Studies acknowledged that some observers have criticized business-school curricula for a lack of attention to production management, over-reliance on quantitative techniques, and inadequate emphasis on strategic entrepreneurship. It responded as follows:

Individual North American business schools vary substantially so [that] such observations might apply to different schools to different degrees and at different times. Some criticism, such as inadequate attention to the concerns of production and the "plant floor", probably applies to most. Better schools of management, as better businesses, have moved and are moving to respond to these concerns as resources permit.

Certainly, traditional ideas about "best management practice" are under substantial attack on many fronts. All of what we teach about management, and the pedagogy we use in so doing, requires continuing, critical examination. Nonetheless, it is important to business school curricula and in North American management practice. Inevitably, still further change will be necessary.

(Canadian Federation of Deans of Management and Administrative Studies, Brief, November 30, 1983, pp. 3–4.)

Whatever the orientation of curricula, severe underfunding of business education has seriously restricted both the numbers who receive a management education and the quality of their training. In a letter to this Commission, W.H. Richardson, President of the Society of Management Accountants of Canada, cited the following indicators:

In student-teacher ratios, professional ranking, research funding and doctoral programs, business faculties continue to place far behind the general university average.

A student/teacher ratio two to three times higher than in other faculties. In accounting programs alone, the 1965/66 ratio was 26:1 and the 1978/79 ratio was 36:1. Overall ratios in 1981 were 13:1 university wide and 30:1 in the business faculties. Given the current pressure on business enrolments, that ratio has probably increased substantially today.

The highest ratio of part-time to full-time faculty, almost 1:1 today. 1981 business school enrolments accounted for about 12% of the total university enrolments, but with less than 5% of full-time faculty. This disproportionate use of part-time faculty suggests that the business student is receiving his/her education from less qualified people than the norm.

Even with 12% of university enrolment, it is estimated that business faculties receive only about 3%–4% of the operating budget of the university system, though this is an average that would fluctuate considerably between schools . . .

The Canadian Federation of Deans of Management and Administrative Studies reports that these kind[s] of problems are not restricted to the accounting streams of business faculties.

The unfortunate fact is that many qualified students are not getting the opportunity they deserve to enter business schools, and those that do are receiving a less than adequate education.

Essential research into such areas as measurement of value, productivity, information management, and the not-for-profit sector is not being done. Even if it were, qualified instructors are not available to teach the new techniques and skills arising out of the research.

I believe that we are past the crisis point in developing tomorrow's accountants and managers. For our own economic survival, we must begin now to put matters right. (Society of Management Accountants of Canada, Brief, November 16, 1983, pp. 2, 4.)

This Commission is of the opinion that Canada must find additional resources for business education. These resources should come from business, from within the university system, and from government.

The international comparison mentioned earlier of Canadian corporate management and its performance leaves no room for complacency; on the contrary, it should be a matter of considerable concern. While government can help to improve the quality of Canadian management – by providing support for business schools, and guidance and training for those involved in smaller enterprises – business must tackle most of the problem itself. It may be, as some have suggested, that the rather unsatisfactory ranking of Canadian management is a result of the sheltered environment in which large segments of the economy have operated in the past. In the far more competitive environment into which we are moving, whether we like it or not, improved management may become essential to the competitiveness of our industries.

Entrepreneurship

As Commissioners emphasized earlier, and as a number of individuals and groups recognized in their submissions, entrepreneurship is a critical element of national economic growth and development. It is difficult to measure the contribution of entrepreneurship to our economic well-being, in contrast to the other elements that contribute to this process, such as human and physical capital and technological advances.

It is sometimes difficult to distinguish between the entrepreneurial and the management functions. A study undertaken for this Commission defined entrepreneurship as part of the process of that innovation:

Entrepreneurship involves the perception of an opportunity to innovate, and the creativity entailed in responding to that opportunity. Some individuals, understanding the potential to alter previous production methods, may implement new techniques or organizational arrangements based upon that understanding, while others may confront the same situation but not share the same insight or creativity. Second, entrepreneurship entails decisions based upon an analysis of uncertainty and risk. An error may occur; an attempt to innovate may fail; there is no guarantee that a new production method will succeed . . . The desire to acquire profit forms a powerful incentive to innovate.[19]

Another study undertaken for this Commission maintains that entrepreneurship is central to economic progress. This survey describes an entrepreneur as an "individual who bets on a new idea and implements it."[20] It concludes that an entrepreneur initiates activities that involve considerable uncertainty, and that could have a profound effect on social relationships by upsetting the existing order and eroding the wealth and privilege of certain groups. In that sense, entrepreneurship is part of the process of "creative destruction".

There are various views on the circumstances that promote or inhibit entrepreneurship. One view is that entrepreneurship may emerge as a consequence of a perception by individuals, firms or nations that they have fallen behind. Another view emphasizes immigration, particularly by minority groups, as a contributing factor:

> *Immigration entails self-selection in that immigrants generally are aggressive and optimistic risk-takers. Furthermore, they may find that avenues to success in their new country are blocked: they are not part of the established culture and their professional qualifications may not be honoured. Their only available route for advancement may be to go into business. Exposure to different production methods in their homeland may spur certain immigrants to take risks and pursue an entrepreneurial career.*[21]

Another view emphasizes a fluid social and political structure and an appropriate reward structure as essential if individuals are to accept the risks of initiating new activity.

The coming together of like-minded individuals may also facilitate entrepreneurship. Former employees of older firms often form new ones. Relations developed between entrepreneurs and financiers may lead to financing of new ventures. Thus it may not be possible to ensure that each region has its *pro rata* share of entrepreneurial activity.

It also seems evident that government policy can encourage or discourage entrepreneurship. Government adjustment assistance, for example, can reduce political opposition to economic change, thus facilitating entrepreneurship. Government policies may also suppress change, either directly or indirectly, by reducing the rewards of entrepreneurship.

Before considering specific measures that governments might take to foster entrepreneurship, it is necessary to gain a clearer understanding of the concept itself. Many Canadians think of it in the context of smaller businesses, particularly new ventures, initiated by one or a few innovative individuals. But many large corporations exhibit entrepreneurship, and, indeed, in many cases, it has been essential to their continuing success. Such entrepreneurship has usually been the product of a team of professional managers, rather than of a few individuals. We can perhaps most readily recognize this process in the larger Japanese enterprises that operate so successfully on the world stage.

One critic claims that U.S. corporations have not moved far enough in this direction:

> *It is becoming clear that America's economic future depends less on lonely geniuses and backyard inventors than on versatile organizations. Our abundance of Nobel laureates attests to American cleverness . . . Our problem is that we are*

not consolidating this technological leadership into enduring commercial leadership because our industrial organization is not adaptable enough.[22]

In the view of this critic and of a number of other observers, adjustment to this new competitive environment will require increased worker participation, political institutions that can link social and economic development, assistance in adjustment, and increased education, training and retraining.

While ongoing entrepreneurship by large corporations is important to the continued well-being of our economy, entrepreneurial activity among existing or new small businesses has been commanding widespread attention recently in both the United States and Canada. A disproportionate amount of employment growth appears to be occurring in small businesses. Indeed, in most industries, including manufacturing, small enterprises account for most, if not all, employment growth. This development applies not only to Canada and the United States, but also to Western Europe.

The most recent data for Canada appear in Table 8-11. Small firms provided 17 per cent of jobs in 1978, but accounted for 66 per cent of employment growth in all sectors between 1978 and 1982. They accounted for the bulk of employment growth in every sector except community services and public administration. In all but two manufacturing categories – electrical products, and food and beverages – most employment growth occurred in small enterprises. (Small enterprises are defined as employing fewer than 20 persons, medium enterprises as employing between 20 and 100 persons, and large enterprises, over 100 persons. The change in employment was measured over the period 1978 to 1982, using employer payroll-deduction accounts from the income-tax files.)

Table 8-12 shows U.S. employment growth by size of enterprise and industry for the period 1980–82. The smallest enterprises (those employing fewer than 20 employees) accounted for most employment growth in most sectors. Employment declined fractionally among medium-sized firms and significantly among large enterprises, but increased substantially in small firms.

What are we to make of these developments? One school of thought considers that these results indicate an increase in entrepreneurship in small enterprises, which in turn has come about because more people want to operate, or work for, a small firm. One presentation to this Commission's Symposium on Small Business gave a number of reasons for this preference:

- Many young people do not wish to work in a bureaucracy, either private or public.
- The economic dislocations of the late 1970s and early 1980s made a larger number of skilled persons available to start new businesses.
- Technology has created many new market niches that did not previously exist.
- Higher general levels of education have enabled individuals to acquire entrepreneurial skills at an earlier age.
- Market fragmentation has reduced the benefits of mass marketing and has created openings for specialists.

TABLE 8-11 Contribution by Size of Enterprise to Sectoral Employment Change in Canada, 1978–82[a]

	Small		Medium		Large		All	
Sector	Employment	%	Employment	%	Employment	%	Employment	%
Unclassified	52 840	7.2	674	0.1	2 735	0.4	56 249	7.7
Primary	10 643	1.4	–3 749	–0.5	–1 620	–0.2	5 274	0.7
Mining	12 665	1.7	5 386	0.7	12 621	1.7	30 672	4.2
Manufacturing	52 434	7.1	–23 938	–3.3	–100 609	–13.7	–72 113	–9.8
Construction	439	0.1	–11 418	–1.6	–12 337	–1.7	–23 316	–3.2
Transportation	18 044	2.5	–2 231	–0.3	11 252	1.5	27 065	3.7
Wholesale trade	32 442	4.4	–7 935	–1.1	5 584	0.8	30 091	4.1
Retail trade	87 894	12.0	–7 208	–1.0	71 869	9.8	152 555	20.8
Finance	23 519	3.2	–5 183	–0.7	15 096	2.1	33 432	4.6
Community services	53 581	7.3	18 125	2.5	97 772	13.3	169 478	23.1
Business and personal services	125 031	17.0	13 536	1.8	42 060	5.7	180 627	24.6
Public administration	13 553	1.8	3 816	0.5	127 383	17.3	144 752	19.7
Total	483 085	65.7	–20 125	–2.7	271 806	37.0	734 766	100.0

Source: Stewart Wells, Assistant Chief Statistician, National Accounts and Analytical Services, Statistics Canada. Presentation to Royal Commission, Small Business Seminar, October 15, 1984. Preliminary figures.

a. Includes changes in part-time employment converted to a full-year equivalent.

TABLE 8-12 U.S. Employment Growth by Major Industry and Enterprise Size Class, 1980–1982

		(data in thousands) Employment Size of Enterprise		
Industry	**Total**	**1–19**	**20–99**	**100 or more**
All industries	984	2 650	–2	–1 664
Agriculture, forestry and fishing	49	72	–7	–16
Mining	278	65	28	185
Construction	97	274	–114	–63
Manufacturing	–1 265	274	–55	–1 484
Transportation, communications, and utilities	33	146	4	–117
Wholesale trade	–82	230	–29	–283
Retail trade	152	364	–40	–172
Finance, insurance, and real estate	494	302	34	158
Services	1 228	923	177	128

Source: United States Small Business Administration, *The State of Small Business: A Report to the President* (Washington, D.C.: U.S. Government Printing Office, 1984), p. 26.

- Development of the computer-software industry, which requires brains, but not necessarily large financial resources, to start a business.
- A demand for custom-produced goods induced by higher per capita incomes.
- Deregulation (in the United States) has allowed new business formations in industries into which entry was earlier denied.[23]

According to this view, changes in labour and product markets and in technology are combining to make the smaller enterprise the preferred institutional form for many productive activities. The growth of employment in the small-business sector is more than merely a response to changes in demand, technology and workers' preferences; it is a reflection of the entrepreneurial character of small businesses:

> *If small firms are creating jobs, they are doing something that large firms are not on average doing; that is to say, they are finding new markets, both domestically and internationally, they are creating new products, new processes, new forms of business endeavour which are proving themselves to be successful and that is reflecting itself in the formation of more jobs.*
>
> (Patricia Johnston-Lavigueur, at Royal Commission, Small Business Seminar, Transcript, October 15, 1984, p. 89.)

While this conclusion is consistent with available facts, Commissioners view it with reservations. The proportion of sales made by small firms has not increased to match employment. Temporary factors prevailing during a turbulent economic period may have produced an upsurge in employment among small firms. U.S. statistics show that over the period 1958–77, the small-enterprise share of employment and sales declined in most sectors. While recent findings perhaps signify a new trend, only time will tell the whole story.

There are others who believe that fundamental forces are leading to a growth in North American entrepreneurial activity. One economist lists these forces as:

- The rapid evolution of knowledge and technology which is creating new entrepreneurial opportunities.
- Demographic trends that encourage the growth of service industries, where the small business form is most appropriate.
- The development of more adequate venture capital delivery systems.
- An increase in the ability of large corporations to undertake entrepreneurial activities.[24]

We turn now to the central issue: What can we Canadians do to foster entrepreneurship?

Encouraging Entrepreneurship

Venture Capital

Questions surround the adequacy of the supply of capital available to finance new ventures and expand existing ones, and of measures to increase the supply. During this Commission's hearings, a number of participants emphasized the importance of venture capital and its scarcity in certain industries and lines of endeavour, and at certain stages of development and levels of finance.

One submission, for example, outlined the problems in the software industry:

> *Because of the small size and newness of companies in this field, and the lack of understanding of the value of the products, conventional financing methods are almost impossible. Typically, a far higher proportion of personal financial resources must be provided by the entrepreneur than in other industries, and this is a particularly prohibitive handicap to the younger (and often more innovative) people. As a result, many valid projects never reach fruition, or reach the market too late because they were undertaken as a "moonlighting" activity, or are not done well enough to compete, or are never started.*
>
> (Software Industry Development Association, Brief, September 2, 1983, p. 8.)

Another brief underlined the difficulty of obtaining venture capital to develop new inventions:

> *[There is a] real problem of [obtaining] start-up money for inventions. The venture capital business does not address that in this country at all. The small business development corporations that Ontario has instituted are a step in the right direction, and certainly that is a help. It still has some constraints which are very limiting. But that whole area of starting up new technologically-based business is one that is very immature in Canada, and needs some support.*
>
> (Frank W. Maine, Transcript, Toronto, December 6, 1983 [vol. 61], p. 12803.)

Yet another submission noted the lack of capital to launch small new enterprises:

Most of the problems that I see are the little start-ups, the fellows who need $100,000 to $300,000 or $400,000 to get off the ground and get going, and it is the step before the institutionalized venture capital companies come into play.

(Calgary Research and Development Authority, Transcript, Calgary, November 7, 1983 [vol. 41], p. 8380.)

Table 8-13 presents evidence on the flow of venture-capital investments by private sector members of the Association of Canadian Venture Capital Companies (ACVCC). The investment flows reported vary significantly over time. While, between 1976 and 1981, venture-capital investment averaged only $35 million a year, it amounted to more than $85 million in 1981 and then dropped to $62 million the following year, reflecting, no doubt, the impact of the recession. In 1983, it rebounded to $86 million.

A presentation to this Commission's symposium on small business presented further evidence on the stock of venture capital:

In terms of sources of venture capital funding or financing in Canada, I do not believe that there is a lack of funds. Industry estimates made indicate that there is currently some $1 to $1.5 billion Cdn. available for venture capital investments. However, a large portion of these funds is available from public sources (particularly provincial) where there may be fewer incentives to sponsor and direct efforts to the best possible ventures than from private source funding. Additionally, in the U.S. a substantial amount of pension and private funds has been directed towards investments in venture capital. U.S.-based pension funds, both public and private, have had a definite impetus in stimulating new product development and start-up venture capital backed firms through direct investments by such private pension funds as AT&T and IBM. U.S. pension fund venture investment dwarfed the total funds invested in venture capital by all pension funds in Canada. For example AT&T pension funds alone invested much more in venture capital than all the pension funds in Canada combined.

(Stuart Feiner, Notes prepared for Royal Commission, Small Business Seminar, October 15, 1984, pp. 2–3.)

Another analyst presents a further insight into the stock of venture capital available in Canada:

*Based on information published in the Sources of Funds Index, it is estimated that some $1.2 billion is now available under the broad definition of venture capital. This compares favorably with the U.S., at least in aggregate, since latest estimates from the U.S. (*Venture Capital Journal*), sets their total at $11 billion . . . If we remove . . . direct government-sponsored funds, as opposed to those which are incentive schemes such as SBDC's [Small Business Development Corporations], the figure for Canada is nearer to $800 million.*

As an indication of the growth of the industry, the full membership in the Association of Canadian Venture Capital Companies, which started only in 1972, has grown from 14 in 1978 to a current 46 full members and 43 associates. In its peak year (1981) the Association reported $121 million of investment, which was distributed 30% to start-ups, 30% to development stage

TABLE 8-13 **Canadian Venture Capital Investments, Domestic and Foreign, 1976–1983**

	1983		1982		1981		Average of 1976–1981	
	Number	$ Millions	Number	$ Millions	Number	$ Millions	Number	$ Millions
Canada	66	86.3	88	61.7	113	85.5	59	34.7
Foreign countries	42	18.7	35	17.2	65	35.4	18	9.4
Total[a]	108	105.0	123	78.9	180	121.2	177	44.1

Source: The Association of Canadian Venture Capital Companies, "Unaudited Information Regarding the Investment Activities of the Association Members", 1983; and Ontario, Ministry of Treasury and Economics, *Economic Transformation: Technological Innovation and Diffusion in Ontario* (Toronto: Queen's Printer, 1984), p. 29.

a. Includes investments with location unspecified.

companies, 28% to expansion, 4% each in turnarounds and buy-outs – 4% was not identified.[25]

Overall, the stock of venture capital seems adequate in relation to the practical opportunities presenting themselves, although some consider that government agencies manage too much of the stock. Any problem with venture capital appears to involve communication between investors and entrepreneurs, rather than funding available.

Tax changes could augment the non-government pool of venture capital. Several participants in this Commission's symposium on small business suggested that the federal government should tax capital gains earned by venture capital companies at the capital gains rate. Possible loss of tax-free status inhibits Canadian pension funds from using the most appropriate vehicle for venture capital investment: the limited partnership. One participant in our symposium described the situation as "absolutely ludicrous".

These tax problems have serious consequences:

Under the current Income Tax Act any investment by a pension fund in a limited partnership is considered to be foreign property regardless of where it makes investments and, is therefore, subject to the 10% limit on foreign investment for the pension funds. Since many of the major pension funds are heavily in the U.S. market, they are already at their 10% limit and, with good reason, are loathe to sell liquid securities in order to participate in non-liquid venture funds. Obviously some modification of this ruling would not be difficult and would certainly help venture capital partnerships raise capital. In the case of North American Ventures Fund II, at least $15 million was "left on the table" because of this foreign content ruling.

Similarly, in the past year, several venture capital companies have been threatened by Revenue Canada with reassessment on some of their earlier capital gains as income . . . The industry has been operating for many years in a state of stability and reasonable expectation of such capital gains treatment. These recent moves by Revenue Canada are having a major disquietening effect, and if they persist, could effectively staunch the flow of capital into the field, as well as increase the already high hurdle rates of return which venture capitalists apply when looking at prospective investments.[26]

What little is known about government venture capital operations does not induce one to argue for their further expansion. A study of the Canada Development Corporation (CDC), a mixed enterprise in which the federal government has a major stake in the venture-capital operation, concluded:

The Corporation has not fared very well by being involved with venture capitalists, certainly less well than it would have fared, on average, by randomly investing in nonfinancial equities.[27]

There is also some indication that the performance of Ontario's venture capital agency, IDEA Corp., has been somewhat disappointing.[28]

One of the foremost problems is the inability of those with promising proposals to convince would-be investors that theirs is a practical and viable business proposition. Subsidies might better be given to assist in converting ideas into practical business proposals, rather than in supporting the supply of venture capital.

Other Forms of Finance

The supply conditions of debt and equity capital have received detailed scrutiny recently in a study undertaken for the Economic Council of Canada. The study concluded:

> *There is no evidence of important market imperfections in the loan market ... In fact, this study shows that it is not true that small firms cannot borrow; they have higher debt-to-assets ratios than the larger ones. One may at least question the wisdom of maintaining several lending institutions, at the federal and provincial levels, without any evidence that they are needed.*[29]

In an earlier report, published in 1982, the Council concluded that there was no generalized credit gap in debt markets, and that the pattern and volume of investment would not have been appreciably different in the absence of government lending programs and institutions.[30] Other observers have cited the continuing need for innovative debt financing, particularly given the nature of the security required.

With respect to equity finance, the Economic Council acknowledged that "small businesses in particular, find it difficult to obtain equity finance".[31] Public policy can amend some of these difficulties. However, the so-called "agency problem" is not so easily remedied. This problem involves the unacceptable way in which an outside equity interest affects the operations of a business.

Difficulties that are potentially amenable to public policy solutions include excessive-issue costs, and "thin" (illiquid) equity markets. The Economic Council suggests that participation in equity markets may be enhanced by changing regulations to encourage increased investments by financial intermediaries in the equities of small and medium-sized firms, and by changing the tax system (that is, the capital-gains tax) to make equity ownership more attractive.[32]

This Commission asked a number of intervenors why the Canadian market for junior equities is so "thin" and what can be done about it. These intervenors answered that the thinness of the market itself discouraged many participants, and that the relatively active U.S. market was, in part, an outgrowth of the long-standing pools of non-government venture capital. In Canada, these pools are of recent origin, and many are government managed. The Economic Council contended that one cause of the equity problem was the tendency of financial underwriters to take an excessive "spread" (that is, the difference between issue price and market price after one month) on junior issues. The Investment Dealers Association provided this Commission with evidence that the spread varies considerably according to economic conditions. We have not been able to determine whether this spread is higher, on average (over many issues and cyclical experiences), than it should be, compared to that prevailing in other areas.

Small Business

The participants in this Commission's small-business symposium suggested some changes in public policy that could benefit small business directly, rather than indirectly through financial markets. One participant argued that deemed realization of capital gains on death of the proprietor made the maintenance of family-owned companies difficult and reduced the incentive of entrepreneurs to build them up. In addition, it was suggested that the tax system should be neutral, as it applies to firms of different size. While debate continues as to whether or not the tax system is neutral, Commissioners agree that it should be so. In this connection, it might be worthwhile to study further the continuing use of flow-throughs and refundability of credits that cannot be claimed against taxable income.

Another participant expressed the opinion that neutrality with respect to firm size should also apply to government-subsidy programs, as the costs of meeting program requirements are simply too high for most young businesses. This is another reason for opting in favour of a tax-based incentive system with refundability.

The symposium produced two other significant points. First, small business would benefit from better-prepared and -screened trainees and from measures that would help to maintain continuity of employment for those being trained. Secondly, we were told:

> *Governments in the past have used the firm as an instrument for the delivery of social policies without realizing how expensive this is. The overhead costs of actually delivering all the unemployment insurance, payroll taxes and the rest, [are] very high . . . I don't think that policy makers have been sufficiently aware of the costs to the small firm of using the firm as the delivery mechanism for these policies.* (Caroline Pestieau, at Royal Commission, Small Business Seminar, Transcript, October 15, 1984, pp. 67–68.)

While, as a general principle, Commissioners believe that it is reasonable to expect business to contribute to the operation of social policies, we also think that it would be desirable for government to examine possible steps to reduce the disproportionately heavy burden that appears to be imposed on smaller-business enterprises.

In addition, Commissioners suggest that the government consider reducing the degree of "planning regulation". This type of regulation may cover such fields as entry into a particular industry, the manner in which the operation is conducted, and the prices that may be charged. In the judgement of the U.S. Small Business Administration, the extensive move towards deregulation has created entrepreneurial opportunities for a great many enterprises in such areas as trucking and warehousing, communications and banking, which are reflected in increased business formations in these industries. Commissioners anticipate that similar opportunities would develop in Canada as a result of reduction in regulatory controls.

Notes

1. Donald J. Lecraw, "Corporate Operation and Strategy in a Changing World Environment", in *Technological Change in Canadian Industry*, vol. 3 (Toronto: University of Toronto Press, 1985).
2. Robert B. Reich, *The Next American Frontier* (New York: Times Books, a division of Random House, 1983).
3. *Ibid.*, p. 231.
4. *Ibid.*, pp. 140–41.
5. *Ibid.*, p. 141.
6. See, for example, T.J. Courchene, "Towards a Protected Society: The Politicization of Economic Life", *Canadian Journal of Economics* 13 (1980): 556–77; and Mancur Olson, *The Rise and Decline of Nations: Economic Growth, Stagflation, and Social Rigidities* (New Haven: Yale University Press, 1982).
7. Michael C. Jensen and Richard S. Ruback, "The Market for Corporate Control: The Evidence", *Journal of Financial Economics* 11 (1983), p. 5.
8. Canada, Royal Commission on Corporate Concentration, *Report* (Ottawa: Minister of Supply and Services Canada, 1978), p. 132.
9. Gordon Donaldson and Jay W. Lorch, *Decision Making at the Top: The Shaping of Strategic Direction* (New York: Basic Books, 1983).
10. "Continuity Makes Top Managers", *Financial Post*, June 27, 1981, p. 15. Report prepared by McKinsey & Company in co-operation with the *Financial Post*. Articles appeared June 6, 13, 20 and 27, 1981.
11. McKinsey & Company in co-operation with the *Financial Post*; and Thomas J. Peters and Robert H. Waterman Jr., *In Search of Excellence* (New York: Harper and Row, 1982).
12. Isaiah A. Litvak and Christopher J. Maule, "The Canadian Aluminum and Steel Industries", in *Technological Change in Canadian Industry*, vol. 3 (Toronto: University of Toronto Press, 1985).
13. Conducted by the European Management Forum, an independent, non-profit foundation based in Geneva. See *Report on International Industrial Competitiveness* (Geneva: EMF Foundation, 1984).
14. Jerry Dermer, "Growing Canada's Threshold Technology-Producing Firms", *Business Quarterly* 49 (Spring 1984), p. 41.
15. *Ibid.*, p. 44.
16. Canada, Federal Cultural Policy Review Committee, *Report* (Ottawa: Minister of Supply and Services Canada, 1982), pp. 138, 163.
17. Donald Daly, "Canadian Management: Past Recruitment Practices and Future Needs", background paper prepared for the conference "Management in the 1980s: The Crisis of Management Education and Research", sponsored by the Canadian Federation of Deans of Business and Administrative Studies, Ottawa, March 1980, p. *i*.
18. McKinsey & Company in co-operation with the *Financial Post*.
19. David Conklin, "Entrepreneurship, Innovation and Economic Change", in *Response to Economic Change*, vol. 27 (Toronto: University of Toronto Press, 1985).

20. Reuven Brenner and Léon Courville, "Industrial Strategy: Inferring What It Really Is", in *Economics of Industrial Policy and Strategy*, vol. 5 (Toronto: University of Toronto Press, 1985).
21. Conklin, "Entrepreneurship, Innovation and Economic Change".
22. Reich, *The Next American Frontier*, p. 279.
23. Patricia Johnston-Lavigueur, at Royal Commission, Small Business Seminar, Transcript, October 15, 1984, pp. 21–24.
24. As discussed by A. Beutel, at Royal Commission, Small Business Seminar, Transcript, October 15, 1984, pp. 104–5.
25. George F. Fells, "Venture Capital in Canada – A Ten-Year Review", *Business Quarterly* 49 (Spring 1984), p. 71.
26. *Ibid.*, pp. 72–73.
27. Abraham Tarasofsky, "The Canada Development Corporation 1973–83", preliminary draft (Ottawa: Economic Council of Canada, 1984), p. 60.
28. Linda McQuaig, "IDEA's Style Brings Disappointment", *Globe and Mail, Report on Business*, November 6, 1984, pp. B1, B19.
29. Jean-Marie Gagnon and Benoît Papillon, *Financial Risk, Rate of Return of Canadian Firms, and Implications for Government Intervention*, study prepared for the Economic Council of Canada (Ottawa: Minister of Supply and Services Canada, 1984), pp. 84–85.
30. Economic Council of Canada, *Intervention and Efficiency: A Study of Government Credit and Credit Guarantees to the Private Sector* (Ottawa: Minister of Supply and Services Canada, 1982), pp. 27–35.
31. *Ibid.*, p. 29.
32. *Ibid.*, p. 35.

CHAPTER 9

Industrial Policy

CHAPTER 9

Industrial Policy

Industrial Policy in a Canadian Context

Commissioners have chosen to define "industrial policy" in a broad sense to cover all government efforts to promote growth, productivity and the competitiveness of Canadian industries. We recognize, however, that industrial policy means different things to different people. Consequently, we believe that it is important to review what Canadians have said to us about this term before we go on to suggest a fundamental realignment of our country's industrial policies.

Some observers see the industrial policy of a nation as nothing more than a general framework for public and private sector co-operation, a framework that includes the accumulated trade, tax, expenditure and regulatory policies of the government. Others use the concept in a more particular sense, associating it with the manufacturing sector as distinct from the resource and service sectors. In this context, some see industrial policy as a blueprint for action: for government support of private sector "winners" and adjustment assistance for private sector "losers".

Still others equate industrial policy with a whole range of general economic development policies: that is, with anything and everything the government does to influence the evolution of the structure of the economy over the longer term. Since private enterprise provides the organizing force for a substantial part of economic activity, a critical prerequisite for successful economic development is the existence of a supportive framework of laws and institutions. Adequate investment in either physical or human capital is unlikely to be forthcoming if the rewards of investment are subject to expropriation or heavy taxation. Similarly, private enterprise is unlikely to flourish and workers are unlikely to be mobile if they are subject to undue red tape. The incentives for aggressive participation in the private enterprise system must be clear. Workers and their families require some sort of basic minimum security if they are to take risks and move to new locations or change careers. Finally, macro-economic policies must also ensure that output and employment grow at a reasonably even pace, and that inflation is held under control.

Economic development policies embrace such diverse areas as education and training, investment in infrastructure such as roads and airports, tax policies that bear on savings and investment, social security, unemployment insurance, resource policies, tourist promotion and regional development. Some of these policies have much broader goals than economic development alone. Education support is first and foremost a response to the social objective of ensuring that all Canadians receive the necessary education to enable them to participate effectively in all aspects of our society, including the economy. Tax provisions that encourage home ownership are motivated as much by social objectives as they are by aims of economic development. Still, the implications of such provisions for economic development and industrial policy are extremely important.

These implications derive from the fact that in general, resources devoted to one sector become unavailable to another sector, although the return in the form of national or regional benefits may be greater if resources are allocated to a sector with greater potential for growth and development than another. Explicit encouragement of growth in one sector often means implicit discouragement of growth in other sectors. The sectors that are not favoured face stiffer competition for inputs or less favourable demand conditions for their outputs. Encouragement to a favoured sector has to be paid for; subsidies for one sector require higher tax rates elsewhere. Subsidization of investment also raises the demand for capital and thus affects interest rates and the exchange rate. Subsidization of labour in one sector causes the contraction of labour inputs and product-output levels in other sectors. Special tariff or quota protection puts upward pressure on the exchange rate, making exports more expensive abroad and imports cheaper at home; the result is a contraction in the exporting and import-competing sectors other than those that benefit from the special protection.

In part, the diversity of opinion about industrial policy reflects ideological differences among groups in Canadian society, but the variation in views also stems from a far-from-perfect understanding of how the economy works, or what will make it work better. The question is not whether a country should have an industrial policy; whether by design or by default, a country will inevitably have an industrial policy of some kind. The relevant question is to what degree industrial policy should favour some sectors over others. Should government endeavour to be, in some overall sense, neutral in setting its trade policy, tax regime, expenditure program and regulatory framework? Or should it attempt to identify and promote the industrial activities in which the country has, or should have, a comparative advantage? Should government go even further and attempt to engineer a trade or competitive advantage? If Canadians conclude that a targeted industrial policy is indeed the best choice, does it follow that our government is well placed to devise and implement such a policy?

Most of the business sector's presentations to this Commission on the subject of economic development held that any attempt by government to undertake a comprehensive and targeted industrial policy would be neither feasible nor desirable:

It is [the Board's] conviction that the thrust of government should be to create an environment in which private enterprise can thrive and prosper. The business of government is to govern not to compete actively in the marketplace.

(Saint John Board of Trade, Brief, September 12, 1983, p. 17.)

The role of the state in the Canadian economy . . . has already reached a level that cannot be surpassed without risk of discouraging private initiative.

(*Conseil du Patronat du Québec*, Brief, October 14, 1983, pp. 8–9.)

We do not believe that a comprehensive national industrial strategy is either feasible or necessary. With respect to the question of feasibility, it must first be shown how an effective, co-ordinated industrial strategy could be developed and implemented on an ongoing basis in such a diverse nation as Canada, in which eleven governments are typically pursuing often divergent policies. Extensive decentralization of economic and industrial policy making powers is simply incompatible with the notion of a co-ordinated national industrial strategy . . .

Another problem that must be addressed in assessing the feasibility of a Canadian industrial strategy is the absence of a clear consensus on what such a strategy would consist of, with the result that various advocates are constantly producing lists of worthy objectives that are in fundamental conflict with each other.

(Business Council on National Issues, Brief, December 6, 1983, pp. 34–35.)

The basis of the business community's argument against government intervention is experience, sometimes bitter experience:

In the past, we have found government policy to be inconsistent, at times contradictory, and not responsive. But more important . . . too much government policy has been developed in isolation without consultation with industry.

(Celanese Canada Inc., Brief, October 14, 1983, p. 10.)

Governments do not have an enviable record in choosing winners or cushioning losers in the marketplace, or managing essentially private sector investments and operations.

(Retail Council of Canada, Brief, November 1, 1983, p. 60.)

The argument goes that if only the government would give the right command – if only it would adopt the right "industrial strategy" – then the country, like a huge army, would get back on the right track again. The advocates of this approach to Canadian economic development do not appear to comprehend that most economic development in this country is taking place despite these kinds of policies, not because of them.

(Andriy J. Semotiuk, Brief, November 3, 1983, p. 3.)

Basically, the business community believes that government should confine its activity to the creation of a positive environment for private sector investment and growth:

Governments have a crucial role to play in economic development . . . Governments must decide the direction the economy is to take and then work with industry to permit it to achieve the desired goals. Governments must create the environment to which entrepreneurs are attracted and in which they will flourish. Successful economic planning should not result in governments doing the investment or acquiring operating assets . . . Similarly, successful economic planning should not provide support or protection for the non-entrepreneurs in our industry even when they are Canadian companies.

(H.N. Halvorson, Consultants Ltd., Brief, August 19, 1983, p. 4.)

The economic problems currently facing Canadians (slower growth, poor productivity performance, structural unemployment, shifts in export markets, etc.) indicate a need for a fundamental re-structuring of the economy . . .

This needed restructuring will require a constructive and co-operative joint effort by business and government. Government definitely does have a role to play in such efforts but this role must be clearly defined. New directions in industrial development must come from the business sector itself.

(Burns Fry Limited, Brief, November 24, 1983, p. 1.)

A second, quite different view is that government's proper role in industrial policy is that of a "guiding hand". Proponents of this view insist that the private sector and the public sector must work together to devise strategy and tactics that will reinforce the competitive position of domestic industry at home and abroad. Some observers attribute Japan's spectacular rise to the close co-operation between its private and public sectors and, particularly, to the catalytic role of government in providing a focused process for the taking of decisions on new industrial initiatives. Several newly-industrialized countries (NICs) have followed the Japanese example, with some apparent success. In the view of those who see a relationship of cause and effect between an active industrial policy and positive economic performance, Canada and the United States cannot afford to be passive bystanders. To meet off-shore competition, they argue, North American economies, too, may have to emulate, at least partially, the co-operative industrial/government relationship practised by Japan.

A number of representations to this Commission suggested that employment considerations, not economic growth as such, ought to be at the forefront of public policy. Many social service and labour groups doubt that economic growth is fully reflected in job creation and job security. They believe that government should play a strong role in guiding industrial policy in order to ensure that employment is a priority:

Private enterprise is only interested in profits and the largest possible return on their invested capital. They are not interested in creating jobs . . .

If the business establishment is not responsible for providing employment, it is obvious that the government must be prepared to make the necessary decisions or recommendations that will benefit all of society, not just a privileged few.

(United Steelworkers of America, Local 6500, Brief, October 3, 1983, p. 2.)

The role of government in economic decision-making must be much more instrumental in the achievements of socially desirable and democratically determined investment and production goals. Private profitability should not be the sole [criterion] for measuring contribution to social need . . . The alternative is a system where community based initiatives and entrepreneurship form the basis of a rational economic policy for full employment. Planning to meet human/social needs becomes the function of economic policy.

(Social Planning Council of Metropolitan Toronto, Brief, November 9, 1983, p. 79.)

The current approach in business circles of advocating a reduced role for government in the economy does not make sense in light of these impending issues. To the extent that business cannot reasonably be expected to promote the public interest at the expense of markets and profits . . . it is the responsibility of government to provide [business interests] with incentives and constraints that will ensure that their actions also serve the public's well-being. When this is not possible, government has to perform these functions itself. That includes making public investments when private investments are insufficient to keep the economy at a high employment level.

(Canadian Mental Health Association, Brief, October 31, 1983, pp. 18–19.)

Those who favour an active role for government in directing industrial policy have seldom been any more specific than those who consider that government's role should be limited. Nonetheless, the following excerpts from briefs to this Commission give some flavour of what the assumption of an activist role by government would involve:

In a democratic political system only *government can have the power, and* only *government can be entrusted with the responsibility to maintain economic stability and employment, and secure a fair distribution of income.*

(United Steelworkers of America, Brief, October 28, 1983, p. 10.)

The impact of new technology is so widespread and impacts in so many ways that it will take government action to create the kind of framework that we think is necessary to cope in the years ahead. In our view, it is really a case of the government acting in advance to maximize our ability to build a fair and just society of opportunity.

(Communications Workers of Canada, Transcript, Edmonton, November 15, 1983 [vol. 46], p. 9421.)

We . . . propose that the Commission clearly recognize the increased role which government must assume in economic affairs in order to ensure a society of equity and security, as well as initiative, from which no one will be left out. Let the Commission clearly define the share of responsibility which should fall to the federal, provincial, and municipal governments respectively. Let the Commission at the same time declare that the federal government must in addition be ultimately responsible for making sure that the provinces, and through them the municipalities, assume and faithfully discharge the share of responsibility which falls to them, and that they do so in such a way that minimum acceptable standards are retained throughout the country.

(Ontario Public Service Employees Union, Brief, November 16, 1983, p. 49.)

A regeneration of dynamism in industry . . . cannot, in our opinion, rest principally on the initiative of private enterprise. To the contrary, the success of such a strategy implies an extension and a deepening of economic intervention by the state.

(*Centrale de l'enseignement du Québec*, Brief, November 23, 1983, p. 61.)

Clearly, Canadians have widely divergent views about the extent to which government should involve itself in the promotion of economic growth and employment. It would seem, in fact, that relatively few observers recognize the existence of any viable middle position between a strict "hands-off" approach to industrial policy and a highly interventionist approach. Yet it is reasonably certain that neither of the extreme positions is tenable. A fundamental change is taking place in the world economy, a change that casts doubt on the wisdom of the hands-off approach. Commissioners recognize that opposition to a more active role for government arises, in no small measure, from adverse experience with the growth in government intervention since the early 1960s. It is precisely because intervention has often been unsuccessful that we have undertaken to consider what can be done to develop a sounder and more fruitful working relationship between government and the private sector.

At the same time, our analysis leads us to conclude that governments generally lack the capability to orchestrate, or even formulate, a comprehensive, detailed, industrial strategy of the kind advocated by the more ardent interventionists. Even if a detailed strategy were possible, it would not be desirable. The world is just too complex, and the need for flexibility and adaptability too great, to justify confining the private sector in such a strait-jacket.

Canadian Industrial Policy in Historical Perspective

Canadian industrial policy has evolved through four general phases in response to changing circumstances at home and abroad. In the period from 1867 to 1914, a substantial emphasis was placed on tariff protection and the subsidization of secondary industry, and major investments were made in infrastructure in transportation and other areas. During the years between the two World Wars, the catastrophic impact of the Great Depression led to a focus on policies aimed at restoring and sustaining demand. Between 1945 and 1957, industrial policy, broadly defined, included macro-economic stabilization policies devised in the Keynesian tradition, concerted moves to reconstruct the peacetime economy, strong incentives for foreign investors, and a second National Policy that relied heavily on a new underpinning of social welfare programs. Finally, the period from 1957 to the present has witnessed a series of moves towards freer international trade and towards continental integration of certain sectors such as the automotive industry, defence production, and crude oil and natural gas production. This period was marked by growing domestic ownership of the Canadian economy and, in the 1960s and early 1970s, by increased government involvement in promoting development in slow-growth regions. In addition, government provided more assistance for industries and for particular companies confronted by severe competition at home or abroad, by obsolescence or by declining demand; it also provided increasing support for existing or new companies to enable them to keep pace with rapidly emerging economic developments around the globe.

Federal Industrial Policies

In the 1950s, federal industrial policy included encouragement to foreign, primarily American, direct investment and a continuation of Canada's efforts, in concert with those of other countries, to entrench a stable international monetary system and a liberal trade regime. These moves generated considerable prosperity, but they also led to growing concern about the extensive degree of foreign ownership in both the manufacturing and the resource sectors.

The election in 1957 of the Conservative government of Prime Minister John Diefenbaker resulted, in part, from the disaffection of some regions that had not shared fully in the post-war prosperity. The Diefenbaker government sought to make industrial policy more directly responsive to regional concerns. The National Oil Policy of 1961 strengthened the petroleum sector in the Western provinces. The government also sought to shift trade away from its growing dependence on the United States. Nevertheless, it quickly became involved in decisions that reflected the changing structural realities of the North American economy. Thus the cancellation of the Avro Arrow aircraft program led ultimately to the Canada-U.S. Defence Production Pact, under which Canada obtained guaranteed access to the American defence-procurement market.

The early and middle 1960s brought a renewed emphasis on the manufacturing sector. This emphasis was reflected in the establishment of a new Department of Industry, and it was made even more evident in the negotiation by the Pearson government of the Canada-U.S. Auto Pact. The 1960s also produced further tariff reductions under the Kennedy Round of negotiations under the General Agreement on Tariffs and Trade (GATT). In the middle and late 1960s, there was a growing debate on the underlying technological competitiveness of the Canadian economy; much of this debate centred on the question of "science policy" and the adequacy of Canada's research and development (R&D) incentives. Fundamental changes were made in the nature and extent of federal support for employment training and education. Before the decade ended, the federal government had created the Department of Regional Economic Expansion (DREE), which was to provide a focus for the development and co-ordination of regional policy. Meanwhile the establishment of the Department of Consumer and Corporate Affairs prepared the ground for a sustained effort to develop more effective competition policies.

The growth in federal support for employment training and education was dramatic. An initial increase in federal grants to universities culminated in a 1967 federal-provincial agreement under which the Government of Canada would provide 50 per cent of the operating costs of post-secondary educational institutions through a combination of cash grants and the surrender of tax points. Under the Technical and Vocational Training Act of 1960 and the programs that succeeded it, the federal government encouraged job training, first through a shared-cost program and then, beginning in the late 1960s, through the purchase of accommodation and courses from the growing provincial certificate- or diploma-granting institutions.

It was only in the 1970s, however, that the federal government came to identify its evolving bundle of policies as an industrial strategy. In 1972, Jean-Luc Pépin, then Minister of Industry, Trade and Commerce, announced that he and his department were embarking on the development of a "better" industrial strategy, which he described as an "ensemble of coordinated objectives and instruments, i.e., policies, programs and institutions."[1]

External shocks of varying orders of rapidity and magnitude confirmed the need for a more closely co-ordinated approach. These shocks included the policies initiated by President Richard Nixon in an effort to deal with pressing U.S. balance-of-payments problems and the 1973–74 crisis imposed by the Organization of Petroleum Exporting Countries (OPEC). Canada's evolving industrial strategy focused heavily on the development of a secondary manufacturing sector. Increasingly, the federal government undertook various kinds of consultation with key interests, including business, labour and the provincial governments.

A number of other political and economic developments during the 1970s had a bearing on industrial strategy and its evolution. The Foreign Investment Review Agency (FIRA) was established to advise the government on whether or not to authorize foreign investments in Canada, and to negotiate terms that would maximize the benefits available to this country from such investment. The Tokyo Round of GATT negotiations, which took place between 1973 and 1979, had a significant effect on the industrial climate, as did the controls imposed on profits and incomes under the Anti-Inflation Program of 1975–78.

The federal government experimented with other policy initiatives, as well. The Canada Development Corporation, which was established in 1971 with a provision for mixed public and private ownership, subsequently acquired assets in many sectors of the economy. In the same year, the Government of Canada sought to devise better policies on science and technology by creating a Ministry of State for Science and Technology. In 1975, with the creation of Petro-Canada, it moved directly into oil and gas exploration, production and marketing.

Despite all these activities, federal industrial policy had little clear focus during most of the 1970s, nor did the exercise launched early in the decade by Mr. Pépin result in the emergence of a comprehensive statement of the government's industrial strategy during the 1970s. Federal support for Canada's economy represented "a patchwork of industry-by-industry and some across-the-board incentives and programs, produced without much consultation with business and labour."[2] Responsibility for industrial policies was scattered across several government departments.

In the late 1970s, the Department of Industry, Trade and Commerce attempted to build a consultative process from the bottom up. This initiative involved discussions of the process at a First Ministers' Conference in February 1978, followed by the establishment of 23 sectoral task forces covering 21 manufacturing industries, plus construction and tourism. The task forces were composed of representatives of business, labour, the federal and provincial governments, and the academic community. In their reports, they proposed a strategy for the development of each sector. Many of them called for increased government assistance for their respective sectors through tax breaks and other measures.

The sector task forces, which became known as "Tier 1 committees", were succeeded by the so-called "Tier 2 committee", which was directed to make recommendations that cut across sectoral lines and involved broad economic policy issues. However, by the time the Tier 2 committee reported, in the fall of 1978, the federal government had embarked on a series of budget cuts and other restraint measures which greatly reduced the prospects for substantial new assistance to industry. The emergence of a powerful small-business lobby further changed the political calculus of industrial policy, since it demanded greater attention to the needs of smaller firms and the fast-growing service sector. The small-business sector was very sensitive to regulatory and tax burdens.

In 1978, the federal government assigned the task of co-ordinating development spending to a new committee of the Cabinet, the Board of Economic Development Ministers (BEDM)[3]. This committee was to be headed by a president and served by a new central agency, the Ministry of State for Economic Development (MSED). In 1980, amid growing economic difficulties, the minister responsible for MSED, Senator H.A. (Bud) Olson, announced an agenda for economic development that attempted to shift emphasis from the needs of specific industries to the strength of basic factors of production, such as human resources, capital and technology.

Internal government debate about appropriate development strategies in light of changing circumstances subsequently gathered new momentum. This debate not only involved renewed concerns about the extent and utility of government intervention, but also reflected the broader controversy taking shape over such matters as the Constitution and federal-provincial relations generally. All of this boiled down to a battle between the proponents of rival concepts of the nature of Canada and the way in which the country should evolve in the future. The outcome of the debate was a statement on economic development presented in the November 1981 budget. The 1981 "Economic Statement" was related to the National Energy Program introduced a year earlier. It was based on the fundamental view that Canada's opportunities lay in the development of its rich bounty of natural resources. The statement did not ignore manufacturing, but it linked future development in this sector to the need for manufactured goods produced by the rapidly growing resource industries. By this means, its proponents sought to bridge the interests of Atlantic, Central and Western Canada. The approach was influenced by the (Blair-Carr) Task Force on Major Projects,[4] which recommended the establishment of an Office of Regional and Industrial Benefits within the Department of Industry, Trade and Commerce.

Soon, however, the worsening of Canada's economic situation brought the new strategy into disrepute. The break in world oil prices after 1981, the escalating federal budget deficit, soaring inflation and record levels for interest rates combined to produce a totally different context for policy measures. The downward movement of world oil prices, in combination with other economic factors, resulted in the abandonment or suspension of many of the energy megaprojects and cast doubt on the fundamental assumption that lay behind the new industrial strategy. This assumption consisted of the view that a permanent improvement had taken place in the terms of trade for natural resources in relation to those for manufactured goods. The Economic Statement seemed to demonstrate the difficulties of attempting to combine political and economic objectives in a concerted industrial strategy and, indeed, of formulating any type of strategy that would prove effective for an extended period in an uncertain and changing world.

Provincial Industrial Policies

During the 1960s and 1970s, industrial policy questions involved federal-provincial relationships of increasing complexity. Alternative strategic approaches – particularly insofar as they meant a choice between giving priority to the manufacturing sector and giving it to the resource sectors – inevitably favoured some regions over others.

Even without the constitutional division of powers between the two levels of government, it would have been difficult to devise industrial policies that would bridge the different interests of different regions and, at the same time, ensure that benefits would be widely distributed. As matters stood, these constitutional divisions complicated the situation even further. First, they enabled provinces to pursue industrial strategies designed to maximize benefits for their own citizens. This consideration naturally raised concerns about interprovincial competition and internal barriers to trade which could reduce the efficiency of the economy as a whole.

Secondly, provincial control over so many of the jurisdictional areas critical to economic development policy, such as natural resources, education, labour relations and securities regulation, meant that a high degree of co-operation and co-ordination would be necessary if effective national policies were to be formulated and implemented. These policies would, in fact, have to be devised jointly by federal and provincial governments, and they would be very hard to develop in the context of the heightened interregional and intergovernmental conflict of the 1970s. The circumstances gave rise to a paradox. Regional diversity required that policies be devised to assist specific regions of the country. However, decisions involving such allocations – whether an auto plant was to be built in Quebec or in Ontario, for example, or how the counterpart of industrial benefits deriving from Canada's acquisition of a new U.S.-designed jet fighter were to be distributed among the regions – became matters of continuing controversy.

During the 1970s, many provincial governments intensified their attempts to promote economic development. They were able to do this because of the growth that had taken place in their financial and bureaucratic resources during the 1950s and 1960s. Massive energy revenues dramatically expanded the resources available to the Prairie provinces, especially Alberta, and became the basis of aggressive strategies to diversify those provinces' economies. The range of policy tools also expanded. In particular, the provinces began to make much more active use of public enterprise to promote regional development. Of 233 provincial Crown corporations identified in 1983, 76 had been created after 1960, and 48 after 1970.

In addition, the provinces introduced policies that were aimed, much more explicitly than any provincial policies in the past, at counteracting the adverse effects on their economies of both the forces of the market-place and the policies of the federal government. The concept of their pursuing only activities in which their own regions had a comparative advantage was partially rejected. More and more provinces sought to use their resources to broaden their economic bases. Moreover, some provincial policies were introduced to counter federal policies that were seen to be discriminatory or ineffective. Throughout the 1970s, it was a matter of vigorous debate whether the condition of the outlying provinces was simply a consequence of impersonal market forces or the result of the misapplication of federal power.

Whatever the cause of regional disparities, provincial policies were directed to redressing them and to forcing changes in the regional distribution of private investment. The champions of this approach saw the province, rather than the nation, as the economic unit in which wealth was to be maximized. As Premier William Bennett of British Columbia told the 1978 First Ministers' Conference on the economy:

> *In listening to my fellow First Ministers here, I must say that what has come out clearly to me, is . . . that we are not a single national economy; we are a country with distinct regions, with distinct economies unique to themselves, that need the attention and cooperation of the governments in meeting their own specific aspirations and needs.*[5]

The provinces' industrial policies varied with their economic conditions and needs, their available resources, the ideologies of their governments, and the pressures that private interests brought to bear on their leaders. The goal of the Western provinces was to use the new revenues provided by the energy boom to strengthen and diversify their economies, to redress their historic economic and political grievances, and to force a shift in political power. Alberta and Saskatchewan had, perhaps, the most explicit and concerted provincial industrial policies of the 1970s.

Alberta's plans for diversification emphasized the encouragement of local processing of energy and agricultural resources. The province hoped that this strategy would result in expansion of industry, growth in employment, and the enhancement of its political power and influence. The provincial government adopted many means to promote these goals. One such means was the Alberta Heritage Savings and Trust Fund, into which the province funnelled about 30 per cent of its annual oil and gas revenues in order to create a large pool of capital for subsequent investment. By 1984, the fund held $13.7 billion in total assets.

Another provincial undertaking was the joint public-private Alberta Energy Company Ltd. In 1974, the province acquired Pacific Western Airlines, a company that it considered could play an important part in reinforcing its position as the "gateway to the North". The government also actively supported the transformation of Alberta Gas Trunk Line Ltd. into Nova, an Alberta Corporation. The original company was established in the 1950s to gather and distribute gas inside the province and to deliver it to other pipelines for transmission beyond its borders. The change of name reflected the company's rapidly expanding interests in major petroleum-related projects across North America and around the world. Two new agencies, the Alberta Oil Sands Technology and Research Authority and the Alberta Research Council, were set up to encourage the processing of Alberta's resources within the province. Through these and other agencies, development funds were channelled into such areas as petrochemicals, tourism, forestry, high technology and medical research. The province encouraged small business through changes in the corporate tax system and other measures; it also promoted the transfer to the province of head-office activity, particularly in the oil and gas industry.

Saskatchewan developed an explicit industrial strategy based on a high degree of public ownership. Its New Democratic Party (NDP) government took control of a significant part of the potash industry in the 1970s, and played a major entrepreneurial role in other resource sectors, including oil, mining and, especially, uranium. It promoted industrial development through the Saskatchewan Economic Development Corporation and a variety of other means, including support for research and for expansion of the West's largest steel maker, Interprovincial Steel. In 1983, Saskatchewan, like Alberta, established a heritage fund.

British Columbia's industrial policy has traditionally focused on the development of such resource sectors as mining and forestry. The province has undertaken major rail and highway projects and aggressive development of its hydro resources. In the 1970s, it, too, began to press for diversification of its economy through stimulation of manufacturing and promotion of high-technology industries. Manitoba governments have been active in promoting forestry and power developments in the North, and have also established a wide variety of programs to aid manufacturing.

On the east coast, Newfoundland has emulated the strategy of Alberta and Saskatchewan, seeking to obtain greater control over its own resources as a means of promoting economic development. After experiencing a series of failures in earlier development projects, such as the Come-by-Chance oil refinery and the Stephenville Linerboard mill, the province's industrial policy now emphasizes the further processing of its resource endowments. In addition, the manufacturing sector is being encouraged to produce goods, such as fishing equipment, complementary to the province's industrial structure. The Newfoundland government has argued that in order to pursue the development of "Newfoundland for Newfoundlanders" and to preserve the fabric of the maritime rural community, it is vital for the province both to control its offshore oil and gas development and to exercise greater control over the fishery.

Nova Scotia's industrial policies have concentrated on the long-standing problems of the Cape Breton coal and steel industry, and on the development of manufacturing, especially in the Halifax-Dartmouth and Strait of Canso areas. The province has sought to link development to the offshore resources of fish and oil, and to promote diversification of its industries into high-technology manufacturing. A similar mix of incentives, subsidies, grants, provision of infrastructure, and procurement policies has been used in Prince Edward Island and New Brunswick, but generally these provinces have not acted as aggressively as a number of others. One indication of this restraint is that in 1980, when Newfoundland had 42 provincial Crown corporations, the largest number in the country, each of the other three Atlantic provinces had fewer Crown corporations than any of the remaining provinces.

If the primary goal for Western and Eastern Canada is to shift economic development in their direction and end their dependent status, the challenge for Central Canada is to preserve and expand its manufacturing economy in a changing world economy. Between 1970 and 1977, Ontario's share of gross domestic product (GDP) dropped from 41.9 per cent to 39.2 per cent; its growth rate was among the lowest in the country. Both Ontario and Quebec experienced major structural shifts as a result of changes in economic patterns in the United States and in the world at large. Measures taken by Ontario to encourage industry have included the founding of an Employment Development Fund which, among its other projects, has helped the Ford Motor Company to build an engine plant in the province and promoted capital investment in pulp and paper. In 1981, Ontario brought all of its industrial development activities under the umbrella of a cabinet committee, the Board of Industrial Leadership and Development (BILD). The province planned to concentrate on resource development, development of rail and urban transit technology, and increased nuclear generation and rail electrification, which would minimize its dependence on imported oil. It also established several technology-development centres to encourage advances in computer technology and related fields. The provincial government, however, has avoided any claim that it is following a grand industrial strategy.

Since the early 1960s, the makers of Quebec's industrial policy have sought both to promote the growth of the province's economy and to increase francophone participation in that economy. In pursuit of these goals, the Quebec government has stressed the function of provincial Crown corporations. Hydro-Québec and the James Bay Development Corporation have made hydro development a major engine for growth. Francophone participation in industry has been strongly encouraged by Crown corporations active in the financial sector. Important Crown corporations include the *Société générale de financement*, an investment and holding corporation; the *Société de développement industriel du Québec*, which provides development loans and grants; and the *Caisse de dépôt et placement du Québec*, which manages the assets of the Quebec Pension Plan (QPP). Through these agencies, Quebec has invested in a wide variety of provincial industries. Besides trying to support traditional industries, the province has done more in recent years to promote technologically advanced industries. It has also gone further than most provinces, through a series of economic "summits" and related activities, in building mechanisms for consultation between government and the private sector.

Financial Support for Industrial Development

Table 9-1 gives an indication of the overall importance of direct financial assistance by the federal government to the manufacturing sector during the 1960–80 period. Federal financial assistance in the form of various subsidies

TABLE 9-1 Federal Grants to the Manufacturing Sector

Year	Total: Millions of Current $	Total: Millions of Constant 1971 $	Grants Relative to Value Added	Grants as a Percentage of Total Federal Expenditures	Grants as a Percentage of Manufacturing Investment
1960–61	4.4	6.2	0.042	0.084	0.177
1961–62	8.0	11.0	0.077	0.139	0.330
1962–63	33.7	45.9	0.295	0.552	1.444
1963–64	64.4	86.2	0.525	1.000	2.985
1964–65	59.5	77.7	0.440	0.827	2.182
1965–66	76.0	96.2	0.509	1.054	2.293
1966–67	81.3	98.3	0.497	1.011	2.028
1967–68	107.7	125.7	0.633	1.177	2.919
1968–69	103.3	116.5	0.563	1.029	3.011
1969–70	159.0	171.7	0.790	1.441	4.071
1970–71	177.7	183.4	0.886	1.349	3.829
1971–72	249.1	249.1	1.146	1.634	5.563
1972–73	258.8	246.5	1.067	1.456	5.620
1973–74	282.2	246.2	0.982	1.366	5.051
1974–75	301.1	227.9	0.858	1.161	4.147
1975–76	295.5	202.0	0.818	0.886	3.709
1976–77	323.9	202.2	0.811	0.929	3.876
1977–78	275.6	160.8	0.625	0.707	2.965
1978–79	287.5	157.7	0.558	0.676	2.942
1979–80	410.0	203.9	0.676	0.866	3.552

Source: André Blais, Philippe Faucher, and Robert Young, "L'Aide financière directe du gouvernement fédéral à l'industrie canadienne, 1960–1980", Notes de recherche 12 (Montreal: Université de Montréal, Département de science politique, 1983).

and grants increased rapidly during the 1960s. Financial assistance in real terms (that is, discounting inflation) peaked in the early 1970s and fell steadily until 1979–80. In that year, direct financial assistance to the manufacturing sector accounted for less than 1 per cent of total federal expenditures; it also accounted for less than 1 per cent of total value added in the manufacturing sector. On the other hand, federal financial assistance constituted as much as 5.6 per cent of manufacturing investment in the early 1970s; in 1979–80, the figure was 3.5 per cent.

The overview of federal financial assistance to the manufacturing sector presented in Table 9-1 incorporates many programs. Almost all of these programs have been substantially modified or restructured over time, but only a very few of them have been phased out. The majority of the programs are discretionary rather than automatic: that is, instead of providing funds on the basis of some prescribed formula, they require firms to persuade the administering department that the project for which assistance is requested could not be undertaken in the absence of support. Most automatic-assistance programs are related to research and development, training and the shipbuilding industry. During the 1960s and 1970s, a disproportionate share of financial assistance went to declining sectors, slow-growth provinces, and big business.

At present, the single most important federal financial assistance scheme is the Industrial and Regional Development Program (IRDP). Assistance under the IRDP is available for each stage of project development: innovation, plant establishment or modernization and expansion, marketing, and restructuring. The program uses an indexed tier system that distinguishes census regions on the basis of a number of economic measures. The rate of subsidy varies between 25 and 75 per cent, depending on the employment and income levels of the census region and the financial capacity of the province. Estimated expenditures for 1984–85 stand at about $470 million. Other major federal subsidy programs include the Defence Industry Productivity Program, the Shipbuilding Industry Assistance Program, the National Industrial Training Program, and the Canadian Industrial Renewal Program.

The estimated value of federal corporate tax incentives is shown in Table 9-2. Over the 1960s and 1970s, the value of these tax incentives increased almost tenfold even in constant dollar terms. Still, their value was small relative to total value added in the manufacturing sector. In the mid-1960s, corporate tax incentives exceeded 2 per cent of total value added, but they fell sharply in importance thereafter. New measures introduced in the 1970s reinforced the importance of corporate tax incentives, returning them to the 2 per cent level by 1979. The contribution of corporate tax incentives to investment decisions is difficult to assess because these incentives often change substantially over time. Indeed, some observers argue that the uncertainty generated by frequent modifications to the corporate tax law significantly discourages investment. Within the manufacturing sector, only industries related to resource processing benefit disproportionately from tax incentives. Furthermore, the effective tax rate does not vary significantly according to the size of the firm. Thus the corporate tax system is largely neutral as an industrial policy instrument within the manufacturing sector, even though some tax incentives are substantial.

At least since the early 1970s, however, the Canadian tax system has tended to favour investment in manufacturing plant and equipment. Investment in most service sectors does not generally bring any special tax advantages. The fact that small business, which does receive relatively favourable tax treatment, accounts for a large share in many service sectors may mean that the average effective tax rates on the return to capital may be no higher in the service sector than they are in the manufacturing sector. Three provisions of the corporate tax system are of key importance: accelerated capital-cost allowances for machinery and equipment used in manufacturing processes; a preferential rate of tax for manufacturing corporations; and the investment tax credit, which varies from 7 per cent to 50 per cent, depending on the region and the nature of the business investment.

Gauging the nature and overall extent of provincial initiatives is difficult. The provinces vary widely in both their fiscal and their political capacity to engage in activist industrial policy. In part, because the Atlantic provinces and Manitoba are more dependent than the other provinces on federal

TABLE 9-2 Federal Corporate Tax Incentives: Manufacturing Sector

Year	General Tax Incentives			Selective Tax Incentives		
	Millions $		Percentage	Millions $		Percentage
	Total: Current $	Total: Constant 1971 $[a]	Tax Benefit Relative to Value Added	Total: Current $	Total: Constant 1971 $[a]	Tax Benefit Relative to Value Added
1960	63.5	88.1	0.61	46.5	64.5	0.45
1961	83.0	115.3	0.80	68.0	93.8	0.65
1962	176.5	239.8	1.54	131.6	178.8	1.15
1963	181.5	242.3	1.48	184.8	246.7	1.51
1964	214.7	279.2	1.59	203.7	264.9	1.50
1965	287.4	362.9	1.93	323.5	408.5	2.17
1966	423.8	511.2	2.59	429.5	518.1	2.62
1967	237.0	275.9	1.39	260.0	302.7	1.53
1968	130.0	146.2	0.71	229.9	258.6	1.25
1969	174.0	187.5	0.86	202.0	217.7	1.00
1970	153.1	158.0	0.76	132.0	136.2	0.66
1971	172.2	172.2	0.79	178.2	178.2	0.82
1972	120.1	144.4	0.49	233.8	213.1	0.92
1973	405.7	354.0	1.41	379.0	330.7	1.32
1974	456.4	345.5	1.30	594.6	450.1	1.69
1975	430.5	294.3	1.19	570.9	390.2	1.58
1976	463.8	289.5	1.16	532.3	332.3	1.33
1977	472.0	275.2	1.07	528.5	308.2	1.20
1978	919.5	503.3	1.79	751.9	411.5	1.46
1979	1085.0	539.5	1.79	1214.8	604.1	2.00

Source: André Blais, Philippe Faucher, Robert Young, and Roger Poupport, "Les avantages fiscaux du gouvernement fédéral à l'industrie manufacturière canadienne", Notes de recherche 13 (Montreal: Université de Montréal, Département de science politique, 1983).

a. Deflated by the Consumer Price Index.

transfer payments, they simply have less financial room for manœuvre. This Commission's research on federal and provincial budgeting shows that the share of provincial spending (in per capita constant dollars) devoted to economic-development activities declined markedly in most provinces between 1960 and the mid-1970s, and has increased only slightly since then.[6] This is a somewhat surprising trend, given the provinces' recent efforts to develop their economies. Many of these efforts, however, have employed regulatory and other instruments, as well as expenditure. Part VI of this report analyses the implications for the economic union of provincial industrial policy initiatives. The analysis concludes that the impediments to the movement of labour, capital, and goods and services within Canada do not, at least as yet, seriously injure our overall competitive position. In any event, national policies, such as the policy of holding domestic oil price below world price, have played a more pervasive role in influencing resource allocation.

Notes

1. As cited in Richard D. French, *How Ottawa Decides: Planning and Industrial Policy-Making 1968–1980* (Ottawa: Canadian Institute for Economic Policy, 1980), pp. 105 – 6.
2. G. Bruce Doern and Richard W. Phidd, *Canadian Public Policy: Ideas, Structure, Process* (Toronto: Methuen, 1983).
3. BEDM was later renamed the "Cabinet Committee on Economic Development" and, still later, the "Cabinet Committee on Economic and Regional Development".
4. Canada, Consultative Task Force on Industrial and Regional Benefits from Major Canadian Projects, *Major Canadian Projects: Major Canadian Opportunities* (Ottawa, 1981).
5. W.R. Bennett, "The British Columbia Position: Towards an Economic Strategy for Canada", opening remarks at the Conference of the First Ministers, Ottawa, February 13, 1978, p. 1.
6. Allan M. Maslove, Michael J. Prince, and J. Bruce Doern, *Federal and Provincial Budgeting*, vol. 41 (Toronto: University of Toronto Press, 1985).

Industrial Policy In Canada and Abroad[1]

The debate over how best to bolster industrial growth and development is by no means unique to Canada. Virtually every advanced country, including the United States, is undergoing the same searching process. Many of the submissions to this Commission expressed an interest in what Canadians might learn from the successes and failures resulting from other countries' efforts to strengthen their industrial bases. It is important, of course, to remember that many approaches which work well abroad might not be successfully transplanted to Canada without considerable adaptation and modification. Even so, it is still well worthwhile to compare with our own the approaches adopted by other nations. Not surprisingly, given Japan's miraculous flowering as an industrial nation, both its national approaches to industrial development and the management practices of individual Japanese companies and industries have attracted considerable attention. Other countries, too, have developed policies and programs that are worthy of study.

Any comparison of industrial policies among countries is complicated by several factors. First, there are many kinds of industrial policy instruments: these can be applied in varying degrees and in different combinations, and the data relating to them can be assembled in different ways. Moreover, as Commissioners have already noted, the distinction between economic-development policy and industrial policy as such is not always clear. Again, in the view of a number of observers, the manner in which policies are determined and implemented is at least as important as the policies themselves.

In the review that follows, Commissioners do not attempt to make a precise distinction between general policies and instruments used to achieve particular goals. We seek, instead, to compare developments in other countries with developments in Canada, in five broad areas of relevance to industrial policy: regional development, policies intended to encourage economic openness to the world economy, technological progress, direct government involvement, and institutional-regulatory/framework areas such as competition policy and banking. Last, but certainly not least, we consider efforts to direct measures to specific firms. Our review ends with an attempt to summarize the overall orientation of various national industrial policies and to relate this summary to the economic performance of Canada and certain other industrial countries.

Regional Policies

National governments differ in the emphasis they place on regional development policies. The United States, for example, offers no explicit regional development incentives, although most other industrial countries do so. The U.S. Congress has used the defence budget and major agencies such as the National Aeronautics and Space Agency (NASA) to pursue the same kind of regional development results as Canada has pursued through explicit regional development programs.

Britain's regional development incentives have their roots in policies formulated in the 1920s to retard the decline of the textile, shipbuilding and coal-mining industries in northern England and Scotland. Since that time, policies of providing aid to depressed regions have been formalized in legislation that has created a hierarchy of assisted regions. The principal tool for regional assistance in the United Kingdom is the non-discretionary regional development grant. The grant is received automatically by any firm in possession of an Industrial Development Certification. Its level is equal to a proportion of qualifying assets, which varies with the location of a given firm. The regions that receive the greatest assistance are called "Special Development Areas" (SDAs); Development Areas (DAs) and Intermediate Areas (IAs) receive lower levels of assistance.

Forty-nine per cent of the aid granted to industries in West Germany is channelled through regional development programs that are funded equally by the federal and state governments. The emphasis of regional development programs has shifted from assistance aimed at sustaining particular enterprises to measures specifically designed to promote increased productivity and investment. All programs are open to both foreign and domestic enterprises. Over the past decade, the average annual budget for regional programs has been $4 billion (in 1980 U.S. $), or 15 per cent of total German industrial investment during this period. Assistance is distributed to regions and not to specific industries, with special emphasis on the Ruhr, the Eastern Border Zone, and West Berlin. The Program for the Improvement of Regional Economic Structure identifies less-developed regions on the basis of employment opportunities, income per capita, and the level of regional infrastructure.

Accelerated depreciation allowances of up to 50 per cent of the value of assets are available to operations in the Eastern Border Zone and West Berlin. The allowance is limited to new depreciable investment. In addition to an investment allowance, projects may also receive a discretionary investment grant. Ceilings for the grant are set at 15 per cent of investment if the project is in a normal growth area, 20 per cent if it is in an area fairly close to the eastern border, and 25 per cent if it is in the border zone. The condition for assistance is that the project create 50 new jobs or provide a 15 per cent increase in the employment level of a firm.

Another West German program provides aid to regional industry associations. Applications for aid must be approved by a bank, and the bank must commit a substantial proportion of the funds required. This condition ensures an important role for private sector institutions in the provision of regional aid. The proposal is reviewed by the Ministry of Economics, and assistance takes the form of a loan made by the firm's bank and guaranteed by the government; the private sector lenders assume the responsibility for administering the investment.

Sweden grants low-interest loans and subsidies of up to 30 per cent of investment in the northern part of the country. France has a detailed set of regional development incentives, including regional development grants tiered by region and by the number of jobs created. A more recent program offers forgivable loans (*prêts participatifs*) for business locating in regions dominated by declining industries. Japan maintains a subsidy system that awards up to 50 per cent of the cost of relocating in one of 3000 designated locations outside the largest metropolitan areas.

The major analysis of Canadian regional policy appears in Part VI of this Report and need not be anticipated here. It is sufficient in this context for Commissioners to make the point that although resources devoted to overt regional policy do not represent a large part of federal spending in Canada, regional policy as an implicit goal of other policies is extensive, as we have seen earlier in this chapter.

Policies Indicative of the Degree of Openness to the World Economy

Three policy areas are particularly indicative of the degree to which countries are prepared to encourage the openness of their economies to the world economy. They are tariff and non-tariff barriers to trade, foreign-investment restrictions, and export-promotion measures.

Table 9-3 summarizes international differences in tariff rates. Australia and, to a lesser extent, Canada have above-average tariff rates. Although nominal Japanese tariff rates are below European Community (EC) levels, the effective protection accorded Japanese industry during earlier periods was relatively high by international standards, and it is probably still higher than the nominal tariff rates suggest. Countries also shield their industries behind non-tariff barriers (NTBs). A complaint frequently levelled against Japan is that its trade and distribution system makes virtually impossible the

TABLE 9-3 Average Industrial Tariff Levels

					"World" Weights[c]			
	No Trade Weighting[a] Simple Average		Own Country Import Weighting[b]		Imports Weights on BTN Aggregates[d]		Import Weights on Each BTN Commodity[e]	
Country	1976 Ave.	Final[f] Ave.	1976 Ave.	Final Ave.	1976 Ave.	Final Ave.	1976 Ave.	Final Ave.
Australia								
Dutiable[g]	28.8	28.0	29.1	28.1	27.8	26.7	26.4	25.2
Total[h]	16.9	16.5	15.4	15.1	13.3	12.8	13.0	12.6
New Zealand								
Dutiable	31.4	28.3	28.6	25.5	33.0	30.4	30.2	27.5
Total	24.3	21.9	19.7	17.6	20.5	18.7	18.0	16.3
European Community								
Dutiable	8.8	6.0	9.8	7.2	9.5	7.0	9.6	7.1
Total	8.0	6.5	6.3	4.6	7.0	5.2	6.9	5.1

TABLE 9-3 (cont'd.)

Country	No Trade Weighting[a] Simple Average		Own Country Import Weighting[b]		"World" Weights[c]: Imports Weights on BTN Aggregates[d]		"World" Weights[c]: Import Weights on Each BTN Commodity[e]	
	1976 Ave.	Final[f] Ave.	1976 Ave.	Final Ave.	1976 Ave.	Final Ave.	1976 Ave.	Final Ave.
United States								
Dutiable	15.6	9.2	8.3	5.7	9.2	5.5	7.6	4.8
Total	14.8	8.8	6.2	4.3	7.1	4.1	5.6	3.5
Japan[i]								
Dutiable	8.1	6.2	6.9	4.9	8.0	5.7	7.9	5.5
Total	7.3	5.6	3.2	2.3	6.1	4.4	5.8	4.1
Canada								
Dutiable	13.7	7.8	13.1	8.9	12.0	7.3	12.9	8.3
Total	12.0	6.8	10.1	6.8	8.9	5.5	9.4	6.1
Austria								
Dutiable	14.2	9.8	18.8	14.5	15.9	12.0	17.0	13.3
Total	11.6	8.1	14.5	11.2	10.5	7.9	10.9	8.5
Finland								
Dutiable	17.0	14.6	11.6	9.2	11.2	9.0	11.5	9.1
Total	14.3	12.3	8.2	6.5	6.7	5.3	6.7	5.3
Norway								
Dutiable	11.1	8.2	10.5	8.0	10.2	7.4	10.0	7.5
Total	8.5	6.3	6.4	4.9	5.8	4.3	5.8	4.4
Sweden								
Dutiable	7.8	6.1	7.7	5.9	7.4	5.3	7.1	5.2
Total	6.2	4.9	6.3	4.8	4.6	3.3	4.5	3.3
Switzerland								
Dutiable	3.7	2.7	4.1	3.3	4.2	3.1	4.0	3.1
Total	3.7	2.7	4.0	3.2	3.3	2.4	3.2	2.4

Source: Mancur Olson, *The Rise and Decline of Nations: Economic Growth, Stagflation, and Social Rigidities* (New Haven: Yale University Press, 1982), p. 134.

a. An average of tariff levels on the assumption that all commodities are of equal significance.

b. The relative weight attributed to each tariff is given by the imports of that commodity in relation to the total imports of the country concerned.

c. The significance of each tariff determined by world imports of the commodity, or aggregate of commodities, to which the tariff applies. World imports are the imports of the countries listed and the European Community.

d. BTN = Brussels Tariff Nomenclature. The weight attributed to each tariff is given by the world imports of the BTN class of commodities in which it falls.

e. Each tariff weighted by world imports of that particular commodity: the maximum attainable disaggregation.

f. "Final" means after the Tokyo Round of tariff reductions.

g. Average tariff rates considering only those commodities on which tariffs are levied.

h. Average tariff levels of duty-free commodities, as well as those to which duties apply.

i. Some anecdotal evidence, as well as casual impressions of the relatively high costs that Japanese consumers must pay for many imported goods, and the fact that agriculture tariffs are not included beg the question whether these figures may give the impression that the level of protection is lower than it actually is. This is a matter in need of further research.

introduction of foreign goods into its market. Alternatively, a country may establish environmental or safety standards for goods that foreign firms find difficult to meet, or it may impose strict quotas on the value or quantity of imported goods. Thus Canada, like many other countries, sets quotas for imports of textiles, shoes and Japanese automobiles.

Like imports, foreign direct investment can be controlled in a number of different ways. Countries can prohibit or limit the participation of foreign-owned firms in specific areas of activity, such as banking or communications. They can screen direct investments and require investors to make certain undertakings regarding local sourcing, exporting, employment maintenance and technology transfer. Finally, countries can control the type of direct investment that is allowed (such as minority-interest or joint-venture investment) or the terms on which direct investment is permitted (say, by imposing dividend restrictions). Moreover, foreign investors are subject not only to national investment-review mechanisms, but also, to general investment regulations, local government restrictions, and implicit restrictions arising from the public ownership of various sectors such as transportation and utilities.

Until recently, Japan was unique among the industrial nations in the extent to which it excluded foreign investment. Its stringency was particularly apparent in areas that its government had singled out as targets for growth, including telecommunications and computer technology. Restraints on foreign investment included the designation of the percentage of foreign ownership permitted any given firm in each industry and of the approval required for each investment proposal. Approval was provided only after certain criteria were met; these included limitations on the scale of output and provisions for the appointment of Japanese directors in joint ventures.

These restrictions were relaxed, however, in response to intense international pressure; among other measures, some countries imposed limits on Japanese investment in their domestic economies. By 1976, Japan permitted foreign ownership in most industries, but it restricted foreign ownership in mining to 50 per cent and severely limited foreign participation in agriculture, forestry, fisheries and petroleum. Validation is still required for foreign investment, but it is usually automatic. The foreign presence in the Japanese economy is increasing with the relaxation of restrictions.

At the other end of the spectrum are Germany and the United States, the only large industrial nations that have not subjected incoming investment to a formal review process at any time during the post-Second World War period. Both countries do, however, sometimes restrict foreign investment in indirect ways, notably under national security legislation. In response to several large investments undertaken in the mid-1970s by interests in the countries that are members of the Organization of Petroleum Exporting Countries (OPEC), West German authorities have established an informal notification system whereby banks and major companies report large impending foreign acquisitions to the government. In a few instances, the government has quietly encouraged a purchase by German investors to forestall foreign acquisitions. Banks have increased their industrial shareholdings for the same purpose.

Australia's method of screening foreign investment is similar to that followed, until very recently, by Canada. The Australian Foreign Investment Review Board (FIRB) advises the government on the desirability of foreign investment ventures in that country. It also ensures that Australian investors will have a chance to participate with foreign investors in the ownership of natural resources and industries. The FIRB has four main tasks: to inhibit foreign investment in real estate/property, except for immediate residential purposes; to screen all foreign investment in non-bank financial intermediaries and insurance companies where the growth rate of assets is in excess of 15 per cent per annum; to examine all new business proposals where the foreign investment is greater than $5 million; and to require minimum Australian participation levels in mining ventures within Australia.

France also reviews all foreign direct investment, although investment from other EEC countries requires only prior notification to the Minister of Economics. Investment originating from non-EEC countries requires the authorization of the Minister of Economics, whether the investment is foreign-based or made by French companies under foreign control. Investment is judged by its contribution to output, employment, exports and improved technology. Foreign direct investment will be prohibited if, because of the amount involved, or of other factors, a specific transaction or transfer would have an exceptionally detrimental effect on the interests of France.[2]

France generally welcomes foreign investment in depressed areas and in growth industries, but resists foreign dominance. In an effort to restrict or reduce the role of wholly foreign-owned firms, the French government has, on occasion, subsidized joint foreign-domestic ventures, such as the computer firm CII Honeywell Bull. Thus France's policy towards foreign investment is highly pragmatic: France imposes restrictions only if such investment raises concerns about national independence.

Foreign investment in Canada and foreign control of sectors of the Canadian economy have long been contentious political issues in this country. Public opinion has shifted several times since the Second World War, and each shift has influenced the broad pattern of our industrial policy. A subsequent section of this chapter outlines in some detail the measures used to control foreign investment in Canada. It is sufficient here to note that during the 1970s and early 1980s, the federal government intensified its efforts to "Canadianize" sectors of the economy. While some observers dispute the efficacy of these initiatives, the degree of foreign ownership and control of the Canadian economy has, in fact, fallen significantly over the past two decades. This fall has been particularly significant in the petroleum sector, but the manufacturing sector, too, has experienced a considerable degree of "Canadianization". More than 50 per cent of all major sectors of the economy is now owned by Canadians. Indeed, in recent years, Canadians have been net exporters of capital. In part, at least, this shift has been a result of the acquisition by Canadian companies of interests previously owned by foreigners. Nevertheless, reinvestment of internally generated funds by foreign-owned corporations operating in Canada continues to be an important factor in maintaining the latter's presence in Canada.

One partial measure of the restrictions imposed on foreign direct investment by a given country is the prevailing level of foreign investment in that country. It should be noted, however, that the level of foreign investment reflects both the restrictions imposed on would-be foreign investors by the country in question and its overall attractiveness to foreign companies as a site for investment.

In 1978, as Table 9-4 shows, Canada absorbed 17.7 per cent of all foreign direct investment in the developed market economies. Some 16.7 per cent was in the United States, 13 per cent in Britain, and 12 per cent in West Germany. Canada's ratio of foreign direct investment inflows to capital formation was above average until 1974 and, as Table 9-5 demonstrates, has been about average since then. By contrast, the stock of foreign-owned assets in Sweden is relatively small, and foreign direct investment provides only a small part of Swedish capital formation. Foreign investment appears to have become relatively more important in recent years as a source of new capital in France.

The government of virtually every industrial country is heavily involved in export promotion. All governments provide industry with the services of trade officers and commercial intelligence gathering. All engage in export financing at concessionary rates. Some countries have gone much further, by such means as treating export income more favourably than other income, for tax purposes.

The proponents of certain new theories of trade maintain that export promotion need not involve the ongoing subsidization of export activity. Domestic procurement policies may provide a local firm with the volume of production it needs to move further up the learning curve than would-be competitors abroad and perhaps, in this way, secure a long-term cost advantage over them. Current export success may correlate less with current export-promotion activities than with past subsidy or domestic market-restructuring policies.

The instruments used by the U.S. federal government to promote exports include the Export-Import Bank, the Overseas Private Investment Corporation, and a provision allowing U.S. exporters to establish Foreign Sales Corporations (FSCs) as a means of securing favourable tax treatment on export earnings. Most U.S. export-assistance programs provide subsidized loans, loan guarantees, insurance and tax reductions, rather than direct subsidies. According to some assessments, the programs have had a minimal effect on the improvement of the long-term competitiveness of U.S. industry. They have made U.S. exports marginally more attractive than they would otherwise be and have helped U.S. manufacturers to conduct business abroad. However, the programs have not been integrated into a coherent export strategy, nor have they been carefully targeted to assist businesses for which such funding would be critical.

The Export-Import Bank was established in 1934 to help foreign buyers purchase U.S. exports. The Bank has recently focused its efforts on facilitating aircraft sales; in the past, agricultural products, communications equipment, electric power plants, and mining and manufacturing equipment have received assistance. The Overseas Private Investment Corporation

TABLE 9-4 Stock of Direct Investment from and in Developed Market Economies[a]

	Stock of Direct Investment Abroad						Stock of Inward Direct Investment					
	1967		1973		1978		1967		1973		1978	
Region or country	$ Billion	Percentage	$ Billion	Percentage	$ Billion	Percentage	$ Billion	Percentage	$ Billion	Percentage	$ Billion	Percentage
North America	60.3	53.7	109.1	52.7	181.7	48.9	29.1	40.4	53.5	38.1	84.0	34.4
Canada	3.7	3.3	7.8	3.8	13.6	3.7	19.2	26.6	32.9	23.4	43.2	17.7
United States	56.6	50.4	101.3	48.9	168.1	45.2	9.9	13.7	20.6	14.7	40.8	16.7
Western Europe[b]	48.2	42.9	84.8	41.0	158.1	42.5	28.7	39.8	66.1	47.1	133.8	54.9
Belgium and Luxembourg	1.3	1.1	2.2	1.1	4.7	1.3	1.4	1.9	3.8	2.7	9.6	3.9
France	6.0	5.3	8.8	4.3	14.9	4.0	3.0	4.2	5.8	4.1	14.9	6.1
Germany, Federal Republic of	3.0	2.6	11.9	5.8	31.8	8.5	3.6	5.0	13.1	9.3	29.2	12.0
Italy	2.1	1.9	3.2	1.5	3.3	0.9	2.6	3.6	6.8	4.8	10.1	4.2
Netherlands	11.0	9.8	15.4	7.4	23.7	6.4	4.9	6.8	7.5	5.4	12.8	5.3
Sweden	1.7	1.5	3.0	1.4	6.0	1.6	0.5	0.7	1.0	0.7	1.3	0.5
Switzerland	3.7	3.3	10.2	4.9	27.8	7.5	0.4	0.5	2.2	1.6	7.7	3.2
United Kingdom	17.5	15.6	26.9	13.0	41.1	11.0	8.2	11.4	17.4	12.4	32.5	13.3
Japan	1.5	1.3	10.3	5.0	26.8	7.2	0.6	0.8	1.2	0.8	2.2	0.9
Southern hemisphere[c]	2.4	2.1	2.7	1.3	5.2	1.4	13.7	19.0	19.7	14.0	23.9	9.8
Australia	0.4	0.4	0.5	0.2	1.1	0.3	5.4	7.5	10.2	5.2	10.9	4.4
South Africa	1.9	1.7	2.1	1.0	3.8	1.0	7.2	10.0	8.1	5.7	10.8	4.4
Total	112.4	100.0	207.0	100.0	371.8	100.0	72.1	100.0	140.5	100.0	243.9	100.0

Source: United Nations Centre on Transnational Corporations, *Salient Features and Trends in Foreign Direct Investment* (New York: United Nations, 1983), p. 34.

a. The estimated stock figures for the Federal Republic of Germany, Italy, Norway, Portugal (until 1975), Spain and the United Kingdom excluded reinvested earnings.
b. Stock estimates for Austria, Denmark, Finland, Norway, Portugal and Spain are included in the estimated stock for Western Europe.
c. Stock estimates for New Zealand are included in the estimated stock for the southern hemisphere.

TABLE 9-5 Flow of Direct Investment into Developed Market Economies as a Percentage of Gross Fixed Capital Formation, 1960–1979

Region or Country	1960	1961	1962	1963	1964	1965	1966	1967	1968	1969	1970	1971	1972	1973	1974	1975	1976	1977	1978	1979
North America	1.0	0.9	0.8	0.4	0.5	0.7	0.8	0.9	30.8	1.0	1.2	0.6	0.7	1.3	1.9	1.1	1.3	1.0	2.1	2.3
Canada	7.9	6.7	5.7	2.9	2.4	4.1	5.1	4.4	3.8	4.2	5.0	4.5	2.7	2.7	2.1	1.7	−0.7	0.9	2.1	2.9
United States	0.4	0.3	0.4	0.2	0.3	0.3	0.3	0.5	0.5	0.8	0.9	0.2	0.4	1.2	1.9	1.0	1.6	1.0	2.1	1.9
Western Europe	1.1	2.0	1.8	1.9	2.0	2.2	2.2	2.2	1.9	2.1	2.3	2.4	2.4	2.6	2.9	1.9	1.4	2.0	2.3	1.7
Belgium and Luxembourg	—	—	—	—	—	3.6	1.8	5.0	5.5	5.5	5.3	6.8	5.0	7.0	8.5	6.3	5.2	7.2	6.7	4.4
France	—	1.3	1.6	1.2	1.1	1.0	1.0	1.2	0.7	1.0	1.9	1.4	1.4	1.8	2.3	1.6	1.0	1.9	2.9	2.1
Germany, Federal Republic of	1.2	1.6	1.6	2.1	2.6	3.1	3.3	2.9	1.8	1.5	1.3	2.0	2.8	2.4	3.1	1.4	1.7	1.3	1.2	0.6
Italy	—	2.0	3.2	2.6	4.1	2.4	2.5	1.8	2.0	2.2	2.8	2.3	2.5	2.0	1.6	1.6	0.3	2.7	1.0	0.6
Netherlands	1.6	2.0	3.8	3.1	3.8	3.3	3.0	4.3	4.9	6.0	6.6	6.2	5.5	6.1	6.3	5.6	1.9	1.5	1.3	2.5
Sweden	0.7	0.4	1.4	2.1	0.8	1.6	2.4	1.6	1.6	2.3	1.5	1.1	0.8	0.6	0.7	0.5	—	0.3	0.2	0.2
United Kingdom	3.2	5.0	2.7	3.2	3.2	3.3	3.0	2.3	3.4	3.7	3.8	4.2	3.5	5.1	5.0	2.6	3.0	3.6	4.2	3.8
Japan	0.1	0.3	0.2	0.4	0.3	0.2	0.1	0.1	0.2	0.1	0.1	0.3	0.2	—	0.1	0.1	0.1	—	—	—
Southern hemisphere	9.1	8.2	7.7	9.3	9.2	9.9	7.5	7.4	8.6	7.4	9.7	10.7	8.9	0.8	7.0	2.1	4.6	5.2	5.8	4.8
Australia	9.1	8.2	7.7	9.3	9.2	9.9	7.5	7.4	8.6	7.4	9.7	10.7	8.9	0.8	7.0	2.1	4.6	5.2	6.6	5.4
Total	1.2	1.4	1.3	1.2	1.3	1.4	1.4	1.4	1.3	1.4	1.7	1.5	1.5	1.6	2.1	1.3	1.2	1.3	1.7	1.6

Source: United Nations Centre on Transnational Corporations, *Salient Features and Trends in Foreign Direct Investment* (New York: United Nations, 1983), p. 44.

(OPIC), established in 1969, seeks to expand direct U.S. investment in developing countries. OPIC encourages capital exports by insuring U.S. investors against political risks such as expropriation in foreign countries. Under the provisions of the Internal Revenue Code relating to Foreign Sales Corporations, certain categories of domestic corporations selling products in foreign markets are to be treated for tax purposes as foreign corporations. The effect is to allow deferral of federal income tax on the corporation's current income.

Australia's Export Finance and Insurance Corporation provides insurance on credit extended by exporters, guarantees loans made for exports, and makes export loans itself. To develop export markets, Australia also makes direct grants to exporters.

Japan makes use of both direct and indirect methods of export promotion. Between the end of the Second World War and the early 1970s, the Japanese government stimulated exports, restricted manufactured imports, and facilitated large-scale imports of raw material. Tax incentives and accelerated depreciation effectively shielded significant portions of export revenue from taxation. The Japan Development Bank and Japan's Export-Import Bank provided long-term credit for export-related investment at reduced rates. High duties and quotas blocked imported manufactured goods where Japan perceived itself as uncompetitive.

Since the early 1970s, international pressure has induced Japanese policy makers gradually to liberalize trade and open their country's economy. Broad export incentives have been curtailed; the tax incentives still in place apply only to exports by small businesses and to overseas investment. The principle arm of the Japanese government in promoting trade, the Ministry of International Trade and Industry (MITI), no longer directly assists exports, although certain other government policies and practices continue to support knowledge-intensive industries. Japan's Export-Import Bank aggressively finances and insures exports of factory systems, a rapidly growing part of trade.

Many observers argue that the basis of current Japanese export-promotion strategy is initial protection of the domestic market for a chosen range of products. The products selected for support are those that have high-income elasticities of demand: that is to say, demand for these products grows significantly faster than the income of potential purchasers. In addition, the products – which may be based on technology imported from other industrial countries – tend to be of a kind that can be turned out with increasing efficiency and, hence, lower cost, as a result of lessons learned from practical production experience. The government provides producers with sufficient protection to enable them to develop large-scale production for the domestic market. By the time the producers move into the export market, they have acquired the experience necessary to give them an advantage over would-be competitors.

France provides both direct and indirect export assistance, although it has not been as successful as Japan with the indirect approach. From 1975 to 1977, the French government directly financed overseas trade (through long-term credits and general interest subsidies) in the amount of some ten billion francs, almost 2 per cent of the value of its total exports in 1977. It also channels subsidized export finance through the banking system (mainly through the *Crédit national*) and credit agencies such as the *Compagnie française d'assurance pour le commerce extérieur* (COFACE). Government assistance extended through COFACE may cover up to 70 per cent of the cost of additional productive capacity for enterprises that undertake to increase foreign sales by a specified amount. A similar role is assigned to the *Banque française du commerce extérieur.* The French government also provides "mixed credits", a combination of commercial credits and development aid for developing nations. Finally, France pursues a policy of exporting complete plants to developing countries. In 1977, sales of these plants, totalling 26 billion francs, amounted to one-third of French capital-goods exports. The plants are usually sold on favourable terms, and their sales may lead to re-exports in sectors such as steel.

Given these developments elsewhere and the importance of international markets, Canada has been obliged to expand its own policies for export promotion. Instruments used to promote and develop export markets include the services of trade commissioners, the international marketing and trade-relations divisions of the Department of External Affairs, the industry-sector branches of the Department of Regional Industrial Expansion (DRIE), and various market-intelligence, promotional and aid-related programs. Both the Canadian Commercial Corporation (CCC) and the Export Development Corporation (EDC) play vital roles in facilitating export transactions. The CCC acts as the principal mechanism for government-to-government sales from Canada, while the EDC acts as the principal mechanism for insuring the export sales of Canadian firms against non-payment by foreign buyers. The EDC also facilitates medium- to long-term export financing for foreign buyers of Canadian capital goods and services. This financing includes *crédit mixte*: export financing which mixes highly concessional financing with conventional export financing to produce very low, blended, interest rates. Canada uses this device to counter *crédit mixte* terms offered by competitors.

Policies Relating to Technological Progress

Governments can support technological progress and innovation directly, through research and development (R&D) grants, contracts and tax incentives, or indirectly, by facilitating the acquisition of technology. These kinds of support are connected with basic policies to assist education, especially to produce qualified scientists and engineers.

Chapter 8 compared Canadian research and development (R&D) expenditures with those of a number of other nations. The data indicated that while total Canadian outlays as a proportion of national output have generally been below those of the other major members of the Organisation for Economic Co-operation and Development (OECD), the disparity appeared to be smaller when R&D expenditures on defence and space were deleted. Table 9-6 indicates the proportion of research and development financed directly by government. Again, Canada's rank is relatively low, while the

United States, the United Kingdom, Norway, and Portugal all provide relatively high levels of direct support.

The Japanese support level for R&D shown in Table 9-6 seems to be fairly low. One reason may be that research support is often conveyed in the form of low-interest, partially forgivable loans. An example is provided by the Very Large Scale Integrated Chip project completed by five Japanese electronic companies in 1979. The project cost $308 million, of which $132 million was a government loan repayable out of profits over a five-year period beginning in 1983. Often, according to one observer, the five-year period is used for product development, and repayment is usually a small fraction of the loan.[3]

Sweden, the United States, Japan, and Singapore currently provide significant R&D tax incentives. Canada has offered an R&D tax incentive of one kind or another since 1962.

An assessment of overall support levels is exceedingly difficult to make because its validity depends on the subsidy element in R&D contracts, the tax treatment of subsidy income, the definition of R&D for tax purposes, and the opportunities for transferring unused tax savings (credits) either to other tax years or to other taxpayers. In general, industry observers conclude that overall support levels, broadly defined, are relatively high in West Germany, Japan and the United States. In testimony before the Senate Committee on National Finance, Bernard Ness, the president of Canada Wire and Cable, stated that:

> *Combined tax and non-tax support covers only 19 per cent of industrial R&D expenses in Canada, compared to 38 per cent in the United States and on a scale between 25 and 34 per cent in Germany, France and the United Kingdom.*[4]

Recent Canadian commentaries have noted that the direction of R&D efforts is as important as the amount spent.[5] There are, however, wide variations in the way in which research and development are directed in different countries. In the United States, which provides little in the way of direct grants, government R&D contracts are driven largely by defence and space requirements, and are generally awarded to individual firms. In France, most R&D assistance is targeted to strategic sectors considered worthy of support by the government. Another program provides forgivable loans to firms with fewer than 200 employees to enable them to introduce new products or processes. The West German government allocates R&D support with the help of an advisory committee from industry and labour. Selection criteria are oriented less to particular sectors than to the relative extent of expenditure and risk that a given project involves. The greater the risk and the R&D cost relative to the applicant's resources, the more likely is approval. Finally, Japanese R&D support in the form of grants and forgivable loans is channelled both to individual firms and to research associations made up of three or more co-operating firms and approved by the Agency for Industrial Science and Technology. R&D priorities are set on the basis of agreement reached between interested firms and the government.

In Canada, the National Research Council (NRC) provides substantial support to industrial development in many forms. Approximately half of its

TABLE 9-6 Resources Devoted to R&D Since 1980 (NSE + SSH)

	United States			Japan		Germany			France		United Kingdom
	1981	1982	1983	1981/82	1982/83	1981	1982[b]	1983[b]	1981	1982	1981/82[c]
GERD											
Million national currency	73 724	82 017	89 522	5 982 356	6 528 700	38 351	41 300	43 000	62 471	73 000	6 205
Million United States dollars PPP	73 724	82 017	89 522	27 104	30 961	15 488	17 353	—	10 827	11 987	11 304
Annual average percentage increase (1975 price)	5.2	4.4	4.7	11.1	7.2	2.8	2.8	1.1	7.0	3.9	2.1
Percentage of GDP	2.52	2.7	2.73	2.38	2.47	2.49	2.58	2.58	2.01	2.06	2.42
Sector of performance (percentage)											
Business enterprise	70.3	72.0	72.1	60.7	—	68.3	69.7	69.7	58.9	59.4	62.9
Government	12.1	11.6	12.0	11.1	—	14.3	13.8	13.9	23.6	—	—
Higher education	14.4	13.4	13.0	24.2	—	16.3	16.0	15.9	16.4	—	—
Private non-profit	3.2	3.0	2.9	4.1	—	0.5	0.5	0.5	1.1	—	—
GERD	100	100	100	100	—	100	100	100	100	100	100
Source of funds (percentage)											
Business enterprise	48.8	49.4	48.5	62.3	—	57	56.9	58.1	40.8	42.2	41.1
Public	49.2	48.7	48.6	26.9	—	41.6	42.1	41.0	37.5	—	49.8
Government direct	46.6	46.2	46.1	15.7	—	—	—	—	—	—	—
General university funds	2.6	2.5	2.5	11.2	—	—	—	—	—	—	—
Other national sources	2.0	1.9	1.9	10.7	—	0.4	—	—	16.5	—	—
Abroad	0	0	0	0.1	—	0.9	1.0	0.9	5.1	—	9.1
GERD	100	100	100	100	—	100	100	100	100	100	100
Total R&D Personnel											
Number in FTE	—	—	—	64 977	—	371 548	—	—	249 000	—	—
Average annual percentage increase	—	—	—	3.1	—	1.1	—	—	3.9	—	—
Per thousand of total labour force	—	—	—	11.4	—	13.6	—	—	10.7	—	—

Sector of employment (percentage)											
Business enterprise	—	—	—	56.1	—	65.3	—	—	51.3	—	—
Government	—	—	—	8.3	—	14.4	—	—	24.8	—	—
Higher education	—	—	—	3.3	—	19.7	—	—	22.2	—	—
Private non-profit	—	—	—	2.6	—	0.7	—	—	1.8	—	—
Total R&D Personnel	—	—	—	100	—	100	—	—	100	—	—
Total RSE											
RSE/University graduates in FTE	691 400	723 000	750 000	392 625	406 042	128 162	—	—	85 500	—	—
RSE/University graduates as % of total R&D personnel	—	—	—	60.5	—	34.5	—	—	34.5	—	—
RSE by sector of employment (percentage)											
Business enterprise	72.3	73.4	74.1	49.1	—	60.1	—	—	41	—	—
Government	9.5	9.1	8.8	7.4	—	15.2	—	—	18.4	—	—
Higher education	14.3	13.8	13.5	41.6	—	23.6	—	—	38.2	—	—
Private non-profit	3.9	3.7	3.6	1.9	—	1.1	—	—	2.3	—	—
Total RSE	100	100	100	100	—	100	—	—	100	—	—

TABLE 9-6 (Cont'd)

	Italy		Canada		Netherlands	Sweden[a]	Norway	Finland	Portugal	Ireland	
	1981	1982[d]	1981/82	1982/83	1981	1981	1981	1981	1980	1981	1982
GERD											
Million national currency	4 055 335	5 080 438	4 244	5 117	6 643	12 740	4 214	2 483	4 119	83	98
Million United States dollars PPP	4 595	5 219	3 423	3 998	2 526	2 227	625	572	126	157	169
Annual average percentage increase (1975 price)	18.3	6.8	8.7	9.5	–0.9	10.0	1.1	8.1	7.6	5.9	0.9
Percentage of GDP	1.01	1.08	1.22	1.39	1.88	2.23	1.28	1.17	0.33	0.79	0.79
Sector of performance (percentage)											
Business enterprise	56.4	56.8	47.2	50.3	53.3	66.6	52.1	57.1	28.6	43.6	43.6
Government	25.7	26.7	25.2	24.6	20.8	6.4	18.4	25.8	47.3	39.3	39.3
Higher education	17.9	16.5	26.8	24.4	23.2	26.8	29	16.5	19.9	16	16
Private non-profit	—	—	0.7	0.7	2.8	0.3	0.5	0.6	4.2	1.1	1.1
GERD	100	100	100	100	100	100	100	100	100	100	100
Source of funds (percentage)											
Business enterprise	50.1	48.7	39.3	41.8	46.3	57.3	40.1	54.2	26.6	37.7	37.7
Public	47.2	49.2	41.4	40.1	47.2	39.9	57.2	43.6	66.8	56.5	56.5
Government direct	—	—	—	—	26.1	21.4	34.4	31.2	—	45.6	45.6
General university funds	—	—	—	—	21.1	18.5	22.8	12.3	—	10.8	10.8
Other national sources	0	0	15.8	14.5	1.3	1.3	1.4	1.2	4.7	1.1	1.1
Abroad	2.7	2	3.4	3.6	5.2	1.5	1.4	1	1.9	4.8	4.8
GERD	100	100	100	100	100	100	100	100	100	100	100
Total R&D Personnel											
Number in FTE	102 836	—	65 712	—	54 470	43 114	14 843	17 650	7 711	5 474	5 449
Average annual percentage increase	7.3	—	7.7	—	1.7	8.8	–1.1	5.1	8.6	–5.7	–0.5
Per thousand of total labour force	4.5	—	5.5	—	10.1	10	7.5	7.3	1.8	4.3	4.2

Sector of employment (percentage)											
Business enterprise	49	—	46.6	—	49.8	63.4	45	47.4	18.4	26.8	28.4
Government	19.8	—	30.7	—	23.4	7.6	21	29.8	48.1	43.4	40.6
Higher education	31.2	—	21.6	—	24	28.8	33.3	22.1	30.8	28.8	29.5
Private non-profit	—	—	1	—	2.8	0.2	0.8	0.7	2.6	0.9	1.4
Total R&D Personnel	100	—	100	—	100	100	100	100	100	100	100
Total RSE											
RSE/University graduates in FTE	52 060	—	29 670	—	19 436	15 235	7 496	—	2 663	2 636	2 774
RSE/University graduates as % of total R&D personnel	50.6	—	45.2	—	35.7	35.3	50.5	—	34.5	48.2	50.9
RSE by sector of employment (percentage)											
Business enterprise	37.4	—	46.5	—	43.4	52.8	41.1	—	14.1	23	23.6
Government	15.1	—	27.2	—	23.4	10.0	19.2	—	31.4	24.2	24.5
Higher education	47.5	—	25.3	—	31.5	36.8	38.7	—	91.8	51.2	49.9
Private non-profit	—	—	0.9	—	1.7	0.4	1	—	2.7	1.6	2
Total RSE	100	—	100	—	100	100	100	—	100	100	100

Source: Organisation for Economic Co-operation and Development, *Science Resources, Newsletter* (Paris: OECD, 1984), no. 8, pp. 4–5.

Note: GERD = Gross Domestic Expenditure on R&D
PPP = Purchasing Power Parity
FTE = Full-Time Equivalent
RSE = Researchers, Scientists and Engineers
NSE = Natural Sciences & Engineering
SSH = Social Sciences and Humanities.

a. NSE only. Growth rates are slighty overestimated because of increased coverage of HE and BE sectors since 1979.
b. National estimates.
c. Preliminary. Partially OECD estimates.
d. Preliminary.

current $400 million budget is directly allocated to industry-related programs (broadly defined); another $100 million provides supporting services and facilities. The NRC undertakes extensive research and development itself and in co-operation with industry. It also provides information about existing technologies (particularly to small and medium-sized companies) through its Technical Inquiry and Field Advisory Service. A number of other federal departments and agencies also provide technical assistance to firms, as do most provincial governments. At both the federal and the provincial levels, technical assistance is primarily directed at small firms.

The Federal Business Development Bank, through its Counselling Assistance to Small Enterprise (CASE) program, provides both counselling and training assistance to managers; in fiscal 1984, more than 13 000 firms benefited from the program. The bank also provides business-management seminars, owner/manager courses, and management clinics; more than 68 000 Canadian business people participated in these activities in 1984.

Japan's technology-acquisition (TA) activities have attracted considerable attention. Japan has promoted the acquisition of new technology from abroad through a variety of means, including the provision of translations of foreign technical literature, the regular dispatch of large missions abroad, international exchanges of academics, industrial co-operation agreements, the licensing of pilot plants, and the approval of foreign direct investment. Its use of such methods enabled it to close many technological gaps between itself and the United States, at a fraction of the cost of the R&D expenditures in the latter country. The Agency of Industrial Science and Technology is responsible both for Japan's technology-acquisition arrangements at the government level and for its national R&D effort. In 1983, it had a budget of $600 million and supported nearly 4000 researchers in 116 institutions. The Japan External Trade Organization is the government's commercial intelligence service. More than 600 of its employees were stationed in 56 foreign countries in the early 1980s.

At the company level, technological acquisition in Japan involves a thorough scanning of foreign technological information from patent offices, trade conventions and academic journals. Almost 1000 Japanese companies are said to engage in these activities; over 500 have stationed or sent research staff offshore, and almost 400 engage the services of universities and research agencies. The most sophisticated information gatherers are the nine general trading companies that operate globally, trading in virtually everything, including technology. Another source of information scanning is provided by government-supported research institutes, which supply subscribers with a continuous flow of information concerning important developments.

The Korean technology-acquisition effort, remarkable for its speed and size, is based in large part on the Japanese model. Nine general trading companies dominate the private sector's technology-acquisition effort. The Korean Technological Development Corporation is a technology venture-capital company that promotes close associations between foreign sources of high technology and Korean manufacturers. Another organization, the Korean Technology Advancement Corporation, arranges technology imports and joint ventures, and exports the technologies developed by the state-run contract-research institute, the Korean Institute of Science and Technology. Both the Korean Trade Promotion Corporation, which forms part of the Ministry of Commerce, and the Ministry of Finance maintain technology officers abroad to provide intelligence on new technological developments.

The technology-acquisition effort in Sweden rests on three pillars: the "Big 13" indigenous multi-nationals that sell, operate and acquire technologies abroad; industrial research institutes and associations, particularly in pharmaceuticals, transport equipment, and electrical machinery; and the government. The Board for Technological Development has the responsibility for promoting the technological development of small and medium-sized firms. With a staff of 125 (1981), it follows foreign technology developments, co-operates with foreign governments and companies, and supports collective research on an industry-wide basis. Sweden also makes extensive use of its patent office and technical universities as information sources. In addition, it maintains technological attachés in eight cities abroad.

France relies largely on indigenous multi-nationals, foreign multi-nationals and government agencies for its technological acquisition. The *Agence nationale de la valorisation de la recherche* has the mandate to commercialize French inventions both within France and abroad and, more generally, to disseminate innovation throughout the French economy. It has a staff of 200 and works closely with the *Centre national de la recherche scientifique*. France also maintains a long-range technology-assessment capacity in the form of the *Centre d'études des systèmes et des technologies avancées*, which has the responsibility to ensure that the nation develops a capability in emerging technologies.

Direct Government Involvement: Public Enterprise and Government Procurement

Among the more direct vehicles of government involvement in industrial policy are public enterprise and government procurement. As Figure 9-1 shows, the use of public enterprise as a policy instrument varies among countries with market economies. At one extreme is the United States, which has very few public enterprises. At the other extreme is Austria, where nearly all of the utilities, oil refineries, coal mines, railways, steel mills, airlines, and motor-vehicle plants are publicly owned. Japan and Canada have relatively low levels of public enterprise. In Japan, complete or partial public ownership is confined to telecommunications, the railways and the airlines; in Canada, electrical utilities, railways, airlines and the telecommunications industry exhibit substantial degrees of public ownership. In both Britain and Italy, by contrast, the level of public ownership is relatively high. Figure 9-1 shows that telecommunications, railways, electrical utilities, and airlines are in state hands in many countries, and that some less-developed countries (LDCs), such as Mexico, Brazil and India, rely quite heavily on state enterprise.

It is worth observing that until recently, public ownership was an explicit component of industrial strategy in Britain, where it was used to sustain declining sectors, such as shipbuilding and coal mining, and to bail out companies in difficulty, such as the automobile and steel industries. The

FIGURE 9-1 The Extent of Public Enterprise in Eighteen Countries

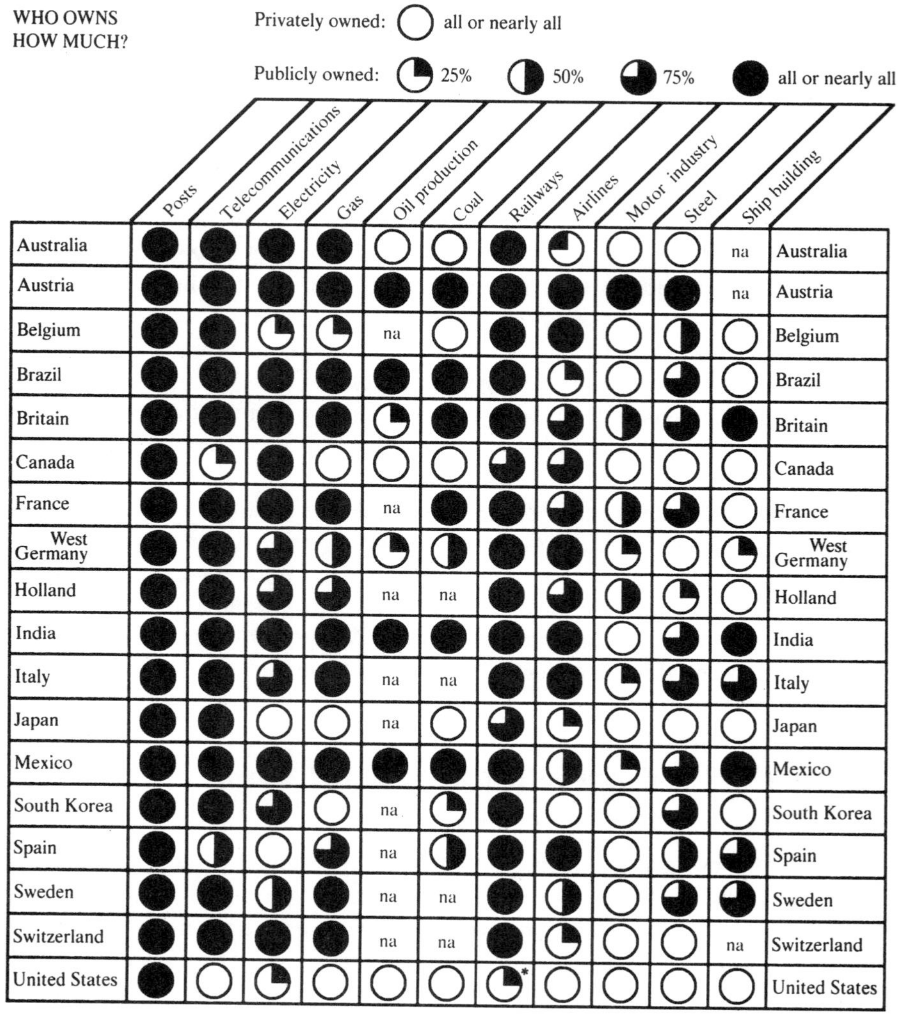

Source: Cited in J.R.S. Prichard (ed.). *Crown Corporations in Canada* (Toronto: Butterworth 1983), p.106.

na - not applicable or negligible production.
* including Conrail.

present Conservative government has embarked on a course of selling off certain of its interests in state enterprises. France has used nationalization to bail out its steel industry and to create a "national champion". Sweden has employed public enterprise to bail out its shipbuilding industry.

In Canada, both the federal and the provincial governments use Crown corporations as instruments of industrial policy. In 1981, Crown corporations had revenues of $40 billion, an amount equal to 13 per cent of Canada's gross national product. Total assets of Crown corporations in the same year amounted to $140 billion, that is, to 11 per cent of total corporate assets. In 1983, Crown corporations accounted for 20 per cent of total investment in Canada and for about 3 per cent of total employment. That they represent a significant element in the economy is readily apparent from these statistics.

Provincial Crown corporations figure more prominently than their federal counterparts, accounting for more than 50 per cent of total public enterprise sales and employment, and about 70 per cent of assets and investment. The most important provincial enterprises are the Crown-owned electrical utilities. Power utilities account for more than 60 per cent of the assets of provincial Crown corporations and more than 40 per cent of the assets of all Crown corporations. Public enterprise has been growing in importance, particularly at the provincial level. The emergence of enterprises owned jointly by government and private interests, such as the Canada Development Corporation, has added to government involvement in investment and asset holding. In 1981, government equity investments in mixed enterprises amounted to about 7.5 per cent of total equity capital in Canada; an estimated 5 per cent of all assets of non-financial corporations were held by mixed enterprises.

Both levels of government have used public enterprises in order to fulfil basic infrastructure requirements. Thus some 50 per cent of the federal government's public enterprises, in terms of assets and revenues, are concentrated in the transportation sector. There is relatively little Crown-corporation activity in the manufacturing sector, although government participation in this sector has been increasing in recent years. Crown corporations such as the Federal Business Development Branch and the Export Development Corporation serve to assist all sectors in business development and marketing.

Government procurement policy can be a powerful tool of industrial policy. Through procurement, governments can guarantee a cash flow to the innovator, provide a demonstration of the innovation in action, and assist private companies by assuming some of the risk associated with innovation. A number of studies have pointed to "procurement pull" as a useful alternative to "subsidy push" in encouraging innovation.

Some analysts have cited government procurement as the principal and, historically, the most effective instrument of U.S. industrial policy. Important – indeed, critical – commercial developments in aircraft, aircraft engines, semi-conductors, and computers have flowed from defence and space procurement. In one view:

> *Government purchases have been used to subsidize and shape the development of emerging products and markets by providing the stimulus of large demand in early stages of products. The impact has been pronounced in the electronics and aerospace sectors. Government purchases in 1977 accounted for 56 percent of total aircraft shipments, and 57 percent of radio and television communications equipment.*[6]

As a rule, procurement practices implicitly or explicitly favour domestic suppliers. The three levels of government in Canada purchase an estimated $40 billion-worth of final goods and services annually, excluding the wages of government employees, but including capital formation; the federal government accounts for about $16 billion-worth of the total amount. All levels of government use their purchases of goods and services to pursue industrial policy objectives, particularly assistance to domestic or local manufacturers. Before the introduction of the recent Agreement on Government Procurement within the General Agreement on Tariffs and Trade (GATT), the federal Department of Supply and Services routinely gave priority to Canadian-based manufacturers. If there were three or more Canadian vendors, they were used exclusively, and the item required was not put to international tender. Even when bids were put to international tender, Canadian bids were given a 10 per cent preference rating. On the whole, only about 20 per cent of total federal procurement was open to foreign suppliers. The incremental cost to the federal government of favouring Canadian suppliers over foreign suppliers has been estimated at an annual cost of $250 million, which is substantially less than the cost of federal direct subsidies or tax incentives to industry.

How the GATT Agreement on Government Procurement will affect federal procurement policy is still uncertain. The agreement excludes defence procurement and certain purchases by Crown corporations. Preliminary estimates indicate that the GATT stipulations will open a further 10 per cent of federal procurement to foreign suppliers. The agreement does not apply to provincial or local governments.

The available information on provincial procurement policy is quite fragmentary. While all provinces extend some degree of preference to local suppliers, only Newfoundland, Nova Scotia and British Columbia grant outright preference under all circumstances. It is not clear to what extent provincial government policies extend to Crown corporations and to provincially funded institutions such as hospitals. Ontario's procurement policies are perhaps the most subtle: for example, its Crown corporation, the Urban Transportation Development Corporation (UTDC) effectively dominates the available markets in Ontario, thanks, in part, to provincial government pressure on municipalities. Quebec's policy is perhaps the most comprehensive: it grants a general price preference to Quebec suppliers and, in certain circumstances, restricts bidding to those suppliers. In general, provincial procurement policies parallel those of the federal government.

Institutional-Regulatory Framework Policies: Competition Policy and Banking Policy

Two types of industrial policy are essentially institutional and regulatory: competition policy and banking policy.

While most observers agree that competition is essential to the proper functioning of a market economy, there is less agreement about the relationship between industrial structure and competition. Some analysts believe that in countries with small domestic markets, such as Canada, the extent of industrial concentration should not be a matter of concern, since only large firms can achieve the economies of scale and muster the financial resources necessary for effective competition with giant foreign companies.

Other analysts argue that a lack of competition from domestic sources, in industries not subject to foreign competition, could very well add to the costs and reduce the competitiveness of industries that are confronted by foreign competition at home or abroad.

There are two basic policy approaches to competition: that of "managed" competition, as practised in Japan and most European countries, and that of "maximum" competition, as practised – at least until recently – in the United States. One observer makes the following distinction between the two approaches:

> *Less obvious perhaps, is the notion of "managed competition" as compared to maximum competition. With the former, a company might be encouraged to give up marginal products or product lines to better concentrate on what it does best while other domestic firms in the same industry were also encouraged to make similar concessions. The result would be a narrower line for all firms, permitting a higher level of resource commitment behind each remaining product-market.*
>
> *"Managed competition" requires government to play a role in mediating decisions about who would give up what, and it or an industry association would monitor compliance ... The continued industrial restructuring in Japan is a case in which government policies combine with corporate strategy to ensure rapid adjustment for targeted industries. It contrasts sharply with American practice which assumes that the maximum degree of competition is best, even if that means five gas stations on a corner instead of four, with decisions to withdraw left to the competitors to be made in isolation.*[7]

The Japanese approach to cartels and mergers has been summed up in this way:

> *In 1953, Japan followed the German lead and amended [its legislation] to permit depression cartels, rationalization cartels and export cartels. Japan was less concerned with a restrictive definition of mergers and a focus on the domestic market structure than with international competitiveness and the exploitation of scale economies. Despite recent tightening of legislation, this attitude persists.*[8]

The American approach is fundamentally different. According to one observer, anti-monopoly law "lies at the heart of the American socio-political philosophy 'which believes in the decentralisation of power and ... the economic freedom and opportunity for new men, new ideas and new organisations to spearhead the forces of progress'."[9]

Canada's competition policy is largely embodied in the Combines Investigation Act, which is administered by the Bureau of Competition Policy of the Department of Consumer and Corporate Affairs. The Bureau investigates such prohibited practices as corporate mergers and monopolies that operate, or are likely to operate, to the "detriment" of the "interest of the public", conspiracies to restrain competition, and other activities that work against competition. The Bureau also monitors resale-price practices, trade discrimination and misleading advertising. Another agency, the

Restrictive Trade Practices Commission, has power to inquire into, and order the discontinuation of, certain potentially anti-competitive trade practices.

In a 1969 report, the Economic Council of Canada stressed the limitations of Canadian competition policy and law.[10] Over the last four decades, the Crown has successfully prosecuted only one monopoly case; no merger cases have been successfully prosecuted. Recent decisions of the Supreme Court of Canada have reputedly made it more difficult to secure indictments involving conspiracies to restrict competition by a variety of means. During the past 15 years, the federal government has made several unsuccessful attempts to revise and strengthen the Combines Investigations Act. A subsequent section of this chapter outlines this Commission's views on the direction that Canadian competition policy ought to take in the future.

In some countries, the banking system plays an important role in industrial policy. One analyst distinguishes between countries (Japan, West Germany and France) in which the banking system holds considerable equity in industrial corporations and countries (the United States, Britain and Canada) in which the banking system holds little or no industrial equity.[11]

Japanese industry is financed primarily by bank loans; only 20 per cent of total investment is held in equity or common shares. Large firms are organized into banking groups in association with one or another of the 13 largest commercial banks. Each banking group has a trading company that acts as a go-between, importing goods and services for sale in Japan and exporting the group's products. Credit is extended with relative ease to the banking group's affiliates. The bank can help nurse a troubled firm back to health by assuming management of the debtor's finances and imposing compromises on other creditors within the group. Ties between the bank and its corporate customers are increased by the bank's ability to invest in shares in non-financial companies, by cross-directorship, and by the temporary assignment of bank employees to the businesses of bank customers. The close affiliation between the banks and industrial companies provides a focal point around which the capital market can design reorganization plans. It is also reputed to serve as a means of reducing the cost of capital to industrial firms. One observer estimates that in recent years, the cost of capital to the Japanese electronics industry has averaged some 4 percentage points less than the cost of capital to that industry in the United States.[12]

West German banks play a major role in industrial investment. Government assistance to industry generally requires bank approval, and the banks themselves usually participate financially in subsidized projects. The interdependence between the banks and industry is enhanced by the presence of bank representatives on the boards of corporations and by extensive bank ownership of company shares. Moreover, almost 85 per cent of the shareholders in Germany deposit their shares with the "big three" banks, Deutsche, Dresdner, and Commerzbank, under trust agreements that assign their proxies to the banks. In 1980, the banks controlled 70 per cent of the shares of the 425 largest firms in Germany. This voting power gives the banks a strong role in crisis management. The banks also serve as an "early warning system", identifying problems in industry as they develop and taking the initiative to resolve them. The banks' role in the reconstruction of failing industries or firms is facilitated by the fact that they face less pressure than does the government to protect employment or to satisfy interest groups.

France has a durable tradition of private bank involvement in the initiation and management of business, and the banks frequently serve as intermediaries in industrial reorganization. Private banks are often shareholders in firms, an arrangement that ensures their interest in helping these companies through times of crisis. For its part, the French government involves itself in both crisis management and business funding generally, through its own financial institutions, which account for 80 per cent of the funding of French industry. Specialized intermediaries under the *Direction du Trésor* (the Treasury), such as the *Crédit national*, the Economic and Social Development Fund, and the French Bank for Foreign Trade, have become the major actors in organizing the funds of new firms. The *Direction du Trésor* is also the agency responsible for implementing government financial instruments such as regional development grants.

Canada's Bank Act secures a capital market in which the banks hold little or no industrial equity. Like American and British banks, Canadian banks are not intimately involved in the management of firms to which they have loaned money.

Canadian governments are quite heavily involved in both direct lending and loan guarantees. The Federal Business Development Bank (FBDB), for example, lends to small and medium-sized businesses that are unable to obtain financing from other sources under reasonable terms and conditions. In March 1984, the FBDB's outstanding loans amounted to $1.7 billion. The federal government also provides loan guarantees through the Small Business Loans Act and the Industrial Regional Development Program. Finally, the Crown-owned Export Development Corporation (EDC) plays a vital role in supporting the export of a number of Canadian products. It provides insurance to Canadian firms against non-payment by foreign buyers, credit guarantees and direct financing. The EDC normally assumes 90 per cent of the commercial and political risks of insolvency or default, blockage of funds, war or rebellion, and cancellation of import licences or export permits. The EDC's total liability on insurance and guarantees outstanding at the end of 1983 amounted to $2.7 billion, while its loans receivable totalled more than $6 billion. Provincial governments also provide loans and loan guarantees in order to promote the growth of secondary manufacturing within their borders.

In 1980, the estimated total stock of loans, loan guarantees and loan insurance made available by government to the private sector came close to $50 billion.[13] However, 60 per cent of this total applied to the housing sector and 10 per cent to the resource sector. Furthermore, the actual value of the subsidy implicit in a $100 loan approximates only $10; that in a guarantee of a $100 loan approximates only $1. The federal government accounts for some 80 per cent of total government assistance in the form of loans and loan guarantees. While its assistance is theoretically geared to small firms, in total dollar-volume terms there appears to be a bias in favour of big firms. Loans and loan guarantees are more widely dispersed across industry sectors than are direct subsidies, and the poorer provinces appear to be favoured.

Firm-Specific Policies

Last, but hardly least, in our review of industrial policies are policies directed to specific firms. Firm-specific subsidies are used both to promote successful firms – that is, as part of a strategy of "picking winners" – and, somewhat more often perhaps, to bail out troubled firms or forestall prospective trouble. Two countries, France and Japan, are notable for directing support to specific firms in pursuit of a strategy of trying to pick winners. Two other countries, Britain and Sweden, have made extensive use of firm-specific assistance, primarily in order to prop up hard-pressed companies.

Britain's case illustrates the danger of providing substantial subsidies to firms confronted by the prospect of a continuously bleak future. The support of ailing industries and firms absorbs the lion's share of Britain's industrial assistance budget, creating a serious drag on the economy and severely impeding the adjustment process that must eventually take place in response to changing economic circumstances. While British government assistance to floundering firms appears to have been motivated primarily by employment considerations, it has also been triggered by trade, defence, technological and regional considerations. According to some observers, however, government-led rescues of the motor-vehicle and shipbuilding industries in the late 1970s failed to stem the tide of competing imports into the country; they merely forestalled inevitable plant closures and worker lay-offs.[14]

In France, a highly explicit targeting mechanism – the *Comité d'orientation pour le développement des industries stratégiques* – directs support to specific products, firms, and industries. The support devices include R&D contracts, procurement (purchase agreements), export financing and promotion, favoured treatment through the largely government-owned banking system, and subsidization. Some analysts conclude that French firm-specific assistance has been only modestly successful, owing to a choice of targets for prestige rather than economic reasons, an unwillingness to abandon failures, and the use of assistance to forestall adjustment.[15]

Japan maintains an explicit system of assistance to smaller businesses faced with trade-, technology- and environment-related adjustment problems or raw material shortages. On presentation of an acceptable adjustment plan, a firm becomes entitled to low-interest loans, guaranteed loans and tax incentives.

Japan assists larger enterprises in a number of ways. Historically, such assistance has involved import protection, but this protection is less rigorous now than it was in the past. Assistance to firms continues to involve procurement preferences, the sanctioning of specialization arrangements and joint research projects, the support (through forgivable loans) of research, and favourable tax treatment of investment. Unlike France, Japan sets its priorities on a collaborative basis: government is the senior, but not necessarily the dominant, partner. There is generally no question of choosing a national champion, as France has attempted to do. When mistakes occur, or when a good choice is undone by events, the Japanese show no hesitation about abandoning or severely curtailing the activity in question. Japan has retreated from ventures in a wide range of industries, including aluminum, petrochemicals, shipbuilding, cement, textiles, coal and steel. Finally, the choice of investments is governed by "rate-of-return" criteria, rather than by prestige, political pressures or employment considerations. By rate-of-return criteria, we mean that investments are channelled into areas where, because of potential market growth and the protection from new entry afforded by the learning curve, sustained high profits are likely.

Governments in Canada are extensively involved in providing assistance to specific firms in distress. Firms in the aeronautics, shipbuilding and automobile industries have received substantial assistance; 25 shipbuilding companies have been granted almost $2 billion over the past ten years. Firms in the textile, shoe and furniture industries have also received direct-grant assistance or other forms of financial support, but the main form of assistance to these industries has been the maintenance of tariffs and quotas. While firms in distress have absorbed the lion's share of government assistance, support has also been given to firms at the forefront of new technology. Three notable successes to date are Spar Aerospace Ltd., CAE Electronics Ltd., and Pratt and Whitney Aircraft. Inevitably, however, some firms that have been supported as potential winners have turned out to be losers.

Overall Policy Orientation and Performance

The range of industrial policy instruments and the combinations in which various countries employ them defy ready summarization. Table 9-7 attempts no more than to indicate, very generally, the degree of emphasis that several countries have given to each of the major types of industrial policy. Certain points that emerge from the table are worth noting. For example, no country other than the United States is classified as having a "strong" competition policy. No country other than Japan has maintained stringent restrictions on foreign investment, and these restrictions Japan is currently relaxing. France, West Germany, Britain and Canada give a higher priority to regional development than do most other countries.

A qualitative assessment of the effects of the various policy choices on national performance points to the following conclusions.

Trade policy. Australia, France and Japan have employed protectionist strategies in the recent past. Australia's economic record has been rather weak over the past decade or so, while Japan has performed relatively strongly. France's performance has been mixed: strong initially, but weaker in recent years. Some observers argue that Japan's trade policies did much to protect infant industries from competition in the domestic market during their development phase and thus prepare them for entry into the international market. Britain, which has generally maintained a free-trade stance, has lost much of both its domestic and its export markets for manufactured goods during the post-Second World War period. West Germany, which has adopted trade policies similar to Britain's, has performed relatively well.

Foreign investment policy. Until recently, Japan has severely restricted foreign investment while maintaining very high levels of domestic savings and

TABLE 9-7 Mix of Industrial Policy Instruments of Selected Countries

	United States		Britain		Australia		Japan		France		Germany		Sweden		Canada	
	Emphasis Strong	Emphasis Weak	Emphasis Strong	Emphasis Weak	Emphasis Strong	Emphasis Weak	Emphasis Strong	Emphasis Weak	Emphasis Strong	Emphasis Weak	Emphasis Strong	Emphasis Weak	Emphasis Strong	Emphasis Weak	Emphasis Strong	Emphasis Weak
Competition policy	x			x		x(?)		x		x		x		x(?)		x
Labour-adjustment policies		x		x		x	x			x	x		x			x
Trade protection		x		x	x		x		x			x		x	x	
Regional development policies		x	x			x		x	x		x			x(?)	x	
Government R&D expenditures	x		x		x			x		x	x		x(?)		x	
Public ownership		x	x			x(?)		x	x			x		x		x
Firm-specific subsidies		x	x			x	x		x			x		x	x	
State influence on credit allocation		x		x		x	x		x			x	x			x
Social security policies		x		x		x		x	x		x		x			x
Foreign investment restrictions		x		x		x	x			x		x		x		x

Source: Marsha Chandler and Michael J. Trebilcock, "Comparative Survey of Industrial Policies in Selected OECD Countries", in *Economics of Industrial Policy and Strategy*, vol. 5, prepared for the Royal Commission on the Economic Union and Development Prospects for Canada (Toronto: University of Toronto Press, 1985).

capital investment. Other countries have been much more permissive in accepting foreign investment; some have performed well, some poorly.

Firm-specific policies. Many analysts point to Japan's apparently successful use of selective strategies to promote high-growth firms and industries. France's use of firm- and industry-specific policies has had very mixed results, including major failures in computers, electronics and aircraft manufacturing. West Germany, which has enjoyed a reasonably high rate of growth, has generally avoided selective support to firms or industries; instead, it has concentrated on promoting conditions conducive to market-led adjustment. In Britain, where growth has been low, the government has tended to use selective support to bail out ailing firms or industries, a policy that has often entailed nationalization. In some instances, the bail-outs have been for basic industries such as steel, autos and ship-building; in others, the assistance has gone to high-technology "industries of the future" such as aerospace, for such projects as those undertaken by Rolls-Royce and the development of the Concorde. Canada's use of selective intervention has been similar.

Research and development. The importance to economic growth of expenditures on R&D is hotly debated. The question of the appropriate public policy for a small country such as Canada, which cannot engage in large-scale technology races with larger economies, is even more controversial. The experience of other countries offers little clear guidance toward a resolution of this issue. Japan has one of the lowest levels of reported government expenditures on R&D among the major OECD countries, and it has spent significantly less, in total, on R&D as a proportion of economic output than has Britain. Making use of others' investments in technology through adoption or adaptation of their innovation clearly has some advantages over domestic investment in original research and development. Of course, such a practice would be counter-productive if all countries followed it.

Competition policy. This is another variable that yields ambiguous results. The United States has traditionally maintained a vigorous anti-trust policy in order to foster domestic competition, while most European countries and Japan have a very weak anti-trust tradition. Indeed, the latter countries have adopted policies in many sectors that encourage mergers, consolidations and concentration.

It is evident that the relationships between these industrial policies and economic performance tend to be conflicting and contradictory. Japan's notably successful performance seems to reflect a variety of factors: the combined efforts of industry and government to enable the nation to catch up with more advanced industrial countries; a high level of capital investment and, in all probability, a unique policy-making system that appears to be very much in tune with the national temperament and ideally suited to achieving national aspirations. The utility of all of these factors may be reinforced by Japan's strategy of concentrating substantial resources on the development of particular industries or sectors which it has singled out as prospective areas of strong growth.

Of course, national strategies alone do not account for the differences in national growth rates. Nor is economic growth the only possible basis for a comparison of national economic policies. One study distinguishes between national strategies that aim primarily at redistributing income and those that encourage work, savings and investment. The study concludes, as Figure 9-2 shows, that the advanced North American and Western European nations tend to be marked by high levels of income redistribution, low rates of savings and investment, and significant disincentives to work, while the reverse is true of countries in the Far East.[16]

FIGURE 9-2 Country Strategy

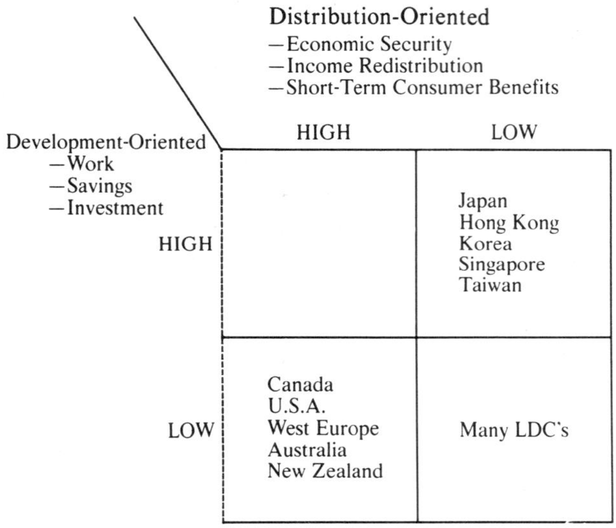

Source: Bruce R. Scott, "National Strategies: Key to International Competition", in *U.S. Competitiveness in the World Economy* (Boston: Harvard Business School Press, 1985), p. 127.

It does not necessarily follow that a high level of income redistribution results in low economic growth. Indeed, some economists have argued that up to a point, income redistribution can help to promote growth by reducing resistance to necessary economic change.[17] A study which relates national economic growth to a country's standing in the industrial hierarchy and to factors such as population growth, income transfers, and the growth of government, concludes that countries with relatively large income transfers tend to grow faster than those with relatively small income transfers.[18] The same study also found a correlation between the age of the political structures of various countries and their rate of economic growth: countries with more mature structures grow more slowly. It is a matter of debate, however, whether much weight should be attached to this conclusion.

Another approach to an international measure of economic performance is to compare not just policy instruments and their effects, but also the links between political institutions *per se* and, therefore, the inherent structure of political representation. Studies on the political dimensions of general economic development policies, deficits and taxation, and labour-market policies suggest a strong association between the degree of sustained representation of labour in government and the degree of concrete policy commitment to training and job-creation programs. The more highly sustained the representation of labour, either indirectly or through political parties, the greater is the relative commitment to employment and employment-adjustment goals.[19]

None of these comparative studies reveals any single policy or any single variable that convincingly explains why some countries succeed in promoting economic development and others do not. Nor does a mix of economic and political factors alone provide an adequate basis of comparison. The list of possible factors is endless, and comparisons between apparently similar practices can be misleading. It is possible, for example, that Japan's commitment to a form of guaranteed employment should be viewed as a unique product of its culture, rather than as a product of its economic or industrial policy.

Whether this review of international industrial policies suggests a need for more (or more intelligent) intervention or for less intervention and a willingness to let market forces guide the economy is a question we shall address later. One thing, however, is clear: if we Canadians are to meet successfully the challenges confronting our industrial sector, future development must be more responsive to international competitive conditions than to internal political pressures to protect the *status quo*. Faced as we are with increasingly strong competition in domestic and international markets, it is in the interest of business, labour and government alike to bolster the ability of Canadian industry to meet and match that competition.

Canada's industrial policy record is mixed. Our overall economic performance since 1945, which has certainly been influenced to some degree by our industrial policies, has been good in some dimensions and poor in others. We have successfully reallocated output and employment among major sectors of the economy in response to changing economic circumstances, paralleling the performance of nations, such as Japan and West Germany, which have been held up as models of adaptability. Within the manufacturing sector, we have reallocated labour in the same direction as the "successful" countries, but not to as great an extent. Furthermore, our employment-growth record has been exceptionally strong. On the other hand, over the past ten years or so, our rate of productivity growth has been low relative to the rates in other industrial market economies. In addition, during the same period, the benefits we derive from our natural resource wealth have continued to wane in importance; the reasons for this decline include slow growth abroad, technological changes that reduced demand for certain commodities, and competition from less-developed countries. This trend, in turn, has placed a greater burden on productive investment in areas where international competition is already tough and is expected to become tougher still.

It has been all too easy to find grounds for criticizing a broad range of government initiatives in the area of industrial policy. The recently amended federal tax provisions that permitted the sale of R&D tax credits by one firm to another proved to be an idea that, however well motivated, was misapplied. Several new ventures which the federal government has backed as potential "winners" have turned out to be "losers", although there have also been some success stories. Efforts to bail out high-profile firms through loans, grants, equity infusions and outright take-overs have produced a few notable successes and some striking failures. Extensive government support, in the form of quotas and subsidies, of faltering industries such as textiles, shoes and shipbuilding has added to the costs of the economy, undermined its international competitiveness in other areas, and impeded the adjustment to changing economic circumstances that is essential if Canada is to maintain a healthy growth of output and incomes.

We Commissioners appreciate the difficulty of the position in which governments find themselves. To allow a company to fail or an industry to wither away without extending a helping hand exposes a government to criticism for ignoring the hardship experienced by the workers in that company or that industry and by the communities in which they live. Yet, as we have just indicated, when governments do extend aid in such circumstances, they become subject to criticism for impeding, often at considerable cost, an adjustment process that ultimately must be undertaken.

A balanced approach is in order, for there is neither an obvious standard of success nor broad consensus on how to achieve it. Indeed, the criteria of success vary from sector to sector. From a national perspective, success does not require the preservation of specific activities or industries, but individuals involved in failing industries may understandably hold a contrary view. What we must acknowledge is that all countries make mistakes in the exercise of industrial policy, for no country has perfected the ideal mix of policy instruments. Resource misallocation is an inevitable consequence of government support programs, just as resource misallocation is an inevitable consequence of private sector decisions. The challenge for Canada is to do at least as well as its major competitors in the exercise of industrial policy.

Notes

1. Much of the material in this section is drawn from Commission research. See Marsha Chandler and Michael J. Trebilcock, "Comparative Survey of Industrial Policies in Selected OECD Countries", in *Economics of Industrial Policy and Strategy*, vol. 5 (Toronto: University of Toronto Press, 1985).
2. Dorothy B. Christelow, "National Policies Toward Foreign Direct Investment", *Federal Reserve Bank of New York Quarterly Review* 4 (Winter 1979–1980), pp. 21–32.
3. William G. Ouchi, *The M-Form Society: How American Teamwork Can Recapture the Competitive Edge* (Reading, Mass: Addison-Wesley, 1984), pp. 116–17.
4. Canada, Senate, Standing Committee on National Finance, *Proceedings*, March 22, 1984, p. 9.

5. See Canada, Ministry of State for Science and Technology, Task Force on Federal Policies and Programs for Technology Development, *Report* (Ottawa: Minister of Supply and Services Canada, 1984) (D. Wright, Chairman); and Canada, Senate, Standing Committee on National Finance (C. William Doody, Chairman).
6. Marsha Chandler and Michael J. Trebilcock, "Comparative Survey of Industrial Policies in Selected OECD Countries", in *Economics of Industrial Policy and Strategy*, vol. 5, prepared for the Royal Commission on the Economic Union and Development Prospects for Canada (Toronto: University of Toronto Press, 1985).
7. Bruce R. Scott, "National Strategies: Key to International Competition", in *U.S. Competitiveness in the World Economy*, edited by Bruce R. Scott and George C. Lodge (Boston: Harvard Business School Press, 1985), pp. 105–6.
8. Chandler and Trebilcock, "Comparative Survey of Industrial Policies in Selected OECD Countries".
9. Martin Edomonds, "Market Ideology and Corporate Power: The United States", in *Industrial Crisis: A Comparative Study of the State and Industry*, edited by Kenneth Dyson and Stephen Wilks (Oxford: Martin Robertson, 1983), p. 71.
10. Economic Council of Canada, *Interim Report on Competition Policy* (Ottawa: Information Canada, 1969).
11. See John Zysman, *Governments, Markets and Growth: Financial Systems and the Politics of Industrial Change* (Ithaca: Cornell University Press, 1983).
12. Ouchi, *The M-Form Society*.
13. Economic Council of Canada, *Intervention and Efficiency: A Study of Government Credit and Credit Guarantees to the Private Sector* (Ottawa: Minister of Supply and Services Canada, 1982).
14. See Chandler and Trebilcock, "Comparative Survey of Industrial Policies in Selected OECD Countries".
15. See, for example, Scott, "National Strategies".
16. Scott, "National Strategies".
17. See, for example, Reuven Brenner and Léon Courville, "Industrial Strategy: Inferring What It Really Is", in *Economics of Industrial Policy and Strategy*, vol. 5, prepared for the Royal Commission on the Economic Union and Development Prospects for Canada (Toronto: University of Toronto Press, 1985).
18. John McCallum and André Blais, "Government, Special Interest Groups and Economic Growth", in *Responses to Economic Change*, vol. 27, prepared for the Royal Commission on the Economic Union and Development Prospects for Canada (Toronto: University of Toronto Press, 1985).
19. See G. Bruce Doern, "The Politics of Economic Policy: An Overview"; David A. Wolfe, "The Politics of the Deficit"; and Leon Muszynski, "The Politics of Labour Market Policy", in *The Politics of Economic Policy*, vol. 40, prepared for the Royal Commission on the Economic Union and Development Prospects for Canada (Toronto: University of Toronto Press, 1985).

Reorienting Canada's Industrial Policies

Commissioners believe that a reorientation of Canada's industrial policies is imperative if Canada is to avoid being out-performed by other industrialized nations or by newly industrializing nations (NICs). We define industrial policy broadly: that is, we include all government efforts to promote growth, productivity and the competitiveness of Canadian industries. While industrial policy must draw constantly from Canadian experience and the experience of Canada's major competitors, it must also adapt constantly to changing circumstances at home and abroad. At the same time, it must exhibit a reasonable degree of stability and predictability.

A Market-Oriented Framework For Industrial Policy

In considering the critical issue of industrial policy, we are mindful of the wide range of views expressed by Canadians to this Commission about the proper role for government in formulating and implementing such a policy for Canada. The fundamental questions are these: Should government confine itself to a rather passive role in facilitating industrial growth and development by the private sector? Or should it intervene actively and directly in private investment decisions, in order to encourage the development of companies or industries that it has singled out as potential winners and the phasing out of demonstrated losers? A research paper prepared for this Commission[1] sums up the arguments for and against the latter approach. It cites objections to a targeted industrial policy on the grounds of:

- The alleged difficulty of picking winners over losers
- The inherent discrimination involved in the process of government intervention in the private sector
- The erosion of the vital market function in the allocation of economic resources.

It argues for a targeted industrial policy on the grounds that:

- Governments have a reasonable probability of success in distinguishing between winners and losers.
- Selection must be made in order to fulfil regional employment objectives and obtain entry into specific markets.
- Necessary scale economies require that the development of a new product or process be undertaken by a single firm.

It is probably true that most Canadian economists have doubts about the ability of governments to pick potential winners and to help them gain a comparative advantage on the international stage. If all countries were to pursue this strategy, the benefits to each nation would, on average, simply match the costs of entering the game. Nevertheless, the study cited above concludes that Canadian governments should intervene aggressively to support firms singled out as potential winners; its rationale is that such help is necessary to overcome the impediments to private sector initiatives that result from Canada's regional diversity and the smallness of its domestic market.

Quite apart from the economic cases for and against a targeted industrial policy, the practical problems of implementation are considerable. The adoption of a targeted industrial policy requires government to establish selection criteria that will identify which sectors or firms should be supported, and which should be allowed to disappear or be deliberately phased out. While many attempts have been made to define selection criteria, no convincing formula has emerged. It is clear in retrospect that if some of the criteria suggested in the past by various government departments had been adopted, they would have led to an unreasonable proportion of bad investments. Picking winners is an extremely difficult business, particularly since enterprises that look promising today may be made obsolete by changing conditions tomorrow.

France and Japan are the two countries that have most explicitly and extensively adopted targeted industrial strategies. As we noted earlier, the French experience has been mixed at best; success has been especially elusive in areas, such as electronics, where international competition is intense. France's industrial targeting appears to have been blurred by considerations of prestige and by a desire to protect declining industries.

Japan's experience with targeted industrial strategies has also been mixed. A number of targeted sectors – the microchip industry, for one example – have experienced a high rate of success. Moreover, Japan has shown no reluctance to abandon losing industries, such as aluminum, petrochemicals and shipbuilding. It is by no means clear, however, how much the Japanese success story owes to the targeting of government support *per se*. It now seems evident that Japan's support for the steel industry was misdirected, in view of the changes in economic conditions that were taking place at the time. Where targeting has been successful, it is not evident that the benefits have exceeded the opportunity costs (that is, the costs of forgoing more lucrative investment opportunities) associated with the targeted support. Most observers conclude that Japan's success is the result of many factors, not the least of which is the quality of management of individual firms.

Experience with targeted industrial strategies provides many illustrations of the difficulties of picking "winners" and the inherent administrative complexity of implementing such strategies. A comprehensive study of alternative support strategies in the United States concludes that U.S. support for applied research of general application has been effective, while research directed more narrowly to the proprietary-commercial area has not. The study extends its conclusions to Europe's experience:

> *The lesson here is a general one . . . There are many other studied cases, most of these European, in which government has tried to identify and support particular products that it was hoped would ultimately prove to be commercial successes. While there are a few successes, the batting average has been very low, except when the government in question has been willing to subsidize or require the procurement of the completed product as well as the R&D on it.*[2]

Some observers argue that the difficulty of picking "winners" arises from a lack of responsiveness and flexibility, and that the problem can be remedied by administrative changes. The view of this Commission is that the failures observed over time are attributable to fundamental problems in the selection system, and that there is no quick administrative solution.

The determination of whether a given activity is a potential winner can also be a very slow business, not because of bureaucratic inefficiency, but because of the nature of the activity itself. The difficulty of targeting industrial policy support for proprietary technologies provides an illustration of this point. Generic technologies, such as those related to producing spring-wheat strains or dryland-cultivation techniques, provide benefits to a readily identifiable group of beneficiaries: for example, farmers who own wheat-growing land. On the other hand, the beneficiaries of the subsidization of a proprietary technology may be as few as one individual: the owner of the firm involved. The choice of generic R&D projects can be guided by sector representatives acting in concert with academics and other researchers. In contrast, it is very difficult to decide which proprietary technology to support on the basis of the agreement of informed, but objective, parties, for the informed parties are not disinterested. Consequently, the decision-making process is almost certain to be ponderous and slow.

In view of the practical difficulties of developing a targeted approach to industrial policy, this Commission does not recommend such an approach for Canada. Rapidly changing international and domestic circumstances demand a highly flexible and adaptive economic system; it is very doubtful whether governments can respond to such situations better than private enterprise can. The fact that many of the components of industrial policy are under provincial or federal-provincial jurisdiction is a further argument against attempting to pursue a closely orchestrated industrial policy.

There can be no argument about the need for closer consultation and co-ordination among governments, business, and labour. Part VI of this Report proposes a number of institutional changes designed to enhance the effectiveness of Canada's economic management. A targeted industrial policy, however, would require a much more intensive involvement of the government bureaucracy in making decisions about private investment than Commissioners are prepared to recommend.

In our judgement, Canada's approach to industrial policy should become more highly market-oriented than it is at present, rather than move toward still more intensive government intervention. Commissioners believe that more reliance should be placed on the ability of basic market forces to determine which industries and companies deserve to prosper. While there are several reasons why a strict hands-off approach is neither feasible nor desirable, governments have, in our view, intervened in the market-place too often and too extensively over the past several years.

Canadian governments should not, of course, close the book on the question of targeted industrial policies. While there is little evidence to suggest that targeted strategies are effective in Canada or elsewhere, we can all be sure that governments around the world will continue to experiment with policies to improve their trade prospects. As the international climate of competition becomes more intense, sometimes as a result of attempts at targeting by other countries, the pressures on Canada to experiment will grow. Such experiments will be high-risk endeavours in a high-risk world. Until we have more confidence in the feasibility and suitability of a targeted approach to industrial policy, and until we have more knowledge of the adjustments likely to arise out of a more open trade environment with the United States, this Commission recommends that Canada place deep reliance on market forces in allocating Canada's human, capital, and natural resources.

In keeping with this emphasis on market mechanisms, Canada should develop a clearly defined framework for an industrial policy that would facilitate both private sector decision making and co-ordination of its decisions with government policies and programs. This framework should identify the objectives of industrial policy, the main factors to be taken into account in devising and implementing industrial policy, and the key initiatives to be undertaken in relation to each of these factors. It is to a consideration of such a framework that we now turn.

Productivity and Competitiveness as Strategic Objectives

In a small, open economy, industrial policy and trade policy are almost synonymous. Both should be anchored in a clearly defined set of objectives or goals. Conventionally, these goals are more or less as follows:

- A high growth rate in average real income
- Stability in real income over time and in all regions
- An opportunity for stable and "meaningful" employment for all citizens
- A reasonably equitable distribution of income.

While we Commissioners endorse this set of objectives, we recognize that it does not provide an operational framework for the implementation of an industrial policy. Thus, we would hope that the four goals outlined above would be furthered by the definition of a common strategic objective that would provide a consistent basis for the policies and programs of the 11 governments across Canada.

What should the common strategic objective be? We believe that it should be related to the fundamental purpose of industrial policy, the collective label given to government efforts to promote the growth, productivity and competitive performance of the Canadian economy. Concern for productivity and competitiveness has been a compelling theme in the hearings and submissions to this Commission, and we are convinced that their significant improvement must be the fundamental objective of our future industrial policy.

The recent resurgence of interest in industrial policy derives, in large part, from the relatively poor performance of the Canadian economy in recent years, particularly its low rate of productivity growth. This poor performance is especially troubling in light of the tough international competition facing Canadian manufacturing firms and some resource sectors, such as forestry and mining. Additional interest in industrial policy stems from deep concern about unemployment which, over the next decade, is expected to fall only slowly from its present high level. While this Commission is of the view that high current rates of unemployment are largely a cyclical problem and, hence, are best resolved through the traditional tools of demand-management policy, complementary industrial and related adjustment policies could help to accelerate the creation of new jobs.

Fears that Canadians are losing out in international markets are fed by an international trading environment that has become increasingly competitive. These fears are also fostered by a growing resort to non-tariff barriers (NTBs), such as quotas and voluntary restraints on exports. This tendency is particularly dangerous to Canada because it is the only major industrialized country without guaranteed access to a market of 100 million people or more. Another source of concern is the success of the newly industrialized countries in building on their labour-cost advantage in the production of standardized products and, increasingly, of more sophisticated products, to become major competitors in the international market-place.

If Canadian industry is to survive and prosper, it must be able to compete effectively with foreign interests both at home and abroad. This means at least three things. In the first place, Canadian firms must look outward on the rest of the world. They must search out markets wherever they can find them. They must undertake research and development (R&D) in areas where Canada has a special edge, and seek out the technological advances being made abroad that we must adopt or adapt in order to remain competitive. Secondly, government must encourage competitiveness in the Canadian market-place, particularly among firms that are shielded from foreign competition, in order to limit the costs of Canadian companies that are competing with foreign firms at home and abroad. Governments must also avoid hampering the competitiveness of Canadian firms by burdening them with excessive taxes or undue regulatory requirements. Thirdly, both industry and government must recognize the many factors that could alter Canada's competitive position. These factors include changes in the exchange rate, which have consequences for the economy as a whole, and changes that affect the fortunes of particular firms or industries. Changes of either kind impose problems of adjustment for which solutions have to be found.

Commissioners are, of course, concerned about competitiveness, not for its own sake, but because it is essential to the growth and development of the Canadian economy: to the expansion of output, the increase of employment, and the rise of real incomes. The same considerations are the basis of our concern about productivity, that is, the efficiency with which Canada produces goods and services; this has an important bearing on the country's international competitiveness. A recent submission to a forum known as the Berkeley Roundtable on the International Economy described competitiveness this way:

> *A nation's competitiveness is the degree to which it can, under free and fair market conditions, produce goods and services that meet the test of international markets while simultaneously expanding the real incomes of its citizens. International competitiveness at the national level is based on superior productivity performance and the economy's ability to shift output to high productivity activities, which in turn can generate high levels of real wages.*

> *Competitiveness is associated with rising living standards, expanding employment opportunities, and the ability of a nation to maintain its international obligations. It is not just a measure of the nation's ability to sell abroad, and to maintain a trade equilibrium. The very poorest countries in the world are often able to do that quite well. Rather, it is the nation's ability to stay ahead technologically and commercially in those commodities and services likely to constitute a larger share of world consumption and value added in the future.*[3]

In the broadest terms, then, competitiveness is simply effective resource use. An empirical approach to the measurement of competitiveness defined in this broad manner can be found in the European Management Forum's *Report on International Industrial Competitiveness*.[4] The report ranked Canada seventh of 22 countries in 1984, eleventh in 1983, and sixth in 1982. Areas in which Canada ranked relatively poorly in 1984 were innovative orientation, outward orientation, socio-political consensus and stability, economic dynamism, state interference and industrial efficiency. The last factor is deemed to depend on employee productivity and costs, price stability, investment rates, employee motivation and turnover, and corporate profits and taxation. While one might quarrel with the mixture of opinion and hard data on which these rankings are based, the report does remind us of the variety of influences that may bear on a nation's competitive position.

A narrower, more specific, measure of a nation's competitive position is its relative cost or unit-cost position. While it would be desirable to assess all of the costs related to production, costs related to labour are the easiest to compare internationally. Since labour costs account for such a large share of total production costs, this is not a major limitation. The competitive position of a country is significantly influenced by its relative labour costs. At the same time, it is necessary to bear in mind that what is important is the combined productivity of all the factors of production. A country that deploys its labour and its capital more efficiently than another country may have lower labour costs and yet sustain a higher wage rate. To account for the productivity factor, international cost comparisons are usually made in terms of unit-labour costs, that is, the cost of labour needed to produce a unit of output.

Since international trade is particularly competitive in the field of manufactured goods, and since trade in these goods is of growing importance, comparisons of manufacturing-unit labour costs among countries are especially pertinent. Unfortunately, the available comparisons do not show very consistent results for Canada.

One of the best-known measures of competitiveness in manufacturing is prepared by the International Monetary Fund (IMF); the Fund shows relative unit-labour costs in manufacturing activity as adjusted for exchange-rate changes and short-term cyclical variations in productivity performance. Table 9-8 provides the IMF indices for Canada and its two most important trading partners, the United States and Japan. According to this table, Canada's competitive position relative to the rest of the world deteriorated sharply – by almost 20 per cent, in fact – between 1980 and 1983. The position of the

United States deteriorated even more sharply, by 33 per cent. The considerable appreciation of the U.S. dollar and the related appreciation of the Canadian dollar against other currencies were the essential reasons for this deterioration. The table indicates that over a longer term – that is, since 1975 or even 1970 – Canada's relative position has not changed materially. The competitive position of the United States has followed a more volatile pattern. Moreover, the table indicates that Japan, too, has suffered a decline in its relative competitive position, albeit a modest one.

TABLE 9-8 Index[a] of Changing Competitive Position of the Manufacturing Sector: Selected Countries

Country	1983 Compared to 1970	1983 Compared to 1975	1983 Compared to 1980
Canada	98.0	98.6	118.4
United States	92.0	130.0	132.9
Japan	105.6	95.4	108.9

Source: International Monetary Fund, *International Financial Statistics January 1985* (Washington, D.C.: IMF, 1985).

a. Index relative to specified base year: less than 100 indicates an improvement in the competitive position; more than 100 indicates a deterioration in the competitive position.

While the IMF data indicate that Canada's competitive position deteriorated quite sharply in the early 1980s, an alternative measure of competitiveness, developed by Morgan Guaranty Trust and highly regarded, suggests that the decline was much less pronounced. Indeed, the Morgan Guaranty Trust index, which measures real effective exchange rates for non-food manufacturers, suggests that since 1975, Canada's competitive position has strengthened appreciably, by some 10 per cent. This finding is consistent with the fact that many Canadian firms and industries are successfully meeting foreign competition in both domestic and international markets. It is also consistent with the substantial increase in Canada's trade surplus since 1979.

Despite the continuing increase in Canada's overall commodity-trade surplus, there is still concern about Canada's international competitiveness, particularly in the manufacturing sector. This concern arises, in part, from certain comparisons of actual unit-labour costs in various countries, as compared to relative changes in such unit costs as those provided by the IMF and Morgan Guaranty Trust figures.

What are the absolute differences in unit-labour costs between Canada and other OECD countries? One submission to this Commission describes Canada as a very high-cost country.[5] According to Table 9-9, which summarizes the findings presented in this submission, unit-labour costs in Canada's manufacturing sector were almost 30 per cent above those in the United States in 1983. Canada has the second-highest unit-labour costs of the nine

TABLE 9-9 Labour Costs per Unit in Manufacturing, Selected Countries, 1983

United Kingdom	136.0
Canada	129.3
Italy	107.2
Belgium	106.3
United States[a]	100.0
Germany	92.3
France	86.5
Sweden	73.3
Japan	61.2

Source: Donald J. Daly, "Cost Competitiveness and Canada's Challenges and Choices", a Brief to the Royal Commission on the Economic Union and Development Prospects for Canada, July 1984, p. 3a.

Methods: These estimates incorporate the net effects of output per hour in real terms, total compensation per hour, and the 1983 exchange rates. This covers a major part of costs for GDP in manufacturing, and costs per unit for capital and depreciation can be approximated for some countries. The results are updates of the methods used in D.J. Daly, *Canada's Comparative Advantage* (Ottawa: Economic Council of Canada, 1979); A.D. Roy, "Labour Productivity in 1980: An International Comparison", *National Institute Economic Review* (August 1982), p. 35; updated by U.S. Bureau of Labor Statistics, *News*. "International Comparisons of Manufacturing Productivity and Labor Cost Trends, Preliminary Measures for 1983" (May 31, 1984).

a. United States = 100.0

countries listed in the table, and these costs are more than twice as high as Japan's. On the other hand, a calculation by Data Resources Inc., presented in Table 9-10, indicates that Canada is a higher-cost producer than Japan, France, Italy and Germany, but a lower-cost producer than the United States. Thus, one study shows that Canada's manufacturing unit-labour costs are higher than those of its major trading partner, the United States, while the other shows that they are not. By one measure, Canada's position appears to have deteriorated seriously since 1980. By another measure, Canada's position has actually improved, a conclusion that seems to tally with the recent growth of Canada's manufacturing export trade. Neither index takes resource exports into account, and therefore neither reflects the major problems that have appeared for our forestry and mining sectors. Both studies agree, however, that unit-labour costs are higher in Canada than they are in most of the other major OECD countries. There can be little doubt that Canada is a high-cost country, at least in comparison with Japan and insofar as the manufacturing sector as a whole is concerned. Nevertheless, we must be very careful in drawing conclusions from this last observation. High unit-labour costs may indicate success, in the form either of strong world demand for our products or of high-wage/employment alternatives outside the manufacturing sector. They may also indicate a past failure to keep wage settlements in line with productivity growth.

For a given firm or industry, failure to keep unit costs in line with those of foreign competitors will result in a declining share of both foreign and domestic markets. Sometimes a firm can remedy the problem by reducing

TABLE 9-10 Unit Labour-Costs Multiples of United States Levels

Country	1968	1975	1982
United States	1.00	1.00	1.00
Canada	0.90	1.03	0.94
France	0.60	0.85	0.63
United Kingdom	0.56	0.88	0.96
Germany	0.52	0.98	0.78
Italy	0.50	0.88	0.62
Japan	0.40	0.66	0.49

Source: Roger Brinner and Nigel Gault, "U.S. Manufacturing Costs and International Competition", *Data Resources Review* (October 1983), p. 1.13.

TABLE 9-11 Trade Balances in Manufacturing

	[(Exports – Imports)/(Exports+Imports)] x 100					
Industry	1966	1975	1980	1982	1983	Average 1966–82
Food & beverage	20.3	1.0	11.9	20.0	15.4	11.6
Rubber & plastics	–59.5	–63.7	–38.0	–11.0	–16.9	–42.4
Leather	–57.3	–74.9	–68.9	–68.9	–72.8	–69.4
Textiles	–73.8	–74.8	–59.4	–58.0	–64.8	–67.8
Knitting mills	–73.9	–93.7	–93.1	–92.9	–94.3	–91.1
Clothing	–41.2	–41.0	–35.3	–45.5	–55.1	–39.4
Wood	76.0	55.4	79.8	84.2	80.9	76.3
Furniture and fixtures	–42.2	–45.5	–9.2	11.1	11.0	–21.9
Paper and allied	88.9	82.0	86.6	83.4	81.0	85.1
Printing and publishing	–82.4	–73.8	–64.4	–64.8	–54.5	–70.3
Primary metals	40.9	35.3	35.4	42.3	35.0	37.6
Fabricated metals	–65.4	–52.4	–38.7	–34.7	–31.9	–45.4
Machinery	–56.9	–49.4	–47.7	–41.7	–41.8	–47.7
Transportation	–17.1	–11.7	–8.4	7.6	3.8	–4.7
Equipment electrical products	–47.0	–47.5	–39.7	–33.9	–37.2	–42.9
Non-metallic minerals	–49.0	–45.2	–33.0	–24.9	–26.3	–33.6
Petroleum and coal products	–84.6	18.2	42.0	39.5	34.8	22.6
Chemicals	–27.7	–36.6	–7.6	–7.0	–14.4	–18.5
Miscellaneous manufacturing	–49.6	–67.2	–57.7	–54.8	–54.5	–60.5

Source: Canada, Department of Regional Industrial Expansion, Economic Analysis and Strategic Planning, "Trade in Manufactured Products 1983" (Ottawa: The Department, 1984).

costs through such means as the rationalization of production, the introduction of state-of-the-art technologies, and the renegotiation of labour agreements. At other times, these measures will not be sufficient to provide a remedy, and the options for government are either to provide some degree of protection from foreign competition or to facilitate the orderly withdrawal of resources from the industry in question. If unit-cost comparisons are interpreted correctly, especially at the product or firm level, they can be an early-warning signal of adjustment problems ahead.

For the nation, failure to keep real unit costs in line with those of our major competitors will result in deteriorating trade balances and, ultimately, in a devaluation of the Canadian dollar and the decline in living standards that devaluation entails. Table 9-11 reports Canadian manufacturing trade balances (calculated as total exports minus total imports, divided by the sum of exports and imports) on an industry basis for the years 1966 to 1983. There is no general deterioration here. Indeed, in 14 of 19 industries, the trade balance was more favourable both in 1982 and in 1983 than it was over the 1966–82 period as a whole. The industries in which trade-balance data indicate a poor and deteriorating competitive position are leather, textiles, knitting mills and clothing. The problems which these industries face have been widely documented.

The trade balances of selected high-technology industries appear in Table 9-12. Most of the balances are negative and some, such as the balance for radio and television receivers, are close to the minimum value of -100, indicating that exports are very small relative to imports. The 1982 balance was more favourable than the 1966 – 82 mean in seven cases, less favourable in one (that is, office and store machinery, which includes computers), and about the same in one.

The trade-balance data appear to reflect a modest improvement, in recent years, in the competitive positions of most Canadian manufacturing industries. It is possible, however, that the data reflect the weak domestic demand – and the consequent weak demand for imports – in 1982 and 1983, rather than any underlying improvement in competitiveness. There is nothing inherently disturbing about a negative trade balance in any particular industry. If, however, the industries in which Canada has a negative balance constitute a growing fraction of our trade, our aggregate trade balance will deteriorate over time, raising the possibility of further depreciation of the Canadian dollar.

Another way to assess changes in national competitiveness is to measure changes in estimated national shares of world markets. An increase in a country's world-market share for a particular product implies an increase in its competitiveness in that product. To measure the size (in terms of sales) of the world market for a particular product is difficult, and so investigators employ a variety of market-share proxies. One proxy is the Canadian share of OECD exports as reported by the Department of Finance in its Economic Review. Canadian shares by broad product group are reported in Table 9-13. It is notable that the Canadian share of all exports declined by 1 percentage point over the period 1972–83. This decline appears to have been a consequence of the relative decline in Canadian exports of fuels and crude

TABLE 9-12 Trade Balances in Selected "High-Tech" Industries

	[(Exports – Imports)/(Exports + Imports)] x 100				
Industry	**1966**	**1975**	**1980**	**1982**	**Average 1966–1982**
Aircraft and parts	14.5	19.0	8.8	19.8	–10.2
Scientific and professional instruments	–39.1	–61.2	–56.6	–51.7	–56.6
Office and store machinery	–56.6	–39.6	–40.8	–48.0	–42.2
Household radio and television receivers	–39.3	–80.4	–77.4	–72.6	–73.2
Communications equipment	–43.1	–24.8	–25.2	–13.7	–25.3
Electrical industrial equipment	–57.7	–58.1	–46.9	–46.2	–53.9
Plastics	–74.1	–79.6	–49.5	–45.8	–62.7
Pharmaceuticals	–43.9	–56.4	–45.0	–41.1	–47.8
Industrial chemicals	–3.7	–8.8	20.8	18.9	9.6

Source: Donald D. McFetridge, "The Economics of Industrial Structure: An Overview", in *Canadian Industry in Transition*, vol. 2, prepared for the Royal Commission on the Economic Union and Development Prospects for Canada (Toronto: University of Toronto Press, 1985).

materials. The Canadian share of OECD-manufactured exports did not change.

Another market-share proxy consists of Canadian exports as a proportion of the exports of the world's three largest exporters, excluding Canada. According to this measure, the relationship between market share and competitiveness is as follows:

> *Relative market share is related to the ability to reduce costs and improve competitive position. Other factors that need to be taken into account are the relative maturity of the industry and the responsiveness of the industry to technology-based cost reduction. High relative share at the country level confers external economies to its firms because it facilitates development of technical infrastructure services such as professional associations and engineering consultants and managerial infrastructure such as international marketing services and strategic management capabilities.*[6]

Table 9-14 shows changes in the average relative market shares of various Canadian industries between the periods 1971–76 and 1976–81. The table appears to indicate a decline in competitiveness between the first period and the second, since Canada lost export share (relative to the largest three

TABLE 9-13 Share of OECD Exports, 1972–83[a]

Year	Canada	U.S.A.	Japan	EEC	Other OECD[b]	Total OECD Exports
			(per cent)			(billions of U.S. $)
Food, beverage and tobacco (SITC 1)						
1972	9	24	2	60	5	27.3
1973	7	31	2	56	4	42.2
1974	8	31	2	55	4	49.5
1975	7	30	1	57	4	55.7
1976	7	30	2	57	4	58.4
1977	7	25	1	62	4	62.8
1978	6	27	1	62	4	77.3
1979	6	27	1	63	4	92.7
1980	6	28	1	61	4	110.5
1981	7	30	2	58	4	112.4
1982	8	26	1	60	4	102.3
1983	9	27	1	59	4	99.1
Crude materials (SITC 2,4)						
1972	23	29	3	30	15	19.0
1973	20	32	3	30	15	28.6
1974	19	32	3	31	15	38.1
1975	19	32	3	31	15	33.2
1976	21	31	2	31	15	38.1
1977	20	33	2	31	13	43.0
1978	18	35	2	32	18	48.7
1979	19	35	2	31	13	64.0
1980	18	36	2	31	13	71.7
1981	19	36	2	30	13	64.0
1982	18	36	2	31	12	57.0
1983	19	35	2	32	12	57.2
Fuels (SITC 3)						
1972	19	17	1	60	3	9.1
1973	18	13	1	64	4	13.3
1974	21	14	1	60	4	24.8
1975	19	16	1	57	6	27.3
1976	18	14	0	60	8	9.1
1977	15	13	0	64	7	33.4
1978	13	10	1	66	10	37.9
1979	12	9	1	66	11	59.9
1980	11	10	1	64	14	83.4
1981	11	11	1	64	13	89.7
1982	11	14	0	61	13	89.9
1983	12	11	1	62	14	85.5

TABLE 9-13 (cont'd.)

Year	Canada	U.S.A.	Japan	EEC	Other OECD[b]	Total OECD exports
			(per cent)			(billions of U.S. $)
Machinery and transport equipment (SITC 7)						
1972	7	21	14	53	6	101.4
1973	6	21	14	53	6	133.5
1974	5	23	15	51	6	169.0
1975	5	23	14	52	7	199.2
1976	5	22	16	51	6	226.0
1977	5	20	17	52	6	256.4
1978	5	19	18	52	6	310.4
1979	5	20	16	54	6	355.9
1980	4	20	17	53	5	413.2
1981	5	23	20	47	5	421.8
1982	5	22	19	49	5	404.8
1983	6	21	21	47	5	397.4
Fabricated materials and manufactured goods (SITC 5, 6, 8, 9)						
1972	4	12	12	63	8	110.7
1973	4	12	11	65	8	151.9
1974	3	13	13	62	8	215.1
1975	3	13	12	63	8	214.0
1976	4	13	12	63	8	236.3
1977	3	13	12	64	8	271.8
1978	4	12	12	64	8	324.1
1979	3	14	11	64	8	408.1
1980	4	14	12	62	8	475.7
1981	4	15	14	59	8	444.4
1982	4	14	14	60	8	415.2
1983	4	14	14	60	8	409.8
Total						
1972	7	18	11	56	7	267.3
1973	7	19	10	57	7	369.6
1974	7	20	11	55	7	496.5
1975	6	20	11	56	8	529.5
1976	6	19	11	55	7	588.5
1977	6	18	12	57	7	668.0
1978	6	18	12	57	7	798.5
1979	6	18	11	58	7	980.7

TABLE 9-13 (cont'd.)

Year	Canada	U.S.A.	Japan	EEC	Other OECD[b]	Total OECD exports
			(per cent)			(billions of U.S. $)
1980	6	19	11	57	7	1 154.4
1981	6	20	13	53	7	1 132.4
1982	6	19	13	54	7	1 069.2
1983	6	19	14	53	7	1 049.0

Source: Canada, Finance Canada, *Economic Review, April 1984* (Ottawa: Minister of Supply and Services Canada, 1984), pp. 235–36.

Note: Balances may not be the sum of detail because of rounding.
SITC = Standard International Trade Classification.

a. 1983 figures are estimates based on partial data.
b. Excludes Australia, Ireland, New Zealand, Portugal, Spain, Switzerland, Turkey and Yugoslavia.

exporters) in most of the categories listed. The largest losses were in crude petroleum, non-ferrous ores, non-ferrous metals and motor vehicles. Gains occurred in three sectors: electric power, canned meats and coal.

Care must be taken in interpreting these results. They do not necessarily imply that in absolute terms, Canada's share of world output or exports has changed, but only that it has changed relative to the largest three exporters in each industry. They may imply that Canadian penetration of a given market has changed relative to penetration by one of the three largest exporters, or that countries historically served by Canada have grown more slowly than countries served by some or all of the three largest exporters. Nonetheless, Table 9-14 suggests that there has been some deterioration in Canada's competitive position. The analysts responsible for the foregoing assessment offer the following conclusion:

> *This analysis of the changes in the Canadian industrial portfolio leads one to conclude that the country's manufacturing industries face a difficult future. There is a heavy reliance on slow (and occasionally negative) growth industries. More importantly, even in these slow growth areas, Relative Market Share has deteriorated, indicating that the country's overall competitive position has weakened. Finally, the relative reduction of the proportion of the portfolio in the high growth/high share area of the matrix is a sign of serious structural weakness.*[7]

A nation with larger shares of rapidly growing markets might expect to see its currency appreciate in real terms and to experience the improvement in living standards that appreciation entails.

TABLE 9-14 Relative Market Shares of Canadian Industries

Industry	Relative Market Share[a] Average 1976–81	% Change[b]
Commodity sector		
Non-ferrous ores	42.8	−13.34
Meat, poultry & fish	13.8	1.03
Basic iron & steel	4.3	1.12
Lumber & wood materials	17.3	0.72
Pulp & paper	35.3	0.13
Coal & lignite	9.9	2.78
Iron ore & scrap	32.7	−1.29
Non-ferrous metals	34.0	−7.13
Petroleum derivatives	6.4	1.32
Sunset sector		
Heavy electrical equipment	2.0	−0.64
Yarn & fabrics	1.2	−0.60
Clothing	0.7	−1.23
Leather products, furs	2.1	−0.82
Confectionaries	3.0	0.42
Hosiery & knitwear	0.2	−0.17
Foundry products	5.7	0.72
Iron & steel products	4.1	0.19
Hi-tech sector		
Light electrical equipment	2.0	−0.85
Telecommunication product	5.5	−1.58
Precision instruments	3.2	−0.89
Chemicals	14.7	1.42
Aerospace	4.9	−1.19
Pharmaceuticals	1.4	−0.24
Computers & office equipment	5.8	−0.48
Consumer electronics	0.9	−0.39
Photographic equipment	1.4	0.26
Special & misc. machines	7.1	−2.06
Transport equipment sector		
Commercial vehicles & railway equipment	16.5	1.26
Agricultural machinery	14.2	−0.65
Motor vehicles (private)	14.4	−8.74
Spare parts (motor vehicles)	17.2	−2.33
Rubber products	0.2	1.54
Capital-intensive sector		
Cigarettes, tobacco products	0.4	−0.03
Metal products	4.8	−0.18
Paints & pigments	0.5	−0.10
Fertilizers	22.7	0.27
Cement	8.2	−0.89
Watches & clocks	0.9	−0.38
Glass & glassware	3.4	−0.47
Canned preserved fruits	3.8	−0.71
Beverages (incl. alcoholic)	6.5	−3.31
Ships & boats	1.4	0.31

TABLE 9-14 (cont'd.)

Industry	Relative Market Share[a] Average 1976 – 81	% Change[b]
Cosmetics & toiletries	1.3	−0.04
Plastics & synthetic fibers	2.7	0.31
Household appliances	1.0	−0.14
Other raw materials	37.7	0.15
Labour-intensive sector		
Clay & pottery products	1.8	0.26
Furniture & misc. wood products	6.4	−3.66
Plastic products	3.4	0.09
Electronic components	1.4	−1.57
Misc. leisure products	2.5	−0.07
Printed matter	3.7	−0.20
Carpets & misc. textiles	2.8	0.62
Miscellaneous	4.4	1.64
Energy sector		
Electric power	37.3	14.50
Coke, coal derivatives	1.4	−0.07
Crude petroleum	21.2 - - 56.64	
Natural gas	39.9	−4.15
Renewable resources		
Canned preserved meat	12.6	3.37
Cereals	14.4	−2.53
Flour, other milled products	16.0	−0.67
Other agricultural products	5.9	−1.17
Dairy products, fats	3.6	0.07
Animal feeds	4.2	−1.85
Fuel wood, charcoal	46.8	−0.09
Raw materials from agriculture	26.1	1.24

Source: Joseph R. D'Cruz and James D. Fleck, "Improving the Competitiveness of the Canadian Industrial Portfolio", *Business Quarterly* 49 (Fall 1984), p. 74.

a. Relative Market Share shows Canada's share of world exports divided by the combined share of the three largest exporting countries for that industry, other than Canada.

b. % Change shows the difference between 1976–81 and 1971–76.

Thus market-share analysis can be useful, in conjunction with other types of analysis, as a tool for forecasting future trends. Such analysis has also been put to prescriptive uses. The authors of the analysis we have just mentioned and other economists argue that an "ideal portfolio" of exports would involve large shares of rapidly growing markets and small shares of slowly growing markets. Moreover, an economy that is properly adjusting to changing circumstances will, in their view, show increasing shares in faster-growth markets and declining shares in slower-growth markets: "What is disturbing is the lack of evidence of change in the composition of the Canadian portfolio.

Over time, a healthy economy should shift away from slow growth, mature industries and towards faster growing industries."[8] While these analysts conclude that Canada should pursue a targeted industrial policy to encourage growth of exports in areas of potential high growth, Commissioners are not persuaded, as we shall explain later, that this is a role governments can play effectively. We are convinced that the private sector will move, in time, into areas of growing opportunity, particularly if governments do not impede the adjustment process and provide a generally supportive environment.

Overall, then, recent analysis of Canada's competitive position suggests the following conclusions:

- Canadian unit costs in manufacturing appear to have stayed in line with the unit costs of our trading partners over the longer term. However, some deterioration in Canada's position may have occurred since 1980, largely as a result of the appreciation of our dollar relative to currencies other than the U.S. dollar.
- Canada's labour costs have generally been higher than labour costs in Japan and in much of Europe. Studies conflict in their conclusions about our cost position compared to that of the United States.
- Manufacturing trade balances expressed as a proportion of total trade were generally more positive (or less negative) in recent years (1982, 1983) than their long-term average. The exceptions are the balances for textiles, clothing and footwear. The pattern of improving, though still largely negative, trade balances also holds in high-technology industries.
- Canada's overall share of OECD exports declined slightly between 1972 and 1983. This decline was concentrated in crude materials and fuel exports.
- Canadian exports declined, relative to those of the three largest exporting countries, in most industries between the periods 1971–76 and 1976–81. The declines were largest in several of the raw-materials sectors.

These observations do not imply that declines in real income or adjustment problems of a catastrophic nature are on the horizon for Canada, but neither do they present a picture of an economy poised for dramatic income gains.

Productivity growth is the ultimate harbinger of things to come. The forecasts for the Canadian economy reviewed in Chapter 7 indicate that productivity growth will average between 1 and 1.5 per cent until the end of this century. This represents a substantial improvement over the 1973–81 period, but it is not guaranteed; in any event, we shall benefit if we can do better.

Commissioners have drawn attention in this Report to new sources of international competition, notably the newly industrializing countries of East Asia. We have also drawn attention to the rapidity with which technological innovation and the mass-production techniques of industrialized countries are being adopted globally. International trade competition is undoubtedly intensifying. We have already argued that Canada should not try to shelter itself from this competition; instead, we Canadians should actively seek a more liberalized trade environment and a more liberal trade arrangement with the United States.

If we are to meet these challenges successfully, the fundamental strategic objectives of industrial policy must be enhanced productivity growth and a stronger competitive position. Accomplishing these objectives means, in turn, strengthening the environment for the efficient allocation of resources and adjustment to new realities. It also means strengthening the basic factors in the economic processes of production and marketing.

A Macro-economic Framework to Support Industrial Development

Private enterprise is the dominant driving force behind our economic system. In order to function efficiently and effectively, however, it must be supported by macro-economic measures, including fiscal and monetary policies designed to promote steady growth of output and employment in a context of relative price stability.

While stable output, employment and prices must be maintained if the private sector is to function effectively, government has only a limited ability to ensure this stability. Canada is subject to external shocks that government can cushion, but that it cannot prevent. The Canadian economy's extreme vulnerability to the international business cycle was emphasized by the 1981–82 recession. Of all the OECD countries, Canada suffered the worst decline in output during that recession. Nor is Canada vulnerable only to swings in the business cycle. Changing commodity prices, exchange-rate fluctuations, the vagaries of weather conditions, and a host of other factors can have a very unsettling and costly impact on Canada's economy. The 1973 and 1979 hikes in world oil prices, imposed by members of the Organization of Petroleum Exporting Countries (OPEC), had and continue to have profound effects on this country. The inflation spiral and the productivity slow-down date from the onset of sharply higher world oil prices, although the price rise was by no means the sole source of these developments. U.S. monetary policy is an external factor that has major implications for interest rates in Canada, which in turn have major implications for the functioning of our economy.

Chapter 10 examines at length the various constraints on the exercise of macro-economic demand-management policy in Canada. The examination points out the limits on what may be achieved through monetary and fiscal policy in an economy as open as Canada's. It also argues that to be effective, demand management should be exercised within a medium- to long-term frame of reference.

While monetary and fiscal policy cannot provide a wholly stable domestic economic environment, they can, on occasion, add to the instability of the environment. For example, of the 19 federal budgets introduced between 1968 and 1984, all but five announced new housing programs or revised existing ones. Many of the programs were designed to stimulate the housing industry and, consequently, overall economic demand. Unfortunately, these programs often drove up new housing starts to an unsustainable level. Slumps in construction followed. Some years ago, the Economic Council of Canada concluded that greater stability in construction activity was important as a means of promoting productivity growth in the industry.[9] A longer-term framework for government housing policy could help to provide the stability required to promote productivity growth and thus complement the objective of industrial policy.

Federal budgets and mini-budgets have appeared with increasing frequency over the past decade. At times they have put forward proposals that were sweeping in concept and complex in administrative detail. The 1980 federal budget, which introduced the National Energy Program (NEP), illustrates this point. The NEP precipitated a considerable outflow of direct-investment capital as Canadians acquired interests, previously held by foreigners, in the petroleum industry. Although interest rates were already high enough to cause serious problems, they were driven still higher by the heavy borrowing undertaken to finance these acquisitions. This was only one of the unsettling consequences of the sweeping changes introduced by the NEP.

The frequency of changes in the tax laws over the past several years may also serve to undermine measures designed to encourage capital investment. It is clear, at least, that the carry-over of proposed tax legislation from one session of Parliament to the next has created an uncertainty about the status of many of the proposed new measures that can only impede capital investment and innovation in the private sector.

The principle that flexibility and adaptability are essential in a rapidly changing world extends to the exercise of macro-economic policies. As much as possible, however, governments should try to provide consistency in the overall macro-economic and micro-economic framework; unnecessary changes should be avoided, and unavoidable changes should reflect a medium- to long-term perspective. By taking this approach, governments would facilitate both decision making in the private sector and consultation between the private sector and the public sector. The private sector, in turn, must be consistent in its proposals for government initiatives.

A Commitment to Freer Trade

Commissioners have already pointed out that commercial policy constitutes a critical part of industrial policy in a small open economy such as Canada's. Part II of this Report outlined our reasons for supporting continued efforts both to reduce multilateral trade barriers and to establish much freer trade – if not free trade – with the United States. We are saying, in short, that a key component of Canada's industrial policy should be a commitment to freer trade, which should be matched by a freer flow of capital investment than there has been over the past decade or so.

The question of whether to opt for free trade or for protectionism is undoubtedly the key issue to be resolved in forming an industrial policy. This issue is brought more sharply into focus by the growing use of import quotas, export subsidies, dumping duties and restrictive government-procurement policies. The post-war trend toward freer trade has been threatened in recent years by a tendency toward "managed" trade. Given the domination of a number of industries by oligopolistic multi-national corporations, this is a tendency that can have a particularly adverse effect on a country such as Canada.

To the greatest extent possible, Canada should avoid engaging in negative defensive competition with other countries in an effort to promote particular exports. Such an approach might serve only to encourage capital investment in areas where Canada has no comparative advantage. Rather than engaging in expensive international contests that depend ultimately on the amount of subsidy each nation is prepared to provide to a given industry – a game in which all contestants are losers – we should continue to work with other nations to build on the remarkable trade-liberalization achievements of the post-Second World War period.

Because the process of revising the framework of multilateral trade is cumbersome, involving as it does so many countries, and because Canada's trade is overwhelmingly with the United States, Commissioners have argued that there would be great merit in making a special bilateral effort to achieve freer trade with our neighbour to the south. In our view, a commitment to freer trade – on a multilateral basis if possible, but at least with the United States – would provide the single most important incentive for private enterprise in Canada to become more efficient, more innovative and, hence, more competitive.

Canadian corporations vary as widely as corporations elsewhere in the world in their ability to anticipate and respond to change and opportunity. The best of these companies are probably as able as the best anywhere, and it is likely that the same comparison also holds true of the worst. Under the protection of tariffs, quotas and other forms of support, some Canadian managements have become complacent. As data to which we shall refer later indicate, many Canadian firms are less subject to competitive market forces than are their American counterparts. As a consequence, Canadian firms may be less prepared to abandon losing operations and more likely to turn to government when they are in trouble. Of course, many Canadian companies have broken out of this pattern, and many American firms exhibit some degree of inertia. In general, however, adjustment in Canada has tended to be slower than is desirable in terms of economic efficiency.

Increased competition from the world in general, and the United States in particular, would work powerfully to induce Canadians to allocate our human, capital and natural resources in ways that would improve the country's productivity. As Commissioners have already indicated, governments in Canada should not attempt to shield domestic industry from the forces of change and the reallocation of resources that change inevitably involves; instead, they should work with industry to help it to adapt to change as easily as possible. The institution by governments of measures to facilitate the adjustment process should constitute a major component of industrial policy.

If Canada is seen to vacillate on its commitment to freer trade relations, its ability to persuade other countries to move forward in this direction will be greatly diminished. Vacillation would also encourage domestic industry to seek shelter from the harsh discipline of international competition by pressing government for various forms of assistance. The message from government should be consistent and fair: the primary objective of industrial policy and trade policy will be to enhance the ability of the Canadian economy to respond to competitive market forces.

Since Canada's industrial policy and trade stance are so closely intertwined, a commitment to freer trade must be accompanied by a commitment to "level the playing field". If we achieve a free-trade arrangement with the United States, Canadian firms must receive effective access to all markets. The Canadian tax structure must allow domestic industry to compete effectively with foreign firms, and the regulatory framework must not unduly impede the restructuring of industry that is a necessary part of the adjustment process. In other words, it would be even more important in an environment of free or freer trade with the United States than it is now for certain of our policies to be sufficiently similar to those of the U.S. government to enable us to be reasonably competitive. This does not mean that all aspects of our industrial policy would have to approximate that of the United States. It is instructive to recall that France and West Germany have very different approaches to industrial policy: France favours a targeted approach, while West German policy is more market oriented. That such different approaches to industrial policy are permissible within a common market should allay fears that Canada would be unable to pursue independent policies in a less binding trade association with the United States. It is necessary to distinguish those areas of policy, such as taxation, where a parallel approach is required for competitive reasons, from those areas where a different approach is required because of differences in the economic structures or the natures of the two countries.

A commitment to freer trade cannot, of course, ignore the realities of the efforts of other countries to promote their exports. A widespread form of promotion is the provision of export insurance and financing, often at subsidized rates. In general, governments play an increasingly active role in international business transactions. They often justify this activity by reference to the similar actions of other governments.

The Export Development Corporation (EDC), established by the federal government in 1969, is the principal Canadian government agency involved in export insurance and financing. The Canadian Wheat Board and other Crown corporations also extend credit to purchasers of Canadian exports. However, the key role in the financing of Canadian trade is played by the commercial banks. Ninety per cent of our export trade relies on short-term financing, an area dominated by commercial bank activity.

The Export Development Corporation, which finances about 5 per cent of exports, concentrates on medium- and long-term financing to maturity, granted at a fixed price. Commercial banks may compete with the EDC in offering medium-term financing and may co-operate with the EDC in offering long-term financing of various types. The EDC directs the bulk of its financing to the support of export sales to countries in Africa, Eastern Europe and South America.

There are clearly dangers in unrestrained competition among countries in subsidizing exports. Recognizing these dangers, the OECD countries have agreed on minimum rates for export financing. In this Commission's view, Canada should continue to support efforts to further limit subsidy activity. Meanwhile, the realities of competition for export markets must be faced. If other countries subsidize the financing of their exports in markets where Canadians wish to sell, the Canadian government must consider similar action. It must be careful, however, to ensure that the amount of the subsidy is consistent with the benefits obtained. It is not desirable to subsidize the exports of Canadian products unable to meet competitive prices even in the absence of export subsidies by other countries.

While export subsidization may be a legitimate defensive action in some situations, other means of meeting competition should be considered. Is there scope, for instance, for a more efficient design of existing programs? A research paper prepared for this Commission argues that private institutions can undertake most of what is now done by the EDC.[10] According to this study, the EDC could leave short- and medium-term insurance to the private sector, while providing re-insurance and acting as an insurer of last resort for large or very risky projects.

A recent federal government consultation paper considers the possible results of increased involvement of the private sector in export finance and insurance.[11] It concludes that the cost of government subsidies to the private financial institutions would likely be greater than the implicit subsidy associated with the working capital extended to the EDC. However, the greater cost could be offset by the increased volume of exports that might accrue to Canadian exporters from the improved services offers by chartered banks.

One possibility, then, would be to channel all subsidies for export finance through private financial institutions. The role of the EDC would be to administer the subsidy mechanism, to monitor the benefits of the subsidies, and to continue to discharge some of its guarantee and insurance functions. While this possibility merits serious consideration, the difficulty of regulating the required subsidies poses tough political and administrative problems. Commissioners therefore recommend caution in moving toward "privatization" of the functions carried out by the EDC. While increased involvement of financial intermediaries would appear desirable, it must be noted that their involvement is already extensive. At issue are those cases in which market failure is likely, and in which national interests are not likely to be served by market forces. Government participation through the EDC and other such agencies would appear warranted; other countries have apparently reached this conclusion, since they have maintained similar agencies.

A Commitment to Strengthening Canada's Labour, Capital, Technology and Management Inputs

Measures for improving the training and adaptability of Canada's labour force are proposed elsewhere in this Report. Commissioners' recommendations include the institution of new means for financing post-secondary education; less emphasis on institutional training and more emphasis on on-the-job training; greater incentives for retraining and mobility; and greater incentives, through gain sharing, for consultation between management and labour on wage levels and productivity initiatives. In Chapter 8, we have already addressed the questions of capital formation, technological progress, management and entrepreneurship. Since in that chapter we did not address these important elements of our economy in the framework of an industrial policy, it may be helpful to summarize briefly here our main conclusions with respect to them.

Capital Formation

While some recent studies have suggested that taxation of savings and investments may impede the growth of the capital stock, the portion of capital investment undertaken in Canada over the past few decades in relation to gross national product (GNP) has been reasonably satisfactory by OECD standards. Commissioners' studies indicate that the government should review the effect of the tax system on savings and investment, to see, in particular, whether it encourages unproductive forms of savings and investment, and to assess the adequacy of allowances for inflation. The reviewers should also consider the effects of shifting the basis of personal and corporate tax from net income to expenditures, as we shall explain more fully below.

Research and Development

A target level of expenditures on research and development (R&D) in relation to GNP would not, in Commissioners' view, be a particularly useful element of industrial policy. The effectiveness of R&D expenditures is much more important than their quantity. To increase the effectiveness of R&D, we have advocated that governments consider several steps. They should ensure that existing incentives are available to all businesses by refunding to taxpayers credits which the latter cannot claim, under present arrangements, if they lack taxable income. They should broaden the definition of R&D, even though the change might cause administrative problems, and reduce the rate of tax subsidy. They should ensure that adequate resources are devoted to obtaining information about foreign technological developments. Canada should maintain a network of contacts with experts in other countries and should establish a more frequent Canadian presence in new technological development. Governments should also increase the exposure of domestic industry to international competition.

Acquisition of Technology

New technologies are being shared more and more on a world-wide basis, and the originating country often has little lead time over other countries to exploit the benefits of its discoveries. Canada draws extensively from the world pool of new technologies, in part through foreign investment by multinationals. Within Canada, new technologies seem to spread more slowly among manufacturing industries than in other countries. One means of speeding up the process is to provide the spur of liberalized trade and increased competition. In addition, minimizing barriers to the flow of direct investment would also encourage early Canadian adoption of new technology.

Public policy in the area of education, together with measures that encouraged the gathering and dissemination of information on new advances in technology, could also contribute to improved technological adaptation in Canada. Greater emphasis on science, engineering and business courses in post-secondary education may be necessary. Universities should be more active in undertaking R&D that has a commercial potential. The National Research Council's initiatives in gathering and disseminating information could provide a model to be followed by other similar organizations. In other countries, technology brokers, contract-research organizations, and "think tanks" have played a pivotal role in the acquisition of technology. Both Canada's private and public sectors should involve themselves more actively in these types of endeavours. The recent establishment of the Canadian Institute for Advanced Research is an example of private sector initiative, undertaken with public sector support, which will help Canada move to the forefront of technological innovation.

Management and Entrepreneurship

Increased international competition would make all the more compelling Canada's need to develop business management that can match the best in the world. In addition, it would itself act as a sharp stimulus to the improvement of the quality of Canadian management. While government can help to up-grade management by reorienting assistance to small business and increasing support to education in business administration, the responsibility for improvement rests principally with business itself.

Entrepreneurship plays a key part in developing our economy. While small business is a vital source of entrepreneurship, there are other sources, too, which require encouragement. Some tax changes might encourage venture-capital activity. Relaxing regulatory restrictions might increase equity investment by financial intermediaries in small and medium-sized firms; in addition, the federal government should change the tax system to encourage companies to issue equity capital (as opposed to debt) and investors to hold such shares.

Other adjustments respecting small business and entrepreneurship include review of the capital-gains tax (especially the deemed realization of capital gains when the proprietor of a family business dies), a greater degree of neutrality in the tax system, and greater awareness of the problems of access to government subsidies. In addition, governments should recognize that requirements imposed in connection with the administration of social benefit programs pose particular problems for small firms.

A Commitment to Framework Policies that Encourage Adaptation and the Efficient Allocation of Resources

We Commissioners have repeatedly urged that governments pursue an industrial policy that relies heavily on the responsiveness of the private sector to market forces, rather than on active intervention by government in the market-place. Moreover, we strongly believe that this approach must be complemented by measures which will encourage the process of adjustment to new competitive forces in a way that is consistent with the efficient use of our scarce human, capital and natural resources.

Tax Policy[12]

The tax system is one of the most important determinants of economic growth over the longer term. When the Royal Commission on Taxation (the Carter Commission) reported in 1966, one of the foremost goals of policy analysts was the establishment of a tax system that was equitable in its treatment of different groups. While equity remains an important goal, tax specialists now stress the need for a system that is calculated to encourage economic efficiency. This shift in emphasis is partially explained by a growing awareness of the constraints imposed by Canada's exposure to large international capital flows, which can be strongly influenced by the tax system.

In designing tax measures, governments must consider their effect on both the allocation of resources and the distribution of income. This Commission has focused its attention on those features of the tax system that appear to detract unnecessarily from the long-run growth of gross national product (GNP), and on those income features that have little to do with distribution goals or that could be altered and still be consistent with such goals. To understand the issues involved, it is necessary to be aware of some very general relationships between the tax system and economic growth. Personal and corporate-income taxes that accrue from income derived from capital may reduce savings and investment and, hence, the capital stock; since the size of the capital stock is an important determinant of potential output, it follows that taxes of this kind can affect Canada's growth.

Tax measures that are biased against risky undertakings may cause investors to direct an undue share of resources toward mature stable industries. Taxes on wage income can influence the incentive to work, while payroll taxes, such as those that support Unemployment Insurance and pension funds, can induce firms to substitute capital for labour. Commodity taxes favour some commodities, and thus some lines of production, over others. Some taxes, such as those on alcohol and tobacco, may be deliberately used to discourage production and consumption. Finally, economic growth can be influenced by the relative complexity of the tax system.

Personal income taxes, including payroll taxes, drive a wedge between the value of output produced by a factor of production and the net return received by the owner. Consequently, less of the factor may be supplied than is desirable. Both the U.S. Treasury's *Blueprints for Basic Tax Reform*[13] of 1977 and the United Kingdom's *Meade Report*[14] of 1978 recommended adoption of a tax system based on consumer expenditures, referred to hereafter as a "consumption tax". A consumption tax, which would replace the existing personal and corporate income taxes, would be based on what one removed from the "social pot" rather than on what one contributed in the form of income. Unlike existing levies on consumption, such as the retail sales tax, a consumption tax would not be imposed on individual items of purchase. It would be calculated on the basis of total income over the year, adjusted for the change in registered savings; the resulting figure would represent total consumption during the period.

Consumption taxation, unlike income taxation, does not distort savings. An income tax, by taxing the returns to saving, raises the "price" of future consumption relative to present consumption and thus favours the latter. Under a consumption tax, present and future consumption bear the same rate of tax. The consumption tax, therefore, does not influence the timing of consumption or the level of savings and investment. Replacement of the income tax by a consumption tax would also result in an increase in the labour supply and in the rate of return on investment. It would appear then, that to move from an income-based tax to a consumption-based tax could result in substantial efficiency gains and a major boost to GNP. One econometric calculation made in the United States has estimated that a switch to a consumption tax could lead to a sustained increase in GNP of as much as 10 per cent.[15] The gains in the more open Canadian economy would probably be smaller.

The consumption tax is often criticized on the grounds that because it would exempt capital income, it would be regressive. This argument overlooks the fact that the rate structure of a tax is independent of the base. The desired degree of progressivity can be achieved through a consumption tax – as it can be achieved through an income tax – by altering the rate structure. During the transition from an income-based tax to a consumption-based tax, some taxpayers would gain and some would lose; transition provisions could moderate this result, but it would remain a problem.

On balance, there appears to be merit in the concept of a consumption-based personal tax system. The present system's provision for Registered Retirement Savings Plans (RRSPs) and Registered Pension Plans (RPPs) has already moved it some distance in the direction of a personal consumption tax, and to ease or remove the present restrictions on RRSPs and RPPs would be a logical step in extending this process. Current restrictions exclude these funds from the benefit of the dividend tax credit, thus creating a significant incentive to hold debt rather than equity. This is an example of a tax disincentive to equity investment in Canada.

Certain features of the current personal income-tax system introduce distortions by unduly favouring particular types of savings. Thus, until the May 1985 budget measures, contributions to a Registered Home Ownership Savings Plan (RHOSP) were sheltered (up to a limit), and withdrawals remained untaxed if they were used to purchase housing. Other provisions of the present system that may be overly generous to capital income are the $1000 pension-income deduction and the Quebec Stock Savings Plan.

A feature of the existing corporate income-tax system that distorts resource allocation is its lack of indexation provisions for inflation. Although *ad hoc* adjustments such as accelerated capital-cost allowances help to offset the effects of inflation on the cost of capital, such adjustments are not sensitive to the level of inflation. Inventories, in particular, have been severely hit by high effective tax rates during periods of rapid inflation. The simple remedy would be to index to the general price level the capital-cost allowance and the first-in/first-out cost of inventory. Alternatively, the problem relating to inventories could be solved by allowing the last-in/first-out approach to inventory accounting.

Because the corporate income-tax system does little to take into account the degree of risk associated with a given rate of return, it is, in effect, biased in favour of "safe" investments. Various measures have been introduced to compensate for this shortcoming, but their effect is selective. For resource industries, these measures include fast write-offs for exploration and development expenses. Other tax measures, such as the investment tax credit and accelerated capital-cost allowances, help to offset risk associated with R&D expenditures and investment in manufacturing. The current provisions of the capital gains tax are, however, biased against risk-taking; this bias is illustrated by the fact that capital gains are fully subject to tax, while limits are imposed on the amount of capital losses that may be claimed against other income.

In view of the extent to which the present corporate-tax system distorts investment, this Commission has concluded that governments, in consultation with business, should consider adoption of an alternative means of calculating the corporate-tax base. Fundamentally, the corporate-tax base is currently defined as accruing revenue less current costs plus the cost of depreciation and interest on debt: that is, the inherent rental cost of a firm's capital. The alternative Commissioners suggest for consideration is adoption of a cash-flow method of defining the tax base. According to this method, the tax base is defined as revenues less all input expenses on a cash-flow basis. Thus capital investment would be immediately deductible, but no deductions would be permitted for interest or depreciation. Achievement of the full benefits of this approach would require a provision for the refundability of "negative taxes": that is, the refundability of any excess of deductions over taxable income. Full refundability would ensure the neutrality of the tax, reduce discrimination against risky ventures, and make it easier for firms to finance investment.

Research carried out for this Commission indicates that other features of the existing tax system have further adverse economic effects. Resource taxes based on production rather than on earnings discourage output from high-cost sources. The federal sales tax on manufactured goods creates an incentive for retailers to undertake the production of the goods they sell, an arrangement which may not serve the best interests of the economy as a whole. Price regulation can be a form of taxation, and its effects are often as distortive as those of the tax system itself. Thus, for example, when provincial utilities sell electricity to consumers at prices below its real value, this effective transfer of resource rents to power users rather than to provincial treasuries benefits larger consumers at the expense of smaller ones, distorting the allocation of electricity. The same point applies to the federal government's policy, now being abandoned, of setting the price of domestic oil sold in the Canadian market below the prevailing world price.

In its broadest form, then, the tax system has a powerful influence on the allocation of resources in our society, and on the extent to which these resources are produced and consumed. This Commission considers it important that the disincentives inherent in the tax system be replaced with measures that will encourage the efficient allocation of productive resources and the adoption of new processes, products and services. In our view, such measures are necessary components of any industrial policy that will enable Canada to meet its strategic objectives. Tax measures, however, are extremely complex and sensitive, demanding a great deal of analysis and consultation before policy changes are formally presented in Parliament.

The Regulatory Framework

Varying kinds and degrees of regulation by government departments and agencies affect extensive sectors of the Canadian economy: financial institutions, investment dealers, transportation, communications, agriculture and energy, to name only a few. The exercise of such regulation has an important bearing on the allocation of economic resources. Regulatory requirements should, therefore, be as consistent as possible with what Commissioners consider ought to be the primary objective of Canadian industrial policy: fostering the growth of productivity and competitiveness.

Over a period of some years, complaints have been growing, in some quarters, that Canada is overregulated. Submissions to this Commission frequently repeated these complaints. These allegations beg certain questions: Is there more regulation in Canada than in most other countries? Has regulation increased at a faster pace in Canada than in other countries in recent years? Do the nature of Canada and our traditions and values suggest the need for a more extensive regulatory framework than that required by other countries, including the United States? The answers are important because excessive or misdirected regulation can constrain competition and restrict improvements in productivity.

Since so much of Canada's trade is with the United States, the most pertinent international comparison of our regulatory framework is with that of our major trade partner. A 1980 study represents the most thorough attempt to determine the extent and/or intensity of economic regulation in Canada compared with that in the United States.[16] The study concluded that the scope of federal regulatory activity in Canada is similar to that in the United States. It found dramatic differences, however, in the statutory restrictions placed on regulators, which are much greater in the United States than they are in Canada. Resources devoted to the enforcement of regulations at the federal level were proportionately higher in Canada both in 1970–71 and in 1977–78. The authors of this study concluded that the intensity of enforcement of regulations was about the same in the two countries. The rate of growth of federal regulatory activity during the 1970s was roughly the same in both countries, although employment growth among federal regulators was greater in the United States.

According to this 1980 report, as of the late 1970s, a moderately larger proportion of the gross domestic product (GDP) was generated in sectors subject to price or entry controls in Canada than was so generated in the United States. Most of the difference was the result of the greater prominence in Canada of regulated sectors, such as transportation, rather than the result of a greater degree of regulation. An exception is the agricultural sector, which is more highly regulated by marketing boards in Canada than in the United States. A survey paper[17] prepared for this Commission estimated that in 1978, 31 per cent of Canadian GDP was subject to price, output or entry controls, and that this proportion had increased to 34 per cent by 1980.

There are other differences, too, between the Canadian and American situations. Canada often regulates largely state-owned industries, such as railways, airlines and telecommunications, while the U.S. Administration does not generally undertake this responsibility. Moreover, although Canadian regulation is at least as broad as that of our neighbour, there may be a difference in the burden it imposes. The types of programs that American business people find the most onerous – occupational health and safety, fair employment practices, and environmental protection – have tended to receive less emphasis in Canada.

Regulatory activities that are more extensive in Canada have usually involved specific industries, such as airline and railway transportation, and areas of agriculture under the control of marketing boards. Many observers have argued that a desire to increase profitability often motivates regulation of particular industries. In this respect, regulation in Canada may be less burdensome, from the point of view of those regulated, than it is in the United States.

Since publication of the 1980 study mentioned above, the regulatory picture has changed considerably: there has been a move toward deregulation in the United States and, to a much lesser extent, in Canada. A more recent study[18] calculated that the proportion of U.S. economic activity carried out under "effectively competitive conditions" rose from 56 per cent in 1958 to 77 per cent in 1980. The study attributed the increase in competition to the decreasing importance of scale economies in manufacturing, rising competition from imports, and anti-trust activity and deregulation. The author was unable to measure the contribution of the decline in scale economies to the increase in competition. He estimated by abstraction, however, that import competition accounted for 37 per cent, anti-trust for 40 per cent, and deregulation for 23 per cent of the remaining increase in competition between 1958 and 1980.

Since the mid-1970s, U.S. deregulation has affected the following industries: telephone equipment, railroad transportation, trucking, air transportation, long-distance telephone service, banking, and security and commodity brokers. The study just referred to concluded that U.S. anti-trust authorities spurred deregulation:

> *It was Antitrust Division pressure that led the Securities and Exchange Commission to abolish the fixing of stock-broker's fees in 1975. New competition in the telephone sector has partly been created by antitrust cases and pressure on the Federal Communication Commission. The deregulation of banking entry and pricing has also been advanced by a variety of antitrust actions.*[19]

Canadian officials have acted in a similar matter. As a result of the 1975 amendments to the Combines Investigation Act, the Director of Investigation and Research can appear before marketing boards and regulatory tribunals to represent the public's interest in competition. The Director's intervention has led to some deregulation. The Economic Council of Canada has argued that the regulatory process may not adequately recognize the public interest in free competition. The Director can, by intervening, help to remedy this shortcoming. The role of the Director in defending freedom of entry into the underwriting of unregistered securities is a case in point. To reduce regulation of some important sectors of the Canadian economy would strengthen competition, a development which Commissioners have strongly advocated.

Some limited deregulation has taken place in Canada over the last five or six years. In its announcement of its new air-transport policy, in May 1984, the federal government mentioned some of the problems created by ill-advised regulation of the private sector. The policy statement concerning the air-transport industry contended that past regulation had hindered the adoption of innovative provisions with respect to both services and pricing; reduced the flexibility of airline management in pursuing new market opportunities and in adjusting their operations to minimize cost; hampered the ability of airlines to respond quickly to changes in circumstances; through undue delays in regulatory decisions required airline management to devote excessive time and energy to essentially unproductive regulatory considerations; and because it is difficult to anticipate regulatory decisions, complicated airline planning.

To date, deregulation has brought liberalization of the terms on which airlines can offer discount fares, licence consolidations that allow airlines some flexibility in route structuring, and a greater willingness to approve additional trans-border services. While this development is not nearly as extensive as U.S. deregulation, it signals a considerable reduction of regulatory control of air transport.[20]

Regulatory control, or planning, goes beyond the enforcement of health, safety and environmental standards to effect decisions about who should offer what service, where, when and on what terms. Deregulation of U.S. airlines triggered rethinking of Canadian policy. In any case, the Canadian regulatory process was becoming too complex and too highly subject to political consideration. To limit regulation of the airline industry to issues of safety and quality will probably be economically beneficial. Deregulation in the United States has not caused, as some had feared, loss of service to small communities; it has resulted, instead, in service more appropriate to the size of the communities served.

Some deregulation has occurred also in Canadian telecommunications. Technological change has made competition on a number of fronts both feasible and desirable. In such areas, governments can no longer justify regulation on the grounds that it protects consumers against exploitation by a natural monopoly. Remaining regulation is now clearly intended to redistribute costs, and therefore income, among various groups of users of telecommunications services; to ensure Canadian sovereignty; and to further national unity.

Telecommunications regulation, for example, redistributes costs by permitting long-distance service to subsidize local telephone rates. The issues are complex, and Commissioners would not argue that the rates charged on these services should necessarily equal their respective costs. If they did, however, local-service rates might rise by as much as 70 per cent, and long-distance rates might decline by 50 to 70 per cent.[21]

While Commissioners will not pursue specific issues in telecommunications currently before regulatory authorities for decision, certain broad issues deserve consideration, as they involve regulation generally. Is there a better way to a transfer income than through cross-subsidization of one service by the users of another? Even if there is a better system, can our political institutions, including the regulatory agencies, see to its implementation? We shall return to these questions later in this chapter.

As we have seen, the federal government has already reduced regulation and infused increased competition into the telecommunications industry. It has allowed attachment of subscriber-owned single telephone lines, key systems and private branch exchanges to the Bell Canada and other telephone systems; permitted the interconnection of the equipment of other telecommunications systems (such as CNCP Telecommunications) with that of the Bell and other telephone systems; let radio-paging services interconnect with telephone systems; and approved the attachment of coaxial cable to telephone-company structures. As one study[22] has noted, however, not all recent regulatory decisions have supported competition. An example is the 1977 approval of an agreement between Telesat and the telephone companies that precluded any long-distance competition among them.

Some deregulation has also occurred in the financial system. The role of foreign banks in the Canadian economy has increased as a consequence of the most recent amendments to the Bank Act. The distinctions among banks, insurance companies, trust companies and investment dealers is becoming less clear day by day as each group begins to hold assets and issue liabilities that formerly represented the province of only one group. The Government of Quebec has announced that it intends to permit, to the extent that its jurisdiction allows, "full services" to financial institutions by 1985. Elsewhere banks are offering discount-brokerage services, brokers are offering "cash-management accounts", and credit unions are engaging in commercial lending.

The trend in the agricultural sector, however, has been in the opposite direction. In 1971, there were 97 federal and provincial agricultural marketing boards. By 1981 the total stood at 124. In 1962, marketing boards received 14 per cent of farm-cash receipts, while by 1983, the proportion had risen to 55 per cent.

The imposition of quality, safety and environmental standards is potentially of mutual benefit to producers and consumers. Realization of this benefit depends on how these standards are set and enforced. Studies conducted by the Economic Council of Canada have found that quality and safety standards have been effective in reducing serious accidents. Problems continue to exist, however, in that standards are often set without proper consideration of compliance costs. A survey conducted by the Council and submissions to this Commission cited a number of examples of burdensome compliance costs. Stelco claimed that regulatory requirements raised the construction costs of its Nanticoke plant by about 11 per cent, and that its operating cost is 8 per cent higher than if "less stringent, but equally effective, environmental requirements had prevailed."[23] It argued that it could have avoided many of these costs without sacrificing environmental standards. Respondents to the Council's survey also reported incurring substantial costs through participating in regulatory proceedings.

Even more burdensome, perhaps, are both the uncertainty regarding specific application of often-vague regulatory provisions and the necessity for dealing with overlapping agencies and jurisdictions. Individuals appearing before this Commission claimed that these problems were of a continuing nature. Respecting regulatory uncertainty, one participant observed:

> *A major part of the problem with regulation is regulatory uncertainty. The unique circumstance of mining is that it is . . . highly capital intensive and when you get through the various regulations which you have with respect to staking claims and that sort of thing and you find a deposit you want to work at, the approvals process that one goes through in British Columbia will probably take two to three years and an expenditure of somewhere between $5 and $10 million to prove not a whole lot.*
>
> (Tex Enemark, Transcript, Vancouver, June 12, 1984 [vol. 8], pp. 1935–36.)

Another intervenor made this comment on overlapping jurisdictions:

> *We believe that performance generally will be most improved by less, not more, government presence in the market-place. Needed are fewer rigidities, a cut-back of counter-productive regulations, and the removal of such obstacles to commercial efficiency as overlapping plant inspections; interprovincial impediments to the mobility of goods and labour; and the restrictive supply management structures.* (George Weston Limited, Brief, September 24, 1984, p. 1.)

The Economic Council has found that the regulatory process was not, in general, among the more important problems facing the small-business community:

> *Rather, their principal headache seemed to be the paperwork associated with taxation, statistics, and customs and excise requirements. Most of their regulatory difficulties involved zoning, planning, building codes, transportation, and labour standards. Their greatest frustrations with regulations were evident when many regulatory jurisdictions intersected, as in the case of land use and construction.*[24]

Many participants in this Commission's hearings, however, believed that regulation constitutes a continuing burden on small business:

> *Business[es], especially (but not only) small businesses, are burdened with non-productive government regulations. An easing of regulations will be beneficial to all Canadians.* (Canada Jaycees, Brief, July 20, 1984, p. 3.)

Participants in this Commission's symposium on small business mentioned the disproportionate burden that regulations, notably those on relations with employees, place on small business:

> *Another problem that we find onerous to small business is the over-regulation . . . In the Province of Ontario where we have the Employment Standards Act and the Human Rights Commission – all of these things don't present too much of a burden to the large business, but they [reduce] . . . the flexibility of a small business.* (Russell Beach, Beach Industries Limited, at Royal Commission, Small Business Seminar, Transcript, October 15, 1984, pp. 79–80.)

For smaller businesses, then, the regulatory framework appears to hamper growth and job creation.

While a great deal of regulation concerns our collective interest in safe products, a safe work place, and a healthy environment, much of it oversees the transfer of income from one segment of society to another. This activity involves provision of services at less than cost to some users and at more than cost to others, and/or monitoring the returns to the producer(s) involved and establishing limits on their charges as means of restricting profits to a "reasonable" level. As Commissioners have stated above, effecting these income transfers often requires a detailed regulatory intervention by government, which we have referred to as "regulatory planning" or "control".

Two survey papers[25] report the size of some income transfers resulting from regulation. There are transfers from one group of consumers to another in the telecommunications, airline, railway and trucking industries. The expense of undertaking these transfers includes the cost of the regulatory process itself; the consumption forgone on purchases deterred by regulated prices higher than they would have been under competitive conditions; the additional production cost incurred as a consequence of substituting less efficient for more efficient producers and techniques; and the costs of seeking and defending beneficial regulatory provisions.

Would society benefit from reduced regulation? One school of thought says that regulatory transfers are not visible to those who must pay for them. Making them more explicit – by including them in the tax-expenditure process, for example – would increase their "political cost" and correspondingly reduce their popularity. In some cases, then, governments would cease to permit transfers that were feasible only by regulation. Society might benefit from this outcome.

Transfers might continue in some areas, by cheaper (if politically more difficult) means such as the tax system:

> *Recognizing that risk adds to the direct costs of redistributing income through regulation leads to a better appreciation of the merit in the economists' dictum that a direct cash subsidy paid out of general tax revenue is a more efficient instrument for redistributing income than is direct regulation.*[26]

One of the research studies prepared for this Commission[27] sounds a proper note of caution. It argues that we often do not know whether a practice of a particular industry is part of a cross-subsidization scheme. Prices are generally the same, for instance, for small and extra-large shirts. Does this represent a cross-subsidy from small to large persons? Or does it reflect the fact that price differentiation would be more bother than it would be worth? Furthermore, even when we identify cross-subsidization, we are not sure of its ultimate beneficiaries. Local telephone rates are higher for businesses than for residences. It is difficult to judge who ultimately benefits from this differential. It is not easy, then, to make regulatory transfers more explicit and more politically visible. Nevertheless, some movement in this direction appears desirable.

In conclusion, regulation involves complex issues. The first fundamental is to determine who should make the regulations, and how they should be made. Given the requirement that the regulator be disinterested, government is the obvious choice. More pressing issues of current concern relate to the regulatory process itself. Commissioners have identified a number of shortcomings and have put forward a number of proposals for correcting them. The problems raised include: an excessive degree of regulation in certain areas, compounded by the existence of conflicting and overlapping regulations; the granting to the regulators excessive discretion, which adds to uncertainty; insufficient consultation on proposed changes in regulatory provisions; and the obscurity surrounding the transfer of costs (income) often inherent in certain regulatory requirements. As a means of reducing or eliminating these problems, Commissioners suggest reform of the regulatory process in several areas.

Suggested Reforms

Sunset Provisions. Commissioners propose a "sunset clause" for major regulatory activities undertaken by federal departments and agencies. The primary purpose would be to require Parliament periodically (perhaps every ten years) to consider whether a particular regulatory function should be continued. If Parliament approves continuation, it could revise the governing legislation to take account of changing conditions and circumstances, as is required every ten years in the case of the Bank Act.

Reducing Regulatory Discretion. Governments usually establish regulatory bodies to undertake functions that require the exercise of judgement. As a consequence, they must give regulators some discretion in carrying out their mandate. Governments may, however, give regulatory authorities too much discretion and thus add unnecessarily to the uncertainty surrounding the process. Commissioners suggest review of the existing mandates of regulatory bodies to determine whether Parliament could more precisely define the responsibilities of the regulator and more accurately describe their routine procedures and proceedings.

Increasing Consultation. Within recent years, public authorities have increasingly recognized their obligation to consult those affected directly and indirectly by the establishment of new regulatory processes or changes in existing ones. This obligation should apply to proposed regulatory provisions made by the government itself and those of a more detailed nature proposed by regulatory bodies. The federal government could give new momentum to the process by requiring the government and/or the regulatory body concerned to consult with the public and other special-interest groups, as appropriate, on proposed changes in regulatory requirements or procedures. Parliament should oversee this consultation process.

Overseeing Regulatory Redistribution of Incomes. Through the exercise of their authority, as Commissioners noted earlier, many regulatory bodies sanction or require redistribution of costs and, thus, of incomes, often through cross-subsidization among various users of a particular service. Each case needs examination on its own merits. Such transfers, however, are often hidden or obscure. Without full knowledge of the extent of such redistribution, it is, of course, impossible to consider whether the redistribution is warranted. To make such assessment possible, we suggest that Parliament require regulatory bodies, or perhaps the Director of Investigation and Research, to report regularly to Parliament and the public on the full extent of all redistribution of costs and income sanctioned by regulatory provisions.

Competition Policy

It has often been argued that markets in Canada tend to be less competitive than those in other countries, particularly the United States. Many Canadian industries are characterized by relatively few producers and relatively little variation in market shares over time. Moreover, most analysts agree that Canadian competition policy is ineffective in preventing the concentration of economic activity.

In the 1970s, it became fashionable in North America to diversify, and a number of large conglomerates were formed. These mergers were financed in a variety of ways, but eventually, sizeable amounts of stock came into the hands of institutional and small investors. Thus the conglomerates were forced to face the discipline of the stock market. In Canada, much of the take-over activity was facilitated by heavy reliance on debt instruments, and the only check on the concentration of power was the obligation to make payments to the banks. Substantial pools of private capital were also involved, accompanied by debt financing from the banks, and the acquisition of control of very substantial assets.

A study, undertaken for this Commission, of the concentration of economic activity in Canada reached the following conclusions:[28]

- Aggregate concentration (that is, the share of corporate assets controlled by the largest 25, 50 or 100 enterprises) has risen since 1968 and, especially, since 1975. The proportion of the assets of the largest 100 enterprises that is accounted for by Canadian or government-owned firms has also risen.
- Concentration increased in most of the major sectors over the period 1975–80 as Table 9-15 shows. Underlying these sectoral changes was a wide variety of changes in concentration ratios of industries within particular

sectors, including mineral fuels (+8.3 percentage points), department stores (+12.2 percentage points), and water transportation (−17.1 percentage points). There was little substantial change within the manufacturing sector.

- The pattern that has evolved in Canada is one of declining concentration in industries that were formerly highly concentrated and increasing concentration in industries that were not. This pattern was particularly evident between 1970 and 1980.
- Individual Canadian industries tend to be more highly concentrated than their counterparts in the United States. That is, the proportion of shipments or sales accounted for by the largest four producers is much higher in most Canadian industries. In total, nearly four-fifths of U.S. economic activity is essentially competitive. The estimate for Canada is substantially lower, amounting to only two-fifths of economic activity as measured by GNP.

The question is: What are we to make of this evidence? Let us begin with the problem of increasing aggregate concentration.

Economists generally assess the consequences of industry concentration within the context of a particular sector. Estimates of aggregate concentration are simply measures of the size of the largest enterprises in a given sector of industry in relation to the size of the sector, but not in relation to the size of a particular market. The fact that an enterprise is large does not

TABLE 9-15 Change in Four Firm Concentration Ratio,[a] 1975–1980

Industry	Change
Agriculture, forestry, and fishing	−0.5
Mining[b]	−1.1
Manufacturing	+0.4
Construction	−3.0
Wholesale trade	−4.1
Retail trade	+5.1
Transportation, communications, and utilities	+7.8
Finance	+4.4
Services	+7.6

Source: R.S. Khemani, "Extent and Evolution of Competition in the Canadian Economy", in *Canadian Industry in Transition*, vol. 2, prepared for the Royal Commission on the Economic Union and Development Prospects for Canada (Toronto: University of Toronto Press, 1985).

a. Change in % shipments accounted for by the largest four enterprises (including government enterprises) 1975 to 1980.

b. Indicates 1976 data.

necessarily imply adverse economic consequences; on the contrary, large enterprises are usually expected to benefit from economies of scale. The report of the Royal Commission on Corporate Concentration offers these conclusions:

> *Our study of conglomerate corporations revealed that their diversification has probably not increased concentration within industries and may even have increased competition. There are some indications that conglomerate diversification has decreased the overall efficiency of the firms involved, as measured by return on assets, and that investors in highly diversified firms have received lower-than-average returns. In theory, diversified firms have a greater ability than other firms to engage in a variety of anticompetitive practices (predatory pricing, cross-product subsidization, tied selling, etc.) but we have found only a few instances in which they have exercised this power. We conclude that the proposed competition law can deal with these problems adequately. Similarly, we see no need for special legislation affecting conglomerate mergers.*[29]

Increases in producers' concentration in a particular market can be harmful, but only under a restricted set of circumstances. The number of domestic producers in an industry will not affect competition if the industry is exposed to international competition, or if there are minimal barriers to the entry of new competitors. Even if new entry is difficult and there is little or no international competition, the consequences are not inevitably harmful. If additional producer concentration results in the creation of larger, more efficient plants or in a more rationalized distribution of output within and among plants, then the benefits to the economy of lower-cost production will generally outweigh the costs arising from the increase in monopoly power.

A study done for this Commission finds that increases in lengths of production runs, which are often the result of rationalization, are generally associated with increases in producer concentration.[30] Thus, if our domestic producers are taking advantage of the economies of large-scale production, we should expect them to be large relative to the Canadian market. Moreover, as the rationalization of production proceeds, a number of Canadian industries may become even more concentrated, which would not be an undesirable development.

The importance of liberalized trade as a guarantee of competition cannot be stressed too often. Given the discipline of international market prices, Canada can obtain the benefits of scale and of rationalization economies without suffering any increases in domestic monopoly power. This point is emphasized in a recent Economic Council of Canada study[31] that compares the concentration of domestic *production* with the concentration of domestic *sales*, including sales of imports. When this import-adjusted measure of concentration is used, Canadian concentration levels are much closer to the levels prevailing in the United States. In addition, because trade increased during the 1970s, import-adjusted concentration in Canadian manufacturing actually fell by about 10 per cent during the decade.

Let us turn now to the more general assessment in this Commission's study[32] that the proportion of GNP produced under effectively competitive conditions is much lower in Canada than it is in the United States. This type of calculation is very difficult to make accurately; other investigators might reach different conclusions. Nevertheless, the estimates contained in the study – that four-fifths of the U.S. economy is competitive, as opposed to only two-fifths of the Canadian economy – do suggest that the difference between the two proportions is significant whatever its precise dimensions.

The study attributes much of this difference to the greater prominence of government-enforced price, output and entry restrictions in this country. For example, it estimates that 86 per cent of the U.S. agricultural sector is effectively competitive, while the corresponding figure for Canadian agriculture is only 53 per cent. The reason for the difference is that Canada makes much greater use of supply-restricting marketing boards than does the United States.[33]

This finding has two implications. First, the power to increase effective competition in the agriculture sector lies almost wholly within the hands of the provinces and the federal government. Governments could do away with supply-management boards or revise their mandates in order to provide greater room for competition, perhaps by raising the limits of permissible supply, by facilitating the entry of new producers, or by allowing for a greater degree of international competition in the domestic market. This point could be applied to many other sectors. The perceived lack of competition in Canada is the result, in many instances, not of an absence of traditional U.S.-style anti-trust laws, but of restrictions on competition put in place by governments themselves.

Secondly, it is important to note that while the United States makes less use of marketing boards than does Canada, our neighbour seeks to achieve many of the same objectives through various price-support systems and other forms of subsidization. It is not difficult to show that while both systems of augmenting farm incomes entail economic costs, marketing boards are often less wasteful than the U.S. price-support methods. The important point here is that competition is a means, not an end: there may be instances in which the restriction of competition is socially beneficial or at least preferable to the available options.

Calculations aimed at measuring the degree of competition by reference to the degree of domestic concentration in any given industry can also be highly misleading. In a study undertaken for this Commission,[34] the mining and petroleum industry in the United States is judged, on this basis, to be 96 per cent effectively competitive, while the comparable figure for Canada is only 7 per cent. The study attributes some of this difference to the controls on Canadian crude oil and natural gas prices. It attributes the balance to the high level of concentration in the Canadian sector. It is difficult to believe, however, that a comparison of domestic sectors provides a true picture of the relative amounts of competition in the two countries. The fact of the matter is that the Canadian sector is extensively exposed to foreign competition at home and abroad.

If Canadian producers actually have some monopoly power, they may well exercise much of it in international markets, and this situation may be beneficial, on balance, to Canadians. The potash industry in Saskatchewan provides an example that illustrates this possibility. The introduction of a prorationing scheme and the subsequent consolidation of the industry under the leadership of the government-owned Potash Corporation of Saskatchewan may have resulted in higher returns on export sales than would have been realized in the absence of these measures. In this context, restrictions on competition benefit the economy, since they result in higher profits for Canadian producers and, perhaps, higher royalty incomes for Canadian governments.

In general, the issue is not whether governments should be more diligent in the pursuit of traditional anti-merger, anti-cartel policies. Governments often restrict competition; indeed, they are likely to be actively involved in any significant and enduring restriction of competition. Once this likelihood is recognized, we can ask the essential questions that follow:

- Which restrictions on competition are functional and should be preserved?
- What is the most effective method of eliminating the remaining restrictions on competition?

There are certain obvious functional restrictions on competition that should be maintained. No one would advocate allowing unrestricted entry into the Atlantic and Pacific fisheries, for example. Nor would anyone advocate completely free entry into some professions, although debate would arise about what the entry requirements should be and who should set them. Restrictions on competition in export markets might also be generally beneficial, even if they carried over, to some extent, into the domestic market. In most cases, however, suppression of competition is in the interest of only a particular group, and not in the interest of the economy as a whole. The question, then, becomes how best to promote, maintain or re-establish competition. The two most important means of promoting competition are:

- Trade liberalization
- Elimination of the regulatory restrictions on price, output and entry that apply to certain industries.

In those sectors of the economy whose goods and services flow freely across national borders, international competition is usually all that is required to ensure that domestic markets are competitive. In these sectors, there is little need for public policy to restrict mergers of domestic companies, concentration within particular domestic industries, or co-operative arrangements among domestic suppliers. Even a well-conceived and effectively administered competition policy is a poor substitute for exposure of domestic industry to the winds of global competition.

Competition policy in many market economies has come to reflect the thesis that the economic benefits of efficient large-scale production will often more than offset the economic costs associated with the increase in market power that is usually inherent in the development of economies of scale. In a small economy, increases in the scale of output are certain to produce net economic benefits when they occur in sectors that are subject to open international competition. It is hard to over-emphasize the central role of freer trade as a force for increased domestic competition. In Canada, the number of combines cases in which removal of trade barriers would have eliminated alleged anti-competitive activities is legion.

The second important condition for greater domestic competition is the elimination of regulatory restrictions on prices, output and entry. Where these restrictions are removed, the possibility of competition from new entrants serves to discipline market participants. Recent theoretical work in industrial organization testifies to the power of potential competition to ensure both competitive pricing and efficient production, even in markets in which there are only a few firms. In Canada, the financial, transportation and professional-service sectors are obvious candidates for partial deregulation of this sort.

Let us now consider competition policy in relation to those areas of the economy that are not subject to direct competition from abroad, either because of their inherent nature (such as construction), or because foreign competition would conflict with other public objectives (such as the protection of communications media for cultural and social reasons). Competition-policy issues also arise where barriers to the entry of potential competitors into an industry (other than the barriers imposed by regulation) are exceptionally high.

Competition policy has traditionally focused on mergers that could be considered to have adverse economic consequences. The present Combines Investigation Act, for example, makes it a criminal offence to engage in a merger "whereby competition . . . is or is likely to be lessened to the detriment or against the interest of the public, whether consumers, producers or others."[35] While this provision, like similar restrictions that applied in earlier years, has proved to be almost totally ineffectual, there is a growing body of opinion that the whole thrust of the policy is misdirected. Since the Economic Council of Canada issued its report on competition policy in 1969,[36] the view has developed that questions relating to mergers should be removed from the sphere of criminal law and be considered on their economic merits by an administrative tribunal as a matter of civil law.

Successive proposals put forward during the 1970s to implement this new approach encountered stiff opposition from the business community, which objected to the extent of the proposed law's application, the discretionary power it would give to the members of the tribunal, the uncertainty it would produce, and other matters as well. Amendments put before Parliament in mid-1984, which were never enacted, would have sought to reduce uncertainty by providing for the courts to adjudicate merger cases on the basis of a fairly simple set of criteria that would have left little or no room for exercising judgement about the economic costs and benefits of a proposed merger.

When the reform measures were first proposed, a number of observers assumed that it would not be difficult for a competent tribunal to distinguish between mergers that would serve the public interest by increasing the efficiency of the economy – a benefit that would outweigh the possible cost of reduced competition in the market-place, which might in any case be avoided by other means, such as tariff reductions— and mergers that would serve only the interests of the participating parties. Over time, however, most observers have come to a better appreciation of the problems involved in developing adequate criteria for determining which mergers should be approved and which rejected.

Horizontal mergers, involving firms that already serve essentially the same market, should be the easiest to evaluate. In all likelihood, the great majority of horizontal mergers considered by an administrative tribunal would be approved with little difficulty if competition could be maintained by the inflow of goods or services from abroad. Even in industries where international competition was non-existent and the barriers to entry of potential domestic competitors were high, mergers would probably be approved if they seemed certain to increase economic efficiency significantly.

None of the legislative amendments put forward over the past several years proposes that conglomerate mergers—that is, mergers which involve companies operating in unrelated markets—should be subject to review either by the courts or by an administrative tribunal. Vertical mergers, which involve firms that operate in different sectors of an integrated supply chain (the merger of a food processing company with a major food retailer, for example), would almost certainly be subject to review, but adequate criteria for determining which of these mergers are in the public interest have never, to our knowledge, been developed. The basic problem is that market power can be defined only in relation to a particular market, but vertical mergers involve creating an entity that operates across several markets. Thus it is difficult to determine whether or not vertical integration by a firm occupying a dominant market position will be economically beneficial.

The reform proposals put forward over the past several years have also sought to remove the provisions of the Combines Act that treat monopolistic behaviour detrimental to the public interest as a criminal offence. Again, earlier proposals provided for such cases to be considered by an administrative tribunal, while the amendments put forward in 1984 would have referred such issues to the courts for consideration as a matter of civil law.

We Commissioners have already emphasized our conviction that whenever possible, Canada should rely on international trade to ensure the maintenance of dynamic competition in the domestic market-place. Canada should also seek to expand significantly the boundaries of competition in industries where that boundary is now restricted by regulation. In other areas of the economy, however, policy instruments should be available that will maintain as much competition among domestic suppliers of goods and services as is practical in economic terms. To achieve this objective would both serve the interests of consumers and place competitive restraints on the costs of inputs required by Canadian companies engaged in competition with foreign firms, at home and abroad.

In our judgement, the vast majority of corporate mergers that are concluded in response to the dynamics of the market-place should not be of concern from the perspective of public policy, particularly not where the inflow of trade from abroad can be relied on to maintain a healthy degree of competition. At the same time, however, a modern nation with an open market economy should have available to it, under civil law, the means to prohibit horizontal or vertical mergers that are contrary to the public interest. By the same token, we believe that means should also be available for dealing on a civil-law basis with flagrant abuses of monopolistic power. Such an abuse might occur, for example, where a firm that occupies a dominant position in the market-place sells a product at an exceptionally low price in an effort to drive an emerging competitor out of business.

Observers who accept the need for reform in the regulation of mergers and monopolistic behaviour are generally divided into two groups: those who believe that these matters should be subject to consideration by an administrative tribunal with a right of appeal to the courts only on matters of law, jurisdiction and natural justice, and those who believe that the same matters should be adjudicated by the courts alone. Those who favour the intervention of an administrative tribunal, such as the present Restrictive Trade Practices Commission, argue that only a body of this kind could exercise the economic judgement required to determine whether a particular instance of corporate behaviour was detrimental to the public interest. Those who oppose adjudication by such a tribunal and favour the use of the courts do so precisely because of the freedom the former approach would provide for the exercise of discretion. Such an approach, they contend, would lend itself to arbitrariness and uncertainty.

As Commissioners indicated earlier, we are well aware of the difficulty of developing criteria for determining whether or not certain types of mergers serve the public interest. We also recognize the difficulty of distinguishing between corporate behaviour that is abusive and predatory in its intent and effect, and behaviour that is innocent in intent and in keeping with acceptable competitive practices. Because it is so difficult to make such distinctions, we conclude that it would be better to call on an administrative tribunal to exercise its best economic judgement in the resolution of merger and monopoly cases than to fall back on adjudication by the courts, which are quite unequipped to exercise economic judgement.

We must also emphasize our view that the proposed administrative tribunal should review mergers, alleged monopolistic behaviour, and related matters such as specialization agreements aimed at industrial rationalization only if they appear to offer a serious threat to competition in the domestic market. While the tribunal must be able to exercise its judgement on the basis of the circumstances surrounding each case brought before it, the law and the regulations under which the tribunal is created should carefully define the tribunal's mandate and provide clear guidelines on the manner in which it is to carry out its proceedings.

A study undertaken for this Commission[37] analyses certain types of restrictions on competition that may be imposed along the vertical chain of supply, including territorial restrictions on sales, exclusive dealing and tied-selling provisions, and resale-price maintenance. Since 1975, the first three forms of restriction have been subject to review by the Restrictive Trade Practices Commission, which has various remedies at its command if it concludes that such practices substantially reduce competition in the market-place. In 1951, Parliament made it illegal for manufacturers or wholesalers to require a retailer to sell a product at a minimum price, although both groups were left free to "suggest" a resale price. Enforcement of this ban against resale-price maintenance has been a major activity of combines authorities over the past three decades. The study undertaken for this Commission contends that there are circumstances in which resale-price maintenance could, in fact, provide significant economic benefits. While Commissioners are not in a position to reach any conclusion on this issue, we do recommend a review of the provision making it illegal in any circumstances to require compliance with resale prices. It might be determined that resale-price maintenance should be illegal only when its detrimental effects on competition demonstrably outweigh its benefits. Alternatively, resale-price maintenance could be made a matter for review by an administrative tribunal, just as exclusive dealing and tied selling are now reviewed by the Restrictive Trade Practices Commission.

For some years, the laws against conspiracies to restrict competition through such means as price-fixing and market-sharing arrangements operated reasonably effectively in achieving their limited purpose. However, recent decisions of the Supreme Court of Canada appear to have undermined the effectiveness of those provisions by increasing the burden on the Crown to prove the intent of the alleged conspirators and the adverse economic effect of their action. In our view, it is important that the law should be amended as necessary to remove these impediments to the Crown.

We agree with the conclusion of the Royal Commission on Corporate Concentration that mergers and acquisitions involving major conglomerates should be dealt with on an individual basis by the federal government and Parliament. As that Commission pointed out in its 1978 report, the decision to prevent a merger is essentially political in nature:

> *The attempted Power-Argus merger was important, not because of its potential effect on competition within industries (which we think would have been minor) but because the prominence of the parties in the economy made their actions significant to the public. Transactions this spectacular will always demand inquiry. We think that conglomerate mergers of this kind should first be analyzed under the competition law, but if (as in Power-Argus) there are no significant competitive implications, or none that could not be dealt with under the competition law, there may still be overriding reasons of public policy that will compel intervention by the state. We do not think it is possible to establish in advance legislative criteria by which unique cases like a Power-Argus merger can be assessed. If the state intervenes to prevent or dissolve a merger like Power-Argus, the decision to do so must be a political one, to be taken by government and Parliament in the light of the circumstances as they see them at the time.*[38]

In essence, the approach taken here leaves the central role of ensuring competitive behaviour to be controlled by the international market-place and the threat of entry of competing interests. It minimizes government manipulation of the structure of domestic industry. While this approach is not in line with the U.S. tradition, it is in keeping with past Canadian practice, certain more recent trends in the United States, and actual practice in most other industrialized countries. Another study[39] made for this Commission suggests that while most industrial countries have affirmed their support for an effective competition policy, they have not practised what they have preached. Quite simply, while such countries have broadly similar competition provisions on the statute books, vigorous enforcement is the exception rather than the rule.

One factor in this lack of enforcement in most industrial countries – a factor that will cause problems for even a limited competition policy in Canada – is the use of the so-called "strategic" or "targeting" approach to industrial policy, in which governments support domestic firms engaged in high-growth, high-barrier-to-entry activities, in the hope of obtaining a world-wide trade advantage. A major study prepared for this Commission notes that in a small country, targeting is almost certain to guarantee control of the domestic market for the chosen firm.[40] The essence of the targeting approach is early entry and quick movement up the learning curve. The latter achievement is facilitated by the guarantee of a domestic-market base, which provides a context in which to build up volume and expert assistance. Thus, pursuit of this strategy means that a government will not only acquiesce in mergers and specialization agreements, but also actively prevent the erosion of the domestic market base of the chosen firm: that is, it intervenes to deter potential entrants. Competition, in short, would be suppressed.

An example of the tension existing between competition policy and the new industrial strategy is provided by the Bell Canada/Northern Telecom/Bell Northern Research vertical integration case, on which the Restrictive Trade Practices Commission recently reported.[41] Competition-policy issues of a traditional nature were involved. A regulated monopoly, Bell Canada, owns a significant proportion of a telecommunications-equipment manufacturer, Northern Telecom, and both own Bell-Northern Research. The regulated monopoly might pay its captive supplier excessive prices and include these in its rate base.

Vertical links that extend to the final point of sale can be defended on the grounds of increased efficiency and, hence, lower costs. There are further efficiency gains to be made from taking advantage of new technologies developed within associated corporate entities. The central issue in the debate, however, was whether Northern Telecom could have achieved its considerable success in export markets if it had not enjoyed guaranteed access for its products to the substantial Bell Canada market.

The opponents in the debate were the Bureau of Competition Policy, which argued that competing suppliers should have unrestricted access to the Bell Canada market, and the Department of Communications, which maintained that the connection between Bell and Northern Telecom was desirable, since it sustained Canadian jobs in the telecommunications industry and promoted Canada's "technological sovereignty". The Department of Communications argued that all of Northern Telecom's European and Far Eastern competitors had some form of preferential access to their domestic telecommunications utilities; consequently, Northern Telecom could not have achieved its considerable success in export markets if it had not enjoyed guaranteed access to the substantial Bell Canada market. The Restrictive Trade Practices

Commission (RTPC) found that Northern Telecom's preferential access to Bell Canada had not resulted in the latter's paying higher prices for equipment. The connection between the two companies, therefore, did not impose excessive costs on domestic users of their telecommunications services. This may have been true of the Bell-Northern relationship; in general, however, a firm that is guaranteed a domestic-market base would be expected to exploit it. Knowing this, should governments initiate, support, acquiesce in, or oppose market-guaranteeing measures?

The link between the uranium cartel, potash pro-rationing and preferential access to Bell Canada should be recognized. All the arrangements have involved restrictions on competition in which a government has been involved. Each may or may not be nationally beneficial. The question is whether domestic-market guarantees or other restrictions on domestic competition should be extended throughout the manufacturing sector (especially the technology-intensive segment) as an element of industrial policy.

One factor to be considered is the possibility that this strategy may be practical only if it can be hidden, since otherwise it invites retaliation. More fundamental is the question concerning the merits of targeting. In most cases, domestic-market guarantees involve significant economic costs. While such costs might be considered justified if they were more than offset by higher-than-usual profits subsequently earnable abroad, the prospects for such an outcome must be regarded as small.

While the Bell-Northern link may have contributed to the emergence of Northern as a major player in world markets – and may have done so without imposing costs on Bell Canada's customers – this fact does not imply that public policy should set out to duplicate this situation elsewhere. Commissioners' conclusion is that unless there are strongly compelling reasons, domestic competition should not be suppressed in order to achieve industrial strategy purposes.

Our assessment of the major competition-policy issues leads us to conclude that the role of the Director of Investigation and Research under the Combines Investigation Act should be recast. In future, the occupant of this office should be less concerned with mergers, monopolies and vertical restrictions imposed along the supply chain and more concerned with reform of the fundamental conditions that determine the state of competition in the Canadian economy. Such reform would involve opposition to demands for continued or increased tariff, quota or equivalent protection. It would involve efforts to dismantle regulatory restrictions on entry and output, including those imposed by professional associations and marketing boards. Finally, it would involve opposition to attempts to "guarantee" to a single producer access to the Canadian market or to a provincial market. While it is true that the Director has pursued these goals since the mid-1970s, Commissioners are suggesting that this activity be greatly intensified. Competition policy should also seek to ensure that the treatment of foreign investment in Canada is consistent with the maintenance of strong competition. Greater freedom of access to the Canadian market for foreign investment interests should help to increase the degree of competition in the Canadian economy.

The serious efforts made between 1971 and 1975 to reform Canada's competition law ran afoul of what one observer has described as a "swift, massive and overwhelmingly adverse" reaction from the business community.[42] It is in the ultimate interests of all Canadians to try again to reform Canada's outmoded competition policy. In pursuit of this goal, it will be important to retain an existing feature of the Combines Investigation Act: the provisions allowing Canadian firms to co-operate in export markets, provided they do not reduce domestic competition. It will also be important to overcome a shortcoming in the present legislation: the apparent exemption of self-regulated professions (such as law and medicine) from the provisions of the act if their conduct is pursuant to authority delegated to them by provincial legislation.

In order better to formulate and administer appropriate competition policy, the government should consider requiring all large corporations and corporate groups – public and private, foreign-owned and Canadian-owned – to make available to the public information relevant to their operations. Given the relatively small size of Canada's domestic market, a high degree of concentration is necessary in certain industries if Canadian participants in these industries are to compete effectively against foreign enterprises at home and abroad. Yet a high degree of concentration may be considerably less acceptable in domestic industries that are largely sheltered from competition with foreign firms. Lack of domestic competition might make the goods and services produced by such industries excessively costly to Canadian firms which must buy from them. Consequently, these firms might find that their ability to compete against foreign firms is reduced. Given this situation, it is clearly important that Canadian competition policy be capable of responding to a variety of conditions and circumstances. The availability of extensive information concerning the functioning of all large-scale enterprises is a prerequisite for exercising a properly balanced competition policy.

Crown Corporations and Privatization

There have been a number of major acquisitions by such Crown corporations as the Potash Corporation of Saskatchewan and Petro-Canada. Share purchases by the Canada Development Corporation (CDC) and government-pension/fund managers such as the *Caisse de dépôt et placements du Québec* have created several new mixed enterprises. The limited data available indicate that government-equity holdings in all mixed enterprises constituted 7.5 per cent of the equity capital in Canada in 1981: a fivefold increase over 1972.

While government ownership of industry has increased in Canada, it is still not large either by European standards or by comparison with governments' industrial holdings in developing countries such as Brazil, Mexico or India. There are countries with much less government ownership than Canada: most notably Japan and the United States. There is little movement generally, however, away from government ownership, except in the United Kingdom. As is evident from Table 9-16, the British government has sold parts or all of a large number of state entreprises to the private sector. To date, it has "privatized" or scheduled for "privatization" approximately 10 per cent of government-enterprise assets.[43]

TABLE 9-16 The British Privatization Effort

The Privatization Program

Year	Up for Sale	Amount (£M)
1979–80	5 per cent of BP	276
	25 per cent of ICL	37
	Shares in Suez Finance Company and miscellaneous	57
1980–81	50 per cent of Ferranti	55
	100 per cent of Fairey	22
	North Sea oil licences	195
	51 per cent of British Aerospace	43
	Miscellaneous and small NEB	91
1981–82	24 per cent of British Sugar	44
	50 per cent of Cable and Wireless	182
	100 per cent of Amersham International	64
	100 per cent of National Freight Consortium	5
	Miscellaneous plus Crown Agent and Forestry Commission land and property sales	199
1982–83	51 per cent of Britoil (first cash call)	334
	49 per cent of Associated British Ports	46
	BR hotels	35
	Sale of oil licences, oil stockpiles and miscellaneous	73
1983–84	Second cash call for Britoil	293
	7 per cent of BP	565
	25 per cent of Cable and Wireless	260
	Miscellaneous	132
Summer 1984	100 per cent of BR Sealink	66
	100 per cent of Jaguar	297
Autumn 1984	50 per cent of British Telecom (Payable 1984 – 86)	3 900
Scheduled for privatization before 1988		
	British Telecom (November 1984)	
	British Airways (1985)	
	British Airports Authority	
	British Steel (profitable parts)	
Approved in principle		
	Rolls Royce	
	British Leyland (esp. Land Rover, Unipart)	
	British Shipbuilders (Naval warship yards)	
	National Bus Company	
	Royal Ordinance Factories	

Source: Speech made by Professor Michael Littlechild to a Conference on Weaving a New Industrial Policy, sponsored by the Institute for Research on Public Policy, Toronto, February 1985.

In the light of the British example, we might ask whether Canada should follow suit. The unfavourable financial results experienced by a number of Canadian government enterprises add force to this question, as does the general perception that many Crown corporations are not sufficiently accountable to the government. Furthermore, privatization, deregulation and competititon are related issues. We might note in passing that privatization can be more difficult to arrange than nationalization.

To determine whether a government enterprise should be privatized, we should first consider whether the enterprise serves as an effective instrument of public policy. In some instances, the answer will be obvious. The purpose of the Cape Breton Development Corporation (Devco) is to promote employment in the area through support to coal mining and other forms of industrial development. In other cases, the public-policy function may be less obvious; indeed, it may no longer exist. If a government enterprise is no longer serving a goal of public policy, then we might legitimately ask why it should not be privatized. In part at least, the answer is likely to depend on one's ideological view of whether government should be involved in a business enterprise except to serve a purpose of public policy. Commissioners are inclined to believe that the majority of Canadians would agree that government should not be involved except for pressing reasons of public policy.

Do the interests of public policy continue to justify the federal government's total or partial ownership of such corporations as Air Canada, Canadian National Railways, Teleglobe, Eldorado Nuclear and the CDC? If we put ideology aside, the primary issue is whether privatization of such corporations would increase their efficiency. The available evidence suggests that private ownership of such corporations will probably not result in increased efficiency in most instances. Rather, it appears that by itself, privatization would produce little or no improvement in productivity.

However, private ownership of such enterprises could be salutary in other ways. A case in point involves the deregulation of the airline industry, which many consider cannot proceed very effectively without a significant change in the status of Air Canada. This change might involve the privatization of the airline to make it subject to the discipline of the capital markets and the removal of existing restrictions on competition from other companies, particularly CP Air.

A government enterprise may operate at a distinct and fundamental disadvantage in relation to its privately owned competitors. In these circumstances, privatization would increase efficiency and profitability. One such field might consist of high-technology, market-oriented industries in which public accountability and the resulting bureaucratic rigidity are incompatible with prompt and flexible responses to changing conditions and circumstances. The commercial aircraft business, in which the federal government is deeply involved through de Havilland and Canadair, may be a case in point.

Finally, privatization might increase the efficiency of government itself. Many observers think that government has become so large, so complex and so centralized that regardless of structural reforms, elected officials cannot manage it. While decentralization may provide at least a partial remedy, it may be incompatible with the accountability requirements of public ownership. A former senior public servant has put the dilemma this way:

> *Besides the difficulty of making public enterprise compatible with international trading and financial policies, there are also real difficulties in making it compatible with our form of democratic government.*
>
> *While this situation has a host of manifestations, its roots lie in four problems: the problem of confict of interest, the problem of accountability, the problem of form and the problem of size.*
>
> *The first problem stems from the fact that the more Ministers and high officals are responsible for actually running an enterprise in business, the more they tend to be in confict of interest with the other duties of their offices. In making decisions on behalf of the enterprise, they are drawn to act either according to the norms of their official functions, which are not the norms of business, or according to the norms of business, which are not the norms required of them in their official functions. Either way they have powers and information not available to business.*
>
> *This problem, compounded by the constraints on the time of Ministers and high officials, plus the fact that they are rarely trained in business much less in the actual enterprise involved, inevitably encourages the delegation of the enterprise to its administrators in a more or less autonomous manner. The result is the second problem, the problem of accountability.*
>
> *The natural inclination of Parliament is to insist upon, and the natural inclination of those managing the enterprise is to assume, the greatest possible autonomy. At the same time, Parliamentarians set, the managers of public enterprise pay lip-service to, and Ministers and officials accept impossibly incongruous levels of responsibility. Government without responsibility risks tyranny; business without a clear chain-of-command risks bankruptcy; and this lack of accountability in public enterprise risks both.*[44]

Thus, while privatization may or may not lead to more efficient operations at the firm or market level, it might result in simpler and more efficient government.

Many Crown corporations have obvious public policy functions. They may, for example, provide employment in depressed regions and services such as transportation facilities, electricity or telecommunications, to various groups, at subsidized prices. Their public policy purpose, such as strengthening national unity, may be more abstract. These functions lead to another question: Could we achieve these public policy goals by other means? The federal government could provide jobs or investment in depressed regions, for example, by subsidizing private firms.

This is an instance where people often confuse means and ends. While the operation of Crown corporations provides one means of meeting the goals of public policy, it is rarely the only means. Where there are other ways to achieve the objective, this consideration may not significantly deter privatization. The privatization of Canadair and/or de Havilland, for example, would not necessarily put an end to the federal government's "presence" in the commercial aircraft industry. That government could provide subsidies for research and development or employment and investment tax credits to the privatized companies. The question should always be: Can public policy goals be more effectively realized by means other than government ownership?

If a government enterprise no longer has a public policy function, or if other means are available to carry out its function, the federal government, in Commissioners' view, should at least consider privatization. This brings us to the question of how to transfer the government's interest to the private sector. To whom should the government sell a Crown corporation? As a general rule, it should not sell a Crown corporation to the corporation's largest competitor, particularly in industries with limited competition and difficult entry for other would-be competitors. The government might resolve this latter problem by reducing regulatory impediments to new entrants; potential competition might then allow the sale of a Crown corporation to one of its existing competitors.

There is also considerable concern in some quarters that foreign buyers might obtain control of a Crown corporation that is being offered for private ownership. In Commissioners' opinion, it would be an error to exclude foreigners from bidding for shares in such firms. In many cases, such a course would exclude firms that could use the assets of the corporation to best advantage and/or exclude all bidders but existing competitors.

Should the government offer for sale all or only part of its interest in a given corporation? The government might well get a better price if it sells its entire interest — though perhaps it should do so in stages. If it retains effective control, purchasers will know that the government can use the corporation for public policy purposes, perhaps at the expense of profits, and will discount their offer accordingly.

The creation of mixed enterprises from private enterprises causes similar problems. The purchase prices of shares will reflect the possibility of a government buy-in and subsequent use of the firm for public policy purposes. In effect, the possibility that any firm might be the target of a government buy-in raises the cost of equity capital for all firms. For this reason, there is great merit in a policy, such as that followed by the Alberta Heritage Fund, of restricting share purchases by government holding companies and pension-fund managers to 10 per cent of the equity in any company. This restriction would assuage fears of a government's purchasing controlling interest in hitherto private enterprises.

As this consideration suggests, the primary problem is not so much the creation of more mixed enterprises by partial privatization as it is the potential creation, in future, of more mixed enterprises by partial nationalization. Indeed, recent Canadian experience suggests that the first item on the agenda is not starting the process of privatization, but stopping the process of nationalization. Some governments have bailed out privately owned companies that have run into trouble by assuming government ownership. Analysis and experience may suggest that complete or partial ownership by government provides a better means of rescuing such companies than loan guarantees or outright subsidies, but this solution begs the question of whether governments should bail out such companies at all.

Thus, the main issue is not what type of firms Canada should sell, but what type of firms it should stop buying. If governments continue to intervene to "Canadianize", to provide or maintain high-tech jobs or jobs in depressed regions, or to provide subsidized services of various kinds, we shall probably see much more, rather than less, government ownership. The value of these forms of intervention is very much open to question. Reducing the incidence of such examples of intervention would be the first and most important step in controlling the growth of government and mixed enterprise.

To re-examine the role of Crown corporations and the value of mixed public/private ownership of enterprises is a logical extension of reforming competition policy and the regulatory framework. Commissioners' emphasis on increased competition to improve Canada's productivity requires a much broader basis for competition policy, one that addresses all impediments to competition. Concerns about merger corporations and conglomerates have received undue attention, although these must continue to be addressed if, indeed, foreign competition does not act as a check to domestic concentration. Commissioners have noted that the regulatory framework is a frequent impediment to enhanced competition within Canada; for this and other reasons, we have suggested that deregulation – especially of regulatory planning – would be desirable. This undertaking would be useful, however, only if accompanied by some privatization of Crown corporations. It makes little sense to argue for extensive deregulation of the air transportation industry when Air Canada so dominates that industry. Governments should avoid continued nationalization of private assets, particularly in cases designed to bail out firms or industries in trouble. Other means should be examined to assist the transfer of resources to more productive uses.

Foreign Investment and the National Interest

Historically, opportunities for investment in Canada have usually called for more funds than Canadians could make available from their savings. Consequently, Canada has imported large amounts of foreign capital directly, in the form of foreign debt and equity capital (that is, through direct foreign investment). We have, in effect, also imported capital in the form of reinvested earnings by foreign-owned firms already established in our country. Both federal and provincial governments have encouraged capital inflows, as these funds allow the Canadian economy to achieve levels of industrial development not otherwise possible. At the same time, foreign investment has produced high levels of foreign ownership and control of certain sectors of the Canadian economy.

In the decades ahead, foreign capital and the new ideas and techniques that often accompany it can contribute to the growth and prosperity of our national and regional economies. Foreign investment, however, does require us to share control over our economic future with non-Canadians, who may sometimes hold values and aspirations that differ from our own. Moreover, the multi-national nature of most foreign-controlled enterprises makes such firms susceptible to the policy directives of foreign governments, which may be detrimental to Canadian interests. During the past two decades, many

Canadians have expressed heightened concern over the relatively high levels of foreign ownership in our manufacturing and resource industries, and both federal and provincial governments have responded with regulations and other policies designed either to limit foreign control or to mitigate its adverse consequences.[45]

Foreign Investment Issues

While data on developments in the recent past provide an uncertain guide to the future, Commissioners would venture a number of observations about the prospective flows and the stock of foreign investment capital. First, the inward movement of foreign direct investment has decreased from the heights reached in the early 1960s. In fact, Canada's share of global direct foreign investment has fallen from 16 per cent in the early 1960s to 3 per cent in the late 1970s and then to a negative figure in the early 1980s. The National Energy Program alone resulted in an outflow of direct foreign investment of about $6 billion as a result of the purchase of foreign-owned companies by Canadian interests.[46]

An analysis limited to transnational capital flows, however, overlooks retained earnings as a source of new investment. Such reinvestment of profits by foreign-controlled enterprises has a cumulative effect on the stock of foreign investment. But to the extent that those firms retain such profits in Canada and reinvest them, they do not appear in data on the balance of payments. Thus, while the net flows of direct investment into Canada may have slowed and, in recent years, even turned negative, the stock of foreign investment in Canada has continued to rise. Foreign control of capital in Canadian industry remains high by international standards, even though, as Figure 9-3 shows, there were considerable declines in levels of foreign holdings in many domestic industries during the 1970s. In 1982, foreign companies held 49 per cent control in Canadian manufacturing, 45 per cent in petroleum and natural gas, 43 per cent in mining and smelting, and 26 per cent in all other industries, excluding agriculture and finance. Firms controlled in the United States own most of these large foreign holdings, and now account for about 80 per cent of the foreign direct investment in Canada.

Few other economies, apart from those of Australia, Belgium and Ireland, have as much as 40 per cent of their manufacturing capital in companies owned by non-residents; Italy, France, West Germany and the United Kingdom have economies that are between 20 per cent and 30 per cent foreign owned; Sweden and Norway are at or over 10 per cent by this measure; while the United States and Japan are approximately 5 per cent foreign owned. Moreover, Canada's intra-firm trade increased steadily during the 1970s: Canadian-based firms that own, or are owned by, foreign-based firms currently account for more than one-half of imports from the United States in a wide range of industries. Thus, while inward flows of foreign capital have been decreasing, Canada's stock of foreign investment remains high when compared with that of other developed nations, with the result that foreign multi-nationals are likely to continue to play an important role in Canada's economy.

FIGURE 9-3 Distribution of Control in Canadian Non-Financial Industry

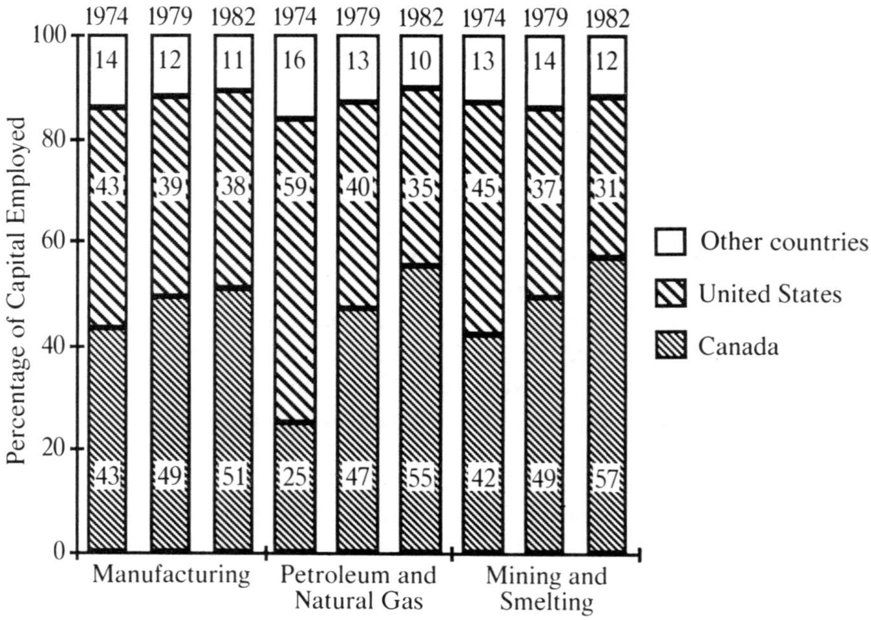

Source: Statistics Canada, *Canada's International Investment Position 1979 and 1982,* Cat. No. 67-202 (Ottawa: Minister of Supply and Services Canada, 1984), p. 32.

As we saw earlier, outward flows of capital have significantly exceeded inward flows on a balance-of-payments basis over the past decade. The stock of Canadian direct investments abroad as a proportion of the stock of foreign direct investment in Canada rose from 25 per cent in 1974 to 54 per cent in 1983. If this trend continues, Canada will soon become a significant exporter of capital, although it will likely remain a net importer. As a result of its favourable current-account position of the last few years, Canada has been a moderate net exporter of capital from a balance-of-payments perspective. This would not be so, however, if we included in the balance reinvested earnings of foreign-owned subsidiaries. This trend toward increasing Canadian investment abroad suggests that our policy toward inward investment must take into account our national interest in securing equitable reciprocal treatment for Canadians investing abroad.

An appraisal of existing policies affecting foreign-controlled firms must take account of the advantages and disadvantages of foreign direct investment. Most general studies of the economic effects of foreign investment conclude that the benefits from inward capital flows are substantial and are likely to increase in the future. The benefits of foreign investment extend beyond the obvious advantages of access to foreign capital at highly competitive rates, as a supplement to domestic savings. Canadian governments gain considerable revenue by taxing gains attributable to foreign investment: between 1.5 per cent and 2.5 per cent of gross national product.[47]

Even more important, foreign investment is a major source of valuable technology, managerial "know-how" and entrepreneurship. Since innovative products, practices and concepts will be the key to Canada's economic success, our policies toward foreign-controlled enterprises must avoid restrictions that impede the importation of these elements. In particular, equity ownership of an enterprise may give foreign innovators more incentive to apply fully their ideas and processes, and to enhance the quality of their products. If innovators have to license the use of their concepts to domestic firms that they do not control, either the licence fees will be much higher, or foreign innovators will take their ideas to other countries where they can pursue them on more advantageous terms.

Those who favour the regulation of foreign investment in Canada complain, first, that many foreign parent companies establish Canadian subsidiaries as branch plants meant exclusively to serve the domestic market. They contend that this intention leads to truncated industrial enterprises that are contrary to Canada's national interest because they cannot try to break out of our own relatively small market by developing a dynamic market for exports abroad. Some analysts have asserted that Canadian subsidiaries of foreign parent firms import more, export less, and conduct fewer managerial and research activities in Canada than comparable Canadian-controlled businesses. In short, those favouring regulation of foreign-controlled firms have maintained that regulation would increase the dynamism, the technological progressiveness, and the export capacity of Canadian industry.

In fact, however, little evidence links extensive foreign control and deficiencies in Canada's industrial performance. For example, while domestically controlled manufacturing firms may spend more on research and development than their foreign-controlled counterparts, the latter tend to have higher productivity. Foreign-controlled firms tend to import more goods than domestic firms, perhaps because suitable "inputs", or components, are not available from Canadian sources of supply or because Canadian inputs are not competitive with imports in price or quality. Thus there may be more logical explanations for Canada's truncated industrial structure than foreign ownership. The National Policy of 1879 and the continuing use of protection since then, the relatively small size of the domestic market, and the tariff and non-tariff barriers created by our major trading partners have all contributed significantly to our current industrial problems. Moreover, both foreign and domestic investors appear to have responded in similar ways to the conditions and circumstances prevailing at home and abroad.

A second argument for regulating foreign-controlled firms arises from the difficulties that national governments sometimes encounter when they seek to influence the behaviour of foreign multi-national enterprises. Firms that conduct the majority of their business activities outside Canada are likely to be more responsive to the general policies or specific directives of foreign governments than are firms based in Canada. Moreover, Canadian-controlled businesses may be more receptive than foreign-owned firms to public-policy initiatives to strengthen cultural autonomy and preserve national security.

American tax and regulatory policies affect the business decisions of U.S.-owned multi-nationals operating in Canada. During the past two decades, many foreign – usually U.S.-owned – multi-nationals in Canada have had to choose between the competing policy demands of two national governments. Disputes have involved trade restrictions imposed by the U.S. government on the trade of U.S.-owned subsidiaries in Canada for national security reasons; the attempted extraterritorial application of U.S. anti-trust and other regulatory laws; and American tax laws that encourage multi-nationals to repatriate their foreign-source income and to expand their production in the United States, rather than increase the size of their operations in this country. While it is easy to exaggerate the economic significance of these bilateral conflicts, their relative frequency and their potential for causing serious friction in Canada-U.S. relations suggest the need to establish regulatory machinery to manage these disputes in future.

A third argument for regulation of foreign investment is that foreign multi-nationals often restrict the authority of their Canadian subsidiaries to export or to experiment with innovative techniques. There is little authoritative evidence to support this claim. To the extent that the claim is valid, the national orientation of parent-company managers or the short-sightedness and inertia of large and complex corporate bureaucracies may be to blame. It is, of course, difficult to determine the motives of management in such situations. For example, there is some hearsay evidence that foreign-controlled firms in the manufacturing and natural resource sectors tend to favour established suppliers located in their home countries over Canadian firms offering goods of comparable quality at competitive prices. Similarly, the managers of a multi-national parent firm may resist proposals for providing its Canadian subsidiary with a world product mandate (a mandate to produce particular products as the sole corporate source of supply for world markets) merely because they stand to gain by maintaining control over all aspects of the firm's management. In the light of these potential conflicts of interest, some form of government regulation would seem reasonable.

This Commission believes that the same tax and regulatory policies applicable to domestic firms should generally govern foreign-controlled firms, except in sectors where cultural or national-security interests predominate. This principle of national treatment or non-discrimination is emerging as a customary rule of public international law, and Canada has recognized it through its formal assent, in 1976, to the Organization for Economic Co-operation and Development's Declaration on International Investment and Multinational Enterprises. The OECD convention recognizes that a commitment to equal treatment for foreign and domestic investors is fully consistent with the maintenance of selective regulatory instruments to deal with situations where foreign-controlled firms take major business decisions averse to national interests. Moreover, the convention authorizes the prior screening of foreign investors and the imposition of special conditions, such as performance undertakings by a foreign-controlled firm taking over an existing firm or setting up a new business. The Foreign Investment Review Act, which the federal government has replaced by the Investment Canada Act, sharply reducing government intervention in foreign investment, is broadly congruent with the selective case-by-case approach to regulatory intervention endorsed by the OECD convention.

The provisions of the General Agreement on Tariffs and Trade (GATT) also constrain Canada. In the early 1980s, the United States raised objections to local procurement requirements and export-performance requirements that Canada's Foreign Investment Review Agency (FIRA) was asking foreign investors to meet. The U.S. Administration believed that these rules were contrary to the national-treatment provision of the GATT: that is to say, the Canadian government did not make the same requirements of Canadian firms investing in Canada. The GATT formed a panel to assist the two countries to resolve the dispute; it found that the "local content" undertakings secured by FIRA during the course of its negotiations with foreign investors violated Canada's GATT undertaking not to discriminate against imported products. Canada agreed to modify its administrative practices to comply with the panel's ruling, which the United States accepted as a resolution of the dispute.

Policies Affecting Foreign Investors

In testimony before this Commission, in May 1984, one intervenor succinctly described some of the main issues confronting Canada with respect to foreign investment:

> *In view of the direction that international trade is taking [and of] its importance, Canadians are exposed more and more to foreign influence, and most of them are ready to see a number of foreign firms enter [Canada] to make a contribution here. It is certain that how these firms are treated must depend on what they do, not who they are, and that they must definitely not be favoured by import incentives that are not granted to our own domestic business concerns. We must keep [our doors] open, and that requires important changes in certain of our present philosophies, both provincial and federal.*
>
> (Guy St-Pierre, Transcript, Montreal, May 31, 1984 [vol. 2], pp. 351–52.)

Two types of regulation are currently employed to control foreign direct investment. First, the government completely or partly closes certain key sectors of the Canadian economy to foreign-controlled firms or allows them to enter and do business on terms less advantageous than those accorded to domestically controlled firms. Secondly, in 1973, Parliament passed the Foreign Investment Review Act, which the government replaced with the Investment Canada Act in 1985. Currently, foreign-controlled firms seeking to take over a Canadian firm, above a threshold level, or to establish a new business in Canada, must obtain prior approval from the federal Cabinet. A brief review of these two types of policies should provide a basis for considering the appropriate design for future regulations aimed at foreign-owned enterprises.

Both federal and provincial laws designate key economic sectors and formally reserve them for firms controlled by Canadian residents. We have seen several of the reasons for regulation. There is a widely perceived need to safeguard our cultural and political autonomy: hence reservation of broadcasting and newspaper publishing for Canadians. Only Canadian-controlled firms may harvest or exploit some types of natural resources. For example, foreign-controlled firms are not eligible to receive commercial fishing licences or leases, or licences to engage in uranium mining. Canadians are to obtain the maximum possible benefit from the exploitation of scarce resources that all citizens own. It is difficult, also, to enforce compliance with detailed regulations governing Canadian operations by resource firms based in foreign countries. Difficulties in ensuring compliance with consumer protection and other regulations or more broadly conceived views of the national interest have led to federal and/or provincial legislation restricting foreign investment in such areas as transportation, communications, insurance and trust operations.

Key-sector regulations also require foreign-owned firms operating in certain industries to compete with domestic firms under special conditions or restrictions. Federal banking law limits the share of the Canadian market that foreign-owned banks may hold. Federal energy laws enacted as part of the National Energy Program of 1980 provided Canadian-controlled energy companies with more favourable regulatory treatment in exploration grants than that accorded their foreign-owned rivals. The government defended its discriminatory treatment of foreign-based banks and petroleum companies on the grounds that exceptional national interests justified retaining Canadian control over the development of these key sectors. To some extent, these restrictions are transitional measures: Parliament has progressively liberalized the market-share limits applicable to banking in recent years. In addition, Ottawa intended the differential incentive measures in the energy sector to encourage foreign-based firms, which had traditionally controlled over 80 per cent of our domestic oil and gas industry, to increase their levels of Canadian equity ownership. In early 1985, the government announced the phasing out of these discriminatory exploration grants.

Closing a sector or type of activity to foreign investors or buying out or eliminating controlling interests in foreign-owned firms is the strongest form of regulatory action that a country can take. Such action depends on the assumption that the potential costs of foreign control clearly outweigh the potential benefits. In other words, this approach recognizes no trade-off between the advantages of domestic ownership and the economic gains that might accrue from the operation of foreign-owned enterprises. A strictly preventive approach to foreign investment might also provide unjustified protection to domestically owned firms and reduce those firms' incentives to improve their competitive performance. Because of these disadvantages, the government should close sectors only to defend compelling national interests. Some existing controls on service and natural resource industries may not meet such a standard. The government will probably review these measures, in any event, as bilateral and multilateral negotiations to liberalize trade in services will almost inevitably confront their use.

The Foreign Investment Review Act established a prior-screening procedure for foreign-controlled firms. Under this legislation, expert staff review all major foreign investments which involve an effective controlling interest. A detailed cost-benefit analysis of the proposed investment determines whether the establishment of the enterprise would confer "significant benefits" on Canada in the light of five rather vague statutory criteria, which identify such factors as job creation, technological innovation and export performance. The staff often negotiates with foreign investors to secure performance pledges designed to make the firm's proposed activities more beneficial to Canadians. These undertakings outline the business objectives of foreign investors and often include specific commitments concerning their likely purchases of goods and services from domestic suppliers, their anticipated export sales, and other probable benefits to Canada deriving from their investment. The staff does not exercise any official decision-making authority, but its recommendations have been highly influential in Cabinet decisions on applications. Since 1973, when the act establishing FIRA became law, the Cabinet has rejected only about 7 per cent of the foreign-investment proposals reviewed by FIRA, but critics have noted that this does not take account of the unknown number of discouraged investors who never applied.

On the strength of submissions that Commissioners received, of testimony put forward during our public hearings, and of analysis provided by our own research program, we believe that the FIRA process has increased the sensitivity of foreign investors to Canadian social values and economic goals. (For reasons explained below, we support some of the modifications in the present system set forth in the proposed Investment Canada Act.) FIRA's formal review procedure has encouraged pragmatic dialogue between public officials and foreign investors, and has given clear advance notice of Canada's standards of good corporate citizenship.

Commissioners believe, also, that recent public debates about FIRA have tended to exaggerate its coercive or restrictive effect. This misconstruction is primarily attributable to the strict ban on public disclosure of concrete information concerning FIRA applications, including the reasons for the Cabinet's disposition of these cases. Although the government has periodically issued policy guidelines governing FIRA applications, these statements of general principle have been a poor substitute for disclosure of the Cabinet's reasons for particular decisions, including those that led to FIRA recommendations. While the secrecy of the existing process may strengthen the bargaining position of FIRA staff in negotiating with foreign investors, it also risks discouraging desirable foreign firms from applying for approval of potentially productive enterprises.

Commissioners believe, moreover, that the government's failure to disclose the reasons for its past decisions has undermined political accountability in the FIRA process, and that reforms to clarify that process would also improve the quality of public debate on foreign-investment policies. There must, of course, be reasonable limits on disclosure to protect the proprietary interests and commercial secrets of FIRA applicants. These problems, however, arise in many fields of economic regulation, and Canadian regulatory agencies have evolved sophisticated procedures to protect the confidentiality of legitimate interests. As a means of overcoming or minimizing some of these problems, we recommend the creation of a quasi-judicial administrative tribunal to replace the existing Foreign Investment Review Agency and to assume the decision-making tasks currently assigned to the minister responsible for the agency and to the Cabinet. The main advantage of the proposed tribunal would be its ability to employ public hearings and to provide written reasons for government action.

In December 1984, the Canadian government tabled draft legislation in the form of Bill C-15 that proposed several significant changes in the existing process. First, foreign investments aimed at creating new businesses in Canada will no longer be subject to regulation, except when their operations may adversely affect certain Canadian cultural activities. Secondly, there will be reviews of foreign take-overs of existing Canadian firms, but applicants will no longer have to prove that their proposed investment will result in "significant benefits" to Canada. Proof of "net benefit" to Canadian economic development will be sufficient to secure approval for take-overs. Thirdly, a new agency known as Investment Canada will replace FIRA. Fourthly, Bill C-15 would make reviews applicable only to direct take-overs of firms with assets in excess of $5 million. (Under the existing legislation, all foreign direct investments involving businesses with assets of $250 000 or more are subject to regulatory scrutiny.) There would also be review of indirect acquisitions involving investments of $150 million or more. Commissioners endorse the government's proposals for scaling down the scope of regulation and lightening the burden on foreign investors of demonstrating that their business projects will be beneficial to Canadians. In view of the intense global competition to acquire new investment and new technology – and of Canada's comparatively poor performance in attracting direct foreign investment during the past decade – these proposed changes constitute a move in the right direction.

Just as Commissioners pointed earlier to the need for a more transparent decision-making procedure, we consider that the principal drawback to Bill C-15 is that it moves the final decision on foreign take-overs from the Cabinet to a single minister. At least, when the decision is subject to approval by the Cabinet as a whole, other departments have an opportunity to scrutinize the proposal, and the central agencies of government also have a chance to raise issues of public policy. While the Cabinet is too busy to examine all proposed take-overs, to assign exclusive decision-making powers to a single minister creates a substantial risk of arbitrary action.

We Commissioners base our preference for a quasi-judicial tribunal to review foreign investment primarily on the need for public proceedings and full public disclosure. Non-government intervenors should have a chance to argue the issues in public. Moreover, the tribunal should publish a report that sets out the economic, or other, policy reasons for its actions. In the past, the government claimed that the secrecy surrounding foreign-investment applications prevented disclosure of valuable proprietary information to existing or future business rivals. While we recognize the need for restricting access to sensitive information, these protective measures can be compatible with public proceedings and a general presumption in favour of full disclosure. Existing regulatory bodies, such as the Anti-Dumping Tribunal, encounter similar problems and have formulated procedures to protect legitimate commercial interests.

In addition, the foreign-investment agency should develop rules of procedure to avoid undue delay in the screening procedures. Perhaps it could usefully adopt a procedure whereby a case would automatically receive approval if the tribunal had not passed judgement within a specified period or had not notified the applicant of a need for delay.

In reviewing future foreign take-overs of Canadian-owned firms, the new agency, Investment Canada, should emphasize the likely consequences of the merger for the cost efficiency and technological progressiveness of the domestic industry. FIRA cases have too often neglected the vitality or intensity of competitive rivalry among both foreign and domestic firms in the many Canadian industries with relatively high levels of foreign participation. The review agency should consider whether a large multi-national may be attempting, through a firm that it controls, to secure an "undue" or excessive position of ownership in the domestic industry. The courts responsible for interpreting the Combines Investigation Act have found it difficult to decide the precise meaning of undue concentration or lessening of competition. Unconstrained by the limitations of criminal law, our proposed quasi-judicial tribunal would possess the requisite specialized knowledge to assess the probable impact of the foreign take-over on competition and other relevant aspects of industrial performance.

Since Commissioners recommend that the new administering authority analyse the competitive and technological conditions surrounding proposed foreign take-overs, it is desirable to raise the threshold for reviewability above the $5 million in assets proposed in Bill C-15. We propose a threshold of $50 million in assets. This modification would focus scarce enforcement resources on the larger and more critical take-overs. We endorse the government's proposal under Bill C-15 not to scrutinize new investments by foreign owners: the anti-competitive effect of these investments on the domestic industry is likely to be much smaller because, unlike take-overs, they increase the number of independent rivals competing in the market. Nevertheless, the government should monitor the effect of this exemption on competition in the Canadian economy generally.

In the future, the take-over/review process should exert a positive influence over the post-entry performance of foreign-controlled firms in Canada. One means of doing so would be through the reporting requirement that Commissioners propose for Canadian directors. Since review precedes actual entry by the foreign investor, its accuracy and effectiveness depend on forecasts and speculative assumptions concerning future economic conditions. Undertakings concerning future performance are invariably conditional on the accuracy of such forecasts and assumptions, and these economic uncertainties limit the reviewing agency's ability to insist on strict compliance. Moreover, the review process does not directly address the adverse consequences of foreign-government policies and informal directives aimed at Canadian subsidiaries or affiliates of multi-national enterprises. While the

Combines Investigation Act provides the federal Cabinet with broad powers to counter foreign policies and directives averse to Canadian interests, there has been no systematic monitoring or investigative effort.

Commissioners believe that the government should invest more resources in the collection and analysis of information that would permit the making of more accurate comparisons between the overall performances of foreign-controlled and domestic firms. The government should also impose standardized reporting requirements on all large firms, both foreign and domestic. We recommend that the directors of all major corporations, both domestic and foreign, be responsible for assessing and reporting on their firms' adherence to a formal code of conduct promulgated by the Cabinet. The federal government has set out a number of codes of conduct in the past, and these should serve as useful models. The 1976 OECD Declaration and its allied conventions recognized the legitimacy of general performance standards regarding, among other matters, technology transfer, export sales and the acquisition of goods and services from domestically owned suppliers.

Most major corporations in Canada now publish extensive annual and quarterly returns relating to their financial status and business activities, pursuant to company and securities laws. Commissioners recommend that in addition to fulfilling existing reporting obligations, all large Canadian and foreign-controlled firms (that is, those with assets of $50 million or more) be required to disclose annually information relevant to the proposed code of conduct, such as R&D expenditures, purchases from affiliated firms, and exports to affiliates and to unrelated buyers. These annual returns should focus on a limited number of quantifiable measures sufficiently standardized to permit comparisons among groups of firms. An amendment to the Corporations and Labour Unions Returns Act would seem the most appropriate strategy for implementing the proposed reporting scheme.

The Canada Business Corporations Act requires that a majority of directors of a Canadian corporation be "resident Canadians", and most provincial company acts incorporate a similar requirement.[48] These federal and provincial company laws do not, however, impose any particular duties or requirements on Canadian directors to ensure that a Canadian, as compared to a foreign, viewpoint affects corporate decision making. Yet surely, Canadian directors should seek to reflect in corporate decisions their beliefs concerning the ambitions and interests of our national community. Commissioners believe that it would be desirable to amend existing company laws to make clear provision obliging Canadian directors to ensure that Canadian interests receive serious and sustained consideration in the making of all important corporate decisions. Legislation should require Canadian directors to file an annual report, which would accompany the informational return just described, setting out their corporation's efforts to promote the performance objectives identified in the proposed general code of conduct. Such a reporting obligation would permit public scrutiny of the extent to which directors have discharged their responsibility to reflect Canadian interests.

Adjustment Policies

As Commissioners have already emphasized, measures to assist Canadians to adjust to the relentless ongoing changes under way in our economy should form an important component of Canadian industrial policy. These changes — massive during the present century — are a vital and unavoidable part of the economy's dynamic response to innovative and traditional forces that have produced substantial growth in our output, employment and standard of living. New industries thrive and grow, and growing competition at home and abroad, as well as pressures created by technological change, drive out older industries or force them to change. Alternatively, an industry may continue to prosper, but technological advances may drastically reduce the numbers of workers it employs, as has happened in agriculture. For the people involved, the process of change can be extremely painful, and thus they may vehemently resist it. Indeed, change is a process that inevitably generates considerable uncertainties which, in turn, have economically adverse effects. There is, therefore, ample justification, on both economic and social grounds, for the institution of policies aimed at facilitating adjustment and easing the hardship of transformation for those who are involved.

Throughout most of 1984 and into early 1985, Britain was embroiled in a bitter and violent strike by coal miners over proposals put forward by the government-owned National Coal Board to close down 20 uneconomic pits and terminate 20 000 jobs. The steel riots in Paris in early 1979 over proposals to phase out steel production and related jobs in regions with obsolete plants precipitated a similar reaction to the prospects of economic change. Both events are in some ways reminiscent of Britain's early-nineteenth-century Luddite movement, which violently protested against unemployment caused by the introduction of new machinery in the textile industry. The similarity of worker concerns over the span of almost two centuries is striking.

From a purely economic perspective, the case for government involvement in the adjustment process is tightly circumscribed. The interests of the economy as a whole are best served by the rapid shift of capital, human and other resources out of areas that provide relatively low value in terms of output of goods and services, into new areas of higher value. In the absence of constraints, this process proceeds in accordance with the dictates of market forces as part of a never-ending pursuit of maximum profits and incomes. It is a process involving a form of economic Darwinism — the survival of the fittest — in which the market-place rewards or penalizes investment and other decisions.

In line with this concept is the view that private-sector participants, who have a strong vested interest in the outcome of the process, are far more likely than governments to identify and respond properly to market developments. Therefore an economist who accepts this point of view can say little in favour of government intervention to alleviate the consequence of private risk taking by the owners of financial or physical capital.

In the case of labour (that is, human resources), the economic and social perspective on adjustment is rather different. The operation of market forces, for example, might result in unduly low expenditures for general education and training. Companies cannot be sure that such expenditures will yield adequate returns in the form of qualified new employees, and individuals not only lack the means to finance their own education or training, but also find it difficult to borrow (without government assistance) against prospective future earnings.

Clearly government must ensure the availability of general education and training. For similar reasons, government could help workers to adjust to change by providing financial support for retraining and relocation. This, of course, is quite a different matter from governments' helping to sustain unproductive enterprises simply to maintain existing employment. To sustain unproductive enterprises only impedes adjustments that must eventually be made.

By helping workers to adjust to change, government might help to reduce resistance to the process of change itself. It might also be argued that society has a social and ethical obligation to share the burden of adjustment. This sharing may require more than merely retraining and/or relocating displaced workers; it may require compensating them for some of the private costs of adjustment, such as the loss of investment in a home.

The political perspective on this matter is quite different in Canada from what it is in many other countries. Regional or local concentrations of firms and workers in hard-pressed industrial sectors often generate strong political pressure on government to intervene in order to sustain the firm or firms involved and to maintain the jobs of the workers they employ. Such intervention frequently retards, rather than facilitates, the process of changes, but since the full cost of impeding the process of adjustment is often not readily apparent, it does not generate much opposition. Trade-protective measures, such as tariffs and quotas, have the political virtue of appeasing both management and labour, while the costs of such protection are spread widely throughout the economy over time.

Where these instruments are not available, political pressures will often compel governments to provide various forms of subsidies to specific firms in order to sustain output and employment. These subsidies also have the political virtues of appeasing investors and workers simultaneously. While the costs are more visible than trade-protection measures, they often can be partially disguised by such off-budget devices as loan guarantees or loans at below-market interest rates. By contrast, government expenditures for labour-adjustment programs, such as retraining, early retirement, severance payments and mobility allowances, entail highly visible costs, as well as a potentially high-cost political acknowledgement that a particular sector cannot or will not be shielded from the adverse effects of market forces.

The political process in this country, therefore, is likely to lead to the adoption of policies that in many respects are quite different from the approach that would be suggested by economic and social considerations alone. Instead of easing the costs of labour adjustment, governments are likely to favour policies that postpone or retard the adjustment process, with concomitant reductions in national income and adverse effects on job creation over time. The effect of these policies has formerly been clearly evident in Canada, in the textile, clothing, footwear, shipbuilding and Nova Scotia coal-mining industries; all of these industries now face adjustment problems that are almost as large as, if not larger than, they have been at any time in the past, despite massive assistance through trade protection and firm subsidies.

The nature and seriousness of the policy dilemma is well illustrated by the textile industry. For 1979 alone, the cost to the economy per job saved by the protection through tariffs and quotas of the Canadian textile and clothing industry was estimated to be $34 500,[49] while in the same year, the average income of Canadian textile workers was $10 000. This suggests that if protection were removed and all Canadian textile workers lost their jobs as a result – an unlikely outcome – the money saved each year would be sufficient to provide income to those workers, amounting to two or even three times their real 1979 earnings for the remainder of the years they were of working age, and still offer some additional savings to benefit Canadian textile consumers in the form of lower prices.[50]

Canadians are confronted with the challenge of devising policies that will facilitate, rather than retard, rapid economic adjustment, while at the same time providing generous assistance to the individuals most affected by change. Economic and ethical considerations require this conjunction of policies. The experience of Japan and West Germany in the post-war period suggests that a strong commitment to rapid adjustment is vital to a healthy economy, while the post-war experience of Britain suggests that the lack of such a commitment is a recipe for serious economic stagnation. The Japanese and West German experiences also suggest the importance of well-conceived adjustment policies to ease the costs of change, particularly for labour. Can we confer on our own political institutions the capacity to generate a similar mixture of policies?

The government must give a high priority to the development and implementation of public policies that will facilitate rapid adjustment. On both social and economic grounds, there are compelling reasons why government should adopt measures that will ease the problems of transition and cover a reasonable share of the costs of adjustment for those workers and their families who are caught up in the process of change. The institution of such policies and programs should, in turn, help to reduce governments' resistance to change.

Governments should not be diverted from adopting effective adjustment measures by the argument that in a recession they cannot be afforded, and that in times of economic growth they are unnecessary. Even in times of high unemployment, growing industries are often impeded by a lack of workers with particular skills. For example, a recent survey of 4012 establishments in Canada discovered that approximately half of the 1354 respondents reported hiring difficulties during 1977 to 1979, and 43 per cent anticipated shortages during the following five years. Conversely, in periods of rapid economic growth and low unemployment, there may still be some declining industries. Workers in such industries may have trouble finding new jobs either because they lack the necessary skills or because of their reluctance to move to another area.

Policy makers must determine whether a particular sector is undergoing only a short-term slump, or whether it is in a long-term decline as a result of underlying economic forces. To determine which sectors of the economy will disappear (or be completely transformed, as has occurred in the agriculture sector over the last half century) is no easier than to forecast the sources of others. Canada's shipbuilding industry, for example, has been confronted by serious difficulties over a period of many years. Does it lack comparative international advantages, or are advantages in certain areas being obscured because of subsidies provided by foreign governments to their own shipbuilding industries? Conceivably, our shipbuilders could meet international competition in certain select areas if other nations would also abandon the granting of trade-distorting subsidies.

In the Cape Breton coal mining industry, the widely-accepted judgement at the end of the 1960s was that the industry was not viable and should be phased out. Following the sharp increase in world oil prices initiated by the Organization of Petroleum Exporting Countries (OPEC) beginning in 1973, coal prices began to rise substantially, and the coal industry has now expanded. Although coal prices have subsequently declined somewhat from their previous peak, it is difficult to predict the future of the industry in view of continuing uncertainty about the price and supply of Middle East oil, and of more guarded predictions about the prospects for nuclear power.

While the domestic textile industry has long been troubled, Canadian exports to the United States have grown significantly in recent years, and the introduction of technological advances that substitute capital for labour suggest that at least some elements of this industry are, or could become, internationally competitive. Within recent years, both the Canadian automobile and farm-machinery/manufacturing industries have faced severe economic difficulties, as have those in the United States, with which our industries are closely associated. In both countries, the farm-implement industry continues to face a severe slump. Is the problem confronting that industry cyclical in nature? Or is it indicative of a long-term structural decline? As a result of substantial cost-cutting economies, the introduction of models more closely suited to market demand, the economic upturn, and the imposition of quotas on Japanese vehicle imports, the Canadian and U.S. auto industries have experienced a strong recovery. Has the automotive industry recovered, or will it again encounter severe difficulties if protective quotas imposed on the import of Japanese vehicles are lifted? Is the recent lifting of U.S. quotas on Japanese vehicle imports sufficient to jeopardize the Canadian auto industry?

Difficult as these questions are for private sector decision makers intimately acquainted with an industry's problems and potential, they are even more difficult for public sector policy makers, who usually lack this detailed knowledge, and who are often confronted by representations from those involved that obscure the realities of the situation. Governments should exercise caution in implementing adjustment policies designed to have long-run structural effects. The goal should be to develop policies that minimize the risk of major systematic errors in judgement. Flexibility, adaptability and reversibility are more easily attainable if decentralized judgements by those affected by an industry's future prospects dominate centralized public sector judgements. The provision of adjustment assistance to displaced workers, for example, leaves each individual free to determine what course to follow in seeking other employment opportunities.

Earlier in this section, we suggested that political forces would tend to invert policy requirements that appear to be dictated by economic and, to a lesser extent, social or ethical considerations. Political forces will tend to favour, in descending order, trade protection to preserve output and employment, individual subsidies to firms to enable them to maintain output and employment, and subsidies to labour to facilitate its mobility. Governments must find policy options that reduce the degree of conflict between policies dictated by good politics and those dictated by good economics and proper social concerns. We shall examine these policy options below.

Trade Policy

When important sectors of the economy face severe import pressures, benign acceptance by government is an unrealistic response. Affected workers and firms may demand various forms of relief: resort to unilateral escape clauses provided in international agreements, imposition of anti-dumping duties, or pressures on particular exporting countries to establish "voluntary" export quotas. Many countries have resorted to protection in recent years, a move that runs counter to the best interests of all nations. One means of restricting protectionism might be an international agreement tightly restricting such actions. The agreement could require that if a government imposes protection, it would have also to institute an adjustment strategy aimed at reducing capacity in the affected sector or at increasing its efficiency through restructuring.

To make institutional changes domestically could also prove beneficial. Governments could make information widely available about the expected costs and benefits of proposed protective measures. The Canadian Tariff Board, for example, could investigate and hold public hearings on proposed restrictions. In its report, the board could estimate the expected costs and benefits, express a judgement on the measures proposed, and recommend other means of assistance that might involve an alternative to trade protection. The government would, of course, be free to accept, reject or modify such recommendations, but the information provided, the submissions made during hearings, and the views of a responsible tribunal would provide an extensive base for judging the course of action adopted by political authorities. The agency charged with this responsibility should have a broad economic focus, as does the Tariff Board, not a specialized mission concerned with particular interests, such as the Textile and Clothing Board. The U.S. International Trade Commission and the Australian Industry Assistance Commission perform functions similar to those proposed.

To offset pressures from producers for protection, it might be desirable to provide financial assistance to consumer-interest groups. It might also be desirable to alter the political dynamics that lead to adoption of policies that are opposed to the long-term economic interests of the nation. New laws governing the financing of political campaigns, for example, could reduce the dependence of political parties on contributions from producer interests, perhaps through providing electoral subsidies.

While the federal government will continue to protect particular sectors against the severe competition of foreign imports, at least for limited periods, we should consider what form this protection should take. To establish long-term quotas on imports from abroad is undesirable, as such quotas virtually guarantee domestic producers a share of the market, whether or not they take any steps to increase their competitiveness. A better course would be to establish a constant tariff duty. The costs of foreign competitors will probably decline, enabling a growing proportion of their product to surmount the tariff barrier. The result will be an orderly contraction in the market share of the domestic industry if that industry is unable to keep pace. An alternative would be gradually to reduce the amount of the tariff, as is the usual practice in implementing international trade-agreement reductions.

Firm Subsidies

If trade-protection measures were more constrained legally and politically, governments might attempt to preserve industry output and employment against stiff foreign competition by granting subsidies to specific firms. Such subsidies, however, tend to block or retard adjustment. Subsidies entail most of the same economic costs as a tariff because they often have a similar effect. In a well-functioning capital system, few shortcomings in the market – sometimes referred to as "market failure" – justify subsidies to declining sectors. Government assistance to modernize may be necessary to make an industry or firm internationally competitive, but an obsolete plant is often the result, rather than the cause, of loss of international competitiveness.[51] Firms able to cover only variable costs must allow their fixed assets to run down, thus reducing their long-term capacity to remain efficient producers. If new fixed assets could produce an adequate return, the capital market would presumably provide the necessary funds. If the government proposes assistance to help a firm achieve long-run competitiveness and profitability, the public should be sceptical, for such assistance is normally dictated by a negative assessment on the part of the private capital market of the viability of the investment target.

Even the effectiveness of industrial subsidies in maintaining jobs is open to some question. To establish such a case, it is necessary to assume that a given number of jobs in a certain firm are of an incremental nature and, therefore, would not be maintained in the absence of a subsidy. Even if this is so, a subsidy to a specific firm will not serve to maintain employment unless its jobs are incremental in nature with respect to the industry as a whole. This would be so if no subsidy were paid to a failing firm, and if other companies in the industry failed to increase output and employment sufficiently to take up the slack caused by such a failure. Even in a situation where jobs are of an incremental nature both in a specific firm and in the industry as a whole, the question that remains is whether they are incremental in the case of the economy as a whole. In other words, if no subsidy were paid, would there be a net reduction in the total number of jobs in the country? Subsidies use resources that might help to create a greater number of more productive jobs elsewhere in the economy. Subsidies to troubled firms in declining sectors often preserve the most marginal and least competitive companies; thus they work against the efficient restructuring of the economy and the creation of new, more enduring jobs.

If political pressures nevertheless dictate that subsidies will be granted to firms in declining sectors, to assist the strongest, not the weakest, firms would seem a superior strategy. Governments could assume some of the costs associated with mergers, consolidations and orderly reduction of physical capacity. Recent bail-outs of failing firms in Canada have overlooked such opportunities. Three farm-machinery companies in financial distress (Massey-Ferguson, Cooperative Implements, White Farm) have received substantial aid from the federal government, although firms and the industry as a whole have serious excess productive capacity. There appears to have been no attempt to facilitate mergers or otherwise rationalize production. A major trucking firm (Maislin Trucking) was bailed out (although it ultimately failed), despite excess capacity in the industry and possibilities of merger with other long-haul carriers with similar route networks. The bail-out of the Atlantic fish-processing companies, while industry wide in focus, still result in the maintenance of many inefficient branch processing plants.

If some firm-directed subsidies are politically unavoidable, they should take a form that minimizes the prospects of recurrent demands for assistance. Governments should attach conditions to the assistance, including orderly contraction of productive capacity or rationalization.

One danger inherent in this proposed approach is that the governments may make an erroneous judgement about the future of an industry. Conditional assistance could induce major structural changes predicated on erroneous projections of how the market will evolve, either because of poor judgement or on account of an unforeseeable change in circumstances at home or abroad. Perhaps governments could reduce this danger by leaving with the industry in question the initiative for making restructuring proposals, rather than imposing a centrally conceived blueprint solution. Moreover, as British and, to a lesser extent, French experience indicates, to induce mergers and consolidations courts the danger of assembling elaborate corporate umbrellas that mask the perpetuation of inefficient multi-branch operations. Orderly contraction and the reinforcement of points of strength in the industry should become the primary object of policy. The use of a buffer body, such as the Canadian Industrial Renewal Board, to implement policies marked by this industry-wide focus may enable political leaders to "distance" themselves from political interests demanding other forms of subsidy.

A further policy refinement would be to discourage the use of low-subsidy instruments that have little or no visibility. A tighter GATT Non-Tariff Barrier Code on Government Procurement could, for instance, require costing of off-budget subsidies such as loan guarantees and the provision of loans at below-market interest rates. Inclusion of these costs in government-expenditure budgets and spending envelopes at the time that the assistance is provided would increase visibility and accountability.

Labour-Adjustment Policies

If the government accomplished these policy changes, political attention would shift to the adjustment costs faced by labour, which is where both economic and social analysis suggest placing the focus. Part V of this Report addresses in depth the key issues respecting labour-adjustment policies. The suggested reforms emphasize help to labour-force participants seeking jobs. Commissioners consider on-the-job training more beneficial than institutional training. Furthermore, suggested reforms to the Unemployment Insurance (UI) system would encourage workers to seek out remunerative and stable jobs as compared to those in which they are constantly subject to lay-offs.

An alternative approach that Commissioners have considered corresponds to the West German and Japanese systems of conditional unemployment-insurance benefits. After a period of unconditional benefits lasting, say, 16 weeks, the government could require a recipient to participate in a retraining program in order to continue to qualify for benefit payments. The assumption is that after a period of time, an unsuccessful job search indicates a need for different or up-graded skills. A significant portion of UI expenditures, therefore, would underwrite the costs of job retraining. Conditional unemployment-insurance benefits also minimize open-ended support to a labour-force participant. As with firm-specific subsidies, it is important that the recipient adopt some course of action that minimizes the prospects of recurrent demands for support.

Notwithstanding these supposed advantages, Commissioners prefer maintenance of an unconditional approach to unemployment insurance. This approach, in our view, is more consistent with reliance on individual judgement about future employment options or retraining. Our proposed reforms would encourage labour-force participants to be more active in exercising such judgements. Improved retraining and mobility programs would complement this approach.

To improve existing retraining and mobility policies, Commissioners put forward several suggestions. The federal government should require all larger employers to register job vacancies with Canada Employment Centres. This would help to overcome the serious problems arising from the lack of adequate information about such vacancies across the country, which, in turn, impairs the ability of the centres to fill vacancies with individuals who are unemployed or about to be laid off. The provision of more detailed data on specific occupations and systematic medium-term forecasts of prospective skill shortages would facilitate better matching of present or future unemployed persons with institutional or on-the-job retraining programs geared to meet their needs.

Government should remedy several shortcomings in present institutional training programs. These programs are often of too short duration to provide significant higher-skills training; too few places are available for qualified and interested candidates; living allowances for trainees are inadequate, and student loans are not applicable to such programs; and federal-provincial financing arrangements give a largely exclusive right of participation in these programs to provincial educational institutions and generally exclude private sector training institutions, thus precluding more diversified judgements about future employment opportunities. Part V also recommends that more emphasis be placed on on-the-job training.

To facilitate the mobility of the labour force, governments should increase the assistance provided to workers who must move to jobs in new locations; this aid now covers only a part of direct costs. In addition, the Government of Canada should use part of the Unemployment Insurance savings generated by proposals outlined in Part V to assist adjustment by broadening early-retirement schemes for older workers (perhaps those between the ages of 60 and 65) as the French have done. At present, this approach eases adjustments in the textile, clothing, footwear and tanning industries. Moreover, federal and provincial governments should consider increasing the portability of private pension plans through requiring early vesting of employer contributions as a further means of increasing labour mobility. Governments might also require major employers to provide time for employees to participate in programs of skills up-grading. Commissioners elaborate on this proposal in Part V.

We Commissioners propose the adoption of these policies in the hope that they will facilitate the redeployment of labour from declining to expanding sectors of the economy, by easing the transition costs of individual workers involved in such shifts. In this respect, the effect of these policies is quite different from general UI programs or programs designed to provide extended unemployment benefits to specific sectors, such as the Canada Textile Adjustment program or the U.S. Trade Adjustment Assistance program. Indeed, many of these latter programs appear to retard, rather than promote, adjustment. The proposals that we recommend here would integrate social policy with economic policy much more fully; Japanese, West German, Scandinavian and, to a lesser extent, French experience suggests that such integration is pivotal to effective employment adjustment.

An important problem that we have not yet dealt with involves the costs to the many Canadians who are directly or indirectly dependent on declining industries in depressed communities. These costs are both financial and psychic, ranging from depreciation in the resale value of a home and increased taxes for municipal and other services to residents who remain behind, to the loss of social amenities. Given the complex politics of intervention, governments often use trade protection or subsidies to avoid facing up to such problems. They might best reconcile political and economic considerations by assisting those communities with the highest adjustment costs; the political costs of failing to intervene there are also likely to be high. Governments should generously subsidize any large-scale exit from a community of workers and their families. This assistance might include generous severance packages for older workers and compensation for the depreciation in the resale value of houses, for loss of social amenities and, through assistance to municipalities, for higher per capita public service costs for those remaining behind in the community.

To concentrate resources on inducing people to leave severely distressed communities can help to limit budgetary expenditures. The Industrial and Labour Adjustment Program, recently terminated, had some of these features. This program designated twelve communities as distressed. However, it was temporary and modestly financed, and it focused excessively on providing financial assistance to firms to remain or to relocate in designated communities. Adjustment assistance to individuals overly stressed creation of temporary jobs in the designated communities. In short, the program appeared to embrace and confuse cyclical and structural concerns. Nonetheless, it suggests productive new policy directions.

A revised community/industry-adjustment program should be made a permanent feature of Canada's industrial policy. Adopting structural adjustment policies only in recessions, when resources are limited, is likely to be much less effective and more costly than adjustment policies directed to declining sectors in a generally more buoyant economic environment. Japanese legislation relating to structurally depressed industries exemplifies a longer-term perspective on adjustment in declining sectors.

In community/industry-adjustment programs, government must judge whether communities or sectors are in long-term decline. If, for example, three years ago, the federal and Ontario governments had designated the automobile industry and communities such as Windsor as distressed, and had induced a major exodus of labour, it is clear, with the benefit of hindsight, that they would have been making a serious mistake. This example suggests the wisdom of using extreme caution in applying radical policies to facilitate a major exodus from supposedly declining communities on the basis of short-term evidence of industrial difficulties.

Transportation, Communications Services and Other Infrastructure Support Services

Canada's vast continental land mass and sparse population has made transportation and communication facilities a political and social necessity, as well as a fundamental part of our economic foundation. Transportation and communication have increasingly become necessary complements of each other in some areas and competitors in others. Efficient inventory control in the manufacturing sector depends on both these sectors. Communication systems also vitally affect modern capital markets, enabling investment capital to move swiftly within the global village.

The transportation and communication infrastructure are both important industries in themselves and also vital to production in all other industries. This infrastructure also determines the extent to which we Canadians communicate with one another, and the way in which we define ourselves as a nation. Canadians in more remote locations are concerned with how southern or urban Canada manages its transportation and communication needs. Those who live in remote areas view these links as vital to their economy and their very definition of being Canadian.

Atlantic Canada has received heavy subsidization for many components of its transportation system. The long debate over the Crow's Nest Pass Freight rate (the Crow Rate) has historically underlined the importance of transportation to Western Canada. Central Canada's concerns include the upgrading of the St. Lawrence Seaway and the effect of U.S. deregulation on trucking and railway industries. While the East-West transportation and communications infrastructures have always been vital, they have – as has the Canadian economy as a whole – been in constant tension with the continental pull both of geography and of the economic strength of the U.S. economy. Approximately 40 per cent of the oil and gas Canadians consume flows through pipelines that pass through the United States. The St. Lawrence Seaway and the Great Lakes system are a shared marine asset. Significant portions of the business of Canadian railways, trucking companies and airlines are continental. The cross-border flow of tourists, and, hence, many large and small local economies, depend on the quality of several modes of transportation. Trade between Canada and the United States amounted to $150 billion in 1984.

Transportation and communications issues are likely to be even more challenging in the future than they have been in the past. Several issues confront policy makers, including the need to respond to the deregulation of transportation in the United States in the rail, air and trucking sectors; the need to develop technologically sophisticated and environmentally safe transportation systems for frontier and offshore oil and gas development; the need to modernize the Western rail and grain-handling systems; the need to respect individual choice while maintaining our national identity, which may be threatened by increased access to American television programming through the use of satellite dishes and other technologies; and the need to deal with the potential growth of interlocking ownership among transportation and communications enterprises, including Crown and mixed public and private enterprises.

While it is essential for Canada to maintain a competitive and efficient transportation and communications system, Commissioners believe that policies governing these facilities must take account of a wide variety of economic and social goals. Basic changes to the system or new large-scale investments inevitably and necessarily raise major political considerations. Controversies over the building of the Canadian Pacific Railway (CPR), the formation of The Canadian National Railway (CNR), the Trans-Canada Pipeline, the St. Lawrence Seaway, the Alaska Highway Natural Gas Pipeline, the Crow rate, and airline deregulation testify to these realities.

The 1967 National Transportation Act is indicative of present dilemmas. At its most basic level, the legislation supports the principle of "intermodal competition". Transport Canada and the Canadian Transport Commission, however, have been primarily concerned, at least until recently, with ensuring that the national transportation system responds to the government's economic objectives of wide-ranging growth, stabilization and income redistribution. Since the 1970s, government policy has increasingly reflected the view that the national transportation system has matured, that intermodal competition exists, and, therefore, that it is possible to meet the needs of the economy without such a high level of government intervention across the entire system.[52] Policy is directed towards maintaining a complex network of "managed markets", as they involve a number of transportation sectors. The same can be said of the overall policy approach to telecommunications and broadcasting.

A study undertaken for this Commission compares intergovernmental regulatory trends in three sectors: airlines, telecommunications, and securities and financial markets.[53] Government regulation in these sectors has evolved from a form of policing to a promotional function, and subsequently to a planning format. The former policing function involved a narrower focus, similar to basic public-utility regulation, while the latter planning format involved decisions aimed at meeting a wider range of goals, including regional and social goals. The former was passive and adjudicative, while the latter required more activity. This active role was a product of a variety of pressures on both the federal and the provincial governments. The provinces have been involved in a threefold sense: as regulators themselves, as representatives of interests in these sectors, and as the owners of their own transportation and communications enterprises. Given the rapidly changing technology in these areas, combined with some of the realities of recent U.S. deregulation measures, this Commission's study suggests that selective deregulation measures be adopted in this country. This does not necessarily suggest that all aspects of these operations should be governed by market forces, but rather that selective reductions should be made in regulation. Commissioners support this general approach.

Our earlier reviews of the regulatory framework referred to the need for selective deregulation in a number of areas because of such factors as the rate of technological change (especially in telecommunications), U.S. deregulation measures (especially in transportation), and the need to enhance competitive forces in the Canadian economy. Our consideration of competition policy suggested that the concern should not be corporate concentration *per se*, but rather public and private actions that tend to restrict competition. Increases in corporate concentration in Canada's transportation and communications sectors have been significant, but whether they have been made at the expense of competition is more questionable.

Our earlier analysis of the role of Crown corporations and mixed enterprise is also relevant, since it is the combined presence of extensive regulations plus public enterprise that distinguishes the Canadian public-policy approach to transportation from that of the United States. Thus, deregulation of air transportation may make only limited sense unless it is accompanied by the sale of Air Canada. Over recent decades, both levels of government have used Crown corporations extensively in the transportation and communications sectors.

Let us consider, also, the role of mixed enterprises such as Telesat Canada. The ownership structure of Telesat Canada is such that this institution has become a vehicle for slowing down, or at least managing, the introduction of new technology potentially useful to its member shareholding firms, but at the same time, threatening to existing land-based telephone systems, many of which are owned by provincial governments that hold shares in Telesat Canada. The 1977 Cabinet decision to allow Telesat Canada to join the TransCanada Telephone System (TCTS), which informally regulated transcontinental rates, further complicates the interlocking public-private/ownership structures. Whatever may be claimed about its role in stabilizing technology, TCTS cannot be said to have aided competition.

A related issue concerns the degree to which a Crown corporation, such as Canada Post, will be allowed to compete and transform itself into a full-fledged communications company. We usually think of Canada Post in terms of its historic labour-relations and deficit problems, but its future viability is inextricably linked to its competitive capabilities. Business critics want its deficit eliminated, but object to its competing in private sector services. At the same time, Canada Post is losing business to competitors, which helps to account for its deficit.

In a very different vein, Commissioners wish to consider key concerns about the future of the Canadian Broascasting Corporation (CBC) in the communications industry. While we Canadians think of the CBC as a cultural enterprise, it is also the key to what a growing telecommunications industry can become. Requiring the CBC to compete in order to obtain revenue is perhaps not the way to proceed. The best policy might be to subsidize the CBC fully so that it need not compete for advertising dollars, thus leaving it free to foster both culture and the arts industry.

Another factor which Commissioners wish to note about policy trends is that federal spending on transportation and communications as a percentage of total federal expenditure, after a short burst of increases in the early 1970s, has steadily declined from 7.3 per cent in 1974[54] to 5.3 per cent in 1982. The expenditures arising from the Crow agreement will result in some increased investment, but the data show that prior to this decision, support for railway infrastructure had been shrinking. Provincial expenditure data show a similar pattern of overall decline in all provinces except Alberta.

Declines in the share of spending are not necessarily causes for concern in themselves. Juxtaposed with probable capital-infrastructure needs over the next two decades, however, the relative decline in public investment becomes a serious problem that must be reversed. In 1981, Transport Canada indicated that the task of replacing aging capital stock in the transportation sector (including pipelines, but excluding passenger-railway facilities) would require more than $90 billion in total public and private sector investment.[55] This figure does not include potential federal transportation investments in energy-resource projects, such as those in the Beaufort Sea, off the Newfoundland shore, and in the Arctic.

These expenditure requirements, apart from the sheer size of the investment involved, illustrate how key transportation decisions must be linked to mega-project resource developments and to the regulatory framework and federal-provincial/overlapping-approval processes. Transportation investments associated with resource developments involve long lead times, as do the resource projects themselves; thus, long-term market stability is important. Resource markets, however, are unstable. Almost invariably, resource mega-projects involve both the federal government and the provinces. The complex consortia of firms involved in a large-scale resource undertaking usually ask governments to provide substantial subsidies or at least to share a significant proportion of the risks involved. Commissioners urge federal and provincial governments to try to achieve the greatest possible co-ordination of the approvals processes governing major new projects. We are also well aware, however, that extensive time may be required to work out risk-sharing arrangements between governments and private sector participants as they apply both to the proposed resource developments and to the provision of associated new transportation facilities.

As we have indicated, the estimated levels of future investment required in transportation do not include those applicable to passenger-rail facilities. While recent attention has focused on the "on again, off again" status of a number of Via Rail's passenger services, there are serious long-term/investment decisions to be made that have major economic and political ramifications. Economically, the best receptor for enhanced passenger-rail service is in the Quebec-Windsor corridor. To provide this service would require a massive government investment to construct the track bed required for high-speed trains to compete effectively with other modes of transport. Much of this very large investment would favour Central Canada, a fact that, of course, displeases other parts of the country. Until these political conflicts of interest are resolved, rail service will probably be based on half-measures that result in poor service and further deficits.

Commissioners consider that there is a need for an increased level of government and private investment in the transportation and communications fields over the next two decades. We see a strong role for Crown corporations continuing in this sector as a whole, but we suggest that privatization might make sense in selected areas. At the same time, we are also concerned about the degree of regulation that persists in certain areas of transportation and communications.

The U.S. move toward deregulation of a number of transportation industries may leave Canada with no practical choice but to follow suit, at least in some measure. In their cross-border business, for example, Canadian railways already face the effects of this deregulation because U.S. railways can make agreements or contracts on a bilateral basis with shippers, without having to register or table their rates before U.S. regulators. Since Canadian railways could be harmed by this competition, selective deregulation should be allowed in Canada for this kind of cross-border traffic. The deregulation of U.S. trucking also affects the Canadian trucking industry. The Economic Council of Canada's study of the Canadian trucking industry[56] argued that considerable deregulation in Canada would be desirable and feasible. We believe that a gradual movement towards partial deregulation of trucking is sensible, keeping in mind the differences in the nature of the Canadian market. Commissioners see a general need for governments to favour a more market-oriented approach in the transportation and communications sector than is currently the practice.

Intervention Guidelines for Industrial Development

Markets are the primary means for allocating resources in the Canadian economy. While Canadian markets do not correspond to the perfect markets usually described in textbooks, many are highly efficient. In most circumstances, it is unrealistic to expect governments to out-perform the market in determining the proper allocation of resources through direct intervention aimed at influencing the activity of any particular sector or firm. Nevertheless, there are certain limited cases in which reasonable economic grounds may exist for considering such intervention. Commissioners have discussed how a well-designed adjustment policy can help the market to transfer labour and capital out of declining sectors and into expanding sectors with a minimum of disruption. We now consider the circumstances in which a more direct form of government intervention can help to promote economic development.

In its broadest terms, government intervention may be warranted in situations in which there exists what economists often refer to as a "market failure". Such failure arises when costs or benefits to third parties are not fully reflected in market transactions. Public goods and services often provide tangible and intangible benefits difficult to price in the market or to charge to those who use them. Defence provides what is regarded as a public good, and certain kinds of knowledge and information could fall into the same category. A case can be made, for example, for government subsidization of research and development through tax assistance, grants and other means. This research may lead to the creation of knowledge that will add to the public good, through the development, for instance, of a new strain of wheat that will significantly increase the crop yields of Canadian farmers.

Government intervention may be required in situations where the technology is such that large-scale operations produce substantial economies. In the more extreme cases, this factor may lead inevitably to the creation of what are often considered to be natural monopolies, particularly where utilities such as telephone and electrical power services are involved. Simply because their monopoly position carries with it substantial economic power, such utilities are almost universally subject to public regulation and/or operated by government-owned corporations. Many transportation facilities are also provided or subsidized by governments. Unfortunately, in many instances, these subsidies have been established at levels substantially in excess of those required to promote the development of an efficient transportation system. The St. Lawrence Seaway is a good example of a transportation project that because of its high fixed costs, could never have been undertaken except by government.

Some economists have argued that private-sector companies are unduly averse to assuming risks, and that as a result they are biased against involvement in large risky projects in which capital investment will be recovered, at best, only over a long period of time. The private sector's discount rate for a high-risk project may include an exceptionally high premium to cover the risk. While a private company or companies might conclude that the resulting discount rate or expected return was unacceptably low, a government might conclude that it was justified to assume some (or all) of the risks involved, because of the high social benefits the project would yield in relation to its prospective costs. This, at least in part, appears to have been the reasoning behind the support governments have provided to certain mega-projects over the past decade or so.

Another reason for government intervention is to assist "infant industries". Governments hope that with a modicum of support, such industries will become self-sustaining and thus create jobs and income. For this type of approach to be successful, long-term gains must exceed initial short-term losses. A great disappointment has been the failure of many infant industries to grow up. This history leads Commissioners to be sceptical about government support of infant industries.

Governments have also cited the small size of the Canadian market in relation to minimum efficient plant size in justifying intervention to rationalize the structure of production. The problem of sub-optimal scale plants which produce only for the domestic market is caused by the tariff. Ironically, therefore, government intervention is required in this sort of situation to undo the effects of its earlier intervention.

There are some industrial policies that do not deal with specific market failures, but do have an economic rationale. The government defends as necessary certain policies to assist industries to compete internationally or to protect domestic industries from foreign competition in order to match the assistance provided by other countries to their own domestic industries. Commissioners believe, however, that a better approach to this problem would be for the government to continue to work to minimize trade-distorting practices. Only if such an approach were to fail, and only if the counter-subsidies appeared to have the potential of inducing the "other side" to desist from its interventionist policy, should our government contemplate intervention.

Many national governments are inclined to support domestic industry, particularly in the manufacturing sector. This inclination no doubt reflects the degree to which manufacturing industries are exposed to international competition. Canadian tax incentives for manufacturing and processing, such as the lower tax rate and capital-consumption/ allowance rate on a two-year basis, as well as the emphasis on manufacturing in most federal government, industrial assistance programs, can be justified in terms of the support other countries give to their manufacturing sectors. Nevertheless, it is Commissioners' conviction that all countries would probably be better off with a more neutral tax and expenditure system.

Small business is another sector that has been favoured by the government. Arguments in favour of such support usually cite the entrepreneurial dynamism of the sector and the benefits to be derived in the form of increased growth in output and employment.

The promotion of regional development is another important goal of government policy. As a general rule, regional development is not designed to compensate for any of the traditional causes of market failure. Instead, it is based on a broader national objective that all areas should share in the benefits of growth in output and employment, and hence, that industrial activity should be spread more equally across the country. The investment tax credit is regionally differentiated to encourage investment in high-unemployment regions of the country. The Industrial and Regional Development Program (IRDP), the federal government's main industrial grants program, is structured to provide greater incentives in high-unemployment regions. However, regionally differentiated tax and expenditure programs can retard overall economic growth and distort the pattern of development.

Objectives other than improving economic efficiency are often the motivating force behind industrial policies. Redistribution of income from one group to another is frequently a prime consideration. As a general rule, industrial policies are not a good means of achieving this objective. Nevertheless, because producers' groups can benefit substantially from many policies, whereas the losses tend to be diffused much more generally among the public, there can be considerable political pressure for industrial policies to be directed towards the redistribution of incomes.

While market failures can result in inefficiencies that may warrant government intervention, the political process itself also has failings that must be taken into account. A government's preoccupation with income redistribution, for example, may cause it to overlook or ignore other measures that could correct the existing failure in the operation of the market-place. The underlying situation may, therefore, be made worse by government intervention intended to improve it. This paradox should give pause to those who call for interventionist solutions for every failing in the market, however minor. It is only in the case of very serious market failings that intervention is likely to be at all helpful.

Since government will inevitably intervene to promote economic development, it is useful to have some criteria for determining where intervention is warranted. The first criterion is that an intervention should be considered only if it is likely to improve the allocation of resources and, hence, real growth; it is necessary that projected benefits exceed projected costs by a significant margin. While cost-benefit analysis is not a precise science, it does offer a variety of useful techniques for evaluating specific industrial policies and programs. The application of this and other evaluation methodologies by the program-evaluation divisions of departments and agencies, with the assistance of the Comptroller General's office, should be important in identifying, and subsequently discontinuing, those programs that are not producing net benefits.

For those interventions which, in addition to improving the allocation of resources, also have non-economic objectives, it is necessary to have a second criterion: that a non-economic objective should be achieved at the least cost. The same evaluation tools mentioned above can be used to analyse the relative effectiveness of programs in accomplishing given objectives.

The government should not allow intervention expenditures to become open ended. Instead, it should establish a strict budgetary limit to serve as a fence around the expenditure of public funds. All too often, an expenditure commitment to support a particular sector, industry or firm has been permitted to escalate far beyond original budget levels.

It is very important that all industrial policies and programs be subject to the closest possible government scrutiny. The presumption must be that in the great majority of cases, the market is the best-available mechanism for resource allocation. The burden of proof must be on those who propose intervention. The economy will be more dynamic and its development prospects better if greater emphasis is placed on the market, and less on government intervention, as the engine of development.

If the case for intervention proves to be compelling, then it is also important that the government choose the most appropriate instrument. Commissioners strongly believe that the instrument which is most consistent with a market-oriented approach should be selected. For this reason, we prefer tax incentives to selective grant programs and both to direct regulation. Tax incentives are more generally available than grants and do not involve the exercise of administrative discretion. They tend, therefore, to have a less distortionary effect on the market-place than do grants. Both tax incentives and grants leave the final production and pricing decisions in private hands, whereas regulation transfers some of the more important of these decisions to government and its agents.

A Commitment to a Strengthened Economic Union

A key component of this Commission's mandate is to make recommendations to secure and strengthen the Canadian economic union. Part VI of this Report addresses this aspiration and advances extensive recommendations. At this juncture, Commissioners simply wish to point out the importance of a strong economic union for the implementation of effective industrial policies. Indeed, a strong economic union and effective industrial policies are interdependent. Given the division of power and authority between the federal and provincial governments in this area, it is not possible for effective industrial support to be provided unless the policies and programs of the two orders of government are reasonably harmonious and mutually reinforcing. It is most unlikely that the economic union will be strong if there is regional disaffection with Canada's industrial policies. Moreover, it is unlikely that Canada's industrial policies will lead to improved productivity growth and competitiveness if the domestic market is hampered by restrictions on the interprovincial mobility of resources. The Canadian Chamber of Commerce made this observation on domestic barriers to trade, investment and the movement of people:

> *We are concerned that existing institutions and policies have reduced the flexibility of the Canadian economy and its abliity to change. This has been done over the years by erecting barriers to the movement of a) labour, b) capital and c) by government policies that inhibit the rationalization of some of our industries.* (Canadian Chamber of Commerce, Brief, October 6, 1983, p. 55.)

These developments threaten to segment Canada's already small domestic market and, in the process, reduce economic efficiency and our ability to meet international competition.

Commissioners have stressed that a more market-oriented approach to industrial policy should guide the allocation of Canada's human, capital and natural resources. While a case can be made for provincial governments to compete among themselves for the location of these resources, to maximize their social benefits once a plant is established, government should not protect its output further, through procurement, for example. In addition, governments should avoid engaging in what might be called "negative sum competition"; this procedure might develop, for instance, in the course of bidding for new investment, especially foreign investment. Intergovernmental consultation and co-ordination are necessary prerequisites for strengthening the economic union and devising effective industrial policies.

Conclusions

Submissions to this Commission have demonstrated the considerable divergence of views held in Canada with respect to industrial policy. The business community generally favours a government "hands-off" approach, while social and labour groups express fear that such a course would result in measures that favour economic growth at the expense of the full-employment objective. Correctly fashioned, however, industrial policy need not involve a trade-off between economic growth and employment. Indeed, Commissioners are of the view that a well-thought-out, consistent framework for industrial policy will result in the economic growth and employment objectives being complementary and mutually reinforcing.

If these objectives have been contradictory in the past, a point which is debatable, the contradiction arose as a result of the undue attention government paid to protecting declining industries and retarding the adjustment of the economy to changing conditions. Far too little attention has been given to putting in place incentives that would contribute to the creation of a flexible and adaptative economy in which human, capital and natural resources are constantly being directed to uses that provide goods and services of progressively increasing value.

While there may have been a time in Canada's past when strong demand for our products abroad and protection for markets at home allowed us the luxury of condoning some misallocation of our economic resources, changes in our present and prospective circumstances now require us to make every effort to improve our productivity and our international competitiveness. The challenges posed by other major industrial countries, such as the United States and the nations of Europe, as well as Japan and the newly industrializing countries, require that we reorient our industrial policies. Commissioners have recommended that Canada pursue the development of a more liberalized trade environment, particularly with the United States. While we believe that such an approach would offer Canada potentially substantial economic benefits, the institution of industrial policies that will enable us to reap these benefits is of vital importance.

There is no panacea for improving the amalgam of instruments that compose industrial policy because so many aspects of our society are involved. Nor is there any facet of international experience that would suggest a grand solution. This Commission has carefully considered the possibility of pursuing a highly-targeted approach to industrial policy under which governments, in co-operation with the private sector, would try to distinguish between industrial "winners" and "losers". We are convinced, however, that problems involved in detailed government efforts to anticipate market forces, administrative complexities, the high risks of failure – particularly in an era of general government restraint – and other considerations weigh against such an approach at this time. This reality is and will remain strong until Canadians gain some experience with the adjustments required by a more liberal trade environment with the United States. Commissioners believe, instead, that the policies Canada establishes to foster industrial growth and development should be governed much more strongly by the dictates of the market-place than they are now.

To argue for a more highly market-oriented approach is not to argue for the continuation of *ad hoc* policies or the implementation of no policies at all. Canada needs a clear and consistent industrial policy to guide the private sector in its investment decisions and to facilitate consultation and co-ordination among governments. Of utmost importance is the adoption of a strategic objective, or set of objectives, that will make possible the charting of a steady industrial policy course. In light of emerging trade and technology developments, Commissioners recommend that industrial policy be firmly directed toward improving Canada's productivity and internationally competitive position.

This achievement, in turn, requires reorienting many major policies and programs, both at the federal and at provincial levels. Foremost among these requirements is that concerted efforts be made to achieve a steadier framework for private decision making and investment policy. Private sector decisions are complicated enough, without those who make them having to contend with gyrations in the relevant government policies. In addition, governments should recognize that more open trade and investment policies will also unleash new forces in the market-place that will further the need to allocate our human, capital and natural resources as efficiently as possible. The opportunities associated with a more closely integrated international environment, together with the demands which tough competition will place on domestic industry, can be expected to do much to remedy Canada's poor productivity performance of the past dozen years.

While tougher international competition will be strong medicine, it is not the only remedy. Governments across Canada must pay close attention to the development of the human and capital resources that our industries need to compete effectively with other countries. Part V of this Report elaborates on the training and educational skills that our labour force will need to ensure that Canada keeps pace with, if not ahead in, the technological "race". In this part of our Report, Commissioners have highlighted two dimensions of our economy that are particularly vital: first-class management and a strong entrepreneurial spirit. Both dimensions require "shots in the arm" because both have been found wanting in some critical ways. Capital formation has, until recently, been relatively strong in Canada, but even here, tax reforms and other measures could help to encourage the private sector to take a more dynamic, risk-oriented approach. Domestic research and development must be more effectively directed to commercial applications, and foreign technological developments should be more rapidly and aggressively adopted or adapted. Both moves will require the institution of a more sophisticated information "network" among Canada's managers and researchers and foreign experts than exists at present.

The whole framework of government policies that so strongly influences decision making in the private sector should be reconsidered with a view to encouraging the pursuit of excellence, the efficient allocation of resources, and the institution of innovative new processes, products and systems. The tax system, for example, has a fundamental bearing on decisions about working and leisure, and about consuming, saving and investing. Competition policy, the monitoring of foreign investment, the regulatory framework, and the scale and scope of Crown-corporation operations also have major implications for private-sector decisions. All these factors have features that Commissioners believe require reform in order to enhance Canada's productivity and competitive performance. Our transportation and communications sectors also require strengthening, for in a country as immense as Canada, they provide the infrastructure that is essential to securing and strengthening the economic union. In addition, governments across Canada must help to secure the economic union by minimizing those policies and programs that impede the free movement of labour, capital, and goods and services across the country.

Industrial policy requires adjustment mechanisms that facilitate the transfer of resources from low-valued use to high-valued use. Flexibility and adaptability in a rapidly changing world should be self-evident requisites for Canada, as we depend heavily on international trade. Commissioners urge that adjustment policy become a central component of industrial policy: declining industries should not be shored-up, but rather rationalized or phased out as circumstances require; assistance should be directed to re-employing the resources of declining industries, especially labour resources, in more productive industrial enterprises.

These components of industrial policy hold the potential for greatly improving Canada's productivity and competitive record. Commissioners are confident that these factors, in turn, will contribute to increases in our Canadian output, employment and real incomes.

Notes

1. Richard G. Harris, *Trade, Industrial Policy and International Competition*, vol. 13 (Toronto: University of Toronto Press, 1985).
2. Richard R. Nelson, "Government Stimulus of Technological Progress: Lessons from American History", in *Government and Technological Progress: A Cross-Industry Analysis*, edited by Richard R. Nelson (New York: Pergamon, 1982), p. 469.
3. Stephen Cohen, David J. Teece, Laura Tyson, and John Zysman, "Competitiveness", Berkeley Roundtable on the International Economy working paper (Berkeley: University of California, 1984), p. 3.
4. European Management Forum, *Report on International Industrial Competitiveness* (Geneva: EMF Foundation, 1984).
5. Donald J. Daly, Brief, November 8, 1983.

6. Joseph R. D'Cruz and James D. Fleck, "Improving the Competitiveness of the Canadian Industrial Portfolio", *Business Quarterly* 49 (Fall 1984), p. 78.
7. Joseph R. D'Cruz and James D. Fleck, *Canada Can Compete! Strategic Management of the Canadian Industrial Portfolio* (Montreal: Institute for Research on Public Policy, 1985), p. 68.
8. D'Cruz and Fleck, "Improving the Competitiveness of the Canadian Industrial Portfolio", p. 79.
9. See Economic Council of Canada, *Toward More Stable Growth in Construction*, report of the Study on Cyclical Instability in Construction (Ottawa: Information Canada, 1974).
10. André Raynauld, "Insuring and Financing Exports in Canada", in *Domestic Policies and the International Economic Environment*, vol. 12 (Toronto: University of Toronto Press, 1985).
11. Canada, Finance Canada and External Affairs Canada, "Export Financing", Consultation Paper (Ottawa, 1985).
12. The review that follows draws from a survey paper prepared for this Commission by Robin W. Boadway and Neil Bruce, "Theoretical Issues in Tax Reform", in *Approaches to Economic Well-Being*, vol. 26 (Toronto: University of Toronto Press, 1985), and from the results of a conference on tax policy held by this Commission, as well as other material prepared by R.W. Boadway.
13. United States, Department of the Treasury, *Blueprints for Basic Tax Reform* (Washington, D.C.: U.S. Government Printing Office, 1977).
14. Institute for Fiscal Studies, *The Structure and Reform of Direct Taxation* (London: George Allen and Unwin, 1978) (J.E. Meade, Committee Chairman).
15. L.H. Summers, "Capital, Taxation and Accumulation in a Life Cycle Growth Model", *American Economic Review* 71 (September 1981): 533 – 44.
16. W.T. Stanbury and Fred Thompson, "The Scope and Coverage of Regulation in Canada and the United States: Implications for the Demand for Reform", in *Government Regulation: Scope, Growth, Process*, edited by W.T. Stanbury (Montreal: Institute for Research on Public Policy, 1980).
17. R.S. Khemani, "Extent and Evolution of Competition in the Canadian Economy", in *Canadian Industry in Transition*, vol. 2 (Toronto: University of Toronto Press, 1985).
18. William G. Shepherd, "Causes of Increased Competition in the U.S. Economy, 1939 – 1980", *Review of Economics and Statistics* 64 (November 1982): 613–27.
19. *Ibid.*, p. 623.
20. See Richard Schultz and Alan Alexandroff, *Economic Regulation and the Federal System*, vol. 42, prepared for the Royal Commission on the Economic Union and Development Prospects for Canada (Toronto: University of Toronto Press, 1985).
21. Another study that attempts to derive "ideal" prices for local and long-distance services under the assumption that some income redistribution via telephone pricing is desirable suggests that local service should be 19 per cent higher in price and long-distance service 50 per cent lower. See J.A. Breslaw and J. Barry Smith, "Efficiency, Equity and Regulation: An Optimal Pricing Model of Bell Canada", *Canadian Journal of Economics* 40 (November 1982): 634 – 48.
22. Stanbury and Thompson, "The Scope and Coverage of Regulation in Canada and the United States".
23. Economic Council of Canada, *Reforming Regulation* (Ottawa: Minister of Supply and Services Canada, 1981), p. 124.
24. *Ibid.*, p. 127.

25. See W.T. Stanbury and George Lermer, "Regulation and the Redistribution of Income and Wealth", *Canadian Public Administration* 26 (Fall 1983): 378–401; and Keith Acheson, "Economic Regulation in Canada: A Survey", in *Canadian Industrial Policy in Action*, vol. 4, prepared for the Royal Commission on the Economic Union and Development Prospects for Canada (Toronto: University of Toronto Press, 1985).
26. Stanbury and Lermer, "Regulation and the Redistribution of Income and Wealth", p. 401.
27. Acheson, "Economic Regulation in Canada".
28. See Khemani, "Extent and Evolution of Competition in the Canadian Economy".
29. Canada, Royal Commission on Corporate Concentration, *Report* (Ottawa: Minister of Supply and Services Canada, 1978), p. 407.
30. John R. Baldwin and Paul K. Gorecki, *The Role of Scale in Canada-U.S. Productivity Differences*, vol. 6 (Toronto: University of Toronto Press, 1985).
31. J.R. Baldwin, P.K. Gorecki and J.S. McVey, "Imports, Secondary Output, Price-Cost Margins and Measures of Concentration: Evidence for Canada", Discussion Paper 263 (Ottawa: Economic Council of Canada, 1984).
32. Khemani, "Extent and Evolution of Competition in the Canadian Economy".
33. Actually, of the 54 per cent of Canadian farm cash receipts handled by marketing boards, only 24 per cent is handled by supply-management boards. The balance is handled by boards that do not limit output.
34. Khemani, "Extent and Evolution of Competition in the Canadian Economy". See also Shepherd, "Causes of Increased Competition in the U.S. Economy".
35. Combines Investigation Act, s. 2.
36. Economic Council of Canada, *Interim Report on Competition Policy* (Ottawa: Information Canada, 1969).
37. F. Mathewson and R. Winter, *Competition Policy and Vertical Exchange*, vol. 7 (Toronto: University of Toronto Press, 1985).
38. Royal Commission on Corporate Concentration, *Report*, p. 407.
39. Marsha Chandler and Michael J. Trebilcock, "Comparative Survey of Industrial Policies in Selected OECD Countries", in *Economics of Industrial Policy and Strategy*, vol. 5 (Toronto: University of Toronto Press, 1985).
40. Harris, *Trade, Industrial Policy and International Competition.*
41. See Restrictive Trade Practices Commission, *Telecommunications in Canada*, Part III, *The Impact of Vertical Integration on the Equipment Industry* (Ottawa, 1983).
42. Irving Brecher, *Canada's Competition Policy Revisited: Some New Thoughts on an Old Story* (Montreal: Institute for Research on Public Policy, 1982), p. 17.
43. This figure is the receipts from privatization (see Table 9-16) divided by the book value of government enterprise capital which Littlechild puts at £80 billion.
44. Michael Pitfield, "The Limits of Public Enterprise", address to the Couchiching Conference, Orillia, Ontario, August 11, 1984, pp. 4–5.
45. See A.E. Safarian, "Government Control of Foreign Business Investment", in *Domestic Policies and the International Economic Environment*, vol. 12, prepared for the Royal Commission on the Economic Union and Development Prospects for Canada (Toronto: University of Toronto Press, 1985).
46. Canada, Finance Canada, *Economic Review, April 1982* (Ottawa: Minister of Supply and Services Canada, 1982), p. 80.
47. See Glenn P. Jenkins, "Taxes and Tariffs and the Evaluation of the Benefit from Foreign Investment", *Canadian Journal of Economics* 12 (August 1979): 410–25.

48. Section 100(3).

49. Glenn Jenkins, *Costs and Consequences of the New Protectionism* (Ottawa: North-South Institute, 1980).

50. William G. Watson, *A Primer on the Economics of Industrial Policy* (Toronto: Ontario Economic Council, 1983).

51. Richard G. Harris, Frank D. Lewis, and Douglas D. Purvis, "Economic Adjustment and Public Policy in Canada" (Kingston: Queen's University, 1982).

52. John W. Langford, "Transport Canada and the Transport Ministry: The Attempt to Retreat to Basics", in *How Ottawa Spends Your Tax Dollars: National Policy and Economic Development, 1982*, edited by G. Bruce Doern (Toronto: James Lorimer, 1982).

53. Schultz and Alexandroff, *Economic Regulation and the Federal System.*

54. Allan M. Maslove, Michael J. Prince, and G. Bruce Doern, *Federal and Provincial Budgeting*, vol. 41, prepared for the Royal Commission on the Economic Union and Development Prospects for Canada (Toronto: University of Toronto Press, 1985).

55. Langford, "Transport Canada and the Transport Ministry", p. 163.

56. Economic Council, *Reforming Regulation.*

CHAPTER 10

Short-Term Stability and High Employment

CHAPTER 10

Short-Term Stability and High Employment

Introduction

As Commissioners have already emphasized, there is good reason to believe that over the longer run, the main determinants of economic growth and development are structural factors related both to the supply of goods and services, such as expansion of the labour force and changes in capital investment and productivity, and also to shifts in world demand for Canada's products. That Canadians' real incomes are now, on average, more than twice as large as they were 25 years ago, that total employment is almost twice as high, and that total employment in manufacturing is 1.3 times as high are among the results of combinations of these structural factors.

At the same time, however, we are also acutely conscious of the fact that our well-being at any given point can be sharply affected by shorter-term fluctuations in the economy. This is particularly obvious at a time when unemployment remains close to its record post-Second World War level, when real interest rates are very high, and when experience with high inflation and even higher interest rates is still very fresh in Canadian minds.

The major elements here – output, employment and unemployment, inflation, and interest and exchange rates – are closely interrelated, although some may be of more fundamental importance than others; most observers, for example, view unemployment as of more importance than the exchange rate. The study of the relationships, levels and stability of these elements over the short term has come to be called "macro-economics". Governments, using a variety of instruments, try to achieve the best possible balance among these factors; the most important and powerful are monetary and fiscal policy, which together constitute "demand management".

Because of the complex relationships among macro-economic elements, the simultaneous achievement of goals involving the levels and stability for each is often very difficult, if not impossible. A growth of output so strong that it strains available human, material and financial resources, for example, may lead to an increase in inflation and interest rates that in time could adversely affect the prospects for the continued growth of productivity and employment. An extended period of high unemployment may be associated with weak investment and thus with a lasting reduction in Canadians' capacity to produce and in our real income levels. Long-run benefits may involve short-run costs, and vice versa. Given these kinds of trade-offs, which directly affect the welfare of different groups in society, the problems of striking the right balance in setting demand-management policy must be both complex and controversial.

In organizing our discussion of demand management and some of its options, Commissioners have faced something of a dilemma in emphasis. For most of the post-war period, Canada, like most other developed Western economies, has experienced relatively high employment. A tendency for the rate of inflation to creep or climb upwards has, however, been a persistent concern. Many of the major developments in economic analysis over this period have centred on inflation and have brought into better focus the limits of demand-management policy in stabilizing the economy and reducing unemployment. Another important strand of development has dealt with the nature of unemployment; it suggests that a significant level of unemployment is a normal phenomenon, associated with the "frictions" of workers moving into the labour force or from job to job.

Canada's economic experience since 1982, however, makes it all too clear that unemployment can rise far above any level that could be considered "normal", and that it can still constitute a severe – currently, the most severe – problem facing our economy. Since 1982, rates of unemployment have prevailed which are higher than 11 per cent overall and, indeed, stand at almost 20 per cent for youths aged 15 to 19. These high rates and the lengthy periods of unemployment experienced by many older workers constitute a grave failure of our economy to provide a reasonable standard of social and economic welfare for all, and to make full and good use of its resources. The prospect that the situation will improve only slowly causes Commissioners deep concern, not merely because of the immediate hardship and current waste of resources involved, but also because prolonged experience with unemployment can sap the morale and the future potential of those affected, including those who are, or should be, at the critical stage of acquiring their first work experience.

For these reasons, a paramount objective of this Commission is to find ways to achieve, on a sustained basis, substantially lower levels of unemployment. Nonetheless, we are a Commission "for the longer term". We believe that the present high unemployment is largely a cyclical phenomenon, though one that may take several years to overcome. When we reach policy conclusions in this chapter, we give full weight to the need to use demand-management policy to alleviate the short-term, but crucial, problem of the high cyclical unemployment current in Canada. We also give substantial attention and weight to historical experience and to analysis arising in the post-war period. These elements offer lessons for the longer run about the level of unemployment likely to be sustainable, on average, through demand-management policy. In light of this Commission's long-term perspective, the question of means available to reduce this *non-cyclical* component of unemployment is of equal importance to, or even greater importance than, the *cyclical* component.

To provide a framework for the analysis of demand management, the first section of this chapter outlines some of the basic notions of macro-economics. Supplementing the general discussion are subsections on recent analytical approaches to unemployment and on recent experience with inflation and policy attitudes towards it. Two specific analyses are important to understanding the macro-economic choices open to the economy: the implications of the openness of the Canadian economy to trade and capital movements, and the extent to which the size of fiscal deficits and government debt constitute a constraint on policy. After reviewing this analytical framework, we shall consider its implications for the conduct of Canada's monetary and fiscal policy. The issues to be considered include:

- The desirability and feasibility of using exchange controls, taxes or other measures to insulate interest rates in Canada from international movements of interest rates
- The desirability and feasibility of going further in providing various forms of inflation adjustment
- Monetary and fiscal policy questions that arise from the federal and regional nature of Canada.

We shall also consider whether incomes policies might serve as means of further improving macro-economic performance, and whether structural changes in wage and price setting might have the same potential and, in particular, might be used to lower the "normal" rate of unemployment without generating new inflationary pressures. A brief concluding section outlines a possible policy approach that includes monetary, fiscal and incomes-policy action in an attempt to achieve a more rapid reduction in unemployment than seems in prospect, while avoiding any resurgence of inflation.

Our Macro-economic Choices: An Analytical Framework

Some aspects of macro-economics – in particular, the linkages of money, inflation, exchange rates and interest rates – have been the subject of study for centuries; the analysis of business cycles also has a long history. However, modern analysis of macro-economic issues, especially the role that demand management can play in stabilizing the economy, really began to take form only after the publication, in 1936, of John Maynard Keynes' *The General Theory of Employment, Interest and Money*.[1]

A highly simplified outline of the main ideas and vocabulary of the evolution of macro-economics since Keynes provides a good means of sketching current issues and the policy-action options that our present understanding suggests are open to us. Our "story" form of presentation is meant to provide a constant reminder of the highly simplified nature of our discussion, which is aimed at underlining the broad considerations that must be taken into account for policy purposes.

The Development of Macro-economics

Perhaps the most familiar name to students of modern macro-economics is that of John Maynard Keynes. For several decades, most theoretical work in this field has expounded, expanded or reacted to *The General Theory of Employment, Interest and Money* and his other works. This is not to say that Keynes created macro-economics. Many concepts fundamental to this field are much older than his works. One, for example, is that of aggregate demand, which refers to total spending in the economy on "final" goods and services.[2] The aggregate demand in a given national economy is, broadly speaking, the sum of spending by consumers on goods and services, by business on new physical capital and net accumulation of inventories, by governments on the goods and services they provide, and by foreign purchasers of the country's exports. The complement of aggregate demand is aggregate supply, which is, basically, the sum of the final goods and services that will be supplied for all of the above purposes at a given average price level. Aggregate demand in nominal terms, that is, in terms of the prices that actually prevail at a particular point in time, is determined by a number of factors; these include the level of the money supply, which is governed by monetary policy, and the levels of government expenditures and revenues, which are determined by fiscal policy. For any given level of nominal aggregate demand, real aggregate demand will vary inversely with the price level: the higher the price level, the lower will be the real demand, and vice versa.

Analysts early developed important points about interdependence of spending (aggregate demand), prices, income and employment. One concept was the multiplier effect: the notion that an initial increase in spending will eventually result in some multiple of the initial increase because the income from the initial spending will be re-spent. Analysts also assumed that in the short run, the prices of goods and services would not vary much with output as long as that output was below the level corresponding to full employment of the labour force. Prices would start to rise only if demand rose beyond this point.

Aggregate demand and aggregate supply together determine the short-term levels of output, employment and prices. Consequently, monetary and fiscal policy will affect these levels as will other influences on demand, such as demand for exports and the amounts people wish to save. In theory, then, monetary and fiscal policy, by influencing aggregate demand, might guide the economy to the output level consistent with relatively full employment and stable prices.

The deep prolonged depression of the 1930s led macro-economists to the view that in the absence of government action, aggregate demand might fail to find a level consistent with full employment of the economy's resources. They concluded, therefore, that demand-management policy had a potentially important role: that is, to keep aggregate demand high enough to sustain relatively full employment.

The widespread acceptance of this theoretical approach in the 1940s and 1950s owed much both to the Great Depression, which came about when aggregate demand fell far short of aggregate supply for an extended period, and also to the Second World War, which demonstrated that government could indeed play a very effective role in stimulating aggregate demand and thereby decreasing unemployment.

By the mid-1940s, economists recognized that this analytical framework applied only to the very short term. It became apparent that in the longer run, capital investment would expand the potential productive capacity of the economy. Furthermore, the accumulation of wealth from savings, such as those invested in bonds issued to finance government deficits, might induce individuals to channel an increased proportion of additional income, not into further savings, but into consumption, and thus add to aggregate demand in the economy. A more complex theory was clearly required, one that could be used to analyse issues involving economic growth over the longer term. This growth theory has evolved continuously since the 1940s, but it has proved difficult to integrate with the theory of shorter-run "cyclical" fluctuations in the economy.

The creeping inflation of the 1950s and a closer scrutiny of the historical record forced economists to conclude that the notion of a sharp dividing line between inflationary and non-inflationary levels of demand was not appropriate, even as a simplified representation of reality. In the real world, prices and wages began to rise before the economy was running "flat out": that is, before the unemployment rate fell to the level which people thought might correspond to the rather vaguely defined concept of full employment.

The analytical response to this phenomenon evolved into the so-called "Phillips curve" originally devised by A.W. Phillips of the London School of Economics, who carried out an extensive analysis of the history of wage behaviour in Britain. The Phillips curve depicts a relationship between inflation, as represented by the *rate of change* of prices or wages (rather than just the price or wage *level*), and the level of unemployment or some other measure of economic activity. Phillips found the relationship between the two phenomena to be inverse: if unemployment were "low" and the economy were, therefore, operating close to the limit of its capacity, upward pressure on costs and prices would be "high", and vice versa.

This framework for viewing demand management implied that the policy problem was more awkward than it had at first appeared. Demand-management policy might be able to move the economy along the Phillips curve, achieving lower unemployment at the cost of higher inflation or achieving lower inflation at the cost of higher unemployment. There was no reason to think, however, that such policy could shift the position of the curve itself and so improve the basic trade-off. Empirical estimates of the Phillips curves for individual nations suggested that in most countries, inflation would, in fact, begin at levels of unemployment higher than the notions of full employment current in the 1950s. In Canada, for instance, full employment was considered to encompass an unemployment rate of 3 to 4 per cent. Not surprisingly, this discovery led to consideration of policy measures that might shift the curve, measures such as price controls, wage controls and other, more voluntary, "incomes policies". It was suggested that the trade-off between inflation and employment might also be improved by increasing the efficiency of labour-market operations. Improving the trade-off might involve reducing regional or occupational labour shortages that put upward pressure on wages and salaries before the economy as a whole was fully employed.

By the early 1960s, the advent of computers and advances in statistical analysis had led to the development of an increasing number of econometric models of the economy. These models were designed to provide reasonably accurate quantitative representations of the economy and its dynamics. In addition to providing useful economic forecasts, they furnished a basis for estimating how possible changes in monetary and fiscal policy would affect aggregate demand, employment and inflation. The development of this capability offered some prospect that judicious, and possibly frequent, changes in monetary and fiscal policy could "fine tune" the economy and thus keep it close to the best possible point of balance between unemployment and inflation on the Phillips curve.

It was also generally realized, however, that monetary and fiscal action tended to influence the economy only after various lags, and that economic forecasting was subject, probably inevitably, to significant errors. Thus the notion that it was possible to keep the economy within a very narrow range on the Phillips curve was never taken very seriously – or, at least, never taken very seriously for very long – by most of those involved in policy making or policy analysis. Indeed, the degree of uncertainty associated with economic developments had led a number of economists to accept the view, advanced by Milton Friedman of the University of Chicago, that governments could probably do no more to stabilize the economy than simply allow the money supply to grow at a constant pace. This view contradicted the accepted notion that government, by varying the availability of credit, could contribute to the stabilization of demand. In part, at least, the alternative view was a product of a developing perception that changes in monetary policy tended to influence the economy after particularly long – and variable – lags, making the effective application of such policy extremely difficult.[3]

Taking the concept a step further, some economists recommended an approach to fiscal policy that would, on average, maintain expenditures on a reasonably steady track over the longer term. The exceptions to this "rule" were expenditures for programs such as Unemployment Insurance (UI), which vary automatically with the business cycle and keep tax rates at levels calculated to balance the budget or produce a target surplus or deficit. This approach would involve an acceptance of the fluctuations in revenues and in the deficit that resulted from fluctuations in the level of economic activity. Such policies would provide automatic fiscal stabilization: the amount of taxes collected and Unemployment Insurance benefits paid would be allowed to vary as required to dampen cyclical fluctuations in the economy. In periods of slow growth, for example, tax liabilities would decline, and UI benefit payments would rise, dampening the decline in aggregate demand, output and employment.

In the 1960s, some economists perceived that changes made by the central bank in the money supply might have a greater effect on nominal demand than the majority of macro-economists had allowed for over the previous two decades, and that fiscal actions might have somewhat weaker effects than had been supposed. The direct longer-run relation between money and prices (that is, between monetary growth and inflation), which had been recognized by many economists in the pre-Keynesian era, was brought forcefully to public attention; again, the most prominent preceptor was Dr. Friedman, the leader of the emerging theory of economics known as "monetarism". Economists who supported this theory also devoted increasing attention to the possibility that the way in which fiscal policy was financed affected its impact. The change in the budget deficit associated with a given fiscal policy action could be accommodated by a change in the money supply, such as the sale of at least some of the government debt to the central bank, or it could be financed entirely by sale of debt to the general public. Use of the latter alternative would put pressure on interest rates, "crowd out" private expenditure, and thus offset part of the action's effect on nominal demand.

In 1968, an address made by Dr. Friedman and an article written by Edmund Phelps precipitated a further development in the economic analysis of inflation and stabilization policy. In essence, both economists argued that the notion of a stable trade-off between inflation and unemployment ignored a fundamental reality: if inflation continues for some time, people begin to expect it to continue, and they adjust their economic behaviour accordingly. If the rate of wage increase starts to rise as unemployment drops below a certain point and labour markets tighten, it is presumably because workers are in a position to earn higher *real* wages.[4] Once the higher rate of wage increase is reflected in costs, however, prices also start to rise more quickly, with the result that workers do not obtain expected increases in *real* wages. If labour markets remain tight, the nominal wage rates demanded and obtained will increase again, to offset the higher rate of price increase. In short, the inflation spiral will continue as long as labour markets are tight.

The short-run Phillips curve might appear to offer a trade-off between inflation and unemployment. It is critically important, however, to recognize that the position of this curve is fixed only for the rate of inflation *expected* by most participants in the economy. If demand-management policy attempts to take advantage of this apparent short-run trade-off by trying to reduce unemployment below the so-called "normal" unemployment rate for any significant period of time, the expected and actual rates of inflation will progressively shift upward. As the expected rate of inflation increases, as it will if unemployment falls enough to add upward pressure, the short-run Phillips curve and the actual rate of inflation will tend to ratchet progressively upward. The argument also holds in reverse: if unemployment is high enough, actual inflation will fall below the currently expected rate, and the actual and expected rates will continue to fall over time.

The longer the period of time under consideration, the steeper is the trade-off curve. Ultimately, there is no trade-off between sustainable levels of unemployment and the rate of inflation.[5] Associated with this "no long-run trade-off" principle is the notion that there is a critical level of unemployment rate that tends to prevail, on average, over the longer run. This critical unemployment rate has been variously called the "natural", "normal" or "full employment" rate, or, more neutrally, the "non-accelerating inflation rate of unemployment" (NAIRU). When unemployment stands above this rate, inflation will tend to decrease continuously. When unemployment stands below this rate, inflation will tend to increase continuously.[6]

Thus a situation in which the unemployment rate is higher or lower than the NAIRU is inherently unstable since it involves continuous change in the pace of inflation and cannot be maintained indefinitely. In principle, if unemployment is at the NAIRU, inflation will tend to persist at its current rate. In other words, the NAIRU represents a stable or "equilibrium" situation for the economy. The level of the NAIRU depends on the structure of labour markets and, possibly, on other institutional features of the economy. Factors that make for a prompt matching of supplies and demands for different types of labour, such as helpful information about job openings, high mobility of labour, and incentives that encourage people to take such jobs as are available, also make for a situation in which the unemployment rate can be quite low without leading to net upward pressure on inflation: that is, they tend to result in a low NAIRU. Factors that make for a mismatch in supplies of, and demands for, labour, including geographical dispersion, fluctuations in demand for different types of labour, and changes in the labour-supply mix, tend to result in a relatively high NAIRU. For the Canadian economy, the NAIRU is currently estimated to stand in the range of 6.5 to 8 per cent. (It is generally believed to have been lower, probably in the 4 to 5 per cent range, from the mid-1950s to the mid-1960s, but to have risen to the current range by the mid-1970s.)

The NAIRU is a critically important concept, and we shall refer to it frequently throughout this chapter. The "no long-run trade-off" principle implies that the NAIRU sets a lower limit to the level of unemployment that expansionary demand-management policy can achieve on a sustained basis. Demand management may still have an important potential function: in general, to stabilize the economy within the range of the NAIRU. Nevertheless, the notion that demand-management policy could achieve even lower rates of unemployment if society were willing to tolerate higher *but stable* rates of inflation evaporated with the general acceptance of the "no long-run trade-off" view. Another key corollary is that the chief way to achieve lower average rates of unemployment over the longer run is to reduce the NAIRU through policies supplementary to demand-management policies. Part V of this Report considers certain structural policies, including reform of the Unemployment Insurance system and other social safety nets that may make it possible to reduce the NAIRU.

General acceptance of the principle of "no long-run trade-off between unemployment and inflation" still left a short-run trade-off. This trade-off was different, however, from the original Phillips-curve concept of a trade-off between lasting reductions in unemployment and the continuing rate of inflation. It was now suggested that the trade-off was between *temporary* periods of unemployment below or above the NAIRU and increases or decreases in the continuing rate of inflation.

The proposition that there is no long-run trade-off between inflation and unemployment is consistent with one contention of the monetarist school: that an increase in the rate of growth of the money supply, beyond the increase required to accommodate the sustainable increase in real output, will eventually result only in higher prices, and not in greater expansion of output and employment. This proposition has now gained wide, though not universal, acceptance. The monetarists' argument marks a return to the classical economic view that money is essentially neutral in the sense that in real terms, it has no long-run effect.

The proposition that no trade-off exists over the long run was put forward in the latter part of the 1960s, just after inflation had risen to a higher level than was consistent with the prevailing unemployment rate, given an "unshifting" Phillips curve. Before long, economists started to work with "extended" or "augmented" Phillips curves, in which the current rate of wage increase was related not only to the unemployment rate, but also to some measure of the *expected* inflation rate or some combination of the expected inflation rate and "catch-up" for past unexpected inflation. Fairly soon, it became evident that expectations about the rate of future inflation were having an effect on wage settlements, consistent with the hypothesis that there was little or no trade-off between inflation and unemployment over the long run.

The concept of "inflationary expectations" is important, not only to the analysis of actual inflation and the inflation-unemployment relationship, but also to the interpretation of interest rates and the analysis of their economic impact.[7] When people refer simply to the "interest rate", they usually mean the *nominal* interest rate, which is the ratio of the flow of money income that accrues to the owner of an asset – say, a savings deposit or a bond – to the money value of the asset in question. The real interest rate is the nominal interest rate adjusted for the effects of inflation in reducing the real purchasing power of the asset in question. Thus, if a $100 bank deposit brings its owner $10 per annum, its nominal interest rate is 10 per cent. If the inflation rate is 6 per cent per annum so that over a year the purchasing power of the deposit falls from $100 to (approximately) $94, the real rate of interest yielded by that deposit is (approximately) 4 per cent. The $6 "inflation premium" must be saved if real wealth is to be preserved. In brief, the real interest rate equals the nominal interest rate minus the rate of inflation.

Decisions to save, invest, borrow or lend are likely to depend more on real than on nominal interest rates. For example, if inflation is continuing steadily at a rate of 20 per cent, an investor will require a nominal interest rate of 20 per cent just to break even in real terms (before taxes), since the interest will be paid in money worth 20 per cent less than the value of the money borrowed. Under these circumstances, a nominal interest rate (on, say, bank deposits) of 22 per cent might be considered low,[8] whereas under steady inflation at 4 per cent per annum, nominal interest rates of 10 per cent might be considered high.

Real rates of interest calculated by adjusting nominal interest rates for actual rates of inflation are sometimes referred to as "actual" or *ex post* real interest rates. Decisions to invest, save, borrow or lend are, however, inherently forward looking, and the real interest rate that affects them is the expected or *ex ante* rate: that is, the nominal rate adjusted for *expected future* inflation. Expected future inflation rates are, therefore, an important determinant of nominal interest rates.

Another determinant of inflation came to be regarded as important in the 1970s. In 1973, the world economy received a severe shock – and a sharp reminder of its vulnerability – from the Organization of Petroleum Exporting Countries (OPEC), which set in motion a fourfold increase in international oil prices. The experience dramatically emphasized the fact that measured inflation is not determined solely by the relationship among aggregate demand, unemployment and wages. Significant "supply shocks" can make both inflation and unemployment more severe.[9] Nevertheless, when allowance is made for supply-side shocks, the Phillips curve, as adapted to take account of inflation expectations, still provides a reasonably satisfactory framework for analysing the inflation experienced by developed Western countries since 1973.

During the early 1970s, there was a further development in thinking about the effects of expectations on the behaviour of the various participants in the economy. Partly as a matter of analytical convenience, it had been conventional to assume that expectations were determined by recent past experience and, therefore, tended to lag behind actual developments. In this "adaptive expectations" view, an expansionary shift in policy would give rise to the following sequence of developments. If the economy were at the NAIRU, the stimulative action would, after some lag, cause a reduction in unemployment. This decline in unemployment would, after some further lag, cause an increase in inflation. The increase in actual inflation would be followed by an increase in the expected rate of inflation. The cost and price hikes initiated in response to the increase in expected inflation would cause further increases in the pace of actual inflation. And so the spiral would continue to mount. As we noted above, this view suggested that inflation would eventually result in the dissipation of any real expansion in output and employment initially generated by expansionary policy measures. The economy would return, perhaps along a cyclical path, to the "pre-expansion" level of unemployment, but at a higher price level or rate of inflation.

In contrast, the new anticipatory view holds that individuals and businesses base their expectations on a "rational analysis" of the future effects of current and prospective economic policy and other circumstances. In particular, participants in the economy may anticipate the ultimate inflationary impact of any expansionary policy measures. This foresight leads them to boost inflation immediately by demanding higher prices, wages and nominal interest rates in order to avoid being left behind. Thus, policy measures can have a perverse effect. For example, a perceived attempt by monetary authorities to increase the money supply in order to reduce interest rates can have the opposite effect if investors are prepared to lend only at increased nominal rates of interest because they expect the monetary policy to raise the future rates of inflation and thus erode the value of their capital.

Behaviour based on such rational expectations, combined with very flexible prices and wages, can dissipate, virtually from the start, any real expansionary thrust of macro-economic measures. However, anticipatory behaviour has another side that provides some room for optimism about the effect of anti-inflationary policy. If participants in the economic process can be convinced of the authorities' firm determination to pursue policies to reduce inflation, achieving this result may require less slowing of the rate of economic growth and a lower rise in unemployment than would be anticipated if expectations adjusted only to changes in actual economic conditions. Private behaviour might become less inflationary immediately after the shift in policy. Ideally, a move by policy makers to contain inflationary pressures by reducing the *nominal* level of aggregate demand would quickly lead to a reduction in the rate of increase of prices and wages, sufficient to prevent any decline in the level of *real* aggregate demand and, hence, any significant rise in the level of unemployment.

This description does not do justice to the subtleties and complexities of the "rational expectations" or "new classical" school of thought. The theory of rational expectations may suggest that demand management can have no impact on real variables such as output and employment. Yet most policy makers would agree that this conclusion goes beyond what happens in the real world. No country in post-war history has been able to reduce embedded inflation through a shift to anti-inflationary demand-management policy without going through a recession, no matter how strongly the authorities have worded their commitment to reducing the growth of the money supply. Nonetheless, the rational expectations analysis at least reminds us of the common-sense tenet that expectations have a critical influence on economic behaviour. It is not safe to assume that people will form their expectations mechanically and retrospectively. Participants in the economy almost certainly tend to react directly to policy and to act on the basis of what they believe about the longer-run effect of policy actions.

A final analytical development over the last decade has been the deeper exploration of the reasons for the relatively slow adjustment that is usually observed in rates of wage increases. The causes seem to be threefold: many wage contracts last for two or three years; many wage contracts "overlap", or expire on different dates; and inflationary expectations generally tend to lag behind actual experience. In turn, the slow adjustment of wages helps to explain why a speed-up or slow-down in the growth of nominal demand, following an inflationary or deflationary shift in policy, initially appears as a change in real growth and in unemployment. Only after an extended lag is the change in nominal demand reflected mainly in a change in inflation, with output and unemployment returning to their trend levels.

Today's Mainstream Economists and Their Differences

The majority of today's macro-economists still use an expanded version of the analytical framework that evolved out of Keynes' theories. They think that both monetary and, at least in the shorter run, fiscal policy can influence nominal aggregate demand, and that changes in nominal demand have at least some short-run effects on real demand, output and unemployment. Generally, they believe that what can be broadly termed "Keynesian policies" have contributed significantly to making economic fluctuations substantially less severe in the post-war period than they were in the preceding hundred years. Finally, many still accept that periodic severe shortfalls of total demand which the operation of "normal" market forces does not solve quickly – the basic Keynesian problem – are a continuing danger and create an important function for active monetary and fiscal policy.

Today's economists do, however, generally stress short- and long-run effects on prices more than did the original Keynesian analysts. Furthermore, the majority now accept the view that there is little or no possibility of using expansionary demand policy to achieve sustained reductions in unemployment that will reduce that factor below the NAIRU, and they are unwilling to tolerate the inflation that would accompany such policy. Although they do not view the work of establishing a satisfactory analytical framework as complete, they sometimes think back wistfully to the "good old days", when it seemed unnecessary for economic analysis to concern itself with such a variable human element as expectations,[10] when the profession's reputation for forecasting economic developments was higher, and when the policy advice it offered tended to be more palatable and more welcome.

These general propositions appear to command the support of a sufficient number of today's macro-economists to be considered as the mainstream view. It would be highly misleading, however, to suggest that this view translates into consensus on a wide range of policy issues. It remains, for example, a matter of considerable controversy – and of considerable importance in terms of future policy – whether it was appropriate for Canada, the United States and most other Western nations to tighten sharply their monetary policies in 1979 and thereafter, in an effort to reduce the inflation that had built up, partly because of the second oil-price shock. The sharp contraction in the growth of the money supply was almost certainly the primary cause of the severe recession experienced around the world during the 1980 – 82 period. The resulting decline in output and the dramatic increase in unemployment did much to reduce the inflationary spiral of prices from double-digit levels. This outcome presumably dispelled any doubts about the effectiveness of monetary policy in influencing aggregate demand and inflation. Lingering questions remain, however: Was the cure worse than the disease? Might not a less stringent application of monetary policy have achieved a similar result? And might other policy options have helped to control inflation with less lost output, lost income and unemployment?

While the United States has experienced a rather healthy recovery from the recession, Canada and Western Europe have not. Mainstream macro-economists are divided on the question of whether Canada and Western Europe will recover fully from the recession in the not-too-distant future (say, within two to four years). They also disagree about whether that recovery will occur on its own or will require assistance from more expansionary monetary and/or fiscal policy. They are divided, too, about whether it will be possible, after the recovery, to maintain unemployment rates in the NAIRU range without engendering new flare-ups of inflation.

Neither is there consensus as to whether attempting to achieve further reductions in inflation (say, going all the way to a zero rate) would be worthwhile, given the economic and social costs of postponing full recovery that such a course would probably involve. Nor is there agreement about whether inflation should be addressed solely through non-inflationary demand management, which relates, primarily, to monetary policy, or by supplementing such policy with some form of incomes policy. Some argue that a temporary incomes policy would lessen the above-average unemployment associated with the process of reducing inflation. A smaller number claim that a permanent incomes policy would make it possible to achieve permanently lower rates of unemployment, without touching off another inflationary spiral: that is, that such a policy would lower the NAIRU. Finally, there is no consensus as to whether monetary and fiscal policy are best conducted according to fixed, relatively simple, publicly stated rules, or whether it is useful to take discretionary action in response to the evolving course of, and outlook for, the economy.

The disagreements among economists on these issues reflect complex combinations of differences in value judgements and in judgements on what are, in principle, matters of fact. The divergences in value judgements range from differences in the importance individual economists attach to avoiding a period of above-average unemployment, to differences in the weight they give to avoiding the interference with personal freedom that an incomes policy would entail. Divergences in empirical estimates are almost as wide. For example, practitioners have come up with substantially different calculations of the amount and duration of above-average unemployment associated with achieving a given reduction in inflation, and of the costs, in terms of efficient functioning of the economy, associated with inflation or application of an incomes policy. Perhaps most fundamentally, there are profound differences in judgements concerning the strength of the private sector's self-correcting forces: that is, about the likelihood that the economy, if left alone, will stay reasonably close to the NAIRU. These differences, which reflect considerable uncertainty about the effectiveness of various policy options and the nature of the trade-offs among them, are important because they underlie the difficulties we Canadians face as we consider means of improving macro-economic performance.

Before turning to these policy issues, however, we must consider the evolution of analysis in several specific areas: the nature of unemployment, and why the NAIRU is generally viewed as having risen significantly over the past two decades; the industrialized nations' recent, but fairly general, shift to the view that controlling inflation is a prerequisite for achieving good economic performance; the implications of the fact that Canada is an open economy with close linkages to the rest of the world through large, and relatively free, flows of goods and services and financial capital; and whether concerns about the size of the government deficit should constrain the exercise of fiscal policy to achieve macro-economic goals, such as a lower level of unemployment.

The Level of Unemployment and the Evolution of NAIRU

A key trend in the post-war period has been the rise in average unemployment rates. Economists' views about unemployment, its causes and its significance have, in turn, undergone important changes. This section briefly reviews this evolution of knowledge, focusing on the components of the NAIRU, the "normal" rate of unemployment, which, as we have seen, is the portion of unemployment that is not directly related to cyclical changes in demand.

In focusing on the NAIRU, we Commissioners are not attempting to downgrade the importance of the hardships created by the cyclical component of unemployment. Indeed, the cyclical component disturbs us deeply, not least because, since 1982, it has accounted for a substantial proportion – probably at least one-third – of total unemployment. Because cyclical unemployment is tied to cyclical changes in demand, however, we deal with it separately, later in this chapter.

The unemployment rate is one of the most widely cited economic statistics. To a considerable extent, the attention it receives reflects policy makers' and the public's concern about the hardship that unemployment imposes on the jobless and their families and, from an economic perspective, about the lost output represented by unemployed workers.

The degree of hardship associated with periods of unemployment is extraordinarily difficult to measure, but for many members of the labour force, it has clearly declined in the post-Second World War period. This decline reflects a number of important trends described in more detail in Chapter 7. Most important, perhaps, has been the very substantial rise in the proportion of Canadian families that have more than one income earner. During the years immediately after the Second World War, an unemployed worker was often the sole or primary source of income for a family, but this situation became significantly less common in the late 1960s and 1970s, as the labour-force/participation rate of youth and, most dramatically, of married women increased. Even when unemployment peaked in December 1982, nearly 70 per cent of families with one or more unemployed members had at least one member who was working. In more than half of these families, the unemployed person was not the primary income earner. Another factor in easing the hardship of unemployment has been the expansion of the coverage and the benefits of the Unemployment Insurance (UI) system and, to a lesser extent, of provincial welfare programs. In addition, both real income and wealth have grown substantially so that many families can finance periods of unemployment more readily now than in the past.

In noting this long-term trend towards reduced hardship, the severity of the current unemployment problem and associated financial hardship must be acknowledged fully. As several studies have confirmed, the burden of unemployment is unevenly distributed among members of society.[11] Thus we make these general statements about the unemployed population as a whole in the full realization that they do not apply in many individual cases.

Given this general easing of hardship in the past few decades, some analysts have challenged the notion that unemployment is largely involuntary. The outcome of the ensuing debate has widely confirmed the very uncertain nature of the distinction between voluntary and involuntary unemployment. Keynes classified unemployment as voluntary if a job is available, but the unemployed worker is not willing to accept it at the existing wage; involuntary unemployment, he said, occurs when the worker is willing to work at existing wages, but no jobs are available. Much popular discussion today uses a simpler distinction: unemployment initiated by a worker's quitting the last job is classified as voluntary, and other unemployment is considered involuntary.

Neither approach is sufficiently subtle to provide ground for analysis of some labour-market situations. Job hunters may have imperfect information about the various jobs available and their rates of pay and working conditions, and their unawareness makes it difficult to draw a dividing line between voluntary and involuntary unemployment. If an individual refuses the first job available, but continues to search for employment, is he or she voluntarily unemployed? Similarly, if a worker joins a firm or enters an industry or occupation known to be subject to lay-offs, in response to fluctuations in demand, is he or she voluntarily unemployed when a lay-off occurs? The unemployment is voluntary in the sense that the worker knew the risk at the time of accepting employment; indeed, the wage received may well have reflected this risk. It is involuntary, however, in the sense that he or she might have preferred continued work, even at a reduced wage.

The extensive debate has not produced agreement on acceptable definitions of voluntary and involuntary unemployment. It has, however, resulted in some new ways of looking at unemployment. One that emerged in the 1970s was the "new unemployment" view, which emphasized the importance of turn-over in the labour market. Its proponents challenged the notion that unemployment can be characterized simply as a shortage of jobs for a stock of unemployed workers waiting for an economic expansion. Rather, they suggested, at least when the economy was at or below the NAIRU, the problem was not a shortage of jobs, but the brevity of many spells of employment, which presumably reflected a large supply of unattractive jobs and a certain amount of experimentation with different types of employment. This situation, said the turn-over analysts, was particulary characteristic of many younger workers and of women, the groups whose labour-force participation was rising significantly. As evidence, they pointed to the substantial flows among the various labour-market categories (employed, unemployed, out of the labour force) and to the relatively brief duration of spells of unemployment.

A considerable amount of subsequent research has shown that while this concept is valid in a number of important respects, it is overly simplistic as a general description of unemployment. Research confirms, for example, that average spells of unemployment are brief, typically lasting two to two-and-a-half months. Furthermore, the groups with the highest unemployment rates, that is, youth and women, undergo shorter durations of unemployment than men. Thus, more frequent, rather than longer, spells of unemployment must account for the higher unemployment rates of youth and women. The research also shows, however, that a sizeable minority of workers suffer long spells of joblessness, and these lengthy spells account for a significant amount of the economy's total unemployment. In other words, individuals unemployed for long periods bear a substantial portion of the total burden of unemployment. Moreover, some of them are "chronically unemployed" because they suffer such repeated spells of joblessness that they are unemployed for a substantial portion of their working lives. For these individuals, the claim that unemployment primarily reflects a shortage of available jobs seems substantially accurate. This conclusion is reinforced by the findings that a substantial proportion of spells of unemployment end in withdrawal from the labour force, that this proportion increases with the length of the spell of unemployment, and that spells of unemployment that end in employment are longer, on average, than those that end in withdrawal from the labour force.

Many analysts decry unemployment as a waste of valuable human resources. Although this description is widely accepted as applicable to unemployment caused by a deficiency of aggregate demand, it is less so to other components of the unemployment rate: frictional unemployment, which results from time lags in workers' moving from one job to another; seasonal unemployment, which results from the seasonal nature of activity in some industries and kinds of jobs; and structural unemployment, which results from basic changes in technology and consumer demand.

In fact, *some* periods of unemployment, rather than being a waste of resources, are a productive investment in the acquisition of information about job opportunities. To a point, job turn-over among young labour-force participants may represent their productive investment in the acquisition of information about types of employment most suitable for the longer term. In addition, for any unemployed searcher always to accept the first job offered is not in the interest either of the individual or of society. The search process, both by employers with job vacancies and by unemployed or underemployed workers, facilitates the efficient matching of workers and jobs. Similarly, temporary lay-offs in response to fluctuations in demand can be an efficient arrangement for employers and employees, especially when workers highly value brief periods of additional leisure time, and when the alternatives to lay-offs, such as inventory accumulation, are prohibitively expensive.

Thus, *some* of the unemployment unrelated to deficient demand is beneficial in the sense that it yields returns both to the individual and to society. The challenge in terms of policy is to ensure that the amounts of seasonal, frictional and structural unemployment are not excessive: that is, that the NAIRU is not too high.

A final observation concerning the waste of human resources applies to the way in which we measure unemployment. The unemployment rate as it is currently calculated does not reflect all unutilized or underutilized labour. The most important exclusion is the group commonly referred to as "discouraged workers": people who could work, but are not searching for employment because they believe that none is available, or because they are still awaiting recall after more than six months on lay-off. Another important group omitted consists of the underemployed people who are working fewer hours than they wish, or who are temporarily performing jobs that do not fully use their skills. The importance of these groups increases significantly in times of recession, but some underuse exists when the economy is at the NAIRU, because of a mismatch of job skills, for example.

The NAIRU is estimated to have risen from the 4 to 5 per cent range in the 1950s and early 1960s, to 6 to 7 per cent in the early 1970s, and to 6.5 to 8 per cent today. (These estimates should be treated with some caution because of the difficulties in allowing for the variety of factors that have affected inflation and unemployment during these years.) A detailed treatment of the various factors that are believed to have caused this rise in the NAIRU is provided in Part V of our Report. Briefly, the two factors that most empirical studies have found important are the very substantial demographic changes that have occurred in Canada since the Second World War and changes in social legislation that have affected the labour market, particularly legislation regarding Unemployment Insurance and, to a lesser extent, minimum wages. A third potentially important factor – one that has received little attention until recently – is the rapidity of structural change in the economy. If the pace of change accelerates, structural unemployment will increase temporarily as the economy and labour markets adjust to increases in demand in some industries and decreases in others. Some evidence indicates that the rate of structural adjustment was higher in the 1970s and early 1980s than in the late 1950s and early 1960s, although it is now probably no greater than it was during the immediate post-war period. However, the extent to which this increased volatility of the economic environment has contributed to a higher NAIRU has yet to be established.

The various factors have different implications for the future course of the NAIRU. Most of the demographic trends should now be leading towards a decline in the NAIRU, albeit a slow one: the growth rate of the labour force has dropped from earlier peak levels; most members of the baby-boom generation have slowly worked their way into the labour market; and the labour-force/participation rate of women is not expected to continue its earlier rate of rapid growth. Similarly, social legislation, particularly amendments to the Unemployment Insurance Act since the later 1970s, has contributed to some reduction in the NAIRU, although the extent to which these developments have been offset by increasing structural adjustment is an unsettled question. To predict the degree of volatility of the future economic environment is, of course, even more difficult.

Thus we see that the evolution of knowledge and belief about unemployment has led to increased recognition of its complexity and of the trade-offs between employment and other goals. The commitment to full employment declared in the 1945 White Paper on Employment and Income[12] has gradually given way to the realization that policy makers must pay attention to the goal of achieving both high employment levels and price stability. The degree to which unemployment results in economic hardship, the extent to which it represents a waste of human resources, and the proportion in which it is involuntary are questions that continue to be debated extensively, and this Commission can draw no simple conclusions concerning them. Unemployment is associated with financial difficulties, but for many unemployed persons, the degree of hardship is less now than it was in the past. Deficient demand and most structural unemployment result in a waste of resources, with associated human and social costs, but some frictional and other kinds of unemployment can be productive, since they can improve the matching of workers and jobs, and facilitate adjustment to economic fluctuations. The degree to which unemployment is voluntary or involuntary is disputed to the extent that agreement has not yet been reached even on the meaning of these terms.

Inflation and Real Economic Performance

One of the most fundamental shifts in policy attitudes over the course of the 1970s was towards inflation. During the early 1970s, governments in countries that belonged to the Organisation for Economic Co-operation and Development (OECD) tended to accept the trade-off view of the relation between unemployment and inflation. Although they wanted to avoid a continual upward ratchetting of inflation, they seemed willing to live with the current rate of inflation, which was then in the 3 to 6 per cent range in most countries, rather than wage an all-out campaign to reduce it. By the end of the 1970s, however, the rate of inflation was nearing, or had passed, the 10 per cent level in many of these countries. Particularly after the second OPEC oil increase, which occurred in 1979–80, most of the Western industrial nations became much less willing to accommodate inflation. What were the causes of this change?

Some analysts have argued that the combination of rising inflation and falling real economic performance (slower real growth and higher unemployment) in the 1970s indicated that inflation *causes* poor real economic performance. This case is not easy to establish because of three strands of the 1970s experience.

Clearly, the relationship between economic performance and inflation during the decade was not causal. The oil-price shocks raised inflation, lowered real demand for goods and services, and probably lowered their real potential supply, as producers economized on the use of petroleum at the cost of some loss to their potential production with any given amount of labour and capital. The slow-down in the underlying trend of productivity growth, which some, though not all, analysts identify, also tended to worsen both real performance and inflation. These adverse "supply-side" shocks, although important to an understanding of economic development in the 1970s, do not imply a causal relationship running from inflation to real economic performance. In particular, few economists think that a more clearly anti-inflationary demand-management policy would have affected the size or the real impact of those supply-side shocks in any basic way, for better or for worse.

A second strand in the relationship between inflation and real economic performance involves the effect of inflation on demand. It is possible that an increase in the rate of inflation, in particular an increase that is not a direct result of a shock such as the escalation of world oil prices, might depress an economy's real demand for goods and services. In the absence of a fully indexed tax system – a system with inflation adjustments for capital consumption allowances, inventory costs, interest deductions, capital gains, and so on – inflation is likely to reduce the real after-tax rate of return on investment. All other factors being equal, this effect will discourage capital investment. Long-term investment is particularly sensitive to uncertainty about future rates of inflation and interest rates, and uncertainty can reasonably be expected to be greater when inflation averages 10 per cent than when it averages 2 to 4 per cent. Moreover, inflation may depress capital investment that depends on financing amortized over a long period of time, such as mortgage financing for construction, because inflation increases "front-end loading": that is, the real cash flow that must be allocated to debt servicing in the early years of amortization.[13] Inflation is also likely to raise nominal personal savings rates, but it simultaneously increases nominal personal interest income. Finally, if a country's rates of inflation are higher than those in competing countries and are not fully offset by exchange-rate depreciation, the result is a loss of competitive strength and thus further weakness in demand.

In these instances, causation runs from inflation to real demand, which, in turn, has effects on economic performance. In theory, the effects can be offset by various institutional adjustments, such as indexing the tax system as it applies to business income, interest and capital gains; introducing indexed or graduated-payment bonds and mortgages; letting nominal government deficits rise both to offset the higher nominal personal savings corresponding to the "inflation premium" component of interest income and to reflect the decline in the real value of government-debt costs; and appropriately depreciating exchange rates.

Some of these adjustments occurred in Canada during the last decade. There were various *ad hoc* increases in investment incentives in the tax system, although economists debate whether they fully offset the interaction between high inflation and the lack of an "inflation-accounting" approach to the calculation of taxable income. There were some limited experiments with graduated-payment debt instruments to alleviate the front-end/loading problem with mortgages. The Canadian government ran deficits during the late 1970s that were probably high enough to offset roughly the inflation component of its public debt costs. Except between 1974 and mid-1976, Canada's exchange rate adjusted in a way that, by and large, offset any excess of domestic inflation over inflation experienced by our major trading partners. The presence of these adjustment mechanisms makes it unlikely that any major portion of the fall-off in Canada's economic performance after 1973 can be attributed to the aspects of inflation that reduce real demand.

A third strand in the relation between inflation and real economic performance is inflation's potential for impairing the functioning of the economic system. History and theory suggest that in situations of very high inflation, savings flows tend to be diverted from investments that have long-run productivity to various "inflation hedges" comprised of real estate and readily storable commodities such as gold and art. Meanwhile, many participants in the economy devote substantial amounts of time, effort and paperwork to keeping up with inflation information, resetting prices, minimizing average cash balances that are earning no return, and comparable activities; yet the complexity and uncertainty of many of these economic calculations presumably lessens the efficiency of the economy. In particular, uncertainty besets longer-term decisions so that investment planners generally shorten their time horizons with a resulting loss of attention to actions oriented to the longer-term future. Causation here clearly runs from inflation to economic performance, although the worsening of the latter may accumulate only slowly and be reflected partly in recorded real-output statistics and partly in unmeasured inconvenience to various participants in the economy. Assessment of the quantitative importance of this category of inflation effects is necessarily speculative, even in the case of hyperinflation. Intuitive judgements of the importance of adverse impacts of this type, which arise from inflation in the 10 per cent range, suggest that the effects were probably slight to moderate and were generally not high enough to account at all fully for the productivity slow-down.

As we have noted, however, most OECD countries did harden their approach to inflation in the late 1970s, and they persisted in doing so even in the face of the severe recession of the early 1980s. Their governments were generally unwilling fully to accommodate even the direct inflationary effects of the second oil shock, whereas a number of countries, including Canada, had provided significant monetary and/or fiscal accommodation at the time of the first oil shock. Even in the spring of 1979, before the second oil shock, the Carter administration was obviously tightening the U.S. policy and thus making reduction of inflation a key medium-term goal, notwithstanding clear recognition that a period of above-average economic slack would likely be initiated in the process. In the United Kingdom, the Thatcher government has, of course, become noted for its severe anti-inflation measures, but the Labour government of Prime Minister James Callaghan had already moved to a basically non-accommodating stance in its last two or three years in office.[14]

It seems reasonable to suppose that in a number of these countries, an intuitive judgement – or fear – that inflation impairs real economic performance along one or more of the lines already suggested was one of the reasons for giving priority to policy meant to contain and reduce inflation. Other factors, however, were probably just as important or even more so. One was the growing recognition that, as explained in the preceding section, any real gains in economic performance resulting from the adoption of inflationary demand policies was likely to be short lived. In fact, given the probable sensitivity of expectations (particularly as they affected interest rates and exchange rates) to an indication that a government was prepared to accept higher inflation, stimulative policy might have accelerated inflation more rapidly than historical relationships suggested, and any gains in real activity levels would have been particularly brief.

The notion of learning to live with relatively high rates of inflation has not been appealing. Neither governments nor the general public have shown a desire to make the institutional changes, including indexation of various types, that would be required to ease at least some of the problems associated with living with, say, 10 per cent inflation. Continuing inflation in this range creates serious inequities. (The largest readily identifiable group of "losers" consists of elderly people whose pension rights are not protected by full indexation, or who have significant savings invested in such a way that they are not able to take advantage of high interest rates.) Furthermore, the political viability of maintaining a fairly high rate of inflation is open to question. If a government is prepared to tolerate 10 per cent inflation, why should people believe that it will take decisive action to prevent a climb to 11 or 12 or 15 per cent or even higher? Sooner or later, the public will reject high inflation, whether it is climbing steadily or intermittently, and demand that it be controlled at what is generally accepted as a low level.

The difficulty of the process of adjustment varies, of course. The higher the rate of inflation, and the more firmly entrenched inflationary expectations have become, the more difficult adjustment becomes. Moreover, the authorities have a range of choices about the degree and pace of the reduction. Most of the major members of the Organisation for Economic Co-operation and Development initially opted to curb inflation gradually. (A partial exception was the United Kingdom, which started its process of adjustment from cost inflation of 15 to 20 per cent.) However, the United States, in 1979, and Canada, in 1980, decided to accept the risk of recession and adjusted their monetary policies in order to reduce inflation more sharply.

In sum, the tendency among the industrial nations to give priority to anti-inflation measures in the late 1970s and early 1980s did not reflect conclusive new evidence of the adverse effects of inflation on economic performance.[15] Neither was it based on carefully calculated comparisons of the likely courses of economic performance under combative and relaxed attitudes towards inflation. Rather, it reflected a widespread judgement – almost, one might say, an instinct – that to accommodate high and rising inflation was simply no way to run an economy. This view was perhaps based as much on fear of the possibility that ever-increasing inflation could, at some unpredictable point, lead to major economic collapse and social and institutional upheaval as on the probability that over some specified period, average real living standards would become x per cent lower if inflation were allowed to continue.

The Implications of an Open Economy for Demand-Management Policy

We have already noted that modern macro-economic analysis had its genesis in Keynes' *General Theory*. As its title indicates, this was a work of economic theory; moreover, it dealt primarily with a closed economy: that is, one that neither trades nor engages in capital-market transactions with the outside world. The subsequent development of Keynesian thought, particularly the systematic explication of its implicit policy conclusions, tended to be dominated by the work of economists based in the United States, where, in the 1940s and 1950s, the hypothesis of a closed economy closely coincided with the nature of the country. For that reason, analysis of the problems of an open economy, which is of particular relevance to Canada, was rather slow in coming.

To adapt Keynes' theories to the dynamics of an open economy required economists to broaden their understanding of issues involving the international balance of payments, as well as to develop a clearer knowledge of the implications of monetary and fiscal policy changes in an economy that is exposed to the world through the trade and capital flowing across its borders. Subsidiary considerations included adapting early ideas about policy in an underemployed economy to a fully employed economy, a process so much more relevant in the first two decades after the Second World War, and in due course, the creation of a body of analysis directed at understanding the inflationary process in an open economy.

Without doing too much violence to historical accuracy, we can begin to describe these developments by examining what is referred to as the "elasticities approach" to the balance of trade: that is, the sensitivity to changes in the exchange rate of the quantity of exports times their price, minus the quantity of imports times their price. In the 1930s, many governments resorted to devaluation of their currencies, in an effort to promote their exports by making them cheaper abroad and to cut back on imports from abroad, many of which competed with domestic goods, by making them more expensive at home. Many economists of the day thought that whether an individual country could sustain such a policy – quite apart from whether many countries could succeed in using the same remedy simultaneously – depended on the sensitivity of home demand for imports and of foreign demand for exports. The explanation of their thinking may be found in the extreme example in which both export and import demands are completely insensitive to price. Devaluation can then do nothing to improve the demand for domestic output and will clearly lead to a deterioration of the trade balance. In terms of foreign currency, for instance, the amount received in payment for exports will decline as a result of the depreciation of the exchange rate,[16] while the amount paid for imports will remain unchanged.[17]

As demand sensitivity to prices increases, this extreme outcome begins to change. The quantity of goods imported will fall as their domestic prices rise, and the quantity of goods exported will increase as their foreign prices fall; thus aggregate demand will certainly expand. Whether the balance of trade will improve, however, depends on the sensitivity of the demand responses in question. If quantities demanded change only slightly in response to price, the balance of trade will continue to deteriorate. If demand is sensitive enough, however, the balance of trade will improve. The sensitivity of demand to price is called "elasticity"; this factor is computed as the ratio of the percentage change in quantity demanded to the percentage change in price. The precise break-even point – the point at which there will be no change in the trade balance – lies where the sum of the price elasticities of demand for imports and exports is unity.

Given the critical function that this analysis ascribed to elasticities of demand (and of supply, in more elaborate versions), it is hardly surprising that from the late 1930s to the early 1950s, there was much debate among economists about the precise statistical degrees involved. Those who were pessimistic about the elasticity of demand to price changes doubted that devaluation could much improve trade balances, while those who were optimistic held the opposite view. The argument was not solely academic. Pessimism about the elasticities of prices must lead to the conclusion that a regime of flexible exchange rates is inherently unstable: because the exchange rate of a trade-deficit country tends to fall under such a regime, it exacerbates the deficit, setting up a vicious circle of falling exchange rates and deteriorating trade balances. Hence, in the political sphere, pessimism about elasticities was strongly associated with interventionism in the exchange market and often with more general economic intervention.

After the Second World War, it soon became apparent that the elasticities approach provided only partial analysis of the balance of trade in a world in which low employment levels were the norm. The unqualified elasticities approach presumes the existence of a stock of unemployed resources that can be drawn on to meet the extra demand for exports and import substitutes that results from a successful currency devaluation. A fully employed economy does not have such a stock; it cannot expand supply for foreign trade without diverting resources from other uses in the economy.

Here we have the fundamental insight of what came to be called the "absorption approach" to balance-of-payments analysis: that a country in which domestic absorption (that is, consumption plus investment plus government expenditure) exceeds the economy's productive capacity is bound to have a balance-of-trade deficit, regardless of the exchange rate, because it must import goods and services to meet domestic demand. Two corollaries follow. One is that a country with a fully employed economy can improve its trade balance through devaluation only if it takes simultaneous measures to reduce domestic demand, thus making resources available for the production of exports. The second corollary is that the successful operation of a regime of flexible exchange rates requires attention to the level of aggregate domestic demand.

That second corollary required economists to extend their analysis of demand-management policy. One of the most important examples of this extension was the Mundell-Fleming model, named for the Canadian and British economists who independently developed it. This model was essentially an open-economy version of the closed-economy macro-analysis popular in the 1950s and early 1960s, which we have already described. Today we see that this model had serious shortcomings; specifically, it concentrated on macro-economic policy's influences on levels of income and employment, using three unhelpful assumptions: that the economy was chronically underemployed; that its price levels were fixed for the foreseeable future; and that people expect the exchange rate to remain static. Nevertheless, this analysis yielded two insights of lasting importance for macro-economic theory. First, it stressed, as earlier analysis had not, that the balance of payments consists of more than the trade balance: it also includes the balance of capital flows, to which economists and policy makers must pay attention in devising economic policy in an open economy. Secondly, the analysis clearly demonstrated the fact that in an open economy, the manner in which domestic policy impinges on purely domestic goals, let alone on the balance of payments and exchange-rate targets, depends on the nature of the country's exchange-rate regime. According to the Mundell-Fleming model, a country with fixed exchange rates could use fiscal policy, but not monetary policy, to pursue domestic income and employment goals. Flexible exchange rates reversed the possibilities.

This conclusion, the precise form of which is nowadays of more academic than practical interest, followed from consideration of the effects of capital flows in determining the balance of payments under fixed exchange rates and in influencing exchange rates under a flexible system. In particular, the model assumed that international capital flows were highly elastic (at the extreme, perfectly elastic) in response to interest-rate differentials. Thus, in a country with a system of fixed exchange rates, any attempt to lower interest rates through an increase in the money supply would be frustrated by the reaction of the international capital market, whose funds would flow out to take advantage of higher interest rates elsewhere. By the same token, an expansionary fiscal policy would not be offset by rising domestic interest rates as it would be in a closed economy. Rather, capital inflows induced by a tendency of domestic interest rates to rise would ensure that expansionary fiscal policy could simultaneously increase domestic income and improve the overall balance of payments. Although domestic credit does not expand in the model, the money supply does, in response to the capital inflow to neutralize upward pressure on interest rates and the exchange rate.

Under a flexible system of exchange rates, however, capital inflows generated in response to the incipient increase in interest rates which results from the expansion of fiscal policy would drive up the exchange rate.[18] This appreciation, which would make exports more expensive abroad and imports cheaper at home, would tend to go on until the effect of expansionary fiscal policy on domestic output was offset by a change in the real balance of exports and imports. An expansionary monetary policy, however, would drive down a flexible exchange rate through its incipient downward pressure on interest rates, affecting domestic income and employment. Therefore, it was argued, a regime of flexible exchange rates would restore the potency that monetary policy was thought to have in a closed economy. The model simply transformed the route by which policy would have its effects; that route would cease to be one primarily involving changes in interest rates and become one primarily involving changes in exchange rates.

The late 1960s and early 1970s witnessed major growth in both the size and the efficiency of world-wide capital markets. The same period also saw the emergence of inflation as a world-wide problem. Macro-economic theorists working on open economies began to incorporate these developments, as they did the subsequent breakdown of the system of (more or less) fixed exchange rates that had been established shortly after the Second World War and the international financial turbulence of the 1970s and 1980s.

Two contemporary ideas profoundly influenced economists' views about the manner in which macro-economic policy should be conducted in an open economy. These were monetarism, which insisted, particularly, on the central importance to the inflationary process of the interaction of the supply and demand for money, and the development of the expectations-augmented Phillips curve, which was important to the understanding of the relationship between inflation and unemployment. The monetary approach to analysis of the balance of payments and exchange rates emerged, in the early 1970s, from the work of Canadian economists Robert Mundell and Harry Johnson, among others. With benefit of hindsight, it can be seen both as a major extension of the Mundell-Fleming model and as an attempt to overcome the shortcomings of that earlier analysis. This new approach focused on a world in which prices were not assumed to be stable, but rather one in which inflation was a central policy problem. Taking up Friedman's insight, this approach identified as the key factor underlying longer-run inflation the interaction of the supply of, and demand for, money, both in the world economy as a whole, under fixed exchange rates, and in individual open economies, under flexible rates.

This analysis also pointed out that the way in which expectations about inflation are formed differs under fixed and flexible exchange-rate regimes. Under a fixed system, an individual economy, especially a relatively small one, cannot long sustain a rate of inflation very different from that prevailing abroad. Therefore expectations about the prospects for inflation in that country must be based primarily on views about the prospective levels of inflation in the rest of the world. A system of exchange rates that are flexible, however, permits participants in the economy to draw their expectations from the domestic scene. In other words, a flexible exchange rate permits an open economy to have not only its own "made-at-home" inflation *rate*, but also its own inflation *expectations*.

A detailed review of current macro-economic theory relating to the open economy is unnecessary, but it is useful to mention one or two highlights. Modern analysis makes it abundantly clear that, contrary to the Mundell-Fleming model, adopting a flexible exchange rate does not turn an open economy into one that for the purposes of conducting policy may be treated as if it were closed. Flexible rates do give an open economy latitude in choosing its own long-run inflation rate, but they do not insulate it from the short-run, but often severe, effects of monetary turbulence abroad. Examples of these often-widespread effects include transmission of pressures on interest rates from one country to another and wide swings in exchange rates that are not directly related to differences in inflation rates, that is, wide swings in real exchange rates. Neither do flexible exchange rates insulate an economy from such real shocks as world-market changes in the relative prices of energy or raw materials. Moreover, since flexible exchange rates are determined in extremely efficient markets, a country has great difficulty exploiting any short-run trade-offs between inflation and unemployment that closed-economy analysis suggests. In fact, there is always a distinct possibility that domestic policy changes in an open economy may have their first effect, not on output and employment, but on exchange rates and, thereby, on domestic prices.

What general conclusions can be drawn from this brief and necessarily oversimplified account of the evolution of the macro-economic theory of the open economy? Above all, this theory increasingly stresses that the pursuit of domestic policy goals is interdependent with actions affecting the balance of payments and exchange rates. Moreover, the complex nature of that interdependence suggests that there are important limits to the actual policy independence possessed by the authorities of an open economy such as Canada. With a flexible exchange rate, we Canadians can choose our long-run inflation rate, and to that extent we can have a "made-in-Canada" macro-economic policy. We cannot, however, insulate our economy from foreign monetary developments in the short term or from real developments.

Moreover, because the workings of international capital and exchange markets can so limit, both in duration and scope, the potential of our monetary and fiscal policies for affecting real demand, the effect of our policy actions on domestic and foreign expectations – that is, on confidence – is especially important.

These conclusions are very different from those formed by macro-economists of the early post-war period, which seemed to suggest that the authorities of a country such as Canada had broad scope to fine-tune the performance of their domestic economies. Views on these matters have shifted for two reasons. First, understanding of the way in which the economy works has changed. To some extent, the current, more pessimistic view of the possibilities of fine-tuning the economy are based on analyses of interactions that have long been at work in the world, but that earlier analyses failed to take into account. However, the second reason – one that encourages Commissioners to take those views seriously – is the changed nature of the world. The international economy is much more integrated now than it was 20 or 30 years ago. In particular, the world capital market has been transformed beyond all recognition, both in size and efficiency, reducing the latitude available to the government of an open economy to pursue autonomous macro-economic policies.

Commissioners have noted at several points in this Report the great benefits that accrue to Canada from its participation in a liberal international economic order, and we have argued that further liberalization of the international economy is highly desirable. Although we believe that the gains of such a policy would outweigh the costs, we must, nevertheless, note that this international integration has imposed costs on Canada in the form of exposure to external shocks and considerable loss of domestic autonomy in short-run macro-economic policy matters.

The Budget Deficit: An Independent Constraint on Policy?

Are budgetary deficits of the magnitude of the current Canadian and U.S. federal deficits in themselves a matter for economic concern? In the past, economists who subscribed to Keynesian views on demand management usually argued that the size of the deficit was not a matter for concern. The important point was "to balance the economy" rather than "to balance the budget". These economists did not argue that the amount of the deficit should be limitless, but rather that the size of the deficit should be determined only by what was required to provide the appropriate amount of aggregate demand in the economy. Such economists also argued that since public debt is often held largely by citizens of the country, a situation which certainly applies to Canada's federal debt, it is an obligation that the people of a country mostly owe to themselves. For this reason, it does not impose a burden on a nation as a whole, comparable to the burden that exists when an individual or a firm is in debt to someone outside the family or corporate group.

The first consideration in looking at deficits is their implications for the growth of government debt relative to the size of the economy. If the ratio of the debt to the size of the economy is constant or decreasing, it is difficult to argue that the deficit presents an imminent crisis or is unsustainable, although it may be cause for continuing concern. Figure 10-1 shows the ratios of net debt of the Canadian federal government to gross national product (GNP), which is a measure of the size of the economy, for the fiscal years from 1927 to the present, plus projected values for fiscal years from 1985 to 1991. At the beginning of the period, the debt/GNP ratio was high, reflecting the large deficits incurred in the First World War; it increased significantly during the Depression and then jumped dramatically as a result of heavy deficit financing during the Second World War. From the end of the war until fiscal 1975, the federal government ran surpluses in some years and relatively modest deficits in others. On balance, the dollar value of the net debt outstanding increased moderately, but it grew much less rapidly than the economy, so that the debt/GNP ratio fell dramatically. By fiscal 1975, it was much lower than it had been at any time since the First World War. Since 1975, however, the size of deficits has driven the outstanding debt up more rapidly than GNP has increased, and the same trend has continued very much more rapidly since fiscal 1982. The current debt/GNP ratio is more than double its 1975 value, though it is still substantially below the levels experienced from the First World War to the early 1950s. The projections for the next seven years, which were based on the tax and expenditure structure in place before the November 1984 fiscal statement and reasonably favourable economic assumptions, show the debt/GNP ratio as continuing to rise. Measures announced in November 1984 and not reflected in the projections shown were expected to moderate, but not reverse, this upward trend.

The debt/GNP ratio will rise as long as the ratio of the deficit to GNP exceeds the rate of GNP growth multiplied by the ratio of the outstanding debt to GNP. With the federal government's net debt standing currently at some 40 per cent of GNP and nominal GNP growth in the 7 per cent range (representing roughly 3 per cent real growth plus 4 per cent inflation), a deficit equal to 2.8 per cent of GNP (that is, 7 per cent of 40 per cent) would entail no change in the debt/GNP ratio. However, the budgetary deficit for fiscal 1985 is projected at $35.8 billion, which is some 8.5 per cent of GNP, and even assuming sustained recovery, the deficit prior to the May 1985 budget measures was projected at about 6 per cent of GNP for fiscal 1991.

Another useful reference point in considering deficits and debt is the budget balance excluding net public debt charges (that is, net of government investment income), which is sometimes called the "primary balance". (See Figure 10-2.) Debt would grow in lock-step with GNP if the primary balance were zero and the average interest rate paid by the government on its debt were just equal to the growth rate of nominal GNP. In fact, however, current interest rates are higher than the expected average rate of GNP growth. Under these circumstances, the primary balance must be in surplus to avoid an increase in the debt/GNP ratio. Nevertheless, the primary balance for Canada is currently in a deficit equal to roughly 4 per cent of GNP, and projections prior to the May 1985 budget showed that even by fiscal 1991, it would decline only to about 1.25 per cent of GNP.

FIGURE 10-1 Government of Canada: Net Public Debt as a Percentage of GNP

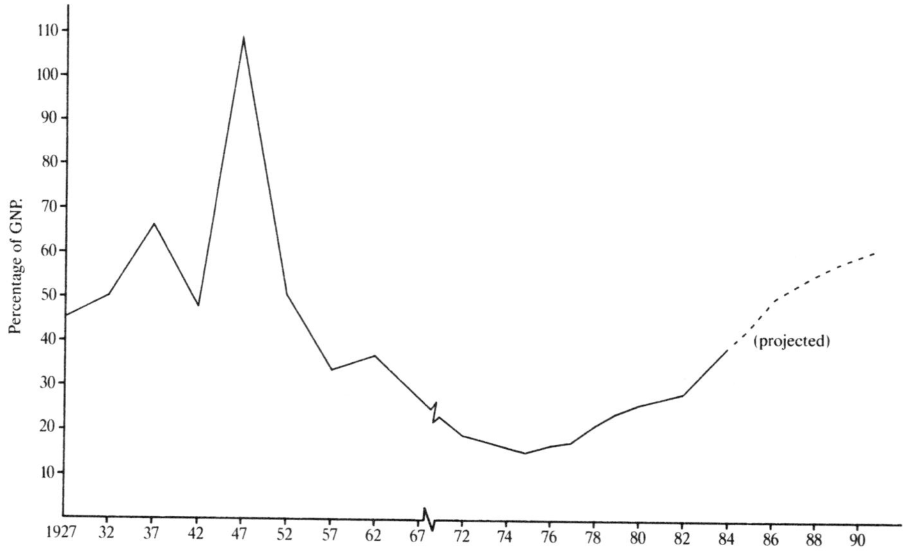

Source: Projections calculated from Minister of Finance, Government of Canada, *A New Direction for Canada*, November 1984.

Notes: The projected values are based on the "status quo" projections in the federal government's fiscal statement of November 1984. These projections assumed the existing tax structure and the expenditure programs and plans that had then been enacted or put before Parliament, but they did not allow for measures introduced in that statement. They also assumed reasonably favourable economic conditions: an average annual rate of real growth of more than 3 percent, a gradual decline in the unemployment rate to 7 per cent by 1990; and a substantial decline in nominal and real interest rates.

The Canadian federal deficit is clearly of a magnitude, even if it should be reduced automatically by further economic recovery, to raise serious questions about its sustainability. The federal budgetary structure prior to the May 1985 budget implied continuing increases in the debt/GNP ratio and, if all other factors are equal, a rising ratio of interest charges to GNP. Just to cover the increases in interest charges would mean continuing increases in tax rates, continuing reductions in expenditures, or carrying still higher deficits. These implications for the government's fiscal position and for future tax and expenditure levels probably provide the clearest reasons for concern about the size of Canada's current and projected deficits.

Another frequent concern is that high deficits or debt tend to "crowd out" private investment, thus reducing future prospects for economic growth.[19] In an open economy, high deficits also tend to crowd out net exports. (The impact of the government deficit on net exports can be offset by other factors, such as high private savings, a phenomen currently apparent in Canada.) Crowding out can occur through upward pressures on interest rates and/or

FIGURE 10-2 Government of Canada: The Primary Deficit and Net Public Debt Charges as a Percentage of GNP

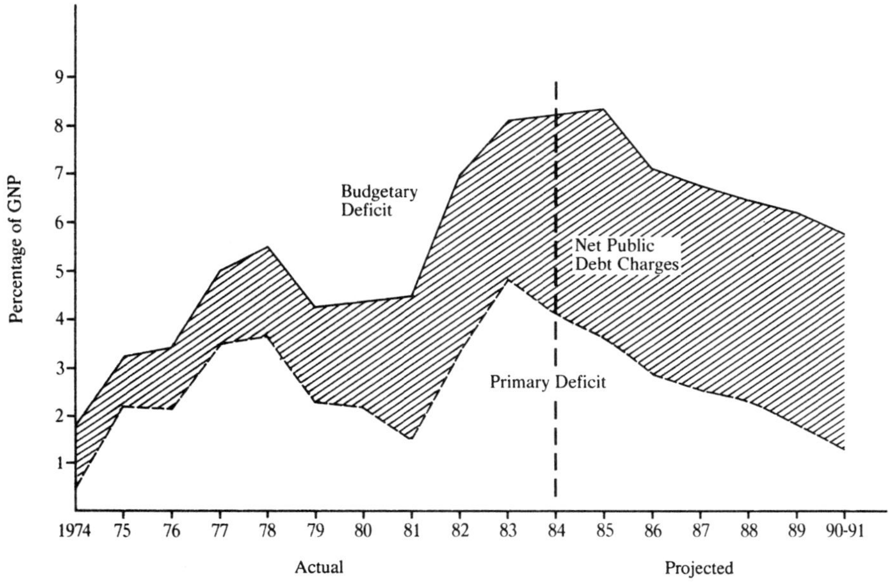

Source: Government of Canada, Dept.of Finance, *A New Direction for Canada*, 1984.

exchange rates deriving from the government's demand for capital financing.[20] Many analysts attribute, at least in part, the high levels of real interest rates that have prevailed internationally since 1982 to the large government deficits being run by many countries, especially by the United States, given its importance in the world's capital markets.

A final criticism of high deficits and debts is that they make governments vulnerable to increases in interest rates and constrain their ability to manœuvre. In particular, they reduce governments' ability to take expansionary fiscal action.

Before leaving this analytical consideration of deficits, it is appropriate to ask why the Canadian deficit has grown to be such a major problem and to examine the circumstances under which it would be reasonable to anticipate bringing it under better control. As we have already noted, at the end of the Second World War, the federal government faced a huge debt, amounting to some 100 per cent of GNP. Over the ensuing 30 years, however, that debt fell almost continuously as a percentage of GNP, and in more than half of these years, it fell absolutely. As a result, by 1975, Canada's federal net debt was only 15.5 per cent of GNP. During the last half of the 1970s, however, the budgetary deficit increased substantially; it averaged more than 3.5 per cent of GNP from fiscal 1976 to 1982 and then ballooned with the severe recession that began in the latter year. These enlarged deficits caused the debt/GNP ratio to rise again; it reached 26 per cent by 1980 and more than 40 per cent in March 1985, a figure higher than that for any year since the beginning of the 1950s.

This pattern is not unique to Canada. Beginning in about 1975, almost all developed countries moved from the relatively balanced budgets of the post-war period to large deficits. As a result, the total government debt outstanding for some 17 OECD countries increased from about 40 per cent of GNP in 1970 to 51 per cent in 1983.

Why did almost all developed countries suddenly experience this shift after three decades in which debt and deficit problems were almost non-existent or, at most, easily manageable? To understand the reason, it is helpful to take into account some simple arithmetic that applies to deficits. If we leave aside for the moment the balance of exports and imports, economic logic dictates a precise relationship between the surplus or deficit of the government and the corresponding surplus or deficit of the private sector. A private sector surplus is defined here as an excess of private sector savings over private sector capital spending. If the government sector is running a deficit of a given size, the private sector must have a surplus of the same size. Thus, the sudden rise in government deficits after 1975 had to be matched by an equal rise in private sector surpluses.

Of course, simple arithmetical relationships do not, in themselves, say anything about causation. Do high private sector savings cause larger government deficits, or is it the other way around? In 1982, at least, the direction of causation seems clear. Private sector capital spending in Canada (including changes in inventory) fell from 21.8 per cent of GNP in 1981, to 16.1 per cent in 1982. That sharp decline caused income to fall, thus reducing government revenues, while increased unemployment produced correspondingly higher government expenditures. Because the fall in private spending was so large, the increase in government deficits was also very large.

Since 1982, savings in the private sector have continued to be relatively high, while its capital spending has remained weak. Necessarily, the government-sector deficit has been large. Thus, the process of restoring Canada's fiscal balance will have to involve a recovery in private capital spending and perhaps some reduction in the relatively high savings rate.

The preceding analysis, however, does not take account of the foreign sector: that is, our imports and exports of goods and services and the differences between them. If we expand our consideration to include the balance on current account, we must modify our simple arithmetic. For example, a government deficit may be partly offset by a private sector surplus and partly by an excess of imports over exports. Such an excess implies that foreign savings are being drawn on to help finance the government deficit. (This is exactly what is occurring on a large scale in the United States at the present time.)

The relationships between the balances in the government sector, the private sector, and the foreign sector are shown in Table 10-1 for the seven major industrial countries in the OECD from 1975 to 1982. As these data show, the foreign sector balances were usually small, and so there was a close relationship between government-sector deficits and private sector surpluses.

Leaving aside Italy (whose data may be distorted by a high inflation rate), Japan, West Germany and the United Kingdom averaged the highest government deficits, along with the highest private sector surpluses, over this period.

A review of the historical record suggests that the primary cause of the growth of government-sector deficits since about 1975 has been a private sector weakness in capital spending in relation to savings rates. We have already noted the Canadian data. Since both Japan and West Germany have long had reputations for high savings rates, it is not surprising to find them running large private sector surpluses.

This view of the cause of larger government deficits is supported by data on the behaviour of gross capital formation in the OECD countries. From 1960 to 1973, real gross capital spending increased at an average of 6.3 per cent per year. Over the following eight years, this growth rate fell sharply to a mere 0.3 per cent; in other words, capital spending levelled out almost completely after 1973. For the European members of the OECD, the decline was even sharper: from 5.5 per cent for 1960–73 to −0.7 per cent for 1973–81. This Commission's research program did not explore the causes of this sudden and severe change in the pattern of capital spending in Europe after 1973. Some analysts have suggested, however, that it resulted, at least in part, from levels of real wages that were excessively high in relation to productivity and thus curtailed the prospective profitability of new investment. As we noted earlier, Canada experienced no downward shift in the investment share of GNP until

TABLE 10-1 Sectoral Balances of the Seven Major Industrialized Countries of the OECD, 1975 to 1982

Country	Government-Sector Deficit (percentage of GDP)	Private Sector Surplus[a]	Foreign-Sector Balance[b]
United States	−1.6	+1.8	0.0
Japan	−4.1	+4.6	−0.3
West Germany	−3.5	+4.2	0.0
France	−1.3	+0.4	+0.9
United Kingdom	−3.5	+3.9	−0.4
Italy	−9.9	+9.6	+0.4
Canada	−2.6	+1.1	+1.0

Source: Calculated from data given in Robert W.R. Price and Jean-Claude Chouraqui, *Public Sector Deficits: Problems and Policy Implications*, Occasional Studies, OECD Economic Outlook (Paris: OECD, 1983), p. 21.

a. Private sector surpluses estimated as the sum of household and corporate sectors.

b. A positive foreign-sector balance indicates a positive foreign contribution to savings: that is, a current account deficit. A negative foreign-sector balance indicates that a portion of national savings was provided to the rest of the world: that is, that the country ran a current account surplus.

after 1981, although our savings have tended to be relatively high since 1973, particularly if the measure includes no adjustment for the distorting effect of inflation on personal savings. We cannot be certain whether the decline in investment in Canada since 1981 has been entirely a cyclical development that is likely to be reversed, or whether a part of it was the result of some fundamental weakness.

Finally, it seems useful to consider what changes Canada would require in the present pattern of private capital spending and savings if the private sector is to return to the balanced position that would eliminate the government deficit, without help from the foreign sector. From 1982 to 1984, private sector capital spending averaged about 16.5 per cent of GNP, that is, about 3.5 percentage points below the average that prevailed during the 1947–81 period. To return to an average 20 per cent level would require an increase in private capital spending in the order of $14 billion (based on the GNP expected by mid-1985). The average private sector savings rate from 1982 to 1984 was 22.8 per cent of GNP. To reduce this amount to match a 20 per cent capital-spending level would require an increase in consumer spending of some $12 billion. Thus, to enable the government to bring its budget back to a balanced position would require a net increase in private sector spending of some $26 billion.[21]

Although the view is widespread that Canada's deficit should be substantially reduced as the economy recovers, there is much less agreement as to whether it would be desirable to reduce the deficit sharply before recovery is further advanced. There is also little agreement on means to promote the increase in private capital spending and the reduction in private savings that are a necessary counterpart of deficit reduction.

An argument can be made that even in Canada's current circumstances, a reduction of the deficit would have significant favourable effects on expectations about inflation and interest rates. Action to reduce the deficit now, so this argument goes, would lessen fears that continuing high deficits may eventually lead the central bank to increase the growth rate of the money supply in order to accommodate the deficit, with inflationary consequences. Fears of such future inflationary dangers may be helping to keep current interest rates high. Under these circumstances, it is conceivable that the favourable effects on interest rates and confidence would have a large enough impact on investment and other components of demand to offset, more or less, the direct negative effects on demand from the requisite expenditure reductions or tax increases.

The more widely accepted view among economists, however, is that deficit reduction could affect interest rates favourably, but not sufficiently, in the short run, to offset direct effects on demand. Given the importance Commissioners attach to avoiding further increases in unemployment, it might be preferable to defer any substantial reduction in the deficit until recovery is further advanced. We would, however, modify our view on the timing of a significant move towards deficit reduction if such a cut-back could be coupled with an easing of monetary policy sufficient to offset, or more than offset, the effect on demand and unemployment in the short term. We shall return to this possibility later in this chapter.

Notes

1. This outline owes more to the simplifications of Keynes, found in the elementary economics texts of the 1950s and 1960s, than it owes to Keynes' own complex and subtle work. We do not wish to create the impression that all macro-economists immediately accepted Keynes' analytical framework. We concentrate on his work because it was vital to the development of macro-economics, and because it gained increasingly general acceptance over the 1940s and 1950s. See John Maynard Keynes, *The General Theory of Employment, Interest and Money* (London: Macmillan, 1936).
2. "Final" goods and services do not include inputs into the production of other goods and services, nor do they include items produced before the current measurement period.
3. Professor Phillips made important contributions to the analysis of the implications of lags for the conduct of policy.
4. According to another view of the short-run relation between higher wage increases and lower unemployment, the causation runs the other way: that is, workers, are more willing to supply labour when wages appear to be higher.
5. The long-run trade-off curve might even become positively sloped (more inflation associated with more unemployment) rather than vertical (more inflation associated with no reduction in unemployment) if higher inflation causes labour markets to function less efficiently.
6. This review of the relation between inflation and the NAIRU disregards sources of inflation (or deflation) other than excess demand. Such other factors may temporarily disturb the relation between changes in inflation and the level of unemployment. For example, an adverse supply shock, such as a sudden rise in the price of oil imports, might cause inflation to increase temporarily, even if the current unemployment rate happened to be at a level generally considered to indicate significant labour- market slack (that is, above the NAIRU).
7. This analysis of interest rates and expected inflation, while mentioned at this point in our account, has long been familiar; it was introduced just before the turn of this century by the American economist Irving Fisher.
8. It might still, however, pose cash-flow problems for borrowers. See the treatment of the "tilt" or "front-loading" effect later in this chapter.
9. Some economists, most recently Michael R. Darby *et al.* in *The International Transmission of Inflation* (Chicago: University of Chicago Press, 1983), argue that the oil-price shock and other large raw-material price increases of the 1972–74 period were not accidental exogenous events; rather they were attributable, at least in considerable part, to excessive demand among the industrialized nations generally, which in turn resulted from excessive monetary growth in the late 1960s and early 1970s.
10. Keynes himself should be held blameless for the lack of attention to expectations. For him, they were of major importance, though not necessarily in the ways emphasized in recent analysis.
11. See, for example, R.P. Shaw, "The Burden of Unemployment in Canada", *Canadian Public Policy* (forthcoming).
12. Canada, Department of Reconstruction and Supply, *Employment and Income* (Ottawa: King's Printer, 1945).
13. If nominal interest rates increase in line with inflation, as they usually do, the nominal repayment stream, which is traditionally constant, tilts, becoming higher, in real terms, in the initial years of the repayment period and lower towards the end. For example, given a 25-year mortgage with a 5 per cent real interest rate, the annual payments per $100 of principal are $7.10 under zero inflation and $15.93 under 10 per cent inflation (15 per cent nominal interest rate). The latter

stream, which has the same real present value as the former, entails a real payment of $14.49 in constant dollars (in which the $100 principal was measured) in the first year, roughly twice the level of the no-inflation case, but that payment falls to $1.47 in constant dollars after 25 years, about one-fifth the level of the no-inflation case. Thus inflation is said to front-load the real payment stream when the interest payments (or the combined interest and repayment-of-principal payments used in a conventional mortgage) are constant in nominal terms.

14. In 1976, Prime Minister Callaghan stated at the Labour Party Conference in Blackpool:

    We used to think that you could just spend your way out of a recession and increase employment by cutting taxes and boosting government spending. I tell you in all candour that that option no longer exists and that insofar as it ever did exist, it worked by injecting inflation into the economy. And each time that happened, the average level of unemployment has risen. Higher inflation followed by higher unemployment: that is the history of the last twenty years.

15. In fact, some countries, such as Brazil, Israel and Iceland, have succeeded, over fairly extended periods, in combining high rates of inflation with real economic performance that is not obviously worse than average.

16. Notice the assumption that export prices are set in the domestic market. If they are set in foreign markets, as they are in a small open economy, devaluation leaves unchanged export prices, export revenues in foreign currency, and the trade balance.

17. Alternatively, viewed in terms of the domestic currency, the deterioration of the trade balance results from an increase in the cost of imports, with no offsetting gain in export receipts.

18. By contrast with the fixed exchange-rate case, this model implicitly assumes that the money supply would remain on some given path that was independent of the fiscal policy action.

19. The combination of the rapid growth in debt resulting from high deficits and of crowding out of private investment with the accompanying reduction in total GNP growth prospects, has the potential to create a vicious circle of low growth and spiralling debt/GNP ratios. Among other economists who have made this point is Professor James Tobin of Yale University, who advocates a sharp reduction in the size of the U.S. federal deficit.

20. In an open economy with a flexible exchange rate, crowding out may well operate to a more important degree through the exchange rates on net exports than through the interest rates on physical capital investment. Thus, in an open economy, crowding tends to be reflected more in decreases in the stock of total assets (physical capital *plus* set foreign assets) owned by residents than in the physical capital stock located in the country.

21. Commissioners do not wish to suggest that a reduction in the government deficit all the way to balance is necessarily desirable.

The Conduct of Fiscal and Monetary Policy

Clearly, a government's overall monetary and fiscal policies exercise a major influence on the growth of the economy's nominal demand. Less obvious is the degree to which demand-management policies result in a change in the volume of output as compared with a change in the overall price level. The current conventional view is that a speed-up or slow-down in the growth rate of nominal demand will initially be reflected largely in a speed-up or slow-down in real output and an accompanying fall or rise in unemployment. As time passes, however, less and less of the change will be reflected in higher or lower output and more and more of it in a faster or slower rate of inflation. Before considering the policy implications of this rule of thumb, it is worth reviewing the post-war record of fiscal and monetary policy.

Retrospective

It takes only a few historical highlights to illustrate the tendency of the Canadian economy to encounter the same problems repeatedly. The same history also indicates the way in which the analytical economic framework and the objectives and application of policy have evolved in response to experience.

In 1945, the Canadian government, in its White Paper on Employment and Income, adopted the maintenance of a "high and stable level of employment and income ... as a major aim of Government policy."[1] Although it did not attempt to quantify this goal, the government, having witnessed the double-digit unemployment rate of the 1930s, might well have expected even "high employment" to involve an unemployment rate somewhat higher than the 2 to 4 per cent level that characterized the first decade following the Second World War.

By the late 1950s, the authorities were troubled by the slow response of inflation to conditions of economic slack. "This tendency toward rising prices, particularly in a period of recession, is a matter for concern," the federal government asserted in the 1959 budget speech. It expressed strong determination to resist inflation and confidence that it was "well within the power of Canadians to achieve reasonable price stability without sacrificing either immediate recovery or balanced growth".[2]

In 1964, the Economic Council of Canada (ECC) published its first annual review, proposing medium-term goals of 3 per cent for the unemployment rate and less than 2 per cent for the average annual rate of price increases.[3] The Council recognized that the combination of high employment and price stability had not been achieved over the 1945–63 period, but thought that this goal might still be attainable, given favourable international developments, advances in productivity, policies to increase mobility and adjustment in the Canadian economy, and "responsible restraint in both wage demands and business pricing policies."

In 1966, the Royal Commission on Taxation (the Carter Commission) advanced the view that the unemployment rate could usually be reduced to 4 per cent without development of any sustained inflationary pressure, but that rates below 3 per cent were unsustainable.[4] It advocated a short-term target of 3.5 per cent and considered the ECC's 3 per cent goal possible in the medium term. It also criticized the policy of the late 1950s and early 1960s for over-concern with inflation.

In 1968, the government, in a White Paper entitled *Policies for Price Stability*, stated, "It is becoming increasingly evident that, with the existing tools of economic policy, we cannot count on simultaneously maintaining the desirable level of employment and reasonable price stability."[5] Stressing a determination to avoid inflation "without awaiting the harsh remedies which economic forces, given time, will otherwise administer", the White Paper specified some of the policy problems involved in controlling inflationary demand pressures:

- Lags in the impact of policy actions, coupled with the speed with which unforeseen demand pressures sometimes arise
- Uncertainty about the precise upper limits at which the economy can be permitted to operate relative to its capacity, before serious demand pressures and inflationary price increases develop
- Bottlenecks in particular sectors arising before high employment is attained generally and thus generating inflationary pressures.

The White Paper also put forward the government's response to inflation, which involved restraint in its spending on goods and services, coupled with tax increases, to achieve reduced deficits (or increased surpluses); structural measures concerning human resources and trade policy; establishment of the Task Force on Labour Relations to study the special problems of wage and salary bargaining in the public sector;[6] and creation of the Prices and Incomes Commission to "inquire into and report upon the causes, processes and consequences of inflation and to inform those making current prices and income decisions, the general public and the Government on how price stability may best be achieved."[7] A special Senate committee was also established.[8]

Monetary policy was tightened, but the fixed exchange rate of the day severely constrained the independence of Canadian monetary action. In 1970, however, the Canadian dollar was allowed to float; it began to appreciate significantly, unemployment increased, and inflation slowed, at least as measured by the Consumer Price Index. Yet initially, little reduction in the rates of wage increases was evident. Meanwhile, the Prices and Incomes Commission had attempted to persuade business and labour to adhere to voluntary wage and price guidelines, but agreement with labour proved elusive, and the attempt was abandoned in the same year.

In 1971, the Special Senate Committee on Growth, Employment and Price Stability reported that it was feasible to apply fiscal, monetary and exchange-rate policies to achieve the medium-term goal both of maintaining unemployment at 4 to 4.5 per cent and of restricting annual increases in the Consumer Price Index to 2 to 3 per cent. It saw little need for imposing general wage and price controls or guidelines, though it recognized that their temporary use, if backed by strong national support, could supplement demand-management policy to "bring about a short-term psychological adjustment towards a less inflationary climate."[9] It recommended that the Prices and Incomes Commission identify "unreasonable" wage or price increases and that Old Age Security (OAS) and Canada Pension Plan (CPP) benefits be fully indexed.

The summary report of the Prices and Incomes Commission, presented in 1972, attributed the increase of inflation in the mid-1960s largely to excess demand; the persistence of inflation after the clear emergence of economic slack in 1970, said the report, resulted both from lags in adjusting inflation expectations to match slower economic growth and from strongly held inflationary expectations. Estimating that the unemployment rate reached a "danger point" of inflationary pressure when it fell below 4.5 to 5 per cent, the Commission was also pessimistic about the possibility of using human-resource/adjustment programs, regional-development or similar types of structural policies to reduce unemployment in a way compatible with price stability. It regarded demand-management policy as the key to countering inflation; however, it also considered that adoption of a temporary incomes policy could provide a useful reinforcement to demand management in "trying to extricate the economy from a major inflationary outbreak originally generated by an overshoot of demand but persisting stubbornly because of widely held inflationary expectations and response lags."[10]

By 1971, the unemployment rate had risen to more than 6 per cent. Budgets which had given priority to reducing the rate of inflation in the late 1960s now had as their first objective the reduction of the unemployment rate. Consequently, federal fiscal action in 1971, 1972 and 1973 was expansionary. The February 1973 budget even noted that the policy might be excessively expansionary, but this risk was judged worth taking at this time, in the interest of dealing more effectively with unemployment. Monetary policy was also expansionary: the narrow measure of the money supply (M1) grew at double-digit rates from 1971 to 1973.

With the benefit of hindsight, monetary and fiscal policy are generally viewed as having been too expansionary from 1971 to the close of 1973 and thus as having contributed to building up inflationary expectations that are perhaps only now being reduced. The period is of particular interest, as it illustrates a number of difficulties to which policy making is subject. For example, Canadian policy makers, academic economists and the interested public initially failed to recognize what the 1972 Unemployment Insurance reform would do to the non-cyclical component of unemployment (the NAIRU). From 1971 to 1972, the unemployment rate remained at an average of 6.2 per cent, although the number of people employed increased at the relatively strong rate of 3 per cent. As already noted, the Unemployment Insurance (UI) reforms are generally estimated to have increased the unemployment rate by one to two percentage points. Thus, although an unemployment rate of 6.2 per cent may have indicated that the labour market was relatively slack before the reforms were made, afterwards it was equal to, or below, the new NAIRU, signalling a moderately tight market. Few people realized, however, the change that had occurred.

Initial National Accounts data also tended to mislead policy makers and other observers of the day. At the time of the February 1973 budget, the published data showed real Gross National Expenditure (GNE) in 1972 below the trend value, another indication of a slack economy. But subsequent revisions to the National Accounts showed the cumulative growth of real GNE between 1969 and 1972 as 2.2 percentage points higher than had the first-published version, a level marginally above the trend.

During this period, the money supply was allowed to increase at a rapid rate, at least partly because of a desire to hold down interest rates and restrict the inflow of capital from abroad so as to limit appreciation of the Canadian dollar. Our dollar had strengthened partly because of a boom in our resource exports. Such a development inevitably poses a difficult policy choice: to dampen inflation by allowing substantial appreciation of our currency at the cost of imposing a difficult adjustment on the manufacturing sector, or to protect the competitive position of Canadian manufacturing by limiting exchange-rate appreciation at the risk of setting off an inflationary spiral.[11]

However, the major increase in domestic inflation in 1973 and 1974 did not come solely from excessively expansionary policy within Canada. It is now apparent that during the previous few years most other OECD countries, acting independently, had been pursuing monetary and fiscal policies that were probably excessive individually and were undoubtedly so in their cumulative impact. (In the United States, these policies dated from the country's growing involvement in the Vietnam War in the mid-1960s.) The synchronized growth that followed in virtually all the advanced industrial countries not only generated internal inflationary pressures, but also led to a sharp increase in international commodity prices, which occurred in response to the substantial increase in world-wide demand. These hikes were compounded, in the early 1970s, by the sharp rise in the prices of a number of agricultural products; that rise was the result of major crop failures in several parts of the world and of the disappearance from the South American coast of the schools of anchovies that had provided a rich source of animal feed. These pressures had especially strong effects in Canada, where the rapid increases in prices of many of our raw-material exports led to high profits that created the potential for high and successful wage demands that proved difficult to bring down when the resource-price boom ended. In late 1973, the system received the first oil-price shock. A sharp global recession followed, accompanied for a time by continuing sharp increases in prices.

Throughout 1972 and 1973, the Canadian government had expressed concern about inflation. Rather than tightening fiscal and monetary policy, however, it had confined its response to encouragement of supply, restraint of particular prices, and assistance to citizens especially hard hit by inflation. In essence, the government's approach was to accept high rates of inflation as likely to continue for some time and to introduce measures aimed at reducing their adverse impacts. The May 1972 budget, for example, introduced full indexing of Old Age Security and Veterans' pensions. The February 1973 budget tried direct price reduction through cuts in the sales tax (on children's clothing) and tariffs, together with a form of budgetary stimulus (tax cuts) that was intended to help contain inflation. In a measure that took effect in January 1974, the same budget introduced indexation of rate brackets and most personal exemptions to offset the effects of inflation on the personal income-tax system, in order to prevent inflation-induced increases in real tax liabilities.

By May 1974, the budget makers were referring to "inflation, world wide in its origin and impact" as being "deeply [disturbing to] our country and this government". Their macro-economic policy stance provided no further stimuli, but they rejected deflation of demand through severe monetary and fiscal restraint as "a cure worse than the disease" and termed general wage and price controls "totally ineffective in overcoming the kind of inflationary problems we have been, and are still facing."[12] They did, however, institute more measures intended to mitigate the effects of inflation on income categories that had not been aided by the 1972 and 1973 measures. One of the 1974 measures was the introduction of the $1000 interest-income exemption in the personal income tax. The government also attempted to restrain particular prices by such means as removing the sales tax from adult clothing and footwear and holding the domestic price of oil below world levels.

In the following months, the outlook for inflation worsened as wage and salary costs accelerated. But the outlook for real output and employment also deteriorated sharply as a result of the recession affecting Canada's major trading partners. The budget of November 1974 introduced income-tax cuts and incentives to construction, to sustain aggregate demand; it also sought to mitigate the effects of inflation, primarily through the exemption of $1000 of pension-annuity income from the calculation of personal income tax. The government appealed for restraint in wage demands and announced that it would try to persuade labour and business interests to agree to such restraint in an effort to ease inflation. No such agreement was forthcoming. Given that failure, as well as the continued strength of inflation, the June 1975 budget provided no further general stimulus to demand. The government, however, still rejected severe fiscal and monetary restraint, and shunned controls because of the lack of widespread public support.

Partly because our policy measures were relatively expansionary and partly because the increase in world oil prices had domestic effects that were favourable as well as unfavourable, the Canadian economy experienced a much milder slow-down from 1974 to 1975 than did the economies of most OECD countries. However, our inflation rate also stayed higher than most of theirs.

In September 1975, the Governor of the Bank of Canada stressed the prime importance of achieving lower rates of inflation and the necessity of keeping the rate of monetary expansion within reasonable limits in order to reach this goal.[13] In the following month, the government introduced its Anti-Inflation Program (AIP), which consisted of:

- Fiscal and monetary policies aimed at restraining growth in total demand and production at a rate consistent with declining inflation
- Government expenditure policies intended to limit the rate of increase in public service employment and the growth of public expenditures to or below the trend in the growth of GNP
- Structural policies to deal with the special problems of energy, food and

housing, to ensure a more efficient and competitive economy, and to improve labour/management relations

- A temporary prices and incomes policy that established controls over prices, wages and other incomes for larger firms, and over wages and some prices in the government sector.

In November 1975, the Governor of the Bank of Canada announced the first explicit targets for the growth of the money supply. For the first year, Ml (a limited definition of the money supply) was to expand 10 to 15 per cent (preferably towards the lower end of the range); thereafter, the growth was to decline, to approach the rate consistent with long-term price stability. This program marked the official start of monetary targeting in Canada.

Soon after introduction of the Anti-Inflation Program, wage and price inflation declined quite sharply, while the Canadian economy continued to avoid a recession as severe as that experienced in the United States and most Western European countries. Unemployment, however, climbed gradually to a new peak of 8.4 per cent in 1978. During the 1976–78 period, analysts judged that the economy had room for some expansion of demand without risking the gains made in lowering inflation. Federal fiscal policy became increasingly expansionary as tax cuts, rather than new or expanded expenditure programs, provided most of the stimulus.

Although unemployment fell during the period from 1978 to 1981, reaching a low of 7 per cent in mid-1981, price and wage inflation started to increase again; it was given an extra boost in 1980 and 1981 as a result of the sharp increase in world and domestic energy prices. The government had made further efforts in 1977 and 1978 to achieve agreement with labour and business on the need for incomes restraint, and in 1978, the Centre for the Study of Inflation and Productivity was established to provide an early-warning system on inflation. In addition, fiscal policy was tightened somewhat between 1978 and 1981.

In November 1979, the United States, faced with rising inflation and a depreciating currency, implemented a monetary policy that was much more aggressively anti-inflationary than Canada's. Although our monetary authorities cushioned the effect on Canadian financial markets of some of the large swings in U.S. interest rates, Canada also moved into a period of much higher nominal and real interest rates.

The world-wide recession of 1981–82, which followed the doubling of international oil prices in 1979–80 and the sharp tightening of monetary policy had particularly severe effects in Canada. The rate of inflation slackened in 1982 and fell sharply in 1983; the result of the recession in slowing the increase of prices and wages was augmented by the application of the federal government's "Six-and-Five" program and by the introduction of similar programs relating to public sector wages and prices in most provinces. A number of private sector prices under federal regulatory control were included in the program.

Another significant development of the 1981–82 period was the apparent breakdown in the historical relationship between nominal GNP and M1. In setting its target band for monetary growth, the Bank of Canada had been using this narrow measure of the money supply, which excludes, among other items, personal savings accounts and term deposits with the chartered banks. The breakdown was caused principally by shifts in personal deposits into the newly available daily interest chequing accounts, which, by definition, were not included in the M1 measure, and by corresponding developments in business deposits. In 1982, the Bank of Canada suspended the practice of defining its policy in terms of a target growth rate for M1.

From mid-1981 to late 1982, the severe recession led to a very sharp rise in unemployment, which has since remained at very high levels. Inflation has continued to decline. Most European countries have experienced a similar pattern of unemployment and inflation; the U.S. economy, virtually alone, has experienced rather strong recovery. The Canadian government began to take expansionary fiscal policy action with the June 1982 "mini-budget". Monetary policy has remained relatively tight, substantially because of the importance given to limiting depreciation of the Canadian dollar relative to the very strong U.S. dollar.

This review of the post-war record suggests a number of conclusions:

- Given current labour and product-market institutions, unemployment rates of about 6.5 per cent at best, and perhaps rising as high as 8 per cent at worst, appear to be required to avoid accelerating inflation. Analysis of this issue is, however, complicated by the large "special" price shocks that the economy has experienced since 1972.
- Wage and price controls do seem to have eased the transition to lower inflation during the 1975–77 period, and the Six-and-Five program probably helped this process in 1982 and 1983. The Canadian experience with such incomes policies differs from that of many other countries, in particular the United States. The U.S. controls instituted from 1971 to 1974, which were not supported by anti-inflationary monetary policy, and which did not pursue a phased reduction in inflation, had little lasting effect; any helpful initial impact tended to be offset by a subsequent snap-back of prices and wages.
- Achievement of general agreement in support of voluntary restraint of incomes and prices is difficult to obtain in Canada, given the country's decentralized wage negotiations, and the fact that many of its important "prices" (including interest rates) are more or less determined in international markets.
- It is unrealistic to hope to fine-tune the economy by applying policies to keep real demand on a narrow path of non-inflationary growth. Attempts are constantly undercut by the uncertainties to which economic forecasting seems inevitably subject, by uncertainties concerning levels of real output and unemployment that are sustainable without setting off renewed inflationary spirals, and by uncertainties about the extent of, and lags in, the effects of monetary and fiscal policy actions.
- Recent experience with instability in the relationship between the demand for money and changes in GNP raises serious doubts about the desirability of setting monetary policy in terms of strict adherence to a simple rule of monetary growth.

- Sufficiently tight monetary restraint can sharply reduce inflation, but the process is likely to involve a severe and possibly extended recession. A gradual approach to controlling inflation will probably involve less severe rates of unemployment, but it will take longer to produce effects and offers less certainty of success.

Policy Issues

General Policy Issues

Any discussion of future policy setting for Canada must first address two general issues: approaches to exchange rates and active, as contrasted with automatic, mechanisms for stabilization. Only then can we turn to issues related specifically to today's circumstances.

The Exchange-Rate Regime

As we have seen, the choice between a fixed and a flexible exchange rate is of fundamental importance. For a small open economy to opt for a fixed exchange rate is to abandon virtually any opportunity to exercise an independent monetary policy. (Recall, however, that such an economy's freedom to manœuvre under a floating-exchange system should not be exaggerated.)

For Canada, choosing a fixed exchange rate would mean, essentially, tying ourselves to U.S. monetary policy, to U.S. interest rates, and, broadly speaking, to the U.S. rate of inflation. Such ties would produce benefits if the United States succeeded in establishing monetary stability and low inflation. Under these circumstances, such a policy approach would help us to establish stable, non-inflationary expectations and to stabilize the environment for decision making in industries for which trade with the United States is important.

These potential benefits are not illusory. The countries of the European Monetary System (EMS) have opted for a fixed regime with regard to one another's currencies, although the "bands" within which rates are fixed permit significant flexibility. The Federal Republic of Germany, as the largest country in the group, exercises an important influence on the monetary policy of the system as a whole, and many observers suggest that the other EMS countries have benefited from this link by "importing" expectations of low and stable inflation.[14]

Despite the merits ascribed to the European example, to tie the Canadian dollar to the U.S. dollar would further limit our monetary independence. Recent experience has demonstrated that Canada might not wish to be bound to developments in the United States. Even under favourable circumstances, however, fixing our exchange rate with the U.S. dollar would deny us the shock-absorbing benefits that a flexible exchange rate can often provide. A flexible exchange rate eases our adjustment in the face of a "boom or bust" in resource exports and, under certain circumstances, provides some temporary insulation from changes in U.S. interest rates, although we remain strongly influenced by U.S. monetary developments.

Commissioners conclude that maintenance of flexible exchange rates and thus of the possibility of independent monetary policy is, on balance, desirable. We shall consider later in this chapter the desirability (or lack of desirability) of attempting to insulate Canadian interest rates from U.S. rates through exchange controls or interest-equalization taxes.

Steadiness or Activism in Macro-economic Policy

During the latter 1970s, a growing number of countries came to favour a strategy of setting macro-economic policy – and particularly monetary policy – on a steady medium-term course estimated as consistent with stable growth in nominal GNP, with stable and low rates of actual inflation, and with non-inflationary expectations. Policy makers were brought to this approach by their growing awareness of several realities: the limits of their ability to forecast developments in the medium term; the lack of long-term trade-offs between unemployment and inflation; and the importance of expectations in influencing economic behaviour. Canada, the United States, West Germany, Switzerland and Britain all chose to set monetary policy by specifying a target growth range for one or more measures of the money supply.

This approach, however, has not been without its difficulties. First, reasonable stability and predictability in the relationship between money and aggregate demand (nominal GNP) is an essential part of the steady approach to monetary growth. Yet in several countries, especially Canada and the United States, the relationship between GNP and the chosen measure of the money supply has not proved as predictable as expected. For example, the 1982 drop in nominal GNP in the United States was more drastic than predicted on the basis of the reduction in monetary growth. In Canada, the breakdown in the historical relationship was so severe that in 1982, the Bank of Canada suspended the monetary-growth/targeting approach.

Secondly, just as adherence to a fixed exchange rate essentially means that monetary policy must be directed to maintaining that rate, so adherence to a money-supply growth rate means that the exchange rate must be allowed to fluctuate freely. Yet countries for which trade is important are often reluctant to accept large swings in exchange rates, especially swings that do not reflect differences in inflation performance. Thus, both West Germany and Switzerland have been prepared to compromise, at least temporarily, their adherence to monetary-growth targets in order to "lean against" swings in the exchange rate that they regarded as excessive.[15]

Thirdly, although monetary policy makers can set a stable and low target for growth of the money supply, fiscal policy admits of no such simple rule. Possible guidelines for fiscal policy do exist; most involve maintaining some "cyclically adjusted" or "high-employment" budget balance, expressed as a percentage of GNP, or some debt/GNP ratio trend. Such an approach permits – indeed, requires – the operation of the automatic fiscal stabilizers: that is, it preserves the automatic counter-cyclical swings in the actual budget balance that tend to dampen swings in the economy. The success of reliance on the automatic stabilizers, however, depends very much on acceptance of their implications for the deficit by the public at large and by the domestic and international investment communities. In essence, these groups must neither be "spooked" by the substantial deficits that automatically result in times of severe recession, nor press for tax cuts or expenditure increases when economic booms automatically generate substantial budget surpluses. Moreover, estimates of the cyclically adjusted budget balance are inevitably somewhat arbitrary. There is always a margin of uncertainty about the true level of the "high employment" or "trend" output path to be used as a basis for calculating the "normalized" or cyclically adjusted budget balance. Even in the absence of such uncertainties, the choice of a target budget balance or debt/GNP ratio involves complex controversial issues, both analytical and empirical.

In addition to these difficulties, at least two considerations raise questions about the suitability of a stable setting for the growth of money supply and a stable approach to fiscal policy. First, economies may occasionally be subject to severe and prolonged recessions caused by substantial weakness in private demand. Such circumstances may well warrant the provision of some stimulus beyond that generated by the automatic stabilizers. Secondly, rigid adherence to steady policy settings precludes the conscious adjustment of the mix of monetary and fiscal policies.

Economists have reached no clear consensus on the advantages and disadvantages of adopting steady guidelines for policy. Generally speaking, the "monetarists", who emphasize the advantages, are those who are particularly impressed by the limits of policy makers' ability to forecast the course of the economy and to estimate the effect of discretionary action; who are concerned about adversely affecting expectations by making discretionary policy changes; and who have confidence in the strength and speed of the economy's self-righting mechanisms. The "neo-Keynesians", who take the opposite view on one or more of these points, tend to be more sympathetic toward discretionary departures from the "steady rules" approach, at least when there are clear shifts in the money-GNP relationship or clear prospects of an extended boom or recession. (Of course, such shifts and prospects are seldom very clear until well after the event.)

A compromise approach, which has recently received attention from some academic economists, suggests formulating demand-management policies in terms of targets for growth of nominal GNP. When the relationship between the money supply and nominal GNP is stable or undergoing a relatively mild, short-lived, cyclical disturbance, this compromise approach might well involve the same settings for monetary and fiscal policy as would the stable monetary and budget-balance guidelines. It would, however, involve a willingness to change the targets and to adjust fiscal and monetary policy in the event of significant prolonged departures of nominal GNP from a steady growth path. It would also provide a framework for considering changes to the mix of monetary and fiscal policy. For example, if it were deemed appropriate to cut the fiscal deficit substantially, in view of concerns over the growth of public debt and the lack of funds required for private investment, it might also be considered appropriate to provide some monetary stimulus to offset the effect of tighter fiscal policy on nominal (and real) GNP growth. This approach tends to be more attractive to neo-Keynesians than to monetarists; to the latter, it verges on a back-door return to the illusions of fine-tuning.

A significant element of the rationale for adopting steady rules to govern monetary and fiscal policy is the potential the policy offers for helping to establish non-inflationary expectations, which, once established, improve the prospects of achieving or maintaining low inflation and reasonably high employment. Ironically, although to establish such expectations firmly may require a period of rather rigid adherence to clearly non-inflationary monetary and fiscal rules, the existence of firm expectations of low inflation subsequently increases the room of authorities for taking *discretionary* action to combat recessions or other economic disturbances. For example, in the late 1970s, when the West German and Swiss central banks temporarily raised the rate of increase of the money supply in their respective countries, in order to counter appreciation of their exchange rates, they may well have judged that they could do so without risking a resurgence of inflationary expectations because of the confidence they had established in their underlying commitment to maintaining low inflation. The recent willingness of the U.S. Federal Reserve System to allow a high rate of increase in M1 in response to an apparent upward shift in the demand for money might be similarly interpreted. In sum, it seems that credibility can be achieved over time at a price, and that once established, it may well permit stabilization policy to operate more effectively than it could in the absence of such confidence. Yet the danger remains that hard-won credibility will be eroded if the public loses faith in authorities' continuing commitment to prevent the development of renewed inflationary spirals.

Commissioners conclude that the difficulties to which fine-tuning is so clearly subject and the potential contribution to stable expectations that governments can make by following steady policies oriented to the medium term provide a strong case for rejecting short-run adjustments of monetary and fiscal policy as long as departures from a non-inflationary growth path are moderate. Granting this, however, we note that the current state of economic analysis falls considerably short of offering clear guidance for developing satisfactory medium-term guidelines for setting policy. For this reason, we think it worth considering an approach based on targeting monetary and fiscal policy in relation to non-inflationary growth of nominal GNP. Furthermore, while we support a medium-term rather than a "fine-tuning" approach, we do not exclude the possibility of supplementing automatic stabilization with discretionary action in times of wide and protracted departures from satisfactory levels of nominal demand. The existing high levels of unemployment and the prospects for their slow reduction suggest that the current situation may constitute the kind of exceptional case just described.

Medium-Term Prospects: Implications for Present Policy

During the last three years, fiscal policy in Canada and the United States has gone well beyond mere acceptance of the upswing in deficits that would have resulted from following a steady, cyclically adjusted, budget-balance approach. Deliberate fiscal measures and unexpectedly high real-interest rates have increased the federal deficits substantially. (This holds true even if we adjust for the effect on the deficit of the cyclical weakness in the economy. What remains after such an adjustment is a high "structural deficit": that is, a deficit that would exist, given actual tax and expenditure structures, even if the economy were operating at a "normal" level of activity.) Monetary policy, however, has generally remained rather tight.

This policy mix has achieved major reductions in inflation in both countries, although there are some doubts as to whether the reductions in inflationary *expectations* have fully matched those in actual inflation. In the United States, this policy mix has also been consistent with a reasonably satisfactory recovery from the recent recession, but many Americans are still concerned about the continuing high level of the deficit. In Canada, the recovery started from a deeper trough and has been rather anaemic, particularly as measured by the unemployment rate. There are fears that unemployment will remain high for an extended period. The level of the Canadian federal deficit also causes much concern to many observers.

Given the broadly similar setting of policy in Canada and the United States, it is not entirely clear why recovery has been so much stronger in one country than in the other and, in particular, why private investment has recovered strongly south of the border, but is still weak in this country, as Figure 10-3 shows. The explanations advanced include the apparently greater rigidity of wages in Canada (and, therefore, our economy's less flexible response to monetary restraint and to changing competitive conditions) and the fact that the cessation of the energy boom and the world-wide weakness in raw-material industries have had stronger effects on the Canadian than on the U.S. economy. In addition, the preceding inflationary boom appears to have been more pronounced in Canada, causing a more severe "hangover" as corporations and individuals have retrenched to reduce the heavy debts incurred when they expected inflation, along with economic prosperity, to continue and, thus, the real burden of debt servicing to be low. That the United States substantially strengthened tax incentives for investment in 1981, whereas Canada had taken similar action in the 1972–77 period, is no doubt of some importance in explaining the relative strength of business investment in the two countries, both in the late 1970s and more recently. Of course, the higher levels of capacity utilization in the United States also help to explain the greater strength of investment in that country, although the difference in capacity utilization is itself part of the puzzle that we are trying to solve. Finally, differences in the two tax systems' treatment of consumer debt and mortgage-interest payments may make the Canadian economy more sensitive to high interest rates.

In both countries, however, demand management is constrained by the fact that projected federal deficits, even if cyclically adjusted, imply ever-higher ratios of debt (and debt-servicing costs) to GNP as long as real interest rates stay relatively high. These high deficits doubtless gave important support to the level of economic activity during the recession. They may also, however, have created expectations that to bring them under control will eventually require substantial tax increases, or that to finance them will induce a shift to more inflationary monetary policies.

FIGURE 10-3 Business Fixed Investment

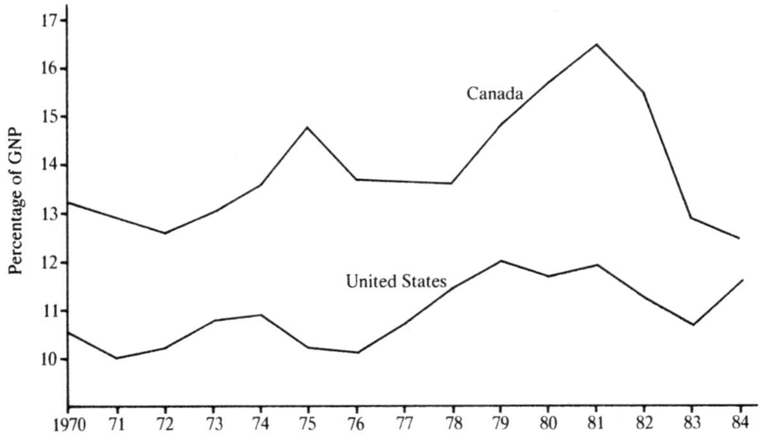

Sources: Canada. Historical Compendium, Table 24,
U.S.A.– The President's Council of Economic Advisors:
Economic Report to the President, February 1984, Table B7.

Inflation and Employment Goals

As we Commissioners have already made clear, we accept the view that given the present structure of the economy, demand-management policies alone cannot reduce unemployment below 6.5 to 8 per cent on a sustained basis. It is for this reason that we attach such importance to structural initiatives which could lower the attainable floor rate of unemployment. Moreover, we think that it would be very unwise to risk our recent reduction in inflation, purchased at such great cost, by attempting to use demand-management policy alone to return unemployment very rapidly to the 6.5 to 8 per cent range. We are still faced, however, with a range of important choices in future fiscal and monetary policies. A fundamental choice concerns the extent to which Canada should push for further reductions in the rate of inflation. That choice means balancing the risks of making slower progress towards further reduction of inflation and of reducing unemployment only slowly to more tolerable levels.

Our current unemployment rate is much higher than most estimates of the NAIRU; other indicators also suggest a substantial degree of slack in the economy. Furthermore, we seem to have made major progress in restoring expectations that inflation will be maintained at moderate levels for the foreseeable future. The prospects for the Canadian economy, considered in Chapter 7, suggest that within the present framework of economic policies, we face a rather extended period of only modest recovery. Under these circumstances, a moderate increase in the projected growth of demand, which would offer the prospect of a significant reduction in unemployment, as well as a strengthening of investment, should be consistent with further reduction in inflation.

Policy with Respect to the Deficit

The earlier analysis of deficits and debts offered in this chapter suggested that deficits are a potential problem if they are of a size that causes an upward *trend* in the debt/GNP ratio. This appears to be the present situation in Canada, even if we adjust for current below-normal levels of activity.

Among the larger OECD countries, as Tables 10-2 and 10-3 show, Canada's deficit/GNP ratio for the total government sector is exceeded only by Italy's. However, while Canada's overall deficit/GNP ratio is higher than that of the United States, when the deficit is expressed as a percentage of net private savings, Canada appears to be in a better position than its neighbour. This fact reflects the much lower level of personal savings in the United States than in Canada.

Commissioners accept the wisdom of lowering the deficit to a level consistent with stabilizing or decreasing the debt/GNP ratio. We shall not put forward a specific target for reduction of the deficit: that is a job for those with access to the latest economic and fiscal projections, and such targets may well require revision over time as the projections change. We recognize, however, that the required deficit reduction is substantial, probably in the order of an annual increment of 1.5 per cent of GNP, which would be equivalent to $10 billion by fiscal year 1991.[16] (According to the government's November 1984 projections, this would reduce the federal budgetary deficit, by the same year, to about 4 per cent of GNP.)

Examples are helpful to illustrate the magnitude of the action we are considering. To achieve a $10 billion deficit reduction by the end of the decade, entirely through an increase in personal income tax revenues, would require that rates be increased by about 20 per cent, and this calculation does

TABLE 10-2 Ratio of Budget Balance to GNP

	(total government sector)					
Country	**1979**	**1980**	**1981**	**1982**	**1983**	**1984**[a]
United States	+0.6	−1.2	−0.9	−3.8	−4.1	−3.2
Japan	−4.8	−4.5	−4.0	−3.4	−3.3	−2.2
West Germany	−2.7	−3.1	−3.8	−3.4	−2.7	−1.7
France	−0.7	+0.2	−1.8	−2.5	−3.4	−3.5
United Kingdom	−3.2	−3.8	−3.1	−2.4	−3.3	−3.1
Italy	−9.5	−8.0	−11.9	−12.7	−11.8	−13.5
Canada	−1.8	−2.7	−1.6	−5.0	−6.2	−6.0
Total of above countries[b]	−1.7	−2.4	−2.6	−4.0	−4.2	−3.6

Source: Organisation for Economic Co-operation and Development, *Economic Outlook, December 1984* (Paris: OECD, 1984), p. 29.

a. OECD estimates and forecasts.

b. 1982 GNP/GDP weights and exchange rates.

TABLE 10-3 Ratio of Budget Balance[a] to Net Private Savings[b]

	(total government sector)										
Country	1974	1975	1976	1977	1978	1979	1980	1981	1982	1983	1984
United States	4.8	52.4	30.4	13.7	−2.6	−9.3	22.0	15.0	71.4	68.2	49.7
Japan	−2.1	17.1	20.6	23.0	31.0	29.8	28.2	26.5	24.7	26.9	20.3
West Germany	12.9	55.9	35.5	28.9	26.2	27.8	35.4	46.2	40.6	30.5	15.8
France	−5.9	20.2	5.8	8.5	16.7	6.7	−2.6	24.2	35.2	47.0	47.2
United Kingdom	61.4	76.1	68.5	37.8	40.7	35.8	42.8	40.5	30.8	56.3	48.1
Italy	48.7	69.4	52.4	47.9	54.2	51.4	47.5	73.0	78.0	82.9	85.1
Canada	−19.1	24.1	16.8	26.7	30.6	15.3	20.8	10.4	50.5	49.8	44.0
Total of above countries	9.1	45.6	30.6	20.5	15.2	10.0	25.2	25.7	54.0	54.8	42.7

Source: Organisation for Economic Co-operation and Development, *Economic Outlook, July 1984* (Paris: OECD, 1984), p. 29.

a. General government financial *deficit* as a percentage of private savings. A minus sign indicates a financial *surplus*.
b. Net private savings are household plus business net savings.

not allow for any effect that tax increases might have in constraining economic growth and, thus, the increase in revenues. To eliminate the deficit entirely, through expenditure reductions, would require an average cut of about 10 per cent of all expenditures, excluding public-debt charges, of about 11 per cent if national defence costs and foreign aid were exempt; of about 15 per cent if transfers to the provinces for equalization and established-program financing, to cover health care and post-secondary education, were also exempt; or of about 20 per cent if, in addition, expenditures on the Old Age Security/Guaranteed Income Supplement (OAS/GIS) were exempt.

We shall not attempt to indicate in detail the form that a package for reducing the deficit should take. We do, however, note several considerations that, in our judgement, should be taken into account in determining the contents of any such package:

- Tax cuts during the 1975–78 period contributed significantly to the build-up of the deficit. Since 1975, expenditures for regular government programs have been kept reasonably stable in relation to trend GNP; growing public-debt charges, plus an increase in UI benefits and the introduction of special programs related to the recession, account for most of the recent increase in federal expenditure relative to GNP.
- Despite the impact of past tax reductions on the government's fiscal position, we are concerned that a large increase in tax rates now would have adverse effects on incentives and thus impair prospects for the development and growth of the Canadian economy. We also note that significant increases in taxes will be necessary, over the medium term, for reasons other than reduction of the deficit. The contribution rates for the Canada Pension Plan (CPP) and the Quebec Pension Plan (QPP) will have to rise as the programs mature, and some increase in general taxes may also be necessary to finance OAS/GIS pensions and health care as the proportion of the elderly in the population increases.
- Given these considerations and the fairness of "spreading the pain", we favour a combination of tax increases and rather broad reductions in expenditure. This recommendation raises the question of which expenditure areas should be spared, at the cost of deeper cuts elsewhere. Everyone, of course, will have particular candidates. We have recommended in Part II a faster pace of increase for foreign aid. We have also called attention to the potential need to expand economic and employment-adjustment programs. Canada's relatively low defence expenditures provide a case for exempting this area. Moreover, given current economic circumstances, we would not wish to see cuts that adversely affected Canadians who are already experiencing hardship as a result of unemployment.
- A possible way to implement broadly based tax increases and expenditure reductions would be to set the indexing factor for the personal income tax and for some transfer programs at x percentage points below the rate of inflation, and to hold the price factor for all other expenditure programs – excepting foreign aid and national defence – at x percentage points lower than the rate of inflation. We calculate that to set these factors 3 percentage points below the inflation rate for a three-year period would generate a deficit reduction in the order of 1.5 per cent of GNP.

This Commission's concern that the deficit be reduced has important implications for our Report: any net expenditure increases or tax reductions we propose would add to the tax increases and expenditure cuts required elsewhere. We also recognize that tight restraint by the federal government creates an environment that could well make federal-provincial fiscal and other relations more difficult.

The Mix of Monetary and Fiscal Policy

Earlier in this section, we Commissioners expressed our judgement that Canada's fiscal and monetary policies should be directed to promoting some increase in the pace of recovery. We have now added the objective of reducing the structural deficit. The only way to achieve both objectives simultaneously is to change the policy mix, moving to a somewhat more expansionary monetary policy that will more than offset the initially restrictive effect of deficit-reducing fiscal measures. This net shift towards expansion would help to bring the unemployment rate down from its current unacceptably high level; it would also help to reduce the deficit by stimulating capital spending and net exports and, perhaps, by reducing private savings.

The kind of monetary policy we favour would probably involve a *temporary* increase in money-supply growth rates followed by a return from the higher base to rates consistent with non-inflationary, nominal GNP growth. It is important that a credible plan for reducing the deficit to sustainable levels be initiated at an early date so that Canada can start to ease monetary policy temporarily, without creating renewed inflationary expectations. Finally, some of us also favour fiscal policy measures that would encourage increased private spending: for example, a temporary reduction in some of the tax incentives for saving.

The prospects for the Canadian economy under such a policy approach depend critically on whether the U.S. Administration follows a similar course of deficit reduction coupled with some "one-shot" monetary easing or continues to use its current fiscal-monetary mix. If the United States were to adopt the former course, its interest rates would decline, and a similar fall in Canadian interest rates would probably not have a major effect on the exchange rate. If, however, the United States persists with its current policy mix, the recommended change in the Canadian policy mix will likely result in a smaller temporary reduction in our interest rates, coupled with some depreciation of the exchange rate. (As we explain below, the exchange rate must depreciate to a level from which it is subsequently expected to appreciate if Canadian interest rates are to be reduced relative to U.S. rates.) Under this second possibility, the export- and import-competing sectors would experience more stimulus than under the first, while the interest-sensitive sectors, particularly residential and non-residential construction, would experience less.

It should be emphasized, however, that although a one-shot easing in Canadian monetary policy must be expected to cause some reduction in the exchange rate, all other circumstances being equal, the decline should be self-limiting if the policy is conducted within a broader framework that includes a clear credible commitment to avoid inflationary pressure. We do not wish to downplay the risks: a loss of exchange-market confidence could turn a limited depreciation into a free fall. We believe, however, that the overall approach we have suggested clearly avoids the prospect of increasing inflation and thus establishes the key condition to ensure that the exchange-rate depreciation will be self-limiting.

Another possibility is a broader policy approach that would combine monetary and fiscal policy action with a temporary incomes policy. Commissioners consider such an approach in the conclusions to this chapter.

Notes

1. Canada, Department of Reconstruction and Supply, *Employment and Income* (Ottawa: King's Printer, 1945), p. 23.
2. Canada, House of Commons *Debates*, April 19, 1959, pp. 2518–19.
3. Economic Council of Canada, *Economic Goals for Canada to 1970*, First Annual Review (Ottawa: Queen's Printer, 1964), p. 189.
4. Canada, Royal Commission on Taxation, *Report*, vol. 2, *The Use of the Tax System to Achieve Economic and Social Objectives* (Ottawa: Queen's Printer, 1966).
5. Canada, Department of Consumer and Corporate Affairs, *Policies for Price Stability* (Ottawa: Queen's Printer, 1968), p. 7.
6. See Canada, Task Force on Labour Relations, *Canadian Industrial Relations* (Ottawa: Queen's Printer, 1968).
7. Canada, Prices and Incomes Commission, *Inflation, Unemployment and Incomes Policy*, Final Report (Ottawa: Information Canada, 1972), p. iii.
8. See Canada, Senate, Standing Committee on National Finance, *Growth, Employment and Price Stability* (Ottawa: Information Canada, 1971).
9. *Ibid.*, p. xiv.
10. Canada, Prices and Incomes Commission, *Inflation, Unemployment and Incomes Policy*, Summary Report (Ottawa: Information Canada, 1972), p. 7.
11. It is important to recognize that if the boom in exports lasts, adjustment in manufacturing must occur, one way or the other.
12. John N. Turner, Minister of Finance, *Budget Speech* (Ottawa: Department of Finance, 1974), pp. 1, 6.
13. Bank of Canada, *Annual Report of the Governor to the Minister of Finance and Statement of Accounts for the Year 1975* (Ottawa: The Bank, 1976), pp. 9–11.
14. Another frequently cited example is that of Austria, which is not a member of the EMS, but has tied its currency closely to the West German Deutschmark. Some 35 per cent of Austria's trade is with West Germany, and many people consider the currency link an important factor in Austria's success in achieving low inflation and low unemployment. Austrian employers and unions are highly conscious of the implications of their pricing and wage setting for competitiveness with their chief trading partner.
15. The experience of these countries is reviewed in the proceedings of a symposium held by this Commission. See John Sargent, *Foreign Macroeconomic Experience: A Symposium*, vol. 24 (Toronto: University of Toronto Press, 1985).

16. In November 1984, the Minister of Finance stated the government's intention of achieving expenditure reductions which, presumably, would largely be translated into a deficit reduction in the order of $10 to $15 billion by fiscal year 1991. Such a reduction would, on the basis of the November 1984 projections, be sufficient to end the growth of the debt/GNP ratio. Professors Neil Bruce and Douglas Purvis of Queen's University, who have also called attention to the government-debt issue in studies for the C.D. Howe Institute and for this Commission, have proposed a deficit reduction of $11 billion by 1988.

Related Institutional Issues

The management of monetary and fiscal policy raises questions about the desirability of Canada's undertaking various institutional changes. Three of these issues are the close ties between our exchange rate and international interest rates, indexation as a means of adjustment to inflation, and the constraints on stabilization policy raised by Canada's regional and federated nature.

The Exchange Rate and International Interest Rates

The steep decline in the value of the Canadian dollar in relation to U.S. currency, which began in the late 1970s and extended into the early 1980s, is regarded by some observers as a measure of Canada's economic weakness. Short-term fluctuations in the exchange rate are also sources of continuing concern in this country. In addition, Canadian interest rates, following the course of U.S. rates, climbed to unprecedented heights in our economy towards the end of 1981, and even after subsequent declines, they are still at high levels, particularly in real terms.

Most economists agree that both Canada's current low level of capital formation and its slow recovery from the 1981–82 recession are attributable, at least in part, to these high interest rates. It is widely recognized that these rates have been a world-wide phenomenon transmitted to Canada through international capital markets. The same high interest rates that have created difficulties in Canada have also done much to exacerbate, though they did not cause, the international debt crisis that emerged in 1982, involving certain developing and Eastern Bloc countries.

Because our system makes possible the virtually free flow of capital across our borders, plus a heavy flow of trade in goods and services, international monetary developments have wide-ranging and profound effects on the Canadian economy. As a result, some observers fear that our continued adherence to present arrangements must involve a substantial sacrifice of our ability to control our own economic destiny. In this section, we shall first consider the extent to which such concerns are justified and then examine various measures that might be adopted to address them.

The Exchange Rate

Although no one could possibly claim that all has been well with our economy over the last decade, Commissioners nevertheless believe that attempts to gauge Canada's economic health by reference to the exchange rate with the U.S. dollar are both misguided and misleading. In our judgement, such a view is an outgrowth of past circumstances that no longer apply.

From the end of the Second World War to the mid-1960s, the U.S. dollar was the key currency of the international monetary system. During this period, the currencies of all our other trading partners were linked to the U.S. dollar by fixed exchange rates. The float of the Canadian dollar from 1950 to 1961 was an anomaly in the international monetary system. In an environment of generally fixed exchange rates, the Canadian dollar moved against these other currencies in lock-step with its movement against the U.S. dollar. Hence, Canadians came to think of the U.S. dollar exchange rate as synonymous with the exchange rate between Canada and the rest of the world in general.

Given the special circumstances of the time, Canadians were correct in this perception. Until the mid-1960s, particularly after the Korean War, the United States was successful in achieving a relatively high degree of domestic economic stability. Its economy during these years was, for the most part, almost inflation free. In consequence, any tendency of the Canadian dollar to depreciate against the U.S. dollar (or for the current account to be in deficit after Canada returned to a fixed exchange rate) could properly be read as a sign either that the terms of trade (that is, the relative values of the goods and services in which we trade internationally) were turning against us, or that undue inflationary pressures were building up internally. A tendency for the Canadian dollar to appreciate indicated the reverse.

These special circumstances no longer prevail, however, and to continue to use the U.S. dollar exchange rate in this way would be inappropriate for two reasons. First, the rest of the world has not pegged its currencies to the U.S. dollar for more than a decade. The U.S. dollar exchange rate, therefore, gives an imperfect reading of what is happening to the Canadian dollar relative to the basket of currencies of the countries with which we trade. Secondly, the macro-economic performance of the United States over the last decade, like that of most other countries, has not provided a stable bench-mark and may not provide one during the next few years.

The difficulty with using the U.S. dollar exchange rate to measure the international performance of our Canadian dollar is illustrated in Figure 10-4, which shows the exchange rate of the Canadian dollar measured against U.S. currency and against two indices of our "effective exchange rate": that is, against two baskets of the currencies of Canada's trading partners. Even though the latter are heavily influenced by the U.S. dollar exchange rate (because the U.S. dollar makes up more than 70 per cent of the baskets of currencies in question), it is clear that the U.S. dollar rate and the effective rate have often behaved somewhat differently. Sometimes, as in the 1982–84 period, the U.S. dollar exchange rate has indicated that the Canadian dollar is a weak currency, while at least one of the trade-weighted rates has told a somewhat different story.

Figure 10-5 plots the trade-weighted exchange rates of major OECD countries from 1969 to 1984. It shows quite clearly that the Canadian dollar, far from being chronically weak, as the U.S. dollar exchange rate alone suggests, was indeed one of the world's stronger currencies during this period. Its depreciation against the U.S. dollar between 1980 and the present was symptomatic of the strength of the U.S. currency against virtually all currencies, and not of any specific weakness in the Canadian economy.

This is not to suggest, however, that the relative changes in the exchange rates of the Canadian dollar against the U.S. and other currencies were of no importance to Canada. Obviously, they were important, and it is reasonable to ask whether they required a concerted policy response by Canadian

FIGURE 10-4 U.S. Dollar and Trade-Weighted Exchange Rates for the Canadian Dollar

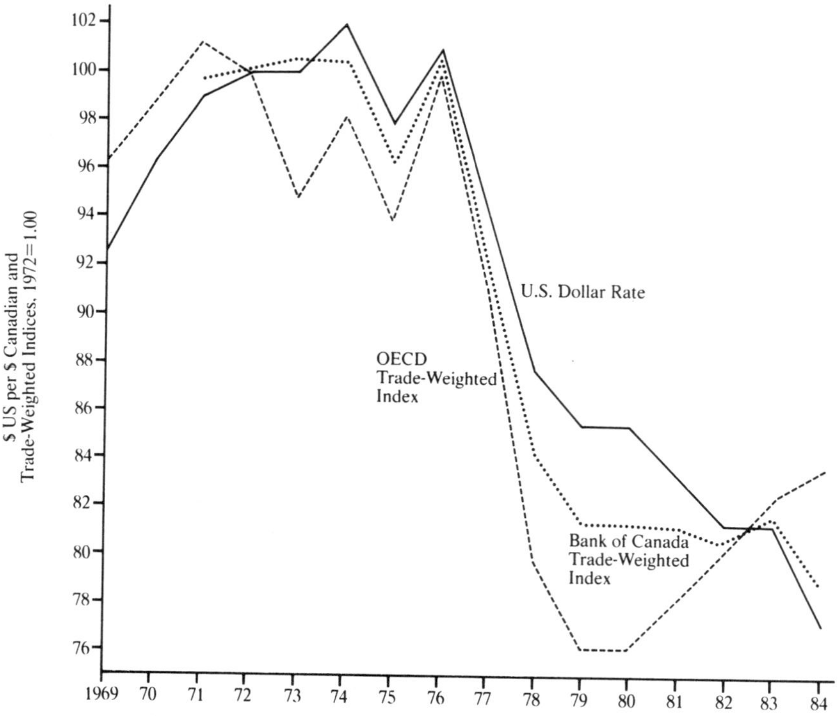

Source: OECD *Economic Outlook,* Dec.1984 Tables 32, R15, R16; *Bank of Canada Review,* Feb. 1985 and Sept. 1984.

FIGURE 10-5 Effective Exchange Rates, Trade Weighted (Average of Daily Rates)

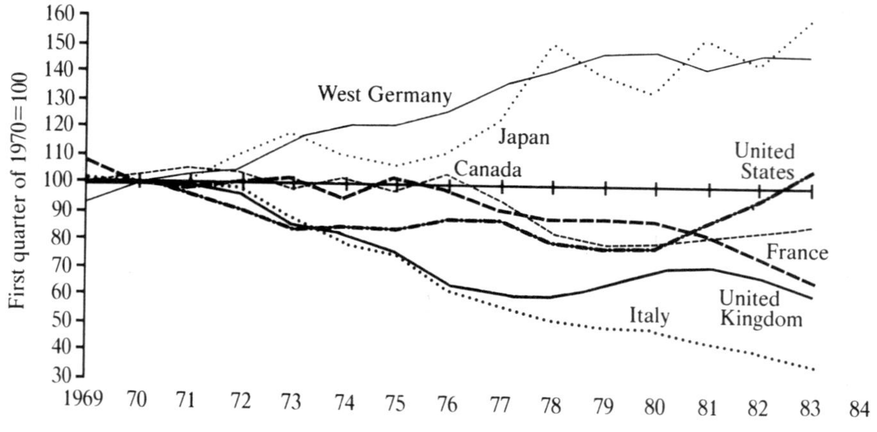

Source: OECD *Economic Outlook,* July 1984, Table R16 and 33.

authorities. Exchange-rate fluctuations, regardless of their cause, have consequences for the producers and consumers of goods traded across national boundaries. In Canada, exports represent more than a quarter of national income, which means that one way or another, exchange-rate fluctuations affect virtually every Canadian. Moreover, since more than 70 per cent of our trade is with the United States, there can be no denying that the U.S. dollar exchange rate is an extremely important variable for all of us. We must, therefore, consider what response, if any, might be appropriate for the Canadian authorities to make to exchange-rate fluctuations.[1]

The Long Run

The primary responsibility of Canada's fiscal and monetary authorities is to achieve a situation in which inflation is low and stable, employment is high and stable, and economic growth proceeds at a reasonable pace. Furthermore, Commissioners do not believe that over the long run, trade-offs are available among these goals. Exchange-rate policy must be judged against this background.

An exchange rate is the relative price of two currencies, a price influenced by factors affecting either of them. This elementary truth has important implications. If the authorities of all countries with whom Canada trades give similar priority to the pursuit of domestic goals, including that of low inflation, exchange rates will maintain long-run stability in the absence of changes in the real terms of trade. If Canada successfully pursues such policies, but some of its trading partners find a rise in domestic inflation tolerable, then their currencies will depreciate against the Canadian dollar, and vice versa.

The Canadian government cannot simultaneously commit itself to the pursuit of domestic economic stability and to the maintenance of a stable exchange rate against the currency of any country unless it can be certain that the other country's authorities will pursue the same domestic goals, and that the real terms of trade and other determinants of trade between the countries will not change. If our government cannot be certain of both points, it must choose between a commitment to domestic goals and a commitment to a constant exchange rate. Commissioners conclude, as we have already indicated, that Canada should opt for a flexible exchange rate against the currencies of other countries, including the United States.

This does not mean, we emphasize, that Canadian exchange rates should fluctuate constantly. It means, rather, that when faced with a choice between pursuing domestic goals and stabilizing the exchange rate over the long run, the authorities should firmly choose the former alternative. The main disturbances to exchange rates would then, in principle, result from monetary-policy initiatives in other countries that it would be unwise to imitate in Canada and from changes in the terms of trade. There is no reason to suppose that such shocks will come frequently or that when they do come, they will always be severe. A commitment to a flexible exchange rate amounts to a contingency plan for lessening the impact on the domestic economy of such shocks as they arise.

The Short Run

The preceding argument is not controversial. Very few people would contend that the Canadian authorities should commit themselves in advance to importing excessively inflationary or deflationary policies from abroad, by attempting to peg the exchange rate. Neither is it difficult to agree that when the terms of trade (or other real factors) move against Canada, it is better to allow exchange-rate changes to effect the required adjustment of relative prices of our imports and exports than to force the change to work its way through the economy by way of internal adjustments, primarily in wages. As experience over the last few years has shown, however, the exchange rate also seems to be subject to all manner of short-run pressures, the origins of which are not obviously to be found in other countries' profound policy changes or in basic changes in the terms of trade.

Many analysts argue that a free market in foreign exchange contains within itself speculative forces that cause rates to move in ways that do not reflect underlying, long-term, economic factors but that, nevertheless, can undermine the efficient operation of an economy as open as Canada's. It is thus tempting to argue that the Canadian authorities, while continuing to give priority to domestic goals, should still leave themselves room to iron out short-run fluctuations in the exchange rate.

Since Canada returned to flexible exchange rates in 1970, the government and the Bank of Canada, through monetary policy and exchange-market intervention, have explicitly adopted such a policy stance on more than one occasion. The abandonment of money-growth targets in 1982, for example, was associated in the minds of many observers with shifting policy emphasis towards stabilizing the U.S. dollar exchange rate. This period was hardly one in which our exchange rate against the U.S. dollar was pegged. None of the policy actions obviously contravened the principles set out above. The exchange-market interventions and some of the monetary-policy actions were geared explicitly to smoothing out the exchange rate's movement towards the long-run value that the pursuit of domestic goals seemed to require. The questions we face here are these: Did such interventions achieve their aims? And will they be productive if governments continue to resort to them in the future?

Commissioners would first point out that such interventions are technically feasible. The pursuit of long-run domestic price stability requires that the growth rates of various domestic monetary aggregates remain within certain bounds. To the extent that attempts to smooth out fluctuations in the exchange rate require the expansion and contraction of the domestic monetary supply, they carry a possibility – but only a possibility – that those bounds might be violated. The links, over time, between the growth of monetary aggregates and the domestic price level are not so precise as to prevent the authorities from influencing the foreign-exchange market.

Intervention may also be desirable, at least in principle. The pursuit of domestic price stability dictates only a range of growth rates for various monetary aggregates, not precise values for the growth of specific aggregates, because the demand relationships for particular aggregates are not entirely stable over time. A temporary drop in the demand for Canadian monetary aggregates will tend to increase the short-term domestic inflation rate implicit in a particular rate of growth of the supply of those aggregates; it will also tend to put temporary downward pressure on exchange rates. Monetary tightening to counter this downward pressure on exchange rates will reduce the growth rate of the monetary aggregates at precisely the right time as far as the pursuit of domestic goals is concerned.

A temporary shift in the demand for monetary aggregates is not the only source of short-term pressures on exchange rates that the Canadian authorities might appropriately offset. Temporary balance-of-payments problems (the result, say, of a bad harvest) might also best be dealt with by Bank of Canada intervention in the exchange market, as might problems caused by movements of short-term capital, based on false information or a speculative bubble. In each case, the source of disturbance is temporary and likely to be removed in the longer run. Yet if it is allowed to affect the exchange rate, the price signals given to the market sectors of the economy might be misleading. Thus, for example, a temporary fall in the exchange rate might lead to a general and inflationary increase in domestic wages.

The case for intervention in such circumstances is strong, but not overwhelming. Temporary fluctuations in exchange rates present the private sector with opportunities for profit; to the extent that speculators exploit these opportunities, their activities will tend to stabilize exchange rates without the aid of the monetary authorities. In fact, because of speculators' knowledge of the forces at work in foreign-exchange markets and their ability to weigh prospective developments, their actions might counterbalance a sharp drop in the exchange rate that would otherwise occur in response to some adverse, but probably only temporary, development in the market-place. Short-term, central bank intervention in the foreign-exchange market needs more to justify it than the existence of temporary pressures on the exchange rate. It requires either that central bank authorities have some systematic monopoly on knowledge that makes them able to judge better than private agents when and to what extent to intervene, or that the private sector cannot muster enough resources to intervene effectively, whereas the central bank can.

It is by no means obvious that either of these conditions holds at present. The private sector is clearly not lacking in resources. In fact, private international capital markets have grown to such an extent that central banks frequently complain that the resources at their disposal are insufficient to resist pressures emanating from this quarter. The private sector's knowledge is more debatable. During the last ten years, on a number of occasions, it has certainly seemed as if speculators were attempting to shift Canadian exchange rates to an inappropriate level. During this period, however, private operators have known full well that the Bank of Canada was ready to intervene in the foreign-exchange markets, and that knowledge must have had two effects on their activity. First, to the extent that the Bank was expected to iron out fluctuations that could otherwise have profited private agents, their incentive to learn about the causes of such exchange pressure and to speculate on its outcome must have been reduced. Secondly, private operators' incentives to second-guess and speculate on the intentions of the Bank must have been increased.

We cannot use evidence generated by central bank intervention to infer how private markets might work in the absence of this activity, although it is worth noting that intervention was often minimal for significant periods, especially in the case of major European currencies. We presume that the actions of the market would be more stabilizing than is apparent when the Bank intervenes, but how much more is a matter about which reasonable people can disagree; so, too, is the question of how often the Bank's intervention is itself well conceived.

Interest Rates

During the last few years, concern about the Canadian dollar's exchange rate, particularly in relation to the U.S. dollar, has become deeply associated in the public mind with concern about high interest rates. High levels of interest charges are widely believed to undermine the private-sector investment on which the long-run growth of output and employment depends. What scope do the Canadian authorities have for insulating the domestic economy from interest-rate levels that are too high to be compatible with these goals?

After 1982, the inflation rate in Canada fell dramatically, but nominal interest rates did not fall to the same extent. Moreover, even allowing for the fact that actual inflation and expected future inflation do not necessarily coincide, real interest rates, which are the chief matter of concern for capital accumulation and hence for growth and employment, have risen substantially since 1981. It is therefore worth considering the extent to which we can control real rates and the extent to which domestic control could be strengthened by institutional change.

One of the most striking developments of the last 20 years has been the internationalization of capital markets. Nowadays the level of real interest rates is determined primarily by the world-wide interaction of the supply and demand for capital. Consequently, a dominant influence on the real interest rates prevailing in any given country is the structure of real interest rates prevailing internationally. Of course, some countries, notably the United States, are bigger than others, both as suppliers and demanders of capital; thus their policies can affect the world-wide level of real interest rates. Canada, however, is simply too small to have any influence in these matters. As long as we permit capital to flow across our borders with almost complete freedom, the level of real interest rates prevailing in the world economy will be a major influence on our rates, especially in the longer run.

To specify the "longer run" is important because the Canadian authorities do have some short-run influence over domestic real interest rates as long as they maintain flexible exchange rates. If interest rates rise temporarily in the world economy, the Bank of Canada can choose whether to match the increase. The choice has immediate consequences for the exchange rate. If the Bank follows the increase, the exchange rate will remain unchanged. (More precisely, it will continue to take whatever path other factors determine for it.) If the Bank does not match the increase, the Canadian exchange rate will fall, initially to the point at which investors conclude that the relatively low interest available on securities in Canada is more than offset by the appreciation they expect in the value of the Canadian dollar between the time at which funds are invested in this country and the time at which they can be converted back into a foreign currency. In other words, there is a short-run trade-off between the domestic level of real interest rate and the exchange rate.[2]

This trade-off is one of the benefits that a flexible exchange rate bestows on Canada, but we must emphasize its short-run nature. Canadian real interest rates cannot sink below those prevailing world wide unless the Canadian dollar is expected to appreciate at some time in the future. A temporary depreciation of the currency – that is, one that the exchange market confidently assumes to be temporary – can stave off temporary increases in world interest rates or delay the effect of more permanent increases. It cannot stave off the latter forever. In the long run – and that period is sometimes better measured in months than in years – real interest rates in Canada are broadly determined in world markets.

Intervention in Capital Flows

Our interest rates are essentially beyond our control because of the freedom with which capital can enter and leave the country. Any attempt by Canadian authorities to establish long-run control over real interest rates in this country would require them to interfere in this free movement. We turn now to a consideration of two methods by which they could do so.

Exchange Controls

Any intervention in the movement of capital across our borders, aimed at reducing real domestic interest rates below the world level would have to rest on a judgement that real international rates are higher than appropriate to our domestic economic circumstances. Since 1982, the view has been widespread that real interest rates are indeed excessively high. But deciding whether their level justifies the creation of the institutional machinery of exchange controls which, in themselves, would have an economic cost depends, at least in part, on a judgement about the permanence of the problem. Inflationary expectations were probably an important factor in creating these high rates, but they are also partly a result of a high rate of borrowing by the public and private sectors of the U.S. economy, in combination with a rather low rate of U.S. domestic savings. This problem is understood within the United States, as elsewhere, and we hope that it will be tackled in due course. To deal with a temporary problem, however, serious though it may be, by making a permanent institutional change is not an appropriate action. Hence, in Commissioners' judgement, the introduction of exchange controls would not be justified for Canada today.

An Interest-Equalization Tax

Temporary problems do sometimes persist for uncomfortably long periods, and they do recur. Sometimes interest rates abroad are too high for too long to be staved off by a short-run depreciation of Canadian currency. Commissioners therefore take seriously suggestions that temporary measures to influence interest rates warrant consideration.

The principal measure to be considered is some form of interest-equalization tax, which would work by taxing at a premium rate all interest income earned outside the country by any person or corporation taxable in Canada. Thus it would tend to make domestic investors willing to lend to Canadian borrowers at a lower rate of return than they would expect to receive from foreigners.[3] In judging such a tax, one must assess both how much effect it would have on domestic interest rates and what other costs, if any, it would impose on Canadians.

Such a measure would reduce interest rates in Canada only to the extent that it diverted more domestic savings from flowing out of the country than it kept foreign savings from flowing in. Given that Canada has a high domestic-savings rate, an effective interest-equalization tax might indeed have this effect. However, it would also have other effects that are not quite so desirable. First, it would mean that all Canadian savers, not just those who had previously held their wealth abroad, would earn a lower rate of return than they would earn in the absence of intervention. Such a tax, then, would, in effect, be levied not just on speculators, but on all Canadian savers.

Secondly, to have any hope of being effective, the tax would have to be levied on all investment income earned abroad, no matter where, including that earned in less-developed countries. Under any other arrangement, it is difficult to see how investors could be prevented from re-routing, through intermediaries located in poorer countries, investments ultimately destined for the United States and Western Europe. There are certainly drawbacks to a measure which, if it is to be effective, would levy excess taxes on Canadian investments in countries that desperately need investment and that Canada wishes to aid.

Moreover, a theme throughout this Report has been that Canada, perhaps more than any other advanced country in the world, depends on maintaining a liberal international trading environment to ensure its future prosperity. Though trade in capital is not quite the same as trade in goods and services, the two are intimately related, and it is not obvious that we could promote further liberalization of our trade relations with the rest of the world at the same time that we were imposing restrictions on capital flows. An interest-equalization tax is, when all is said and done, a form of protectionism.

Finally, an interest-equalization tax would, by design, drive a wedge between international interest rates, which represent the return that the Canadian economy earns on savings supplied to the rest of the world and the interest rate facing individual Canadian decision makers. When decision makers act on the basis of a trade-off that differs from the trade-off actually facing the economy as a whole, the result is usually some distortion or cost in terms of economic efficiency.

Automatic Adjustment to Inflation through Indexation

Although the approach Commissioners recommend for monetary and fiscal policy should be consistent with further reductions in inflation, the possibility that inflation may continue in the 3 to 4 per cent range cannot be ruled out. Such a rate of inflation, although moderate compared to the levels experienced over the past decade, nevertheless remains a potential source of inequity and economic distortion. Uncertainty about future inflation can produce further inequity and distortion. In principle, these problems can be alleviated by a set of institutional changes, most of which involve indexation in one form or another.

A study prepared for this Commission outlined the many institutional and private adjustments to inflation that have already been made.[4] The personal income tax has indexed exemption levels and rate brackets to avoid making taxpayers liable for higher effective tax rates if their real incomes do no more than keep up with inflation. The Consumer Price Index (CPI) has been used as an index for a number of government transfers to individuals: the OAS/GIS payments and Family Allowances. Unemployment Insurance (UI) benefits and accruing CPP/QPP pension rights are indexed to measures of earnings. Cost of living adjustment clauses (COLAs) have become quite common in wage contracts, especially those of fairly long duration. Many analysts see the increasing popularity of shorter maturity terms for financial instruments over the past decade as, at least in part, a response to increased uncertainty about inflation and, thus, about the real value of fixed dollar amounts maturing some distance into the future. Finally, the sharp rise of nominal interest rates in the 1970s is generally viewed as an adjustment to the considerably higher levels of actual and prospective inflation.

Despite discussion and tentative experiments, there is little or no formal provision for automatic inflation adjustments in four areas:

- Lack of inflation adjustment in business accounting reduces the usefulness of conventional financial statements as indicators of the ongoing viability and value of a business; it may bias a firm towards excessive dividend payments and mislead the public about the true level of profits. Accountants have, therefore, engaged in much study and discussion of alternative approaches to adjustment, and the accounting professions in the United States and Britain have taken initiatives to introduce inflation accounting, which involves adjusting inventory and depreciation allowances from the traditional "historical cost" basis to a "current" or indexed basis. It also involves adjusting nominal interest payments to reflect the decline in real value of outstanding liabilities that are fixed in dollar terms (which include virtually all business debt).

  The Canadian Institute of Chartered Accountants recently made a start in this direction by issuing experimental standards for adjusting for the effects of changes in prices. It asked large firms to use these standards to provide supplementary information in their financial statements. These supplements are, however, voluntary, and so far, the number of firms issuing them has been insufficient to allow a clear assessment of their usefulness.

- The tax treatment of business income, interest income, and capital gains requires inflation adjustments similar to those needed for accounting purposes.[5] The tax authorities have introduced certain *ad hoc* offsets to the lack of formal inflation adjustment, such as accelerated rates of depreciation, the 3 per cent inventory allowance, and the $1000 interest-income deduction. The extent to which these measures have offset the tendency of effective tax rates to rise under inflationary conditions is not entirely clear. It is clear, however, that the degree of offset they provide differs from one industry to another and among firms in the same industry. Formal inflation adjustment would result in a more neutral tax system. It would also lessen the incentive, which the unindexed system creates because of the full deductibility of nominal interest costs, to finance through debt rather than equity.

  To introduce inflation adjustment would result in a loss of tax revenue, but the loss could be offset, at least partially, by eliminating the *ad hoc* provisions.
- Indexed financial instruments, such as bonds and mortgages, the principal value of which is linked to a price index, have received considerable academic attention. The British government successfully introduced bonds of this type in 1981, but no such instrument has been seen in Canada or the United States. In their absence, savers and borrowers inevitably face uncertainty about the impact of inflation on the real value of their assets and loans. In addition to eliminating this uncertainty, indexation would provide a straightforward way of eliminating the front-loading of real payment streams that is characteristic of conventional bonds and mortgages under inflationary conditions.
- Some limited indexing of private pensions exists in Canada, and the federal government has put forward proposals that would require at least a degree of indexation to be applied more broadly in the future. The lack of fuller indexation of private pensions is partly related to the absence of indexed financial instruments; private pension plans cannot guarantee fully indexed payments as long as they are not able to invest in indexed assets. Partial indexing might be achieved, however, by relating benefit levels to interest-rate levels, as under the federal proposal.

We Commissioners recognize the complexities that reform in each of these areas would entail. We recognize, as well, that indexation would not be an unmixed blessing. In addition to adding complexity, widespread use of indexing, particularly of wages and salaries, is destabilizing under some circumstances with some types of indices. For example, if Canada experienced a rise in import prices with no corresponding rise in export prices, the CPI would rise, although the economy's ability to pay for goods and services, domestic and foreign, would not have increased. In these circumstances, indexation would preserve some real incomes and not others, thus tending to create an inflationary spiral and concentrating the necessary downward adjustment on the unindexed sectors.

Nevertheless, we judge that the greater use of inflation adjustment or indexation would, on balance, be beneficial in all four of the areas listed. Use of indexed bonds, for example, could lower the real cost of public-debt charges (because current, long-term, nominal interest rates appear to include a premium against the risk of renewed inflation). A period of low inflation and low inflationary expectations is, in our view, the least disruptive time to make this institutional change.

Moreover, the risks associated with certain inflation-adjustment mechanisms can be reduced by using indices more appropriate than the unadjusted CPI. The ideal index would not be sensitive to supply shocks, shifts in the terms of trade, or changes in indirect taxes. The National Accounts use a deflator to show price changes of the gross domestic product (GDP) at factor cost; the CPI can be adjusted to eliminate the impact of changes in import prices, indirect taxes and possibly food prices. Either might be an appropriate measure for the indexation of financial instruments, such as bonds or mortgages, of pension benefits, and of the taxation of business and investment income. These measures might also be considered as replacements for the CPI in providing standards for indexing personal income-tax exemption levels and tax brackets, and for at least some indexed transfer payments, such as Family Allowances.

The Regional and Federal-Provincial Aspects of Stabilization Policy

Both the federal nature of Canada and the broad diversity of its several regions raise a number of issues about economic stabilization policy. Should the federal government differentiate stabilization policy by region? Do stabilization-policy actions discriminate against some regions? Has the postwar decrease in the federal share of total government expenditures and revenues diminished the federal government's ability to apply effective stabilization measures? Do we need greater federal-provincial co-ordination of stabilization policy?

Regional Differentiation of Federal Policy

We turn first to the recurring question of whether the federal government should attempt to differentiate its fiscal and monetary policies regionally. At the most general level, substantial differentiation already exists if "regional fiscal policy" is taken to include all government revenues and expenditures. Such differentiation is effected explicitly through equalization grants and through expenditures by the Department of Regional Industrial Expansion (DRIE). The federal income tax and the system of transfer payments to persons also involve implicit regional differentiation, which is created by the relationship of the income tax and some transfer payments to per capita incomes, and by the relationship of UI benefits to unemployment rates. Notice that differentiated tax rates (or the depreciation provisions of the corporate income tax) provide an alternative means of achieving the objectives of current expenditures by the Department of Regional Industrial Expansion. This was the practice in the early 1960s, and it is currently a feature of the investment tax credit.

Regional Fiscal Policy

Many people use the term "regional fiscal policy" in a more restricted sense, referring to regional differentiation of temporary variations in taxes or expenditures that are motivated by considerations of stabilization policy. Canada's experience with regionalization of this type of policy has been limited. The most significant use has been the allocation of funds under direct employment programs.

Should this type of regionalization be expanded? Basic to any consideration of this issue is the fact that cyclical conditions in Canada's regions generally vary in a similar way. (If this were not so, there would be few grounds for any stabilization policy at the national level.) When exceptions occur, it is usually because some export-oriented industry that is important in the region is experiencing particularly favourable or unfavourable conditions. Such a situation may well require fundamental structural adjustment rather than smoothing of a cycle. Moreover, the federal personal income-tax and personal transfer systems (particularly Unemployment Insurance) automatically help to stabilize fluctuations in regional conditions, regardless of whether they coincide with average conditions across the nation. Moreover, when unfavourable regional conditions obtained, the federal government has on occasion provided assistance directly to the industries involved.

Some observers suggest that the above-average unemployment rates that almost always prevail in certain regions indicate a continuing state of inadequate demand.[6] Their calls for a response of differentiated stabilization measures amount to advocating either:

- More-than-average stimulus to a "poor" region when general economic weakness leads to stimulative fiscal policy nation wide
- Exemption of a "poor" region from restrictive national policies when the national average of economic activity is strong.

Proponents of regionally differentiated stabilization policy have not reached consensus on which option they prefer. In fact, it is sometimes less than clear which of the two an individual proponent favours. Such lack of agreement is not surprising, since each option has its advantages at different points in the cycle. If the federal government provides "extra-strength" stimulus to a depressed region during a recession, there will be outcries when assistance is evened out as the economy recovers that "Federal assistance is being cut back more here than in prosperous regions." Moreover, if a depressed region is exempt during periods of national restrictive policy, there will be criticism as the economy swings into recession that "Less is being done here to prevent the slide than in more prosperous regions." Furthermore, although the second option might increase the average level of activity in the region affected, it would lead to less stabilization of activity there than would a policy of making no differentiation.

In sum, given Canada's pattern of broadly similar cyclical conditions across regions, a region could gain from a differentiated fiscal stabilization policy during some phases of a cycle, but it would appear to lose from such a policy during other phases. Thus, the attractiveness, political or economic, of either option is doubtful from any longer-term perspective.

Implementation of both options, on the other hand, would go beyond stabilization policy. Together they would amount to permanent differentiation in favour of a given region: in other words, to an enlarged version of what is already done through the Department of Regional Industrial Expansion, equalization, and the national tax-transfer system. And although the pursuit of both options might raise the average level of activity in a region, it would do nothing to increase its stability. If such a permanent regional policy is considered desirable, it seems unlikely that differentiation in the types of taxes and expenditures generally used for national stabilization policy would prove the most effective instrument.

Monetary Policy

Regional differentiation of monetary policy presents a rather different problem. Apart from any questions about its desirability, it is simply not a practical possibility within a common currency area. Given the mobility of financial capital, we cannot expect to maintain differential interest rates on general loans of the same risk class. This practical consideration does not, of course, rule out the use of interest-rate subsidies tied to the location of physical activity. Such subsidies could be provided through explicit government-expenditure measures; in principle, they could also be achieved through implicit subsidies, such as variations in banks' reserve requirements tied to their patterns of lending for investment in specific regions. In this Commission's opinion, however, such interest-rate subsidies are more usefully viewed as a part of fiscal policy rather than of monetary policy.

Regional Complexities

Another issue here is whether national policies impinge in unintended ways on particular regions. Critics sometimes suggest that because tight monetary policy causes exchange-rate appreciation (or reduces depreciation than would occur under a mix of looser monetary and tighter fiscal policy), it has particularly severe effects on regions where raw-material exports are of above-average importance, particularly the West. Alternatively, heavy fiscal restraint tends particularly to affect Ontario and Quebec, where manufacturing industries are the most directly oriented to the domestic market.

These points seem to have some substance. It is never possible to find policies, alone or in a mix, that achieve perfect neutrality across regions. Nonetheless, the broad regional effects should be a factor taken into consideration in determining the monetary-fiscal policy mix.

The Relative Size of the Federal Sector

Whether the growing size of the provincial-local sector has impaired the potential effectiveness of federal fiscal action for stabilization is an issue that has been considered at length in two discussion papers prepared for the Economic Council of Canada.[7] The author points out that while the provincial-local sector has grown significantly, relative to the economy and relative to the federal sector, the federal sector has also grown slightly relative to the economy. Thus, as long as provincial-local spending is no less stable than the private sector spending it has displaced — and it is probably more stable — there are no grounds for concluding that the federal sector is less able to achieve any given degree of stabilization than it was in the 1950s.

This is not to deny that enhanced co-ordination of federal- provincial action would be helpful. The issue seems to be whether more formal approaches to co-ordination, perhaps in the form of formal agreements, would be superior to our current informal approaches: annual or more frequent meetings of Canada's eleven finance ministers plus occasional First Ministers' Conferences. The answer depends, in part, on whether we can realistically aim for more co-ordinated outcomes, given a system in which both levels of government have full responsibility for their own budgetary actions. (Institutional arrangements that might enhance federal-provincial consultation and co-operation are discussed in Part VI.)

A final issue is whether there are areas in which new institutional mechanisms for federal-provincial co-ordination might be particularly advantageous. A research study prepared for this Commission suggests that greater co-operation might enhance stabilization by achieving a countercyclical pattern of public spending on capital projects.[8] Capital expenditures constitute an attractive instrument of stabilization policy because their effects are concentrated in the particular areas in which the projects are located. The advantages of a co-operative approach arise because most such projects are carried out by provincial or local governments, but the responsibility for stabilization is viewed as primarily federal. More co-ordination in this area might be achieved either through a formal stabilization fund or through *ad hoc* measures, such as those that the federal government initiated in the early 1970s to stimulate provincial and local capital spending.

Notes

1. Clearly nothing can be done, in a relatively free-trade world, about the fact that our real exchange rates may move differently from those of our individual trading partners. This fact poses particular problems of competition for individual industries and regions even when the average or trade-weighted real exchange rate can be viewed as reasonably appropriate.
2. This analysis can be summed up by the so-called "interest parity" relation, which suggests that under conditions of full capital mobility:
   - Interest rates in Canada = U.S. interest rates + expected change in Canadian $ price of the U.S. $.
   - An expected depreciation is represented by a positive value in the second term on the right-hand side (an expected rise in the price of U.S. $ measured in Canadian $) and thus leads Canadian interest rates to exceed U.S. rates. An expected appreciation is shown as a negative value in the same term and thus leads Canadian interest rates below U.S. rates.
3. Such a measure would, in principle, permit real interest rates in Canada to be maintained at lower levels than those ruling in the world at large. However, the fact that Canada, although currently running a balance-of-payments surplus, is still a net debtor on international account somewhat qualifies our ability to reduce domestic interest rates by this means.

4. Peter Howitt, "Indexation and the Adjustment to Inflation in Canada", in *Post-War Macroeconomic Developments*, vol. 20 (Toronto: University of Toronto Press, 1985).
5. Substituting the expenditure basis for the present income basis of personal taxation (and the cash-flow basis for the income basis of business taxation), as discussed earlier in Part III, would obviate the need to index the tax system.
6. However, as two research papers prepared for this Commission suggest, most of these long-lasting divergences in unemployment appear basically non-cyclical in nature. See Yves Rabeau, "Regional Stabilization in Canada" in *Fiscal and Monetary Policy*, vol. 21; and Robert L. Mansell and Lawrence Copithorne, "Canadian Regional Economic Disparities: A Survey" in *Disparities and Interregional Adjustment*, vol. 64 (Toronto: University of Toronto Press, 1985).
7. Pierre Fortin, *The Comparative Size of the Federal and Provincial Budgets and Economic Stabilization*, Discussion Paper 211 (Ottawa: Economic Council of Canada, 1982), and *Provincial Involvement in Regulating the Business Cycle: Justification, Scope and Terms*, Discussion Paper 213 (Ottawa: Economic Council of Canada, 1982).
8. Rabeau, "Regional Stabilization in Canada".

A Role for Incomes Policies?[1]

Commissioners use the term "incomes policy" broadly, to refer to policies of intervening in wage and price setting in order to influence the overall rate of inflation.[2] This definition covers a wide range of policy initiatives, including exhortation or "jaw-boning"; guidelines for, or agreements on, acceptable levels for wage and price increases; statutory controls on wages and prices (or profits); and tax-based incomes policies (TIPs), which provide incentives for restraint through taxes or subsidies. It is usually governments that undertake such interventions, but in some countries, especially those which practise centralized bargaining between national labour and business organizations, incomes policies are privately administered under the government aegis.

The industrialized world has a rich post-Second World War history of experience with incomes policies from which we can draw some conclusions about their advantages and disadvantages. In Canada, these experiments included a number of attempts at voluntary restraint, one of which involved the creation of a special agency, the Prices and Incomes Commission of 1969 to 1970. In addition, mandatory wage and profit controls were a key part of the Anti-Inflation Program of 1975 to 1978, and wage controls were applied to public sector employees in the federal "Six-and-Five" program and in associated provincial programs which began in 1982, and some of which are still in effect. The United States employed incomes policies during the Korean War period (the Wage Stabilization Board of 1950 to 1953), during the Kennedy and Johnson administrations (the guideposts of 1962 to 1966), during the Nixon administration (the wage-price controls of 1971 to 1974) and during the Carter administration (the guidelines of 1978 to 1980). In many European countries, since the Second World War, periods with incomes policies of some form have been more common than periods without them.

The Potential Contribution of Incomes Policies

A variety of proposals for incomes policies have been put forth. One distinction useful to make at the outset is between measures to be designated as permanent and those to be designated as temporary. The distinction is important because the underlying rationale is different for each approach.

Is There a Case for a Permanent Incomes Policy?

Adoption of a permanent incomes policy is typically advocated on the grounds that the economy has an inflationary bias which makes price stability difficult or impossible to maintain. Two distinct arguments have been advanced:

- The decentralized setting of a vast multiplicity of wages and prices is socially inefficient because the workers and managers in individual firms do not take into account the inflationary costs that their actions impose on the rest of society. According to this view, a permanent incomes policy is required to deal with the divergence between private costs and social costs.
- The market power of large corporations and unions biases the economy towards inflation, making price stability and full employment incompatible.

> Thus, a permanent incomes policy is required if full employment is to be maintained over time without generating inflationary pressures which would eventually make it impossible to maintain full employment.

Each of these arguments is worth examining in more detail.

The Prisoners' Dilemma

The view that decentralized wage and price setting results in social costs is based on the following rationale:

> *When business firms grant wage and salary increases in excess of the average growth rate of productivity in the economy, they impose a cost on society by producing the "public good" ("bad") called inflation. Yet they are not charged for doing so, and therefore do not take this social cost into account when they make their wage-salary decision.*[3]

Another explanation of the inflationary process is that individual wage and price setters are in what is often called a "prisoners' dilemma" situation. In one version of this story, two criminals are arrested, charged with murder and locked in separate cells. The police have sufficient evidence to convict both of a lesser crime, such as breaking and entering, for which they would each receive a five-year prison sentence. Without a confession, however, the Crown will be unable to obtain a conviction on the murder charge. Each prisoner is informed individually that if he alone confesses and testifies against the other, he will receive a light sentence, while his accomplice will receive the maximum 30-year sentence. If both confess, the prosecution will recommend 20-year sentences.

If the two prisoners could collude, their joint optimal strategy would be for both to remain silent and accept the five-year sentences. But they are in separate cells, and each must act independently. Each individual's optimal strategy is to confess because, by doing so, he will obtain a lighter sentence *whatever the other prisoner chooses to do.* Thus, although both recognize that they would be better off if they could co-operate, neither will do so because each is forced to make an independent decision about his action. In these circumstances, both would be likely to welcome any means that would allow co-operation for their mutual advantage.

There are many real-life examples of prisoners' dilemma situations. A simple, but telling, example can be observed in the baggage-receiving area of the Vancouver airport. On the floor around each carousel is a white line. If everyone stood behind the line (the co-operative action), each individual would be able to see her or his luggage arrive without pushing, crowding or undue waiting. Once one individual edges forward, however, the others will follow in order to see. Individual decision making leads to a tight crowd around the carousel station; those in the front line are being shoved and those behind are unable to see their baggage; thus everyone is worse off.

U.S. President Jimmy Carter once used a vivid simile to describe the prisoners' dilemma aspects of the inflationary process: "Inflation is like a crowd at a football game. No one is willing to be the first to sit down."[4] The group as a whole prefers the co-operative outcome (everyone sitting down) to the non-cooperative outcome (everyone standing up), yet the non-cooperative outcome obtains.

Similarly, no one is willing to be the first to stop in an ongoing inflationary spiral of wage and price setting. Suppose that inflation has been running at approximately 10 per cent for some time, and the general expectation is that it will continue to do so in the future. Firms that wish to maintain constant relative prices for their products will, therefore, raise their prices by 10 per cent. Firms and workers who have agreed on a 3 per cent increase in real wages will settle on a wage increase of 13 per cent. With an average price increase of 10 per cent, real wages rising, on average, at the rate of productivity growth, the economy at the NAIRU, and a monetary growth rate per unit of output of 10 per cent, inflation will continue at the 10 per cent rate.[5]

This spiral could, in principle, be ended if all wage and price setters would simply not incorporate the expected inflation. For example, the firm planning no change in its relative price would maintain the current price, while the workers seeking a real wage increase of 3 per cent would accept a wage settlement of 3 per cent. Because the average increase in prices would be zero, there would be no subsequent pressure for higher wages to maintain living standards. Because wages increased at the rate of productivity growth, there would be no upward pressure on prices. The inflationary spiral would have ended. Without some co-ordinating or co-operative mechanism, however, all the wage and price setters will incorporate expected inflation in their behaviour, and the wage-price spiral will continue.

Clearly, the prisoners' dilemma applies to the inflationary process, but only with some restrictions. It is apt only if inflation is ongoing and the expected inflation rate differs from the desired rate. Furthermore, it only applies to the process of reducing the underlying rate to the desired rate; once the two rates are equal, the co-operative and unco-operative outcomes coincide. Individual wage and price setters are not permanently trapped in a prisoners' dilemma game. This suggests that the argument is stronger as a rationale for temporary controls than for permanent ones.

Secular Inflation

The second rationale for a permanent incomes policy, sometimes called the "theory of secular inflation", is based on the view that the market power of large corporations and unions gives the economy a built-in inflationary bias that makes full employment and price stability incompatible.

Although this theory cannot be completely rejected on the basis of existing knowledge, it appears to be inconsistent with the proposition, accepted by monetarists and Keynesians alike, that the economy has a natural unemployment rate, a NAIRU. It also appears to confuse high prices with rapidly rising prices; market power might well raise prices or wages for some goods or types of work above the levels that they would otherwise reach, but it cannot result in their rising more rapidly. Furthermore, it contradicts empirical evidence which indicates that price stability can be achieved when there is extensive underutilization of plant capacity and unemployment.

Presumably, the proponents of the theory of secular inflation are suggesting that the market power of large firms and unions has pushed the NAIRU above what they regard, under the circumstances, as a realistic level of "full employment". Thus, to prevent inflation from increasing, it may be necessary to maintain levels of unemployment and excess capacity that are higher than is socially desirable.

A permanent incomes policy is one option for reducing the NAIRU. This Commission's view, however, is that in the Canadian setting, this option is unattractive compared to others available, such as structural changes designed to improve the functioning of the labour market. Some countries, of which Austria is probably the best example, do appear to have used a more-or-less permanent incomes policy to achieve comparatively low unemployment rates without steadily rising inflation. However, the conditions that enable these essentially voluntary and privately administered policies to function do not exist in this country. A permanent incomes policy in Canada would have to be imposed and administered by government, either through statutory wage and price controls or through tax incentives. Co-operation of the federal and provincial governments would be required, for intervention in wage and price setting on a permanent basis lies outside federal jurisdiction. Such continuing intervention in our market economy would become extremely costly to our long-run prospects for income and employment growth. This Commission, therefore, rejects the institution of a permanent incomes policy as a means of dealing with inflationary pressures in Canada.

Is There a Case for a Temporary Incomes Policy?

Although the case for a permanent incomes policy may be weak, the rationale for a temporary incomes policy under certain circumstances appears to be considerably stronger. Winding down an inflationary spiral, for example, requires a prolonged period of economic slack, especially if inflationary expectations are deeply entrenched. These high costs provide the rationale for alternative or supplementary approaches. If an incomes policy will help to achieve reductions in inflation that are not purely transitory, then actual and expected inflation will tend to decline more rapidly than would otherwise occur for any given level of unemployment at or above the NAIRU. The transition from high to low inflation will thus have lower costs in terms of unemployment, bankruptcies and lost output. Figure 10-6 compares the transition paths of demand restraint and an incomes policy in moving from a high to a low inflation rate.

The view that a temporary incomes policy could successfully aid the transition to lower inflation rates appears, at the present time, to be widely held in Canada (but less so elsewhere) among laity and experts alike. Indeed, one knowledgeable observer terms it a "middle-of-the-spectrum view, which may perhaps by now be seen as the conventional Canadian wisdom".[6] The fact that econometric studies indicate that the 1975–78 Anti-Inflation

FIGURE 10-6 Alternative Approaches to Inflation Reduction

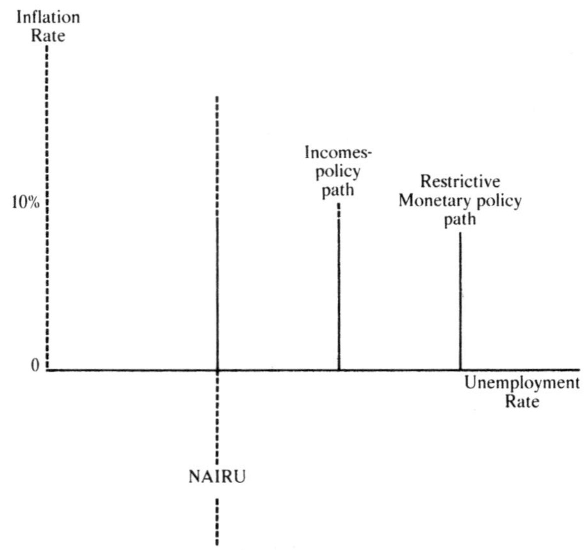

Program had a significant independent effect on wage settlements has undoubtedly contributed to the development of this conventional Canadian wisdom.

Complementary Demand-Management Measures

An important part of the rather sanguine view outlined above is the proposition that an incomes policy must be carefully co-ordinated with a program of monetary and fiscal restraint. This proposition has two parts:

- To maintain the economy at existing levels of output and employment, the rate of monetary growth must be reduced by the expected reduction in price inflation. Thus, for an economy at the NAIRU, with an ongoing inflation of x per cent, an incomes policy intended to reduce inflation to y per cent should be accompanied by a reduction from x to y per cent in monetary growth per unit of output. If this does not happen, monetary and incomes policies will be working at cross purposes. One of the errors of some control programs instituted in several other countries was the belief that incomes policy could, by itself, reduce inflation while monetary and fiscal policies remained expansionary.
- The credibility of an incomes policy will be enhanced if monetary policy goes further and makes some independent contribution to reducing inflation. Credibility is important in affecting inflationary expectations,[7] which suggests the need for operating the economy somewhat above the NAIRU. (The incomes policy path in Figure 10-6 illustrates this case.) The fact that the 1975–78 Anti-Inflation Program combined a gradual reduction in monetary growth with gradually declining norms for wage

increases may well account for its success relative to that of most incomes policies instituted elsewhere.

Incomes-Policy Options

Although we have suggested that an incomes policy is likely to be a useful component of a package designed to make the transition from a high to a low inflation rate, we have not yet discussed the form of such a policy. Yet it is important to do so because an incomes policy can take one of a number of forms, each with a distinctive blend of positive and negative features. In this section, we examine the various possibilities, from voluntary mechanisms to wage-and-price controls and tax-based incomes policies, in order to determine the real options available to Canada.

Voluntary Mechanisms[8]

One form of incomes policy is simply to establish broad national agreement among business, labour and government on the rate of change in wages and prices. The form of such an agreement is a guideline, or set of guidelines, that all three parties will respect in the general process of collective bargaining and determining prices.

A system of voluntary restraint along these lines would clearly have tremendous advantages for Canada today. It would avoid the conflicts and tensions often generated by mandatory controls and would accord with the desire of many Canadians, including the members of this Commission, to avoid, as much as possible, extending state intervention into our economic life.

Other countries have been able to rely on voluntary mechanisms for lengthy periods. During the post-war period, a number of European countries devoted considerable effort to developing institutions and decision-making processes that encourage ongoing collaboration between government and major economic interests. Countries such as Austria, Sweden, Norway, Denmark and, for a briefer period, West Germany established tripartite systems, which emphasize central negotiation and accommodation among the three "social partners" – government, business and labour – on a wide range of economic policy issues. Although these systems differ in important details, the heart of each was the development of a voluntary incomes policy.

In the view of a number of observers, the success of these economies, particularly during the 1970s, has rested substantially on the effectiveness of these mechanisms in achieving social consensus. This section, therefore, examines the European experience with incomes policies and the prospects for developing such voluntary co-operation in Canada.

The Tripartite Experience

In assessing the European experience, it is important to focus on two basic points. The first is the economic and political conditions under which voluntary incomes policies have been established and have flourished. The second is the actual effect of such policies on the economic performance of the countries that have used them.

Virtually every student of European tripartism stresses the extent to which its mechanisms depend on features of the economic and political structures of the societies that rely on them. One such pre-condition seems to be the centralization of both economic and political authority. National federations of employers and trade unions cover the great majority of enterprises and the work-force, and these federations are capable of negotiating and concluding agreements that bind their members. Similarly, government authority to reach and to fulfil understandings about public policy is not fragmented among different bodies or different orders of government.

Certainly, the countries with the most experience in voluntary incomes policy are centralized societies. Politically, they are either unitary states or, like Austria and West Germany, centralized federations in which authority over economic policy is concentrated at the national level. They are also centralized in the practice of collective bargaining. The Scandinavian countries and West Germany have well-established employer federations; Austria achieves a similar concentration through compulsory membership in official "Chambers". A parallel pattern has developed within organized labour. Countries such as Austria, Sweden, Norway and Denmark have both high levels of unionization and trade-union movements that are the most highly centralized in the Western world, in terms of the national federations, financial resources and authority over their affiliates and members. This framework complements a highly centralized process of wage formation; direct or indirect government involvement in the negotiations is a common feature.

A second factor that facilitated the emergence of consensus mechanisms in these countries was political alliance between the governing party and the major economic interests. Although conservative-leaning parties in some countries were sympathetic to tripartite initiatives, modern tripartism, for the most part, was the creation of Social Democratic parties that were closely allied with organized labour. Social Democratic governments (or coalitions of which they were a part) gave a high priority to full employment and expansion of the welfare state. In addition, they brought with them to power a faith in economic planning and a determination that labour should participate more equally with business and government in the processes of policy formation. Indeed, Social Democrats often appealed to the electorate on the ground that their special relationship with labour made them uniquely able to deal with trade unions, to generate wider social consensus, and to minimize social conflict over the directions of economic change.

The presence of institutional and political factors conducive to tripartite decision making has not, however, meant that in these countries, consensus on incomes policy was easy to achieve or to maintain. Rather, voluntary collaboration is subject to continuing internal strains and to occasional collapse. In general, tripartism reduces the autonomy of all three of the parties and can thus generate severe tensions, not only between the main participants, but also within the organizations that represent them. Such conflicts can become particularly strong if a significant segment of the membership of any participating organization perceives its leadership to be co-operating in the adoption of unpopular measures. This danger is greatest for labour organizations. Leaders of even the most highly centralized federations often discover that the price of acquiescence in unpopular courses is erosion of their membership levels or serious challenges from below.

Because of these strains, the tripartite approach in Western Europe has gone through a number of phases, each characterized by an active search for consensus on an incomes policy, and each marked at its close by instability or breakdown of participatory arrangements. The first phase covered the period of post-war reconstruction. A second phase, which began in the mid-1950s, eroded – and in some instances, collapsed – in the late 1960s, in reaction to the effect of wage restraint. In the words of a recent study by the U.S. Brookings Institution, the policies of this period:

> *... failed to provide significant rewards for cooperation. In particular, the distributional implications of most of the policies were not advantageous to labor, and efforts by national union officials to cooperate with the incomes policy objectives of their governments eroded the institutional authority of the officials over the rank-and-file membership. In fact, cooperation ... in several countries brought about reductions in real wage growth that were followed by grass-roots revolt, wildcat strikes, and the wage explosions of the late 1960s.*[9]

The third phase of tripartism, which began in the very different economic circumstances of the 1970s, was often a complement, rather than an alternative, to deflationary policies. Thus, negotiations broadened beyond simple wage policy to a wider "social contract" in which governments offered workers various forms of compensation for their co-operation: wage indexation, price controls, tax reductions or increased social benefits, participation in management, improved legal protections for unions. These new arrangements, however, were unable to contain all the tensions. Breakdowns occurred in several countries, including Sweden and West Germany. Some countries, such as Britain, which had experimented repeatedly, if often unsuccessfully, with such initiatives, subsequently elected governments resolutely opposed to such forms of economic policy making. The predisposition to consensual forms of decision making may indeed be stronger in parts of Europe than in North America, but even in Europe, success is not guaranteed.

Over the last 20 years, however, no system of economic management has avoided periodic crises. The question remains, therefore, whether the voluntary approach, with all its internal strains, represents a better means than ours of managing a modern economy. An answer requires a judgement of the economic records of tripartite countries, and, unfortunately, systematic examination of the results of the consensus-seeking process is a difficult task. Existing studies tend to compare different countries over different time periods, and they often disagree on the contribution of incomes policies to the economic patterns they discover.

Some early examinations gave optimistic readings of the economic performance of countries that had adopted the tripartite approach. Recent studies, however, have produced important qualifications. One study conducted for this Commission compared the performance of Austria, Sweden, Norway and several other countries with that of all the OECD nations over the last 20 years.[10] As a group, the tripartite countries do not seem to have performed better systematically, according to a wide range of economic indicators including economic growth, profits and rates of return, investment levels and productivity. Nevertheless, on the two measures central to this section, inflation and unemployment, these countries did fare better, although the experience of individual countries differed. Austria's record is impressive by any standard, but in Sweden and Norway, inflation was above the OECD average throughout most of the 1970s and early 1980s. Unemployment rates in each of these countries were consistently below the OECD average, though the record has eroded recently. The present rates are still enviable by Canadian standards, but they are high by the norms established in those countries during the 1970s and early 1980s.

Perhaps the most decisive effect of economic tripartism has been that on the frequency of strikes. During the years between the two World Wars and the period that followed the Second World War, the decline in rates of strikes, in countries such as Austria, Sweden and Norway, was truly spectacular, especially given their previous histories of conflict. Indeed, it is possible that tripartism's major contribution has been that of reducing the levels of industrial and social conflict.

What conclusions can be drawn from this brief survey? Clearly, tripartite co-operation should be a serious contender for the management of a modern economy. Tripartite mechanisms have served some countries well, especially in particular periods. If, in the future, Canada were to face major new inflationary pressures, a voluntary incomes policy would offer real attractions. Nonetheless, important qualifications are in order. The success of this approach in various European countries has been facilitated by economic and political structures and relationships embedded in the fabric of their societies, and, even then, the process has not always been easy to implement. Moreover, voluntary restraint has not proved a magic formula yielding guaranteed economic success.

Consultative Approaches in the Canadian Environment

Clearly, the distinctive set of factors which have facilitated incomes policies in some European countries is, for the most part, not replicated in Canada. In the first place, Canadian institutions are characterized by the fragmentation of power, not by its concentration. In both economic and political institutions, authority is dispersed across competitive groups in ways that inhibit the centralized interaction that lies at the heart of tripartite systems.

In the political realm, our federal system divides authority over economic matters between the two orders of government. As a result, economic policy evolves through the independent, and often competing, actions of 11 governments. This constitutional division does not, of course, prevent federal authorities from discussing a voluntary restraint program with business and labour, but it does limit the prospects for reaching comprehensive agreement.

The federal government could not, for example, enter into any commitment concerning the salaries of provincial employees (who constitute a significant component of public sector unions) or the wide range of provincially regulated prices. A fully comprehensive agreement would, therefore, require discussions among business, labour, and Canada's 11 senior governments. The history of federal-provincial conferences does not encourage high expectations of such deliberations.

Fragmentation of authority also characterizes the institutions representing both business and labour in Canada. Business in this country certainly does not lack representatives. Some 480 nationally oriented business associations are in operation today; there are 102 associations representing various interests in the agricultural sector. In contrast to the European pattern, however, Canadian associations are fragmented, pluralistic and often competitive. The vast majority represent special-product interests, and they are not integrated into a central association that can speak for business as a whole. Even general associations, such as the Business Council on National Issues, the Canadian Chamber of Commerce, the Canadian Federation of Independent Business, and the Canadian Organization of Small Business, represent different elements of the business community. Moreover, these general groups are direct-membership associations that have no formal relationship with sectoral organizations, such as the Canadian Manufacturers' Association, or the many subsectoral associations; thus they cannot speak authoritatively for all business groups. (The closest Canada comes to central organizations is at the provincial level, where the Business Council of British Columbia and Quebec's *Conseil du Patronat* represent their constituents.) Most important, given their voluntary nature, these organizations would be hard pressed to bind their members to specific norms or even to commit the business community as a whole to a general course. We Commissioners believe that business associations have an important role to play in consultations on economic policy (a theme to which we return in Part VI of this Report), but they could do no more than encourage their members to adopt guidelines on wages and prices.

This pattern of dispersed authority is repeated in Canadian organized labour, which lacks the comprehensive centralized structures that sustain tripartism in Europe. In the first place, the proportion of the work force that is unionized is substantially lower in Canada than it is in Europe, and the problem of how to represent the interests of unorganized labour in any negotiations is controversial. Even more important is the pluralistic nature of the Canadian labour movement. Whereas West Germany, for example, has a total of 16 unions, Canadian unions are highly fragmented, and most of them are small. In 1980, the labour movement in Canada comprised 734 unions; two-thirds of these had fewer than 10 000 members, and 40 had fewer than 22 members. This organizational fragmentation is the counterpart of highly decentralized processes of collective bargaining. Although there is some variation from industry to industry and from region to region, most collective bargaining in Canada takes place between a single union and a single employer, in a single location. Even in spite of informal linkages among units, the system ranks among the most decentralized in the world. Certainly it is in stark contrast to the centralized structures of nations that have adopted the tripartite approach. As one commentator says of Canadian labour:

> *[Centralization] is minimal when compared to the nations of Scandinavia and Continental Europe ... where multi-employer structures are the rule. In Canada, only about 8 per cent of units covering 25 per cent of the workers in the sample bargain under multi-employer structures, and a significant portion of these units are local in scope. Again, this contrasts with Scandinavia and Continental Europe where industry wide bargaining at the regional or national level is common. Only the United States and the United Kingdom exhibit comparable levels of decentralization.*[11]

This fragmented structure generates a parallel pattern at the national level. The Canadian Labour Congress (CLC) is certainly the predominant central federation and the one best positioned to engage in broad national discussions. Nevertheless, the CLC cannot claim to speak for all organized labour because Canada has several separate federations. Moreover, the real economic power of most unions – the power to organize and bargain collectively – rests firmly with their locals and is exercised within a tradition of considerable local autonomy. The central federation remains a voluntary association of unions, regulating relations among affiliates and representing their collective interests to governments. Neither the executive of the CLC nor the executives of most of the affiliated unions have much ability to commit locals to movement-wide courses of action.

The implications of this dispersed authority become clear as soon as attention turns to a voluntary incomes policy. The discussions of 1976–77, on ending the mandatory wage and price controls then in place, foundered partly on this very point. As the author of a study prepared for this Commission observes:

> *There was no precedent in Canada for a union central adopting a wage negotiating guideline. The CLC does not have the internal machinery for assessing any such standard or for generating consensus around it. Thus, even if the CLC leadership had seen such a standard as being in the interest of its members, they would have been making a radical change in their practices by endorsing it, and would have done so at considerable risk to themselves. They had no mandate from the 1976 convention to engage in this kind of activity, and would have been held accountable for their actions at the 1978 convention.*[12]

In contrast to the European pattern, then, the fragmented nature of our Canadian political and economic institutions constrains development of a voluntary incomes policy. The underlying political relationships among business, labour and government are different here as well. As we noted earlier, a key factor in the emergence of tripartism in Europe was the formation or control of governments by Social Democratic parties which were closely allied with organized labour. Union leaders tended to be in broad agreement with the overall direction of economic and social policy, which encouraged their co-operation in the risky business of incomes restraint. In Canada, however, the close relationship between organized labour and the

New Democratic Party (NDP), which has yet to win power nationally, complicates the process. Organized labour faces an enduring tension between its longer-term political objectives and co-operation with the government of the day, a tension that contributes to considerable ambivalence about the value of consultative arrangements generally. Indeed, within the labour movement as a whole, there remains considerable scepticism about whether anything that goes beyond the collective bargaining process will protect the interests of its members.

Given this institutional and political context, it is perhaps not surprising that attempts to develop a voluntary incomes policy have been unsuccessful in Canada. In 1969, the federal government appointed the Prices and Incomes Commission, which attempted to negotiate a package of commitments to restraint among business, labour and governments. After a series of exploratory meetings, however, the CLC and the Confederation of National Trade Unions jointly rejected the call for voluntary guidelines. The Prices and Incomes Commission continued its efforts, and at a national conference in February 1970, it managed to secure broad agreement from the business community to restrain price increases. However, a subsequent attempt to develop a guideline of 6 per cent for wage and salary increases failed, in the face both of continued opposition from organized labour and of the federal government's own acceptance of several public sector settlements that exceeded the guideline. Without meaningful commitments on wages and salaries, the program of price restraint expired at the end of 1970.

In response to another acceleration in inflation in 1974, the then Finance Minister John Turner attempted to achieve consensus with business and labour on the necessity of exercising voluntary restraint. He initiated a round of discussions which extended into a series of 20 meetings that came to be known as the "consensus talks". The exercise took place at two levels. At the political level, it involved the minister, business leaders he had selected, and officers of the CLC. The intent, on the government's side, at least, was to reach a common understanding of Canada's economic situation as a foundation for an agreement on appropriate measures of restraint. However, in April 1975, when the government proposed a voluntary guideline for wage increases of 12 per cent (up to a maximum of $2400), with parallel limitations on increases in prices and profits, the CLC quickly rejected the proposal. In October 1975, the government imposed a mandatory controls program.

In September 1976, on the government's initiative, another round of consultations, known as the "post-controls talks", began to explore the possibilities of an early exit from controls (scheduled to run until 1978) and of agreement on post-controls policy. At the outset, the government, which was represented by the Prime Minister, several ministers, and a very few senior officials, met separately with business and with labour. In early 1977, however, business and labour leaders discovered that they had shared interests in an early end to controls and an improved system of consultation with government; thereafter, the meetings were tripartite. In June 1977, the government made specific proposals: controls would end in 1977, one year ahead of schedule, if business and labour would make certain commitments on wages and prices; if these sectors did not respond within two weeks, controls would run their course. The CLC rejected the proposals and effectively terminated the consultation process.

The Scope for Voluntary Mechanisms

Despite the undeniable attractions of relying on voluntary agreement in developing an incomes policy, the structure of our institutions and the complexities inherent in our political relationships limit the applicability of the tripartite model in this country. There is undoubtedly great scope for consensus-building mechanisms, especially mechanisms to support a continuing national dialogue about our economic problems and prospects. Nevertheless, our expectations for incomes policies must be conditioned by our experience. The desirability of consensus in a democratic society suggests that a voluntary program should always be the first preference of Canadian governments. Moreover, there are signs that the experience of the recent recession is promoting reconsideration of traditional attitudes towards incomes policies; if Canada once again faced serious inflationary pressures, incomes restraint might well receive much more sympathetic consideration than it has evoked in the past. Nevertheless, the prospects for developing an effective, purely voluntary, incomes policy remain uncertain at best.

Statutory Wage and Price Controls

Given the lack of past success with voluntary mechanisms as a means of restraining inflationary pressures in Canada, government is left to choose among other policy options: statutory wage and price (or profit) controls; a tax-based incomes policy; or the application of macro-economic policy alone (a course that will almost certainly involve recession).[13] None of these courses is very appealing, but they are the options from which a government must choose.

Statutory wage and price controls are at least easy to conceptualize. They attempt to achieve by fiat what the structure of the economy makes difficult to obtain otherwise: a reduction in the actual rate of inflation, without a substantial increase in unemployment. They are often part of an inflation-reduction package that also includes monetary policy geared to reducing the growth of the money supply in step with reducing inflation.

If the public can be convinced that the reduction in inflation achieved by controls is not simply temporary, inflationary expectations will decline, and this development will result in less inflation for each level of unemployment. As long as appropriate monetary policy accompanies the controls, there is no reason for higher inflation to resume after the controls end and, therefore, no reason why the public should expect it to resume. In other words, using controls as part of a package to enable the economy to make the transition from a high inflation rate to a low rate does not involve "fooling" the public in any way. This point is important because potential success over the longer term depends on public expectations that inflationary pressures will not erupt again following the removal of controls.

The Benefits of Controls

The potential benefits of temporary wage and price controls are clear. How well have these programs worked in practice? Attempts to control rising prices by government fiat have been made since Biblical days. The majority were largely unsuccessful because the source of inflationary pressures – an increase in the quantity of money or some other cause of excess demand – was not removed. Here, however, we are reviewing a much more sophisticated form of incomes policy, one in which the stipulation of norms for wage and price increases is accompanied by appropriate reductions in the rate of growth in the money supply.

The experience of Western nations, including the United States and the United Kingdom, with statutory incomes policies in the post-war period has not been overwhelmingly favourable. In many instances, the policy appears to have had little effect. In others, the results were only temporary, and the removal of controls was followed by a wage or price "bubble". In many of these unsuccessful cases, however, the controls were not combined with the appropriate monetary restraint. To date, Canada's 1975–78 Anti-Inflation Program (AIP) is probably one of the best examples of a statutory incomes policy introduced as part of a package that included restraint on monetary growth. Thus, the case for using wage and price controls rests, to a considerable extent, on this experience.

How successful was the AIP? To assess the effect of a controls program is not an easy task. Any reduction of inflation that occurred during the program could have had other causes. Alternatively, even if inflation did not decline (perhaps because of unavoidable increases in import prices), prices might have increased more without the controls. In other words, to establish the effects of the controls, analysts must determine what would have happened in their absence under otherwise identical circumstances. A number of empirical studies have addressed this issue. Most conclude that the AIP lowered wage increases by 2.5 to 4 per cent per year during the three years it was in operation. It is estimated that a comparable reduction in wage inflation by means of monetary restraint alone would have required unemployment rates of approximately 12 to 13 per cent, as compared with the 7 to 8 per cent actually experienced.[14]

The AIP's effect on price increases was less impressive. The controls, which affected prices only indirectly, by putting restraints on profits, influenced only about 60 per cent of the commodities that make up the Consumer Price Index. The annual rate of change in the CPI declined from about 11 per cent in the two years before the introduction of the AIP to 7.5 per cent in the first year of the program and to 8 and 9 per cent respectively in its second and third years. The substantial drop during the first year came primarily from a reduction in food prices that had little to do with controls. In the second and third years of the program, on the other hand, substantial increases occurred in the prices of food, energy and imports, which were uncontrolled, and which offset the downward pressure on controlled prices. As a result of these unanticipated inflationary shocks in 1977 and 1978, the program did not fully achieve its objectives. However, these shocks would have tended to raise the inflation rate in any event: estimates indicate that in the absence of controls, price inflation would have been 1 to 2 per cent higher in each of 1977, 1978 and 1979. The lag is notable. Although the program had little independent effect on prices in its first year because existing wage contracts were not abrogated, its effect on price inflation became greater as time went on; it peaked in 1979, the year following the end of the program.[15]

Profit margins declined during the AIP, but the fall appears to have resulted, primarily, from the slow-down in economic activity. In other words, the program's profit controls do not appear to have exerted any significant independent effect, at least for the economy as a whole. Thus, the AIP's effect on price inflation resulted chiefly, if not entirely, from the lower rate of increase it induced in labour costs through lower wage inflation. Empirical studies also indicate that no wage or price bubble developed in the post-controls period. The AIP experience, therefore, supports the view that direct wage and price controls can aid the transition from high to low inflation rates, a view in line with conventional Canadian wisdom.

No studies have yet been published about the effectiveness of the Six-and-Five program of wage controls in the public sector, implemented by the federal and most provincial governments in 1982 and 1983. There is no doubt that wage settlements in the public and private sectors did decline markedly in 1982. The difficulty is to determine how much of the decline was associated with the severe recession and how much with the AIP controls. A complete answer must await careful econometric research, but a simple inspection of the data suggests that the 6 per cent ceiling imposed in the first year of the federal program had some independent effect on public sector wage settlements. However, the 5 per cent ceiling used in the second year of the program was, in retrospect, probably too high; it seems to have resulted in some settlements that were higher than they would have been in its absence. This phenomenon illustrates one of the problems inherent in setting wage or price norms far in advance: these norms may turn out to be inappropriate for the economic conditions prevailing at the time they take effect.

The Costs of Controls

Since virtually every Western industrialized country has adopted some form of incomes policy at various times, the cost of these policies is well documented. The costs associated with direct wage and price controls are by no means trivial. The administrative costs alone are considerable. Controls require a bureaucracy to monitor wage and price increases and to ensure compliance with the guidelines. (One of the most difficult and expensive tasks this agency faces is the costing of non-wage benefits.) Reporting procedures also impose a cost burden on the private sector. In addition, there are the costs of distortions associated with general wage and price limits, which block the relative changes that otherwise would have been made in response to economic forces in the market-place. A simple example illustrates this point.

Suppose that the economy has five commodities, each providing 20 per cent of GNP and each subject, in the absence of an incomes policy, to different future price increases. An ideal incomes policy would scale down all the prospective increases by some common percentage, thus preserving the relativity of the planned changes and ensuring that no adverse effects interfered with the normal functioning of the economy. If the goal of the incomes policy were to reduce the inflation rate from 6 per cent to 3 per cent, the distribution of price changes would look like this:

Commodity	1	2	3	4	5
Proportion of GNP	20%	20%	20%	20%	20%
Planned percentage increase in price	2	4	6	8	10
Non-inflationary price increase	−1	1	3	5	7

The downward pressure would be proportionately the same at all points, maintaining the relative distribution of prices that would have occurred without controls.

In a normal program, however, the limits imposed are absolute. Suppose that the program sets a 3 per cent limit on price increases for all commodities. The distribution of price changes will look like this:

Commodity	1	2	3	4	5
Planned percentage increase in price	2%	4%	6%	8%	10%
Price increase under controls	3	3	3	3	3

The distribution of prices is now skewed from what the market-place would have achieved in the absence of the program. The control ceiling becomes a floor for some commodities and, for others, seriously undercuts proper value. Without controls, any given year sees considerable variation in negotiated wage settlements and price increases. A controls program that sets upper limits, even with allowance for costly administrative exceptions, is bound to alter this distribution in undesirable ways. Moreover, application of the ceilings to all settlements is bound to involve some inequities, which can undermine support for the program.

Constitutional and Political Issues

Considering statutory wage and price controls for Canada raises various constitutional and political issues. Some of these issues stem from the division of powers between the federal and provincial levels of government. In effect, the division of powers limits the federal government's capacity to mount a statutory controls program, although the limits it imposes may not be as extensive as they seem at first thought.

Under normal circumstances, prices and incomes lie largely within provincial jurisdiction, as matters of "property and civil rights" fall within the powers of a province pursuant to section 92(13) of the Constitution Act, 1867. (The federal Parliament may, of course, legislate incomes policies in the federally regulated sector, which includes banks, airlines, railways, and federal Crown corporations, and in the federal public sector.) However, the Anti-Inflation Act, passed in 1975, gave the federal government regulatory authority over prices, profit margins and wages in selected areas of the private sector. It also applied directly to the federal public sector, and it authorized the government to enter into agreements with the provinces to apply the AIP to the provincial public sectors. Administered by a federal tribunal, the Act was to be in place until 1978 unless the AIP was terminated earlier.

Several trade unions challenged the constitutionality of the Act. Responding that the legislation was grounded in its emergency powers, the federal government, in 1976, referred to the Supreme Court of Canada for a ruling. In a seven-to-two decision, the Court held that the Act was valid under the federal power to make laws for the "Peace, Order, and good Government of Canada" in an emergency situation, even in peacetime.

The case seems to have established several key points for the future. First, the Court will not ask whether there is evidence of an emergency, but rather whether there is a "rational basis" for the legislation. Secondly, extrinsic evidence, such as economic briefs or government white papers that bear on the issue, will be admissible as evidence that such a rational basis exists. Thirdly, the onus is on the opponents of the legislation to show that it has no rational basis. Fourthly, the Court will not consider the wisdom or likely success of the legislation. Thus, this case indicates that the federal Parliament may introduce a statutory wage- and price-control program in an emergency, provided that the legislation has a rational basis. Furthermore, the Court is unlikely to question the government's assessment of emergency conditions.[16]

One important limitation, however, is that emergency legislation is inherently temporary as the majority of judges firmly indicated in 1976. A permanent system of federal wage and price controls would have to be created by both levels of government or sustained through an amendment to the Constitution. Moreover, if the federal government resorted to a succession of "temporary" emergency programs, the nature of the "emergency" would become legally suspect, and difficulties in federal-provincial relations would certainly be exacerbated.

The Canadian Charter of Rights and Freedoms may also have some implications for the conduct of incomes policy. Such a policy restricts what collective bargaining can achieve, but it does not interfere with an individual's right to join or form a union. Thus temporary wage controls would not appear to contravene the freedom of association that the Charter guarantees. Most incomes policies, however, are selective in their coverage. For example, the AIP guidelines applied only to firms with 500 or more employees; firms whose employees bargained in an association with employees of other firms; construction firms with more than 20 employees; federal government and Crown-corporation employees; employees of participating provincial governments; and members of professions. A policy that covers only part of the labour force could be challenged under the equality provisions of the Charter.

Political complications also surround statutory programs. Controls are more likely to succeed if both business and labour support them, but to attempt to gain that support raises the same set of constraints and tensions examined in our consideration of voluntary mechanisms. The fact that wages are easier to control than many prices may increase suspicions that the program is essentially anti-labour in nature. Even if a program is not intended to slow growth in real wages, it may have this effect if unanticipated inflationary shocks hit the uncontrolled-prices sector. Each occurrence of differential treatment makes it more difficult to obtain the co-operation and, at the extreme, the compliance of labour in future anti-inflationary efforts. (This was the fundamental logic of a wider and wider range of public policies that underlay the extension of the "social contracts" negotiated in Europe during the 1970s.)

Another problem arises from the fact that it may be politically difficult to lift established controls from certain sectors. Rent controls still exist in some provinces, for example, as a legacy of the "temporary" 1975–78 AIP.

More generally, incomes policies extend political authority over a wide range of private activity, dramatically increasing the state's responsibility for the fate of the economy. They also transfer more of society's distributional function into the public realm. Government has long been involved in income redistribution through the tax and social-benefit systems, but an incomes policy makes the state much more clearly the final arbiter of income differentials. The psychological difference is important. Although the allocative outcomes of markets may not always seem fair, the process is reasonably anonymous. An incomes policy, on the other hand, places distributional questions at the very centre of the government agenda and inevitably injects conflicts over these questions into the political process. The difficulty is that without broad social consensus on the ideal distribution of the nation's resources, governments are hard pressed to fine-tune income differentials, especially in a period of stagnant or even declining real incomes. The danger is that the conflicts generated by the effort may seriously exacerbate political tensions throughout society.

There is no inevitability here. A number of European countries have managed to contain the pressures; indeed, incomes policies have probably helped to reinforce political stability in some: Austria is a case in point, although the contrary experience of Britain should also be noted. In Britain, the collapse of incomes policies, both statutory and voluntary, has often inflicted drastic consequences on their political authors: we cite the experience of the Conservative government of Prime Minister Edward Heath in February 1974 and that of the Labour government of Prime Minister James Callaghan in March 1979.

In addition to all these considerations are the costs deriving from interference with individual freedom. The fact that these are difficult to measure does not mean either that they are insubstantial or that they are unimportant.

The Case for Temporary Controls

As part of a package including moderate demand restraint, temporary statutory wage and price controls are probably a better choice for society than is severe demand restraint for a limited period or prolonged moderate demand restraint. Government may, however, be reluctant to choose statutory controls because of uncertainties about its constitutional authority to do so and because of objections from opposition parties and other groups, particularly organized labour. If inflation rises again, however, the government might do well to institute controls and so avoid the recession that must result from reliance on demand restraint alone. If it does initiate controls, it would do well to emphasize that the major beneficiaries of a successful wage- and price-control program are the workers who would otherwise have been laid off, the owners of firms that would otherwise have gone bankrupt, and the many others whose income and employment prospects would otherwise have been reduced. Recognition of these benefits would contribute to support for such policies.

Tax-Based Incomes Policies

The difficulties associated with demand restraint and statutory controls provide the rationale for proposals of tax-based incomes policies (TIPs). The measures suggested vary in several ways, but their central feature is that they create incentives for moderation in wage and price increases. On the one hand, like direct controls, these policies promise to avoid the high unemployment and lost output associated with controlling inflation solely by means of monetary and fiscal restraints. On the other hand, these policies attempt to use, rather than supplant, decentralized mechanisms of individual decision making and collective bargaining, preserving informational advantages and permitting freedom of choice.

Where statutory controls impose limits or norms on wage and price setters, TIPs would impose a set of rules within which firms and workers would be free to determine wages and prices. The rules would acknowledge the principle that moderation is in the self-interest of the wage and price setters and would likely include norms or guidelines for percentage increases in wages, prices, profit margins or some combination of these factors. The mechanisms could be taxes (the "stick" approach), subsidies (the "carrot" approach), or both. The taxes might be levied on firms through the corporate-profit tax or through a payroll or value-added tax; they might be levied on employees through the personal income tax or through a payroll tax. Whatever the rules, they would presumably apply only to the private sector. In the public and quasi-public sectors, the norms could be applied directly.

Both discrete and continuous TIPs have been proposed. A discrete TIP would apply the same penalty to all increases above the norm or the same reward to all increases below it. A continuous TIP need not have a specific norm; rather, it would provide a schedule of tax or subsidy rates that varied with the rate of wage or price increase. For example:

Observed Percentage Price Increase	Tax Rate on Corporate Profits
10	54
8	52
6	50
4	48
2	46
0	44
−2	42
−4	40

Combinations of discrete and continuous schedules are possible; for example, the policy could provide a schedule of tax rates for increases above a norm and a flat rate below it.

One often-cited TIP scheme would use the corporate income tax to stiffen firms' resistance to wage increases above a norm: the size of the penalty (the tax rate) would depend on the difference between the increase granted and the norm. TIPs which are more elaborate (and thus more costly to administer) would apply both to wages and to prices or profits. For example, employees who accepted wage increases within the guidelines might be granted a tax rebate, as might employers whose price increases or profit margins did not surpass a norm.

Fiscal neutrality (a net revenue of zero) would probably be a desirable feature of a TIP so that its purpose might be seen strictly as controlling inflation, rather than as raising revenues or providing a fiscal stimulus. The design could accomplish this goal by including both reward and penalty elements that approximately offset each other. Alternatively, a TIP providing a pure reward could be combined with an increase in the general tax rate to achieve fiscal neutrality.

The Advantages and Disadvantages of TIPs

In considering the choice between statutory controls and TIPs, the point that deserves most emphasis is the similarity in their underlying rationales and in the difficulties they face. Both systems are appropriately viewed as complementary to, rather than substitutes for, policies of demand restraint intended to wind down an inflationary spiral. Thus both face the difficulty that apparent early success may tempt a government to abandon or reduce the demand-restraint part of the package. Both involve similar administrative tasks: measuring wage and price changes and non-wage benefits, and monitoring compliance with the policy. Since neither is likely to cover all wages and prices in the economy, some of the inequities and inefficiencies associated with partial coverage are bound to occur. Finally, both should be used infrequently and on a temporary basis to deal with serious inflationary pressures.

In contrast to the extensive experience with various forms of statutory controls, experience with TIPs is limited. A number of countries have seriously considered implementing such a policy, but only Hungary has actually done so. Studies indicate that its TIP has succeeded in restraining inflationary pressures, but the implications of the Hungarian experience for economies that are not centrally planned are not clear. Thus, there is some uncertainty in the matter of how effective a TIP would be in reducing inflation, and in the matter of which design features are most desirable.

Of course, Western industrialized nations have accumulated considerable experience with tax incentives of various kinds that is clearly useful in predicting the effectiveness of a TIP. Furthermore, despite extensive experience with statutory controls, uncertainty remains about the probable effectiveness of such programs.

Although the effects of a TIP are more problematical than those of statutory controls, some of the doubts about both have the same roots. As we have seen, an ideal incomes policy would scale down all wage and price increases proportionately, preserving relativity and ensuring that the policy would have no adverse effects on resource allocation. To design a TIP that would preserve relativity would be difficult even if wage and price setting were fully synchronized. Some TIPs, however, would be more likely to approximate this result than others. In particular, a continuous TIP would exert downward pressure at all points of the wage- and price-change distribution, although equal pressure at each point would be difficult to achieve. In our earlier illustration of a continuous TIP schedule, for example, a firm anywhere on the range of distribution could lower its tax rate by lowering its price increase.

Most proposed TIPs, however, are discrete, with a schedule of tax rates for increases above a norm and a lower rate for increases below the norm. Such a policy could not preserve the wage- or price-change distribution because it would exert no downward pressure on increases that, in the absence of the TIP, would have been below the norm.

If we compare the effects of a discrete TIP with those of direct controls, we see that both policies alter the distribution of wage and price changes: direct controls cut off the upper part of the distribution, and a TIP cuts out a segment from the middle. It is difficult to say which effect is more serious, since both distort relativity to some extent. The advantage of the TIP is that it does permit large increases, which allows wage and price setters to deal with serious shortages or inequities.

Although a continuous TIP should cause little distortion in the relative wage or price structure, it penalizes firms with higher wage or price changes even if they reduce their increases from what they would have been without the TIP, and subsidizes those whose increases would have been at the lower end of the distribution continuum. Both fairness and allocative efficiency, therefore, argue against a substantial penalty (that is, a steep tax schedule), which limits the potential effectiveness of the program.

As in the case of direct controls, a TIP that does not abrogate existing contracts can achieve only modest reductions in the inertia affecting wage inflation. One source of this inertia is the long-term and overlapping nature of wage contracts. Another is the slow response to anti-inflation policies of expectations of future inflation. Theoretically, a TIP could reduce these expectations, but the people involved in wage and price setting are likely to be quite uncertain about the effects of an untried program. They are unlikely to lower their expectations until there is some demonstration that the program is reducing inflation. This argument suggests that the effectiveness of a TIP would be somewhat less than that of direct controls.

Several supporters of a TIP claim that its administrative costs would be much lower than those of direct controls because the program could be accommodated within the bureaucracy that administers the tax system. Commissioners believe, however, that the costs of administering a TIP are likely to be very similar to those of administering direct controls. First, there is no reason to believe that the relationship between the number of firms covered and the effectiveness of the program would be different for the two policies. Therefore, the degree of coverage judged appropriate would be quite similar. Secondly, both programs would involve monitoring wage and price increases and assessing compliance with the guidelines laid down; these are not currently activities of the tax authorities. Thirdly, the most difficult and expensive parts of these activities, the valuation of non-wage benefits and the measurement of price increases, would be common to both programs. For these reasons, it appears likely that a TIP on wage and price increases in Canada would involve a bureaucracy similar in size and requirement of skills and knowledge to that of the Anti-Inflation Board of the 1970s.

The social and political costs of a TIP are the most difficult to assess, but they may also be the most important. For statutory controls, as we have seen, these costs are likely to involve a general reduction in goodwill and a co-operative spirit; harm to the collective bargaining system; increased animosity and distrust of government on the part of the private sector; the direction of the efforts and resources of business and labour away from collective bargaining and towards the political arena; and the possible increased acceptance of government intervention as a method of solving economic problems. Because of its "voluntary" nature, a TIP might involve lower costs in relation to these last elements than would statutory controls. Although it would complicate collective bargaining and decentralized wage and price setting, it would not displace these important institutional features of our market economy.

A potentially important offset, however, arises from the reliance of a TIP on the tax system. Many observers are concerned that the tax system is already too complex. They believe that it must be simplified and made more equitable if it is to retain the social acceptance so important to a system that relies, to a considerable extent, on voluntary compliance. Whether a TIP would further erode confidence in the system is not clear, but the risk should be kept in mind. From the perspective of the federal government, a TIP has a clear advantage over statutory controls in that it could be implemented in the private sector without invoking emergency powers.

Commissioners see little reason, then, to expect that a tax-based incomes policy would be more effective in reducing inflation than statutory wage and price controls. On the other hand, a TIP has some advantages in that it allows collective bargaining and wage and price setting to proceed, and thus interferes less with individual freedom and market forces.

Conclusions

On his 90th birthday, George Bernard Shaw was asked how he enjoyed old age. Shaw replied, "It's not bad when you consider the alternative." The issue of choosing the best policy for dealing with inflation and unemployment has to be approached in a similar fashion. Each of the incomes policies reviewed in this section, voluntary mechanisms, statutory wage and price controls, and tax-based incomes policies, has significant adverse aspects. We Commissioners have important reservations about all three. But to reduce inflation by demand restraint alone has, as we have recently been reminded, very substantial costs, many of which are borne by the weakest members of society. The most important conclusion of this section, therefore, is that there are sound reasons for carefully examining structural reforms that would facilitate the control of inflation and unemployment. In the absence of these structural reforms, governments will have to rely on fiscal and monetary restraint, possibly combined with periodic incomes policies, to counter inflationary pressures.

Commissioners have further concluded that incomes policies can help to reduce inflation provided that these policies are part of a larger package incorporating appropriate restraint in aggregate demand. Such a combination of policies can reduce the very substantial costs associated with the reduction of inflation through pure demand restraint; it might well be regarded as a more equitable way of spreading those costs across the entire population.

Living with inflation is not a viable option. The experience of the recent recession has again confirmed that it is possible to reduce inflation primarily by demand restraint, but only at high cost. Should a serious inflationary spiral again emerge, it would be desirable for business, labour and government to seek agreement on adopting voluntary norms for wage and price restraint. If such an agreement cannot be reached (as has been our past experience) consideration should be given to the temporary adoption of either statutory controls or a tax-based incomes policy.

Notes

1. Much of this section draws on a study prepared for this Commission by Craig Riddell, "Dealing with Inflation and Unemployment in Canada: Options and Their Consequences", in *Dealing with Inflation and Unemployment in Canada*, vol. 25 (Toronto: University of Toronto Press, 1985).
2. As opposed to policies that attempt to control or prevent price increases in particular sectors, such as rent controls.
3. L. Seidman, "A New Approach to the Control of Inflation", *Challenge* 19 (July/August 1976), p. 40.
4. U.S. President Jimmy Carter, October 25, 1978, televized address.

5. In this and other examples in this section, we assume a constant average velocity of circulation of money.
6. J. Vanderkamp, "Wage and Price Controls: Some Basic Macro Issues", in *Wage and Price Controls*, edited by Greg Mason (Winnipeg: University of Manitoba, Institute for Social and Economic Research, 1983).
7. Indeed, some analysts claim that a credible commitment by the central bank to reducing monetary growth will lead to substantial reduction in inflation without causing the pain of a recession. The argument is associated with the "rational expectations" position reviewed earlier; if citizens believe that the central bank is committed to a restrictive monetary policy, they will realize that inflation will fall; thus their inflationary expectations will decline, leading to a decline in actual inflation.

   At the present time, this theory lacks substantial empirical support, although its proponents argue that the absence simply reflects the fact that the public has not viewed commitments to restrictive monetary policy as credible. Perhaps the experience of the 1981–82 recession, in which a restrictive monetary policy clearly results in a substantial reduction in inflation, will help the "rational expectations" mechanism to work better in the future.
8. This section draws on several studies carried out for this Commission. See Ken G. Waldie, "The Evolution of Labour-Government Consultation on Economic Policy", in *Labour-Management Co-operation in Canada*, vol. 15; and Leo Panitch, "The Tripartite Experience", William D. Coleman, "Canadian Business and the State", and Pierre Fournier, "Consultation in Canada: Case Studies and Perspectives", in *The State and Economic Interests*, vol. 32 (Toronto: University of Toronto Press, 1985).
9. Robert J. Flanagan, David W. Soskice, and Lloyd Ulman, *Unionism, Economic Stabilization, and Incomes Policies: European Experience* (Washington, D.C.: Brookings Institution, 1983), p. 4.
10. Panitch, "The Tripartite Experience".
11. Robert J. Davies, "The Structure of Collective Bargaining in Canada", in *Canadian Labour Relations*, vol. 16, prepared for the Royal Commission on the Economic Union and Development Prospects for Canada (Toronto: University of Toronto Press, 1985).
12. Waldie, "The Evolution of Labour-Government Consultation on Economic Policy".
13. Theoretically, the federal government could also choose to live with inflation. However, as Commissioners argued earlier, this is not a true option because in the long run, the goals of stable prices and full employment cannot be traded off.
14. See, for example, David A. Wilton, "An Evaluation of Wage and Price Controls in Canada", *Canadian Public Policy* 10 (June 1984): 67–73. The experience of 1981 to 1983 suggests that these estimates many overstate the extent of unemployment likely to be associated with this degree of reduction in the pace of wage increases.
15. *Ibid.*
16. The division of powers under ss. 91 and 92 remains intact during an emergency, but the range of concurrent federal powers is enlarged; this means that parallel provincial laws are more likely to be found to be inoperative. Under the doctrine of paramountcy, where a provincial and a federal law conflict, the federal law is paramount.

Structural Changes in Wage Mechanisms[1]

If inflation should begin to rise again, Canada's choice of economic policy options, in the absence of structural reforms, is not highly appealing, as the previous sections have made clear. Accordingly, this section examines certain structural changes in our system for determining wages that could lead to improvements in our economic performance, especially in price stability and levels of employment. Commissioners' concern here is with the long term, and not with the short- to medium-term problem of how to accelerate the current recovery from recession. In keeping with this long-run perspective, we focus largely on an economy that initially is assumed to be operating in the NAIRU range.

For conceptual purposes, it is helpful to divide potential reforms into two groups. The first comprises structural changes designed primarily to reduce fluctuations in output and employment resulting from economic shocks, and thus to enable the economy to be maintained close to the NAIRU and its natural level of output, without generating rising levels of costs and prices. Most of the structural changes considered in this section belong to this first group. The second set of reforms consists of those that would lower the NAIRU, and the most important of these are reforms to Unemployment Insurance. These UI reforms are considered in Part V of this Report.

It is important to recognize at the outset that these structural reforms would have costs as well as benefits, and that their effects cannot be predicted with complete certainty. To decide which reform, if any, should be implemented is not an easy task. To neglect that task, however, might be most unwise: George Bernard Shaw's dictum about the alternative must be kept in mind. The key question is: Which alternative is likely to yield the mix of costs and benefits most advantageous to Canadian society?

Earlier, we outlined "prisoners' dilemma" situations in which decentralized decision making by individual actors cannot achieve the outcome that is in the best interest of society as a whole. Several of the institutional reforms dealt with here would probably not be in the individual interests of particular consumers, employees or employers. For this reason, these reforms are not necessarily those that a decentralized market economy will adopt independently. Their implementation, therefore, may depend on government's taking the initiative.

Full Employment in the 1980s and Beyond

The consideration of potentially important structural changes is best begun by outlining the constraints that govern Canada's choices. This framework is necessary to an understanding of the effects of these changes, as well as to give some indication of those improvements in performance that can realistically be achieved. As we have seen, most economists now accept the proposition that in the long run, there is no trade-off between inflation and output or employment. The implication is that to accept somewhat higher inflation will not result in lower levels of other than temporary unemployment. In this sense, the NAIRU, the "non-accelerating inflation rate of unemployment", stands as a realistic definition of full employment. To aim to maintain the economy below the NAIRU would require continual increases in inflation. Thus, if we consider that the current NAIRU range of 6.5 to 8 per cent unemployment is unacceptably high in terms of economic hardship, wasted resources and social costs, we must adopt structural measures to reduce the NAIRU. If we accept this constraint, we can say that a full-employment goal is feasible, and that it is consistent with price stability.

At this point, it is worth recalling John Maynard Keynes' dictum: "In the long run we are all dead." To a considerable extent, what matters most for economic performance is the sequence of short periods during which the economy can, and typically does, deviate from full employment. The extent and duration of these deviations must be another concern of full-employment policy.

After the Second World War, the Western industrialized world gained confidence in the ability of governments to protect citizens from the vicissitudes of the business cycle by stabilizing output and employment. At least until 1980, the post-war period generally compares very favourably, by this standard, with the pre-war era. However, two points have emerged from our accumulated experience with Keynesian macro-economic policy. First, as we have seen, we lack the ability to fine-tune the economy by means of discretionary monetary and fiscal policy. It may be possible to avoid serious recessions, especially if inflation has been held in check, but the notion that governments can improve performance by attempting to smooth out cyclical fluctuations completely is open to serious question. Secondly, the commitment to using aggregate demand policy to prevent even minor downturns may well have imparted an inflationary bias to the economy. (This notion is part of the theory of secular inflation reviewed earlier.) One U.S. economist made these points in 1974:

> *The present inflation is rooted deep in the nature of the mixed economy . . . We live in the age after Keynes. Electorates all over the world have eaten of the fruit of the tree of modern economic knowledge and there is no going back to an earlier age. High employment or full employment is everywhere a goal insisted on by the electorate of all political persuasions. A half-century ago there was no comparable political sentiment effective against incurring prolonged depression or even stagnation; rather there was often a preoccupation with the perils of inflation, of budget and foreign trade deficits. This shift in populist attitudes of governments necessarily shifts the odds against stable prices (and of course against falling prices). No longer can one expect half of the peace-time years to experience falling prices. If general price levels rarely stand still and often rise then the secular trend of prices must be upward on the average.*[2]

Recognition of these two points has turned economists' attention from the use of stabilization policy for fine-tuning towards the structural characteristics of the economy that may contribute to the extent and length of deviations from full employment. This very useful change of focus has increased awareness of the fact that economies with different institutional characteristics differ in the extent of deviations from their normal levels of output and employment. This means that increased recognition of the limited ability of governments to foresee economic shocks and offset them, in order to prevent cyclical fluctuations, as well as the possible inflationary consequences of doing so on a continuing basis, has given rise to the opinion that fiscal and monetary policies should be directed more towards longer-term goals. This proposition, in turn, implies that we should seek structural changes to bring the system to shorter and less severe deviations from full employment.

Change is the most pervasive feature of modern economic life; the economy is continually being affected by various disturbances, some of which are partially anticipated, while others are quite unexpected. The nature of the economy's reaction to these disturbances depends on its institutional features, as well as on other factors. Initial reactions to shocks can give rise to cumulative effects that result in cycles of overall economic activity. A change in aggregate demand, for instance, can be the result of any one of myriad circumstances: an increase in the quantity of money, increased expenditure on plant and equipment by firms, increased expenditure by consumers, or increased demand for our exports in foreign markets can provide a positive stimulus. Other circumstances can result in negative shocks. Thousands of positive and negative disturbances in aggregate demand occur weekly. Some of these disturbances cancel one another so that despite their importance for individual products, markets, firms and workers, they have no net effect on aggregate demand. In most instances, however, the net effect is not zero.

When a net increase or decrease occurs in aggregate demand, it partly affects wages and prices and partly affects output and employment. The result of a fall in aggregate demand of, say, 10 per cent may be a 10 per cent decline in output and a corresponding decline in employment with no change in prices; a 10 per cent fall-off in prices, with no change in output and employment; or some combination of the two. The extent to which the effect changes wages and prices (that is, has nominal effects) or output and employment (that is, has real effects) depends on a number of factors.

One of these factors is the position of the economy relative to its potential output or full employment. The effect on output and employment of an increase in aggregate demand is typically stronger if the economy is initially below potential output than if it is above potential output. A second factor is the extent to which participants in the market-place anticipate the change in aggregate demand. An important general proposition, though one that evokes considerable controversy, is that the more the public anticipates changes in aggregate demand, the less the effect those changes will have on output and employment, and the greater the effect they will have on wages and prices.

The relative time horizon also affects the division between real and nominal effects. Assuming that the economy is operating at the NAIRU, any permanent change in aggregate demand will, in the long run, alter wages and prices alone, but it may affect employment and output in the short run.

As we have mentioned, major supply shocks, such as the increases in energy or food prices that occurred in the 1970s, can also cause output and employment to deviate from their usual levels. These shocks are particularly troublesome in that they tend to raise prices and to reduce output and employment; that is, they can lead to stagflation. In addition, they may require a downward adjustment in real wages to maintain full employment.

The proposition that greater wage and price flexibility would lead to greater stability in employment and output has a long history. It is clearly valid where there is a change in demand in a single market, but, as Keynes noted, the effects on aggregate demand must be taken into account. If wage reductions made in response to a decline in aggregate demand lead to a further decline in aggregate demand, they may make employment and output less, rather than more, stable.

This is a complex issue, and it is not possible to explore it in detail here. We do note, however, that modern Keynesian and monetarist economists alike hold that greater wage and price flexibility would contribute to greater stability in employment and output, given stable monetary and fiscal policies. In addition, more flexible wages and prices would clearly reduce the costs of fighting inflation by demand-management policies. They would also weaken the case for using statutory wage and price controls or tax-based incomes policies to deal with inflationary pressures.

Reform of Wage- and Price-Setting Arrangements

The response to demand and supply shocks depends to an important extent, on the manner in which the economy determines wages and prices. We turn, therefore, to a consideration of the influence of existing institutional mechanisms on the setting of wages and prices.

One of the most important institutional arrangements affecting the economies of Canada and the United States is the system of collective bargaining between unions and management. Among its important implications for wages and prices is the considerable rigidity or inertia it creates in both. The result of this rigidity is that the short-run effect of changes in aggregate demand falls primarily on output and employment, rather than on wages and prices. Wide and lengthy deviations from full employment, therefore, can and often do occur. If we effected structural changes that made wages and prices more responsive to demand, we could achieve greater stability in employment and output.

The inertia in wages and prices and its implications for employment have not gone unnoticed by policy makers. In his annual report for 1982, the Governor of the Bank of Canada raised the issue:

> *Our economic system has exhibited stubborn resistance to a reduction in the rate of cost and price inflation. Why has the resistance been so stubborn?*
>
> *Let me say first of all that I doubt that anybody is able to give a definitive answer to this question. It involves an aspect of the functioning of Canadian society that has received far too little consideration . . . I think it likely that a thorough examination of the question would point to policy initiatives of one kind and another that would improve appreciably the prospects for employment and output in Canada.*[3]

Recent research by macro-economists identifies several features of North American wage contracts as an important source of inertia in costs and prices. Union contracts in Canada and the United States often run for two to three years. They typically specify the wage rates to be paid throughout their term; thus these wages are not contingent on the economic conditions prevailing at the time the wage is paid. The main exception is cost-of-living/adjustment provisions, which make wage levels contingent on only one dimension of economic conditions, that is, the increase in the Consumer Price Index. In addition, collective bargaining agreements overlap one another; in an average year, about half of all settlements are renegotiated, with only a modicum of seasonality in the bargaining calendar.

In brief, we are interested here in three components of collective bargaining in North America:

- The overlapping of contracts
- Predetermined duration of contracts, which is often considerable
- Predetermined or non-contingent wages.

For a number of reasons, these features are believed to be an important source of persistence in wages and prices.

First, an obvious factor in the sluggish response of the average wage to changes in economic conditions is that only some wages are reset in each contract period. The observed change in the average wage is affected, not only by new settlements reached during the period and by increases under cost-of-living/allowance (COLA) provisions, but also by the proportion of wages that do not change and by implementation of deferred increases as provided for under existing contracts. (The size of the deferred increases was determined earlier, when the relevant contracts were negotiated.)

The second obvious way in which these institutional features cause wage rigidity results from the long-term nature of contracts. The economic conditions prevailing at the time of negotiations have considerable influence because they can shift relative bargaining power by affecting the cost of a strike or lock-out to the firm and to the workers. However, negotiators also look to the conditions that they expect will prevail during the term of the contract. Thus changes in current economic conditions, especially those that are regarded as temporary rather than permanent, exert less influence on long contracts than on short contracts.

The third and most subtle, but possibly also most important, reason that these institutional features appear to be a major source of inertia consists of the interaction between the overlapping of union contracts that cover different workers in similar or related industries or occupations and the importance attached by firms and their employees to relative levels of compensation. In setting wages, firms and workers take into account the compensation levels prevailing and expected to prevail in similar industries and occupations. This process implies looking both backwards at wages set previously and forward to negotiations that will occur during the course of the group's present contract. It tends to produce considerable persistence in the pattern of wage settlements, which, in turn, significantly affects the level of employment and output. If recent wage increases have been running at, say, 10 per cent, and a decline in demand occurs, it will be difficult, at least initially, for firms to persuade union leaders and workers that substantially reduced settlements are now in order. As a result, much of the decline in aggregate demand will be met by reductions in output and employment.

The fourth source of inertia is the fact that contracts both extend for a predetermined period and provide for rates of compensation that are not contingent on all relevant economic factors. Whatever negotiators' expectations about the future, they almost always prove incorrect to some extent. Yet a contract with a predetermined duration and pre-set wage rates means that any adjustment for unanticipated economic conditions must normally be postponed until it runs its course.[4] Empirical evidence indicates that this lag makes "catch up" important in many subsequent contract negotiations.

The problem of unanticipated economic conditions can, of course, work both ways. Many wage contracts signed in the late 1960s and early 1970s clearly failed to anticipate subsequent large increases in inflation. Thus, real wages were lower than anticipated, and employees were dissatisfied. The opposite occurred in the early 1980s: contracts negotiated just before the beginning of the recession anticipated both a higher level of inflation and stronger economic activity than actually occurred. Employers were squeezed as they paid higher real wages and faced weaker market conditions than they had expected.

These two cases point to one of the disadvantages of a long-term, fixed-wage contract. The terms agreed to at the time a contract is negotiated may turn out to be inappropriate to the economic conditions over the life of the contract. The negotiation of subsequent contracts must then provide adjustments. As a consequence, the process of adjustment to the original change in economic circumstances is spread over time.

The foregoing considerations indicate that long-term overlapping contracts cause the short-run effect of changes in aggregate demand to fall primarily on output and employment, rather than on wages and prices. Empirical evidence also supports this view, as illustrated by differences in wage-setting institutions in industrialized nations. Canada and the United States are unique in their reliance on long-term overlapping contracts. Japan and several European countries make use either of shorter contracts or of more closely synchronized bargaining; labour relations in the United Kingdom are characterized by short contracts without a predetermined expiry date and by non-synchronized negotiations. If long-term overlapping contracts are an important source of inertia, the response of wages and prices to aggregate demand should be more sluggish in North America than in Europe and Japan. Furthermore, if sluggish wage adjustment results in greater variation in output and employment, these real variables should deviate more from their trend or normal levels in North America. Similarly, if synchronization is important, Japan and the United Kingdom should show significant differences in degree of responsiveness of wages, prices, output and employment.

The general conclusions of several cross-country comparisons confirm these expectations. Nominal wages display substantially less variability in the United States than they do in either Britain or Japan, while output and employment display substantially more variability. In Canada, where the degree of wage inertia resembles that of the United States, the variability of output and employment is more like that of the United States than it is like that of Japan or the United Kingdom. Japan, with its short contracts and synchronized negotiations, displays the greatest variability in nominal wages relative to the variability in employment and hours worked.[5]

That North America's long-term contracts are a post-war phenomenon suggests that analysis of the historical record might also cast light on the relationship between wage flexibility and economic performance.[6] The empirical evidence tends to confirm the suggestion of many observers that wages and prices have become less responsive to variations in aggregate demand during the past 40 years. The most striking study is that of a U.S. economist who finds that wage and employment variability in the United States before the Second World War was similar to that of Japan and the United Kingdom. Only in the post-war period did the United States display less variability in wages and greater variability in employment and hours worked.[7]

Other cultural or institutional differences among countries appear to account for some of the observed differences in wage, price, output and employment variability. As we have previously noted, several European countries have more centralized bargaining structures than Canada and put greater reliance on voluntary incomes policies. In Japan, an important factor is the substantial use of bonus payments. Nonetheless, the evidence suggests that long-term, overlapping, wage contracts are an important factor in creating wage and price rigidity.

Additional evidence comes from macro-economic models. Simulations carried out in 1982 showed that a policy of shortening contract lengths was significantly more effective in lessening the unemployment costs of reducing inflation than either statutory wage and price controls or a tax-based incomes policy.[8] In a study carried out for this Commission, two different econometric models indicated that in general, greater wage and price flexibility would reduce the deviations from equilibrium levels of output and employment caused by a change in aggregate demand.[9]

Thus, the analysis suggests that we could use shorter wage contracts and/or synchronized negotiations to decrease the inertia in our wages and prices, and to permit greater stability in employment for the future. Of course, such a change would also reduce stability in nominal wages and prices. This is the nature of the trade-off that we face in a world in which the economy is often hit by disturbances that governments, central banks and the public can anticipate only very imperfectly.

Should these structural changes be made? Let us examine a number of factors that need to be taken into account in attempting to reach a judgement. First, as already noted, decreasing contract duration and synchronizing negotiations would have symmetrical effects: they would make inflation-reducing measures less painful in terms of unemployment, but they would also make the economy more prone to rapid increases in wages and prices. Our view is that the symmetrical nature of these changes is not a strong argument against them. Indeed, their adoption would make more quickly apparent the consequences of overly expansionary policies. An unfortunate consequence of the existing institutional arrangements is that the short-term costs of such policies are deceptively low and so create a temptation that the economy would be better off without.

This point deserves some elaboration. With the output of the economy initially at its potential, the first result of a rise in aggregate demand – especially an unanticipated rise – would primarily be increases in output and employment. Since the inflationary consequences would be small at this point, a government might be tempted to pursue such a policy, especially as an election approaches. However, the gradual overheating of the economy sets in motion forces that tend to raise wages and prices and to lower output and employment. The stronger state of product and labour markets leads to some initial increases in prices and earnings, which then feed into higher wages, either directly through COLA clauses or indirectly as "catch-up" pressures affect new settlements. The higher wages, in turn, raise the costs of production, causing further price increases. The seeds of an inflationary spiral have now been sown.

Shorter wage contracts and/or synchronized negotiations would make wages and prices respond more quickly to a situation of excess demand, thus signalling more rapidly the inflationary implications. As a consequence, the costs of excess demand would be obvious sooner. Policy makers would be supported by tangible evidence as to why restraint measures were required. Structural changes in wage settlements, then, could help to arrest inflation more quickly than it could otherwise be halted. Thus the fact that the proposed structural changes would make the economy more prone to increases in wages and prices does not constitute an argument against their adoption.

Before we seriously consider changing these institutional arrangements, however, we need to ask why labour-market participants continue to choose overlapping fixed-wage contracts. Obviously, these institutional arrangements reflect firms' and unions' preferences; otherwise they would choose an alternative. One obvious reason is a desire to economize on the costs of negotiations. From 1967 to 1981, negotiations in all Canadian industries lasted an average of six to ten months.[10] Although negotiating periods would undoubtedly be reduced if contract periods were shorter, these data do suggest that the direct costs of negotiations may be large, and that contracts covering a period shorter than one year are not likely to be feasible.

Another explanation for the wide use of long-term contracts is that they constitute a method of avoiding or reducing industrial disputes. Canadian labour laws prohibit strikes and lock-outs during the term of a collective agreement, and since the expiry date of the contract is known, the firm and its customers can take such action as inventory accumulation, to minimize the potential costs of a strike; with shorter contracts, negotiations would occur more frequently. The probable effects on collective bargaining disputes need to be considered. Recent evidence indicates, however, that the probability of a strike's occurring varies directly with the length of the previous agreement.[11] Thus, to shorten contracts would reduce the probability of a strike's occurring in any set of negotiations, although it would increase the number of negotiations. Employers also seem to prefer long-term wage contracts to assist their planning and to facilitate use of the marketing advantages of security of supply.

Thus, overlapping multi-year agreements seem to have become an enduring feature of North American labour markets. In using them for wage-setting, however, individual firms fail to take into account the social costs of the wage and price inertia they generate. That is, in negotiating a long-term, fixed-wage contract, the two parties do not take into account the costs imposed on society as a whole through macro-economic instability in employment and output. Furthermore, no single firm or union has any incentive to deviate from this type of contract. To do so would neither help the individual parties nor contribute much to aggregate employment stability. Improving employment stability would require a co-ordinated change by a significant number of firms and unions.

What we have here is another prisoners' dilemma: a co-ordinated change could make all parties better off, but individual parties cannot achieve the same result independently. This suggests that there is a public policy case for altering the institutional arrangements. To make the case convincing, however, it must be shown that the change would decrease the costs to society as a whole, without substantially decreasing benefits to the parties involved in wage and price determination. This seems to be the situation. Although the private benefits of long-term contracts are not small, including as they do such items as reduction in the costs of negotiation, avoidance of disputes, and contributions to long-term planning and security of supply, they must be compared to the costs imposed by wage and price inertia, which are clearly large.

Thus there seems to be a case for public policy to encourage shorter contracts or possibly more closely synchronized wage negotiations. An intermediate possibility is a flexible wage provision within the context of a long-term contract. The entire contract need not be renegotiated each time wages are discussed. Rather, employers and employees could negotiate long-term contracts on working conditions, non-wage benefits, and other particulars, but negotiate wages more frequently.

Wage Indexation and Gain Sharing

That wage rates are predetermined in most collective agreements suggests another way to reduce wage and price inertia: make wages or earnings contingent on realized economic conditions, rather than set them in advance. Two kinds of contingent-compensation systems can serve. In wage indexation, employees are paid an hourly wage, the size of which is contingent on some measure of realized economic conditions. In a "gain-sharing" or "shared-compensation" system, employees receive a share of the profits or revenue of the firm. As we shall see below, the latter is a more fundamental reform.

Wage Indexation

The most common form of wage indexation is the COLA clause, which links wages to changes in the cost of living. Much less common are schemes that index wages to variables related to the employer's ability to pay: the wages of gold miners, for instance, might be related to the price of gold or those of steel workers to the price of steel.

Wage indexation is one way of dealing with uncertainty. Uncertainty about future economic conditions means that both employers and employees face risks. Wages set in advance will turn out to be too high for some economic conditions and too low for others. If both employers and employees observe economic conditions that they agree are relevant, both parties can gain from making wages contingent on realized outcomes. Thus a wage-indexation system has potential benefits.

Offsetting these benefits are the additional costs of negotiating, writing up, and enforcing an indexing arrangement. Although these costs may not be trivial, especially for the first such arrangement, they do not appear to form a serious obstacle. A more serious difficulty seems to be finding observable variables that are closely related to the conditions relevant to the firm and its workers. There are two problems here. One is the inevitability of imperfect information: neither party will have complete information about all the relevant economic conditions. Thus, the wage cannot be made fully contingent on realized conditions. The parties are restricted to a second-best arrangement in which the wages are made contingent on some specified variables. This clearly reduces the potential benefits of an indexed system. Another frequent problem is asymmetrical information: one party has better information than the other about some key aspects of the relevant conditions. Typically, the firm has superior information about demand-side or "ability-to-pay" variables, such as revenues, profits, output or labour productivity. The more widespread use of wage-contingency schemes would require more sharing of information among employers and employees and their representatives than currently takes place.

Increased risk for workers might constitute another cost. Certainly workers dislike the risks associated with an uncertain income. However, flexible compensation is not inherently more risky for all workers. Fixed-wage contracts also involve income risks in that employers may use temporary lay-offs in response to fluctuations in demand. Whether contingent-wage/compensation schemes are more or less risky than fixed-wage systems depends on how much the former reduce the risk of lay-offs: that is, to what degree these schemes affect the variability of employment.

Empirical evidence supports the view that more flexible wage-payments systems imply a lower risk of lay-offs. The evidence of cross-country comparisons has already been cited. Additional evidence comes from comparing temporary lay-offs and wages in unionized firms, where fixed-wage contracts are common, with the same conditions in non-union firms, which can, and often do, adjust wages upward and downward to reflect changes in the state of the economy. Studies confirm that unionized companies rely more on temporary lay-offs to respond to fluctuations in demand than do non-union companies.[12]

Flexible systems do, however, change the distribution of risk among workers. In any given firm, workers are not affected equally by the risk of lay-off. Unionized firms and, to a lesser extent, non-union firms usually make lay-offs in reverse order of seniority. Thus, under a fixed-wage system, the risk of lay-off is very low for the majority of workers, except during an unusually severe recession. The risk is high, however, during even moderate downturns in economic activity, for workers at the bottom of the seniority ladder. To change to a more flexible wage-compensation system would result in a somewhat higher risk of income fluctuations for the majority of workers, but in substantially reduced risk for those with little seniority.

Gain Sharing

Compared to wage indexation, gain sharing, or shared compensation, has considerably stronger tendencies to stabilize employment and output in response to economic shocks. Such a system can operate in two general ways. One is to negotiate or otherwise determine a sharing formula in advance. The most obvious base for making this determination is revenue (or profits) per employee: the parties would agree ahead of time that each employee would receive, say, two-thirds of the revenue per employee and the employer would receive the remainder. The second method is to determine the shares after the fact. This second system is used in Japan, where bonus payments are negotiated semi-annually for most regular industrial workers. The bonus is not related to profits or revenue by an explicit formula, but it does vary somewhat with the company's market performance. Either system is likely to involve a fixed salary or wage, with the share or bonus as a supplement. In Japan, the bonus component of income is substantial, averaging more than one-quarter of a worker's total earnings.[13]

The author of a recent book argues that an economy in which a share-compensation system is widely used will exhibit a strong tendency to maintain full employment of labour.[14] He sees a fundamental difference between an economy in which workers are paid a fixed hourly wage and one in which they are paid a share of revenue or profit. In the wage economy, the labour market is in equilibrium when the demand for labour equals the supply of labour. In the share economy, on the other hand, there is always unsatisfied demand, in the form of unfilled vacancies, at the prevailing negotiated shares. This excess demand for labour acts as a cushion, protecting the economy from significant deviations from full employment. Any reduction in labour demand will be offset by the existence of unfilled vacancies. The reason for this important difference between compensation systems is that with share compensation, a firm can reduce unit-labour costs and increase profits by expanding employment and output to any degree desired. With the wage system, the firm will expand employment only to the point at which the additional revenue generated by the extra workers equals the additional cost represented by their wages.

The main empirical evidence supporting the view that widespread use of a share-payments system will stabilize employment and output comes from post-war Japan. Japan weathered the economic contractions of 1954, 1957–58, 1962, 1965, 1971, 1974–75, and 1981–83 with relatively little change in registered unemployment. Of course, it would be a mistake to attribute this remarkable performance to the use of the bonus system alone. Japan's annual synchronized bargaining, as we have already noted, contributes to stability in employment and output. In addition, the country has a large number of workers who move out of the labour force whenever the economy turns down, and who therefore do not show up in normal measures of unemployment. Nevertheless, analysis of the Japanese experience lends support to the proposition that a share-payments system can make a positive contribution to a country's economy. Like Japan's other key wage-setting institutions, substantial bonus payments were adopted in the post-war era. Before that time, the Japanese economy suffered substantial fluctuations in employment and output.

The Case for Contingent Compensation

Given the potential benefits of contingent-compensation arrangements, why are they not more common? One answer may be that the transactions and monitoring costs that arise from imperfect and asymmetric information are simply too large to make worthwhile indexation to variables other than the CPI. This answer presumes that the people involved in wage determination have assessed gain-sharing or wage-indexation schemes and decided that the expected costs exceed the expected benefits.

Nonetheless, there is a case for policy intervention to promote gain-sharing arrangements. Like the case for shorter contracts and synchronized negotiations, it rests on the macro-economic benefits to Canadian society of greater employment stability. The multiplier effects associated with business cycles mean that lay-offs in one industry reduce total output demand and, consequently, employment in other industries. Yet individual firms and unions do not take these macro-economic effects fully into account in making choices about wage setting. The situation is another prisoners' dilemma in which co-ordinated change could benefit society as a whole.

In addition, the move to widespread use of fixed-wage contracts may have been partly based on the assumption, common in the 1950s and 1960s, that governments could substantially reduce cyclical fluctuations through discretionary use of monetary and fiscal policy and through built-in stabilizers. We now recognize, however, that our ability to anticipate and offset economic shocks is much more limited. The experience of the recent recession may well encourage firms and unions to reconsider wage-setting arrangements. Despite evidence that labour-market participants are in the process of re-examining compensation schemes, significant change has yet to occur in Canada. If substantially more widespread use of gain-sharing arrangements is considered desirable for society, it seems likely that some form of government intervention will be required.

A final point should be emphasized about the function of public policy in promoting flexible payments systems. Commissioners assume that such a policy would be intended to be neutral for the *average* compensation level: that is, it would make compensation more responsive to changes in economic conditions that affect particular firms and industries, but on average, over time, wages under the new system would be neither lower nor higher than they would be under the existing system.

Conclusions

In this section Commissioners have reviewed four options for increasing stability in employment and output in Canada: shorter contracts, synchronized wage setting, indexation of wages, and gain sharing. Each would lead to increased flexibility and variability in wages and prices. They would not, however, necessarily cause real wages to be any more variable overall.

As we stated at the outset, we cannot make precise predictions about the effects of these reforms, which are currently the subject of considerable research and debate. Of the changes described, gain-sharing/compensation arrangements seem likely to yield the best mix of benefits and costs. A further, and not entirely unrelated, advantage is that contingent-compensation reform would probably be the easiest to implement. To achieve synchronized wage negotiations or uniformly shorter contracts would require federal-provincial agreement on the wisdom of these reforms. Moreover, it would involve governments' imposing these changes on the private sector, which is a consequence Commissioners would prefer to see avoided.

The federal government alone could bring about greater use of gain sharing by offering employees more favourable tax treatment of earnings they receive in the form of a share of profits or revenue.[15] Such a scheme should not favour any particular form of gain sharing, such as profit sharing, but rather, should provide equal incentives for a variety of flexible wage-payments systems. Nor would any compulsion be applied. Employers and employees who prefer not to take advantage of the more favourable tax treatment accorded this type of income should be free to make this choice, just as individuals are now free not to take advantage of the more favourable tax treatment given to income from capital gains.

A serious obstacle to the more widespread use of gain sharing, especially for employees of firms that are privately owned, is the inadequate exchange of relevant information between employers and employees. However, as we point out in Part V of this Report, Commissioners consider a more open exchange of information a key element for improving labour/management relations and reducing the incidence of strikes and lock-outs.

Notes

1. This section draws on a study carried out for this Commission by Craig Riddell, "Dealing with Inflation and Unemployment in Canada: Options and Their Consequences", in *Dealing with Inflation and Unemployment in Canada*, vol. 25 (Toronto: University of Toronto Press, 1985).
2. From the writings of the Massachusetts Institute of Technology's Paul Samuelson.
3. Bank of Canada, *Annual Report of the Governor to the Minister of Finance* (Ottawa: The Bank, 1982), p. 10.
4. It is noteworthy, however, that during the recent recession, a number of contracts were re-opened with the consent of union members, and compensation was adjusted downward as a means of enhancing job security.
5. See Robert J. Gordon, "Why U.S. Wage and Employment Behaviour Differs from That in Britain and Japan", *Economic Journal* 92 (March 1982): 13–44; and W. Craig Riddell, "The Responsiveness of Wage Settlements in Canada and Economic Policy", *Canadian Public Policy* 9 (March 1983): 9–23.

6. The pioneering multi-year settlement was the 1948 agreement between General Motors and the United Auto Workers. In Canada, one-year contracts were widely used until the late 1950s; the move to two- and three-year agreements took place between 1956 and 1959 in manufacturing, the sector in which multi-year agreements remain more popular than elsewhere. For the economy as a whole, the move towards multi-year contracts took place gradually throughout the late 1950s and early 1960s.
7. See Gordon, "Why U.S. Wage and Employment Behaviour Differs from That in Britain and Japan". See also Robert J. Gordon, "A Century of Evidence on Wage and Price Stickiness in the United States, the United Kingdom, and Japan", in *Macroeconomics, Prices and Quantities: Essays in Memory of Arthur M. Okun*, edited by James Tobin (Washington, D.C.: Brookings Institution, 1983).
8. William M. Scarth, "An Evaluation of Tax-Based Incomes Policies", in *Tax-Based Incomes Policies: A Cure for Inflation?*, edited by Michael Walker (Vancouver: Fraser Institute, 1982).
9. Brian O'Reilly, W.R. White, and Robert Ford, "Price Flexibility and Business Cycle Fluctuations in Canada: A Survey", in *Post-War Macroeconomic Developments*, vol. 20 (Toronto: University of Toronto Press, 1985).
10. Canada, Labour Canada, *Major Wage Settlements* (Ottawa: The Department, various years).
11. Jean-Michel Cousineau and Robert Lacroix, "Why Does Strike Activity Vary over Time and Between Industries?" (Montreal: Université de Montréal, Département des sciences économiques, 1983). The relationship between contract length and strike activity is treated further, later in this Report.
12. James L. Medoff, "Layoffs and Alternatives under Trade Unions in United States Manufacturing", *American Economic Review* 69 (June 1979): 380–95.
13. Although we are concerned primarily with the implications of gain sharing for employment stability, it is worth noting that many observers recommend such a system as a method of improving employee morale and productivity. Some analysts also view gain sharing as an important part of a package for the development of a labour-relations environment that involves increased co-operation and consultation. These aspects are considered in Chapter 17.
14. Martin L. Weitzman, *The Share Economy: Conquering Stagflation* (Cambridge, Mass: Harvard University Press, 1984).
15. The February 1984 budget proposed a measure along these lines, but it no longer appears to be under active consideration.

The Challenge to Expedite the Reduction of Unemployment

Before we turn to our main conclusions and recommendations on the broad range of issues of economic growth, employment and economic stability that we have been examining, we should consider further the critical short- to medium-term challenge confronting Canada: How are we to improve this country's prospects of achieving substantially lower levels of unemployment over the next several years, without putting at risk the progress Canadians have already made in reducing inflation? In other words, how can we expeditiously reduce unemployment to the present NAIRU range? (The longer-run challenge of reducing the NAIRU itself is taken up again in Part V of this Report.)

In our examination of macro-economic policy, we Commissioners have indicated our conviction that as one means of furthering this shorter-run objective, the government should change the mix of monetary and fiscal policy. It should take fiscal measures to reduce the deficit, and simultaneously, if temporarily, increase monetary expansion enough to more than offset the effect of fiscal restraint on aggregate demand. Such a combination of moves would raise the prospective growth of output. This development, in turn, should contribute to a reduction in unemployment that is more certain and decisive than that currently anticipated, while achieving the reduction in the deficit that is necessary to provide room for stronger growth of capital investment and output in the private sector.

We would be fortunate, however, if this approach, taken by itself, resulted in reducing unemployment by as much as one percentage point a year, starting in 1986, a pace that would not take us to the NAIRU range until 1989 or 1990. Yet to use monetary and fiscal policy to push the reduction in unemployment much faster would be to put at risk our progress in reducing inflation; bottlenecks could develop during rapid expansion, and overactive policy could adversely affect confidence and, thus, the exchange rate, interest rates, and wage and price behaviour.

Commissioners believe that the challenge is not just to the federal government and the Bank of Canada. The onus is on all participants in Canada's economy – in particular on business and labour, as well as government – to follow courses that will maximize the extent to which growth in aggregate demand is translated into growth in output and employment, and to minimize the extent to which the former slows the pace of reducing inflation.

Earlier in this chapter, Commissioners rejected the idea of establishing a permanent incomes policy in Canada. We also noted the potentially adverse effects of adopting a temporary incomes policy. At the same time, however, we concluded that the benefits of such a policy could outweigh its costs, particularly when it is used to reinforce fiscal and monetary measures aimed at checking inflation. In the absence of such a complementary measure, as Canadians have learned from recent harsh experience, fiscal and monetary policy alone may succeed in controlling inflation only at high cost in terms of lost output and employment.

The situation that now confronts Canada is somewhat different from that in which adoption of a temporary incomes policy is ordinarily contemplated. At the moment, inflation appears to be reasonably well under control. Given, however, the extraordinary challenge that confronts us as a nation to do everything possible to reduce unemployment from its present unacceptable level as quickly as may be practical, Commissioners believe that a temporary incomes policy should be instituted to reinforce the downward trend in inflation and so make possible a temporary acceleration in the rate of economic growth, with minimal risk of renewed inflation. With such an incomes policy in place and with a change in the monetary-fiscal mix of the type already outlined, we believe that it would be feasible to accelerate the average reduction in unemployment as much as two percentage points annually, in order to achieve the NAIRU level by about 1988. Although Commissioners are well aware of the costs and inconvenience of employing an incomes policy, the institution of such a policy for a period of, say, three years or so would, in our judgement, be a small price to pay for the major social and economic benefits Canada would reap from a faster reduction in unemployment.

Commissioners' overwhelming preference is for a voluntary incomes policy based on agreement among the principal players, about guidelines for wages and prices (or profit margins) consistent with further reduction in inflation. We recognize, however, that it might well prove difficult – as it has in the past – to arrive at an effective agreement under which all major groups would voluntarily bind themselves to abide by guidelines. The prospects may be better for achieving consensus in support of mandatory guidelines introduced by federal and provincial governments.

Commissioners believe that governments, as well as implementing a temporary incomes policy, should act to reinforce the prospects for relatively strong growth in demand. Specifically, we advocate that federal, provincial and municipal governments move forward on the basis of at least some informal co-ordination, and, if possible, increase the capital expenditures they have planned for the rest of the decade, especially those expenditures that could contribute directly to creating jobs and improving the economic infrastructure.

Policy makers might be disturbed by the effects on the deficit of this temporary increase in capital expenditures, although economists draw important distinctions between capital and current expenditures in assessing the suitability of any given deficit level. If policy makers judge it desirable to offset some or all of these effects, Commissioners would support the introduction of a temporary income-tax surcharge. We also recommend a review of tax expenditures as a further possible means of increasing revenues. Reductions in inflation subsequent to the introduction of some measures may have obviated the rationale for implementing them: the $1000 investment-income deduction, the $1000 pension-income deduction, and the Registered Home Ownership Savings Plan deduction are obvious examples.

Commissioners are convinced that it is eminently worthwhile and clearly in the best interest of all the groups concerned to work openly, co-operatively, and in a spirit of substantial willingness to ask and grant concessions, in order to meet the challenge of reducing the unemployment rate by two percentage points a year from now until 1988, without undercutting our gains against inflation.

Conclusions and Recommendations

General

Canada's growth and employment prospects depend heavily on developments in trade and in the use of our human and natural resources. Regional development policy and the institutional framework of our federal form of government also affect our growth and employment prospects. Part III of this Report addresses other components that affect these prospects: the role of capital, technology and management; the choice of industrial policy; the demand management or setting of monetary and fiscal policies; and the flexibility of wages and prices in responding to the vagaries of the business cycle. While the following recommendations are addressed separately, their strength depends significantly on their integration with the recommendations in the rest of this Report.

Governments must be prepared to vary their role in the allocation of human, capital and natural resources in response to changes in external and domestic pressures. In general, however, governments should endeavour to facilitate the operation of the market mechanisms of our economy, rather than to seek occasions for further intervention.

■ In the management of the economy, governments must acknowledge the considerable international and domestic constraints on policy. They cannot provide quick solutions to every economic difficulty. Rather, they should set the medium- and long-term framework within which solutions can be worked out.

Although economic growth is a key means of increasing the welfare of all members of society, Commissioners do not advocate the pursuit of maximum growth at all costs. The claims of growth must be balanced against those of equitable income distribution, employment security and environmental quality. □

Recent Performance and Prospects

Canada's post-Second World War performance was strong until 1973; after that date, inflation began to climb rapidly, and productivity growth declined. Since the 1981–82 recession, unemployment has been our most serious policy concern.

This Commission has examined four independent projections of Canada's likely economic performance in the absence of major policy changes. These forecasts suggest that Canada's growth rate in real gross national product over the next two decades will closely parallel the U.S. rate. Annual real growth in Canada should average 3 per cent during the late 1980s, and decline to about 2.5 per cent during the 1990s, in keeping with a decline in the rate of labour-force growth. The growth prospects for natural resource-based production seem weak, especially in mining and forestry.

■ Most analysts predict that unemployment will remain at relatively high levels in Canada throughout the 1980s. Current high rates of unemployment are associated with insufficient total real demand relative to total supply. In addition to this critical problem, there are major structural problems which, unless addressed, will not allow unemployment to drop below 6.5 to 8 per cent over the long term. This level is unacceptable by this Commission's standards, and the problem of reducing the structural unemployment rate must be addressed. □

Employment growth and productivity growth are essentially independent. Growth in the labour force is the principal cause of employment growth. Productivity growth increases both the supply of output and real demand to roughly equivalent degrees. Thus, growth and employment goals are not in substantial conflict over the longer run. We can improve productivity without harming long-run employment growth; more generally, technological unemployment is unlikely to become a major problem. Rather, increased productivity and technological change are the key to longer-term growth in real income and economic welfare.

Some fields have experienced an increase in the rate of technological innovation over the past two decades, but the overall rate is difficult to estimate. The decline in productivity growth since 1973 might suggest a decline in the pace of technological innovation. However, the recent increase in the share of gross national expenditure spent on research and development (R&D) in the United States and Canada will raise the pace of technical change and contribute to a recovery in productivity growth.

Industrial Policy

Canada's industrial policy has shifted since 1945, emphasizing, in turn, nationalistic goals or trade liberalization, development of the manufacturing sector or development based on natural-resource wealth.

Industrial policy in Canada incorporates a wide range of policy instruments, some of which have purposes related to trade or to general economic policy. Neither the federal government nor the provinces have blueprints for industrial policy. This omission reflects a fundamental reliance on market forces and private-sector enterprise as the engine of growth.

Commissioners' review of foreign industrial policy indicates that policies that work in some countries may not work in others. Despite Japan's low expenditure on R&D, that country has been successful in the knowledge-intensive industries. France and Germany have very different industrial policies, despite being members of the European Community. France has a highly targeted interventionist approach, while Germany's approach is more market oriented. There would seem to be no particular mix of industrial policy instruments that ensures success.

Canadians differ on the proper role of government in promoting economic growth and employment. The polar extremes of a strictly hands-off approach and a highly interventionist, targeted, industrial policy appear to overlook the complexities of policy formation and practice.

■ Relative to current practice, Commissioners favour a more market-oriented industrial policy. More particularly, we favour letting the market work and placing less emphasis on government intervention to protect declining industries. We have reviewed the possibility of a more specifically targeted approach – the strategy of "picking winners" – but we believe it unlikely that such a highly interventionist approach would meet with greater success overall than would a more neutral policy.

For several reasons, some modes of intervention make sense; hence Commissioners do not favour a strictly hands-off approach. Furthermore, while there is little evidence in Canada or abroad that a targeted industrial policy is more effective than a market-oriented approach, other countries will continue to experiment. Canada should monitor these experiments carefully and consider strategic ways of strengthening its areas of comparative advantage. In our judgement, however, Canada has relied on intervention too often, too extensively and in too *ad hoc* a fashion.

Canada's industrial policy should emphasize broad-based support programs that work in tandem with basic market forces. To the extent that government involvement is required as, for example, in R&D support, benefit/cost criteria should guide it.

This Commission does not propose a blueprint for industrial development; indeed, to attempt a detailed formulation would be counter-productive. We believe, however, that consistent with our emphasis on market mechanisms, there should be a clearly stated framework for industrial policy. Such a framework would facilitate both private-sector decision making in Canada and the co-ordination of government policies and programs. This stated framework should express the strategic objective for industrial policy. Commissioners believe that the productivity of Canadian industry should predominate over other concerns, and that we should concentrate on improving our competitive position.

Commissioners believe that industrial policy should fortify incentives for excellence, for the efficient allocation of resources, and for adjustment to new economic realities. Such a policy would produce increases in real income, fuller employment and the means to address income distribution.

To improve the productivity of Canada's human, capital, and natural resources, and the competitive position of Canadian industry, industrial policy should include the following elements:

- A supportive macro-economic framework that while controlling inflation, promotes growth of output and employment at a reasonably even pace, in accordance with the economy's capacity

- A commitment to freer trade and the freer flow of investment. We favour both multilateral freer trade and bilateral free-trade negotiations with the United States.
- A commitment to strengthening Canada's labour, capital, technology and management resources.

Capital, Technology and Management

Recommendations respecting education and training are addressed in Part V of this Report.

■ With respect to capital, technology and management, this Commission makes the following recommendations.

Capital Formation

- International comparisons suggest that Canada has not suffered from any serious lack of investment over the last two decades. However, some recent economic analyses indicate that the tax treatment of savings and investment may result in a capital stock that is too small.
- While this Commission has not reviewed the tax system in detail, it does appear to us that government should examine the effect of this system on savings and capital formation. This examination should consider the adequacy of the current allowances for inflation in the tax treatment of savings and investment. It should also consider the desirability of altering the current personal tax system by substituting an expenditure base for the income base.

Domestic R&D

The effectiveness of R&D expenditure is more important than setting a target level in relation to GNP.

- To increase the effectiveness of domestic R&D, governments should consider the following measures:
  - Ensure the availability of existing incentives to all business through some type of refundability of tax losses.
  - Broaden the definition of R&D while lowering the rate of tax subsidy, even though we recognize that such a broadening could give rise to administrative problems.
  - Ensure that adequate resources are devoted to obtaining information about foreign technological developments and to disseminating information on technological developments to domestic industry.
  - Encourage excellence by concentrating Canadian effort on projects, research and development of world-scale value

through "networking" between experts within Canada, as well as internationally.
- Reduce protection of domestic industry and encourage it to be more competitive internationally.

Technological Acquisition

New technologies are increasingly shared on a global basis, and the originating country has little lead time over others to exploit its advantage. Canada draws extensively from the world pool of new technologies, in part through investment in Canada by multi-nationals. New manufacturing technologies spread more slowly in Canada than they do in other countries.

- A potential solution is to liberalize trade and to reduce the existing barriers to the flow of equity capital.
- Public policy in education and the gathering and dissemination of information could improve technological adaptation in Canada. Post-secondary institutes should place more emphasis on science, engineering and business courses. Universities should be more active in the commercialization of inventions. The National Research Council's initiatives on information gathering and dissemination could be a model for other agencies. Technology brokers, contract-research organizations and think-tanks have assisted technology acquisition in other countries. Both the private and public sectors in Canada should consider more activity of this nature.

Management and Entrepreneurship

- Increased international competition demands that Canada draw on world-class management. We should have greater exposure to competition, a reorientation of small-business/assistance programs, and strengthened business schools. Closer bonds between business and the arts community would improve product design.
- Entrepreneurship is another key component of national economic development. While small business is a vital source of entrepreneurship, other sources also require encouragement. Governments should consider changing regulations to stimulate equity investment by financial intermediaries in small and medium-sized firms, and change the tax system to make equity ownership more attractive.

Framework Policies

Another element that is needed to improve Canada's economic position is a commitment to framework policies that encourage the private sector to adapt to change and the efficient allocation of Canada's human, capital and natural resources. Framework policies include tax policy, competition policy, general regulatory policy, foreign investment and adjustment policy.

■ Our recommendations in each of these areas are as follows.

Tax Policy

- While Commissioners have not undertaken a comprehensive review of tax policy, they have investigated the issue in general terms and looked at some specific problems. Tax policy has a fundamental influence on economic and social choices.
- We recommend a thorough review of the influence of the tax system on decisions that distinguish work and leisure, and consumption, savings and investment. Policy makers must become more aware of the efficiency costs of the tax system. In addition, Canadian tax policy must recognize the fluidity of capital flows.
- There appears to be merit to building on recent changes that moved personal income tax in the direction of a personal consumption tax.
- Governments should review non-neutralities in the corporate tax structure and consider indexing of capital assets for inflation. Alternative accounting methods of defining the corporate tax base, such as the cash-flow approach and the refundability of negative taxes, are also worthy of review. Such provisions could replace fast write-offs of exploration and development expenses in the resource sectors, and accelerated capital-cost allowances in the manufacturing sector.

Competition Policy

Canadian industry appears to have become more concentrated at the producer level over the past decade. However, trade liberalization and deregulation have reduced concentration at the seller level. Mergers and conglomerates can result in undue concentrations of economic power; they can also improve efficiency and competiveness internationally.

- Canada's competition policy should better reflect both of these realities. Commissioners recommend that Parliament empower the Director of Investigation of the Combines Investigation Act to report on all developments that impede competition in Canada, including trade protection and regulatory provisions. We recommend further that governments exercise greater discretion respecting mergers and conglomerates, directing restraining provisions to those cases where a clear threat to competitive practices is evident. With increased trade liberalization, the primary area of concern could be the non-internationally trading sectors of the economy. Canadian firms should retain the right to co-operate with one another in export markets, provided that they do not reduce domestic competition, and clarification should be offered through advance rulings. All large corporations, public and private, Canadian owned and foreign owned should be required to file annual reports with the government.

The Regulatory Framework

Commissioners do not accept the simplistic notion that regulation should always be kept to a minimum. Some current problems, such as those associated with the environment, can probably be addressed only through an increase in regulatory activity. In many other areas, however, a reduction in regulation, and a concomitant increase in competition, would substantially increase economic efficiency. Even where regulation is necessary, it could in many cases be made simpler and more responsive to changing conditions.

- We recommend that government undertake to review and reform the regulatory framework as a whole. Regulatory agencies should be subject to closer Parliamentary scrutiny than they are at present, and their mandates should be more clearly and closely defined. Whenever possible, regulatory activity should be subject to a "sunset clause": that is, it should be limited in advance to a specific term.

Crown Corporations and Privatization

- The sale of some Crown corporations to the private sector would be a logical concomitant of deregulation, since it would enhance competition. By the same token, the federal government and the provinces should arrest the tendency toward nationalization or mixed enterprises, particularly insofar as this tendency is associated with industry bail-outs. Both levels of government should reassess the functions of these Crown corporations and mixed enterprises. If the functions or objectives of a given Crown corporation could be met more effectively by other means, the enterprise in question should be either phased out or sold to the private sector. If a Crown corporation is to be privatized, foreign buyers should not normally be excluded from bidding for the assets. Exceptions to this rule include cases where purchase by a foreign buyer would result in barriers to entry by other competitors, or where the industry in question should be reserved for Canadians.

Foreign Investment

Over the past 15 years or so, Canadian ownership of our industries has increased substantially. It is now appropriate to re-examine mechanisms for monitoring foreign investment in Canada. Bill C-15 provides some useful guidelines, but further innovations are required to balance the need for international equity funds and the need to foster good corporate citizenship.

- The review of foreign-investment proposals should be conducted by a quasi-judicial tribunal to ensure full public disclosure and political accountability. Fast-track procedures and practices for the handling of commercial confidences would need to be developed. Commissioners believe that new foreign investments need no longer be reviewed; the tribunal should review acquisitions only. The threshold for review should be raised from $5 million in gross assets to at least $50 million in order to focus resources on the larger and more critical take-overs. The review process should emphasize the competitive and technological conditions surrounding the proposed foreign take-over. The government should clarify the standards governing the post-entry behaviour of foreign investors by promulgating a general code of conduct applicable to all major firms, domestic and foreign, operating in Canada. To promote compliance with the code of conduct and to improve our understanding of the consequences of foreign control, the government should legislate an annual reporting requirement for all major firms or for corporate groups operating in Canada with assets in excess of $50 million. Firms should be required to disclose specified types of information relevant to their observance of these guidelines. Canadian directors should be required to file an annual statement detailing their firm's efforts to achieve the objectives of enterprise performance set out in the proposed code of conduct.

Adjustment Policy

- Whenever possible, adjustment assistance should be provided to workers rather than to firms. Commissioners recommend the institution both of tougher international agreements and of mandatory reference to a neutral agency, such as the Tariff Board, in order to make it more difficult for governments to resort to protection of declining industries. By the same token, we also recommend that it be made more difficult for governments to resort to the use of firm-specific subsidies; this could be done by attaching conditions to the recipients, and by requiring the costing of off-budget subsidies. If firm-specific subsidies are given in declining sectors, the assistance should go to the most viable, and not the weakest, firms. Part V deals at length with our recommendations regarding labour adjustment policies. Declining single-industry communities require special labour-adjustment assistance.

If the economy is flexible and adaptable, adjustment will probably be much easier, and involve less unemployment. In addition, real income levels will be improved. Flexibility in prices and wages – or, more generally, the development of successful incentives – is the key to achieving a flexible and adaptable economic structure.

Infrastructure Support Services

This Commission views policies regarding transportation, communications and infrastructure generally as vital components of an industrial policy designed to enhance Canada's productivity growth and overall competitiveness. Commissioners note with concern the shrinking share of government expenditure devoted to such infrastructure.

■ We urge both the public and the private sector to view investment in the transportation and communications field as a priority. While Commissioners recognize that a strong public role in this field is both inevitable and desirable, we conclude that deregulation and a more market-oriented approach is desirable.

The private sector should be encouraged, through the tax system and government programs, to adopt the technological and other measures necessary to establish a first-rate transportation and communications network across the country. Canada needs better mechanisms for accommodating divergent regional-investment policies and regulatory policies that have national implications.

Government Intervention

■ Government should provide itself with a clear set of guidelines to determine the nature of its intervention at the sectoral or firm level. Given the difficulty of measuring the costs and benefits of intervention, Commissioners recommend that selective intervention be used sparingly. Few cases warrant special attention, and the burden of proof should be on those that propose intervention at the sectoral or firm level. A strict limit on the funds budgeted for intervention is essential. Intervention should be undertaken only where there is clear evidence of market failure, or in industries that exhibit substantial economies of scale, or where high risk and large size make it difficult for market forces to operate adequately. Where these considerations prevail, the following guidelines should apply:

- The benefits of intervention must demonstrably exceed its costs.
- If efficiency is not the overriding objective, the objective should be achieved at the least cost.
- There must be sufficient consultation with business and labour to ensure that the chosen means of intervention are appropriate.
- International obligations must not be jeopardized.

The Economic Union

■ A commitment to a strengthened economic union is a vital element of a healthy Canadian economy. Barriers to the free flow of labour, capital goods and services should be minimized, and integration of policies should be harmonized. □

Stabilization and High Employment

For structural and institutional reasons, the rate of unemployment consistent with stable inflation in Canada is in the range of 6.5 to 8 per cent. Expansionary monetary and fiscal policies cannot sustain levels of unemployment below this range over the longer term. A permanent reduction in such "structural" unemployment would require structural changes, by which we mean such policies as freer trade, labour-market adjustments, and new mechanisms for labour-management relations.

The current rate of unemployment (about 11 per cent) is well above the rate consistent with stable inflation. This unacceptably high rate is the result of an insufficiency of total demand relative to total supply. Impediments to reducing unemployment by even 3 to 4.5 percentage points are the large federal government deficit, the high real current rates of interest and the extraordinarily complex role played by expectations.

Limitations in forecasting and lags in the effect of policy action argue against moderating short-run fluctuations in economic activity through discretionary action. The federal government should use stabilization policy to achieve non-inflationary growth in demand in the medium term, while preserving automatic fiscal stabilizers. However, economists disagree about the strength of the self-righting forces in the economy, that is, the forces that will drive unemployment toward its "natural" or full-employment level. Commissioners believe that discretionary stimulus or restraint can help in periods of major extended divergence in demand from a non-inflationary growth path.

Global interdependence, especially in capital markets, limits the degree to which policy can insulate an open economy such as Canada's from foreign developments. Given our flexible exchange rate, we can choose our inflation rate in the long run, and to that extent, we can have a made-in-Canada macro-economic policy. But the influence that we can hope to have on real demand in our own economy is likely to be short term in nature and rather limited in scope.

■ To preserve independence in domestic policy for Canadian authorities, this Commission recommends a flexible exchange rate. We do not recommend exchange controls or an interest-equalization tax to control capital outflows.

Commissioners share the widespread concern about the size of the federal government's deficit. We recognize that if the government does not reduce the current structural deficit, it will have to increase taxes just to pay interest costs and will find its flexibility seriously constrained.

■ Commissioners recommend a strategy of gradual deficit reduction, given the current outlook of slow recovery. To stabilize or decrease the debt/GNP ratio, the government will need to reduce the deficit by about 1.5 per cent of GNP, which would be equivalent to $10 billion by 1990–91. The practice of laying out an explicit medium-term fiscal plan, introduced in the December 1979 budget and continued since, is useful. We favour using a combination of tax increases and rather broad expenditure reductions to reduce the deficit. The precise means of achieving this reduction are a matter for shorter-term government policy, but Commissioners offer one possible means for consideration. This would be to set the indexing factor for the personal income tax and for some transfer-payment programs at *x* percentage points below the rate of inflation and to hold the price factor for all other expenditure programs – except foreign aid and national defence – at *x* percentage points below the rate of inflation. Setting these annual indexing factors three percentage points below inflation for a period of three years would generate a reduction in the deficit of about 1.5 per cent of GNP, thereby reducing the deficit and by that amount the deficit/GNP ratio from the 6 to 7 per cent range projected for the late 1980s.

■ Under present circumstances of high unemployment, a shift to a less expansionary fiscal stance, so as to reduce the deficit, should be more than matched by a temporary shift to a less restrictive monetary stance. A moderate increase in the projected growth of demand, which might significantly reduce unemployment and strengthen investment, should still be consistent with a further reduction in inflation.

While Commissioners recognize that adherence to a steady monetary-growth guideline can help to ensure that a stable, non-inflationary environment will be maintained, shifts in the demand for money during the past few years have made this approach difficult to apply. Furthermore, such an approach might lessen governments' ability to adjust the mix of monetary and fiscal policy in order to balance consumption and investment, and to balance the sectors of the economy that are strongly influenced by the exchange rate and the sectors that are not.

■ As a compromise solution, the government could relate demand-management/policy targets to the growth of nominal GNP. This policy would require a willingness to adjust monetary-growth targets to nominal GNP, in the event of significant shifts in relation of the money supply, and monetary and/or fiscal policy in the event of severe prolonged departures of nominal GNP from a steady growth path. Commissioners recommend that the joint setting of monetary and fiscal policy be consistent with non-inflationary growth of nominal demand.

Commissioners have also considered potential adjustments to lessen the distortions and damage that any continuing inflation imposes. We share what seems to be a general preference, that has emerged over the last few years, to emphasize low and stable inflation, rather than structural adjustments that would make it easier to live with inflation.

■ Despite the preceding conclusion, Commissioners believe that serious consideration should be given to indexation of financial assets, accounting systems and tax systems. To adjust the tax system to take inflation into account would improve its neutrality in general and lessen the incentive to rely on debt financing in particular.

In Commissioners' judgement, permanent wage and price controls or even a permanent tax-based incomes policy would probably not prove acceptable to Canadians and would not be consistent with our general approach of promoting a flexible, adaptable and growth-oriented economy.

■ We do, however, recommend the temporary use of controls or incentive-based incomes policies if the country needs to reduce inflation again. Furthermore, the use of temporary controls could bring about a more rapid reduction of unemployment than presently seems to be in prospect. Such temporary controls should be the subject of negotiation with business and labour groups.

Commissioners believe that a formal voluntary incomes policy, which would involve commitments to respect common guidelines for wage increases and for price or profit patterns, will be difficult to achieve, given the structure of labour and product markets in Canada.

■ We recommend, however, continued informal and formal consultation on a broad range of economic issues, and increased openness about the bases of economic policy formation. Such an approach might assist public understanding and encourage realistic attitudes about wages and prices. It might also contribute to lower unemployment.

■ Commissioners believe that gain sharing—that is, making compensation more dependent on the current performance of the firm or industry—offers the most promising approach to achieving greater cyclical stability in employment and productivity growth. Gain-sharing would be viable only in an environment of greater trust and openness, and thus we tie our recommendation for its use to our position on consultation noted above.

■ Commissioners recommend to labour, business and governments that they consider some form of incomes policy, coupled with supportive monetary and fiscal action, to increase employment. Without such a comprehensive approach, reduction of unemployment to the level of 6.5 to 8 per cent may be a lengthy and difficult process. Furthermore, without such a demonstration of political will by all major groups in society, and by individuals as well, the prospects for undertaking major structural changes to reduce unemployment below 5 per cent would appear to be less bright. This basic challenge of political will is the central determinant of improved economic performance. □

PART IV

NATURAL RESOURCES AND ENVIRONMENT

PART IV

Contents

PART IV

Introduction

The natural environment and its resources are special to Canadians. We usually describe our economic history as the exploitation of a sequence of resource products: fish, fur, timber, wheat, minerals, and, most recently, oil and gas. Each product has left its distinctive stamp on Canada's economy, its politics, and even the Constitution. In short, natural resources have been the basis upon which our country was built.

Our natural resource endowment has also shaped this country in a more fundamental sense. Canada's status as a resource-rich nation contributes in significant ways to our culture and our international identity. The pursuit of resources opened each of the country's several regions and created most of its thousands of communities, and always the nature of the resource and the character of the environment in which Canadians found it contributed to a uniqueness of the region or the community. All Canadians have certain qualities in common, but the expression of these qualities will not be precisely the same in a Newfoundland outport, a mining town in northern Ontario, and a farming community in Saskatchewan. The many aspects of our environment – and the many different uses we have made of it – are responsible for much of our national diversity, of which we are justly proud, and for not a little of our regional friction, which we have sometimes had reason to regret.

Although resources and environment have contributed so largely to Canadian development, they have not been without problems. Resource industries are notoriously cyclical, and it is partly, at least, on this account that our economy has alternated between "boom" and "bust", often over very short periods. Moreover, we have tended to rely on foreign capital and expertise to develop mineral deposits, while at the same time we have worried about the consequences of foreign control of so much of our natural endowment. Almost from Canada's beginning as a nation, we have been dissatisfied with our role as primary producer, and we have sought ways to increase the local processing of products. In addition, intergovernmental relations touching on resource issues have not always been smooth; nor have our goals for the resource industries always been clear. Finally, while we still think of Canada, as does the international community, as a vast and unspoiled land, we are also aware, at the same time, that many parts of the country show the scars of a sometimes-wanton disregard of the fragility of our natural endowment.

If we Canadians have sometimes had doubts about the role that our resource endowment has given us, we have nonetheless retained a confidence that it is indeed our role. Even now, we ourselves and the world at large perceive Canada as a country whose economy is based on an abundance of natural resources. Yet however great the contribution of those resources to Canada's social and economic development in the past, can we safely assume that they will make a dominant contribution to our future? Are we, in fact, losing our historic comparative advantage in natural resources? If so, then two further questions arise. First, does this loss of advantage apply to resources in general, or only to particular sectors or commodities? Secondly, does it mean that Canada will be forced to undergo a process of major economic adjustment? In particular, must Canadians create a fundamentally new economic basis for our country, one that relies less on natural resources and more on human resources?

There are many developments in both our domestic and our international economies which signal a change in the function of resource industries. While our resource industries are still important – indeed, often vital – and will remain so to many regions and localities, we are becoming relatively less dependent on resources *as a nation*. Moreover, although there is certainly much that we can do to retard this tendency, we may not be in a position to reverse it. Although our natural resources are still abundant by world standards, they are by no means as boundless as perhaps they once seemed to be. In some resource sectors, such as forestry, we are approaching – in fact, some would say have passed – the practical limits of growth. It seems to this Commission that our confidence in the plenitude of our resources has made us wasteful. In other sectors, such as mining, we find that changing technologies and slower growth have reduced world demand for some of our key minerals. Foreign competition, especially from developing countries, poses another and a growing threat to our traditional role as a leading exporter of resource products. Our resource sector's declining relative importance is not entirely the result of changing demand and physical scarcity, however; to a considerable extent, it is also the result of poor management. We have failed in many ways to make the best of what we have, so great has been our confidence that we shall always have it.

The lesson is that Canadians can no longer take natural resources for granted. We can no longer expect them to provide either the leading edge for future economic growth or an automatic solution to our troubles in times of economic difficulty. To the extent that we continue to rely on resources, we shall have to ground that reliance in responsibility. In general, the issue will not be how quickly we can exploit our resources, but how well we can manage and sustain them. Resource policy will have to take into account not only our needs ten or 15 years from now, but also the needs of generations to come.

Resource issues are prominent in this Commission's mandate to examine Canada's prospects. Not only are they important to our economic prospects, but they are also important because of what they imply about Canada and Canadian institutions generally. The questions associated with resources and the environment have become bound up with almost every other issue that presently concerns Canadians, from education to federal-provincial relations, to the role of government in our economy. This suggests that it will not be possible to address the problems of individual resource sectors in isolation. If particular solutions are to work, they must be carried out in a context of broader co-operation and institutional change. Before we can design such a context, however, we must accept the fact that many of our traditional assumptions about Canada, our institutions, and our role in the world may no longer be accurate.

Canadians have begun to adjust to a more realistic view of the place for resources in Canada's future growth. During this Commission's cross-country hearings, more than a few intervenors expressed the opinion that our natural resource endowment will not yield the same proportion of benefits in the future as it has done in the past. The Machinery and Equipment Manufacturers' Association spoke bluntly:

> *We must accept that the potential for resource industry expansion has now become limited for reasons over which we have no control. The expansion of our manufacturing industries, however, if nationally well managed, can be assured.*
>
> (Machinery and Equipment Manufacturers' Association of Canada, Brief, August 27, 1984, p. 5.)

According to Polysar, "Canada should encourage the exporting of Canadian expertise rather than the exporting of our resources." (Polysar Limited, Brief, September 13, 1984, Attachment B, p. 3.) The Mining Association of Canada took a pessimistic view of its own sector's situation:

> *Canadian production for most metals . . . as well as the volume of [proved] ore reserves, declined; Canada's share of world markets decreased; and . . . employment stagnated. Moreover, the industry is no longer discovering and opening new mines at rates sufficient . . . to maintain present output.*
>
> (Mining Association of Canada, Brief, November 23, 1983, p. 2.)

Agreement with such sentiments was far from unanimous, however. David Culver, President and Chief Executive Officer of Alcan Aluminium Limited, confronted the issue head on:

> *There is a growing perception that Canadian resource-based industries are industrial "losers". I think we would be making an enormous error if we subscribed to this thinking. Canada's natural resources continue to be in demand – whether it be coal in B.C. or oil off Newfoundland.*
>
> (Alcan Aluminium Limited, Brief, August 2, 1984, p. 4.)

The Canadian Chamber of Commerce supported this view:

> *We do not believe ... that Canada's primary resource industries ... stand condemned. As industrialization spreads among the three-quarters of the global population now classed as economically developing, the world's need for abundant resources at reasonable cost will increase. This will provide continuing opportunities for Canada as a producer of food, energy, minerals and other resources.* (Canadian Chamber of Commerce, Brief August 23, 1984, p. 40.)

These two points of view are not irreconcilable. No one doubts that our Canadian resource sector continues to be important, or that it possesses opportunities for future growth. However, the resource sector is no longer alone, or nearly alone, in its importance; nor can it be, if we are to maintain an economy that will sustain us in the future. The point Commissioners would emphasize is that unless major efforts to manage our natural resources better are made a national priority, the relative decline in the importance of resources to Canada will be needlessly and irresponsibly hastened.

Chapter 11 presents the main points of the evidence from which Commissioners derive these conclusions. Our emphasis in this chapter is on the role of resources in the national economy. But Chapter 11 does not tell the whole story, as there are hundreds of communities whose well-being still depends on the health of one or another of the resource sectors. Many intervenors talked about the problems, prospects and policy needs of particular resource industries. Their concerns were not long-term and general, but immediate and personal. They saw their livelihood or their communities threatened by land salinization, or by the depletion of timber stocks, or by a loss of foreign markets, or by what they saw as inappropriate taxes or government directives. Our second task, then, is to address these more specific concerns. In Chapter 12, we assess the prospects and policy needs of the individual resource sectors and propose some remedies. In each instance, we have been guided by the general analysis in Part III of this Report, which suggests that there will be a greater need in the future to encourage flexibility and adaptability in the economy and to give greater weight to concerns of efficiency in designing government policy and the incentive structure for the private sector.

As we Canadians learn not to take our resource endowment for granted, we become increasingly aware of the fragility of that endowment. This Commission had no mandate to mount large-scale research efforts into particular environmental matters such as acid rain and land salinization. Nevertheless, we Commissioners were very much struck during our hearings by the breadth and intensity of concern expressed by many Canadians about environmental issues. Moreover, we are convinced that to manage the natural environment in accordance with constructive environmental principles will improve the prospects for our resource-based industries. Accordingly, Chapter 13 assesses the scope of the regulatory task and the ability of our institutions to respond to current and future environmental issues. We do not mean to suggest that the problems of the environment are solely, or even primarily, linked to the resource sector. The other sectors of the economy and the new urban environment they have produced are at least equally culpable in this regard. We voice our concerns about the environment at this point in our Report simply because, wherever the specific blame may lie, it is Canada's natural endowment that suffers the consequences of our neglect. This endowment has been the source of much that makes our nation Canadian, and we have a responsibility to pass it on, substantially intact, to future generations.

CHAPTER 11

Resources and Canadian Economic Development

CHAPTER 11

Resources and Canadian Economic Development

The Role of the Natural Resource Sector

There are two senses in which the natural resource sector – and every other sector – contributes to the economic well-being of Canada. In the first place, natural resource goods are part of what we produce as a nation, either for our own consumption or for export in exchange for other goods. What matters in this context is the extent of our resource production and its value relative to other goods and services. By this measurement, we face economic dislocation in the future if the contribution of resources to aggregate output is reduced, or if the terms of trade are to turn against primary goods.

The other perspective on resources and the economy looks at the sector not as a producer of goods, but as an employer of capital and labour. The important point in this instance is the number of jobs a particular natural resource project will provide or, conversely, how many jobs will be lost if a given mine or mill should close. As a source of income from direct employment and investment, the natural resource sector will only contribute to our economic future if it is able to absorb significant numbers of new workers.

Let us begin with output. Table 11-1 gives the current dollar values and percentage shares of the natural resource industries' contributions to gross domestic product (GDP) for various years since 1926. Note that in absolute terms, output in all sectors has expanded substantially and, for the most part, continuously. Overall, the resource sectors have expanded their value of output more than forty-fold since 1926, and more than twenty-fold since the Second World War.

As the percentage figures show, however, the value of output of the primary industries has not kept pace with the rest of our economy. Resources accounted for about 24 per cent of total GDP in 1926. Mobilization caused its relative contribution to drop to 16.5 per cent by 1941, but by the war's end it was back above 20 per cent. By 1971, however, only about 10 per cent of

TABLE 11-1 GDP at Factor Cost by Industry, Canada

(millions of dollars and percentage of total)

Year	Agriculture $	Agriculture %	Forestry, Fishing and Trapping $	Forestry, Fishing and Trapping %	Mines, Quarries and Oil Wells $	Mines, Quarries and Oil Wells %	Electric Power (Gas and Water) $	Electric Power (Gas and Water) %	Total $	Total %
1926	884	18.2	107	2.2	154	3.2	—	0.0	1 145	23.5
1941	670	9.1	156	2.1	391	5.3	—	0.0	1 217	16.5
1946	1 305	12.2	350	3.3	364	3.4	224	2.1	2 243	20.9
1951	2 322	11.8	562	2.9	814	4.1	410	2.1	4 108	20.9
1956	1 839	6.4	588	2.1	1 219	4.3	691	2.4	4 337	15.1
1961	1 498	4.2	462	1.3	1 398	4.0	1 036	2.9	4 394	12.4
1966	2 886	5.3	629	1.1	2 203	4.0	1 489	2.7	7 207	13.2
1971	2 791	3.4	743	0.9	2 840	3.4	2 385	2.9	8 759	10.6
1976	6 100	3.5	1 631	0.9	7 377	4.3	5 058	2.9	20 166	11.6
1981	10 399	3.3	3 037	1.0	18 649	5.9	11 032	3.5	43 117	13.7
1982	10 846	3.3	2 990	0.9	19 050	5.8	13 947	4.2	46 833	14.2

Source: Statistics Canada, *Historical Statistical Compendium*, prepared for the Royal Commission on the Economic Union and Development Prospects for Canada (Ottawa: Statistics Canada, 1985), Tables 12.1 and 12.2.

national output originated in the resource sector. This trend was reversed after 1972 as rising values for most primary materials, especially energy, along with an increase in electrical power generation, caused their shares to rise again, by nearly 4 percentage points. By 1982, the resource sector's share of total output (14%) was essentially what it had been 25 years earlier. Thus while resources have fallen from the position they held in the early decades of the century, there has been little decline recently.

What has changed in recent decades is the relative importance of the various resource sectors. Agriculture's share of GDP has declined more or less continuously over the post-war period. Its contribution had fallen to approximately 6 per cent of total national output by 1956, and it has since been halved again. In the forestry, fishing, and trapping categories, most of the decline had also taken place by the early 1960s, with less significant decline since then. On the other hand, electric power and mines, quarries, and oil wells have improved their relative positions somewhat in recent years.

The provinces vary widely in their degree of direct dependence on resource industries. Those that rely most on resource production[1] are Saskatchewan, with its agriculture, and Alberta, with its agriculture and oil and gas. In 1982, as Table 11-2 shows, more than 20 per cent of Saskatchewan's gross provincial product (GPP) came from the primary sector, as did nearly 15 per cent of GPP in Alberta. Newfoundland and Prince Edward Island are also quite heavily dependent on resources, while Quebec and Ontario are the provinces least dependent. In keeping with the national pattern, there has been relatively less decline in most provinces' degree of reliance on the resource sector since the 1960s than there was earlier. However, the resource share has been halved in Ontario and Quebec since the 1960s, and there has also been a marked decline in the sector share in Newfoundland, Nova Scotia, and British Columbia.

TABLE 11-2 Sector Shares of Gross Provincial Product

(per cent)

Province	Agriculture	Forestry	Fishing and Trapping	Mining[a]	Total Resource
Newfoundland					
1961	1.0	2.4	2.7	11.4	17.4
1971	0.7	1.3	2.1	13.5	17.7
1982	0.4	0.9	2.2	6.7	10.2
Prince Edward Island					
1961	9.3	0.0	3.1	0.0	12.4
1971	6.9	0.0	3.0	0.0	9.9
1982	9.9	0.0	2.5	0.0	12.3
New Brunswick					
1961	2.7	2.1	1.0	0.9	6.8
1971	1.6	2.0	0.7	3.0	7.4
1982	1.4	1.2	0.5	2.9	6.1
Nova Scotia					
1961	2.0	0.5	2.4	5.4	10.3
1971	1.4	0.6	1.9	2.7	6.5
1982	1.4	0.3	1.7	2.8	6.3
Quebec					
1961	2.7	0.9	0.1	2.1	5.8
1971	1.8	0.7	0.0	1.7	4.2
1982	1.4	0.5	0.0	0.8	2.7
Ontario					
1961	3.0	0.4	0.0	2.9	6.3
1971	2.0	0.3	0.0	1.9	4.3
1982	2.1	0.2	0.0	0.7	3.1
Manitoba					
1961	5.1	0.1	0.2	3.2	8.7
1971	7.0	0.1	0.1	4.1	11.4
1982	6.0	0.1	0.1	1.6	7.8
Saskatchewan					
1961	13.4	0.2	0.2	7.0	20.8
1971	23.5	0.2	0.1	8.1	31.8
1982	15.3	0.1	0.0	5.4	20.8

TABLE 11-2 (cont'd.)

(per cent)

Province	Agriculture	Forestry	Fishing and Trapping	Mining[a]	Total Resource
Alberta					
1961	8.4	0.2	0.1	10.1	18.7
1971	6.2	0.1	0.0	14.7	21.0
1982	4.6	0.1	0.0	10.0	14.6
British Columbia					
1961	2.0	4.2	0.8	2.6	9.6
1971	1.2	3.9	0.4	3.0	8.6
1982	1.6	2.2	0.4	2.4	6.7

Source: Conference Board of Canada, *The Provincial Economies* (Ottawa: The Board, 1984).

a. Includes hydrocarbons.

Much of the contribution that resources make to Canada's economic well-being arises from our opportunities to trade them for the goods and services of other nations. Two trends appear in Table 11-3. First, the value of resource exports has grown significantly over time, from less than $2 billion at the end of the Second World War to nearly $50 billion currently. Secondly, there has been a quite dramatic downward shift in the share of Canada's total export trade accounted for by resources. As late as the mid-1950s, the products of Canadian farms, mines, forests, and oceans provided 84 per cent of the value of the goods we sold abroad. Our *relative* dependence on resource exports began to decline with the sharp increase, in the early 1960s, in shipments of manufactured products, mainly autos and auto parts under the Auto Pact. By 1983, the resource sector's share of exports had fallen to about 51 per cent. Still, it is clear that our ability to export an ever-increasing value of resource products has been instrumental in giving us the standard of living we now enjoy.

Another dimension of the situation emerges if one looks at employment patterns. Table 11-4 shows both total employment in the natural resource sector for various years from 1921 to 1983 and each sub-sector's share of that total. At the onset of the Great Depression, one Canadian in three worked in resource industries, mainly in agriculture. The ratio was much the same 15 years later, at the end of the Second World War. Then came the shift of labour out of agriculture. Because of this shift, by 1956 the resource sector's share of total employment had dropped to slightly more than half of its pre-Depression level. By 1966, 10.7 per cent of the work-force was employed in resource industries. The decline since 1966 (to about 7 per cent of total employment in 1983) has been steady, but less spectacular, and most of it continues to occur in agriculture. The shares of the other sectors are much closer to what they were at the end of the war.

TABLE 11-3 Export Shares by Resource Sector

(millions of current dollars and percentage of total)

	Agriculture		Fishing and Trapping		Forestry		Mining[a]		Total Resources	
Year	$	%	$	%	$	%	$	%	$	%
1931[b]	—	218	33.8	—	170	26.3	113	17.5	501	77.7
1941[b]	—	410	22.3	—	340	18.5	448	24.3	1 198	65.1
1946	771	31.5	118	4.8	626	25.6	451	18.4	1 966	80.3
1951	986	24.3	147	3.6	1 454	35.8	947	23.3	3 534	86.9
1956	988	20.4	133	2.7	1 496	30.9	1 471	30.4	4 088	84.5
1961	1 160	19.6	141	2.4	1 622	27.5	1 861	31.5	4 784	81.0
1966	1 790	17.3	217	2.1	2 239	21.7	2 933	28.4	7 179	69.5
1971	1 891	10.6	288	1.6	3 085	17.3	4 767	26.8	10 031	56.3
1976	3 832	10.0	597	1.6	6 534	17.0	11 424	29.7	22 387	58.2
1981	8 329	9.9	1 502	1.8	12 855	15.3	24 476	29.2	47 162	56.3
1982	8 885	10.5	1 597	1.9	11 961	14.1	23 025	27.2	45 468	53.8
1983	9 008	10.0	1 560	1.7	13 148	14.5	23 104	25.4	46 900	51.6

Sources: 1931–1951, 1983, *Bank of Canada Review, Statistical Summary* (Ottawa: Bank of Canada, various issues); 1966–1981, Statistics Canada, *Historical Statistical Compendium*, prepared for the Royal Commission on the Economic Union and Development Prospects for Canada (Ottawa: Statistics Canada, 1985), Tables 6.9 and 6.10.

a. Includes hydrocarbons.
b. In 1931 and 1941, agriculture, fishing and trapping were one category.

In some resource sectors, absolute decline in employment has accompanied relative decline. In 1931, 1.1 million Canadians worked on farms. By 1961, the figure had fallen to less than 700 000 and in 1983 only 476 000 Canadians were employed in agriculture. The decline has been absolute in forestry as well (from 86 000 in 1961 to 75 000 in 1983). On the other hand, the number of fishermen and trappers has increased, particularly since the mid-1970s (from 18 000 in 1961 to 19 000 in 1976 to 36 000 in 1983). Employment in mining rose from 80 000 in 1961 to 210 000 in 1981, falling again to 170 000 in 1983.

As Table 11-5 shows, the variation in resource employment across provinces is marked. Nearly a quarter of Saskatchewan's labour force still works in the primary sector, while in Quebec, the proportion is less than one in 20. Resource employment in many localities and municipalities – Sudbury and Port Alberni, for example – remains high. Resource dependence is a concept that must be qualified to suit the geographical area one has in mind, a point to which we return below.

The employment and output figures reported in the tables in this section represent only a part of the resource sector's economic impact. Significant indirect effects arise from the sector's links with other industries. Backward-linked industries provide inputs to the resource industry itself, in the form of

TABLE 11-4 Employment by Natural Resource Sector, Canada

(thousands and percentage of total employment)

Year	Agriculture		Fishing and Trapping		Forestry		Mining[a]		Total Resources		Manufacturing	
	#	%	#	%	#	%	#	%	#	%	#	%
1921	1 042	32.8	34	1.1	40	1.3	52	1.6	1 167	36.8	530	16.7
1931	1 128	28.7	48	1.2	50	1.3	72	1.8	1 298	33.1	665	16.9
1941	1 082	25.8	51	1.2	94	2.2	93	2.2	1 320	31.5	917	21.9
1946	1 186	25.4	27	0.6	84	1.8	74	1.6	1 371	29.4	1 214	26.0
1951	939	18.4	30	0.6	115	2.3	79	1.5	1 163	22.8	1 350	26.5
1956	776	13.9	20	0.4	118	2.1	117	2.1	1 031	18.5	1 435	25.7
1961	681	11.2	18	0.3	86	1.4	80	1.3	865	14.3	1 452	24.0
1966	544	7.6	26	0.4	76	1.1	121	1.7	767	10.7	1 744	24.4
1971	510	6.3	22	0.3	72	0.9	129	1.6	733	9.1	1 795	22.2
1976	472	5.0	19	0.2	70	0.7	145	1.5	706	7.4	1 921	20.3
1981	485	4.4	35	0.3	78	0.7	210	1.9	808	7.3	2 122	19.3
1983	476	4.4	36	0.3	75	0.7	170	1.6	757	7.1	1 886	17.6

Sources: Statistics Canada, *Labour Force Annual Averages, 1975–1983*, Cat. No. 71-529 (Ottawa: Minister Supply and Services Canada, 1984); and *Historical Statistics of Canada*, 2d ed. (Ottawa: Statistics Canada, 1983).

a. Includes hydrocarbons.

excavation machinery, transportation services, fishing boats and agricultural machinery. Forward-linked industries, such as smelting and refining, fishpacking, and food processing, use the output of the resource sector as inputs. While not all of the resource sector's indirect effects on the economy are readily ascertainable, it is certain that the sum of these effects is large. The food and beverages industry alone employed 14 per cent of all workers in Canada's manufacturing industries in 1982. And, of course, incomes earned in the resource industries themselves are spent on consumer goods and services such as housing, food, and entertainment.

In some parts of Canada, resources also contribute significantly to government revenues. In 1981, resource revenues constituted 45 per cent of gross general revenue in Alberta, nearly 20 per cent in Saskatchewan, and 6

TABLE 11-5 Employment in Natural Resource Sector by Province

	(per cent of total provincial employment[a])				
Province	**Agriculture**	**Forestry**	**Fishing**	**Mining[b]**	**Total Resources**
Newfoundland					
1966	—[c]	3.0	16.5	5.0	N.A.
1976	—	1.2	16.3	3.9	N.A.
1982	—	1.1	15.8	2.3	N.A.
Prince Edward Island					
1921	59.5	— 4.0[d] —		—	N.A.
1966	19.7	—	9.1	—	N.A.
1976	13.2	—	4.6	—	N.A.
1982	12.7	—	6.6	—	N.A.
Nova Scotia					
1921	26.5	— 8.0 —		7.8	42.3
1966	4.6[e]	1.0	5.5	3.1	14.2
1976	2.7	0.6	3.4	1.5	8.2
1982	2.1	0.7	3.5	1.7	8.0
New Brunswick					
1921	35.4	— 5.4 —		0.6	41.4
1966	5.4[e]	4.0	3.0	1.4	13.8
1976	2.6	2.5	2.1	1.2	8.4
1982	2.8	1.8	2.4	1.3	8.3
Quebec					
1921	28.1	— 1.9 —		0.5	30.5
1966	5.0[e]	1.1	0.2	1.3	7.6
1976	3.0	0.6	0.2	1.0	4.8
1982	3.0	0.5	—	0.8	N.A.
Ontario					
1921	26.4	— 0.9 —		0.8	28.1
1966	4.5[e]	0.5	0.4[f]	1.2	6.6
1976	3.1	0.2	0.1[f]	0.9	4.3
1982	3.2	0.3	0.1[f]	0.7	4.3

Table 11-5 (cont'd.)

Province	Agriculture	Forestry	Fishing	Mining[b]	Total Resources
	(per cent of total provincial employment[a])				
Manitoba					
1921	40.1	—— 0.3 ——		0.1	40.5
1966	14.0[e]	0.4	0.4[f]	1.6	16.4
1976	8.9	0.2	0.1[f]	1.6	10.8
1982	9.1	0.3	0.1[f]	1.1	10.6
Saskatchewan					
1921	65.4	—— 0.3 ——		0.1	65.8
1966	28.4[e]	0.1	0.4[f]	1.6	30.5
1976	24.6	0.2	0.1[f]	1.7	26.6
1982	20.0	0.2	0.1[f]	2.2	22.5
Alberta					
1921	52.8	—— 0.4 ——		4.0	57.2
1966	14.2[e]	0.5	0.4[f]	3.4	18.5
1976	13.9	0.2	0.1[f]	4.1	18.3
1982	6.8	0.2	0.1[f]	5.3	12.4
British Columbia					
1921	16.0	—— 7.8 ——		4.9	28.7
1966	3.1[e]	2.9	1.8	1.4	9.2
1976	1.8	2.1	1.6	1.3	6.8
1982	2.5	1.4	1.4	1.3	6.6

Sources: Statistics Canada, CANSIM (Ottawa: Minister of Supply and Services Canada, 1983); *Labour Force Annual Averages, 1975–1983,* Cat. No. 71-529 (Ottawa: Minister of Supply and Services Canada, 1984); Department of Fisheries and Oceans, *Annual Statistical Review 1982* (Ottawa: The Department, 1984). For 1921, Census of Canada 1931 (Ottawa: Dominion Bureau of Statistics), vol. VII, Table 8.

Note: N.A. = not available because of missing sub-totals.

a. These figures do not include employees engaged in the further processing of natural resources, for example in pulp and paper and metal products.

b. Includes hydrocarbons.

c. Information not released by Statistics Canada for reasons of confidentiality: small employment figures.

d. In 1921, forestry and fishing employment were covered by one category.

e. 1966 agriculture figures are for males only.

f. Fisheries estimates are averages for Ontario and Prairie provinces.

per cent in British Columbia. However, the other provinces derive only very limited revenues from natural resources, and only in Alberta, Saskatchewan and British Columbia have these revenues grown in importance over time. In most of the other provinces, the revenue share from natural resource rents has declined substantially in the last 30 years.[2]

Two conclusions follow from this brief overview of past performance. First, in relative terms, our natural resource sector contributes much less to national economic activity now than it did in the past. This decline began in earnest immediately after the Second World War and was largely complete by the mid-1960s. In the 1970s, many observers believed that the pattern of decline was about to be reversed, partly because of the resource boom in western Canada. Indeed, in 1981, the federal government proposed a medium-term strategy based on Canada's resource strengths.

Output in the natural resource industries has continued to grow absolutely, and in a few instances, employment has continued to grow as well. Other sectors, however, have grown so much more rapidly that the relative share of output and employment accruing from resources has shrunk significantly. The relative decline of employment is especially pronounced because of productivity increases in the resource industries. The mix within the natural resource sector has been altered somewhat, with agriculture continuing to slip and energy and hydro expanding, particularly in recent years.

Secondly, while the natural resource sector no longer looms as large in the national economy as it once did, it continues to dominate the economic life of some provinces, some areas within every province, and many localities. Grain prices are still important in Saskatoon, as are fish landings in St. John's. And many Canadians are only too familiar with the fact that in one-industry towns, a downturn in demand for minerals or plywood can mean the death of the community. In many ways, it is misleading to talk in general or national terms about dependence on resources.

What does the foregoing analysis tell us about the place of resources in future Canadian economic development? The long-term forecasts made in Part III presented an overview of the resource sector and warned of serious problems. Our own sectoral analysis suggests the same conclusion, at least in some respects. In an absolute sense – dollar value of production, for example – resources will be at least as significant as ever. Entire industries are not about to shut down, although individual mines, farms, or fishing enterprises might. Large numbers of Canadians will continue to work as farmers, loggers, fishermen, miners, and roughnecks. We shall also continue to find markets for our resources abroad that will provide us with ongoing access to the products of other nations.

In an absolute sense, then, Canadians will continue to see resources as a fundamental part of our economy. There are problems with dependence on resources, most notably cyclical instability and the tendency for employment to grow only very slowly over time or even to decline, but there are many positive features as well. Resources do provide skilled jobs. It was pointed out to Commissioners repeatedly in our hearings that resource industries are some of the highest-technology concerns in the world. They can therefore provide employment, and hence a "stay option", in regions of the country that are unlikely to attract manufacturing or service industries.

In a relative sense, however, it is likely that the resource sector as a whole will continue to decline, albeit more slowly than in the immediate post-war period. Output is unlikely to grow as quickly as that for manufactured goods and services so that the share of GNP attributed to these activities will fall further. Exports of resource products will continue to expand, and the terms of trade are unlikely to turn against us in any dramatic fashion. Nevertheless, this trade orientation will increasingly need to be supplemented by more highly processed products in order to maintain our access to the goods and services of other nations.

Where employment is concerned, the pattern of relative decline will be even more pronounced. Overall, resource industries are unlikely to provide any net new jobs in the future. As in the early 1970s, this may not be true in all cases or in every year. Generally speaking, however, Canadians will have to find more and more of their jobs and sources of income on the factory floor or in the office tower. It is in this sense more than in any other that the fear is justified that resources are no longer the engine of growth they once were.

What do these conclusions portend for future adjustments? Are we at a turning point as regards the role of resources in Canadian economic development? From the perspective of the national economy, we have dealt, in the past, with much larger dislocations stemming from structural changes in the resource sectors than we are likely to face in the future. To argue that we now face special problems in this respect requires demonstration either that the costs of adjustment in the immediate post-war years were so large that even to repeat them on a much reduced scale is unthinkable, or that the economic climate is so different now that even much smaller dislocations will be more difficult to absorb. On the former point, it is, in fact, commonplace to remark on how smoothly we moved in such a short time from a predominantly rural to a largely urban society.

The second consideration is more substantive. Is it true that our capacity to adapt to even small economic shocks is now so much reduced? Could we not handle another off-farm exodus of the extent seen on the Prairies in the 20 years following the war? Our conclusions in Part III indicate that our ability to adjust remains high. However, to the extent that Canadians have elevated place-prosperity to a position above that which it occupied previously, relocation becomes more difficult. If we no longer accept that displaced farm workers from one province will take up jobs in another, or that resource towns will close as mineral deposits become uneconomic, it becomes that much more important to maintain the resource base. If, however, the resource-related economic base is truly inadequate, this adjustment, though painful, is probably inevitable and best proceeded with promptly. If, on the other hand, the inadequacy stems from the needless deterioration of resource-industry prospects, government actions to restore the balance may well be justified.

These prospects do not provide justification for neglecting the resource sectors. Indeed, for reasons of national comparative advantage, local and regional development, and national self-esteem, it is important to address problems that do exist. We may not have maximized our potential for natural resources in the past, but it is important that mismanagement not be the cause of any future decline. While the bulk of adjustment took place in the post-war years, we have continued to think and act as though resources guaranteed our prosperity. They may no longer do so.

There *are* problems, in fact, in each of our main resource sectors, in some instances, quite serious ones. Often, however, they are problems that can be overcome by appropriate policies. Finally, it is important to address problems quickly because resource industries discharge a function in our society that is far in excess of what mere statistical indicators of jobs or value added can convey.

It must be stressed that the following review of specific sectors[3] and the policy prescriptions Commissioners have to suggest are necessarily brief. The breadth of our mandate precluded us from undertaking detailed and specialized studies of individual industries. We attempt only to flag what we see as important problems, and to indicate how reform might proceed in a direction consistent with the main themes of this Report.

Notes

1. Not including electricity, for which no consistent statistical series is available on a provincial basis.
2. Statistics Canada, *Provincial Government Finance: Revenue and Expenditure*, Cat. No. 68-207 (Ottawa: Minister of Supply and Services Canada, various years).
3. Much of the background material contained in the sectoral profiles presented was adapted from a study prepared for this Commission. Interested readers are referred for further details to Bruce Wilkinson, "Canada's Resource Industries: A Survey", in *Canada's Resource Industries*, vol. 14, prepared for the Royal Commission on the Economic Union and Development Prospects for Canada (Toronto: University of Toronto Press, 1985).

CHAPTER 12

The Natural Resource Sectors

CHAPTER 12

The Natural Resource Sectors

Agriculture

Profile

It is not easy to draw a profile of Canadian agriculture. The Canadian farmer is the Prairie wheat grower with over 1000 hectares of land, hundreds of thousands of dollars' worth of equipment, and annual sales of more than $250 000; the Canadian farmer is also the small vegetable grower or orchard operator with 40 hectares and sales of a few tens of thousands of dollars. Agriculture varies almost as much within a given region of Canada as it varies from one region to another. What is common to Canadian agriculture in all of its forms, however, is the characteristic production unit, the family farm. The last Census indicates that in 1981, 87 per cent of the 318 000 farms in Canada were operated by sole proprietors and 9.3 per cent were partnerships. Fewer than one-half of 1 per cent were owned by corporations whose shares were not held by a single family. Two-thirds of operators (based on average farm size) owned all of the land they farmed. These figures were much the same in 1971. As Table 12-1 shows, the largest farms are in Saskatchewan and Alberta, and the smallest are in Newfoundland and central Canada.

In 1982, the agriculture sector contributed 3.3 per cent of Canada's gross domestic product (GDP); the figure was not much different in 1971. The importance of agriculture varies greatly from province to province. In 1982, agriculture's share of gross provincial product (GPP) was highest in Saskatchewan (15 per cent) and Prince Edward Island (10 per cent) and lowest in Newfoundland (less than 1 per cent). During the 1970s, agriculture grew in relative importance in Prince Edward Island, and to a lesser extent, in British Columbia, but declined in nearly all other provinces.[1] Agriculture remains the economic basis of many rural communities all across Canada which serve as supply, service and distribution centres for the industry.

Primary agriculture currently employs 476 000 people, a figure that represents less than 5 per cent of total national employment. The agri-food system as a whole, however, employs 1.45 million Canadians and accounts for 15 per cent of total employment. For example, the food-processing and beverage industries employ 255 000 people, the food service industry employs 359 000, and food stores currently employ 221 000. A number of other important industries, such as rail and water transportation, depend to a significant extent on the agri-food sector.

Figure 12-1 summarizes the commodity composition of Canadian agriculture in 1984. Grains and oil-seeds together accounted for over one-third of total farm cash receipts of $20 billion. Cattle and dairy receipts made up a second third. The other important commodities are fruits and vegetables, hogs, and poultry and eggs. Production of grains, especially wheat, and oil-seeds is concentrated in the Prairie provinces, while corn production is concentrated in Ontario and Quebec. Soybeans are grown only in Ontario, dairy production is highest in Ontario and Quebec, and fruits and vegetables are grown chiefly in southern Ontario, the Fraser and Okanagan valleys of British Columbia, and Nova Scotia. Prince Edward Island and New Brunswick are important potato producers, Alberta and Ontario are important producers of beef, and Quebec and Ontario produce significant quantities of pork. (See Table 12-1.) Ontario is Canada's premier agricultural province, with an annual value of farm output of about $5 billion. Saskatchewan, Alberta, and Quebec, in that order, are the next-largest producing provinces by value.

Canada is self-sufficient in many agricultural sub-sectors: grains, oil-seeds (except soybeans), most dairy products, potatoes, and livestock and meat products (except lamb). There is, however, as Table 12–2 shows, a substantial trade deficit in fruits and vegetables. This deficit is partly the result of an increase in demand of 11 per cent per year, on average, over the past decade for products not grown in Canada; these include citrus and tropical fruits, coffee, and cocoa. But it is also the result of an 8-per cent average annual increase in imports of products that are grown in Canada. For all non-tropical fresh fruits and vegetables, the import share is two-thirds of Canadian consumption.

The bulk of Canada's output of all agricultural commodities, except grains and oil-seeds, is absorbed by our domestic market. The net trade balance on grain amounted to $4.8 billion in 1983. That year, Canada enjoyed a net surplus in all agricultural trade of $3.7 billion. The agricultural sector was thus responsible for more than one-quarter of our country's total trade surplus in all commodities. (See Table 12-2.)

Canada's share of the world market in grains and oil-seeds declined somewhat during the late 1970s. The decline was a function of reduced production, bottlenecks in the grain-transportation system, and concentration on traditional but relatively slow-growing markets in the developed world. The use of export subsidies and aggressive marketing techniques by competitor countries also challenged our position. Canadian grain exports have rebounded during the 1980s, thanks, in part, to improvements in the Canadian grain-handling system. However, a more important factor in the

TABLE 12-1 Structure of Agriculture by Province

Province	Number of Farms	Average Farm Size (hectares)	Farm Cash Receipts 1984 (million $)	Top Three Commodities by Value of Farm Cash Receipts		
Newfoundland	679	49	40.9	Poultry and eggs	Dairy	Hogs
Prince Edward Island	3 154	90	186.7	Fruit and vegetables	Dairy	Cattle
Nova Scotia	5 045	92	261.2	Dairy	Poultry and eggs	Fruit and vegetables
New Brunswick	4 063	108	229.4	Fruit and vegetables	Dairy	Poultry and eggs
Quebec	48 144	79	3 073.2	Dairy	Hogs	Cattle
Ontario	82 448	73	5 284.3	Cattle	Dairy	Small grains (excluding wheat)
Manitoba	29 442	263	1 926.4	Wheat	Cattle	Small grains
Saskatchewan	67 318	394	4 221.2	Wheat	Cattle	Small grains
Alberta	58 056	348	3 863.8	Cattle	Wheat	Small grains
British Columbia	20 016	123	964.5	Dairy	Fruit and vegetables	Poultry and eggs
Canada	318 361	214	20 051.6	Wheat	Cattle	Dairy

Sources: Canada, Agriculture Canada, *Handbook of Selected Agricultural Statistics 1984* (Ottawa: Minister of Supply and Services Canada, 1984); and Statistics Canada, *Farm Cash Receipts* (December 1984), Cat. No. 21-001 (Ottawa: Minister of Supply and Services Canada, 1985).

FIGURE 12-1 Canada's Farm Cash Receipts by Major Category, 1984

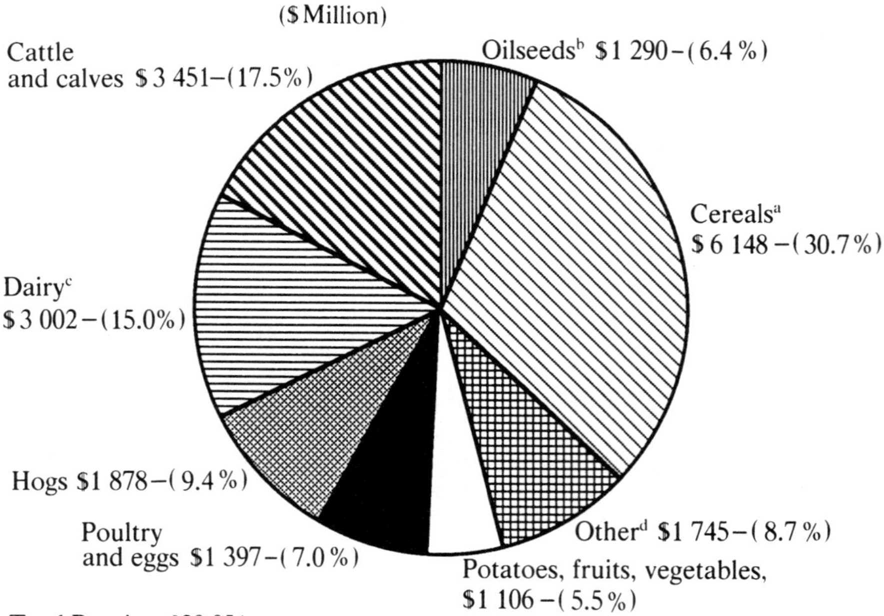

Total Receipts $20 051

a. Includes wheat, oats, barley, rye, corn, Western Grain Stabilization Payments, Canada Wheat Board Payments, crop insurance payments, Canada Wheat Board cash advances and liquidation of deferred grain receipts; minus Canada Wheat Board Cash Advance Repayments and deferred grain receipts.

b. Includes flaxseed, canola and soybeans.

c. Includes dairy supplementary payments.

d. Includes sheep and lambs, wool, honey, fur farming, miscellaneous livestock, forest and maple products, provincial income stabilization program, deficiency payments, supplementary payments, floriculture and nursery, tobacco, mustard seed, sunflower seed, clover and grass seed, hay and clover, dry beans, dry peas, miscellaneous crops, net non grain cash advances.

e. Addends do not sum to exactly this total because of rounding.

Source: Statistics Canada, *Farm Cash Receipts,* No. 21-001, February, 1985, (Ottawa: Minister of Supply and Services Canada, 1985).

growth of exports has been increased sales to the centrally planned economies, which now account for over 50 per cent of our wheat exports and 35 per cent of our barley exports. Because of the European Community's (EC) common agricultural policy (CAP), exports to Europe and the United Kingdom have declined.

In 1982, Canada's production of wheat, amounting to 27 million tonnes, was exceeded by only four other nations: the Soviet Union, the United States, China, and India. Canadian wheat exports currently account for approximately 22 per cent of world trade, but other nations have lately emerged as significant competitors. The EC, for example, has increased its world-market

TABLE 12-2 Net Trade Balance For Agricultural Commodity Groups

	(millions of constant 1981 $)				
	1971–75 (average)	1976–80 (average)	1981	1982	1983
Grain and grain products	3 478	3 706	4 827	4 796	4 813
Oil-seeds and oil-seed products	272	331	498	332	312
Animal feeds	102	128	136	123	150
Animals, meat and other animal products	14	241	400	728	558
Dairy products	30	39	115	162	118
Poultry and eggs	(9)	(46)	(17)	(30)	(33)
Fruits and vegetables	(1 036)	(1 408)	(1 487)	(1 388)	(1 319)
Other	(1 125)	(1 398)	(1 299)	(872)	(844)
Total agricultural commodities	1 726	1 594	3 173	3 851	3 715
All commodities	1 029	2 424	1 855	12 665	11 108

Sources: Canada, Agriculture Canada, *Handbook of Selected Agricultural Statistics 1984* (Ottawa: Minister of Supply and Services Canada, 1984); and R. Daviault, *Selected Agricultural Statistics for Canada* (Ottawa: Agriculture Canada, Economics Branch, 1976).

share for wheat from 8 per cent in the early 1970s to nearly 16 per cent in recent years; France alone currently accounts for more than 10 per cent of world wheat exports.

Although Canada is still the world's largest producer of barley (14 million tonnes in 1982–83), our share of world exports has declined over the last decade from about 27 per cent to 23 per cent. Meanwhile, the Community's share of exports has risen from 45 per cent to 52 per cent. Oil-seeds, particularly canola, have become an important Canadian export (2 million tonnes in 1981–82). Canola accounts for about 7 per cent of total world oil-seed output, while soybeans constitute over one-half of world oil-seed output. Canada's position as the world's largest producer of canola has recently been taken over by China: our share of world production declined from about one-third in 1979 to one-sixth in 1982–83.

Canadian exports of live animals, beef, and pork are also significant. The United States is still Canada's major market: Americans buy 70 per cent of our pork exports and 90 per cent of our beef exports. Since 1970, Japan has become increasingly important as a market for Canadian meat, especially for pork. Exports to Japan fluctuate considerably, and therefore various provincial hog-marketing boards and private processors have been attempting to develop exports to Japan through long-term contracts.

Prospects

Global Projections

Global projections of future prospects for agricultural production vary with the assumptions made about population growth, increases in productive capacity, income and price elasticities of demand, and the agricultural and commercial policies of both importing and exporting nations. The *Global 2000* report to the President of the United States, the United Nations Food and Agriculture Organization's (FAO) *Agriculture: Toward 2000*, and other reports conclude that developing countries will continue to accept large increases in agricultural imports over the next few decades, provided that they can finance them. According to the FAO's projections, agricultural imports by developing nations will grow at a rate of 3.8 per cent annually to 2000; the average annual rate of increase between 1961 and 1980 was 5.7 per cent.[2] It is expected that the centrally planned economies will depend even more heavily on grain imports, although the change will be slower than it has been in the past.[3] The Soviet Union's grain imports are expected to level out. Various studies indicate that by 2000, North America will be the largest available source of imported cereals and oil-seeds for the developing world.

Table 12-3 shows recent projections of growth rates of world consumption and production to 2000 and 2020 for the major agricultural commodity groups. For cereals, the 1.8 per cent expansion rate to 2000 represents a considerable decline from the 2.6 per cent annual growth rate of the 1970s. The projected 2.1 per cent growth rate for oil-seeds is about one-half the rate of the 1970s. For the period from 2000 to 2020, the expected rates of growth are lower again. It is expected that most of the twenty-first/century increases must come from improved yields, rather than from increased land use.

Opinions vary about price projections of agricultural products, and recent projections tend to be more conservative than those made a few years ago. Some observers foresee growing scarcities of food and a concomitant rise in real food prices. The *Global 2000* report and the subsequent Canadian "Agri-food Strategy" predicted that real food prices would rise by about 1 to 2 per cent per year to 2000.[4] Other observers suggest that real prices for grains could continue their historical decline.[5] More recent predictions by Agriculture Canada foresee that real prices will remain much as they are or, possibly, will decline by up to 1 per cent per year to 2000.[6] The most certain prospect is that price instability will be common, as it has been in the past.

TABLE 12-3 Projections of World Production and Consumption, 1980 to the Years 2000 and 2020

	(annual compound percentage growth rates)	
Products	**1980–2000**	**2000–2020**
Cereals	1.8	1.4
Oil-seeds	2.1	1.9
Meats	2.4	2.0
Milk products	1.5	1.1

Source: Kenneth R. Farrell, Fred H. Sanderson, Trang T. Vo, and Michael F. Brewer, "Meeting Future Needs for United States Food, Fiber and Forest Products", in Joint Council on Food and Agricultural Sciences, *Reference Document: Needs Assessment for Food and Agricultural Sciences* (Washington, D.C., 1984).

Projections for Canada

How will these projected global developments affect Canadian agricultural prospects in international markets? Commissioners heard a variety of views on this question. The Alberta Wheat Pool, for example, was cautiously optimistic:

> *In the case of the prairie provinces: a) The outlook for increasing volumes of grain exports continues to be bright. b) The outlook for meat product exports is modest. c) The prospects for vegetable oil exports are promising in the long run, though undefined in this decade.*
>
> *Considering these circumstances, it is clear that Canada must maintain a viable economic climate for the production, handling and exporting of grain. Steps should be taken to protect the infrastructure now in place which will permit western Canada to be an effective world trader in vegetable oils. The future of livestock feeding, meat processing and exporting deserves immediate and special study in order to determine a recommended course of action from a national standpoint.* (Alberta Wheat Pool, Brief, October 24, 1983, p. 6.)

The Christian Farmers Federation of Ontario (CFFO) expressed a much more pessimistic view:

> *The CFFO does not share the optimism of the Federal government's agri-food strategy: Challenge for Growth, published in July 1981. We see around us mounting difficulties such as soil degradation, the industrialization of agriculture, erratic international markets and deteriorating food quality.*
>
> *We do not expect major increases in our agri-food production because of the limits of our foodland resource, the growing cost of our technology, and the disturbing side-effects of many of our current farm practices.*
>
> *Exports are an increasingly unreliable solution to Canadian food marketing problems. Export markets are becoming more unstable and are often dependent upon some form of export subsidy . . .*
>
> *A Canadian strategy should be based on import replacement, resource stewardship, a family farm structure and nutritional improvements.*
>
> (Christian Farmers Federation of Ontario, Brief, December 6, 1983, p. 2.)

Projections of annual growth of global grains trade to 1990 and 2000 vary between 1.2 per cent and 5 per cent: a wide range indeed! Whatever projection proves correct, it appears that grain exports will not expand as rapidly in the 1980s as they did between 1960 and 1980.[7] The Canadian Wheat Board anticipates, as Table 12-4 records, that Canadian grain and oil-seed exports will expand to 37 million tonnes annually by 1990. This projection appears to be not unreasonable: in 1983–84, exports of wheat alone already amounted to nearly 22 million tonnes, less than 1 million tonnes short of the 1990 target, and these levels were reached even though much of the world was experiencing a recession. Nevertheless, to achieve the exports projected to 2000 will require a substantial effort to bring new land under cultivation, reduce the land presently put into summerfallow, and improve yields.[8]

Grain and oil-seeds projections to the year 2000 are more tentative. The expansion of wheat exports to 44 million tonnes, projected by Agriculture

Table 12-4 Canadian Grain and Oil-seeds Exports, Actual and Projected

	(millions of tonnes)			
	Actual		Projected	Projected
	1978–79[a]	1983–84	1990[b]	2000[c]
Wheat	13.0	21.8	22.0	44
Coarse grains	4.1	6.8	8.5	12
Oil-seeds	2.8	2.1	6.5	N.A.

Sources: Historical numbers: Statistics Canada, *Cereals and Oilseeds Review* (Ottawa: Minister of Supply and Services Canada, 1984); and W.E. Jarvis, "Market Demand and Production Requirements for Prairie Grain", in Canadian Wheat Board, Advisory Committee, Prairie Production Symposium, October 1980; and Stewart Borland and Gerald Robertson, "A Sectoral View of the Longer-Term: Agriculture", in *Long-term Economic Prospects for Canada: A Symposium*, vol. 23, prepared for the Royal Commission on the Economic Union and Development Prospects for Canada (Toronto: University of Toronto Press, 1985).

Note: N.A. = not available.

a. Exports at the time the 1990 projection was initially set.

b. 1990: Jarvis.

c. 2000: Borland and Robertson.

Canada, implies an annual growth rate from 1990 to 2000 of 7.5 per cent. The estimate for barley assumes a more modest growth rate of 3.5 per cent. Such exports, even at current nominal prices, would mean an increase of 70 per cent by the turn of the century over 1983 levels in the value of these agricultural exports.

In general, future growth in agricultural trade surpluses will occur in the traditional wheat and course grain sector, and to a lesser extent, in the canola and red meats sectors. We can expect to import increasing amounts of fruit and vegetables, and to face serious competition in pork, poultry, and eggs. In order to take advantage of the opportunities – or to beat the competition – we must improve the performance of Canadian agriculture. In spite of Canada's past success as a producer and exporter of agricultural commodities, there is some reason to be apprehensive about our ability to meet these challenges adequately.

Issues and Recommendations

The Future of the Family Farm

> *The family farm is at one and the same time an economic unit and a social unit. It is together a business, generating a family income and a life style generating human qualities of individual initiative, co-operation and leadership . . . It is a farm in which the decisions regarding production and marketing are made by the family which operates the farm. The household is the centre of the farming operation, providing the bulk of the labour, making the farm decisions and interacting with the community.*
>
> (Family Farm Foundation of Canada, Brief, October 24, 1983, p. 2.)

The traumatic economic events of the 1980s have increased Canadians' concern about the continued viability of the traditional production unit, the family farm. The Family Farm Foundation described the dimensions of the problem:

> *Family farms have [proved] themselves extremely efficient producers of agricultural products. Despite weather, changing technology, economic stress ranging from poverty to prosperity, the family farm has stood the test of time over 80 years and indeed has led the way in many, many areas.*
>
> *Today, the family farm is being threatened. Inflation, the price of farm inputs, high interest rates, [and] falling commodity prices ... are placing serious economic and social strains on the family farm. The family farm deserves protection, both as a family unit and as an economic unit.*
>
> (Family Farm Foundation of Canada, Transcript, Regina, November 23, 1983 [vol. 50], p. 10325.)

It is clear that farmers are currently experiencing economic difficulties. Farmers' net income as a percentage of their gross income fell from 30 per cent in 1972 to less than 20 per cent in 1982. Statistics Canada's index of prices of total farm-input costs rose by 76.5 per cent between 1976 and 1983, while its index of prices for all farm products rose by only 47.5 per cent. Since 1981, a weighted index of farm-product prices has actually fallen, while input costs have continued to rise.[9] For the last 30 years, in fact, productivity gains in agriculture have largely been captured by consumers, who have been able to meet their food needs with a decreasing proportion of their incomes. As a proportion of income, the food bill of the average Canadian is the second-lowest in the world; only American consumers pay less.

Agriculture is a notoriously cyclical industry. Prices for most products are set in world markets, and they are susceptible to myriad climatic and political influences beyond the producers' control. Moreover, it is difficult for farmers to make rapid adjustments in production. On the other hand, input costs – with the exception of costs for land and, recently, for fuels and fertilizers – have risen more or less continuously. The result of this fluctuation in revenues and the continuous increase in costs is a highly variable income stream. While the boom in commodity prices in the 1970s raised farm income to record levels, the price declines and cost increases of more recent years have severely eroded these gains.

There is an additional element in the "boom-bust" cycle of agriculture. High incomes tend to become quickly capitalized into higher land values. Consequently, established farmers who add to their landholdings and farmers who are starting out incur large debts. If interest rates are high as well, the burden of debt becomes even more onerous. Net revenues will decline, but the carrying charges on acquisitions of land (and on any machinery purchased to farm it) will continue.

The number of Canada's farm bankruptcies tripled between 1979 and 1982, although in proportionate terms the number is still small, standing at 0.13 per cent of all farms in 1982. However, bankruptcy rates are not necessarily a good indication of the financial health of farming, since many farmers "voluntarily" liquidate their assets before the bankruptcy stage, and many others struggle with severe cash-flow problems. A study released by the Farm Credit Corporation in October 1984 stated that 39 000 or 17 per cent of Canadian farmers were under severe financial stress.[10]

Canadian farmers have consistently proved themselves to be among the best in the world at adopting new technologies and new methods, and this Commission sees no reason to doubt that they will maintain this record in the future. The problem is how to keep the financial erosion of family farms to a minimum, in the face of the worst agricultural recession since the 1930s. Canada's productive farmland is a national asset of great value, and it should be passed on intact to future generations. The survival of the Canadian family farm is also justified on grounds of regional equity, since single-proprietor agriculture is the economic mainstay and social basis of much of non-urban Canada. While the scope for massive movement off the farm is far more limited today, it nevertheless remains true that cyclically induced departures, based on financial losses, are socially disruptive. Moreover, it can be argued – although Commissioners have seen little evidence on this point – that support for the family farm is warranted on general economic grounds: that is, on the grounds that an owner/operator can be expected to husband his resources better and to use less energy and fewer chemical fertilizers than the operators of a corporate farm.

How should we Canadians support our agriculture sector? The sections that follow set out recommendations for much larger research and development (R&D) expenditures, to be funded in part by producers, and an aggressive international trade policy. In this present section, Commissioners wish to draw attention to other problems that invite government attention: the problem of farmers' limited access to capital markets and the closely related question of intergenerational land transfers.

The viability of the single-owner farm depends more and more on the farmer's ability to expand his hectarage and to engage in capital-intensive production. As farmers' capital requirements grow, they become less able to meet them out of the returns to their own equity and more and more dependent on access to capital markets. Relative to other businesses, however, farm enterprises are generally at a disadvantage in capital markets since the variability of the weather compounds the uncertainties of the farmers' business cycle. Because farming is generally a riskier undertaking than other business ventures, operators of non-farm businesses can usually obtain bank financing more easily than farmers. In recent years, for instance, banks have been unwilling to provide long-term farm loans at fixed rates of interest. The advantage that other businesses enjoy in capital markets contributes to their ability to buy agricultural land – for industrial-park development, for example – at prices that are unrelated to the price of agricultural land, making it ever more difficult for the family farmer to compete for land resources.

There are, however, several programs, both federal and provincial, aimed at increasing small farmers' access to financial markets. Among them are subsidized credit schemes such as the Special Farm Financial Assistance Program (SFFAP) of the federally funded Farm Credit Corporation (FCC), the Saskatchewan Farm Purchase Program (FPP), and Ontario's Beginning

Farmer Assistance Program (BFAP). Before the mid-1970s, the FCC was the major source of fixed-rate long-term funding for land acquisition and the purchase of capital equipment. Over the past decade, however, much of this lending has shifted to the private banking sector at floating rates.

A variant of the capital-access problem arises when farmers wish to transfer farm property to their offspring. Typically, the assets represented by land, buildings and machinery are the only provision farmers have been able to make towards retirement. Regrettably, farmers' children may find it impossible to raise the funds necessary to buy out their parents and keep the farm in the family.

In view of these problems, Comissioners support the maintenance of effective special credit arrangements for farmers, but the special schemes should not subsidize the sector by providing access to capital at less than market rates. Indeed, we do not believe that policies should be designed specifically to keep marginal operations permanently in business. Nevertheless, the design of special credit arrangements should take into account the unusual features of agriculture: its volatility, its lack of access to equity capital, and the need to transfer ownership intergenerationally. The specifics of any such policies can be left to the experts. We wish only to endorse the general point that special programs are necessary and to urge constructive action by governments and farm groups.

Land Supply and Quality

Many participants in this Commission's consultation process put forward the view that Canada faces potentially serious problems in maintaining its supply of productive agricultural land:

> *Even in the recent past Canada's legislators and the Canadian public believed that Canada has almost inexhaustible supplies of land for farming. Also, they were convinced that improved agricultural technology and its application would ensure the availability of farmland forever.*
>
> *These misconceptions have created a misleading impression of abundance and have resulted in land use practices which are precipitating some major concerns . . .* (Agricultural Institute of Canada, Brief, November 29, 1983, p. 5.)

> *Soil salinity affects an estimated 5.4 million acres (2.2 million hectares) or 4.1 percent of the cultivated and range land on the prairies. Conservative estimates put the monetary losses resulting from salinization at $29 million annually and this will increase to $465 million by the end of the century.*
>
> (Canadian Organic Producers Marketing Cooperative Limited, Brief, November 3, 1983, p. 8.)

> *Subtle deterioration of the inherent productivity of prairie farmland is also of great concern. In the eight decades since cultivation began, the humus content of the Prairie soils has decreased by nearly 50%.*
>
> (Lethbridge Research Station, Brief, October 31, 1983, p. 4.)

Nor did intervenors limit their attention to soil quality. They also expressed concern about the conversion of rural land – often land of high agricultural capability – to urban uses:

We are shocked at the disappearance of much of Canada's agricultural heartlands as cities like Toronto, St. Catharines, Winnipeg, Regina and others expand. We wonder at the wisdom of continued expansion of major cities, especially those surrounded by prime farmland.

(Thompson Industrial Commission, Brief, October 6, 1983, p. 6.)

Industrial development centred around large urban communities, coupled with urban sprawl, has already gobbled up much of the best agricultural land in Canada, as in other countries ... If this trend is not controlled, millions more acres of the most productive farm land in this country will be covered with concrete and lost as a food resource base for future generations.

(National Farmers Union, Brief, November 21, 1983, p. 22.)

Are these concerns justified? During the 1960s and 1970s, the federal government and the provinces carried out a detailed inventory of Canada's land resources.[11] According to this inventory, only 11 per cent of Canada's land is capable of sustaining agriculture of any kind, less than 5 per cent is capable of producing crops, and less than 0.5 per cent is valuable class-one land capable of sustaining the whole range of Canadian crops. Although Canada is the second-largest country on earth, the amount of Canadian land available for crop production of any kind is approximately equal to the area of Sweden. Canada's whole stock of class-one agricultural land is smaller than the area of New Brunswick. For obvious historical reasons, most of the best agricultural land in Canada is located near our largest cities: 37 per cent of Canada's class-one agricultural land and 25 per cent of our class-two land can be seen from the top of Toronto's CN tower.

A federal government study of urban centres with populations greater than 25 000 documents the quantity and quality of land converted to direct urban use between 1966 and 1976.[12] During this decade, rural lands equal in area to the city of Hamilton were built over. Of all the rural land converted to urban uses, 63 per cent was rated in the top three classes for agriculture. In Ontario, 79 per cent of the rural land converted to urban uses was prime farmland. In Manitoba, the figure was 91 per cent; in Prince Edward Island, it was 99 per cent.[13]

The pursuit of leisure and recreation imposes further demands on land resources. Recent years have seen an explosion in demand for campgrounds, cottage sites, highway picnic sites, ski trails, parklands. Car graveyards, race tracks, gravel pits and quarries, and other urban-related undertakings take an additional toll of rural lands. Once farmland is appropriated for urban or urban-related use, it seldom reverts to agriculture.

The continued loss of farm land to urbanization has important implications for Canada's production potential. In considering this loss, we must be chary in taking comfort from the increases in total hectarage that come from improving land. There is no benefit in replacing land that can grow fruits, vegetables and corn with land suitable only for barley or hay. In areas such as the Golden Horseshoe, between Toronto and St. Catharines, and the Okanagan Valley of British Columbia, one-third of improved farmland has been converted to other uses in the last 25 years.[14] Some of the crops grown in these areas, such as tender fruits and hybrid or vinifera grapes, cannot be produced commercially in any other part of Canada.

Commissioners support the call for a comprehensive study of the loss of prime farmland to urban development. How rapidly is this loss proceeding? Does it represent a failure of the private-land market? That is, are we ignoring important social considerations in tolerating a situation in which urban developers can consistently outbid farmers for agricultural land? Is a development freeze – a solution that has been tried in some jurisdictions – an adequate solution, or are there better avenues to try? Commissioners agree with the many intervenors who argued that we cannot put off much longer finding firm answers to these questions.

Most agronomists agree that the deterioration of Canadian soils threatens the expansion of our agricultural production. About one-third of the productivity of Canada's prairie soils has been lost since cultivation began, making them more susceptible to erosion. Excessive salinity results when unused water absorbs salts, moves down through the soil, and then seeps to the surface in other, lower areas. Salinity affects an estimated 2.7 to 4.0 per cent of all dryland in Western Canada and more than 20 per cent of irrigated hectarage, mostly in southern Alberta. The area affected by salinity is increasing by about 10 per cent annually. It is not known how much soil Canadian agriculture loses to wind and water erosion, but estimates are available for some localities. In the southern Prairies, for example, losses to wind erosion are substantial in dry years. Excess soil acidity, caused by the use of fertilizers (especially nitrogen) and by emissions from natural-gas/processing plants, thermal power plants, and smelters, now affects more than 2.5 million hectares in the Prairies; 70 per cent of the affected land is in Alberta.[15] Significant topsoil losses have been recorded in Prince Edward Island (20 tonnes per hectare on potato land) and Ontario (as much as 50 tonnes per hectare on corn land). Sixty to 70 per cent of all sediments in the Great Lakes originate from agricultural land.[16]

The problems of soil deterioration are serious but not unmanageable, given a concerted effort to solve them. Initial research suggests that the problem of acid soils can be dealt with in a relatively straightforward manner, although more investigation is needed. As for salinity, one important cause of the problem is summerfallowing. This practice began primarily as a means of storing moisture in the soil for a year so that a better crop could be produced the following year. Yet summerfallowing retains only a relatively small percentage (7 to 14 per cent) of the year's precipitation for the following year's crop. The remainder passes down through the soil, often forming a salt seep elsewhere. Continuous cropping helps to absorb the excess moisture, reduces erosion, and, if an annual legume crop is included in the rotation, restores organic matter and nitrogen to the soil.

Even without improvements in farming technology, it appears that summerfallowing could be substantially reduced on at least 50 per cent of the total cultivated hectarage on the Prairies. Given additional research and a program of education designed to make farmers more aware of the long-term adverse effects of summerfallowing, it should be possible to improve on this estimate. On the other hand, it may be unreasonable to expect many farmers to change their practices in the absence of improvement in the farm economy. No farmers set out to follow practices that will cause deterioration of their land, but financial restrictions may make it impossible for them to apply all available knowledge.

Marketing Boards

Agricultural marketing boards constitute a contentious subject. This became evident at this Commission's hearings:

> *Agricultural marketing boards which restrict the supply of agricultural output should be eliminated.* (Campeau Corporation, Brief, November 24, 1983, p. 2.)

> *Marketing Boards of all descriptions should be discontinued. The point has been reached in Canada that because of government regulation there is so much distortion in the market place that no one knows what the true value is for many food items, commodities, or utilities.* (Charles W. Houston, Brief, July 14, 1984, p. 3.)

Understandably, producers' organizations did not agree:

> *The Canadian Federation of Agriculture unequivocally supports ... supply-management programs [for the poultry and milk industries]. They are necessary for the healthy survival of these sectors. They are extensively supervised in the public interest. They are productivity-increasing in their operations.*
> (Canadian Federation of Agriculture, Brief, September 22, 1983, p. 13.)

What effect do marketing boards have on agricultural performance? In order to answer this question, it is necessary to distinguish between agencies that control the supply of their product (eggs, chickens, turkeys, tobacco, and milk) and agencies that simply facilitate farmers' common marketing (of hogs, fruits and vegetables). With respect to the latter, the Economic Council of Canada has concluded that:

> *These boards have worked to the advantage of producers, who are now able to secure a fair return formerly denied them because of their insufficient bargaining power. To the extent that markets function better, that additional detailed information is provided, and that quality is controlled, both the consumer and the producer benefit. No doubt, as in the case of other institutions, the operation of the boards could be improved. Nevertheless, the Council endorses their activities and sees no need for radical changes in their mandates.*[17]

For boards with supply-management capabilities, the evidence is very different. Numerous studies have demonstrated that such marketing boards insulate domestic producers from foreign competition, often to the point of eliminating foreign supplies altogether. They also reduce interprovincial trade in agricultural commodities, with the frequent result that these commodities are not produced in the provinces that can produce them at the lowest cost. Finally, supply-management marketing boards raise the prices of agricultural products above the level that might be achieved in a market where common marketing took place, but supply control did not.

There are several studies that attempt to estimate the extent of the excess return extracted from consumers by supply-management marketing boards.[18] One study sets the annual excess payments at $56 million for eggs, $97 million for broilers, and $33 million for turkeys.[19] Another study sets the annual excess payments for fluid and industrial milk at $366 million and $629 million respectively.[20] These excess payments show up as quota values, which are essentially payments for the right to produce. One study estimates that the value of quota for five commodities – milk, eggs, broiler chickens, turkeys, and tobacco – increased by more than 33 per cent in the two-year period from 1978 to 1980.[21]

The supply-management marketing boards do not extract these excess returns without imposing an efficiency loss on the Canadian economy. The loss can take a number of forms, but most studies restrict their estimates to the surplus forgone as a result of diminished consumption and the cost of replacing foreign suppliers by Canadian suppliers. These studies find that of each dollar transferred from consumers to farmers, approximately 25 cents is wasted. A study of egg marketing in British Columbia attempted to estimate the value of every type of waste induced by the egg-marketing board.[22] It concluded that it costs $3.3 million annually in lost output to transfer $5.3 million to B.C. egg producers; this sum represented an efficiency loss of 60 cents per dollar transferred. Still other studies calculate that it may cost as much as $3 to transfer one dollar from consumers to farmers.[23]

In sum, by restricting foreign and domestic supply, supply-management marketing boards raise the prices of agricultural commodities and thus augment farm incomes. They appear to accomplish this, however, at a significant efficiency cost to the Canadian economy as a whole. Nor do they benefit all producers equally. They bring very little benefit to new farmers, who must buy their quota. Indeed, it may be that few of the beneficiaries of marketing boards are still on the land; many have sold their quota and retired. Again, Commissioners would repeat that these criticisms are levelled at national supply-management marketing boards controlling the supply of agricultural products such as eggs, chickens, turkeys, tobacco and milk; we are not criticizing those marketing boards which do not restrict supply, many of which operate at the provincial level.

Commissioners assume that in general, Canadians support the goal of augmenting and stabilizing farm incomes. Nevertheless, national supply-management marketing boards represent an expensive way to meet a perfectly acceptable social goal. One alternative would be a scheme that reduced the extent of income fluctuations experienced by the producers, instead of supporting their level of income, as such marketing boards do. Unlike the boards' methods, an income-stablization scheme would smooth out market risks without generating efficiency losses. The Western Grain Stabilization Act and the Agricultural Stabilization Act might serve as models for a program of this kind. This Commission recommends that the federal government, the provinces, farm groups and consumer associations commit themselves to the task of designing and implementing other possibilities such as an income stabilization scheme. We further recommend that Canada move gradually to phase out supply-management marketing boards.

Pending replacement of marketing boards by an alternative scheme, Commissioners recommend that such boards be made more flexible and accountable. Specifically, we suggest that governments exercise caution in authorizing additional supply-management boards; that existing boards increase their production quotas so that quota values fall to more reasonable levels; that quantitative import restrictions be used only as a last resort; that quota be freely transferable between individuals (that is, not tied to farms) and across provinces; and that consumer groups be more adequately represented on the boards.

The Western Grains Economy

Grain Handling and Transportation. If Western grain producers are to retain their share of world markets, there must be improvement in the grading, handling, storing, and transporting of grain. Some adjustments have been made, and there have been a few very modest changes in the grading system. By and large, however, the rate of improvement has been glacial. The country elevator system is much what it was before the First World War. Nearly two decades ago, a recommendation was made that the number of grades of grain be reduced, a step that would have reduced the number of separate storage bins in country elevators and speeded up the filling of hopper cars. A freeing-up of elevator-bin space would have given farmers an opportunity to grow and sell other products through the elevator system. The recommendation is still valid today, indeed, it was reiterated in a major study by the Canada Grains Council in 1982.[24] As yet, major changes have not been forthcoming.

Another source of inefficiency in the grain-handling system is the practice of charging farmers, rather than the grain-handling companies, for leakages of grain that occur between the producer and the final sale at the terminal or the shipping port. This custom lessens the incentive to reduce shrinkage. In short, there is much that could be done to reduce the costs per tonne of grading and mixing grain and of moving grain from farmers' fields to ocean-going ships. Steps should also be taken to increase the system's efficiency in coping with greater farm output. For all of these purposes, substantial new investment and major technical innovations in the handling of grain will be necessary, both before rail transport and during rail transportation itself.

The Statutory Grains Freight Rate (the Crow Rate) is, of course, another very important factor in the efficiency of grain handling and marketing. During our hearings, Commissioners heard both vigorous defences of the historic Crow Rate and just as vigorous condemnations.

The matters at issue in the Crow Rate debate have been discussed extensively in recent years. For a variety of complex historical and political reasons, the rail-freight rates for grain shipments in effect at the beginning of the 1980s were the rates that had been in effect in 1897. This arrangement had two important implications for the Western grains economy and, by extension, for the Canadian economy as a whole. First, since railway costs had obviously increased significantly since 1897, the revenues derived from hauling grain were not compensatory. The predictable result was that the railways had ceased to invest in rail lines and infrastructure for the export grain trade. No new lines were being built, and existing ones were deteriorating. Planned increases in grain shipments were impossible; even more worrying was the fact that existing export levels were threatened.

The other result was a distortion in the relationship between the costs of shipping grain and the costs of shipping grain products and animal products out of the Western provinces. Since freight rates for grain exports were artificially low, while those for grain and animal products were set in the market-place, there was less processing, feedlot, and meat-packing activity in the Prairies than there might have been if all rates had been set on the same basis.

The solution to the problem of deteriorating infrastructure was clear: the railway companies had to be induced to upgrade existing rail facilities and to invest in new ones. This inducement could take one of two forms. The companies could be given direct subsidies, which might, perhaps, be linked to performance guarantees. Alternatively, rail rates could be allowed to move to compensatory levels, so that the railways would receive the normal return from investing their own funds in infrastructure improvement. Each solution had its advantages and disadvantages, but basically, either solution would stimulate the necessary investment. If direct subsidies were paid, however, rail rates would stay at their existing level and the disincentive to locate grain-processing and meat-processing facilities in Western Canada would remain. If rates were allowed to rise to compensatory levels, this disincentive would disappear, and interregional comparative advantage would dictate the location of processing activities.

The problem was further complicated by equity issues. If the government subsidized the railways directly, Canadians in general would pay for rail-line investments. If rates were to rise to compensatory levels, Western farmers would pay the costs. To many Western Canadians, the latter solution represented an abrogation of a fundamental historical concession, which they had received in return for the costs imposed on them by the other features of the National Policy. Since the federal government seems to have accepted from the beginning that the Western grain producers were entitled to a continuation of an historical "Crow Benefit", the issue became: to whom and how should that continuing benefit be paid?

It was not just Western farmers who were interested in the outcome of the Crow Rate debate. The subsidization of Western grain farmers was a contentious issue in other parts of the country, particularly in Quebec, but sentiment outside the West was not altogether hostile to the Crow Rate. As Commissioners were told at our hearings in the fall of 1983, at the height of the Crow Rate debate in Parliament,

> *The death of the Crow would have serious consequences for the Maritimes. If the Crow goes, it would be a matter of a short time before the Maritime and Atlantic subsidies would be taken off. Primary producers in the Maritimes could not survive the extra costs of transporting their product to the markets.*
>
> (National Farmers Union, Prince Edward Island, Brief, September 2, 1983, p. 10.)

Opinion outside the agriculture sector did not universally favour retention of the historic arrangement:

> *While our original attention was focused on the effect that these arbitrarily low freight rates might have on the movement of other commodities, such as lumber and pulp, we are now looking at the even more alarming prospect of the railways being unable to finance future capacity needs in the system. A crunch in the form of railway equipment shortages or rationing would eventually have impacts on the forest industry that would include losses of earnings, losses of jobs, as well as taxes and capital investment.*
>
> (Council of Forest Industries of British Columbia, Transcript, Prince George, September 13, 1983 [vol. 7A], p. 1775.)

There were two choices for the federal government. It could transfer sufficient funds directly to the railways to cover the full cost of moving the grain to export positions, leaving freight rates at the 1897 levels. Alternatively, it could let rates rise to market levels and make the same subsidy payments directly to Western producers. Under either option, provision would have to be made for future cost increases.

In 1983, after considerable study and negotiation, the federal government passed legislation that payments of the Crow Benefit would go directly to the railways, in return for performance guarantees on infrastructure development. This position was favoured by a major part of the Western farming community. The federal government's decision to make payments to the railways rather than to the farmers was also determined, in part, by the fact that the feedlot industry in central Canada depends to a considerable extent on subsidized shipping rates for feed grains. The new scheme, however, would also permit freight rates to rise as railway costs rose. A complicated sharing formula was developed, a variety of safeguards were introduced, and provision was made to review the entire situation in a few years.

This compromise solution still leaves intact major distortions, both in the location of grain-processing industries and in the structure of the Western grains economy. As this Report is being written, the effectiveness of the new system is the subject of a thorough study initiated by the federal government under the chairmanship of Mr. Justice Gordon Hall of Manitoba.[25] In view of this ongoing review, this Commission does not recommend any specific formula. We do, however, support further adjustment on the payment of the Crow Benefit, as provided for in the Western Grains Transportation Act, in line with market principles and the need for flexibility, and the promotion of modernization and efficiency.

International Markets for Grains. Canada depends on relatively few buyers for its grain exports. The two largest buyers of Canadian wheat are the Soviet Union and China, both of which have rather unpredictable buying patterns.[26] If Soviet agriculture were reorganized, the country's imports might decline substantially. Projections suggest that annual imports of grain into the Soviet Union and Eastern Europe will decline substantially to the year 2000.[27] Similarly, if China continues to improve incentives to its farmers, its demand for Canadian grain could decline or shift from wheat to feedgrains. Indeed, China is now an exporter of wheat.

It is obvious that Canada should diversify its markets for grains, especially wheat. Diversification will require a shift in the mix of wheat produced in Canada. Canada's main wheat crops are hard spring-wheat varieties. Some nations, such as Japan and the United Kingdom, demand this kind of wheat and are willing to pay a premium for it. Canada does have a special niche in these markets, but growth in demand for high-protein hard wheats is not anticipated. Demand is expanding, however, particularly in the developing world, for high-yield wheats of the "Triple-M" type.[28] Canadian exports of wheat to less-developed countries (LDCs), except China, are very small. Canada must develop production of these kinds of wheats if we are to share in this expanding market.

Before the 1980s, uncertainties in the world grain markets often led to a situation where Canada carried the burden of shortages and excess inventories. In recent years, the United States has carried that burden, as Canadian grain stocks have been minimal. Since 1971, major importing and exporting countries have lived under an International Wheat Agreement which has no economic provisions such as a buffer-stock provision or export-quota commitments. In 1979, the last attempt to renegotiate such economic provisions failed, and there is little reason to believe that member countries, particularly the United States, would come to an agreement in the short term. Nevertheless, a renewal of an International Wheat Agreement with economic provisions would be of general benefit to Canada, as well as to other major exporters and importers of grain because it would promote stability and market growth. Canada has generally supported such international undertakings and should continue to do so.

Commercial Policy

World agricultural policy is substantially interventionist. Most nations use a striking number and variety of tariff and non-tariff barriers (NTBs) to protect their farming communities, even when international treaties seem to preclude such measures. There is virtually no country that does not, as a matter of established policy, seek to preserve and expand its domestic agricultural base.

In most cases, Canadian agriculture can compete effectively with other producers anywhere in the world if it is allowed to compete on a fair basis. But Canadian farmers cannot, and must not be expected to, compete with farmers who are heavily subsidized by their governments or in markets where they face a wide range of tariff and non-tariff barriers. As the Canadian Food Processors Association stated to this Commission:

> *We are in a world market game which doesn't abide by the rules of GATT by any manner or means. Unless Canada is prepared to take the same actions as some of these other countries, we are going to be left out in left field.*
>
> (Transcript, Winnipeg, November 30, 1983 [vol. 54], p. 11486.)

Commissioners are loathe to recommend that Canada emulate its trading partners by increasing barriers to trade. It would, in our opinion, be better to work towards a true free-trade environment for agricultural products, especially given Canada's comparative advantage in many of these products and its status as a major exporter. Care should be taken, however, in any trade negotiations dealing with farm products that Canada's special interests are met.

Fruits and Vegetables

Over the past decade or so, there has been a substantial increase in the per capita consumption by Canadians of fresh produce. A wide range of imported fruits and vegetables are directly competitive with domestic sources of supply. For heavily consumed items such as tomatoes, celery and lettuce, the foreign share is over 80 per cent. For tomatoes alone (excluding greenhouse production), the foreign share is 96 per cent. For all non-tropical fresh fruits and vegetables, the foreign share is well over 50 per cent. When potatoes are excluded from this total, the foreign share rises to nearly two-thirds of our domestic consumption of fresh produce.

At first glance, it might appear that Canadians have major opportunities for increasing the domestic share of fruit and vegetable sales. Canada has vast supplies of land and water. Moreover, horticultural production does not depend entirely on class-one land. The technology exists for large-scale greenhouse production and for proper storage of many basic fruits and vegetables to provide produce outside the usual field-crop season.

Yet any move to import-substitution will not be simple. Capital costs of field-crop production are substantial. Because our Canadian growing seasons are fairly short, suitable storage facilities would be essential to any expansion of domestic output in this sector. To undertake either a 100-hectare potato operation or to invest in a 50-hectare vegetable farm with the appropriate storage facilities involves an investment of about $1 million, a capital intensity higher than that required for grain farming. Labour is cheaper both in the southern United States and in Mexico. There are obstacles to expansion of output on the marketing side as well. Canadian growers would have to break into supply channels of wholesalers (and accompanying retail chains) with long-established contacts in Florida, California, and Arizona. To do this, they would have to be able to provide guaranteed quantities and qualities of produce. On the other hand, some factors favour Canada over our competitors: lower outlays for insecticides because of the cooler climate; lower costs of transportation to market; the depreciated Canadian dollar; and cheaper water. This last factor will become especially important in the future.

While detailed costing studies are not available, there is some evidence that Canadian producers are not yet making the best of what appear to be expanding opportunities. Lack of attention to reliability of supply and, especially, to quality are frequently cited weaknesses in the practice of Canadian growers.[29] Nor do Canadian growers always make use of the latest developments in storage, even though some provincial governments have supportive loan programs. Canadian farms are too often small-scale operations. In recent years, however, Canadian growers have gained experience in using the most modern greenhouse technologies as well as hydroponics. In most provinces, too, there are commercial greenhouse operations using excess industrial heat. Nonetheless, in general, Canadians have not yet taken full advantage of these technologies in producing vegetables.

In summary, although there may be some cost advantages for producers in the southern United States over producers in Canada, there is potential for Canadian producers to expand. Provincial governments should encourage growers to practise more efficient methods and should work together to establish Canada-wide policies. Additional research to develop improved seed varieties, better insect and disease control, more efficient use of space, and new vegetable products could yield satisfactory returns to Canadian horticultural producers.

Research and Development

The need for enhanced research and development efforts was a theme common to many of the agricultural submissions Commissioners received. We were reminded, correctly, that it is scientific achievement rather than unaided nature that has made Canada a leading agricultural nation. Important social, as well as economic, benefits accrue from agricultural research:

> *Research and innovation are essential to future growth and competitiveness of agriculture and the food industries . . . Perhaps it is not sufficiently appreciated that it is publicly funded research that has made Canada a leading agricultural country in the world . . . Our failure to keep up, let alone lead, in this field would greatly undermine our long run competitive position.*
>
> (Ontario Federation of Agriculture, Brief, November 2, 1983, pp. 14–15.)

> *Agricultural research is one of the best investments the people of Canada can make. Net return on investment is estimated to be 40–50% per year, far higher than most commercial ventures.*
>
> (Lethbridge Research Station, Brief, October 31, 1983, p. 5.)

> *Between now and the year 2000, the federal government ought to increase the funds earmarked for research in agriculture. However, the producers would like to be involved, in order to contribute their views, and they are even prepared to contribute financially, taking into account, of course, their financial abilities. They are convinced that their participation would make for the better application of the research to the real need of agriculture to become more and more competitive.*
>
> (*La fédération de l'UPA du Saguenay-Lac-St-Jean,* Brief, November 2, 1983, p. 22.)

Tragically, Canada has allowed its emphasis on such research to diminish, relative both to gross national product and to our competitors. Federal government outlays are now about one-half the proportion of GNP spent on agricultural research in the United States or Japan.[30]

There can be no debate about Canada's need to increase its commitment to agricultural research and development, and to increase it at a rate that will allow us to catch up with our competitors. There can be no debate, either, about the necessity for government support. Individual producers, even producer groups, are simply too small and too widely dispersed to undertake sophisticated basic research. A check-off system, under which a levy of so many cents per unit of output would be assessed for research purposes, should certainly be considered wherever it is feasible. Producer groups might welcome such a system as a means of gaining some control over the ways in which R&D dollars were being used. But ultimately it is governments, acting for Canada as a whole, that must make the commitment. Given returns to research as significant as they have been in the past, such a commitment would be a productive use of the nation's resources. Commissioners do not wish to make recommendations, beyond the ones we have already mentioned, about specific amounts or particular directions for this research effort. These questions are best left to the network of granting agencies, research scientists, and farm groups involved. In nearly every area we have surveyed, however, we see major opportunities for Canadian agriculture if new and better products are developed, or if improved production, handling, and marketing techniques are devised.

Conclusions

The potential exists for continued expansion of Canada's exports of grains, oil-seeds and red meats, but there are major uncertainties in world markets. Although some of these are not within Canadians' control, there are a number of steps than can be taken to enhance our competitive position. These include:

- Significant improvements in the production, handling and transportation of grains, supported by amendments to the Western Grains Transportation Act
- Making steady progress towards freer trade in this difficult area
- Supporting, over the longer term, a renewal of an International Wheat Agreement including economic provisions
- Greatly increasing public commitment to research and development
- Exploring alternatives, such as income stabilization, to national supply-management boards. Failing outright replacement, we urge substantial reforms of such marketing boards.

Steps must also be taken to ensure that Canadian farmland and the family farm are preserved into the next century. We recommend a careful study of the loss of prime farmland. We do not advocate farm-support programs which will keep marginal operations in business, but because of the special risk factors associated with farming, we support the retention of special credit arrangements for farmers.

Notes

1. Conference Board of Canada, *The Provincial Economies* (Ottawa: The Board, 1984).
2. United States, Council on Environmental Quality and the Department of State, *The Global 2000 Report to the President: Entering the* Twenty-First Century (Washington, D.C.: U.S. Government Printing Office, 1980); and Food and Agriculture Organization of the United Nations, *Agriculture: Toward 2000* (Rome: FAO, 1981).
3. Kenneth R. Farrell, Fred H. Sanderson, Trang T. Vo, and Michael F. Brewer, "Meeting Future Needs for United States, Food, Fiber and Forest Products", in Joint Council on Food and Agricultural Sciences, *Reference Document: Needs Assessment for Food and Agricultural Sciences* (Washington, D.C., 1984); and

David Cole and S. Horton, "World Grain Trade and Its Financing: Past Patterns and Future Prospects", paper prepared for the Institute for Research on Public Policy, Montreal, 1983.

4. *The Global 2000 Report to the President*; and Canada, Agriculture Canada, *Challenge for Growth: An Agri-Food Strategy for Canada* (Ottawa: The Department, 1981).
5. See, for example, Terry Veeman and Michele Veeman, *The Future of Grain: Canada's Prospects for Grains, Oilseeds and Related Industries* (Ottawa: Canadian Institute for Economic Policy, 1984).
6. Stewart Borland and Gerald Robertson, "A Sectoral View of the Longer-Term: Agriculture", in *Long-Term Economic Prospects for Canada: A Symposium*, vol. 23, prepared for the Royal Commission on the Economic Union and Development Prospects for Canada (Toronto: University of Toronto Press, 1985).
7. Based on models discussed in C.A. Carter, "International Trade Opportunities for Canadian Agriculture", paper presented at the Canadian Agricultural Economics and Farm Management Society 1984 Workshop, Ottawa, July 5, 1984. Models discussed were: International Wheat Council, "Long Term Grain Outlook", Secretariat Paper No. 14 (London, 1983); Australia, Department of Trade and Resources, "The World Food Economy in the 1980's" (Canberra, 1982); and Michigan State University, Department of Agricultural Economics, "Long Term Forecast" (East Lansing, 1982).
8. Veeman and Veeman, *The Future of Grain.*
9. Canada, Agriculture Canada, *Handbook of Selected Agricultural Statistics 1984* (Ottawa: Minister of Supply and Services Canada, 1984).
10. Canada, Farm Credit Corporation, Research Division, *Farm Survey* (Ottawa: Minister of Supply and Services Canada, 1984).
11. This survey, the Canada Land Inventory, divided Canada's land resources into seven categories: class one land is the best for agricultural purposes, and class seven land is of no use for agriculture. Once complete, the Canada Land Inventory yielded the first clear picture of just how much of Canada's land resource could produce agricultural products.
12. C. Leigh Warren and Paul C. Rump, *The Urbanization of Rural Land in Canada, 1966–1971 and 1971–1976* (Ottawa: Environment Canada, Lands Directorate, 1981). In the 1971–75 study, comparisons are made with 1966–71 data from an earlier federal government study.
13. David M. Gierman, *Rural to Urban Land Conversion*, Occasional Paper No. 16, Lands Directorate, Environment Canada (Ottawa: Minister of Supply and Services Canada, 1977), pp. 48–49. As cited in Wendy L. Simpson-Lewis and Edward W. Manning, "Food for Thought: Can We Preserve Our Agricultural Land Resource?", *Alternatives* 10 (Spring–Summer 1981).
14. Simpson-Lewis and Manning, "Food for Thought".
15. P.B. Hoyt, M. Nyborg, D. Penny, and H. Ukrainetz, "A Degradion by Acidification", paper presented to the Alberta Soil Science Workshop, 1981.
16. The Honourable Eugene F. Whelan, Brief, November 24, 1983.
17. Economic Council of Canada, *Reforming Regulation* (Ottawa: Minister of Supply and Services Canada, 1981), p. 65.
18. These studies were surveyed and evaluated for the Commission by Wayne Thirsk, "Interprovincial Trade and the Welfare Effects of Marketing Boards", in *Perspectives on the Canadian Economic Union*, vol. 60 (Toronto: University of Toronto Press, 1985).
19. M.M. Veeman, "Social Costs of Supply-Restricting Marketing Boards", *Canadian Journal of Agricultural Economies* 30 (March 1982).

20. Richard R. Barichello, *The Economics of Canadian Dairy Industry Regulation*, Technical Report No. E/12 (Ottawa: Economic Council of Canada and Institute for Research on Public Policy, 1981).
21. Economic Council, *Reforming Regulation*.
22. T.E. Borcherding and G.W. Dorosh, "The British Columbia Egg Marketing Board: Monopolistic Restrictions and Social Costs", Discussion Paper 80-03-1 (Burnaby: Simon Fraser University, School of Administration and Economies, 1980).
23. W.T. Stanbury and George Lerner, "Regulation and the Redistribution of Income and Wealth", *Canadian Public Administration* 26 (Fall 1983): 378–401.
24. Canada Grains Council, *Prospects for Prairie Grain Industry, 1990* (Winnipeg: The Council, 1982).
25. Committee of Inquiry on Crow Benefit Payment.
26. Borland and Robertson, "A Sectoral View of the Longer-Term".
27. For example, see Organisation for Economic Co-operation and Development, *Prospects for Soviet Agricultural Production and Trade* (Paris: OECD, 1983); and International Wheat Council, *Long Term Grain Outlook*, Secretariat Paper No. 14 (London: The Council, 1983).
28. Medium hard kernel, medium gluten strength, and medium protein content.
29. Ted Hole, "Production and Marketing of Fresh", and John Wiebe, "The Alberta Industry", in Alberta Agriculture, *Proceedings of Alberta Horticulture Conference, 1980* (Edmonton: The Department, 1980).
30. Veeman and Veeman, *The Future of Grain*.

Forestry

Profile

The forest-products sector, which embraces both logging and manufacturing, is a major component of the Canadian economy. In 1982, logging shipments amounted to $4.0 billion, and shipments of paper and processed-wood products totalled $22 billion. The forest industry accounted for 13.5 per cent of all manufacturing shipments and nearly 15 per cent of manufacturing value-added. In 1982, the sector employed 260 000 people, of whom about 40 000 worked at logging.

Although most of the provinces have important forestry activity, the industry is largely concentrated in British Columbia, Ontario, and Quebec. British Columbia produces about one-half the value-added in both the logging and the wood-products industries. Forest products account for half the value of British Columbia's manufacturing shipments, 60 per cent of the province's exports, and 10 per cent of its labour force. Ontario and Quebec account for nearly two-thirds of Canadian manufacture of pulp and paper.

Canada is a major player in the world market for forest products. In 1981, we accounted for 20.2 per cent of world exports (a slight decline since the mid-1960s); British Columbia's share alone amounted to 7.9 per cent. By comparison, the United States accounted for 12.7 per cent of world forestry product exports in that year.[1] Approximately half of total forest-industry shipments in Canada are exported, accounting for nearly 15 per cent of Canadian merchandise exports and making a major contribution to Canada's trade balance. The United States buys over 70 per cent of our exported forest products; Western Europe and Japan are Canada's other significant customers.

Table 12-5 summarizes changes over the last three decades in the relative importance of each major type of forest product export. Like the steep jump in the dollar value of our exports of forest products in the 1970s, the substantial decline, since 1950, in the relative importance of newsprint is of particular interest (although newsprint exports have increased in absolute terms over the same period). This shift is also evident in the figures for Canadian shares of world production and world exports, which are given in Tables 12-6 and 12-7. Canada's share of world newsprint production fell from 53 per cent in 1951–55 to 32 per cent in 1980–81. Although our share of world production of woodpulp also declined, we maintained our share of world exports. Our share of world lumber exports rose during the 1970s, from 37 per cent to 44 per cent; however, the latter figure represents a decline from a peak, in 1978, of nearly 50 per cent. Canada's share of the U.S. newsprint market has dwindled to 57 per cent in 1984, from 72 per cent in 1965, although, again, absolute volume has risen slightly. On the other hand, Canada's share of the U.S. lumber market increased from one-fifth to nearly one-third between 1974 and 1984.

Prospects

Although projections of world consumption of paper and paperboard vary considerably, one fact seems clear: the growth rate will be slower in the future

TABLE 12-5 Canadian Forest Products Exports: Selected Years 1950–1983

Year	Softwood Lumber	Woodpulp	Newsprint	Other	Total	Millions of $
		(percentages)				
1950	24.3	19.0	44.3	12.4	100.0	1 102
1960	20.4	20.5	47.8	11.4	100.0	1 587
1970	21.8	26.8	37.9	13.5	100.0	2 929
1980	25.7	30.5	29.0	14.8	100.0	12 697
1983	29.7	28.3	30.5	16.6	100.0	13 148

Source: *Bank of Canada Review* (various years).

TABLE 12-6 Canadian Volume Shares of World Production, Selected Years

Years	Softwood Lumber	Woodpulp	Newsprint
		(annual average percentages)	
1951–55	9	22	53
1961–65	8	17	41
1971–75	9	16	36
1980–81	13	14	32

Sources: Forest Products Research Society, *Proceedings: Timber Demand: The Future Is Now*, p. 62; FAO, *1981 Yearbook of Forest Products Reports* (Rome: FAO, 1983).

TABLE 12-7 Canadian Volume Shares of World Exports

Years	Softwood Lumber	Woodpulp	Newsprint
		(annual average percentages)	
1970–71	37	32	69
1980–81	44[a]	33	61

Sources: Forest Products Research Society, *Proceedings: Timber Demand: The Future Is Now*, p. 62; FAO, *1981 Yearbook of Forest Products Reports* (Rome: FAO, 1983).

a. The Canadian share of softwood lumber exports reached a peak of 49.7 per cent in 1978 and it has been declining gradually since then.

than it has been in recent decades. The downward trend began in the 1970s, when the annual growth rate in the world pulp and paper industry fell from an average of 5.6 per cent in the 1960s to an average of 3.0 per cent.[2] The prime reasons for expecting this shift to continue into the future are an anticipated lower rate of income growth in the future and increased competition from substitutes. By the mid-1990s, technological developments, particularly new computer applications and advances in the electronic transmission of information, may further reduce the volume of paper used. Various forecasts predict that in the 1985–90 period, the growth rate for paper and paperboard will average 2.7 per cent, while for the years 1990–95 it will decline to 2.3 per cent.[3]

Global demand for lumber and wood products has grown at about 2 per cent annually over the past 25 years. For the years to 2000, world demand is projected to expand, at most, about half as rapidly as demand for paper products: that is, at an annual rate of 1 to 1.5 per cent.[4] However, some intervenors at our hearings argued that the outlook beyond 2000 is brighter:

> *As the population of the world increases, you are going to see a tremendous increase in the demand for forest products . . . They say that nobody will be able to meet the world demand for forest products after the year 2000.*
>
> (Association of British Columbia Professional Foresters, Transcript, Vancouver, September 8, 1983 [vol. 3], p. 502.)

It is not certain that the Canadian industry will maintain even its current share of this slowly growing market. Access to the American market may be eroded by competition from lower-cost sources of softwoods, both in the southern United States and overseas. Recent U.S. estimates predict that until 2000, annual imports of softwood forest products will be no greater than they were in 1980, and that by 2010 they will be 9 per cent lower, although they will rise again by nearly 2 per cent per year over the subsequent 10 years to 2020.[5] While new chemical/mechanical pulping technology is making the production of softwood pulp in Canada cheaper, the southeastern United States is expected to remain a lower-cost producer of softwood market pulp and newsprint than the northwestern United States or Canada.

Changes taking place in other parts of the world may further limit our ability to compete. Even a decade ago, there were as many as 90 million hectares of plantation forests in the world. The higher-quality ones can produce 15 to 20 cubic metres of timber growth per hectare per year. In Brazil, timber growth is 40 to 60 cubic metres per hectare per year. Success stories in nations such as Brazil, Chile, and Zambia suggest that while development and transportation costs are likely to be prohibitive in the medium term, new industrial plantations can be financially successful and could eventually reduce developing countries' imports of forest products from developed nations by as much as U.S. $10 billion a year.[6] As both developed and developing countries move forward rapidly with afforestation and plantation programs, long-term European and Japanese demand for Canadian natural forest products may also decline.

New technology allows the production of low-cost pulp from hardwoods, the major forest reserve of many tropical and Southern Temperate Zone nations. This development and the fact that hardwood is much cheaper in these countries (recently in the order of U.S. $50 per tonne in Brazil as compared to U.S. $105 in Canada),[7] adds another negative element to the situation. However, work on fast-growing hardwood poplar that matures in 10 to 12 years suggests that Canada may eventually become competitive in this area.

Another factor that makes future markets for Canadian forest products uncertain is the possibility of an increase in trade barriers in the United States and other markets. In 1983, American producers attempted to block the unrestricted access that Canada enjoys in the U.S. softwood-lumber market. Several hundred American companies and nine trade associations argued that Canadian federal and provincial policies and practices violated the U.S. countervailing law. This attempt failed, but the possibility of eventual success remains.

Since January 1, 1984, the Scandinavian countries have had unrestricted tariff-free access to the European Community (EC), Canada's second-largest market. As a result, the EC has reduced its 1.5 million-tonne tariff-free quota on newsprint imports from outside the European Free Trade Association (EFTA), even though this amount was stipulated in the GATT as compensation to Canada for the United Kingdom's entry into the Community. Over the last three or four years, the devaluation of the Swedish kroner by more than 40 per cent, relative to the Canadian dollar, has made Swedish products in that market highly competitive.

Finally, Canada's efforts to remain competitive in world markets are hampered by two domestic factors: high labour costs and inadequate investment. Labour costs account for about one-half of the cost of wood delivered to mills, and labour costs are higher in Canada than they are in the southern United States and the tropics. For newsprint, our labour costs are currently about 20 per cent above those in the southern United States. Moreover, Canada has had an unenviable record of labour strife in this sector.[8]

Investment in the Canadian pulp and paper industry was sluggish through most of the 1970s as compared to investment in the rest of the world, particularly in the United States. Much of the machinery now in use in Canada is technologically obsolete, and hence less productive than our major competitors' machinery. Over 50 per cent of our paper-making machines were built before 1950, as compared with 25 per cent in the United States and 5 per cent in Scandinavia. The Canadian average for employee-hours required per tonne of newsprint is 50 per cent above the average required in Scandinavia, and 25 per cent above the U.S. average. Moreover, Canadian plants for fine papers and other specialized products are relatively small and inefficient. It will take substantial investment to bring this sector up to a world-competitive level.[9]

Large investments are also necessary in many areas of the wood-products sector. In British Columbia, for example, much of the existing equipment now in use was bought when first-growth timber was still plentiful, and it is unsuited to the smaller diameter of second-growth timber. Consequently, unit production costs are high. The Canadian Forestry Service informed this Commission:

> *The industry has a very good history of generating inventions in the processing of wood and developing wood products. However, limited empirical studies of the sector's technological productivity suggest that it has not been particularly innovative in implementing new technologies . . . In brief, the capital plant of the sector has been heavily run down and has simply not kept pace with international competitors.* (Canadian Forestry Service, Brief, February 10, 1984, p. 4.)

All projections of Canadian production and exports must be considered tentative. Table 12-8 summarizes one set of projections. Exports are expected to grow somewhat more slowly than domestic shipments, that is, at annual rates of about 2 per cent for woodpulp, and paper and allied products, and 2.2

per cent for lumber and other wood products. Even these estimates will prove overly optimistic if the United States realizes the projections mentioned earlier for growth of its domestic supply. To compensate for this loss, Canada would have to find huge new markets in the rest of the world. Given the current and prospective development of plantation forestry in the southern hemisphere, this would be a difficult challenge. Of a range of estimates provided by British Columbia's Ministry of Forests, the Economic Council of Canada considers as "most likely" a scenario, based on future demand as well as on supply factors, in which provincial harvests expand at only 1 per cent per year until 2000.[10]

Finally, there is the matter of future employment levels in the forest-products industry. The prospect is not encouraging. The Department of Regional Industrial Expansion (DRIE) estimates that employment cuts may be kept to 10 per cent from currently depressed levels, given possible new investment and modernization of the industry. If such investment is not undertaken, labour-force reductions could approach 20 per cent. Other sources predict still higher unemployment effects for some regions and for some sectors of the industry. The forestry subsector least likely to experience declines is pulp production.[11]

Issues and Recommendations

Although the predicted industry-growth rates are less than those experienced in earlier years, they nevertheless represent substantially increased consumption of Canadian forest products. A 2 per cent annual compound growth rate for the forest industry implies that the demand for Canadian products will increase by more than 37 per cent by the year 2000, and by more than 67 per cent by the year 2010. A 2.5 per cent growth rate would require increases in output of nearly 50 per cent and 90 per cent respectively.

In fact, our ability to meet even the minimum projected increases in market potential is by no means assured. Contrary to the belief of many Canadians, we do not have limitless supplies of high-grade accessible timber. There are

TABLE 12-8 Canadian Projections for the Forestry Industries, 1980–95

	(per cent per year)		
Industries	**Total Shipments**	**Domestic Shipments**	**Exports**
Logging	2.0	2.0	N.A.
Lumber and other wood products	2.4	2.7	2.2
Paper and allied products (including woodpulp)	2.2	2.4	2.0

Sources: Interim Report of the Forest Industries Advisory Committee (Ottawa: Minister of Supply and Services Canada, 1983); and John Wansbrough, "Sectional View of the Longer Term: Forest Products", in *Long-term Economic Prospects for Canada: A Symposium*, vol. 23, prepared for the Royal Commission on the Economic Union and Development Prospects for Canada, (Toronto: University of Toronto Press, 1985).

also grounds for concern about the age of the capital stock in the industry, as well as about labour relations, government policies and the state of research and development. It is clear that we face some real problems in this sector, problems that need attention soon if we are to continue to prosper as a significant international producer.

Timber Supply

> *Our supply of softwoods is declining rapidly, and in many regions of Canada, it will not be possible to sustain our present levels of production, even if the current decline is arrested.* (Canadian Institute of Forestry, Brief, October 31, 1983, p. 9.)

> *[The lumber industry's] problem is going to be one of supply. Our fibre is limited. Unless we husband it extremely well and use every management tool, we are going to be short of fibre.* (Maritime Lumber Bureau, Transcript, Fredericton, September 23, 1983 [vol. 15], p. 3553.)

Forests cover 44 per cent of our country's total area and represent 15 per cent of the world's forest lands. Quantity, however, is one thing and quality another. Less than half of Canada's forest area consists of stocked and productive lands. Furthermore, much of our productive forest land supports understocked forests of low quality. A unit of forest land in Canada supports much less wood than the same unit supports in Europe or in the United States. Finally, the forest-land base in Canada has been declining in the face of agricultural expansion, growing recreational land use, overharvesting, and poor management practices. Therefore, Canada's timber supply is not nearly as large relative to annual harvests as was once thought.

The peak harvest year to date was 1979. The difference between the harvest that year and the regulated annual allowable cut (AAC) is the theoretical timber reserve, or the amount by which the industry could theoretically expand the annual harvest. The size of the theoretical reserve for softwood timber (37 per cent above the AAC) would appear to suggest that the predicted 2 per cent annual increase in the softwood harvest could be achieved. However, a host of factors reduces the amount of timber worth harvesting, given existing and anticipated price and cost factors. These factors include inaccessibility; small size, poor quality or inappropriate mix of trees in relation to the available processing facilities; and inferior land bases for which reforestation is uneconomic. In addition, the AAC estimates for some areas are gross figures that ignore losses arising from forest fires, disease and insect destruction. Such losses are substantial: in the late 1970s, they were equal to about 80 per cent of the annual harvest.

When reserves of softwood are realistically evaluated, only Alberta has much scope for increased production on the basis of existing forest stands. Alberta's potential is almost double its 1979 harvest level.[12] For the nation as a whole, 2 per cent annual growth in the rate of softwood harvesting would create a deficit by 1995. Hardwood is another matter: projections indicate that reserves will still be substantial in 1995, amounting to nearly 160 per cent of requirements. Hardwood harvests, however, currently represent only a small proportion of total wood production in Canada.

Forest reserves have dwindled because the current forest-management policies of governments and the forest industry have failed to ensure adequate levels of reforestation. Canadians cut over an area of about 770 000 hectares annually. The area replanted or seeded annually is approximately 240 000 hectares.[13] The Canadian Forestry Service estimates that 25 to 50 per cent of the area harvested annually fails to regenerate or reverts to non-commercial stocks. According to the Science Council of Canada, 25 million hectares of formerly productive forest land are now in a waste state.[14] This area is equal to one-eighth of Canada's surviving productive forest land.

Poor harvesting and management practices are not the only cause of shrinking forest reserves. For every hectare of wood harvested between 1975 and 1979, nearly two hectares were consumed in forest fires, amounting to an average annual loss of 1.46 million hectares of forest. No more than half the total area of burned-over land will return naturally to commercially productive forest. Yet little of this land is being reforested. Other stands of timber are lost to insects, disease and windthrow. During the 1970s, the spruce budworm damaged nearly 75 million hectares of forest in the Atlantic provinces, Quebec, and Ontario, an area almost three-quarters of Ontario's size. And, of course, some productive forest land is converted each year to other uses.

In total, we are losing coniferous forest alone at a rate of about 1 million hectares per year.[15] This figure does not take into account the significant damage by acid rain that is likely to occur in future decades. Research sponsored by the federal government has confirmed that acid rain reduces the germination rate and early growth of a variety of tree species. Over 38 million hectares of forest in eastern Canada may be subject to damage from this source.

The problems of our forests are not insoluable. Intensive silviculture, which involves genetic improvement, proper site preparation, prompt reforestation, fertilization, removal of brush and weeds, and commercial thinning, can produce average annual timber growth several times greater than the current average AAC per hectare for all of Canada. Any major reforestation and management programs undertaken in the near future, however, will not result in enhanced yields until well into the next century. As one intervenor suggested, the redemption of our forests is both an urgent task and one that will require great patience:

> *To work for the development of our forests is to work today for a distant future. Actions taken in 1984 will not produce results for 30, 40, 50, or even 80 years, but they have to be taken now if we don't want to sacrifice our forests. If it isn't done today, we'll lose them.*
>
> (Canadian Federation of Professional Foresters' Association, Transcript, Hull, December 14, 1983 [vol. 71], p. 14697.)

It will be difficult to design a policy that will embody enough patience to wait for trees to grow to maturity. Nevertheless, a policy of intensive forest management, that is, of forest husbandry, is essential. The Commissioners would invoke the familiar adage that a forest is not a gift we inherit from our ancestors, but rather a resource we borrow from our children and our grandchildren.

Land Tenure

One serious obstacle to proper long-term forest management in Canada is our system of forest-land tenure. In the United States, Sweden and Finland, about three-quarters of commercial forest land is privately owned. While private ownership is extensive in some provinces – 73 per cent of Nova Scotia's forest land is in private hands, for instance – the figure for Canada as a whole is only 6 per cent. The remainder is Crown land controlled chiefly by the provinces, which delegate responsibility for forest-lands management to the private sector under various term licensing arrangements. From the public's point of view, this system has the advantage that it gives ultimate control over resource exploitation and management to government, and yet makes use of the labour and capital resources, organizational skills and operational efficiency of the private sector. The province's right to compensation for use of the publicly owned resource is upheld through the collection of stumpage fees on harvesting.

This system has a fundamental disadvantage: it is extremely difficult to design a tenure arrangement that will create sufficient economic incentives to ensure the efficient long-term management of timber resources. A private company will harvest timber at an optimal rate only if it bears the full opportunity costs of holding the timber as uncut inventory and has security of tenure for at least the period necessary for the forest to mature. Similarly, a private company will invest in reforestation and stand-improvement projects only if it can be certain that its tenure will be upheld over a term of several decades. Although forest tenure is usually renewable, the terms of tenure are subject both to periodic revision and to statutory amendment. For example, British Columbia granted Forest Management Licenses "in perpetuity" in 1947, only to reduce their term to 21-years renewable a mere 11 years later. Given that in Canada a stand of softwood trees takes 50 to 80 years to mature, the uncertainties generated by this system are obvious.

Because licensees have little inducement to engage in good management, government is obliged to intervene. Most licensing agreements specify harvest rates and recovery standards and require reforestation to some minimum standard. The Crown meets the costs of these contractual obligations by providing credits against stumpage payments. As a rule, it also extends credits for approved silvicultural management beyond the contractual minimum. In practice, however, these credits rarely provide an incentive sufficient to encourage licensees to pursue a standard higher than the minimum.

A recent Economic Council of Canada report[16] rejects one alternative: selling Crown forest lands to the private sector; it gives several grounds for doing so. This action would result in an unacceptably high level of concentration in the ownership of the resource. It would leave some problems of market failure unsolved. The transition from public to private ownership would bring dislocation and uncertainty and thus delay required investment. Finally, in the Council's judgement, "privatization" of our forests would be politically unpopular and therefore, presumably, politically infeasible.

It should be possible to design systems of land tenure short of private ownership that would provide some incentive to licensees to practice more efficient forest management. One simple improvement would be an increase in the duration of leasing agreements. This Commission recommends that leases be extended to coincide with the average maturation periods of the various tree species to which they apply, thus giving lessees a long-range incentive to protect and maintain the forest. This arrangement would not end the responsibility of government foresters to oversee the forest-management practices of the private occupier. Nor would this task exhaust the role of government. Commissioners see a need for a dramatic increase in public expenditure for forest renewal, forest protection and forest management.

Investment in Forest Renewal and Management

What scale of investment, public or private, would be needed to upgrade our forests and guarantee their future productivity? Estimates vary, but all are in the range of hundreds of millions of dollars. The Association of British Columbia Professional Foresters gave Commissioners an annual figure of from $700 million to $1 billion.[17] The 1981 National Forestry Conference in Banff recommended that expenditure on silviculture be raised to $600 million annually, approximately the expenditure required to raise the practice of silviculture in Canada to the level of practice in Sweden.[18] Currently, annual spending in Canada on silviculture, public and private, amounts to $240 million.

Commissioners recommend that provincial governments dramatically increase their expenditures for reforestation, for forest protection, and for silviculture generally, in keeping with the scope of the problem. Management of the resource falls squarely within provincial jurisdiction, and it is the provinces that will receive the direct benefits of investment in the form of higher stumpage fees. The monies should be dispensed on a case-by-case basis and only after careful study of the project's costs and potential benefits.

If Canada is to increase its standard of forest management, then we must also increase our expenditure for forest-service staff and for research. We lack enough professional and scientific personnel to carry out adequate forest management. The Scandinavian countries and the United States employ one professional forester for every 15 000 hectares of forest land. Canada employs one forester for every 43 000 hectares of forest land, and only a very small proportion of these are actively engaged in the field, making the actual ratio one forester to 380 000 hectares of forest. This Commission recommends major assistance for Canada's schools of forestry.

Canada also lags behind other countries in forestry research. In the fiscal year 1981–82, the federal government and the provinces together spent $56 million on research related to forest management. The benefits that arise from forestry research can be very large: the U.S. Forestry Service has estimated that the average benefit-to-cost ratio for its forestry research is 50:1.[19] A few case studies in Canada indicate that the ratio in this country is even higher.[20]

Increased research is needed in two broad areas. First, Canadians must seek new ways to protect and improve the resource base: to limit insect damage, control disease and increase yields. This research should be modelled on a systems approach, to include overall management strategies designed to put the Canadian forest back on a sustained-yield basis. Research should also be directed to the development of new varieties of trees. Development of fast-growing hardwoods would clearly benefit the Canadian industry. Softwoods take 50 to 80 years to mature; the hybrid poplar can be harvested in about 12 years. Hardwood fibres, which are much shorter than softwood fibres, cannot be used with current newsprint technology. At present, hardwood pulp is used on only a very limited basis, mostly for waferboard and fine papers. However, in view of the indications for future softwood supply and our substantial surplus of hardwoods, research that led to wider use of hardwoods could bring high returns. Given the importance of our forest industry and the obvious market failures described above, a case can be made for government participation in general research, such as an effort to develop faster-growing trees. Here we see a continuation of the traditional role of the federal government, in association with industry and provincial governments.

The private sector should bear the main responsibility for product and process innovation. Innovation characterizes any viable industry, and there is no more reason for government to subsidize innovation in forestry than there is reason for it to subsidize innovation in other sectors. In fact, government aid in the areas of reforestation, silviculture and basic research should be contingent on industry investment both in product and process innovation and in modern plant and equipment. If the public is to direct hundreds of millions of dollars annually toward the forestry sector, it must have some guarantee that the companies involved will carry their share as well.

While most of the Canadian forest is owned by the Crown, there are important holdings in private hands, particularly in the Great Lakes-St. Lawrence region and in New Brunswick and Nova Scotia. Private landowners, like the lessees of Crown lands, must be encouraged to carry out good forest practices. At present, certain aspects of public policy work against such practices and, in particular, fail to recognize the multi-generational nature of forestry. For example, the income-tax system encourages a private landowner to sell a forest stand outright to a jobber who will then clear-cut it, with no reforestation. The landowner who takes this course is subject to a capital gains tax at half the regular tax rate, whereas careful management and judicious harvesting would involve him in annual expenditure and potentially subject him to his full personal or corporate tax rate at the time of harvest. Stumpage would be sounder than a continuing property tax as a way of securing a return to provincial and local governments. Some provinces have recognized this situation: Ontario's Woodlands Improvement Act, for example, provides for a rebate of taxes on lands that are maintained in forest condition. Commissioners recommend that provincial governments actively pursue such policies, which can do much to assure proper management of existing stands and a rapid return to forest status of lands best suited to that use.

Given that private forest holdings are generally more accessible than most Crown lands to both markets and recreational use, and that they are capable of sustaining a wider range of tree species than lands within the boreal forest region, the policies of all three levels of government should encourage the practice of good forest management on private landholdings.

This example illustrates the close link between taxation and the issues of forest management and development. Obviously, the taxation system is one important channel through which government could provide increased incentives for productive forest management to the forestry sector. As we move into a new era in Canadian forestry that will place more emphasis on proper husbandry, it will be necessary to re-examine the taxation structures now in place. A tax system that worked in an era of relatively cheap and plentiful timber may not work now.

Federal-Provincial Co-operation

In the course of the consultative process, Commissioners found broad support for some sort of nation-wide forestry plan or strategy:

> *Both levels of government must pursue a policy of investment in the development of our forests, private and public.*
>
> (*Fédération de l'UPA du Saguenay-Lac-St-Jean*, Transcript, Chicoutimi, October 27, 1983 [vol. 35], p. 6855.)

> *It is imperative for federal-provincial agreements to be established to provide for commitment and continuity for forest management in a more meaningful and rational manner than heretofore.*
>
> (Canadian Forestry Association, Brief, September 26, 1983, p. 18.)

Commissioners agree that forestry is an area where enhanced federal-provincial co-operation is called for. We have already indicated the ways in which we see responsibilities being divided in the areas of reforestation, silviculture, and basic research. Other opportunities for co-operation will occur in the context of regional development policies involving forestry projects. The future of our forests is so critical to so many Canadians living in so many locations that jurisdictional issues cannot be permitted to hold up progress.

Conclusions

The forest products sector is typical of the state of natural resources in Canada. The sector is extraordinarily important to our country and especially so to some regions. The future seems bright enough, but not as robust as the past. In any event, there are serious and obvious failures of management which, if corrected, would provide a greater degree of assurance in the period of slower growth and tough competition ahead.

Much greater federal-provincial co-operation will be necessary to undertake policies that will:

- Increase substantially the investment in forest renewal, protection and management by the public sector, in return for performance and modernization guarantees by the forest companies
- Enhance the timber supply through a more intensive system of forest husbandry. Additional research funds will be required.

- Modify the forest-land/tenure system by extending the duration of leasing agreements
- Adjust the tax system so as to encourage proper maintenance of private woodlots.

Notes

1. Economic Council of Canada, *Western Transition* (Ottawa: Minister of Supply and Services Canada, 1984), p. 43.
2. Canadian Pulp and Paper Association, Brief, October 14, 1983, p. 17.
3. Peter Graff, "Paper Consumption – A Global Forecast", *Pulp and Paper International* (May 1983), p. 58.
4. Kenneth R. Farrell, Fred H. Sanderson, Trang T. Vo, and Michael F. Brewer, "Meeting Future Needs for United States Food, Fiber and Forest Products", in Joint Council on Food and Agricultural Sciences, *Reference Document: Needs Assessment for Food and Agricultural Sciences* (Washington, D.C., 1984).
5. *Ibid.*
6. John Spears and Edward S. Ayensu, "Sectoral Paper on Forestry", background paper prepared for the conference The Global Possible: Resources, Development and the New Century (Washington, D.C.: World Resources Institute, 1984).
7. Claes G. Hall, "Brazil and Its Economy – A Few Highlights" (mimeo, 1984).
8. Raymond R. Pinard, "The Forest Industry: Main Driving Force of Quebec's Industry", 1983–84 Hautes Études Commerciales Lectures (Montreal: DOMTAR, 1984).
9. Canada, Department of Regional Industrial Expansion, "Canadian Forest Product Industries: Vol. 1, An Assessment of the Pulp and Paper Industries; Vol. 2, An Assessment of the Lumber and Panel Industries" (Ottawa: The Department, 1984).
10. Economic Council, *Western Transition*, p. 45.
11. Department of Regional Industrial Expansion, "Canadian Forest Product Industries".
12. F.L.C. Reed and Associates Ltd., "Recent Reductions in the Canadian Timber Base", in Proceedings of the Canadian Forest Congress, Toronto, 1980, Appendix 4, p. 171.
13. Canadian Forestry Service, *Selected Forestry Statistics* (Ottawa, 1984).
14. Science Council of Canada, *Canada's Threatened Forests* (Ottawa: The Council, 1983).
15. Canadian Institute of Forestry, Brief, October 31, 1983, p. 8.
16. Economic Council, *Western Transition*, p. 53.
17. Association of British Columbia Professional Foresters, Brief, September 23, 1983, p. 7.
18. See Barry Sadler, ed., *Canada's Forests: Transition to Management*, proceedings of the National Resources Conference 1981 (Banff: Banff Centre, School of Management, 1982), p. 103.
19. Science Council, *Canada's Threatened Forests*, p. 12.
20. *Ibid.*

Fisheries

Profile

Fishing is Canada's oldest industry. Portuguese boats were visiting the bountiful Grand Banks regularly by 1450, a half century before the lands of what we now know as Canada were officially "discovered". Today Canada is the world's largest exporter of fish, although the total Canadian catch represents just 2 per cent of the world total. The catching and processing of fish contributed nearly $1.3 billion to Canadian gross domestic product (GDP) in 1982 and employed 100 000 people.

There are three separate fisheries in Canada. The largest, the Atlantic coast fishery, accounted for 82 per cent of total tonnage and 71 per cent of total value of output in 1983. The catch is dominated by groundfish, mostly cod, and by luxury species of shellfish, in particular scallops and lobster. On the Pacific coast, the catch consists largely of herring, most of it destined for the Japanese roe market, and of highly valuable salmon. Though the commercial catch of freshwater fish in Canada is small in relation to the catch of marine fish, it is by no means insignificant. In 1983, it accounted for 3.6 per cent by weight and nearly 5.5 per cent by value of Canada's total fisheries harvest. Freshwater fisheries are especially important to Native communities throughout Canada.

Approximately 80 per cent of Canada's total annual fish catch is exported. Table 12-9 shows that our largest customer is the United States, followed by the countries of the European Community (EC) and Japan. Although we rank first in value of exports in world markets, earning nearly $1.6 billion in 1984, our shipments make up only about 8 per cent of total value of trade in fish products. As a result, most of the Canadian industry has little market power in world fish markets; the exception is the British Columbia roe-herring industry. Control of markets for Canadian fish generally lies in the hands of American buyers.

TABLE 12-9 Canadian Fish Products Exports 1975–84

	1975–76	1983–84
Average annual value of exports (current dollars)	$459 million	$1 559 million
Percentage of total Canadian exports	1.4	1.4
Distribution of trade (%)	**1976**	**1984**
United States	67.9	60.9
Japan	1.7	14.8
European Community	18.3	13.2
Other	12.1	11.1
	100.0	100.0

Sources: Statistics Canada, *Summary of External Trade* (December 1976 and December 1984), Cat. No. 65-001 (Ottawa: Minister of Supply and Services Canada, 1977, 1985).

Fishing and fish processing provide only 0.4 per cent of Canada's GDP and employ approximately 1 per cent of our labour force. In British Columbia, the fishery accounts for less than 2 per cent of total employment. In the Atlantic region, however, fishery employment ranges from nearly 3 per cent of the labour force in New Brunswick to 20 per cent in Newfoundland. More than one-quarter of the total population of the Atlantic provinces lives in 1339 small fishing communities. At least half of these communities have essentially single-sector economies in which fishing and processing plants employ 30 per cent or more of the labour force.[1] These facts highlight the cultural, economic, and community significance of the fishing industry throughout the Atlantic region. As the President of the Canadian Saltfish Corporation stated at this Commission's hearing in St. John's:

> *In terms of Canada's GNP, [the fishery] is not of great consequence in total figures. In terms of the social and political and economic realities of Newfoundland, it is of tremendous significance. That must be recognized.*
>
> (Bill Wells, Transcript, St. John's, September 21, 1983 [vol. 12], pp. 2821–22.)

Prospects

The United Nations' Food and Agriculture Organization (FAO) has projected that the global demand for fish protein in 2000 could be more than double the demand in 1980 if relative prices for fish were to remain stable. It expects the demand for fish (and for food commodities generally) to expand most rapidly in the developing nations.[2]

If recent growth in the world catch is any indication of future supplies, we can anticipate a global shortfall by 2000. The world fishing industry experienced a dramatic decline in the rate of growth in landings during the 1970s. Throughout the 1950s and 1960s, the total saltwater and freshwater catch grew at an average annual rate of almost 6 per cent, from 22 to 71 million tonnes, but since the mid-1970s, the ocean catch has grown at a rate of about 1 per cent per year. The freshwater harvest in 1981 was 12 per cent lower than the harvest in 1970. The main reason for the decline is simply that global fish stocks are limited: some species are already over-fished and others are nearing that point. The dramatic reduction in 1973 of the Peruvian anchoveta harvest, from 13 million to 1.7 million tonnes, was the result both of over-fishing and of a great drop in the supply of plankton in 1972. This catch is still at least 80 per cent below the catch in 1970.

In Canada, too, over-fishing caused a severe decline in landings for some species in the 1970s. The greatest declines were in the Atlantic coast's gulf-herring fishery and in the catches for some types of Pacific salmon. The rebuilding of stocks has begun, but problems remain. Gulf herring is coming back only very slowly. In British Columbia, the management of salmon stocks is increasingly complicated by the effects on upstream spawning areas and downstream transit areas of forestry, irrigation, flood control, hydroelectric power generation, pollution, and urban and industrial development. Effective salmon-fishery management requires a highly sophisticated and carefully co-ordinated management plan for entire river basins. This represents an expensive and a politically sensitive undertaking, not least because it involves both the federal government and the province.

On balance, however, the volume of most Canadian fish stocks, if effectively managed, should be more than sufficient to reach predicted levels of future domestic and export demand. Although the biological limits of prudent harvesting have been reached, or nearly reached, for some stocks, other stocks are still well above their equilibrium populations. Cod landings are expected to increase by perhaps 75 per cent over 1982 levels by 1987, and the potential for yield increases in some salmon stocks is also very large.[3] Other potentially commercial stocks – redfish and Greenland halibut, for example – are now only lightly fished because of persistent weakness in traditional markets. Thus, while dwindling supplies constitute the long-term problem for the world as a whole, the principal problem for Canada, particularly in the next decade, is how to secure access to foreign markets and deliver the product to meet the quality and taste features demanded. For a few important high-value species such as scallops, lobster and Pacific roe herring, there is no shortage of demand. One intervenor described the situation as follows:

> *I think that fish, unlike the forest industry and the agriculture industry in Atlantic Canada still has considerable growth potential . . . The problem in the Atlantic fishery tends to be more a superabundance of fish and an inability to market it profitably, than it is a threat to the resource.*
>
> (Peter J. Nicholson, Transcript, Halifax, June 5, 1984 [vol. 5], pp. 1166–67.)

The potential for expansion in the Canadian market is relatively small. Our annual consumption of fish is very low – less than 7 kilograms per capita – but amounts vary substantially across regions. Domestic consumption amounts to about 20 per cent of domestic production. In the future, it is very unlikely to rise enough to match potential expansion in output; however, better distribution, particularly to regions with below-average per capita consumption, would improve the delivered product and increase consumption. Higher volumes of exports are the only viable solution.

The United States is Canada's largest export market. However, fish accounts for only 5.5 per cent of American consumption of animal protein. Groundfish, including cod, the major source of Canada's anticipated growth in supply, accounts for only 1.7 per cent. In order to absorb the anticipated expansion in Canadian cod output, Americans would have to increase their consumption of fish by one pound per capita, or about 7 per cent. If prices for fish products increase only modestly in the future, consumption may increase, and the development of new fish products might attract new buyers. In addition, a substantial and sustained advertising program could help to shift consumer demand from red meats and chicken to fish products. Larger and more dependable supplies of good-quality fresh fish offer by far our greatest market opportunity. It should be noted, however, that Canadian fresh fish exports, particularly of cod, haddock, and flounder, face perennial protectionist agitation by segments of the American fishing industry, a factor that could constrain future exports.

Japan has provided an increasingly important export market for Canadian fish in recent years: its share of Canadian exports increased from less than 2 per cent in 1976 to 14.8 per cent in 1984. On the other hand, increases in exports to Europe are likely to be limited by tariffs and quotas that give the Scandinavian countries privileged access. Expanded market access for Canadian groundfish in Europe is important. The strategy of several European fishing nations appears to be to limit or deny Canadian access to the European market in order to force Canada to concede quotas inside the 200-mile zone. European freezer trawlers produce for the higher-value portion of the market, confining Canadian exports largely to salt cod and some frozen products.

If Canada is to increase its share of markets, domestic and foreign, it must build a reputation for superior quality and quality consistency, particularly in frozen groundfish products. In the past, a reputation for inconsistent quality has damaged our country's position in the world market to some degree. One result has been Iceland's capture of most of the "high quality" frozen cod market in the United States, although Canada has recently made encouraging strides towards gaining a share of this market. The Japanese and western European markets are extremely quality-conscious, and they have come to expect a number of products to possess a freshness that is possible only if the fish has been processed and frozen at sea.

Canadian fisheries policy has forbidden the use by our own fishermen of the freezer-factory trawlers that are routinely employed by the Japanese, the West Germans, the French, and, recently, the Americans. The purpose of the prohibition has been to protect on-shore plant employment, but this objective must now be weighed against the increasing cost of missed opportunities to diversify our markets and take maximum advantage of currently underutilized species. Unless we open significant new outlets for increased production, we can only expect continuing price depression in our traditional market, the United States, with the effect that the future of existing shore-based employment will remain precarious and confined to traditional species.

What of the rapidly growing markets for fish products in the developing nations? While there will certainly be some opportunities for increasing Canadian exports of fish to these markets, they will be limited by the perishability of the product, given current technology and delivery systems, and by the relative poverty of many of the developing countries.

Issues and Recommendations

The dominant theme of those who appeared before this Commission to discuss the fishery was one of missed opportunity. Many intervenors doubted the sector's ability to take full advantage of the great opportunities that do exist, and there was no hesitation in identifying where the problems lie:

> *The current crisis in our fishery is perhaps an excellent example of the economic enterprise allowed to flounder because of lack of management, innovation, productivity and market development.*
>
> (Sandy Cameron, Transcript, Halifax, October 13, 1983 [vol. 24], p. 4621.)

With the extension of jurisdiction, when [we] finally had a nation that was prepared and had the capability to control the resource, to husband it and farm it and then develop a pattern of harvesting production and marketing to take advantage of the resource, for the first time in 400 years of history, that opportunity presented itself and we completely blew it.

(Bill Wells, Transcript, St. John's, September 21, 1983 [vol. 12], p. 2824.)

Fishing has been the object of a series of inquiries that stretch back into the last century. Two recent inquiries undertaken by the Commission on Pacific Fisheries Policy (the Pearse Commission) and the Task Force on the Atlantic Fisheries (the Kirby Task Force) have identified the major problems facing the industry on each coast and have made many recommendations for reform. Much of the analysis that follows has been adapted from the reports of these bodies.[4]

Overcapacity

Overcapacity abounds in both the harvesting and the processing sectors of the fishing industry. There was a rapid increase in capital investment and employment in the fisheries just before and again after the introduction of the 200-mile limit in 1977. The increase was based on an expectation, encouraged by both the federal government and the interested provinces, that Canadians would now have access to greater fish stocks, and that export demand would increase as a result of the exclusion of foreign fleets. Notwithstanding its own dire warnings that the fishery resource could not sustain many of the grandiose schemes being proposed, the Department of Fisheries and Oceans permitted the number of licensed fishermen on the Atlantic coast alone to increase by 45 per cent between 1974 and 1981. Between 1977 and 1981, the number of east coast processing facilities, under provincial jurisdiction, but with financial encouragement from programs delivered by the federal government's Department of Regional Economic Expansion (DREE), rose by 35 per cent. In the same period, employment in the fishing sector on the Pacific coast increased by 37 per cent. On neither coast, however, did the anticipated export boom occur, although a few markets, such as the Japanese market for Pacific salmon, did create a market for increased Canadian exports. It is clear, in the circumstances, that expansion has been excessive.

The basic source of overcapacity lies in the common-property aspect of the resource. The lack of identifiable ownership of the fish stocks both encourages a higher than optimal number of participants to remain in the industry and provides an incentive for each participant to maximize potential catch through investment in gear. A more powerful vessel enables an individual fisherman to anticipate a larger share of a common quota. Since everyone reasons similarly, the result is a fleet of more powerful and more expensive vessels, without any increase in each fisherman's share of the quota. In some fisheries, the result of intensive competition for limited stocks has been a depletion of the resource. In most fisheries, the result is excess capacity and thus lower profitability. Appropriate regulation of the fisheries requires both allocation of the stock and prevention of overinvestment in gear on the part of individuals.

Overcapacity in processing plants also arises, unavoidably, from the seasonal nature of the inshore fisheries. Because plants are built to handle peak capacity and are idle for much of the year, profitability is lower than it would be in less seasonally oriented sectors. The seasonal peaking also strains quality control.

Possible solutions to the problem of overcapacity in the harvesting sector will be taken up below. As for overcapacity in the processing sector, the Kirby Report advances a number of recommendations aimed at increasing off-season use of processing facilities. These recommendations include the establishment of specific allocations for "resource-short" plants in the off-peak season, the freezing of a portion of the summer inshore catch for off-season processing, and the introduction of an intermediate-sized vessel, the so-called "Scandinavian longliner", that would be able to operate almost year round off the northeastern coast of Newfoundland.

Income

Another important issue in the Canadian fishing industry, one obviously related to overcapacity in the harvesting sector, is the generally inadequate level of income earned from fishing. In the Atlantic industry, in particular, many fishermen must supplement their income from fishing with income from other sources, of which Unemployment Insurance (UI) is the most important. In 1981, the average income of full-time east coast fishermen was approximately $16 000; 75 per cent of this amount was derived from fishing and 16 per cent from UI. In the smaller Pacific-coast fishery, the average fishing income was roughly twice as high. The difference was partly a result of the higher value of Pacific species such as salmon and roe herring.

The Pearse Report urges review of the Unemployment Insurance provisions for fishermen. Contributions to Unemployment Insurance by fishermen fall far short of benefits received, a situation that encourages participation in an overcrowded activity. The Pearse Commission found that because of the shortness of the fishing season for most fishermen, the contributions of west coast fishermen amount to less than 5 per cent of the benefits received. Furthermore, the criteria for eligibility for seasonal benefits can result in pressures to alter fishing periods in order to comply with UI requirements. Average weekly catches, which determine benefits, usually decline near the end of the season and so have the effect of reducing benefits. Naturally, the fishermen tend to quit early to avoid this penalty.

The Kirby Report proposes a scheme that would replace Unemployment Insurance for fishermen with new production-bonus and income-stabilization programs. The federally funded production bonus would consist of cash credits paid in the off-season and determined by criteria such as gross value of landings, fish quality, season of catch, and gear used. The gross-income/stabilization plan (based on a rolling five-year period) would be funded by the federal government and the participants in the program. The Kirby Report suggested that pilot projects be designed to test these ideas.

Commissioners' general recommendations about unemployment insurance appear in the section of Part V that deals with social support. Fishing

Benefits, however, constitute an entirely separate program, only 10 per cent of which is financed from premium contributions of fishermen and 90 per cent from consolidated revenues.[5] It is therefore more appropriately dealt with here.

This Commission believes that both the general economic foundation of the fishery and the ultimate welfare of those remaining in fishing will be better served if the fishing-benefits provision of the UI program is terminated and replaced by an income-stabilization scheme of the type recommended in the Kirby Report. The substitution of such a scheme was envisaged at the time of the 1971 amendments to the Unemployment Insurance Act, yet implementation has been repeatedly delayed by considerations very far removed from those of either efficiency or equity. After termination of Fishing Benefits, fishermen would be eligible not only for an income-stabilization scheme, but also for income supplementation under the Universal Income Security Program (UISP) proposed in Part V. Income from fishing and from the stabilization plan would be taken into account in determining UISP benefits. Consequently, lower-income fishermen would receive income support from UISP, while higher-income fishermen, many of whom now qualify for full UI benefits, would no longer receive assistance. The proposal would not reduce the total value of transfer payments to fishermen, but it would reallocate these funds according to criteria designed to promote more economically efficient behaviour.

Fleet Licensing and Allocation of Stocks

Both the Pearse and the Kirby Reports conclude that "quota licenses" or "enterprise allocations" are the preferred licensing practice where they are feasible. Quota licenses are similar to techniques used to regulate the use of other renewable resources (such as timber, water, and grazing land) in that the licence assigns a specific catch to each licensee. This system eliminates the basic cause of overcapacity (the common-property aspect of the fishery) and encourages participants to adapt their vessels and fishing methods in order to take the licensed catch at the lowest cost.

However, the effective use of quota licensing requires reliable information on fish landings. In addition, it is difficult to adjust quotas in fisheries where stocks fluctuate widely and unpredictably. These considerations preclude the use of quota licensing in the salmon and roe-herring fisheries. Consequently, the Pearse Report recommends the use of a revised limited-entry licensing system based on gear capacity in these two fisheries and a quota-licensing system in most other west coast fisheries. As noted above, the licensing procedure is an effective means of controlling fleet size. The Pearse Report recommends resort to a buy-back scheme to reduce the salmon and herring fleets by 50 per cent.

On the Atlantic coast, quota licensing is most feasible for trawlers longer than about 18 metres, for herring seiners, and for scallop draggers. Since the inshore fishery includes approximately 8000 smaller vessels, the monitoring of individual catches that a quota system requires would not be practical in this sector. It would be better to control the landings of inshore fishermen by setting a limit on the amount of gear that each fisherman is allowed to use. The Kirby Report advises that licences should not be transferable between inshore and offshore sectors, but that "enterprise allocations" should be divisible and tradable within sectors. Since the report was received, the enterprise-allocations scheme has been formally implemented throughout the Atlantic offshore-trawler fishery and, on an experimental basis, for boats in the 16- to 19-metre range on Newfoundland's western coast. The method has been well received by fishermen and has not produced any serious practical problems.

The issue of inshore versus offshore allocation of stocks is contentious. At present, the two fisheries share the total catch about equally. Because of the employment patterns, however, the Atlantic inshore fishery (estimated at 85 to 90 per cent of fishermen, including the mid-shore fleet) is seen as the "social" fishery, while the offshore fishery, which covers 10 to 15 per cent of employment, is considered more efficient economically. However, as the Kirby Report notes, there are many particular situations that reverse this pattern. For example, the inshore fishery of southwestern Nova Scotia has had more economic success than the trawler-based fishery on Newfoundland's southern coast. Ultimately, the economics are determined by the practical length of the fishing season, the cost of catching, the inherent value of the stocks available, and the number of fishermen sharing the landed value of the catch in any given region.

Since the 200-mile limit was set in 1977, the inshore and offshore sectors of the Atlantic fishery have been engaged in a tug-of-war for allocations of fish stocks. While the conflict is real, the terms used to characterize it are misleading. At stake is not the distance from land at which fish are caught, but rather the control of resource supply and the timing of its delivery to processors.

Integrated, trawler-owning companies (the offshore sector) have sought the security of a year-round fish supply. This purpose has led them to oppose the award of larger allocations to independent fishermen (the inshore sector), who are generally unable to deliver fish throughout the year because of environmental factors, that is, the weather and fish migrations, and who are not bound to deliver their catches to any particular plant. The seasonal peaking of deliveries from the inshore fishery also causes difficulties in marketing.

While the struggle between fleet sectors and between provinces for larger shares of the resource is bound to continue, its intensity is likely to abate. In the first place, the rate of quota growth has slowed substantially, which means that there is much less "new fish" to fight over. Moreover, it has finally become widely recognized that the preoccupation with larger and larger catches is inappropriate in light of limitations in the market. Again, following the Kirby Report, the Department of Fisheries and Oceans has divided all Atlantic groundfish quotas into inshore and offshore percentage allocations that have been guaranteed to remain fixed for at least five years. Canadians may hope that this arrangement has eliminated most of the remaining potential for "inshore/offshore" conflict, at least for the medium term.

International Considerations

Fisheries policy and management are subject to influence by a variety of factors in the international environment. Foreign (mainly European) governments continue to seek permission to fish, particularly for cod, within the Canadian 200-mile limit. As a rule, these governments back up their requests both with an offer to give Canada preferred access to their own markets and with a threat to close their markets to our fish products unless we accede to their request.

The Kirby Report recommends that Canada develop and expand its markets by conventional means, rather than by making allocations to foreign fleets in return for access to their markets. It also calls for re-examination of Canada's traditional hostility toward foreign investment in our fishery. Foreign investment could afford access to new markets and new technology, as well as to badly needed capital. Ultimate government control of the resource provides a measure of protection of sovereign interests that is not available in many other sectors of the economy. However, little capital, Canadian or foreign, will be forthcoming as long as the currently available technology is barred from the Canadian fishery and access to the United States market remains insecure.

Some of Canada's fishery-development and management problems, particularly in the Pacific salmon and halibut fisheries, arise from conflict between Canadian and American fishery policies and programs, both at the federal level and the state or provincial level. These problems demand the bilateral negotiation of politically sensitive issues and the successful administration of bilateral commissions, such as the International Pacific Salmon Fisheries Commission (IPSFC) and the International Pacific Halibut Commission (IPHC). In addition, because Canada is a major coastal nation, it is both our responsibility and in our interest to maintain an active role in the negotiation of international issues under the Law of the Sea. By and large, the effect on the Pacific fishery of the 1982 United Nations Convention on the Law of the Sea (UNCLOS), or the UNCLOS III "enclosure movement", has been to reinforce the vulnerability of Canadian fishery development and management to the vagaries of Canada-U.S. diplomacy and transboundary-management arrangements. Thus international pressures have reduced the Canadian halibut fishery. Some difficult diplomatic issues relating to the salmon fishery have been resolved: after 14 years of negotiation, the Pacific Salmon Treaty was signed in March 1985.

Aquaculture

Opportunities both for growth of supply and for reduction of seasonal unemployment in the fisheries may arise from the development of aquaculture (the raising of fish stocks within enclosures) and the culturing of shellfish. Salmon farming is in an early developmental stage in a few operations in British Columbia and on the Atlantic coast. The results so far are mixed, but many observers are optimistic about the future of these technologies.

Aquaculture has long been practised in Asia and Europe. Some European nations have now moved into aquaculture as a large commercial venture. In 1982, Norway and Denmark each produced about 20 000 tonnes of salmon and trout by aquaculture, a tonnage that Norway hopes to double shortly. In contrast, Canada's production by aquaculture of these two types of fish for 1982 was less than 800 tonnes. Oyster farming by Japan in 1982 amounted to about 250 000 tonnes, compared with Canada's 2000 tonnes.

The greatest advantage of aquaculture is that it enables producers to supply fresh fish of uniformly high quality on a regular basis. Aquaculture is also a means of providing alternate employment to some of the workers who withdraw from traditional fishing as excess capacity is reduced. Norway's aquaculture demonstrates both these features: it has at once moved strongly into European markets and provided direct employment (about 2000 person-years in 1983) in small seaside communities.

Aquaculture will probably be the area of greatest future growth in the world's fisheries. Like expenditure for basic agricultural and forestry research, expenditure for aquacultural research is not something that private producers undertake naturally. The amounts involved are too large, and the possibility of a direct pay-off is too small. Consequently, a substantial portion, but certainly not all, of the contribution must come from governments at both levels.

Employment, Efficiency, and Regional Development

Fisheries employment on both coasts is expected to decline over the next decade in response to reduction of excess capacity, modernization and rationalization. On the east coast, particularly in Newfoundland, these factors may be partly offset by greater production as cod stocks continue to increase over the next few years, but elsewhere the tendency is unambiguous. The challenge is to devise policies that will allow the number of people employed in the fishery to decline slowly. If the decline is gradual, it should be possible to ensure adequate incomes for those who remain and to develop other employment opportunities for those out of work. We deal elsewhere in this Report with adjustment assistance, and our recommendations there apply to the fisheries.

Fishery-policy issues in the Atlantic region have invariably had a political and cultural, as well as an economic, significance. Rationalization measures will unavoidably have implications for the coastal settlement pattern and for the rural way of life. It is difficult to envisage any formulation of fishery policy for the Atlantic coast that does not attempt to accommodate these concerns. Canadians have come to recognize the inevitability of balancing efficiency and social considerations. As Commissioners were told at our hearings:

> *This unique problem of, in some cases, a single industry dependence, and fluctuations in its economic environment can lead to social disruption and the constant debate between the industry's social goals and its economic efficiency.*
>
> (Fisheries Council of Canada, Brief, September 13, 1983, p. 4.)

The Kirby Report recognized this duality in setting out what it saw as two important objectives for the Atlantic fishery:

1. *The Atlantic fishing industry should be economically viable on an ongoing basis, where to be viable implies an ability to survive downturns with only a normal business failure rate and without government assistance.*
2. *Employment in the Atlantic fishing industry should be maximized subject to the constraint that those employed receive a reasonable income as a result of fishery-related income transfer payments.*[6]

The debate centres on the specific terms of the trade-off, that is, on the public cost implied by the trade-off in relation to both the resources of government and the values that Canadians assign to the preservation of certain traditions. Out of this implicit balance evolves a view of the proper role of government in fisheries policy and of the fishery in the social and economic development of the region.

There is little that this Report can add to the technical material already available in the reports of the Pearse Commission and the Kirby Task Force. We can only reiterate what is already obvious to many Canadians: that any change in fisheries policy is extraordinarily difficult to achieve because the industry has become inextricably bound up with regional development, employment policy and profound desires to preserve lifestyles and communities.

This Commission is convinced that Canadians are forgoing significant economic benefits from the fishing industry because of the way it is operated. The real issue may not be whether economic efficiency should override social objectives. Rather, it may be whether Canadians are prepared to implement the recommendations discussed in this section, applying the discipline required to facilitate adjustment and so attain a longer-term gain for both the "social" and the "economic" fisheries.

Conclusions

We Commissioners shall not attempt, at this point, to summarize the many recommendations we have referred to, but we shall make some suggestions which strike us as vital for the medium- and longer-term success of the Canadian fisheries. A secure access to export markets, particularly that of the United States, will require considerable attention. Quality and technological factors, including freezer ships, quality-related pricing, aquaculture, and less-perishable delivered products, will be important for the development of the fresh-fish and other markets.

Problems of overcapacity ought to be addressed along the lines of the Pearse and Kirby recommendations, a few of which are already being implemented to some extent. An income-stabilization scheme should replace the Fishing Benefits provision of the Unemployment Insurance program. The results of declining employment opportunities should be dealt with according to the proposals set out in Parts III, V and VI of this Report, where adjustment assistance and regional development are discussed.

Commissioners believe that if Canadians and their governments move in these directions, the fishery should continue to show potential for growth on a national basis. It should also have a pre-eminent part in preserving and enhancing the network of small communities of Canada's coastal regions.

Notes

1. Canada, Task Force on Atlantic Fisheries, *Navigating Troubled Waters: A New Policy for the Atlantic Fisheries* (Ottawa: Minister of Supply and Services Canada, 1982), p. 23 (Michael J.L. Kirby, Commissioner).
2. Food and Agriculture Organization of the United Nations, *Agriculture: Toward 2000* (Rome: FAO, 1981), p. 82.
3. See Task Force on Atlantic Fisheries, *Navigating Troubled Waters*, p. 49; and Canada, Commission on Pacific Fisheries Policy, *Turning the Tide: A New Policy for Canada's Pacific Fisheries* (Ottawa: Minister of Supply and Services Canada, 1982) (Peter H. Pearse, Commissioner).
4. Commission on Pacific Fisheries Policy, *Turning the Tide*; and Task Force on Atlantic Fisheries, *Navigating Troubled Waters.*
5. The financing for the national UI program is split 25/75, on average, when unemployment approximates 10 per cent; that is, 25 per cent is paid from consolidated revenue, and 75 per cent is paid from premiums. Fishermen represent an anomoly in the UI program, since many are self-employed and thus have no "employer contribution". The proportion of UI benefits paid from consolidated revenue would naturally tend to be higher than the national average.
6. Task Force on Atlantic Fisheries, *Navigating Troubled Waters*, p. 60.

Minerals

Profile

In the period leading up to the First World War, railway construction and the discovery of new deposits led to the establishment of the first permanent mining communities in Canada. These were places such as Glace Bay, founded in 1901; Kimberley, in 1892; Thetford Mines, in 1892; and Timmins, in 1912. In the 1920s, improved exploration and mining techniques, coupled with a sharp increase in the demand for minerals, stimulated more development. The greatest growth in mining occurred during the 25 years after 1945, and it was in those years that Canada attained its present prominence in the international minerals trade.

Table 12-10 shows Canada's output, our share of world output, and our rank among world producers for 14 major minerals (excluding oil and gas) in 1973 and 1983. For all of these minerals, except coal, Canada is among the top seven producing nations in the world. Overall, we are the world's largest exporter of minerals, selling over 80 per cent of our total production abroad. Nevertheless, Canada has not had for some time, and cannot now expect to have, much market power in mineral resources, with the possible exception of nickel. Competition from new sources has substantially reduced Canada's share of world production for several minerals. Between 1973 and 1983, nickel's share slipped from about 42 per cent to 19 per cent, asbestos slipped from about 42 per cent to 20 per cent, and silver dropped from over 16 per cent to less than 9 per cent. Smaller, but by no means trifling, declines occurred in our production shares for copper, zinc and lead. Only in the production of potash and sulphur has Canada's role increased significantly in recent years. Representatives of the Quebec mining industry told this Commission that:

> *The situation of the mining industry in Quebec is particularly gloomy. Over the past 10 years, copper production has dropped by 36 per cent, zinc production by 54 per cent, and asbestos production by 56 per cent. The production of iron ore has decreased by 25 per cent in the last five years. Only the production of gold has increased—by 145 per cent—in the course of the last decade.*
>
> (*Association des mines de métaux du Québec Inc.*, Transcript, Quebec City, October 25, 1983 [vol. 33], p. 6415.)

While Canada sells minerals to more than 100 countries, in 1983, Canada's most important foreign customers were the United States (60 per cent of exports), the European Community (15 per cent), and Japan (7.5 per cent). In 1983, the metallic and non-metallic minerals (excluding hydrocarbons) that brought the largest export revenues were aluminum, copper, iron ore, potash, nickel, zinc, asbestos, molybdenum and lead, in that order.

The minerals industry has played a pivotal role in the economic and regional development of our country. Today, the mining industry dominates economic activity in some 140 communities in every part of Canada,[1] although those employed directly in mining account for less than 2 per cent of the labour force. In value of mineral production (excluding hydrocarbons), Ontario ranked first among the provinces in 1984; it was followed by Quebec, British Columbia, Saskatchewan and Newfoundland.

TABLE 12-10 Canadian Production and World Rank of Major Minerals

Minerals	Canadian Production 1983 (1973)	Share of World Production 1983[a] (%) (share in 1973)	Canadian Rank in 1983[a] (rank in 1973)	Major Producers 1983 (rank)
Iron ore (mine production)	33.5 million t[b] (47.5 million t)	4.5 (5.7)	7 (4)	U.S.S.R. (1) Brazil (2) Australia (3) China (4) India (5) U.S.A. (6)
Copper (mine production)	653 000 t (824 000 t)	7.6 (11.3)	4 (3)	Chile (1) U.S.S.R. (2) U.S.A. (3) Zambia (5)
Nickel (mine production)	125 000 t (249 000 t)	19.1 (42.5)	2 (1)	U.S.S.R. (1) Australia (3) New Caledonia (4) Cuba (5)
Zinc (mine production)	988 000 t (1 226 000 t)	16.5 (22.4)	1 (1)	U.S.S.R. (2) Australia (3) Peru (4) U.S.A. (5)
Lead (mine production)	272 000 t (342 000 t)	7.3 (10.0)	4 (4)	U.S.S.R. (1) U.S.A. (2) Australia (3) Peru (5)
Gold (mine production)	73 512 kg (64 650 kg)	5.1 (4.7)	3 (3)	South Africa (1) U.S.S.R. (2) China (4) USA (5)
Silver (mine production)	1 197 t (1 477 t)	8.9 (16.3)	5 (1)	Mexico (1) Peru (2) U.S.S.R. (3) U.S.A. (4)
Molybdenum (Western world)	10 194 t (13 785 t)	16.7 (16.5)	4 (2)	Chile (1) U.S.A. (2) U.S.S.R. (3) Mexico (5)
Aluminum[c] (primary metal)	1 094 000 t (941 500 t)	7.6 (7.5)	3 (4)	U.S.A. (1) U.S.S.R. (2) West Germany (4) Norway (5)
Asbestos	858 000 t (1 690 000 t)	20.3 (41.5)	2 (1)	U.S.S.R. (1) South Africa (3) Zimbabwe (4) Brazil (5)

TABLE 12-10 (cont'd.)

Potash (K_2O equivalent)	6 294 000 t (4 453 000 t)	23.6 (19.9)	2 (2)	U.S.S.R. (1) E. Germany (3) W. Germany (4) France (5)
Sulphur (elemental)	6 631 000 t (4 168 000 t)	17.9 (14.5)	2 (2)	U.S.A. (1) U.S.S.R. (3) Poland (4) France (5)
Uranium[d] (U concentrates)	6 823 t (3 661 t)	19.2 (18.7)	2 (2)	U.S.A. (1) South Africa (3) Namibia (4)
Coal	44 787 000 t (20 473 000 t)	N.A.	N.A.	N.A.

Sources: Canada, Energy, Mines and Resources Canada, *Canadian Minerals Yearbook*, 1973, 1983, (Ottawa: Minister of Supply and Services Canada, 1975, 1984), Table 8, and *The Canadian Mineral Industry, Monthly Report* (January 1985), Table 3.

Note: N.A. = Not available. Canada does not rank in the world's top ten coal producers. The top five producers are the United States, the Soviet Union, China, Poland, and West Germany.

a. Preliminary figures.

b. t = tonnes.

c. Shipments rather than production.

d. Western world only.

As Table 12-11 shows, employment in metal and non-metal mining increased steadily in the 1960s to include about 87 000 persons by 1970. The 1970s saw fluctuations in metal-mining employment, but overall, mining employment in 1980 was the same as it had been in 1970. The recession of 1981–82 caused a significant shrinkage in mining employment. The job total had fallen below 79 000 by 1982, the lowest level since the mid 1960s. Certain regions, such as Quebec-Labrador and Yukon, were particularly hard hit. Employment in mineral-manufacturing industries grew more steadily between 1960 and 1980, reaching 180 000 in the latter year. The recent recession had an impact here, too: by 1982, the job total was 161 000.

Market structure in the minerals sector is dominated by a few multi-national corporations that often set prices among themselves in an oligopolistic style, and pre-empt the market through vertical integration and long-term contracts. For instance, the world prices for aluminum, asbestos, sulphur, uranium, and potash are set by multi-national corporations, as are the American, Canadian and South American prices for copper and zinc, and the European price for zinc. Because of weak demand, oligopolistic pricing of nickel and molybdenum has not been possible. Long-term contracts are very important for copper, iron ore, coal, manganese, bauxite, aluminum, and uranium.

TABLE 12-11 Number of Persons Employed in the Minerals Sector

	Mining-Industry Employment 1961–82[a]						
	1961	**1966**	**1970**	**1976**	**1980**	**1981**	**1982**
Metals	58 591	61 670	66 590	68 269	66 118	68 712	61 503
Non-metals	16 238	18 734	20 660	21 334	21 440	20 574	17 171
Total	74 829	80 404	87 250	89 603	87 558	89 286	78 674
	Mineral-Manufacturing/Industry[b] Employment 1963–82[a]						
	1963[c]	**1966**	**1970**	**1976**	**1980**	**1981**	**1982**
Primary metal industries	91 621	110 303	116 545	117 041	126 450	125 168	113 215
Non-metallic mineral products industries	44 487	51 144	49 428	55 021	56 086	55 269	47 949
Total	136 108	161 447	165 973	172 062	182 536	180 437	161 164

Source: Canada, Energy, Mines and Resources Canada, *Canadian Minerals Yearbook 1970, 1975, 1984–85* (Ottawa: Minister of Supply and Services Canada, 1972, 1977, 1985), Statistical Summary.

a. Includes production, administrative and office workers. Excludes fuels, except for petroleum refining.

b. Includes metal rolling, casting, iron foundries, iron and steel mills, cement, lime and clay products, glass manufacturing, petroleum refining.

c. Figures for 1961 are unavailable.

World output of most minerals grew rapidly during the 1950s and 1960s. In the same period, average prices declined. In the 1970s, however, growth in output fell sharply, while prices reversed their long decline and underwent a significant rise. The price increases of the 1970s were not caused by a failure to provide new reserves, for reserves continued to swell. They were caused, in part, by the sharp rise in the price of oil during the 1970s, since energy cost is a sizeable factor in the cost of minerals production. Rising concern about the environmental and health hazards associated with the production of minerals has also resulted in higher costs for producers.

Prospects

Commissioners encountered a wide range of views about the future prospects for Canada's mining industries. Some intervenors were quite optimistic:

> *This isn't the end of the world for the mining business. We have properties of merit [for example,] . . . Canada is very rich in potential. God, we are one of the richest countries in resources in the world!*
>
> (Falconbridge Limited, Transcript, Sudbury, October 20, 1983 [vol. 31], p. 5993.)

Many others were decidedly more pessimistic:

> *As many of you know, the mining industry in Canada is experiencing its most severe economic downturn since the 1930s. This malaise, however, is not merely the result of cyclical metal markets or the deep recessions that have affected most western economies. It is attributed also to the deep-seated changes that have taken place in international metal markets.*
>
> *The last several years have seen rising energy costs which have the twin effects of raising production costs for most industrial manufacturing operations and of reducing the consumption growth rate for most base metals.*
>
> *In addition, many mineral producers have remained in the market largely as a result of subsidies or other support they receive from their respective countries. The outcome of all this is heightened competition . . .*
>
> (Prospectors and Developers Association, Transcript, Regina, November 24, 1983 [vol. 51], p. 10746.)

> *Canada ranks third amongst the world's mineral producing countries; but while it is still the largest producer of several minerals, its market share is slipping badly, and the world mineral market in which it shares is a stagnant or contracting one.* (BP Selco Inc., Brief, December 14, 1983, p. 4.)

Generally, the sentiment seemed to be that while there is genuine cause for concern, mining is not a "sunset" industry; it can be improved if both government and the private sector take the appropriate steps:

> *Contrary to common perception, we do not have a very rich mineral endowment by world standards . . . What we do have in Canada is a mineral endowment that is ample enough, given the application of Canadian exploration and mining skills and a supportive governmental environment, to continue to generate new wealth for most of Canada's less advantaged regions.*
>
> (BP Selco, Brief, December 14, 1983, pp. 8–9.)

Opinion varied, however, about whether the problems we face are endemic to the industry as a whole or apply only to particular commodities. Inco Limited told us that "whatever ails the copper industry, ails to various degrees our Canadian mining companies" (Inco Limited, Transcript, Thompson, October 19, 1983 [vol. 30], p. 5808), but the Canadian Chamber of Commerce tended to the second view:

> *Within the mining sector there are going to be some areas where obviously we are going to have a very rough time. Copper is certainly one. But there are others where we have an edge, and where in regard to our productivity, we believe that we can compete. And potash, coal and . . . zinc, as well, where we have the majority production in the world in the developed countries.*
>
> (Canadian Chamber of Commerce, Transcript, Hull, December 14, 1983 [vol. 70], pp. 14861–62.)

The present problems of the Canadian mining industry are largely the result of three inseparable factors: the recent recession, structural changes in world production and trading patterns, and technological change. The impact of the recession on world mineral consumption was dramatic. Like other major producers, Canada found itself saddled with large excess reserves and unused capacity in virtually every mining sector. World consumption of some minerals has yet to return to the peak levels of a decade ago.

Structural changes in world mineral markets began to have a noticeable effect at the same time that the world economy slowed down. Thus, the maturation of industry in Western countries has resulted in a decline in the intensity of metals use, a trend not offset by high rates of economic growth in some industrializing countries. Other factors of change are the entry of new producing countries in particular mining sectors; the substitution of plastics, ceramics and even glass for copper, steel, lead and nickel; the substitution of one metal, such as aluminum, for another, such as copper or nickel; the development of new uses for some metals, such as the use of copper for solar heating and air-conditioning; reduction in demand, as cars become smaller, for iron and steel, zinc, copper, nickel and lead; a reduction in demand for lead and asbestos because of their threat to health; and more recycling of metals. On balance, these changes suggest that one of the main challenges to the world mining industry will be to develop and market new uses for its output.

The more recent the projections of demand growth and price increases, the more modest they tend to be. Nearly all studies completed before 1980, or even before 1982, now look unrealistically high. The September 1984 projections from the World Bank, shown in Table 12-12, suggest that in general, world demand for minerals will grow much more slowly over the next decade than it did during the two decades before 1973, although not quite as slowly as it grew between 1973 and 1980. The World Bank expects the greatest growth in demand to occur in the developing nations. These countries, however, may not provide a market sufficient to absorb a large expansion of exports from the mining sector of developed countries such as Canada.

As for prices, the future is mixed. Column 6 of Table 12-12 presents the World Bank's predicted rates of real price change over the next decade. Only the prices for lead and potash are expected to rise from their 1983 levels by 1990. The World Bank anticipates some recovery in real prices after 1990 for all the minerals listed, except iron ore and potash; even so, only copper, aluminum, and zinc are expected to reach prices even modestly above the 1981 levels by 1995. In general, then, the next decade promises prices for minerals that are not much different, on average, from the prices that were obtained before 1970.

What do these projections imply for specific Canadian minerals? It seems clear that a number of metal-mining, smelting, and refining industries are under considerable competitive pressure. This is particularly true of industries that depend on copper, which is losing many of its traditional markets to other materials. As for nickel, even though Canada is the lowest-cost producer in the world, subsidized protection in less-developed countries (LDCs) and among members of the Council for Mutual Economic Assistance (COMECON) means that excess capacity and depressed prices will likely be characteristic of this industry for years to come. Canadian production costs have declined substantially in recent years, but even with the Canadian dollar below $.75 U.S. our costs are still somewhat above prevailing world prices.

TABLE 12-12 Global Projections of Demand

	Demand Growth Rate (% per year) by Economies				Real Price Changes	
Minerals	Industrial	Centrally Planned	Develop- ing World		(1983/1981) x 100	1984 Projection (% per year)
Iron-ore[a]					102.5	
1983–90						−1.12
1990–95						0.00
1985–95	0.1	1.1	5.3	1.0		
Aluminum[b]					107.1	
1983–90						−0.75
1990–95						0.79
1985–95	2.6	2.0	4.7	2.9		
Copper					95.8	
1983–90						−0.14
1990–95						1.72
1985–95	0.9	2.1	3.4	1.6		
Nickel[c]					97.8	
1983–90						−0.22
1990–95						1.69
1985–95	1.6	0.7	3.6	1.5		
Zinc					94.6	
1983–90						−0.22
1990–95						1.69
1985–95	2.2	1.9	3.1	2.3		
Lead					61.3	
1983–90						3.21
1990–95						0.63
1985–95	0.7	2.6	3.0	1.6		
Potash					60.6	
1983–90						5.75
1990–95						0.00
1985–95	1.6	3.1	4.6	2.8		

Source: World Bank, "Price Prospects for Major Primary Commodities" (Washington, D.C.: World Bank, Economics and Research Staff, 1984), Vol. I, II, IV.

a. Projected growth rates for gross imports (1985–1995).

b. U.S. producers' list prices are used.

c. Merchant market prices as published by *Metals Week* are used.

Lead has lost a significant portion of its traditional market through the discontinuation of its use in paint and the decline in its use in gasoline. The most important market for lead, accounting for about 50 per cent of sales, is the lead-acid battery industry. To date, no substitute for the lead-acid battery has appeared, although the down-sizing of cars has reduced demand for the metal. Zinc sales depend greatly on zinc's use in steel alloys. Thus the degree to which improved steels, such as the new High Strength Low Alloy and Dual

Phase steels, can compete successfully with plastics and other new materials that are encroaching on steel's traditional markets will affect not only the iron and steel industry, but the zinc industry as well.

Projections for iron ore forecast a surplus on world markets until the early 1990s, primarily because of decreasing demand for steel. This chronic overcapacity suggests that high-cost producers, including those in Canada, may face financial difficulties. Inco Limited told this Commission that "Australia and Brazil alone could satisfy the world's iron-ore requirements for more than 50 years at current rates of consumption." (Inco Limited, Brief, October 11, 1983, p. 7.)

Canada's share of world aluminum production has risen modestly over the last decade, largely because our electric power is relatively cheap. Moreover, in contrast with most of its competitors, the Canadian industry is opening new energy-efficient plants. Consequently, the future of aluminum production in Canada appears quite satisfactory.

Gold is the major focus of exploration and development activity in the Canadian mining industry at this time. In 1983, 70 per cent of all new capital investment in mining was directed to gold production.[2]

Canada produced 19 per cent of the Western world's total output of uranium in 1983. We may soon replace the United States as the world's leading producer. At present, Canada generates only 11 per cent of its electricity with nuclear power. This figure is expected to increase to 19 per cent in 1990 and to 22 per cent in 2005.[3] Although domestic use of uranium will increase, Canada will require only about 15 per cent of domestic uranium production for its own use.

The difficulty, in the short term at least, will be to find markets for our own surplus output in a world which tends to over-supply. Since, over the next few years, the United States is expected to account for about half of the non-communist world's requirements for uranium which is not already covered by domestic production or long-term contracts, new sales to that nation are important.[4] Over the years, moreover, American producers have attempted to embargo Canadian uranium imports through Congressional action. So far, as with timber, these efforts have been unsuccessful. The next-most-important market for new sales is Western Europe, where the Canadian product is already well represented.

Both of these obstacles to uranium production and export may prove to be temporary. Nuclear power production in the Western world is expected to double over the next decade. It will probably do so even in the United States, where the growth of nuclear capacity has been retarded by cancellations and delays. In the long term, then, the value of Canada's uranium exports is expected to rise substantially.

For the four major non-metallic minerals – asbestos, potash, sulphur and coal – the outlook is mixed. The industry likely to face the most difficult time is asbestos, whose prospects are reduced by serious health concerns about its use. World demand for potash will grow substantially in the longer term, although there will be excess supply for the next few years. Saskatchewan has the largest and lowest-cost reserves of potash, and it will undoubtedly take a major place in world markets in the years ahead. It is expected that the province's potash production will rise by 7 per cent annually. The most likely markets for Saskatchewan's potash are the United States, China, India and Brazil.[5] An important question is whether Canada's potash industry should be content to suffer the ups and downs of a marginal supplier, or attempt to dominate markets through long-term contracts.

Most of the sulphur produced in Canada is a by-product of the natural gas industry. Sulphur is removed from the gas in order to "sweeten" it. World consumption of sulphur increased in 1983 and 1984 after a sharp drop in the United States and a smaller decline in Western Europe in 1982. In the short term, world consumption should exceed production. As a result, sulphur inventories in Canada should continue to decline and prices should rise. Natural gas-price deregulation in Canada is expected to result in increased production and sales of gas to the United States and consequently, in higher sulphur production.[6]

Coal reserves have a wider global distribution than those of most other minerals, and so international trade in coal is relatively limited. Metallurgical coal for steel making has long been the main world coal export. In recent years, however, trade in thermal coal – that is, coal burned to generate electric power – has been increasing as countries strive to diversify their energy supply sources. Meanwhile, growing efficiency in steel production and substitution of other materials for steel has reduced demand for metallurgical coal. The Canadian metallurgical coal industry, which still accounts for about 85 per cent of Canada's coal exports, is burdened with substantial excess capacity and faces numerous foreign competitors. Just as huge new developments came on stream in northeastern British Columbia in 1984, producers in southeastern British Columbia were shutting down some of their production. Projections of export demand suggest that it will not be necessary to develop much new capacity beyond what will become available during the mid-1980s. Nevertheless, the National Energy Board (NEB) predicts that exports will expand sufficiently to constitute 38 per cent of total demand for Canadian coal in 2005, compared with 29 per cent in 1983.[7]

Although Canadian coal costs at the minehead are generally in line with those in other producing countries, our costs of transportation over the long distances from minehead to port are relatively high. Thus Canadian thermal coal, in spite of its low sulphur content, is often at a noticeable cost disadvantage in European markets, relative to supplies from the eastern United States, Poland, South Africa and even Australia.

Japan is the nation with the largest appetite for imported coal. Canada holds a 15 per cent share of the Japanese market for metallurgical coal, and opinions vary as to whether the Japanese portion of Canadian exports will grow or decline. The future Japanese demand for coal imports from all countries is also uncertain. It may be necessary for Canadian producers and provincial governments to develop a united front in negotiating with Japan as their Australian counterparts are now doing. Japan is financing new mines in northeastern British Columbia and other places around the world. These developments are depressing the prices which all producers can get for their exports to that country.

The NEB expects Canadian demand for coal to grow about 2 per cent annually, on average, betwen 1983 and 2005. The mix of demand will remain about the same as it was in 1983, with electrical generation accounting for about 74 per cent. The share of coal in domestic electricity generation is projected to decline from 17.3 per cent in 1983 to 14.3 per cent in 2005. However, the total use of coal in terms of the energy it will provide (for electricity generation and all other uses) is expected to increase by 53 per cent by 2005.[8] It is often suggested that if Ontario Hydro were to buy more thermal coal from Canada's Western sources and less from the United States, the market for Western coal could be expanded. On efficiency grounds relating to transportation costs and energy value, it is more expensive to shift to Canadian sources. On the other hand, American coal has a higher sulphur content than Canadian coal and creates larger social costs in increased emissions. In sum, although growth in production and exports of coal will not match the rapid pace of the last decade, coal production should continue to expand.

Clearly, unless unforeseen changes occur on the world scene, it is unlikely that the Canadian mineral sector as a whole will soon – or, perhaps, ever – re-experience the buoyant conditions it enjoyed in the 1950s and 1960s. Some minerals, such as potash, aluminum and gold, will continue to do well. For many other minerals, however, gains will be harder to achieve than they were in earlier decades. If our Canadian industry is to maintain its current world market shares, that is, if it is to expand at the same rate, at least, as world demand, it will have to cope effectively with world competition.

Issues and Recommendations

World Marketing Issues

There are several important obstacles to the expansion of Canadian mineral exports. Many developing nations have used domestic subsidies and international aid to exploit their mineral resources. In spite of slack demand, these countries will continue to produce minerals and to export them, at subsidized prices if necessary, in order to maintain employment and to earn vital foreign exchange. There is some evidence that some COMECON nations are also following subsidized export strategies. Much of world trade in minerals is tightly controlled by governments: about 50 per cent of world copper trade and 40 per cent of nickel trade, for example.

Trade barriers, too, are often detrimental to Canada's minerals trade. Most developed countries grant preferential access to non-ferrous metals from most developing countries under a Generalized System of Preferences. In addition, some markets are difficult to enter because of special regional trade-and-aid arrangements, such as those the European Community maintains with former African colonies. Furthermore, many countries allow free entry to raw materials, but maintain high effective tariffs on processed minerals. U.S. protectionism is a threat to Canadian exports of steel, copper, uranium and, possibly, aluminum exports because of Canada's cheap and allegedly subsidized hydro-electricity rates.

Canada does bring some advantages to the competition for world minerals trade. Because Canada is a price taker, rather than a price setter, even a one-cent decline in the value of the Canadian dollar in relation to the U.S. dollar can give Canada a more competitive position or, alternatively, raise the profits of Canadian firms. If depreciation is to be helpful to the industry, however, a lower Canadian dollar must not simply result in offsetting increases in costs. Other factors that improve our position in world minerals trade are the country's political stability, a well-educated labour force, technological know-how, and developed transportation systems. These factors help to offset Canadian disadvantages, relative to many developing nations, of less rich deposits and higher wages.

Success in international markets will require renewed effort on the part of both the mining industry and our government. We can continue to be an important mineral-producing nation, but we cannot assume that this will come about naturally. We shall obviously need to maintain and secure access to international markets, but there are other, more specific measures that need to be taken as well.

Industry Performance

The biggest difficulty presently facing many Canadian mining companies is their financial predicament: specifically, their high ratio of debt to equity and hence their high interest costs. Although this ratio has been evident since the late 1960s, it reached serious proportions with the advent of very high interest rates and a world recession in the early 1980s. The debt-to-equity ratio rose from 0.60 in 1979–80 to 1.04 in 1982, and the cashflow-to-debt ratio dropped, during the same period, from 0.54 to 0.04.[9] This situation, however, was largely a result of the companies' own decision to shift their reliance from equity and long-term bonds to bank loans with floating interest rates. This decision apparently represented an attempt to prevent dilution of shareholders' equity and raise the return on this equity. It was not forced on the industry by any increase in its capital requirements: the ratio of capital to value added in mining actually decreased between 1941 and 1976.[10] Neither was it purely a consequence of economic recession, for the trend to greater dependence on debt financing has continued over several business cycles.

In the past, expenditure for research and development (R&D) in exploration, mining, smelting and refining techniques did much to keep the Canadian mining industry competitive. In recent years, however, only the aluminum industry has invested significantly in R&D for process innovation. In the other mineral sectors, R&D expenditure has been very small, nor is much work being done to develop new product uses for metals, a crucial need in light of the many substitutes for metals being introduced.

Many critics of mining management emphasize its inadequate and short-range view of corporate planning, which has led to rapid reversals of policy and erosion of longer-term cost and efficiency improvements; its lack of attention to market and product diversification; and its tendency to substitute higher pay for the appropriate development of human resources and employer-employee relations. Intervenors at this Commission's public hearings admitted to these problems:

> *The first onus is on the mining industry to put its house in order. (a) It must expand and make more efficient the exploration process in Canada ... (b) It must expand research into exploration and mining technologies ... (c) It must re-direct its efforts towards smaller, high grade, low cost mines ... (d) We must look for new markets and new applications for our projects.*
>
> (BP Selco Inc., Brief, December 15, 1983, pp. 16–17).

Thus, although many of the changes in world circumstances are beyond the control of Canadian firms, it would appear that the industry itself could do much to improve its performance. The industry should place less reliance on bank loans and more on equity capital, even if this step means that new shares are priced below book value. It should also pay more attention to employee relations and human resource development. While depreciation of the dollar enhances the international competitiveness of the Canadian mining industry, it is important that wage and executive-salary costs do not become unrealistically high. Finally, increased research and development would make the industry both more competitive and more environmentally sound.

Obviously these measures will not be efficacious in every case. We must accept the fact that some mines will face increasing difficulties over time, and we must be prepared to see them phased out, intervening to provide adjustment assistance only when necessary. Governments cannot, and should not, intervene to bail out failing operations. If a deposit is truly viable, the private sector can be counted on to refinance and reorganize the operation and resume production. If it is no longer profitable, we must let it go.

Taxation

A frequent theme in mineral industry representations to this Commission was the complaint that, in general, taxation of the industry is at once too high and of the wrong type. The industry argued that governments have failed adequately to recognize the cyclical nature of returns on minerals, particularly metals. Thus many of the tax measures now in place are based on a temporary improvement in profitability in the 1970s and the widespread assumption that there were very substantial economic rents to be collected by governments. In the present context, the effect of these measures is punitive.

Among the variety of views we Commissioners heard during our hearings were:

> *Value based royalties are inefficient because they arbitrarily reduce the net value of ore in the ground regardless of the price it can command. Dual tax jurisdictions resulting in a variety of anomalies and differing classifications are difficult to administer from the tax payer's point of view and have resulted in unduly high effective tax rates relative to profits.*
>
> (BP Selco Inc., Brief, December 15, 1983, p. 18.)

> *The principle of economic rents coming off the top as opposed to a residual is one the Commission should examine with respect to other mineral products as*

well as gas and oil. I happen to know of a situation currently where the fact that the economic rents come off the top is stifling a further investment and expansion in a mining industry in Canada which then provides advantages to world wide competitors.

(Dr. Lloyd Barber, Transcript, Calgary, June 19, 1984 [vol. 11], p. 2816.)

The two essential features of mineral resources are that they are limited in supply and that deposits vary in quality. If the revenue from the highest-cost source exploited (that is, the marginal source) equals the owner's costs for labour and materials, plus a normal return to the capital in use, then lower-cost sources will generate revenues in excess of the costs and the normal return. This surplus is called "economic rent".

Governments capture economic rents from non-renewable resources through leases, auctions, Crown corporations, regulation and taxes. Among the taxes that have been used to secure resource rents are those on the units sold or value of output (such as the Petroleum and Gas Revenue Tax), export taxes, property taxes, profit taxes and royalties. The prevalent form of royalty is a fixed levy on each unit of output.

Three factors need to be taken into account in any evaluation of a tax designed to capture resource rents: the efficiency aspects of the tax, its equity aspects, and its effect on government revenues. A tax introduces inefficiency into the pattern of resource use to the extent that it causes the resource to be allocated in a way that it would not be allocated in the absence of the tax. A tax that is expressed as a fraction of economic rent should not affect resource allocation. However, a tax per unit of output, which constitutes a gross royalty, can distort allocation by making it unprofitable to exploit deposits that, in the absence of the tax, would be profitable to exploit. If the royalty exceeds the potential rent from a deposit of a given quality, the producer will have no incentive to exploit that deposit. The royalty thus induces the producer to raise the cut-off grade and to reduce the amount of resource extracted in order to maximize profits. A number of provinces now permit the producers of many resources to deduct some operating and other costs from their royalty payments, an arrangement that reduces the cut-off/grade effect.

Taxes on returns to equity, that is, profit taxes, make no distinction between the normal return to the capital in use and the rent; consequently they generate some disincentive to efficient use of inputs, especially at high rates of taxation. In general, however, a profit tax reduces efficiency less than does a gross royalty system. Royalties are appealing to governments because they are easy to administer: the rate of tax is simply multiplied by the output of the producer. The computation of a tax on profits is more complicated, since allowances must be made for production costs. In some circumstances, moreover, the greater allocative efficiency associated with a profit tax can be a disadvantage: since a profit tax does not affect output, it does not favour conservation over extraction.

Because non-renewable resources are seen as society's property, taxing economic rents away from the producers does not violate any notion of equity. Nevertheless, it is difficult, in the absence of a conclusive definition of a "normal return to capital", to determine what proportion of the returns to the producer consists of economic rent. Even if this proportion could be determined to the entire satisfaction of producers and governments alike, gross royalties would not be an equitable way to extract the rent: because the royalty rate under a gross royalty system is uniform, firms with the same income can face different tax bills. A tax on profits is more equitable than a gross royalty system; so is a net royalty system, which allows the deduction of certain costs from gross royalties.

A royalty system is a more stable source of government revenue than a tax on profits. Profit taxes are paid only when an operation becomes profitable; they stop when losses are realized. Royalties, on the other hand, are paid on a continuous basis from the moment the operation begins. Moreover, profit taxes are affected by both changes in price and changes in output, while the amount of royalties paid depends on output alone (though output may fluctuate more under a royalty system than under a profit-tax system). The latter point is not necessarily an argument in favour of royalties: it may be that governments are better equipped than are firms to support cyclical variations in income.

The choice between the two tax systems depends, then, on the weights assigned to their respective costs and benefits. A profit tax has no effect on output; however, the higher the tax rates associated with a profit tax, the smaller the incentive to the firm to lower its production costs. A gross royalty system, on the other hand, is easier to administer than a profit tax and generates a steadier flow of government revenues; it also provides some incentive to resource conservation, which a profit tax does not. By the same token, a gross royalty distorts allocative efficiency to a greater extent than does a profit tax, and it might also be seen as less equitable.

Commissioners recommend that the federal government and the provinces collaborate in the establishment of a tax system that is more closely related to profits, while retaining a minimum gross royalty. After collection of a low-level gross royalty, taxes should be levied on profits rather than on output. For income-tax purposes, gross-royalty payments should be deductible from income. Exploration costs and other expenses necessary to bring properties to the stage where capital expenditures for production facilities become necessary should be deductible from current income, or it should be possible to carry them forward for deduction in future years. An amortized portion of capital expenditures, including property-acquisition costs, should also be deductible or carried forward.

Since minerals are a non-renewable resource, the provinces, as owners, are entitled to compensation. Royalties based on output have long been a part of the Canadian rent-collection structure and they should continue to be so. The argument has been made that to maintain a minimum gross royalty on non-renewable resources would ensure that some lower-grade ores will not be produced because they would not contribute to a profit. So be it: what is not produced now will be available for production in the future.

Regulation

Regulation ranked next after taxation in the list of the mining industry's concerns. Intervenors complained about the sheer number of regulations, the costs of complying with them, and the unpredictability with which they are implemented and then altered:

> *A further burden on our industry is the cost to us of the regulatory environment in which we are asked to operate. The Federal Government uses 25 different departments and agencies to administer 35 separate Acts and 78 separate sets of regulations which govern mining activities. This is largely duplicated at the Provincial level in each province in which we choose to operate.*
>
> *The costs of this are twofold. Not only do we incur the loss of productivity and direct costs of our side of the regulatory interface, but the sheer size and complexity of government means that there is no longer an effective government/industry interface.* (BP Selco, Brief, December 15, 1983, p. 8)

> *In the development stage government intervention can be a heavy burden. Assurances of stable regulation and security of tenure are essential in order to enable a company to finance the project and negotiate long term contracts for its product.* (Saskatchewan Mining Association Inc., Brief, October 25, 1983, p. 4)

This is not an area in which it is easy to make recommendations. It is understandable that the industry should find frustrating the multiplicity of boards, hearings and regulations. At the same time, it must be remembered that each of these interventions exists for a reason, however unreasonable the overall structure of intervention may sometimes seem. Many regulations are aimed at protecting the environment, and this is a purpose that Canadians generally support, for it is of critical importance in the long term. Many people argue, indeed, that even economic development is eventually threatened if the natural environment is not safeguarded. Other regulations seek special employment advantages for groups that have not always fared well in the minerals sector. Still others attempt to maximize the economic spin-offs to the province, region or municipality; again most Canadians support this practice in principle.

As Commissioners will point out below, in our review of environmental issues, a case can be made for imposing more and tougher environmental regulations. In general, however, we are sympathetic to the claim that the regulatory process for mining properties is cumbersome and slow, and that it is hampered by unnecessary duplication of regulations by different jurisdictions. Clearly, there is room for improvement. It would be helpful if governments were to sit down with industry representatives and relevant public interest groups and work out a mutually acceptable set of procedures. Companies must have reasonable assurance that they will face substantially the same regulatory environment over the lifetime of a planned investment. We urge governments to undertake a systematic review of their regulatory regimes affecting the mining industry, with a view to simplifying and streamlining them and to removing interjurisdictional duplication. Given the evidence that the industry will face a harsh competitive climate over the next 20 years, it is all the more important to undertake a review of this type now.

Conclusions

It is generally expected that average annual growth in demand for non-fuel minerals in the next two decades will run at less than half the rates attained since the close of the Second World War. Global structural changes and mineral substitution have left a legacy of surplus productive capacity that for Canada's non-ferrous metals may take five, ten or even more years to correct. The minerals industry is not without its bright spots, however: the outlook is encouraging for aluminum, potash, the precious metals and, perhaps, uranium.

In the minerals area, this Commission recommends that:

- After collection of a minimum royalty, taxation be based on profit rather than output
- Canadians take a more realistic attitude towards the economic adjustments that will be necessary. Commissioners have suggested that criteria be established for government intervention.
- Governments undertake a systematic review of their regulatory regimes with the intent of streamlining the processes.

Given suportive public policies, the minerals sector will remain a significant, if relatively declining, contributor to the Canadian economy in the forseeable future.

Notes

1. A 1979 DREE study identified 142 communities in which 30 per cent or more of the total labour force depended on metal and non-metal mining, smelting, and refining. See Task Force on Mining Communities, established by Federal, Provincial and Territorial Ministers with Responsibilities for Mining, *Report* (Ottawa, 1982).
2. Canada, Energy, Mines and Resources Canada, *Canadian Reserves as of January 1, 1983* (Ottawa: Minister of Supply and Services Canada, 1984), and *Canadian Mines: Perspectives from 1983* (Ottawa: Minister of Supply and Services Canada, 1984).
3. National Energy Board, *Canadian Energy: Supply and Demand 1983–2005*, Technical Report (Ottawa: NEB, 1984).
4. Noel O'Brien, "A Canadian Viewpoint on the Outlook for Uranium", paper presented at Mineral Outlook Conference, Ottawa, 1984 (Toronto: Denison Mines Limited, 1984).
5. Economic Council of Canada, *Western Transition* (Ottawa: Minister of Supply and Services Canada, 1984).
6. Canada, Energy, Mines and Resources Canada, *1983–84 Sulphur Review* (Ottawa: The Department, 1984).
7. National Energy Board, *Canadian Energy*, p. 95.
8. *Ibid.*, pp. 49 and 95.
9. Canada, Energy, Mines and Resources Canada, *Medium-Term Outlook for Minerals: A Preliminary View* (Ottawa: The Department, 1984).
10. Ralph Sultan, "Financing the Future", in *Financing Canadian Mining in the 1980s: Strategies for Action*, edited by David Yudelman (Kingston: Queen's University, Centre for Resource Studies, 1984).

Oil and Gas

Energy issues loom large in the affairs of most nations, and Canada is no exception in this respect. Over the last decade, energy policies have been the subject of protracted and sometimes rancorous debate among Canadian governments and between Canada's private and public sectors. Much of the rancour is now past, but many questions remain.

Retrospective

From Leduc to the National Oil Policy

Canada's modern oil and gas industry began with the discovery of Imperial #1 at Leduc, Alberta, in 1947. This find led to a basic re-evaluation of the geology of the Western Sedimentary Basin, and soon other oil and gas fields were discovered, most of them in Alberta, but some in Saskatchewan and British Columbia. Western Canadian oil needs were quickly met, and the search began for markets to absorb the surplus capacity. The Interprovincial Pipeline reached Manitoba in 1949. It was extended to Sarnia in 1953, and eventually, to Toronto. Another pipeline, the Transmountain, took Alberta crude oil through the Yellowhead Pass to Vancouver and Seattle. The pattern was repeated for natural gas. After much political debate, the Trans-Canada Pipeline was completed to carry natural gas to eastern Canadian markets. Westcoast Transmission brought gas from Alberta and the Peace River district of British Columbia to Vancouver and the northwestern United States.

Even with these pipelines in place, the Western oil and gas industry operated well below capacity. Pressure soon developed in the West for import restrictions that would reserve the eastern Canadian market for Western producers. The federal government referred this and other energy issues to the Royal Commission on Energy (the Borden Commission). Its report, issued in two parts in 1958 and 1959, set the stage for the next era in Canadian energy policy.

The National Oil Policy

The federal government announced the National Oil Policy (NOP) on February 1, 1961. Following the report of the Borden Commission, it drew the "Ottawa Valley Line", as it came to be known, west of Ottawa and along the Quebec-Ontario border. All oil purchased west of this "Borden line" had to come from western Canada. Quebec and the Maritimes, on the other hand, were allowed to continue to import lower-cost off-shore supplies. In exchange for a Canadian agreement not to restrict imports of Venezuelan crude, which was controlled in large measure by American companies, U.S. authorities agreed to open up the important Chicago market to Western producers. The National Energy Board (NEB) was created to oversee this marketing arrangement, and to monitor and approve natural gas-export contracts.

With the fillip of the NOP and the general economic expansion of the times, the Canadian oil and gas industry continued to grow. The main purchasers of crude oil in eastern Canada were a highly concentrated group of refiners, owned in large part by the same companies that supplied the oil and in some instances owned the pipelines through which it travelled. Alberta instituted a pro-rationing system in order to exert some influence on the price. Canadian oil prices were also affected at this time by the fact that Ontario prices were not to rise to the point where they encouraged the "smuggling" of refined products from Quebec. (They did rise to that point eventually, and "smuggling" did begin.) Import restrictions drove up prices in the United States, and gradually Canadian supplies to the Chicago market became cheaper than comparable U.S. deliveries. The net result of these influences was a remarkable stability in Canadian crude oil prices throughout the NOP years. This stability provides a vivid contrast with what was to come.

From 1971 to 1980

The Organization of Petroleum Exporting Countries (OPEC) had existed for some time before it was able to exploit its market power effectively. Growing international shortages and agreements between OPEC and the multi-national oil companies began pushing prices up in 1971, but it was the Arab-Israeli war in 1973 that led to a truly dramatic price rise. Canada, as a small importing *and* exporting country, was affected by these developments in two quite different ways. As an importer, we faced the same new economic burdens as other oil-importing nations. As an exporter, however, we found that our petroleum supplies had suddenly become much more valuable. Oil, which had been freely marketed at less than four dollars a barrel, was now to quadruple in price.

Because of geography and past marketing arrangements, losses were concentrated in one part of the country – central Canada, the Atlantic Provinces, and Manitoba – and gains in another – the three Western provinces. Westerners were able to view this assymetry without any great alarm, but Easterners and the federal government were not. Relative regional welfare levels rise and fall continuously in Canada as economic circumstances change, but this shock appeared to be too large and too sudden simply to ride out.

The situation facing Canadian policy makers was complicated. It was not clear exactly what was happening in world oil markets. Many analysts were predicting the imminent collapse of OPEC. There was understandable reluctance to force a costly adjustment to a situation that might well be reversed. Moreover, most of the economic rent that would result from moving Canadian prices to world prices, assuming that the world-price level was stable, would accrue, in the first instance, to multi-national oil companies with reserves and production in western Canada. Neither the provincial royalties in place nor corporate income taxes would capture more than a small portion of the windfall gain. Under the terms of the existing equalization scheme, the entitlements of the recipient provinces rose each time Alberta's revenues increased. Since even Ontario would soon become a "have-not" province under the formula, the potential drain on federal revenues was enormous. The Arab nations' embargo on oil exports, a consequence of the

Arab-Israeli war, emphasized the vulnerability to loss of supply of the market in Quebec and the Atlantic provinces. Serious doubts began to arise about the adequacy of our remaining reserves of oil and gas. We spoke of exhausting our reserves in 13 years, rather than in hundreds of years. Oil-price increases of the extent occurring in the world market would certainly add to what was already considered a serious inflation problem.

The National Oil Policy died in the fall of 1973. In September, as part of its anti-inflation program, the federal government temporarily froze the domestic price for Canadian crude at the then-current level of $3.80 per barrel. Export prices were to rise to the world level, and the federal government would collect as an export tax the difference between the Chicago price and the frozen Canadian price. Revenue from this surcharge would be used to subsidize the costs of importing OPEC oil into eastern Canada. The announcement in December of a single national price structure below world levels consolidated this policy.

The second part of the strategy was to address the threat of supply disruption in Quebec and the Atlantic provinces. The provinces and the federal government set up task forces to monitor the supply situation on a daily basis. Eventually, legislation was introduced to permit emergency allocation of supplies in the event of another disruption. While some shipments of western crude were made to Canada's east coast by way of the Panama Canal, the government's longer-term solution to the problem was an extension of the Interprovincial Pipeline to Montreal. Since the Western industry was already operating at capacity, supplies to Montreal had to be diverted from elsewhere. Thus crude oil exports to the United States were to be reduced to zero in 10 years. The NEB had already begun to adopt a more restrictive position on natural gas exports, and this policy was to continue as well.

As a short-term reaction to the situation and from a national perspective, the plan had much to recommend it. The reservation of domestic oil for domestic use did reduce the threat of supply disruption and decrease Canada's dependence on imported supplies. The price freeze provided some stability while the market power of OPEC was being tested. It also provided temporary insulation against the stagflation that was affecting other countries, although many would now argue that the approach was too gradual and of doubtful efficacy. As a rent-collection device, the package was superb. The export tax captured all of the economic rent on remaining shipments to the United States. The use of these receipts to subsidize oil imports into eastern Canada complemented the price freeze on domestic oil consumed west of the Ottawa Valley. Together, these measures spread the rent across the country and kept it from accumulating in the hands of the multi-national oil companies and the Western provincial governments. Since Alberta's revenues would not rise as rapidly as they would do in the absence of the freeze, equalization entitlements, and hence federal obligations, would not rise as rapidly either.

The problem with the 1973 program was that from longer-term and Western provincial government perspectives the measures were inappropriate. Freezing oil and gas prices for lengthy periods worked against the desired goal of energy self-sufficiency. Canadians continued to waste valuable petroleum supplies long after other nations were implementing conservation measures. Exploration and development, particularly development of frontier and non-conventional supplies, were not encouraged precisely when they were most needed. Canada's long-term energy requirements would not be met with $3.80-a-barrel oil. To Western Canadians, the policy seemed discriminatory. It addressed one energy sector and ignored others, such as hydro, although special arrangements were eventually made for synthetic oil plants.

Reaction in the producing provinces was immediate. In order to capture the economic rents and reassert their constitutional rights of ownership, the provinces scrapped existing royalty agreements and imposed a higher royalty based on a sliding scale. Much of what the provinces gained, the federal government lost, since the increase in companies' deductions for royalty payments reduced the income-tax base. The federal government responded, in 1974, by disallowing deductions of royalty payments for purposes of calculating corporate taxable income and ending a number of other long-standing tax breaks to the oil industry. The result was a squeeze on producer profits and a threatened flight of capital, whereupon both levels of government drew back somewhat. While the compromise did not restore the deduction for royalties, it provided a special "resource-allowance" deduction in its place. Overall, taxation of the industry was somewhat reduced.

The following six years provided a period of relative calm. Canadian oil prices moved in a series of steps toward the world level, and every adjustment but one was agreed to by both parties. (See Figure 12-4, below.) By 1978, the Canadian price was more than 80 per cent of the world price. The federal government, Alberta, and Ontario acted together to ensure that the Syncrude operation proceeded as planned. With the help of federal subsidies, the Interprovincial Pipeline was extended to Montreal. Ottawa implemented *ad hoc* revisions to the equalization formula to restrict entitlements arising from growing Western energy revenues.

In retrospect, it is clear that over these years Canadian energy policy was developing into a long-term strategy. It was also becoming less discriminatory toward regions. The question remained, however, whether this new rationality could stand the test of another dramatic increase in world oil prices.

The National Energy Program

The next chapter in the story of Canada's energy policy is a dramatic one. World oil prices doubled in 1979–80. The Canadian price dropped from 80 per cent of the world price in 1978 to 45 per cent by 1980. The 1973 energy-policy dilemma had to be faced anew. Economic efficiency suggested that Canadian prices should follow international prices upwards, and the producing provinces echoed this notion. But the federal government had as yet no formal mechanisms in place with which to capture part of the economic rents that this price movement would generate. In spite of excluding one-half of non-renewable resource revenues from the equalization formula in 1977, the federal government would not be able to meet the full amount of the increase in equalization entitlements that would arise from a substantial increase in the rents collected by the Western provinces. Moreover, federal officials were again worried about the inflationary effect of allowing an energy price increase of the extent demanded. They also wished to keep energy prices below world levels in order to give the Canadian manufacturing sector a competitive advantage in world trade and, in any event, once again to soften the adjustment shocks for both labour and capital.

After intensive negotiations between federal and provincial governments and the public and private sectors and after two federal elections, the Government of Canada unveiled the National Energy Program (NEP) at the same time that it disclosed the federal budget, in October 1980. Ottawa's solution was a bold one. The program had three stated objectives: security of supply through ultimate independence from the international market; Canadianization of the industry through increased domestic ownership; and fairness in the determination of prices and the assignment of revenues. These objectives were pursued in several ways. First, Ottawa unilaterally imposed a schedule that provided for a gradual increase in the domestic prices of oil and natural gas. Under this schedule, Canadian crude oil prices were not to exceed 75 per cent of world price, though some major projects were excepted. Natural gas prices were to be tied to oil prices, on a ratio of 65 cents to the dollar, in order to encourage substitution of gas for oil in eastern Canadian markets. This policy did redistribute Western petroleum rents across the country, in keeping with the "fair share" objective of the NEP. Some observers argued, however, that it encouraged consumption and discouraged exploration and development, a policy directly at odds with the NEP's self-sufficiency goal.

The second major feature of the NEP was a host of new and complex taxation measures designed to increase federal revenues from the oil industry. These measures included the Petroleum and Gas Revenue Tax (PGRT), the Natural Gas and Gas Liquids Tax (NGGLT), the Petroleum Compensation Charge (PCC), and a Canadian Ownership Charge. The first tax was a flat levy of 8 per cent on net operating revenue – not net income – from oil and gas production; the 1981 Canada-Alberta Agreement increased this levy to 16 per cent. The tax on natural gas was a flat levy per million cubic feet, so that it, too, bore no necessary relationship to producer income. The Petroleum Compensation Charge was a standard excise tax designed to raise revenue to cover the cost of subsidizing the importation of expensive off-shore crude oil into eastern Canada. The Canadian Ownership Charge was a similar levy on petroleum products. Its purpose was to finance takeovers of foreign oil companies.

The NEP also made substantive changes in the incentive structure. The consumer was offered inducements to substitute natural gas for oil and to undertake energy conservation measures such as home insulation. Producers were offered direct subsidies for exploration and development activity, the Petroleum Incentive Payments (PIPs), which would replace depletion and "super-depletion" allowances. The NEP extended preferential treatment to firms on the basis of their degree of Canadian ownership, and to activity carried on offshore and in the Territories ("Canada Lands") rather than in the provinces. It also made provision for the federal Crown oil company,

Petro-Canada, to take over one or more of the large multi-national oil companies operating in the country, with the help of the "Canadianization" levy. Finally, the federal government reserved for the Crown a 25 per cent interest in development rights on Canada Lands, including pre-NEP discoveries (the so-called "back-in provision"). This provision was controversial and much debated, but it was not without a history or precedents in the evolution of land-management arrangements. In 1961, for example, the federal government had introduced the Canada Oil and Gas Lands Regulations, which established tests for granting leases based on Canadian ownership, and which provided for the surrender to the Crown, on a chequerboard basis, of a sizeable portion of the area of any oil or gas discovery.

The NEP did attain many of its objectives. It moved Canadian energy demand away from oil to substitutes, particularly natural gas; it gradually increased prices for Canadian oil and gas; it distributed economic rents throughout the country; it encouraged extensive exploration in frontier areas; and it created opportunities for more extensive Canadian ownership of the petroleum sector in frontier areas and for participation of Canadian firms in exploration from which they had previously been shut out by the multinationals. To many observers, however, federal policies seemed overly concerned with the costs of adjusting to higher energy prices and too little concerned with realizing the potential economic benefits. Many Westerners saw the NEP as a policy that slighted their region and its interests.

The ten months following the announcement of the NEP provided one of the low points in federal-provincial relations. Alberta reacted to the NEP by reducing deliveries to eastern Canada. Ottawa responded by implementing a special excise tax to cover the cost of additional imported oil. Alberta also held up progress on an oil-sands project, in an effort to strike at federal concerns about self-sufficiency. The Canadian public was the loser in the dispute, and in the end it was public opinion that forced the two governments to resolve their differences.

The September 1981 Agreement and After

Agreement between Alberta and the federal government was reached in September 1981. Oil prices were still to be set by government rather than in the market-place, but they were now to rise substantially faster than they had risen under the NEP. The 75 per cent ceiling on "old" oil was retained, but oil from recent discoveries and non-conventional sources was guaranteed the international price. Existing taxes underwent considerable adjustment, and a new tax was introduced: the Incremental Oil Royalties Tax. The Petroleum and Gas Revenue Tax was restructured and its rate increased to 16 per cent, but new deductions reduced the effective rate to 12 per cent. The tax on exports of gas and gas liquids was reduced to zero; in exchange, Alberta took over the PIP program in that province. The NEP's special provisions for new and non-conventional oil were retained.

The new agreement was important in several respects. It established that Alberta and the other Western provinces were willing to turn over substantial amounts of oil and gas revenue to other Canadians. The Western provinces would turn these revenues over directly, through special federal taxes on petroleum, and indirectly, through agreeing to accept less than world prices for their output. The agreement explicitly recognized the link between prices and incentives for exploration and development, and it re-established the practice of setting price and taxation arrangements by negotiation and agreement.

The NEP and even the September 1981 agreement were based on highly optimistic price projections. Almost before the ink was dry on the 1981 accord, international oil prices began to slip. Consequently, neither revenues nor drilling activity developed as expected. In the face of soft oil markets, both Alberta and the federal government adjusted prices and taxes. The domestic price of old oil rose above the 75 per cent ceiling, and by the fall of 1984, more than 50 per cent of Canadian production was receiving the international price. In 1985, the federal government and three Western provinces agreed to dismantle crude-oil price controls and allow oil to follow world prices.[1] Under this agreement, a more market-sensitive price system for natural gas is to be implemented later in 1985. In addition, the fiscal regime is to be adjusted downwards in hope of stimulating exploration and development.

Prospects

Energy Use

As Table 12-14 (below) shows, oil accounted for nearly 32 per cent of primary energy demand in Canada in 1983. Natural gas accounted for another 18 per cent. Oil's share is down by more than 10 percentage points from 1973, but the natural gas share has remained roughly constant. Primary consumption of oil and natural gas in Canada varies across regions, depending on the availability and relative prices of competing energy sources. In the Atlantic region, oil accounts for over two-thirds of energy consumption, although there has been a shift over the past decade in favour of hydroelectricity and coal. In Quebec, off-oil substitution has been particularly marked: oil's share of consumption declined from nearly 56 per cent in 1973 to 38 per cent in 1982. The shift has been largely to hydro-electricity, which now accounts for 56 per cent of Quebec's primary energy consumption. In Ontario, where oil accounts for 35 per cent of energy demand, its share has declined by only 5 percentage points over the same period. The significant shift in Ontario has been the increase in the share of nuclear-generated power at the expense of hydro-electricity. In the Prairie provinces, oil's share has changed relatively little. In Saskatchewan and Alberta, there has been a decline in the share of natural gas and an increase in the use of coal in electricity generation. In Manitoba and British Columbia, hydro-electricity is the largest source of energy.[2]

Oil

Domestic production of crude oil, including synthetics and pentanes plus, is lower than it was in the early 1970s, as Figure 12-2 shows. Figure 12-3 demonstrates that production of conventional crude oil has consistently outstripped additions to reserves since the late 1960s. Over 70 per cent of the 1983 average daily crude oil output of 241 500 cubic metres was conventional light oil; conventional heavy oil and supplies from non-conventional sources made up the balance. Alberta produces over four-fifths of Canadian oil, and Saskatchewan contributes nearly all the rest.

FIGURE 12-2 Production and Trade of Crude Oil and Equivalent, Canada, 1972–83

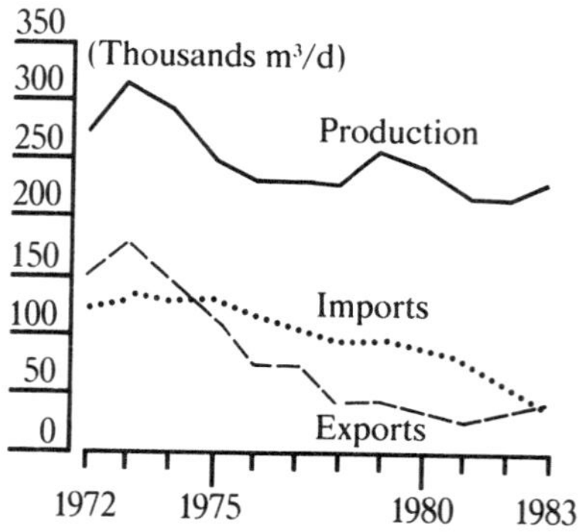

Source: Based on data from Energy, Mines and Resources Canada. Taken from Economic Council of Canada, *Connections: An Energy Strategy for the Future* (Ottawa: Minister of Supply and Services Canada, 1985), p. 33.

FIGURE 12-3 Established Reserves and Cumulative Production of Conventional Crude Oil, Canada, 1957-83.

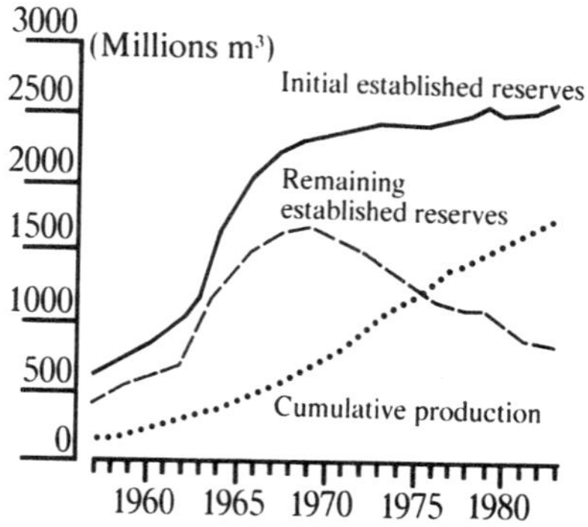

Source: Based on data from the Canadian Petroleum Association. Taken from Economic Council of Canada, *Connections: An Energy Strategy for the Future* (Ottawa: Minister of Supply and Services Canada, 1985), p. 31.

A net exporter through most of the 1960s and the early 1970s, Canada became a substantial net importer by 1975. As Table 12-13 indicates, however, trade in crude petroleum and fuel oil was roughly in balance again by 1984. This balance was the result both of a continuous decline in imports and of an increase in exports. The vast majority of our crude oil exports go to the United States; they earned $1.8 billion (net) in 1982. Venezuela, Mexico, and Iran supplied 63 per cent of Canada's total imports in 1983.

The growth rate of energy consumption during the 1970s has been declining in the world as a whole as a consequence of OPEC's success at raising oil prices. During the 1960s, consumption expanded at an annual average rate of 6.0 per cent; in the 1970s, that rate was only 3.1 per cent.[3] It is expected to continue to grow only slowly over the next 20 to 30 years. Generally speaking, the more recent the projections, the lower are the anticipated growth rates. Most countries are expected to continue to move toward greater self-sufficiency in energy and to rely increasingly on alternative sources of energy. The National Energy Board's projection for Canada to 2005 shows an increase, recorded in Table 12-14, in the importance of natural gas, hydro, and nuclear power, at the expense of oil. The primary basis for this projection is an assumption that these other energy sources will be cheaper than oil. As we indicated earlier, and as Figure 12-4 illustrates, Canadian oil prices have remained well below international prices over most of the past decade. In recent years, however, the gap between domestic and international prices has been closing, and the present Canadian government approves of a move to parity.

Like estimates of future energy consumption, estimates of future world oil prices have become more moderate since the 1970s. In September 1984, the National Energy Board offered two scenarios: under its low-price scenario, there would be no real increase in the world price of oil before 2005; under its high-price scenario, which allowed for such events as an escalation of the

TABLE 12-13 Canadian Trade in Energy Products, 1984

	(millions of dollars)		
	Imports	**Exports**	**Balance**
Natural gas	—	3 886.4	3 886.4
Crude petroleum	3 375.6	4 390.5	1 014.9
Fuel oil	962.3	—	−962.3
Coal and other crude bituminous substances	1 095.2	1 846.6	751.4
Other petroleum and coal products	608.8	3 192.7	2 583.9
Electricity	—	1 378.7	1 378.7
Radioactive ores and concentrates	—	333.7	333.7
Total	6 041.9	15 028.6	8 986.7

Source: Statistics Canada, *Summary of External Trade* (December 1984) Cat. No. 65-001 (Ottawa: Minister of Supply and Services Canada, 1985).

TABLE 12-14 Current and Projected Fuel Shares in Primary Energy Demand in Canada

	(percentages) Primary Energy Demand[a]	
	1983	2005
Oil	32	21
Gas	18	21
Coal	10	10
Nuclear	5	11
Hydro	28	31
Other	7	6
Total	100	100

Source: National Energy Board, *Canadian Energy: Supply and Demand 1983–2005*, Technical Report (Ottawa: NEB, 1984), p. 101.

a. Hydro and nuclear are converted at 10.5 petajoules per terawatt hour.

Middle East War between Iran and Iraq, there would be annual real-price increases of 2.5 per cent from 1983 to 1990, and of 2.4 per cent from 1990 to 2005.[4] Energy developments must be planned with these more modest price increases in mind.

FIGURE 12-4 Canadian Crude Oil Prices 1973–84

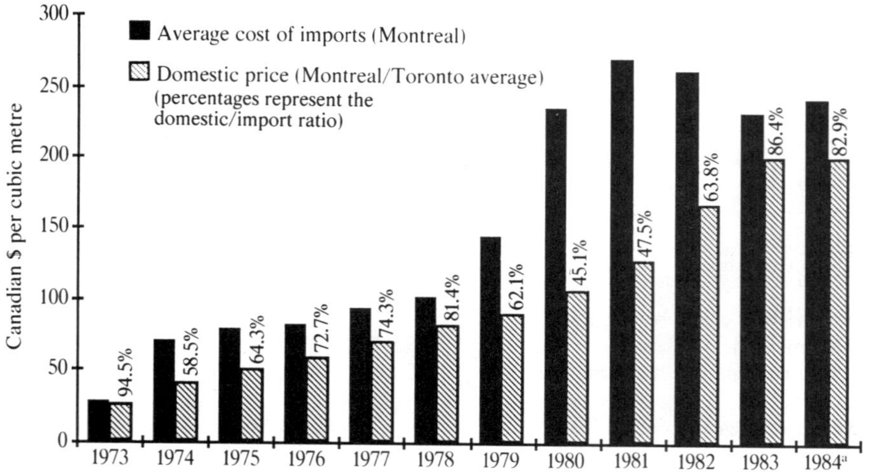

Source: Canada, Energy, Mines and Resources Canada, *Energy Statistics Handbook* (Ottawa: The Department, 1984).

a. Average prices to second quarter.

Future Canadian demand for oil is difficult to predict with any certainty: it will depend on the rate of economic growth, the extent of the continuation of conservation measures, the amount of excess capacity in the hydro, nuclear and thermal electricity industries, and the pricing policies of these industries. To forecast future oil supply is even more difficult. Many intervenors were cautiously optimistic:

> *We have opportunities in the frontiers; we have opportunities still remaining in the western Canada basin. Again, to enhance the recovery of oil, there have been initiatives by both governments to make this possible. We have a tremendous resource in the oil sands of Alberta, which, if we put these things in place, [would give us] self-sufficiency. I don't think we would be responsible if we said that the east coast is going to do it or the Beaufort Sea or the Arctic Islands. All of these areas have potential, and we should be working to see which ones benefit us in terms of the industrial spin-offs for Canadians.*
>
> (Canadian Petroleum Association, Transcript, Calgary, November 4, 1983 [vol.41], pp. 8291–92.)

In one respect, the answer to the question of future supply is clear. Our reliance on conventional oil from the Western Sedimentary Basin, including oil from enhanced recovery projects, will diminish. The volume of oil already recovered from this basin is larger than its known and its anticipated reserves. Consequently, non-conventional sources of supply will become increasingly important.

Table 12-15 summarizes the National Energy Board's 1984 projection of changes in the relative importance of the different sources of oil over the next two decades. Synthetic light crude oil, frontier light, and blended heavy crude and bitumen accounted for 28 per cent of total supply in 1983; the NEB expects this figure to swell to 77 per cent by 2005. It also expects conventional light crude to account for less than 25 per cent of Canadian production by the same date.

The Economic Council of Canada has recently assessed the costs of recovering oil from various non-conventional sources.[5] The figures in Table 12-16 are social costs: that is, the total costs experienced by industry, excluding all taxes and royalties. Estimates that included taxes and royalties would be higher. The Council's study suggests that regardless of the method used to increase Canadian oil production, projects will have to be virtually free of taxes if they are to succeed. Economic rents cannot be extracted if there are none to be had. Yet even projects that yield no economic rents can be of immense benefit to the economy if, while yielding a reasonable return to the operators, they provide employment and produce oil that is competitive with world prices, thus reducing our reliance on imports.

Natural Gas

Table 12-17 summarizes world natural gas reserves and gas consumption. Canada's proved gas reserves of about 3484 billion (10^9) cubic metres seem immense, but they account for only 4 per cent of proved world reserves. Canadian share of world consumption amounting to 3.3 per cent is also small.

TABLE 12-15 Estimated Sources of Crude Oil Production, 1983–2005

	(thousands of cubic metres per day)		
	1983	**1990**	**2005**
Conventional light and pentanes plus	174.1	117.5	49.9
Oil sands synthetic (including upgraded heavy crude)	23.5	42.5	63.5
Frontier	—	1.9	44.0
Total light	197.6	161.9	157.4
Blended heavy crude and bitumen	43.9	39.1	59.2
Total	241.5	201.0	216.6

Source: National Energy Board, *Canadian Energy: Supply and Demand 1983–2005*, Summary Report (Ottawa: Minister of Supply and Services Canada, 1984).

Because of current prices and transportation costs, much of the world's natural gas cannot be marketed at long distances from the source of supply. The huge figures for world reserves suggest that even after the year 2000, when gas prices may be considerably higher than they are now, gas from the Canadian Arctic and other frontier areas is not likely to have any market power abroad except, perhaps, in the United States. Therefore any increase in exports must come primarily from sales to the United States, where our product will have to compete with U.S. gas and alternate sources of energy.

Unlike our reserves of conventional oil, our established reserves of natural gas have increased almost continuously since the Second World War. (See Figure 12-5.) Canada's domestic sales of natural gas rose substantially during the 1960s, but they have remained fairly constant since the early 1970s. Exports of natural gas to the United States have followed the same pattern. At present, Canadian gas accounts for approximately 4 per cent of total U.S. gas consumption. Because the United States' own capacity for production exceeds current domestic demand, and because Canadian export prices are higher than U.S. domestic prices, we have been able to sell, in recent years, only about 40 per cent of authorized export volumes. Since November 1984, in an effort to bolster these sales, the federal government has permitted greater flexibility in gas-export pricing, and the matter of domestic and export-pricing policies is under study.

Additions to reserves in the United States are, however, unlikely to keep pace with future demand in that country. Consequently the NEB expects that by 1987, gas exports to the United States will reach 68 per cent of committed volumes. By 1990, they will be up to 90 per cent of authorized sales.[6] Annual export revenues in the peak years are expected to reach $7 to $8 billion, more than double the current revenues.

TABLE 12-16 Summary of Social Supply Costs[a] for Alternate Oil Supplies

Source	Social Supply Costs ($1983 per barrel)	Comments
Western Canadian conventional light oil	$16	Although risk and costs are relatively low, supplies are limited, even with the New Oil Reference Price. Reductions in taxes could expand additions to reserves beyond National Energy Board forecasts.
Western Canada enhanced oil recovery from existing known reserves	$13–25	Some projects are profitable; others will be quite marginal under existing price and tax regimes. Lower taxes would enlarge the number of profitable projects.
Large-scale surface mining of oilsands to produce synthetic high quality oil	$47	Based on Alsands data. High financial risk.
In situ oilsands production of bitumen (without upgrading)	$28	Wolfe Lake data; still at experimental stage.
East coast Hibernia oil	$15	Delivered to Montreal. Costs count *only* the development and production stages, so this source is not fully comparable to other sources of supply because exploration costs are not included. High technological risk (including iceberg problems, for example).
Beaufort Sea oil (assuming a commercial discovery)	$15–40	Delivered to Montreal. Costs count *only* the development and production stages, so this source is not fully comparable to other non-frontier supply sources. Considerable environmental risk.

Source: Adapted from David H. Slater, "Submission" by the Chairman of the Economic Council of Canada to the Standing Senate Committee on Energy and Natural Resources, May 24, 1984.

a. Social supply costs = total costs experienced by industry excluding all taxes and royalties. Calculations based on 10% rate of discount.

Whether we will, in fact, increase our U.S. exports and export revenues to this extent depends on a variety of circumstances, including future gas-pricing policies in the United States, the extent of new reserves discovered there, the rigour of future U.S. clean air legislation and enforcement, and the extent to which other exporters to the United States, such as Mexico, reduce their export prices.[7] Although the United States did not object to Canada's partial

FIGURE 12-5 Established Reserves and Cumulative Production of Marketable Natural Gas, Canada, 1955–83

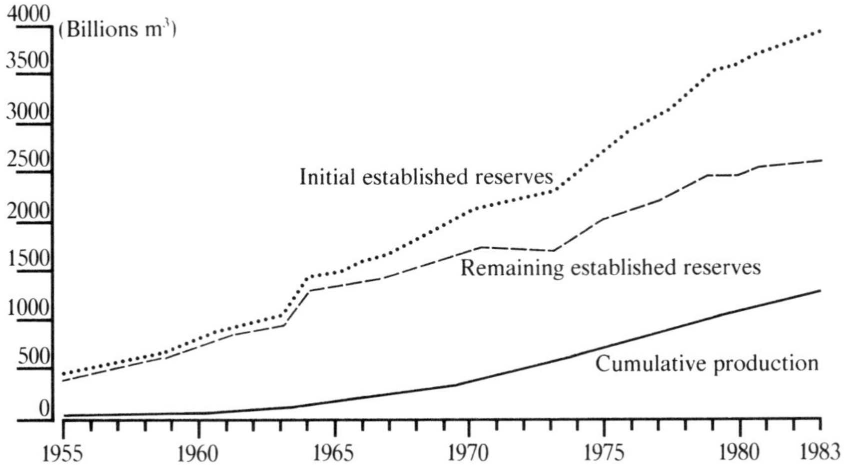

Source: Based on data from the Canadian Petroleum Association. Taken from Economic Council of Canada, *Connections: An Energy Strategy for the Future* (Ottawa: Minister of Supply and Services Canada, 1985), p. 57.

deregulation of export prices when it was introduced, the prospect of growing imports, at a time when U.S. demand for gas is not increasing, has since raised concern about Canadian competition in that country. U.S. demand is so nearly static that it now appears unlikely that the Alaska Natural Gas Transportation System (ANGTS) will be used in this century to move Alaskan gas to the lower 48 United States.

Gas-export growth will also depend on the Canadian supply situation. According to projections released by the Canadian Energy Research Institute (CERI) in early 1984, surplus gas from non-frontier sources – that is, gas from these sources that will not be committed under existing licenses or required for domestic consumption – will be available for export up to the early years of the coming century. Projections published by the NEB in September 1984 indicate that Canada's conventional reserves alone are sufficient to sustain export growth until at least 2000.[8] Surplus supplies from the Arctic and from offshore projects might allow us to increase our gas exports for a few years longer.

These projections assume that future returns to producers will be high enough to stimulate exploration and development. In recent years, however, drilling for gas in Canada has declined substantially: in 1983–84, estimated exploratory and development gas-well drilling was only 40 per cent of the 1976–80 average. The decline had several causes: the difficulty of increasing exports to the United States, a slow-down in the growth of domestic demand owing to the recession, mild winters, fierce competition from electricity utilities, and a decline in gas producers' net revenues. Some of these causes, or similar ones, could affect supply growth in the future. For example, any

TABLE 12-17 World Natural Gas Reserves and Consumption (1982)

	Proven Reserves (10^9 cubic metres)	Percentage of World	Consumption (10^9 cubic metres)	Percentage of World
OPEC	28 834.9	33.3	69.4	4.5
North America	8 359.5	9.6	575.3	37.5
of which Canada	3 484.3	4.0	50.7	3.3
Western Europe	4 243.5	4.9	207.1	13.5
Eastern Europe	35 169.0	40.6	541.1	35.2
of which U.S.S.R.	34 514.6	39.8	445.6	29.0
Other	10 098.9	11.6	143.1	9.3
Total world	86 705.9	100.0	1 535.4	100.0

Source: Adapted from Bijan Mossover-Rahmani, "The OPEC Natural Gas Dilemma", in *Proceedings of the International Gas Markets Conference*, edited by Shane S. Streifel (Calgary: Canadian Energy Research Institute, 1983).

Note: Canadian reserves are from NEB estimates. Canadian consumption figures are from NEB estimates.

significant increase in the value of the Canadian dollar relative to the U.S. dollar would depress our export revenues and therefore discourage drilling.

New export licenses are granted only if current reserves exceed the sum of commitments under existing export licenses, plus 25 times the present year's domestic demand for gas. Some observers argue that the requirement of 25 years' domestic supply inhibits exports unduly. Others defend the requirement, arguing that supply from conventional sources will satisfy projected domestic demand and existing export contracts for some 20 years only, that alternative supplies from the Arctic will be substantially higher priced, and that gas is cleaner than coal and safer than nuclear power.

One prospect beyond the U.S. market should be mentioned: the export to Japan of Canadian Arctic gas in liquified form. Japan expects liquified natural gas to make up about 13 per cent of its total energy demand by 1990–95 and is moving ahead with plans to import it from a number of countries. The Japanese anticipate that Canada will supply about 6 to 8 per cent of their gas imports between 1990 and 1995.[9]

A New Energy Framework

Encouraging Future Supply

The most important energy issue facing Canada is that of future supply. How shall we meet our energy needs, particularly our need for oil, over the next 20 to 30 years? What portion of our needs can we reasonably expect to supply from Canadian sources? And what policies must accompany whatever objectives we set for ourselves? The question facing policy makers is not whether we have oil and gas. We clearly do. What we do not know with any certainty is the extent to which it will be profitable to develop new sources of oil and gas under the economic conditions that are expected to prevail over the next two to three decades. The ultimate issue is whether the economic incentives will be sufficient, or can be made sufficient, to encourage the industry to meet the targets we set.

An Economic Council of Canada study published before the 1985 energy accord was struck shows the effects of price deregulation under various taxation regimes.[10] It concludes that deregulation of oil and gas prices would encourage substitution of gas because of the change in relative prices that would follow. On average, oil imports would decline by about 9 per cent per year over the period 1985–90, and total oil demand would fall by an estimated 4 per cent. Demand for natural gas, on the other hand, would increase by nearly 13 per cent. On the supply side, the Council's results suggest that the deregulation of oil and natural gas prices would stimulate domestic oil production and exploration over the next few years. Gas production would also increase, but gas exploration and development would decline.

The Council also considered the results of simultaneous price deregulation and modificiation[11] of the Petroleum and Gas Revenue Tax (PGRT); it found another significant positive effect on discoveries of oil and gas reserves. Under price deregulation alone, additions to oil reserves would average 2.3 per cent per year between 1985 and 1990; under price deregulation plus modification of the PGRT, additions would average 8.4 per cent annually. Gas-exploration activity would still fall under the latter regime, but by only 3.8 per cent, instead of by 6.6 per cent.

Prices and taxes are only the most obvious determinants of exploration and development activity. Two other factors are important as well. One is the regulatory regime that governs the industry. The other is the stability or predictability of any administered prices, taxes and regulations. The following sections review each of these factors in turn, setting out Commissioners' recommendations for public policy.

Crude Oil Pricing. The first longer-term issue is the relationship that Canadian oil and gas prices should bear to the international price. The determination of prices for Canadian oil and natural gas has rarely been left to market forces alone. The National Oil Policy of the 1960s, by keeping foreign crude oil out of Ontario and the West, pushed prices in those regions higher than they would otherwise have climbed. Since 1973, the federal government has set prices below the world level.

A number of submissions to this Commission held that Canada should continue to keep domestic petroleum prices below world prices. The rationale for this policy was the argument that the world price is an artificial one, based not on international costs of production, but rather on an exercise of market power by a few oil-producing nations. Commissioners disagree with this argument. The world price is the real opportunity cost for Canadian supplies, even if it is only the "artificial" creation of OPEC's market power.

The difference between the world price and the domestic Canadian price is the value that is forgone every time a barrel of oil is consumed domestically rather than sold abroad. Likewise, it is the cost of replacing this same oil if we are forced to turn to the international market. To assign any price to oil other than the world price is to distort both supply incentives and demand incentives as well.

Accordingly, Commissioners recommend that Canadian crude regularly be sold within Canada at world prices. We welcome the recent "Western Accord", an agreement between the federal government and three Western provinces, which adopts this policy. In extraordinary circumstances, however, we would reserve to governments the right to put a temporary freeze on domestic petroleum prices. There are real economic costs involved in forcing Canadians to make a sharp adjustment if it is only to be reversed shortly thereafter. Given a sharp upward movement in the world price, such as occurred in 1973–74 and in 1979–80, a temporary freeze or sliding scale of prices should be contemplated. Similarly, if the OPEC price were to tumble dramatically, we would be well advised to keep a floor under the domestic price through a tariff or import-pricing regime. Even then, the decision to depart from world prices should only be taken by federal-provincial agreement. If it became clear – as clear, at any rate, as these things can ever be – that the price rise or decline was permanent, we would have to be prepared to see our prices follow the international ones.

This recommendation does not mean that Canada must necessarily sacrifice marginal frontier or non-conventional operations. It simply means that we should not use artificially high prices to support such projects. If we judge continued development of these projects to be valuable, as we would under currently foreseeable circumstances, and if international price trends are rendering them increasingly unattractive, other measures are available to support them. For example, governments could defer royalties and taxes on a given project until that project achieved a reasonable rate of return, or they could provide tax credits or other subsidies.

Natural Gas Pricing. It is not possible to make such a simple recommendation for natural gas pricing. Because there is no international market for gas, such as there is for oil, there is no handy reference price. There are two separate markets for western Canadian gas: domestic sales and exports to the United States. Prices within Canada have been set so that gas selling at the Toronto "city gate" has cost approximately 65 per cent of the price of crude oil. The price paid to producers, however, was an Alberta border price, set by federal-provincial agreement. Any difference between the two, beyond transport costs, has been made up by federal taxes or subsidies. Since November 1984, export prices have been set by negotiation between gas exporters and customers, but they can never be less than the Toronto level. The Western Accord requires the implementation of a more flexible, market-sensitive pricing mechanism by November 1985, and this direction is one Commissioners endorse. Our recommendation is that natural gas prices be allowed, over time, to find their own levels in *both* domestic *and* export markets. This policy will entail a substantial deregulation of gas markets over a period of years, both at the producer and the consumer ends of the system. In particular, there would be no attempt to set the price of gas in relation to the price of oil. Given the relatively greater endowment of natural gas as compared with oil from conventional producing regions and given, too, the competitive markets for gas in the United States, it is likely that natural gas prices will continue to be lower than oil prices. To assure more flexibility in the domestic market, more large consumers should be encouraged to buy directly from Western producers. This shift will be facilitated if the pipeline companies carry such gas under no more onerous tariffs and conditions than those which apply to their own gas.

The current system of export regulation, under which the National Energy Board monitors supply and demand in Canada and approves export sales negotiated privately, should remain in place. Although the Western Accord does not deal with this issue, we would expect it to become an important one in 1985. Security of supply should remain an important objective, but the reserve period, presently standing at 25 years, should be re-evaluated now and periodically in the future.

Taxation and Subsidies. As our historical review has shown, the gas and oil sector has been the target of a bewildering succession of federal and provincial tax and subsidy schemes. A number of intervenors argued that the present range of such programs is confusing, inappropriate and unfair, and that the federal-provincial disputes it engenders are harmful to the industry and, ultimately, to the country.

> *Under the terms of the National Energy Program and the Federal/Provincial Energy Agreements of 1981 and 1983, the oil and gas industry has been subjected to a heavy burden of taxes and royalties and does not receive the full price for the largest portion of its oil production. These government policy decisions reduce the confidence of industry investors and impair financing capability for investments. Industry should not be faced with discriminatory taxes which other forms of energy are not required to pay.*
>
> (Canadian Gas Association, Brief, December 1, 1983, p. 7.)

> *The third area I would like to touch on is the area of incentives. Again, these have changed from being income tax related incentives to the grant form. Whatever one may say about the grant form, it produces far more capability on the part of the government giving the grant, to direct who will get the grant and where the grant will be spent, than an income tax related system of stimulation does. So, there has been a pronounced movement in recent years from a system of encouragement of exploration and development of energy in this country that was primarily related to the tax system, and therefore had a very commercial economic analysis and bias connected with it, to a system that was a good deal less dependent on normal economic analysis.*
>
> (R.R. Latimer, TransCanada PipeLines Limited, Transcript, Ottawa, December 15, 1983 [vol. 72], p. 15107.)

> *The constitutional division of resource jurisdiction has resulted in deepening rifts and confrontation between governments and industry and has harmed*

Canada's economic performance. Oil and gas sector activity has particularly suffered from this situation.

(Canadian Petroleum Association, Brief, October 24, 1983, p. 7.)

It is time to establish some basic principles with respect to taxation and subsidy of the petroleum industry, to develop a system that is compatible with these general precepts, and to make a commitment to leave the new system as it is for the forseeable future, barring any disruptive developments. Commissioners therefore propose three principles to govern taxation of the oil and gas sector. The provinces' rights as landlords must continue to be recognized. The treatment of the oil and gas sector under the tax system should not differ from the treatment of any other non-renewable resource industry. Taxation above a minimal provincial royalty should be based on profits rather than on the value of production.

This Commission specifically recommends that:

- The producing province would continue to levy an incentive-based royalty to reflect the compensation due to the owners of a non-renewable resource, up to a maximum level set by federal-provincial agreement. Royalty payments would be deductible as business expenses for the purposes of calculating corporate income tax. The present system, which does not permit the deduction of royalty payments from income for tax purposes, and which specifies a special resource allowance as a general deduction, would be scrapped. Royalty payments would be the province's first, but not its only, claim on the industry's revenues. We would suggest that the royalty level be lowered: the collection of rents by governments must be based largely on profits, rather than on output volumes and gross revenues, if the development of marginal supplies is not to be discouraged.

If the provinces were to agree to an incentive-based royalty approach, it would follow that the income-tax share would increase at the expense of the royalty share. As noted below, some adjustment in the division of revenue between the two levels of government may be required.

Commissioners further recommend that:

- Governments collect the remainder of their share of the rent in the form of corporate income taxes, both provincial and federal. Taxes on the value of production would be avoided. We welcome the phasing-out or elimination of such forms of taxation as those announced in the Western Accord. Deductions permitted would be royalty payments up to the agreed maximum and the business expenses normally allowed in other industry sectors. These would include operating expenses (including exploration expenses) and an amortized portion of all capital costs, including acquisition and development costs. Depletion, earned or otherwise, would not be deductible. Deductions not used in any tax year could be carried forward. To promote exploration and investment in the petroleum industry, unused deductions arising from exploration expenditures or investment in the industry would result in refundable tax credits, replacing the Petroleum

Incentive Payments (PIP) system being phased out under the Western Accord.

- There be provision for a temporary windfall-profits tax to be levied, after agreement with the provinces concerned, in the event of a major disruption in international oil markets.
- With respect to non-conventional petroleum resources and conventional resources outside the Western Sedimentary Basin (including heavy oil and oil sands, tertiary recovery of conventional resources, Beaufort near-shore and on-shore, and eastern offshore), we believe some continuing "tilt" in incentives is appropriate on two grounds: regional economic development and security of supply. Accordingly, as PIP is phased out, a more modest incentive ought to be introduced in the form of a refundable tax credit for exploration. This measure would both encourage exploration generally and allow smaller firms to participate in frontier and non-conventional projects. As we said earlier, where the continued development of such projects is deemed to be valuable to Canada, and where international price trends are rendering these projects increasingly unattractive, we believe that taxation and royalty levels should be adjusted downward or that refundable tax credits, royalty or tax holidays, or other forms of subsidy should be made available.

The Regulatory Environment. The petroleum industry operates under a wide variety of regulatory provisions. This plethora of rules was described to Commissioners at our public hearings:

> *The following quotes from the annual report of a very successful small Canadian oil company illustrates the degree of present day frustration with government intervention . . . NEP, FIRA, PIP, APIP, EDIS, DDIS, SOOP, COOP, NORP, IORT, COGLA, PGRT, NGGLT, COSC, and on and on it goes. This list of unintelligible acronyms is only a sample of government taxes/programs presently active in the oil industry. The interference and increased involvement by both levels of government over the past 10 years has been crippling.*
>
> (Formula Growth Limited, Brief, October 24, 1983, p. 3.)

In any sector, the subject of regulation imposes a dilemma. In isolation, each requirement or condition is nearly always eminently justifiable; taken together, however, regulations can become an insurmountable barrier to the progress of a given project. There is no simple solution to this problem. Commissioners can only enter a plea that governments make their regulations as simple and as inexpensive to implement as possible. We provide some suggestions below, in our review of environmental regulation, about the streamlining and co-ordination of regulations.

A final point is in order here. We Canadians must recognize that if a project dies because it fails to meet regulatory procedures (assuming these are properly designed), its death is natural and not to be impeded. Regulations are meant to stop marginal ventures; not every blocked proposal signifies regulatory overload.

Predictability. The best policies in the world can be harmful if the industry cannot assume that they will be in place long enough to allow it to calculate and compare expected returns from particular resource projects. Commissioners were told that:

> *In the oil and gas industry the policy . . . has been very, very unpredictable. The oil and gas industry is one that requires a stable, clear, long-term policy for development.*
>
> (F. Gordon Dixon, Transcript, Calgary, November 7, 1983 [vol. 41], p. 8337.)

Other intervenors addressed the issue of predictability in the following terms:

> *Major energy projects have a long 10–30 year, planning horizon best supported by a fiscal regime of royalty, and other taxes and incentives which [are] relatively predictable but flexible and adaptive to changing business circumstances. Alteration of the "rules of the game" at frequent 2–3 year intervals in response to short term shifts in public policy and cyclical world energy situations only serves to increase uncertainty and add to project development risk.* (Dome Petroleum Limited, Brief, October 25, 1983, p. 5.)
>
> *What is needed [in the energy sector] is a combination of long-term goals, which enjoy a wide-spread consensus among the key sectors of our community (governments, the petroleum sector and consumers), and short-term adaptability in terms of tactics so that we can respond quickly to a changing energy environment. Short-term pragmatism will allow us to react in a timely manner to changing circumstances while a longer-term strategy will prevent us from over-reacting to new circumstances.*
>
> (Petro-Canada, Brief, November 15, 1983, pp. 9–10.)

Commissioners can make but one recommendation here, and it is the obvious one: Governments must establish a simplified taxation and regulatory regime and leave it in place. They should alter it only in unusual circumstances, and only after consultation with those affected and with other orders of government.

Canadianization. Another major issue is the extent to which the country wishes to continue to pursue the goal of Canadianization of the oil and gas sector. The NEP set a target of 50 per cent domestic ownership by 1990. In order to achieve this goal, the federal government instituted a special Canadian Ownership Charge and scaled PIP grants in favour of Canadian-owned companies.

The results of the Canadianization measures can be gauged from Figure 12-6. Canadian-owned firms accounted for about 38 per cent of petroleum industry reserves in 1983, compared with about 27 per cent in 1977. Figures on control are lower, but the rate of increase is even higher. The changes reflect the greater participation in the industry of companies that were already locally owned, as well as some high-profile take-overs of foreign companies.

The costs and benefits of foreign ownership are considered in general terms elsewhere in this Report. The question here is whether a special case can be

FIGURE 12-6 Ownership and Control of the Petroleum Industry, Based on Petroleum-Related Revenues, Canada, 1977–83

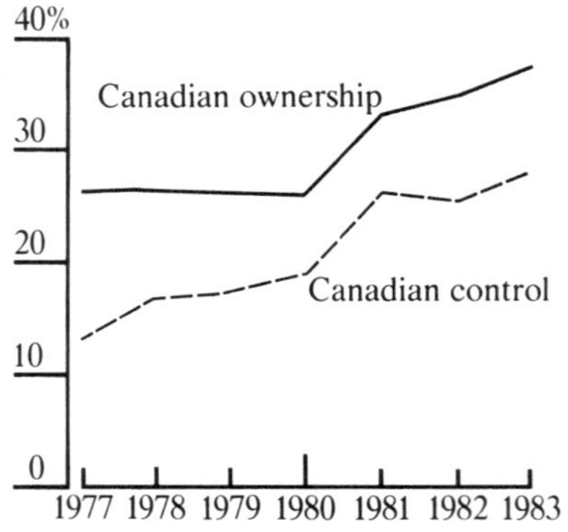

Source: Based on data from the Petroleum Monitoring Agency. Taken from Economic Council of Canada, *Connections: An Energy Strategy for the Future* (Ottawa: Minister of Supply and Services Canada, 1985), p. 22.

made for encouraging Canadian ownership in the oil and gas sector. We Commissioners think that it can. A secure supply of oil and gas is vital to a country's well-being, yet the international petroleum market-place has been dominated by OPEC, whose interests are often at odds with those of Canada. Furthermore, it would be dangerous to leave our fate entirely in the hands of multi-national oil companies. The actions of Canadian-owned firms – especially public firms – are more likely to be consistent with expressed Canadian goals. In addition, it is a matter of national pride to have a robust domestically-owned presence in this high-profile international sector. For these reasons, this Commission favours tilting both the land-tenure system for Canada Lands and the incentives system in favour of Canadian firms, to the extent that that policy is compatible with our international obligations.

Revenue Sharing

The final major issue is the question of the division of economic rents between the federal government and the provinces. As Commissioners have already indicated in our review of taxation, we recommend that the producing province be given first pass at the economic rents by virtue of its status as landlord. Thereafter the two governments would share taxation revenues as they would share those from any other sector: through the complex of corporate and excise taxes already in place.

The question remaining is how much lower will be the maximum level of royalties to which the federal government and the producing provinces will agree so that royalties may be deductible for federal income-tax purposes. Any recommendation on this score must be tied to federal government responsibilities in the area of equalization payments. If energy revenues are to be more fully equalized than they are now, the federal share must be increased to reflect this fact. If not, there is a case for letting the provincial share rise instead. We refer the reader to Part VI for further discussion and recommendations.

Conclusions

Canada's oil and gas sector has, not surprisingly, dominated national discussion of resources over the past dozen years. The sector is fundamental to the functioning of any modern economy and so large in Canada as to make a major difference in setting a wide variety of public policies, whether directly related or not. At the time of writing this Report, the sector is once again the focus of major reform, although to date, no legislation has been presented to Parliament or to provincial legislatures.

This Commission has given the oil and gas sector a good deal of attention and has presented for consideration as a long-term policy a new energy framework based on the principles of efficiency, fairness and predictability. This new framework is designed to accomplish two particular objectives: to allow the energy industry to make a full contribution to Canada's economic development; and to put in place a system sufficiently resilient that future shocks, which will invevitably come, will be absorbed more easily than they have been in the past.

Notes

1. In March 1985, the federal government and three Western provinces signed an accord which is to form the basis for a major reform of the National Energy Program. At the time of writing this Report, the accord has not been translated into legislation. Government of Canada, *The Western Accord* (Ottawa, 1985).
2. Economic Council of Canada, *Connections: An Energy Strategy for the Future* (Ottawa: Minister of Supply and Services Canada, 1985), p.103.
3. World Bank, "Price Prospects for Major Primary Commodities" (Washington, D.C.: World Bank, Economies and Research Staff, 1984), vol. 5.
4. National Energy Board, *Canadian Energy: Supply and Demand 1983–2005*, Technical Report (Ottawa: NEB, 1984).
5. David, Slater, "Submission" by the Chairman of the Economic Council of Canada to the Standing Senate Committee on Energy and Natural Resources, Ottawa, May 24, 1984.
6. National Energy Board, *Canadian Energy*, p. 64.
7. *Ibid.*, pp. 62–65.
8. *Ibid.*, p. 67.
9. Shun-Ichi Shimizu, "Characteristics of the Japanese LNG Market and Keys to Success in LNG Projects", in *Proceedings of the International Gas Markets Conference*, edited by Shane S. Streifel (Calgary: Canadian Energy Research Institute, 1983).
10. Economic Council, *Connections*. The Council assumed that world oil prices would remain stable; projections would change slightly under a different world price.
11. Modified PGRT "becomes a tax on production revenues, net of operating costs and of investment expenditures on oil and natural gas exploration, development and production in each year." (Economic Council, *Connections*, p. 182). The 1985 Western Accord specifies removal of the PGRT.

CHAPTER 13

The Environment, Society and the Economy

CHAPTER 13

The Environment, Society and the Economy

The review of global prospects at the beginning of this Report included an agenda of significant environmental issues that the citizens and the policy-makers of the world must confront in the years ahead. The items on that agenda – forest depletion, the greenhouse effect, acid rain, soil degradation, nuclear waste, the extinction of species, water quality – touch, in some way, every aspect of this Commission's mandate. The present section examines the nature of the environmental challenges that Canadians face, the effects of our rising awareness of those challenges, and the institutional means available to us for meeting them.

The Environment: Changing Attitudes and Responses

The International Dimension

Canada's status as a prominent middle power has been sustained in no small measure by our contributions to international initiatives related to the environment, particularly those associated with the United Nations. Canada's participation in the multi-session United Nations Conference on the Law of the Sea (UNCLOS) is one such contribution. The inclusion in the 1972 United Nations Declaration on the Human Environment of two important legal principles put forward by Canada is another:

> *States have ... the sovereign* right *to exploit their own resources ... and the* responsibility *to ensure that activities within their jurisdiction or control do not cause damage to the environment of other states or of areas beyond the limits of national jurisdiction.*
>
> ...
>
> *States shall co-operate to develop further the international law regarding liability and compensation for the victims of pollution and other environmental damage caused by activities within the jurisdiction or control of such states to areas beyond their jurisdiction.*[1]

Recent developments in multilateral trade negotiations offer another example of the growing importance of environmental concerns in traditional economic areas at the international level. A perception that some environmental protection standards may be disguised attempts to restrict import competition is at least partially responsible for the Code of Conduct for Preventing Technical Barriers to Trade (the Standards Code) that emerged from the Tokyo Round trade negotiations. The code requires its signatories not to use environmental, health, safety and consumer-protection standards to create unnecessary obstacles to international trade. Application of the code will not be easy. The question of whether a given regulation is an "unnecessary" barrier to trade is, of course, a matter of judgement. Moreover, many environmental standards are set, not by national governments, but by provinces (states) or municipalities. For this reason, the code requires central governments to use "such reasonable means which may be available to them"[2] to see that other jurisdictions within their boundaries adhere to its principles.

As a prosperous nation that occupies an extensive portion of the earth's surface, Canada has a major responsibility in many areas of environmental concern. Because the effects of human activity on the global environment are often cumulative and long-term, and because so many causes of environmental damage and degradation operate across national boundaries, this responsibility extends beyond the life of the present generation and beyond the boundaries of our own vast land. The measure of our civilization will be determined in no small part by the extent to which we live up to our responsibility at home and continue to offer assistance and leadership abroad.

The Environment versus Economic Growth

Many observers argue that measures taken to protect the environment often work at the expense of economic performance. According to this view, the competitiveness of Canadian firms is inhibited by the costs of compliance with domestic environmental standards, especially where these standards exceed the requirements that firms face in other countries. Concerns are often raised about the delays associated with obtaining environmental approval for projects, sometimes from several jurisdictions with differing standards. A further common complaint is that environmental controls reduce employment by diverting capital from "productive" investment to non-essentials. Particularly when economic growth is slow, as it has been recently, environmental controls can retard new capital investment, including investment in more environmentally sensitive technology, or discourage it altogether. These criticisms have not gone unremarked; the last few years have seen a decline in real per capita government spending on research and compliance.

In this Commission's view, efforts by industry to improve its short-term competitive position by avoiding or delaying environmental and resource-management costs simply defer these costs or leave them for the public to assume in the form of government expenditure, ecological damage, or forgone earnings and lost options. The lack of attention to reforestation illustrates this point only too well. Canadians must establish an accounting approach that recognizes all of the costs of economic activity, however difficult it may be to express some of these costs in dollars. As the representative of the Saskatchewan Environmental Society remarked to this Commission:

> *The gross national product is, in a sense, a false measure of how far ahead we have been able to get because it does not take into account such things as depleted soils and the cost of restoring them [or] contaminated food chains and the health effects.* (Saskatchewan Environmental Society, Transcript, Saskatoon, November 21, 1983 [vol. 48], p. 9869.)

It will be essential in the decades ahead to integrate environmental decisions and economic decisions, for there is, in Commissioners' view, no ultimate conflict between economic development and the preservation and enhancement of a healthy environment and a sustainable resource base. We agree with the similar conclusion expressed in the *European Community's Environmental Policy*:

> *The desire to avoid imposing additional costs on industry has led to a reluctance on the part of some Community governments to agree to tougher pollution controls, land-use requirements and curbs on potentially dangerous materials or production processes. The tangible short-term costs to the economy of such measures have all too often outweighed the frequently intangible and longer-term benefits to society of a healthier environment and substantial longer-term economic costs of failure to prevent pollution.*[3]

The Environmental Challenge: Changing Perceptions

Environmental issues first became a matter of general concern, in Canada and elsewhere, in the 1960s. Over the years, the definition of these issues has become increasingly broad and complex. The initial focus of concern was local pollution: that is, site-specific, single-source, environmental problems, the causes and effects of which were relatively easy to identify. The devastation of a stretch of English seashore that resulted from the sinking of the oil tanker *Torrey Canyon* in 1967 is a familiar example of a problem of this type. Such "classic" pollution problems are now widely recognized, and efforts have been made to bring them under control. While disasters of the *Torrey Canyon* variety are still all too possible, we have at least improved our techniques for cleaning up after them. On land, factories that spew out black smoke are less equably tolerated now than they were in the past, and emissions have been made subject to ever-more-careful monitoring. Nevertheless, many factories continue to pollute the air, just as oil spills and deliberate dumping continue to contaminate the oceans.

The 1970s brought growing concern about our capacity to manage the earth's resources on a sustainable basis. The first oil crisis of 1973 and the Club of Rome's study *Limits to Growth*[4] made major contributions to global awareness of potential resource depletion and launched an important continuing debate. If "running out" was the problem – and there was serious dispute on this point – "finding more" or "using less" were the solutions. The "conserver society" movement, stimulated in Canada by the work of the Science Council of Canada and by energy-conservation projects such as Prince Edward Island's Ark, was one response to the depletion challenge. Renewed alarm about the state of Canada's forests was another.

The 1970s also saw the emergence of a distinction, though by no means an absolute one, between the problems of pollution and the far more complex and difficult problems of long-term hazard which, at their worst, may be both unquantifiable and irreversible. The events at the Three Mile Island nuclear generating station and at the Bhophal chemical plant in India dramatically illustrate problems of the latter kind. Occupational health and safety issues, such as the possibility of detrimental effects of video-display terminals (VDTs) on the unborn, introduce similar concerns into the daily lives of ordinary Canadians.

The problems of long-term environmental hazard are less well understood and more difficult to remedy than the problems of "classic" pollution. The causes and consequences of long-term hazards are less readily linked, and the problems tend to be more serious as the example of chemical contaminants that pose carcinogenic and mutagenic threats demonstrates. Long-term contaminants tend to have a variety of sources and are difficult to identify, partly because they are often present only in trace elements. For this reason, they often accomplish serious damage before their presence is noticed or their effects are determined. Even when their presence has been confirmed, they are more difficult to break down or neutralize than the more familiar pollutants. Indeed, the damage wreaked by many kinds of long-term contaminants is irreversible: as far as human knowledge extends, once done, it cannot be undone. The effects of the long-term hazards tend to be more widely dispersed geographically and are more significant ecologically than the effects of simple pollution. The damage done by an oil spill is primarily local and of relatively short duration; but the destructive effects of acid rain are obviously international and may persist for decades.

Thus, while the environmental issues of the 1960s and early 1970s usually involved the management of non-persistent pollutants from industrial and municipal sources, the focus now is on environmental damage that threatens the long-term sustainability of the planet.

Environmental Values and the Environmental Movement in Canada

Canadians' changing perception of the environmental challenge at once reflects and reinforces changes in our values, aspirations and expectations. Before the 1960s, interest in conservation centred on the efficient management of resources for consumption. While concern about the efficient use of resources persists, the old emphasis on consumption has yielded considerable ground over the past quarter-century to a new emphasis on "the quality of life". According to this new reckoning, the environment is a source, not of wealth alone, but of other, less tangible satisfactions as well. Moreover, abuse of the environment is seen to threaten not only our prosperity, but also our health, our safety and, ultimately, our society.

If the environmental movement of the 1960s was vulnerable to the criticism that it reflected the aesthetic preferences of affluent North Americans whose interest in preserving threatened landscapes and endangered species was not always representative of world public opinion, it is considerably more difficult to dismiss current expressions of concern about the environment, which emphasize health and safety issues and which often arise from a strong sense of obligation to future generations. The importance of these issues is difficult to quantify; it is impossible to disregard. Indeed, some would argue that a firmly entrenched environmental consciousness is becoming a basic characteristic of Canadian society. Certainly, as Canadians' view of the environment changes, opposition to public policies that address the environment declines. It is now more common to hear arguments – even economic arguments – in favour of environmental protection measures than it is to hear arguments against them. From the environmental hearings of the past decade has emerged a sense of the importance of integrating economic and social concerns, of seeking both managed economic development and a high quality of life.

Public participation is increasingly significant at every stage of environmental decision making, from the definition of issues to the selection of policies. The Canadian environmental movement has its roots in the 1960s, when neighbourhood associations, concerned citizens' committees, and individuals began to work actively to identify the environmental consequences of industrial activity. Meanwhile, many communities directed their attention to matters such as municipal waste disposal sites, contaminated swimming beaches, non-returnable containers, and littered campsites and portage trails. With the realization that environmental problems were wide-ranging in their effects, local associations gradually formed larger and more formal groups in order to express their concerns in broader forums. The formation of Pollution Probe at the University of Toronto in 1969 was a particularly significant landmark in the evolution of environmental interest groups in Canada. Many less widely-known organizations came into being in the same period, and some existing organizations, such as camping associations and naturalists' groups, added environmental issues to their traditional concerns. Today, the environmental issues of concern to Canadians are often articulated by "coalitions" and "umbrella" groups that operate at the national and provincial levels, while local associations continue to perform important practical and educational functions.

Government Responses to Environmental Issues

Since the 1960s, Canadian governments have responded to the problems of the environment with both legislative and institutional reforms. Government did not start with a blank slate: remedies to some types of environmental abuse were already available either under common law or under existing resource-related statutes.[5] However, the new response was distinctive both in the prominence it accorded environmental matters and in the form it took. In the period from 1968 to 1972 alone, Parliament enacted several significant pieces of environmental legislation, including the Canada Water Act, the

Clean Air Act, the Arctic Waters Pollution Prevention Act, and the Northern Inland Waters Act. It also added new environmental provisions to the federal Fisheries Act and the Canada Shipping Act. In 1971, the federal government created the Department of the Environment, in order to consolidate in one ministry all agencies responsible for environmental protection, management and research. In most provincial jurisdictions, too, environmental regulation and institutions became matters of increasing priority during this period.

Today, the range of measures employed by governments to discourage or constrain conduct that is harmful to the environment includes educational programs and guidelines, regulations governing standards and licensing, prohibitions and sanctions, financial incentives, and reporting requirements. This Commission's interest here is not in the details of individual environmental programs, but rather in the ability of our system of environmental management to respond to emerging environmental concerns and evolving public values.

The success of educational measures directed at the general population or at particular industries is not easy to assess. By extending awareness of environmental issues and the availability of remedial measures, educational initiatives may contribute indirectly to environmental protection. On the other hand, the educational approach has been criticized because it can be used as a substitute for stricter measures and more practical actions. Exhortations, voluntary guidelines and good behaviour standards do suffer the obvious limitation that compliance places the "responsible" corporate citizen at a disadvantage in relation to competing firms.

Regulation is widely used both by the federal government and by the provinces to modify or control environmentally harmful conduct through standard setting. The federal Fisheries Act, for example, permits the minister to designate substances "deleterious" and to prohibit their discharge either into the sea or into interprovincial inland waters unless the operator has obtained approval. Similarly, the Clean Air Act authorizes the federal government to establish national air-quality objectives and to regulate emission standards at an air-pollution source. Expert sub-committees of the Federal-Provincial Committee on Air Pollution define "desirable", "acceptable" and "tolerable" levels of national air quality and develop objectives for the control of major contaminants such as sulphur dioxide and nitrous oxides.

To set general standards through regulation is often an administratively simple way of dealing with non-persistent pollutants. Nevertheless, this approach has been the subject of considerable criticism. When a single strict standard is applied uniformly over an extensive area, the level of environmental protection provided may be higher in some regions than a site-specific assessment would require.

Non-statutory policy and review procedures are an important part of environmental decision making. The Environmental Assessment and Review Process (EARP), which the federal Cabinet established in 1973, has no statutory basis. Its purpose is to ensure that the likely environmental effects of federal programs and of projects that involve federal money or land are taken into account in the earliest stages of planning. EARP operates in two phases. First, the agency responsible for the project determines whether the project is likely to have significant environmental consequences. If it is, then a panel of experts appointed by the Federal Environmental Assessment and Review Office (FEARO) and the Department of the Environment undertakes a public review, including hearings, of a detailed impact-assessment document which the proponent agency has prepared in accordance with guidelines specified by the review panel. Since 1974, EARP has reviewed several major federal projects. In the view of some critics, EARP is little more than the voice of the federal government's ecological conscience, since its authority is based on moral suasion rather than on statutory force.

The limitations of the approaches outlined above have stimulated thinking about new methods of environmental decision making and about ways to integrate this process more effectively with the planning activities of public and private actors. Experiments with environmental mediation have been carried out, notably in the United States, with a view to reducing the costs of conflict resolution and facilitating the participation of a wide range of interested individuals and groups. Such "alternative dispute-resolution" techniques do have attractions in some circumstances. Questions persist, however, about the choice of interests that should be involved in the process and the identification of those persons who can most effectively represent them. Moreover, the permanence of mediated environmental agreements may be uncertain, since it depends on the ability of the parties involved to monitor and enforce compliance, through the courts if necessary.

More than one observer has proposed the introduction of an environmental bill of rights for Canada as a means of ensuring for citizens the maintenance of a safe and clean environment in which to live and work. The authors of one work on the environment list a number of principles that might be embodied in such a bill of rights:

- The right to a healthy and attractive environment
- The right to use the law to defend the environment in courts and tribunals
- Environmental impact studies
- Access to information
- Public participation in setting environmental standards
- An environmental ombudsman
- Class actions
- The right to defend the environment at a reasonable cost
- Restrictions on agency decisions
- Judicial review of administrative action
- The burden of proof to be on the pollutor.[6]

Dissatisfaction with the effects of many existing regulatory approaches to pollution has prompted some economists to urge that more market-oriented policies be used to control environmental damage. They suggest that in certain circumstances, options such as fees for the right to discharge effluents would be both more effective and more economically efficient than regulation. An "effluent charge" is basically a payment per unit of pollution discharged from a designated source. An "effluent-rights" program would involve a distribution of the rights to discharge pollutants, based on an understanding of total allowable pollution emissions from all sources in a particular jurisdiction. The rights could be distributed by means of an auction, or they could be assigned on the basis of emissions from existing sources. Such rights could then be transferred at prices determined by the relationship between the total rights available and the demand for those rights.

The Dynamics of Environmental Policy Making

The multiplicity of forms and agencies of government intervention in environmental management demonstrates the complexity of our Canadian governments' responses to public concern with environmental protection and standards. A brief examination of the dynamics of the policy-formation and implementation processes will reinforce that impression of complexity.

Information, scientific, technological, economic and regulatory, is vital to the environmental-protection process. Obviously, effective pollution control requires a measurement of pollution. For example, an agency responsible for water quality must translate criteria for fishing, recreational use and safety into standards for, say, suspended solids and biochemical oxygen demand. In order to set totals for allowable emissions, the agency must also determine the absorptive capacity of the water. Where there are several sources of emissions, the agency must devise a system for assigning individual quotas, the sum of which will not exceed the allowable total. It may be necessary to adjust totals and quotas as new information becomes available, since many of the effects of pollutants reveal themselves only after a long interval.

The scientific information required for effective environmental control is costly and difficult to accumulate and evaluate. It takes continuous effort simply to gather the base-line data needed to improve our understanding of the interaction of environmental and industrial processes in the circumstances peculiar to Canada. Scientific information must not only be gathered; it must also be made accessible to concerned parties: researchers, industry representatives, environmental groups, and the general public.

Like scientific information, information about the regulatory process and its results is difficult to obtain and to assess. Very little environmental regulation consists of across-the-board rules or standards. For the most part, the regulatory apparatus consists of discrete, and usually confidential, agreements made with individual firms, by federal or provincial departments, at the discretion of the minister. While environmental interest groups have tried to monitor environmental regulation, their resources are far too thin, and the decision-making arenas are far too numerous, to permit them to act as an effective third presence.

Both industry and environmental interest groups are given to deploring the complexity of the environmental-regulation process. This complexity is especially evident in project- and product-approval procedures, which often involve hearings. The time between the initiation of a proposal for a major resource-development or industrial undertaking and the date the project comes on stream is significant to the proponent, whose expenditures during this period must be financed from other revenue sources. Extended and costly hearings are therefore a source of considerable concern and frustration, particularly when approval must be sought from more than one jurisdiction. Regulatory "lag" is thus often said to deter economic development, particularly where major projects are concerned.

Environmental interest groups, too, derive considerable frustration from the hearings process. The fragmentation of the process among several jurisdictions may deflect attention from major issues by emphasizing technical particulars. Moreover, the burden of participation in the assessment process is often severe, a circumstance that emphasizes a difficulty widely familiar to public interest groups: the "free-rider" problem. Environmental interest groups find it much more difficult to secure permanent membership, and hence resources, than do producer interests and manufacturing associations. The reason is that non-members can obtain the benefits of the environmental groups' activity without having to contribute to it. Consequently, environmental groups, which by definition have a stronger institutional interest in environmental performance than have other kinds of organizations, face extraordinary obstacles in trying to promote and monitor environmental issues. When one adds to this fundamental weakness the fact that there are numerous venues for decision making, the extreme difficulty of the task that such groups undertake becomes apparent. Commissioners do not mean to suggest that none of the other participants in the environmental/economic equation have a serious interest in environmental improvement. Obviously, they do. But the reality is that private companies, and indeed governments, vary widely in their degree of commitment to the environment.

The free-rider problem and the complexity of the regulatory process make it clear that environmental decision making suffers from serious institutional weaknesses that should be addressed. This Commission sees a need for greater public funding of environmental groups so that they can serve as a more continuous presence in environmental hearings and in monitoring and compliance activity.

It will be a delicate undertaking to design a decision-making process that permits a sufficient degree of public participation and yet avoids excessive regulatory "lag". For major projects, which almost always require the approval of more than one government, a key reform would be movement toward a single joint-hearings process. Another important reform would be the establishment of the federal government's environmental assessment process on a statutory basis. Obviously, there would have to be some limit to the applicability of such a statute; otherwise, any project, however minor, that involved federal property or federal financing could not proceed without hearings. The answer to this problem would be to define a threshold: for projects of less than a certain size, assessment would not be compulsory.

While, in some instances, the decision-making process consumes too much time, in others it does not consume enough. Environmental issues often exhibit great technological complexity and provoke considerable scientific debate. One advantage of consolidating the review procedures of two or more jurisdictions is that more time would be available for the proper exposure of technical and scientific controversy. The assessment process must not only give more time to such controversy; it must also develop better procedures than it now possesses for clarifying and resolving it. In clarifying the scientific debate, such procedures would also expose the economic and political motives that often underlie "scientific" arguments. A more intense and exacting hearings process would probably be more time consuming than the present arrangements, but the decisions it produced would be better informed and therefore less costly, at least in the long run.

Concerns about the complexity and uncertainty of the environmental protection process also arise in connection with day-to-day compliance and enforcement procedures. Governments' failure to develop consistent approaches to compliance, to standards for assessing performance, and to shifting economic conditions contributes to the difficulty of sustaining overall progress in environmental matters.

Critics of the present regulatory system argue that Canadian governments cannot possibly be neutral regulators, considering that their own Crown corporations are often the promoters of projects that are under regulation. Some observers believe that even now the American regulatory regime is superior to the Canadian regime, since the former provides more opportunities for private litigation and involves the possibility of stiffer penalties. Others see the American arrangement as a recipe for costly and excessive procedural wrangling throughout the regulatory and judicial systems.

Many observers also object to government's avoidance of universal compliance and enforcement standards in favour of individual – and generally confidential – agreements with companies. A case could be made that invididual agreements are necessary, since no two industrial projects have precisely the same effect on the environment. Many of the objections to such agreements could be overcome by a system of very stiff penalties that would be known publicly, and that would come into effect automatically if compliance failed to materialize. Alternatively, there could be somewhat milder penalties and a requirement that compliance schedules be made public.

A brief examination of two industries will illustrate the mechanics of regulation under existing formulae. In the pulp and paper industry, the basis of regulation is the determination of an allowable effluent requirement for each mill. The federal government and the provinces share jurisdiction, although their concerns are different: the federal government has authority over fish, the provinces over water.

The federal authorities prescribe allowable levels of effluent for the component processes relevant to each mill, while the provincial guidelines are based on the mill's attributes and the absorptive capacity of the water. In both areas, the guidelines give little, if any, consideration to the costs of compliance. A reasonable degree of co-operation exists between the two levels of government, which generally agree to recognize the more stringent of the two sets of guidelines. For the past two decades, the federal government has granted special capital-cost allowances for pollution-abatement equipment in existing plants. In 1979, approval of adequate provision for pollution abatement was a condition for receiving special financial assistance under a joint federal-provincial program. Apparently, these have proved to be weak incentives.

Our second example concerns the sulphur dioxide emissions from Inco's smelter at Sudbury, Ontario. After passage of the Ontario Air Pollution Control Act in 1967, Inco was required to build a new taller stack to replace three shorter chimneys. Sulphur dioxide emissions were to be reduced to 4716 tonnes per day by July 1, 1970; to 3991 tonnes per day by December 31, 1974; to 3265 tonnes per day by December 31, 1976; and to 680 tonnes per day by December 31, 1978. Inco could not meet the third target, and extensive negotiations followed. In 1980, the province issued a new directive that imposed an immediate limit of 2267 tonnes per day; emissions were to be reduced to 1769 tonnes per day by 1983. Inco officials asked why the guidelines issued were so optimistic, since performance is bound to be judged with reference to those guidelines. Perhaps, they suggested, the regulators had significantly overestimated the economic prospects of the industry. Then it became clear that strict enforcement of the Air Pollution Control Act might put some pulp and paper mills and smelters out of business.

Obviously, the tailoring of compliance guidelines to fit the economic circumstances of each mill or smelter leads to variations in the quality of air and water at different sites, and to an uneven responsibility for the costs of environmental improvement. In the extreme, marginal mills or smelters are not expected to take any action; profitable operations are. New mills face tougher standards than old ones. Some commentators have even argued that existing producers sought the tailoring of requirements and subsidies through accelerated capital-cost allowances because that approach would give them an advantage over possible entrants.

These examples show that there is considerable "give and take" as the regulator and the regulated enterprise seek to balance environmental and other goals. The complexity of the regulatory task calls upon all of the devices of governing: the carrot, the stick, persuasion and public information. The key to success is to devise a combination of decisions that produces sustained implementation, which is the result of real changes in behaviour. All participants in the environmental issue have now had more than a decade of experience: although there has been progress, we have seen that sometimes both governments and private firms have been able to pull back from earlier levels of commitment. It is for this reason that Commissioners support a movement toward the consolidation and the legal entrenchment of the many forums in which environmental decisions are made.

To attain the goal of sustained implementation also requires that a new political and economic maturity be applied to the use of policy devices such as effluent charges. This is not to argue that the levying of effluent charges is in itself a sufficient solution to the problem of pollution. Rather, this Commission argues that when used with other policy instruments, the levy can contribute to sustained improved behaviour. Effluent charges internalize the costs of pollution to the company involved and give the firm practical incentive to change its economic behaviour.

The interaction of scientific, institutional and economic factors in environmental policy making and implementation subjects these complex processes to many forms of discontinuity. Decisions about investment in environmental research can be influenced by many unrelated factors. Regulatory processes do not operate consistently, or they take place in several forums, taxing the patience of the participants and inhibiting effective exposure to, and analysis of, fundamental issues. Compliance and monitoring efforts are subject to modification in accordance with the shifting budgetary concerns of government and industry. All of these phenomena are natural enough in what is still an early stage of our progress towards proper maintenance of the environment. If it is true, however, as Commissioners believe it is, that there is no long-term conflict between economic growth and environmental concerns, and if it is also true that decisions which affect the environment generally look to the short term, then there must be some permanent arrangement for monitoring decisions of these sorts. Otherwise Canadians cannot be sure that decision makers are, in fact, taking them along a long-term path that they broadly support.

It is in this sense that environmentalists are right in calling for a form of "non-GNP" social accounting that captures some non-economic indicators of well-being. Having made this statement, Commissioners must also acknowledge that agreement on what a system of environmental monitoring should include will not be easy to achieve. The basis for such a system could be an independent national body equipped with the scientific expertise to identify existing and potential hazards and to lay the groundwork for preventive action. The monitoring system could embody national, regional and sectoral environmental criteria: it would monitor pollutants and hazards of high national or regional priority, large bodies of water, and major companies and Crown corporations in each sector.

Notes

1. Cited in Canada, Environment Canada, *Conference on the Human Environment* (Ottawa: Information Canada, 1972), p. 10.
2. Seymour J. Rubin and Thomas R. Graham, eds., *Environment and Trade: The Relation of International Trade and Environmental Policy* (Totowa, N.J.: Allanheld, Osmun for the American Society of International Law, 1982), p. 9.
3. *The European Community's Environmental Policy*, 2d ed. (Luxembourg: Office for Official Publications of the European Communities, 1983), p. 19.
4. Donella H. Meadows, Dennis L. Meadows, Jorgen Randers, and William W. Behrens III, *The Limits to Growth*, a report for the Club of Rome's Project on the Predicament of Mankind (New York: Universe Books, 1972).
5. Related issues are surveyed in D. Paul Emond, "Environmental Law and Policy: A Retrospective Examination of the Canadian Experience", in *Consumer Protection, Environmental Law and Corporate Power*, vol. 50, prepared for the Royal Commission on the Economic Union and Development Prospects for Canada (Toronto: University of Toronto Press, 1985).
6. David Estrin and John Swaigen, *Environment on Trial: A Handbook of Ontario Environmental Law*, rev. ed. (Toronto: Canadian Environmental Law Research Foundation, 1978), Chapter 21.

Canada's Environmental Agenda

Several major environmental issues merit special reference here because of their importance, and because a long-term commitment must be made if they are to be resolved. Solutions will require both prompt action and sustained effort, and neither will be easy to achieve. Commissioners set out this agenda as our contribution to increasing Canadians' awareness of the importance of dealing with a series of very large environmental issues on an urgent basis. We have not, however, been able to delve deeply enough into items on this agenda to recommend specific solutions. Such action is beyond the scope of our mandate.

As human capacity to alter the environment has grown, humanity has too often abused the natural world in which we all live. The potential for wide-ranging environmental catastrophes that would seriously harm global habitats is growing. In these circumstances, how much do we wish to gamble? As people usually learn best through experience, convenient ways for us to achieve our immediate economic ends are frequently at odds with nature and natural processes. We must read the preliminary signs of environmental damage quickly and try to take wise action. Sometimes, however, even by the time that the visible signs of environmental deterioration are detected, they may represent processes which are well advanced and almost impossible to reverse.

We have reviewed, in Chapter 2, major problems threatening the earth's ecological systems. Of the problems outlined, we would single out acid rain, other forms of air pollution, hazardous-waste disposal, water quality and forest conservation as areas for immediate attention by Canadian governments, corporations and citizens. Other environmental issues of special significance in Canada include the restoration of the Great Lakes, the export of water, the preservation of Canadian wildlife, and protection of the Arctic.

Acid Rain and Other Forms of Air Pollution

Canadians are experiencing a host of air-pollution problems as a result of the combustion of fossil fuels in power plants, factories and automobiles. Acid rain is causing large-scale destruction of forests, streams and lakes. Levels of ozone in the atmosphere are already high enough to damage valuable crops such as corn, wheat and soybeans. Gaseous sulphur and nitrogen oxides are known to cause serious damage to paint, paper and textiles, and to contribute to the erosion of building stone. Possibly the most serious consequence of fossil-fuel combustion is the long-term accumulation of carbon dioxide (CO_2) in the atmosphere. Scientists expect the build-up of this substance to raise global temperatures significantly by the middle of the next century. These developments pose complex, systemic, environmental threats requiring a co-ordinated institutional response. Canada's experience with acid rain shows how difficult it is to evoke such a response. Because acid rain, ozone and the build-up of carbon dioxide in the atmosphere are problems with a common origin, they are also susceptible to common solutions. Strategies to date most often address issues in isolation. Present control systems for reducing emissions are expensive, but not prohibitively so. If we procrastinate, however, effective action may be beyond the capacity of future generations.

The Great Lakes and Water Management

The Great Lakes provide an unequalled natural endowment for Canada: the largest chain of freshwater lakes in the world, containing 18 per cent of the total amount of fresh water on earth. At present, one in three Canadians and one in seven Americans depend on the Great Lakes for their water supply. Currently, water demand on these lakes amounts to 140 000 litres per second. A Board of the International Joint Commission (IJC) predicted, in a report issued in 1981, that demand could rise to one million litres per second by 2035, an amount that could result in a dramatic drop in the water level of Lakes Michigan, Erie and Huron. This development would occur because most of the renewable supply of fresh water in the Great Lakes – that is, water that falls as rain and snow and passes through the Great Lakes system – is already in full use. A permanent lowering of lake levels would create economic losses amounting to hundreds of millions of dollars annually. In light of predictions of lower demand for water and forecasts of lower growth for the economy generally, the IJC has recently stated that estimates beyond the year 2000 are unreliable. It does, however, believe that water quantity *is* an issue in Canada, and that demand for water should be monitored carefully.

Water quality has, of course, long been a problem for Canada, particularly in the Great Lakes basin. Canadians appear to be firm in their demands for tougher legislative standards to protect the quality of drinking water, yet Quebec is the first province to enact legally-enforceable standards for quality. In the years since Canada and the United States signed the 1972 Great Lakes Water Quality Agreement, significant achievements have been recorded, particularly in the point-source control of phosphorus and a number of other conventional urban and industrial pollutants. Nevertheless, substantial efforts have not eliminated the serious pollution problems in the Great Lakes. Unfortunately, little progress has been made in 18 population centres identified by the IJC in 1981 as exhibiting significant environmental degradation. There has also been limited success in coming to grips with the overall problem of toxic chemicals poisoning the Great Lakes basin. New chemicals are continually being introduced into the water. Even if only a few are harmful, it is becoming more and more apparent that their individual, combined and long-term effects do present serious environmental problems. The International Joint Commission has questioned the adequacy of present environmental risk-assessment techniques and the degree of confidence placed in them. It has also urged both the Canadian and the American governments to increase their efforts to support a co-ordinated and well-researched strategy to reduce the use of toxic substances and to pay serious attention to the development of monitoring methods for groundwater resources in the Great Lakes region.[1]

The Great Lakes Water Quality Agreement (1978) is a milestone document because it was one of the first international statements that promoted the integration of human activity with the realities of the biota, land, water and air phenomena of the environment. The IJC maintains that because, in many jurisdictions, existing environmental and resource programs are compartmentalized and spread across several departments, a comprehensive approach requires, at the very least, a reorganization of thinking and, perhaps, a reorganization of institutional arrangements.

It is important that Canada increase vigilance over acid rain and the monitoring of the quality of the Great Lakes and other major river basins and lakes. It is equally important that we put in place more comprehensive plans for preserving the ecology of our river basins and coherent regulatory arrangements for water use and management, in particular, for waters north of the sixtieth parallel. The lack of a management framework for water, along with water-pollution and conservation issues, were the dominant concerns in submissions to the Inquiry on Federal Water Policy.[2] To manage water resources is not an easy task. Costly infrastructure generally requires long-term commitments to water availability, and allocations among users involve many trade-offs. To develop a master plan for this handling of a fundamental resource may involve a repetitive and slow consultative process, but it must include consideration of the interests and hopes of the current users of the water systems, as well as attention to the maze of federal, territorial, provincial and state jurisdictions governing them.

Water Export and Diversion

Water export from Canada and the transfer of water between drainage basins within Canada are expected to be major policy issues of the next few decades. These issues sparked considerable interest at the recent hearings of the Inquiry on Federal Water Policy. Pressure is mounting to divert or transfer water from and within Canada – particularly from northern Canada and the Great Lakes – to southern Canadian urban centres and the water-short states of the American southwest. There is evidence, however, that water diversions might be avoided if, for example, residents of Canada and the United States take steps to manage water resources more efficiently. One measure worth consideration would be the establishment of a pricing system for water that more accurately reflects its value.

Two water-diversion projects which have been on the drawing board for many years are the $150-billion North American Water and Power Alliance (NAWAPA) scheme and the $100-billion Grand Canal Company plan. The NAWAPA scheme was to have dammed rivers in Yukon and Alaska and flooded part of the Rocky Mountain Trench. A canal linking Alberta with the Great Lakes was also part of this mammoth plan. The Grand Canal scheme, which has gained more attention recently, would turn James Bay into a freshwater lake, then channel a portion of its water through various Quebec and Ontario river systems and canals down to the Great Lakes; from there further diversion would be engineered to serve other distant regions of Canada and the United States.

Only one in ten intervenors appearing before the Inquiry on Federal Water Quality spoke of water export as an opportunity. The overwhelming majority rejected, out of hand, consideration of export or added conditions so restrictive as to make approval unlikely for many years. Concern about water transfers centred on three issues: doubts about economic gains generated by such projects, concern about social disruption and, most strongly, concern about environmental effects.[3]

The environmental effects of major water diversions would be felt both during and after the construction phase. Disturbance of rivers and lakes could damage or destroy fish habitats and further harm the fish populations by siltation. Flora and fauna around the sites of construction could also be adversely affected, and the permanent loss of agricultural or forest land is a real possibility. Once construction is completed, permanent environmental effects would ensue: flooding or stream-flow reduction, drying up of marshes and lakes, and the transfer of harmful foreign species into river basins. While some effects are predictable, it is impossible to foresee all the environmental effects of a large project.[4]

In 1982, the eight Great Lakes States, along with Quebec and Ontario, produced a resolution that would prohibit water diversions from the Great Lakes basin before thorough impact studies were made and agreement was obtained from all provincial, state and federal governments concerned. In 1985, a Great Lakes Charter was signed by the same governments. It embodied the intent of the earlier resolution and promised further consultation and co-operation in the use of water in the Great Lakes basin. The Government of Canada has supported fully the efforts of Ontario and Quebec in designing this agreement.

The Arctic Environment

Canadians have a rich and diverse northern heritage, a landscape of incredible beauty, fragility and hostility. The ice-covered ocean is of global importance because of its profound influence on world climate. It is also an essential breeding ground and refuge for marine mammals, migratory birds and other wildlife.

In recent decades, the establishment of defence installations, the discovery of oil near and beneath the Arctic Ocean, and increased exploration for mineral wealth brought about the realization that economic development in these regions can quickly become an engineering and scientific challenge of great proportions. The technical problems are real, and our ability to adjust to them depends on how well we understand the characteristics of the rigorous climate of the Arctic environment. Project development in the North must be guided by the dual criteria of environmental soundness and balanced social and economic development.

Fish and wildlife have long formed the basis of the traditional economy and culture of northern Canada's aboriginal peoples. Failure to protect and manage adequately these renewable resources could lead to the collapse both of the northern environment and of the societies associated with it. Although the Government of Canada has talked of "balanced development", not enough has been done to protect areas of outstanding natural significance. A system of protected conservation areas does not exist in our North, even though the legislative capability to form one has existed for several years. Only a few of the 151 ecological sites identified in the International

Biological Program are protected, and there is only one national wildlife area in the North: Polar Bear Pass, designated in 1982.

Seventy per cent of the Canadian coastline, the longest in the world, borders on the Arctic Ocean. We share this marine territory with five other nations. Except for a number of single-purpose bilateral treaties, there is no international agreement defining states' rights and responsibilities in the Arctic Ocean region. Indeed, there is uncertainty about almost every aspect of national jurisdiction in the Arctic Ocean: the location of marine boundaries; the measurement and extent of territorial waters; the status and control of shipping lanes; the limits of the continental shelf; rights to seabed minerals; protection of the environment; and regulation and conservation of the fisheries. Canada's claims to its Arctic offshore must be affirmed and protected by national legislation.

Hazardous Wastes

The presence and safe handling of hazardous wastes is another important issue on our environmental agenda. In addition to a variety of potentially adverse effects on human health, the consequences of chemical contamination of the environment include a loss of food species, curtailment of important economic activities and a variety of irreversible ecological changes that threaten humanity's future use and enjoyment of the living world.

Although some hazardous substances are found in municipal and domestic waste, the majority are residues from the industrial and nuclear power processes. These wastes contain oil, phenols, arsenic, mercury, lead, radioactive materials and a large number of human-made chemicals. Estimates put Canada's hazardous waste production at about one million dry tonnes per year, nearly half of it produced in Ontario. Polychlorinated Biphenyls (PCBs) provide a good example of the insidious threat of these chemical contaminants, as well as the essentially political nature of the decisions required to control them. Because PCBs are extremely mobile, the point where they are emitted has little relation to their danger. PCB compounds have been found in all the oceans, in Arctic bears, in Great Lakes fish, in rainfall and in human beings. It is estimated that more than half of the PCBs produced have been discarded in landfill sites and dumps, in the form of junked plastics, paints and electrical equipment. Contaminants washed out from such sites can enter groundwater or can be carried by rain and snow into nearby streams and rivers, and so find their way into lakes and oceans. Destruction of PCBs is preferable to long-term storage. Numerous technologies exist to destroy PCBs effectively, and many countries have used them. In Canada, however, no facilities exist to dispose of these contaminants safely. The failure of Canada's governments, industries and citizens to agree on the location of such facilities has contributed to the current stalemate.

Canada is indeed entering a period in which environmental damage caused by toxic wastes, the safe disposal of wastes, and the choice of sites for their disposal will constitute a major divisive force in our society. The problem will never "just go away". Hazardous-waste/treatment facilities will have to be built in or near communities, and public resistance will be high. The problem is compounded by the fact that traditional landfill sites are no longer considered acceptable disposal dumps for these substances. The result is that untreated wastes, some highly corrosive, are being stored in drums and tanks until treatment becomes available. Wastes are also being stored permanently in deep wells where porous rock layers below the water table absorb liquid contaminants. To ship wastes to Canada's "remote" areas in not a solution. Today, even the least-densely populated areas of Canada are someone's backyard.

The ideal system to work towards is one which minimizes production and use of hazardous substances and tracks any that are produced through all stages of use, transport and disposal. Modern treatment facilities are needed. We must move from the present situation of management-by-crisis to management-by-planning. In the long run, to do nothing about the haphazard handling of chemical wastes is far more dangerous than to resort to controlled transport, treatment and disposal. Hazardous wastes and their elimination or disposal constitutes an area where it is clear that increased regulatory procedures, as well as continuing research, are well warranted.

Wildlife Protection

Wildlife and plant life help to provide us Canadians with our daily requirements of food, fibre, shelter, fuel, chemical and biomedical products. Wildlife species are also important as a recreational attraction, for the general economic benefits they provide and for other contributions they make to the quality of life. Economic activity associated with wildlife has been valued by the Canadian Wildlife Association at over $7 billion in 1977.[5]

The management of wildlife and plant life, and the management of human use of these resources, are complex matters. Because there are a number of different, and sometimes competing, ways in which wildlife is enjoyed and used, the art of management is to provide for the most broadly acceptable mix of activities, taking account of the variety of cultural values and of the paramount need to conserve the resource heritage for future generations.

Guidelines for Wildlife Policy[6] in Canada was developed between 1980 and 1982 by a committee of the Federal-Provincial Wildlife Conference. The *Guidelines* outline three fundamental goals:

- To maintain the ecosystems on which wildlife and people depend
- To preserve the genetic diversity of wildlife
- To ensure that the enjoyment and use of wildlife is sustainable.

Commissioners support these goals, as well as the principles that the cost of management essential to preserving viable populations of wildlife should be borne by all Canadians, and that special management measures required to permit intensive uses should be supported by the users.[7] Wildlife policies, like air pollution policies, must be broadened from the current single-purpose approach to include, for example, habitat protection and management.

Notes

1. International Joint Commission, *Second Biennial Report Under the Great Lakes Water Quality Agreement of 1978 to the Governments of the United States and Canada and the States and Provinces of the Great Lakes Basin* (Ottawa, 1984).
2. Canada, Inquiry on Federal Water Policy, *Hearing About Water: A Synthesis* (Ottawa, 1985).
3. *Ibid.*, pp. 15 and 50.
4. Anthony Scott, "The Economics of Water Export Policy", in *Canada's Resource Industries*, vol. 14 (Toronto: University of Toronto Press, 1985), prepared for this Commission jointly with the Inquiry on Federal Water Policy, 1985.
5. Estimated by the Canadian Wildlife Federation in 1981.
6. Minister of Environment, *Guidelines for Wildlife Policy in Canada* (Ottawa: Minister of Supply and Services Canada, 1982). The *Guidelines* are based upon the World Conservation Strategy, prepared for the International Union for Conservation of Nature and Natural Resources with the support of the United Nations Environment Program and the World Wilfdlife Fund.
7. *Ibid.*

Conclusions and Recommendations

Integrating the Environment and Economic Development

Institutional arrangements that are designed to deal with clear-cut disputes or problems are often unsuited to the resolution of environmental issues. More and more, environmental decisions depend on the application of ambiguous or provisional scientific and technical evidence to very long-term questions that involve, or potentially affect, the interests of many parties, not all of whom are even identifiable. Moreover, environmental policy making must also take into account the personal values and aspirations of Canadians, which are even more difficult to quantify, though not less important, than the scientific issues.

Commissioners perceive a vital need to integrate environmental decisions with decisions about economic development. In the process of industrial adjustment, opportunities should not be lost to introduce environmentally oriented technological advances. Environmental concerns should receive sustained attention despite the obvious desire to enhance short-term/growth prospects, for, as we have argued, there is no long-term conflict between economic development and the preservation of a healthy environment and a sustainable resource base. Our perceptions of wealth and well-being ought to incorporate environmental, health, and safety considerations. In other words, environmental goals should not be treated as incidental to the other goals of resource and industrial policy. Commissioners seek a sustainable form of development that acknowledges the interdependence of society, the economy and the environment at both the national and the international levels.

In light of Canadians' tendency to make decisions on the basis of short-term considerations, it is important that we strengthen our institutional capacity to monitor decisions. We must have grounds for confidence that decision makers are actually taking steps consistent with the long-term goals defined by public opinion.

The environmental decision-making process illustrates the difficulty of combining public participation with technical expertise, and of reconciling long-term imperatives with powerful and immediate pressures for short-term economic gains. As we have seen, the results of our decisions must also coincide with important international obligations.

Taking Preventive Measures

- Commissioners recommend greater use of a preventive approach to environmental decision making, an approach that reflects and reinforces the growth in public support for policies that contribute to the regeneration of ecological systems. The concern for environmental values should be incorporated into a variety of decision-making processes, such as those that affect the work-place, the regulation and approval of large-scale projects, and the introduction of new products into the market-place.
- Greater consideration should be given to the development of a combined social and economic accounting system that covers not only the conventional economic indicators, but also such matters as soil depletion, forest

degeneration, the costs of restoring a damaged environment, and the effects of economic activity on health.

Formalizing the Environmental Framework

Although many of our recommendations elsewhere in this Report call for reductions in government intervention, Commissioners believe that the environmental field is one in which greater government intervention will prove to be necessary. Successful intervention will require a significant degree of federal-provincial co-operation. We anticipate, too, over the long term, a quantum leap in the size of the environmental task facing Canadians. If we are to deal ably with this task, we must make more effective use of the significant legislative framework that is now in place.

We therefore recommend that:

- Efforts be made to establish, on a sustained basis, the institutional arrangements through which environmental decisions are made
- Governments give greater emphasis to the scientific and analytical capacity of their environmental departments and increase the resources available for the enforcement of environmental policy
- A national body with a core of independent scientific expertise be created to identify hazards that are, or are likely to become, seriously injurious. It would be the responsibility of such a body, styled the "Environmental Council of Canada", to provide information and advice about hazards that are of high national or regional priority: those, for example, that involve major water systems, significant industrial groups, and the actions of federal and provincial Crown corporations.
- In recognition of the important role that research and development play in support both of the environmental regulatory function and of self-monitoring by concerned private sector businesses and associations, funding should be made available to permit research to be undertaken on a continuous basis.

Environmental Review and Assessment

This Commission recommends that:

- Project-approval hearings be co-ordinated or consolidated as a remedy for the excessive "regulatory lag" that results from multiple-hearings requirements. Major projects, in particular, almost always require the approval of more than one government and, frequently, more than one agency in the same government. Consequently we urge that efforts be made to harmonize requirements when multiple hearings are unavoidable and to develop common federal-provincial-municipal/review procedures whenever possible.
- The federal environmental-assessment process be placed on a statutory basis, and that threshold sizes be established for compulsory project assessment so that for smaller projects, assessment would not be compulsory

- Hearings procedures give greater attention to the effective analysis of technical and scientific controversy, not only to improve our understanding of complex scientific questions, but also to expose more clearly the underlying economic and political dimensions of what sometimes are cast as purely scientific decisions.

Visibility and Participation

Commissioners recommend that:

- Measures be implemented to ensure a sustained public monitoring of environmental progress involving government-industry negotiations on environmental performance standards. Visibility and accountability should be increased.
- Increased public funding be made available to environmental groups to enable them to provide a more continuous presence in hearings and in monitoring activity.

Conclusions and Recommendations

The natural resource sector's contribution to Canada's economic well-being, cultural life, and political traditions and institutions has been immense. Because natural resources have been so important to Canada's past, however, we tend to exaggerate their importance to our future. In fact, the resource sector has not grown at a rate commensurate with the economic expectations we have developed in the years since the Second World War; nor does its projected growth match our hopes for the decades to come.

It has become clear in recent years – if it was not clear before – that Canada's natural resource endowment is not unlimited. We are losing our agricultural land to suburbs and shopping centres. Our stands of readily accessible, high-quality timber are largely gone, and our richest and most accessible deposits of ore and fossil fuels are already in production. Our mismanagement of the fishery has meant that we have not been able to reap the potential benefits of the designation of the 200-mile offshore zone in 1977. These problems of supply are compounded by prospects of lower demand in world markets for forest products and most non-fuel minerals. Moreover, our forestry and minerals industries can expect increasingly stiff competition from countries with lower production costs, and this competition will be made all the more difficult by the rapid advances in products and process technology.

These problems do not mean that our basic resource industries will disappear. Relative to other nations, Canada remains well endowed with natural resources. The outlook for oil and gas, a few minerals, hydro-electricity, and Western grains is favourable. The dollar value of production in the resource sector will continue to grow. Nevertheless, the share of output in this sector will decline, relative to the share of output in other sectors of our economy, although the decline will not be as rapid as it was in the first two post-war decades. Total exports of resource products will continue to expand, and the terms of trade are unlikely to turn against us in any dramatic fashion. Increasingly, however, we shall have to supplement resource exports with exports of more highly processed products if we are to maintain our capacity to buy the goods and services of other nations. The pattern of relative decline will mean that we can generally expect no net gain in resource-sector employment in the future: a growing proportion of Canadians will find their jobs in factories or offices. Indeed, the decline in the resource sector's share of total employment is the clearest indication that the sector will not be the engine of economic growth that it was in the past.

The prospect of a decline in the relative importance of the resource sector in relation to our national economy is no reason to neglect that sector's problems or its claims. Resource industries are still essential to the economic life of many regions of Canada. Moreover, we have an obligation to pass on to future generations a variety of viable resource industries founded on a natural endowment that is as secure and as healthy as we can make it. Canada's success in resource production owes as much to human ingenuity as it does to the resource endowment itself, and many of the problems of the sector can be overcome, or at least diminished, by appropriate applications of that ingenuity. We must apply new methods, new processes, new public policies, and new thinking to the problems of maintaining both the competitiveness of the resource industries and the integrity of the natural environment that is their base.

■ Chapter 12 set out this Commission's detailed recommendations for the individual resource sectors. The thrust of our recommendations for dealing with the challenges ahead in each resource sector is as follows:

- For agriculture, we recommend a range of measures, from expansion of foreign markets, to increased R&D, to reform of national supply-management marketing boards, planned to enhance the efficiency of a sector which has great potential over the long term.
- For forestry, we recognize a legacy of mismanagement and recommend significant changes in the way the forest sector operates, as well as a major infusion of public and private investment.
- For the fishery, what has been lacking is political will, and we recommend measures to build on the fundamental reforms of the Kirby and Pearse Reports to shift the balance in public policy toward building a viable economic base in Canada's coastal regions.
- For minerals, we recognize generally the more limited possibilities. We recommend a more realistic approach to adjustment and a movement towards a profit-based tax system.
- For energy, we recommend a new framework based on the principles of efficiency, fairness and predictability, and a complete overhaul of the fiscal regime for oil and gas.
- For the environment, we recognize the growing challenge and the need to integrate decisions related to environment and economic development. We recommend a series of measures to correct the incentives which are aimed at protecting the environment; and, in general, we propose strengthening the regulatory framework.

Commissioners believe that it is important, however difficult, to assess the problems and opportunities of the resource sector in a more comprehensive way, just as, for example, governments focus from time to time on the general issues of the manufacturing sector.

■ The following general principles briefly relate Commissioners' detailed recommendations to the management of the resource sector as a whole:

- We conclude that in Canada, with all its rich resource heritage, there is no conflict, in the long term, between the stewardship, preservation and enhancement of the natural resource base and growth prospects for the traditional resource industries. Consequently, we perceive a vital need to integrate environmental decisions and decisions related to economic development, and our proposals for action in each of the particular resource sectors reflect this perception. Thus we recommend a study of the loss of prime farm land to non-agricultural uses and emphasize our concern about the problems of soil deterioration and soil salinity. We support the infusion of large sums of both public and private monies into reforestation and silviculture, and we recommend that the duration of leasing agreements between governments and forest companies be increased in order to provide an incentive for long-term management of forest tracts. Finally, in recognition of the fact that natural resources belong to the Canadian people and must be passed on to future generations, we believe that private developers should continue to pay governments a royalty based on production for oil and gas and minerals.

- In many other places in this Report, we call for less government intervention; in the area of environmental regulation, however, we are obliged to call for more. Over the long term, the task of environmental regulation promises to be immense. We shall have to deal with growth in the number and size of projects that may adversely affect the environment, with an increasing number of pollutants and hazards, with the irreversible, and sometimes unquantifiable, effects of a growing range of industrial substances and processes, and with the emerging international aspects of our environmental responsibility. Consequently, we recommend that governments increase their spending to provide the analytical resources needed to support the long-term regulatory task. We further recommend that federal environmental processes be put on a statutory basis, and that federal and provincial review processes be brought into greater harmony.
- Changes in the pattern of world trade have offered new opportunities and new challenges to the Canadian resource sector. Our ability to realize the opportunities – and to survive the challenges – will depend on our ability to design resource strategies suited to a global context. This consideration has led us to recommend that the grains sector and the fishery sector pursue marketing and production strategies that will give them access to the new and rapidly growing markets in the developing countries. Whether it is a question of expanding our markets or of beating the competition, we believe that it is within Canada's interest to work for free trade, both at the multilateral level and at the bilateral level, with the largest purchaser of Canadian resource products, the United States. The adjustment problems that would derive from freer trade and the bargaining tactics

that would be necessary to bring it about would vary with each resource.

- We believe that in many instances a stricter adherence to market principles and an increase in the incentives to the private sector would brighten the prospects of Canada's resource industries. Thus we consider that a commitment to market pricing for both oil and gas would provide the incentive essential to increased exploration and development. For oil and gas and minerals, we believe that the establishment of a taxation scheme based largely on profits rather than on output volumes would both promote the development of marginal supplies and allow the industry to make more rational resource-allocation decisions. Although we do not advocate transferring ownership of forest tracts to private industry, we do suggest that such modifications to the land-tenure system as increasing the duration of leasing agreements would promote more responsible forest management. Finally, we recommend a phasing-out of national agricultural-supply/management marketing boards and their replacement by an income-stabilization scheme designed to moderate large fluctuations in farmers' incomes.
- We believe that there is room for significant improvement in the efficiency of both the regulatory framework and the handling, licensing and transportation infrastructure that supports the resource sector. We underline the important effect of the Crow Rate on the transportation of all bulk commodities, especially Western grains. We support further movement in the direction of market-rate principles when the Western Grains Transportation Act comes up for review, but we leave it to the Committee of Inquiry on Crow Benefit Payment (Hall Committee) to advise on specific adjustments to the payment of the Crow Benefit. In the minerals area, we recognize that the regulatory structure is cumbersome and slow, and we recommend that governments undertake a systematic review of their regulatory processes with a view to streamlining them. We would also draw attention to the fact that fisheries management has all too often led to overcapacity, unnecessary tensions, uneven product quality and, thus, lost opportunity. For oil and gas, we recommend a simpler taxation regime and a simpler pricing formula, both of which would decrease medium- and long-term uncertainty.
- The resource sector has undergone far-reaching adjustments since the Second World War. Further adjustment will be both essential and unavoidable, although perhaps less dramatic than it has been in the past. We believe that if a given operation has failed to realize a profit over a sustained period, adjustment is inevitable and should be allowed to take its course; governments should not intervene to support uneconomic activity. Mines that

can no longer produce an ore competitively should be phased out, and we believe that in general, the same principle holds for the fishery. As we pointed out above, however, government action is necessary in some areas to guard against deterioration in the quality of our renewable resource base. In particular, we recommend a substantial increase in both public and private expenditures for the renewal of the Canadian forest.

There must be and can be a balance in the adjustment process between efficiency and fairness to people whose livelihoods or communities have long depended on traditional resource industries. In the case of the family farm, we recognize the special problems created by farmers' limited access to equity capital, by the volatility of farm prices, and by the principle that the land is to be passed to future generations. We therefore support the retention of special credit schemes for agriculture and, as mentioned above, we urge consideration of an income-stabilization scheme to replace national supply-management boards. By the same token, we support replacement of Unemployment Insurance for fishermen by a new production-bonus and income-stabilization program, a scheme that would promote more efficient behaviour without reducing total benefits. Fishermen would also be eligible for income supplementation under the Universal Income Security Program (UISP) proposed in our recommendations on social security. In the minerals sector, we recommend the provision of adjustment assistance for communities and individuals affected by mine closures.

- Research has a large pay-off, but often the benefits seem too distant to the producer of the resource to justify the expenditure. We recognize that there must be renewed Canadian effort in fundamental research, especially in the traditional resource industries, if Canada is to match progress in competitor countries. Research into soil deterioration and new crop varieties warrants long-term funding by government. So does research related to aquaculture and to maintenance and improvement of the forest base. We have also called for an increase in expenditure on training in forestry. Finally, we support a stepped-up research effort in the field of environmental management, where we believe that the institutional capacity to provide scientific advice on a systematic basis is essential.
- In view of the importance of resources to Canada's future economic prospects and of the need to take a more integrated view of the problems and opportunities in the resource area as a whole, we recommend the establishment of a Council of Resources Ministers to provide leadership for increased federal-provincial co-operation. We recognize that various ministerial groups (for example, on agriculture and mines) now exist, but

we believe that it is important for a co-ordinated strategy across the range of resources to be developed, based on the principles we have outlined above. We also recommend the development within the federal government of a greater capacity to analyse the contributions and problems of the resource sector as a whole. □

PART V

HUMAN RESOURCES AND SOCIAL SUPPORT

PART V

Contents

PART V

Introduction

The Goals of Social and Human Resource Policies

Throughout much of this Report, Commissioners have focused on aggregates: on the economy or sectors of it, on corporations, on groups or on the institutions of government. In this part of our Report, we wish to focus on those programs that bear directly on individual Canadians: the programs of our human-resource and social-policies sector. In approaching these topics, we have searched through the records of our hearings and the submissions made to us, in an attempt to identify common goals and values with which Canadians approach these programs. There is no doubt that when Canadians assess social- and human-resource policies, they place a high value on efficiency in the use of scarce resources; in this respect, social policies are no different from others. We have found, however, that Canadians also bring a broader set of values to bear when they consider social programs.

First, we Canadians value equity. To our way of thinking, equity implies that the distribution of rewards in our society should reflect not just the ownership of resources and not merely the operations of chance, but also need, effort, merit and the taking of risk where that risk may lead to benefits for others. To our mind, equity is not identical with equality, and yet it often implies a somewhat greater degree of equality than is to be achieved by market mechanisms alone.

Secondly, we Canadians value security. While different people assign different values to security, we all require assurance that in the face of illness, loss of employment, family breakdown or the sometimes inexorable workings of a complex and dynamic economy, we will receive some protection. Security need not and should not be absolute, and there will naturally be wide debate about what degree is adequate, but it seems unquestionable that we all value it and expect our governments to provide it.

Thirdly, we Canadians seek opportunity. To most of us, opportunity is tied to labour-force participation; for most of us, a job represents our avenue of upward mobility and is often an essential element of our sense of self-identity. We therefore want our human-resource programs to be structured in such a way as to help us to find opportunities, to take advantage of them when they come, and to gain some economic headway when we do so. The other side of opportunity is responsibility. We have a corresponding responsibility to provide for ourselves whenever we can and to be willing to adjust our behaviour so as to minimize our dependence on government.

Finally, we Canadians believe in sharing. Whether we are sharing risk or reward, adversity or wealth, we believe that it is our responsibility not merely to help ourselves, but also to help those who, through disability or, perhaps, the hand of fate, cannot provide fully for themselves. To this end, we believe that the benefits provided by social programs should be tailored so that those who, through no fault of their own, have profited less fully than others by the many opportunities provided in our economy should receive at least some of the rewards.

Equity, security, opportunity, responsibility and sharing: these concepts are not put forward in any particular order, for different Canadians will attach different weights to each. Commissioners believe, however, that these are the goals and values that Canadians would wish us to use when we examine those programs which bear most directly upon us all as individuals.

The development of major social-security and social-service programs, the rapid expansion of educational and training systems, the augmentation of a framework for labour relations, the assimilation of millions of immigrants into Canadian society, and the improvement of some aspects of our labour markets all stand out as important achievements of the post-Second World War era. Yet despite broad agreement concerning the values and goals outlined above, the basic means by which we should seek to accomplish them have been increasingly debated. The arguments about the universality of our social programs constitute one such debate. Another relates to the adequacy of our educational and training systems and the continual discussions of how best to structure our unemployment insurance plans. Still another revolves around the nature of our immigration policies. Controversy surrounds the entire area of labour relations, and as a nation, we are far from determining how best to provide equal opportunities in the work-place. A careful examination of these areas of interest is essential to determining Canada's future development prospects.

Achieving Our Social Goals

In striving to achieve the best possible combination of equity, sharing, opportunity, responsibility and security, we Canadians must also remain mindful of our need to achieve an appropriate degree of economic efficiency, for this contribution to the well-being of us all is vital in an increasingly competitive world. To improve economic efficiency is, in effect, to increase the output available to meet the needs and wishes of Canadians, including the poorest and most vulnerable groups within our population, as well as the richest and most secure. It is obvious, therefore, that we must pay due regard to the economic efficiency of all our program designs.

This concern for economic efficiency underlies Canadians' general preference to pursue our goals primarily through formal instruments of social insurance and income redistribution, and through governments' provision of essential social services which the market would not adequately provide, rather than by imposing constraints on the functioning of market mechanisms. Thus, for example, the need to develop a more efficient, flexible and adaptive labour market undergirds Commissioners' analysis of intervention in wage setting, our approach to meeting labour-force requirements, our consideration of existing constraints on part-time work, and our proposals for the reform of aspects of our Unemployment Insurance (UI) system and our major income-transfer programs. We are well aware, of course, that there are many instances of market failure, of situations where the labour market does not operate to ensure efficient allocation of human resources. Where such market failures do exist, we have not hesitated to recommend interventions to correct them.

Just as we Canadians have a range of goals to aim for in considering our human-resource and social-support programs, so also we have a variety of instruments through which to achieve these goals. Broadly speaking, these mechanisms may be divided into two categories: the *direct delivery of services* by government or public institutions such as schools or hospitals and the provision of *transfer payments or the use of tax mechanisms* which redistribute money from one member of society to another. Transfer programs may be further subdivided into those intended to serve primarily as a social-insurance instrument, helping to insulate Canadians from unexpected declines in income, and those which redistribute income on the basis of some definition of need. Unemployment Insurance is the primary example of the former type of program, and social assistance is an example of the latter.

As we assess our current programs, it is important to keep in mind both our multiplicity of goals and the possibility of using various means to achieve them. For example, we may criticize our income-transfer programs for being insufficiently redistributive: that is, for inadequately serving the goals of sharing and security. Equally, however, we must take into account that those programs must fit prevailing concepts of equity, must encourage people to grasp opportunities, and must be delivered in such a way as to maximize the overall efficiency of our economy. We must seek, therefore, to find the best possible balance among those goals.

It is equally important to distinguish among instruments when designing individual programs. For example, attempts to blend the two instruments of insurance and redistribution in a single program may reduce the efficiency of each. Thus Unemployment Insurance is not well suited to serve as an instrument of equitable income redistribution because the program pays benefits on an individual, rather than a family, basis; excludes people who have not paid premiums; fails to test for all sources of income; and applies a very short accounting period to benefits. Yet, intentionally or inadvertently, Canadians use Unemployment Insurance as a redistributive instrument; we do so, for example, by applying a surtax to workers whose annual income is greater than $30 000 and by maintaining a regional benefits structure which is not related directly to individual risk. General acceptance of the desirability of separating insurance and redistribution would therefore provide the basis of important reforms in the UI program, and we Commissioners have based some of our reform proposals on that proposition. Yet, because we are mindful of the multiple goals which the income-security system as a whole should attain, we shall recommend that such an option not be pursued in isolation but, rather, that it be accompanied by a stronger reliance on the tax-transfer system for redistribution of income.

When the focus of the welfare state does shift to these tax-transfer mechanisms, the change also makes major improvements possible. During the decades that immediately followed the Second World War, it was widely assumed that rapid economic growth and the development of social programs had eliminated widespread poverty from modern societies. From the 1960s onward, however, a growing body of evidence and experience has steadily eroded that view. The extent of poverty in Canada continues to stand as a tragic problem, but one which Commissioners believe is susceptible to substantial amelioration through improvements in our income-security programs and tax systems. Moreover, we view the constellation of our tax and transfer programs as seriously flawed with respect to the incentives and opportunities which it provides for low-income Canadians to improve their economic situation. The suggestions we make below are intended, in part, to deal with these problems.

Commissioners believe, too, that the time is opportune to consider major changes in our higher-education and training programs. In some respects, these have served Canadians well, but we are concerned that the programs of financial support now in place will not promote the excellence our nation has every right to demand from publicly financed institutions and the flexibility which those institutions will require to deal with the challenges and opportunities that lie ahead. We therefore canvass a number of reform proposals relating to this part of government activity.

We have already emphasized our conviction that for most Canadians, the primary source of income and opportunity resides and must continue to reside in the labour markets. The efficiency and equity with which those markets operate is therefore vital, not only to our national economic prospects, but also to the prospects of the vast majority of individual Canadians. In many respects, Canadian labour markets deserve a positive evaluation, but there are also many respects in which they can be improved. We devote considerable space in this chapter to an examination of their structure and functioning and to suggestions for their improvement.

We have looked very briefly, too, at a few of our social services, at Canadian immigration policy, and at the role of the voluntary sector in providing services. We have focused less on these issues than on others, not because we consider them less important, but rather because in attempting to narrow slightly what is already an exceedingly broad mandate, we have chosen to concentrate on the economic and income-distribution aspects of the welfare state. For rather similar reasons, we have not attempted to deal with health policy and programs in Canada, although in this case our decision is also based on Canadians' high levels of satisfaction with the health-care system.

Implementing Major Reforms

The reforms proposed in this section are extensive. They will affect the lives and livelihood of virtually every Canadian. They are also both highly complex and closely interrelated. These attributes are particularly important with respect to those proposals dealing with income security, unemployment insurance and transitional adjustment. In those areas particularly, we

Commissioners must emphasize our view that the benefits of reform will be greatly amplified if governments treat our proposals as a single package. We shall be recommending a significant set of changes to our unemployment-insurance system and our income-security system. The UI changes will make our economy more dynamic by encouraging the expansion of more efficient industries and avoiding the payment of inappropriate cross-subsidies to less efficient firms and sectors. These are important changes, well worth considering in themselves, but used alone they would cause substantial hardship to some Canadians. If, however, they are implemented in conjunction with a Universal Income Support Program (UISP), the combination will offer substantial compensation for any negative effects, while most of the desirable effects will be retained. If the net savings generated by our basic changes in unemployment insurance are also redirected into a Transitional Adjustment Assistance Package (TAAP) – a very important step, in this Commission's view – individuals will be even better able to cope with the economic adjustments which we foresee.

The most desirable package, Commissioners believe, would include the following components.

- Personal income tax and transfer programs would:
  - Provide a Universal Income Security Program which would pay a basic income supplement to all Canadians. The supplement would be progressively reduced as income rose.
  - Fund that program by means of eliminating the Guaranteed Income Supplement for the elderly (but not Old Age Security); Family Allowances; Child Tax Credits; Married Exemptions; Child Exemptions; Federal Social Housing Programs; and Federal Contributions to the Canada Assistance Plan.

  If these programs were eliminated, the Universal Income Security Program would be essentially self-funding.
- With respect to unemployment insurance, there would be changes such as the following:
  - Introduction of experience rating introducing a relationship between premiums and the risk of unemployment
  - Reduction of benefit levels from 60 per cent to 50 per cent of insurable earnings
  - Extension of the employment period required to qualify for UI benefits from the present 10–14 weeks
  - Provision of one week of benefits for every two or, possibly, three weeks' labour-force attachment
  - Termination of regional extended benefits.

  These changes will substantially reduce program costs and encourage more efficient allocation of labour resources. The resulting savings could be used to finance the third major component of the package.
- The Transitional Adjustment Assistance Program would provide adjustment assistance for Canadians who have exhausted their UI benefits, or to those for whom no immediate job opportunities can be identified, provided that they are willing to move in order to accept employment or to undertake retraining to improve their labour-market prospects. The program would provide greatly expanded support for:

    - Portable wage-subsidy programs
    - Mobility grants
    - Training programs
    - Early retirement
    - Compensation for losses in assets (housing) as a result of decline of communities
    - Employee purchase of plants which might otherwise close or of other forms of local economic development projects.
- With a Universal Income Security Program in place, it becomes less important, in dealing with poverty, to maintain high levels of minimum wages, since the UISP will provide a wage subsidy for very low-wage workers. This arrangement will allow governments to de-emphasize minimum wages as a policy device, with the consequent possibility of encouraging higher levels of employment for low-skill workers and providing more employer-employee/financed, on-the-job training.

Commissioners recognize the extensive nature of the changes proposed, but consider that Canada must make a very important "package" of integrated changes to our nation's human resource and social support programs. We make this judgement in the belief that this undertaking is essential to Canadian adjustment to the requirements of our advance into the twenty-first century. In this vein, the authors of a recent study of our government and our economy have pointed out that:

> *One of the biggest defects in the present 'industrial policy' of Canadian government is precisely the absence of an adequate system to help, support, induce and (to some extent) force workers to adjust to . . . changing economic circumstances. The failure of our existing enormous transfer system to accomplish this task satisfactorily is indeed a serious condemnation of that system . . .*[1]

Not all of the proposals presented in this section need to be considered as parts of a package approach. Commissioners' recommendations on labour-management relations or occupational health and safety, for example, are only very indirectly related to income-security or UI-program changes, and the same is true of most of our suggestions concerning post-secondary education. We shall, therefore, make it clear as we move through the text which pieces had better be considered the basis of a package approach, and which can be considered alone.

Finally, we wish to emphasize that our proposals would do little to increase the net cost of Canada's social programs. The major elements of our suggested reforms are either self-financing (as with the UISP) or financed by expenditure reductions mentioned elsewhere in the package (as with UI and TAAP programs). We have not proposed reductions in the programs in this sector because it is our view that Canada's expenditures in this area are not excessive. For this reason, our financial objective has been to suggest appropriate reallocations of funding within existing expenditure levels.

Note

1. Richard Bird and Christopher Green, *Government Intervention in the Canadian Economy* (Toronto: University of Toronto, Institute for Policy Analysis, 1985).

CHAPTER 14

The Evolution of Policy: *Major Trends and Issues*

CHAPTER 14

The Evolution of Policy: *Major Trends and Issues*

Before we plunge into a detailed consideration of specific proposals for reform, it is important to examine the broad patterns of development in social policy and labour relations. Accordingly, this section focuses on three dimensions of Canadians' collective experience. We shall examine the historical development of these sectors, assess the current network of policies, and only then attempt to peer into the future and to anticipate the major forces that are likely to shape those policies in the years to come.

The Retrospective View

The transition from the predominantly agrarian community of the nineteenth century to the urban society of contemporary Canada exposed Canadians to a new and unfamiliar social environment. The expansion of industrial production created a large industrial work-force and generated a wide set of enduring tensions between labour and management. The policy issues posed by these sweeping changes in our economy and our society dominated our country's political agenda throughout much of the twentieth century, especially during the pivotal decades of the 1940s, 1950s and 1960s.

The Welfare State

The economic developments of this century have brought a prosperity undreamed of by earlier generations of Canadians, but these same developments also set in motion forces of social change which simply overwhelmed the rudimentary provisions for public relief which prevailed during the nineteenth century. The new economic and industrial order left people particularly vulnerable to the loss of earnings of the primary breadwinner during periods of unemployment, illness, disability and old age. At the same time, traditional social institutions, such as the family, the church and the local community, were less and less able to cope with Canadians' social needs. The traditions of private charity, which were an important part of the small, stable and closely knit communities in rural areas and small towns, eroded steadily in the face of a mobile and increasingly urban population. The intense economic and social dislocation of the 1930s graphically demonstrated the inadequacies of traditional welfare mechanisms and the need for a more comprehensive system of social security.

The pressures for social reform thus flowed, in the first instance, from economic development. Canadian experience in this regard paralleled that elsewhere: industrial nations, often with widely differing traditions and systems of government, created increasingly elaborate forms of collective provision for their social needs. There was, however, no simple determinism at work, for the social programs of these various nations also showed tremendous diversity. Each Western nation developed its own version of the welfare state in light of its cultural traditions and the balance of political forces within it.

In the context of Canadian culture, the welfare state reflected a broad evolution in the dominant beliefs about the proper role of government and about the rights and duties of citizens. The twentieth century witnessed a growing acceptance of the legitimacy of social security and, more generally, a deepening belief in the importance of a wider set of social rights which would complement the legal and political rights already established. In the period that followed the Second World War, these ideas were reinforced by the spread of economic theories that were much more compatible with significant income redistribution than earlier orthodoxies had been. Yet in Canada, at least, the advance of collectivist views has always been constrained and challenged by the enduring strength of individualist political values, with their emphasis on personal achievement and responsibility. The tension between collectivist and individualist beliefs has continued to fuel welfare politics and to shape our social security system, both in its overall scope and in the design of specific programs.

This battle of ideas was fought out in the political arena. During the first half of the twentieth century, support for the welfare state grew steadily. Intellectuals, social reformers and the developing profession of social work often led the way in documenting the severity of social problems and outlining blueprints for their solution. The emergence of left-wing political protest in the form of the Co-operative Commonwealth Federation (CCF) generated a third force in Canadian politics that was strongly dedicated to social change. Organized labour, which grew rapidly after the mid-1930s, also became a consistent champion of the expansion of the welfare state. In addition to these external pressures, reformist elements developed within the major political parties and in parts of the senior civil service. Moreover, established political leaders were clearly sensitive to the broad current of public support for social spending. When the question of pensions became prominent, for instance, "many M.P.'s in Canada were convinced that the pension issue was a significant, even decisive, factor in electoral choice, especially at certain critical junctures in the development of pension policy."[1]

The actual policy responses to these economic and political changes spanned a 50-year period. Indeed, the welfare state stands as a classic testament to the Canadian preference for incremental, rather than wholesale, reform. In many significant areas, the basic principle of state intervention was actually established during the inter-war period. Workers' Compensation was initiated in Ontario in 1914 and progressively adopted by other provinces; Mothers' Allowances for widowed mothers with dependent children spread quickly after their introduction in Manitoba in 1917; income redistribution in favour of the aged became a fact between 1927 and 1936 as the provinces opted, one by one, into the federal Old Age Pension Act; pensions for blind persons over 40 years of age followed in 1937; and the principle of a federal contribution to support for the unemployed had been acknowledged – albeit grudgingly – in the early 1920s and, again, in the 1930s. All of these benefits were means-tested and were often inadequate. Certainly it was impossible to speak of a "right" to support in that period. Nevertheless, by the time war broke out in 1939, collectivism was already established on firm ground in Canadian welfare politics.

This base grew rapidly in the decades that followed. Firmer political support, economic growth and, after the war, declining defence expenditures provided a favourable context for change. The range of social needs covered was expanded, while demogrants and social insurance reduced reliance on means-tested programs, establishing a clearer right to support. In the income-security field, Unemployment Insurance, introduced in 1941, was followed by Family Allowances in 1944, Old Age Security in 1951, several conditional grant programs in the social assistance area during the 1950s, Youth Allowances in 1964, the Canada and Quebec Pension Plans in 1965, the Canada Assistance Plan and the Guaranteed Income Supplement in 1966, the Spouses Allowance in 1975, and the Child Tax Credit in 1978. In the health field, the National Health Grants, initiated in 1948, supported a major expansion of hospital construction by provincial governments throughout the period, and health insurance was introduced on a nation-wide basis following the introduction of the Hospital Insurance and Diagnostic Services Act of 1957 and the Medical Care Act of 1966.

By the end of the 1960s, then, the main structure of the Canadian model of the welfare state was in place. The 1970s, by contrast, turned out to be a decade of transition. The early years of the period saw the continuation of the reformist momentum, with a significant enrichment of the Unemployment Insurance and Family Allowances programs, and a major debate over the introduction of a guaranteed annual income (GAI) during the sweeping Social Security Review initiated in 1973. The second half of the decade, however, seemed to mark the end of a generation of expansion. Some social programs were cut back, and a whole range of fundamental questions emerged about the future of the welfare state.

Income security, health and education represent central supports of the welfare state, and the expansion of each has been a central feature of Canadian life during the last 40 years. The historic growth of the welfare state throughout the post-war period can be traced in the tables that follow.

The first three tables highlight the expansion and importance of Canada's income-security programs. Table 14-1 demonstrates the relative size of the major components of the system and the way in which each of these components has expanded since 1956. Tables 14-2 and 14-3 illustrate the importance of these programs to Canadians. In many policy areas, government action affects the general public indirectly, by influencing the nature of economic activity or the operations of major institutions in the private sector. Income security, however, represents a direct contact between government and citizen, and for millions of Canadians that contact is central to the maintenance of their standard of living and their general well-being. Table 14-2 documents the large number of recipients of the major national programs. Table 14-3 provides another view of the importance of the transfer system, especially to Canadians in lower-income groups.

These transfer programs represent the most visible component of our redistributive system. Governments also provide assistance to individuals and families through the increasingly elaborate set of exemptions and credits which permeate the income-tax system. The cost of these "tax expenditures" is now sizeable indeed. In 1984–85, for example, the combination of the personal, marriage and age exemptions, the child exemption and the child tax credit, the employment deduction and the tax assistance with pensions and retirement savings cost the federal government approximately $25 billion in revenue forgone. Critics have pointed out that our tax and transfer programs are not well integrated, and that tax exemptions, in particular, provide the greatest benefits to higher-income earners. This Commission agrees that transfer programs and tax expenditures should no longer be treated as conceptually distinct elements of pubic policy, but as integrated components.

The next group of tables illustrates the growing importance of health-care programs in Canadian society. Table 14-4 tracks the dramatic post-war expansion of the health-care sector, as measured by the number of hospital beds, physicians and dentists available to Canadians. The two figures that follow examine the expenditure implications of this growth. Figure 14-1 shows the substantial increase in the role of government in the health-care sector as a whole: the public share of total health expenditures rose steadily from 43 per cent at the beginning of the 1960s to about 75 per cent by the mid-1970s; it has since remained stable at that level. Table 14-5 indicates the expansion of health spending as a proportion of gross national product (GNP). Between 1960 and 1970, the share of health spending in our GNP rose sharply, from 5.6 per cent to 7.3 per cent, coincident with the implementation of the hospital-insurance and medicare programs. Equally remarkable, however, was the relative stability of health spending during the 1970s. Despite all the controversy about rising health costs of that decade, it is now clear that their increase was no greater than the growth in the productive capacity of the economy during ten consecutive years. Since 1980, health costs have begun to rise again, but it is too early to know to what extent this growth represents a new trend, and to what extent it is a result of the recession.

The cycles of educational expansion are represented in Table 14-6, which tracks enrolment patterns at each level of schooling over four decades. In

TABLE 14-1 Expenditure on Major Income Security Programs, 1956–1982

Programs	1956	1960	1964	1968	1972	1976	1980	1982
	($ millions)							
Federal								
OAS-GIS[a]	376	587	871	1 478	2 430	4 305	7 020	9 304
Unemployment Insurance	210	482	344	438	1 869	3 332	4 332	8 454
Family Allowances	394	502	559	615	611	1 942	1 812	2 204
Canada Pension Plan	—	—	—	11	190	775	1 903	2 873
Provincial								
Social Assistance Direct Relief	20	24	59	381	751	1 392	2 414	3 164
Old Age and Blind Pensions	60	80	116	40	23	334	565	681
Mothers and Disabled Allowances	37	73	93	69	41	64	116	171
Workmen's Compensation	70	92	124	177	280	701	1 192	1 726
Quebec Pension Plan	—	—	—	4	58	261	664	1 006
Local								
Direct Relief	24	57	80	131	244	270	394	522
Total	1 191	1 897	2 246	3 344	6 497	13 376	20 412	30 105

Source: Statistics Canada, *National Income and Expenditure Accounts*, Cat. No. 13-201 (Ottawa, various years).

a. Old Age Security-Guaranteed Income Supplement.

TABLE 14-2 Number of Recipients of Major Income Security Programs, 1971–1981

(thousands)

Year	Old Age Security	Guaranteed Income Supplement	Spouses Allowance	CPP/ QPP	Family Allowances[a]	Unemployment Insurance	Social Assistance[b]
1971	1 720	860	—	331	3 024	N.A.[c]	1 622
1972	1 763	974	—	449	3 063	1 904	1 533
1973	1 808	1 045	—	564	3 110	2 007	1 370
1974	1 858	1 076	—	690	3 344	2 068	1 347
1975	1 916	1 082	—	822	3 446	2 454	1 436
1976	2 011	1 087	54	1 008	3 510	2 401	1 500
1977	2 086	1 115	72	1 164	3 561	2 479	1 508
1978	2 149	1 136	74	1 304	3 595	2 524	1 502
1979	2 220	1 162	75	1 426	3 611	2 333	1 548
1980	2 317	1 191	81	1 558	3 631	2 274	1 334
1981	2 388	1 245	85	1 680	3 645	2 432	N.A.

Sources: Statistics Canada, *Social Security: National Programs, 1982* (Ottawa, various volumes); *Benefit Periods Established and Terminated Under the Unemployment Insurance Act* (Ottawa, various years), pp. 73–201.

a. Number of families receiving Family Allowances (excluding youth allowances).

b. Number of persons assisted through the Canada Assistance Plan.

c. N.A. = Not available.

TABLE 14-3 Transfer Payments as a Proportion of Income within Income Quintiles, All Units

Quintile	1971	1976	1981	1982
Lowest	53.3	57.7	57.3	61.4
Second	18.2	22.7	22.7	28.0
Third	5.7	8.4	8.8	11.8
Fourth	3.4	5.1	5.0	6.5
Highest	2.0	2.7	2.6	3.3
Total	6.6	8.6	9.0	10.9

Source: Statistics Canada, *Income Distributions by Size in Canada*, Cat. No. 13-207 (Ottawa: Minister of Supply and Services Canada, various years).

TABLE 14-4 Expansion of the Health-Care System: Hospital Beds, Physicians and Nurses, 1941–1975

Year	Total Hospital Beds	Population per Each Physician	Population per Each Nurse
1941	103 541	968	441
1951	145 950	976	325
1961	192 939	857	258
1971	210 974	659	146
1975	208 345	585	129

Source: Statistics Canada, *Historical Statistics of Canada*, 2d ed. (Ottawa: Statistics Canada, 1983), pp. B82–92, B177–188.

these figures, we can see the flow of the post-war "baby boom" through the elementary and secondary schools, during the 1950s, 1960s and 1970s, and the decline in student numbers in the 1980s. The figures also follow the expansion of the post-secondary educational institutions, illustrating the creation of a major system of community colleges during the 1960s and the significant expansion of the university sector. The expenditure implications of these changes can be seen in Table 14-7.

FIGURE 14-1 Share of the Public Sector (Federal, Provincial, and Local) in Total Health Expenditures, Canada, 1960–1981

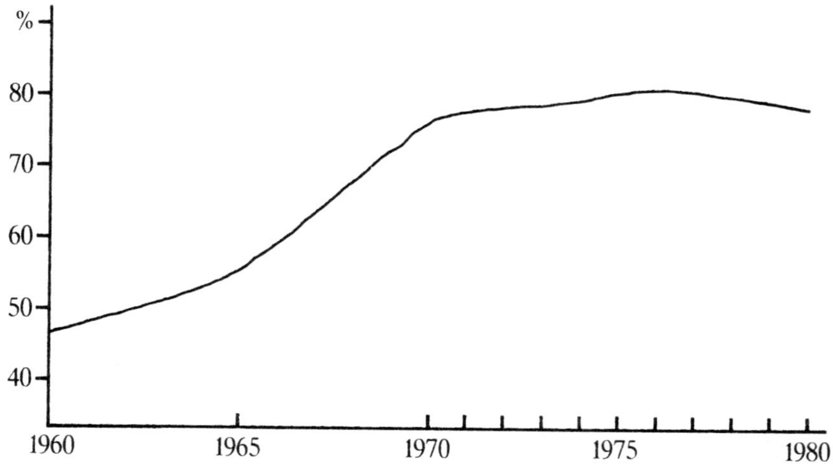

Source: Canada, Health and Welfare Canada, Health Economics and Statistics Division, preliminary unpublished figures.

TABLE 14-5 Health Expenditures, by Category, as a Percentage of the Gross National Product, Canada, 1960–1982

	1960	1965	1970	1975	1980	1981[a]	1982[a]
Total health expenditures	5.67	6.07	7.30	7.49	7.48	7.60	8.44
Personal health care	4.62	5.11	6.36	6.61	6.55	6.65	7.41
Other health costs	1.00	0.96	0.94	0.88	0.85	0.85	1.03

Source: Canada, Health and Welfare Canada, Health Economics and Statistics Division, unpublished figures.

a. Figures are provisional.

TABLE 14-6 Education: Full-Time Enrolment, by Level, Selected Years

	(thousands)				
Enrolment	**1941–42**	**1951–52**	**1961–62**	**1971–72**	**1981–82**
Elementary and secondary school	2 143	2 625	4 413	5 806	5 032
Community college	19	28	53	174	273
University	36	63	129	323	402

Source: Statistics Canada, *Historical Statistical Compendium*, prepared for the Royal Commission on the Economic Union and Development Prospects for Canada (Ottawa: Statistics Canada, 1985), Table 15.3.

TABLE 14-7 Educational Expenditures as a Proportion of GNP, 1950–1974

Year	Percentage
1950	2.4
1960	4.4
1970	9.0
1974	7.5

Source: Statistics Canada, *Historical Statistics of Canada*, 2d ed. (Ottawa: Statistics Canada, 1983), p. W61–80.

Note

1. Kenneth Bryden, *Old Age Pensions and Policy-Making in Canada* (Montreal: McGill-Queen's University Press, 1974), p. 184.

The Contemporary Pattern

The expansion of the Canadian welfare state constitutes one of the major accomplishments of the post-war generation. Much of the political energy of the last 40 years has been devoted to this task, and Canada has clearly become a fairer society as a result. Nevertheless, now is a time for taking stock, for re-examining the structure which has been put in place, for assessing its adequacy in light of contemporary social needs, and for anticipating its prospects for the future.

In assessing Canada's existing policies, Commissioners have adopted two broad perspectives. The first compares Canadian social policies with those of other Western industrial nations, and the second examines more directly the welfare of Canadians.

Canada in Comparative Perspective

A comparative perspective is of invaluable service in any evaluation of the Canadian welfare state. To concentrate solely on social expenditures in this country might lead to suggestions that Canada's rate of growth has been exceptional and necessitates major economic or social adjustments not faced elsewhere. Even a brief examination of the experience of other countries puts such concerns in a fuller context. In fact, the expansion of the Canadian welfare state – so dramatic when viewed in isolation – seems much more modest by the standards of Western industrial nations generally.

As Figure 14-2 illustrates, a comparison of Canadian expenditures on social programs with those in other countries belonging to the Organisation for Economic Co-operation and Development (OECD) shows Canada ranking in the lower third, with expenditures of 21.7 per cent of gross domestic product (GDP) in 1981, compared to the OECD average of 25.5 per cent of GDP. Expenditures in the United States, standing at 21 per cent, were almost identical to those in Canada. In general, Canada stood ninth out of twelve major OECD countries in 1981. In the same year, the Netherlands and Denmark, with expenditures of 36 per cent of GDP, led all other OECD countries; they were followed by Sweden and Germany. Italy, France, Norway and Britain devoted slightly more of their national resources to social programs than did Canada. Australia and Japan lagged behind Canada, with expenditures of 3 and 4 per cent, in company with such smaller OECD countries as Finland, New Zealand and Greece.

Canada's position relative to this standard has remained fairly constant over time, changing from eighth place in 1960 to ninth in 1975. Between 1960 and 1981, social expenditures in all OECD countries grew from 13.4 per cent of gross domestic product to 25.5 per cent. Canada participated in this surge, with a growth rate almost identical to the OECD average, although our growth did occur later than that of many countries. The Scandinavian countries, for example, as well as France and Japan, experienced above-average growth in the early 1960s, while Canada and the United States made their increases in the mid-1960s. All countries, however, experienced a slowing of the rate of increase in real expenditure between 1975 and 1980.

FIGURE 14-2 Social Expenditure as Percentage of GDP

(in current dollars)

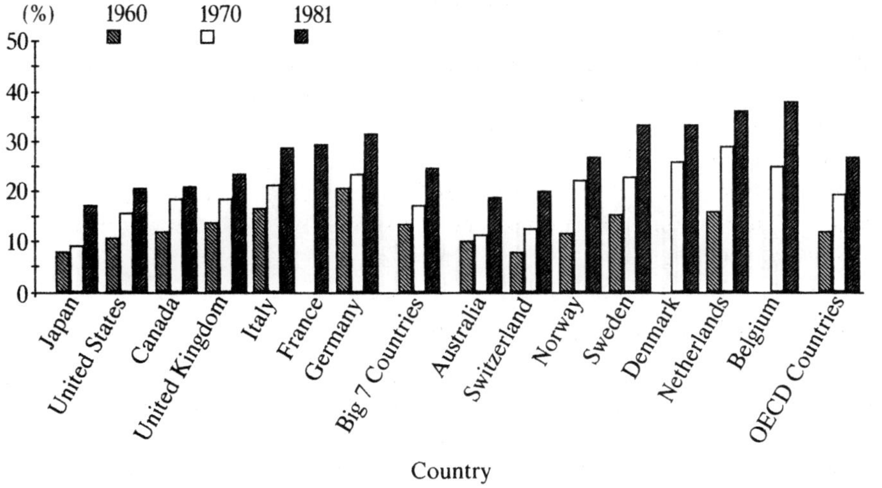

Source: Organisation for Economic Co-operation and Development, *Social Expenditure 1960–1990: Problems of Growth and Control* (Paris: OECD, 1985), Appendix C.

Note: Social expenditures include direct federal, provincial or state, and local costs of health, education, unemployment insurance and income-maintenance programs, but exclude housing and community programs. Tax expenditures are not included. Unless otherwise stated, percentage shares of GDP are based on current dollars. Data for all countries in all years did not appear in source.

a. Data are for 1981, except: Belgium, 1980; Denmark, 1979; and Switzerland, 1979.

Industrial countries differ, not only in the overall proportion of their national resources that they devote to social spending, but also in selecting their priorities within the social sector. Indeed, relative expenditures in specific policy areas vary widely. By comparison with other OECD nations, Canada spends proportionately less on pensions, about average amounts on education and health, and more on unemployment benefits. In expenditure for pensions, as Figure 14-3 shows, Canada has consistently trailed other countries, standing last of twelve countries in 1981, with direct expenditures of 4.6 per cent of GDP, compared to a twelve-country average of 8.8 per cent.

Part of the explanation for Canada's relatively low expenditures on pensions can be found in the age profile of our population, as the elderly represent a smaller proportion of the total population here than elsewhere. Canada's ratio of pensioners to workers, for example, stood at 21.2 per cent in 1980, as compared to 28.4 per cent in other OECD countries; in fact, our rate was lower than that of every other country except Japan. Demography, however, does not tell the full story. Our expenditures are lower because Canadian benefits, too, are lower. The average OECD expenditure per pensioner is 14.8 per cent of average GDP per worker; Canada, on the other hand, spends only 11.6 per cent; again, this proportion is smaller than that of

FIGURE 14-3 Social Expenditure on Pensions as a a Percentage of GDP

(in current dollars)

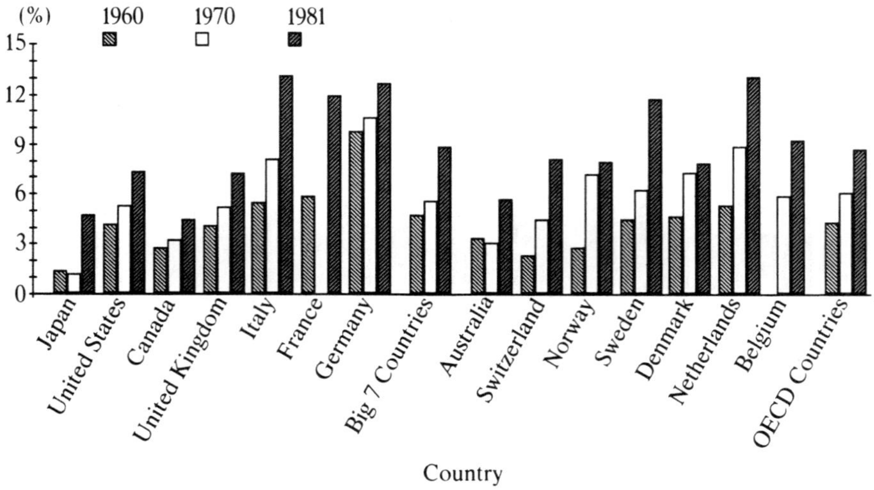

Source: Organisation for Economic Co-operation and Development, *Social Expenditure 1960–1990: Problems of Growth and Control* (Paris: OECD, 1985), Appendix C. Data for all countries for all years did not appear in source.

a. Data are for 1981, except: Belgium, 1980; Denmark, 1979; and Switzerland, 1979.

every other OECD country but Japan. Canada did spend an additional $6.6 billion in 1983–84 on tax expenditures, primarily in the form of tax exemptions for contributions to Registered Retirement Savings Plans (RRSPs), the Canada and Quebec Pension Plans (CPP/QPP) and private pension plans. Nevertheless, even if tax expenditures for Canada are included and similar expenditures in other countries disregarded, our nation moves up only to tenth place, still well behind European countries and the United States.

Canadian expenditures on education and health, by comparison, stand much closer to the average level of funding in other OECD countries. In 1981, Canada devoted 6.2 per cent of its GDP to education, compared to the OECD average of 6.1 per cent. In fact, this position reflected a considerable change for Canada. In 1960, our expenditures ranked us eighth out of ten OECD countries, but a rapid increase in the second half of that decade brought Canada's standing to fifth out of 12 in 1975. The Scandinavian countries have consistently ranked as top spenders in these areas, while Germany and Japan have lagged behind. Figure 14-4 also demonstrates another important trend: educational spending dropped in all major OECD countries except Italy, Sweden and Japan, between 1975 and 1981, largely because of declining enrolments in educational institutions.

Health care is another sector in which Canadian spending hovers close to OECD average. Canada ranked seventh of 12 OECD members in 1982, devoting 5.9 per cent of GDP to public health expenditures, compared to the

FIGURE 14-4 Social Expenditure on Education as a Percentage of GDP

(in current dollars)

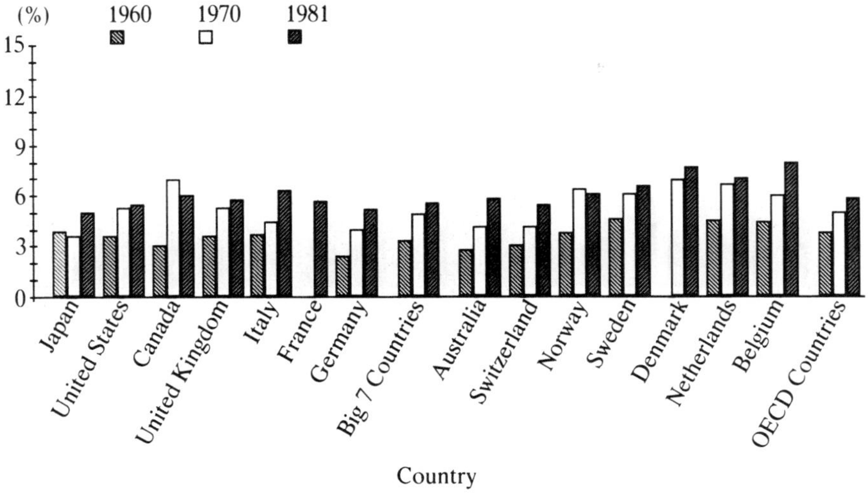

Source: Organisation for Economic Co-operation and Development, *Social Expenditure 1960–1990: Problems of Growth and Control* (Paris: OECD, 1985), Appendix C. Data for all countries for all years did not appear in source.

a. Data are for 1981, except: Belgium, 1980; Denmark, 1979; and Switzerland, 1979.

average expenditure of 6.1 per cent. The United States has consistently stood last in *public* health expenditures – spending 4.5 per cent of GDP, for instance, in 1982 – while Sweden ranks first. However, in terms of total share of GNP devoted to public and private health-care expenditures, the United States ranked at or near the top throughout most of the post-war period. Most major OECD countries, including Canada, experienced their greatest growth in health costs during the 1960s, but Canada's growth rate did drop below the average from 1970 to 1981, reflecting the stabilization in health-care expenditures noted earlier. (See Figure 14-5.)

When attention turns to unemployment benefits, Canada's international position changes dramatically, since our spending in this sector, as Figure 14-6 illustrates, has been consistently high compared to that of other OECD countries. In 1981, with expenditures of 2.3 per cent of GDP, Canada stood second only to Denmark, and well above a 12-country average of 1.25 per cent. In comparison, the United States spent only 0.5 per cent on unemployment payments.

Canada's relatively large expenditures on unemployment compensation are not the result of higher benefit levels or of longer average periods of benefit. Indeed, from 1975 to 1980, Canada's benefit levels were almost identical to those in the United States, while benefits in Japan and Germany were 30 to 50 per cent higher. Moreover, the average benefit period in Canada, between 1975 and 1980, was only slightly shorter than that in the United States, while France, Italy and Japan had, on average, significantly longer benefit periods.

FIGURE 14-5 Social Expenditure on Health as a Percentage of GDP

(in current dollars)

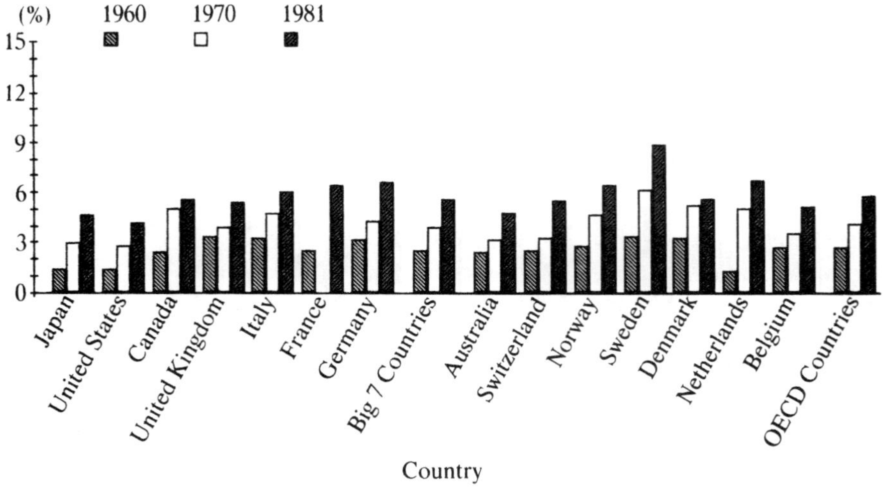

Source: Organisation for Economic Co-operation and Development, *Social Expenditure 1960–1990: Problems of Growth and Control* (Paris: OECD, 1985), Appendix C. Data for all countries for all years did not appear in source.

a. Data are for 1981, except: Belgium, 1980; Denmark, 1979; and Switzerland, 1979.

FIGURE 14-6 Social Expenditures on Unemployment Compensation as a Percentage of GDP

(in current dollars)

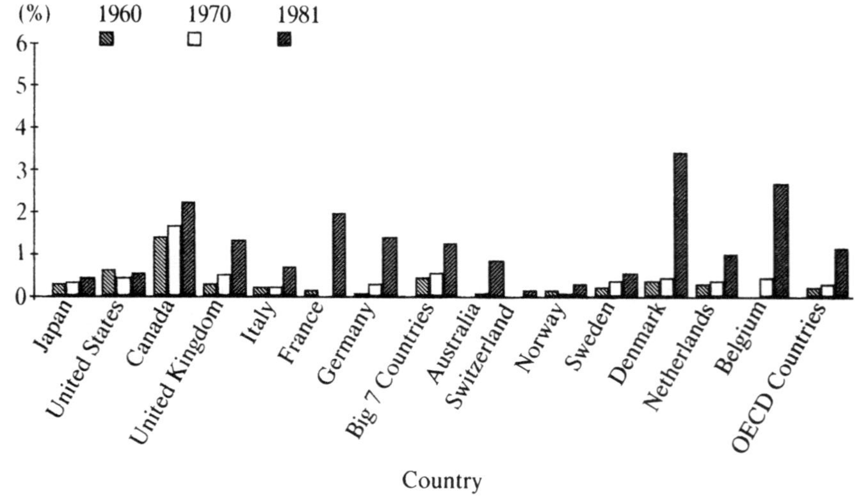

Source: Organisation for Economic Co-operation and Development, *Social Expenditure 1960–1990: Problems of Growth and Control* (Paris: OECD, 1985), Appendix C. Data for all countries in all years did not appear in source.

a. Data are for 1981, except: Belgium, 1980; Denmark, 1979; and Switzerland, 1979.

The primary explanation of Canadian expenditure levels seems to lie in Canada's higher unemployment rates and its higher percentage of workers covered by unemployment compensation. Between 1975 and 1980, Canada had an average unemployment rate of 7.5 per cent, compared to an OECD average of 5.4 per cent, and 6.7 per cent of our working population received unemployment benefits, compared to only 2.2 per cent in the other major OECD countries.

The Welfare of Canadians

When we focus directly on Canadian experience, two major elements stand out. Plainly, the overall welfare or well-being of Canadians as a whole has risen dramatically over the post-war period. The economic difficulties of recent years should not blind us to the distance we have come as a community since the Second World War. It is equally clear, however, that the distribution of welfare among Canadians has changed much less.

There is no simple standard for measuring the overall level of welfare in a society. People disagree fundamentally, both on the range of social indicators relevant to our well-being and on the relative importance to be attributed to each one. The consideration presented here is therefore confined to three dimensions of welfare which virtually everyone would accept as important: income, health and education. By and large, Canadians have made substantial progress in each of these dimensions during the post-war period. Certainly, our incomes have risen sharply. Table 14-8 presents the basic data from 1951 to 1981: nominal income increased more than nine-fold, while real income rose by almost 175 per cent.

Canada's standard of living remains one of the highest in the world. Table 14-9 measures the gross domestic product on a per capita basis for nine OECD countries. The simple nominal measure shows Canada ranking fifth, in a tie with Austria. Such a nominal measure, however, provides a distorted view of living standards because it does not take into account differences in

TABLE 14-8 Income of Canadians, 1951–1981

	(per capita income)			
	1951	1961	1971[b]	1981
Current	$989[a]	$1 459[a]	$2 891	$9 636
Constant (1951 $)	989[a]	1 281[a]	1 908	2 685

Source: F. Vaillancourt, "Income Distribution and Economic Security in Canada: An Overview", in *Income Distribution and Economic Security in Canada*, vol. 1, prepared for the Royal Commission on the Economic Union and Development Prospects for Canada (Toronto: University of Toronto Press, 1985), Table 2.

a. Non-agricultural population only.

b. The Northwest Territories are excluded in 1961, but included in 1971 and 1981. Income of individuals residing in collective dwellings is excluded in 1981 and included in 1971.

price levels in the countries being compared. Focusing more directly on the "real" GDP per capita requires the use of purchasing-power parities, which measure the cost of a standard basket of goods and services in each of the countries involved. By this measure of real GDP per capita, Canada enjoys the second-highest standard of living among the countries examined.

As well as being generally better off, Canadians are also much healthier today. Table 14-10 reports data on two important indicators, life expectancy and infant mortality, from 1961 to 1976. Both these reflectors of public health have improved steadily, in response to advances in medicine, readier access to health-care services, and better health habits, including life-style changes such as increased physical activity and decreased consumption of cigarettes. Once again, this pattern compares favourably with international standards, as Table 14-11 documents.

Finally, Canadians are more highly educated than ever before. Young people are staying in school longer and, as Table 14-12 shows, the proportion of our population with less than Grade-9 education has fallen sharply since 1941. A more complete breakdown of educational attainment during the past decade is provided in Table 14-13, which demonstrates that over one-third of Canadians have some post-secondary education.

Comparative studies of educational participation rates are particularly difficult to construct because of differences in educational systems across countries. Once again, however, Canada appears to be among the leaders. There is now considerable debate, however, over the degree of success that our educational system is achieving in preparing Canadians to deal with the problems they are likely to confront in the years to come. Even so, it is important to remember that by these measures of welfare Canadians have made considerable progress.

TABLE 14-9 Gross Domestic Product per Capita, 1980

	(in nominal and real terms)			
	Nominal Measure		Real Measure	
Country	GDP per Capita[a]	Rank	GDP per Capita[a]	Rank
Austria	$10 270	6	8 040	7
Canada	10 760	5	11 430	2
France	12 180	2	9 010	4
Germany	13 240	1	9 400	3
Italy	7 000	9	7 180	9
Japan	8 910	8	8 140	6
Netherlands	11 970	3	8 590	5
United Kingdom	9 390	7	7 610	8
United States	11 450	4	11 450	1

Source: Peter Hill, *Real Gross Domestic Product in OECD Countries and Associated Purchasing Power Parities*, Working Paper No. 17 (Paris: OECD, 1984), Table 1.

a. Expressed in U.S. dollars.

TABLE 14-10 Life Expectancy and Infant Mortality in Canada, 1951–1981

Life Expectancy[a] (years)	1951	1961	1971	1981
Men	68.33	69.50	69.76	71.67
Women	72.33	74.98	76.56	78.65
Infant mortality (per 1000)	38.5	27.2	17.5	9.6

Sources: *Canada Year Book 1975* (Ottawa: Ministry of Industry, Trade and Commerce, 1975), pp. 182–83; *Canada Year Book 1980–1981* (Ottawa: Minister of Supply and Services Canada, 1981), pp. 149–50; Statistics Canada, *Life Tables, Canada and Provinces, 1980–82*, Cat. No. 84-532 (Ottawa: Minister of Supply and Services Canada, 1984), pp. 16–18; Statistics Canada, *Vital Statistics III: Mortality 1981*, Cat. No. 84-206 (Ottawa: Mnister of Supply and Services Canada, 1983), p. 11.

a. Life expectancy at one year of age; infants are less than one year old.

When attention turns to the distribution of welfare, however, a different pattern emerges; it is one in which stability, rather than change, is the dominant theme. Health care, indeed, does stand out as one area in which Canadians have come to receive more nearly equal services. Here the

TABLE 14-11 Life Expectancy and Infant Mortality in Selected Industrialized Countries, 1960 and 1981

	Life Expectancy[a]				Infant Mortality (0–1 year)			
	1960		1981		1960		1981	
Country	**Level**	**Rank[b]**	**Level**	**Rank[b]**	**Level[c]**	**Rank[d]**	**Level[c]**	**Rank[d]**
Canada	71	2	75	3	27	6	10	4
Australia	71	2	74	4	20	3	10	4
Austria	69	4	73	5	58	10	13	9
France	70	3	76	2	27	6	10	4
Germany (Fed. Rep.)	70	3	73	5	34	9	13	9
Italy	69	4	74	4	44	11	14	11
Japan	68	5	77	1	30	8	7	1
Netherlands	73	1	76	2	18	2	8	3
Sweden	73	1	77	1	17	1	7	1
United Kingdom	71	2	74	4	23	4	12	7
United States	70	3	75	3	26	5	12	7

Source: *World Development Report 1983* (New York: Oxford University Press for The World Bank, 1983), Table 23.

a. Life expectancy at birth.

b. From highest to lowest.

c. Per thousand.

d. From lowest to highest.

TABLE 14-12 Distribution of the Population 15 Years of Age and Over, by Level of Schooling, 1941–1981

	(percentage distribution)			
Year	Less than Grade 9	Grades 9–13 and Other post-Secondary	University Degree	Total 15 Years and Over
1941	56.8	42.2	1.0	100.0
1951	51.9	46.2	1.9	100.0
1961	44.1	53.0	2.9	100.0
1971	33.3	61.9	4.8	100.0
1976	26.7	66.9	6.4	100.0
1981	21.9	70.1	8.0	100.0

Source: Statistics Canada, *Historical Statistical Compendium*, prepared for the Royal Commission on the Economic Union and Development Prospects for Canada (Ottawa: Statistics Canada, 1985), Table 15.1. See original source for notes to this table.

expansion of the welfare state has had a clearly egalitarian effect: Canada's introduction of universal hospital and medical care insurance removed financial barriers to health-care services and increased the share available to low-income earners.[1]

Other elements of the post-war expansion of social spending have not had this equalizing effect. The increased incidence of post-secondary education does not appear to have made that experience more accessible to children of poor families. Indeed, the pattern of educational attainment continues to descend from one generation to another: the higher the education of parents, the more likely their children are to attend university. Table 14-14 reports the relevant data for 1982. Less than 20 per cent of children whose fathers received elementary education or less entered college or university, whereas 68 per cent of children whose fathers were university graduates did so. Unfortunately, there are no national data, compiled over a period of time, on changes in the socio-economic background of university students. It seems unlikely, however, that the proportion of university students from poorer economic backgrounds has increased greatly over the last few decades.

Lack of change appears even more starkly in the distribution of income. As Table 14-15 confirms, the overall distribution of income has changed remarkably little during the past 30 years. The poorest fifth of Canadian families and individuals continues to receive about 4 per cent of all income, while the most affluent fifth receives about 40 per cent. Comparisons among countries are particularly difficult to construct in this area. Nevertheless, studies completed for the OECD and the British Royal Commission on the Distribution of Income and Wealth both agree that Canada ranks approximately midway in terms of degree of inequality in the distribution of income. (See Table 14-16.)

This surface stability, however, masks a wide range of underlying social changes. In the period between 1951 and 1981, for example, the proportion of

TABLE 14-13 Level of Schooling of Canadians 15 Years of Age and Over, 1971, 1976, 1981

Year	Level of Schooling			
	Less than Grade 9	Grades 9–13	Some post-Secondary	University Degree
1971	32.3	45.9	17.1	4.8
1976	25.4	44.1	24.1	6.4
1981	20.7	43.6	27.6	8.0

Source: Statistics Canada, *1981 Census of Canada, Population: Historical Tables for Census, Education Data 1971, 1976 and 1981* (Ottawa: Statistics Canada, 1984), Table 1-1.

Canada's farm population fell from 20 per cent to about 4.5 per cent of our entire nation. The family structure has continued to evolve: large numbers of elderly people and young adults now live independently, and single-parent families are increasing in number. In addition, female participation in the labour force has risen from a rate of 17 per cent in 1951 to about 52 per cent in 1981. Given these and other important social trends, it seems surprising that the distribution of income appears so stable, and existing research has not fully discovered the reasons for this phenomenon. Part of the explanation seems to be that the various social changes have offset one another's effects. According to one study, for example, changes in family composition have worked to increase inequality of income, whereas changes in female participation in the labour force have worked to reduce it. Their effect has combined to produce only limited change in the overall distribution of income.[2] Whatever the full explanation may be, the gap between the affluent and the poor in Canadian society remains as wide as ever.

The effect of government activities on the distribution of income is also difficult to measure. To determine precisely who benefits from each expenditure program, and who finally bears the burden of each tax is by no means an exact science, and specialists in the field continue to debate these questions. The best evidence available, however, suggests that government does exercise a mildly redistributive effect that is particularly important to low-income Canadians. The most recent comprehensive analysis concluded that in 1969, there was redistribution from the higher- to the lower-income classes.[3] This redistributive effect was not the product of taxation, since low-income earners appeared to pay a larger proportion of their income in taxes than did high-income earners. The redistributive effect of expenditures, however, was in favour of low-income groups, and it outweighed the tax effects. As a result, the overall effect of taxes and expenditures was progressive.

Tables 14-17, 14-18 and 14-19 provide more recent, but more partial, views. Table 14-17 confirms that transfer payments continue to be important in reducing income inequality, and have become more so since 1971. Table 14-18 indicates the additional effect of personal income taxes, but not

TABLE 14-14 Highest Education Attained relative to Education of Respondent's Father for Canadians Aged 17–64, 1982

Highest Education Attained by Respondent	Education of Father[a]					
	Elementary or less	Some Secondary	Completed Secondary	Some post-Secondary	Completed College	Completed University
No college or university education	80.3	69.2	53.6	49.0	47.3	31.7
College education	12.6	17.9	21.2	27.0	26.8	23.1
University education	7.1	12.8	25.0	23.9	25.8	45.3
Total college and university education	19.7	30.7	46.2	50.9	52.6	68.4

Source: Statistics Canada, *Supplement, Labour Force Survey, 1982* (Ottawa).

Note: Totals may not sum to 100 per cent because of rounding.

a. Figures represent percentage of respondents in each category.

TABLE 14-15 Income Inequality in Canada, 1951–1981

	(pre-tax income, all units) Quintile Shares					
Year	First (lowest)	Second	Third	Fourth	Fifth (highest)	Gini Coefficients[a]
1951	4.4	11.3	18.3	23.3	42.8	0.390
1961	4.2	11.9	18.3	24.5	41.1	0.371
1971	3.6	10.6	17.6	24.9	43.3	0.400
1981	4.6	10.9	17.6	25.2	41.8	0.377

Source: F. Vaillancourt, "Income Distribution and Economic Security in Canada: An Overview", in *Income Distribution and Economic Security in Canada*, vol. 1, prepared for the Royal Commission on the Economic Union and Development Prospects for Canada (Toronto: University of Toronto Press, 1985), Table 7.

Note: Based on the Survey of Consumer Finances.

a. A Gini coefficient is a measure of inequality such that a decline in coefficient signifies a decline in the degree of inequality.

of other taxes. To establish the redistributive impact of health and educational services is a more complex task, and Table 14-19 provides an estimate of the redistributive effects of those services in 1974, the last year for which estimates are now available.

Another negative impression of the distribution of income comes from focusing on the plight of the poorest members of our society. Canadians disagree about the extent to which broad equality of income is a desirable goal. Nevertheless, there is undoubtedly strong social consensus on the need to help the poorest and most vulnerable Canadians. Over the last 15 years, poverty has re-emerged as a fundamental issue on Canada's social policy agenda, and much debate and experimentation has been devoted to this compelling social problem.

To assess the extent of "poverty" in Canada requires the adoption of a working definition of the term, and much depends on the framing of that definition. Considerable attention has been paid to these points in recent years; indeed, the re-emergence of poverty as a social issue depended heavily on advances in the prevailing conceptions of poverty and on the establishment of modern "poverty lines". Despite these initiatives, the definition of poverty remains inherently subjective, and different approaches to dealing with its problems have been proposed.

The "needs" approach to reducing poverty establishes a minimum income to provide basic necessities such as food and shelter. Statistics Canada adopts this approach in developing its "low-income cut-offs". In effect, the agency defines as "poor" a family that spends more than a given percentage of its income on food, shelter and clothing. That figure was originally set at 70 per cent, but it was adjusted to 62 per cent in 1973 and to 58.5 per cent in 1981, in order to reflect changing patterns of consumption. The "relative" approach, on the other hand, defines poverty in relation to the income of

TABLE 14-16 Income Inequality in Canada and Selected Industrialized Countries

Country	(pre-tax income, various years)								
	OECD Study			Royal Commission Study					
	Economic Families			Economic Families			Individuals		
	Year	Rank	Gini	Year	Rank	Gini	Year	Rank	Gini
Canada	1969	4	0.382	1975	2	0.379	1974	3	0.472
Australia	1966–67	10	0.313	—	—	—	1973–74	2	0.477
France	1970	1	0.416	—	—	—	—	—	—
Germany (Fed.)	1973	3	0.396	—	—	—	—	—	—
Japan	1967	9	0.335	—	—	—	—	—	0.0
Netherlands	1970	5	0.385	—	—	—	—	—	—
Norway	1969	6	0.354	—	—	—	—	—	—
Sweden	1972	7	0.346	—	—	—	1974	5	0.434
United Kingdom	1973	8	0.344	1975	3	0.355	1972–73	4	
United States	1972	2	0.404	1975	1	0.423	1974	1	0.501

Sources: Malcolm Sawyer, "Income Distribution in OECD Countries", in *OECD Economic Outlook, Occasional Studies* (Paris: OECD, 1976), Tables 3 and 5; Thomas Stark, *The Distribution of Income in Eight Countries*, Royal Commission on the Distribution of Income and Wealth, Background Paper No. 4 (London: H.M.S.O., 1977), pp. 211, 218.

TABLE 14-17 The Effect of Transfer Programs on the Distribution of Income, 1971–1981: Gini Coefficients

Units	Income before Transfers		Income including Transfers	
	1971	1981	1971	1981
All units	0.447	0.439	0.400	0.377
Families	0.386	0.375	0.343	0.320
Unattached individuals	0.558	0.529	0.465	0.405

Source: F. Vaillancourt, "Income Distribution and Economic Security in Canada: An Overview", in *Income Distribution and Economic Security in Canada*, vol. 1, prepared for the Royal Commission on the Economic Union and Development Prospects for Canada (Toronto: University of Toronto Press, 1985), Table 9.

Note: All figures refer to pre-tax income.

TABLE 14-18 Effect of Transfer Programs and Income Tax on the Distribution of Income, 1981

Income	Quintile Shares					Gini Coefficients
	First	Second	Third	Fourth	Fifth	
Income before transfers	1.4	9.6	17.8	26.4	44.9	0.439
Total money income	4.6	10.9	17.6	25.2	41.8	0.377
Total income after income tax	5.3	11.8	18.0	24.9	40.0	0.351

Source: F. Vaillancourt, "Income Distribution and Economic Security in Canada: An Overview", in *Income Distribution and Economic Security in Canada*, vol. 1, prepared for the Royal Commission on the Economic Union and Development Prospects for Canada (Toronto: University of Toronto Press, 1985), Table 5.

society as a whole. The Canadian Council on Social Development, for example, basically defines as "poor" a family of three with an income of less than half of the average Canadian family's income. Table 14-20 presents these two poverty lines for 1983. While there is no consensus on the appropriate poverty line, the Statistics Canada lines are most widely used; Commissioners adopt them in this analysis.

As Table 14-21 shows, the extent of poverty did decline steadily from 1961 to 1981, but it has begun to increase again, as a result of the recession. Canada's social progress clearly depends on its economic strength. As the National Anti-Poverty Organization (NAPO) has emphasized, the increase in family poverty in 1982 and 1983 wiped out the gains that had been registered

TABLE 14-19 The Effect of Transfers and Education/Health Services on the Distribution of Income, 1974

Income	Quintile Shares					Gini Coefficients
	First	Second	Third	Fourth	Fifth	
Income before transfers	1.3	9.8	18.0	25.8	45.2	0.441
Total money income	4.0	10.9	17.7	24.8	42.5	0.389
Total money income plus in kind transfers	4.6	11.7	18.2	24.9	40.6	0.375

Source: Statistics Canada, *Distributional Effects of Health and Education Benefits, Canada, 1974* (Ottawa), Table 1.

TABLE 14-20 Poverty Lines in Canada, 1983

Family of	Statistics Canada[a]	CCSD[b]
One	$ 9 538	$ 8 625
Four	19 397	20 125

Source: Canadian Council on Social Development, Task Force on the Definition and Measurement of Poverty in Canada, *Not Enough: The Meaning and Measurement of Poverty in Canada* (Ottawa: The Council, 1984), p. 25.

a. Urban families.
b. CCSD = Canadian Council on Social Development.

in the previous six years.[4] Large numbers of people stand behind these cold statistics. In 1982, some 2.8 million Canadians fell below the poverty line, leading lives hemmed in on every side by inadequate resources.[5]

A closer look at the profile of poverty in Canada reveals some critical issues. Table 14-22 examines the incidence of poverty among various social groups, highlighting, in particular, the plight of elderly women living on their own and the problems confronting single-parent families with female heads. Poverty is a central fact of life for far too many Canadian women. Table 14-23 broadens the focus by detailing the composition of the "poverty population" as a whole. Clearly, poverty is not simply a problem for the elderly and for single-parent families. Indeed, the largest number of poor people live in families consisting of a couple with children. Poverty is as much a problem of children as of the elderly. Moreover, many of the poor are

TABLE 14-21 Percentage of Canadians with Low Income, 1961–1983

Year	Unattached Individuals	Families	Persons
1961	49.2	27.9	N.A.[a]
1971	43.1	18.3	20.6
1981	37.8	12.0	14.7
1982	37.4	13.2	16.1
1983	41.1	14.6	17.9

Sources: For 1961–1981, F. Vaillancourt, "Income Distribution and Economic Security in Canada: An Overview", in *Income Distribution and Economic Security in Canada*, vol. 1, prepared for the Royal Commission on the Economic Union and Development Prospects for Canada (Toronto: University of Toronto Press, 1985), Table 12. For 1982 and 1983, Statistics Canada, *Income Distribution by Size in Canada, 1982* (Ottawa), *Income Distribution by Size in Canada, Preliminary Estimates 1983* (Ottawa), and *Statistics Canada Daily* (Ottawa, September 14, 1984).

a. N.A. = not available.

TABLE 14-22 The Likelihood of Poverty in Canada, 1981

	Percentage of each Category with Incomes below the Low-Income Cut-off	
Characteristics	**Families (Head)**	**Individuals**
Age		
Less than 24	22.7	38.4
25 – 34	12.6	18.2
35 – 44	10.7	22.4
45 – 54	9.0	30.3
55 – 64	10.5	40.9
65 + (Male)	12.9	48.4
65 + (Female)	24.7	62.2
Education		
0 – 8 years	18.9	62.9
High school	11.6	33.3
Post-secondary, no diploma	8.4	34.2
Post-secondary, with diploma	7.0	22.8
University degree	4.7	17.3
Sex/Family Structure		
Children		
Married couple	8.3	—
Married couple, child	8.9	—
Married couple, children and/or relatives	8.0	—
Male-single/parent family	13.8	—
Female-single/parent family	42.8	—

Source: Canadian Council on Social Development, Task Force on the Definition and Measurement of Poverty in Canada, *Not Enough: The Meaning and Measurement of Poverty in Canada* (Ottawa: The Council, 1984).

TABLE 14-23 Composition of Canada's Poor Population, 1982

Family Type	Percentage of All Poor Persons
Unattached Individuals:	
Over 65	13.9
Under 65	20.1
Families:	
Couples, no children	10.9
Couples, with children	35.3
Single parent, male	3.5
Single parent, female	11.8
Other	4.5
Total:	100.0

Source: Canada Employment and Immigration Commission analysis of data from the Survey of Consumer Finances, 1982 (unpublished).

"working poor", who struggle to meet their needs despite low wages and little help from the social security system. Theirs is a plight too often ignored. The extent of poverty in Canada has been reduced, to be sure, but its persistence stands as a continuing challenge to the welfare state.

Notes

1. For a survey of the evidence on this point, see Gilles Grenier, "Health Care Costs in Canada: Past and Present", in *Income Distribution and Economic Security in Canada*, vol. 1, prepared for the Royal Commission on the Economic Union and Development Prospects for Canada (Toronto: University of Toronto Press, 1985).
2. David P. Ross, *The Canadian Fact Book on Income Distribution* (Ottawa: Canadian Council on Social Development, 1980), chapter 2.
3. W. Irwin Gillespie, *The Redistribution of Income in Canada* (Toronto: Gage, 1980), p. 170.
4. National Anti-Poverty Organization, "Poverty in Canada", statement issued in September 1984.
5. Canada Employment and Immigration Commission analysis of data from the Survey of Consumer Finances, 1982 (unpublished).

The Future: A Crisis of the Welfare State?

Peering into the future is as hazardous a venture as it is important. Canadians' ability to anticipate the developments which will influence the evolution of the welfare state is obviously limited, the more so, the further into the twenty-first century we look. Nevertheless, the future of Canada's social programs will also be affected by the choices that Canadians make now. It is therefore essential that we make the best-informed decisions possible about the major factors likely to affect ourselves and our compatriots in the years to come.

This contention holds true, especially, in light of extensive speculation about a "crisis of the welfare state". A wide variety of observers have argued that the social security systems of Western nations, including Canada, have entered a new and inimical phase and are likely to erode steadily over the decades to come. The prospects for the welfare state, it would seem, can no longer simply be taken for granted.

Can we Canadians continue to count on the full range of social security programs that have become such an integral part of modern society? Recent experience puts the question even more forcefully. The exciting era during which we built our welfare state and rapidly increased our social spending has come to an abrupt end, to be succeeded by a dreary process of restraint and retrenchment. For almost a decade now, the federal government has been struggling to slow the rate of increase in its health and education transfers to the provinces; spending on Unemployment Insurance has been somewhat tightened; and the indexing of major programs such as Family Allowances or Old Age Security has been suspended or capped on several occasions. During the recent recession, in particular, the gap between our social aspirations and our performance has widened as governments have struggled to balance expanding case-loads and declining resources. Social assistance benefits, in particular, have been restrained in virtually every province, sharply in some; and Canadians have witnessed the expansion of food banks and soup kitchens, unwelcome reminders of an earlier era.

Will these pressures ease as Canada and other Western nations recover from the recession? Or are they, in fact, harbingers of an even grimmer future? Those who foresee a deepening crisis of the welfare state point directly to the likelihood of the second possibility and stress trends in Western societies that will last much longer than the current recession.

The "crisis of the welfare state" is a phrase more often used than precisely defined. When people refer to this "crisis", they tend to weave together a variety of concerns about the future. Some see the crisis in terms less of current deprivation than of future difficulties which will steadily worsen over the next decades as the Canadian population ages and makes greater and greater demands on our welfare system. Others fear that modern social spending has become so extensive that it seriously jeopardizes our prospects for investment, productivity and economic growth. The fiscal problems of the welfare state, they insist, will not disappear with the recession. Still others see the crisis in more specifically political terms, suggesting that a growing disenchantment with the changes (or the lack of them) which the welfare state has brought on Canadian society is undermining the political consensus which sustained its development over the last 50 years. Social spending, they suggest, has once again become the object of ideological controversy, and its future is increasingly in doubt.

Commissioners are far from complacent about either the current performance or the future prospects of our social programs. Although we do not believe that the Canadian welfare state is in danger of collapsing under its own weight, still, the various concerns expressed in crisis scenarios do touch important issues and tensions inherent in modern welfare capitalism. Canadians' capacity to respond effectively to these problems will depend heavily on the performance of Canada's economy. If, over the next decades, Canadians fail to achieve a pattern of at least moderate growth, as envisaged in Part III of this Report, then the tensions that exist between our social commitments and our economic capacity will be exacerbated. In general, however, Commissioners anticipate that governments should be able to maintain their social commitments to the Canadian people.

Let us turn to the first element of the "crisis" concerns: the implications of the aging of the Canadian population. A careful reading of Canada's foreseeable demographic future suggests that Canadians face no inevitable crisis. The changing age structure of our population certainly represents a formidable challenge to which it would richly pay our nation to begin to respond now. The situation, however, does not warrant alarmist visions of an intolerable social burden inevitably growing over the coming years. It is, of course, important to anticipate our demographic future, but our governments now have the unusual luxury of time to plan.

The salient fact which underpins these concerns about the future viability of our welfare state is that the "baby-boom" generation is aging. This large group will enter retirement during the second decade or so of the next century, and it will then depend heavily for its well-being on the productive capacity of the Canadian economy in general and on the redistributive capacity of the welfare state in particular. How large a burden this development will represent for the Canadian people will depend on myriad factors, including our future patterns of productivity growth, immigration, fertility and mortality. We can, however, obtain some initial idea of the extent of the potential problem from looking at population figures tabulated by Statistics Canada.

Table 14-24 presents two projections of the proportion of Canada's population aged 65 and over, at decade intervals, between 1981 and 2030; these projections are based on different assumptions about fertility and immigration. The first is based on expectations of low fertility and low immigration, while the second is based on assumptions of high fertility and high immigration. In effect, the first projection is designed to obtain a reasonable upper estimate of the proportion of old people in our population into the early twenty-first century, while the second is designed to establish a reasonable lower estimate.

A note of caution is in order here: the further into the future we stretch the projections in Table 14-24, the more sensitive to particular assumptions and the more speculative they become. Nevertheless, two particular properties of

TABLE 14-24 Projections of Proportion of Population Aged 65 and Over, 1981–2030

Year	Projection A % of population	Projection B % of population
1981	9.7	9.7
1990	11.7	11.5
2000	13.8	12.7
2010	15.8	13.5
2020	20.5	16.1
2030	26.2	18.8

Sources: Statistics Canada, *Components of Population Growth, 1983–2006* (Ottawa); and Statistics Canada, Demography Division, *Components of Population Growth, 1983–2031* (Ottawa, unpublished).

Note: Projection A is based on assumptions of low fertility and low net immigration. Projection B is based on assumptions of high fertility and high net immigration.

these projections stand out. The first is that regardless of assumptions, the proportion of old people in Canada's population increases very modestly until the turn of the century; the second is that, again regardless of assumptions, this proportion increases rapidly after 2000, reaching a level that is roughly either double or triple the current proportion by 2030. Given the demands that old people inevitably make on pension programs and health services, it does appear, at first sight, that the Canadian welfare state will have to carry a heavy burden indeed 30 to 50 years hence.

Even if we take Table 14-24 at face value, however, it is extremely misleading as a guide to the size of the future burden likely to be imposed by the growing proportion of old people in our population. While the data it presents are based on various assumptions about immigration and fertility, these expectations also have implications for the proportions of young people in the population. The relevant statistics are presented in Table 14-25. As immediately appears, the very assumptions which put an upper limit on the proportion of old people in our population produce a lower limit for the proportion of younger people, and vice versa. Overall, as shown in Table 14-26 the "dependency ratio", that is, the proportion of our population under 15 and over 65, grows between 1985 and 2030 by less than 25 per cent, no matter what assumption we make. Moreover, the proportion of our prime working-age population (Canadians between 25 and 64 years of age) hardly changes, or even rises slightly over the same period. In addition, as projections in Chapter 7 indicated, the proportion in the labour force of 25- to 64-year-olds will likely increase over the period, from 65 to 68 per cent.

Whatever else one might say about these figures, they are hardly the stuff of which crises are made. The dependency ratio will increase by a substantial amount after 2010, if our projections are accurate, but it will hardly move before then. Moreover, even in the year 2030, Canada is unlikely to experience a higher dependency ratio than it did in 1961, when the post-

TABLE 14-25 Projections of Proportion of Population Aged 24 and Younger

	Projection A	Projection B
Year	% of population	% of population
1981	41.6	41.6
1990	34.9	35.6
2000	30.5	34.5
2010	26.4	33.2
2020	23.4	33.5
2030	22.1	33.5

Sources: Statistics Canada, *Components of Population Growth, 1983–2006* (Ottawa); and Statistics Canada, Demography Division, *Components of Population Growth, 1983–2031* (Ottawa, unpublished).

Note: Projection A is based on assumptions of low fertility and low net immigration. Projection B is based on assumptions of high fertility and high net immigration.

TABLE 14-26 Dependency Ratios: Projections of Proportion of Population Aged 0–14 and 65+, 1981–2030

	Projection A	Projection B
Year	% of population	% of population
1981	32.2	32.2
1990	32.1	32.7
2000	30.9	34.5
2010	30.0	34.1
2020	33.9	36.4
2030	38.4	39.5

Sources: Statistics Canada, *Components of Population Growth, 1983–2006* (Ottawa); and Statistics Canada, Demography Division, *Components of Population Growth, 1983–2031* (Ottawa, unpublished).

Note: Projection A is based on assumptions of low fertility and low net immigration. Projection B is based on assumptions of high fertility and high net immigration.

war/baby-boom generation was still young. In that year, our dependency ratio was 41.6, a figure which represents its probable peak for the entire twentieth century.

The implications of demographic change for the overall expenditures of government are less clear, but the basic message is similar. The changing age structure of Canada's population will undoubtedly lead to large increases in the cost of social security and health-care programs, but they should also allow for decreases in educational spending and the cost of other child-related programs such as Family Allowances. Thus, for example, the combination of Family Allowances and Old Age Security accounted for 2.6 per cent of our gross national product in 1950, at the height of the baby boom. That proportion rose, somewhat erratically, to 3.4 per cent in 1970, but has declined to 3.3 per cent in 1985 and is projected to stand at 3.2 per cent in 1990.

The overall net effect will be an expansion of total spending, since on a per capita basis, expenditures are considerably greater for the elderly than for the young. But present projections of these net increases do not necessarily point to a severe fiscal crisis in the future. Over the next couple of decades, certainly, the expenditures needed to maintain social programs at their current levels should be manageable in the face of population changes. Expenditures will begin to mount more sharply in the third and fourth decades of the twenty-first century, and existing studies differ somewhat on how serious the burden of costs will become. Even the most pessimistic assessments, however, emphasize that the situation then confronting Canada will be comparable to that already in place in many European countries at the beginning of the 1970s; and by the time Canada reaches that point, it is likely to be enjoying a much higher per capita real gross national product. Fundamentally, the degree of strain that a higher proportion of old people in our population will put on the economy 40 years hence will depend a great deal on the extent of economic growth over the intervening period. Given the numbers involved and the time that will elapse before marked changes in the dependency rate set in, even a quite modest, but sustained, rate of increase in our economy's productivity will enable us to accommodate the projected burden.

Accordingly, Commissioners see no reason to conclude, at this stage, that the aging of Canada's population, in itself, represents a crisis of the welfare state. Important decisions about the Canada and Quebec Pension Plans must be made in the next few years, in order to preserve their fiscal integrity, and the adjustments needed will involve significant increases in contribution rates. Indeed, some of the adjustments required in the future will be difficult to implement. To transfer resources between sectors of the social service system is never easy, and the shifts will challenge the adaptability of our institutions. These trends will also have important implications for our federal system, since the balance of federal, provincial and municipal government action in providing services differs as between the young and the old. Education is largely provided by municipalities and provinces. The costs of health care, on the other hand, are shared by the provinces and the federal government, while pensions are mainly a federal responsibility. Thus, as the majority of our dependent population comes to be composed of the old, rather than the young, the costs of supporting the welfare state will be transferred increasingly from municipal and provincial governments to the federal government.

The second element of the "crisis" is the fear that there is a fundamental incompatibility between a mature welfare state and a healthy economy. Throughout the post-war period, the majority of Canadians assumed that social programs would complement the market economy, making it more productive, stable and harmonious. Social spending would be an instrument of automatic, counter-cyclical stabilization; it would contribute to a healthier, better-educated work-force; it would provide the social infrastructure essential to an increasingly urban economy; and it would secure broad social consensus and stability by integrating poorer groups in the larger national community. During the long period of sustained economic growth that marked the post-war decades, these assumptions seemed plausible, and earlier fears of a basic tension between economic growth and social equity subsided. The economic problems of the 1970s and 1980s, however, have stimulated fresh debate about the fundamental compatibility of the welfare state and the market economy.

In responding to these concerns, it is critical to distinguish between the general question of the overall level of social spending, on the one hand, and the design of specific programs on the other. The broad conclusion of Commissioners is that the overall level of social spending does not constitute a crisis, but that the design of a few of Canada's social programs does create undesirable incentive structures and constrains the productivity of the economy.

At the most general level, Commissioners see no reason to believe that the Canadian welfare state cannot be sustained, or that it creates an unbearable burden for our economy. Comparative evidence suggests that if there is an upper limit to social expenditures in a market economy, Canada has not yet reached it. Other Western nations have managed to combine higher social expenditures as a proportion of GNP with impressive levels of economic performance. Indeed, some observers have argued cogently that social spending has actually made a positive contribution to economic growth.[1] Others have suggested that a well-developed social security system is a precondition of adjustment in the economy: without such protection, workers in declining industries and communities might well redouble their political pressure for subsidies, quotas and other policies designed to prop up their means of livelihood.

Still others have replied, however, that there are clear limits to any positive relationship between economic growth and social spending, and that in certain European countries with very high social expenditures – Belgium and the Netherlands, for example – the welfare state has contributed to difficult economic problems.[2] Commissioners know of no evidence, however, to suggest that such conclusions are justified in relation to Canada, where total social spending represents a much smaller proportion of gross domestic product. Canada's long-term ability to avoid such a painful dilemma certainly depends on at least moderate economic growth in future decades. However, we see no signs of the imminent collapse of the Canadian economy because of the burdens which the welfare states creates. We Canadians might choose to reduce our social spending in order to ease the deficit or to meet other spending priorities, but we are under no compulsion to do so. Economically, we seem free to choose our social future.

This reality does not mean that no tensions exist between the claims of social programs and economic efficiency. In the first place, the income which the welfare state redistributes must be raised by taxation, and it costs society more than a dollar to provide a dollar's worth of income in the form of services or cash to a needy person. Taxation bears certain efficiency costs; these result from the ways in which individuals allocate their time and efforts in order to cut down on their tax obligations. If, in the process, they distort the pattern of economic activity so that the resources available to society produce less output, the resulting effect on efficiency is negative. It is exceptionally difficult to reckon efficiency costs precisely. In addition, of course, there are the administrative costs imposed on tax payers by the tax system, and the administrative costs to the public sector of collecting revenues and managing the various social programs in which money is actually spent. However, none of these hidden costs means that social programs are so expensive that they should never be expanded. Even with a full understanding of the costs, the Canadian public might well support expansion of important parts of our welfare state. Nevertheless, the costs do reinforce the need to make the most effective use possible of our social expenditures.

In the second place, there are a number of problems inherent in the operation of individual social programs. It is important to recognize the points at which social programs and economic efficiency conflict and to minimize the conflict wherever possible. The tension between efficiency and economic equality, which some observers see as a sharp two-dimensional trade-off, is, in fact, a good deal more subtle than that. It is possible to provide a given amount of insurance or redistribution of income with varying degrees of efficiency. Plainly, there is scope to increase the economic efficiency of particular programs without exposing Canadian society to greater risk and inequality.

The final element in the "crisis" of the Canadian welfare state is fundamentally political. According to some observers, the broad consensus which sustained the steady expansion of social spending throughout the post-war period is disintegrating, and our welfare state is facing a crisis of legitimacy, as the Canadian public becomes increasingly restive about the fiscal burden generated by welfare-related programs. Once again, this contention does capture important strands of contemporary social debate. Nevertheless, the core of public support for our basic social programs seems solid: Commissioners see no convincing evidence of the emergence of new political consensus among Canadians that would mandate a dismantling of the welfare state.

Clearly, however, the post-war consensus on social policy has weakened. Although debate on the specifics of Canada's social policy was occasionally vigorous during the 1950s and 1960s, there was fairly broad agreement on the desirability of expanding the social service sector, and governments of all political persuasions and at both levels of our federation participated in the development of our social security system. The 1970s and 1980s, however, have witnessed considerably stronger debate. Criticisms have come from both ends of the political spectrum: on the right, a resurgent neo-conservatism is challenging the underpinnings of our social welfare system; on the left, a quieter disillusion has diminished faith in social policy as an effective instrument of reform.

Neo-conservative critics weave together a complex set of arguments. In economic terms, they insist that modern welfare and its associated taxes distort incentives, stifle entrepreneurship, hinder the operation of labour markets, and generally undermine economic growth. In social terms, they assert that reliance on social services reflects an exaggerated view of the capacity of government to engage in social engineering; the unintended consequences, they maintain, include the undermining of the family, the reinforcement of dependency among the population, and the growth of elaborate bureaucracies which, primarily, advance the interests of the professionals who staff them. Generally speaking, neo-conservatives lament the erosion of personal responsibility, which they see as the moral basis of a healthy society.

The criticism from the left is less dramatic, but no less significant. During the post-war years, social reformers placed great faith in the capacity of the welfare state to usher in a fairer society. Indeed, for some social democratic parties in Europe, educational and social policy displaced nationalization of the economy as the key to economic equality. This faith in the potency of the welfare state was shaken, however, by the rediscovery of poverty during the 1960s, as well as by the growing realization that the overall distribution of income had remained remarkably stable, and that many social programs did not confer most benefit on the poorest members of society. For some observers on the left, the welfare state looked less and less like an instrument of social reform, and more and more like a mechanism for preserving the legitimacy of an unequal society. While this criticism seldom generated explicit political attacks on social security, it did sap the enthusiasm of many who had earlier ranked among the welfare state's most stalwart champions.

This revival of ideological dispute came at the time of decreasing enthusiasm among groups holding mildly reformist and centrist opinion in social policy debates. The developments of the 1950s and 1960s largely fulfilled the social policy agenda of the post-war generation, an agenda that had been fashioned during the Depression and its aftermath. With the major elements of the welfare state in place, a loss of momentum and a growing uncertainty about the next steps were perhaps inevitable. But this hesitancy was reinforced by economic difficulties of the last decade and the criticisms from both right and left. As a result, centrist opinion has been more preoccupied with defending the gains of the past than with charting brave new courses.

Clearly, in recent years, political consensus on social policy has given way to more active ideological debate and uncertainty. This change, however, has not, as yet, generated a crisis in the form of a marked erosion of public faith in the welfare state. There is no evidence of a major shift in the broad views of Canadians about the role of social security in modern society. The Canadian public does not support across-the-board cuts in our social services. Its support for the Canadian welfare state has survived the recent recession, and widespread discussion of government deficits is a testament to the basic legitimacy of our social policy framework. While there have been no tax revolts on the order of that initiated by Proposition 13 in California, Canadians polled in 1982 expressed a clear preference for reductions in government services, rather than tax increases, as a means of reducing deficit levels; but social programs did not automatically head the list when respondents were asked where cuts should fall.[3]

To be sure, Canadians do differentiate among social programs. Universal public health insurance already seems to be deeply entrenched in our national culture, and periodic proposals for limitations on this service have elicited little enthusiasm, to say the least. In 1973, for example, 78 per cent of Canadians polled rejected the idea that routine annual medical examinations should not be covered by medicare,[4] and a decade later, over 80 per cent of those canvassed objected to the practice of extra billing.[5] Support for many other components of our welfare state is equally solid. Pensioners and disabled persons retain a special place in the affections of Canadians, and opinion polls consistently find wide endorsement of the view that benefits for these groups are inadequate, and that more should be done for them.

Conversely, the concept of individual responsibility continues to condition the Canadian public's attitudes towards programs which support employable people. The Unemployment Insurance program vividly illustrates this view. No other income-security program provoked more controversy during the 1970s. Canadians continued to accept the basic legitimacy of the UI program, agreeing overwhelmingly that "Unemployment Insurance is necessary in today's society." They were just as strongly convinced, however, that stricter controls were essential, as Table 14-27 shows. Today the recent recession has softened these feelings somewhat. Canadians' views about the causes of unemployment changed in the 1980s, and the public preference for restrictions in these benefits eased marginally, as Table 14-28 indicates.

Belief in individual responsibility similarly shapes attitudes towards recipients of social assistance. A requirement that employable men receiving welfare accept "any available work" was endorsed by 78 per cent of those polled in 1962 and by 85 per cent in 1976; in 1979, two-thirds of the Canadian public supported a similar requirement for mothers with children 13 years of age or over.[6]

This tough-mindedness about employable UI recipients mingles with a clear concern for the poor and needy generally, and an apparent willingness to reallocate expenditures to make social security more redistributive towards this group. During the past 15 years, polls have consistently found public support, in principle at least, for greater selectivity in administering the Family Allowance program, while the idea of a guaranteed annual income received substantial support even in the midst of a recession. (See Table 14-29.) Whether such generalized support would continue in response to specific proposals is not clear, of course. In 1971–72, the federal government's proposal to base Family Allowances on an income test met substantial opposition from women who stood to lose their monthly benefit if the change were effected. Again, during the federal-provincial Social Security Review, some governments were nervous about the potential public reaction to the actual implementation of a form of guaranteed income. Nevertheless, Canadians would seem open to a discussion of more selectively managed welfare programs.

Yet, when all is said and done, there is little evidence of a serious erosion of public faith in Canada's welfare state. The uneasy amalgam of collectivist and individualist values which has characterized public preferences during recent decades does not seem to have changed dramatically. In an open society, public attitudes evolve in response to ongoing political and social debate, and it remains possible that Canadians will change their opinions

TABLE 14-27 Public Attitudes towards Unemployment Insurance, 1977–1978

	Agree Strongly or Somewhat (%)		Disagree Strongly or Somewhat (%)	
	Sept. 1977	**Sept. 1978**	**Sept. 1977**	**Sept. 1978**
Unemployment Insurance is necessary in today's society.	82	84	11	10
Stricter controls are needed to ensure that Unemployment Insurance benefits do not go to people who will not take a job.	84	88	6	5
Many people take unfair advantage of Unemployment Insurance.	81	87	9	8

Source: Employment and Immigration Canada, *Statistics on Advertising for Unemployment Insurance: Reports of Three Studies* (Ottawa, 1978); and *Fourth Marketing Research Study on Unemployment Insurance* (Ottawa, 1978).

TABLE 14-28 Public Attitudes towards Unemployment and Unemployment Benefits during the 1980s

1. Responsibility for Unemployment: Responses to statement, "People don't have jobs because they don't want to work."

	1980	1981	1982	1983
	(per cent)			
Disagree	28	31	44	53
Depends	19	18	22	21
Agree	51	50	33	26

2. Public Attitudes Towards Eligibility Requirements for Unemployment Insurance

	1981	1982	1983
	(per cent)		
Loosen	20	29	34
Tighten	66	56	55
No Opinion	14	15	11

Sources: 1. *Decima Quarterly Report on Public Affairs Trends*, Quarters 1, 5, 9, 13 and 17. Data apply to the spring of each year.

2. *Decima Quarterly Report on Public Affairs Trends*, Quarters 7, 11, 15. Data apply to the fall of each year.

TABLE 14-29 Public Attitudes toward a Guaranteed Annual Income

Attitude	Summer 1980 (per cent)	Spring 1981 (per cent)	Fall 1982 (per cent)
Favour	66	75	67
Oppose	26	21	28
No opinion	7	4	4

Source: Decima Quarterly Report on Public Affairs Trends, Quarters 2, 5, 11.

more decisively in the future. Viewed from the perspective of the mid-1980s, however, the support of Canadians for the broad parameters of the welfare state seems reasonably clear.

Each of three elements of the crisis of the welfare state – demographic, economic and political – raises serious issues or points to enduring tensions in our social security system. In combination, these elements represent a formidable set of challenges. Clearly, difficult choices will have to be made. Moreover, our capacity to respond effectively to them will continue to depend heavily on the strength of the Canadian economy during the coming decades. None of this means, however, that the Canadian welfare state is entering a terminal phase. Rather, it means that the pressures to use our resources as effectively as possible will be greater than ever.

Notes

1. See for example, John McCallum and André Blais, "Government, Special Interest Groups and Economic Growth", in *Responses to Economic Change*, vol. 27, prepared for the Royal Commission on the Economic Union and Development Prospects for Canada (Toronto: University of Toronto Press, 1985).
2. See Organisation for Economic Co-operation and Development, *Economic Surveys: Belgium/Luxembourg 1982–1983* (Paris: OECD, 1983); and *Economic Surveys: The Netherlands 1983–1984* (Paris: OECD, 1984).
3. Public opinion data on these issues are discussed in Richard B. Johnston, *Public Opinion and Public Policy in Canada*, vol. 35, prepared for the Royal Commission on the Economic Union and Development Prospects for Canada (Toronto: University of Toronto Press, 1985), chapter 2, especially Tables II-13 and II-14.
4. Canadian Institute of Public Opinion (July 1973), N = 701.
5. *Decima Quarterly Report on Public Affairs Trends* (Fall 1983), N = 1434.
6. Canadian Institute of Public Opinion (September 1962; June 1976; and March 1979, N = 690, 1060 and 1056).

CHAPTER 15

Work and Pay: *The Functioning of Labour Markets*

CHAPTER 15

Work and Pay: *The Functioning of Labour Markets*

Labour-Force Trends, Past and Future

The Canadian labour force grew very rapidly in the period that followed the Second World War and particularly during the late 1960s and the 1970s. In the 1980s, that rate of growth has slowed and, according to predictions, will continue to do so. Rapid growth has reflected both a very substantial increase in the source population[1] and some increase in the percentage of that population which participated in the labour force.[2] As Commissioners demonstrated in more detail in Part III of this Report, however, such aggregate trends may conceal more than they reveal. For example, much of the growth in the source population resulted from the coming to working age of the "baby-boom generation". The number of 15- to 24-year-olds in the source population reached a peak of nearly 4 600 000 in 1980 and is now declining. The labour force of the near future will be aging, as well as growing, less rapidly.

The story of labour-force/participation rates is more complex. The modest overall increase in those rates is a composite created by a dramatic rise in the participation rate of women aged 25 and over, a moderate decline in that of adult men, and a slight upward trend in that of youth. As a result of these changes in demography and participation rates, youths and adult women became a much larger proportion of the labour force, and adult men became a smaller one.

It is projected that the trends in participation rates of all three groups will continue, although some considerable uncertainty exists on this point. If, for example, Canadian courts find that compulsory retirement at age 65 is illegal, some elderly persons may choose to prolong their participation in the labour force. Canada's labour force will become significantly larger, too, if female-participation rates continue to rise. This possibility creates a complex situation, and one that is difficult to project. While more women of all ages have been joining Canada's work-force since 1956, very distinct age profiles characterize female participation: the figures peak sharply for women in their early twenties and drop off sharply for those beyond the age of 50. If that pattern continues as the population ages, the combination of the two processes will reduce overall female participation rates.

A whole range of other factors also affects labour-force participation. These demographic, sociological, generational, attitudinal and other components are even more difficult to forecast, and their effect in determining the numbers of Canadian women who will decide to participate in the labour force is only partly understood. Conditions of work, availability of child care, and other circumstances probably influence these numbers as well.

Not surprisingly, the demographic characteristics of the Canadian labour force have been a principal focus of discussion. Other features however, are also important. Employment in the service industries and, with it, part-time and white-collar jobs expanded rapidly between 1956 and 1979, especially before 1973. The manufacturing sector accounted for a declining share of labour-market activity, and employment in primary industries declined in absolute numbers. Women were, and remain, employed principally in services, manufacturing and trade, though the proportion of female employees in all industrial groupings has increased substantially. Women and youths are far more likely than adult men to seek or to hold part-time jobs. The number of households with more than one member in the labour force also increased greatly over this period.

Notes

1. Roughly speaking, the civilian, non-institutional population 15 years of age and over, excluding inhabitants of the Territories and of Indian Reserves which are not covered by the Labour Force Survey.
2. In general, those who are working or actively searching for employment.

Labour-Market Imbalances and Unemployment[1]

Unemployment is often discussed in terms of labour-market imbalances. There are two basic types of imbalance: structural and aggregate. Structural imbalance occurs in situations where there are mismatches between the characteristics or circumstances such as skills, experience, or location of individuals seeking work and the requirements of vacant jobs. Aggregate imbalance is usually cyclical, occurring as a result of an excess supply of, or excess demand for, labour in general, regardless of individual characteristics or circumstances. Unemployment resulting from aggregate imbalances is often termed "cyclical" or "demand deficient".

A complicating factor in dealing with unemployment is that even when the labour market is in overall balance, the result is not a neat, day-by-day "fit", with each worker in a job and no job vacancies or unemployment. Gaps and dislocations are characteristic of the constant flux of any "real life" labour market. Jobs and firms open, change and expire. Workers enter the labour force and leave it, re-enter, and change jobs, employers and locations. Each of these adjustments takes time. Unemployment that results from this labour-market turnover and from the time workers need to adjust to it is referred to as "frictional". In practice, of course, frictional, structural and demand-deficient, or cyclical, unemployment are not always easy to separate from one another.

The rates of frictional plus structural unemployment constitute, at any given point in time, the non-accelerating inflation rate of unemployment (NAIRU): the extent of unemployment remaining when that caused by deficiencies in aggregate demand is eliminated. Cyclical unemployment must be dealt with by appropriate demand-management measures, as discussed in Chapters 7 to 10 of this Report. However, any policies which can reduce the NAIRU by lessening structural and frictional unemployment serve as very important means of increasing both the efficiency of our economy and the earnings of individuals.

It is very important for those who are genuinely concerned with alleviating the impact of high levels of unemployment on individual Canadians not to misunderstand the concepts involved. The NAIRU is not a fixed figure. It can be lowered by the intelligent application of policies such as training, education, mobility grants and other adjustment programs, and by the careful design of our major income-transfer systems. The currently estimated NAIRU of 6.5 to 8 per cent is too high, and it is essential that any government that wishes to deal with the real problems of unemployed Canadians seek to lower it very substantially. That is the major objective of Commissioners' recommendations with respect to the structural and frictional unemployment problem in Canada.

Structural unemployment and the policies which will help to alleviate it are fairly well understood. We deal with them in other sections. Frictional unemployment is a more recent and less well understood concept, but to understand it is important for those who wish to deal effectively with the unacceptably high levels of unemployment of the 1980s. Commissioners deal with it at some length here, since it is our conviction that the easy nostrums of the past will not provide effective guideposts for the future.

Frictional unemployment has been the subject of important analytical and empirical research in the past decade. In practice, it reflects the effects of such factors as the scarcity of information about job openings or employee availability, and the time and other resources it takes to acquire such information and to act on it. While some frictional unemployment is not only inevitable but desirable in a changing economy, an efficient labour market requires that its extent not be excessive. This requirement, in turn, means that government programs must be reviewed to ensure that they do not inadvertently promote excess frictional unemployment. The analysis of what has come to be called "the new unemployment" bears on this policy need. As with many new branches of analysis, its proponents sometimes overstate this case. Commissioners therefore note that our conclusions with respect to the "new unemployment" analysis are that it is a significant contribution to our knowledge of the phenomenon of unemployment, but that it is important to balance that awareness with a broader understanding of labour markets.

The Analysis of the New Unemployment

In what most analysts would now agree is rather an overstatement, one of the first persons to draw attention to "the new unemployment" wrote in 1973:

> *Most macroeconomic analyses of unemployment are based on ideas about the causes and structure of unemployment that are inappropriate and out of date . . . The conventional view of postwar unemployment might be described as follows: "The growth of demand for goods and services does not always keep pace with the expansion of the labor force and the rise in output per man. Firms therefore lay off employees and fail to hire new members of the labor force at a sufficient rate. The result is a pool of potential workers who are unable to find jobs. Only policies to increase the growth of demand can create the jobs needed to absorb the unemployed."*
>
> *This picture of a hard core of unemployed workers who are not able to find jobs is an inaccurate description of our economy and a misleading basis for policy. A more accurate description is an active labor market in which almost everyone who is out of work can find his usual type of job in a relatively short time.* The problem is not that these jobs are unavailable but that they are often unattractive. *Much of the unemployment and even more of the lost manpower occurs among individuals who find that the available jobs are neither appealing in themselves nor rewarding as pathways to better jobs in the future.*[2]

The Economic Council of Canada in its more balanced 1982 analysis of labour markets in the 1980s notes:

> *This conclusion has led many labour market analysts to suggest that appropriate measures to reduce unemployment should focus on facilitating rapid job search and increased job holding, rather than on increasing the number of available jobs.*[3]

It seems, then, according to supporters of the "new employment" view, that some of the unemployment originally thought to have been caused by deficiencies in aggregate demand, was, in fact, frictional. This means that the best method of dealing with it is not through monetary and fiscal policies, as had been thought at first, but through labour-market policies. Indeed, as we noted in Chapter 10, to try to deal with frictional unemployment by the former means would amount to an attempt to lower the general level of unemployment below the NAIRU. The eventual result, according to many economists, would be failure to lower unemployment and increased inflation.

This school of analytic thought developed two sub-branches, which are known as "search theory" and "implicit contract theory". We shall consider them briefly here.

Search Theory and Evidence

Theory

The basic premise underlying search theory is that knowledge of the characteristics of available jobs and workers is neither perfect nor free. As a consequence, and because of the very substantial differences among workers and jobs, any labour market offers a variety of wages and job characteristics. Thus, when an employee becomes dissatisfied with a particular situation, it must be because of a possibility that the job she or he holds is inferior to others that might be available. Alternatively, it might be said that workers know their actual wages and, at least in a general way, the distribution of wages in the market. They do not know where jobs of a particular kind, paying particular wages are to be found. Thus, having resolved to find other jobs, they seek a "good", or relatively well-paid, position. The process of search continues as long as the expected returns from keeping on at it exceed the costs. These costs can be reckoned as the sum of additional forgone earnings, out-of-pocket expenses, and psychic discomfort experienced as a result of unemployment.

Given that people search for employment, the question arises: Why might they choose to do so while unemployed, rather than before leaving a previous job or after accepting a temporary one? The suggested answer is that a person can sometimes gather and disseminate information more efficiently while unemployed and thus able to specialize in collecting information.[4]

Answers to several different questions would have to be obtained in order to evaluate the importance of search behaviour in relation to overall unemployment. These questions might include the following: Does the improved access to generally available sources of labour-market information offset the loss of information that is available only in the work-place? Does it also make up for loss of access to internal promotion ladders? Is the additional efficiency of unemployed search, plus the value of any additional leisure that may be enjoyed, great enough to compensate for the forgone earnings, plus the adverse signals to employers and any psychic discomfort that may result from being unemployed? The answers to the first two questions will probably depend on the characteristics of the particular labour market. As for the third, income-maintenance schemes such as unemployment insurance (UI) affect the individual's choice, for such payments reduce the costs of unemployed search and so can be expected to increase its duration.

Evidence

In view of the nature of search theory and related behaviour, one would expect to find both unemployed and employed job searchers, depending on the circumstances of the persons looking for work. One would also expect wage demands to decline as a period of unemployment lengthens. The authors of a recent analysis of employed and unemployed job search found evidence of both types of search behaviour.[5] (See Table 15-1.) They find that employed search is most prevalent among men, part-time workers, the highly educated, and workers in managerial, professional and service occupations. Among a group of unemployed searchers, there was also some evidence that wage demands were lowered as the period of unemployment lengthened. The study also showed that UI beneficiaries search longer than non-beneficiaries, and that search duration declines as unemployment rates rise. These last two results suggest that job searchers have some control over the duration of their search. Other studies have confirmed this effect of UI entitlements on the duration of periods of unemployment; these are examined below.

TABLE 15-1 Employed and Unemployed Job Searchers

	(Canada's annual averages, 1975–1983)			
	(1) Employed	(2) Unemployed	(3)=(1)/(2)	Unemployment Rate
Year	(thousands)		(per cent)	
1975	266	596	44.3	6.9
1976	247	642	37.9	7.1
1977	268	765	36.0	8.1
1978	300	828	36.0	8.3
1979	348	762	45.5	7.4
1980	360	783	45.7	7.5
1981	389	811	48.1	7.5
1982	387	1200	37.9	11.0
1983	435	1359	32.0	11.9

Source: Statistics Canada, *Labour Force Annual Averages, 1975–1983*, Cat. No. 71-529 (Ottawa: Minister of Supply and Services Canada, 1984), pp. 342–50, 369–77, 412–20.

Table 15-1 also demonstrates that the ratio of employed to unemployed job searchers changed abruptly between 1976–78 and 1979–81. In 1979, the unemployment-insurance program was amended to reduce benefits and tighten qualification requirements. These revisions had a demonstrable effect on rates of unemployment.[6] It is estimated that NAIRU dropped by nearly half a percentage point after 1979.[7] The discontinuity between 1978 and 1979, as shown in Table 15-1, suggests that searchers, faced with an increased relative cost of unemployment, tended to substitute employed for unemployed search. In 1982 and 1983, the proportion of unemployed job searchers rose dramatically. The increase paralleled the marked economic decline of that period and may well mean that many Canadians no longer had the option of employed search and were engaged in involuntary search for any job, rather than a better one.

There are also a number of less intensive or "discouraged" searchers outside the labour force as defined by Statistics Canada. These people have not searched for jobs within the past four weeks, as required of those classified as unemployed; nevertheless, they indicated, in response to special labour-force surveys, that they wanted and were available for work, but were not seeking it for "labour-market/related reasons". The data suggest that the number of "discouraged" searchers, although smaller than the number of employed searchers, is hardly negligible. Both the number of discouraged workers and the proportion who believe that no work is available seem to be positively related to the unemployment rate.

The authors of one study have concluded that search theory contributes to an understanding of labour-market behaviour in Canada, but that it cannot account for more than half of the unemployment recorded in 1977. They expressed concern that individuals are too prone to quit their jobs and to search too long for new ones, and that too much search is unproductive, leading to no job or no wage gain.[8] A more general and safer conclusion, however, might be simply that the insights of search theory contribute to Canadians' understanding of the labour-market behaviour of both the employed and the unemployed. The importance of voluntary search varies with time, with macro-economic conditions, and with individual circumstances.

Implicit Contracts

The theory of implicit contracts was developed to explain an aspect of the new unemployment phenomenon that search theory cannot explain: instead of embarking on a job search, some employees simply wait for re-employment during lay-offs. This theory is concerned with attempts by firms and their workers to reach an understanding about variations in wages and employment in the face of economic uncertainties. Whenever a firm invests in the search for workers, or workers invest in search and preparation for employment, an incentive is created for the firm and the worker to remain together in order to realize returns on their investment. Temporary lay-offs, with appropriate understandings about recall, can be viewed as a device for keeping employees and employers together while they adjust to temporary reductions in demand.

A firm facing fluctuations in the demand for its goods and variations in the price it receives for its products can adjust in a variety of ways: it can produce steadily and use inventories as a buffer; it can rent (or buy) its non-human inputs on a variable basis; or it can adjust its labour costs by reducing either working hours or the number of employees. Under what circumstances, then, will variations in employment (lay-offs) be preferred to other forms of adjustment? The theory of implicit contracts suggests that under some special, but not improbable, circumstances, both employers and employees might consider that lay-offs can represent the best choice.

As with search theory, unemployment insurance again enters the picture because it lowers the costs of being "on lay-off". This development, in turn, may lower the wage which must be paid to workers who risk lay-off and increase the likelihood of their waiting for a recall. Moreover, with a few exceptions such as "developmental" uses, UI is available to laid-off workers, but not to support other means of adjustment such as reduced hours. Thus, when UI payments involve a subsidy, that is, when the premiums of a given group of employers and employees do not cover the full costs of their unemployment benefits, there is an incentive for the subsidized firms to adjust through lay-offs.

While implicit contract theory contributes to our understanding of certain labour-market behaviour, it has limited application for lay-offs, which account for a relatively small proportion of total unemployment. Moreover, only 30 per cent of lay-offs end in an employee's return to the original employer.

Search and Implicit Contract Theory: Conclusions

Inevitably, there will be some frictional unemployment arising from job-search, and as long as demand for particular products fluctuates, there will also be periodic lay-offs. The extent of job-search unemployment depends on the availability of labour-market information, customs with respect to hiring, the relative cost and efficiency of employed and unemployed search, and the level of turnover in employment. Temporary unemployment because of lay-off depends on the extent of cyclical and seasonal variations in demand; price and wage flexibility; the amount of subsidy provided by unemployment insurance; and the relative costs of adjusting to variations in sales through changes in inventory and production, rather than by varying labour and other inputs.

Unemployed job search is, indeed, partly a process of productive investment in information. In that sense it differs to some degree from both demand-deficient and structural unemployment. There is a desirable level of search behaviour, and too little may be as costly for society as too much. Given demand fluctuations in particular markets, lay-off unemployment, too, may perform a useful economic function when adjustment by other means, such as inventory accumulation, is very costly or even impossible.

While the "new unemployment" analysis cannot be used to explain all aspects of frictional unemployment, it does focus attention on specific labour-market policies to reduce employment instability, and to ease and speed job search. In particular, it has ensured that perverse incentives deriving from some features of unemployment insurance and minimum wages have been subjected to especially searching scrutiny.

Labour-Market Turnover and Duration of Unemployment

When considering the nature and effect of unemployment, it is particularly important not merely to look at the total numbers of unemployed people, but also to consider the rate of movement of people into and out of jobs and the labour force. The data now available to us demonstrate that the "flows" of people into and out of the ranks of the unemployed are very much larger than the total "stock" of unemployed at any given time. In 1977, for instance, an average of 850 000 persons were unemployed in Canada, but there were over 4 000 000 entries into, and exits from, unemployment. This record implies, of course, that the average completed spell of unemployment must have been fairly short: something in the order of two to three months. Similar results were obtained for each of the years from 1976 to 1980.

To measure the duration of periods of unemployment is a large and complex task which cannot be fully explored here. However, the length of spells of unemployment as reported directly in periodic surveys, such as the Labour Force Survey, is seriously misleading for two reasons. The surveys intercept spells of unemployment in progress, thus underestimating the complete duration of the period they interrupt; they also under-represent the number of very short spells which may be started and completed in the interval between surveys. Research designed to overcome these problems suggests that the average duration of completed unemployment spells is short, lasting, on average, two-and-a-half months, but it also emphasizes that a good deal of unemployment is accounted for by those unemployed for long spells.[9] An example will help to illustrate this. Suppose that five people experience unemployment. Four of these are unemployed for one month, and one for eight months. The average duration of their periods of unemployment is thus 1.8 months, but two-thirds of the total extent of unemployment is accounted for by the one person's long spell without work.

The duration of periods of unemployment differs by age-sex and regional groupings, with younger persons and women experiencing shorter stretches of unemployment than adult men.[10] This record implies that observed higher unemployment rates for young persons and women are the result of higher frequency or incidence of unemployment that more than offsets their shorter periods of joblessness.

The length of periods of unemployment depends on such economic variables as unemployment levels, labour-force/participation rates, and changes in Unemployment Insurance regulations.[11] There is a considerable tendency for unemployment to be concentrated among relatively few people, since some persons suffer long and/or repeated spells without work.[12] These chronic sufferers are found in all demographic and regional groupings.

The brevity of the average spell of unemployment has been cited in the United States as evidence that unemployment was voluntary during a time when jobs were readily available.[13] More recently, however, other American observers have argued that this inference is unwarranted because many unemployment spells did not end in employment, but in exit from the labour force. Unemployment that ended with the finding of a job lasted, on average, much longer. The total period of joblessness – of being unemployed and out of the labour force because of discouragement – might be much longer than the average "duration of unemployment" as measured by standard labour-force surveys, and for those involved, the two states may well be indistinguishable.[14] In Canada the pattern is similar. Some 45 per cent of all unemployment spells end in withdrawal from the labour force. Here, too, spells ending in employment are longer, on average, than those ending in labour-force withdrawal. A large proportion of unemployed workers drop out of the statistically measured labour force. Moreover, unemployment is highly concentrated: that is to say, a relatively "small number of workers out of work a large part of the time" bear a large proportion of it.[15]

Commissioners consider this last finding highly important for purposes of labour-policy formation, particularly when it is combined with the findings that chronic unemployment particularly affects prime-age and older workers and is not highly concentrated by region. It is partly for this reason that we lay so much stress on the need to expand programs that will facilitate major labour-force adjustments, particularly when the adjustment to change is likely to involve a lengthy period of unemployment.

Increases in Unemployment in the 1960s and 1970s

As Commissioners have stated, in Part III of this Report, the standard explanation for the rise of unemployment in Canada in the 1960s and 1970s was that it reflected, in part, an increase in the NAIRU. That rise, in turn, was attributed to the rapid growth in working-age population, to rising work-force/participation rates, particularly of women, and to increases in frictional unemployment, stimulated by social legislation, particularly by amendments to the Unemployment Insurance Act. As the labour force grew during the 1960s and 1970s, our economy did generate additional jobs at a fairly rapid rate, but the supply of jobs did not quite keep up with the growing supply of labour. As a result, both employment and unemployment grew. Indeed, over the 1970s, the employment-to-population ration (an alternative to the unemployment rate as an indicator of economic performance) actually rose. As our analysis in Part III indicated, over long periods, the unemployment rate will be virtually independent of the rate of labour-force growth. In the short term, however, a rapidly growing population and labour force can present difficult challenges for a nation as it tries to create an adequate supply of jobs.

The 1960s and 1970s also saw a change in the demographic composition of the labour force. Women and youths became a much larger proportion of the total work-force and adult men a smaller one. In this period, the unemployment rates of women and, particularly, of youth have typically been higher than those of adult men. Thus, even if every other circumstance had remained the same, this expansion of groups with higher unemployment rates would, by itself, have raised average unemployment rates. Investigators have found that the effect of this change in labour-force composition has been positive, but small: something in the order of 0.3 percentage points.

Not all of these changes occurred wholly independently of social legislation. A number of researchers have shown that work-force participation rates, especially those of youths and women, increase with the generosity of unemployment insurance payments,[16] and that teenage participation in the labour force responds to changes in minimum wages.[17]

There is, however, another aspect of the rapid growth of the female- and youth-labour force that may be important in analysing labour-force trends. If job requirements are characterized by age-sex differences, demographic groups that grow more rapidly will experience greater difficulty in finding work, and their unemployment rates will rise. This will occur if characteristics that are genuinely relevant to the production process are associated with sex and age. Young entrants into the labour force, for instance, however energetic or well educated they may be, must, of necessity, be inexperienced. Women, too, have, on average, skills and occupational characteristics that differ from those of men, and females seek full- and part-time work in different proportions from males. If the production process is designed, at any given moment, to use fairly rigid mixes of different skills and occupations, structural unemployment can result from disproportionate growth among various elements of the labour force, especially if relative wages do not adjust to changing supply conditions in the labour market. This structural demographic problem may have been quite important over the past decade, adding approximately one percentage point to the average rate of unemployment.[18]

There were other changes in the 1970s that empirical evidence would indicate have raised the NAIRU. One which has been extensively examined is that of labour-market legislation, particularly that governing unemployment insurance and minimum wages. Minimum wages can make permanently unemployable some workers whose contribution to output falls below its level. They can also make it difficult for young unskilled applicants to obtain jobs with a large training component which, initially, represents a cost, rather than a source of income to the employer. This reality forces such entrants into unpleasant, dull, dead-end jobs which they quit and change frequently, and between which they are unemployed or out of the labour force. In Canada, minimum wages rose rapidly, relative to the prevailing average level of wages, in the early 1970s, and as a result, unemployment increased.[19]

We have already seen how unemployment insurance makes unemployment less costly to those covered. That result is, of course, a primary objective of the program, but taken too far, it can also have deleterious effects. Despite some offsetting influences, this protection can increase both employee turnover and the duration of unemployed job search, and it can encourage lay-offs as a form of adjustment to a firm's demand fluctuations. The 1971 revisions of the Unemployment Insurance Act, which increased the generosity of the UI scheme in several respects, are generally considered to have increased unemployment by some 1 to 2 percentage points.

Thus, in consequence of both demographic and legislative developments, the NAIRU rose in the late 1960s and the 1970s. The forces involved, however, largely spent themselves during the 1970s. The rate of growth of the labour force, both domestic and immigration-related, has declined, and a further decline is projected, quite aside from cyclical circumstances. Offsetting this decline are projections that women's participation rates will continue to rise, though perhaps less quickly. The baby-boom generation has now largely reached working age, and its successors are a smaller cohort of youth. Minimum wages have been declining in relation to the average wage and in relation to prices. The 1971 Unemployment Insurance revisions were soon followed by a gradual tightening of both law and administrative regulations that culminated in the 1979 revisions. In brief, most of the forces which caused the NAIRU to rise from 1966 to 1977–78 should now be causing it to decline, albeit slowly.

Rapidity of change can also affect the extent of frictional and structural unemployment. When change occurs rapidly, there will be a temporary increase in structural unemployment as the labour market adjusts. Recently economists have started to examine whether the increased volatility of the economic environment since the late 1960s has contributed to a rise in structural unemployment.[20] There is some indication that this has, in fact, occurred, although there is so far no agreement on the importance of this factor relative to other factors such as demography and social legislation.

This review of economic theory and empirical evidence is somewhat optimistic in that it suggests that even with the current range of policies, the NAIRU should, in the future, go no higher, at least, than its present level. There are less-optimistic possibilities, however, and the most common is that rapid economic and/or technological change will raise the level of structural unemployment. In this Commission's judgement, the evidence in favour of these less-optimistic possibilities is weak, though it cannot be dismissed entirely. Nevertheless, even if these latter possibilities are given some weight, they strengthen, rather than weaken, the very strong case that we see for labour-market policies that will reduce the NAIRU from its current excessive level of 6.5 to 8 per cent.

Notes

1. This section draws on the paper by S.F. Kaliski, "Trends, Changes, and Imbalances: A Survey of the Canadian Labour Market", in *Work and Pay: The Canadian Labour Market*, vol. 17, prepared for the Royal Commission on the Economic Union and Development Prospects for Canada (Toronto: University of Toronto Press, 1985).
2. Martin Feldstein, "The Economics of the New Unemployment", *Public Interest* (Fall 1973), pp. 4 – 5 (emphasis in original).
3. Economic Council of Canada, *In Short Supply: Jobs and Skills in the 1980s* (Ottawa: Minister of Supply and Services Canada, 1982), p. 48.
4. See A.A. Alchian, "Information Costs, Pricing, and Resource Unemployment", in *Microeconomic Foundations of Employment and Inflation Theory*, by E.S. Phelps *et al.* (New York: Norton, 1970), p. 29.
5. Abrar Hasan and Surendra Gera, *Job Search Behaviour, Unemployment and Wage Gain in Canadian Labour Markets* (Ottawa: Economic Council of Canada, 1982).
6. C.M. Beach and S.F. Kaliski, "On the Design of Unemployment Insurance: The Impact of the 1979 Unemployment Insurance Amendments", *Canadian Public Policy* 9 (June 1983): 164–73; Pierre Fortin and Keith Newton, "Labor Market Tightness and Wage Inflation in Canada", in *Workers, Jobs, and Inflation*, edited by Martin Neil Baily (Washington, D.C.: Brookings Institution, 1982), pp. 243–78; and W.C. Riddell and P.M. Smith, "Expected Inflation and Wage Changes in Canada", *Canadian Journal of Economics* 15 (August 1982): 377–94.
7. See Riddell and Smith, "Expected Inflation and Wage Changes in Canada", p. 390. See also Beach and Kaliski, "On the Design of Unemployment Insurance".

8. Hasan and Gera, *Job Search Behaviour, Unemployment and Wage Gain.*
9. See C.M. Beach, S.F. Kaliski, and V.H. Skulmis, "Analyzing Unemployment Durations for the Annual Work Patterns Survey", paper presented at the Canadian Economics Association meeting, 1983. Another data set – a sample of the Longitudinal Labour Force Data Base covering workers insured by Unemployment Insurance – also largely confirms these findings: S. Magun, "Unemployment Experience in Canada: A Five-Year Longitudinal Analysis", paper presented to the Canadian Economics Association meeting, 1982.
10. See C.M. Beach and S.F. Kaliski, "Some Aspects of Labour Market Behaviour in Canada: A Study Based on Gross Flows Between Labour Market States, 1976–80", paper presented to the Eastern Economic Association meeting, 1982; and A. Hasan and P. de Broucker, "Duration and Concentration of Unemployment", *Canadian Journal of Economics* 15 (November 1982): 735–56.
11. See C.M. Beach and S.F. Kaliski, "On the Design of Unemployment Insurance: The Impact of the 1979 Unemployment Insurance Amendments", *Canadian Public Policy* 9 (June 1983): 164–73.
12. See Hasan and de Broucker, "Duration and Concentration of Unemployment". Some of their results are based on two sets of longitudinal data: the Labour Force Tracking Survey (LFTS) and the Annual Work Patterns Survey (AWPS).
13. See M.S. Feldstein, "Temporary Layoffs in the Theory of Unemployment", *Journal of Political Economy* 84 (October 1976): 937–57.
14. See Kim B. Clark and Lawrence H. Summers, "Labor Market Dynamics and Unemployment: A Reconsideration", *Brookings Papers on Economic Activity* 1 (1979): 13–60.
15. See Hasan and de Broucker, "Duration and Concentration of Unemployment".
16. See, for example, Tom Siedule, Nicholas Skoulas, and Keith Newton, *The Impact of Economy-Wide Changes on the Labour Force: An Econometric Analysis* (Ottawa: Economic Council of Canada, 1976).
17. Robert Swidinsky, "Minimum Wages and Teenage Unemployment", *Canadian Journal of Economics* 13 (February 1980): 158–71.
18. See Frank Reid and Douglas S. Smith, "The Impact of Demographic Changes on Unemployment", *Canadian Public Policy* 7 (Spring 1981): 348–51.
19. See Pierre Fortin and Louis Phaneuf, "Why Is the Unemployment Rate so High in Canada?", paper presented to the Canadian Economics Association meeting, 1979.
20. See M.F. Charette and B. Kaufmann, "Short Run Variations in the Natural Rate of Unemployment" (mimeo, 1984). An analysis of these studies appears in the Commission paper by S.F. Kaliski, "Trends, Changes, and Imbalances: A Survey of the Canadian Labour Market", in *Work and Pay: The Canadian Labour Market*, vol. 17 (Toronto: University of Toronto Press, 1985).

Youth Unemployment

The problem of youth unemployment warrants special attention because of the serious nature of the employment difficulties facing Canadians under twenty-five. Concern about youth unemployment grew during the 1970s as the number of young workers (15- to 24-year-olds) and the unemployment rate of this group rose. The increase was particularly large for young females, a factor which reflects, in part, the general rise in female-unemployment rates.

The youth-unemployment rate has typically exceeded that of adults because entry into the labour force often involves a period of "search" unemployment and because the transition from school to work involves experimentation with a variety of jobs and the accumulation of job-related skills and experience. These relatively constant factors could scarcely account, however, for the increase in the ratio of youth to adult unemployment: that ratio rose from about 1.8 in the early 1950s, to 2.1 in the mid-1960s, to 2.5 in 1976–77. To make matters worse, this increase occurred at a time when unemployment in general was rising. The greater rise in youth unemployment primarily reflects the fact that the various forces – demographic factors and changes in social legislation – accounting for the rise in the non-accelerating inflation rate of unemployment (NAIRU) had a proportionally greater impact on the youth-labour market. As a result, throughout the 1970s, youth accounted for approximately one-quarter of the labour force, but about half of the unemployment.

Since 1977, the ratio of youth to adult unemployment has fallen significantly – from about 2.5 in 1977 to 2.1 in 1983 – though this improvement is offset by the higher unemployment rates of both groups. In part, this change may reflect the reversals noted earlier in demographic trends and social legislation. However, the decline appears to reflect cyclical, in addition to secular, forces. The recent recession resulted in a significant decline in the youth work-force/participation rate as many 15- to 24-year-olds remained in, or returned to, schools, colleges and universities. Furthermore, although young workers are particularly susceptible to cyclical economic downturns – they are often among the first to be laid off, and new entrants into the labour force, because of their limited work experience, have difficulty competing for the available jobs – the recession was severe enough to affect many adults as well.

Future employment prospects hinge on this combination of secular and cyclical influences. The longer-term prospects for youth employment appear favourable. Projections of future unemployment rates for different age-sex groups are, of course, subject to considerable uncertainty. Nonetheless, most projections indicate significant declines in the unemployment rate of youths, relative to that of adults, and some forecast very substantial declines.[1] The most important factor in this respect is the declining size of the youth cohort entering the labour force. The demographic trends which worked to the disadvantage of the "baby boom" generation will work to the advantage of future cohorts of young workers.

On the other hand, the medium-term prospects for youth unemployment appear much less favourable. This situation reflects several factors: the currently high unemployment rates among today's youth; the cyclically depressed work-force/participation rate, indicating that a significant number of young people will be entering or re-entering the labour force as employment expands, thus keeping the unemployment rate high; and the projections of a slow return to more normal levels of employment. Because of these circumstances, employment policy should focus more on the current generation of youth, many of whom have little experience of stable work, rather than on the smaller cohorts of youth expected to enter the labour force in the future. The most important contribution which policy can make to the labour-market prospects of the current generation of 15- to 24-year-olds is a more rapid return to full employment, an issue Commissioners addressed in Part III of this Report. In addition, proposals we make with respect to adjustment assistance and education and training are intended to contribute to improved prospects for this group.

Many Canadians considered that the "new unemployment" view, presented earlier in this section, was particularly relevant to youth, a group with high labour-market turn-over and short spells of unemployment. Subsequent research has shown, however, that this assessment of youth unemployment was overly simplified, as it was for unemployment in general. It is true that the average duration of completed spells of unemployment is shorter for youth than for adults, and thus the higher youth-unemployment rate is accounted for by more frequent spells of unemployment. Nevertheless, these averages tell only part of the story. As with adults, youth unemployment is highly concentrated. While a majority of young people find jobs relatively quickly after becoming unemployed, an important minority do not, and this group accounts for much of the sector's unemployment. Furthermore, a significant fraction of youth-unemployment spells end in withdrawal from the labour force, which means that the total duration of joblessness is understated by our usual measures of labour-force status.

Youth unemployment tends to be highest among the least educated, particularly school drop-outs. For example, in 1982, the unemployment rate among 15- to 24-year-olds stood at 18.8 per cent, but at 32 per cent among those with less than eight years of education and at 10 per cent among those with university education. Other factors accounting for prolonged periods of unemployment are location in areas of slow growth and high unemployment, and lack of success at finding a first job. These factors suggest the need for structural policies relating to education and training, the transition from school to work, and regional mobility; these issues are addressed in subsequent parts of this chapter.

Commissioners have noted that, from the long-term perspective which is this Commission's primary responsibility, youth unemployment is a current problem which is expected gradually to disappear. An issue of potential concern for the medium to long term, however, is the prospects for the current generation of youth. Will this group become the unemployed adults of the future? The central question here is whether individuals who suffer unemployment as teenagers or young adults are to some extent permanently "scarred" in the sense of having relatively high probabilities of adult unemployment or less-rapid earnings growth. Unfortunately, research on this important question is limited to the U.S. experience and is generally inconclusive.[2] Improved general employment prospects are clearly necessary, and the improvement, when it materializes, may be sufficient to reduce unemployment within this cohort. Still, continued monitoring of its labour-market situation will be needed. It would be unfortunate to have in place a range of special programs for youth at a time when the groups facing the greatest labour-market difficulties were the 25- to 34- or the 35- to 44-year-olds.

Notes

1. For example, one recent study projects youth unemployment rates falling below those of adults before the end of this decade. See David Foot and Jeanne Li, "The Demographic Determinants of Unemployment in Canada", paper presented at the conference "Unemployment: Can It Be Reduced? An International Perspective", sponsored by the Centre for Industrial Relations, University of Toronto, Toronto, November 28–30, 1984.
2. See the studies in R.B. Freeman and D.A. Wise, eds., *The Youth Labor Market Problem: Its Nature, Causes, and Consequences* (Chicago: University of Chicago Press, 1982).

Unemployment Insurance[1]

The Unemployment Insurance (UI) system was established in 1940, following the recommendations of the Royal Commission on Dominion-Provincial Relations and the resolution, through a constitutional amendment, of the difficulties which had caused the Employment and Social Insurance Act of 1935 to be declared *ultra vires* the British North America Act. From 1940 to 1971, gradual and modest changes were made in provisions governing the coverage, eligibility, benefits and financing of the Unemployment Insurance Act. Dramatic changes to these key features of the Act were made in the 1970s, primarily in 1971, but also later in the decade. After 1971, the size of the UI system grew dramatically. Expenditures increased from approximately $700 million in 1970, to almost $2 billion in 1972, and further to almost $12 billion in 1983. With current and projected expenditures of approximately $11 billion per year, Unemployment Insurance is the largest operating program of the federal government.

Unemployment insurance is intended primarily to provide income protection for those who suffer loss of earnings because of unemployment. In addition to its contribution to economic security, however, UI can affect the attainment of other basic goals: in particular, income distribution or equity and economic efficiency. Furthermore, there will generally be trade-offs among these goals, so that designing an optimal system involves difficult choices. Because of its size and the extent of its coverage, the UI system has numerous effects on the functioning of the labour market. Some of these are consistent with the objectives of the program, while others are chiefly unintended adverse consequences. It is Commissioners' intention, in proposing certain changes to the existing UI and other income-support programs, to encourage higher levels of employment, while easing any difficulties of transition for Canadians who will have to seek out new employment opportunities.

Objectives of the UI System

While the primary goal of the UI system is to provide insurance against the loss of income associated with unemployment, other objectives have also been pursued or recommended. These include facilitating labour-market adjustment, redistributing income, and contributing to macro-economic stability. In addition, the program has important effects on economic efficiency and equity.

Unemployment insurance can improve the operation of the labour market if its benefits help workers to find stable employment or contribute to a better matching of abilities with job requirements. Similarly, UI benefits may help unemployed persons to finance job search in locations where employment prospects are more favourable. On the other hand, the program may impede labour-market adjustment if it encourages labour-force participants to remain in regions or occupations with poor employment prospects.

UI can contribute, too, to overall economic stability by acting as an "automatic stabilizer", although this achievement is not a primary objective of the program. It performs this function by contributing to a government deficit and increasing aggregate demand in recessions, and by contributing to a surplus and decreasing aggregate demand in "booms". At the same time, it has become better recognized in recent years that social programs financed by payroll taxes can contribute to economic instability if their financing provisions result in increases in premiums during recessions, when program expenditures rise.[2] For example, the substantial increase in UI-premium rates in 1983, when the economy was just emerging from the most severe recession of the post-Second World War period, probably contributed to a slower recovery.

Should the UI system be used to redistribute income and wealth in Canada's economy? Views differ, and the issue has been the subject of debate. Of course, at any point in time, UI redistributes income from those who are currently employed and paying UI premiums to those who are unemployed. The fulfilment of this insurance function, however, does not necessarily imply that a broader redistribution among income classes, regions or occupations is in process.

Some Canadians believe that the UI program should concern itself strictly with social insurance, leaving income redistribution to programs specifically designed for that purpose. Others have suggested that unemployment insurance should contribute to our accepted social objectives relating to income distribution. The UI system has gradually moved in this direction, by such means as extending coverage to workers in seasonal industries, relating benefits to regional unemployment rates, and imposing a surtax on higher-income UI recipients.

This Commission is vitally concerned with poverty and, more generally, with the distribution of income and opportunity among Canadians. Our view, however, is that income redistribution does not constitute an appropriate application of the UI system. There are several reasons for this conclusion. Canadian income-distribution objectives focus on family income and need, while UI benefits are directed to the individual worker and are unrelated to other income or assets. To contribute to redistributive goals, UI benefits would have to be related to family income, and this adjustment would involve testing for other income and assets. In addition, the accounting period (the period over which benefits and income are reconciled) would have to be substantially lengthened, since the weekly accounting period presently in use is much shorter than that usually considered appropriate for income-support programs intended to reconcile income and needs. To change the UI system along these lines would be bound to interfere significantly with the program's social insurance objective which, in Commissioners' view, should be the primary focus of unemployment insurance.

This emphasis on the social insurance function of the UI program does not imply that this Commission opposes programs with redistributive objectives. On the contrary, our view is simply that unemployment insurance is an inappropriate means by which to attempt this important objective, and that explicit income-security programs are much more likely to be effective for this purpose. Yet although Commissioners place primary emphasis on the insurance objective, the benefit and financing provisions of the UI system should also facilitate, rather than retard, labour-market adjustment; they should contribute to economic stability and be designed to promote equity and economic efficiency within the Canadian economy.

If Canadians accept the social insurance function as the primary purpose of the UI system, a fundamental issue arises: Should unemployment insurance be provided by our governments or by the private sector as are most other forms of insurance? Commissioners believe that there is a sound rationale for publicly provided unemployment insurance. This rationale follows from the fact that private insurance companies are unlikely to offer comprehensive insurance against the risk of unemployment, except possibly in very narrowly specified circumstances. For this reason, there is a place for state-supported unemployment insurance. Society as a whole benefits from a comprehensive scheme which allows the risk of unemployment to be diversified, to some degree, across employers and employees, across regions and over time.

For two reasons, private insurance companies would not find it profitable to offer comprehensive insurance against the risk of unemployment. First, it is often impossible for the insurer to determine the risk that a particular insuree represents. Since low-risk individuals are less likely to purchase insurance, the company might find that only high-risk individuals would buy protection, thus making the sale unprofitable. If, to circumvent this possibility, an insurance company raises its premiums, it might attract a smaller group of customers with an even higher risk of becoming unemployed. Compulsory UI coverage avoids this "adverse selection" problem.

Secondly, individuals can control, to some extent, the risk of becoming or remaining unemployed. To deal with this "moral hazard" problem, insurance companies would seek to obtain the sorts of broad monitoring and surveillance powers that our Canadian society does not wish to grant to private companies. Under our present system, the relationship between unemployment insurance and Canada Employment Centres makes it relatively easy for our society to deal with the moral hazard problem.

Unemployment Insurance and Unemployment

Earlier in this chapter, we Commissioners noted that changes in the UI system have been identified as a factor contributing to rising unemployment rates, and we observed that UI reform would be one way of lowering the non-accelerating inflation rate of unemployment (NAIRU). To demonstrate, however, that making unemployment insurance less generous would lower the NAIRU is not, by itself, a sufficient reason to make such changes. If the Canadian government's sole objective were to lower the NAIRU, it could eliminate unemployment insurance. The issue, rather, is whether UI reforms would benefit Canadian society as a whole. Fortunately a number of the changes that this Commission has to suggest would, in our opinion, both benefit Canadian society *and* lower the NAIRU.

Empirical studies provide very strong support for the view that changes in the UI system – in particular the very substantial changes made in 1971–

72 – have had a significant effect on Canada's unemployment rate. Prior to 1971, the UI benefit rate (benefits as a proportion of previous earnings) varied between 43 and 53 per cent, depending on the existence of dependents; it was raised, in July 1971, to 66.6 per cent of actual insurable earnings, subject to a ceiling on those earnings. Claimants with dependents, who had made low earnings or suffered prolonged unemployment, received 75 per cent of insurable earnings. Whereas the legislation formerly required a minimum of 30 weeks of employment during the two preceding years, the new provisions lowered this requirement to eight weeks for the preceding year. The regulation that every two-week period of employment qualified the claimant for one week of UI payments was changed to a maximum entitlement of 44 weeks of payments for a minimum employment period of eight weeks. The program's coverage was expanded significantly, and extension periods were established on a regional basis. Thus the UI program's eligibility criteria were broadened to cover far more people than ever before, and its benefits were made more "generous". The effects of these changes on expenditures and financing requirements were soon evident. In 1970, UI expenditures stood at approximately $700 million; in 1972, they approached $2 billion. Expenditures have continued to grow very rapidly.

Another important set of changes occurred in 1979.[3] These lowered the benefit rate to 60 per cent and raised qualification requirements for new entrants and re-entrants into the labour force and for repeat users (that is, claimants who had already drawn substantial benefits in their qualifying periods). Their effect was therefore to make the UI program somewhat less generous. These changes, although much less extensive than the 1971–72 revisions, have also had a significant effect on unemployment, in this instance, reducing the NAIRU.

Unstable Employment: Seasonal and Cyclical

Our Canadian government's current method of financing the unemployment insurance system tends to subsidize industries with unstable employment patterns and to tax those with stable employment patterns. As Table 15-2 demonstrates, the extent of this cross- subsidization is very large. The reason is that premium rates are the same for all industries and employees, although employees in some industries draw much more extensively on unemployment insurance than do others. Without an unemployment insurance system, industries with unstable employment, either seasonal or cyclical, would have to pay a wage premium to attract workers, while industries with very stable employment patterns could pay lower wages and still attract employees. The existence of unemployment insurance as currently funded makes industries with unstable employment patterns more attractive than they would be in the absence of cross-subsidization and thus allows them to pay a smaller wage premium. Conversely, industries with unusually stable employment become relatively less attractive and thus have to pay comparatively higher wages. These differences in wages paid in various industries affect labour costs and, ultimately, product prices. Costs and prices rise in industries with stable employment and decline in industries with unstable employment. Purchasers of the products react to these changes in relative prices by buying less of a higher-priced product and more of a relatively lower-priced product. Thus, as a consequence of cross-subsidization, a larger proportion of output and employment will be characteristic of industries with unstable employment patterns, and a smaller proportion will characterize industries with stable employment patterns.

TABLE 15-2 Benefit/Contribution (Benefit/Cost) Ratios of Unemployment Insurance, by Industry, Canada, 1977

Industry	Ratio above 1	Ratio below 1
Agriculture	1.50	
Forestry	5.09	
Fishing and hunting	2.10	
Construction	2.46	
Non-durable goods (food and beverages, etc.)	1.24	
Recreation (sports, tourism, etc.)	1.67	
Personal services	1.40	
Teaching		0.38
Public services		0.15
Communications		0.36
Mining		0.67
Finance, insurance, and real estate		0.75
Retail trade		0.84
Commercial services		0.91
Transportation		0.58
Durable goods		0.87
Total	1.00	

Source: Canada, Task Force on Unemployment Insurance, *Cost Ratio Analysis of The Insured Population*, Technical Study No. 12 (Ottawa: Employment and Immigration Canada, 1981), p. 7.

Because premium rates are the same for all firms and industries, there is less incentive for firms to "smooth out" their employment patterns to attract workers. In Canada's dynamic and open economy, changes are continually occurring in the demand for various goods and services. Our climate, too, causes important seasonal variations. Firms can adjust to these fluctuations in various ways: through controlling inventories; diversifying product lines; altering the time lag between receiving orders and making shipments; saving work for slack periods; adjusting employees' working hours; or laying off and rehiring employees as a means of adjusting their numbers. Firms will choose the least-cost method of adjustment. Unemployment insurance, of course, lowers the cost of adjusting through lay-offs and "rehires", relative to other methods of controlling for demand fluctuations.

A disproportionate share of unemployment is generated by Canada's seasonal industries, often concentrated in depressed regions, and by individuals with unstable work attachments in all industries and regions. For this reason the income-security problems of many Canadian workers are intimately tied to the seasonality of economic activity. We Canadians cannot alter our climate, but we can ensure that our economic policies do not add to the effect of the the forces of nature in creating high unemployment. The unemployment-insurance subsidies that are an integral part of the infrastructure of Canada's forestry, construction, and other industries make them larger, less stable, and more attractive to workers than they would be without this support. Similarly, the intrinsic taxes on stable-employment industries make these industries smaller than they would be without this drain on their resources. Moreover, there are some workers in all industries and regions who prefer a lifestyle of intermittent work punctuated by regular spells of unemployment subsidized by UI benefits. All of these effects raise our economy's average rate of unemployment and lower its level of real output.

The results of one study[4] of the effect of UI provisions on Newfoundland and Alberta indicate that if the "generosity" of the program in the high-unemployment regions were extended to the whole of Canada, the extent of unemployment and short-term employment would increase significantly. The authors conclude that the main differences in regional unemployment stem from the fact that individuals in regions with high unemployment rates experience many short periods of unemployment as compared to the other regions, where unemployment more commonly occurs during one long period or a few. Such conclusions tend to confirm the hypothesis that the UI program reinforces the concentration of unstable and short-term jobs in regions with high unemployment and a heavy concentration of seasonal industries.

An earlier study[5] found that for the great majority of industries and provinces, the trend toward reduced seasonality moderated or even reversed after 1971. The estimated decrease in seasonality was particularly large for construction, the industry most heavily subsidized by unemployment insurance.

A general method of dealing with these effects is to relate premiums to a firm's lay-off rate or to the rate at which UI benefits are paid to its workers. Most other insurance systems, both those applied by private sector firms, such as automobile insurers, and those used in the public sector, such as the worker's compensation system, are based on "experience-rated" financing structures. (These firms, however, are experience rated by group rather than individually.) Experience rating of premiums would also reduce the incentive which now exists for firms to use lay-offs as a means of responding to demand fluctuations instead of resorting to employment sharing, inventory accumulation, and reserving work for non-peak periods.

In the United States, where various experience-rating programs operate in different States, a number of empirical studies[6] have been conducted. They generally agree that inadequate links of premiums to risks explain a significant proportion both of short-term employment and of unemployment. Thus American analysts substantially agree about the effect on job instability of the UI schemes currently in place in their country.

The degree to which Canada's UI system should be experience rated is a matter which will require more detailed analysis and discussion. It seems clear, however, that some such modification of our current UI financing system would improve the incentive structure of the program and lower the NAIRU.

Duration of Job Search

Adjustments in the benefit structure of the UI system would change Canada's unemployment rate in a number of ways. They would affect the duration of job search, for higher benefits lower the cost of search for the individual. Table 15-3 shows that the effect of UI benefit payments on the duration of unemployment has been investigated quite extensively in both Canada and the United States. Commissioners consider the results of U.S. studies in this Report for two main reasons. One is that American UI programs differ from one State to another, and this circumstance provides a clear advantage for research into the ways that different schemes affect the duration of unemployment. The second is that the U.S. studies, especially those conducted since 1976, deal with data on individual UI claimants. This information is of prime importance to any attempt to determine the effect of the system on work incentives. The Canadian studies are also very helpful in that they provide estimates of the effect of the profound changes made in Canada's UI program in the 1970s.

TABLE 15-3 Estimated Impact of an Increase in UI Benefits on Duration of Unemployment in Canada and the United States

Studies[a]	Additional Weeks of Unemployment
Canada[b]	
Green and Cousineau (1976)	+1.4
Rea (1977)[c]	+1.5
Maki (1977)	+2.0
Lazar (1978)	+2.0
United States[d]	
Chapin (1971)[e]	+0.4
Marston (1975)	+1.0
Ehrenberg and Oaxaca (1976)	+1.5
Classen (1977)	+1.1
Holen (1977)	+1.0
Burgess and Kingston (1977)	+1.0

a. These studies are listed in the notes to Chapter 15, except as noted.

b. Increase from 43 per cent (before 1971) to 67 per cent (1972) in the earnings-replacement ratio.

c. For the overall impact, Rea obtained a maximum estimate of four weeks.

d. Simulated impact of an increase from 50 per cent to 60 per cent in the earnings-replacement ratio.

e. Gene Chapin, "Unemployment Insurance, Job Search, and the Demand for Leisure", *Western Economic Journal* 9 (March 1971): 102–7.

The first part of Table 15-3 shows, in condensed form, the effect that the 1971 changes to the UI program had on the duration of unemployment as estimated in four Canadian studies. Two of these studies[7] estimate that the changes prolonged the duration of unemployment by two weeks. The other two, using a somewhat different approach, obtained slightly lower estimates of 1.4 and 1.5 weeks.[8]

More recently, a study examined the effect on duration of unemployment of the 1979 UI amendments.[9] The authors found that the reduction in the benefit rate from 66.6 to 60 per cent shortened periods of unemployment for all age-sex groups. Other recent studies[10] also found evidence of significant UI effects on the duration of job search. A study[11] prepared for this Commission notes that the ratio of employed to unemployed searchers rose between 1976–78 and 1979–81. This suggests that faced with the increased costs of unemployment initiated by the 1979 amendments, searchers looked for work while employed, rather than while unemployed.

One U.S. study[12] compared UI claimants with those unemployed persons who receive no UI benefits. This approach has *prima facie* appeal, but it suffers from considering populations with characteristics that are not easily comparable. Three independent studies[13] using micro-economic data on the duration of unemployment for UI claimants estimated that the average duration of a spell of unemployment is extended by one additional week for each 10 percentage/point increase in the earnings-replacement ratio of UI benefits. The methodology used in these studies consists in studying differences in the length of unemployment among a number of American States with various UI programs, taking into account the particular characteristics of the population and the economic situation. An earlier study[14] had appeared to obtain a slightly higher estimate of 1.5 weeks, but this result applied to one specific group, that of men over 45. For the other groups considered, the estimated impact was lower.[15] Given the diversity of the data and methods used, the results are robust: in the United States, a rise of 10 percentage points in the earnings-replacement ratio between two States can result in an unemployment period that is longer by one week; in Canada, the 1971 increase, which was almost double that percentage figure, led to an increase of nearly two weeks in the duration of unemployment. U.S. and Canadian results therefore appear to be consistent. For the authors of two other works[16] in the same field, the empirical results are so conclusive that they consider the matter to be resolved.

Consequences of Longer Duration

The longer duration of unemployment inherent in a more generous UI benefit structure may be socially beneficial if it leads to more productive job search. That is to say, the UI benefits represent an investment in job search, and it is important to evaluate the returns from this investment. Greater investment may be justified if it leads to more intensive job search, to higher post-unemployment earnings, or to obtaining a more stable job.

Less is known about these questions than about the effect of benefit levels on unemployment duration. One study,[17] however, has addressed the issue of search intensity. Its authors, using a large sample of American UI claimants, estimated that prolonging the benefit period by one month or increasing the earnings-replacement ratio by 8 percentage points results in a *reduction* of 6.5 per cent in the average number of hours devoted each week to job search: that is, the intensity of the search diminishes. Thus, the total amount of search is affected by two UI-related factors that offset each other: the number of search weeks increases, but the number of search hours per week decreases.

The empirical results for the effect of UI programs on post-unemployment earnings are diverse, varying between 0.0[18] and 12.3 per cent.[19] Given the significant methodological difficulties associated with this question,[20] it is difficult to draw firm conclusions from the evidence. As for the effect of UI benefits on post-unemployment job stability, only one study is available,[21] and the method it uses is crude. It finds no evidence of a link between the level of UI benefits and the subsequent job stability of the claimants. Thus the empirical studies do not succeed in identifying the benefits of the UI program as clearly as they do its costs.

Interregional Labour-Market Adjustment[22]

The general historical pattern of interregional migration has been for movement to occur from regions with relatively low earnings and poor employment opportunities to regions with relatively high income and good employment opportunities. Since the 1930s, Ontario, Alberta and British Columbia have generally experienced net in-migration, while our other provinces have generally experienced net out-migration. These migration flows constitute an important part of adjustment to economic change. Since the movement generally travels out of regions with low wages and/or poor employment prospects into regions with higher wages and better prospects, migration increases the overall level of income in Canada and reduces structural unemployment.

Unemployment insurance can be expected to slow this adjustment process, as it makes location in regions with poor employment prospects relatively more attractive than it would be otherwise. In 1971, the UI program was regionally differentiated: shorter qualification periods and longer benefit entitlements periods were introduced in regions with high unemployment rates. Thus it is likely that the UI program has retarded migration from high-unemployment regions even further since 1971.

Parallel to the 1971 reform of our federal UI program, a historic change occurred in interprovincial migratory flows. Whereas, before that date, the four Atlantic provinces had experienced net out-migration, they began to experience net in-migration from 1971 onwards. Some authors have tried to determine whether at least part of this change in migratory patterns could be explained by the revisions of the UI program. One study[23] restricted to the flows between New Brunswick, Nova Scotia and Ontario, did confirm that there was a significant reduction in out-migration from the two Atlantic provinces, where earnings are low and unemployment rates are high, toward Ontario, where incomes and job prospects are more attractive. The estimated reduction in out-migration associated with the reform of the UI program amounted to 3000 individuals per year. The author rejected the hypothesis that the program also caused return migration.

A more general study,[24] covering the impact of all regional transfer payments on the interprovincial allocation of Canada's human resources, focused particularly on our UI program. On the basis of a very large and detailed micro-economic sample, it also concludes that the post-1971 reduction in out-migration from the Atlantic provinces into the rest of Canada corresponds to a change in the major elements of the UI program. For the Atlantic provinces as a whole, the effect is estimated as constituting a reduction of 8000 out-migrants per year, other circumstances being equal. A more recent Canadian study,[25] the only indigenous one to examine the pattern of migration between Census metropolitan areas, also finds strong effects of unemployment insurance on migration, especially after 1971.

Overall, then, it would appear that Canada's UI program does slow labour-market adjustments, in particular, out-migration from lower-income, high-unemployment regions. This effect seems to have become especially strong since the 1971 amendments of the UI Act, which introduced regional differentiation into the program. This relatively new factor contributes to the level of structural unemployment in Canada and to lower living standards for our population as a whole. Commissioners recognize the important equity objectives embodied in the regional differentiation of the UI system. Nevertheless, we believe that these objectives can be attained through other policies which would have fewer adverse effects on unemployment and income.

Summary and Conclusions

Comissioners believe that the present unusual extent of unemployment in Canada is caused by insufficient aggregate demand. Under the circumstances, the UI program is of great help to many Canadians. Moreover, at the macro-economic level, it can stabilize the economy's consumption by automatically supporting the income of the unemployed during a recession. Although its role in automatic stabilization has been reduced in recent years because of changes in the financing of the program, unemployment insurance probably stopped unemployment from reaching an even more dramatic level in the recent severe recession.

On the other hand, it is evident that certain UI provisions affect the incentive structure and adjustment mechanism of our national labour market. On reviewing the evidence compiled by a number of researchers, Commissioners have concluded that the unemployment insurance program:

- Contributes to an increase in the duration of unemployment
- Increases the volume of temporary lay-offs
- Reinforces the concentration of temporary and unstable jobs in high-unemployment and low-wage regions
- Provides too generous a subsidy to Canadians whose labour-force behaviour is characterized by repeated unstable employment.

We are convinced, therefore, that Canada's UI program does not fully satisfy the objectives of facilitating adequate adjustment in the labour market and developing stable and productive jobs. Consequently, the UI system should be revised to make it more efficient in the coming years. We would recommend, however, that these revisions be implemented gradually as the Canadian economy returns to full employment.

On the financing side, an important reform would be to relate premiums more closely to the risk of lay-off. This process of experience rating should be done on a firm-by-firm, rather than on an industry-group, basis. This Commission views experience rating as the most important change that should be made to Canada's existing UI system. This reform would obviate the need for special programs to encourage work-sharing.[26] Unemployment insurance financed by common premium rates biases employers and employees towards lay-offs, rather than reductions in working hours, as a form of response to temporary fluctuations in demand because UI benefits are programmed for persons out of work for a whole week. To offset this unintended bias, a short-term compensation policy was introduced in 1982. While the program has succeeded in encouraging work-sharing, it has cost considerably more than common UI benefits, and its administrative costs are high. Each work-sharing project must be certified on an individual basis by the employer, the employees and the Unemployment Insurance Commission. To remove the bias against work-sharing by introducing experience rating is thus a more sensible approach than the existing system comprised of a financing structure which discourages work-sharing combined with an expensive special program designed to counteract that effect.

While little is known about the degree to which unemployment insurance has contributed to Canada's macro-economic stability, the system's stabilizing properties deteriorated as UI financing was modified between 1976 and 1980. The result of these changes is that most cyclical variations in program costs fall on the private sector. Amendments should be made to the financing arrangements to improve the stabilizing properties of the UI program.

The other unemployment-insurance reforms Commissioners propose relate to benefits. We intend only to indicate the general nature of these changes, since precise details would require further analysis and discussion. In our opinion, an appropriate set of reforms would comprise an approach such as the following:

- Reduce the benefit rate to 50 per cent of earnings
- Raise the entrance requirement to 15 to 20 weeks of insured work over the preceding year
- Tighten the link between the maximum benefit period and the minimum employment period: for example, establish a ratio of two or three weeks of work to qualify for one week of benefits
- Eliminate the regional differentiation of the Unemployment Insurance program.

To eliminate the regional differentiation of the UI program would encourage rather than discourage — as does the present system — labour movement towards regions with higher levels of employment. The existing system tends to perpetuate regional unemployment differentials, and this situation, together with the absence of experience rating, tends to reinforce the concentration of temporary and unstable jobs in high-unemployment and low-wage regions.

The other suggested changes to the benefit structure are meant to encourage steadier job attachments, more intensive job search during periods of unemployment, and a higher proportion of job search while employed. The recommended benefit ratio of 50 per cent is based on an estimate of the costs and benefits of unemployment insurance, and a subsequent calculation of the rate which would yield the greatest net benefits.[27]

The proposed changes to the benefit structure also reflect this Commission's view that the UI program has become too large relative to other labour-market programs, and that the employment opportunities for Canadians would be improved by switching some funds from UI support to programs organized to facilitate adjustment to technological and economic change.

The net effect of such changes on the present incentives for unstable work patterns would be dramatic. Under the current scheme, workers with as little as ten weeks of insured work can draw as much as 40 weeks of benefits at 60 per cent of their average insured earnings. Thus they can obtain benefits equal to 240 per cent of their individual earnings. Under the proposed changes, such persons could draw benefits equal only to 17 per cent of earnings from a pattern of repeated unstable work. At the same time, the system preserves a full year of benefit entitlement for individuals who have worked steadily for the preceding two or three years.

The main intent of Commissioners' proposals is to redistribute the funds provided by premiums and by general taxation to more productive ends such as the creation of durable and well-paid employment, better labour-market adjustment, and adequate protection of workers experiencing difficulty in the labour market. We firmly believe that these changes should be considered as part of a package of income-security and labour-market/program reforms. In particular, proposed changes to the UI system should be examined in the context of the Transitional Adjustment Assistance Plan (TAAP), described in the next section, and the Universal Income Security Program (UISP) described in Chapter 19, below. The UISP would provide income-supplementation benefits which would offer additional support to low-income Canadians, whether their basic income derived from work or from work and unemployment insurance. Thus the impact of the UI changes would be cushioned, especially for low-income Canadians with family responsibilities who lose their jobs. In these circumstances, the UISP, in combination with UI, would actually provide more income than current arrangements during the UI entitlement period. It would also provide continuing income supplements for individuals and families who must accept lower pay to re-enter the labour force. We must emphasize, however, that our reformed package would never make it more financially advantageous to avoid work than to participate in the labour force as some income-security programs and some combinations of UI and social assistance may do today.

The suggested changes to UI benefits would have a significant effect on benefit costs. The reduction in benefit rates from 60 to 50 per cent of insurable earnings would result in program savings of at least 17 per cent of basic benefits. The extended benefits, currently financed from consolidated revenues, are equal to about 21 per cent of regular benefits. It is not possible to calculate the savings from heightened entrance requirements and the closer link between the maximum benefit period and the length of employment, since these factors depend on complex behavioural assumptions. Use of the UI system would also be reduced somewhat by the experience-rating component, the reduction of benefit levels, and the closer link of benefit periods with qualifying periods. Overall, the costs of UI benefits would likely be reduced by not less than 35 to 40 per cent or about $4 billion at 1985 levels of unemployment. Commissioners believe that these monies should be used to facilitate labour-market adjustments through the creation of a Transitional Adjustment Assistance Program.

Notes

1. This section draws on five research papers prepared for the Royal Commission on the Economic Union and Development Prospects for Canada: J.M. Cousineau, "Unemployment Insurance and Labour Market Adjustments", and Jonathan R. Kessleman, "Comprehensive Income Security for Canadian Workers", in *Income Distribution and Economic Security in Canada*, vol. 1; S.F. Kaliski, "Trends, Changes, and Imbalances: A Survey of the Canadian Labour Market", in *Work and Pay: The Canadian Labour Market*, vol. 17; Morley Gunderson, "Alternative Mechanisms for Dealing with Permanent Layoffs, Dismissals and Plant Closings", in *Adapting to Change: Labour Market Adjustment in Canada*, vol. 18; and John Vanderkamp, "The Efficiency of the Interregional Adjustment Process", in *Disparities and Interregional Adjustment*, vol. 64 (Toronto: University of Toronto Press, 1985).
2. See, for example, M. Ellman, "Recent Dutch Macro-Economic Experience", in *Foreign Macroeconomic Experience: A Symposium*, vol. 24, prepared for the Royal Commission on the Economic Union and Development Prospects for Canada (Toronto: University of Toronto Press, 1985), and "The Crisis of the Welfare State – the Dutch Experience", in *The Economics of Human Betterment*, edited by K.E. Boulding (London: Macmillan, 1984).
3. Since 1971 there have been frequent changes to the UI Act, the regulations it imposes, and the administrative practices that relate to it. For details see G. Dingledine, *A Chronology of Response: The Evolution of Unemployment Insurance from 1940 to 1980*, Task Force on Unemployment Insurance, Technical Paper 2 (Ottawa: Employment and Immigration Canada, 1981); and J. Kesselman, *Financing Canadian Unemployment Insurance* (Toronto: Canadian Tax Foundation, 1983).
4. G. Glenday and J. Alam, "The Labour Market Experience of Individuals: Unemployment Insurance and Regional Effects" (Ottawa: Employment and Immigration Canada, Task Force on Labour Market Development, 1982).
5. S.F. Kaliski, "Some Aspects of the Nature and Duration of Unemployment in Canada", in *Issues in Canadian Policy (II), Proceedings of a Conference*, edited by R.G. Wirick and D.D. Purvis (Kingston: Queen's University, Institute for Economic Research, 1979).
6. See, for example, Martin Feldstein, "The Effect of Unemployment Insurance on Temporary Layoff Unemployment", *American Economic Review* 68 (December 1978): 834–46; Robert H. Topel, "On Layoffs and Unemployment Insurance", *American Economic Review* 73 (September 1983): 541–59; Arlene Holen, "Effects of Unemployment Insurance Entitlement on Duration and Job Search

Outcome", *Industrial and Labor Relations Review* 30 (July 1977): 445–50; Frank Brechling, "Unemployment Insurance Taxes and Labor Turnover: Summary of Theoretical Findings", *Industrial and Labor Relations Review* 30 (July 1977): 483–94; Henry Saffer, "The Effects of Unemployment Insurance on Temporary and Permanent Layoffs", *Review of Economics and Statistics* 65 (1983): 647–51; and Harry C. Benham, "Unemployment Insurance Incentives and Unemployment Duration Distributions", *Review of Economics and Statistics* 65 (February 1983): 139–43.

7. See Dennis R. Maki, "Unemployment Benefits and the Duration of Claims in Canada", *Applied Economics* 9 (September 1977): 227–36; and Fred Lazar, "The Impact of the 1971 Unemployment Insurance Revisions on Unemployment Rates: Another Look", *Canadian Journal of Economics* 11 (August 1978): 559–70.
8. See Christopher Green and Jean-Michel Cousineau, *Chômage et programmes d'assurance-chômage* (Ottawa: Economic Council of Canada, 1976); and Samuel A. Rea, "Unemployment Insurance and Labour Supply: A Simulation of the 1971 Unemployment Insurance Act", *Canadian Journal of Economics* 10 (1977): 263–78.
9. Charles M. Beach and S.F. Kaliski, "Measuring the Duration of Unemployment from Gross Flow Data", *Canadian Journal of Economics* 16 (1983): 258–63.
10. See Abrar Hasan and Surendra Gera, *Job Search Behaviour, Unemployment and Wage Gain in Canadian Labour Markets* (Ottawa: Economic Council of Canada, 1982); and Glenday and Alam, "The Labour Market Experience of Individuals".
11. S.F. Kaliski, "Trends, Changes, and Imbalances: A Survey of the Canadian Labour Market", in *Work and Pay: The Canadian Labour Market*, vol. 17, prepared for the Royal Commission on the Economic Union and Development Prospects for Canada (Toronto: University of Toronto Press, 1985).
12. Stephen T. Marston, "The Impact of Unemployment Insurance on Job Search", *Brookings Papers on Economic Activity* 1 (1975): 13–48.
13. See Kathleen P. Classen, "The Effect of Unemployment Insurance on the Duration of Unemployment and Subsequent Earnings", *Industrial and Labor Relations Review* 30 (July 1977): 438–44; Holen, "Effects of Unemployment Insurance Entitlement on Duration and Job Search Outcome"; and Paul L. Burgess and Jerry L. Kingston, "The Impact of Unemployment Insurance Benefits on Reemployment Success", *Industrial and Labor Relations Review* 30 (October 1976): 25–31.
14. Ronald G. Ehrenberg and Ronald L. Oaxaca, "Unemployment Insurance, Duration of Unemployment, and Subsequent Wage Gain", *American Economic Review* 66 (December 1976): 754–66.
15. *Ibid.*, p. 765.
16. Benham, "Unemployment Insurance Incentives"; and Robert H. Topel and Finis Welch, "Unemployment Insurance: Survey and Extensions", *Economica* 47 (August 1980): 351–79.
17. John M. Barron and Otis W. Gilley, "The Effect of Unemployment Insurance on the Search Process", *Industrial and Labor Relations Review* 32 (April 1979): 363–66.
18. Classen, "The Effect of Unemployment Insurance on the Duration of Unemployment and Subsequent Earnings".
19. Burgess and Kingston, "The Impact of Unemployment Insurance Benefits on Reemployment Success".
20. Finis Welch, "What Have We Learned from Empirical Studies of Unemployment Insurance?", *Industrial and Labor Relations Review* 30 (July 1977): 451–61.
21. Classen, "The Effect of Unemployment Insurance on the Duration of Unemployment and Subsequent Earnings".

22. For a detailed review of the empirical studies on migration in Canada see the paper by J. Vanderkamp, "The Efficiency of the Interregional Adjustment Process", in *Disparities and Interregional Adjustment*, vol. 64, prepared for the Royal Commission on the Economic Union and Development Prospects for Canada (Toronto: University of Toronto Press, 1985).

23. Jean-Michel Cousineau, "La mobilité interprovinciale au Canada: le cas de l'Ontario, du Nouveau-Brunswick et de la Nouvelle-Écosse", *L'Actualité Économique* 55 (1979): 501–15.

24. Stanley L. Winer and Denis Gauthier, *Internal Migration and Fiscal Structure: An Econometric Study of the Determinants of Interprovincial Migration in Canada* (Ottawa: Economic Council of Canada, 1982).

25. Paul Shaw, *Inter-metropolitan Migration in Canada: Changes and Determinants over Three Decades* (Ottawa: Statistics Canada, 1984).

26. For a more detailed discussion of the relationship between UI and work-sharing see the paper by Frank Reid, "Reductions in Work Time: An Assessment of Employment Sharing to Reduce Unemployment", in *Work and Pay: The Canadian Labour Market*, vol. 17, prepared for the Royal Commission on the Economic Union and Development Prospects for Canada (Toronto: University of Toronto Press, 1985).

27. See Martin Neil Baily, "Unemployment Insurance as Insurance for Workers", *Industrial and Labor Relations Review* 30 (July 1977): 495–504, and "Some Aspects of Optimal Unemployment Insurance", *Journal of Public Economics* 10 (1978): 379–402; and J.S. Flemming, "Aspects of Optimal Unemployment Insurance", *Journal of Public Economics* 10 (1978): 403–25.

The Transitional Adjustment Assistance Program (TAAP)

We Commissioners remarked in the previous section that while unemployment insurance (UI) constitutes an essential centrepiece of modern labour-market policy, some elements of the UI program create important barriers to labour-market adjustments. We noted, too, that any steps the Government of Canada can take to lower structural and frictional unemployment by helping Canadians to adjust to new labour-market opportunities will assist efforts to develop high levels of employment at low levels of inflation. To this end, we believe that it is important for the government to consider reinforcing the UI reforms suggested above by means of a program that will encourage positive adjustment to labour-market requirements.

The Transitional Adjustment Assistance Program (TAAP) would assist members of the Canadian labour force to adjust to emerging employment opportunities. To this end, it should focus on skills development and on helping Canadians to achieve labour-force mobility. It might also have occasional use in support of changing development opportunities in communities otherwise subject to serious declines. TAAP benefits would generally be available to workers who had exhausted UI benefits or whose lay-offs appeared to be permanent even if their benefits were not exhausted. Commissioners recommend that the main elements of the TAAP should include:

- *More funding of on-the-job training programs* or, when new jobs can be identified, of programs offered in institutional settings. TAAP beneficiaries might carry with them to new employment an on-the-job/training subsidy or a combination of training-place/purchase money plus larger training allowances. Given that TAAP beneficiaries would usually have experienced considerable uncertainty and frustration in the labour market, it is doubly important that TAAP-related training be associated with real job prospects and not mere make-work projects.
- *Portable wage-subsidy programs*. Since TAAP beneficiaries might often have been without jobs for some time, and since most would probably belong to older age groups, they might often be at a competitive disadvantage in seeking employment. This disadvantage could be largely or entirely overcome by providing them with a portable wage subsidy.
- *Early retirement plans* are often attractive to workers in their late 50s or 60s and might be preferable to other arrangements which would uproot older workers. TAAP benefits should be available for this purpose.
- *Mobility grants* have not so far constituted a major part of Canadian government interventions in the labour force. They might, however, provided that they are large enough, be a very important means of encouraging workers with family responsibilities to search for new job opportunities in new locations. For prime-age workers (those between 25 and 54 years of age), one of the greatest impediments to mobility is often the potential loss of equity in their homes. This is a particularly acute problem when workers face a move from a declining one-industry town to a

more economically successful region, usually associated with a relatively large urban centre. For workers facing such a situation, TAAP benefits should provide some support in the form of compensation for equity loss. TAAP mobility grants might therefore cover removal costs and provide some compensation for lost-asset value in housing.

- *Special projects financing*. Occasionally it might be possible for laid-off workers, faced with a plant closure, either to purchase the plant and reopen it on a co-operative basis or to band together to create new economic development opportunities in the affected community. In some instances, TAAP assistance could be used to support such activities. Nevertheless, this Commission urges the utmost caution in using this approach. TAAP benefits might be available only once in a lifetime or after a very long requalifying period. It would therefore be tragic for many Canadians if they were to lose their TAAP benefits in hopeless economic enterprises.

While it is not possible within the limits of this Report for Commissioners to spell out in detail how the TAAP might operate, we would recommend the following general structures and procedures:

- Eligibility for UI should not be affected by TAAP. Workers should retain their normal UI-benefit entitlements under the reformed UI provisions recommended above. This Commission does not recommend that basic UI entitlements be made contingent on undertaking some form of adjustment-related program such as on-the-job training, although we do support the current developmental uses of unemployment insurance. Instead, we believe, the current "active job-search" requirement is appropriate.
- Eligibility for TAAP benefits might be established on the basis of length of time in the labour force or according to age, or by some combination of these requirements. In general, Commissioners believe that TAAP should be directed to prime-age and older workers (between 25 and 64 years of age), with a labour-force attachment of at least five years.
- Canadians' entitlement to use TAAP must be based on their willingness to undertake adaptive behaviour. TAAP benefits would be provided after UI benefits were exhausted provided that the recipient used the income transfer in one of the ways outlined above. They would be directly related to the costs of adjustments to the recipients and their families and could cover the full costs of adjustment up to a maximum amount. Total benefits available would be proportional to length of time in the labour force up to a maximum of about 15 to 20 years' labour-force attachment. UI recipients might opt to undertake TAAP programs before their benefits were exhausted; if they did so, their basic UI benefits might be added to the TAAP entitlement. TAAP benefits would not be made available if a high probability existed of recall to a previous job. Probably, therefore, they should not be made available in the first few weeks of a period of unemployment unless it were very clear that no opportunities for reasonable employment would open up locally.
- TAAP programs could be delivered through UI/Canada Employment offices, where counselling support would also be available. It might also be possible to contract out the delivery of TAAP, but it would be important to ensure

that contractors, who would also provide counselling, had access to accurate labour-market information and were carefully monitored.

In order to finance the TAAP, Commissioners recommend that UI savings financed from the employer/employee premium accounts of the unemployment-insurance system be passed along, initially as reduced premiums. These savings would accrue from reduced benefit levels, extended entrance requirements, and the closer link between weeks of employment and the maximum benefit period. The government should then raise personal income taxes by an amount sufficient to equal the premium savings and contribute that money to a special Transitional Adjustment Assistance Fund. The fund should be further augmented by the value of the Regional Extended Benefits program. Any other UI cost reductions created by the effects of the benefit changes and of the improved labour-force adjustments which, we hope, would result from the TAAP could simply be passed on to the public in the form of lower premiums.

Since the federal government occupies, on average, only about 66 per cent of the personal income-tax field, it could not automatically capture the equivalent of all of the reduced UI premiums without resorting to a tax increase substantially larger than the UI reduction would offset. For the same reason, provincial governments would capture about one-third of the extra personal income tax as a tax "windfall". The total TAAP funds available to the federal government would therefore be in the order of $3.3 billion, and the provinces would gain about $650 million in additional tax revenue. Commissioners hope that provincial governments, too, would earmark these funds for labour-market/adjustment programs, and that joint federal-provincial TAAP arrangements would be funded on an approximate basis of an 80 per cent federal contribution and a 20 per cent provincial contribution.

Alternatively, it might be preferable for the federal government to capture all of the value of the UI premium reduction and to operate TAAP as a purely federal program in order to minimize federal-provincial entanglements. If this arrangement should prove to be desirable, it would be appropriate to introduce a federal-tax surcharge to finance the TAAP. In this way the recaptured funds would be excluded from the base on which provincial taxes are collected, and all of the funds saved would accrue to the federal government. Since this tax would have a specific purpose, it might be appropriate to refer to it as the "TAAP surcharge".

The Transitional Adjustment Assistance Program could make a very substantial difference to many Canadians and could contribute very considerablly to the flexibility of our country's labour markets. In 1984, there were an average 253 000 Canadian workers over 25 years of age who had been unemployed for a year or longer. Under the arrangement Commissioners suggest, these people would be the primary TAAP beneficiaries. If the $4 billion TAAP pool were targeted primarily to help these workers, the benefits available to each would average $13 700. If only 150 000 Canadians took advantage of the program, the benefits would average $26 700. Amounts of this size would often be enough to cushion the costs of adjustment very substantially.

In addition, benefits accruing from the Universal Income Security Plan (UISP), described fully in Chapter 19, below, would be available to supplement the incomes of Canadians. These would cushion the effect of lower wages that might be paid in new jobs as TAAP workers "started again" in new locations. Of course, UISP and TAAP portable wage subsidies could combine virtually to eliminate the effect of lower wages for many workers undertaking adjustments.

The individual elements of the TAAP package are not new. Governments have experience in dealing with each of them, and that experience should make it possible to deliver the proposed program efficiently and effectively. What is new is the extent of the adjustment effort, which is larger by a significant margin than current government efforts, even though no net increase in the dollar size of the public sector is inherent in this program. Commissioners believe that an effort of this degree is needed to assist Canadians to make the adjustments required to move our economy successfully into the twenty-first century. We suggest that there is one positive advantage of making the UI changes we propose and initiating the TAAP program: the two undertakings would have a cumulative effect. Our proposals, we believe, would replace the anti-adjustment features of unemployment insurance with the positive adjustment features of TAAP. This double effect should serve greatly to enhance labour-force flexibility and adaptability.

Minimum Wages

Another factor which might have contributed to the rise of unemployment rates in the 1960s and 1970s was changes in the minimum wage. Legislation specifying minimum wages has been in existence for over 40 years. Its stated objectives have varied over time, but the most important and enduring aim has been to reduce poverty. Originally, minimum-wage laws applied only to women and children, but coverage was later extended to most of the labour force. Today, the main exclusions are domestic service and farm labour.

Table 15-4 shows the existing minimum-wage provisions in the various Canadian jurisdictions. The minimum wage for experienced adult workers varies from $3.50 to $4.30 per hour. Most jurisdictions also have a minimum wage for younger workers and students, and this varies from $3.00 to $3.85 per hour.

Significant numbers of Canadians are still ranked as "working poor", despite the substantial growth in well-being that has occurred since the Second World War. This Commission is vitally concerned with the problem of Canada's working poor, and Commissioners have therefore examined various methods for raising their incomes. Low incomes among these people result from two causes: low wages and poor employment prospects. Clearly, policies which operate to improve both the income and the employment prospects of low-wage earners will be most effective. The minimum wage must be evaluated on the basis of these criteria.

The fundamental difficulty with using a minimum wage as a tool to reduce poverty is that increases in that figure can be expected to reduce employment opportunities for low-wage earners. There are two main reasons for this. Firms faced with raising the wages of low-paid, low-productivity labour, relative to the price of other inputs into the production process, will find substitutes for the relatively more expensive element. This usually involves the more extensive use of machinery and equipment, though it may also require greater use of higher-wage, higher-productivity labour, which is made relatively more attractive by an increase in the minimum wage. The other reason for reduced employment opportunities derives from the higher labour costs faced by firms accustomed to using low-wage labour. While, initially, a firm may absorb these higher costs by taking lower profits, it will eventually pass them on in the form of higher prices to the consumer of the product, which will lead, in time, to reduced sales and production. This reduction in the scale of operation typically involves an eventual – if not immediate – reduction in employment. Firms employing low-wage labour are typically small and operate in highly competitive industries. Increases in labour costs relative to those of substitute products can have substantial effects on employment, sometimes forcing firms out of business. In addition, labour costs usually amount to a significant proportion of total costs in these industries, which makes employment rates quite sensitive to changes in labour costs. Increases in minimum wages will benefit some low-wage earners: those whose employment opportunities are not reduced. Others, however, will suffer from the reduced employment opportunities. The ones who suffer may well be those with the least skills and the fewest opportunities.

A number of empirical studies have confirmed the "disemployment" or job-loss effects of increases in the minimum wage. The reduction in employment opportunities typically increases the unemployment rate and reduces the labour-market/participation rate of low-wage workers. That is, in response to reduced employment opportunities, some affected workers search for work, while others drop out of the labour force. A recent Canadian study, which examined the effects of changes in the minimum wage on six age-sex groups (males and females in the 15–19 year, 20–24 year, and 25-plus age groups) concluded:

> *The minimum wage exerts a significant negative effect on the employment and labour force levels of most of the age-sex groups analysed here. Taking the employment and labour force effects together, our results indicate that the minimum wage has a significant positive effect on the unemployment rates . . . of all six age-sex groups. The employment and labour force effects of the minimum wage are neither sufficiently small nor sufficiently offsetting to prevent significant increases in unemployment in face of higher minimum wages. It is important to emphasize that the minimum wage adversely affects not only the unemployment rates...of teenagers, but also those of adult workers. Thus, the analysis here indicates that the effect of the minimum wage on employment and unemployment is stronger and more pervasive than heretofore appreciated.*[1]

Earlier Canadian studies also found significant effects of changes in the minimum wage on employment, unemployment and labour-force participation. On the basis of these studies, it is estimated that a 10-per cent increase in the minimum wage, relative to the average wage, will raise the unemploy-

TABLE 15-4 **Minimum Wages for Experienced Adult Workers and Young Workers and Students**

Jurisdiction	Experienced Adult Workers	Effective Date	Young Workers and Students[a]	Effective Date
Federal	$3.50	01/05/81	Employees under 17: $3.25	01/05/81
Alberta	$3.80	01/05/81	Employees under 18 not attending school: $3.65	01/05/81
British Columbia	$3.65	01/12/80	Employees 17 and under: $3.30	01/05/81
Manitoba	$4.30	01/01/85	Employees under 18: $3.85	01/01/85
New Brunswick	$3.80	01/10/82		
Newfoundland[b]	$3.75	01/01/83		
Nova Scotia	$4.00	01/01/85	Under-age employees 14 to 18: $3.55	01/01/85
Ontario	$4.00	01/10/84	Students under 18 employed for not more than 28 hours in a week or during a school holiday: $3.15	01/10/84
Prince Edward Island	$3.75	01/10/82	Employees under 18: $3.54	01/10/82
Quebec	$4.00	01/10/81	Employees under 18: $3.54	01/10/81
Saskatchewan	$4.25	01/01/82		
Northwest Territories	$4.25	01/08/82	Employees under 17: $3.75	01/08/82
Yukon[c]	$3.60	01/05/81		

Source: Compilation by the Commission.

a. New Brunswick, Newfoundland, Saskatchewan and the Yukon Territory have no special rates for young workers or students.
b. Sixteen years of age and over.
c. Federal rate plus ten cents.

ment rate by 0.2 to 0.5 percentage points.[2] The disemployment effect is even greater than these figures indicate, for some of the reduction in employment leads to reduced labour-force participation in addition to that which leads to increased unemployment.

Raising minimum wages also affects the training opportunities available in the labour market. This effect is particularly important for younger workers whose training and labour-market experience is limited. The expense of providing on-the-job training is often covered by the payment of low wages to employees undergoing a training period: in effect, the training is partly financed by the trainee. Higher wages and higher productivity come into play in the post-training period. High minimum wages tend to discourage such financing methods and, with them, on-the-job training and subsequent wage increases. European countries such as Germany, Austria and Switzerland rely much more on apprenticeship programs than does Canada, for smoothing the transition from school to work. Apprentices' wages are typically quite low compared to those of trained workers: in Germany, for example, the average wage for first-year apprentices is about one-fifth the economy's average industrial wage. However, as the data in Table 15-4 confirm, youth minimum wages in most Canadian jurisdictions are equal to a substantially higher proportion of average industrial wages. Several analysts have suggested that this factor accounts for much of the apparently-low incidence of apprenticeship programs and other on-the-job training in Canada.

The setting of minimum wages also tends to discourage wage flexibility in our economy. Changes in labour-market demand occur in particular regions, occupations or industries and minimum wages inhibit wage adjustment as a mechanism for responding to decreases in demand in particular labour markets, especially those with wages at, or just above, the minimum. As a result, adjustment to change slows down, and unemployment rises, more job vacancies occur, and living standards fall.[3]

This Commission fully accepts the important social objectives of minimum-wage legislation. Good intentions, however, do not necessarily lead to good policies. The evidence that disemployment resulted from the rapid increases in minimum wages of the 1970s suggests that Canadian governments should be careful in the future not to allow minimum wages to rise too quickly. Because increases in the minimum wage can be expected to have several adverse consequences, Commissioners prefer other approaches to reducing poverty among low-wage earners. We favour two chief options: supplementing the income of the working poor and improving opportunities for employment training in order to raise productivity and earnings.

Notes

1. Joseph Schaafsma and William D. Walsh, "Employment and Labour Supply Effects of the Minimum Wage: Some Pooled Time-Series Estimates from Canadian Provincial Data", *Canadian Journal of Economics* 16 (February 1983), p. 96.
2. See Pierre Fortin and Keith Newton, "Labor Market Tightness and Wage Inflation in Canada", in *Workers, Jobs, and Inflation*, edited by Martin Neil Baily (Washington, D.C.: Brookings Institution, 1982), p. 253.

3. For a detailed discussion of this point in the context of regional adjustment, see J. Vanderkamp, "The Efficiency of the Interregional Adjustment Process", in *Disparities and Interregional Adjustment*, vol. 64, prepared for the Royal Commission on the Economic Union and Development Prospects for Canada (Toronto: University of Toronto Press, 1985).

Equal Opportunity and Equal Pay in Canada's Labour Market

Equality in the Labour Market

The efficient use of Canada's human resources requires not only flexibility and adaptability in our labour markets, but also the assurance of equal opportunities for all Canadians. In the absence of equality of opportunity, the skills and talents of some Canadians will be underused, and the total income produced by our economy will be lower than it need be. At least as important as the combined effect of these deficiencies is the effect of inequalities of opportunity on individual Canadians. In this Commission's hearings, representations were made on behalf of groups as diverse in their needs as women, the physically disabled, Native people, visible minorities, youth, and the elderly, against all of whom society directs discrimination and prejudice. Commissioners heard many tales of opportunities denied for reasons that have nothing to do with inherent ability or motivation. We were told that for many decades, there have been substantial differences in the earnings of men and women, and that over the years, these differences seem to have resisted change. In 1911, for example, employed women earned 53 per cent of the income of employed men. In 1982, women employed on a full-time, full-year basis still earned only 64 per cent of the income of men employed on the same basis. Clearly, issues relating to discrimination in the labour market must be an important concern of this Commission, just as they must be of all Canadians.

While problems relating to equal opportunity have always affected a large number of Canadians, the dramatic growth in the numbers of women in the labour-force has increased concern about equal opportunity and equal pay. In particular, since the numbers of Canadian women working outside the home began to rise rapidly, more attention has been paid to the differences in the earnings of men and women, as well as to the distinctive employment patterns between the sexes. In keeping with the depth of concern about differences in male/female employment opportunities, we Commissioners have focused much of our attention on that aspect of the equal-opportunity problem. However, many of the same points can be made about other aspects of inequality in the work place, and our comments should not be considered applicable to women's issues only.

Empirical Evidence[1]

The most important factor in carrying out empirical work on discrimination is to allow for the influence of productivity-related characteristics, such as education, training and experience, which can cause legitimate differences that are not based on discrimination in earnings and employment opportunities. The difficulty of distinguishing between discriminatory and non-discriminatory differences is compounded by the fact that while data exist on many wage-determining factors such as education and training, they are not always available for such factors as labour-market experience and types, not merely years, of education. Furthermore, because of data limitations, studies carried out to investigate discrimination focus on measures of income or earnings and do not deal with fringe benefits or other factors such as the pleasantness of the working environment, the risk of job-related injury or illness, and the flexibility of working hours. Thus, even the most careful empirical studies need to be interpreted with caution.

There are a number of ways to standardize, or control for the influence of, productivity-related factors, and variations of most of these different procedures have been used in the various Canadian empirical studies. Table 15-5 gives the ratio of female to male earnings, both before and after the adjustments were made (by means of the different procedures) for

TABLE 15-5 Female/Male-Earnings Ratio Unadjusted and Adjusted for Various Productivity-Related Factors in Various Canadian Studies

Study	Year and Data	Gross Unadjusted Ratio	Net Adjusted Ratio
Ostry (1968)	1961 Census	0.59	0.81
Robson & Lapointe (1971)	University faculty 1965/66	0.80	0.90
Gunderson (1975)	Narrowly-defined occupation same establ., 1968/69	0.82	0.93
Shrank (1977)	University faculty 1973/74	0.83	0.95
Robb (1978)	1971 Census, Ontario	0.60	0.76
	males *cf.* single females over 30	N.A.[a]	0.94
Gunderson (1979)	1971 Census	0.60	0.77
Stelcner (1979)	University faculty 1976/77	0.91	0.94
Walmsley *et al.* (1980)	Sask. organization, 1980	0.80	0.87
Gunderson (1980)	1971 Census, Ontario	0.60	0.76
Shapiro & Stelcner (1980)	1971 Census		
	Canada public	0.65	0.83
	Canada private	0.57	0.72
	Quebec public	0.66	0.87
	Quebec private	0.56	0.74
Stelcner & Shapiro (1980)	1971 Census, Quebec,	0.60	0.82
	single over 30	0.83	0.82
Kapsalis (1980)	1975 Survey of Cons. Finance	0.61	0.87

Source: Morley Gunderson, "Discrimination, Equal Pay and Equal Opportunities in the Labour Market", in *Work and Pay: The Canadian Labour Market*, vol. 17, prepared for the Royal Commission on the Economic Union and Development Prospects for Canada (Toronto: University of Toronto Press, 1985).

a. N.A. = not available.

differences in productivity-related factors. While the range of estimates is fairly substantial, reflecting, among other variations, the different data sets and methodologies used, a number of generalizations can be made.

In most studies[2] that look at the full-time/full-year earnings of individual Canadians across different establishments, occupations, industries and regions, the basic unadjusted ratio of female to male earnings is about 0.60. Adjusting for differences in such measured productivity-related factors as education, experience and broad occupational groups tends to raise the ratio in this comparison to approximately 0.80. Of necessity, however, the adjustments in these studies are often crude, since data limitations preclude controlling for differences in the detailed industrial or occupational distribution. By contrast, studies based on hourly wages in narrowly defined occupations in the same establishment or on case-studies (which automatically control for establishment, region, industry and, sometimes, for occupation) show unadjusted ratios of about 0.80 or higher and productivity-adjusted ratios of 0.90 to 0.95.[3] Thus adjusting for differences in productivity-related factors tends to raise the ratio of female to male earnings, although a wage gap of 5 to 10 per cent still seems to prevail within the same establishments. This differential, involving comparisons within the same establishment and occupation, can be thought of as representing narrowly-defined wage discrimination. It does not, however, include the portion of the male-female/earnings difference that can be attributed to occupational segregation.

The component of the 0.40 overall-earnings gap that can be attributed to occupational segregation is more difficult to establish. It is difficult, too, to determine how far that wage gap reflects discrimination inside, as compared to outside, the labour-market, and to decide what career, educational and other choices may or may not indicate discrimination. Empirical studies limited to using broad occupations and industry groupings cannot capture the occupational segregation within such groupings. However, studies based on job-evaluation point scores can provide some information, since they compare or evaluate different occupations. In such studies, differences between wages paid for predominantly male-performed jobs and predominantly female-performed jobs of the same value, as measured by a job-evaluation score, can be taken as a measure of the extent of pay differences arising from the occupational segregation of women into predominantly low-paying jobs traditionally performed by females.

Of course, with respect to occupational segregation, job-evaluation procedures do not enable observers to determine the importance of labour-market as compared to pre-labour-market discrimination or the significance of occupational "choices" that may or may not reflect discrimination. Women may be assigned to low-paying, predominantly female-performed jobs by their employers. Alternatively, they may apply for those jobs in disproportionate numbers because they were streamed into them by their educational and training choices; or because they have little choice, given their household responsibilities; or because such jobs are compatible with a preferred life-style. In all likelihood, the explanation is a combination of all of these factors, and the readily available supply of women to do these jobs means that employers may not be under pressure to raise wages in the predominantly female-performed jobs. Job-evaluation analysts do not consider such supply factors in determining the job-evaluation point scores; these point scores are administratively determined, while wages may well be market determined, because of the influence of supply and demand.

Job-evaluation studies tend to find that females are paid approximately 80 per cent of what males are paid for the same productivity, as measured by a job-evaluation point score. This finding indicates the existence of a gap of 0.20, which reflects the occupational segregation of females into lower-wage jobs. This situation suggests that occupational segregation is likely to be more important than wage discrimination as a source of discriminatory-earnings differentials.

The 0.20 portion of the earnings gap attributable to discriminatory occupational segregation applied to predominantly female-performed occupations (that is, about half of the entire gap of 0.40) is likely, for several reasons, to constitute an overestimate. Not all of the differences apparent in the occupational distribution are likely to reflect discrimination. Moreover, it is difficult to contend that a gap as large as 0.20 is sustainable under the forces of competition, since employers would be under profit-maximizing cost pressures to do most of their hiring to fill positions in the low-paying occupations (assuming that employee functions are at least somewhat interchangeable across the segregated occupations), and this demand pressure should serve to close the discrimination gap. Again, a pay gap of 0.20 for equal productivity, as measured by equal job-evaluation point scores, reflects not only the "undervaluation" of predominantly female-performed jobs, but also the "overvaluation" of male-performed jobs. In addition, job evaluations are more likely to be carried out when there is a wide difference in earnings between predominantly male- and female-performed jobs, and they are less likely to be carried out when there is a small difference.

In sum, evidence suggests that approximately half the earnings gap of 40 per cent can be attributed to non-discriminatory productivity-related factors. Most of the remainder appears to be the result of occupational segregation, and narrowly defined wage discrimination accounts for 5 to 10 percentage points of this portion of the gap.

To some observers, this assessment, which reckons that approximately half of the overall earnings gap of 40 per cent reflects discrimination in the labour market, will seem an insultingly low estimate of a phenomenon which they consider of manifestly greater proportion. To others, it will represent a gross overestimate, failing to account properly for unmeasured characteristics and for choices that reflect the comparative advantage of the groups compared, and entirely inconsistent, in the long run, with competitive economic forces.

Neither of these perspectives can or should be dismissed out of hand as so often happens when this issue is debated. An extremely wide discrimination gap is unlikely to exist, given the forces of competition, but a gap of something like 15 to 20 per cent, reflecting both wage discrimination and occupational segregation, does seem to be credible in a labour market riddled by other imperfections.

In saying that existing evidence indicates that the discriminatory wage gap is approximately 15 to 20 per cent, a proportion equal to, or slightly less than half of, the overall earnings gap, Commissioners do not mean to minimize the problem. A discriminatory earnings difference of this extent is certainly neither inconsequential nor, in our view, tolerable. Nor is it the only disadvantage operating against women in the labour force. However, it is important to recognize the implications of this assessment for policies such as equal pay and equal opportunity, designed to remove discrimination in the labour market. In particular, if our assessment is approximately correct, such policies, if successful in fully eliminating this type of discrimination, would narrow the overall earnings gap from the current 0.60 to approximately 0.80, leaving a remaining gap of 0.20 attributable to non-discriminatory factors.

Changes over Time

Earlier, Commissioners noted that substantial earnings differences between men and women have existed for decades. One of the most controversial aspects of documenting the extent of the discrimination problem pertains to changes in the earnings gap that have occurred over time. It is important to identify such changes, not only to determine if the problem is growing, but also to establish whether competitive and other forces are reducing the extent of discrimination. Unfortunately, little empirical work has been done on this subject, partly because of the lack of consistent time-series data on the unadjusted and productivity-adjusted earnings gap.

It has been determined, on the basis of narrowly defined occupational wage-rate data for Ontario[4] that the earnings gap tended to widen over the 1950s and 1960s; however, it narrowed somewhat over the 1970s, even after control for the effect of equal-pay policies. It has also been documented, on the basis of 1981 census data,[5] that the wage and earnings gap narrowed throughout Canada during the 1970s, partly because of the predominance of younger workers where the gap is smallest. The narrowing of the gap in recent years has also occurred in most other OECD countries.

A rigorous analysis of the extent to which the *discriminatory* wage gap is changing is complicated by the variety of other factors that are also changing over time. One might have expected the gap to widen over time, since the influx of women associated with the dramatic increase in the female labour force could have served to depress the wages of female workers. This outcome might quite well have happened because new entrants into the labour force are likely to be less experienced than the average worker, and therefore paid less.

On the other hand, the gap might have narrowed for a number of other reasons: competitive forces might have dissipated discrimination; increasing female participation in the labour force might have led to the accumulation of work experience, as well as to the reduction of sex stereotyping and prejudice; the larger proportion of youths in the labour force might have reduced the average earnings gap, since the gap is smaller among youths; the increased demand for white-collar workers and their greater degree of unionization might have helped females disproportionately; policy initiatives might have made discrimination more costly. The fact that many of these factors were operative in the 1970s, and that many of the factors giving rise to a widening of the gap were more prominent in the 1960s, might account for the possibility that the gap widened in the 1960s, but narrowed in the 1970s. However, in the absence of a thorough empirical analysis of the trends and the relative importance of myriad offsetting factors that are at work, it is possible, at this stage, only to speculate on what is happening today and why. It may be, for example, that policy initiatives and competitive pressures are working to narrow the earnings gap, but that they have been able barely to offset the expanding pressure associated with the dramatic influx of women into Canada's labour force.

Expected Future Patterns

The future is even more cloudy than the present. Technological change may help women to the extent that they are less affected than men by the possible decline in job opportunities in the manufacturing sector. Women, however, may also be adversely affected by office automation.

If deregulation occurs on any substantial scale, it is likely to benefit minorities by opening up new jobs (possibly at lower pay) that may devolve to the new entrants into Canada's labour market. Trade liberalization, on the other hand, is likely to affect women adversely, given their predominance among workers in textiles and light manufacturing; but if the process is accompanied by positive adjustment assistance, workers may have the opportunity to leave low-wage, declining sectors of employment for expanding ones. Public sector retrenchment is likely to bear disproportionately on women, both because of their predominance in public sector jobs, and because there tends to be less discrimination in the public than in the private sector. An expanding economy, by contrast, is likely to help break down discriminatory barriers and to provide a disproportionate number of job opportunities for women and minority groups.

Future labour-market developments then, are likely to have substantial implications, both positive and negative, for the future of women in our Canadian labour market. On the one hand, changing circumstances are likely to open up new opportunities for women. On the other hand, there is also likely to be resistance from incumbent workers whose own jobs and pay are threatened. These developments seem to Commissioners to highlight the importance of policy initiatives that will work to establish employment opportunities which will ensure that women have at least equal access to the new jobs. These initiatives are likely to prove more important than policies to encourage equal pay, at least to the extent that wage discrimination is less likely to occur in new jobs where traditional hierarchies are less firmly established.

Dramatic changes which have occurred in the educational and career choices of younger women in the last 15 years will also have important implications for the future. During this period, the numbers of women attending university and continuing their studies past the undergraduate level rose much faster than the comparable figures for men. Thus, in 1966, women comprised 33.7 per cent of undergraduate registration and 18.0 per cent of graduate enrolment; by 1981, these proportions had increased to 46.6 and

37.3 per cent respectively.[6] Table 15-6 shows the very substantial increases in the proportion of women receiving bachelor's and first professional, master's and doctoral degrees from 1966 to 1980. Table 15-7 illustrates the dramatic increases in female enrolment in the traditionally male-dominated areas of engineering and applied science, medicine, law, commerce and business administration. These statistics supply evidence of a very significant decline in occupational segregation, at least as indicated by university enrolment.

TABLE 15-6 Women as a Percentage of Total Recipients of Degrees Awarded by Canadian Universities and Colleges

Year	Bachelor and First Professional	Master's	Doctorate
1966–67	34.1	20.0	8.1
1967–68	35.2	20.0	9.7
1968–69	36.9	22.0	7.9
1969–70	38.4	21.6	9.3
1970–71	38.1	22.0	9.3
1971–72	39.4	24.8	9.3
1972–73	39.8	26.8	11.2
1974	41.5	27.2	12.3
1975	44.4	28.2	16.1
1976	46.3	30.5	18.8
1977	47.7	31.3	18.0
1978	48.5	32.8	18.2
1979	49.2	36.0	20.5
1980	49.6	37.4	23.0
1981	50.3	39.2	24.2

Source: Thomas H.B. Symons and James E. Page, "The Status of Women in Canadian Academic Life", in *Some Questions of Balance* (Ottawa: Association of Universities and Colleges of Canada, 1984), p. 192.

These developments clearly augur well for the future reduction both of the earnings gap and of occupational segregation. As stated in a recent study published by the Economic Council of Canada, "Over the next few years, it will be mainly the young women who, between 1971 and 1981, succeeded in changing traditional female labour patterns who will be able to move up the promotional ladders in their places of work."[7]

As with many predictions about future developments, however, analysts differ about how large these reductions in the earnings gap and in occupational segregation will be, and about how quickly any change will occur. Any optimistic assessment should not be allowed to obscure the fact that the equalization of earnings and opportunities has been an extremely slow process, and that even the potential acceleration referred to here is unlikely to produce a fully satisfactory rate of progress.

TABLE 15-7 Women as a Percentage of Total Full-Time University Undergraduate Enrolment for Selected Fields of Specialization, Canada

Year	Fine and Applied Arts	Engineering and Applied Science	Medicine	Law	Commerce and Business Administration
1966	61.8	1.4	13.0	6.3	7.8
1967	61.2	1.5	13.8	7.3	8.4
1968	57.4	1.6	15.1	8.8	8.2
1969	56.9	1.6	17.1	10.9	8.5
1970	56.8	1.8	18.1	12.7	10.2
1971	53.9	2.4	20.3	14.9	13.9
1972	57.8	2.6	22.3	18.0	16.1
1973	58.2	3.3	24.3	20.3	18.1
1974	59.1	4.5	26.2	23.7	19.9
1975	60.8	5.5	27.2	26.7	22.3
1981	62.3	10.6	38.5	39.9	37.2

Sources: Statistics Canada, *Historical Statistics of Canada*, 2d ed. (Ottawa: Statistics Canada, 1983), Series 444, 443, 446, 451 and 441); and Thomas H.B. Symons and James E. Page, "The Status of Women in Canadian Academic Life", in *Some Questions of Balance* (Ottawa: Association of Universities and Colleges of Canada, 1984), p. 206.

Implications for Public Policy

The persistence of at least some discrimination in the labour market suggests that there is considerable scope for policy initiatives to create improvements. Such initiatives might move in the direction of equal pay and equal employment opportunities.

Conventional equal-pay legislation dealing with substantially similar work which basically involves the same occupation has some potential function. That function is limited, however, by the fact that its maximum effect is likely to be on the 5 to 10 percentage points of the earnings gap that can be attributed to narrowly-defined wage discrimination within the same occupation and establishment.

Recruiting and promotion policies that deal with equal-employment opportunity could have a broader function, since they can affect occupational segregation, which is generally believed to occur more often and to affect more workers, possibly accounting for 10 percentage points or more of the overall earnings gap. Even though the principle of "equal pay for work of equal value" deals with pay and not with employment opportunities, it could also have a broader function, since it, too, can deal directly with earnings differentials based on occupational segregation. In fact, "equal-value" policies have been advocated specifically to enable comparisons across occupations and thus to overcome the limitations of conventional equal-pay policies which are designed to apply to substantially similar jobs. The scope for equal-value legislation is likely to correspond to about 10 percentage points of the earnings gap, a figure that is consistent with cases of the actual implementation of the equal-value principle; the correspondence could, however, range as high as 20 percentage points if the legislation ultimately addressed pay increases as high as those applied to "overvalued" male-performed jobs. Of the two policy approaches, the equal-pay principle has been given more emphasis in Canada. This initiative has evolved through a variety of forms, each with a different potential effect.

Equal Work

The earliest legislative initiatives relating to the equal-pay principle – that of Ontario in 1951, for instance – required equal pay for "equal work". This stipulation significantly hampered the application of the equal-pay principle, since it was interpreted to allow even minor job differences to negate the assertion that equal work was being performed. Comparisons were also restricted to "equal work" within the same company.

Substantially Similar Work

The legislation was then broadened to allow comparisons to be made when there were minor differences in work, as long as that work was "substantially similar". That expression was often defined in terms of the inputs of skill, effort and responsibility, and according to working conditions, but these criteria were usually assessed independently of one another. This meant that the work had to be substantially similar in *each and every* area of comparison. It was not possible to compensate for a slight shortcoming in one area with a greater amount of some other component.

Composite Approach

The "composite" approach to job evaluation, by contrast, requires only that the work be substantially similar in the *composite* of components of skill, effort, responsibility and working conditions. This broader approach allows a shortcoming in one component to be compensated for by a greater amount of another. It makes the assessment of comparability more difficult, however, because it is often necessary to make trade-offs among the components: to know, for example, whether a bit more responsibility exactly offsets a little less skill.

The composite approach is consistent with the way in which economic forces determine the value of a job. Market forces, for example, do not require two jobs that pay the same to correspond identically in skill, effort, responsibility and working conditions, but only that the market's evaluation of each of these components sum to the same total. While this approach is consistent with basic economic principles, it does add the requirement that somehow the value of each of these components must be traded off against another.

The composite method of assessing equal work begins to approach the "equal-value" or "comparable-worth" concepts, except that the former usually requires that comparisons be limited to jobs involving substantially the same kind of work. If it allowed for the comparison of dissimilar jobs, then the composite approach would be an equal-value approach.

Equal Value

The principle of equal pay for work of equal value allows dissimilar jobs to be compared and evaluated as equal as long as the "value" of the job, as determined, for example, by a job-evaluation scheme, is the same or sufficiently close to be considered so. The procedure allows comparisons across dissimilar occupations and, in fact, is often supported on the ground that this broadened scope enables it to deal both with wage differences arising from occupational segregation and with unequal pay within the same occupation. In that respect, its scope is much broader than that of conventional equal-pay legislation. However, while comparisons across quite dissimilar jobs are possible in theory, in practice those carried out to date have not involved highly dissimilar jobs, partly because job-evaluation procedures become more tenuous as the jobs under examination become less similar.

Equal-value comparisons tend to be regarded as the strongest form of intervention in support of the equal-pay principle. This is primarily because they cover the broadest range of types of work that can be compared.

Proportionate Value

If, however, there is a logic to using the administrative concept of value as determined by a job evaluation scheme – and this is a possibility that remains to be discussed later – then it would seem illogical (except on grounds of expediency) to allow comparisons between jobs only when they are of *equal* value. Such a restriction would preclude any adjustment, for example, if a job-evaluation scheme found that although a given female-dominated job had a job-evaluation score of 90 per cent, compared to a given male-dominated job, yet its pay ratio was only 80 per cent. It would appear that if the job-evaluation procedure were competent to determine the relative values of jobs, workers performing the female-dominated job should be paid at 90 per cent of the rate for workers performing the male-dominated job.

The principle of proportionate pay for work of proportionate value seems to be a logical extension of the principle of equal pay for work of equal value. Even if the equal-value principle entails excessive allocative or administrative costs, political pressures are likely to push in the direction of proportionate pay if equal value becomes the established norm.

Equal-Pay Legislation in Various Jurisdictions

Table 15-8 summarizes the various forms of equal-pay legislation in Canadian jurisdictions. All our jurisdictions have some form of equal-pay legislation, usually established during the 1950s, following the International Labour Organisation's Equal Remuneration Convention No. 100, adopted in 1951. Most jurisdictions require that substantially similar work be the basis for comparison, and most allow the composite approach that enables trade-offs to be made among the components of skill, effort, responsibility and working conditions. Five jurisdictions allow for some groups to be exempt from the legislation, and seven allow comparisons to be made across different locations, but require that the comparisons always be made within the same company. Most jurisdictions stipulate that individuals make a complaint if they consider themselves entitled to do so under the legislation. Only three allow for the legislative agency to initiate some investigations, and of these, only Ontario and, to a lesser extent, Saskatchewan seem to follow that practice. The number of investigations is extremely small in many jurisdictions; Ontario and, to a lesser extent, Saskatchewan are by far the most active. It appears that equal-value initiatives, which may be taken only in the federal jurisdiction and in Quebec, are being applied in a cautious fashion.

Additional Issues Pertaining to Equal Value

Since equal-value legislation is likely to be the "wave of the future" with respect to initiatives on the equal-pay front, it is worth examining this concept in more detail.

Job-Evaluation Procedures

Equal-value assessments are invariably based on job-evaluation procedures. Basically, these procedures involve an assessment of a job in terms of its components of skill, effort, responsibility and working conditions. Persons opposed to the equal-value principle have raised a number of arguments against job-evaluation procedures. Many of these arguments contain an element of truth, though they sometimes overstate the case. Perhaps the most common objection is that job-evaluation procedures try to compare "apples and oranges", although this is also done implicitly by market forces.

In addition, job-evaluation procedures face important difficulties in attaching weight to the different components of skill, effort, responsibility and working conditions. For this reason, the comparisons become more difficult, but not necessarily impossible, when they apply to disparate jobs. It is difficult to attach an objective notion of value to a job (that is to say, a concept of value that is independent of the market valuation). Nevertheless, the equal-value principle does relate to the value of the inputs of skill, effort, responsibility and working conditions, and not to the value of the outputs; the latter can still be determined by market forces.

Economic, as Compared to Administrative, Concepts of Value

The equal-value principle focuses on the valuation of job *input* of skill, effort, responsibility and working conditions. The efficient use of labour resources, however, requires that wages adjust to demand and supply conditions in the

TABLE 15-8 Canadian Equal Pay Legislation by Jurisdiction, 1981

Jurisdiction	Date of 1st Law	Concept of Equality	Composite or Trade-off Approach Allowed	Exempt Groups[a]	Same Company in Different Locations[b]	Agency Initiate Investigations[c]	Number of Investigations
Nfld.	1971	Similar	Yes	Yes	Yes	Yes	N.A.
P.E.I.	1959	Substan. same	Yes	Yes	N.A.	No	1980–82
N.S.	1957	Substan. same	Yes	Yes	Yes	No	1 per year
N.B.	1961	N.A.	Yes	No	Yes	No	1980–81: 5 to 7
Que.	1964	Equal value	Yes	No	Yes	Rare	32 settled since 1976
Ont.	1951	Substan. same	No[d]	No	Yes	Yes	1980–82[e]: 374
Man.	1956	Substan. same	No	No	No	Rare	1978–81: 1
Sask.	1952	Similar	No	Yes	No	Yes	1980–81: 17 1981–82: 12
Alta.	1957	Substan. similar	Yes	Yes	No	No	1980–81: 5
B.C.	1953	Substan. similar	No	No	Yes	Rare	N.A.
Fed.	1956	Equal value	Yes	No	Yes[f]	No	7 settled since 1977[g]

Source: Extracted from Ontario Manpower Commission, *The Employment of Women in Ontario* (Toronto: The Commission, 1983), Appendix XI, p. 198.

a. "Yes" implies that some groups are exempt. These usually comprise domestics, sometimes foreign labourers and occasionally members of non-profit organizations.

b. "Yes" implies that comparisons can be made in the same company across different locations.

c. "Yes" implies that the enforcement agency, usually an employment-standards division or a human rights commission, can initiate an investigation. "No" implies that an individual must make a complaint before an investigation can occur. "Rare" implies that although the legislation allows the agency to initiate an investigation without a formal complaint this seldom if ever occurs.

d. Proposed Bill 141, before legislature as of December 1984, contains composite.

e. Between April 1980 and February 1982, 374 investigations (115 routine audits, 259 arising from complaints), with 86 violations for 1054 employees, who received average settlements of $519.

f. Comparisons can be made in same company in different locations, but within an established geographic area.

g. Including two major group settlements involving 3480 workers. Approximately 20 complaints were under investigation in or close to 1983.

labour market. Administrative assessments are made by job-evaluation agents who, in assigning point scores to each job, need not take into account conditions of labour-market supply and demand. Their assessment will be based on their perception of the "objective" worth of the various tasks required to perform a given job. That is to say, supply conditions (which are established by the willingness of workers to work in certain jobs) and demand conditions (which are established by the need of employers to fill those jobs) do not enter directly into the job evaluator's assessment of the point score to be assigned to each job. They may enter in an indirect fashion in that, for example, certain working conditions may be assigned a higher point score because few people are willing to accept them. Nevertheless, the point-score evaluations of each job are based, in the main, on an administrative (that is, a job evaluator's) concept of the value of a job.

In our current system, supply and demand conditions are important factors in determining the pay rates associated with different jobs. For example, females, on average, may be willing to supply their services in certain jobs because they prefer the working conditions associated with those jobs or because of off-the-job constraints such as family commitments. Similarly, if there were little demand on the part of employers for some of the skills required in predominantly female-performed jobs, then wages of female workers in those jobs might be low. These factors do not necessarily contribute to the point scores for these jobs.

If, for the same job-evaluation point score, wages were lower in the predominantly female-performed jobs than in the predominantly male-performed jobs, equal-value legislation would mandate an adjustment. This adjustment would occur even if the predominantly female-performed jobs were held by persons who willingly supplied their services at the lower wage. It is because job evaluators may ignore such supply factors, which might reflect legitimate preferences, that much of the concern arises over the use of administrative, rather than market, procedures for determining pay. Another cause of concern is the administrative cost associated with the job-evaluation procedure itself.

The administrative determination of wages might also inhibit the adaptability of the labour force to change. At present, market forces and collective bargaining raise wages in rapidly expanding sectors and lower wages in declining or slow-growth sectors. These wage differentials are important initiators of economic adjustment, providing the signal and incentive for some members of the labour force to move out of declining employment sectors into expanding sectors. This process, which is significant over the long run, would be inhibited in an economy in which wages were administratively determined. The debate about the viability of equal-value legislation must deal directly with the issue of which wages should be determined by the economic forces of supply and demand, along with collective bargaining, and which should be determined by job-evaluation procedures.

The choices need not be mutually exclusive. That is, the use of equal-value/job-evaluation procedures in select cases may supplement the action of market forces by providing information to the parties and, perhaps, by removing unintended discrimination. After all, job-evaluation procedures are used extensively in private industry; hence they must have some value in terms of the information they provide and the preservation of such realities as internal equity. Conversely, the broad application of the equal-value principle based on administrative job-evaluation schemes, without any attention to market forces, is likely to create significant allocation problems, as well as to engender market adjustments that may offset, in part at least, the intended effects of the entire process.

Theoretical Effect

Any policy that raises wages relative to those paid for other inputs into production of goods and services will result in an adverse employment effect, both because firms will raise prices and reduce their output in response to a cost increase, and because they will find substitutes for an input that has become more expensive. Where female labour, subject to equal pay, is a cost factor, this adverse employment effect is likely to be fairly substantial, at least in the long term, because there is likely to be a fairly abundant supply of available substitute inputs, and the ratio of female-labour cost relative to total cost can be high in a number of female-dominated labour markets. This effect may be offset, however, by the fact that many of these jobs are in the public and quasi-public sectors, and hence administrators can pass on the cost increase to taxpayers without seriously reducing the demand for the output.

In addition to the direct effect of higher wages on the employment situation, there may also be a number of indirect effects. Opportunities to obtain training and experience in return for lower wages may be reduced, and this consequence may, in the long run, inhibit wage growth. Employers may react by raising job requirements, and working conditions may deteriorate, since higher wages add to production costs. On the credit side, however, recipients of equal pay may welcome the increased requirements and the additional responsibilities, especially if they expand future opportunities for advancement.

Other more subtle adjustments are also likely to occur in response to equal-value legislation. Firms may engage in subcontracting, especially for those functions where they are most susceptible to charges of unequal pay, and where the firms or individuals receiving the contracts are less amenable to legislative initiatives. Certain product lines may be segregated, and certain tasks may be differentiated to some degree, so as not to give the appearance of being substantially similar and thus subject to equal-pay comparisons. In addition, firms may try to avoid hiring applicants whom they regard as ultimately likely to pressure them to introduce equal pay for large groups of workers. They may also avoid making internal evaluations of their own wage structure (especially job evaluations and equal-value comparisons) for fear that the data obtained might be used against them if they did not fully rectify any wage imbalances discovered. These examples are only meant to illustrate some of the adjustments that can occur in response to legislative initiatives relating to employment practices.

Equal-Employment/Opportunity Legislation

While equal-pay policies work to prevent discrimination in matters of pay, equal-employment/opportunity policies are designed to prevent discrimination pertaining to the various dimensions of employment opportunities. Such discriminatory practices might relate, for example, to recruiting, hiring, training, promotions, transfers and termination of employment.

Legislation in Various Jurisdictions

All Canadian jurisdictions have similar equal-employment/ opportunity policies, usually embodied in a Human Rights Code. These policies are part of a broader policy restricting discrimination on the basis of such factors as race, age, religion and national origin. In most jurisdictions, the prohibition against sexual discrimination was added during the 1960s and 1970s, following the International Labour Organisation Discrimination (Employment and Occupation) Convention No. 111, adopted in 1958.

The process of invoking the pertinent legislation usually requires that an individual party complain to a Human Rights Commission. If the Commission decides to act on a complaint, there often follows a lengthy procedure involving investigation, conciliation and, ultimately, a trial-type hearing which may involve appeals to the courts. This lengthy procedure and the requirement that an individual lodge a complaint can obviously inhibit the process that exists to protect Canadians from discrimination.

Affirmative Action

Affirmative action is based on the view that it is not sufficient to make specific acts of discrimination illegal. Rather, positive steps are needed to relieve the effects of past discrimination, eliminate present discrimination and help to prevent future discrimination. These positive steps focus on the results of the intervention, not just on the opportunities themselves.

Affirmative action is a flexible policy which can take many forms. It typically involves setting targets for the hiring of disadvantaged groups, but it can go further and involve quotas and "reverse discrimination". In addition to establishing targets and a timetable for their achievement, affirmative action typically involves the founding of a data base that records such information as the sex, occupational distribution and pay of the work-force.

There are several rationales for affirmative action programs. These programs may compensate for the cumulative effects of a past history of discrimination; in such circumstances, given unequal starting positions, equal opportunity may involve remedial measures, providing specific preferential benefits to a designated group. These time-limited measures might include management training for women and special recruitment programs for underrepresented groups. Affirmative action programs may also be a necessary means of breaking a vicious circle of entrapment which, when broken, will enable women or other groups to acquire experience, training, confidence and responsibilities that will ultimately remove the necessity for affirmative action. Again, the affirmative action approach to the problems of inequity and inefficient use of target-group workers is based on the concept of systemic discrimination. This approach identifies discrimination in the workplace in terms of the way employment practices affect the employment of target-group members, rather than in terms of the purpose of those practices. It may also be particularly suited to breaking down segregation, since it creates an incentive for firms to reach down into the "job ghettos" and demolish the barriers that confine workers to particular forms of work.

All provinces in Canada, except for Quebec and Newfoundland (and Alberta, unless Cabinet approval is obtained), allow voluntary affirmative action programs and relieve them of being considered in contravention of the relevant anti-discrimination legislation.[8] Moreover, both the federal jurisdiction and Saskatchewan can impose affirmative action as a remedy when a court has found discrimination; Saskatchewan can even order, on its own initiative, that such programs be instituted. With respect to Native Canadians, compulsory affirmative action through contract compliance has been required in a number of joint public-private mega-projects. Voluntary affirmative action programs, often worked out with the assistance of the government, also exist in a number of large private sector organizations, as well as in various elements of the public sector.

Expected Effect

Equal-employment/opportunity policies can be expected to increase the labour-market demand for females and hence their employment opportunities and, indirectly, their wages. This expectation stands in some contrast to equal-pay policies which, by raising wages, might be expected to decrease employment opportunities. If this prospect of policies that create effective equal-employment opportunities becomes a reality, there could eventually be less need for equal-pay policies. This application of basic economic principles significantly qualifies the notion that equal pay is a necessary complement to equal-employment/ opportunity legislation, a notion which is based on the view that such legislation alone would simply lead to the hiring of females at unequal wages. The notion ignores the demand pressures emanating from equal-employment/opportunity policies, which can serve to increase both wages and employment opportunities. In this area, however, market forces seem to grind with considerable slowness, and social justice would seem to dictate the use of policy instruments to accelerate their working.

Evidence Concerning the Effect of Equal Pay in Canada

It has been determined,[9] on the basis of data for Ontario, that the transfer in 1969, of equal-pay legislation from the Human Rights Code to the Employment Standards Act – a transfer which was carried out in order to enhance the legislation's effectiveness – had no statistically significant effect of narrowing the male-female/wage gap. It is possible, however, that any change was not recorded, since the data were collected for only one year before and after the passage of the legislation. However, an analysis of another data set, limited to Ontario occupations, also failed to find any significant difference in the time pattern of male-female/wage adjustments in response to the legislative change. This conclusion has been reinforced by a more recent study[10] of the impact of the legislation, which was carried out over a longer time period (1946–1979), and which used a slightly different set of occupations.

While the extent to which these conclusions should be generalized remains open to question, it seems safe to say that empirical analysis has not shown that conventional equal-pay legislation has significantly narrowed the male-female/earnings gap. This conclusion, of course, does not imply that the legislation has not had an effect on some groups; rather, the indication is that the Acts do not seem to have narrowed appreciably the *overall* male-female/earnings gap.

Evidence Concerning Equal-Value Initiatives

The effect of anti-discrimination legislation on specific groups can be illustrated by a number of equal-value cases that have occurred. A job-evaluation study for the State of Washington[11] found, for example, that the pay in predominantly female-staffed occupations was approximately 80 per cent of that in predominantly male-staffed occupations of the same job-evaluation point score. Subsequent analysis suggested that the cost of raising the pay of the predominantly female-performed "undervalued" jobs to the average pay line would be \$37.9 million; a later court decision indicated that approximately 15 500 employees were involved, for an average adjustment of approximately \$2445 per worker.

A job evaluation of municipal workers carried out in San Jose, California, also found that female-performed jobs were paid at rates of 2 to 10 per cent below the comparable-worth line; predominantly male-performed jobs were paid at rates 8 to 15 per cent above comparable worth, creating an overall gap of 10 to 35 per cent of pay rates between jobs of the same point score. The actual settlement to bring the pay of 750 women in "undervalued" female-dominated jobs to the pay line was \$1.4 million, representing an average individual adjustment of \$1867.[12] A job evaluation for Minnesota State employees also led to a budgetary appropriation of approximately \$21.7 million to raise the pay of its 8225 employees in undervalued female-performed jobs. This sum represented an average per-employee adjustment of \$2638.

In Canada's federal jurisdiction, most equal-value cases have involved only a small number of persons, or have dealt with discriminatory classification systems; alternatively, they could have been handled under conventional equal-pay legislation. In 1980, however, 475 librarians received a settlement that involved an annual ongoing adjustment of approximately \$1 million or \$2105 per person when their jobs were compared to those of predominantly male historical researchers. Again, in 1982, 3300 general service workers received a settlement that involved an annual ongoing adjustment of approximately \$8 million, or an average of \$2424 per person. This represented a 20 per cent increase in the wages of the female-dominated subgroups, an increase that was larger than those awarded in most U.S. equal-value adjustments because the Canadian adjustments involved raising the female-pay line to the male-pay line rather than to the average (composite sex) line.

These figures illustrate the size of the adjustments that have been involved in the actual implementation of the principle of equal pay for work of equal value. These adjustments typically involve raising the pay of "undervalued" female-performed jobs by about 10 per cent and typically involve adjustments in the $2000 to $3000 range. What difference these changes have made to the overall earnings gap in each of the relevant jurisdictions remains unknown.

Evidence from the United States

The actual effect of various forms of equal-employment/opportunity legislation has been extensively analysed in the United States. This legislation includes both Title VII of the Civil Rights Act of 1964, the Equal Employment Opportunity (EEO) title, and Executive Order 11246 and its amendments; the latter legislation requires affirmative action on the part of employers involved in federal contracts. The EEO legislation forbids both wage and employment discrimination, while the federal contract-compliance legislation requires affirmative action with respect to employment and upgrading opportunities in those firms that receive federal contracts.

U.S. evidence has been mixed on the effect of the equal-employment/opportunity function of Title VII of the Civil Rights Act. Affirmative action under the Federal Contract Compliance Program has produced significant improvements for black males, but there have been frequent set-backs for white females. Recent evidence also suggests that affirmative action has improved the occupational position of Blacks, in part because of more aggressive enforcement procedures and in part because of a wider availability of more highly educated Blacks. Enforcement procedures do seem to be important to the effect of the policy as does an expanding growing economy. Equal-employment/opportunity procedures increased both wages and employment opportunities, while equal-pay procedures reduced the latter.

Conclusions

This overview suggests that there is both a scope and a role for policy initiatives. Equal-employment/opportunity or employment-equity policies have a number of possible advantages over conventional equal-pay policies. The scope of the former is likely to be larger than the scope of the latter, since occupational segregation is more important than narrowly-defined wage discrimination. Equal-employment opportunities can also increase both the wages and the employment opportunities of women, while equal-pay policies, by themselves, are likely to decrease their employment and training opportunities. Employers cannot avoid applying equal-employment/opportunity legislation simply by not hiring particular groups, though this evasion is more often possible under equal-pay legislation. Affirmative action components of equal-employment/opportunity legislation can also break down work-place barriers and demolish job ghettos, and eventually act to correct misinformation about the capabilities of those groups to whom it applies.

This predisposition towards policies in support of equal-employment opportunities reflects Commissioners' preference for initiatives that expand choices and opportunities, that minimize distortions in market prices, and that facilitate market adjustments and the matching of the right people with the right jobs. Yet although the analysis offered in this section leans towards equal-employment/opportunity policies rather than towards equal-value policies, this Commission does not advocate the abandonment of the latter. We do suggest, however, that the adoption of the principle of equal pay for work of equal value should not be undertaken on a wider scale until Canadians achieve a better understanding of the probable consequences.

Equal-pay/equal-value legislation represents a quantum change in policy orientation because such laws involve administratively determined concepts of value that can be quite independent of market forces; they also involve administrative costs associated with job evaluation. Partly for this reason, its current application has been largely restricted to the public sector, where the impact of market forces is already blunted. To enlarge and extend the concept to the private sector would constitute a dramatic move. Job-evaluation assessments would override not only those wages determined by market forces, but also those determined by collective bargaining. Furthermore, pressure would emerge to apply the concept more broadly: to different groups of workers of the same sex, for example.

Before such a move is made, therefore, it would seem sensible to obtain more information concerning a number of factors, such as the effect of this legislation in those few instances where it has been applied. In addition, it is important that a reasoned debate be held to discuss the pros and cons of administrative, as contrasted with market and collective bargaining, procedures for wage determination. Finally, equal-pay/equal-value policies must be assessed according to a broad set of program-evaluation criteria: the control of administrative costs; the attainment of target efficiency (which requires helping a target group without spilling benefits into the hands of a non-target group); the attainment of allocative efficiency; the provision of non-demeaning benefits; and, over time, the attainment of flexibility.

While equal-pay/equal-value legislation, effectively applied to the private sector, would constitute a significant change in policy, affirmative action is amenable to a staged approach under which its effects could be monitored. In addition, it has the advantage of working through employment-opportunity mechanisms, and the considerable American experience offers Canadians an excellent chance to use its best features and abandon its worst. Furthermore, there are good reasons to believe that affirmative action would be needed only temporarily.

Recommendations

Commissioners generally approve the approach suggested by the Royal Commission on Equality in Employment, and we note the supportive approach taken by the federal government in its response to the Abella recommendations. In general this approach will require:

- Maintenance of existing equal-pay/equal-value policies
- Legislation that requires all employers covered by the Canada Labour Code, including federal Crown corporations, to take affirmative action
- Contract-compliance requirements for contractors working for the federal government
- Encouragement of provincial governments to follow suit.

We are concerned, however, that, as often before, governmental actions will turn out to be "toothless". In order to ensure compliance, these approaches should be firmly legislated rather than merely set out in guidelines. Moreover, the Human Rights Commission should be given more resources so that it can strengthen its monitoring and enforcement activities.

Notes

1. A more detailed discussion of the empirical evidence is provided in Morley Gunderson, "Discrimination, Equal Pay and Equal Opportunities in the Labour Market", in *Work and Pay: The Canadian Labour Market*, vol. 17, prepared for the Royal Commission on the Economic Union and Development Prospects for Canada (Toronto: University of Toronto Press, 1985), on which much of this section is based.
2. For example, Sylvia Ostry, *The Female Worker in Canada* (Ottawa: Queen's Printer, 1968); Roberta Robb, "Earnings Differentials Between Males and Females in Ontario, 1971", *Canadian Journal of* Economics 11 (May 1978): 350–59; Morley Gunderson, "Decomposition of Male/Female Earnings Differential: Canada 1970", *Canadian Journal of Economics* 12 (August 1979): 479–85; Morley Gunderson, *Labour Market Economics: Theory, Evidence and Policy in Canada* (Toronto: McGraw-Hill Ryerson, 1980); M. Stelcner and D. Shapiro, "The Decomposition of the Male/Female Earnings Differential: Quebec 1970" (Montreal: Concordia University, 1980); C. Kapsalis, "Sex Discrimination in the Labour Market" (mimeo, 1980).
3. For example, Reginald Robson and Mireille Lapointe, *A Comparison of Men's and Women's Salaries and Employment Fringe Benefits in the Academic Profession* (Ottawa: Information Canada, 1971); Morley Gunderson, "Male-Female Wage Differentials and the Impact of Equal Pay Legislation", *Review of Economics and Statistics* 57 (November 1975): 426–69; William Schrank, "Sex Discrimination in Faculty Salaries: A Case Study", *Canadian Journal of Economics* 10 (August 1977): 411–33; M. Stelcner, "Male-Female Faculty Salary Differentials: A Case Study – Concordia University" (Montreal: Concordia University, 1979); P. Walmsley, M. Ohtsu, and A. Verma, "Measuring Wage Discrimination Against Women: An Alternative to the Human Capital Approach" (Saskatoon: University of Saskatchewan, 1980).
4. M. Gunderson, *The Male-Female Earnings Gap in Ontario: A Summary* (Toronto: Ministry of Labour, Research Branch, 1982).
5. Jac-André Boulet and Laval Lavallée, *The Changing Economic Status of Women*, study prepared for the Economic Council of Canada (Ottawa: Minister of Supply and Services Canada, 1984).
6. See Alice Nakamura and Masao Nakamura, "A Survey of Research on the Work Behaviour of Canadian Women", in *Work and Pay: The Canadian Labour Market*, vol. 17, prepared for the Royal Commission on the Economic Union and Development Prospects for Canada (Toronto: University of Toronto Press, 1985).

7. Boulet and Lavallée, *The Changing Economic Status of Women*, p. 3.
8. H. Jain, "Human Rights: Issues in Employment", in Human Resources Management in Canada, edited by N. Agarwal et al. (Toronto: Prentice-Hall, 1983).
9. Morley Gunderson, "Male-Female Wage Differentials and the Impact of Equal Pay Legislation", *Review of Economics and Statistics* 57 (November 1975): 426–69.
10. M. Gunderson, "Spline Function Estimates of the Impact of Equal Pay Legislation" (mimeo, 1984).
11. Norman D. Willis and Associates, *State of Washington, Comparable Worth Study* (1974), and *Comparable Worth Study, Phase II* (1976).
12. John H. Bunzel, "To Each According to Her Worth?", *The Public Interest* 67 (Spring, 1982), pp. 77–79.

Time Spent Working

This Commission has stressed the importance of the growth in employment and real earnings as factors contributing to the increased well-being of Canadians. Another key factor is the reduction in time spent working and the increased time thus made available for leisure and other activities. In this century the reduction in Canadians' working time has been dramatic. It has occurred on three fronts: hours worked per week, weeks worked per year, and years worked over a lifetime. A shorter work-week, more holidays, and later entry into, and earlier retirement from, the labour force have produced significant increases in the time available for non-work activities.

There are two sets of issues relating to time spent working. The first involves working time when the economy is operating at normal levels of employment. Here Commissioners' central concern is that working time reflect, as closely as reasonably possible, the preferences of employees. The second issue involves the way hours of work and employment adjust in response to cyclical fluctuations in the economy. This matter was raised earlier when we dealt with unemployment insurance, and we return to it below.

Weekly and Annual Work Schedules: Current Patterns and Historical Trends

Patterns in weekly hours of work can be examined in terms of actual hours of work, paid hours or standard hours. Actual hours of work in any given week are affected by factors such as the proportion of part-time and full-time employees, the structure of industry, the proportion of office and non-office employees, cyclical fluctuations in labour demand, industrial disputes and the occurrence of holidays and vacations. Paid hours, defined as the total number of hours for which employees are receiving pay, including holidays, vacations and paid sick leave, respond to all these factors, except the occurrence of paid holidays and vacations. Standard hours, defined as the number of hours beyond which overtime is normally payable to full-time employees, are affected, among the factors listed above, only by the industrial mix and the proportion of office and non-office workers.

There is considerable diversity in actual hours worked per week by Canadian employees. Data from Statistics Canada's Labour Force Survey, presented in Table 15-9, indicate that during 1983, just over half of all employees worked "typical" work-weeks of between 30 and 40 hours. Nearly one-fifth of all employees were part-time workers, defined by the Labour Force Survey as employees who usually work less than 30 hours per week. Even during that year of severe recession, however, when Canada's unemployment rate averaged 11.9 per cent, over 20 per cent of employees worked more than 40 hours per week; 12.6 per cent worked more than 50 hours per week.

Some of the employees who work the long hours recorded in Table 15-9 hold more than one job. However, since policies relating to work time apply to the job rather than to the employee, it is useful to examine hours worked on

TABLE 15-9 The Distribution of Employed Persons by Hours Worked at All Jobs, Canada, 1983

	Both Sexes		Male		Female	
Hours	**000s**	**%**	**000s**	**%**	**000s**	**%**
0	797	7.4	442	7.1	355	7.9
1–29	1 982	18.5	680	10.9	1 302	29.0
30–34	1 038	9.7	541	8.7	497	11.1
35–39	1 656	15.4	720	11.5	937	20.8
40	2 932	27.3	2 021	32.4	912	20.3
41–49	973	9.1	720	11.5	253	5.6
50 or over	1 356	12.6	1 116	17.9	240	5.3
Total	10 734	100.0	6 240	100.0	4 495	100.0

Sources: Statistics Canada, *Labour Force Annual Averages 1975–1983*, Cat. No. 71-529 (Ottawa: Minister of Supply and Services Canada, 1984), p. 269; and tabulations by the Commission.

the main job. Table 15-10 shows that in any case, hours worked at part-time jobs add little, overall, to the average of hours worked at all jobs. It also records that full-time employees usually work 41.5 hours per week on their main job.

For most purposes, however, the most relevant concept is the length of the standard work-week (and work-year) for full-time employees. Table 15-11

TABLE 15-10 Average Weekly Hours Worked, Canada, 1983

Employee Category	Actual Hours	Usual Hours
All jobs		
All employees	37.3	37.8
Full-time employees	41.3	42.0
Part-time employees	15.3	14.9
Main job		
All employees	36.8	37.3
Full-time employees	40.8	41.5
Part-time employees	15.1	14.7

Source: Statistics Canada, *Labour Force Annual Averages 1975–83*, Cat. No. 71-529 (Ottawa: Minister of Supply and Services Canada, 1984), pp. 287, 296.

Note: Averages are calculated excluding persons who were employed, but not at work, during the reference week.

reports the distribution of standard hours for office and non-office employees, according to the most recently published data from Labour Canada's annual survey of wages and working conditions in establishments of 20 or more employees. The most common standard work-week in all industries is 40 hours for non-office personnel and 37.5 hours for office workers. The average work-week for employees in all industries is 39.5 hours for non-office employees and 36.7 hours for office personnel; the overall average stands at 38.2 hours worked per week.

TABLE 15-11 Standard Weekly Hours, Canada, 1982: Manufacturing and All Industries

Hours per Week	All Industries %	Manufacturing %
Office employees		
Fewer than 35 hours	3	2
35 hours	29	21
Between 35 and 37.5 hours	15	11
37.5 hours	43	39
More than 37.5 hours	10	27
Average for office employees	36.7 hrs.	37.4 hrs.
Non-office employees		
Fewer than 37.5 hours	6	5
37.5 hours	10	3
Between 37.5 and 40 hours	7	2
40 hours	68	82
More than 40 hours	6	7
Average for non-office employees	39.5 hrs.	39.8 hrs.
Office and non-office employees		
Average	38.2 hrs.	39.2 hrs.

Sources: Canada, Labour Canada, *Working Conditions in Canadian Industry 1982* (Ottawa: Minister of Supply and Services Canada, 1983), pp. 4, 6; and tabulations by the Commission.

Note: Averages are calculated using the method specified in Chan F. Aw, "Standard Hours of Work: Trends, Determinants and Implications" (Ottawa: Labour Canada, Economics and Industrial Relations Research Branch, 1982).

Data available for standard hours in manufacturing cover a much longer period than data for the economy as a whole. Table 15-12 records data pertaining to standard weekly hours in manufacturing, for intermittent years from 1870 to 1946, and annually, for the years from 1949 to 1982; figures for the latter period are based on Labour Canada's survey of working conditions.

The evidence shows that the standard work-week diminished fairly steadily over most of the current century, but the reduction became very gradual during the 1960s and 1970s. Relatively sharp declines in the standard work-week were observed immediately after both the First World War and the Second World War. It has been suggested that during those periods, the fear of a substantial rise in unemployment, as a result of soldiers returning from active service, generated increased pressure to reduce the work-week.[1] Another possibility is that the long gradual reduction of the work-week was halted by the need to maintain output during the two wars, but that the process resumed its normal course after each one.

TABLE 15-12 Standard Weekly Hours in Canadian Manufacturing, Selected Years, 1870 to 1982

Year	Hours	Year	Hours
1870	64.0	1962	40.4
1901	58.6	1963	40.3
1911	56.5	1964	40.2
1921	50.3	1965	40.2
1926	50.2	1966	40.2
1931	49.6	1967	40.0
1936	49.2	1968	39.9
1941	49.0	1969	39.9
1946	48.7	1970	39.8
1949	43.5	1971	39.8
1950	43.2	1972	39.7
1951	42.6	1973	39.6
1952	42.3	1974	39.5
1953	42.0	1975	39.4
1954	41.5	1976	39.4
1955	41.3	1977	39.3
1956	41.1	1978	39.3
1957	40.0	1979	39.3
1958	40.7	1980	39.2
1959	40.6	1981	39.2
1960	40.6	1982	39.2
1961	40.4		

Sources: 1870 Calculations by O.J. Firestone, cited in S. Ostry and M. Zaidi, *Labour Economics in Canada*, 3d ed. (Toronto: Macmillan, 1979), p. 80.

1901–46 Calculations by G. Saunders and S.M.A. Hameed using unpublished Labour Canada data, reported in Ostry and Zaidi, *Labour Economics in Canada*, p. 80.

1949–79 Calculations by Chan F. Aw, "Standard Hours of Work: Trends, Determinants and Implications" (Ottawa: Labour Canada, Economics and Industrial Relations Research Branch, 1982) for Labour Canada, using *Working Conditions in Canadian Industry*.

1980–82 Calculations by the Commission using Labour Canada's *Working Conditions in Canadian Industry*.

Data relating to standard hours for industries other than manufacturing and for the all-industry composite are available only for the years from 1963 on. Tabulations for the period from 1963 to 1979 show that the reduction rate of standard hours did not level out in all industries during the 1960s and 1970s.[2] Between 1963 and 1979, the standard work-week for the manufacturing sector decreased by one hour; there was a similar or smaller reduction of working time in transportation and communication, trade and finance. The standard work-week decreased, over this same period, by more than two hours in forestry and mining, and by five hours in service employment. The average reduction in weekly hours for all industries was 1.8 hours. Empirical analyses of the Canadian post-war data on weekly work-hours suggest that one of the most important factors in the long-term reduction is the rise in the real-wage rate over time.[3]

Gradual decreases in the standard work-week have been accompanied by decreases in the work-year, resulting from more holidays and longer annual vacations. Table 15-13 indicates that over the 30-year period from 1949 to 1979, holidays in the manufacturing sector have increased from 6.9 days per year to 11.1 days per year, and annual vacations have extended from 2.3 weeks per year to 3.6 weeks per year. Taking account of the increase in holidays and vacations, the manufacturing sector's net standard work-week, that is, the (gross) standard work-week minus the average hours per week deducted for holidays and vacations, dropped from 40.4 hours to 34.9 hours, between 1949 and 1979. For all industries, it dropped from 36.7 hours to 34.0 hours, between 1964 and 1979. These declines are close to the trend in process over the last century, representing a decrease in the work-week of about two hours per decade.

Determinants of Working Time

In non-union environments, work schedules, like wages and other working conditions, officially appear to be set unilaterally by the employer. Employers have an economic incentive, however, to take account of the work preferences of their employees, and as a result, work schedules are actually determined by interaction that involves both employers' and employees' preferences. An employee's preference for the number of hours of work in each time period will depend on demographic factors such as the individual's age, health and number of dependents; environmental factors such as the temperature and cleanliness of the work site; the physical nature of the work; and monetary factors such as the wage rate and the individual's other sources of income.

A change in the real wage has offsetting effects on preferred working time. On the one hand, an increase in the real wage makes work more attractive relative to leisure, and this change influences the employee's preference to work more hours. On the other hand, the larger income associated with an increase in real wages makes employees better off and usually induces them to "consume more leisure", that is, to work less. Empirical evidence suggests that for most workers, the latter effect tends to dominate: this means that

TABLE 15-13 Trends in Holiday and Vacation Time, Canada, Selected Years, 1949–1979

	Manufacturing				All Industries	
Year	Gross Standard Hours	Holidays in Days per Year	Vacation in Weeks per Year	Net Standard Hours	Gross Standard Hours	Net Standard Hours
1949	43.5	6.9	2.3	40.4	—	—
1954	41.5	7.4	2.4	38.4	—	—
1959	40.6	7.8	2.7	37.3	—	—
1964	40.2	8.0	2.8	36.8	40.1	36.7
1969	39.9	8.8	3.1	36.2	39.5	35.8
1974	39.5	10.1	3.4	35.4	38.8	34.8
1979	39.3	11.1	3.6	34.9	38.3	34.0

Source: Chan F. Aw, "Standard Hours of Work: Trends, Determinants and Implications" (Ottawa: Labour Canada, Economics and Industrial Relations Research Branch, 1982), pp. 16, 64.

increased real-wage rates generally reduce the number of hours a person wishes to work. Indeed, over extended periods, the main source of reductions in working time has been increased real wages.

An employer's need for interaction among employees may require that working hours be standardized to some degree; each employee, therefore, cannot simply be allowed to work his or her preferred number of hours each week. Other considerations being equal, however, the firm has an incentive to offer its staff a work schedule which corresponds as closely as possible to the typical employee's preferred hours of work each week. The greater the divergence of actual hours and preferred hours, the greater the tendency for employees to leave the firm to obtain their preferred hours elsewhere, and the higher the wage the employer must pay to attract and retain the desired work-force.

The employer must also consider certain person-specific costs of employment. Costs such as those for dental insurance premiums, which are set at a fixed amount per employee, belong in this category as do the costs of hiring and training employees, amortized over some expected term of employment at the firm. An employer must pay certain person-specific employment-related costs for each staff member. This requirement creates an incentive for the employer to keep the staff as small as possible and thus keep the firm's person-specific costs to a minimum. This incentive might well induce an employer to increase the number of hours of work per employee beyond the work-time preferred by employees. Longer hours, however, may reduce job satisfaction, increase employee fatigue, and necessitate payment of premium-wage rates for hours worked beyond some standard level set by legislation or collective agreement. The wise employer, then, will choose a work schedule which minimizes costs, based on the net effect of these various factors.

Barriers to Work-Time Reduction

Because work schedules reflect the wishes of both the employer and the employee, they may not be ideal from the perspective of either party. This Commission's view is that work schedules should reflect the preferences of employees as far as this is reasonable and possible, given the requirements to achieve output. Thus any factors, other than those related to production requirements, which may cause employers to prefer more working time than their employees desire, should be examined. Several instances of such barriers have occurred as a result of employment-standards and labour-relations legislation, which has generally been written with full-time employees in mind.

One problem is caused by the ceilings on payroll taxes. Workers' Compensation legislation in all jurisdictions and legislation relating to the Canada (or Quebec) Pension Plan, which covers all employees, requires employers to contribute a specified percentage of each employee's annual earnings, up to a ceiling level per employee. For Unemployment Insurance (UI), employers are required to pay UI premiums on earnings up to a weekly ceiling level per employee. (In 1985, this ceiling represented 3.29 per cent of earnings, up to a maximum insurable-earnings level of $460 per week for each employee.[4]) The purpose of the ceilings is to prevent benefits, which are also proportional to earnings up to the ceiling, from reaching an inappropriately high level for high-income earners.

An unintended effect of the ceilings, however, is to create a person-specific cost for individuals earning above the ceiling. If work hours are reduced and additional employees are hired, the proportion of earnings subject to contribution will rise. The annual ceilings on CPP and Workers' Compensation thus create a barrier against those working less than a full year; the weekly ceiling on UI creates a barrier against those working less than a full week. Simulations indicate that, as a result of the ceilings on these statutory benefits, the replacement of one full-time worker by two half-time employees would increase labour costs by up to 2.5 per cent, depending on the initial earnings level.[5] The effect is directly related to the proportionate reduction in hours.

It would be desirable to eliminate these artificial barriers, since employer bias towards longer hours and fewer employees results in work schedules which do not entirely reflect employee preferences; in addition, this bias reduces opportunities for Canadians seeking work. Simply to eliminate the ceilings on contributions is inappropriate, however, since the ceilings have a social purpose. A better solution would be to base premiums for Unemployment Insurance, Workers' Compensation and Canada Pension Plan on *hourly* earnings, with a ceiling to limit the amount subject to contribution. This action would eliminate the bias against those working fewer hours, while maintaining the function of the ceilings. Of course, it might be necessary to retain the weekly or annual earnings basis for premiums when it was impractical to measure weekly hours of work. This would not be a serious drawback, however, because policies to reduce weekly hours of work would also prove impractical in such situations.

Employment-standards legislation typically requires employees to have worked for a minimum continuous period to establish their eligibility for benefits such as paid public holidays and the right to receive notice of termination of employment. The Canada Labour Code, for example, entitles an employee to nine paid holidays a year, provided that he or she has been employed for at least 30 days and has worked at least 15 of the 30 calendar days preceding the holiday. This provision would disqualify an employee who worked only three days a week, although it would not affect one who worked only four hours a day. The bias against some categories of reduced hours could be eliminated, while the purpose of the requirement for continued employment could be retained. This might be done, for example, by specifying that an employee must have worked at least 60 per cent of his or her normally scheduled hours in the preceding 30 days.

Another bias stems from the administrative practice of some Labour Relations Boards of specifying separate bargaining units for part-time employees. The Ontario Labour Relations Board, for example, excludes from a bargaining unit for full-time workers any employees who work fewer than 24 hours a week. Groups of part-time employees are entitled to certification as separate bargaining units. One possible effect of segregating part-time employees is that a full-time employee who opts to reduce his or her weekly work to 20 hours may no longer be covered by the wages and benefits provided in the collective agreement.

The Ontario Labour Relations Board has expressed a view that full-time and part-time employees do not share enough interests to make it practical for them to be included in the same bargaining unit. The recent Commission of Inquiry into Part-time Work, however, found that the practice of segregating part-time employees contributed to inequitable wages and working conditions for that group. That Commission therefore recommended that Labour Relations Boards include all part-time employees, both regular and casual, in the same bargaining unit as full-time employees.[6] To adopt this recommendation would help to eliminate any bias there might be against reduced work time in the Canadian economy.

Privately negotiated fringe benefits can also create an unintended bias against reduced working time. Table 15-14 shows expenditures on fringe benefits in Canada during 1978, the most recent year for which published data are available for Statistics Canada's occasional survey of compensation costs. The table indicates that fringe benefits add almost 33 per cent to workers' straight-time pay. Although many of these benefits are proportional to hours worked, some, such as medical, dental and life insurance, represent person-specific costs which might make employers prefer to schedule longer hours of work for their employees. If employer contributions to these plans were pro-rated according to the number of hours worked, the plans would no longer represent a barrier. Since such a change would not significantly increase administrative costs, Canadian governments should encourage such pro-rating through collective bargaining, personnel policies or legislation.

TABLE 15-14 Fringe Benefit Expenditures per Employee, Canada, 1978, (Statistics Canada data)

Item	Average Annual Expendi- ture per Employee	Percent- age of Total Employee Compen- sation	Percent- age of Basic Pay for Regular Work
Basic pay for regular work	12 301	74.6	100.00
Commissions, incentive bonuses	263	1.6	2.14
Overtime, including premium pay	522	3.2	4.24
Shift-work premium pay	46	0.3	0.37
Other premium pay	53	0.3	0.43
Total pay for time worked	13 185	80.0	107.18
Paid absence			
Paid holidays	586	3.6	4.76
Vacation pay	794	4.8	6.46
Sick leave pay	170	1.0	1.38
Personal or other pay	27	0.2	0.22
Total paid absence	1 577	9.6	12.82
Miscellaneous direct payments			
Floating COLA	61	0.4	0.49
Bonuses (Christmas, etc.)	51	0.3	0.42
Severance pay	30	0.2	0.24
Taxable Benefits			
Provincial medicare	82	0.5	0.67
Other benefits	57	0.4	0.46
Other payments	28	0.2	0.23
Total miscellaneous direct payments	310	1.9	2.52
Gross payroll (total direct payments)	15 071	91.4	122.51
Employer contributions to employee welfare and benefit plans			
Workmen's Compensation	186	1.1	1.51
Unemployment Insurance	209	1.3	1.70
Canada/Quebec Pension Plan	161	1.0	1.31
Private pension plans	558	3.4	4.53
Quebec Health Insurance Board	59	0.4	0.48
Private life and health plans	203	1.2	1.65
Other benefit plans	33	0.2	0.27
Total	1 410	8.6	11.46
Total Employee Compensation	16 481	100.0	133.97

Source: Statistics Canada, *Employee Compensation in Canada, All Industries, 1978*, Cat. No. 72-619 (Ottawa: Minister of Supply and Services Canada, 1980), pp. 16–19.

In this section Commissioners have identified a number of labour-market policies and privately negotiated arrangements which result in work schedules that do not fully reflect employee preferences. It makes sense to change these polices and arrangements even when the economy supports full employment. In times of above-normal unemployment, these changes might prevent a situation in which some Canadians are working longer hours than they wish, while others are not working at all.

A related issue is the way employment and hours of work respond to cyclical fluctuations in the economy. The choice between lay-offs and reduced hours (or, if both are used, the proportion of each) depends on a variety of factors that reflect employer and employee preferences. In general, employees and employers can assess these costs and benefits and make the appropriate choices, and there is little need for public policy involvement. However, existing policies may unintentionally bias the choice. Thus it is important to examine policies for potential biases.

The existing Unemployment Insurance system represents an important obstacle to reduced hours because it provides benefits to individuals out of work for a full week, but not to individuals whose income falls because of reduced working hours. This arrangement makes employers and employees more likely to prefer lay-offs to reduced hours of work as a means of responding to temporary reductions in labour demand. Such an unintended bias toward lay-offs can be eliminated by changing either UI financing or benefit provisions. As noted earlier concerning the UI system, experience rating of the financing of unemployment insurance would have several advantages; one of these would be that it offsets the tendency to choose lay-offs by making them costly to the firm. The alternative is a short-term/compensation program which operates on the benefits side.

A short-term/compensation program was introduced in Canada in January 1982. Essentially, the program involves redistributing the UI benefits that would have been paid to laid-off workers. Thus persons whose hours of work are reduced receive some additional income in the form of UI benefits. The combination of an increase in leisure time and a relatively small reduction of income makes the program attractive to most employees. Employers face somewhat higher costs than they would face with lay-offs; the additional costs take the form of fringe benefits and administrative expenses associated with the program. However, benefits, too, accrue to employers: reduced costs associated with lay-off and recall; less reduction in employee productivity because of loss of work experience; and less possibility of loss of experienced employees who do not return on recall. Experience with the program suggests that these costs and benefits roughly offset one another.[7]

UI expenditures have been considerably higher – by a factor of 1.35 – under the program compared to those of conventional unemployment insurance. The two main reasons were the waiving of the normal two-week waiting period, a device to make the program more attractive to senior employees whose risk of lay-off was low, and the provision that the program was not to reduce eligibility for conventional UI. As a result of the second provision, about half the employees originally designated for lay-off were laid off after the short-term/compensation agreement was terminated, thus raising the overall costs of the program.

Because of the higher cost of the short-term/compensation program, in the form both of additional UI expenditures and of extra administrative costs, this Commission prefers to operate on the financing side to offset any tendency toward lay-offs made possible by the design of the Unemployment Insurance system. Experience rating brings several other important benefits, as well. Until implementation of experience rating is complete, however, it will be useful to retain the short-term/compensation program, although it might possibly be modified to some extent in order to reduce the unemployment-insurance costs and administrative complexity.

Notes

1. Lise Poulin-Simon, "Le loisir industriel, variable d'ajustement économique aux crises de l'emploi", *Loisir et Société* 6 (1983): 187–207.
2. Chan F. Aw, "Standard Hours of Work: Trends, Determinants and Implications" (Ottawa: Labour Canada, Economics and Industrial Relations Research Branch, 1982), p. 64.
3. S.M.A. Hameed, "Economic and Institutional Determinants of the Average Work Week in Canada", in *Work and Leisure in Canada*, edited by S.M.A. Hameed and D. Cullen (Edmonton: University of Alberta, Faculty of Business Administration and Commerce, 1975), pp. 1–18; Keith Newton and Norm Leckie, "Determinants of Weekly Work Hours in Canada", *Industrial Relations* 34 (1979): 257–71; and Aw, "Standard Hours of Work".
4. Canada, Employment and Immigration Canada, *Benefit Rate and Duration* (Ottawa: The Department, 1984).
5. N. Meltz, G. Swartz, and F. Reid, *Sharing the Work: An Analysis of the Issues in Worksharing and Jobsharing* (Toronto: University of Toronto Press, 1981).
6. Canada, Commission of Inquiry into Part-time Work, *Part-time Work in Canada: Report of the Commission of Inquiry into Part-time Work* (Ottawa: Labour Canada, 1983), p. 31.
7. For a more detailed discusison, see the Commission study by Frank Reid, "Reductions in Work Time: An Assessment of Employment Sharing to Reduce Unemployment", in *Work and Pay: The Canadian Labour Market*, vol. 17 (Toronto: University of Toronto Press, 1985).

CHAPTER 16

Immigration Policy

CHAPTER 16

Immigration Policy

Introduction

Over the years, Canada's immigration policies have done much to shape the nature of modern Canadian society: its cultural texture and ethnic composition, and the ever-expanding stock of its traditions, aspirations and potential antagonisms. Today, with increasing population pressures around the globe, these policies are becoming even more important. To determine how they should be shaped, we must find answers to a number of questions: How open a society do we wish to be? How large a flow of new migrants can we absorb? How do our immigration policies fit within a principal-power role? What is the function of immigration in adjusting our economy to the competitive pressures of the late twentieth century?

In recent years, the Canadian government's long-standing post-Second World War policy on immigration has changed. The 1966 White Paper on Immigration took the position that "Immigration has made a major contribution to the national objectives of maintaining a high rate of population and economic growth."[1] Just eight years later, the government's Green Paper took a much different stance. It stated that "to many Canadians, living in a modern industrialized and increasingly urbanized society, the benefits of high rates of population growth appear dubious on several grounds."[2] More recently, and especially since 1982, Canadian immigration policy has become more restrictive.

Since the Second World War, Canadian immigration policies have also altered the predominately Western European character of most of Canada's provinces and large cities. Today, Canadians are no longer a people of only two languages and cultures; instead, we are increasingly multi-racial and multi-cultural. Reforms in immigration policies in 1962 eliminated all references to racial and ethnic characteristics as criteria for admission of new permanent residents, and policy makers evolved an objective "points" system to ensure even-handed consideration of all applicants. Similar changes in the admission criteria applicable to stateless or displaced persons have enabled refugees from outside Western Europe to apply for, and gain, entry to Canada during the post-war period. It seems likely that in future years, a substantial proportion of newcomers will be attracted from non-European nations, and these new Canadians will continue to expand the diversification of our cultural and ethnic mix. These important changes in Canada's racial and ethnic composition will continue to transform our economic and political life in the coming decades. They are also likely to generate a certain amount of social conflict, and future generations of Canadians will need to invent new policies and techniques for coping with the stresses of a vibrant and dynamic multi-cultural society.

Notes

1. Canada, Minister of Manpower and Immigration, *White Paper on Immigration* (Ottawa: Queen's Printer, 1966), p. 7.
2. Canada, Department of Manpower and Immigration, *Immigration Policy Perspectives*, a report of the Canadian Immigration and Population Study (Ottawa: Information Canada, 1974), p. 5.

Canada's Present Immigration Policy

Canada's immigration policy is currently conducted under the legislative authority of the 1978 Immigration Act. The federal and provincial governments share jurisdiction over immigration, although provincial legislation has effect only insofar as it does not conflict with federal legislation. The two levels of government consult each year in the process of determining planned immigration levels, since immigration has wide-ranging consequences for several areas of provincial interest: housing, health care, education, regional labour markets and social services.

Current legislation specifies three classes of immigrants: family class, convention refugees and designated classes, and economic (or independent) classes. Data on numbers admitted under each of these classes are detailed in Table 16-1. Family-class immigration is intended to reunite families; immigrants in this category are not assessed according to their suitability for the Canadian labour market. The relative importance of family-class immigration has increased in recent years.

The refugee class is identified on the basis of the United Nations Convention and Protocol relating to the Status of Refugees, but other "designated classes" are authorized under the Canadian Act in times of crisis.

TABLE 16-1 Immigration by Class, 1966–1983

Year	Family Class (%)	Assisted Relatives (%)	Independent (%)	Refugees and Designated Class (%)	Total Number of Immigrants
1966	34.2	—	65.8	—	194 743
1970	21.8	23.8	54.4	—	147 713
1971	27.4	24.1	48.5	—	121 900
1972	27.1	25.2	43.5	4.2	122 006
1973	22.6	24.0	52.1	1.3	184 200
1974	24.8	24.3	50.1	0.8	218 465
1975	34.1	24.3	38.6	3.0	187 881
1976	40.7	21.8	29.6	7.9	149 429
1977	44.7	22.7	26.2	6.4	114 914
1978	52.8	19.9	22.4	4.9	86 313
1979	41.7	10.2	23.2	24.9	112 096
1980	35.7	9.4	26.7	28.2	143 117
1982	41.3	37.7		14.0	121 147
1983	54.6	29.7		15.7	89 157

Sources: Canada, Employment and Immigration Canada, *Annual Report To Parliament on Immigration Levels* (Ottawa: The Department, 1981), Table 11, p. 42; *Background Paper on Future Immigration Levels* (Ottawa: Minister of Supply and Services Canada, 1984), p. 4, and *Immigration Levels, 1985–1987: Analytical Considerations* (Ottawa: The Department, 1984), p. 9.

As is indicated in Table 16-1, the number of immigrants admitted under this category fluctuates from year to year. Recently, the number of refugees has been relatively large because Canada has accepted significant numbers of people in this category from South-East Asia. In fact, Canada has one of the world's biggest refugee-resettlement programs, relative to the size of its population. This is a commendable record, and one which our country should strive to maintain.

The final group of immigrants consists of those in the "economic" or "independent" class. These include "selected" workers (selected, that is, according to job-market criteria), entrepreneurs, the self-employed, and assisted relatives of Canadian citizens. Prospective immigrants in this class become eligible for admission by way of a points system. Points are awarded, for example, according to levels of education and training, occupational demand and arranged employment, work experience, area of destination within Canada, relatives within Canada, knowledge of our official languages, and personal characteristics. The number of points necessary for admission varies, depending on the applicant's category: entrepreneur, self-employed, retired, assisted relative, or independent. As of May 1982, except for entrepreneurs and self-employed persons, only those applicants with pre-arranged employment approved in advance by a Canada Employment Centre are eligible for entry. This requirement has resulted in a sharp decrease in the numbers of applicants admitted under this category, compared to earlier years. It is in this sense that our immigration policy has lately become more restrictive.

Designing Our Immigration Policy

Canada's immigration policy has several goals, some of which conflict and require trade-offs. Demographic objectives involve our federal government in choices concerning the size, rate of growth, and age structure of the Canadian population. Social or humanitarian objectives focus on family reunification and the admission of refugees. Economic objectives are general, fostering the development of a strong and viable economy and the prosperity of all regions of Canada.

Our immigration policy has long been tied to the concept of "absorptive capacity" which, in turn, has become more closely linked to labour-market conditions. Before May 1982, labour-market analyses and forecasts, based on unemployment and vacancy rates, were used to estimate demand in almost 500 occupational categories. Occupational rating determined the number of points assigned to a given occupation in processing the application of a prospective immigrant. This procedure, however, was not entirely satisfactory. Subjective judgement played a significant part in determining individual ratings, and although, ideally, the method of selecting immigrants should have been forward looking, it relied, in fact, on data showing the past state of our labour market. Moreover, if an occupational category was opened during any given period, there was no way to control the numbers of immigrants who could enter by way of that opening.

Recent research has shown that workers admitted to specific employment suffer the same unemployment rate as other immigrants.[1] Thus, while attempts are currently being made to develop a better forecasting system for job vacancies, the present immigrant-unemployment statistics raise the fundamental issue of whether this class of immigrants should be targeted to specific jobs at all, or whether greater flexibility in the matter of job selection is a preferable basis of choice. Relatively young, well-qualified and well-educated applicants could be better suited to exercise this greater flexibility than applicants preferred because of more specific occupational qualifications.

Canadians gain when persons with valuable training and education immigrate to Canada. Over the post-war period, the education and skills levels of immigrants have enriched our society and improved the performance of our economy. The result, however, is that while we may save on the expense of providing education and skill-development opportunities for recent immigrants, other countries lose some of the benefits of their investment in their citizens' education. The fact that an increasing proportion of Canada's immigrants are coming from developing countries adds further weight to this Commission's belief that Canada should improve our foreign-aid and development-assistance record.

While Canada gains by following an occupationally selective system of immigration, this course runs the risk of making us more dependent on immigration for certain types of skilled workers. Canadians may find that particular occupations become difficult to enter, for training and apprenticeship programs may become scarce if employers can rely on pre-trained immigrants. To prevent "bottlenecks" in the supply of specific skills, it is certainly useful for Canada to have the option of allowing skilled workers to enter our country when an equivalent domestic group cannot be developed quickly. The same result can often be achieved just as effectively, however, through short-term methods such as employment visas or authorizations. Indeed, the existing employment-visa system is now quite extensive: it provided an estimated 47 000 person-years of labour to our economy in 1983. This is a considerable number when one considers that net immigration in 1982–83 totalled only 61 000 persons, not all of whom would join the labour force. Whatever system is adopted, employers, labour and government must co-operate very closely in identifying Canada's specific needs and openings for particular skills.

Note

1. Canada, Employment and Immigration Canada, "Seminar on Immigration Levels for 1985–1987" (Ottawa: The Department, 1984), p. 7.

Setting the Level of Immigration

Currently, the numbers of immigrants in each category are planned separately. The refugee category is planned only one year ahead, because of the volatility of the refugee situation; the other categories are planned on a three-year horizon, subject to an annual review. The Act requires the minister to report to Parliament on the way in which demographic considerations have been taken into account in determining planned immigration levels. The current projection is that given an unchanged fertility rate and a net immigration of approximately 50 000 persons per year, Canada's population will reach 27 to 28 million people by the end of this century.[1] About 2020, however, if present fertility and net immigration rates continue, our population will peak at about 29 million and then begin a slow decline. As yet, there has been little public debate about the implications of a diminishing population, but in the decades ahead, this trend will become an important issue for Canadians to ponder. For a fuller review of demographic trends, a variety of forecasts are included in Chapter 7.

If one takes a very long-term view and considers the levels at which our population will eventually stabilize, provided that present assumptions about fertility and net immigration prove true, then our current fertility rate and our net immigration flow of about 50 000 persons per year would leave Canada, after about 200 years, with a stationary population slightly above 10 million. To maintain our current population level of about 25 million people with our current fertility rate, net immigration would have to more than double to about roughly 125 000 persons per year. This projection gives some indication of the importance of immigration levels in determining the size of Canada's population in the long term. Of course, the fertility rate is an even more important variable in such calculations, and historically, ours has varied substantially. At the moment, fertility rates across the countries of the developed world, including Canada, are at low levels, but it is impossible to tell whether these levels will remain constant for a long time to come.

In Canada, the implications of low fertility have so far received relatively little public attention. The government of Quebec, in a document issued recently,[2] notes that province's rapid decline in fertility and calls for public debate on the policies needed to maintain an acceptable demographic equilibrium. In Europe, several countries have adopted explicit pro-natalist policies to boost their flagging birth rates; the policies range from generous family allowances and tax exemptions to prolonged maternity leave. Because most of these European measures are of relatively recent origin, and because it is too early to obtain an accurate assessment of their impact on fertility rates, most expert observers believe that they have made only modest contributions to slowing down the rate of decline in birth rates.[3]

These longer-term demographic concerns would be difficult to incorporate into the present process of determining immigration levels. For the economic category, admission is closely linked to labour-market considerations which, in turn, are linked to domestic business cycles. To incorporate explicit, long-term, demographic objectives for immigration levels requires a longer planning horizon and a change of criteria for determining eligibility.

The present rate of aging of Canada's population is a related demographic problem for which immigration has been suggested as one possible policy response. The projected eventual decrease in the relative size of the labour force will leave an increased tax burden on the economically active Canadians, who will have to fund pensions and social services. Population projections suggest that higher levels of immigration can contribute modestly towards increasing the size of our labour force and thus towards reducing the proportion of that segment of our total population which is over 65 years of age. For example, a population projection which assumes a constant fertility rate of 1.7 children per woman and a net immigration of 80 000 persons per year would result in a population of which 21.5 per cent would be aged 65 or older by the year 2030. (In 1980, the proportion of this age group in our population was 9.5 per cent.) A net immigration of 140 000 persons per year from 1986 onwards would reduce this proportion to 20.3 per cent; a net immigration of 20 000 persons per year would increase the proportion to 23.1 per cent.[4]

Notes

1. Canada, Employment and Immigration Canada, *Background Paper on Future Immigration Levels* (Ottawa: Minister of Supply and Services Canada, 1984).
2. Quebec, Ministère du Conseil exécutif, Secrétariat au Développement social, *L'Évolution de la population du Québec et ses conséquences* (Quebec: le Ministère, 1984).
3. Statistics Canada, *Current Demographic Analysis: Fertility in Canada: From Baby-boom to Baby-bust*, by A. Romaniuc (Ottawa: Minister of Supply and Services Canada, 1984), p. 117.
4. Frank T. Denton and Byron G. Spencer, "Prospective Changes in the Population and Their Implications for Government Expenditures", in *Ottawa and the Provinces: The Distribution of Money and Power*, edited by David W. Conklin, Gail Cooke, and Thomas J. Courchene (Toronto: Ontario Economic Council, 1985, forthcoming), Table 1.

Other Considerations

Aside from its demographic importance, immigration contributes to the expansion of productive resources in Canada's economy. This contribution can also have consequences for the level of per capita income that our economy can generate, although these consequences are difficult to determine both in theory and in practice. There seems, for example, to be a public perception that there has been a strong positive link between aggregate growth and growth of per capita income because, historically, the one has been associated with the other. The reality, however, may be that higher real incomes induce increased immigration.

While increased immigration is unlikely to have any dramatic effect on per capita incomes in Canada, the removal of all restrictions on migration throughout the whole world would have notable effects. Though, clearly, this possibility is politically infeasible, economists have long recognized that the flow of goods across borders is a substitute for the flow of people and capital. Changes in barriers to the international flow of goods, therefore, have to be considered alongside changes in restrictions on immigration. Through multilateral trade liberalization, per capita incomes in all countries would be improved. Thus, if a further objective of our immigration policy is, in a small way, to relieve population pressures in the developing world and to raise its countries' real incomes, Canada should adopt less restrictive trade policies towards these nations.

Living in a Multi-racial/Multi-cultural Society

The dramatic impact that immigration policies have had on the increasingly multi-racial composition of our national community appears clearly in recent census data. During the post-war era, the total proportion of the population of non-British/non-French origin rose substantially, from less than 20 per cent in 1941 to 33 per cent in 1981. Whereas, in 1960, the ten leading sources of Canadian immigrants were Italy, Britain, the United States, Germany, the Netherlands, Portugal, Greece, France, Poland and Austria, in 1982, the list of countries of origin was dominated by newcomers such as India, Hong Kong, Vietnam, the Phillipines, China and Guyana. Only the United States, Britain, Poland and Germany retained their significance from the earlier period. And if one pushes the comparison even further back in time, the contrasts between the sort of political community that Canada has been and the one we Canadians are fast becoming stand out all the more starkly.

While many Canadians are understandably reluctant to encourage public debate on policies framed to deal with racial and ethnic conflicts, it is essential that we recognize and come to terms with one of the most potentially explosive sources of political conflict in our increasingly multi-racial community. While the large influx of Canadian immigrants of non-European origin has not led to anything like the racial strife that the United States experienced in the late 1960s, or that Britain suffered just a few years ago, it would be imprudent to ignore early signals indicating the possibilities of racial strife in the years ahead. Problems experienced by Haitian taxi drivers in Montreal, by Sikhs and Hindus in Vancouver, and by West Indians in Toronto indicate a need for all Canadians not only to help "settle" our new immigrants, but also to promote their full integration and participation in all occupations and walks of life. To this end, the recent *Report of the Special Committee on Visible Minorities in Canadian Society*[1] has advanced almost eighty recommendations which merit serious consideration. The creation of a harmonious multi-cultural and multi-racial society will require a high degree of tolerance and civility from all Canadians, reinforced by policies aimed at preventing foreseeable conflicts. The political viability of a less restrictive immigration policy will depend on our capacity to deal with the domestic challenges which are likely to flow from it.

Note

1. Canada, House of Commons, Special Committee on Participation of Visible Minorities in Canadian Society, *First Report to the House* (Ottawa: Queen's Printer, 1984).

Recommendations

This Commission has consciously avoided making precise recommendations about the flow of immigrants that Canada should allow to enter our country over the next few years. The matter calls for careful numerical calculations and firmly based demographic and economic models. It represents an area of Canadian policy which Commissioners perceive as little debated, under-researched, and extremely important. Commissioners are prepared, however to make several somewhat general recommendations:

- Canada should set its immigration levels on the basis of long-term objectives, rather than on that of short-term considerations. Therefore we recommend that a major study be done on Canadian demographic trends and their implications for future government policies relating to immigration, health care, education and pensions, to name only a few of the most obvious areas of concern. We Canadians need to learn much more about the problems of managing our country in the circumstances of a declining and aging population.
- Given the uncertainties involved in deciding both on an appropriate population size and on its age composition, Canada should follow that course which, in the past, has served our country well: that is, a less restrictive policy than that currently in place.
- Canada should support some increase in immigration flows closer to the historical average in post-war years. Recognizing that sudden shifts in immigration policy are undesirable, and that the current high unemployment rates in Canada make it difficult to adjust to higher levels of immigration, we propose that the Government of Canada establish a long-term plan for immigration and consider moving gradually towards higher levels of immigrants over a number of years.
- Canada should now place more weight on the general labour-market skills of potential immigrants and less on narrow occupational requirements. In Commissioners' view, given the objectives of current immigration policies, many of the weaknesses of present screening procedures are inevitable. Nevertheless, we recommend close liaison between business, labour and governments, as well as other parties interested in identifying particular needs. It is important that the criteria for selection of immigrants facilitate their absorption into Canadian society.
- In recommending this approach to immigration policy, this Commission is fully aware of the cultural, linguistic, economic and racial implications. Indeed, Commissioners recommend that immigration policy be debated more openly among Canadians, and that governments in Canada actively consider the "management" implications of a return to the more open-door policy of the 1960s.

CHAPTER 17

Labour/Management Relations

CHAPTER 17

Labour / Management Relations

Labour/management relations vitally affect the income and employment opportunities of individual Canadians, as well as the quality of Canada's work environment. During this Commission's hearings, many complaints were put forward about the state of these relations, and a wide variety of remedies was proposed. To analyse these issues requires, first, that we determine what the problems are, and then, how they can best be resolved.

Unionization and Collective Bargaining[1]

The most common measure of the extent of collective bargaining in an economy is the proportion of the non-agricultural labour force that is unionized. This measure of union density generally understates the effect of union organization, for not all workers covered by collective agreements are union members. The post-Second World War period has seen significant growth in the importance of collective bargaining in Canada. The unionized proportion of non-agricultural paid workers has increased from about 24 per cent in 1945 to about 40 per cent in 1983. By way of contrast, the unionized proportion of non-agricultural paid workers in the United States declined from about 35 per cent in 1945 to about 19 per cent in 1984, and it seems likely to continue to fall. Existing data do not provide comparable statistics on collective bargaining coverage,[2] but a recent study estimates that in 1977, about 86 per cent of employees covered by collective agreements were union members.[3] By extension of this estimate, in 1983, between 45 and 50 per cent of non-agricultural paid workers were probably covered by collective agreements.

The increased importance of collective bargaining in Canada in this period reflects several forces. One is the substantial increase in the unionization in the public and quasi-public sectors,[4] in which there was also substantial growth in employment. In addition, there has been steady but slower growth in unionization in the private sector, primarily because the area of most rapid growth in employment was that of services, a sector with a low proportion of unionization. Industries with a high propensity to unionize – manufacturing, mining, forestry, for example – experienced relatively slow employment growth.

Changes in Canadian law have provided an important impetus for the growth of unionization. Roughly speaking, the law governing collective bargaining in Canada has passed through three main stages. Phase one was the period, mostly prior to Confederation, in which the law discouraged collective bargaining. Judges interpreted the common law to hold that collective action by employees constituted a criminal conspiracy. Other criminal and civil constraints, as well, were applied to both individual and group action by workers. In the second phase, which began in the 1870s, the law took a largely neutral view of collective bargaining. In particular, the Trade Unions Act of 1872, amendments to criminal law, and other legislative actions removed many of the restrictions on union formation and the collective withdrawal of labour. This neutrality lasted until the passage of the Wartime Labour Relations Orders (P.C. 1944-1003) in 1944; since this event, our government's stance towards collective bargaining has been favourable.[5] P.C. 1944-1003, which was modelled on the Wagner Act, passed in the United States in 1935, gave most private sector employees the right to union representation and collective bargaining, provided a code of unfair labour practices, and established a labour-relations board to administer the law. A similar set of changes occurred in the mid-1960s, with respect to the public and quasi-public sectors. With the passage of the federal Public Service Staff Relations Act in 1967, and the enactment of similar legislation at provincial levels, governments encouraged collective bargaining and union formation in these sectors, which were also areas of rapid growth in employment. Thus, the post-war period became the era in which legislation provided a favourable environment for the spread of collective bargaining.

This crude division of the evolution of labour legislation into three main phases is useful, as such simplifications often are, but necessarily omits some important aspects. One is the evolution of the division of powers between the federal and provincial governments over labour-relations matters. This aspect is divisible into two main phases: pre- and post-1925. Until 1925, jurisdiction over labour-relations matters was assumed to rest with the federal government. In that period, the chief law regulating labour relations was the Industrial Disputes Investigaton Act of 1907, which made a strike or lock-out illegal in certain important industries until after an inquiry had been conducted into the dispute, and the conciliation-board report had been forwarded to the minister and made public. The Snider case (*Toronto Electric Commissioners* v. *Snider*) of 1925 changed this presumed division of powers. Labour relations, the Privy Council decided, fell under property and civil rights, and thus under provincial jurisdiction.

After the Second World War, during which our federal government exercised jurisdiction under emergency powers, each province developed its own legislation governing industrial relations. Initially, most provinces adopted legislation similar to P.C. 1944-1003. Since the late 1960s, however, provinces have experimented more with labour legislation, and provincial labour codes now vary considerably. An important advantage of the existing jurisdictional division, from a national perspective, is this ability to experiment with labour legislation, as well as to tailor the legislation to the conditions in each province.

Modelling the Wartime Labour Relations Orders P.C. 1944-1003 on the Wagner Act of the U.S. government resulted in the evolution of a unique North American industrial relations system, a system which has important structural differences from those of Europe, Japan and Australia, the other countries with which we Canadians most often compare ourselves. Of course, there are also important industrial relations differences between Canada and the United States, but the similarities are greater than the differences.

Most provinces also adopted this Wagner Act type of legislation, and in most jurisdictions there have been further legislative changes which have generally facilitated union organization. The extension of collective bargaining rights to employees in the public and quasi-public sectors is the most obvious example. Others include the broadening of the definition of "employee", which made more workers eligible for unionization; numerous changes to the certification process, which have facilitated union organization; increased restrictions on the termination of bargaining rights; and developments such as compulsory dues check-off, imposition of first contract, and stricter enforcement of the requirement to bargain in good faith, which have helped unions, once certified, to maintain their position.

The response to this favourable legislative environment has been dramatic. Table 17-1 compares growth rates for union membership and union density in seven countries, Australia, Canada, Japan, Sweden, the United Kingdom, the United States, and West Germany, between 1961 and 1980. Canada had the highest growth rate of these seven countries and, by the end of the period, had moved ahead of Japan and the United States in the ranking of countries by union density. (In 1961, Canada was at the bottom of this ranking.)

This dramatic difference in union growth in Canada relative to that in other countries is important in terms of some of the policy concerns of the last several decades: the level of strikes and lock-outs, and wage settlements, for example. The Canada-U.S. difference is especially striking, and is worth further examination.

As Figure 17-1 illustrates, union-growth patterns in Canada and the United States were similar from the 1920s to the 1960s, but they have diverged sharply since 1965. To fully assess the reasons for this sharp divergence is not possible here. One potential factor, which does *not* appear to have been an important cause, is the growth of public sector unions. There has been strong and roughly similar growth of these unions in both countries. The main difference has been that private sector unionism has declined in the United States, but grown in Canada. A study carried out for this Commission, points out that growth rates in the chief U.S. public sector unions were higher than those of their Canadian counterparts, while growth rates in the main private sector unions were significantly higher in Canada.[6]

One factor which appears to have played an important part in distinguishing Canada-U.S. union growth since the mid-1960s is the differences in laws – and their administration – governing union certification and the duty to bargain collectively in good faith. Another is the existence of a significant number of states, primarily in the South and West, with strong anti-union

TABLE 17-1 Union Membership Growth and Density in Selected Countries

Countries	Membership (in thousands)			As per Cent of Wage and Salary Earners			Average Annual Percentage Change		
	1961	1971	1981	1961	1971	1981	1961–80	1961–71	1971–81
Australia	1 895	2 437	2 994	59.0	53.1	55.8	2.4	2.5	2.1
Canada	1 447	2 231	3 487	29.5	31.1	35.3	4.6	4.4	4.6
Japan	8 154	11 684	12 355	34.3	34.2	30.6	2.2	3.7	0.6
Sweden	1 922	2 622	3 055	62.5	75.6	88.8	3.1	3.1	2.8
United Kingdom	9 916	11 126	12 182	43.4	50.3	57.5	1.4	1.2	0.9
United States	16 303	21 327	22 396	30.2	29.9	24.7[a]	1.7	2.7	0.5
West Germany	6 306	8 105	9 340	30.9	37.0	41.9	2.0	2.5	1.4

Sources: Union membership: Australia, Commonwealth Bureau of Census and Statistics, *Official Yearbook of the Commonwealth of Australia*; Canada, Labour Canada, *Labour Organizations in Canada*; Japan, Statistics and Information Department, *Yearbook of Labour Statistics*; Sweden, National Bureau of Statistics, *Statistical Abstract of Sweden*; United Kingdom, Department of Employment, *Employment Gazette*; United States, Bureau of Labor Statistics, *Directory of National Unions and Employee Associations*; West Germany, Federal Republic of Germany, *Statistiches Jahrbuch*. Wage and salary earners: OECD, *Labour Force Statistics*.

Note: International comparisons should be approached with caution in view of the different statistical methods and criteria used in compiling the figures.

a. 1980 estimate.

FIGURE 17-1 The Trend in Union Density Growth in Canada and the United States, 1921–1980

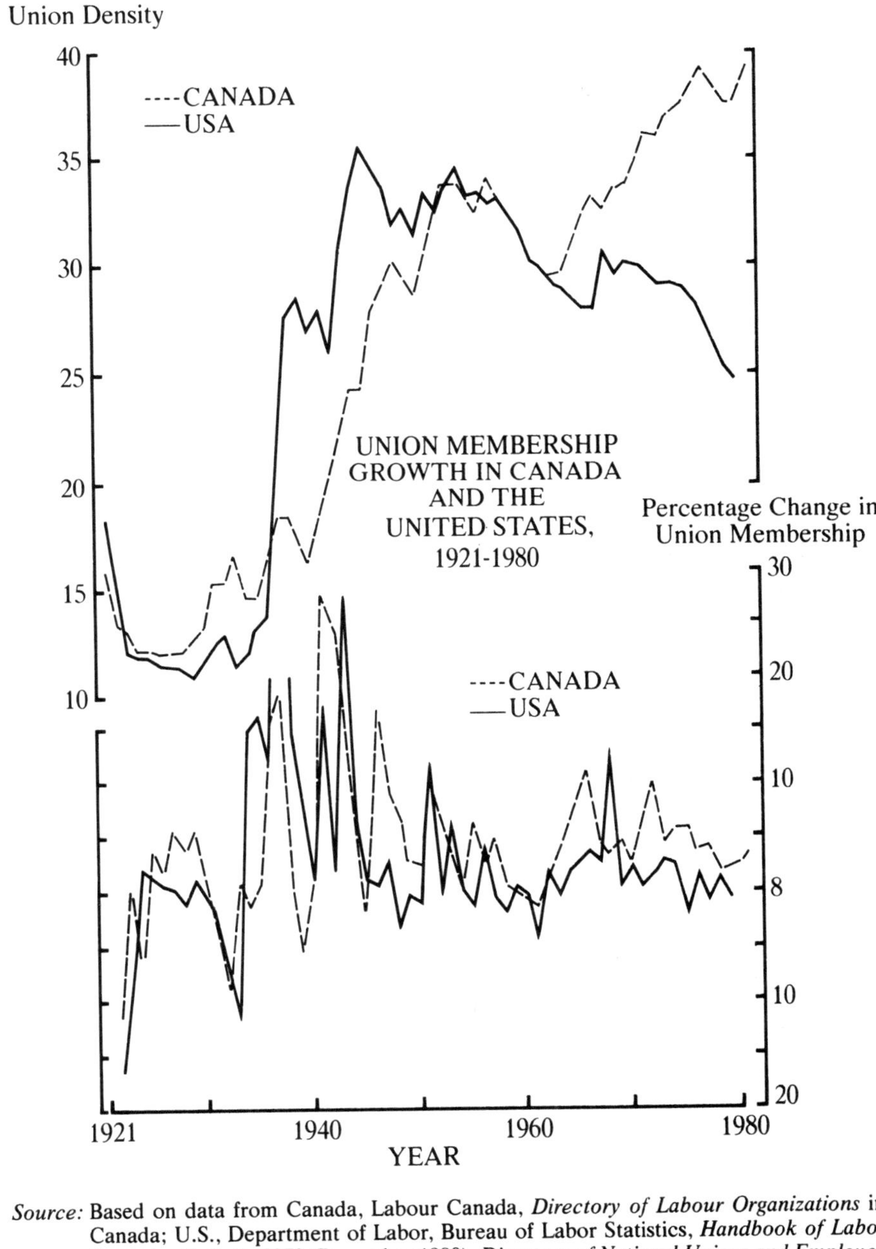

Source: Based on data from Canada, Labour Canada, *Directory of Labour Organizations* in Canada; U.S., Department of Labor, Bureau of Labor Statistics, *Handbook of Labor Statistics,* Bulletin 2070 (December 1980), *Directory of National Unions and Employee Associations, 1979,* Bulletin 1079 (September 1980) and *News* USDL 81-446, September 18, 1981.

attitudes and laws which are less favourable to union organization. The U.S. system, for instance, requires an election some time after application for union certification has been made, whereas certification is automatic in most Canadian jurisdictions once a certain percentage of the employees have signed cards indicating their desire for union representation. U.S. unions lose many of these elections, and the proportion lost has been steadily increasing over the post-war period. The anti-union stance taken by employers in these elections appears to have been relatively strong in the United States, and its strength may reflect lengthy delays in remedying unfair labour practices and related gaps in legal enforcement. In respect to the administration of the law, an important difference is the relatively weak arsenal of remedial measures against violations of the requirement to bargain in good faith that is available to the U.S. National Labor Relations Board as compared to Canadian labour-relations boards. Responding to these incentives, many American employers have extended their anti-union stand beyond the certification process to the negotiation of the first contract, with the result that only about 60 per cent of certified unions are successful in negotiating a first contract with the employer. As for the final factor, the most rapid employment growth in the past several decades has been in the southern and western States. This rapid employment growth appears to contribute to a tendency for companies opening new plants to locate in areas that minimize the risk of union organization.

While the U.S. trend away from the union movement results from numerous additional factors, it clearly reflects, in part, an environment that has become increasingly hostile to collective bargaining. One of the concerns of the union movement is that a similarly hostile environment may develop in Canada. Such a development would require reversing many of the legislative changes made in the post-war era, and is, in this Commission's view, unlikely.

Examination of Canadians' attitudes towards unions is worthwhile, for policy makers will no doubt take into account public opinion.[7] According to the Decima Quarterly Report on Public Affairs Trends, Canadians who were asked to rate their confidence in the leaders of twenty institutions (including banks, schools, provincial governments, oil companies, the federal government, multi-national corporations, newspapers, and the tobacco industry) consistently expressed less confidence in the leaders of labour unions than in those of any other institution. Even in union families, confidence in labour unions is low, although not as low as it is in non-union families. In response to a Decima question (asked in summer 1981 and summer 1982) forcing respondents to choose between "Unions in Canada have become too powerful" and "Unions are necessary in Canada to protect workers from exploitation", over 55 per cent of respondents chose "too powerful". Another Decima question (posed in summer 1980 and summer 1982) asked respondents whether they favoured or oppose greater government control over labour-union activity. Over 60 per cent of respondents favoured greater control; even among union members, a majority favoured greater government control over labour-union activity.

There is some evidence which suggests that Canadians' attitude toward labour unions has become less favourable over time. As the Honourable

André Ouellet, former Minister of Labour, pointed out in his brief to this Commission, the Gallup Poll has, since 1950, asked respondents whether they think labour unions are good or bad for Canada. In the 1950 – 58 period, between 10 and 20 per cent answered "Bad" and between 60 and 70 per cent "Good". (The rest gave a qualified answer or expressed no opinion.) However, in the 1976–82 period, between 30 per cent and 42 per cent of respondents answered "Bad", and between 42 per cent and 54 per cent answered "Good".

The responses to these questions are, of course, open to a variety of interpretations. During the course of our meetings with the public, Commissioners found no strong anti-union attitudes among Canadians. In our experience, the role of the union movement in representing its members is respected and accepted. The focus of public concern is the creation of less adversarial labour-management relations and development of a better process for resolving industrial conflicts. The recommendations Commissioners make later in this section are intended to contribute to this outcome.

Notes

1. Further details on much of the material in this section are available in two studies prepared for this Commission: Pradeep Kumar, "Union Growth in Canada: Retrospect and Prospect", in *Canadian Labour Relations*, vol. 16, and Joseph M. Weiler, "The Role of Law in Labour Relations", in *Labour Law and Urban Law in Canada*, vol. 51, (Toronto: University of Toronto Press, 1985).
2. Data on collective bargaining coverage indicate coverage, in 1982, of 58 per cent, in establishments of 20 or more employees. However, because unions are much more common in establishments with 20 or more employees than in smaller establishments, and because the survey on which these data are based was limited in several other respects, these data overstate the importance of collective bargaining in the Canadian economy.
3. See R.J. Adams, "Estimating the Extent of Collective Bargaining in Canada", Research Paper No. 223 (Hamilton: McMaster University, Faculty of Business, April 1984).
4. The term "public sector" refers to employees of federal, provincial and municipal governments. "Quasi-public sector" refers to employees in education, health, and related sectors which are primarily publicly funded.
5. Of course, this characterization of the evolution of collective bargaining law in terms of three main phases omits important developments within each phase. During the second phase, in particular, there were a number of legislative changes which made union organization somewhat easier. Furthermore, prior to the Second World War, some provinces passed legislation which could be considered forerunners of P.C. 1944-1003.
6. Kumar, "Union Growth in Canada".
7. The following dicussion of attitudes is primarily based on a Commission study by Richard Johnston, *Public Opinion and Public Policy in Canada*, vol. 35 (Toronto: University of Toronto Press, 1985).

Public Sector Labour Relations

Legislation permitting collective bargaining by government employees first appeared in Saskatchewan in 1944, but the process of extending collective bargaining rights to public sector employees began in earnest with amendments to the Quebec labour code in 1964. Three years later, in 1967, the federal government passed the Public Service Staff Relations Act (PSSRA), permitting employees of the federal government and its agencies to bargain collectively. This innovative legislation seems to have encouraged the other provinces to extend collective bargaining rights to their employees. At present, all Canada's jurisdictions grant collective bargaining rights to their public sector employees, but these rights range from the right to bargain collectively over a narrow range of issues, without the right to strike, to full collective bargaining including the right to strike. Public sector wage-restraint programs, which were initiated in 1982, and which remain in force in some jurisdictions, place additional restrictions on collective bargaining.

The legislative initiatives undertaken in the 1960s by our federal and provincial governments have been described as a "bold experiment". Certainly, Canada has gone further than most of the other countries with which we often compare ourselves in giving employees of the public and quasi-public sectors the right to bargain collectively and the right to strike. To construct detailed comparisons in this regard between Canada and other countries would be a difficult task, but a skeletal summary may be useful. The United States and the United Kingdom are the most obvious choices for comparison, since the United States shares with Canada a common private sector model for collective bargaining, and both the United States and the United Kingdom have exercised important, though unequal, influence on our industrial relations system.

Virtually all public sector employees in Canada are covered by comprehensive statutes which grant them the right to organize themselves into unions and to engage in collective bargaining. This right is not as well defined in some other countries. In the United States, for example, federal employees are permitted to form or join unions, but they lack the right to bargain with their employer. Compensation is set, primarily, according to comparability with the private sector. At the state level, the individual's right to form and join a union is protected, but the right to bargain collectively is not guaranteed in the absence of statutory provisions. Many States have been reluctant to provide such legislation. In Britain, while there are no statutory requirements that public sector employers must engage in collective bargaining with representatives of their employees, it would be unusual for employers to refuse to do so. The pay rates for employees of the central government (civil servants) are determined primarily by "fair comparisons" with the private sector.

The scope of bargaining in Canada's public sector is generally more limited than that in the private sector, but such limitations are also common in the United States. While Britain has no such statutory limitations, bargaining through a centralized structure tends to impose limits on issues that are normally subject to negotiation.

There are major differences, especially between Canada and the United States in the area of dispute-resolution procedures. Canada's federal sector is marked by a unique feature in that the employees' bargaining agent alone may select either the conciliation-strike or the arbitration route as the means for resolution of an interest dispute, should negotiations fail to produce an agreement. Our provinces tend to rely extensively on binding arbitration as the ultimate method of resolving interest disputes in the public sector. Nevertheless, the Canadian system goes far beyond that of the United States in permitting the use of the strike weapon. While limitations on the right to strike do exist in Canada, they fall far short of the outright ban that is in effect for most public sector employees in the United States.

The response to the legislative initiatives of the 1960s was indeed dramatic. Unionization of employees of federal and provincial governments increased markedly, and today almost 100 per cent of eligible employees are covered by collective agreements. In the 1970s, the unionization of teachers, nurses, hospital workers and related quasi-public/sector employees added momentum to the rate of union growth. During this period, employment growth was also strong in the government sector and in education, health and related services.

The very rapid growth in unionization in these sectors can be explained, in part, by the fact that most of these employees had previously been represented by associations which engaged in consultation with employers on wages and working conditions. Thus, in many instances, an organizational structure already existed. Nonetheless, the change from consultation with an employee association to collective bargaining was more than cosmetic in nature.

The rapid growth in collective bargaining within the public sector has led to considerable controversy. Wage settlements in the public and quasi-public sectors have been a prominent policy concern since the late 1960s. Large wage settlements by high-profile public and quasi-public sector employees, such as Seaway workers, public servants, teachers and postal workers, have been blamed by some observers for contributing to the inflation problem of the past twenty years. Thus they were responsible, partly at least, and possibly to an important extent, for the two major intrusions of government into collective bargaining in the post-war era: the 1975–78 Anti-Inflation Program and the wage-restraint programs introduced in 1982. The "Six-and-Five" scheme and related wage-restraint programs reflected, in part, a concern that public sector wage settlements were not being modified downward in response to the weak labour-market conditions brought on by the 1981 recession. Several analysts have attributed much of the responsibility for the 1975 Anti-Inflation Program to the spill-over effects of public sector wage settlements.

Public sector labour disputes have also generated controversy. Public opinion polls indicate that Canadians are becoming increasingly intolerant of strikes, especially in certain public services. The issues of which public and quasi-public sector workers should have the right to strike, and how disputes should be resolved for those denied that right have been at the forefront of policy debates.

Another trend, apparent since the mid-1960s, has been the increased use of back-to-work legislation. Table 17-2 shows the number of instances in which the federal and provincial governments have employed emergency back-to-work legislation during each five-year period since 1950. Most of the disputes terminated in this way have occurred in the public or quasi-public sectors. Those in the private sector have occurred primarily in the transportation sector. The dramatic escalation adds to the concern noted above about increased government involvement in the collective bargaining process, and this Commission views it as a serious issue.

Recent developments suggest to some observers that the federal and provincial governments are rethinking the changes made in the 1960s about collective bargaining and the right to strike in the public and quasi-public sectors. To the labour movement, this shift seems part of an attack on the institution of collective bargaining. To many others, including much of the business community, it represents necessary movement away from the overly permissive environment surrounding public sector-wage determination in the past two decades. It is probably accurate to state that governments are caught in a dilemma. On the one hand, they favour collective bargaining, under conditions reasonably close to that of the private sector, for their own employees and workers in the quasi-public sector. On the other hand, they are reluctant to live with the consequences: higher wages and more collective bargaining disputes, which are unpopular with voters.

This situation suggests that public sector labour relations may now have reached an important turning point. One view is that the current public sector-restraint programs are indeed temporary, and that there will be a return to collective bargaining along the lines that existed prior to 1982. An alternative view is that some of the present restrictions on public sector bargaining will remain. An extreme version of this second view holds that the period from 1964 to 1982 constituted an experiment with public sector

TABLE 17-2 Back-to-Work Legislation, 1950 – 84

Years	Federal Jurisdiction	Provincial Jurisdiction	Total
1950 – 54	1	—	1
1955 – 59	1	1	2
1960 – 64	2	1	3
1965 – 69	2	8	10
1970 – 74	4	9	13
1975 – 79	6	16	22
1980 – 84	1	18	19

Source: Unpublished data from Labour Canada, Federal-Provincial Relations and Liaison Branch.

collective bargaining along private sector lines, and that the experiment has now been concluded and judged a failure. To assess these views and their implications for collective bargaining in Canada, we must examine the Canadian experience with public sector labour relations.

The issue which has perhaps generated the most controversy has been that of public sector compensation. There is a strong conventional wisdom that the forces which influence wage determination in the private sector are not operative in the public sector or are, at least, distinctly muted. Most Canadians view these purported differences between the determinants of compensation in the two sectors as giving public sector employees, in the long run, a wage advantage over comparable private sector employees. This claim is reinforced by a general view that public sector employees enjoy greater job security than their private sector counterparts and therefore, if any distinction is to be made, should earn lower wages. In addition, it is often stated that public sector wages are less responsive to changes in economic conditions than are wages in the private sector. A related set of hypotheses involves the influence of public sector compensation on that in the private sector. These "spill-over" hypotheses can take two forms. One theory is that higher wage levels or higher rates of increase for wages in the public sector will affect wages in the private sector, possibly to the extent of imparting an inflationary bias to the economy. The second theory is that a lower sensitivity to economic conditions displayed in public sector-wage settlements suggests that in economic downturns, public sector settlements will decline less rapidly than those of the private sector. If public sector settlements affect those made in the private sector, the sensitivity of wage changes to economic conditions will be reduced in both sectors. The increased wage rigidity that results will make it more difficult to control inflation through demand restraint and will contribute to increased instability in employment and output. These hypotheses can be tested empirically. In Canada, economists and policy analysts have conducted a significant amount of research into these matters. The results of this research are briefly summarized here as they relate to two sets of comparisons: wage levels and wage changes.[1]

Comparison of wage levels indicates that public sector employees typically enjoy a compensation advantage over "comparable" workers in the private sector. "Comparability" is generally established by one of two methods: comparing workers in the same occupation where the nature of the work is assumed to be similar, especially if the occupations are narrowly defined; and using data on earnings of individual workers, while controlling for other factors which affect compensation, such as age, education, sex, skill level and training. (Unfortunately, it is generally impossible to control for differences in employment security, nor is it certain that such differences exist.) The size of this compensation advantage is in the order of 5 to 10 per cent overall, though it varies considerably across groups of employees. It is largest for females and low-wage workers, and smallest – often, indeed, a disadvantage – for employees at higher salary levels.

This public sector-compensation advantage has not always existed. Studies indicate that in the 1950s, public sector employees were paid slightly less than comparable private sector employees. The opposite differential emerged in the

1960s and 1970s. Evidence indicates that this emergence primarily reflects two factors: the rapid growth in employment during this period and unionization. The first factor reflects the reality that in a sector characterized by rapidly growing labour demand, most employers are willing to pay somewhat higher wage increases, and most employees have the market or bargaining power to obtain increases that are somewhat higher than those typical of sectors growing at average rates. In short, wage increases are needed to attract additional workers into rapidly expanding sectors. This is a reality which operates in private industry, as well. The resulting compensation advantage will tend to disappear once employment growth slows to the average rate. Accordingly, the public sector-compensation advantage may decline somewhat in the future, as current forecasts indicate that employment growth in the public sector is likely to fall below average.

The second factor is unionization. It is well established that unionized workers are paid more than they would earn in the absence of unionization and more than comparable non-union workers. This union-wage differential primarily reflects the increased bargaining power accruing to employees from co-ordinated action (the strike threat) as compared to individual action (the quit threat). It is not surprising, then, that the very rapid growth of unionization in the public sector would produce something of a wage advantage, for union density is higher in the public than in the private sector. That is, even if unionized private sector employees were found to earn wages equal to their unionized public sector counterparts, and even if the same differential applied to non-union workers in the two sectors, public sector employees would be found to earn more, on average, than their private sector counterparts because the proportion of unionized workers is higher in the public sector. Since unionization of that sector is now virtually complete, this factor should not lead to any further broadening of the public sector-wage advantage. Indeed, it is likely to narrow somewhat because of projected slow employment growth in the public sector, relative to the private sector. The most recent evidence suggests, indeed, that the public sector-wage advantage peaked in the late 1970s and has declined modestly since that time. This evidence is consistent with the two factors mentioned above, for employment growth and unionization growth in the public sector have slowed considerably since the latter 1970s. Governments also have taken a stronger stand against increasing public sector wages, beginning with the agreement reached at the 1978 First Ministers' Conference.

A serious limitation of the empirical studies of private/public compensation is that they are based on wage rates or earnings, and do not take into account fringe benefits and other non-wage aspects of compensation. The large and growing importance of fringe benefits makes such comparisons highly significant. Unfortunately, Canadian evidence on fringe benefits and working conditions is very limited. Cost estimates of benefits such as payment for time not worked, unemployment insurance, pension, health and welfare coverage, bonuses and profit sharing suggest rough comparability in fringe-benefit costs among municipalities, hospitals, education, government and large private sector firms. However, these comparisons do not take into account working conditions such as job security or deferred compensation such as early retirement and indexed pensions. It is highly likely that valuation of such aspects would show that public sector employees have the more advantageous fringe benefits and other non-wage aspects of employment, adding to the wage advantage outlined above.

Examination of wage changes over an extended period provides a useful supplement to the comparisons of wage levels at a particular point in time. The primary source of information on Canadian wage changes is Labour Canada's data bank of base-rate changes in major collective agreements. Figure 17-2 shows the average annual negotiated wage change for contracts without cost-of-living/allowance (COLA) clauses in the commercial and non-commerical sectors, a division that corresponds very closely to the private and public sectors. Between 1968 and 1983, settlements in the non-commercial sector have averaged slightly below those in the commercial sector. The difference averaged 0.4 per cent per year over this period. Figure 17-3, taken from the brief submitted to this Commission by André Ouellet, the former Minister of Labour, breaks down the non-commercial sector by federal, provincial and local administrations. Since the end of the Anti-Inflation Program in 1978, similar patterns of wage settlements appear in all four sectors. However, before the introduction of the Anti-Inflation Program (AIP) in October 1975, there were significant differences: wage increases in provincial administration rose dramatically higher than those in the private sector, while wages in the local and federal administrations as Figure 17-3 shows, were higher than those in the private sector, but lower than those paid by provinces. Table 17-3 indicates that to include wage increases obtained under COLA clauses (which are much more widely used in the private than the public sector) maintains the record of similar wage patterns since the end of the AIP in 1978.

Comparison of wage changes over time indicates that there is little basis for the view that public sector-wage settlements are less responsive to changes in economic conditions than those in the private sector. Indeed, as Figure 17-2 illustrates, the cyclical behaviour of wage settlements in the two sectors is remarkably similar. In addition, empirical studies find that other determinants of wage changes, such as inflationary expectations and catch-up for unanticipated inflation, have very similar effects in the two cases. Thus, there is little evidence to support the view that the determinants of wage settlements operate differently in the two sectors to any significant degree. The one exception to this conclusion is that arbitrated awards, which are virtually non-existent in the private sector, but much more prominent in the public sector, do behave differently from those of private sector- and negotiated public sector-wage settlements. In particular, arbitrated awards exhibit less sensitivity to economic conditions than do negotiated settlements, but they show more sensitivity to the past effects of inflation and to movements in wages of similar workers elsewhere. However, arbitrated awards are not numerous enough to make the overall behaviour of public sector-wage changes different from that of corresponding private sector changes. Studies of wage changes have also concluded that there is relatively little support for

FIGURE 17-2 **Annual Average Wage Changes Provided by Major Collective Agreements (without COLA)**

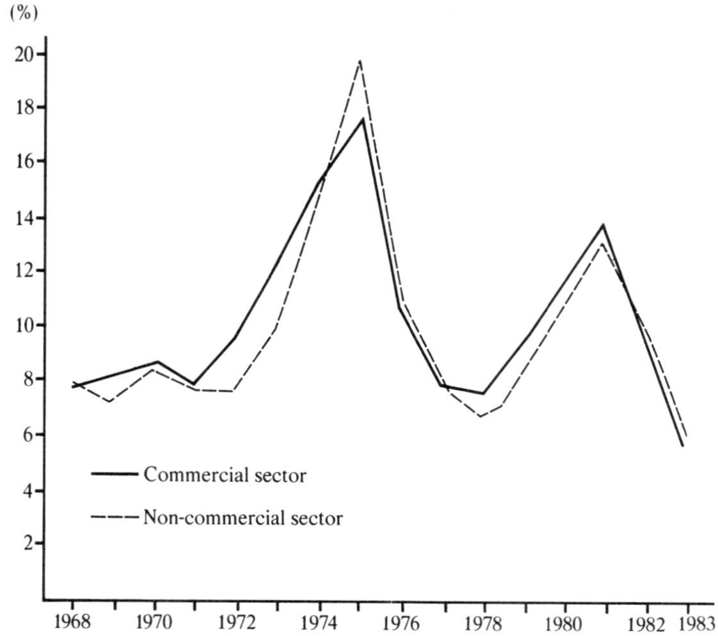

Source: Canada, Labour Canada, Wage Developments Resulting from Major Collective Bargaining Settlement.

Note: The non-commercial sector includes federal, provincial and municipal governments, plus highway and bridge maintenance, water systems and utilities, welfare organizations, education and related services, and hospitals. The commercial sector includes all other enterprises. Thus the commercial sector includes some enterprises, primarily Crown corporations, which some would include in the 'Public Sector' (e.g., CBC, Canada Post). To include these in the non-commercial sector would not significantly alter the averages.

the view that public sector settlements spill over in a general way into the private sector. There is, however, evidence of wage spill-overs from the public to the private sector in specific urban areas and particular occupations.

Two caveats should be noted. First, while wage increases in the public and private sectors have been very similar, on average, over the 1968–83 period, there is no certainty that this outcome would have occurred if the government had not intervened in the wage-determination process. The Anti-Inflation Program of 1975–78 was introduced, to a considerable extent, because of concern over the consequences of high public sector settlements in 1974 – 75. Empirical studies have found that the AIP imposed stricter restraint on public sector than on private sector settlements. Further, the wage controls introduced in 1982 applied only to the public sector. They may have had a "demonstration effect" on private sector settlements, but this effect was probably very modest if, indeed, it existed at all. Thus both interventions into the wage-bargaining process have apparently had a stronger effect on public sector settlements than on private sector ones.

FIGURE 17-3 Wage Settlements, Federal, Provincial and Local Administrations and in the Private Sector

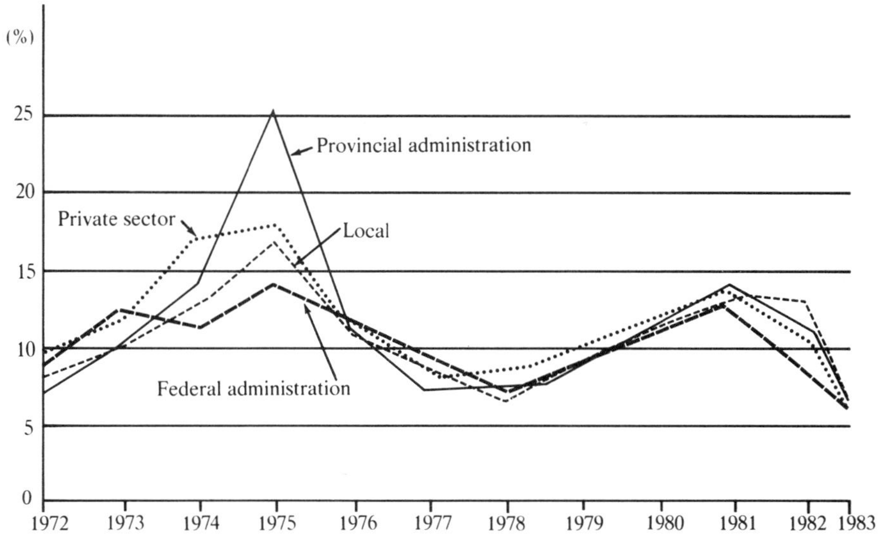

Source: Unpublished data, Labour Canada. Note: the data cover only non-COLA settlements.

Secondly, the data are seriously limited. They exclude non-union wage increases, which are more important in the private sector; they generally employ the base-wage rate: that paid to the lowest classification in the bargaining unit; they exclude the value of fringe and non-wage benefits; and they fail to take into account the possibility of "classification creep", a process by which individuals receive wage increases through promotion and reclassification. Each of these limitations may bias the comparison.

After comparing the evidence relating to public and private sector wages, Commissioners' chief conclusion is that it is not necessary, because of concern about the pattern of public sector wages, to make drastic changes in the legislation governing collective bargaining rights. It is true that unionization gives rise to higher compensation levels than would otherwise exist, and this development somewhat elevates the costs of providing schools, hospitals and other public services. This is one of the effects of collective bargaining, and it exists in the private sector, as well as in the public sector. Just as extensive unionization in the auto industry raises the price of cars, so extensive unionization among government employees raises the cost of public services. There does not, however, appear to be any reason to treat one group differently from another on these grounds alone.

This Commission notes, nevertheless, that there are important differences in the economic forces which affect wage settlements in the private and public sectors. While some differences may operate in the other direction, the overall effect of these forces is likely to raise public sector wages to some degree. Governments will therefore wish to continue to monitor wage developments in

TABLE 17-3 Weighted-Average Annual Wage Increases in Major Collective Agreements

	1978	1979	1980	1981	1982	1983	1978–1983 Average
Commercial Sector							
Non-COLA contracts (888)	7.6	9.5	11.5	13.9	9.6	5.5	9.62
All contracts (1465)	8.2	10.8	11.6	12.9	10.1	5.7	9.88
Federal Government							
Non-COLA contracts (244)	6.6	8.2	10.8	12.6	7.8	5.5	8.58
All contracts (254)	7.1	8.4	11.3	12.7	8.6	5.5	8.93
Provincial Government							
Non-COLA contracts (195)	7.3	8.4	11.2	13.6	10.6	6.6	9.62
All contracts (222)	7.8	9.2	11.3	13.5	11.8	5.0	9.77
Local Government							
Non-COLA contracts (199)	6.4	8.7	10.4	13.2	12.9	5.7	9.55
All contracts (251)	7.3	9.3	10.8	12.8	11.9	5.8	9.65
Education, Health & Welfare							
Non-COLA contracts (829)	6.7	7.9	9.7	13.7	11.3	6.7	9.33
All contracts (1002)	6.8	8.2	9.9	13.4	11.4	6.7	9.40

Source: Canada, Labour Canada, E.I.R. Research File

Note: COLA wage increases are calculated on the basis of actual Canada Price Index (CPI) movements for the 1978–83 period, using a forecast 5 per cent CPI increase for 1984 (and beyond).

their jurisdictions, in order to ensure that these do not contribute to the development of another inflationary wage-price spiral in Canada.

Are Canada's public sector labour relations at a turning point? As with many controversial questions, two answers are offered. The Canadian Labour Congress (CLC) in its brief to this Commission made the following observation:

> *The collective bargaining system is one of the basic institutions of a democratic system. In Canada it is under a serious attack from governments and business. The most visible examples of this threat are in the public service, both federal and provincial.* (Canadian Labour Congress, Brief, December 12, 1983, p. 18.)

A more sanguine observation recently referred to the "doomsday" and "optimistic" hypotheses: the former implied that a retreat from the existing public sector collective bargaining system is at present under way in Canada:

While the arguments advanced to support the doomsday hypothesis deserve careful attention, there is a considerable body of evidence to support the optimistic hypothesis. Even during the period in which public sector bargaining was expanding, there were attacks on the practice from several sources. Private sector employers not only complained about the cost of public services to the taxpayer, but were especially vehement when they believed that wages in the public sector exceeded those paid to employees in their sector. In addition, public reaction to strikes by public sector employees was almost uniformly negative. Periodically, governments and neutral observers suggested that public sector compensation be determined by direct linkage to the private sector, on the basis of parity between the two. In these circumstances, it would have been easy for most governments in Canada to restrict bargaining rights severely or not to grant them at all. But the federal government and a majority of provincial governments did give reasonably complete bargaining rights to public sector employees. Once the legislative framework was established, few changes were made in response to individual disputes. When a strike caused widespread inconvenience or threatened public safety (as with stoppages by municipal transit workers or hospital employees), ad hoc *legislation was enacted . . . Whatever the merits of [such] legislation, it did not change the fundamental structure of bargaining . . .*

In short, Canada's governments since the mid-1960s have supported the principle of collective bargaining, both by the extension of bargaining rights to public employees and by making only marginal changes in the permanent legal framework once legislation was enacted. Since there is little evidence that this long-term commitment changed in the early 1980s, the optimistic hypothesis is supported.[2]

Earlier in this section, Commissioners mentioned that Canada has gone further than other countries in granting collective bargaining rights and the right to strike to its public sector employees. It is possible that our governments are presently reassessing their position, but it is important to note that any changes would be made from a position of relative "permissiveness", at least compared to the position of other countries. The central issue in contemplating any move is whether Canadian experience to date with public sector collective bargaining indicates that a major change in policy is warranted. Our conclusion is that the evidence on the patterns of public sector wages does not justify a major retreat from the existing system of collective bargaining. Canada's experience with the current labour-relations system in the public sector is limited, however, to the past two decades, and because there are important gaps in our collective knowledge (especially with respect to the value of fringe benefits and other non-wage aspects of employment), it is entirely appropriate that Canadians continue to assess the existing system. Increased attention to criteria used by arbitrators, to the costing of non-wage benefits, and to the use of compensation-comparability surveys will contribute to this assessment.

Notes

1. This summary is based primarily on two surveys of this literature: Morley Gunderson, "The Public Private Sector Compensation Controversy", in *Conflict or Compromise: The Future of Public Sector Industrial Relations*, edited by Gene Swimmer and Mark Thompson (Montreal: Institute for Research on Public Policy, 1984); and David A. Wilton, "Public Sector Wage Compensation", in *Canadian Labour Relations*, vol. 16, prepared for the Royal Commission on the Economic Union and Development Prospects for Canada (Toronto: University of Toronto Press, 1985).
2. Mark Thompson and Gene Swimmer, "The Future of Public Sector Industrial Relations", in *Conflict or Compromise: The Future of Public Sector Industrial Relations*, edited by Mark Thompson and Gene Swimmer (Montreal: Institute for Research on Public Policy, 1984), pp. 443–44.

Collective Bargaining Disputes

The amount of strike and lock-out activity is probably the most commonly used measure of the state of a country's labour/management relations. In Canada, the view that the state of those relations has deteriorated in the last 15 to 20 years is based, to a considerable extent, on the increased incidence of collective bargaining disputes.[1]

Canadian policy makers have long displayed considerable concern with strikes and lock-outs. Each of the steps along the road to the Canadian collective bargaining system which emerged in the 1940s was taken in response to some sort of industrial crisis, usually a strike. The first major piece of labour legislation in Canada was the Industrial Disputes Investigation Act of 1907, which made work stoppages illegal until after a conciliation board had investigated the dispute and submitted a report. This Act was Parliament's response to strikes by workers in coal mines, railways and sawmills. The Wartime Labour Relations Orders (P.C. 1944-1003) is arguably Canada's most important piece of labour legislation. Its passage appears to have been prompted as much by the need to minimize work stoppages during the Second World War as by the desire to encourage collective bargaining and unionism. The post-war period has seen further additions to regulations governing strikes and lock-outs.

Concern about the number of collective bargaining disputes in Canada has been expressed in many quarters. For example, an editorial in the Financial Post noted that in 1980 – 82, "there was proportionately more time lost in Canada as a result of strikes and lockouts than in any other Western nation". The editor went on to observe:

> *The cost of this abysmal record is devastatingly high: lost wages and hardship for workers, reduced business for other businesses because of fewer orders and less consumer spending, disrupted delivery schedules for the struck company that often means permanent loss of orders (sometimes to foreign competitors), soured management-labor relations, setbacks in product development, and a less-attractive investment environment. In today's harshly competitive world, these are costs to society we can less and less afford to bear.*
>
> *The damaging effects of labor strife are apparent to management and labor – and to government, which has a crucial role to play both as employer and as author of labor legislation . . . there seems little evidence that these interested parties are sufficiently agitated about our appalling strike record to get some needed changes in the works . . . Clearly, ours is a system desperately in need of revision.*[2]

Other observers have argued that too much attention is paid to collective bargaining disputes as compared to other aspects of labour/management relations or to economic concerns in general. Time lost in labour disputes is small in absolute terms: it amounts to roughly 0.33 per cent of total work time, or about one day per year, a total roughly equivalent to the time given to celebrating Canada Day. Moreover, as the Minister of Labour pointed out in his brief to this Commission, time not worked because of industrial disputes is consistently less than that lost to occupational accidents and illness, and to absenteeism from other causes.

Methods of measuring the amount of strike and lock-out activity depend on the purpose at hand. If that purpose is to assess the economic costs associated with collective bargaining disputes, then the sum of person-days lost to strikes and lock-outs offers a rough, but probably reasonably valid, estimate. If the purpose is to compare strike and lock-out activity across countries, time periods, regions or industries, then the comparison should take into account differences in strike and lock-out potential. The most obvious factors accounting for differences in this area are differences in unionization (for almost all strikes and lock-outs occur in the organized sector) and differences in the number of contracts in process of negotiation (for most strikes and lock-outs occur during contract renegotiation). The ideal measure of strike activity is the degree of probability that a dispute will occur in a given round of contract negotiations: that is, the propensity to strike or lock out.

While there are substantial variations from year to year, it is clear that the extent of strike and lock-out activity (as measured, for example, by the percentage of paid workers involved in disputes or by the person-days lost as a percentage of total working time) was greater between 1965 and 1983 than between 1946 and 1965. Person-days lost as a percentage of working time averaged 0.17 per cent from 1946 to 1965, and 0.34 per cent from 1966 to 1983, an increase of 100 per cent.[3] The average loss of 0.34 per cent of working time for the post-1965 period is also high by historical standards. During the period from 1919 to 1945, working time lost to strikes and lock-outs averaged less than 0.12 per cent. It would be a mistake, however, to conclude from these statistics that the labour-relations climate has worsened since the mid-1960s, without first examining the causes for these trends.

It must be recognized that the strike potential of the Canadian economy has also increased in the period since 1965. In particular, union density (the unionized proportion of the non-agricultural labour force) was approximately the same in 1965 as in 1946, whereas it has increased significantly since 1965, primarily because of the growth in unionization in the public and quasi-public sectors. Furthermore, union density was considerably higher in the post-war period than in earlier periods. Even if a constant proportion of negotiations resulted in strikes or lock-outs (that is, if strike propensity were constant), there would be an increase in the number of collective bargaining disputes if more of the labour force joined unions. Adjusting for the increase in unionization reveals that some, but certainly not all, of the increase in time lost to strikes and lock-outs – a loss that rose from about 0.17 per cent of working time in 1946–65 to 0.34 per cent in in 1966–83 – can be accounted for by increasing unionization.[4]

Unfortunately, even this simple adjustment is not as uncomplicated as it might appear because much of the growth in unionization was in the public sector. Although public sector strikes have come to represent an increasingly large proportion of total strikes (rising from 2.4 per cent of strikes and 1.1 per cent of time lost in 1962–65 to 17.8 per cent of strikes and 20 per cent of time lost in 1978–81), the public sector's propensity to strike is lower than that of the private sector. In part, this difference reflects the fact that arbitration is much more extensively used as a dispute-resolution mechanism in the public sector than it is in the private sector.

Does the increase in time lost to strikes indicate that strikes are more numerous or that they last longer? The answer is clear: Average strike duration has not changed significantly over the post-war period. Between 1946 and 1965, strikes lasted 19 days, on average; between 1966 and 1981 they lasted an average of 18 days.

Canada has not been the only country to experience an increase in the number of collective bargaining disputes since the mid-1960s. Nevertheless, the increase does seem to have been larger in Canada than in most other countries, and this situation means that our relative position has deteriorated compared with that of other countries. If, for example, we compare 11 countries (Belgium, Denmark, France, West Germany, Italy, the Netherlands, Norway, Sweden, the United Kingdom, the United States and Canada) on the basis of days lost to labour disputes per employed person, we find that Canada's relative position deteriorated from seventh place in the years between 1948 and 1957, to ninth place from 1958 to 1967, and to tenth place from 1968 to 1981. In the last period, only Italy's record exceeded Canada's.[5] These data do not, however, take into account differences in union density, the structure of collective bargaining, the frequency of negotiations, the definition of strikes and lock-outs and other differences across countries, which can affect their ranking.

Table 17-4A shows the number of labour disputes per worker and Table 17-4B the number of labour disputes per unionized worker, thus adjusting for differences in union density across countries. Table 17-5A and 17-5B show respectively the number of working days lost per worker and per unionized worker. Clearly, Canada stands among the more dispute-prone countries. On the basis of number of disputes per unionized member, France has the worst record, followed by Italy and Canada, and then the United States, the United Kingdom and Denmark. The remaining countries have low levels of strike and lock-out activity. In terms of working days lost per union member because of labour disputes, Canada has the worst record, followed closely by Italy and then by the United States, the United Kingdom and France. Both Canada and the United States fare poorly in international comparisons of strike and lock-out activity, based on working time lost to labour disputes. The reason is that disputes tend to last longer in North America than in most European countries and in Japan. For the period from 1977 to 1981, for example, the average duration of work stoppages was about 20 days in Canada and the United States, seven days in the United Kingdom and Norway, five in Germany and Sweden, and fewer than four in Denmark, France, Japan and Italy.

International comparisons of the number of labour disputes are very difficult to make because of differences in the way such disputes are defined and measured, and because of substantial differences in collective bargaining institutions among countries. The most significant comparison is that between Canada and the United States, because of the similar nature of their collective bargaining institutions and measurement procedures. Thus a good test of the view that our labour-relations climate (as measured by strike and lock-out activity) has deteriorated relative to that of other countries would involve a Canada-U.S. comparison.

TABLE 17-4A Number of Strikes and Lock-outs per 1000 Workers, 1960–1981

Country	1960–64	1965–69	1970–75	1976–81	1970–81	Rankings 1976–81	Rankings 1970–81
Belgium	0.013	0.018	0.053	0.056	0.054	5	5
Denmark	—	—	0.044	0.088	0.067	7	6
France	0.106	0.092	0.175	0.147	0.161	10	9
Italy	0.177	0.164	0.244	0.123	0.181	9	10
Netherlands	0.017	0.006	0.006	0.006	0.006	1	1
Norway	0.007	0.004	0.008	0.011	0.010	2	2
Sweden	0.005	0.005	0.019	0.028	0.024	3	3
United Kingdom	0.102	0.096	0.114	0.081	0.098	6	8
United States	0.052	0.064	0.065	0.046	0.055	4	4
Canada	0.050	0.077	0.094	0.099	0.096	8	7

Sources: *International Labor Profiles* (Detroit: Grand River Books, 1981); and E.M. Kassalow, "Industrial Conflict and Consensus in the U.S. and Western Europe", in *Labor Relations in Advanced Industrial Societies*, edited by B. Martin and E.M. Kassalow (Washington, D.C.: Carnegie Endowment for International Peace, 1980).

TABLE 17-4B Number of Strikes and Lock-outs per 1000 Unionized Workers

(using average number of strikes and lock-outs 1976 – 81 and union-membership data for 1978)

Country	Union Membership 1978	Number of Strikes and Lock-outs per 1000 Members	Ranking
Belgium[a]	2 621 000	0.08	4
Denmark	1 553 000	0.138	5
France	5 320 000	0.580	10
Italy	8 000 000	0.311	9
Netherlands	1 700 000	0.017	1
Norway	976 000	0.022	2
Sweden	3 240 000	0.036	3
United Kingdom	12 376 000	0.161	6
United States	22 798 000	0.195	7
Canada	3 278 000	0.306	8

Sources: *International Labor Profiles* (Detroit: Grand River Books, 1981); and E.M. Kassalow, "Industrial Conflict and Consensus in the U.S. and Western Europe", in *Labor Relations in Advanced Industrial Societies*, edited by B. Martin and E.M. Kassalow (Washington, D.C.: Carnegie Endowment for International Peace, 1980).

a. Based on union membership in 1976.

TABLE 17-5A Number of Working Days Lost to Labour Disputes per 1000 Workers, 1960–81

Country	1960–64	1965–69	1970–75	1976–81	1970–81	Ranking 1970–81
Belgium	80.0	72.3	227.6	182.8	205.3	6
Denmark	—	—	306.2[a]	109.0	206.4	7
France	148.3	125.5	169.1	140.4	154.7	5
West Germany	18.4	5.6	40.8	36.2	38.5	2
Italy	632.1	822.2	1 128.9	880.0	999.0	11
Netherlands	28.1	4.9	57.3	22.7	39.5	3
Norway	103.9	7.4	41.1	32.6	36.6	1
Sweden	4.5	25.1	61.3	195.1	130.2	4
United Kingdom	128.9	158.1	522.1	465.0	493.4	9
United States	277.4	490.8	501.9	353.5	422.1	8
Canada	191.8	663.0	835.5	786.1	808.7	10

Sources: *International Labor Profiles* (Detroit: Grand River Books, 1981); and E.M. Kassalow, "Industrial Conflict and Consensus in the U.S. and Western Europe", in *Labor Relations in Advanced Industrial Societies*, edited by B. Martin and E.M. Kassalow (Washington, D.C.: Carnegie Endowment for International Peace, 1980).

a. 1972–75

TABLE 17-5B Number of Working Days Lost to Labour Disputes per 1000 Unionized Workers

(using average number of days lost 1976 –81 and union membership data for 1978)

Country	Days Lost	Ranking
Belgium[a]	259.1	6
Denmark	169.6	4
France	555.0	7
West Germany	100.9	3
Italy	2 221.6	10
Netherlands	64.4	2
Norway	62.3	1
Sweden	250.3	5
United Kingdom	923.0	8
United States	1 486.8	9
Canada	2 440.5	11

Sources: *International Labor Profiles* (Detroit: Grand River Books, 1981); and E.M. Kassalow, "Industrial Conflict and Consensus in the U.S. and Western Europe", in *Labor Relations in Advanced Industrial Societies*, edited by B. Martin and E.M. Kassalow (Washington, D.C.: Carnegie Endowment for International Peace, 1980).

a. Based on union membership in 1976, and average days lost during 1976–80.

Table 17-6 shows the working time lost per 1000 workers in the two countries since 1960. Clearly, both strike and lock-out activity have grown more in Canada than in the United States. Once we adjust for the divergent trends in union growth, however, the outcome is more equivocal. As Table 17-6 shows, the number of strikes and lock-outs per union member has not been consistently higher in Canada than in the United States, though time lost per union member has typically been higher here since 1972.

One factor that complicates a Canada-U.S. comparison is that many unionized public sector workers in the United States lack the right to strike, while their Canadian counterparts enjoy this right. Thus a valid comparison of the two countries should examine the private sector alone. An examination of private sector strike and lock-out activity per union member in Canada and the United States since 1960 indicates some increase in these activities in both countries, but the increase is greater in Canada. In our country, for example, the number of private sector work stoppages per 1000 union members averaged 0.40 per cent in 1966–76, as compared with 0.23 per cent

TABLE 17-6 Strikes and Lock-outs in Canada and the United States, 1960 – 83

	Strikes and Lock-outs per 1000 Union Members		Time Lost to Strikes and Lock-outs per 1000 Union Members	
Year	Canada	U.S.A.	Canada	U.S.A.
1960	0.184	0.195	506	1 120
1961	0.188	0.207	923	1 000
1962	0.204	0.218	996	1 121
1963	0.219	0.203	633	974
1964	0.219	0.217	1 059	1 360
1965	0.301	0.229	1 479	1 347
1966	0.335	0.246	2 983	1 416
1967	0.259	0.250	6 069	2 292
1968	0.278	0.267	2 529	2 591
1969	0.273	0.299	3 736	2 252
1970	0.231	0.295	3 009	3 427
1971	0.245	0.267	1 285	2 477
1972	0.233	0.258	3 247	1 393
1973	0.261	0.270	2 229	1 408
1974	0.429	0.301	3 376	2 376
1975	0.382	0.257	3 783	1 598
1976	0.303	0.288	3 817	1 928
1977	0.235	0.277	1 050	1 800
1978	0.306	0.209	2 255	1 824
1979	0.297		2 347	
1980	0.280		2 642	
1981	0.270		2 546	
1982	0.168		1 602	
1983	0.162		1 247	

Sources: Canada, Labour Canada, *Directory of Labour Organizations in Canada* (various years); United States, Bureau of Labor Statistics, *Handbook of Labor Statistics* (1983); and *Directory of National Unions and Employee Associations* (1979).

in 1960 – 64, an increase of 74 per cent. The comparable statistics for the United States were 0.31 per cent in 1966–76, as compared with 0.23 per cent in 1960 – 64, an increase of 35 per cent. The comparison of time lost per union member is even less favourable to Canada's economy: an increase of 287 per cent in the Canadian private sector, as compared with a growth of 86 per cent in the United States over the same periods.

Commissioners' examination of the evidence on work stoppages leads us to conclude that strike and lock-out activity has been significantly greater during the last 20 years than in earlier periods of Canada's history. This increase cannot be attributed simply to the increase of collective bargaining in our economy, for the amount of strike and lock-out activity per union member has also risen significantly. Several other countries have experienced a higher incidence of strikes and lock-outs, beginning in the mid-1960s. The increase has been relatively greater in Canada, however, so that we Canadians are now among the most dispute prone of the industrialized nations. This record suggests to this Commission that Canada may have room for improvement with respect to the number and length of work stoppages.

In order to determine what we Canadians can or should do about strike and lock-out activity, we need to understand the causes of collective bargaining disputes. Undoubtedly, as with any complex phenomenon, there may be multiple causes of labour/management dissension. Nevertheless, it is useful to ask whether there is any general framework which might help us to understand collective bargaining disputes, and which might serve as an aid to forming work-life/policy decisions.

A simple explanation is that strikes and lock-outs result from bad personal relations between employers and employees and/or management and union leaders. These poor relations lead one or both sides to adopt unrealistic bargaining positions, reducing the likelihood of concessions that would lead to a settlement. This explanation is difficult to verify, for even if "bad personal relations" could be measured, how would one know whether the bad relations caused the strike or vice-versa? Nonetheless, poor relations may well be a factor, since the ability to see things from the perspective of the other side is an important ingredient in any negotiations.

Alternatively, union militancy or bargaining power has been seen as the primary source of strikes and lock-outs. If this view is correct, labour disputes should be more frequent at times when unions enjoy greater bargaining power, and work stoppages should occur more often in those industries, firms or regions where union bargaining power is greater. This theory is at least consistent with the general finding that strike and lock-out activity tends to increase in "booms" and decrease in recessions. There is, however, a serious logical difficulty with this theory: As long as both sides recognize that an increase in bargaining power has occurred, why should this increase make a strike more likely? In other words, variations in bargaining power should lead to variations in the size of wage settlements, other conditions being equal, rather than to variations in strike and lock-out activity. For this reason, more recent and more widely accepted explanations of collective bargaining disputes have tended to focus on the information available to the two parties and on the costs of a work stoppage to both sides.

Strikes and lock-outs impose costs on both parties. During a work stoppage, workers lose income, and a firm loses profits. More permanent losses may also accrue: some of the firm's customers who have turned to competitors during the shutdown may not return. If this happens, profits will be lower, and jobs will be fewer even after production resumes. If, then, strikes and lock-outs are costly to both sides, why do they occur?

In a world of certainty and of perfect information, resort to strikes and lock-outs should rarely, if ever, be made. Both sides would anticipate their point of settlement; thus, barring irrational behaviour, they would agree to that outcome and avoid the costs of a shutdown. In any bargaining situation, however, each side will be somewhat uncertain about the willingness of the other to make concessions and about the other's "true" minimum demands. This lack of certainty leads to strategic behaviour, such as bluffing, since it is in the interest of each side to convince the other that they are less willing to yield than, in fact, they are. Imperfect information will result in divergent expectations that will elicit different responses to changes in the external economic environment. Moreover, it will usually not be in either side's interest to reveal its own private information, as this revelation might make its behaviour more predictable.

These factors indicate that collective bargaining is a complicated "game" in which uncertainty and imperfect information can lead to impasses, despite the costs to both sides. In choosing whether or not to make a concession, each party will weigh the risk of an impasse against the possibility of a relatively unfavourable outcome for its own side.

The repetitious nature of collective bargaining situations can also be important. Today's strike or lock-out, despite its costs, might enhance one side's reputation for "toughness", making its threats more credible in the future. Through repeated bargaining, the two sides might learn about each other's preferences and behaviour. Both these factors suggest that work stoppages should be more likely to occur in relatively new collective bargaining situations, rather than in mature established ones. The first factor tends to this conclusion because there is a stronger incentive for both parties to invest in their reputations when those reputations are not yet established. The second factor tends in the same direction because the gradual accumulation of each side's knowledge about the other should make impasses less likely. The dramatic growth in unionization that has taken place since the mid-1960s brought many new participants into the collective bargaining process. This explanation may account for the escalation of employment-related disputes that has been observed during the same period.

A further complication of collective bargaining is that there are three parties involved: management, the union leaders, and the union membership. Information flow among all three groups can be important. One well-known explanation of strikes devolves from the workers' expectations of a settlement. If these expectations are higher than the firm can afford, the union leaders, who are likely to be better informed than the members about the firm's ability to pay, may recommend a strike rather than attempt to persuade the membership to lower its expectations. The latter is a risky strategy for the union leaders to follow, as it makes them appear to be taking the firm's part in the negotiations.

Information-based explanations thus treat strikes and lock-outs as a hazard of collective bargaining in the same sense that accidents are a hazard of travelling. Just as more accidents occur under poor driving conditions, so more strikes and lock-outs occur under poor economic "driving conditions". When economic conditions are stable, impasses are less likely to occur. Both sides will recognize at what point they are likely to settle, and both will prefer to reach that point without incurring the cost of a work stoppage. When economic conditions are rapidly changing, however, it is more difficult for the two parties to anticipate the likely point of settlement, and a strike or lock-out becomes more probable, despite the costs it represents to both sides. While uncertainty and imperfect information do play an important part in the occurence of impasses, both parties, in coming to their negotiating decisions, will nonetheless take into account the potential costs of a strike or lock-out. Thus, the greater the possible costs to both sides, the less likelihood there is that an impasse will develop.

Alternative explanations have quite different implications for policy with respect to strike and lock-out activity. Explanations that focus on bargaining power or union militancy typically lead to recommendations for reducing union power. If bad personal relations are an important cause of labour disputes, policies such as preventive mediation, which attempt to improve relations between employer and employee representatives, should reduce the number of work stoppages. Explanations which cite imperfect information typically lead to recommendations for increasing the quality and quantity of information available to the bargaining parties. Emphasis on the joint costs of strikes and lock-outs leads to the recommendation of policies that will raise the costs of reaching an impasse.

A study prepared for this Commission concludes that Canada's relatively high number of strikes and lock-outs and the increased incidence of work stoppages over the past 20 years can be explained in terms of several factors relating to the information required of, and available to, the negotiating parties.[6] The openness of the Canadian economy, the importance of cyclically unstable industries, such as mining, which have high strike/lock-out rates, the large number of items covered by North American collective agreements, the decentralized nature of collective bargaining, and the absence of institutional mechanisms for the exchange of information among employers, employees and the union leadership all contribute to a high level of work stoppages compared to that of other countries, which generally do not share all of these characteristics. According to this explanation, the increased extent of strike and lock-out activity since the mid-1960s is partly the result of the increased volatility of the economic environment, which has been evident over the same period. Canada's strike and lock-out activity has increased more than that of the United States because of the greater openness of our economy and our greater sensitivity to fluctuations in resource and commodity prices.

This Commission recognizes that these various structural features of the Canadian economy and labour-relations system may well contribute to

Canada's high levels of strike and lock-out activity. Some of these features, such as our nation's industrial structure, should clearly not be altered in order to reduce the number of collective bargaining disputes. Other features, however, are worth examining to this end. Commissioners have therefore examined a number of means of reducing the incidence of work stoppages.

Labour/Management Co-operation and Improved Sharing of Information

In this Commission's view, increased co-operation and consultation among management, workers and their union representatives would improve their personal relationships and thus reduce the number of strikes and lock-outs; these improvements would also confer other important benefits on those directly involved and on Canadian society in general. Because of the importance that this Commission attaches to this proposition, we shall deal fully with the topic in "Labour/Management Co-operation", later in this chapter.

Shorter Contracts

Shorter contracts, requiring more frequent negotiations, would allow fewer problems to accumulate during a contract period. Negotiations of such contracts would be subject to less uncertainty about the future, for economic conditions two or three years ahead are usually much less predictable than those of the next year. While more frequent negotiations would increase the number of opportunities for engaging in strikes and lock-outs, they could also be expected to reduce the propensity to strike or lock out and the length of such impasses as would occur.[7] They would thus reduce the extent of strike and lock-out activity.

In Commissioners' opinion, the higher propensity to strike and lock out associated with longer contracts can be reduced through more frequent contact between labour and management during the contract period; this result would come about through greater use of joint consultation and other mechanisms for improved labour-management co-operation. This Commission, therefore, does not favour restricting contract length as a means of reducing strike and lock-out activity.

More Centralized Collective Bargaining Structure

The structure of collective bargaining in Canada is highly decentralized and fragmented. Most negotiations occur between an individual union and an individual employer, often at the level of an individual establishment. Many employers deal with several unions in the same establishment. Some analysts have suggested that this fragmentation of bargaining units is one factor accounting for our poor strike and lock-out performance, and they have proposed the remedy of broader-based bargaining: that is, bargaining on a plant-wide, industry-wide, or even province-wide basis. There is a two-fold logic behind their proposal. Its first aspect has to do with the number of strike or lock-out opportunities, and the second has to do with the costs of a work stoppage to the two sides. More broadly-based bargaining obviously reduces the number of strike or lock-out opportunities by reducing the number of separate sets of negotiations. If a work stoppage does occur, however, it will involve more employees and, if it requires industry-wide or province-wide bargaining, more employers. Thus while broadening the bargaining bases should reduce the number of work stoppages, the effect on time lost to work stoppages is less clear. Still, the fact that a work stoppage involving more employees and employers would raise the costs of a strike or lock-out to both sides should increase the pressure on both to negotiate a settlement.

At first glance, international comparisons do seem to support the view that more-centralized collective bargaining structures would reduce the number of strikes and lock-outs. Countries with centralized bargaining systems, such as Austria, Norway, Sweden, Germany and the Netherlands, have also been characterized by a low incidence of strikes and lock-outs. France, Italy, the United Kingdom, the United States and Canada, which have less-centralized bargaining systems, are characterized by relatively high levels of collective bargaining disputes, as Table 17-4 shows.

Before we Canadians draw any firm conclusions from these data, however, we must recognize that the countries with centralized bargaining systems also have other characteristics which contribute to their low incidence of strikes and lock-outs. These attributes include highly developed welfare states, high levels of unionization, a labour movement with significant political influence, and extensive use of tripartite incomes policies. In these countries, the scope of collective agreements is much less extensive than in Canada; that is, many non-wage employment benefits are regulated by the state rather than negotiated with employers. One well-known view is that the combination of these attributes has reduced strike and lock-out activity by transferring conflict over income distribution from the industrial to the political arena.[8]

Experience with more broadly-based bargaining in Canada indicates that centralization cannot be expected to achieve favourable results in all cases, but that it can do so in particular situations. Broader-based bargaining structures are relatively more common in British Columbia and Quebec than in the rest of Canada. The British Columbia Labour Code allows the province's Labour Relations Board to create councils of unions if the Board believes that to do so would be in the public interest. Provincial legislation also facilitates consolidation on the employer's side by allowing for the common accreditation of groups of employers as bargaining agents, and a number of employers have followed this route. In other jurisdictions, such accreditation legislation is usually confined to the construction industry. In Quebec, province-wide negotiations between employers and unions, relating to the staffing of hospitals and schools operating under supportive legislation, largely account for the degree of centralization.

In response to the problems of the construction industry, which were evident both in escalating conflict and in inflationary wage settlements, several provincial governments introduced accreditation legislation during the late 1960s, in order to facilitate employers' acquisition of countervailing power. Following this process of consolidation, construction-wage increases fell more into line with those of other industries. This change suggested that broader-based bargaining had some effect in moderating wage increases, even in the face of strong construction demand. A detailed case study concluded that centralized bargaining in the industry has been associated with more stable wage scales and across-the-board settlements which apparently reduced "leapfrogging" among trades.[9] The effect on strikes and lock-outs was, initially at least, less favourable. While the number of labour disputes within the construction industry declined during the 1970s, following consolidation, working-days lost increased dramatically. Although strike activity increased generally during the 1970s, the problem in the construction industry became notably worse as work days lost rose to three times the all-industry average. British Columbia and Quebec, where structural change was greatest, had the worst construction-strike records of the 1970s. Recent studies suggest, however, that greater stability has returned to the construction industry in these two provinces as broader-based bargaining has gained acceptance.

A highly negative assessment of centralization emerges from a recent study of public sector bargaining in Quebec.[10] On the one hand, bargaining between a union common front and provincial government management has eliminated the potential fragmentation of separate negotiations by 12 unions, five centrals and at least five separate management organizations. The "hypercentralization" of the present system has not, however, eliminated fragmented action in the form of wildcat strikes. Intra-organizational conflicts have broken out on both sides, and the distance separating workers, local managers and the collective bargaining process has increased. Collective bargaining has also become an important political event. Moreover, strikes in every bargaining round since the early 1970s (representing over six million lost work days) have sparked discussions of restrictions on the right to strike and challenge the whole system of collective bargaining in Quebec's public sector.

These cases paint a less-than-optimistic picture of the general effect of centralization on time lost to strikes and lock-outs. Nevertheless, some public policy experience, notably in British Columbia, does point to the value of consolidation in specific areas. The experience with the formation of multiple unions in the shipyards of Vancouver in 1966 and the creation of a union council for the BC Rail Ltd. in 1976 appear to have turned out more favourably. The latter move was the most significant factor in reducing the frequency and length of work stoppages, as well as securing their easier resolution.[11]

Railways, shipyards and construction all represent examples of strike-prone interdependent operations historically characterized by craft fragmentation. In such operations, a strike by any one group can produce a total shut-down. These cases would seem to constitute the most promising area for selective intervention. As a general goal of public policy, however, centralization does not appear to be a panacea and may actually be detrimental to industrial peace. In fact, centralization can be expected to have largely negative consequences for the representation and bargaining processes. These consequences include a reduction in local flexibility and autonomy for both management and workers, and restriction of the scope for worker participation. As a result, workers may become alienated and frustrated. Intra-organizational conflict also becomes more likely, making negotiations a longer and more costly process.

The limited evidence that is available from case studies broadly supports this negative perception. One study, based on an investigation of the public service in Saskatchewan, concluded that centralization generally slowed the bargaining process by lengthening negotiations.[12] The slow-down occurred partly because of the need to consult with more people, and partly because of the greater visibility of centralized settlements and a reluctance of bargaining units to settle before other groups. Intra-organizational bargaining problems also intensified as negotiations became more highly centralized, and bargaining was based on smaller understanding of day-to-day operating problems. Local management handled grievances with less flexibility, for instance, and this reduction caused problems in local labour/management relationships. This result was attributable, to a significant extent, to a decline in management interest and willingness to devote time to matters now seen as others' responsibility. Centralization also appeared to narrow the range of issues discussed at the bargaining table. Another study of a sample of public mass-transit organizations in the United States reported equally negative consequences of centralization for worker participation.[13]

Evidence taken from international comparative analyses also suggests that under centralized bargaining systems, shop-floor workers and union members lack influence in the collective bargaining process. This problem appears to be particularly acute among minority groups within unions, including women, younger workers and "guest" workers. In Europe and especially in Sweden and Germany, dissatisfaction with lack of representation has been advanced as one explanation for the outbursts of wildcat-strike activity that occurred in the late 1960s.

Legal Regulation of Strikes and Lock-outs

The right to strike or to lock out is heavily regulated in Canada as compared to other countries. This regulation takes three main forms. One, common to most jurisdictions in the post-war period, makes strikes or lock-outs illegal during the term of a collective agreement and imposes grievance arbitration for resolving disputes relating to the interpretation of that agreement. This situation is different from that in the United States, for example, where the parties are usually free to strike or lock out during the term of a collective agreement or to negotiate an agreement which provides for grievance arbitration of any disputes which may arise. The second regulation relates to disputes which arise in negotiating a collective agreement; it typically requires resort to compulsory conciliation before a strike or lock-out can occur. Such provisions have been a feature of Canadian legislation since the early 1900s. In addition to the time requirement of the conciliation process, several jurisdictions impose a "cooling-off period", after which a strike or lock-out becomes legal, and some jurisdictions provide for the arbitration of a first contract in the event of an impasse. Most jurisdictions also stipulate a mandatory strike vote, which requires that the union members vote in favour of a strike before it can occur. Some jurisdictions also allow the employer the option of requesting a vote on the employer's last offer prior to a strike. The third regulation makes strikes over the issue of union recognition illegal in most jurisdictions.

In the first section of this chapter, Commissioners noted that most of the legislative changes made to Canadian collective bargaining law in this century were intended to control or avoid work stoppages, and that the right to strike or lock out is heavily regulated in Canada, relative to other countries. Yet, as we have seen, our incidence of collective bargaining disputes is very high by international standards. This might suggest that our law has been ineffective, perhaps even perverse, in attempts to reduce work stoppages. This conclusion should not, however, be hastily accepted. It is possible that the level of work stoppages in Canada would have been even higher in the absence of these various regulations controlling the use of the strike or lock-out weapon. We noted earlier that a number of structural features of the Canadian economy and the world economic environment since the mid-1960s may account for Canada's relatively high level of work stoppages. Moreover, a recent empirical study has concluded that certain features of Canadian labour legislation had a significant effect on strike incidence.[14] In particular, compulsory conciliation was found to reduce strike incidence in those jurisdictions and time periods in which that requirement obtained. The effect of compulsory conciliation was found to be stronger when it involved a conciliation board, with its power to recommend a settlement. The requirement for a mandatory strike vote also reduced significantly the probability of a strike, while the cooling-off period and the employer-initiated strike vote tended to increase the likelihood of strikes.

Some of the existing labour legislation, such as compulsory conciliation, may well be having its intended effect. Commissioners believe, however, that the scope for further legislative initiatives to reduce the incidence of collective bargaining disputes is probably very limited. Lower levels of collective bargaining disputes are more likely to result from increased co-operation, consultation and exchange of views and information between labour and management than from additional legislated restrictions on the use of the strike or lock-out.

Reassigning the Third-Party Costs of a Dispute

Can governments reassign the costs of strikes and lock-outs? The costs of some disputes are borne primarily by the two parties involved, in the form of reduced income and profits, so that there is little reason for public policy involvement. In other instances, the dispute will result in significant costs being borne by third parties, often customers or suppliers. Again, there may be costs to society as a whole if the stoppages affect Canada's reputation as a dependable supplier, or if they change the decisions of firms to locate and invest within our borders. In these circumstances, the social cost of the dispute exceeds the private cost to the negotiating parties. These are the situations in which there is a clear role for public policy, which could deal with these situations in a variety of ways. One is to require the disputing parties to compensate the affected third parties, thus ensuring that the disputing parties take more fully into account the social costs of their decisions and actions. Although this procedure is appropriate in principle, it runs into serious practical difficulties which make it appear impracticable. Governments could try, instead, to reduce the third-party costs of such disputes. They could accomplish this aim and confer other significant benefits, as well, by encouraging competition and thus increasing the availability of substitute goods or services for consumers. This option, therefore, has considerable appeal. In some situations, governments are responsible for the erection of barriers to competition in the first place. The postal service provides a useful example here: to allow greater competition in the delivery of mail and parcels would confer important benefits on our society, including reduction in the social costs of labour disputes within the postal system. Indeed, it appears that the third-party costs of a disruption in postal service have declined in the past decade, because of the growth of other delivery services.

When labour disputes are significantly affecting third parties and it is neither possible nor socially desirable to encourage competition, governments stand in a difficult position. On the one hand, intervention to end the dispute will undermine the collective bargaining process in the long run. On the other hand, governments will come under severe pressure from the affected public to "do something". Most of these situations occur in the public and quasi-public sectors. Commissioners' concern is that if a method is not found for dealing with these situations, governments will retreat from the existing right-to-strike provisions and possibly even from the right-to-collective-bargaining provisions.

Governments' current method for dealing with these situations is to allow the dispute to continue until public pressure builds sufficiently to mandate intervention and then to use back-to-work legislation. As Table 17-2 demonstrates, the use of such emergency legislation has been increasing dramatically in recent years. This pattern of response has the unfortunate effect of making such disputes more likely in the future because it reduces the expected cost of the strike or lock-out to the negotiating parties. That is to say, if the firm or the workers expect that they will be legislated back to work, they will anticipate a short strike or lock-out that will cost them relatively little. Such expectations are quite reasonable, given the pressures on governments and, indeed, their past behaviour, as evident in Table 17-2. In these circumstances, it is reasonable to ask whether there is a viable alternative to the strike or lock-out as a method for resolving impasses. The alternative that has been chiefly employed is arbitration.

Interest Arbitration

The use of interest arbitration has grown substantially in Canada over the past 20 years, simultaneously with the growth of unions in the public and quasi-public sectors. Although its use varies across jurisdictions, arbitration is widely used among hospital workers, police, firefighters, teachers and government employees. In some instances, arbitration is imposed by statute; in others, the parties may choose it; and occasionally, it is employed on an *ad hoc* basis as part of back-to-work legislation in particular disputes. Its two main forms are conventional arbitration, in which the arbitrator chooses an award after hearing arguments and evidence from the two parties, and final-offer arbitration, in which the arbitrator, after receiving briefs and hearing evidence, must choose either the employer's or the union's final offer. Conventional arbitration is by far the most widely employed system in Canada. In the United States there has been more experimentation with final-offer arbitration and its variants.

Arbitration, like the strike or lock-out, is intended to be used infrequently, in those circumstances where the two parties are unable to reach agreement. An important consideration, then, is the effect of arbitration on the incentives of each side to make concessions and, ultimately, to converge on a settlement. One concern is that the availability of arbitration as a dispute-resolution mechanism would reduce the parties' incentives to reach a negotiated settlement; this possibility is referred to as the "chilling effect" of arbitration. It would occur, for example, if arbitrators tended to "split the difference" between the two parties' positions. Another concern is that when arbitration represents the ultimate mechanism for choosing a settlement, one or both parties will simply "go through the motions", but withhold the time and effort required for serious negotiations. Over time, both might rely more and more on arbitration to determine wages and working conditions; this possibility is referred to as the "narcotic effect" of arbitration.

Evidence for the validity of these concerns is inconclusive. There is some which suggests that the parties might experience the narcotic and chilling effects of arbitration. If these effects do occur, however, they advance so slowly and mildly that their very existence is still debated. Thus there is little evidence to support the view that collective bargaining will disappear when arbitration is used as a dispute-resolution mechanism.

Final-offer arbitration has the advantage of offering the disputing parties greater incentives to reach a negotiated settlement, for the longer they delay doing so, the greater the risk that the arbitrator will choose the other side's final offer. This method, however, has disadvantages as well as advantages. There are a clearly identified "winner" and "loser", and the arbitrator may be forced to choose between two extreme and unworkable awards. Experiences with final-offer arbitration (most of them in the United States) suggest that these negative concerns are largely unfounded, and that a higher proportion of negotiated settlements is achieved under final-offer arbitration than under the conventional type. Nevertheless, experience of final-offer arbitration is limited, and more experiments will be needed before a more conclusive judgement on the merits of the two types can be reached.

Another important consideration relating to the use of arbitration is the effect on wages. Evidence on this matter is mixed: several studies show no systematic difference on this score between arbitrated and non-arbitrated settlements, although most indicate that a slight upward bias in wages does occur in arbitrated awards. Assessors of this evidence should keep in mind, however, that the existence of arbitration as a dispute-resolution mechanism can be expected to change negotiated settlements. That is to say, in the process of negotiation both disputing parties will consider what an arbitrator is likely to deem an appropriate award. Thus arbitration will effect not only arbitrated awards, but also settlements negotiated under the threat of arbitration. As a result, arbitration could be affecting wages even if no systematic difference is observed between arbitrated and non-arbitrated wage settlements.

Debate continues on the question: To which factors should arbitrators give the greatest weight to in devising an award? The main criteria used by arbitrators, in decreasing order of importance, appear to be comparability with wages earned by similar workers, changes in the cost of living, and the employer's ability to pay. Other factors, such as productivity of the workforce and the achievement of minimum living standards, receive little weight. The emphasis given to comparability and living costs is probably greater than that assigned by settlements negotiated under the threat of strikes or lockouts. Similarly, arbitrated awards probably place less emphasis, in comparison to other factors, on the employer's ability to pay and on productivity.

We Commissioners recognize that Canadian experience with arbitration as a dispute-resolution mechanism is limited, and that the practice is continuing to evolve. Nevertheless, experience to date indicates that arbitration does provide a viable alternative to the strike or lock-out in those situations where the third-party costs of a work stoppage are deemed by society to be excessive. Predictions that collective bargaining would wither away with the use of arbitration have not been realized. Wage settlements negotiated under arbitration or under the threat of arbitration are likely to depend more on factors such as compensation comparability and the cost of living, and less on the relative bargaining power of the two sides. Experience to date does not suggest, however, that arbitrated awards are likely, on average, to be excessive. In this Commission's view, therefore, repeated use of back-to-work legislation is probably more harmful to collective bargaining than the requirement that disputes be resolved by arbitration.

Notes

1. The well-publicized but less-than-fully-understood slow-down in productivity growth has probably played a part as well. There is, however, no conclusive evidence to link the productivity slow-down to a deterioration in labour/management relations.
2. "We Can't Afford This Strike Record", *Financial Post*, August 27, 1983.
3. For more detailed statistics on strike and lock-out activity, see Robert Lacroix, "Strike Activity in Canada", in *Canadian Labour Relations*, vol. 16, prepared for the Royal Commission on the Economic Union and Development Prospects for Canada (Toronto: University of Toronto Press, 1985), on which several parts of this section are based.
4. Time lost per union member averaged 2.5 days per year over the 1966 – 83 period, compared to 1.5 days per year for 1946 – 65, an increase of 67 per cent.
5. See Table 14 in Lacroix, "Strike Activity in Canada".
6. See Lacroix, "Strike Activity in Canada".

7. A recent Canadian empirical study by Jean-Michel Cousineau and Robert Lacroix, "Why Does Strike Activity Vary Over Time and Between Industries?" (Montreal: Université de Montréal, 1983) found that the shorter the length of the previous contract, the lower was the probability that a strike or lock-out would occur in a particular set of negotiations, if other factors were held constant.
8. Douglas A. Hibbs, "On the Political Economy of Long-Run Trends in Strike Activity", *British Journal of Political Science* 8 (April 1978): 153–75.
9. See Joseph B. Rose, *Public Policy, Bargaining Structure and the Construction Industry* (Toronto: Butterworth, 1980).
10. See Gérard Hébert, "Public Sector Bargaining in Quebec: A Case of Hypercentralization", in *Conflict or Compromise: The Future of Public Sector Labour Relations*, edited by Gene Swimmer and Mark Thompson (Montreal: Institute for Research on Public Policy, 1984).
11. See K. Strand, "Altering Union Bargaining Structure by Labour Board Decision", in *The Labour Code of British Columbia in the 1980s*, edited by J.M. Weiler and P.A. Gall (Vancouver: Carswell, 1984).
12. See Daniel G. Gallagher and Kurt Wetzel, "Centralized Multi-Employer Negotiations in Public Education: An Examination of the Saskatchewan Experience", *Journal of Collective Negotiations* 9 (1980): 281–95.
13. See J.L. Perry and H.L. Angle, "Bargaining Unit Structure and Organizational Outcomes", *Industrial Relations* 30 (1981): 47–59.
14. Morley Gunderson, John Kervin, and Frank Reid, "The Effect of Labour Relations Legislation on Strike Incidence" (Toronto: University of Toronto, 1985).

Labour/Management Co-operation

There is a widespread view that Canada's labour-relations system is too adversarial in nature, and that Canadians should move toward a more co-operative system marked by stronger emphasis on problem solving, more consultation, and deeper mutual respect and trust. This view was expressed many times at this Commission's hearings, by individuals and groups with a wide variety of backgrounds and perspectives. It is also held by many Canadians involved in collective bargaining, and by many who devote much of their time and energy to the study and analysis of that process. Our history in this area reveals several attempts and failures to make labour relations less controversial, and any objective assessment of prospects must take this history into account.

At present, in Canada and elsewhere, there is considerable interest in, and experimentation with, various forms of employer/employee interaction that depart from the traditional authoritarian and adversarial mould. Some of this increased interest is undoubtedly a result of the recent severe recession and the pressures for adjustment it brought; increased interest in improving the general climate of industrial relations seems to be characteristic of times of economic stress. It appears, however, that some of these pressures are more permanent in nature.

This Commission shares the view of many Canadians that increased consultation and co-operation between labour and management should be an objective of Canada's labour-relations policy, as well as of employers and employees generally. While there will always be some adversarial aspects to labour/management relations, Commissioners consider that there has been too strong a focus on "dividing up the pie" and too weak a concern about the "size of the pie". Increased co-operation and consultation, although not without some costs, can yield significant benefits in the form of a more enjoyable work environment for employees. Broader employee involvement in planning and decision making can result in improved productivity, better product quality and more competitiveness. Each of these improvements can benefit both employers and employees by producing higher profits *and* wages, as well as more employment opportunities. In addition, the need for flexibility and adaptability in our economy is more likely to be met in an open labour-relations environment. Finally, reductions in labour/management conflict, expressed through strikes, lock-outs, grieving and other procedures, should also occur.

To examine the prospects for bringing about a less adversarial labour-relations climate requires that we consider the incentives for, and obstacles to, increased co-operation and consultation, the role of government in labour relations, and institutional mechanisms for dealing with this important area of our national life. There is a variety of mechanisms for achieving a less-adversarial labour-relations environment that is more directly oriented to problem solving. We turn now to a consideration of some of these mechanisms.

Preventive Mediation Programs

These programs attempt to improve relations between union and management representatives. Conciliation officers and mediators, who are assigned to assist parties involved in collective bargaining disputes, see numerous instances of poor relations among representatives of labour and management. They may recommend, therefore, that these two groups take part in a preventive mediation program, which helps the parties to achieve a more mature and constructive relationship. This process takes place in the absence of the pressures involved in negotiating a particular contract.

The Ontario Ministry of Labour's Preventive Mediation Program[1] has three components: establishment of Joint Action Committees, made up of representatives of labour and management, to improve communication between the two groups; a relationship-improvement program to develop the attitudes necessary for rebuilding strained relationships; and a joint training program to provide stewards and supervisors with improved methods for maintaining better relations.

Experience with these programs is limited, and the degree of their success is difficult to measure. Generally, however, the participants in, and administrators of, the programs consider them effective, and there have been some notable successes. To some extent, of course, success may be related to the fact that programs are implemented only when the two parties demonstrate a commitment to improving their relationship. At any rate there appear to be no serious obstacles to the use of these programs, in which governments are involved as facilitators and neutral third parties.

This Commission judges that preventive mediation programs can contribute to improved labour/management relations and can help to reduce collective bargaining disputes. These programs might also help to create the conditions needed for adoption of innovative approaches to improving labour/management relations such as Quality of Working-Life programs.

Quality of Working-Life Programs

Quality of Working-Life (QWL) programs involve employer-employee collaboration in the planning and structure of the work-place and the work process. They focus on employer/employee interaction, rather than on interaction between union and management representatives. Their primary purpose is to improve job satisfaction by enabling employees to achieve more variety, scope and autonomy in carrying out their tasks. QWL programs require a change in management attitudes and practices, away from an authoritarian style towards a more facilitative, consultative and advisory one. They proffer one strategy for achieving worker participation at the level of the individual or small group, and for extending collective bargaining beyond its traditional union-leader/management-representative type of interaction. Further, they are intended not just to improve labour/management relations, but also to engage employees and supervisors or other managers in efforts to improve total organizational effectiveness.

Some governments have enhanced the expanding public interest in QWL programs. The Ontario Department of Labour, through Ontario's Quality of

Working Life Centre, disseminates information to workers and employers about the potential benefits of employee involvement at the work-place and has fostered new innovative work arrangements in the province. Labour Canada, through its QWL Division, supports initiatives, disseminates information, and sponsors conferences and studies.

There are a number of outstanding examples of particular QWL projects in Canada. The Shell Canada Limited chemicals plant in Sarnia provides one famous example. In 1975, the company decided to discontinue traditional methods of organization and job design in order to increase organizational effectiveness and meet the needs of workers. Its QWL program is based on the belief that workers are responsible, trustworthy, capable of self-regulation, and interested in grasping opportunities for decision making and growth. Design objectives included the reduction of shift work, a modification of pay systems, the elimination of artificial jurisdictional boundaries, the improvement of communications systems, and the adoption of more effective problem-solving practices. The union was involved in the entire program. So far, the results of the program have been excellent. The effectiveness of the work force has been enhanced by training a given employee to perform in a number of skill areas, by improving communications and problem-solving practices, and by involving workers in significant consultation on all matters. Labour/management relations in the plant are said to be highly satisfactory.

While several QWL programs have produced successful results, many have been failures. Measures of overall success are not available, but the experience of Ontario's Quality of Working Life Centre suggests that the attrition rate of these programs is high, probably about 50 per cent. Moreover, diffusion is slow, suggesting either that there are few circumstances in which these programs are likely to give successful results, or that there are obstacles to their adoption. The main obstacles appear to be scepticism on the part of management, together with a reluctance to deviate sharply from traditional methods of decision making and organization, and concern on the part of organized labour that QWL programs may be an attempt to discourage unionization in a non-union setting.

A certain amount of scepticism and reluctance to alter traditional methods is natural, and probably even desirable, in an uncertain world. Nonetheless, this Commission believes that the evidence to date, while limited, suggests that QWL programs can help to improve employee morale and job satisfaction, and promote organizational effectiveness and productivity. To the extent that this is so, these programs should come into wider use, since employers and employees will find them to their common benefit. Governments can play a useful supportive role, providing information on the likelihood of implementation and success of these programs. The Ontario Quality of Working Life Centre can serve as a useful model of this facilitating role.

Japanese-Style Human-Resource and Management Practices

The remarkable success of the Japanese economy, especially with respect to productivity and real-wage growth, has focused attention on various features of the Japanese economic system, including its human-resource and management practices. Compared to North American ways, these practices involve greater emphasis on achieving consensus within an organization and much broader use of consultation with employees and union representatives at all levels within a firm, in advance of key decisions affecting the well-being of employees.

The Japanese labour market and labour-relations system has a number of other unique features which have contributed to its remarkable performance. These include lifetime employment for a significant fraction (about one-third) of the labour force, the seniority-wage system, extensive use of bonus payments, enterprise unionism, and annual wage bargaining. While these features are very important and have numerous consequences, we shall consider here primarily the extensive use of consultation between employers and employees in Japan. It is important, however, to keep in mind that these other institutional features interact with and support the widespread use of consultation and consensus formation.

The Japanese employ a variety of mechanisms for achieving co-operation and employing consultation at various levels of their economy.[2] At the shop-floor level, there are quality-control circles. At the plant level, there are union-management consultations, collective bargaining procedures, and grievance-handling mechanisms which do not rely on third parties. In addition, joint labour/management consultation is common in non-union firms. At the industry level, industrial union federations and employer federations for that industry meet regularly to exchange information and views and to engage in annual wage negotiations. At the national level, unions, employers and government engage in tripartite consultations. In addition, union and management representatives jointly operate the Japan Productivity Centre.

Quality-control circles consist of informal discussion sessions in which small groups of workers (usually eight to ten employees along with the relevant supervisor) make suggestions for improvements to the organization of work, the production process, the product line, and so on. These sessions have been found to contribute, not only to higher productivity, greater profitability and improved product quality, but also to the quality of industrial working life. They thus share important features with QWL programs in that they are focused on employee-employer interaction at the small working-group level and on discussing methods for improving the organization of work to the benefit of both employees and employers.

Joint consultation is widely used in both unionized and non-unionized firms. In unionized firms, this practice complements and overlaps with collective bargaining. Matters such as the health of the enterprise, investment plans, the introduction of new technology, changes in organization, mergers and sub-contracting are not usually covered by collective bargaining, but are dealt with under joint consultation if they significantly affect the work-place and working rules. Japanese employees thus operate in an environment in which they are informed and consulted about matters which might materially affect their well-being. In Canada, by way of contrast, most employers are considerably less open with their employees.

The development of Japan's joint consultation system is worth reviewing. Joint councils were set up by the Allied Occupational Forces following the Second World War, as part of an attempt to democratize Japanese enterprises and encourage the formation of unions and the process of collective bargaining. Unions within the joint council structure pressed for an equal role in the running of the enterprise, and a number of significant strikes took place over this issue. The result of these and later legislative changes was the emergence of a system of "management rights" similar to those common in North America: that is to say, management took responsibility for making decisions about the introduction of new technology, production and employment matters, and other important concerns.

At this point, the Japanese industrial relations system might well have begun to evolve along the adversarial lines of the North American system, on which the Allied Occupational Forces had partly modelled it. However, beginning in the mid-1950s, when the government initiated the "Productivity Movement" and moderate leaders of labour and management formed the Japan Productivity Centre (JPC), joint labour/management consultation entered a phase of substantial growth and development. The JPC played an important part in this development by promoting joint consultation as a means of bringing about the co-operation between labour and management that was necessary for the introduction of new and more productive technology into the work-place.

In the mid-1950s, the initial efforts at joint consultation focused on the attempts to modernize Japanese industry. In those years there were numerous, often violent, labour disputes because unions considered these issues to be threats to job security, and employers held them to be production matters within their own discretion. Nevertheless, labour/management consultation became more widespread, and at the same time, it broadened in scope to include discussion of details of corporate operations, medium- and long-range plans, recruitment and personnel practices, and many other aspects of working life.

While joint consultation is conducted within a framework wherein the employer is assumed to have the final power of decision over matters that are not incorporated into a written collective agreement, in the majority of instances, there is considerable effort to achieve consensus before any significant change is implemented. In addition, surveys indicate that only about 10 per cent of firms act unilaterally when management and labour fail to reach consensus.

The JPC has played an important role in improving labour/management co-operation in Japan over the past three decades. Initial funding for the JPC was provided by government, but it was understood that the Centre was to be run by labour and management representatives, along with prominent academics. The JPC's activities were to focus not only on the improvement of technical and managerial efficiency, but also—and primarily—on the improvement of labour/management relations in Japan. Initially some unions were reluctant to participate in the JPC and to join the Productivity Movement, fearing loss of jobs from the rationalization of plants and apprehensive that increased productivity simply meant working harder and faster for the benefit of the owners and managers of the firm. Other unions, however, foresaw long-term benefits in the Productivity Movement and agreed to participate when it became clear that the union movement could do much to develop the Centre's beliefs and activities. The formal statement of these guiding principles was instrumental in overcoming the suspicions of unions and persuading almost all private-sector unions to participate actively in the Productivity Movement. The Centre stressed the importance of long-term employment gains from increased productivity and the need to minimize any short-term/employment consequences; the need for co-operation and consultation concerning the introduction of measures to increase productivity; and the advantage of making a fair distribution of the fruits of improved productivity among management, labour and consumers.

The JPC promoted technical exchanges between Japan and the United States, educated management about ways of improving productivity, and championed the development of joint consultation as a means of improving labour relations. This last contribution may well have been its most important. Joint consultation now exists in approximately 95 per cent of Japanese firms employing over 300 workers.

Joint consultation represents only one aspect of the Japanese labour relations system, and it is difficult to assess its effect, independent of other aspects, on Japan's remarkable economic performance. Nonetheless, most observers believe that the joint consultation system and the Japan Productivity Centre have made an important contribution to Japan's post-war economic experience, especially in facilitating the process of technological innovation. Lifetime employment and seniority-based wages, however, may be equally important factors.

There are different views about the extent to which Japanese human-resource and labour-relations practices can be implemented with similar success in other countries. At issue is the extent to which Japan's success depends on cultural factors as compared to the nature and structure of the policies themselves. An examination of Japan's industrial relations system in the post-war period suggests that the importance of cultural factors to the Japanese experience may have been overstated. A study team representing the Organisation for Economic Co-operation and Development (OECD), while placing considerable emphasis on cultural differences between Japan and Western countries, nonetheless concluded:

> *This is not to say that other countries cannot learn from the Japanese experience. In this respect perhaps the most important observation is to appreciate what can be accomplished towards both national prosperity and improvement in workers' conditions by the single minded co-operation of labour and management within the enterprise. Coupled with this, at least in the best Japanese enterprises, is the confidence that important decisions, even if they do not satisfy everyone, will be reached by consensus and are not likely to result from management using a strategically powerful position to achieve something at the expense of the workers, or workers using their power to make management accept a policy which may be detrimental to efficiency.*[3]

A more recent assessment by a Canadian observer concluded:

> *I am not convinced that some of the worthwhile aspects of the Japanese industrial relations system are so culture-bound that we [Canadians] could not adopt them. My reading of the history of the development of the Japanese system is that many of these features were direct responses to economic problems the Japanese encountered in the fifteen years after World War II. I am sceptical about the claims that the key features of the Japanese labour relations system are based on cultural and spiritual traditions unique to Japan and thus qualitatively different from the situation in the West. Rather, I am persuaded that the various union-management cooperation mechanisms now operating in Japan were adopted by the parties precisely because it was to their advantage to do so. In other words, these devices were the product of the exercise by the parties of rational economic decision-making and organizational behavior analysis which I hope are not unique to the Japanese archipelago.*[4]

There are several parallels between the JPC and the recently established Canadian Labour Market and Productivity Centre (CLMPC). The funding of the CLMPC is provided by government, but the institution will be run by representatives of business and labour. At first the union movement was reluctant to participate, especially if the Centre's primary focus was to be on productivity, and some unions remain reluctant. Nevertheless, the CLMPC has survived the difficulties of birth and now has the potential to do much to improve Canadian labour/management relations to the benefit of employers, employees and consumers.

In assessing the possibility of implementing in Canada features of the Japanese labour-relations system, observers should keep two additional considerations in mind. First, an important structural feature of Japan's society is enterprise unionism. Enterprise unions are better suited to focus on concerns and issues at the level of the individual firm. Secondly, joint consultation is only one part of an integrated system. It is unlikely that Canadian employers could use quality-control circles to obtain results such as improved productivity and product quality without also adopting some other features of the Japanese system. These features include a more open and communicative management style; greater attention to employment stability and other aspects of employee well-being; more open sharing of information; and plant-wide bonuses.

Commissioners believe that there is considerable potential for, and great advantage to be gained from, the more widespread use of certain features (such as joint consultation) of the Japanese system in Canada. These features will, of course, need to be adapted to unique aspects of the Canadian setting. Further, we consider that the Canadian Labour Market and Productivity Centre can do much to facilitate these changes.

Gain-Sharing/Compensation Arrangements

Gain-sharing/compensation arrangements tie compensation to the economic performance of a plant, firm or industry. Besides the advantages accruing to this type of compensation in terms of greater stability of employment and output, gain sharing has also been a means of achieving more effective work incentives, greater employee commitment and involvement, and improved productivity. Some observers see these arrangements as an important part of a package that includes a more open and participatory management style.

Gain-sharing plans are commonly of three types: profit-sharing, productivity-sharing and employee stock-ownership plans. Profit-sharing arrangements may be further divided into current-distribution and deferred-distribution plans. Current-distribution plans offer a cash (or other liquid-asset) payment shortly after profits are determined, while deferred-payment plans involve payment into a trust fund. Distribution usually occurs on retirement or termination of employment. It is possible to arrange combinations of current- and deferred-distribution plans.

Although considerable attention is being devoted at present to gain sharing, plans of this sort are by no means new. In 1887, Procter and Gamble established one of the first profit-sharing plans in the United States. Eastman Kodak followed in 1912, and Sears Roebuck and Company in 1916. The Scanlon Plan, a productivity-sharing arrangement which also emphasizes employee participation, began in the Depression as a means to save financially troubled companies and maintain employee earnings, though it became much more widely known when it was successfully applied to a profitable company in 1945.

Profit sharing is a fairly widespread practice in the United States. At present, there are about 285 000 deferred-distribution plans and approximately 80 000 current-distribution plans. According to the Profit Sharing Research Foundation, 26 per cent of U.S. manufacturing firms with 50 or more employees, over 30 per cent of retailers, and 44 per cent of banks and trust companies operate profit-sharing plans, and the number of these plans is apparently growing rapidly.

In Canada, profit-sharing plans are much less common. Since current-distribution plans need not be registered with Revenue Canada, their number is unknown, but it has been estimated at fewer than 1000.[5] Revenue Canada estimates that there were 26 000 deferred-profit/sharing plans in operation in December 1982. Many of these are "top hat" plans: that is, they pay benefits only to the principal shareholders of a corporation. According to the Institute of Profit Sharing, there were only about 1500 broadly based profit-sharing plans operating in Canada in 1978.

Productivity-sharing plans involve measuring the productivity of a plant or firm and then sharing the benefits of any productivity gains among participating employees and the firm according to some pre-arranged formula. The three commonly used productivity-sharing plans are Scanlon, Rucker and Improshare. Scanlon and Rucker both involve, in addition to financial incentive, an active committee system through which employees participate in the business. It is estimated that there are 200 Scanlon Plans in the United States and 10 in Canada. Improshare differs from the other two plans in linking employee bonuses to gains in physical output per person-hour, rather than to some measure of dollar savings, and in operating without an employee-participation system. In Canada, this plan is marketed by Woods

Gordon. The Improshare Plan operates in approximately 100 firms in the United States and in 16 firms in Canada.

Most employee stock-ownership plans (ESOPs) involve options that allow employees to make deferred purchases of company stock at current prices or serve as stock-bonus plans. The latter type involves benefits that are distributed in the form of company stock. Most of the interest in ESOPs exists in the United States, where tax incentives, enacted since 1970, have resulted in considerable development of these plans. In Canada, no tax incentives exist for ESOPs, and the extent of employee stock ownership is believed to be small.

Most of the research on the effects of gain-sharing/compensaton arrangements consists of case studies. Rarely have quantitative analyses been made which control for other factors, including the more open and participatory management style and labour/management-committee arrangements which often support gain-sharing plans. The available evidence does suggest, however, that these plans are associated with improved productivity and/or profitability, more satisfactory communication between employers and employees, improved labour/management relations, and better employee morale.

Conclusions

Several general conclusions emerge from the preceding consideration. Clearly, there are incentives for employers and employees and their representatives to adopt a more consultative and co-operative mode of interaction. For employees, the potential benefits of such a change are improved job satisfaction; better quality of work; the possibility of higher wages and better employment prospects if the firm's market prospects improve. For employers, benefits take the form of improved productivity and profitability, fewer labour disputes, and the lower rates of employee turnover and absenteeism that come with a better work environment. The existence of these incentives is important, for it implies that competitive pressures and rational decision making will push employers and employees in the direction of increased co-operation and consultation. There are, however, obvious obstacles, as well as benefits, for the movement in that direction is occurring slowly.

There is a need for more continuous contact between labour and management. At present, too much attention is focused on rule making: the periodic negotiation of a collective agreement. Commissioners anticipate considerable benefits from frequent contact between employers and the representatives of employees for the exchange of information and views on issues of common concern, away from the pressures of collective bargaining. The appropriate institutional mechanisms for such consultation will vary according to the circumstances, which sometimes involve neutral third parties. Whatever the circumstances, however, the importance of frequent contact is clear.

A serious obstacle to many of the changes discussed in this section and, therefore, to better use of Canada's human resources, lies in the attitudes of labour and management, and in the roles they have selected for themselves in our economy. In many instances, management has unilaterally made decisions on matters vitally affecting the interests of employees because these matters fall under "management rights". Yet prior consultation on such matters would undoubtedly improve employer-employee relations significantly. Not all management personnel has accepted the existence of unions; nor, conversely, have all representatives of employees' unions taken a positive stance toward management. Indeed, the latter have often seen their function as one of opposing management, and, in many instances, they have not co-operated in attempts to improve the efficiency of the organization of which they were part.

In this Commission's view, changes in these attitudes, which have persisted over long periods, are unlikely to occur quickly. Nevertheless, the institutional mechanism most likely to succeed in bringing about desirable changes is a bipartite labour/management organization such as the Canadian Labour Market and Productivity Centre.

Notes

1. For more details, see Ontario Department of Labour, "Ontario Initiatives with Respect to Preventive Mediation and Quality of Working Life", in *Labour-Management Co-operation in Canada*, vol. 15, prepared for the Royal Commission on the Economic Union and Development Prospects for Canada (Toronto: University of Toronto Press, 1985).
2. For details of these mechanisms, see the Commission study by Joseph Weiler, "The Japanese Labour Relations System: Lessons for Canada", *in Labour-Management Co-operation in Canada*, vol. 15, (Toronto: University of Toronto Press, 1985).
3. Organisation for Economic Co-operation and Development, *The Development of Industrial Relations Systems: Some Implications of Japanese Experience* (Paris: OECD, 1977), p. 40.
4. Weiler, "The Japanese Labour Relations System".
5. Donald V. Nightingale, "Gainsharing", presented to the Third John Deutsch Roundtable on Economic Policy, Declining Productivity and Growth: Explanations and Outlook, Kingston, Queen's University, July 11, 1984.

Occupational and Work-Place Health and Safety

The safety of the work-place clearly affects the well-being of virtually all Canadians. Numerous observers have expressed concern about the number of job-related injuries that occur in Canada. In addition, awareness has been growing of the serious nature of the problem of industrial or occupational disease. The increasing use of new chemical and biological agents in the work-place, experiences such as that with the mining and industrial use of asbestos, and advances in medical knowledge have contributed to this new awareness.

Policy makers have responded to these concerns. Indeed, in the past decade, probably no area of Canadian employment law has undergone as much change as that of occupational health and safety. Yet a recent assessment concluded that "the response of the Canadian legal system to the challenges of a hazardous work environment displays serious deficiencies."[1]

The Dimensions of the Problem

In 1983, job-related injuries or illnesses killed 761 Canadians and caused the loss of 15 million working days in Canada. There were 952 000 work-injury claims, a figure indicating that roughly one worker in nine was hurt on the job in the course of the year. The costs of these deaths, injuries and illnesses are clearly very high. While the main cost is obviously the suffering of the victim and the victim's family, the employee also loses income, the employer incurs economic costs, and there are costs to society as a whole. To put these figures in perspective, 4.4 million work-days were lost because of work stoppages in 1983. Furthermore, lost working time on account of injuries and illnesses has been increasing, relative to that associated with strikes and lock-outs. Time lost through disabling injury increased from 9.8 million person-days in 1972 to 15.1 million person-days in 1983, an increase of 54 per cent; by contrast, time not worked because of work stoppages fell from 7.75 million person-days to 4.4 million person-days in the same period, a decrease of 44 per cent.

How does the Canadian experience with work-place injuries and illnesses compare with that of other countries? Unfortunately, available data do not permit a satisfactory answer to this important question.[2]

Table 17-7 shows the Canadian experience with non-disabling and disabling work-place injuries and illnesses between 1972 and 1983. Table 17-8 gives similar information relating to work-place fatalities; their rate has declined significantly from 1972 to 1983. Furthermore, because the decline has occurred in each industry, the decline in the total private sector is not simply the result of changes in the composition of employment. (Rapidly growing industries such as finance and services have low fatality rates, so that as their share of employment increases the overall fatality rate will tend to decline.) In fact, over 90 per cent of the decline in the overall fatality rate is the result of the decline in fatalities in each industry, and less than 10 per cent is because of changing industrial structure.

TABLE 17-7 Workplace Injuries, Illness and Fatalities, Canada, 1972–83

Year	Non-disabling Injuries per 100 Workers	Disabling Injuries per 100 Workers	Total Injuries per 100 Workers	Fatalities per 100 000 Workers
1972	6.88	5.51	12.39	17.4
1973	7.31	5.85	13.16	18.4
1974	7.29	6.03	13.32	18.1
1975	6.86	5.53	12.38	14.7
1976	7.02	5.81	12.83	13.2
1977	7.00	5.46	12.46	11.3
1978	6.95	5.69	12.64	11.9
1979	7.13	6.08	13.21	12.4
1980	7.18	6.29	13.46	12.5
1981	6.66	6.27	12.93	11.4
1982	5.49	5.75	11.24	10.7
1983[a]	5.26	5.59	10.85	8.7

Source: Canada, Labour Canada, Occupational Safety and Health Branch.
a. Preliminary figures.

As is evident from Table 17-7, the injury and disabling-injury[3] rates have been roughly constant over the past 12 years, though there is some suggestion of a decline since 1980. During the period, mechanisms for dealing with problems of occupational health and safety have radically improved in most Canadian jurisdictions. In light of this improvement, the corresponding improvement in work-place statistics, except for the decrease in fatalities, is disappointing. It is possible, however, that the improved mechanisms have caused a larger proportion of accidents to be reported.

Traditionally, the focus of concern, in relation to the safeguarding of Canadians in the work-place, has been on problems of safety rather than of health. In part, this is because safety issues are more easily identified. When a faulty guard-rail causes a worker to fall and break a leg, it is not difficult to establish the cause of the accident. It is harder to establish that the work-place is responsible for a disease with a long latency period, to which a worker's extra-employment activities might also have contributed. For example, lung cancer might develop from exposure to an unknown carcinogen in the work-place or from personal habits such as smoking, or from a combination of both causes. More and more attention is being paid to the causes of industrial disease as interest is attracted by the rapid proliferation of disease-generating substances into the work-place, as well as into the general environment. However, traditional means of dealing with industrial illnesses, such as workers' compensation, may not be the most efficient. For example, fewer than 2 per cent of the claims submitted to the Ontario

TABLE 17-8 Fatality[a] Rate[b] by Industry/Canada, 1972–1983 (revised)

Year	Agri-culture	Forestry	Fishing	Mining	Manu-facturing	Construc-tion	Transport	Trade	Finance	Service	Public Admin.	All Industries
1972	24.2	136.3	98.8	141.3	15.5	51.7	32.5	6.2	1.8	5.6	13.0	17.4
1973	24.8	157.5	164.8	144.2	14.8	53.1	37.4	6.9	1.6	4.9	19.4	18.4
1974	27.0	131.2	137.5	155.3	17.0	52.1	33.2	8.9	1.7	4.7	11.3	18.1
1975	9.5	124.6	325.3	121.7	12.7	48.6	28.3	5.4	0.7	3.6	14.3	14.7
1976	13.4	116.1	360.0	120.1	11.3	41.8	27.9	4.5	2.3	2.6	8.9	13.2
1977	11.2	91.6	236.8	90.3	10.1	36.6	22.1	5.2	1.9	2.6	7.9	11.3
1978	6.1	130.6	144.2	85.9	10.4	38.3	25.9	4.4	1.2	2.2	12.3	11.9
1979	10.6	155.3	125.0	96.7	8.8	39.6	26.6	4.7	1.0	3.1	10.6	12.4
1980	5.1	114.4	160.0	108.1	8.5	42.2	27.2	5.3	1.2	3.4	6.8	12.5
1981	13.9	96.0	147.1	76.4	8.7	38.9	24.7	4.2	2.1	3.3	10.8	11.4
1982	12.8	121.5	157.9	94.5	10.3	34.9	21.3	4.3	1.1	2.8	8.5	10.7
1983[c]	13.5	110.5	100.0	62.8	8.1	31.1	16.2	4.0	0.8	2.4	8.1	8.7

Source: Canada, Labour Canada, Occupational Safety and Health Branch.

a. Includes deaths arising out of occupational illnesses, and deaths of workers who were on pension for an earlier disabling injury.

b. Fatality incidence rate equals number of cases per 100 000 workers. Rates calculated using Statistics Canada employment estimates. The rates may be understated because only 80 per cent of workers in the Statistics Canada employment estimates are covered by Workers' Compensation.

c. Preliminary figures.

Workers' Compensation Board in 1980 related to disease. Yet occupational illness accounted for over 12 per cent of fatalities in that year.

Dealing with the Problem

In dealing with occupational health and safety, the central issues are prevention and compensation. Three separate, but interrelated, mechanisms exist for coping with the problem: competitive market forces, the collective bargaining process, and regulation through legislation. What combination of these three mechanisms provides the most socially desirable method for dealing with prevention and for ensuring equitable compensation for victims?

Market Mechanism

If workers are aware of the risk of job-related injury or illness, market forces will cause employers to pay a wage premium for hazardous work. This wage premium performs three key functions: it provides some compensation to the employee for the risk encountered in the work-place; it provides the firm with an incentive to reduce the risk of injury and thereby lower labour costs; and it ensures that the price of the product reflects the risk of injury or illness associated with its production, since a rise in the costs of production raises product prices. Even though the market mechanism may not operate in a fully satisfactory way, these functions are important in the prevention of, and compensation for, work-place injuries and illnesses.

The most fundamental problem with the market mechanism is the lack of complete information about the risks associated with various jobs. Furthermore, employers may not reveal information at their disposal to employees or to governments, as doing so would lead to increased costs of production. These costs would rise either because firms would have to install, and governments monitor, safer production methods, or because companies would have to pay higher wages in order to continue to attract workers.

These realities suggest that the operation of market forces would be improved by increased collection and dissemination of information to all concerned parties. However, there is a more serious problem when disabilities relate to occupational disease. Most occupational diseases are characterized by long incubation periods. With asbestosis, for example, the latency period between exposure to the hazard and manifestation of the disease usually lasts between 20 and 30 years. The problem is compounded by the fact that most diseases are multi-causal in nature, and thus it is impossible to determine the contribution of the work-place, as distinct from the other aspects of the worker's lifestyle, to the appearance of a particular illness.

The dimensions of the information problem are large. Some figures provided by the U.S. Assistant Surgeon General establish that 500 000 chemicals are produced and used in the United States; 3000 new chemicals are developed annually; and each year 500 of the new chemicals are employed in American industry.[4] Given the proximity and industrial integration of the two countries, Canadian figures must be similar. To determine the exact health consequences of such a large number of chemicals, used separately and in combination, would be a monumental task for our industrial scientists and doctors even if the necessary resources were available. It is often difficult to extrapolate from tests on animals the likely effects on humans. The few epidemiological studies that have been conducted have found long and variable latency periods for occupational diseases that may differ for different persons.

These informational problems can lead to a divergence between the social costs of production and the costs faced by private producers who operate a hazardous technology. The burden of this discrepancy falls partly on the workers employed in hazardous occupations and partly on society, which must also bear the costs of having some of its members injured and diseased. The workers and society in general are subsidizing the employer and the consumer of the hazardous product. For example, substitute materials to replace asbestos in brake linings and insulation are in use in Europe, yet asbestos is still the predominant material used in North America, despite its known health consequences. If the product price were higher (reflecting the social cost of producing hazardous materials), it would encourage the use of substitutes.

This kind of undesirable situation is especially prevalent in the case of work-place illnesses. A firm may be unlikely to concern itself with diseases that will first manifest themselves 20 years into the future, knowing that the victim will find it impossible to establish liability, given the latency period and the multiple causes of most of these diseases. The worker will fail to receive a sufficient wage premium, given the uncertain state of knowledge surrounding the multitude of chemicals employed in industry today. A firm which is put out of business following a discovery that one of its inputs is lethal, may legally owe the victims nothing in compensation.

Collective Bargaining

Unions and the collective bargaining mechanism may improve occupational health-and-safety standards through a number of channels. Health-and-safety provisions beyond the minimum standards provided by legislation are often negotiated collectively. The union may facilitate the flow of information to the shop floor and can play an important part in informing workers of their rights. Evidence suggests that the union bolsters the efficacy of joint labour/management health-and-safety committees and provides a good support system for the administration and enforcement of safety regulations. Recent empirical studies indicate that compensating wage differentials are higher in union than non-union working environments.

Work-Place Health-and-Safety Regulation

Legislation and the degree of involvement of government agencies in occupational health-and-safety issues vary from province to province. There are two aspects to the legislation: prevention and compensation. Most jurisdictions have been concerned with both these aspects.

The process of industrialization in Canada was initially characterized by a shocking absence of concern for the risks and dangers it inflicted on the workforce. Virtually no attention was paid to the health, safety or sanitary conditions of the work-place. Early Factory Laws forbade the use of child labour, set working-hour limits, established health and sanitation standards, and appointed an inspectorate with powers to enforce the Act's provisions. However, compensation for an injury sustained at the work-place was attainable only through the (common law) tort-liability system, where the onus was on the employee to establish that fault rested with the employer. Employer's Liability Acts, adopted by many provinces between 1886 and 1911, required the employer to insure risks with a private insurance company, but continued to require employees to establish negligence in order to receive compensation. The exception was Quebec which, in 1909, legislated that the worker had the right to no-fault compensation.

Ontario set up a no-fault insurance scheme in 1914, and similar legislation followed in other provinces. In return for assured compensation, employees surrendered the right to sue their employers and to collect full damages for injuries, including pain and suffering. These no-fault insurance schemes are administered by Workers' Compensation Boards (WCBs) and are financed by employer contributions to an accident fund. Fund assessments are a function of the work-injury experience of the industrial rating group to which the employer belongs. Subsequent amendments to these compensation programs have acknowledged that any work-related disease should be compensable. The burden of establishing the cause of the disease, however, is still borne by the victim.

Preventive legislation requires that governments set standards for work-place safety, sanitation, ventilation and health. A factory inspectorate monitors compliance with these standards, usually under the auspices of the Ministry of Labour. Preventive legislation has been amended and expanded by our federal and provincial governments as more information has come to light concerning health-and-safety issues. Industrial Hygiene Divisions were created in the various Health Departments to assist the existing factory inspectorate, and these groups work in co-operation with the WCBs and other organizations involved with work-place health and safety. In the last two decades, concerns regarding the rapid introduction of toxic and carcinogenic chemicals into production processes have necessitated on-going research into the ability of existing legislation and institutions to cope with the more insidious problem of industrial disease. In recent years, several studies and commissions of inquiry have variously identified many of the problems and deficiencies relating to existing protective legislation, the inspectorate, the WCBs, and incentives for employers whose methods of production generate occupational health-and-safety hazards.

Legislation regarding workplace health and safety has changed considerably in the last decade. Saskatchewan has provided a model which many jurisdictions have adopted, though in a modified form. Its legislation, introduced in 1972, emphasizes the contribution of worker participation to the prevention of work-place injuries and illnesses. This model is now often called the "internal responsibility system". The system confers three rights on employees:

- The right to be represented by joint labour-management/health-and-safety committees
- The right to refuse hazardous work without penalty
- The right to information, as it becomes available, about the hazards of employment.

The first right is based on the premise that co-operation of employees and employers is vital to reducing work-place injuries. Table 17-9 summarizes the existing provisions relating to occupational health-and-safety matters in each Canadian jurisdiction. As it indicates, a work-place/health-and-safety committee may be established by law in every province except Prince Edward Island and Nova Scotia. Alberta has provisions for committees to be organized on a voluntary basis. In Manitoba and throughout our federal jurisdiction, committees are mandated at the discretion of the Minister of Labour. In other jurisdictions a committee must be formed if the number of persons employed in a work-place exceeds a certain limit.

Such a committee is more likely to be effective if vested with broad powers, such as the responsibility to take an active part in refusal-to-work cases; the right to accompany an investigating inspector; access to correspondence between the investigating agency and the employer; the right to receive a response from the employer on questions of health and safety; power to shut down unsafe work-places; adequate training in air monitoring and other safety checks; and compensation for worker members for time spent on committee business. These powers, as Table 17-9 shows, are legislated in Saskatchewan and, to varying degrees, in other jurisdictions, as well.

The right to refuse hazardous work is the second element of the internal responsibility system, and all jurisdictions except Prince Edward Island and Nova Scotia provide protection from retaliation when an employee refuses to work on reasonable grounds. (See Table 17-9.) The extent of this protection depends on the interpretation of "reasonable grounds", which varies across jurisdictions.

The right to refuse unsafe work is fundamental, yet it is important to consider giving employees the means to forestall this action, short of a work stoppage, if they can. Manitoba permits an employee who has a reasonable belief that a hazard may exist to summon a factory inspector to carry out an investigation prior to a work stoppage. This type of provision may avoid a costly work stoppage, allow employees to allay or confirm their fears, and spare employers and employees the inconvenience of processing a claim for time not worked. To deter frivolous complaints, the provision might require that inspections must be initiated by a worker member of the health-and-safety committee.

The third aspect of the internal responsibility system is the right of employees to receive all information relevant to health and safety in the work-place. The right to representation on joint committees and the right to refuse unsafe work become largely ineffective if employees lack access to all

TABLE 17-9 Canadian Occupational Health and Safety Legislation

Issues Addressed by Relevant Statute	Canada	B.C.	Alberta	Sask.	Man.	Ontario	Quebec	N.B.	Nfld.	P.E.I.	N.S.
1. Employer has a duty to provide precautions to ensure health and safety.	*	*	*	*	*	*	*	*	*		
2. Employee must take due care of self and co-workers.	*	*	*	*	*	*	*	*	*		
Joint Committees											
3. Joint committee *may* be established by law.	*	*	*	*	*	*	*	*	*		
4. Worker and manager must co-chair the committee.	*		*	*	*						
5. Employer must co-operate with committee.				*	*		*		*		
6. Employee must co-operate with committee.					*		*		*		
7. Worker member may participate in work-refusal dispute.	*	*		*		*	*		*		
8. Worker member may accompany inspector.		*	*		*				*		
9. Worker representation may be appointed where no committee exists.					*	*	*		*		
10. Committee members are remunerated for work outside office hours.	*		*	*	*	*	*		*		
Right to Refuse											
11. Protection is provided from retaliation for declining to do unsafe work.	*	*	*	*	*	*	*	*	*		
12. Investigation by workers and management is mandatory following refusal to work.	*	*		*		*	*		*		
13. Worker with reasonable perception of danger is protected even though no hazard exists.	*	*		*	*	*	*		*		
14. Worker may appeal decision that job is safe.						*	*				

15. Inspectors are empowered to ensure direct adherence to regulations.	*	*	*	*	*	*	*	*	*	*	*
16. Inspectors may halt work until compliance.	*	*	*	*	*	*	*	*	*		
17. Substitute worker must be informed of earlier refusal.						*	*		*		
Right to Information											
18. Employer must provide all information to ensure health and safety.				*	*	*			*		
19. Employer must identify all dangerous substances used or emitted.	*	*		*		*	*		*		
20. Employer must indicate threat to health on container label.	*	*		*					*		
21. Workers are entitled to see accident and inspection reports.	*	*		*	*	*	*				
22. Standard setting must involve public participation.		*				*	*				
Health Services											
23. Medical examinations must be provided for miners.	*	*	*	*	*	*	*	*	*	*	*
24. Medical examinations must be provided for those exposed to silicone.		*		*	*		*		*		
25. Medical examinations must be provided for those exposed to asbestos.			*	*	*		*		*		
26. Medical examinations must be provided for those exposed to high level of noise.		*					*				
27. Designated employer must provide health service.					*	*	*		*		
28. Worker may be required to undergo examination.	*		*	*	*		*	*	*		

Source: Richard M. Brown, "Canadian Occupational Health and Safety Legislation", *Osgoode Hall Law Journal* 20 (March 1982): 90–118.

Note: Even where a regulation explicitly addresses work-place/health-and-safety issues, the effectiveness or scope of the provision varies from one jurisdiction to another.

available information pertaining to hazards in the work-place. This third right, however, is barely addressed in much of the labour legislation, and the pertinent provisions that do exist are vague and difficult to enforce. The Canadian Centre of Occupational Health and Safety was established by the federal government in 1978, to act as a clearing house for information and to provide an advisory service to employers, labour leaders and other interested parties in this field. From its inception, however, it has provided relatively little information, chiefly because of low funding.

The internal responsibility system might have more success in dealing with safety as distinct from health. Regulations and specification standards that set critical exposure levels might be more successful in preventing health hazards; for example, to restrict the number of asbestos fibres permitted per cubic centimetre of air would effectively reduce a known health hazard. In the future, Canada might integrate aspects of the two systems more thoroughly. Most disease-generating substances must be carefully monitored so that worker exposure does not exceed certain levels. Joint committees could bolster the effectiveness of the health-and-safety legislation by ensuring that affected employees have access to, and understanding of, the standards set, and that they exercise their right to refuse to work if exposure levels go above the legislated limits.

While most jurisdictions have adopted aspects of the internal responsibility system, there are important differences in the approach to work-place health and safety. In British Columbia, occupational health-and-safety programs are consolidated under the Workers' Compensation Board, except in the mining industry. This agency is thus responsible for all aspects of compensation and prevention: standard-setting, inspections and enforcement. In Prince Edward Island, the Workers' Compensation Board is also responsible for all matters pertaining to occupational health and safety. In other jurisdictions, the issues of prevention generally fall to a government ministry. The Alberta system, more than those of the other provinces (except Prince Edward Island and Nova Scotia), relies primarily on self-compliance and self-enforcement. A limited inspectorate exists, but penalties for non-compliances are rarely imposed. But even where a regulation explicitly addresses work-place/health-and-safety issues, the effectiveness of the provision typically varies from one jurisdiction to another.

Addressing the Occupational Health-and-Safety Problem

This Commission believes that employers, employees and policy makers should give increased attention to occupational health and safety. We do not deny that progress has been made in the past decade: the decline in the fatality rate is its most obvious sign. We consider that changes in the legislative framework, especially the increased emphasis on the internal responsibility system, are favourable developments. Nevertheless, the Canadian record still leaves much to be desired. Improvements can be brought about by concerted action of all those directly involved with occupational health and safety: employers, employees and their representatives, governments, and the regulatory agencies.

This Commission was impressed by Du Pont Canada's demonstration that an excellent job-safety record can be achieved when work-place safety is given a very high priority by an entire organization, and when it receives strong emphasis at the highest levels of management. As Du Pont Canada pointed out in its brief to this Commission, its performance, as measured by the frequency of disabling injuries or illnesses, has consistently been better than the industry average by factors of 25 to 35. Table 17-10 shows the disabling-injury rates for the 1977–82 period. The performance on non-disabling injuries is equally impressive.

Du Pont credits its success in preventing injuries to the following main features of their safety program:

- Safety has a top priority and the commitment of the entire organization.
- The objective of preventing injuries and containing identified health risks is a common objective held by management, employees and labour unions, where they are present.
- Safety is a line organization's responsibility. Management at all levels, top to bottom, is held accountable for safety.[5]

This Commission recommends that other organizations attach the same importance to occupational health and safety as do Du Pont Canada and other companies with outstanding safety performance. An excellent safety record may well be profitable for a corporation, in addition to its obvious benefits to society at large. Again, this point was made by Du Pont in its Brief:

> *Apart from the important humanitarian aspects of a good safety record, accident and injury prevention is good business, and as good business, is reflected on the balance sheet. There is an excellent return on the money spent for safety. There are at least five sound economic reasons for operating safely:*
>
> *1. A good safety record helps reduce the cost of insurance and Workers' Compensation.*
>
> *2. Every time we have an accident, we face an array of problems, each with a dollar cost.*

TABLE 17-10 Du Pont Canada Compared to Chemical Industry and All Industry

	(disabling injuries/200 000 exposure hours)					
	1977	**1978**	**1979**	**1980**	**1981**	**1982**
Du Pont	0.04	0.04	0.09	0.12	0.08	0.06
Chemical Industry	1.06	1.10	0.88	0.69	0.74	0.64
All Industry	2.48	2.56	2.67	2.79	2.21	2.11

Source: Du Pont Canada Inc., Brief, August 7, 1984, p. 3.

3. *One of the most important benefits of a good safety program is the impact on employee morale, a benefit which is reflected in turn by a lower turnover rate, higher productivity, improved operational efficiencies, and a better product.*
4. *All companies strive for something called "good will". We are sure our safety record has helped us to attract new employees.*
5. *Our customers know when they deal with Du Pont, they deal with a company vitally concerned with safety.*

(Du Pont Canada, Inc., Brief, August 7, 1984, pp. 7–8.)

In addition to these benefits from a superior safety record, Commissioners note another incentive. Unless management begins to give occupational health and safety a higher priority, government regulation in this important area will surely increase. This Commission recommends continued and even increased reliance on the internal responsibility system for work-place safety, rather than increased direct regulation by government. From the victim's point of view, revisions in the allocation of the accident fund to compensate serious injuries more fully, at the expense of small accidents causing temporary disability, might be a more equitable use of limited funds.

This Commission also recommends stronger economic incentives for job safety through more complete experience rating of workers' compensation premiums. The present system is not fully experience rated so that a firm with a particularly poor record passes this liability on to all other firms in the industry group and bears only a fraction of the increased compensation payments for which it is responsible. Experience rating is important for two reasons. Fundamentally, it provides the incentive for employers to prevent work-place accidents. It also ensures that the price of a product reflects the social costs associated with a hazardous work environment. Employers often object that they cannot afford the higher costs associated with more complete experience rating. Ultimately, however, these costs will be reflected in higher prices to the consumers of the product. From society's point of view, it is important that the price of a product reflect the risk associated with its production. If substitute products can be produced at lower risk, the risk reflected in the product price will help consumers to make the appropriate choice.

Joint health-and-safety/labour-management committees are mandated, in one form or another, in nine of eleven Canadian jurisdictions. If the internal responsibility system is to be successful, it is essential that functional authority be vested in these committees. The committees will be effective to only a limited extent if they are restricted to an advisory role. A variety of options is available for increasing the responsibilities of these committees. They could take a more active part in planning and implementing changes and additions in the work-place. Decisions about building specifications and types of machinery have traditionally been considered the prerogative of management, but many work-place hazards are intrinsically linked with modes of production. A safety committee's advice on plant design could be beneficial to both employer and employees.

Committees could also have the power to arbitrate between a worker and the employer in the matter of refusals to do a hazardous job. In addition, a worker-member of a committee should accompany an investigating inspector through the work-place. Members should be trained to monitor the work-place environment so that they can detect any change in the risks to employees. Unions and the joint committees have a substantial responsibility to inform the work-force of the various hazards and rights of workers. The right to information pertaining to the hazardous nature of a job appears to be the least-addressed aspect of the internal responsibility system. Lack of information and asymmetry of information also inhibit the functioning of market forces. In this Commission's view, more specific management-disclosure requirements are needed. Employees and their representatives should also have access to third-party information about the danger of a job, whether the third party is a research agency or a former employee.

The most important contribution the government can make to occupational health and safety is to ensure continual revision of legislation and standards as new evidence comes to light. This involvement is critical in the area of industrial disease, given that new and potentially lethal chemicals and materials are being introduced daily in the work-place. Whereas other mechanisms may be more useful for dealing with industrial safety, occupational health problems can probably be controlled most effectively by the imposition of standards. These standards must take into account economic, as well as technical, feasibility. This requirement calls for the introduction of more general studies on the economic effects or cost benefits of proposed legislation. Canada can learn from the U.S. experience in accumulating many unnecessary, bureaucratic, legal and administrative costs. The Canadian Centre for Occupational Health and Safety might be the agency to develop these health standards most practicably, supported by direct input from the provincial agencies. The Centre would require adequate funding for this purpose and the other duties it was mandated to perform, such as the collection and dissemination of national statistics.

The long development periods and multiple causes of many diseases pose an insoluble problem for Workers' Compensation Boards, which attempt to compensate workers for illnesses or injuries sustained "out of and in the course of employment". The present system is unable to accommodate the fact that many seriously disabling diseases have multiple causes. Various cancers, for example, are the product of many factors operating at different stages in the development of the disease. Epidemiological studies and evidence of exposure may demonstrate the presence of carcinogens in the work-place, but they fail to determine whether a particular employee has acquired the disease as a result of employment conditions or as a consequence of personal habits or a toxic environment. "The statutory hurdle of establishing that the workplace was the cause of a disease is equally as onerous as was the common law requirement of proof that the employer's fault produced an accident."[6] The latter obligation was removed by the introduction of workers' compensation/no-fault insurance, and the problem of compensating victims of industrial disease may not be resolved without introducing a general social insurance/disability scheme which would compensate victims irrespective of source of injury. Certainly, proposed modifications of the current system of compensation do little to increase the ability of the WCBs to determine which disease-related claims are legitimately occupational in nature.

One solution to this problem would be to expand substantially the current disability benefits provided under the Canada Pension Plan, as proposed, for example, in the federal government's 1982 discussion paper *Better Pensions for Canadians.*[7] An alternative solution would be to absorb the existing workers' compensation system into a comprehensive disability-insurance scheme, as one author has proposed in his examination of the Ontario system.[8] Although Commissioners have not considered these options in detail, we recommend that the federal and provincial governments examine these and other options for dealing with industrial disease.

The past decade has seen considerable change in public policy relating to occupational health and safety. In addition, there is considerable diversity in the policy initiatives taken in various jurisdictions. Yet virtually nothing is known about the effects of these policy changes, or which of the various approaches has proved most successful. This situation is likely to continue unless more effort is devoted to the compilation of satistics which would facilitate interprovincial and international comparisons and other research. This Commission regards the available data as inadequate, given the importance to all Canadians of occupational health and safety.

Recommendations

Commissioners recommend the following courses of action to improve occupational health and safety in Canada:

- Greater emphasis on work-place health and safety at higher levels of corporate management
- Stronger economic incentives to increase the safety of the work-place through more complete experience rating of workers' compensation premiums
- Continued reliance on, and strengthening of, the internal responsibility system
- Recognition that workers' compensation cannot adequately deal with industrial disease, and that alternative mechanisms are needed
- Recognition that occupational health and safety is a matter of national concern, and that more adequate data and research are required.

Notes

1. Richard M. Brown, "Canadian Occupational Health and Safety Legislation", *Osgoode Hall Law Journal* 20 (March 1982), p. 118.
2. Statistics from the International Labour Organisation (ILO), *Yearbook of Labour Statistics*, suggest that Canada's work-place/injury rate (number of reported injuries in proportion to total employment) is high by international standards. A comparison of eight countries for which injury statistics are reported over the

1976–81 period shows Canada with the highest injury rate (approximately 1 worker in 9 injured on average), followed by France (1 in 10), Switzerland (1 in 13), West Germany (1 in 13), United States (1 in 17), Sweden (1 in 35), Netherlands (1 in 50), and Norway (1 in 100). These data should, however, be used with extreme care. The minimum duration of incapacity to which an accident must give rise in order to be included in the statistics varies widely from one country to another. This factor is important because the number of minor accidents is large. In addition, there are other important differences in the nature of the sources, in their scope and in methods of compiling or reporting statistics on work-place injuries and illness. Thus it is possible that the high injury rate in Canada reflects differences in measurement and reporting rather than a more dangerous work-place.

Canada also fares poorly in international comparisons of work-place fatalities. West Germany has the worst record for fatalities, with approximately 15 to 18 fatalities per 100 000 workers over the 1976–81 period, followed by Canada (9 to 11), Switzerland (7 to 12), France (7 to 9), Norway (5 to 9), Japan (5 to 6), the United States (4 to 5), Sweden (3 to 4), and the Netherlands (1 to 3). Again, however, these statistics should be treated very cautiously because of differences in reporting and classification of fatalities across countries.

3. Disabling injuries are defined as injuries which require absence from work for at least one day in addition to the day of the injury, or which result in dismemberment or permanent impairment of a body function. Non-disabling injuries are minor injuries which do not require missing a full day of work.

4. See Pran Manga, Robert Broyles, and Gil Reschenthaler, *Occupational Health and Safety: Issues and Alternatives*, Technical Report No. 6 (Ottawa: Economic Council of Canada, 1981), p. 41.

5. Du Pont Canada Inc., Brief, August 7, 1984, p. 11.

6. Paul C. Weiler, *Protecting the Worker from Disability: Challenges for the Eighties* (Toronto: Ontario Ministry of Labour, 1983), p. 55.

7. Canada, Health and Welfare Canada and Finance Canada, *Better Pensions for Canadians* (Ottawa: Minister of Supply and Services Canada, 1982).

8. Weiler, *Protecting the Worker from Disability*. In order to provide incentives for prevention, the system would be partially financed by a levy on employers, based on the estimated contribution to the cost of the disability scheme.

CHAPTER 18

Education and Training

CHAPTER 18

Education and Training

Introduction

In 1982, Canadians spent nearly 8 per cent of our gross national product (GNP) on education and institutional training programs. In view of the scope of these programs, their importance to Canada's future and, most of all, their importance to individual Canadians, we Commissioners believe that our work would be incomplete if we did not consider the future of education and training programs in Canada. We must acknowledge, at the outset, the difficulties faced in dealing with these programs. Given the importance of this sector to Canada's future, relevant data and analyses are very scarce. Beyond figures that record expenditures and enrolments, little information about programs or students is available at the national level. Curricula vary from province to province, and small attempt has been made to define interprovincial differences or to relate the efficacy of the programs to varying circumstances. A few detailed surveys of post-secondary students have been conducted on the basis of national samples, and these provide essential information for policy makers, but they are not complemented at the primary or secondary levels of education. Educational institutions and local boards continually conduct evaluations of courses, curricula and programs, but little of this material is aggregated at the national level. As a result, Commissioners must develop proposals based on far less information than we would wish.

Several issues tend to dominate discussion of the future of Canadian educational and training programs. One of the most pervasive of these provides the ground for debate between two groups which might be described as "generalists" and "specialists". The generalists hold that the primary, although not the exclusive, function of the educational system is to sharpen the individual's proficiency in critical reasoning, in problem solving, and in learning. They therefore maintain that the core of the curriculum should be a firm grounding in English and French, Mathematics, Science, Social Studies and, possibly, basic Computer Science. This view was well expressed by the Toronto Board of Education in its submission to this Commission:

> *What does seem patently clear is that the school's role cannot and should not be limited to skill training for the labour force. Students must be provided with opportunities that enable them to be active participants in an educational process which increasingly must become life-long... Schools must bear a major responsibility for the development of language and communication skills, for the exploration and development of our culture and for encouraging our young people to become compassionate, conserving and critical members of a democratic society.* (Toronto Board of Education, Brief, November 29, 1983, p. 1.)

In contrast to the generalists, the specialists hold that the labour market is beginning to require skills that are fairly specific and technical. They argue, therefore, that educationists should place more emphasis on practical preparation for specific occupations or clusters of occupations. For instance, several representations to this Commission, stressed the need for Canada's educational system to emphasize technical training, especially in skill areas affected by the micro-electronics "revolution". In addition, a recent study, conducted by the Ontario Institute for Studies in Education (OISE) found that 58 per cent of respondents thought that Canadian universities should place more emphasis on job-oriented programs.[1]

These positions need not, however, be considered as totally opposed. As one intervenor told this Commission:

> *Of course the two points of view may be not irreconcilable: To raise the question of training or of vocational as opposed to basic training with generalists or specialists is [to start] a pointless argument. Sound basic training is a necessity for enabling anyone to profit from training in a special field. Similarly, worthwhile vocational training is only possible to the extent that its recipient has a good general grounding. If there is an important objective to reach, it is that of developing these concepts of training and education that complement each other.* (Monique Simard, Transcript, Montreal, May 30, 1984 [vol. 1], p. 186.)

Other issues are also important. Not least of these is the question of how much to spend for education and training programs. We Commissioners were often told in the course of our hearings that Canada spends too little on post-secondary education and job-related training. The opposite view, that Canada overspends, was expressed less often, but higher-education programs do tend to be offered as a popular target for government restraint.

Closely related to the problem of establishing budgets for education and training is that of determining the appropriate balance between these two elements. Do Canadians, as is often alleged, spend too much for higher education and too little for vocationally-oriented training programs? Do we spend too much on institutional programs compared to on-the-job training? How might we accommodate, within our major post-secondary institutions, the need to provide programs directly oriented to economic development, while retaining another historic function of our universities as major repositories of culture and the primary centres of pure research in our society?

Another major issue – many would say the primary issue – is that of standards of education. Are Canadian educational standards declining? Are we failing our students and ourselves by not insisting on excellence both in the performance of institutions and in the performance of students? If there is a decline in standards, does it apply "across the board"? Or is it more severe in some parts of our system than in others?

Finally, among the foremost concerns which this Commission wishes to consider is flexibility. Canada's colleges and universities and, to a lesser degree, its primary and secondary schools are often accused of failure to adapt to present requirements. The accusation raises a number of questions: Is this charge true? If it is even partially true, can Canadians deal with it without abrogating institutional autonomy? How is our society to handle the training needs of students who leave school early and of mature persons who wish to return to training or education programs later in life? In the pages that follow, we shall turn our attention to all of these important questions.

Note

1. D.W. Livingstone and D.J. Hart, *Public Attitudes Toward Education in Ontario* (Toronto: Ontario Institute for Studies in Education, 1981), p. 31.

Primary and Secondary Education

We Canadians have a tendency, in considering education and training at the national level, to ignore primary and secondary education. This is understandable, given our federal government's heavy financial participation in post-secondary education; the very considerable attention paid to primary and secondary education at the local and provincial levels; the lack of national aggregate data; and, of course, the fact that we have always considered primary and secondary education to lie entirely within provincial jurisdiction. In view of the importance of these levels of education to Canada's future, however, some consideration of them is called for here.

Indeed, it is often suggested that primary and secondary schooling are more important to our nation's future than are higher levels of education. This Commission believes that all three categories are important and thus, although we have devoted the bulk of our analysis to post-secondary education and training, we also wish to make some comments on lower levels of education. The fundamental reason for paying careful attention to educational programs at the primary and secondary levels is simply that for the majority of Canadians, formal education and training does not extend beyond the latter level. Only about one-third of Canadians ever study in post-secondary institutions. Tests of achievement in core subjects and skills taught at primary and secondary levels (mathematics, reading, vocabulary and language expression, abstract reasoning and creativity) forecast future earnings more accurately than do other forms of assessment that measure personal attributes. Tests administered early in a student's academic career appear to predict occupational and educational attainment as accurately as later testing. Cost/benefit analyses generally attribute higher net benefits to additional dollars spent on primary and secondary education than to those spent on post-secondary education. These data suggest that whether Canada's policy makers see formal education as intended primarily to help people to adjust to the effects of technological or other types of change, or as a means of creating a generally more literate and adaptable population, they should direct particular attention to the "quality" of basic education provided in our primary and secondary schools.

Until a few years ago, Canadian educators seemed to be moving towards a more "liberal" education: a wider choice of courses, a greater flexibility of curricula, new teaching methods and de-emphasis of formal exams were the norm. This Commission's hearings would suggest that the results of that trend are now widely perceived as undesirable. However, while Canadians seem to favour a more structured educational format, they also show considerable ambivalence about whether curricular changes should emphasize a "back-to-basics" approach or place greater emphasis on direct preparation for the labour force. Thus 59 per cent of a sample of Canadians polled in 1983 opted for a "back-to-basics" program, while 73 per cent of respondents polled in another survey, conducted by the same firm in the same year, agreed that "our education system places too much emphasis on purely academic education."[1]

While the popular perception, well represented to this Commission in briefs and hearings as well as through popular surveys, is that standards have deteriorated in our schools, the evidence does not unequivocally support this view. One major survey of these studies[2] found that student performance had improved almost as often as it had declined. The authors also reported that chief educational officers surveyed across the country believed that standards had risen in the sciences, remained almost steady in mathematics, and declined somewhat in literature and language. Little evidence exists, however, based on nation-wide testing in Canada. In the United States, widely used scholastic aptitude tests have demonstrated a long decline in the achievement levels between 1960 and 1980; there has been some recovery during the last four years, but standards have not yet risen to pre-1960 levels.

Concern with the quality of primary and secondary education is hardly new. One historian of Canadian education notes that even prior to 1960:

> *What the delegates did discuss at conference after conference was the threat of declining academic standards ... As the continuing debate at the NCCU [National Conference of Canadian Universities] meetings during these decades illustrated, there were wide-spread complaints about the inadequate preparation of matriculants in all subjects ... The main bone of contention was the poor preparation of the students entering universities, which was attributed to poor teaching in the elementary and secondary schools, and, by extension, to the failure of the universities to assume any responsibility for the adequate preparation of the teachers in these schools.*[3]

Commissioners wish to express particular concern about the educational curricula often followed by female students, particularly at the secondary level. For various reasons, these students appear to take fewer courses in science and mathematics than do their male counterparts. This situation reinforces the tendency for women to be under-represented in technology-based jobs. To rectify it may require special attention, but that requirement does not necessarily translate into an extensive range of government programs. Changing student, parental and societal attitudes, combined with attention by teachers and counsellors to achieving a better female-male balance in these areas of study, may be more appropriate responses.

For well-established reasons both of tradition and of jurisdiction, the federal government has not intervened in primary and secondary education, except to mount relatively small official-language programs, to provide supplementary or remedial education as part of job-training programs and to support English as a Second Language and Heritage Language programs. Federal equalization payments can also be viewed as providing indirect support for all levels of education in poorer provinces; indeed, the original justification of equalization payments was based, in part, on the importance of providing adequate standards of education across Canada.

Commissioners do not believe that the federal government should become more deeply involved in primary and secondary education, but we are convinced, in view of general public concern about educational standards and quality, that there is need for a national body to develop achievement-testing procedures and to monitor standards of achievement across Canada. Nowhere does this need appear more plainly than in this Commission's inability to find reliable comparative data, kept over time and across provinces, by which to compare educational attainment and standards.

Our situation with respect to this lack contrasts sharply with that of the United States. There the federal Department of Education conducts research itself and sponsors such semi-autonomous institutions as the National Institute of Education. There have been numerous national task forces on education, and private foundations regularly sponsor independent studies. In particular, studies which trace student performance over time and in different teaching situations are readily available in the United States and virtually non-existent in Canada.

The national body we recommend for Canada should consist of some members who have direct experience in education and some who have had no direct connection with the sector. It must represent both Canada's charter-language groups, and it must be sensitive to the importance of formal education in maintaining the cultural integrity of French Canada. It should have a substantial independent research capacity, and it should report publicly, preferably each year. It must have a sufficiently large permanent staff to provide continuity in its operations, but it would also benefit from secondment of education officials employed by provincial and local governments. Although it could be formed under the aegis of the Council of Ministers of Education, its credibility might be enhanced if it were not directly financed by government. In the United States, private foundations have supported such bodies, and a similar funding base would be ideal in Canada. Indeed, by providing active financial and planning support for such an institution, the private sector could demonstrate in an admirable way its concrete interest in matters of educational policy. Alternatively, since it has typically been quite difficult in Canada to obtain financing for public policy-research institutions from the private sector, an endowment fund provided by the provincial and federal governments might be an appropriate way to guarantee such a body a suitable degree of independence. Commissioners do emphasize, however, our preference for private sector funding.

Notes

1. Information supplied by Decima Research Ltd., Toronto.
2. See Verner R. Nyberg and Brigitte Lee, *Evaluating Academic Achievement in the Last Three Years of Secondary School in Canada* (Toronto: Canadian Education Association, 1978).
3. Robin S. Harris, *A History of Higher Education in Canada 1663–1960* (Toronto: University of Toronto Press, 1976), pp. 376, 377, 384.

Post-Secondary Education

While jurisdiction over post-secondary education (PSE) rests with the provinces, and jurisdiction over occupational training is shared by the provincial and federal governments, total federal expenditures for post-secondary education and occupational training were approximately $8 billion for 1984–85. In the same period, 330 000 students were in full-time attendance at Canadian community colleges, 462 000 students attended university on a full-time basis and 283 000 on a part-time basis.

There is a variety of reasons to account for the broad support that Canadian governments have given post-secondary education and training. They have supported training programs in order to provide employers with a skilled labour force and would-be employees with the skills necessary to participate to the fullest extent possible in our economy. The objects of supporting post-secondary education are more diffuse; they involve teaching, research, the maintenance of cultural values, and the provision to the community of a broad range of information and advisory services. The weight which different observers attach to the achievement of each of these objectives will vary, but most would agree that our universities should serve them all, and that our community colleges should concern themselves primarily with teaching and training.

Since education is an acknowledged area of provincial responsibility, the heavy federal financial involvement in post-secondary education may appear anomalous. It was not so viewed, however, by most intervenors who appeared before this Commission, for the great majority of those who spoke on this subject believed that there was a national role to be played in post-secondary education, and that in consequence, the federal government should be involved.

The reasons for this belief were many. Some intervenors held that the tendency of the Canadian labour force to cross provincial boundaries made higher education a national concern. Some noted that the federal government's overall responsibility for economic management would demand that it play a greater role in education and training in the future as the nature of our economic base becomes significantly more knowledge intensive. Others considered that the out-of-province benefits devolving from the research and cultural activities of Canada's universities made federal involvement imperative. Some were concerned that smaller provinces would be unable to provide appropriate levels of services without federal help. Still others expressed the view that students should be free to attend any Canadian institution of higher learning they might wish and voiced the concern that fee differentiation for out-of-province students might preclude this possibility if the federal government were not to be involved. These views were expressed by people from all provinces and from both major language communities. Where there was opposition to the federal presence, it seldom precluded federal participation, but rather advocated that the federal role be restricted to unconditional financial support.

This Commission agrees with virtually all of these reasons for federal involvement and firmly believes that there is a major part for the Government of Canada to take in supporting post-secondary education and training. While Commissioners would certainly stop short of suggesting that universities should become national institutions under the jurisdiction of the Government of Canada, as some of the intervenors who appeared before us proposed, we do believe that it is important for our national government to maintain its presence in post-secondary education, and we wish to review the form that that involvement should take.

Prior to 1951, our federal government shared in the cost of some occupational training delivered by provinces and provided direct support for education of veterans. From 1951 to 1967, the Government of Canada provided our universities with a flat subsidy per student. Grants were proportionate to enrolment figures and were delivered directly to the institutions through the agency of an inter-university granting council; they were not channelled through provincial governments. In contrast, between 1968 and 1977, the federal government transferred to provincial governments 50 per cent of the operating costs of post-secondary educational institutions or, in 1968, $15 per capita, escalated. From 1972–73 onward, it limited year-over-year increases in the contribution rate to 15 per cent. The actual disbursement of funds to Canadian universities was then handled by the provincial governments.

In 1977, under the Federal-Provincial Fiscal Arrangements and Established Programs Financing (EPF) Act, federal support was once more radically transformed, taking on, essentially, its present form. In place of open-ended grants based on institutional expenditures, provincial governments were to receive block payments based on provincial populations and made up of cash and tax-point transfers. These payments were ostensibly intended to support post-secondary education. They were, however, only distantly related to actual levels of post-secondary spending in each province. Thus, although the size of the total national transfer was originally related to the overall operating costs of post-secondary institutions in 1975–76, provinces were not required to spend any particular amounts on post-secondary education in order to qualify for the federal grant. Moreover, the entitlement was increased annually by an amount related to increases in population and gross national product, rather than to PSE operating costs.

Whether in consequence of the EPF Act transfer mechanism or not, the years since 1977 have seen a decline in constant dollar-per-student expenditures on post-secondary education in almost all provinces; the most extreme examples of this trend have occurred, over the long term, in Ontario and, very recently, in British Columbia. It should be noted, however, that because of the very large numbers of post-secondary students in Ontario, that province's per capita expenditures on PSE are relatively high, in spite of its low per-student transfers. Overall, federal cash and tax-point transfers, nominally in support of PSE, made up 70 per cent of provincial government operating grants to universities and colleges in 1977–78, and 80 per cent in 1984–85. In five provinces, Newfoundland, Prince Edward Island, New Brunswick, Manitoba and British Columbia, the nominal federal transfer for PSE is actually greater than the provincial operating-grant transfer to institutions.

This situation has led to accusations that provincial governments have been diverting to other uses large sums that Parliament intended to be spent on PSE. As a result, many people, both inside and outside post-secondary institutions have expressed concern that the EPF mechanism may not offer the most appropriate means of providing future federal support for post-secondary education.

Provincial governments have developed a wide variety of systems and procedures for disbursing funds to institutions of higher education. Most university funding therefore tends to be discretionary: provinces distribute whatever funds they can "afford" on the basis of relative historical levels of support for different institutions, modified somewhat to reflect recent changes in enrolment. In this situation, the tuition fees paid by students often represent almost the only financial incentive for universities to respond to changes in enrolment demand. Even this incentive is limited, however, because provincial governments exercise heavy control over fees, which, in any case, cover only about 15 per cent, on average, of the universities' general operating expenditures. Under these circumstances, Canadians might well anticipate some lack of response to enrolment demand at the post-secondary level.

Yet in spite of this situation, some fairly significant changes in the composition of enrolment at Canada's universities and colleges have occurred over the last two decades. During those years, there has been a steady rise in part-time enrolment. Thus, between 1962–63 and the present, the proportion of part-time students has risen from 23.7 per cent of total post-secondary enrolment to 37.6 per cent. Over the early and mid-1960s, enrolment in both Arts and Sciences increased considerably, relative to that in other faculties. After 1970, however, the proportion of students in Arts faculties began a decline which has continued to the present. In 1970–71, 14.6 per cent of Canadian undergraduates were enrolled in Humanities programs, a figure which declined to 8.5 per cent by 1982–83. In 1965–66, almost 32 per cent of undergraduate enrolments were in Faculties of Education. While the absolute numbers of students enrolled in these programs has not declined, these faculties did not share in the remarkable growth of the universities that occurred in the 1970s. Thus, by 1983–84, only 12.9 per cent of undergraduate enrolments were in Education. Since the early 1970s, undergraduate enrolment in Science has risen only from 10 to 11 per cent in proportion to overall enrolments, while Business Administration has greatly increased its share of total registration. In 1983–84, for example, 15.7 per cent of full-time undergraduates were registered in Business or Commerce programs, while in 1970–71, the corresponding figure was just 8.3 per cent. Commissioners find this increase encouraging.

Before the recession of 1981–83, many Canadians believed that enrolments in Engineering and Computer Science were not growing quickly enough to meet the needs of our economy. Indeed, intervenors have argued before this Commission that Canadians should still be concerned about this problem. Between 1977 and 1981, however, the number of Canada's engineering graduates rose at an average annual rate of 9.1 per cent. In those same years, overall university-enrolment increases averaged about 1 per cent per year.

It would seem from these figures that in spite of funding rigidities and public perceptions, the universities were at least somewhat responsive to broad changes in enrolment demand during the 1960s and 1970s. Whether they were sufficiently responsive, however, and whether the quality of instruction rose along with enrolment numbers are harder questions to answer. It is even more difficult to evaluate the responsiveness of community colleges, where reliable data are even scarcer.

Whether or not the performance and adaptability of Canada's post-secondary sector has been adequate during the past two decades, we must realize that much of what it achieved was accomplished while the system was expanding. If our PSE systems contract because enrolment decreases or funding is restricted, their future adaptability is likely to be considerably more limited. Thus the potential effect of enrolment trends on the adaptability and, indeed, on the very nature of our post-secondary institutions is both very important and potentially difficult to deal with.

Currently, 86 per cent of Canada's full-time undergraduates are 18 to 24 years of age. That "source population" for our post-secondary institutions peaked in 1982–83; it will decline steadily until 1997 and remain constant thereafter. Whether enrolment will also decline will depend on participation rates, particularly of 18- to 24-year-olds. Twenty-four per cent of Canadians in that age group now attend post-secondary institutions, and 13.5 per cent of these students are studying at universities. Only the United States has a higher rate of university attendance, at 18.5 per cent.

By the mid-1990s, Canada's 18- to 24-year age group will number 2.6 million persons, representing a reduction from the present 3.3 million. If we assume a constant PSE participation rate, there would then be approximately 168 000 fewer full-time post-secondary students than the current total of 792 000. About a 6 per cent increase in participation rates or a compensating increase in enrolment of older age groups would be required to maintain a constant student population.

There are several important caveats to be noted here. First, assumptions are built into any enrolment projections. It is quite possible that enrolment rates of over-24-year-olds will increase. Indeed, Commissioners hope that they will, since we believe that lifetime learning is highly important. Female participation rates, which already come very close to equalling those of males, may continue to rise. Since children of parents with degrees are about three times as likely to enter university as children of parents without degrees, total participation rates for 18- to 24-year-olds may increase as the children of the growing numbers of parents with post-secondary education reach the 18- to 24-year age group. Unless some of these possibilities actually occur, however, enrolments will decline. In any event, given the very great importance of enrolment-trend data for post-secondary educational planning, it will be essential to maintain a sound data base and substantial analytical capacity.

Secondly, adaptability has more to do with the resources available to the education sector and with the flexibility of the institutional base than with the total number of students. There is no reason why the overall resources available to educational institutions must be directly related to that number. Indeed, in the past few years, funding increases have not kept pace with growing student enrolment, perhaps because of the assumption that registration will decline, and that there should not, therefore, be a major build-up of resources in the sector.

The issue of whether or not the Canadian PSE and training sector is currently "underfunded" received a lively airing in this Commission's hearings. To assess whether government's current overall scale of support for education and training is the "right" size is an extremely difficult policy problem, one, indeed, which can have no definite solution. While some features of the Canadian tax system discourage investment in human capital, and some students and trainees still have difficulty in financing their studies, there are, in total, very large subsidies supporting education and institutional training. It is even conceivable that the overall result of government action in this sector is to encourage too much investment in education and training relative to that in physical plant.[1]

Comparison with other countries provides no definite answer. Canada spends on education close to the average amount spent by other members of the Organisation for Economic Co-operation and Development (OECD): OECD figures indicate that our expenditures in 1981 represented 6.2 per cent of gross domestic product (GDP), compared to the OECD average of 6.1 per cent.[2] While Canada ranked eighth out of ten in 1960, well-above-average growth rates from 1965 to 1970 brought our standing to fifth out of twelve in 1975. The Scandinavian countries have consistently ranked as top spenders, while Germany and Japan have lagged behind; the United States spends slightly less than Canada. Expenditures dropped in all major OECD countries, except Italy and Japan, between 1975 and 1981, chiefly, apparently, in response to declining enrolments.

The suggestion is often put forward that greatly increased expenditures on education and training will be necessary in order to help Canadians adapt to the labour-force implications of new technologies. There is considerable uncertainty about the probable employment effects of the new technology likely to be introduced over the next ten or 15 years. Thus, according to one school of thought, the occupations and industries where the new technology will be most heavily applied include almost all office work, much manufacturing, financial services, communications and, perhaps, wholesale and retail trade. Employment may shift from these areas to others such as personal services (the provision of restaurant meals, for example), health care (because of the eventually higher proportion of the elderly in our population), construction, and leisure industries. While some of these areas of employment may require a fairly high level of education, it is far from obvious that the *average* educational requirement is likely to be higher than in the past. In fact, it may well be lower.

A further indicator of the uncertainties to be dealt with in this field is to be found in the implications of a recent Canada Employment and Immigration Commission (CEIC) projection of medium-term labour requirements. Those projections suggest that workers in occupations likely to experience the highest employment-growth rates include analysts of organizations and methods, chemists, physicists, architects, several types of engineers, advertising salespersons, and business-service salespersons. Such occupations start from a relatively small employment base, however. For example, in 1983, only 9000 Canadians were employed as organization-and-methods analysts, and only 4700 as business-service salespersons. Thus high rates of growth do not necessarily produce many new jobs, and they do not necessarily indicate requirements for much more advanced levels of higher education. The largest absolute numbers of new job openings are likely to occur in occupations such as secretarial and stenographic services, bookkeeping, truck driving, janitorial services, public dining services or nursing. Similarly, while there will certainly be significant shifts in Canada's labour force, engendered by the increasingly competitive international environment, it is highly uncertain whether their specific effects on the requirements for particular kinds of education can be predicted.

Very considerable uncertainties confront predictions of specific educational requirements, and many, if not most, Canadians will have to undertake considerable retraining during their lives. These realities lead Commissioners to emphasize the value of a solid general education – of learning how to learn – so that Canadians may be well equipped to adapt quickly and efficiently to the changing realities of the labour market. With this consideration in mind and with full awareness of the continuing need for very considerable levels of specialized training, Commissioners were deeply concerned to hear so many intervenors state that under current levels of funding, PSE institutions are experiencing very great difficulty in maintaining the general quality of their teaching, the quality of research, and the viability of their physical plants. Provincial governments, as we noted earlier, have been very reluctant to increase the funding of these institutions, because of the current need for restraint and the belief that enrolments are likely to decline in the future. Moreover, all levels of government have tended to take the position that the total amounts of funding for all types of education and training should be either fixed or reduced in proportion to GNP. This view has meant that spending increases in one part of the sector have had to be financed from decreases in another part, at the same time that the proportion of GNP devoted to education is static or declining. While this policy is understandable, it is not necessarily desirable. There are many benefits to be gained from a strong post-secondary educational system, and Canadians did, in the 1960s, make a major national effort to build up a system of very high quality. In retrospect, that decision still seems to have been correct, and it may now be very short-sighted to allow that system to decay to the point where it becomes second-rate.

Most of this consideration of the post-secondary sector has focused on changes that have occurred over the past ten to 20 years, but in one respect, change has been lacking during this period. A much larger proportion of young people from high-income families than from low-income families has always participated in post-secondary education. In 1974, for example, Statistics Canada found that "55 per cent of children from well-off families (annual income over $25 000) attended post-secondary institutions while only 11.6 per cent of children over 18 from poor families (*i.e.*, income under $5000) did so."[3] A more recent study of the distribution of benefits from the Ontario university system concluded that:

The principal net gainers from the university system are the middle- and upper-income groups at the expense of the lower-income groups. In this sense the university system is a large public expenditure program in which the relatively poor groups tend to subsidize the relatively rich.[4]

While the final data were not available at the time this Report was written, it is this Commission's understanding that the 1983 Student Survey by the Secretary of State found that essentially the same distributional pattern persists in the 1980s. This finding was further corroborated in the brief presented to us by the Association of Universities and Colleges of Canada:

Much remains to be accomplished if members of all socio-economic strata in our society are to enjoy equal opportunity of access to higher education. Despite the federal and provincial programs of loans and grants for needy students, members of the lower socio-economic groups are still under-represented in universities. Recent reports indicate that economic considerations are only one of many factors influencing a student's decision to undertake work at the postsecondary level. The home environment, place of residence, ethnic group membership and gender all are significant factors which affect a person's likelihood of attending university.

(Association of Universities and Colleges of Canada, Brief, November 1, 1983, p. 6.)

Increasing the funding of training programs, which are more frequently used by lower-income Canadians, might compensate to some extent, for this situation. The provision of higher levels of support to low-income Canadians who wish to attend post-secondary institutions might also help to rectify the present imbalance. It would not, however, in Commissioners' opinion, be appropriate to increase funding for training programs by reallocating money from universities. Moreover, family-socialization patterns will remain a significant barrier to post-secondary education for many low-income students, regardless of the financial support to which they may have access.

Finally, while Commissioners were concerned to hear of the difficulties created for the PSE sector by low levels of funding, we were also concerned that representatives of the sector itself tended to deal less with how they could help Canadians adjust to a changing world than with how badly they needed more money. Representatives of the sector devoted considerably less attention than we had hoped to suggesting how that money might be spent to solve the very real problems of the sector. Any innovative ideas we did hear about post-secondary education tended to come from outside the sector. Thus we feel obliged to observe that significant problems seem to lie within the sector itself. The combination of faculty unions, the tendency to draw administrators from within the institutions, an aging and tenured faculty, uncertainty about the role of PSE institutions in society, all combined with a somewhat defensive attitude toward the *status quo* does not seem to us to provide a healthy situation. We were disappointed not to hear more creative ideas about its own future from a sector which must be at the creative forefront of society.

Commissioners are well aware from studying public-opinion data that Canadians generally support post-secondary education and do not believe that its programs, facilities and funding should be cut back. We suspect, however, on the basis of our hearings, that the person-in-the-street would wish to see our PSE sector undergo more significant reforms than would the incumbents of the institutions themselves. For this reason, we have considered a broad range of reform options for the sector, and we have analysed in some detail relatively radical reform possibilities.

Reform Options for post-Secondary Education

A good number of the many concerns about post-secondary education expressed to this Commission cannot be rigorously evaluated; others are not properly the concern of the federal government. However, the financing mechanisms used by the federal government to support post-secondary institutions have an important effect on the actual operation of the sector and constitute the chief means by which federal influence may be exercised. There are four major interrelated sets of issues with which PSE-funding mechanisms may deal: levels of funding, quality of the system, flexibility and adaptability, and accessibility. Among these issues, the most difficult to handle are probably those related to flexibility and adaptability of the institutions, and the achievement of excellence within the system. If these are the areas of greatest concern, and if Canadians believe that major improvements are necessary, then quite significant changes in funding mechanisms may be needed.

While educators' sense of responsibility and the threat of government action may induce considerable response to present problems, these forces may fail in critical ways. Institutions may fail to recognize or adapt to the educational implications of rapidly changing technology, or they may be unable to make the difficult internal reallocations of resources required. They may also tend to make adjustments which governments or the public can easily monitor, while sacrificing quality or neglecting other dimensions of service which are harder for outsiders to observe. In view of Commissioners' concerns in these matters, it seems appropriate to consider ways in which methods of financing post-secondary institutions may be adjusted to encourage the attainment of greater flexibility and excellence.

Provincial governments may be able to encourage universities and colleges both to achieve excellence and to become more adaptable by allowing them to raise tuition fees without facing a corresponding reduction in provincial subsidies. The most important effect of "freeing-up" tuition fees in this way could be to induce much greater response to enrolment demand: universities could charge higher fees for higher-demand or higher-cost programs, and the prospect of acquiring additional revenue by this method will induce them to provide more places in such programs. Another likely consequence, however, would be a considerable increase in average fees. Such increases would erode equality of access to post-secondary education if countervailing action were not taken. To prevent such erosion, borrowing limits under the Canada Student Loans Program (CSLP) might be extended, or a contingency loan-repayment program might be established and more generous scholarship and bursary arrangements offered.

To give PSE institutions greater control over their fee structure might also induce greater variation in fees across programs and, particularly, among institutions, reflecting differences in costs and in the nature of programs provided. Some institutions would be likely to offer low-cost "no-frills" education, while others would provide more intensive, higher-level education intended to set very high standards of achievement. Both approaches are entirely appropriate and desirable, since both serve a real social need. Some institutions would serve large numbers of average students and do that job well. Others would serve smaller numbers of exceptional students and perform high-level/research functions, again, doing their job very well. In short, a much more heterogeneous post-secondary system, efficiently serving the highly varied needs of different categories of post-secondary students could well evolve over time. It could be politically difficult, however, for any one provincial government to take unilateral action to allow a substantial increase in tuition fees. For this reason, such changes on any but a national scale are rather unlikely. Means of ensuring federal-provincial co-operation would therefore be a crucial consideration in planning such a move.

If a variable fee structure were to be introduced, the effect could be considerably augmented by channelling federal support to post-secondary education through students, rather than through provincial governments. By funding students rather than provinces, the federal government would automatically direct its support to the programs that students demand. Provincial governments would be able, simultaneously, to permit tuition-fee increases, thus allowing post-secondary institutions the flexibility to respond effectively to enrolment demands.

What form should direct federal support to students take? One option might be for the federal government to institute a partial tuition-fee voucher or tax credit as a form of direct income transfer to students. The basic federal transfer would cover some fixed proportion of all tuition costs of formal schooling, including occupational training in institutions, between some minimum fixed deductible and a ceiling. This arrangement would be equivalent to making cash grants to students, differentiated according to program costs. An education-expense tax credit or transfer would divert federal PSE support from lump-sum EPF grants to direct aid to students, in such a way that provinces would have an incentive to respond by increasing tuition fees. To a ceiling level, a large proportion of each increase in tuition fees would be offset by increased federal aid to students. While it would not necessarily be politically easy for a province to allow tuition-fee increases, such an arrangement should make it quite possible.

There is no reason to believe that the average net cost to students would *necessarily* increase. In general, the federal transfer payment could compensate for fee increases. It is quite possible, however, and perhaps even desirable, that some increases could occur. Private sector contributions (including student-tuition fees) are now extremely low by historical standards, and it may not be inappropriate to expect the direct beneficiaries of post-secondary education, including students and employers, to bear directly somewhat more of the cost. This increased cost could be expected to constitute a heavier burden for some universities than for others. It would presumably reflect such market factors as the expected return to the student of receiving an education in that institution. The essential factor is that low-income students who are academically qualified not be excluded from the system by financial barriers. To this end, it would be particularly important that the CSLP or its income-contingent/repayment replacement be readily available to support qualified low-income students.

The federal credit would replace the cash-transfer portion of EPF. In 1985–86, that transfer will amount to approximately $2 billion. However, the Province of Quebec also receives a tax-point remission for post-secondary education, and if the federal government were to provide a comparable remission to other provinces, the funds it could allocate for direct-to-student transfers would be reduced by approximately $450 million. In that academic year, there will be approximately 850 000 full-time post-secondary students to receive the equivalent of the transfer payments in direct aid. The average size of the individual educational credit could therefore amount to approximately $1850.

Commissioners also recommend that the federal government consider a somewhat different version of direct-to-student funding. It might be argued that graduate students, because of the high level of their training, make a disproportionately large contribution to our national economic and cultural development. Graduate students and alumni of graduate programs are also likely to be more mobile than undergraduates and alumni of first-degree programs. Thus it may be appropriate for the government to consider providing considerably higher levels of support for students enrolled in graduate programs and proportionately less support for undergraduates. For example, if the credit or voucher available for undergraduates were reduced to an average of $1500 per student, then about $450 million would be available for transfers to over 53 000 full-time and 34 000 part-time graduate students. If we assume that these groups are equivalent to 64 000 full-time graduate students, the voucher amount per student could approach $7000. This distinction would greatly fortify the consumer power of these students and thus strengthen the competition among universities to attract them and consequently encourage the development of centres of excellence. Given the generosity of such provisions, it would be important, of course, to monitor these programs carefully in order to ensure that academic standards are maintained and that too many students do not undertake graduate studies. While we make no recommendation concerning the appropriate level of graduate-student vouchers, we do recommend that this possibility receive some consideration.

Commissioners' proposal for direct-to-student funding is congruent with the assumption that support for post-secondary institutions is provided, primarily, to underwrite teaching costs, although the graduate-student option would also add significant support to research projects. In fact, as we noted earlier, post-secondary institutions, particularly universities, provide a variety of other benefits to society, of which the most important are research, the maintenance and development of culture and knowledge, and the provision of other community services, such as those offered by public speakers or paid and volunteer consultants. A funding formula based strictly on undergraduate enrolment would not fully reflect the value of these services. Extra grants could therefore be provided to institutions with higher-than-average publication rates or with greater-than-average success in obtaining research grants from the private sector. Alternatively, funds provided by the various granting Councils might cover the overhead costs of research projects, as now happens in the United States, or the universities themselves might be able to work out a national formula for the distribution of funds to support research and student services. Of course, transferring money from the direct-to-student grants for these purposes would raise the effective cost of education for students and, to some extent, shift the balance of emphasis in universities towards research.

In order to retain, and perhaps improve, the access of low-income students to PSE institutions, the Canada Student Loan Program would have to be retained and its loan limits increased for those students who qualify academically for higher-cost programs. Alternatively, the CSLP could be replaced by an income-contingent/loan-repayment scheme of less universal nature than that referred to above. The income-contingent/repayment loan, while not an attractive option to cover all direct-to-student financing, does have advantages for providing support to students who require extra financial assistance. It lowers the financial risk of post-secondary education for lower-income Canadians by assuring them, in effect, that if their increased education does not produce a relatively higher income, its cost to them will be reduced correspondingly. Perhaps equally important, it removes the necessity to consider, before the terms of the loan/grant arrangement are settled, whether or not a student could be supported by his or her parents. The provision in the current CSLP arrangements that requires this information has always been difficult to administer, and many students have learned to manipulate it to minimize the cost of loans to themselves, whatever their family financial situation. The income-contingent/repayment feature does not require any "needs" test before the loan is granted, since repayment will be tailored automatically to post-education income, and not to current need.

Not surprisingly, a shift to direct-to-student funding has significant ramifications affecting the distribution of revenues among provinces. Table 18-1 indicates the extent of the changes (interprovincial dollar shifts) which would have occurred in the flow of funds to provinces if the program proposed had been in effect in 1982–83. If 1984–85 figures were available, the current dollar amounts would be about 11 per cent higher, but the initial distribution shown in Table 18-1 would be essentially unchanged.

Ontario, Quebec and Nova Scotia would each receive somewhat more money if the relative numbers of students remained unchanged. The largest percentage gain of 5.1 per cent would occur in Ontario. British Columbia would lose about 9 per cent of its current federal funding, while Newfoundland, Prince Edward Island and Saskatchewan would lose about 8 per cent each. These changes would occur because of the real distribution of students for, unlike the current EPF formula, a direct-to-student/funding arrangement would distribute the money across Canada on the basis of student population, rather than on that of a simple per capita formula. Moreover, funding figures

TABLE 18-1 Interprovincial Dollar Shifts from Replacement of EPF by Direct-to-Student Funding

	1982-83 EPF ($ 000s) Cash	Tax	Total	Notional Cash[a] After Equivalent to Abatement Distribution	1982-83[b] Full Time PSE Enrolments	Total Direct Transfers to Students in Province[c]	Total Gain (Loss) in Province	Percentage Change from Current Cash Transfers	Percentage Change from Current EPF Total Entitlement
Newfoundland	47 186	37 339	84 525	29 400	11 470	22 221	(7 179)	−15.2	−8.5
P.E.I.	10 150	8 032	18 182	6 300	2 500	4 843	(1 466)	−14.4	−8.1
Nova Scotia	70 486	55 777	126 263	43 900	23 870	46 236	2 336	+3.3	+1.9
New Brunswick	57 932	45 842	103 774	36 100	15 320	29 675	(6 425)	−11.1	−6.2
Quebec	334 843	623 129	957 972	334 800	181 280	351 139	16 339	+3.0[d]	+1.7
Ontario	667 834	610 188	1 288 022	448 200	265 100	513 499	65 299	+9.8	+5.1
Manitoba	85 621	67 752	153 373	53 400	23 400	45 326	(8 074)	−9.4	−5.3
Saskatchewan	84 179	61 124	145 303	50 600	20 100	38 934	(11 666)	−13.9	−8.2
Alberta	130 854	211 913	342 767	119 300	57 740	111 842	(7 458)	−5.7	−2.2
British Columbia	195 062	217 024	412 086	143 400	54 910	106 361	(37 039)	−19.0	−9.0
Yukon & N.W.T.	5 160	5 263	10 423	4 900	0	0	(4 900)	—	—
Total	1 699 307	1 943 383	3 642 690	1 270 300	655 690				

Source: Canada, Secretary of State, *Support to Education by the Government of Canada* (Ottawa: Minister of Supply and Services Canada, 1983).

a. "Notional Cash" is calculated by assuming that the federal government surrenders to all provinces the equivalent of the Quebec Abatement for post-secondary education. Its value is calculated by multiplying the total entitlement by the ratio of Quebec cash to total entitlement.

b. Part-time students are not included. They add approximately 10% to the total of students in each province.

c. The value of the transfer is approximately $1937. Inclusion of part-time students will reduce this to about $1750 (in 1982 $). The total dollars going into a province will be equal to the transfers to students, plus the value of the abatement. The abatement value will be equal to current cash, minus the Notional Cash.

d. To calculate this percentage, the Quebec cash figure was adjusted to include the approximate value of the abatement. The adjustment value is approximately $537 275 000.

would change in response to fee differentiation and shifting student population; these changes would be both inevitable and intentional in a more directly market-oriented system.

On the basis of this review of the present problems and possibilities relating to post-secondary education and its financing, options open to Canadians include:

- A return to the pre-EPF funding formula whereby the federal government transferred to provincial governments 50 per cent of the operating costs of PSE institutions. This move would produce a decrease in federal contributions, but would exert some leverage on provincial governments to increase contributions, since larger provincial transfers to universities would elicit larger federal transfers to the provinces.
- Provision by the federal government of an amount equal to provincial "own source" funding, exclusive of the tax points transferred under EPF. This action would reduce federal contributions by $600 – $900 million, and at least part of this decrease might well be passed on to the PSE institutions in the form of cuts by the provincial governments. After the initial decrease, this formula, too, might be expected to exert upward leverage on provincial expenditures.
- A freeze of basic federal contributions at current or slightly lower-than-current levels, with 50/50 federal matching of incremental provincial PSE spending. Since provincial spending increases would be accompanied by equal federal increases, this arrangement, also would exert upward leverage on provincial expenditures.

While the third option is perhaps preferable, it also has significant disadvantages. It tends to fix federal contributions at the historically high current level. It allows those provincial governments which have provided relatively less to PSE institutions to retain a very high share of federal funding, while financing any increments from this very low base level on a 50/50 basis. In effect, therefore, it may tend to consolidate the benefit to provincial treasuries of what some would regard as previous provincial government underfunding. If it triggers an initial reduction in contribution levels, that reduction might be passed on to the PSE institutions by provincial governments. All of these options rely on the premise that provincial governments will respond to "fifty-cent dollars" by increasing spending in areas where those dollars are available. While this possibility has undoubted theoretical appeal, empirical evidence in its support is derived from a period when public sector budgets were expanding, and when spending on educational programs was highly popular.

Commissioners have also considered a variant of the third option outlined above. The freezing of federal cash contributions to provincial governments at 1984–85 levels would generate quite substantial savings: these would be in the order of $130 million in 1984–85 and, depending on rates of nominal growth of GNP, over $200 million in 1985–86, and well over $300 million in 1986–87. If the federal government used this money to support research activities in Canadian universities by covering the overhead costs of research, freeing accomplished researchers from teaching loads, and underwriting purchases of capital equipment, a very substantial impetus could be provided for Canadian research efforts, and very important centres of specialization and excellence could be created. Commissioners believe that this option also deserves serious consideration, although the shifting of such sums from general support to research support might have negative effects on undergraduate programs and on community colleges. It may be more desirable, therefore, to provide one-half the incremental funding to support university-based research and to use the other half to match, on a 25/75-federal/provincial basis, provincial increases in transfers to post-secondary institutions.

Since all the options for changing funding formulae have flaws, the temptation becomes very strong to accept the *status quo*. That temptation must be offset, however, by the high levels of dissatisfaction with the current situation expressed during this Commission's hearings, both by those within the system and by the broader interested public. Since all the standard intergovernmental mechanisms of fiscal transfer that are available have been tried in this sector, and since all have been found wanting, Commissioners recommend that Canadians seriously consider more significant reforms involving direct-to-student transfers by the federal government and "freed-up" tuition fees in PSE institutions. To cover the overhead costs of research, we recommend that some of the funds currently transferred under EPF be shifted to the granting councils: the Medical Research Council, the Natural Sciences and Engineering Research Council, and the Social Sciences and Humanities Research Council; we further recommend that the Councils award research grants generous enough to provide full funding for the overhead costs of research. We believe that the other options, too, merit serious consideration. Most particularly, however, we are convinced that it is important for federal and provincial governments to begin a serious set of negotiations with respect to post-secondary education. For too long now, Canadian governments at both these levels have been avoiding the very serious need to reconsider the financing and structure of PSE institutions and programs.

Finally, Commissioners wish to make two further comments on this subject. First, we wish to draw attention to the wide range of means of delivery of higher education made possible by modern communications technology. While there are undoubted advantages to on-campus training, this experience is not possible for millions of Canadians who do not live near a PSE institution. The provision of television courses, whether satellite- or cassette-based, the transmission of educational information through on-line home computers, and the supporting use of correspondence material, all constitute noteworthy innovations in providing education to many Canadians who could not otherwise expect to have access to it. We wish to express our admiration and support for those Canadians who have pioneered in these areas, and to recommend that governments continue to underwrite their efforts and encourage the expansion of their work.

We also wish to comment on the state of university-based social science research in Canada. We do so on the basis of our own experience, for it is largely from this source that we recruited our research personnel and the research expertise which is one of the corner-stones of this report. We discovered, as we inaugurated our research effort, that Canada has available a very substantial body of researchers with a remarkably extensive knowledge of Canadian society and the economy. We found no shortage of people capable of conducting research into Canadian topics and of expressing their findings in ways accessible to this Commission. We found a lively interest in almost all of the major issues this Commission wished to confront. But we also became aware of some shortcomings.

Canadian social science appears to be characterized by considerable parochialism. While there exists extensive knowledge of things Canadian, the ability to compare Canadian situations or policies with those of other nations often seemed to Commissioners to be distinctly limited. We have had some difficulty, for example, in finding Canadian academics who could provide up-to-date information on foreign domestic developments. We have learned that Canadian academics do not always participate as extensively as they might in international research networks, and there appears to be relatively little "leading edge" Canadian research in some of the fields with which we were most concerned. It seemed surprising to us that we could find rather few economists deeply concerned with resource policy and almost no political scientists specializing in the politics and government of the United States. In part, this general parochialism might be explained as a reaction against the domination of Canadian social science by U.S. concepts and by American-trained social scientists of the 1960s and 1970s. Nonetheless, that consideration does not make it a desirable feature of Canadian academic life. We have also discovered a considerable degree of disciplinary isolation. Economists, political scientists and lawyers working with this Commission were happy to try to work together, but it became obvious at an early stage of our project that they had had little experience in doing so. This situation left Commissioners and staff with significant problems in trying to devise an integrated approach to the materials available.

Commissioners' suggestions emanating from these concerns are almost self-evident. Canadian scholars and institutions should be encouraged and supported in pursuing interdisciplinary research and in conducting investigation which will extend our nation's horizons beyond our own borders. Government granting Councils and programs designed to encourage research in the social sciences should pay particular attention to developing this aspect of Canadian university-based research.

Notes

1. In the 1960s and 1970s, economists devoted considerable effort to estimating rates of return on education. Their chief purpose was to see whether there was overall under- or over-investment in education. Such studies typically suggest that the rate of return on education is quite high (for example, between 10 and 15 per cent), although a decline in rates of return is believed to have occurred in the 1970s. While such estimates had a considerable impact in the 1960s, their influence declined in the 1970s.
2. Organisation for Economic Co-operation and Development, *Social Expenditure 1960–1990: Problems of Growth and Control* (Paris: OECD, 1985). Note that OECD comparative data are for educational expenditures. When publicly financed training is added, total expenditures approach 8 per cent of GNP.

3. Cited in Lars Osberg, *Economic Inequality in Canada* (Toronto: Butterworth, 1981).
4. O. Mehmet, *Who Benefits from the Ontario University System: A Benefit-Cost Analysis by Income Groups* (Toronto: Ontario Economic Council, 1978), p. 45.

Training

In our earlier discussion of general labour-market issues, Commissioners emphasized the need to help individual members of the labour force to adjust to changes and dislocations, whether caused by economic and market forces or by technological change. Governments may provide this help in the form of direct financial support, by facilitating the flow of information about opportunities, or by supporting training activities.

Governments have tended to provide most of their employment-training assistance through institutional training programs based primarily in *Collèges d'enseignement général et professionnel* (CEGEPs) and community colleges. Most such training, however, is, provided on the job without government support. The costs of this type of training are largely shared by employers, in the form of temporarily forgone production, and by their employees, in the form of temporarily forgone wages. What, then, is the appropriate balance between on-the-job and institutional training? No unequivocal answer to this question is possible, but a case can be made for some movement toward on-the-job training and away from institutional programs. Fortunately, federal policy is already progressing in that direction.

There are other important questions too, that need to be asked and, if possible, answered. For instance, how much training is required? What should be the level of specialization and sophistication of that training? Where should the balance lie between training early and later in life?

Commissioners raised the issue of the degree of specialization and sophistication of training required when we considered post-secondary education. There, we noted that the evidence that technological and economic change would require a more highly-skilled and sophisticated labour force was not necessarily compelling. Rather, it seemed that the skills required of our labour force over the rest of the century might be somewhat different in content from the current mix, but not a great deal more sophisticated. Nevertheless, there is no question but that Canadians should expect and plan for a continuing general increase in the education levels of our society.

We have already noted at many other points in this Report that economic forces will require Canadians to face significant and rapid changes, not least in the structure of opportunities for our labour force. When this reality is applied to post-secondary education, it argues for a solid and rigorous generalist approach, with some degree of specialization for some people. When it is applied to occupational training, it argues for something quite different: the need to be prepared to undertake some specialized training at more than one point in one's career. Commissioners believe, therefore, that both governments and the private sector must, in the future, be willing to devote a larger portion of resources to the training of Canadians.

Institutional Employment Training

The federal government, under the Adult Occupational Training Act (AOTA) of 1966 and its successor, the National Training Act (NTA) of 1982, has provided a significant portion of Canada's institutional occupational training.

Under the AOTA, it provided courses of training primarily for those Canadians who had discontinued formal schooling for at least 12 months; these courses, which were provided in provincial institutions, mainly community colleges, were limited to a year's duration. After 1974, each province was given a guaranteed minimum of funds for such training, indexed to the Statistics Canada Education Price Index. Under the National Training Act, the old Canada Manpower Training Program (CMTP) was replaced by a new National Training Program (NTP) to offer more flexible institutional training.

Until the inauguration of the NTP in 1982, the federal response to criticism of CMTP took two main forms. A decision was taken to reduce the proportion of CMTP trainees enrolled in the low-level Basic Training for Skill Development (BTSD) courses. In addition, the number of CMTP trainees relative to trainees in on-the-job industrial training programs was steadily reduced. Thus there was a shift of resources toward higher-level skill development and from institutional to industrial training.

The National Training Act has made several important changes in institutional employment training. For example, if there is a skills shortage, or if a trainee has no other opportunities to acquire a particular skill, he or she may enrol within fewer than 12 months of leaving school. Thus, in future, employment training may serve to provide young people with an additional bridge between school and work. In addition, the maximum length of a course offering instruction in higher-level skills has been increased from 12 to 24 months. Higher-income/support rates are now provided to encourage laid-off apprentices to continue training and to assist laid-off workers to retrain in "demand occupations". More extensive use of unemployment insurance (UI) benefits in lieu of the lower-level/training allowances has also supported this approach.

A further element is the development of a new system for overall allocation of training resources: the Canadian Occupational Projection System (COPS). This computer-based system draws on forecasts of occupational demand and supply, provided by employers, unions, governments, and educational institutions, to put together projections of the "balance" among a detailed list of occupations. Users access the system through computer links and may experiment with other combinations of the information available, using the data to assist them in making their career or training plans. Occupations in which there is a high level of demand, either nationally or regionally, will be designated "national occupations", and training resources will be directed to these on a priority basis.

Systems such as COPS may, in the future, become more widely available to individuals planning careers. It is important, however, to acknowledge that in the past, neither Canada's nor any other nation's attempts at occupational-demand projection have been very successful. Moreover, there are some dangers in using planning systems that are too broadly based, for today's "demand occupations" may be overwhelmed by new entrants if the same information governs too many training decisions.

On-the-Job Training

While there exists no precise way to measure expenditures for on-the-job training, some estimates suggest that they are as high as those for formal schooling, particularly for male workers. Recently there has been an increase in government support for this sector of our training system. One important impetus for this increase was the disappointing experience with institutional employment training in the 1960s and 1970s. More recently, a number of serious shortages of skilled workers in particular fields (machinists, machinery mechanics, tool and die makers, for example) and the fear that industry, unassisted, will be unable to retrain workers as necessary to meet the rapid technological changes of the 1980s have resulted in greater public interest in employment training.

Throughout the 1970s and into the 1980s, there was a gradual shift of federal training resources away from institutional training and towards the subsidization of on-the-job training. Programs specifically aimed at alleviating apparent shortages of labour in certain trades were also introduced. Finally, various other wage-subsidy programs have been initiated. These contribute to training by helping young people and other targeted groups to obtain jobs that will assist them to "get started" in the labour market.

Wage-subsidy programs to stimulate on-the-job training have also been introduced by provincial governments. The Ontario Career Action Program, for example, is intended to put to work, for up to 16 weeks, trainees from among unemployed 16- to 24-year-olds, at zero cost to their employers. The trainees receive training allowances (in effect, a full-wage subsidy) of $100 per week, in lieu of salary. Another variant, the Ontario Training Incentive Program (OTIP) is intended to provide payments of $1000 each to any employer and employee when the former keeps the latter in an on-the-job training course for a full year.

Although one ostensible purpose of diverting resources from institutional training to on-the-job training is to exploit the informal learning opportunities of the job situation, it has been alleged that the design of current federal programs restricts the extent to which this aim is realized. The programs provide a combination of wage subsidies and support to employers to cover the cost of training programs. However, support is provided only for formal instruction, that is "classroom" training within the firm, and not for the costs of informal instruction at the work station. This kind of support may therefore be less effective than lump-sum support as provided under some provincial programs in which employers are free to propose other ways of providing instruction.

Finally, it has been widely suggested that the diversion of training resources from institutions to on-the-job training and the intention, under the National Training Act, to concentrate on training for high-demand occupations represent a major change in the purpose and probable effects of federal support for employment training. Many analysts believe that the pursuit of "distributional" objectives, such as offsetting regional differences in unemployment rates, are beginning to take second place to an "efficiency" focus, which directs resources to the areas where the largest possible increases in output can be generated per training dollar. This approach is consistent with the approach Commissioners have taken in this report. In general, we believe that distributional objectives should be pursued through programs intended specifically to provide income security, and that training programs should focus as directly as possible on improving the efficiency of our labour force.

Broadly speaking, then, the directions set out in the National Training Act, the agreements signed pursuant to that Act, and the increased emphasis given to on-the-job training seem quite appropriate, and Commissioners do not recommend any change of course. Nevertheless, a system as large and complex as that administered by the NTA typically suffers from a very substantial degree of inertia, and changes within it come only slowly and with difficulty. The federal and provincial governments will have to put forth a considerable continuing effort if this redirection is to be consolidated.

Employment Training for School-Leavers

While Canadian governments typically devote considerable attention to institution-based education and training programs, they have traditionally paid less attention to on-the-job training and to non-institutional vocational education for early school-leavers. Commissioners agree, in general, with the Chairperson of the Toronto Board of Education who commented to us:

> *What I believe we do is to make a significant public policy commitment to those students whose transition to adulthood is going to be fulfilled through the post-secondary education sector, either universities or colleges. What I believe we fail to do—our record is appalling—is to nurture the transition of those students that choose to leave school either before or immediately following the acquisition of a secondary school graduation diploma.*
>
> (Penny Moss, Transcript, Toronto, June 26, 1984 [vol. 13], p. 3245.)

Actually, both federal and provincial governments have already begun to change this situation. Not only has more support been made available for general industrial training programs, but there has also been some expansion of wage-subsidy plans to help young people obtain work. Under the National Training Program, the federal government has also moved to increase the scale of support for industrial and apprenticeship training, some of which goes to young labour-force entrants. In addition, for the first time, this support allowed early school-leavers to enter directly into non-apprenticeship employment training, without first spending a year in the labour force. However, the great majority of those entering the labour force directly from school still receive no government help in obtaining training.

More adequate encouragement for school-leavers to take on-the-job training might include expanding existing programs for these young people, particularly in apprenticeship training; encouraging them to participate to a greater extent in institutional employment training; and spending more on wage-subsidy programs to promote "career action". The institutionally-based programs have the potential flaw of substituting formal institutional training for practical on-the-job training that might prove more productive. Moreover, the institutional approach is selective: a minority of school-leavers receive intensive assistance, but the majority must do without help. This type of program also increases the danger that government assistance will encourage young people to crowd into high-demand occupations when it might actually be desirable for them to choose from a broader range of employment possibilities.

In view of the drawbacks of opting for selective support for vocational training of school-leavers, it may be desirable to consider a "universal" plan. The Swiss, West German and the British systems provide examples. Under the Swiss and West German systems, all young people between the ages of 15 and 18 who are not in regular schools or post-secondary institutions are engaged in some form of vocational training. Some of their training is provided by the state institutions, and some is offered by firms, in the form of apprenticeship programs. These schemes have their attractions. They may, for example, reduce the need for "remedial" employment training, on which Canadian taxpayers spend so much, by arranging to train people properly in the first place. However, they are unquestionably very expensive. Less-costly options should therefore be considered.

One universally applicable proposal would be to offer wage subsidies inversely related to age for all young workers. A program might, for example, pay $1.50 an hour on behalf of 15-year-olds, $1.00 an hour on behalf of 16- to 17-year-olds, and so on. A precedent for this type of scheme was the employment tax credit introduced into the corporate tax in 1978. This credit provided a $1.50-per-hour wage subsidy (higher in designated areas) for new full-time employees hired for at least three months. Some will object that this scheme would merely lead to more "dead-end" jobs for the young because the jobs subsidized would lack a required training component. Some subsidy funds would no doubt go to support such jobs, but this disadvantage must be weighed against the benefits of the scheme: among these are reduced youth unemployment and more on-the-job training. The subsidy is particularly useful in rectifying situations where the minimum wage severely reduces on-the-job training for workers in the target age brackets. A general subsidy would have some of the same effects, but it would not provide a targeted advantage for those newly entering the labour force.

In a fiscally unconstrained world, Commissioners would recommend a generalized job-apprenticeship program along the German lines. Given the reality of fiscal constraints, however, we recommend reinstatement of the employment tax-credit program of 1978, which was targeted at youth, and the elimination of all specifically youth-targeted, direct, job creation. The tax-credit program should also be made available on behalf of women entering the labour force for the first time and of those who are re-entering the work-force, after dropping out for reasons of family responsibility. During phase-in, the program should be monitored to determine whether it displaces existing workers to an unacceptable degree.

Retraining and Paid Educational Leave

The new insight of our times, we suggest, is that education is not a program which can be added to or subtracted from the other patterns of national activity. Education is instead, a way of life within the community, a continuum of experience that progresses from pre-schooling to elementary and secondary schooling, to college and university, on to continuing education, *éducation permanente*, as our French colleagues wisely term it. Education must truly become education-for-life: that is, "life-long educational experiences, fitting Canadians to live in swiftly changing environments." (David Johnston, Transcript, Montreal, May 30, 1984 [vol. 1], pp. 20–21.)

This Commission's research has indicated that the tax system provides more liberal treatment for on-the-job training than for part-time or full-time formal education for prime-age workers and older Canadians. Given a stable technological and economic environment, this fact might be of little concern. After completing a formal education in their early years, Canadians would acquire general and specific skills through on-the-job training. The time devoted to such training would be reduced until, by late middle age, workers would be almost entirely engaged in earning a return on their accumulated skills and would spend little time augmenting them. Whether taxes and subsidies for highly-paid prime-age workers discouraged the acquisition of formal education in comparison to on-the-job training would be of little concern. Very few prime-age workers would, in any case, wish to return to formal schooling.

In fact, changes in technology and the structure of work often necessitate retraining and re-education at various points in an individual's lifetime. Job-related changes can wipe out the value of a worker's skills or create new opportunities, not originally present, for investment or human capital. Provided that a worker is not too old, such changes will often make a period of re-education a paying proposition. They may even make profitable a full-time return to study. Two recent proposals for assisting adult education and training are a levy/grant scheme of the type used for a time in Britain in the 1960s and 1970s, and the proposal for earned educational leave made recently in *Learning for Life*, the report of the National Advisory Panel on Skill Development Leave.[1]

While there are strong proponents of a levy/grant scheme, many analysts have questioned its suitability. The 1981 report of the Canada Employment and Immigration Commission (CEIC) Task Force on Labour Market Development suggests several problems with the levy/grant system:

> *The original intention of the levy/grant system was to redistribute funds (i.e., the costs of transferable skill/training) from firms which did no training themselves but relied on recruiting skilled workers trained by others, to those firms which actually did the training. In practice, the system operated in such a way as to also redistribute funds for other reasons.*
>
> - *Firms within the same industry and which paid the same amount of levy (because their total payroll or employment was identical) recovered greatly*

differing amounts in grants because differences in the skill mix in their enterprises affected their ability to earn training grants.

- *Firms which had low turnover among their skilled staff and hence did little training (because it was not necessary) recovered little from their levy and saw themselves as subsidizing less well-managed firms which had high turnover, conducted a great deal of training and hence attracted relatively large training grants.*
- *Highly specialized firms, with training carefully geared to their own requirements, received a low return on their levy (in the form of grants) because their training did not fit the training boards' grant criteria which were geared to common training standards for the industry as a whole.*
- *Some firms received a high return on their levy because they could arrange "training" activities which satisfied the boards' grant criteria, even though there was no real need for the training. (In this respect, a system intended to improve allocation of resources to training actually promoted a misallocation of resources.)*[2]

Another important recent proposal for support of re-education and retraining is that for earned educational leave. Such an arrangement might, for example, provide every worker with the right to paid educational leave at the rate of one day off for every 30 days worked. Employers would be compensated by means of tax credits for the costs of hiring replacements. This earned time-off proposal put forward in *Learning for Life* offers high rates of subsidy for a short period of time. For example, an employee who had worked for five years would have earned about two months' fully paid leave. For workers who have access to satisfactory opportunities for re-education, however, this length of leave is insufficient, while for those with unsatisfactory opportunities, it is too long.

A third option proposed is the "Registered Education and Training Savings Plan" (RETSP) of *Labour Market Development in the 1980s*, or the "Registered Educational Leave Savings Plan" (RELSP) of *Learning for Life*.[3] Under the RELSP, workers could save for re-education in the same way that first-time home buyers could once save for their first house. Each year, contributions up to a certain limit could be used to reduce taxable income, with resulting tax relief. Later, when the individual took time off to go back to school, the savings of the RELSP could finance educational and training costs.

RELSPs offer some major advantages over the earned educational-leave proposals in *Learning for Life*. The RELSP would provide approximately the right level of subsidy, given nearly equal marginal tax rates before and after training. It could be made even more flexible by allowing workers on leave to borrow against a RELSP account if educational/training opportunities occurred suddenly before sufficient funds had been accumulated to cover fully the costs of leave. It appears, therefore, that RELSPs deserve much closer attention than they have so far received as a possible device for increasing incentives for prime-age workers to return to formal schooling or to training on the job.

Notes

1. Canada, National Advisory Panel on Skill Development Leave, *Learning for Life: Overcoming the Separation of Work and Learning*, a report to the Minister of Employment and Immigration (Ottawa: Minister of Supply and Services Canada, 1984).
2. Canada, Employment and Immigration Commission, Task Force on Labour Market Development, *Labour Market Development in the 1980s* (Ottawa: Minister of Supply and Services, 1981), pp. 225–26.
3. See also Canada, Task Force on Skill Development Leave, *Learning a Living in Canada*, 2 vols. (Ottawa: Minister of Supply and Services Canada, 1983).

Recommendations

Post-Secondary Education

A number of options are available for dealing with post-secondary education. To some, the *status quo* will seem a satisfactory blend of federal financial support and provincial control. However, the majority of intervenors appearing before this Commission did not find the *status quo* acceptable. Commissioners therefore believe that reforms must be considered, and that serious federal-provincial negotiations to promote this end should begin immediately. Four major and related sets of issues call for discussion: accessibility, levels of funding, quality of the system, flexibility and adaptability.

Commissioners believe that financial problems should not be permitted to prevent otherwise-qualified Canadians from receiving post-secondary education. We therefore support the Canada Student Loans Program and its provincial equivalents, and we recommend that loan limits be changed, in consonance with other policy changes we propose, to remove any financial barriers that might exclude otherwise-qualified low-income students. We are concerned, however, that some aspects of the CSLP are not consonant with family structures currently developing in Canada: in particular, the tendency for university students to become, or claim to become, independent of their parents at an earlier age. An income-contingent/loan-repayment scheme, by treating all applicants alike and by avoiding the need to investigate parental income, could significantly alleviate this problem. It should be seriously considered during the course of the federal-provincial negotiations we have recommended. We also wish to emphasize the importance of continuing to grant scholarships for students who excel, no matter what their income level, and of offering bursaries for low- or moderate-income students with above-average grades who might otherwise be reluctant or unable to continue their education.

If Canadians see the quality and flexibility of our education/training system as a key concern, and if they are convinced, as are commissioners, that the infusion of more money will not automatically ameliorate these problems, then, in the view of this Commission, a series of reforms designed to create a more competitive and adaptable system should be considered. The main leverage of governments in dealing with the PSE system is financial. The following financing changes should therefore be considered:

- The federal government should terminate the PSE-cash portion of its EPF grants to the provinces, replacing it with an education-expense tax credit or grant.
- Provincial governments should be encouraged to deregulate the fee structure of PSE institutions.
- Provinces may wish to consider basing their transfers to institutions on an equal grant/per-student figure which would be related directly to enrolment, and which would not differentiate among particular programs.
- The student should be responsible for a portion of education costs. Beyond that point, the federal credit should vary with the amount of expenses and

tuition fees, up to a given limit. The amount of the grant should vary only to correspond to fees and expenses directly related to education, and no attempt should be made to direct students into "demand" programs by means of a variable grant structure.

- A portion of the current EPF transfer should be reallocated to granting Councils such as the Medical Research Council, the Natural Sciences and Engineering Research Council or the Social Sciences Research Council, which should begin to cover overhead costs by means of research grants.

As a variation of this approach, it may be desirable to consider an alternative system in which much larger payments are made to graduate students than to undergraduates. Commissioners' preliminary calculations suggest that undergraduate and community-college grants, averaging about $1500 per year, could be accompanied by graduate stipends in the order of $7000 per year.

Commissioners' recommendation relating to direct-to-student financing is consistent with either increasing or decreasing the amount of funding for the education sector. If Canadians are persuaded that the major problem of the PSE system is underfunding, that the current intergovernmental-transfer mode of funding presents no problem, and that provincial governments have reduced their grants to educational institutions primarily because of the EPF funding formula, then other options should be considered. These include:

- A return to the pre-EPF funding formula
- Provision by the federal government of an amount equal to provincial "own source" funding, exclusive of the tax points transferred under EPF
- Freezing of *basic* federal contributions at current or slightly lower-than-current levels with 50-50/federal-provincial matching of incremental provincial spending on post-secondary education.

Variants of this last option would be either to direct the incremental federal dollars wholly to university-based/research funding or to dispense one-half for increasing research funding and one-half for matching increased provincial funding to PSE on a 25/75-provincial/federal basis.

Among all of the above options, Commissioners would recommend that the direct-to-student/funding variants deserve most serious consideration as the basis of federal support for post-secondary education. We also believe that if intergovernmental transfers remain the dominant mode of funding, then serious consideration should be given to freezing the basic federal contribution and dividing equally what would have been its incremental amounts between research and a fund to match increments in provincial contributions to PSE institutions, on a 25/75-provincial/federal basis.

Other Education and Training Programs

With respect to primary and secondary education, Commissioners recommend that:

- The private sector take the initiative to establish an independent national commission to monitor quality and standards in primary and secondary education, and to conduct and record research in related areas.

With respect to training, Commissioners recommend that:

- Progress be continued in the directions established by the National Training Act, with particular emphasis on on-the-job and job-related programs
- A special wage subsidy be provided for labour-force entrants who have not received other forms of vocational training or post-secondary education. The subsidy would normally be provided to persons 15 to 18 years of age and to people entering the labour force after absence for family-related reasons. The subsidy could be financed by eliminating other job-creation programs for young people.
- A Registered Educational Leave Savings Plan be authorized under the Income Tax Act, to be used by workers to help finance the cost of training. Careful consideration must be given to the type of program eligible for RELSP financing and to the possibility of requiring some performance standards such as successful completion of the program.

CHAPTER 19

The Income-Security System

CHAPTER 19

The Income-Security System

Overview

Canada's income-security system is a complex mix of federal, provincial, and municipal programs comprising social insurance, direct government expenditures, and tax expenditures. The major programs in this system and their estimated 1984 – 85 gross expenditure levels are Unemployment Insurance ($11.6 billion), Old Age Security ($11.4 billion), tax exemptions and deductions for pension purposes ($7.6 billion), Social Assistance ($6.6 billion), Family Allowance ($2.4 billion), Child Tax Exemptions ($1.4 billion), the Child Tax Credit ($1.1 billion), and married exemptions ($2 billion). The personal Tax Exemption ($14 billion) is sometimes included as well. Many other programs such as Veterans' Allowances, Training Allowances and Social Assistance to on-reserve Natives could also be included. A complete list is shown in Table 19-1.

If we except the personal tax exemption, the combination of tax expenditures, Unemployment Insurance (UI) account payments, and federal and provincial expenditures on direct transfers added up to approximately $60 billion in 1984 – 85. Since this sum is equivalent to over 13 per cent of Canada's gross national product (GNP), it is obvious that income-security programs have very important macro-economic implications. Commissioners, having dealt with these implications and with Unemployment Insurance elsewhere in this Report, are concerned here with the design of the other income-security programs, for it is our conviction that the implications of program design are just as important as the questions relating to overall expenditure levels.

Commissioners believe that a review and revision of Canada's income-security programs is an essential adjunct to the changes suggested elsewhere in this Report. Government income-security programs are a fundamental part of the social consensus by which Canadians live. They express, perhaps better

TABLE 19-1 Estimates of Government Social Security Programs in Canada, 1984 – 85

Target Group	Costs in billions $ Federal	Provincial	No. of Persons ('000)
Poor			
Canada Assistance Plan	4.1	4.1	3 000
Provincial Tax Credits	—	1.6	107
Veterans' Allowance	0.5	—	—
Social Assistance to on-reserve Indians	0.2	—	—
Guaranteed Income Supplement & Spouses' Allowance	3.1	—	1 440
Child Tax Credit	1.1	—	5 000
Social Housing	1.1	—	—
Total	10.1	5.7	
Families			
Child Care Expense Deduction	0.1	0.0	370
Family Allowance	2.4	—	370
Child Tax Exemption	0.9	0.5	6 600
Married & Equivalent to Married	1.4	0.6	3 230
Total	4.8	1.1	
Employment Assistance			
Unemployment Insurance	11.6	—	3 200
Training Allowance	0.1	0.1	64
Workers' Compensation	—	1.6	620
Employment Expense Deduction	0.8	0.4	—
Total	12.5	2.1	
Elderly			
C/QPP	4.4(CPP)	1.6	2 330
OAS	8.3	—	2 700
Tax Assistance RRSP, RPP, C/QPP	4.7	2.3	—
Age Exemption	0.3	0.2	0
Pension deduction	0.1	—	903
Veterans' Pensions	0.7	—	655
Total	18.5	4.1	
Total income security	45.9	13.0	
Grand total	61.6		

Source: Calculations supplied by Ministry of State for Social Development, based on 1984 – 1985 estimates and Department of Finance figures.

than any other collective activity, our commitment to equity, security and sharing. They should contribute to our ability to take advantage of opportunities, and they should lead us to take responsibility for our own support whenever that is possible. They are a foundation of support for millions of Canadians and the safety net for millions more. If we are to achieve growth and a better society, we must not fail to ensure that these programs operate both efficiently and fairly.

The changes Commissioners propose elsewhere will call for major and sometimes difficult adjustments, and the effects of these will be felt by millions of Canadians. Many will gain in the short run; most will gain in the longer term. For those of us whose lives are altered by economic change, reasonable protection and security must be provided in such a way as to encourage us to grasp our opportunities. The gains to be reaped from economic growth must be shared with those who would, in any event, require income support, and a generous measure of assistance must be provided to help them live their lives in security and dignity.

Objectives

Commissioners noted earlier that two broad objectives underlie most of Canada's income-security programs:

- The sharing of our resources so as to provide an adequate income in relation to community standards
- The maintenance of an appropriate degree of income security or stability.

In keeping with the fundamental values outlined at the beginning of this chapter, income-security programs must also achieve four other broad goals. These are:

- The equitable treatment of individuals and families in different situations and with different levels of need
- The provision of an incentive to encourage people to take advantage of their opportunities
- The encouragement of people to take responsibility for their own lives and livelihood when they are able to do so
- Respect for the personal dignity of the beneficiaries.

There are other purposes, too, which Canada's income-security programs may be explicitly or implicitly intended to fulfil. These may include the maintenance of political support, the regional redistribution of funds, and support for newly formed families and for families raising children. Since not all of these goals are consistent with one another, the design of income-security programs necessarily involves compromise and a balancing process.

More concrete administrative considerations, too, will determine the effectiveness of programs to a significant degree. These include ensuring:

- The appropriate degree of responsiveness to income change
- A minimum of program abuse
- A high rate of use of the programs by eligible beneficiaries
- Administrative ease and economy.

Achieving the Objectives: Considerations in Program Design

Adequacy of Income

The provision of an adequate income to all citizens is perhaps the goal most commonly associated with modern income-security systems, and virtually all transfer programs address it to some degree. Some programs, such as social assistance, examine family or individual needs quite closely in order to determine appropriate levels of benefits. Others, such as the Child Tax Credit or the Guaranteed Income Supplement (GIS), simply ask for reports of income as a substitute for proof of need. Still others, such as Unemployment Insurance, Canada Pension Plan (CPP), or Old Age Security (OAS), assume that need will arise in certain circumstances such as retirement, older age or unemployment, and therefore make benefits available to all eligible residents in those circumstances. Relatively few transfer programs, however, have the alleviation of low incomes as their only major objective. The exceptions are Social Assistance, the Guaranteed Income Supplement, the Child Tax Credit, and various provincial "top-ups" to OAS/GIS.

Income Stability

The second fundamental goal is the protection of income stability or continuity. In Canada that objective is treated by a variety of more or less appropriate program designs. Since almost everyone faces declining income at retirement, this objective may be partially served by providing a universal payment, in the form of OAS, to all Canadians over age 65. OAS is now accompanied by the CPP, which is currently available to members of the labour force who have contributed to the latter plan. CPP payments to eligible beneficiaries start at retirement for those who are over age 60. The CPP, therefore, is specifically related to income stability, since contributions and benefits are related to earnings.

Drops in income are also, of course, associated with unemployment, and Unemployment Insurance is intended to deal with that source of income instability. Where the decline in income is related to a definite event such as retirement, contribution levels can be related solely to income, for everyone bears the same "risk" of requiring the benefits. Where the probability of decline in income varies from individual to individual, however, the pure insurance principle would require a contribution rate related to the risk of a given event's occurrence. (In this case, of course, the "event" is unemployment.) At present, however, the UI program does not vary its premium rates according to degree of risk, even though the risk of unemployment varies from job to job; in that sense, therefore, it is not a pure social insurance program.

Equity

A requisite in the design of any income-security system is to ensure that the net effect of its programs is equitable. The net effect of the income-security system on an individual or family results from the interaction of both tax and transfer programs. Equity in income-security design has two aspects:

- Horizontal equity, which involves applying the tax and transfer-payment system differently to different individuals or families, according to the various needs created by their particular characteristics or situation
- Vertical equity, which involves treating individuals and families with different incomes, but otherwise similar characteristics or situations, in proportion to the differences in their incomes.

The Family Allowance program, for instance, ensures that at any income level, families with children have more resources than those without children, thus contributing to horizontal equity. By contrast, the Child Tax Credit provides greater benefits to lower-income families with children than to higher-income families with the same number of children, thus contributing to vertical equity.

Equity considerations can become highly complex and are, by their very nature, value laden. Such considerations raise any number of questions. Does ownership of a home, for example, increase the "real" income of an elderly person in a way that should result in a reduction of transfers to that person? If it does, how are program designers to define the appropriate level of income to attribute to the value of the home? How much support should be provided to families with children, compared to couples and individuals with the same incomes, but without children? How much more tax should richer individuals pay than poorer individuals? The more program designers attempt to deal with equity considerations, the more they must consider the characteristics of claimants. To achieve a high degree of equity, particularly horizontal equity, requires a very considerable exercise of bureaucratic discretion and therefore may involve significant administrative costs.

Incentives and Opportunities

Income-security programs must not impair incentives for individuals to improve their own situation. This is important both to avoid impeding people's own efforts at self-improvement and to maximize the efficiency of Canada's labour force. Programs should therefore be designed to provide incentives that will encourage employable beneficiaries to try to find employment, participate in job-training and skills-upgrading programs, make appropriate use of occupational and geographic mobility, and form stable work attachments. Particular care must also be taken not to build into income-security programs incentives which may diminish family formation or lead to breakdowns in family structure.

Responsiveness to Income Changes

Income-security benefits must respond reasonably quickly to the changing incomes of individuals. It may be considered more important, however, for programs to respond more quickly to certain kinds of income loss than to others, both to encourage flexibility in the labour market and to protect beneficiaries from extreme hardship. In general, the less predictable the source of income change, the more quickly the program should be able to respond.

What is the appropriate level of responsiveness for programs intended to provide temporary income replacement during periods of involuntary unemployment? What payments should these programs make to beneficiaries? The answers to these questions will depend on the respondent's views about personal responsibility for saving to bridge temporary income losses. A program which is highly responsive to recent income changes, and which distributes a high level of benefits may discourage personal savings and will certainly require a higher expenditure of public funds. In that vein, another question arises: Should individuals whose incomes are reduced for short periods and who later regain their usual higher incomes be required to repay some portion or all of the benefits they have received?

Accessibility

If a program is worth providing at all, then it is desirable that its benefits be readily accessible to those persons who fulfil the eligibility provisions. If administrative or discretionary barriers to program use must be erected, the program's fundamental benefit structure is flawed, and its administrative costs will be disproportionately high. Universal transfer programs, of course, generally have very high take-up rates, but the ideal selective or targeted program would also have a very high take-up rate among those who are eligible for its benefits. High take-up rates in targeted programs result from ready public access to program information and application procedures, ease of compliance with program conditions, program responsiveness to income changes, and absence of administrative "hassles" in establishing eligibility.

Discouraging Program Abuse

While eliglible persons should be encouraged to take up the benefits of an income-security program, governments should discourage abuse of the program both by those not eligible to use it and by qualified beneficiaries who claim too high a benefit. It is obviously difficult to estimate abuses of income-security programs, since the essence of program abuse is that it be unreported. However, the highest estimates for social assistance abuse are in the 5 per cent range, and similar estimates are probably appropriate for Unemployment Insurance. This figure is almost certainly no higher than corresponding estimates for the abuse of the personal and corporate income-tax systems. Moreover, it is virtually impossible to abuse some of Canada's major income-security programs such as Family Allowances or Old Age Security (OAS), since it is obviously very difficult to "fake" eligibility in these instances, and since initial-benefit levels are independent of any factor other than eligibility.

Much abuse of income-security programs is the result of inappropriate program design, and it can be much more easily dealt with by correcting a program's structure than by employing more people to police its beneficiaries. By far the most common abuse of social assistance programs, for instance, is the receipt of small amounts of unreported income by recipients. Commissioners believe that any person who is able to earn a small income to "top-off" benefits should be strongly encouraged to do so, even though the current program design explicitly discourages such initiatives. Indeed, any social assistance recipients who do find part-time work are likely to be penalized by dollar-for-dollar reduction of their benefits, after a small exemption for "work-related expenses". The solution, in our view, does not lie in more strenuous policing, but rather in a change of program design.

Inappropriate program design can, in fact, cost our economy far more and raise our governments' expenditures higher than any level of abuse. Very few of the thousands of Canadians who are presently taking advantage of the ease of re-establishing eligibility for Unemployment Insurance or of UI regional extended-benefits structure and very few of the businesses which employ these people are engaged in anything which could be called "program abuse". Yet the effect of their use of program benefits is to encourage the continuation of quite inefficient industries so that the real economic cost of this aspect of program design is very high.

When levels of social abuse are low, the extent to which it is worthwhile to pursue abusers is questionable. Often it costs governments as much – or more – to catch abusers as they could save by identifying them. This is not to argue that governments should take no interest in discouraging abuse of social welfare programs, and that no enforcement provisions should be implemented. No doubt the threat of detection is a powerful deterrent to abuse that governments cannot afford to surrender. It is important, however, to keep in perspective assessments of the cost-effectiveness of anti-abuse mechanisms.

Respect for the Dignity of Beneficiaries

Income-security programs should impose no unnecessary stigma or harassment on beneficiaries or potential beneficiaries. In general, social insurance, universal benefit- or income-tax/related schemes create the least stigma. As most employable beneficiaries are imbued with the work ethic, their dignity may be enhanced by providing support through employment programs or through premium-financed social insurance; for employable people, there is far less stigma attached to receiving Unemployment Insurance than to accepting Social Assistance. Programs are also likely to be more acceptable if establishing eligibility is simple and requires little probing into the personal lives of applicants. In the past, demeaning procedures have been imposed on applicants in response to taxpayers' concerns about work effort and budgetary economy. It therefore bears repeating that if reasonable incentives can be built directly into the benefit structures of appropriate programs, there should be no need to retain such expensive and inappropriate "safeguard" features.

Administrative Ease and Economy

Income-security programs should be as simple and economical to administer as their other objectives allow. They should not require vast bureaucracies and shelves of program manuals describing the delivery systems. Moreover, readily observable criteria should be used to determine the initial and continuing eligibility and benefit rates of claimants.

This Commission recognizes, however, that while this standard of program design should be held constantly in view, factors exist which must lead to some administrative complexity. The requirements for equity in the selection of program beneficiaries will sometimes require complex judgements about real similarities or differences in various situations. Again, since some abuse of social programs is inevitable, some policing will always be required. Moreover, no matter how adroit the program design, there will always be special cases. These must be dealt with individually, and that necessity, too, requires some administrative complexity.

The Current System

By the standards set out above, the Canadian income-security system demonstrates some serious shortcomings. Before we can deal with these deficiencies, however, we must note several of the major characteristics of the current system.

Categorization and Incentives: Employable and Unemployable Recipients

The current Canadian income-security system is essentially categorical, differentiating between groups which are not generally expected to be part of the labour force and those which are either part of the labour force or expected to be. The categories of people whom Canadians do not expect to participate in the labour force currently include the elderly, the disabled, and single parents with young children. These omissions probably reflect accurately prevailing Canadian values and do not, by themselves, impose unnecessary administrative complexity. Age is very easy for administrators to determine and very difficult for claimants to falsify. Disability can be assessed by means of physical and psychological tests, though some cases fall into an unavoidable "grey" area. Views differ about the point at which a single parent can be deemed employable: some Canadians maintain that the youngest child should be of day-care age, while others argue for school age or even older; the decision hinges, too, on the availability and cost of child-care facilities. Regardless of the different viewpoints expressed, it is feasible to establish reasonably clear-cut criteria for categorizing single parents as employable or unemployable, even if the grounds of decision vary slightly from one jurisdiction to another.

One of the most difficult questions for Canadians to face in dealing with reform of the income-security system is whether or not to provide, for employable persons, benefits other than those provided by Unemployment Insurance. Benefits to employable recipients could take various forms, including "demogrant" or work-related supplementary provisions for the working poor, and the arrangement of special public or subsidized private employment for unemployed workers. The most important argument in favour of providing some benefits to employable recipients is simply that very great need characterizes this group. In 1985, there are over one million Canadians in families where one-half or more of total family income is derived from work, yet where total family incomes fall below Statistics Canada's low-income cut-off points. Many of these people would be as well-off, or even better-off, financially to live on social assistance, and it is a tribute to their tenacity and to the strength of the work ethic that they continue at their jobs. They may well be forced into social assistance, however, by even small financial reversals.

There are many reasons based both in equity and in economics to consider providing more significant assistance programs for Canada's "working poor". There is, of course, the obvious humanitarian issue of sharing to provide for the needs of these people. Again, over one million Canadian children – one in every five – are members of low-income families, and the majority of these are in working-poor families. We may help these children now and all Canadians later if we provide a better standard of living for their families. We also stimulate our economy when we help working-poor families. They will, perforce, spend almost all of any income they receive, and they will tend to spend it on Canadian goods and services, rather than on imported luxury items.

This Commission believes that in an ideal system, programs would be designed to provide appropriate benefit structures for both employable and unemployable categories of recipients, and we are persuaded that this goal can be achieved. Unemployable persons, for instance, require benefits with a relatively high basic value, for transfers are their basic source of income. For them, program costs might be controlled by a relatively high, but not pre-emptive, reduction rate (that is, the rate at which benefits are reduced for each dollar of other income), since work incentives are less important for groups which society does not expect to work on a full-time basis than for employable persons. Benefits for low-income employable beneficiaries might have a lower basic value because we expect these people to receive some earnings from employment. These benefits should also be reduced at a relatively low rate as earned income increases, so that the effective tax rate on low-income earners – a "tax" rate made by combining income tax and reduction of benefits – does not become prohibitively high. In this way, the use of categories can be made to facilitate a desirable balance of work incentives, adequacy of benefits and program economy.

Delivery Mechanisms: Universality and Selectivity

The current system represents a mixture of "universal" and "selective" benefits. In keeping with the most widely accepted convention, we shall define selective programs as those which impose a test of need, usually based on the beneficiary's income and situation, *before* the payment of a benefit, with the benefit rate then inversely related to the recipient's income level. Universal programs, in contrast, will be defined as those which distribute the same level of *gross* benefits to all persons with specified traits, irrespective of their incomes. In Canada, all such "universal" programs define their benefits as taxable income. For those programs, the income-tax system performs what is, in effect, an income test after the payment of benefits. If the regular marginal tax rate is not appropriate, then special tax-recovery or "claw-back" devices can be applied to the benefits, although no universal programs in Canada currently do this. Hence, by this definition, a universal program can be as highly redistributive in its net benefits as a selective program, and while it distributes greater amounts of gross benefits, its net budgetary requirements need be no larger than those of the selective program. All major Canadian income-security programs are subject to variation of benefit levels according to income either before or after taxes.

On purely economic or distributional grounds, there is no clear-cut case for preferring one payment method over the other. The issue is essentially one of delivery-system design. This conclusion differs from the popular view that selective programs are inherently more efficient, better targeted, and less expensive than universal programs – a view which fails to consider the taxation provisions that accompany the income-security system.

Since the economic factors are not decisive, other factors should determine the payment methods for benefits. Universal programs are usually superior for ease and cost of administration and compliance, but these advantages could be offset by complexities in the associated tax-back devices if other than normal marginal rates of taxation are considered necessary. Indeed, with special categorical benefits such as partial disability benefits, it will often be easier to apply the income test in advance of payments, using selective methods. The reason is that to be effective, a holdback must be integrated with tax withholding at source, and employers then have to know which of their workers are receiving the categorical benefits. This requirement would add to the complexity of the system, creating a problem which would bear particularly heavily on small business.

Other considerations tend to promote the use of universal programs. Universal payments are better suited to preserving the dignity of beneficiaries, and they have higher take-up rates. Recipients face no delays in the processing of benefit claims because gross benefits are paid on a continuing basis. Net benefits can respond quickly to income changes, since any income testing is performed often, through tax withholding at source. There are, of course, some advantages in selective programs. They reduce the visible cost of government services since, by performing their income-testing function before benefits are delivered, they minimize cash flows. They may also prevent the addition of some complexities to the tax system, and if governments are willing to establish the appropriate administrative structures, they can be made rapidly responsive to clients' needs.

The more purely political pros and cons of universal programs are more difficult to assess. Some observers argue that universal programs improve social cohesion and engender broad support because initial benefits are paid to very large numbers of people. Others suggest that while this was true in a period when "big government" was acceptable and even popular, universally delivered benefits now serve as frequent reminders of the size of government for a middle class no longer supportive of very large-scale administration. While Commissioners are mindful that the public view of government is more uncertain than it once was, we think, on balance, that the arguments in favour of universality are more persuasive than those against it, for most types of program.

The preceding analysis of the principles of universality and selectivity pertains to income-support programs other than social insurance. This latter group of programs, including UI and the CPP, is based on a different rationale which makes a different type of benefit structure generally appropriate. The essential purpose of governments in paying social insurance benefits is not to redistribute income. Rather, in their classic form, these benefits are intended to provide a form of insurance, under which individual workers and their employers pay premiums which approximate the cost of the workers' *expected* future benefits. Individuals collect benefits by meeting pre-specified conditions, such as being unemployed or reaching retirement age; the benefits they receive, at least up to a maximum limit, vary directly with their previous income and are taxable as income.

Taxes and Transfers

Just as the current system of income support is a mix of universal and selective programs, it is also a mix of tax and transfer payments. We shall examine the relationship between Canada's income-tax and transfer-payment systems by using family benefits as an example. The family-benefits system consists of a mixture of tax exemptions, tax credits and universal or demogrant payments.

Child tax *exemptions* in the income-tax system perform horizontal equity functions by relieving families with children of some tax liability and by differentiating taxes according to family size. On the basis of a progressive set of tax rates, however, the exemptions provide larger tax savings for households with higher incomes and hence reduce vertical equity among families.

The refundable child tax *credit* is a selective program which has a more explicitly redistributive effect by paying out funds, or offsetting taxes due, for low- to middle-income families with children. Child tax credits are an example of "refundable" tax credits, payable even to families who actually pay no taxes. They are structured so that maximum benefits are paid to all families with children, up to a specified annual income (currently, just over $26 000); above that point, they are reduced by $5 for every $100-increase in income. Since they pay higher net benefits to lower-income families, they are defined as "progressive" in their effect, and they contribute to vertical equity among families with children. They are selective, since income is considered before the size of the benefit is determined.

As "demogrants" or universal payments, Family Allowances are payable to all family units with dependent children, regardless of income, subject only to being accounted as taxable income. Since Family Allowances are subject to taxation in a progressive income-tax system, they provide smaller net benefits to higher-income families and are hence moderately progressive in their impact.

The three fiscal provisions for dependent children are a microcosm of Canada's current income-security system. They use three different delivery systems, which differ in their distributional effects. They are highly complex in their interactions so that families have great difficulty in sorting out overall effects. One major component, the tax exemption, is strongly regressive in effect.

If we add to this arrangement the effect of another component of what might be called the "family-benefits system", the overall result becomes even more curious. Canada's personal income-tax system currently provides a "married" exemption with a value, in the 1984 taxation year, of $3470. The married exemption is a deduction from the income of the breadwinning spouse in a single-earner family, apparently in recognition of the dependent status of the other spouse. In 1917, at the time that this exemption was put in place, Canadian society consisted largely of single-earner families with a dependent spouse at home. In these circumstances, the effect of the married exemption was beneficial; its effects are much less so, however, in a society where some 66 per cent of married women are members of the labour force. In effect, this exemption creates a situation where the first $3470 of a second earner's income is taxed at the first earner's higher marginal tax rate, a factor only partially corrected by the personal exemption available to the second wage earner. Moreover, because this benefit is an exemption rather than a credit, it provides no help at all to really poor families which have incomes below tax thresholds. It cost the federal treasury approximately $1.4 billion in 1984 with a further cost of $0.75 billion to provincial treasuries.

Finally, the personal exemption deserves comment. In 1984, this feature of our tax system allowed a basic deduction of $3970 from the taxable income of each individual taxpayer. The exemption does raise the tax threshold for individuals so that poorer Canadians may escape personal income taxation altogether. However, if it is intended to provide support or relief to individual Canadians, it has rather perverse effects. In fact, it delivers an effective benefit of nearly $2000 to all higher-income individuals who are in the 50 per cent marginal tax bracket, while to very low-income individuals whose marginal tax rates are more likely to be in the 20 per cent range, it gives an effective benefit of only $800. For very poor Canadians who have no income subject to taxation, it provides no benefit at all. It costs the federal treasury $9.4 billion annually and provincial treasuries $4.7 billion. As we shall see below, the vertical equity effects of the personal exemption might be considerably improved by converting this "benefit" to a refundable tax credit – in effect, a guaranteed income.

When the whole-family/personal-benefit structure is taken together, its effect is regressive. This fact, however, does not emerge clearly unless we view the structure as a combination tax and transfer-payment system. That system provides less benefit than it might to those poorer families and individuals who really need help, and it distributes unnecessary benefits to high-income earners. Thus, for example, the combination of personal, married, child and work-expense deductions, Family Allowances and the Child Tax Credit yields a net benefit of approximately $5035 per year to the $100 000 single-earner/two-child family in Ontario. By contrast, a two-earner/two-child family with $25 000 in total earned income receives from the system only $2240 in net benefits. Moreover, the system constitutes a real disincentive to labour-force participation by lower-income second earners, generally women. It is an example of a piecemeal program put in place when our labour-force structure, based on single-earner families, was far different from that of the 1980s.

Overview

Canada's present income-security system has been criticized on a number of highly significant counts. In brief:

- It is ineffective. In spite of an expenditure of billions of dollars there are still many Canadians living in poverty, while many income-security payments are made to people who are not poor.
- It is too complex. There are too many programs and too many people administering them. It is often difficult for Canadians to discover what benefits they qualify for, and the interaction of programs results in many unforeseen pitfalls for beneficiaries.
- It creates work disincentives. This situation may derive from three problems. Benefits are unrealistically high for some recipients or are paid for too long a period. The marginal tax or reduction rate of the system is extremely high, sometimes over 100 per cent. The benefits paid may encourage people to remain tied to unproductive or non-competitive industries and may actively discourage them from taking advantage of better employment opportunities.
- It is inequitable. Because significant parts are based on tax exemptions rather than on direct transfers or tax credits, more benefits go to some high-income than to some low-income families. This anomaly appears, particularly, when the entire tax and transfer system is taken into account, including all of the tax breaks generally used by middle- and upper-class Canadians.
- The sustainability of the system is sometimes claimed to be uncertain because of the age structure of our population, projections of continuing high levels of unemployment, and assumed perverse effects of demographic change.

In sum, these considerations suggest that our Canadian income-security system is badly flawed. This is hardly surprising. Its provisions were constructed piecemeal, in combination with sometimes unco-ordinated adjustments to Canada's personal income tax. The amalgam may have been partially suitable for the Canadian society of 1950, but it is much less appropriate for that of the later 1980s. The issue is not whether reform is necessary, but rather, how deep and rapid that reform must be.

Reforming the System

There are a number of features which Canada should strive to incorporate in a better system of income-security. On the basis of the considerations raised above, the following aims should be among them:

- Better matching of benefits to needs
- More appropriate incentives for Canadians to participate in work, training or education
- Simplification of the system so that it becomes easier for Canadians to comprehend
- Appropriate integration of tax, income transfer and social insurance systems
- Ease of administration
- Provision for the personal dignity of the individual
- Rapid responsiveness to changes in situations.

Commissioners have not included lower cost among the imperatives just listed. While it is possible that a system rationalized along the lines suggested above could cost somewhat less than our present system, it must be remembered that there are a great many Canadians who do need some form of assistance. Moreover, as we have indicated earlier, while we do see short-term budgetary problems, we do not fear for the future sustainability of our income-transfer programs, and we do not believe that those short-term budgetary problems should be solved by large reductions in the resources redistributed through income transfers. Indeed, we view continued adequate levels of funding as essential to the achievement of those adjustments which will ensure a more prosperous future for all Canadians.

The features suggested might be achieved through a set of comprehensive reforms of the income-security and personal income-tax systems or through a more incremental series of reforms. They might depend on a demogrant delivery system which makes basic payments to everyone, regardless of income, and then adjusts net benefits to needs by way of taxation. Alternatively, they might be delivered through the tax system, by adjusting the taxes of members of the labour force and by providing refundable credits to those outside its bounds or those not subject to tax withholding at source. We have already seen that the difference between a demogrant and a tax-based delivery system is essentially one of mechanism; the benefit structure can be the same under either arrangement.

Partial Reforms

While Commissioners believe, for reasons to be detailed below, that it is desirable to consider a comprehensive reform of Canada's income-security system, the reform of several of its components or sub-systems could prove effective in bringing Canadians closer to achieving a number of the objectives set out earlier. For this purpose, the overall income-security system may be broken down into sub-systems directed to help:

- The elderly
- Families with children

- Unemployed, but employable, Canadians who are not receiving UI benefits
- Persons in need who are not expected to work.

The last two sub-systems are dealt with on a joint federal-provincial basis under the Canada Assistance Plan (CAP). Smaller sub-systems also exist to assist groups such as veterans or Native people, and a number of quite specialized programs and services provide help to relatively small numbers of individuals. While such programs are vitally important to those falling within their purview, this Commission cannot deal with them here; indeed, more general reform may make some of them unnecessary.

Pension Policy and the Elderly

No element of our income security system has been more actively debated in recent years than pensions. Since the late 1970s, a long series of reports by task forces, advisory bodies and Royal Commissions have analysed our retirement-income system and highlighted its deficiencies. Business associations, labour organizations, representatives of pensioners, welfare groups and women's organizations have all pressed their views on government. A National Pensions Conference was held in 1981, and government deliberations have continued since then. Canadians have, in effect, been engaged in a "great pension debate" for the better part of the decade.

This debate has been fuelled by a wide variety of concerns: the present financial plight of many elderly Canadians; the impact of inflation on private pension benefits; the long-term implications of demographic change for the financing of future pensions; the need to adapt our pension arrangements to the evolving role of women in modern society. Because of the diverse concerns underlying it, the debate has ranged widely, touching on both public and private pensions and on the appropriate balance between them. In the case of private or occupational plans, attention has focused on the incomplete coverage of the labour force, vesting and portability, and on the protection of benefits from inflation. Issues relating to public programs have ranged from the adequacy of benefit levels to the financial consequences of the aging of Canada's population over the next half century.

The scope of the pension debate itself has posed a major challenge, since pension reform in this country requires a particularly high level of consensus. This is because the division of authority over pension policy between the federal and provincial governments is exceedingly complex, even by Canadian standards. Most occupational plans are subject to provincial regulations; but the federal Pension Benefits Standards Act applies to sectors of the economy subject to direct federal jurisdiction, and the provisions of the federal Income Tax Act are critical to all private plans. In the area of public pensions, the federal government is responsible for Old Age Security and the Guaranteed Income Supplement. But amendments to the Canada Pension Plan require the approval of two-thirds of the provincial governments, representing two-thirds of the total population – a requirement even more exacting than the general amending formula for the Constitution. Moreover, the Quebec Pension Plan falls under the exclusive jurisdiction of the Quebec government.

It is not surprising, therefore, that the debate has been a protracted one, and that actual changes have been limited. Nevertheless, there are signs of emerging consensus. While the package of likely reforms is much more limited than the champions of major change have been advocating, it does represent an important advance on existing arrangements.

Points on which agreements seem possible include reforms to the minimum standards for private pension arrangements. Some of these are:

- Earlier vesting. Employees should have a right to benefit from their employers' contributions as well as their own. In most jurisdictions, the present regulations do not require vesting until an employee has ten years of service and has reached 45 years of age. There is widespread agreement on the need for earlier vesting although not, perhaps, on the exact formula. For the most part, the debate revolves around proposals for vesting after either two or five years. Most participants in the debate would seem to agree that the age standard should be eliminated.
- Portability. Important improvements in the portability of pensions are possible through such mechanisms as locking funds into personal retirement savings accounts, or devising better protection for deferred pension benefits. Both portability and vesting improvements seem particularly important to Commissioners, since we believe that in the future, Canadians are likely to face stronger requirements to change jobs or careers more frequently.
- Inflation protection. While this issue remains more controversial, the proposals for partial indexing of future pensions, advanced by the federal government and the province of Ontario in 1984, represent a solid basis for progress.
- Survivor benefits. Survivor pensions are not required under most of our pension-standards legislation, and many plans do not provide them. This is one reason for the financial plight of many elderly women, and any reform package must require adequate protection for survivors.
- Credit-splitting. The splitting of pension credits on marriage breakdown, unless the courts or the parties themselves provide otherwise, is in keeping with the contemporary principle that marriage is a partnership.
- Part-time employees. Pension benefits should be extended to regular part-time employees. This principle accords with Commissioners' earlier emphasis on flexibility of working time.

In addition, there is scope for greater flexibility in the provisions governing tax assistance to personal retirement savings.

Similarly, agreement seems possible on important elements of our public pension plan, especially the Canada and Quebec Pension Plans. These include:

- Maximum pensionable earnings. Government should ensure that these earnings reach the target level of the average industrial wage within the next two years.
- Credit splitting. Credit-splitting on marriage breakdowns, which is now voluntary, should be compulsory, unless both spouses formally waive the right.

- Contribution rates. Federal and provincial governments should agree to a schedule by which increased contribution rates can be phased in slowly, in order to avoid particularly sharp increases at the turn of the century.

Other proposals in this area, including the introduction of a pension for homemakers, are more controversial, and early agreement on them is less likely.

In light of the present extensive debate over the pensions system, this Royal Commission did not attempt another intensive study of this topic. The emerging consensus among governments will certainly not solve all the problems in our pensions system, but it does represent a step forward. Commissioners urge that the federal and provincial governments proceed as rapidly as possible to agree on reforms. It is time to move from debate to action on pensions.

With respect to OAS/GIS, this Commission believes that current provisions are only minimally adequate. The most recent round of GIS increases, raising the incomes of single elderly people to Low-Income Cut-Off levels should have relieved the most extreme cases of hardship. We do note the anomalous situation created by the pension income and the "over-65" deduction from income for taxation purposes. Like all deductions, these deliver benefits disproportionately to the better-off, but the scarcity of high incomes among Canadians over 65 makes their effect relatively minor.

Commissioners do wish to emphasize, again, however, that Canadian public pensions are very low by international standards. The combination of low income among the elderly and the low level of these benefits means that most governments should not look to these areas to effect reductions in government expenditures.

The Family-Benefits System

In discussing the interrelationships between our tax and transfer systems Commissioners noted a number of faults in the family-benefits system. This system, it will be recalled, consists of Family Allowances, the Child Tax Credit and the Child Tax Exemption. The Child Care Expense deduction and the "married exemption" may also be considered part of this system. The former is a very small program by income-security standards, with a budget of $100 million and 370 000 beneficiaries; we shall consider it briefly below when we look at daycare. We shall also suggest the elimination of the married exemption as part of our comprehensive reform package. We might note in passing that to roll the tax expenditures from the married exemption into child-benefit reforms considered below would enrich the child-benefit package by nearly 30 per cent.

A range of options for dealing with family benefits has been discussed publicly, and in its 1985 discussion paper on benefits for children and the elderly,[1] the federal government has suggested two possibilities for reforms. Commissioners present here two examples of the type of change that has been under consideration. Option 1 is very close to the "alternative option" put forward by the federal government in its consultation paper.

Option 1: Providing Maximum Assistance to Low-Income Families. The set of options most often discussed for achieving change in the family-benefits system is one in which Family Allowances and Child Tax Exemptions are sharply reduced. The savings effected would be put into an increased Child Tax Credit. Let us consider, for example, changes which:

- Reduce Family Allowances from $360 to $240 per year
- Reduce the Child Tax Exemption from $710 to $240 per year
- Increase the Child Tax Credit from $343 to $770 per year
- Reduce the turning point (at which eligibility for program benefits commences) from an annual income of $26 330 to one of $20 000.

This option would target the system more sharply and still permit a Government of Canada cheque to be delivered monthly to all eligible mothers. Table 19-2 indicates the effect on one-earner/two-children families in Ontario. Single-earner families with annual incomes under $29 000 would gain from this option, while higher-income families would lose.

TABLE 19-2 Illustration: Effects of More Selective Program on One-Earner/Two-Children, Ontario Family, 1983

Family Earnings ($)	Family Allowance ($)	(net) Child Tax Exemption ($)	Child Tax Credit ($)	Total Benefits ($)	Change in Benefits ($)
6 000	480	0	1 540	2 020	+650
12 000	359	121	1 540	2 020	+465
18 000	345	135	1 540	2 020	+443
24 000	338	142	1 340	1 820	+232
30 000	302	178	1 040	1 520	−17
36 000	302	178	740	1 220	−24
42 000	267	213	440	920	−111
48 000	267	213	140	620	−391
48 000+	267	213	0	480	−531

Source: Commission calculations based on Survey of Consumer Finances.

Overall, the distribution of "winners" and "losers" is about 50/50, with a fairly equal balance between amounts lost and gained. The system's changes allow families with $6000 or less in earned annual income to gain $650 and families in the $10 000- to $20 000-income range to gain about $450. Families with single earners and incomes over $50 000 will lose slightly over $530 per year.

Other variants of Option 1 might be developed by manipulating the various programs. For example, the elimination of Family Allowances and Child Tax Exemptions or the application of sharply increased tax-back rates to above-average incomes would greatly reduce program costs and improve overall targeting, but sharply reduce benefits for families in middle-income ranges. Conversely, increasing Family Allowances while eliminating the tax exemptions and credits would permit some increase in net benefits to low-income earners and would also preserve some transfers, even to higher-income families with children. This arrangement would maintain some element of horizontal equity.

Option 2: Protecting Poor Families While Achieving Fiscal Savings. An option similar to Option 1, but also incorporating reductions in government expenditure, can easily be derived. Let us consider, for example, changes which would:

- Reduce Family Allowances from $360 to $240 per year
- Reduce the Child Tax Exemption from $710 to $240 per year
- Increase the Child Tax Credit from $343 to $563 per year
- Reduce the turning point (at which eligibility for program benefits commences) from an annual income of $26 330 to one of $20 000.

This option would reduce government spending by $380 million per year, while maintaining most of the other features of the system. Table 19-3 indicates the effect on one-earner/two-children families in Ontario, and Figure 19-1 illustrates the same effect in graphic form: single-earner families with annual incomes under $22 000 would gain from this option, while higher-income families would lose.

Figure 19-2 complicates the issue further – but makes it more realistic – by including two-earner families. These families do not become net losers in the system until they reach an income of $34 000 per annum, and their losses are insignificant until they earn $40 000 per annum. Overall, the distribution of "winners" and "losers" is about 60 to 65 per cent losers and 35 to 40 per cent winners. Many of the winners gain rather little; many of the losers forego

TABLE 19-3 Illustration: Effects of an Expenditure Saving Program which Protects the Poor in One-Earner/Two-Children, Ontario Family, 1983

Family Earnings ($)	Family Allowance ($)	Child Tax Exemption ($)	Child Tax Credit ($)	Total Benefits ($)	Change in Benefits ($)
6 000	480	0	1 126	1 606	+236
12 000	359	121	1 126	1 606	+51
18 000	345	135	1 126	1 606	+30
24 000	338	142	1 026	1 506	–282
30 000	302	178	626	1 106	–431
36 000	302	178	326	806	–438
42 000	267	213	26	506	–525
48 000	267	213	0	480	–531
48 000+	267	213	0	480	–531

Source: Commission calculations based on Survey of Consumer Finances.

FIGURE 19-1 Family Benefits, Option 2, One Earner/Two Child Ontario Family (Changes in benefit levels in relation to family income, 1984)

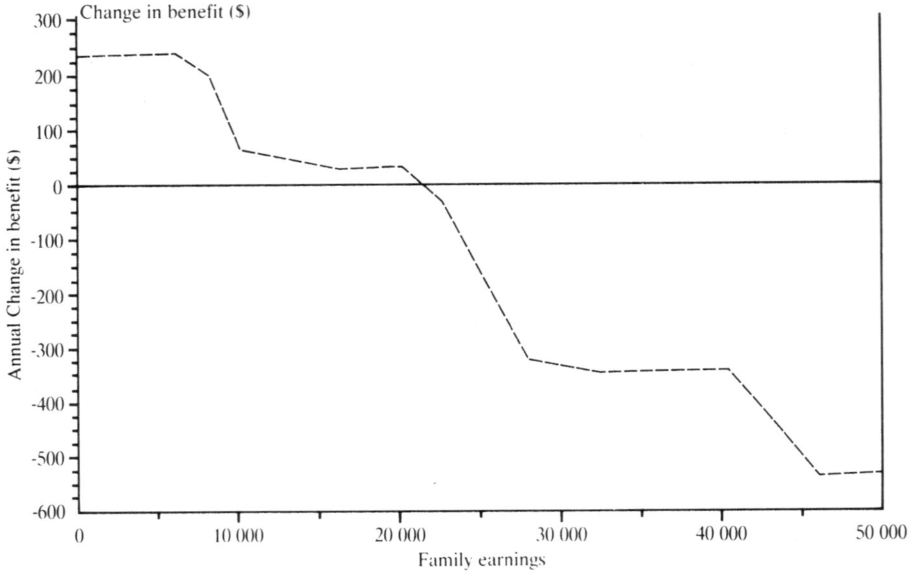

Source: Commission calculations based on Survey of Consumer Finances.

FIGURE 19-2 Family Benefits, Option 2 (Changes in benefit levels in relation to family income, 1984)

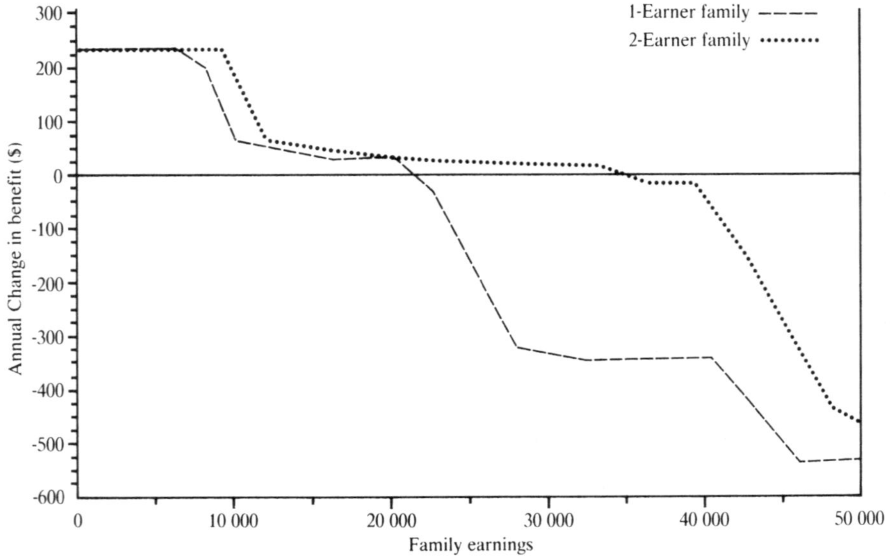

Source: Commission calculations based on Survey of Consumer Finances for Ontario families.

substantial amounts. As we saw with Option 1, to create a system where winners and losers are about evenly balanced, we must move very close to the point of fiscal neutrality where savings are eliminated. Given the relatively small amounts which can realistically be saved by systems such as Option 2, and given the very favourable redistributive effect of the previous option, this Commission favours Option 1. However, this and the other reforms suggested in this section are really relatively minor in an income-security system which could be much improved.

Option 3: The Wrong Way to Reform. Option 3 offers an extreme example of the Option-2 variant just described. It is presented here to illustrate what happens when simplistic "solutions" are applied to complex systems. It consists, very simply, of cutting off all child benefits from families with above-average earnings. To illustrate this measure graphically, we offer two figures. Figure 19-3 shows before-and-after-tax income for families with average annual earnings ($32 000). Figure 19-4 demonstrates the effect of cutting off all child benefits when annual family income reaches $32 000. The result is that disposable annual income (after tax) drops to $24 500 from $25 900 as the total family income rises from $32 000 to $32 001 and then climbs at the same rate as before from the new lower level. The result is that until family income rises above $34 500, the family is worse off than it was with annual earnings of $32 000. This "notch" effect was a common problem of early welfare systems, and it is still significant occasionally. For example, a family trying to earn its way off social assistance may face real "tax" rates which are greater than those faced by families earning over $100 000 per year. The problem is created by a combination of reductions in their cash payments and elimination of their eligibility for some services such as non-insured medical programs. These "notches" in income security and social support systems are the classic example of the "poverty trap" which many low-income Canadians face.

Option 3 could be improved by applying graduated reductions in benefit levels to those whose incomes are above the average family level, but this modification would make it identical in effect to Option 2. In its simplest form, Option 3 does generate very large savings, amounting annually to approximately $1.3 billion, but most of these savings are generated in the notch area. One might question the desirability of reducing the disposable income of the "average" Canadian family by over 5 per cent in order to implement a program design which creates no net winners, offers no redistribution of income to those who need it most, and establishes a potentially significant work disincentive. For these reasons, only options similar to Option 1 or 2 should be considered.

Social Assistance and the Canada Assistance Plan

Under the Canada Assistance Plan (CAP), Canada's federal government contributes 50 per cent of the cost of social assistance, welfare services and work-activity programs delivered by provinces and municipalities. Approximately 73 per cent of the federal transfer ($3.1 billion) goes to support

FIGURE 19-3 Current Income Before and After Taxes and Transfers

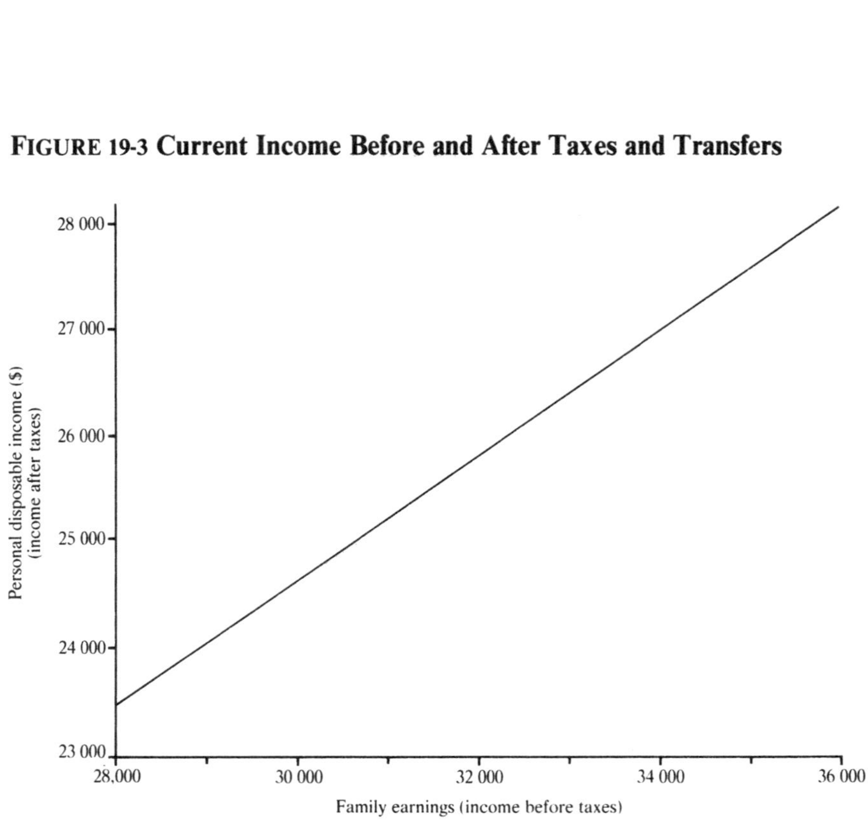

Source: Commission calculations based on Survey of Consumer Finances based on a 1-child Ontario family.

FIGURE 19-4 Impact on Disposable Income of Cutting off Child Benefits from Families with Above-Average Income

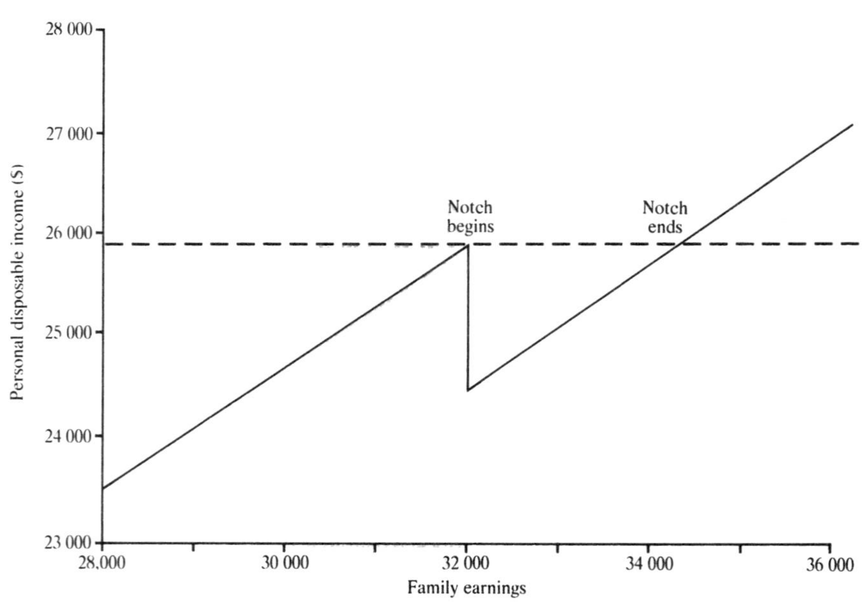

Source: Commission calculations based on Survey of Consumer Finances based on a 1-child Ontario family.

income-security programs which supply basic needs such as food, shelter, clothing, fuel, nursing-home and some health-care needs to approximately two million persons. The remaining federal and provincial expenditures in this area ($1.1 billion) support child welfare, children's institutional care, and such welfare services as day care, home care for the elderly, counselling, and community programs for the disabled and aged; they also fund research and administration.

Commissioners believe that there may be considerable scope for reform of the income-transfer (social assistance) component of CAP programs. Since social assistance is the recourse for many Canadians who are unable to gain income from employment, it is the ultimate "safety net" in modern income-transfer arrangements.

The Canada Assistance Plan was intended to contribute towards the costs of provincial social assistance programs that provided adequate assistance to persons in need, regardless of the cause of need. The exercise of wide discretion in the application of this criterion, however, has brought about an uneven and, for some groups, an inadequate system of assistance across our country. The result has been:

- Wide variation in assistance levels
- Significant increases in the numbers of people relying on charitably financed food banks and hostels
- Discriminatory treatment of some classes of recipients of assistance, which may contravene Sections 15 and 36 of the Canadian Charter of Rights and Freedoms in the Constitution Act, 1982.

In addition, social assistance benefits under CAP normally produce strong work-disincentives. Above a low exemption level, benefits are generally reduced, dollar for dollar, as earned income accrues, an arrangement which effectively imposes a 100 per cent tax rate on earnings. While this policy is in some ways consistent with a "last resort" program for beneficiaries who are not expected to work, the majority of social assistance recipients are single mothers and the disabled. Many of these people could earn modest amounts and would no doubt prefer to do so, but they are discouraged by the fact that, in contrast to better-off Canadians, they cannot really improve their situation by working. A number of reform possibilities should be considered for the CAP.

The social assistance components of CAP should be made somewhat more uniform from coast to coast. Variations in benefit levels of up to 100 per cent are not uncommon among provinces. In 1983, for example, average monthly social assistance levels for two-adult/two-children families varied from $1171 in Alberta to $689 in New Brunswick; for single employable recipients, these levels ranged from $535 in Saskatchewan to $103 in New Brunswick, $180 in Quebec and $226 in Newfoundland. While there are considerable discrepancies in cost of living and net per capita income for non-welfare recipients across Canada, they are far less extreme than variations in social assistance.

It seems clearly desirable to amend the current CAP stipulation that beyond the exemption level ($190 per month for a two-adult family), federal cost-sharing will assume a 100 per cent/tax-back rate. A more appropriate procedure would be to establish lower boundaries for the tax-rate (perhaps 75 or 50 per cent) of shareable benefits. Since social assistance programs are provincially controlled, the federal government should try to negotiate with provinces satisfactory arrangements to this effect; failing that, it might require provinces wishing to be eligible for federal cost-sharing to submit plans that would feature tax-back arrangements which would create work incentives for beneficiaries.

Twice in the late 1970s, federal and provincial governments came very close to agreeing to divide the social assistance and social service components of the CAP into separate financing arrangements. This was a worthwhile initiative, and Commissioners recommend that renewed attempts be made to achieve agreement so that the somewhat different program-design features required to deal appropriately with each of the two components may be accommodated, although Health and Welfare Canada has, by the creation of separate guidelines for cost-sharing under the social service provisions of the Act, already moved some distance towards this approach.

Comprehensive Reforms: The Universal Income Security Program

All of the proposals considered so far are essentially piecemeal reforms of a system built up over some 60 years. While there is much to be said for incremental reform, it also creates a number of problems. If, for example, only the family-benefits system is reformed, with the primary objective of distributing more money downwards to lower-income groups, the effect will be to shift money among different income classes of families with children, while single persons and families without children will share none of the burden. This rather narrow approach to equity and sharing may be undesirable unless Canadians believe that middle- and upper-income families with children should bear all the costs of reform.

The narrow base of most partial reforms limits the options available. If reforms are made only to the family-benefits system as narrowly defined, the total amount available for reallocation, provided that the married exemption is left untouched, is $3.4 billion. While this is hardly a trivial sum, it represents only 5.5 per cent of the total of transfers and tax expenditures listed in Table 19-1, and it improves the system only for low-income families with children. While such a step is laudable enough, Commissioners believe that it is possible to do better.

A narrow base naturally limits the number of programs which can be reformed or replaced. A more "rational" set of social programs would replace many of our present tax exemptions (because they are regressive) and would perhaps apply higher-than-usual marginal tax rates at the high end of the scale to several universal transfers, in order to tax back the benefits accruing to high-income earners. This action would considerably simplify the system and effect a better distribution of benefits.

Commissioners believe that in view of these considerations, a more complete rationalization is a worthwhile target in the reform of our income-transfer system. This will mean replacing much of the present complex range of programs with one transfer, delivered either through the tax system, adjusted to pay out benefits monthly, or through separate cheques, a method similar to that used in current Old Age Security programs. For design reasons to be considered below, where recipients depend wholly or almost-wholly on transfer income for survival, it will be necessary to add a second program or "tier" of benefits to "top up" payments. In keeping with our earlier analysis, Commissioners suggest that this system should provide:

- An adequate survival level of benefits to those who cannot be expected to work
- Income supplements for workers whose earned income is not sufficient to meet their family needs
- A simple, more easily understandable system of taxes and transfers
- A tax-back structure which will not discourage those who are able to work their way out of the need for benefit payments
- No increase in the costs of transfers and tax expenditures
- Assurance to Canadians that they will have an adequate "safety net" as Canada undertakes the adjustments necessary to compete successfully in the modern world
- Basic equity among Canadians in different family and life situations.

Comprehensive income-transfer/reform packages are usually described as "Guaranteed Annual Incomes" (GAIs). That term, however, is not entirely appropriate for the type of reform this Commission wishes to suggest. The term 'Guaranteed Income' often connotes a program with a very high "guarantee level" (that is, a high level of benefits for those who have no other income) and a relatively high reduction rate (effective tax rate) for beneficiaries. Commissioners believe that an option which delivers a relatively low guarantee level, but which also has a lower reduction rate combined with a special "top-up" for those who cannot be expected to work, will produce a more desirable combination of income support and work incentives. Such an option would not provide a payment high enough to encourage employable people to rely wholly on it, and it would not tax back benefits on earnings at a rate high enough to discourage the earning of income. We prefer to describe such a package as a "Universal Income Security Program" (UISP).

A wide variety of options of this type is available. It is not the purpose of this Commission to determine which is the best of them, but rather to indicate the direction in which we believe government might move. That direction might see the elimination of:

- The GIS (but not OAS)
- Family Allowances
- Child Tax Credits
- Married exemptions
- Child exemptions
- Federal contributions to social assistance payments
- Federal Social Housing Programs.

Commissioners believe that these programs should be replaced by a universally available income transfer. We note particularly, however, that current levels of OAS should be maintained. Among programs for the elderly, only GIS is replaced in this proposal, since it is the more directly income-tested component of the Old Age Security system. OAS payments themselves should be maintained since the vast majority of Canadians have based their retirement planning upon them. By way of example of overall reform packages, we provide here two possibilities, defined imaginatively as Option A and Option B.

In Option A, the personal income-tax exemption would also be eliminated, and changes would be made to programs as listed above. Based on mid-1984 figures, a guaranteed income of $3825 per annum for each adult and for the first child in a single-parent family, and $765 for any other child can then be provided for all Canadians, without incurring any extra costs. In Option B, the personal income-tax exemption is left in place, which means that the guaranteed income would drop to $2750 per adult (and for the first child in a single-parent family) and $750 per child. In order to maintain at least the current income level of those elderly with no source of income other than OAS benefits, the basic guarantee for single persons over 65 years of age should be the same as that in Option A ($3825); a tax-back rate of 20 per cent is applied to benefits in both systems, and the current personal income-tax/rate structure is assumed to remain intact. For those over sixty-five, the fifty per cent tax-back rate currency applied to GIS benefits could continue.

Figure 19-5 illustrates that in Option A, one- or two-earner/two-children families with earned annual incomes below $30 000 will gain. Gains of $5000 to $7000 are possible among those families with earned incomes in the $8000 to $10 000 range. However, gains at zero or very low incomes may well be overstated because the effects of loss of housing benefits and of part of social assistance are not included here. The losses can be quite substantial, approaching $5000 for families with incomes over $50 000. Figure 19-6 (Option B) illustrates that to leave the personal exemptions in place reduces this loss for upper-income families to the $1000 range, but also reduces net gains in the $8000 to $10 000/earned-income family to $4000 to $5000.

Figure 19-7 illustrates that in Option A, two-earner/two-children families with earned annual incomes below $30 000 will gain. Maximum losses of about $3800 occur for families earning over $40 000 annually. Most important, families in the "working-poor" range, with earned incomes of between $8000 and $12 000, will also gain amounts in the $5000 to $7000 range. Figure 19-8 illustrates that if we leave the current personal exemption intact, gains in the "working-poor" range are reduced somewhat, to the $4000 to $5000 range, but upper-income losses are sharply reduced to the $1000 range.

These options are meant as illustrations only. An almost infinite variety of guarantee levels and tax-backs can be considered, and experience with the programs will doubtless lead, over time, to design changes. Indeed, it is an important feature of these comprehensive reform proposals that they are flexible, and that the parameters can be amended to provide predictable patterns of income redistribution which will contribute to the achievement of

FIGURE 19-5 Option A: Change in Personal Disposable Income in One-Earner/Two-Children, Two Adult Family, 1984

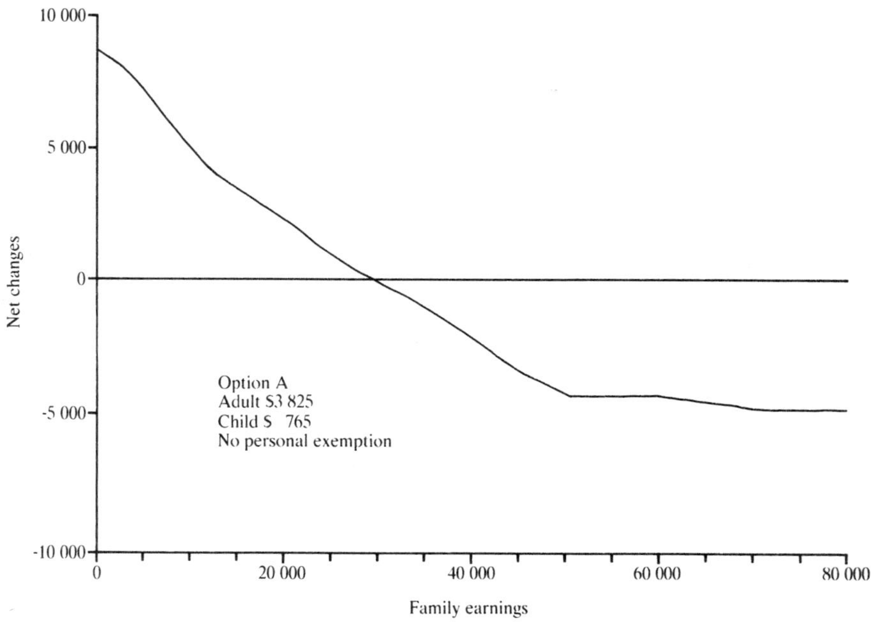

Source: Commission calculations based on Survey of Consumer Finances for Ontario families.

our goals of equity, security, sharing and opportunity, and hence to growth through consensus. The examples also illustrate that within existing cost limits, it is possible to design programs which will provide substantially enhanced levels of security for low-income Canadians, without necessarily imposing prohibitive costs on high-income earners. They also make quite clear another immutable fact: it is not possible to provide higher benefits at the bottom of the income scale without reducing net incomes at the middle and higher levels.

The income guarantees operative at very low-earnings levels are not necessarily adequate to meet all family needs unless some additional support is provided. This occurs because our preferred design options use relatively low levels of guaranteed incomes combined with relatively low tax-back rates in order to give desirable work-incentive features and in order to extend benefits to working-poor families. Individuals and, particularly, families, who have very little income except that provided by the UISP, would still be eligible for provincial or municipal social assistance top-ups as a second tier of benefits, since the funds that those governments currently contribute to social assistance are unaffected by our proposals. These top-ups could continue to be subject to high tax-back rates because they would constitute only about half the benefits for extremely low-income families; the other half would come from the federal supplement, with its low tax-back rate. Thus, for a two-

FIGURE 19-6 Option B: Change in Personal Disposable Income in One-Earner/Two-Children, Two Adult Family, 1984

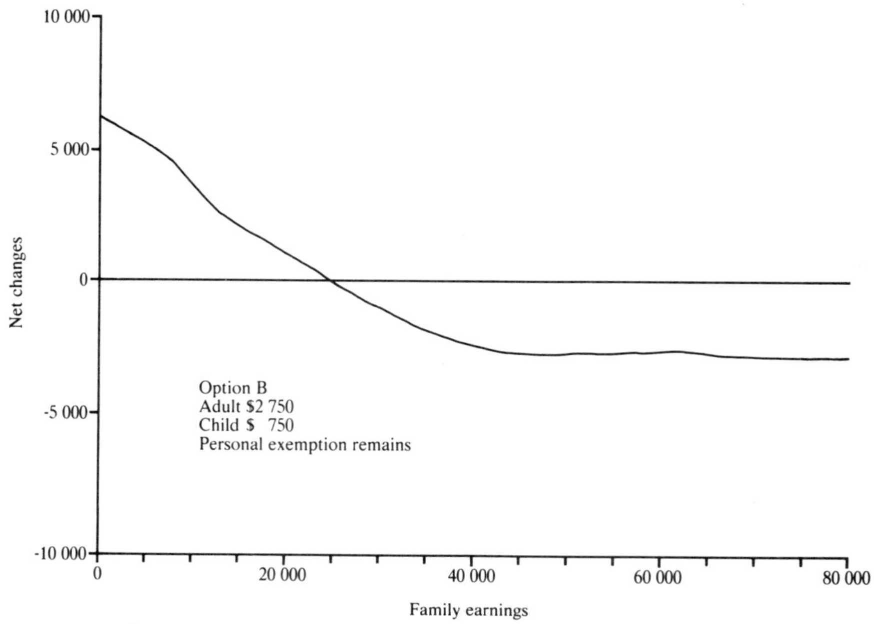

Source: Commission calculations based on Survey of Consumer Finances for Ontario families.

adult/two-child family with no other income, Option A would guarantee a basic annual income of $9180 provided by the federal government and Option B a basic income of $7000, under corresponding circumstances. Provinces might continue to provide social assistance top-ups in the amounts they now provide from their own funds, under CAP-supported social assistance. If they did so, provincial payments would add, on average, approximately $3500 to $4500 to the basic levels, making $12 500 to $13 500 available to Canada's poorest families under Option A or $10 500 to $11 500 under Option B.

Even with relatively low guarantee levels, there still may be concern about the work-incentive effects of these proposals, particularly with respect to young single recipients. If this is a public concern, it is possible to make receipt of benefits contingent on active participation in the labour force in the form of active job search, as defined by the Unemployment Insurance Commission (UIC), or by demonstrating some level of earned income or by participation in locally administered job-creation projects. In the mid-1970s, during consideration of such system designs, planners envisaged that provincial governments might share in these proposals and hence administer some form of "employment-availability" tests. A combination of UIC offices and National Revenue Taxation offices might also undertake appropriate screening. In pure efficiency terms, the cost of such screening is unlikely to be worth the money saved, but it might be difficult to mobilize public support for

FIGURE 19-7 Option A: Change in Personal Disposable Income in Two-Earner/Two-Children Family, 1984

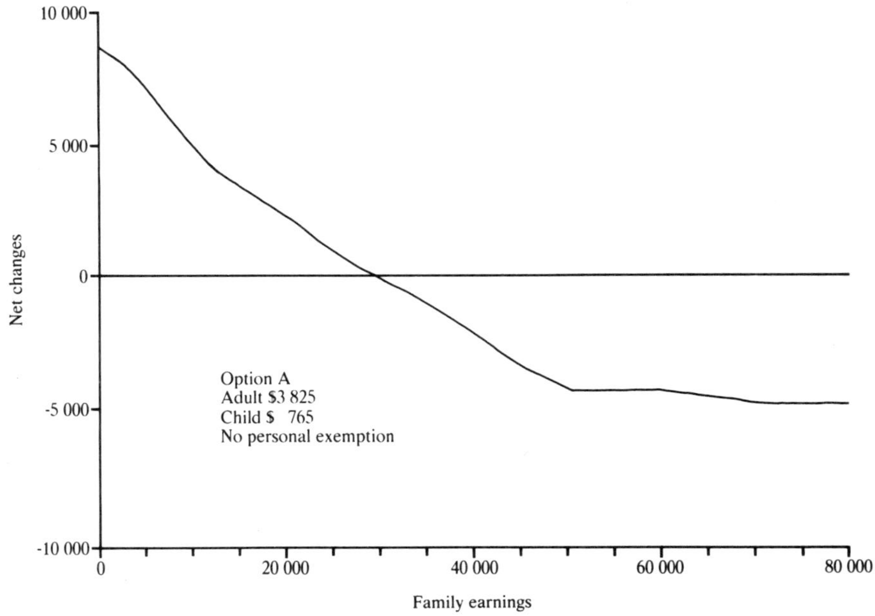

Source: Commission calculations based on Survey of Consumer Finances for Ontario families.

any program which does not include some form of work testing. Concern that younger people might tend to be program "abusers" might also be tempered by varying the guarantee levels for adults by age. Thus, for example, benefits for people 18 to 35 might be restricted to half of those for adults over 35 years of age.

Although the danger that there may be some work-disincentive effect for all classes of beneficiaries may be a public concern, evidence derived from U.S. experiments, which used program designs with larger work disincentives than those we have presented here, suggests that it is small. Nonetheless, Commissioners, too, are acutely conscious of this possibility, and it is partly for this reason that we suggest relatively low guarantee and tax-back levels. This concern also leads us to express a slight preference for some form of Option B, with somewhat smaller guarantees than Option A, even though vertical equity considerations might make A preferable.

There may also be a related concern that a general income supplement will constitute an impediment to labour-force mobility. Commissioners believe, however, that the combination of the changes to Unemployment Insurance and the Transitional Adjustment Assistance Program recommended earlier will have, on balance, highly beneficial effects on labour mobility, while also providing a fully adequate measure of income protection. The UISP will add substantially to this effect by guaranteeing to Canadians who do find new

FIGURE 19-8 Option B: Change in Personal Disposable Income in Two-Earner/Two-Children Family, 1984

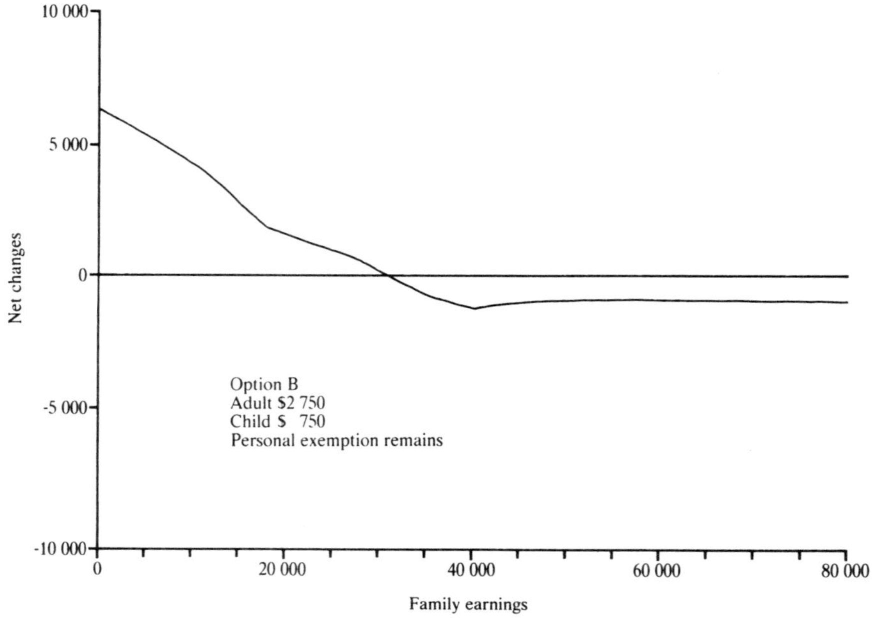

Source: Commission calculations based on Survey of Consumer Finances for Ontario families.

work opportunities that their incomes will be supplemented in a manner which will enable them to fulfil their obligations to their families.

For reasons considered earlier, Commissioners recommend a universal demogrant-based delivery system, rather than a strictly tax-based system, although either one is workable. There is also a variety of far-from-trivial design considerations involved in implementing any such system. Care must be taken, in defining the eligible family unit, not to create incentives to family breakdown. A single benefit level for all children of all ages might prove insufficiently sensitive to family needs. The accounting period (that is, the period over which income and benefits should be reconciled) should not necessarily be annual. In our examples, we have used a 20 per cent basic reduction rate for benefits, in order to avoid unnecessarily pre-emptive levels of overall "taxation" as a client gains sufficient income to pay taxes. Integration of the arrangements with broader tax reform could produce more desirable benefit structures.

Federal-provincial considerations are particularly important in moving towards the UISP. Since the federal and provincial governments share the personal income-tax field, any reduction or elimination of exemptions provides increased revenues for both levels of government. Conversely, because family allowances are defined as taxable income, their elimination would reduce provincial revenues somewhat. As a rule of thumb, the effect on provincial governments of federal income-tax changes is equal to one-half the effect on the federal government or one-third of the total. Moreover, because Quebec operates its own tax system, federal tax changes would not automatically affect the Quebec treasury.

The calculations used in the presentation of the UISP assume that *all* of the net yield from elimination of the various exemptions and family allowances is available for application to the program. Of course, this will not happen automatically as the federal government carries out its tax changes. In fact, without some alternative arrangement, only about two-thirds of the money can be captured by the federal government and converted to UISP benefits. Commissioners believe that virtually all of the available funds should be put into income-security programs; for their successful operation, a co-operative federal-provincial approach is, in our view, absolutely essential.

Two general options can be suggested. The provincial governments might actually withdraw from some percentage points of personal income tax, vacating that tax room so that the federal government might collect the income. Although this approach is unprecedented in the recent history of federal-provincial/tax-collection agreements, yet at various times, many provincial governments have suggested that direct income transfers of the UISP type are a highly appropriate initiative for the federal government to take. Thus, surprising levels of provincial support for such a proposal may exist.

The second general approach would see provincial governments retain the $5 billion in additional tax yield and use it to enrich their own top-up arrangements according to the configuration they consider most desirable. Some provinces might simply wish to follow the federal configuration, while others might take somewhat different routes. It would be important, in this Commission's view, to ensure that all of the available revenues remain in the income-security system, and federal-provincial negotiations should deal with that aspect, as well as ensuring proper co-ordination of the federal and provincial plans. This might be done through incorporating both federal and provincial benefits in a single cheque. While the problems of complexity which bedevil our current systems would not be cured under this arrangement, Commissioners recognize that some degree of provincial differentiation might be a necessary, and perhaps not an excessively high, price to pay for general agreement.

It is this Commission's view that all the problems we have considered can be solved. Given the importance of the other adjustments Canadians must make in the coming decades, and given the massive size and acknowledged deficiencies of Canada's current transfer and tax programs, we consider it important for the Canadian goverment to consider a bold step such as we have outlined here.

Phasing In Reforms

It may prove impossible for a government to move in a single step to a rationalized system of the type suggested here. In that case, Commissioners wish to recommend that the following two-stage approach be considered. In the first stage, the Family Allowance, Child Tax Credit and Child Tax

Exemption programs would be eliminated, to be replaced with a single, large, Family Allowance-type payment or a larger child tax credit, payable monthly. For the year 1985, an amount of $1000 annually would likely be in the appropriate range. The choice between demogrant- and tax-system delivery should be made very carefully, since it would probably form the prototype for the second stage of reform. The tax-back structure on the enlarged child benefit would have to be somewhat different from the system used for the current child tax credit. The application of its 5 per cent reduction rate, which would start at a family-income level of $26 000, to a benefit of $1000 per child, would result in the payment of at least some supplement to all two-child families with annual incomes of less than $65 000. A 10 per cent tax-back rate would reduce the application of this supplement to families with incomes in the $45 000 range, and a 25 per cent rate to families earning in the $35 000 range. The social assistance benefits covered by the Canada Assistance Plan should also be changed in structure, to permit the application of a lower tax-back rate, in the 75 per cent range, to those recipients who have some earned income beyond the current, very low, exemption levels.

At the second stage of program reform, all relevant exemptions should be eliminated from the tax system; the federal government would discontinue payment of its portion of social assistance; and the GIS would be incorporated into the system. The federal government or the federal and provincial governments in co-operation would institute the Universal Income Security Program, and provincial governments would provide social assistance top-ups, where necessary, for Canadians with little or no employment income.

The phasing in of UI systems and the TAAP should proceed in concert with the other changes that Commissioners have proposed. If our government is not to create undue hardship, however, it must ensure that the major elements of UI reform, aside from experience rating, are not fully applied before TAAP provisions can be implemented and, preferably, before UISP is in place. Since we believe that these reforms are a very important part of the changes necessary to help Canadians adjust to emerging realities, we urge that there be little delay in promoting them. We therefore strongly recommend that the first-stage reforms be implemented immediately, that the UISP/TAAP proposals be phased in over two to three years, and that the entire package be in place by the end of 1987.

Commissioners wish to repeat that we recommend these changes as representing the basic directions to be followed. We leave vital details of program design to the federal and provincial governments, for those details depend on two factors: the levels of benefits in the existing income-transfer programs at the time reforms are put in place; and decisions about the features of program design which can only be made by governments in close touch with the people of Canada, at the time the reforms are implemented.

Note

1. Canada, Minister of National Health and Welfare, *Child and Elderly Benefits*, Consultation Paper (Ottawa: The Department, 1985).

VOTE 5—FINANCIAL ASSISTANCE FOR SUPERVISED PERSONAL CARE

SUMMARY BY ELEMENT

Reference No.	Element Title	1986-87 Estimates	% Change From Comparable 1985-86 Estimates	Comparable 1985-86 Estimates
		$	%	$
5.1	PROGRAM SUPPORT			
5.1.1	Extraordinary Maintenance	150,000	275.0	40,000
5.1.2	Specific Programs	15,844,130	...	—
5.1.3	Operational Commissioning	633,227	- -	65,000
5.1.4	Other Program Support	6,454,300	66.2	3,883,084
	Total Sub-program	23,081,657	478.8	3,988,084
5.2	DISTRICT NURSING HOMES			
5.2.1	Operating Grants	38,324,926	8.6	35,294,821
	Total Sub-program	38,324,926	8.6	35,294,821
5.3	PRIVATE NURSING HOMES			
5.3.1	Operating Grants	51,035,093	4.4	48,887,974
	Total Sub-program	51,035,093	4.4	48,887,974
5.4	VOLUNTARY NURSING HOMES			
[illegible]	[illegible]	[illegible]	5.4	20,578,080

Recommendations

This Commission believes that the provision of a Universal Income Security Program with relatively low guarantee levels and tax-back rates is an appropriate long-term goal for the Government of Canada and the provincial governments to pursue, in order to reform the current income-security system. Such a system should replace the majority of current transfer programs and personal and family tax credits and exemptions.

The provision of the federal supplement is an appropriate long-range objective. In the shorter term, Canada's federal and provincial governments should:

- Rationalize the family-benefits system by redirecting money from the child tax exemption either to the child tax credit or to the Family Allowance and by adjusting the tax-back rates on those programs so as to ensure a uniformly progressive benefit system
- Improve the social assistance aspects of the Canada Assistance Plan by permitting the application of lower reduction rates to beneficiaries with earned incomes above exemption levels.

These latter changes, in combination with the experience rating of Unemployment Insurance premiums, should constitute the first stage in phasing in the general income supplement recommended above and should be implemented immediately. Commissioners believe that in view of the benefits to be gained from rationalization of the income-security system, the Universal Income Security Program should follow quickly upon this first stage and should be in place by the end of 1987. At this time, the remaining UI reforms and the TAAP should also be in place.

CHAPTER 20

Social Services

CHAPTER 20

Social Services

General Services

Canada's social services comprise a broad range of programs dealing with child welfare, children's institutional care and welfare services, day care, home care for the elderly, counselling, community programs for the disabled and aged, distress centres, and a host of other services. They are delivered, in part, by provincial and municipal governments, but to a very large extent, through a range of voluntary agencies using a combination of professional and voluntary workers, as well as through other private profit-oriented and non-profit organizations. It has not been the purpose of this Commission, in preparing our Report, to provide an extensive analysis of Canada's social services. However, their importance to the future of many Canadians is critical, and there are, therefore, some aspects on which we do wish to comment.

Two potentially antithetical themes were expressed by groups and individuals who appeared before this Commission to present their views on social services. One was a call for more encouragement of the activities of the voluntary sector which participates in service delivery. The other was a fear that government was reducing its commitment to social services, partly through devolving responsibility to the private and voluntary sectors, and that significant damage to our social services could result.

Of course, these themes need not necessarily conflict: governments might go on providing financial support for social service agencies and, at the same time, continue to exercise regulatory or supervisory authority over them, while devolving the actual delivery of services to less bureaucratic and therefore potentially more responsive, structures. Commissioners believe that such a policy constitutes an appropriate resolution and direction for the future.

Other important themes relating to social services were also brought forward. If many Canadians considered that services should be more frequently delivered by the voluntary sector, they often coupled that statement with a call for service delivery to be de-institutionalized; they prefer that service delivery be based in the local community and, where possible, on existing family structures. Some intervenors promoted this view as a means of saving money in providing service-program delivery. Others saw the suggestion as a way to improve the services themselves. The latter reason was proffered in presentations by several groups of users of the services.

The best judges of how a service ought to be delivered must be the users themselves. Not least for this reason, Commissioners find highly persuasive the suggestion that devolution of services can create improvements, provided that the transfer of responsibility involved is accompanied by adequate funding. The contention that this move could also make it cheaper to provide community- and family-based services gives us considerably more difficulty, however. Little solid empirical evidence exists to uphold this view as it relates to child care, adult psychiatric care and care for the disabled. While institutional costs will, of course, decline if people are removed from the institutions, direct and indirect costs to the community might increase. Most important, if patients are released before adequate community services are available to replace those currently in use, institutional expenditures will certainly decline, but at tragic cost to those who need the services and with considerable disruption to family and community life.

Information is more readily available on the costs of providing community-based care for the chronically ill and the elderly. The data seem to indicate that Canadians cannot expect to achieve really major cost reductions from turning to this type of care; under such an arrangement, indeed, costs often seem to be marginally higher. On the other hand, it must be emphasized that the clients themselves seem very pleased with the community-based service, and assuming that costs remain nearly equal or are not vastly increased, that itself would seem to be ample reason to encourage this arrangement.

A closely related theme was the call to provide services which would help users to become more self-reliant and to move completely from the need for service support. While this goal is ostensibly the objective of most forms of social services, it is one which, in practice, is not always given precedence. Although it seems obvious that governments and agencies which provide services should keep that objective constantly in mind, the frequency with which intervenors mentioned it as a reform needed in our service-delivery system leads Commissioners to emphasize it here.

This view was put to us very strongly in our Vancouver hearings:

> *As for social services, I believe in self-help groups. I work in the anti-poverty field; I work with a lot of self-help groups. There is a lot we can do for ourselves if we're allowed to do it . . . If you are going to have a group of poor people performing their own self-help, then you have got to give them the money . . . to do it. There are many things that we can do for ourselves much better than professionals can do for us. One of the things I really hate about the social services system is that they design their programs without any input from the people that they are supposed to be helping. They seem to have the feeling that they know what is best. It is a very paternalistic system, and I object to that.* (Gus Long, Transcript, Vancouver, June 11, 1984 [vol. 7], pp. 1705–6.)

Intervenors often stated, too, that continuing and increasing attempts should be made to achieve better integration of various types of social and medical services. While the Province of Quebec has tried to integrate medical and social services on a broad scale, elsewhere in Canada, examples of the "one-stop/shopping" approach to service delivery are more rare. Since many of the Canadians who need the assistance provided by social or medical services require more than one type of intervention, it is important that there be better communication among different types of service and, perhaps, that the services be brought closer together.

Another theme which emerged, though less frequently, was the potential value of privatization of service delivery on a supervised, but profit-making, basis. Some advocates of this approach assured Commissioners that market mechanisms could work the same magic in this area as in others. We must, however, express some reservations about an overly enthusiastic application of this approach. The delivery of services for profit is currently applied most widely in day care and, particularly, in nursing-home care. While there is no conclusive evidence of the effect of privatization on users of these services, staff/patient and staff/child ratios are lower in private facilities than in public ones. Moreover, some researchers have expressed reservations about services supplied on a profit-making basis. Particularly with respect to nursing-home facilities, private markets work best when consumers are both well informed about alternative sources of service and mobile. Since neither condition usually obtains for nursing-home residents, governments must, at the very least, continue to play a major supervisory role.

Another theme was the call for broader access to social services. The Canada Assistance Plan (CAP) allows the federal government to share in the provision of services to Canadians "in need or likely to become in need". This expression is interpreted to mean financial need, and in the past, it has had the effect of restricting the free availability of many government-supported social services to the poor, even though the requirement for these services is certainly not wholly related to income. In recent years the federal government has developed new cost-sharing guidelines for CAP-assisted social services. These will allow provinces to support the entire costs of social services used by recipients with incomes up to the Old Age Security (OAS) level plus twice the Guaranteed Income Supplement (GIS) level for adults and one-third of that amount for children. This means that in March 1985, full subsidy for a two-adult/two-child family may be made available, up to $26 818 of annual, after-tax, family income. After that point is reached, recipients must pay 50 cents of each additional dollar of earned income to cover the costs of services. These guidelines appear to be fairly generous, but it remains true that in Canada, higher-cost medical services are "free" to all users, while the use of social services, which are often more cost-effective, involves a charge for middle-income clients. This anomaly often induces clients to substitute the higher-cost service for the lower-cost one. In addition, many provinces do not take full advantage of the guidelines, preferring, instead, to pass on a larger portion of the costs to clients.

Of course, calls for wider access to social services do contradict calls to limit the size of government expenditures. In the end, whether or not one supports universal free access probably depends on how important one believes those services are, compared to the strength of one's views about limiting the size of government. It is difficult to estimate the cost to the public sector of any move towards broader access to services. In 1977, an attempt to renegotiate the social services component of the Canada Assistance Plan in order to provide more open access to its services put the program's cost at about $225 million for the federal share. A realistic 1984–85 figure probably runs close to $500 million.

Various individuals and groups have proposed, for a wide variety of reasons, that more use be made of volunteers and voluntary agencies. Such a change would:

- Provide more community involvement in service delivery
- Provide a more "human face" in service delivery
- Allow users and clients to have a more direct "say" in the provision of services
- Allow taxpayers to have a better view of what their dollars are providing
- Reduce citizen dependency on government
- Reduce the cost of service delivery
- Reduce general government involvement in the community.

This Commission also heard some arguments against greatly increased reliance on the voluntary sector. Governments, it was feared, might be seen as shirking their present mandate to help Canadians directly. Their ability to impose province-wide and national standards might be reduced. On the one hand, funding of services would be more haphazard and stand at greater risk, especially if it were dependent on volunteer donations alone. On the other hand, if government did continue to finance social services, fear might mount that the voluntary sector could forfeit its independence of government. Job security and existing wage levels for employees of service agencies could be reduced, and public access to services could be further restricted. Moreover, the ability of non-professionals to make optimal choices, maintain standards, and fulfil public-sector/accountability requirements might be questionable. Some consumers fear a return to "charity": that is, a system in which services are defined by the rich and given selectively to those in need. Finally, the voluntary sector itself has expressed mixed reactions to any such proposed set of changes. For instance, the President of the United Way of Canada told this Commission:

> *I find it very hard to say, in black and white terms, "It is* either *government services* or *services initiated or managed by volunteer organizations." I could say, "Yes, volunteer organizations have developed a capacity to be close to the people they serve and ability in administration, but I would say that that is [the result of] a developmental process and experience that is gained in business. Here again, I should probably be obliged to qualify my statement, depending on the volunteer organizations involved, just as one would make qualifications depending on the ability of this or that ministry to manage these programs. I find it hard to come down definitely on one side or the other by saying, "This*

isn't the business of the government any more; this the business of volunteer organizations."

(André Mailhot, Transcript, Montreal, May 30, 1984 [vol. 1], pp. 99–100.)

Again, the United Way of Greater Toronto declared:

The choice related to the voluntary sector ... is presented incorrectly as an either/or proposition ... Given the emergence of the self-help movement, along with the climate of fiscal restraint, prevalent cynicism about government and large institutions, we can expect a continued shift towards voluntary delivery of services. This raises, though, some issues that ... are important to address ... First, the risk that reliance on the voluntary sector to deliver services will be used as an excuse to withdraw support for services genuinely the responsibility of government. Second, the risk that the benefits of volunteerism argument will be exploited and lead to the use of volunteers to displace paid workers, recently exemplified out of the Canadian Labour Congress convention and experienced in British Columbia. Third, the tendency apparent in some government departments to seize on the concept of voluntary action and introduce programs which rely on volunteers at the delivery level, but which have high overhead costs and are therefore not financially efficient ... The key to working our respective roles in the delivery of social services is meaningful consultation in advance of policy decisions.

(Gordon Cressy, Transcript, Toronto, June 26, 1984 [vol. 13], pp. 3246–48.)

While these remarks counsel caution, they do not seem to constitute deep reservations about further use of the voluntary sector in service delivery. Commissioners believe that the balance of evidence indicates that governments should support and nurture such activity. The reservations expressed by these United Way representatives do, however, make a compelling case that governments must not adopt a totally "hands-off" approach to service delivery, but continue to provide extensive funding for, and careful supervision of, this process. We can find no justification for suggesting that the services themselves should be considered a primary hunting ground for reductions in government expenditure. We therefore propose that devolution to the voluntary sector of responsibility for social service delivery be accompanied by the maintenance of public funding levels. This recommendation is based on Commissioners' belief that by using the voluntary sector more, our governments ensure that public funds go further and are more effectively spent.

Commissioners believe, too, that in spite of the improved federal guidelines described earlier, the tying together of federal support for social assistance and social services in a simple "needs-based" funding mechanism, the Canada Assistance Plan, no longer permits the federal or the provincial governments the flexibility required to deal with either of these areas of responsibility. A strong incentive exists, therefore, for renewed federal-provincial discussion about the future of social service delivery and the appropriate funding mechanism to cover it.

Commissioners would be more than remiss if we left this section without making a more general comment about the voluntary sector. We have dealt here with its specific role in the delivery of social services, but we wish to exphasize its much broader role in Canadian society. In Canada, volunteers form the backbone of our activities in a variety of fields from young peoples' sports leagues to political parties. Indeed, except for the United States, in no other society in the world is the level of voluntary activity as high as in Canada. This valuable asset of Canadian society is one that governments should take care to nurture and support.

Commissioners also wish to emphasize that the voluntary sector made many representations to us on a range of subjects far broader than their own specific interests. We found these views particularly valuable, since they were so obviously free from self-interest, and we have leaned heavily on them in preparing all stages of our Report. In view of the voluntary sector's broad range of interests and the strength of its views, it would be no exaggeration to say that their perceptions suffuse our work.

Day Care

One of the most essential of Canadian social services is the provision of day-care facilities for children. Given the massive scale on which women have entered the labour force over the last two decades, more and more families now use day-care facilities for their young children, for all or part of each working day.

Many groups and individuals appearing before this Commission recognized the importance of day-care facilities. The provision of these facilities has also been of increasing concern to governments as they have felt the pressures generated by labour-market changes and evolving expectations about the role of women in Canadian society. Two major task forces on day care, one federal and one parliamentary, are currently at work in response to this concern. Since they can investigate the issues involved in much greater depth than we Commissioners have been able to do, it is not our intention to comment extensively here. We do, however, wish to make a number of points.

Canada's present day-care system is a complex mix of publicly provided, publicly funded and private sector arrangements. In some parts of Canada, municipal authorities provide day-care services, while in many areas, municipal or provincial governments fund community groups set up for this purpose. In several provinces, private-sector corporations provide day care. However, the great majority of children in day care are served by unregulated forms of care supplied by relatives and "sitters". Governments are willing to cover the cost of some publicly provided day care for lower-income and some middle-income families. The funding for this service is covered by the Canada Assistance Plan and is subject to the same income-testing guidelines as other social services. The federal and provincial governments also provide an annual tax exemption for day care, amounting to $2000 per child, but like all tax exemptions, this one provides the greatest benefit to Canada's highest-income families. Families in the middle-income range therefore receive relatively little support, with the result that organized day-care facilities which cost several thousand dollars per year often serve a mixture of lower-income and quite well-off families, but very few in the middle-income range. Of course, the greatest access problems are caused simply by the lack of places in supervised day-care centres.

Overall, this situation has the effect of driving the majority of Canadian parents into the unsupervised private sector to find baby-sitting or day-care services at reasonable cost. While the majority of such arrangements may be satisfactory, and while many parents will continue to prefer to use them, the cost to some parents and children, both in financial and in other terms, can be quite high.

Day care is a provincial responsibility, and therefore any solution to related problems must be provincial or federal-provincial in nature. Commissioners are concerned that without some federal involvement, poorer provinces will be unable to afford satisfactory arrangements, and some richer provinces may not be motivated to try to find solutions. We are, however, highly aware that day care could constitute a very costly social service area in which government is not now heavily involved. The cost of an even greater degree of government involvement would be higher still, and we Canadians must consider carefully whether or not we wish our governments to spend more public funds on providing day-care services.

Commissioners wish to make no specific suggestions, beyond recommending that the federal government convert the current child-care tax deduction to a tax credit (from which the value of any subsidized day care received should be deducted, in order to avoid double subsidies at the bottom end), and that the federal and provincial governments consider day care an area of high priority for future discussion. We propose the conversion to tax credits in order to alleviate the perverse distributional effects of the present tax exemption. If any tax provisions are to be retained after federal-provincial review, the tax-credit mechanism is to be preferred. We refrain from making more specific recommendations about the nature and desirability of any federal-provincial cost-sharing mechanism to support day-care services, pending public consideration of the two task-force reports mentioned above.

Conclusions and Recommendations

This Commission wishes to make a number of general observations concerning some of the issues we have reviewed in this part of our Report. Several of the major recommendations proferred in this section are best considered as a package. Thus the reforms Commissioners propose for Unemployment Insurance (UI), the new Universal Income Security Program (UISP) and the new Transitional Adjustment Assistance Program (TAAP) would have maximum efficacy if they were implemented together. The savings generated by the UI changes would finance the TAAP, and the UISP would provide financial assistance if some incomes were lowered by the adjustments. The TAAP would support the effect of changes in the UI system that would promote economic adjustment, while the UISP and some elements of TAAP would cushion any resulting difficulties experienced by individual Canadians.

Since the overall level of social policy expenditures in Canada is low by OECD standards, there is no strong general case for attacking the deficit by reducing social expenditures. However, reallocation and restructuring could greatly improve the system and would be valuable in providing help to those who most need it, while containing overall costs.

Looking forward, Commissioners can see no trends that will inevitably undermine the fundamental viability of social programs. Such factors as the aging of the Canadian population or the demands imposed by technological and economic change require careful planning, but none is likely to prove so large as to make our programs unsustainable, particularly if the reforms suggested in this part of our report are carried out.

We Commissioners are of the opinion that tax and transfer systems cannot be given valid consideration in isolation from each other. Thus, major reform of our income-security programs also requires reform of some aspects of personal taxation.

Labour Markets and Unemployment Insurance

After considering Canadian labour markets, Commissioners are of the view that Canada's most important goals are to create more jobs and to improve the situation of individual Canadians by eliminating any inappropriate incentives in current programs. We undertook our analysis on the assumption that current trends in participation rates will continue, bringing a steadily increasing proportion of women into the labour force. While these trends are basically manageable, particularly given our assumption, detailed in Part III, that labour supply itself creates demand for labour, they do portend continuing high levels of unemployment – and continuing preoccupation of policy makers with that problem – for the next five to eight years, and they do add significantly to the training requirements Canadians must face.

We note in our analysis of labour markets that the highest proportion of current unemployment is either created by deficiency of aggregate demand or by structural factors such as mismatches between available job requirements and skills. A significant amount of unemployment is also created by "frictional" effects, that is the inevitable lags and delays as workers move from one job to another. We have dealt in Part III with aggregate demand deficiency. Here we recommend several measures to facilitate adjustment and training, thus reducing structural unemployment. We also recommend changes in unemployment-insurance and income-security programs which will lower frictional unemployment. Without undertaking changes such as those we are recommending, it will be almost impossible, even in the long run, to reduce unemployment below 6.5 to 8 per cent of the work-force, the current non-accelerating inflation rate of unemployment (NAIRU). Since we consider even those levels to be unacceptably high, we lay great emphasis on these types of reform.

Some increase in unemployment is also engendered by our existing UI programs. First, by making unemployment relatively "cheaper" for individuals, it has, in some cases, a negative effect on job search. Secondly, by providing, through its benefit structure, that individuals in some areas may qualify for 40 weeks of benefits by 12 weeks of work, it encourages regular cyclical unemployment; a feature taken advantage of by both employers and employees. Again, by providing extended benefits in some areas but not others, it discourages labour-force adjustment, while providing no extended benefits to large numbers of unemployed Canadians. Moreover, because its premium structure is unrelated to the risk of unemployment, it penalizes steady employers and employees and shifts benefits towards firms and employees with unstable employment patterns.

■ With respect to Unemployment Insurance, Commissioners recommend that the federal government consider a package of changes such as the following:

- Experience rating which establishes premium rates that are proportional to the risk of unemployment. These rates should generally be calculated on a firm-by-firm basis.
- A reduction of the benefit rate to 50 per cent of insurable earnings
- An increase of the entrance requirement to 15–20 weeks of insured work over the preceding year
- Tightening of the link between the maximum benefit period and the minimum employment period; for example, establishing a ratio of two or three weeks of work as qualification for one week of benefits
- Elimination of the extended benefit period based on regional unemployment rates.

These changes would reduce UI benefit costs by at least one-sixth in respect of the reduction in benefit rates and approximately one-sixth in respect of the elimination of regional extended benefits. The cost reductions that could be achieved by the other changes are too sensitive to behavioural change even to be estimated by methods available to this Commission. However, total savings of at least $4 billion at April 1985 rates of unemployment are probable.

- Commissioners therefore recommend that:
  - The savings in respect of the first three UI reforms be passed along as reductions in overall premium levels. (The regional extended benefits are financed from consolidated revenues.)
  - Personal and corporate taxes be raised by an amount equivalent to premium reductions to create a Transitional Adjustment Assistance Fund. The government savings from termination of extended benefits should be added to the fund.

■ This Commission recommends that the Transitional Adjustment Assistance Fund be used to finance a Transitional Adjustment Assistance Program. This program would provide adjustment assistance for Canadians who have exhausted their UI benefits, or whose lay-offs appear permanent, provided that they were willing to move or to undertake retraining to improve their employment prospects. The program would provide greatly expanded support for:

- Portable wage-subsidy programs
- Mobility grants
- Training programs
- Early retirement.

In addition, the TAAP could be used to provide compensation for losses in assets, such as housing, which occur as a result of the decline of communities. It should also be possible for TAAP funds to be used on a pooled basis to assist workers to purchase equity in plants which would otherwise shut down or in other forms of local economic development projects. In general, the extent of entitlement of workers to TAAP funds should be proportional to their length of attachment to the labour force, since older workers will typically experience greater transitional difficulties than younger workers.

■ Commissioners recommend that existing policies promoting equal pay for work of equal value should be maintained. However, these may involve some negative consequences. If they are used apart from affirmative action programs, for instance, they may actually result in reductions of employment opportunities for disadvantaged groups. Moreover, they can serve to move Canadians too far away from a market-determined to an administered wage system. Commissioners therefore recommend that legislation emphasize creation of equal employment opportunities through affirmative action, rather than the principle of equal value. Commissioners generally approve the approach put forward by Judge Rosalie Abella. This would involve:

- Legislated requirements for affirmative action by all employers covered by the Canada Labour Code
- Encouragement of all provincial jurisdictions to follow suit
- Contract compliance action by the federal government and Crown corporations.

We are not convinced, however, that sufficient attention has been paid to the costs of equal employment-opportunities programs or, particularly, to the issues of equity among the various disadvantaged groups in Canadian society.

- We therefore recommend that the program be phased in following:
  - A three year experimental program of affirmative action in Crown corporations
  - Extensive consultations with the private sector to ensure effective but least expensive implementation to begin in three years' time.

This Commission believes that the programs are more likely to be effective if they are supported by legislation and backed by an adequate enforcement agency.

- We therefore recommend:
  - Legislated equal employment-opportunities provisions, rather than guidelines
  - Establishment of fully adequate levels of funding for the federal Human Rights Commission and equivalent provincial institutions.

■ Work schedules are necessarily established on the basis of understandings between employer and employees that will express a balance between the requirements of the work process and the desires of the employee. This Commission has found, however, that some factors exist which may interfere artificially with the achievement of this understanding. Any such factors should be eliminated in order to achieve fuller flexibility of labour-market arrangements, thus enhancing both employee satisfaction and productivity.

- Commissioners therefore recommend such changes as:
  - Basing Unemployment Insurance, Worker's Compensation and CPP premiums on hourly earnings, with a ceiling on contributions that applies to hourly rates rather than to weekly or annual compensation
  - Eliminating the bias against some categories of reduced hours in creating eligibility for paid holidays or termination notice
  - Encouragement of pro-rating of fringe benefits. □

Immigration

In the past decade, Canadian immigration policy has become more restrictive than our historical norm, both with respect to numbers of immigrants and with respect to the criteria for admission. We Commissioners do not believe that this narrowing is necessary or appropriate, given the long-term projections for Canada's population growth. We are concerned, however, about the overall implications of a more open immigration policy.

■ We therefore recommend:

- A major examination of Canadian demographic trends and their implications for our government's future immigration policies
- That the same study examine, by means of open debate and other methods, the cultural, linguistic and racial implications of other forms of immigration policy
- Establishment of a long-term plan for immigration that, depending on the results of the study described above, will move to higher numbers of immigrants over a number of years. This new plan should place less emphasis on narrow occupational requirements and more emphasis on broadly skilled and generally capable immigrants. □

Labour/Management Relations

■ This Commission notes the very great importance of the labour movement in Canada and throughout the developed world in improving the pay and working conditions of workers. To this end, we wish to recommend generally that all Canadian governments provide a supportive legislative environment for the labour movement and for collective bargaining.

The adversarial system of union-management relations needs to be re-examined. Management must respond to employee concerns about job security and job satisfaction, and to the often-untapped capability of all employees to contribute to improved productivity and product quality. Unions must find new ways to facilitate and to participate in this process; they should have and take the opportunity to do so, not by relinquishing their representation of employee interests, but by adding to it a responsibility for helping to achieve the levels of competitiveness essential to the survival of the enterprise.

Since reductions in strikes and lock-outs could be achieved by the following measures, Commissioners recommend that:

- Labour-relations boards be permitted to create multi-employer and multi-union bargaining units when this is likely to facilitate the bargaining process. Such units should not be imposed but, rather, could be permitted on the application of one or both sides.
- More information be shared by the parties to industrial disputes.

Commissioners are not persuaded that shorter contracts or forced centralization of bargaining structures are likely to improve labour-management relations significantly. Changes in these areas should therefore proceed on a voluntary basis. The right to strike or lock out must be rationally limited by the need to maintain the health and safety of the public.

Employer-employee relations in Canada seem likely to be most responsive to improvement at the level of individual firms, plants and union locals.

Overall solutions proposed at the provincial or national level seem unlikely to be as effective as local solutions.

- Commissioners therefore recommend that governments support, on a local and voluntary basis, such features as:
  - Preventive mediation programs
  - Quality-of-working-life programs
  - Gains-sharing/compensation arrangements.

■ Occupational Health and Safety is an area of important and growing concern. Since great improvements can still be made, this Commission recommends:

- Greater emphasis on these issues at higher levels of corporate management. Management failure in this area is bound to result in higher levels of government intervention.
- More complete experience rating of Workers' Compensation premiums in order to provide direct financial incentives for firms to minimize health and safety problems, in order to ensure that the full social costs of hazardous work environments are reflected in prices
- Continued and increased reliance on the internal responsibility system rather than increased government intervention. This requires:
  - Mandatory, joint health-and-safety/labour-management committees in all eleven jurisdictions, such as currently exist in nine
  - Vesting real responsibility in those committees rather than leaving them with only an advisory role.
- Continual revision of standards by governments as new information about hazards becomes available. This is most important in dealing with occupational health problems. At a national level, these standards could most appropriately be developed by the Canada Centre for Occupational Health and Safety. The appropriate jurisdictions would then apply the standards.

Commissioners are particularly concerned with occupational health issues. Because occupational diseases typically have long incubation periods, it is often difficult to evaluate the effects of industrial processes on workers. That same factor makes it difficult to establish a direct link between occupational factors and specific diseases, and therefore current worker's compensation programs are not well adapted to handling occupational disease.

- In addition to our recommendation of continual development of standards and monitoring of processes, Commissioners also urge that:
  - The federal and provincial governments consider the immediate implementation of a comprehensive social insurance disability plan to deal with the longer-term effects of occupational health problems, as well as with other forms

of disability in the working-age population. This plan could be implemented either by expanding worker's compensation into a comprehensive disability scheme or by extending the present disability provisions of the Canada and Quebec Pension Plans. A federal-provincial working party is currently considering this measure, but progress in developing this idea has been slow. □

Education and Training

In Canada education and training programs discharge multiple functions. They constitute an important way in which young Canadians learn to live together in our community, and they are the most important means by which labour-force skills and knowledge are adjusted to labour-market demands. They also provide a major means of upward mobility. Our post-secondary educational institutions are also the major source of basic research and of much applied research, and they are important repositories of our culture.

Commissioners anticipate no diminution in the general importance of post-secondary education and training. Indeed, PSE is likely to increase in importance as the demand grows for high levels of knowledge and research. Training programs, particularly those relating to industrial training, are likely to become more important as Canadians adjust to the shifting realities of the labour market. The Transitional Adjustment Assistance Program, by providing greatly increased support for training, may be a particularly important factor in this adjustment.

Commissioners are concerned about several features of our educational and training system. In particular we are convinced that:

- Higher levels of excellence are desirable and achievable.
- More flexibility is desirable.
- Use of the PSE system by low-income Canadians is insufficient.
- The current federal-provincial transfer arrangements are inappropriate.
- The current balance between industrial and institutional training is still tilted too far towards the latter.
- There is inadequate provision for retraining and re-education in adult years.

With respect to post-secondary education, Commissioners believe that it is desirable to consider substantial changes in financing mechanisms in order to create a more competitive, dynamic and diversified system. The current EPF transfer arrangements are quite inappropriate for achieving those objectives. They should be changed to encourage reform of the system, but in a way that will minimize direct federal intervention in this area of provincial jurisdiction, while still allowing for the achievement of national objectives.

There has been very considerable informal discussion of the intergovernmental transfer arrangements for post-secondary education over the last five years, but there have been no formal federal-provincial negotiations. Commissioners believe that it is important for federal and provincial governments to enter immediately into serious discussion of other methods of funding than the current mechanism both because the present arrangements are less than satisfactory, and because the uncertainty about possible future arrangements may be impeding necessary reforms to the sector. Several broad options are available. Our federal government could:

- Withdraw completely from this sector and cede enough tax points to the provinces to cover its current contributions
- Return to the pre-EPF funding formula
- Provide an amount equal to provincial "own source" funding, exclusive of the tax points transferred under EPF
- Freeze its basic contributions at current or slightly lower-than-current levels while matching on a 50/50 basis incremental provincial spending on education. Alternatively, incremental funding could be earmarked to support high-level university-based research.
- Undertake a form of direct-to-student financing, allowing for variable PSE fee schedules.

This Commission does not recommend federal withdrawal from PSE involvement. Many of the benefits of post-secondary education are national in scope, and provincial governments might tend to undersupply this sector unless there were some federal presence, particularly if they believe that graduates are likely to leave the province. Many representations and briefs emphasized the importance of involvement of the Government of Canada in this field.

Among the cost-sharing options are:

- A return to pre-EPF arrangements. This would be a step back to a basically unsatisfactory system.
- Provision by the federal government of amounts equal to provincial "own source" funding. This move would constitute a massive cut-back by the federal government, part of which would probably be passed on by provincial governments to already hard-pressed institutions.
- Freezing of basic federal contributions with cost-matching of increments. This stance would exert relatively little "leverage" on provincial government expenditures in this sector and would mean starting from a basically unsatisfactory base point. However it is probably the most desirable of the cost-sharing options, particularly if some of the incremental funds are used to support research.

With the possible exception of the final choice, none of the cost-sharing options seems likely to be satisfactory. None is likely to improve the incentives for institutions to achieve the flexiblity and excellence which Commissioners think desirable. We believe that the complex institutional arrangements for PSE have created very considerable inertia in the system, to the detriment of the student and society as a whole. We therefore believe that the direct-to-student/funding option, although it is the most radical and thus difficult for PSE institutions and governments to accept, may be a preferable approach. In order to institute that approach, the following changes would be required:

- The federal government should terminate the PSE cash portion of its EPF grants to the provinces, ceding the EPF tax points plus further equalized tax points in an amount equivalent to the Quebec abatement. All of the cash portion of EPF, including transitional adjustment payments, should be replaced with an education-expense tax credit or grant, to be increased annually at a rate equal to nominal GNP increase.

- Provincial governments should be encouraged to deregulate the fee structure of post-secondary institutions.
- Provincial transfers to institutions might appropriately be based on an equal per-student figure, without differentiation for particular programs, and be related directly to enrolment.
- Students should be responsible for a portion of education costs. Beyond that point, the federal credit should vary with the amount of expenses and tuition fees, up to a limit. The amount of the grant should vary only with fees and expenses directly related to education, and no attempt should be made to direct students into "demand" programs by means of a variable grant structure.
- A portion of the current EPF transfer (and some additional funding) should be reallocated to granting councils, which should begin to cover overhead costs of funded research.

A variant of this approach would provide much higher grants to graduate students than to undergraduates. This approach would greatly increase the "value" of graduate education for institutions and thus encourage specialization and excellence.

■ Commissioners strongly recommend that federal-provincial discussions aimed at rectifying an unsatisfactory situation should begin immediately, that they should consider a range of options such as we have suggested here, and that they should proceed with all urgency toward a conclusion. We believe that close further attention is merited for the options which:

- Replace intergovernmental transfers with direct-to-student transfers. Careful consideration should be given to the variant which makes much larger transfers to graduate students.
- Freeze current federal cash contributions. The federal government would match provincial expenditure increases on a 50/50 basis.
- Freeze current federal cash contributions while redirecting considerable amounts (perhaps one-half) of what would have been the incremental amounts into funding of university-based research. The rest of the funds should be used to match, on a 25/75 federal-provincial basis, larger provincial government contributions to universities.

■ With respect particularly to primary and secondary education, this Commission recommends the formation of an independent national commission to monitor quality and standards in primary and secondary education and to conduct and record research in related areas. We urge that the private sector take the lead in establishing and financing this commission. With respect to occupational training programs, Commissioners believe that the direction of reform presently being followed by the federal government is generally appropriate. Increased attention to on-the-job and job-related training is to be encouraged.

■ This Commission also recommends that the federal government:

- Provide a special wage subsidy for labour-force entrants who have not had other forms of vocational training or post-secondary education. The subsidy would normally be provided to persons 15 to 18 years of age and to women entering the labour force after discharging family responsibilities. The subsidy could be financed by eliminating other job-creation programs for young people.
- Provide, under the Income Tax Act, for a Registered Educational Leave Savings Plan which workers could use to help finance the cost of training. Careful consideration must be given to the type of program eligible for RELSP financing and to the possibility of requiring completion of any training or education undertaken in order to qualify for the advantage.

Commissioners wish to point out that the TAAP described earlier might significantly increase training requirements in Canada.

Access to higher education by low-income students should be an important avenue of upward mobility in Canada. However, for a variety of reasons, low-income students make far less use of higher education than do middle-income students, thus impeding both their own upward mobility and Canada's labour-force efficiency. Several of the barriers faced by low-income students are not susceptible to immediate government reduction. Family-socialization patterns and peer pressures can be influenced only very indirectly. But governments can and should ensure that undue financial barriers are not blocking the educational prospects of low-income students.

■ This Commission therefore recommends strongly that further attention be paid to improving access for low-income students. At the least, therefore, we recommend continued support for the Canada Student Loans Program and its provincial equivalents, and we recommend that loan limits be changed in consonance with other policy changes proposed in this Report, to remove any financial barriers that might exclude otherwise-qualified low-income students. We also wish to emphasize the importance of continuing to grant scholarships for students who excel, no matter what their income level, and of offering bursaries for low- or moderate-income students with above-average grades who might otherwise be reluctant or unable to continue their education.

Commissioners are concerned, however, that the CSLP is increasingly unable to deal with the issue of student independence of parental support. Therefore we do not reject the concept of contingent-repayment loan schemes, and we recommend that governments continue to consider that possibility. □

Income-Security Programs

While this Commission does not view Canada's problems over the next quarter-century as unmanageable, Commissioners do believe that many – perhaps most – Canadians will have to face the need to make adjustments that will maximize their own opportunities in the face of the effects of economic change. For most Canadians, these adjustments will not be severe, but for some they will be very difficult. This is particularly true for low-income Canadians, families with children that lack income adequate to meet family needs, and workers in peripheral regions or peripheral jobs. Economic change has always caused these Canadians more difficulty than middle-income Canadians and it will continue to do so. Moreover, even without the impact of change, there are over one million Canadian families whose incomes are inadequate to cover any but the barest necessities, and many of these can be considered the "working poor": families where one or more breadwinners are employed all or most of the year, but where incomes are still inadequate to meet their needs.

Middle- and upper-income Canadians get a great deal of public and private support as they adjust to economic change. They receive tax-supported education and training, and their employers often foot a substantial portion of their adjustment costs. Low-income Canadians receive relatively little such support. In general, it often seems true that the poorer one is, the more one is left to one's own devices to cope with the forces of change or destiny.

For these reasons, among others, Commissioners believe that all Canadians have a duty and a right to share the costs of adjustment and to provide help to those who need it. That has always been the basic rationale for many of Canada's income-security programs and it should remain so.

We Commissioners are also persuaded that there is enough money in our current personal tax-expenditure and transfer-payment programs to provide a comprehensive program of support for all deserving Canadians, but that current programs are often fundamentally flawed so that the current safety net is inappropriate. We believe that Canada can do much better than it has done in providing income support for our working poor and for those undertaking adjustments in their own lives in order to build a better future for themselves and their children.

■ The Transitional Adjustment Assistance Program would go some way towards providing assistance, but other reforms, too, are required. Thus Commissioners believe that the provision of a Universal Income Security Program with a universally available income guarantee, subject to reduction at a relatively low "tax-back" rate, constitutes the most appropriate foundation for Canada's income security programs.

- We therefore recommend that the UISP replace existing federal tax and transfer programs including:
  - GIS
  - Family Allowances
  - Child Tax Credits
  - Married Exemptions

- Child Exemptions
- The Federal Share of CAP Social Assistance Programs
- Federal Social Housing Programs.

- The replacement of these programs would make possible a universally available guarantee, in 1985, of approximately $2750 per adult (and for the first child in a single-parent family) and $750 per child with benefits reduced at a 20-per cent rate as other income was available. The elderly should receive an enriched option. A substantially larger guarantee of $3825 per adult could be provided if the personal income-tax exemption were also included.
- The UISP should be put in place at the same time as the broad Unemployment Insurance reforms described above. The entire package should be in place in 1988. The package should be phased in, however, with a two-stage approach. In the first stage, which should begin immediately, the Family Allowance, Child Tax Credit, and Child Tax Exemptions should be eliminated and replaced with a single demogrant or tax credit of approximately $1000 per year in 1985, payable monthly. The total amount should be available to families with a total annual income of up to $26 000. Beyond that level, benefits might be reduced at a 25 per cent rate. Experience rating for UI should also begin immediately, and social assistance payments under the CAP should be restructured to replace the present pre-emptive reduction of benefits above the current work-related/expenses level with a 50 per cent reduction rate. At the second stage of implementation, to be completed by the beginning of 1988, the full range of UI, UISP and TAAP changes outlined above should be in place.

Commissioners wish to emphasize that recommended benefit levels and structures are indicative only. While we believe them to be correct and appropriate levels in mid-1985, they will change with time. Moreover, the interrelationship among such features as basic guarantees and tax-back levels can be varied to achieve a number of effects.

We also wish to emphasize that while the federal government could implement most parts of this proposal unilaterally, these reforms are likely to be far more effective if they are carried out in co-operation with provincial government changes. The major reason for this is that provincial governments automatically receive larger tax revenues whenever the federal government eliminates tax exemptions and deductions. If the full value of these programs is to be maintained for the social policy sector, it will be necessary for the provincial governments either to provide harmonized transfers or to cede some tax points back to the federal government in return for delivery of the income-transfer arrangements.

- Commissioners recommend, therefore, that these proposals be the subject of urgent and serious federal-provincial discussion. We urge the Government of Canada to introduce them to the federal-provincial agenda at an early federal-provincial ministers' meeting and to move forward quickly towards implementation.

The UISP is not intended to provide fully adequate benefits for all Canadians who have no other earnings or income; it is primarily a supplementation program intended to compensate for the fact that there is often a considerable mismatch between earnings and needs. Commissioners therefore recommend that provincial governments continue to provide needs-tested social assistance as a top-up to UI and UISP benefits where these do not fully meet pertinent needs. The equivalent of the current provincial share of social assistance payments should be adequate for this purpose. In addition, provincial governments could reap a substantial increase in tax revenues from some of the tax changes which would accompany the inception of the UISP. It is desirable that these funds should also be used to support income-security programs; that arrangement would make provision of topping-up arrangements financially easy.

The UISP seems to Commissioners to be the essential building block for social security programs in the twenty-first century. Should governments not be able to implement it, a series of less complete reforms would at least ameliorate some of the worst features of the existing systems.

- Thus, failing the implementation of the UISP, Commissioners recommend:
  - Reform of the family benefits program to reduce or eliminate the child tax exemption and the family allowance program and to increase the child tax credit, which should also be made payable on a monthly basis
  - Reform of social assistance provisions of the Canada Assistance Plan to eliminate pre-emptive taxation of social assistance benefits as other income from employment, training allowances or similar sources is received. □

We wish to emphasize that these are partial reforms only, and that the more comprehensive UISP is a preferable choice.

Social Services

This Commission did not undertake an extensive review of Canada's social service programs. We did, however, receive many representations about them, and we did develop several recommendations.

■ Commissioners support the continuing devolution of responsibility for delivering social services to the community level and to non-profit associations. We strongly recommend, however, that this devolution not be handicapped by a reduction in funding, and that governments retain sufficient staff to exercise their monitoring responsibilities. The maintenance of funding is particularly important, since we could see no evidence whatsoever that social services, which include support for children, the elderly, the disabled and those with shorter-term social problems, are overfunded. Indeed, considerable evidence of underfunding was presented to us in our hearings.

- The major social services will also benefit from:
  - Further forms of assistance which will help users to become more self-reliant
  - Better integration of various forms of social and medical services at the community level.

Access to many social services in Canada is now impeded by the "needs-based" approach of the Canada Assistance Plan. Only those "in [financial] need or likely to become in need" have free access to services, so that many Canadians just above the poverty level are effectively precluded from receiving such important support as family, marital and financial counselling or child support services.

- This Commission recommends that the current federal-provincial financing arrangements be severed from social assistance financing and renegotiated to provide Canadians with broader access to these services.
- This Commission is not persuaded that extensive delegation of responsibility for social services to the profit-seeking part of the private sector is likely to improve significantly the services provided to Canadians. Where such privatization is practised, we recommend that it be done in the context of very careful government regulation of the provision of services. Profit maximization, in our view, is not always the best motive whereby to govern human transactions.

There are currently two major task forces working at the national level to review day care in Canada; therefore this Commission has not conducted research in this area. Commissioners do, however, wish to note that the current CAP day-care guidelines actually serve to make access to publicly supported day care quite difficult for middle-income Canadians and that the current $2000 tax exemption for child-care expenses is much more valuable to upper-middle/class Canadians than to the majority of Canadian families. Both these provisions require reform.

- Finally, Commissioners wish to pay tribute to the hundreds of thousands of Canadians who work through the voluntary sector to help their fellow citizens. We recommend that all levels of government should continue to support and nurture such activity by providing fully adequate support and supervision for the programs dispensed through the voluntary sector. □

Report of the Royal Commission on the Economic Union and Development Prospects for Canada

Report

Royal Commission on the Economic Union and Development Prospects for Canada

VOLUME THREE

Minister of Supply and Services Canada

COVER DESIGN: Will Rueter
INTERIOR DESIGN: Brant Cowie

Available in Canada through authorized bookstore agents and other bookstores or by mail from
Canadian Government Publishing Centre
Supply and Services Canada
Ottawa, Canada K1A 0S9

Also available in French

Printed in Canada

Catalogue No. Z1-1983/1-3E

ISBN 0-660-11873-4 (Vol. 3)

ISBN 0-660-11850-5 (Set)

Canada: $45.00
Other countries: $54.00
Price subject to change without notice.

CONTENTS

Detailed Contents lists appear at the beginning of each chapter.

VOLUME TWO

VOLUME THREE

PART VI

The Institutional Context:
Citizenship, Parliament and the Federation

PART VI

Contents

Introduction

The Canadian Constitutional Heritage and Directions for Reform

The three essential elements of Canadian constitutional government – responsible parliamentary government, federalism and citizens' rights, which culminated in the recently adopted Canadian Charter of Rights and Freedoms – are not disposable pieces of machinery to be subjected to narrow instrumental calculations based on cost efficiency. These three pillars represent the historic arrangements through which we govern ourselves, formulate economic policy, preserve social peace, shift the boundaries between the public and the private sector, and make claims on one another as individuals, as members of communities, and as residents of distinctive regions. That subtle blend of institutions and norms, fashioned over more than a century of our existence as a nation, defines our political identity, shapes our collective existence, and helps us to address problems that require our collective response. Our institutional arrangements must be both true to our evolving concepts of ourselves as a people and useful for the collective tasks we have taken on and will take on in the future.

The institutional arrangements bequeathed to us by history are not, therefore, a burden to be borne. Rather, they represent a heritage that we must nurture and refine in response to successive challenges emerging from the domestic and international environments. Canada's institutional arrangements are part of a living Constitution that evolves and that we continuously reshape. Canadians have challenged the particulars of these arrangements for their biases, insensitivities and inefficiencies, and we shall continue to do so.

Profound transformation has taken place in our institutions of government, in response to a sequence of changing pressures. Yet the transformations in

responsible government, federalism and citizens' rights have occurred within a recognizable line of development. If Sir Georges-Étienne Cartier or Sir John A. Macdonald were alive today, they would sense much that was reassuringly familiar along with much that was disorienting, the result of cumulative and incremental change.

Political systems change in complex and obscure ways. Change is partly the result of deliberate and conscious choice, but much change is subtle and informal, the result of slow modifications of behaviour. The constitutional order engages in a constant dialectic with its environment. Political institutions are a meeting point for the diverse social forces that affect the modern state. These forces include international economic interdependence and international tensions, popular expectations of government's responsibilities, social and economic change and the evolving aspirations of diverse internal communities. These forces, along with numerous other factors, change the working nature of institutions and the functions they perform.

Even deliberate change often produces unanticipated and sometimes perverse results. Except at the founding of nations, changes in political systems are typically piecemeal and rarely comprehensive. The cumulative effects of these changes can unbalance the structure of interdependent institutional arrangements and can thus lead inadvertently to a departure from basic values. Our task as Commissioners requires us to consider the institutional adjustments that Canadians have made in response to changing circumstances. Continuing on the path of *ad hoc* gradual change has consequences for the components of constitutional government that we in Canada must address.

As we look back on the transformations in our system of government since the end of the Second World War, the picture that emerges is neither one of chaos, nor one of serenity, but of something in between: a somewhat disorderly procedure evolving piecemeal, in response to pressures of the day, options available and partial visions of the future. The basic institutional framework remains, but there are also discontinuities, false starts and deviations from the principles of constitutional government that we have inherited.

The modifications in our processes of government since 1945 testify to the system's flexibility. These adjustments are remarkable in light of the common view that federal systems are rigid, and of the absence, until 1982, of a comprehensive procedure for amending the Constitution. Commissioners have concluded, nevertheless, that while parliamentary government, federalism and the Charter are appropriate to Canadian values and to the handling of future demands, our institutions since 1945 have not yet successfully adapted to major changes in the environment. Indeed, there have been such significantly negative effects that co-ordinated reform is required to ensure that Canada's constitutional order is both effective in managing the nation's collective affairs and sensitive to the values of liberal democracy.

These are large claims, and Commissioners, in making them, do not wish to be misunderstood. We believe that the essential components of our constitutional system — responsible government, federalism and the Charter — continue to provide firm foundations for the Canadian constitu-

tional order. We also believe, however, that the variety of *ad hoc* accretions that we have inherited or recently added to the system have distorted it. In particular, we fear that some recent developments threaten the function of governments as servants of the people.

Commissioners' proposals for institutional reform are directed toward three basic and closely related objectives. We wish to secure the democratic foundations of Canadian government. We hope to strengthen the capacity of Canada's institutional arrangements to accommodate the internal social, economic and political diversity found within Canadian society. We seek to increase the responsiveness and effectiveness of public policy making in a changing domestic and international environment. Each of these objectives has implications for the operation of responsible government and the federal system, and for the recognition of citizens' rights.

Commissioners' first objective – securing foundations for democracy – derives, in part, from the historic tradition in which Canadians have participated. We are citizens of one of the oldest enduring systems of constitutional government in the world. Maintenance of that heritage is an important task and an essential element of the "institutional and constitutional arrangements to promote the liberty and well-being of individual Canadians" (P.C. 1982-3438) to which our terms of reference directed us. In a complex and uncertain world, where domestic and international actions of the state in the social and economic realm affect each one of us, it is essential that our basic institutions – the three pillars of the Canadian constitutional order – enhance the quality of Canadian democracy.

To strengthen the foundations of democracy, Commissioners' concern is to reinvigorate the practice of responsible government. That form of government is the democratic vehicle by which Canadians keep legislative bodies sensitive to their values, render them accountable for their actions, and install and dismiss governments at periodic intervals. Because of the enhanced role of the state today, a healthy system of responsible government is more important than in the past, when a narrower state agenda, a smaller bureaucracy, and a stronger sense of personal ministerial accountability made the norms and practices of responsible government easier to sustain. The challenges we face are two-fold: first, to strengthen our elected legislatures as forums for legislative debate and scrutiny and for holding governments responsible for their conduct of public affairs; secondly, to ensure that the political executive, the Cabinet, is able to control the bureaucracy so that it operates as the instrument of citizens' representatives.

In any consideration of the democratic tradition in Canada, we must also address the implications of federalism, in particular the relation of federalism to responsible government. Our operational definition of Canadian federalism is a two-level system of responsible governments. To strengthen responsible government at the national and provincial levels, as Commissioners would wish, is therefore to flesh out federalism, and not to undermine it. Through interdependent responsible governments, federalism enhances opportunities for democratic participation by increasing the avenues through which citizens may express their policy preferences.

Although federalism and parliamentary government have co-existed in Canada for more than a century, relations between them have produced tension and will continue to do so. Federalism, with its division of powers, constrains legislative majorities and, in emergent policy areas where clearly defined jurisdictional limits are absent, it also raises questions about which majority, federal or provincial, should take precedence. Frequent resort to intergovernmental bargaining also contributes to the tension between federalism and responsible government, involving consequences for democracy. Intergovernmental bargaining tends to take place among executives, to involve complex agreements and tax-transfer arrangements which blur accountability and, on occasion, to confront legislatures with a *fait accompli*. The intergovernmental process, with its closed sessions and its stress on the interests of governments themselves, lessens the already-limited capacity of legislative bodies to control the political executive and is generally hostile to citizens' involvement. In the complex trade-off required here, Commissioners would favour the enhancement of the parliamentary side of our existence in both orders of government.

Intergovernmental relations are not the essence of federalism. Their undoubted significance is a by-product of the operations of contemporary federalism and reflects the co-existence of two orders of powerful government. That these governments exercise some of their responsibilities interdependently does not change the essential nature of Canadian federalism as a system of 11 responsible governments. The situation, does, however, raise major issues about managing that interdependence. We must address these issues within the context of the primacy of responsible, that is, accountable, government. Competitive elections to determine the partisan composition of legislatures through open discussion and freedom of association are an essential means whereby we keep government the servant of the people. This, our historic method of calling governments to account, will depend increasingly on the public availability of the information upon which decisions can or ought to be based. The availability of that information is often limited by our complex of institutions.

Commissioners' second objective is to strengthen the capacity of Canadian institutions to accommodate and reconcile Canada's internal social, economic and political diversity. We emphasize here arrangements for representing these varied interests and perspectives in public decision making.

Commissioners have sought to keep distinct the issues of regional representation in the national government and the machinery of intergovernmental relations, although these topics have occasionally been linked. For example, in the flurry of constitutional proposals leading up to the Constitution Act, 1982, there were calls for a reformed Senate to be made up in whole or in part of delegations appointed and controlled by provincial governments. In ways that were never fully explained, this second chamber was to perform some of the functions of intergovernmental conferences and simultaneously to compensate for regional insensitivities of the national government to matters directly under its jurisdiction. Commissioners distinguish these two functions, believing that the influence of provincial governments on national policies is best left to the intergovernmental arena.

Reform of the institutions of federalism concerns the questions of how responsibilities should be divided among governments, and how those governments should manage their inevitably overlapping relationships. It does nothing to ensure the legitimacy and representational capacity of national institutions in fulfilling their obligations to Canadians. Equally, reform of national institutions can do little to meet the need for co-ordinating the actions of two strong orders of government. We need both an appropriate relationship among governments and a regionally responsive central government. We believe, therefore, that the best way to inject the concerns of regional and provincial communities into the national Parliament is through the direct representation of their citizens, rather than through representation of provincial governments. Both electoral reform and Senate reform have been suggested as means to this end.

The electoral system appeared on the institutional reform agenda in the 1960s as the Liberals proved less and less able to obtain representation from the West and the Conservatives from Quebec. Some Canadians saw these failures as threatening the legitimacy of the federal government at a time when provincial governments were becoming more prominent in the federal system. Provincial governments, stressing a provincialist definition of Canada, presented themselves as the most legitimate representatives of Canadians, and elaborated this claim in proposals for reform of central-government institutions. Some argued for a reformed Senate appointed primarily or wholly by provincial governments. The opening up of the constitutional issue itself and the noticeable influence of provincial governments on that process gave prominence to provincial views on institutional reform.

Although the Government of Canada accorded priority to the Charter in its constitutional objectives, it also responded to the growth of provincialism. If the constitutional system were to respond to the prevailing view of the relative strength of social forces in the country, there would have to be either devolution of authority to the provincial governments or greater sensitivity at the centre to provincial concerns. Two choices were available to accomplish the latter option: express provincialism at the centre through provincial-government appointments, or incorporate provincial sentiments more directly. Electoral reform was one example of the latter approach.

The debate over the form of provincial participation in national institutions was an elemental controversy about the appropriate relations between the governments of the federal system and the national and provincial communities on which they are based. It was a debate, also, about the definition of the national community. Advocates of inserting a provincial component into Parliament, especially by means of a reformed Senate, were implicitly criticizing the historic principle of representation by population and the insensitivity, particularly to the smaller provinces, which that principle involved.

Commissioners' view of federalism accepts that the national government must have a capacity to represent and to respond to regionalism and provincialism. We believe that either reform of the Senate or, our second choice, reform of the electoral system of the House of Commons is necessary to accomplish these objectives. We prefer Senate reform, as we believe that

the most successful accommodation of regional interests in the formation of national policy requires a modification of the majoritarian principle of representation by population. We propose a Senate elected by proportional representation, with distribution of seats weighted toward the smaller provinces. This change, the significance of which we do not underestimate, would modify the basis of political power in the national government: it would supplement representation by population in the House of Commons with the more federalist principle of representation by region in a democratically elected Senate. We believe that our proposal would make every political party more representative, in caucus and in Parliament, of the provinces and regions. Better regional representation in national institutions should not only contribute to reconciliation of regional and national interests within the national jurisdiction, but should also increase the legitimacy of the national government in intergovernmental affairs.

The third general objective of Commissioners' proposals, that is, responsive and effective economic policy making in a changing domestic and international environment, involves a more direct focus on the function and operation of Canada's institutional framework. Canadians have a number of economic objectives including growth, high employment and low inflation. We cannot, however, divorce pursuit of these goals from the political process of governing and the institutional arrangements that channel it. Our economy, including its international dimensions, is a political economy. Political institutions have economic consequences. Changes in governing arrangements can influence our economic performance and prospects, just as can technological advances, the emergence of new markets, and changes in the international competitive environment.

Commissioners' attitude to conflict – its positive functions and its negative features – is central to our position on the making of policy, economic and other. We neither expect nor seek to achieve the elimination of disagreement, controversy and competition. In an open pluralistic society where state policies deliberately or inadvertently distribute advantages and disadvantages, conflict and competition among private actors seeking to influence governments are inevitable and functional. These actors provide governments with the information necessary for devising new policies and modifying old ones.

Regulated conflict among partisan adversaries is the essence of our parliamentary system. We appreciate the significance of the phrase "Her Majesty's Loyal Opposition", which would be incomprehensible in political systems where imprisonment rather than honour greets those who oppose the government. Moreover, we believe that the expression of choices and alternatives through this mechanism increases the quality and acceptability of the public policies that emerge. Our system of adversarial politics, linked to elections and freedom of speech and assembly, allows the people, however imperfectly, to rule.

The competition between government and opposition parties is only one example of institutionalized conflict within the Canadian state. Competition takes place, also, between governments in the federal system and within each of the governments of that system, for no government is monolithic. On the

contrary, government in Canada, as elsewhere, is comprised of competing and co-operating departments, bureaus and agencies.

Conflict, in other words, is inherent in our system and reflects real differences. We Commissioners, however, neither worship conflict nor view all its manifestations as healthy. A Darwinian jungle is not our ideal nor that of Canada. Our common existence means that we are connected to one another. We must therefore regulate conflict and frame rules to limit its destructive effects and enhance its constructive consequences. Commissioners are searching for a new balance. We wish to see more effective policy making. We wish to see policies that are sensitive to the concerns of the affected interests, that are practicable and feasible, and that can be integrated with other programs of the state. Conflict, appropriately restrained, can help Canadians to achieve responsive government.

To be more specific, Canadians should look carefully at the way our governments make economic policy, in order to make that process more responsive and effective. We must consider relations between citizens and the state and relations between governments. We should look first at leadership, information and consent, key features of effective policy making. We should then look at federalism: we might form better economic policies by introducing more flexible arrangements and clearer regulation of intergovernmental conduct.

Commissioners' concern for democracy does not ignore the consideration that Canada has representative, not direct democracy. There is an accepted and appropriate division of responsibility between citizens and the legitimate wielders of public authority. Citizens do not govern, and governors must make hard choices: *Gouverner, c'est choisir*. Accordingly, in our desire to keep governments accountable and responsible, we must not forget the functional necessity for executive leadership to set goals and to confirm clear directions and encourage their pursuit. Canadians adopted the British system of responsible government and rejected the American doctrine of separation of powers and the suspicion of government on which that doctrine is based. Responsible government was to sustain an "energizing executive", able to lead in the creation of a new country. Similarly, the executive at the provincial level came to act vigorously as provincial aspirations, power and administrative capacity expanded.

Commissioners believe, also, that effective policy making requires a continuous flow of information between the democratic state and its citizens. Sensitivity to the interdependence of issues and thus to the ideas and experience of those caught up in their complexities is essential. Democracy can serve economic performance by providing the state with the information necessary to ease the constant adjustment that economic change requires. The state is so deeply involved in the market-place that the functioning of the economic change it initiates depends heavily on the quality of the information on which it acts. We make recommendations concerning consultative arrangements designed to improve the exchange of information between governments and private actors.

It is true, also, that the state cannot successfully implement public purposes by issuing orders without the consent of the public. Successful implementation requires not only compliance, but also co-operation. We can no longer take these for granted as the growing underground economy indicates. Commissioners' goal is to harness the creative energies of the Canadian people in the process of economic policy making, for we deny that government has a monopoly on relevant knowledge and expertise.

Canadians and their governments live in an international environment which is the source of both economic growth and dislocation, and from which ideological, technological, scientific, military and other forces impinge on us. Citizens and their governments need to communicate effectively if they are to manœuvre together successfully in the world system. This requires consultation about citizens' needs and expectations, and discussion of governments' plans as they unfold. Moreover, the growing international responsibilities of the state threaten democratic controls by strengthening the power of the executive. We seek to check that development. In general, therefore, we seek an enhancement of democratic citizenship.

Economic performance depends on effective management of relations between the federal and provincial governments. In our concern to establish means by which to manage more effectively the inescapable interdependence among governments, we Commissioners do not anticipate or seek perfect harmony and equanimity as the chief goals for the federal system. The two orders of government are legitimate representatives of different constellations of interests and concerns. With this in mind, Commissioners wish to encourage a more functional approach to federalism. Rather than focusing on centralization or decentralization, or on increased federal or provincial power, discussions should stress responsiveness to citizens' needs and effective management of social and economic policy. We propose recommendations, therefore, to increase flexibility of response to problems introduced by governmental interdependence.

Concerning barriers within the Canadian economic union, Commissioners do not consider formal constitutional change other than the extension of section 121 of the Constitution Act, 1867 to cover interprovincial trade in services. Other decisions to be made concerning the economic union involve sensitive trade-offs between economic and political considerations; we believe that intergovernmental forums can best handle these trade-offs at this stage. Clearly, Canadians must establish rules to control barriers to interprovincial trade, in order to check government behaviour that is inconsistent with more open world trade and the need for a more flexible and efficient economy. We propose formulation of a code governing interprovincial trade, the principles of which might ultimately become part of the Constitution. To advance this effort and to render it more visible to Canadians, we suggest, below, institutional procedures for governments.

These, then, are our fundamental goals for institutional reform: to enhance the quality of Canadian democracy, and to strengthen the linkages between citizens and their state; to improve the capacity of our institutions to reflect, accommodate and reconcile the divergent interests in Canadian society; to

enhance the capacity of our governing institutions to generate and implement economic and social policies and programs through which Canadians can achieve policy goals such as those set out throughout this Report.

Confederation

The Canadian state is a complex assemblage of institutions and norms. To understand it, we must look at the principles underlying its institutional features. These principles include, most notably, the three pillars of the constitutional order: responsible parliamentary government, federalism and, more recently, the Canadian Charter of Rights and Freedoms. They provide the framework through which we govern ourselves and shape collective goals. It is through that framework, modified by historical evolution and made more important by the recent dramatic growth of state responsibilities, that the relations of state, society and economy play themselves out. The institutional framework defines what we can achieve through state action. It facilitates the achievement of some purposes and frustrates others.

Our federal arrangements distribute different jurisdictional capacities to two orders of government. We employ both orders to pursue goals, sometimes as members of a provincial community and at other times as citizens of a national community. The selection of goals depends, in part, on which order of government has jurisdiction in a given field. Provincial boundaries determine the relevant population base for policy responses to specific matters under provincial jurisdiction, according to prevailing constitutional interpretation. Decisions of the past affect the existence of political communities today; and our decisions may do the same in the future. Thus, the federal government's arbitrary division of the former Northwest Territories into the Provinces of Alberta and Saskatchewan, in 1905, determines today's beneficiaries of the Alberta Heritage Trust Fund and the Saskatchewan Heritage Fund. So, too, any contemporary division of the Northwest Territories may affect our descendants many years hence. The new Charter of Rights and Freedoms also affects our capacity, through the state, to pursue particular goals.

All political systems are tied to the past, including those that attempt a revolutionary departure from it. Commissioners' starting point for understanding the Canadian system of constitutional government is, therefore, the Confederation agreement of 1867, although it, too, was the product of previous experience.

Federal systems with written constitutions develop from a particular set of decisions reached at a precise moment in history. The act of founding necessarily requires one set of choices about institutional arrangements that foreclose the possibility of others. If the arrangements withstand the battering of future challenges, they deny basic options to future generations. Just as the decision to become a ballet dancer or a nuclear physicist eliminates the possibility of pursuing other careers and determines a lifestyle that may last for years, so the consequences of basic institutional choices remain in force over lengthy periods, for such choices cannot be made, unmade or remade in

response to every passing fancy. As the German sociologist Max Weber observed, once we toss the historical dice to determine basic social arrangements, we cannot easily throw them again. The founding act of constitutional choice establishes the structure of state power and basic relations among core institutions, and initiates the rhetoric of subsequent political debate. It defines the boundaries of community within which we make claims on one another and respond to such claims. It shapes the language we employ in defending those claims, and the arrangements we employ to fulfil them.

The first pillar of constitutional government in Canada, responsible government, is an inheritance from Great Britain. The British North American colonists had begun to achieve representative and responsible government prior to Confederation. In such a system, the Cabinet, or executive council, is responsible for its actions to a representative elected legislature. This system structures the relations between legislature and executive in both federal and provincial governments. It is intended to ensure that government is servant rather than master and, at the same time, to endow the political executive with the capacity for leadership necessary to mobilize resources in the pursuit of agreed objectives.

The bias toward executive authority following Confederation was implicit in the link between the Cabinets and the legislatures. There was a convention that the Cabinets in office would remain as long as they were supported by a majority of the members of the House of Commons or of the provincial legislative assemblies. As the national party system developed, there emerged a convention that support in the legislature would be based on partisan majorities.

The absence of distrust or fear of executive authority was, in part, a product of the monarchical tradition: power flowed from the Crown rather than from the people. Most Canadian politicians of the 1860s, including the Fathers of Confederation, were not "democrats" as that term was popularly understood in the United States, and were anxious to stress the "Britishness" of Canada and hence its distinctiveness from our American neighbours. The United States was just recovering from a Civil War, which some of the Fathers of Confederation attributed to the excesses of democracy and to the American conception of the rights of the people. They believed that these arrangements fatally weakened governing authority. Accordingly, they envisaged that representative and responsible government would more effectively combine democratic control and executive leadership.

The Fathers of Confederation had inherited responsible parliamentary government. To it they added the second pillar, federalism. Federalism was an appropriate institutional response to the existing colonial diversities in the Maritimes and the Province of Canada. In Lower Canada – the future Quebec – a francophone majority had its own civil code, language, culture, history and religious background. It insisted on and received significant powers of self-rule at the provincial level in matters pertaining to cultural survival and growth. Upper Canada – later Ontario – with its British heritage, also required a federal arrangement. The Maritime colonies of Nova Scotia and New Brunswick also had distinctive traditions and histories, and joined

the federation with their own recently established systems of responsible government.

The Act of Union of 1840 had united Upper and Lower Canada. Its implementation had proved to both French and English that collaboration of both language groups within the framework of a single colony with one government would produce recurrent stalemate and deadlock. The British North America Act of 1867 (now renamed the Constitution Act, 1867) brought together into one constitutional system Nova Scotia, New Brunswick and the united Province of Canada, and at the same time, divided that Province. It thereby disentangled the local affairs of the respective francophone and anglophone majorities in the new provinces of Quebec and Ontario. By providing for both disengagement and consolidated action, federalism was, from the beginning, essential to the harmonious co-existence of the French- and English-speaking peoples within a common country.

Confederation, of course, not only created four new provinces out of three British colonies, but also established a new national government. That government would preside over and, indeed, build the new nation, extending its jurisdiction to the Pacific, populating the prairies and integrating the expanded country by means of railways. While creation of the provinces protected existing diversities and community arrangements, creation of the federal government was a response to the challenge of building a new nation. No national community existed in 1867, and there was relatively limited intercolonial trade and exchange. Only a common experience of constitutional development within the British tradition originally united the colonies. Provincial communities, or at least their colonial antecendants, predated Confederation. Sections 91 and 92 of the Constitution Act, 1867 set out most of the powers of the two levels of government. The new constitutional arrangements were based on separate systems of responsible government, each with generally distinctive jurisdictional authority.

French Canadians in Quebec tended to assess federalism in terms of the powers assigned to provincial governments. Many English Canadians, though by no means all, supported a strong central government and its expansionist ambitions. In our post-Confederation history, national policies, especially concerning foreign affairs and conscription, deeply divided the two linguistic communities, and the general insensitivity of the political majorities and provincial governments of English Canada to the francophone minorities in their midst reinforced that division. By the 1970s, these two developments had led to the emergence of a government in Quebec committed to sovereignty-association. Commissioners will return in a subsequent section to French-English relations and their effect on Canadian federalism, and to our proposals concerning a *rapprochement* with the government of Quebec, which has not accepted the Constitution Act, 1982.

Another aspect of the original understanding of 1867 requires emphasis in the light of recent constitutional controversies. Originally, the federal Cabinet was to represent the regions: ministers would speak for their provinces when national policy was being determined. Nevertheless, representation by population was to be the basis of the House of Commons; the Senate, with

federally appointed membership based on regional equality, was to be weak, and has become progressively weaker. From the beginning, therefore, we have had a national government in which citizens are represented on the basis of population. Yet the inevitable consequence of weighting voters equally is to weight provinces unequally. The overriding premise has been that the House of Commons, and the Cabinet power derived from it, represent and make laws for all Canadians as members of a national community.

The third pillar of the Canadian constitutional order, citizens' rights, was also part of our British heritage. The founders of Canada did not reject that heritage of civil liberty. The preamble to the British North America Act of 1867, which established the new nation, stated that Canada was to have a "constitution similar in principle to that of the United Kingdom." Such a constitution was to include responsible government and the civil liberties and freedoms that had come to be viewed as the rights of British subjects. In Britain, no formal written constitution enshrined the ancient and highly-valued rights of persons or limited the powers of Parliament; nevertheless, those rights were not only considered compatible with the tradition of parliamentary supremacy, but were deemed best protected by it.

In keeping with the concept of parliamentary supremacy and the fact that Confederation was the achievement of a small Canadian élite, no ringing declaration of the rights of citizens accompanied the birth of our nation. The Fathers of Confederation attributed no sovereignty to the new Canadian people, who were to exercise their influence through elected representatives. The British Parliament passed the British North America Act; there was no popular ratification of Confederation. Canada remained linked to Europe by virtue of Britain's continuing role in Canadian affairs. Yet, subject to continuing imperial ties, we Canadians had significantly adjusted the arrangements by which we governed ourselves. We had responded to the imperatives of space, of linguistic and cultural duality, and of distinctive colonial histories by establishing provinces. We had also set ourselves the demanding task of building a nation, and we were commencing a journey in the course of which we would gradually shed our links with Britain. The Constitution Act, 1982, by which we set up a comprehensive procedure for amending our Constitution here in Canada, has further reduced the significance of the British connection which earlier had been central to the identity of many English Canadians.

Protection and expression of provincial and regional diversities were never the sole concern of Canadian federalism. From the beginning, federalism was intended also to facilitate emergence of a new national community. That community emerged as successive generations of Canadians and their governments proceeded to build a nation. The choice of federalism presupposed and permitted the evolution of a complex, interdependent relationship between provincial and national communities.

Responsible government, with clear lines of accountability between Cabinets, legislatures, and electorates, logically assumed a type of federalism with little interdependence of policies between governments, a reasonable assumption in 1867. The national government had large and impressive responsibilities, for which it received appropriate powers; provincial

governments were to play a more limited role and therefore had less extensive powers. In general, at least by our contemporary standards, direct government intervention had little effect on society and the economy. Although partisan politics was often heated, and patronage was significant for party supporters, for most Canadians, government was a distant affair.

The social context in which the Constitution was drafted did not involve the pervasive presence of government. The Constitution Act, 1867 inevitably reflected prevailing attitudes about the function of government, assumptions long since gone. Canadians have built the massive bureaucratic apparatus of the modern state on the foundation of a formal division of powers that has changed little since Confederation. One out of five Canadians now works for some level of government. There are few areas of our lives untouched by the state in its performance of its many responsibilities. As one consequence, rather than governments that function independently of each other, we have intimate, and often discordant, interdependence.

The growth of the state and of interdependence gives rise to new requirements for managing relations between governments. It also complicates the working of responsible government, which is central to our Canadian practice of democracy, by blurring the chain of accountability that stretches from Cabinets to legislatures to citizens. The widened involvement of the state in new areas of social and economic regulation also raises new issues with respect to the status of citizens in the constitutional order.

Clearly we need to reassess the principles of responsible government, federalism and individual rights in the light of the complex co-existence of big governments in Canada today. The accomplishments of the Fathers of Confederation constitute a heritage that we must both honour and adapt.

The Evolving State in a Changing World

Since the Second World War, two new primary forces have challenged our traditional constitutional arrangements: the growth of the state and the increased impact of the international environment. Given the multiple functions of the modern state, Commissioners see no evidence that a significant overall decrease in government activity is possible. We see, in particular, a high probability that Canada's international involvement will increase, and that external forces will have an increasing effect on the quality of Canadians' lives. These assumptions will shape our analysis of Canada's constitutional arrangements. We wish to determine, in the light of these assumptions and of the continuing evolution of Canada's social composition, how to provide government that responds democratically to Canadians' wishes and efficiently manages our collective affairs.

The dialectic among state, society and economy, domestically and internationally, defies easy comprehension. Yet we Canadians must understand the many functions performed by governments in our federal state if we are to have informed discussion about the appropriate division of labour between the state and the economy, and about the other functions of the state in Canada. It is essential to keep in mind that government itself is far from being a single-minded actor.

Since the Great Depression of the 1930s, many people have believed that domestic economic management is one of government's major responsibilities, second only to preservation of civil order. Management of the welfare state derives from, and is closely integrated with, the task of economic management. The welfare state is government's response to the failures of the economic system to distribute equitably income, risk and life chances. It is the product of evolving concepts of social justice and citizens' rights, worked out through political processes. Although it is also related to economic stabilization, we can logically consider it the equity side of government's responsibilities in economic management. The two functions are complementary: the state is held responsible both for performance of the economy and for the social consequences of fluctuating patterns of economic activity. These two interrelated tasks require a complex division of labour: although the state must seek to steer the economy, most basic, day-to-day, economic decisions must be taken in the market-place. The state intervenes to adjust the distributive consequences of the market in accordance with evolving criteria of social justice. The welfare state preserves social stability by collectively compensating for inequalities generated by the market.

In addition to discharging its responsibilities in economic management and social welfare, the modern state seeks to maintain social cohesion, symbolizes the community's unity and diversity, and operates on the international stage. It has a responsibility to foster social integration. This "social role", as we have termed it, includes government responses to issues of sexual equality, ethnicity, language, regionalism, Native rights, alternative life-styles and ecology. While the relevant government policy responses clearly affect the economy, the issues derive their impetus from the social pluralism and multiple divisions characteristic of "post-industrial" society. We are witnessing the extension of concepts of equality to new spheres and a consequent willingness to use governments to resolve problems that those concepts define.

A healthy political and social order requires symbolic official affirmation of our identity as Canadians. Official recognition and confirmation of the diverse characteristics of a national society through representative practices and in government policies is essential to that society's definition and perception of itself as a people. Canada's official languages policy, for example, symbolizes our linguistic dualism. Our policy of multiculturalism is a recognition of the contribution of all ethnic groups to Canadian society. The appointment of women to the offices of lieutenant-governor and governor general speaks to sexual equality. Special constitutional conferences on aboriginal rights affirm that Canada's aboriginal peoples are a distinctive component of our modern society.

To dismiss these symbolic functions of the state would be a grievous mistake. The social and symbolic roles of the state have a special capacity to excite the passions of each of us as citizens, for they address our moral beliefs, our feelings of self-worth, and our identities. With its prominence in recognizing status, as well as distributing income, the state must seek to enable citizens to identify with the moral, symbolic order of a highly politicized society. This is no easy task. The emotionally divisive issues of the

last quarter-century in Canada have not been concerned only with class divisions or labour/management conflict, but have frequently emerged from the symbolic and social realms.

The Canadian state also has major international functions and responsibilities. These responsibilities are so much greater than they were before the Second World War that they represent a qualitative change. Since 1945, there has been a proliferation of new states with varying degrees of control over territory and populations. A small club of actors has become a crowd, thus complicating the international system by increasing the number of participating states. Simultaneously, international organizations have become important forums for the attainment of domestic goals. Canada, as a trading nation, depends heavily on a liberalized international order to encourage the flow of goods, capital and services. Various institutional arrangements, which involve the General Agreement on Tariffs and Trade (GATT), the International Monetary Fund (IMF), and other bilateral and multilateral accords, manage this international economic system. Conversely, the international arena also provides ground for the arms race and the playing out of international political rivalries. Canada is not merely an observer of all these developments: we have taken and shall continue to take a prominent part in the resolution of international problems.

The breadth and complexity of the state's relations to its domestic and international environments defies easy comprehension. The domestic and international context is so exceptionally complex that historic patterns of thought — communism, capitalism, socialism, liberalism, conservatism and other intellectual ordering devices of yesterday's politics — do not provide coherent answers to the range of issues that agitate us. Several of those traditional perspectives may help to guide policy in selected areas, but if our concern is for the whole, as it must be, we must be creative.

No consensus exists in today's intellectual and political milieux for Commissioners to ratify and adopt. The frequently lamented decline of political parties and the resulting tendency of interest groups to deal directly with governments are in part a product of that lack of consensus. Without some coherent framework of ideas, it is difficult for political parties to offer direction, integrate the multiple divisions in Canada and deal with the vast demands put upon the state.

The International Environment, Responsible Government and Canadian Federalism

Increased international interdependence in the modern world involves new challenges for Canadians. It also puts new or stronger pressures on Canada's institutional and constitutional arrangements. For instance, a crucial problem throughout the world involves the appropriate relations between the global political structure of geographically fixed states and the international forces — economic, cultural, ideological, scientific, technological and military — within which they exist. States cannot move, and neither can peoples. Accordingly, this Commission has been deeply concerned about Canadian responses to the many external forces that shape our private and

public lives, and that may even alter the delicate balance between federal and provincial governments. The manner in which we Canadians respond can affect the quality of Canadian democracy and the effect of our institutions on economic performance.

There is an inherent contradiction in administering foreign affairs within a parliamentary democracy. International negotiations, participation in complex alliances, and the need for quick responses to international crises may encourage, even require, prompt executive action with little or no public or parliamentary consultation. Some matters, such as deliberate adjustment of the exchange rate, require secrecy for their effective implementation. Executive branches usually have more expertise at their disposal than have legislatures, and legislatures enjoy access to more expertise than citizens. The imbalance is much greater in international matters than on purely domestic issues. Our treaty-making practices, which do not require parliamentary debate, accentuate the imbalance of information and expertise.

Commissioners do not intend to suggest that the executive acts with ease and precision and without institutional controls in the international domain. Managing international economic policy is difficult for the federal government, for example, because it involves blending the "low politics" of economic life with the traditional "high politics" of war and peace. Significant internal reorganizations to achieve that blending have been constantly on the agenda of Western states, including Canada, in recent decades.[1] Bureaucratic politics pervades the making of international economic policy because the process involves numerous departments and agencies with foreign economic interests or responsibilities.[2] Thus the state is far from being a unitary actor, even in foreign affairs. The internal controls on government resulting from this situation are undoubtedly powerful, but they are qualitatively distinct from the discipline of responsible government in our domestic constitutional tradition.

Global interdependence is often viewed primarily from the perspective of economics, a field where it is defined in terms of liberalization of international trade and the flows of international capital. Economic interdependence, however, is only one of the external forces that play on people and states. Many contemporary social movements reflect the interaction between domestic and international forces. Movements seeking to enhance the status of women and aboriginals and to protect the environment, and groups favouring new or "alternative" life-styles are simultaneously national and international. Social movements gain strength from their international counterparts and have an increasing influence on domestic affairs.

The traditional concerns of Canadian foreign policy — war and peace, military contributions to the Western alliance, and procurement to sustain the infrastructure of defence — are major responsibilities of the national government. These responsibilities are relatively immune from fluctuations in the federal-provincial balance in domestic areas.

The federal government is the primary regulator of our growing social and commercial transactions with the rest of the world; it creates policy on tariffs, exchange rates, immigration, citizenship and culture. It is responsible for our

national borders, and their defence, and for the regulation of transactions across them. It may execute this responsibility through domestic legislation, such as the Foreign Investment Review Act (FIRA), or by means of international treaties on tariffs. The media, particularly electronic media, can easily penetrate national borders. Most Canadians live within 300 kilometres of our border with the United States, with which English-speaking Canadians share a common language. Our national government is the only institution in Canada with the ability to regulate the flow of U.S. electronic media into our country. This is one reason for its major role in the fostering of Canadian culture.

The national government's greater involvement in the international arena makes it more sensitive than the provinces to a variety of international concerns and to the interdependence of international and domestic interests. This difference in exposure and awareness complicates the intergovernmental process within Canada as various parties emphasize different concerns in domestic discussions. This situation has been evident in our experience with acid rain, for example, and in provincial adherence to Canadian commitments in international trade.

The provinces obviously lack international contacts equivalent to those exercised by the national government. Nevertheless, in response to international events affecting their residents or businesses within their jurisdiction, provincial governments have become actively involved in international matters. Provincial activity in the international sphere focuses largely on trade. Quebec has, in addition, extensive cultural contacts with France and *la francophonie*.

Manœuvring in the international political economy on behalf of domestic economic interests, therefore, has become a functionally shared responsibility, and provincial governments have become prominent in international trade missions. Because many non-tariff barriers (NTBs) of key interest to our trading partners are under provincial jurisdiction, federal-provincial co-operation is essential if Canadians are to participate effectively in this aspect of international relations. Given the new importance of NTBs, provincial agreement and compliance are essential if the terms of treaties negotiated by Canada are to be fulfilled. At the moment, no arrangement exists to achieve such agreement. That gap in our institutional machinery is a major impediment to negotiation and implementation of bilateral and multilateral arrangements to reduce international trade restrictions.

The need for federal-provincial co-operation in international trade is parallel to the need for federal-provincial co-operation in domestic matters for which both levels of government have a measure of responsibility. We can apply some of the principles governing co-operation in domestic matters to the international realm. The provinces would wish international economic policy to be as sensitive to regional and provincial interests as is domestic policy. And, of course, it is desirable that the provinces be sensitive to the national interest and respect the federal government's international responsibilities.

Growth of the State and Canadian Federalism

The growth of the state in Canada at both federal and provincial levels has generated an additional set of problems: managing the interdependence of governments in the federal system. Interdependence was a concern in 1867. Disallowance, reservation, the declaratory power and federal appointment of the provincial lieutenant-governors – early drafts called them "Superintendents" – all indicated that the national government could intervene directly in provincial affairs.

These federal instruments were not manifestations of intergovernmental partnership. Disallowance and reservation were essentially negative. They could prevent provincial governments from proceeding with particular measures. The declaratory power allowed the federal government to remove certain "works" from provincial jurisdiction. The federal government applied these instruments unilaterally and frequently in the early years. The Constitution Act, 1867 also provided for federal payments to the provinces to compensate for their relinquishment of tariff powers and to bridge the gap between their revenue-raising capacities and their expenditures. Relative to the present situation, however, the interdependence of governments in the federal system was minimal in 1867 and remained so into the twentieth century.

The modest elaboration of the conditional-grant technique between the two World Wars brought the two orders of government into closer collaboration in pursuit of common purposes. Even in the Depression of the 1930s, however, prevailing opinion held that the division of powers was the defining element of Canadian federalism. Flexibility was to come, not from transcending the division of powers by co-operative arrangements, but by constitutional amendment. That amendment, unfortunately, was more easily advocated than accomplished. Hence a constitutional impasse emerged in the 1930s. Many Canadians came to see an inflexible federal system as an obstacle to a leading role for the national government, especially in economic management, which they considered essential in those desperate times.

Wartime conditions after 1939 gave the federal government the dominant role that had been impossible for it to assume in the Depression. In the post-war period, the constitutional impasse was circumvented by means of a growing network of fiscal agreements and conditional grants, especially in the various programs that constituted the welfare state. In the interdependent federalism of the late 1940s and early to mid-1950s, the federal government was still the dominant player. Provincial governments, however, began to enhance their bureaucratic capacity and to amplify the number and increase the subtlety of the governing instruments at their disposal. Seeing themselves as entrepreneurs developing their own economies, they began to challenge the national government's leadership. Nation-building and province-building had to find ways to co-exist.

Provincial governments continue to occupy a prominent place in the nation's public life. Commissioners consider this situation an unalterable feature of the foreseeable future. The co-existence of two orders of government actively involved in the same society and economy has created a

high degree of interdependence among governments. Managing the federal system has thus emerged as a new and difficult responsibility for governments that wield much more power than they did in 1945.

A complex network of intergovernmental agreements and machinery testifies to the shared responsibilities of the two orders of government, and to their inability to pursue their objectives in isolation from each other. The division of powers proves an imprecise guide in determining where responsibility resides when new areas of activity emerge. Thus there are always intergovernmental skirmishes at the margin. These conflicts deflect attention from the ongoing process of working out *rapprochements* in other areas.

The intergovernmental process is both political and bureaucratic. There is no hierarchy. Participants can make demands, strike postures, and threaten and use unilateral action. There is no price system to regulate competition, nor is there any invisible hand to transform competition into a universally recognizable version of the public interest. Nevertheless, there is self-restraint. There is recognition of the legitimacy of other governments. There is a common citizenship linking governors and electorates that distinguishes intergovernmental relations from those among independent states in the international system. Furthermore, there has been a halting development of intergovernmental machinery to manage federal-provincial interdependence. In recent years, both levels introduced departments, bureaus, and agencies of intergovernmental affairs — a number of which they have since disbanded — to manage interdependence.

Be this as it may, Commissioners see considerable room for improvement in intergovernmental relations. We accordingly recommend new institutions to manage interdependence. We suggest the need for a more highly developed sense of constitutional co-existence and of comity, to moderate the excesses of rivalry and competition. Over time, governments, like other organizations, do acquire interests of their own that are divorced from the purposes they were originally intended to serve. Thus the concerns of government often come to override the interests of citizens.

Citizens sometimes see themselves as pawns in the hands of contending governments, neither of which represents their views of how and by what policies they should be governed. Squabbling and rancour can frustrate our desire as citizens for a sense of security that our affairs are well handled in intergovernmental discussion and negotiation. Therefore, Commissioners seek more effective handling of relations between the governments of the national and provincial communities that co-exist as the base of the federal system. We Canadians all belong to both types of community. These communities are alternative manifestations of one people, which is provincial for some purposes and national for others. Governing ourselves within the federal system is thus a more complex task than in a unitary state. The activist role of government at both levels enhances this complexity.

Growth of the State and Responsible Government

Responsible government is the primary vehicle by which Canadians hold governments accountable. Despite the difficulty of encompassing and

controlling the activist state, the institutions of responsible government remain the key to keeping government our servant, rather than allowing it to become our master. The increasing activities of government complicate the functioning of responsible government in several ways.

As we have already noted, intergovernmental networks linking federal and provincial governments weaken the ability of legislatures to control executives and hence of the electorate to control governments. The proliferation of regulatory agencies and Crown corporations outside executive control lessens accountability. The many and increasing activities of the state in the international arena are less subject to influence by legislatures and electorates than are its more domestic functions.

We have seen as well the effect of changes in economic theory. New ideas have emerged about the management of inflation, growth and employment. These ideas influence not only the function of the state and the division of labour between state and economy, but also the relative power of institutions within government. Such influences may affect democratic institutions. Monetarist ideas, for example, enhance the role of the Bank of Canada, which is highly independent of direct government control, and thereby lessen the ability of the electorate and of Parliament to hold the government responsible for an important instrument of economic policy.

More generally, the state's agenda is extensive; the imbalance of expertise and resources between cabinets and legislatures is pronounced. Limitations of time are extreme, and incentives for secrecy are strong. Public exposure, scrutiny, debate and discussion of policy are inevitably spotty and haphazard. The vast apparatus of the administrative state continues to apply earlier policies around which programs have been built, agencies constructed and relations with clienteles established. There is considerable scope for discretion, and policies evolve in the nooks and crannies of the bureaucratic structure, far from the gaze of parliamentarians and voters, but often closely monitored by interest groups. Even Cabinet ministers who are responsible for managing vast bureaucracies, cannot claim to monitor everything their departments do. To assert greater political control over the bureaucracy we have created a host of "central agencies". These, too, are bureaucracies which must also be controlled.

Political parties have not been able to eliminate these difficulties. Canadian parties have a limited capacity to draw interests together effectively and to provide the coherence derived from an integrated party philosophy. With the growth of government, parties have faced even greater challenges to encompass the full range of affected interests. Interest groups therefore interact directly with the bureaucracy. Demands on the state, accordingly, come from many directions, and the absence of an effective system to discipline them means that interest groups have no need to make compromises with other interests, public or private.

Commissioners have no panacea for these ills, but we have suggestions for alleviating them. The direction of our proposals is straightforward. The bias in favour of executive dominance in our system has gone too far and needs redress. We must secure the foundations of responsible government through which Canadians practise democracy in both the federal and provincial spheres.

However desirable it may be to disentangle federal and provincial functions and responsibilities, interdependence and interaction between the two orders of government will continue. This is an unavoidable consequence of vastly increased government intervention since 1867. It often reflects a beneficial competition among governments as politicians vie with one another to satisfy the expectations and demands of citizens and to secure the political recognition this brings. Commissioners would prefer to see interdependence managed well. We would like a system that helps to clarify disputes over jurisdictional boundaries, renders intergovernmental processes more visible and therefore more accountable, and moderates the excesses of competition. We intend our proposed reforms to increase the ability of national institutions to represent and respond to regional concerns, and to increase the capacity of those institutions to integrate national and provincial concerns in the intergovernmental arena.

We Commissioners advance our proposals for institutional reform in the belief that the more government we have, the more democratic we must become. We believe, also, that in a complex society in which the state, the economy and society are closely linked, effective government is incompatible with the isolation, secrecy and aloofness of our governors. Both idealism and realism suggest that the Canadian state requires more democracy, not less. Those who argue to the contrary must come to grips with the consequences of unchecked state power and an uninformed citizenry.

We Commissioners base this essentially democratizing position on a fundamental distinction between markets and governments. Although markets need a secure environment of rules and property rights, and the support of a complex infrastructure, they do not require central direction of the innumerable decisions of individual economic actors: co-ordination of economic activity takes place with or without individuals' understanding the market's overall functioning. Individuals respond to cues from the market as they pursue their particular economic goals; there is co-ordination without hierarchy.

With governments, it is otherwise. In government, sensitivity, trade-offs and co-ordination do not occur automatically. Governments intervene directly in society and the economy. Those participants in government who would alter social and economic arrangements in pursuit of public objectives should be knowledgeable and sensitive. Democratization, therefore, is a prerequisite to effectiveness in the long term. We must strengthen the processes of democratization through parliamentary institutions, both federal and provincial.

Political Community in Canada

The image that a people has of itself has a major influence on the way it lives. No Royal Commission can pronounce *ex cathedra* what that image is to be. Commissioners can explore the critical issue of our collective identity, hoping to clarify the debate and contribute to discussion. In the final analysis, however, Canadians will work out their own answer, within an institutional and constitutional framework, the evolution of which is, in part, a response to the changing pressures of community.

The complexities of community in Canada have grown, not diminished, from the time of Confederation. With the addition of new territory, the original four provinces based on distinctive communities have become ten, and the number may further increase as the North develops.

Canadians emerged as a distinctive people in the post-Confederation process of nation building. For many English Canadians, that evolving sense of collective self fitted comfortably with continuing, but slowly declining, allegiance to Britain. French Canadians were politically less oriented to Europe and identified more with North America; almost all were descendants of the *habitants* who settled Quebec in the seventeenth and eighteenth centuries. The different orientation of English and French Canadians toward Europe sometimes produced French-English tensions over foreign policy, most notably those inherent in the conscription crises of the two World Wars. Extensive immigration from central and eastern Europe to the West, in the years preceding the First World War, laid the foundation for the multicultural heritage which our nation recognized in later years.

The evolutionary maturation of Canada from colony to nation as portrayed by liberal nationalist historians of English Canada, and the concomitant transformation of Empire into Commonwealth are well-known staples of Canadian history. The Balfour Declaration of 1926 and the Statute of Westminster, enacted in 1931, need no elaboration here. Continuing internal development of a Canadian political identity after the Second World War was codified in the Canadian Citizenship Act of 1946, the abolition of civil appeals to the Judicial Committee of the Privy Council in 1949, domestication of a formula for amending part of the Constitution in the same year, and appointment of the first Canadian Governor General in 1951.

In 1951, the Report of the Royal Commission on National Development in the Arts, Letters and Sciences in Canada (the Massey Commission) argued that the state should foster Canadian culture, in part to counter "Americanization". This concern was to recur in numerous areas of policy as the capacity of the British connection to differentiate Canadians from Americans diminished. Although we Canadians were acquiring an autonomous international presence, we were simultaneously becoming, both practically and psychologically, a North American people. The nature of our coexistence with the United States was a recurrent concern for Canadian policy makers. How to combine political autonomy and a distinctive identity with the increasing integration of the North American economy continues to be a fundamental dilemma for Canadians. The difficulty transcends purely domestic concerns and requires delicate handling of our international role. The United States is the world's strongest military and industrial power, and leads the network of alliances arrayed against the Soviet Union and its allies. In these circumstances, the dilemmas and difficulties of Canadian statehood and nation-building are permanent features of our national condition.

In the first decade after the Second World War, Canadian nationalism and elaboration of a national community developed rapidly. Links with Britain, no longer an impressive imperial power, became weaker. While many other nations struggled to recover from war or to emerge from colonial dependence, Canada was becoming a middle power. The federal government, building on foundations of its authority laid down during the Depression and the war, assumed a leading role in the processes of demobilization and reconstruction. The shared experience of depression and war had changed public expectations of government: the federal government, working closely with the provinces, became the central actor in the evolution of the welfare state.

The Government of Quebec was defensive, concerned more with defending provincial powers generally, and Quebec's specifically, than with the search for enhanced status and jurisdiction pursued by its successors. The Report of the Quebec Royal Commission on Constitutional Problems (the Tremblay Report), tabled in 1956, was a vigorous sociological and philosophical defence of federalism and of its special virtues for Quebec. It described Quebec society as spiritual, anti-materialist, rural and anti-statist. Quebec, it argued, preferred to handle important functions, including education and welfare, primarily through private religious institutions, although industrialization, urbanization and secularization were already undermining the Commission's analysis.

In the mid-1950s, the Canadian state at the national level remained symbolically and practically an expression of English Canadians, and primarily of those of British background. A complex set of domestic pressures, however, accompanied increasing autonomy from Britain. The non-British component of English Canada asserted itself. Prime Minister John Diefenbaker, who held office from 1957 to 1963, made his Cabinets more ethnically heterogeneous than had his predecessors; he also named Canada's first woman Cabinet minister. His government gave status Indians the vote in 1960, even though many status Indians opposed the franchise, and appointed an Indian, James Gladstone, to the Senate. Diefenbaker had a vision of "One Canada", derived from the ethnic mosaic of life in the West, his own German and Scots ancestry, and a commitment to parliamentary tradition. His major effort to translate his vision into practice was the Bill of Rights of 1960.

A dramatic change in the role of Quebec's provincial government followed the death of Premier Maurice Duplessis in 1959. The election of Jean Lesage's Liberals in 1960 furthered the transformation that came to be called the "Quiet Revolution". During the 1960s, the provincial government dramatically increased the scope of its activities, replacing the church as the directing force in the evolution of the French-speaking majority in Quebec. Links between francophones in Quebec and elsewhere in Canada eroded as the former came increasingly to define themselves as Québécois. The political allegiance and identity of the Québécois focused on their own province. French-speaking Quebec became increasingly secular and materialist as well as nationalist. This provincial nationalism of Quebec's francophone majority revealed the inadequacies of the federal government's representation of French Canada and the insensitivity of the national community to the needs of French Canadians inside and outside Quebec.

One element of the federal government's response to Quebec's discontent was the creation, in 1963, of the Royal Commission on Bilingualism and Biculturalism. In response to its *Report*, which began to appear in 1967, the federal government, in 1969, enacted the Official Languages Act. Prime

Minister Trudeau's government pursued a vision of a Canada of two linguistic communities, in which French-speaking Quebecers would see both the federal and Quebec governments as their own, and all of Canada as their country. The implementation of this vision required state support to ensure the survival of official-language minorities, francophone outside Quebec and anglophone within. With the redefinition of Canada as officially bilingual, significant increases in the use of the French language developed in the federal bureaucracy. Many Canadians of non-French background saw these transformations as threatening. The federal government responded with the policy of multiculturalism, which recognized Canadians of all ethnic origins as contributors to and participants in a Canada that was to be multicultural as well as bilingual.[3]

In this period, Canadians could not assume the continued presence of Quebec in a united Canada. The people of Quebec engaged in a passionate debate over whether to sunder political links with other Canadians and the national government; the Parti québécois proposed a relationship of "sovereignty-association", an economic association of Quebec and Canada. The basic issue was whether Quebec could be accommodated within a framework of "renewed" federalism.

The Quebec referendum of 1980 resolved the issue of separation. It was won by those opposed to independence, including a small majority of French-speaking voters. The language provisions of the Canadian Charter of Rights and Freedoms followed, along with patriation and an amendment process, as part of the Constitution Act, 1982. The language provisions of the Act obliged the provinces to provide education in their own language for official-language minorities in specified circumstances. These constitutional provisions, an objective of the federal government from the late 1960s, required provincial governments to provide services they were assumed to be unwilling to provide as a matter of choice. In the interest of the evolving definition of the national community the Constitution Act, 1982 thereby foreclosed certain provincial diversities in language policies, based on the division of powers and on different views of the nature of provincial communities.

The obligation to provide education in the languages of official-language minorities results from a prolonged evolution of relations between the two orders of government and the national and provincial communities. It is essential to comprehend that evolution in order to become fully aware of our national identity.

While the federal government was refashioning the image of Canada at the national level to provide for linguistic dualism and multiculturalism, provincial governments were becoming more powerful actors in Canadian federalism. In the constitutional discussions undertaken after the victory of the Parti québécois in November 1976, a number of provincial premiers stressed their view that provincial communities shared parity with the national community. Some even spoke of the priority of provincial communities.

Initially, the four founding provinces of the Canadian federal system consisted of historic, territorially grouped, diverse communities. The

allocation of powers to provincial governments was an appropriate response to these sociological facts. Assigning the more significant responsibilities to the new national government was not a response to a pre-existing national community; rather, this act represented a practical response to a set of nation-building tasks best undertaken in common by that new government. The national community was to emerge as the process of nation building proceeded.

The post-confederation growth of the state at both levels has profoundly affected the evolution of the national and provincial communities. At a time when the public sphere had few functions and the private sphere was comparatively large, the federal/provincial division of powers was irrelevant for most social and economic activity. In federal systems, expansion of the state's role does not merely displace the private by the public sphere. Rather, there occurs a more complex parcelling out of formerly private interests to a public sphere divided between two orders of government. Thus expansion of the state in Canada has meant that the division of powers now affects society and the economy much more deeply than it did in earlier years. As the private sphere contracted in proportion to the more extensive use of national and provincial jurisdictional capacities, the practical significance of provincial and national communities correspondingly increased.

Canadians belong to national and provincial communities whose significance in their lives increases with every increase in the activity of government. In these conditions, citizens can no more divide their national and provincial identities and concept of community than they can expect a classical division of powers to create watertight compartments for the two orders of governments.

The national community that federalism fosters and sustains limits the potential distinctiveness of the provincial societies that are also fostered and sustained by federalism. Membership in, and identification with, the national community are, in part, products of our common life and history as Canadians. In addition, modern conditions tend to erode differences among the provinces. But identification with the national community also results from the efforts of federal leaders, who have often tried to protect and nourish an expanding sense of "Canadianism" against what they have viewed as provincial threats to the integrity of a common citizenship.

In the last decade, in particular, the federal government has attempted to deter the process of "provincialization" of the Canadian community, a process that results from the more prominent provincial government role of recent years. With the emergence of a more active provincial state, inducements developed for the federal government to set common national standards. The federal government encourages provincial compliance in areas of provincial jurisdiction where national standards and relatively uniform performance seem appropriate for the citizens of a common country.

Federalism does not imply that provincial jurisdiction, provincial governments and provincial communities are immune from the imperatives of Canadian citizenship. The national government, representing all Canadians, has a clear responsibility, which is not confined to the areas over which it has explicit constitutional authority, to play a leading role within the federal

system on behalf of the Canadian community. Commissioners do not intend these remarks to provide the national government with a rationale to undermine the obligation of the provincial governments to respond to their own communities. We do not sanction unconstitutional means to gain national ends. Nor do we intend these remarks as criticism of provincial governments, which cannot, of course, undertake national leadership. We simply note that to deny the contribution of federal leadership and initiative is to deny the history of the last 50 years.

During the last half-century, federal-provincial fiscal agreements have produced relatively co-ordinated tax and transfer systems. The welfare state has reduced interprovincial differences in the availability of social benefits. The Canadian Charter of Rights and Freedoms, particularly through the provisions for minority-language/education rights, has helped to set Canada-wide standards of performance. Provincial support or acceptance was critical to the attainment of each of these developments, but without the catalytic efforts of the national government, our tax system, our welfare program, and our rights would be much less integrated than they are.

Our national government has sought to preserve and foster national objectives and common treatment for Canadian citizens, not only within its own jurisdiction, but also in matters within provincial jurisdiction. Commissioners believe that it will continue to do so. Provincial governments will continue to provide different packages of services outside the areas in which those standards operate, and will apply them in different ways. As Canadians question the appropriateness of national standards already in place, relaxation will occasionally occur. Bilateral agreements between the federal government and particular provinces, most notably Quebec, will, as in the past, facilitate differences of treatment. Our basic point, however, remains. The provinces of Canada are not independent states. They operate within a constitutional order the integrity of which depends on recognition that governments are responsible to citizens whose preferences and expectations derive from membership in both national and provincial communities. The provincial diversities of policy that federalism encourages are subject to the constraints of membership in a national community, and the national community is not indifferent to the policy preferences of provincial communities.

In addition to reconciling the multiple social cleavages to which the modern world gives rise – a task equally applicable to the government of a unitary state – the national government of our federal system must also represent and respond to the provincial dimensions of our collective existence. Just as provincial governments and communities cannot ignore national citizenship and the national community, so the national government cannot be oblivious to the provincial dimension of our existence. The psyche of citizens of a federal country is not compartmentalized in terms of the division of powers. The average citizen is simultaneously and comfortably both a Canadian and, say, a British Columbian or a Nova Scotian. Many Canadians therefore find very unsettling overt federal-provincial conflict, particularly that based on primarily governmental concerns. They are disturbed that the co-existence of national and provincial communities, to which they are generally accustomed,

is often not reflected by the interaction of the governments which represent them in the intergovernmental arena.

The subtle interdependence between the federal system and the national and provincial communities which that system reflects and moulds has an additional important dimension that must be understood if we Canadians are to govern ourselves effectively. The individuals who make up the national community differ by sex, ethnic origin, age, economic status and province of residence. Commissioners have already noted the historic French-English dualism of the country and the move to recognize Canada's multicultural character. Our nation's developing multi-racial composition is now on the national agenda. These various cleavages also have provincial manifestations, and Canadians must bridge and reconcile these gaps within provincial communities, as well as within the national community. We have made remarkable progress: 40 years ago, an observer could have mistaken the national government – and by inference the society it represents – as the government of a British, white and male community. The federal government's representation of the real composition of the Canadian people has broadened, but much remains to be done.

Canada, like other internally diverse societies, must try to accommodate those diversities and bind them together in common enterprises. Contemporary states seek to foster an inclusive citizenship and a comprehensive sense of nationhood. While the state must provide leadership, consent is the basis of its legitimacy. As the state makes use of more representative structures and policies, it must become more finely tuned to the complexities of a heterogeneous society.

Commissioners have surveyed the evolution of Canada's national and provincial communities, the emergence of diversity, and the roles of both levels of government in the federation. This survey confirms the importance of making appropriate institutional arrangements for the national government. In a diverse national community, the political process and institutional arrangements, especially their representative elements, should encourage the national government to take broad views.

To complete Commissioners' picture of the Canadian community, we must approach the subject from the vantage point of a new institutional development. Canadians now have a Charter of Rights and Freedoms. For more than a century of government in the parliamentary tradition, we put our trust in political authority and the federalist dimensions of the Constitution. We saw little need to define various categories of rights as beyond the reach of Cabinets and legislatures, and little necessity for such rights to be protected by the courts. We regarded that conscious choice of parliamentary supremacy by our predecessors as a symbol of our political distinctiveness from the United States. The decision to adopt a Charter constitutes a transformation of that tradition.

Antecedants of the Charter are significant. Critics often underestimate the historical import of the Bill of Rights of 1960. Its provisions did not apply to the provinces. The bill itself was a statute of Parliament and not constitutionally entrenched. It contained a clause that allowed Parliament to by-pass its

provisions by simple declaration. Moreover, the Supreme Court of Canada did not use it as vigorously as some Canadians had hoped to defend citizens' rights. Nevertheless, the Bill of Rights represented a significant advance. The Canadian Charter of Rights and Freedoms is a logical next step in the process that the Bill of Rights began.

In the 1960s and 1970s, the national government sought to provide a compelling official definition of Canada responsive to our ethnic pluralism and linguistic dualism. John Diefenbaker was concerned with our ethnic pluralism, and he hoped that the 1960 Bill of Rights would help to include those outside the circle of founding peoples. His successors were anxious to refashion the national government and national community to express our French-English duality. Although the Official Languages Act of 1969 accomplished much, only provincial action, particularly in official-language education, could provide opportunities for French Canadians outside Quebec. The language provisions of the Constitution Act, 1982 were the product of lengthy and bitter constitutional struggles following Quebec's 1980 referendum. They give judicially enforceable positive rights to official-language minorities in education.

The Charter also recognizes the rights of individual Canadians who, as citizens, are a fundamental element in the constitutional order. It recognizes, too, the community dimension of our diversity: in particular aboriginal rights, language rights and multiculturalism.

Over time, a people possessed of a charter will come to view their rights differently from a people without a charter. For a parliamentary people, tradition and practice are the basis of rights; it is not easy to catalogue these rights, and citizens may not be particularly aware of them. For such a people, the protection of rights occurs in the interstices of judicial and political processes; citizens' rights are less likely to be central to its self-definition.

A charter creates a different set of circumstances. It identifies rights that people hold in common. Unless the rights are a dead letter, they become one of the standard ingredients of political rhetoric. In Canada, over time – and adaptation to the Charter will take time – the focus on rights will contribute to a clearer understanding of the meaning of political community and of the citizen's place within it. The Charter, and federal and provincial codes of human rights, with which we have had longer experience, reflect the involvement of the state in relations among citizens and groups as well as between citizens and their governments. The courts, unless they ignore their obligations under the Charter, will have to spell out a clearer philosophy of citizen-state relations and community. In so doing, they will draw on legal commentaries, legal precedents – Canadian and foreign – the academic community more generally, and public opinion, to assist in their deliberations. The long-term consequence of the process set in motion by the Charter should be a much more specific comprehension and a much more subtle sense of citizenship and community in Canada.

In the years to come, interpretation and implementation of the Charter's principles, through judicial decision or parliamentary action, will alter our understanding of the institutional framework through which we Canadians

govern ourselves. Already, the Charter is a fundamental addition to the instruments that govern citizen-state relations. It elevates the status of citizens symbolically and practically by carving out a sphere of rights. It imposes obligations on the state with respect to language rights. It authorizes affirmative action by the state to ameliorate the conditions of disadvantaged individuals or groups. Thus the Charter links citizens with the constitutional order much more explicitly than ever in our history.

Canadian government links cabinets and legislatures, federal and provincial governments, politicians and regulatory agencies and Crown corporations, interest groups and the state, and citizens and the state. Citizens are the ultimate source of authority in a representative democracy such as Canada's, and we must all give sustained attention to these complex interdependencies if we are to govern ourselves democratically and efficiently into the twenty-first century.

Canadians cannot implement the reforms Commissioners propose automatically or easily. There is no "clean slate" on which reformers can write as they wish. They must pursue change through the existing network of institutional relationships and power, and the interdependencies between state and society produced by past policies. Reform will emerge from the interaction of compelling analysis and the political process. We Canadians must involve ourselves and harness the skills and dedication of politicians and bureaucrats to achieve the ends we hope to accomplish.

Notes

1. See Robert Boardman, "The Foreign Service and the Organization of the Foreign Community: Views from Canada and Abroad", in *Selected Problems in Formulating Foreign Economic Policy*, vol. 30, prepared for the Royal Commission on the Economic Union and Development Prospects for Canada (Toronto: University of Toronto Press, 1985).
2. See Gerald Wright, "Bureaucratic Politics and Canada's Foreign Economic Policy", in *Selected Problems in Formulating Foreign Economic Policy*, vol. 30, prepared for the Royal Commission on the Economic Union and Development Prospects for Canada (Toronto: University of Toronto Press, 1985).
3. See Raymond Breton, "Multiculturalism and Canadian Nation-Building", in *The Politics of Gender, Ethnicity and Language in Canada*, vol. 34, prepared for the Royal Commission on the Economic Union and Development Prospects for Canada (Toronto: Univerity of Toronto Press, 1985).

CHAPTER 21

The Institutions of National Government

CHAPTER 21

The Institutions of National Government

National Institutional Reform: Introduction

This Report has previously described the uncertainty of institutional transition in the post-Second World War period: it was a feature that reflected the absence of a clear and consistent sense of direction. There was no broadly based consensus as to the nature of the new patterns of institutional arrangements that were to emerge. Today, demands both for greater co-ordination of public policies and for more decentralization exist simultaneously. Similarly, Canadians seek a number of other paradoxical developments: decisive leadership together with increased public participation and consultation; regional representation alongside national integration; reduced party discipline in the legislature at the same time that proposals are being made for increased executive responsibility. And other examples are not far to seek. In some important aspects, of course, these demands do not exclude one another; rather, the test of effective institutional arrangements is the balance of their political values.

We Commissioners, having regard to our mandate to respect the spirit of the Constitution of Canada, focus our consideration of the national institutions of government on the performance of the parliamentary system in relation to the constitutional norms of representation and responsibility. Thus we give particular consideration to the structures and processes of Parliament: the House of Commons and the Senate; legislative/executive relations; the structures and processes of the Cabinet and the public service, including Crown corporations and regulatory agencies; the place of political parties within the system of parliamentary government. We are concerned, too, with state/citizen relations, including the roles of organized interest groups.

This Commission's public hearings and debates revealed considerable public concern about the present state of Canada's national institutions.

Three major areas for reform are identifiable: responsible government and public accountability; representative government and interest groups; national government and regional interests. These areas we now address.

Responsible Government and Public Accountability

Responsible government is the fundamental basis of democracy within a parliamentary system. In Canada, this system has two essential requirements: first, that Cabinet be effectively in control of the federal government in all its organizational forms, and secondly, that Cabinet be accountable to Parliament for all executive actions, including the management of the administrative state. Logically, the latter requirement depends on the former. A number of factors associated with the growth of government and the operation of modern political parties make it increasingly difficult to meet these two requirements of responsible government, on which our democracy depends.

The requirement that Cabinet be accountable to, and thus maintain the confidence of, Parliament has been interpreted by Canadians to mean that the former body must have the confidence of a legislative majority in the House of Commons. To secure this support, our parties have functioned in a highly disciplined manner: adherence to party policies and positions has permitted little independence for members of the House of Commons. There are those who support the practice of party discipline on the grounds that it serves to promote party unity and thus to establish clear alternatives between our governing and opposition parties; nevertheless, the practice has come under increasing criticism in recent years. This criticism is not new; since the emergence of party government, there have been concerns about the effects of party discipline, as well as occasional efforts to curb and even eliminate, the practice. Such concerns were especially widespread in the various agrarian movements and parties on the Prairies before the Second World War. The supporters of these movements perceived party discipline as a device to subordinate their regional economic interests to central-Canadian majorities in the privacy of caucus.

Responsible government which includes a cabinet accountable to the legislature can be defined narrowly or broadly. From a narrow, technical perspective, it simply means that a Cabinet which loses the confidence of the House of Commons either must resign and be replaced by an alternative Cabinet which secures the confidence of a House of Commons majority or must go to the people. A broader perspective goes beyond this view of responsibility and raises questions about the quality of the accountability relationship. From this vantage point, responsible government is seen as healthy to the extent that Members of Parliament bring to their assessment of the executive's performance an adequate knowledge of the diversity of interests extant in our national politics and an effective capacity to represent that diversity. This in turn, requires some relaxation of party discipline in selected areas so that the representative role of MPs can have public expression. It also requires that Parliament serve as a central forum for the interaction of interest groups and governments. If the former, however, view

Parliament as an irrelevant arena and deploy their resources in private settings with ministers or public servants, much of the substance of responsible accountable government is eroded.

Commissioners prefer a broad construction of the meaning of responsible government. This broader construction requires that the legislature have a greater capacity to represent openly the multiplicity of interests which exist in an advanced industrial society such as Canada. It also requires the legislature to serve as an arena in which organized interests bring their expertise to policy discussions and, in turn, are challenged to represent their particular interests in the context of the competing interests of others and the larger interests of the nation.

From Commissioners' perspective, there have been, in recent years, both negative and positive developments in the representative capacity of our government. The increased significance of relations between governments in which participants are confined almost exclusively to ministers and public servants, weakens the relative status of legislatures in Canadian federalism. The proliferation of interest groups, more and more of which have bypassed both political parties and legislatures, further contributes to that relative weakening. But there are positive signs, as well. At times, particularly fairly lately, parliamentary committees and task forces have provided opportunities for private members to function relatively independently of party discipline and to investigate subjects of national importance, set out policy options, and recommend policy responses to issues of public concern. These instances provide a model for those calling for parliamentary reform. Reformers also hope that party discipline, more generally, could be restricted in its application to major issues of partisan dispute, including, of course, the major policies of the government. This restriction, they believe, would provide greater scope for independent action by individual MPs and their parliamentary committees and task forces, and would enhance the representative capacity of parliamentarians.

Commissioners recognize that Cabinet leadership is an essential component of responsible parliamentary government and, consequently, we accept the need for party discipline. We believe, nonetheless, that there are important roles to be performed by Parliament in holding the government accountable and in representing the diversity of interests in national politics that exists in Canada. Moreover, in our view, Parliament is not only a forum in which Cabinet is held accountable, but also a forum for national debate. Conflicting demands, which the policy process is intended to accommodate and reconcile, should be publicly debated in Parliament. Parliament must be a national body for deliberation, for open and public consultation, and for scrutiny of executive action.

The second requirement of responsible government is effective Cabinet control of the bureaucracy. The development of an "administrative state" poses a direct challenge to our concept of a responsible executive. In some instances, departmental bureaucracies have had too much influence in determining public policy and too much discretion in its implementation. Moreover, the institutional response to this situation has been to create another level of bureaucracy, in the form of "central agencies", which, when

unchecked, can have excessive influence in the management of Cabinet decision making. Consequently, political direction and responsibility for the management of government may be further reduced. If the Cabinet does not control the administrative state, it can be held accountable neither by Parliament between elections nor by the public at elections.

Concern about the perceived power of the bureaucracy is by no means unique to Canada. The Canadian reaction, however, is compounded by three distinct circumstances. First, our national government has been characterized by an administrative system that is highly centralized in its decision making, despite the fact that a large number of its employees operate outside the national capital region. For this reason, the reaction against it is reinforced by the regional alienation which is, to some degree, unavoidable in a far-flung federal state. Secondly, many Canadians perceive our national administrative system to be the creation of the dominant governing party of recent decades. For this reason, the reaction against it is buttressed by the criticisms of those who have considered it to be less than neutral in its policy orientation. This reaction occurs despite the fact that merit-based processes govern most of the senior appointments in the public service. The same criticism is also directed at Crown corporations and regulatory agencies, the governing boards of which are appointed by Cabinet, and which comprise a significant part of our administrative state. Thirdly, the proliferation of Crown corporations and regulatory agencies has produced a growing component of the public sector, whose factual or legal independence seems to symbolize public authority which is beyond the effective control of Parliament and the executive. The irony here, of course, is that while opposition parties have been critical of the dominance of partisanship in effecting appointments to such boards, even members of the governing party – until recently the Liberal Party – have been critical of the independence of those agencies which are governed by its appointees. Whether this concern will be shared by the present Progressive Conservative government, with respect to those whom it appoints to such boards remains to be seen.

There are those who argue that as a consequence of the complexity of public administration in the modern state, we Canadians must reduce our expectations with respect to this dimension of responsible government. Commissioners believe, however, that reforms can be introduced to ensure that the administrative state is subject to tighter Cabinet direction and control. We remind Canadians that the basic concern, to preserve and strengthen the practices of responsible government, is not an abstract preoccupation with principles devoid of meaning for citizens. Rather, responsible government is the means through which Canadians practise democracy and maintain respect for fundamental values in our society. Responsible government therefore deserves our attention and must be constantly nurtured if it is to thrive.

Parliament and Public Accountability

As we have noted, the accountability function of Parliament has led to the emergence of disciplined parties and, in turn, has been compromised by them,

at least to some extent. Our institutional design of responsible government has assumed that parties would constitute the mechanism whereby this accountability would be secured. At the same time, however, the actual operation of parliamentary government as party government has led to the increasing cohesiveness of legislative parties and the virtual elimination of independent MPs. Central to these developments has been the enhancement of party discipline, a feature of party government within the parliamentary system which was, and still is, often misunderstood as consisting in nothing more than the exercise of power by legislative party leaders over their legislative colleagues. Although it is usually recognized that this exercise of power involves both positive incentives and negative sanctions, the focus on "power" more often than not misses what has probably been the essential feature of party discipline. That discipline has been, first and foremost, a function of organized parties in pursuit and maintenance of power; it is a discipline which has been accepted by leaders and followers alike as a prerequisite to success in party competition in a parliamentary system. The positive incentives and negative sanctions which are available to party leaders, especially but not exclusively to the leaders of the party in power, have merely served to supplement the general acceptance of the need for party discipline. They rarely have been effective when this general acceptance was lacking. When a common partisanship was not sufficient to maintain unity within a legislative party, discord and thus independence have soon appeared.

In recent years, a number of features of Canadian politics and parties, separate from the need for the governing party to maintain the confidence of the House of Commons, have contributed to the strengthening of party discipline. It is important to understand these developments, as we wish to suggest means of improving accountability and the representation of diverse interests while accepting the basic role of party discipline in our parliamentary system.

The pre-eminent position assumed more and more by party leaders, partly reflecting the attention given to leadership by the mass media, has enhanced party discipline. The selection of party leaders through extensive campaigns and nationally televised conventions contributes to the prominence of the leader. Furthermore, the mass media treat national elections as contests between party leaders, whether or not the parties have campaigned on leadership. Wider separation of the federal and provincial wings of the two leading parties has limited the number of elected members with independent regional power bases. Thus, in fact, Prime Ministers, whose prestige is enhanced by media exposure, have had greater opportunity to exercise discretion in their leadership roles, even though the formal powers of the office are essentially as they were in the original constitutional design. An additional factor is the tremendous growth of the state in terms of organizational scope and structure which has resulted in a situation where only Prime Ministers are well briefed on all aspects of public policy. Their access to information affords them an advantage not possessed by their Cabinet or caucus colleagues.

Prime Ministers – indeed, any popular party leaders – thus develop a national constituency and can use this base to strengthen their position in the

party. Party leadership, therefore, looms large in Canadian politics. The increased autonomy of national leaders not only makes our parties more oligarchic and personal, but also increases the need for party discipline. Because of the discretionary authority derived from their pre-eminence, party leaders, especially Prime Ministers, need not accommodate all the factions within their caucuses, as they play to a national constituency which is the ultimate basis of their leadership. Since the need for party unity is in no way reduced as a consequence – indeed it is increased, given the need to project a strong leadership image as an element in electoral success – party discipline is essential.

The second factor contributing to stronger party discipline has been the rapid growth of the national state and its consequences for the operation of parliamentary government. The broader scope of government intervention has increased the work-load of Parliament, necessitated longer sessions, and led to the imposition of time constraints on parliamentary debate. As a result, party discipline has received greater emphasis.

A comprehensive system of legislative committees has evolved in the House of Commons over the last two decades. Through committee work, Members of Parliament are now more deeply involved than formerly in debate and in scrutiny of legislation and expenditures. While the new system has enabled the government to accomplish more, it has been accompanied by an extension of party discipline from the floor of the House of Commons to the legislative committee room. An arrangement that many parliamentarians hoped would constitute a break from the strictures of such discipline has failed to materialize. The reason is that legislative standing committees are simply an extension of the House, and the principles of party government and partisanship apply there as well.

The pervasive electronic mass media, particularly television, have encouraged party discipline and perhaps have increased the need for its exercise. They have become the principal vehicle by which government and parties communicate with the public and, in particular, with the electorate. They have promoted visible partisanship and competition among the parties, for they demand drama, conflict and controversy. With media in search of news and politicians in search of exposure, party competition has occurred on a regular, even daily, basis: the bearpit of Question Period reveals it all.

The media have often criticized party discipline, primarily because it has restricted their access to controversies within parties, particularly within the governing party of the day. However, precisely because the electronic media pursue all breaches in party discipline instantaneously and nationally, parties have had every incentive to pay strict attention to discipline.

The factors outlined above have enhanced and reinforced the need for party discipline in the conduct of parliamentary government. Legislative parties have used party caucuses to meet this need, and as a result, over the past two decades, the caucuses have become important influences on party policy. Paradoxically, relaxing the strictures of party discipline in private settings strengthens that discipline in public. The caucus has served as a forum for considering regional and other interests, not all of which can always be fully accommodated within the parameters of party policy. Discussion within

caucus is more frank about the relative winners and losers on a particular policy issue than the party's public treatment of the same questions. The caucus has thus been more than simply a safety valve for the expression of discontent with party policy. It also has provided the mechanism that enables its members to ensure that party policies are developed in full recognition of their political implications, both in the strategic sense and in accord with the fullest expression of political representation within the constraints of party government. This Commission's research indicates that caucus has become more active and influential in recent decades; party MPs argue vigorously in the privacy of caucus for regional and other interests in matters of policy, though they may have to suppress their personal views in public in the interest of party discipline.[1]

Given all these features of modern party government, the capacity of Parliament to hold the Cabinet to account requires that parliamentary structures and processes be organized in ways that enable MPs to perform their representative responsibilities, while recognizing the essential demands of party government. The ability of Parliament to hold the Cabinet accountable and to serve as a national forum for public debate and representation of concerns depends on individual MPs. Members of Parliament must have adequate opportunities to deliberate on issues of national significance, to consult special interest groups and discuss policy options with them openly, and to scrutinize executive and bureaucratic actions.

The need for party discipline has restricted the opportunities for MPs to participate independently and publicly in policy deliberations. In addition, organized special interest groups have not only challenged Members in their roles as representatives of the body politic but have often bypassed them completely.

Despite a comprehensive committee system and increased support in terms of personnel, office facilities and research services, restriction on the involvement of MPs in policy-making deliberations has occurred. Members have limited scope for policy initiatives outside the strictures of party discipline largely because the legislative committee system has evolved as a mirror image of the Commons itself. Only rarely have committees been able to function in a non-partisan manner. The exceptions, however, show how MPs, in committee, could help to provide Parliament and the government with policy analysis and guidance in addition to that given by administrative officials or extra-parliamentary sources.[2]

To enable Members of Parliament to perform a greater public role, investigative committees could be established to study emerging matters of public interest before party positions have been determined. In committees, MPs could investigate, deliberate and make recommendations free of party considerations. Legislative committees should be distinguished from the investigative committees we Commissioners propose to encourage. This distinction is required because legislative committees must be subject to party discipline as they are examining and debating the merits of government legislation and spending intentions. Experience to date with parliamentary investigative committees and task forces does not suggest that partisan

considerations will be totally absent. Nevertheless, it does indicate that if parties are willing to use parliamentary committees for the purpose of investigating matters which have not yet become subjects of partisan division, they can achieve serious and productive results.

Another development has become an important limiting factor in enabling MPs to maintain accountability: an increasing number of interest groups now claim to be the legitimate representatives of large parts of the political community. Their representations have tended to focus on the Cabinet and the bureaucracy, however, and not on Parliament, thus indirectly weakening Parliament's control of the executive. Nevertheless, in recent years, the regular parliamentary proceedings and special public hearings of parliamentary committees have induced many of these groups to participate more fully in public debate. For many interest groups, parliamentary committees impose unwelcome demands on scarce resources of time, money or personnel by requiring them to participate in activities which are not always considered influential in determining government policy. Moreover, even though committee hearings are conducted in public, they rarely result in the media exposure such groups often seek for the purpose of communicating their views to a broader audience. Only rarely, in instances where committee enquiries are held on future policy directions and options, for example, are the demands that parliamentary participation makes on interest groups considered to be worth the effort that would be required to meet them.

If elected representatives are to be in a position to hold government accountable on the basis of the public interest and the expectations of citizens, then Parliament should be the principal public forum within which interest groups are challenged to define their special interests and to explain their particular policy preferences in light of broader interests in national policy development. To the extent that partisanship dominates committee proceedings and hearings, however, MPs, and therefore Parliament as an institution, will be constrained in their efforts to resolve the conflicting demands of special interest groups or to pursue the attempt to reconcile their concerns with the general public interest. To further this process of reconciliation, rather than to reduce or eliminate the activities or interest groups, is Parliament's role.

To reassert the primacy of Parliament as Canada's principal forum for public debate, while acknowledging that partisan considerations will not be entirely eliminated from parliamentary discussion of issues which affect competing special interests, requires structures and procedures whereby major interest groups will be involved in public examination and discussion of their demands. Such proceedings should not be confined to standing committees structured along highly differentiated policy lines. Instead, this process of discussion and examination should occur not only within the investigative committees we propose, but also within a small number of committees which focus on several comprehensive policy matters that do not ordinarily come under scrutiny by committees: the budget, regulatory policy, Crown corporations, and federal-provincial or intergovernmental relations, for example. We would expect the media to be more likely to cover the proceedings of these committees, further increasing the potential for such

parliamentary activity to broaden general understanding of the issues and to increase public awareness of particular concerns.

These committees would certainly not be uninfluenced by party considerations, since they would concern themselves with subjects relating to important political issues on which the parties will have general positions if not detailed policies. Thus in questioning representatives of major interest groups, they would not be free of partisan perspectives. However, critical examination of witnesses is not foreign to our parliamentary process and may appropriately be used with interest groups which seek, through political activities, to influence public policies.

Such public processes offer several benefits. Interest groups will become more aware of the constraints within which public policies are developed. Parliamentarians will become better-informed decision makers as a result of more regular access to the special expertise which interest groups possess. More thorough exposure of the complexities of policy formation will help to advance the education and understanding of the public at large. With an enhanced knowledge base, legislatures will enjoy an increased capacity to advise, challenge and control Cabinets.

Even if interest groups achieve a more visible and open relationship which will help them to bring their views forward, consideration should be given to the use of advanced technology to ensure that Members of Parliament always have the opportunity to be familiar with their constituents' concerns and with broad patterns of public opinion. To date, party and special interest-group politics have created a much wider distance between government and citizens than was originally intended. Our system of representative, party government does not always provide the party in power with sufficient information about the views and preferences of citizens on the broad range of issues of the day. New means of communication between elected representatives and members of the public, made possible by modern technology, could make Parliament a more effective entity in its relations with the bureaucracy and the executive, and thereby help to improve the responsiveness and accountability of government.

Commissioners believe that if Parliament is to have the authority to hold the Cabinet and individual ministers accountable for their administration of public affairs, there must be a reassertion of the primacy of elected representatives over various administrative bodies. In principle, these bodies are meant to assist Parliament in maintaining accountability, and administrative institutions that have been established to help Parliament to hold Cabinet responsible for its exercise of authority should be servants and not masters of Parliament. A number of agencies reporting to Parliament, including the Public Service Commission, the Office of the Commissioner of Official Languages, the Privacy and Information Commissioners, and the Office of the Auditor General, investigate, appraise and audit implementation of legislation, and program management. We Commissioners consider that our elected representatives in Parliament have not always given sufficient direction to, and retain inadequate control of, these agencies. Thus, an important order of bureaucracy, much of which has developed in recent decades, operates independently of the executive, which it is meant to

scrutinize, and of the legislative branch, which it is meant to serve in performing this function of executive scrutiny.

To ensure that accountability is, and is seen to be, an integral function of parliamentary government, our elected representatives must more clearly define the criteria, the procedures, and the basic strategies that these agencies use in fulfilling their responsibilities. To put MPs in a position where they can establish the necessary guidelines will require sustained forums in Parliament. Accordingly, Commissioners suggest that a new Parliamentary Committee on the Public Service should consolidate review of the work of the Public Service Commission, the Office of the Commissioner of Official Languages, and the Privacy and Information Commissioners. The new committee would study reports of these agencies about the performance of the public service in meeting various criteria, which politicians themselves would define and rank in importance. This same committee would review the spending estimates and approve the budgets for these parliamentary agencies. The Public Accounts Committee should provide guidance to the Office of the Auditor General and review its estimates, in order to promote the effective operation of this office.

A further consideration if Parliament is to be able to maintain Cabinet accountability for executive actions is associated with the state's expanded international responsibilities. The growing complexity and scope of international treaties and agreements, and the influence of international forces on domestic issues have conferred more influence on the political executive than it has ever had before. The executive exercises this influence, through foreign policy and foreign affairs initiatives, on the overall range of political decision making in Canada. A process of internationalization of domestic policy making is under way. It is vital that Parliament's role in reviewing foreign policy initiatives and international agreements be strengthened.

The act of ratification represents formal acknowledgement by a state of its consent to be bound by treaty or international agreement. Present arrangements do not require parliamentary involvement, although as a matter of practice, the government of the day often seeks parliamentary approval prior to ratifying an agreement. In light of the accelerating challenge to democratic controls presented by the increasing international responsibilities of the state, Commissioners believe that it is desirable to provide secure foundations for parliamentary ratification of international treaties and for other measures to strengthen parliamentary scrutiny of executive action in the international domain. The international arena is increasingly important to Cabinets and senior public servants. This expansion of the scope of executive action must be matched by Parliaments whose vision has become equally broad. This development, in turn, will help to educate Canadians in the international realities which will increasingly influence our future.

Responsible Government and the Administrative State

Canada's system of responsible parliamentary government requires that ministers, collectively and individually, exercise authority in the administration of public affairs. This necessity, in turn, requires that ministers control

the vast administrative apparatus that is the Government of Canada. Past concern that Cabinet has had less than the desired degree of control over the bureaucracy has already resulted in changes. Cabinet structures and processes have been altered and formalized, and various support services have been added in recent years, in response to the challenge of the modern administrative state. A brief review of reforms to the executive arm of government will promote consideration of further measures intended to assist the Prime Minister and Cabinet to control the expanded and complex administrative arm.

A chief executive officer (CEO) at the apex of any complex organization is essential if there is to be overall executive control and direction of the organization's activities. Government, like other organizations, can be effective only if it embodies principles of integration and coherence; to promote these, the Prime Minister has assumed characteristics of the CEO function. The expansion of state activity has made public policies and programs increasingly interdependent. Planning and co-ordination thus assume more importance in the context of executive responsibilities. By constitutional convention, the Prime Minister has the ultimate authority and responsibility for planning and co-ordination at the executive level. Recent Prime Ministers have responded to this challenge in three ways: by reinforcing their authority through a more hierarchical Cabinet structure; by reducing their span of control in working primarily through an inner Cabinet; and by expanding their staff support to assist them in discharging their responsibilities as chief executive officer.

There has also been a steady evolution of Cabinet structures. This process was put in motion to deal both with the complexities of policy making in the modern state and with the problem of achieving political control over the state's large administrative bureaucracies. The use of *ad hoc* Cabinet committees can be traced back to the years before the Second World War, and the committee structure was formalized during the mid-1960s. Prime Ministers have always had smaller groups of very close advisers among their senior staff, and this arrangement, too, became increasingly formalized during the 1960s and 1970s as the Priorities and Planning Committee became the real centre of executive power, second only to the Prime Minister. Although, in theory, the full Cabinet may still have the final word over executive action, the full Cabinet has come to accept the decisions of the "inner Cabinet", the Priorities and Planning Committee.

As party leader and the government's Chief Executive Officer, the Prime Minister requires some independence even of the Priorities and Planning Committee. Prime Ministers from the time of Lester Pearson to the present have therefore relied heavily on their advisory staffs in the Prime Minister's Office (PMO) and the Privy Council Office (PCO), devolving considerable influence to a small number of senior officials in these two offices. The PMO and the PCO constitute, in effect, the Prime Minister's "departments" for conducting political strategy, on the one hand, and for determining policy priorities and developing administrative co-ordination, on the other.

Besides providing assistance with the Prime Minister's increasingly complex and difficult responsibilities as chief executive officer, an hierarchi-

cal Cabinet structure built on an elaborate support base was to serve other purposes. This structure and the introduction of a formal committee system congruent with policy fields were intended to ensure that all ministers would be better informed about policy options and better able to co-ordinate initiatives in related policy fields and agencies. These organizational changes were expected to help Cabinet members to retain control of the interdependent policies for which they are collectively responsible.

In some respects the committee system decentralized Cabinet decision making. Within the framework of the priorities and plans established by the "inner Cabinet", Cabinet committees now, in effect, may make decisions on behalf of the full Cabinet. The various committees, including the Priorities and Planning Committee, also introduced checks on some elements of the exercise of power within the executive system; in particular, they strengthened the processes of collective decision making and checked the independence of individual ministers. The committee system has provided an opportunity for the ministers involved to assess their colleagues' proposals more thoroughly than they could do in meetings of the full Cabinet. In large measure, indeed, it was introduced for this very purpose. The rationale was that given the increased interdependence of national policies and programs, individual ministers should not have the sole power to make decisions when a more co-ordinated government response would be more effective.

Formalized Cabinet committees were intended to check the influence on their ministers of departmental officials, as much as to reduce the discretion of individual ministers and thus strengthen the means for the political executive to scrutinize bureaucratic conduct. In Cabinet committees, Cabinet colleagues assess one another's proposals as, indirectly, do colleagues' departmental officials. These assessments can provide ministers with a measure of independence of their own officials and of the "client" groups associated with particular departments. Similarly, the central agencies, such as PMO, PCO, FPRO, Treasury Board, Finance, and, from 1979 to 1984, MSERD, MSSD, were expected to provide the Prime Minister and the Cabinet with administrative support and expertise to counter the institutional autonomy of the departmental bureaucracies and to assist in the process of policy integration. These "super-bureaucrats" can, in theory, check and co-ordinate line departments and agencies in order to permit ministers collectively to assert political control over the administrative state.

The Cabinet's increased formalization, its committee system and the support provided by central agencies have improved the ability of ministers to manage public affairs. These developments, however, have not fully brought under control an increasingly complex and, as some Canadians have described it, unmanageable bureaucracy, nor have they proved to be without their own costs. In Commissioners' view, there is a limit to the degree of support that agencies can give to the processes of Cabinet decision making and co-ordination. Bureaucratic structures and mechanisms are no substitute for effective political direction and control. They do not create the elusive "political will"; they can only reinforce it if it is already in place. We acknowledge that the central agencies constitute a necessary, if not a sufficient, check on the inevitable dispersal and diffusion of power to

bureaucrats in the modern administrative state. They make an important contribution to integrated control over the vast range of government departments, agencies and Crown corporations. Central agencies, however, can serve their purpose effectively only under the close direction of ministers and, particularly, under that of the Prime Minister. In the absence of such ministerial direction, they become another layer of bureaucracy to be controlled. Furthermore, central agencies with overlapping mandates often compete with one another. In short, individual ministries or departments of government must also be organized to ensure that they are shaped by the required degree of internal political direction and control.

The use of junior ministers or ministers of state has sometimes enabled the Cabinet to exercise more effective control over various specific aspects of public policy and administration. However, the appointment of such ministers has been, at best, unsystematic. Commissioners believe there may be merit in adopting and formalizing a more complex ministry system, comprising a smaller number of senior ministers to whom a larger number of junior ministers would report. At a minimum, clarification is needed to reduce the present uncertainty about the relation of junior ministers or ministers of state to the senior ministers with whom they are affiliated and to senior ministers in general. Some observers have expressed concern about the growth of the Cabinet over the past two decades, a growth to which the use of junior ministers has contributed. Given the complexity and scope of the organization comprising the Government of Canada, however, the achievement of genuine political control with the concomitant accomplishment of a reasonably coherent set of government policies requires a relatively large Cabinet with some degree of hierarchical structure, both among committees and within each large portfolio headed by a senior minister.

Such steps as the appointment of junior ministers, taken to increase the control of political representatives over departmental bureaucracies, have had a measure of success. Insufficient progress has been made, however, in securing greater control over Crown corporations and regulatory agencies. These bodies, particularly major regulatory agencies, have assumed political importance in many vital areas of Canada's economic activity. Not only has the scope of regulatory activity broadened considerably since the Second World War, but such areas as broadcasting, telecommunications and transportation, which have been federally regulated for a longer period, have become more important. Successive governments have commissioned studies and prepared legislation to control such agencies. They have not yet, however, found a fully satisfactory resolution. Without adequate executive direction and control, these non-departmental forms of government organization threaten to undermine our principles of responsible government. Canada has erred in the direction of allowing these bodies too much autonomy and discretion, and they have become virtually separate branches of government.

Admittedly, it is difficult to establish appropriate instruments or procedures to direct and control Crown corporations and regulatory agencies. They are not all alike. They are not departments of government, and they serve different purposes that require different management regimes.

Commissioners are concerned, as we noted in Part III of this Report, that there has been a tendency to manage Crown corporations in a strategic vacuum, without a well-formulated rationale for continuing public participation. Thus, more effective management systems and governmental control can only be assessed within the broader framework of competition and regulatory reform. In our view, the call for greater control has been translated too simplistically into a tangle of bureaucratic red tape surrounding Crown corporations, rather than into the development of a more effective strategic management system serving both the government and its holding operations once it has been determined that those operations are key instruments of public policy.

It is essential, especially for commercial Crown corporations, that the zeal for accountability not lead to a "paper war" among bureaucracies, leaving ministers on the sidelines and Parliament still wondering just what it is that these corporations are expected to be doing. Commissioners have not investigated alternative management systems in any great depth. We would encourage the government to experiment with models which may be closer to private sector holding companies.

In particular, we recommend that the executive have appropriate statutory powers to issue policy directives to Crown corporations and regulatory agencies, except where Parliament, for cogent reasons, explicitly prohibits such powers, as it might, for example, in the case of certain cultural bodies. We also endorse the practice of making capital budgets of Crown corporations subject to Cabinet approval. In addition, we suggest that Cabinet continue to seek means to strengthen its review of regulations formulated by regulatory agencies.

This description adopts as its perspective the traditional concept of public servants as the implementors of public policy, but the public service has been the object of policy as well. The one-fifth of working Canadians employed in the administrative state have rights that must be preserved and, perhaps, expanded or clarified.

In the 1960s, the introduction of collective bargaining at federal and provincial levels represented increased recognition of the public servant as citizen and employee. However, collective bargaining rights in the public sector never equalled those of the private sector. For most of the 1960s and early 1970s, there was no apparent conflict between the responsibility of government as manager of the public service and as manager of the economy. From then on, however, the conflict between the two functions increased greatly. Public servants became the object of new economic management policies which, in some instances, were intended to end or reduce their rights. Although extensive debate about public sector wages and strikes began before the mid-1970s, direct wage controls came into effect only with the 1975–77 anti-inflation program and the 1982–83 "Six-and-Five" program. The former imposed controls on the public sector, as well as on major sections of the private sector, and sought to control both wages and prices. It applied at both the federal and provincial levels. The "Six-and-Five" program applied only to federal public servants. The federal government sought, however, to extend its coverage to other sectors through exhortations directed at recipients of federal grants.

These measures should be related to a series of other steps by means of which governments also sought to reduce bargaining rights previously granted. The Treasury Board took more stringent views about the numbers of workers designated as essential during strikes. This action weakened the efficacy of strike action in the public sector, and the courts later upheld the Board's practice. Some provinces resorted more often to "back-to-work" legislation. Bargaining rights were maintained only if they were not exercised too often or too vigorously. Certain provincial retrenchment and restraint programs further eroded the position of public workers.

Commissioners conclude that since, over the last two decades, the bureaucracy has grown at the same rate as the labour force, and since public sector wages are responsive to economic forces, there is no reason to regret the existence of rights to bargain collectively in the public service, subject to the overriding right of the community in matters of public health and safety.

Issues surrounding political rights, as well as collective bargaining rights, of public servants are also being debated, for in some circumstances these, too, are properly related to the scrutiny of bureaucratic conduct that is central to the general principles of responsible government. Commissioners believe that senior government-policy officials in the permanent public service should have no right to engage in partisan political activity. Other public servants, however, should be free to engage in the full range of political expression, except where conflict of interest could arise. The degree of difficulty in distinguishing senior from junior officials for this purpose is no greater than that of devising criteria for selecting persons who may or may not strike, and a similar means could be used to distinguish the two groups.

"Merit" and "patronage" are two different grounds of appointment. Each helps politicians to achieve some measure of control over the bureaucracy, boards, agencies and Crown corporations. It has been suggested, however, that the upper ranks of the federal public service have become too heavily politicized. Although there have been instances where prominent political appointments violated the ideal of a neutral public service, the argument that the senior bureaucracy has become politicized is misplaced when it is used as a general criticism. The system of appointments based on merit and subject to the recommendation of the Clerk of the Privy Council has worked well.

On the other hand, appointments to a large number of boards and agencies have traditionally been made on the basis of political advice provided to the Prime Minister. This category of appointments may be too large, and the public might be better served if more of these appointments were based exclusively on merit. An all-party group designated by the proposed Parliamentary Committee on the Public Service should review the current practice of Governor-in-Council appointments to boards, agencies, foreign posts, top-level departmental positions, and ministers' staffs, in order to identify positions where the advantage of partisan sensitivity is clear. Commissioners believe that this general review process should be continuous, and that appointments where partisanship is of no clear value should be made on the basis of merit. Further, Governor-in-Council appointments of a non-traditional public service nature should be made in a more open manner. In a parliamentary system, the right of the executive to make these appointments is beyond dispute, but the Cabinet could first inform a parliamentary

committee about potential appointments. Open discussion of the criteria used to guide selection would seem particularly useful in filling senior policy advisory positions.

Notes

1. See Paul G. Thomas, "The Role of National Party Caucuses", in *Party Government and Regional Representation in Canada*, vol. 36 (Toronto: University of Toronto Press, 1985).
2. See Peter Dobell, "Some Comments on Parliamentary Reform", in *Institutional Reforms for Representative Government*, vol. 38, prepared for the Royal Commission on the Economic Union and Development Prospects for Canada (Toronto: University of Toronto Press, 1985).

Representative Government and Interest Groups

Representation by population and representation by region shape parliamentary government in Canada. These principles do not, however, determine what is represented or how. Canada's political parties have traditionally competed to represent citizens. Parties, at the national and provincial levels, present citizens with various definitions of the public interest and various means of achieving it. Implicitly, therefore, they signal the ways in which socio-economic interests should be represented. The way in which parties formulate their choices reflects the internal structures of their decision-making processes. Public funds support certain party activities, and laws regulate some, but parties themselves decide their own positions on public policy and choose their own leaders, candidates and officers.

In recent decades, representatives of numerous groups affected by state intervention and public policies have become more directly involved in government decision making. Such groups make vigorous efforts to represent and articulate their views on policy issues, both general and specific. Their involvement in public decision making has implications for party, Parliament and Canadian constitutionalism in general.

Parties, Interest Groups and Political Representation

The dominance of parties has made Canadian politics highly organized. Government by party has disciplined Canadian politics, extensively in Parliament and less so in the various levels of party organization. Our parties are not centralized organizations, but party members share a common collective interest in the pursuit and attainment of governmental power. This collective interest in securing electoral support introduces discipline to party organization. However, several developments have affected the organization and operation of parties and the capacity of the party system to function as the exclusive instrument of political representation in Canada.

First, televised politics has accentuated the personalized character of our parties. Party leaders, particularly the Prime Minister, have become more significant than their colleagues and the party in general because electoral competition, as presented and viewed on television, has focused on leadership. Secondly, public opinion surveys and polls have assisted governments to design policies in response to the preferences of various interests, be they region, class, sex, religion, age or general ideology. Television and the use of polls have significantly undermined two of the most important roles of rank-and-file party members. Television undermines their role in communicating party policies to the voter; polling undermines their role in communicating grass roots opinion to party leaders. Thirdly, well-organized special-interest groups have involved themselves in the processes of political representation. Taken together, these three developments have had important consequences for party government.

Technological change in the form of television and the means of recording public opinion has profoundly affected politics. Established parties have adjusted to it, perhaps because this change does not challenge their place in the institutions of representative government. Indeed, parties have begun to

use the media and polling results to "target" particular sections of the population through selective broadcasting and direct mailing. They have not adapted successfully, however, to the proliferation of organized special-interest groups: such organized advocates of particular interests present a challenge to parties and party government.

Reference to "interest groups" calls to mind widely divergent images. On the one hand, they can appear as essential building blocks of democracy. They provide the opportunity for citizens to articulate their views. They allow like-minded people to combine their resources to ensure a hearing. They provide the regular avenues for participation in general elections. They are also essential for effective policy making.

The other image is that of the "special interest". It suggests narrow, selfish, self-interested concerns at odds with the "public interest", or powerful, wealthy groups which use the "inside track" to gain special privileges for themselves and frustrate the popular will. The term also suggests a cacophonous fragmented chorus of limited, sometimes self-righteous groups which frustrate the building of consensus and paralyse effective decision making. Both images, of course, are partly right and partly wrong. In evaluating fundamental institutional reform, it is necessary to come to terms with the emergence of interest-group politics and with the need for more effective means of consultation between governments and private interests.

Political parties in Canada have, of course, attracted differential electoral support from the broad range of socio-economic and regional interests found in the country. Ideology has been a factor in political success and failure, but leadership and positions on policy and political issues have clearly been more critical, especially for the Liberals and Conservatives. However, except for the relationship of organized labour to the New Democratic Party, organized interest groups and parties have not established formal associations. Interest groups have functioned largely in a non-partisan way, pursuing their aims through contacts with the government, the public service and Parliament. Prolonged periods of one-party dominance have contributed to this pattern. One-party dominance has discouraged particular interests from fostering close attachments to parties consigned to long spells on the opposition benches; links with the party in government are based on its possession of office, rather than on its partisan complexion.

Organized Interests and Political Representation

Organized interests pursue their goals in a wide variety of forums. Many special-interest groups have often forged particularly close relations with the administrative structures of the national government. Increasing state intervention has contributed to the proliferation and, in some instances, to the fragmentation of these organized interests. Indeed, the state has encouraged a number of such interests to organize in order that they may assist in the development and implementation of national policies. Various mechanisms facilitate consultation in relation to this process. Consultative committees,

advisory committees and councils, all comprised of interest-group representatives, have flourished over the past two decades. These forums generally have the effect of linking groups to the administrative branch, and not directly to individual ministers or the Cabinet.

Some interest groups advance their positions in a more public manner, through the mass media, although they may also approach individual Members of Parliament or the Cabinet. Representatives of interest groups often compete with opposition-party spokespersons in criticizing government actions. More and more interest groups seek closer relations with the Cabinet itself. In part, those developments may be explained by the frustration which many groups have experienced in their dealings with administrative agencies.

Public visibility and private access are thus alternative routes to greater influence on policy making. Most groups pursue both "public" and "private" strategies: the full-page advertisement in the daily paper, the press conference, the delegation to the minister, the private phone call between lobbyist and official are all employed. In general, however, groups with wide social acceptance which pursue limited, material goals, and which have a permanent bureaucratic structure of their own prefer the "quiet diplomacy" of well-tended private networks and personal contacts. "Outsider" groups with less legitimacy, more controversial positions, and goals which are more symbolic or ideological tend to pursue the more public strategies, from marches to petitions. Some groups, of course, make a successful transition from "outsider" to "insider". Ministries and other agencies are created to respond to their interests; they become more integrated into the administrative processes of government.

Governments, however, are becoming less able to satisfy the many conflicting demands made on them by special interests. The increasing complexity of society is reflected in an increasing fragmentation of interests which become more and more difficult for "normal" political processes to accommodate. Efforts to restrain government expenditures have increased the problem: the politics of "zero sum" are inherently more conflictual than the politics of growth. At the same time, there are demands for comprehensive policies to encompass broader interests and concerns. These demands take the form of calls for greater stability in financial and economic policies; for reduction of the discretionary powers of ministers, administrative officials and regulatory boards to make decisions without advance notice to the affected parties; and for greater coherence in policies and practices that affect large segments of the public. These trends are frequently at odds with a political process geared to incremental responses to a shifting set of discrete special interests.

What measures and procedures, then, will best facilitate involvement of Canadian interest groups in public decision making, especially as it concerns economic policy? Commissioners wish to encourage those interests involved to interact with one another more frequently and more openly and visibly, and to take greater account of the broader concerns and conflicts of Canadian society. We look to Parliament itself to determine the final resolution of those conflicts.

The Contributions of Consultation

In all modern industrial societies, the representation of private-sector interests in public decision making has become an important issue. Pervasive interdependence between the public and private sectors has created a situation in which what major economic interests can achieve depends not only on their own initiatives, but also on the sensitivity of the state to their concerns. Conversely, the success of government policies depends heavily on the response of private interests to them. This fundamental interdependence has produced intense pressures for new mechanisms for consultation between the public and private sectors, inevitably involving business and labour, but extending, to an even greater degree, to other organizations in the social and voluntary fields.

Canada has not gone as far as some countries in the direction of comprehensive national consultations. Our consultative practices tend to be fragmented, informal and episodic. Are such practices adequate in light of recent Canadian experience and anticipated future needs, such as the continuing pressures of economic adjustment? Commissioners' terms of reference invite us to examine and report on "means for improving relations between governments, business, labour and other groups". This mandate reflects a widespread perception that these relations have involved unnecessary conflict, and that failure to resolve the tension has incurred undue costs. Relations between the federal government and the Canadian Labour Congress have been seriously strained for almost a decade, and intense disputes between government and labour have erupted in recent years in several provinces. Contact between business and government has been less generally antagonistic, but consultation has been irregular. Sharp disagreements have occurred in some sectors, and there has been evidence of continuing frustration and suspicion.

The tensions of the last decade are at least partly a consequence of fundamental disagreements about the appropriate directions for Canadian economic policy to take. No amount of consultation would have resolved these disagreements. Nevertheless, representatives of business, labour and the general public expressed to this Commission strikingly similar sentiments about their sense of exclusion from economic policy formation. They repeatedly emphasized the need for more effective consultation. The Voluntary Planning Board, for instance, stated:

> *We see consultation, during conception, planning, implementation and evaluation of programs and policies as crucial to effectively dealing with our economy.* (Voluntary Planning Board, Brief, October 19, 1983, p. 3.)

No one expects new mechanisms alone to produce an all-embracing social consensus. Many Canadians hope, however, that these mechanisms might contribute to more common understandings of our economic problems and shared expectations about our prospects. This could increase the effectiveness of government economic policies, to the advantage of all concerned.

Consultation refers to a wide range of practices, from casual telephone conversations to elaborate institutions for formal decision making. To clarify

what is meant by consultation in any particular context and what is expected of any consultative process will help to prevent disappointment and recrimination.

Basic consultation consists of the exchange of information and opinion about issues of common concern. Participants can learn about one another's views, explore areas of agreement, and clarify areas of disagreement. Consultation involves common education: while it may not result in agreement, it can influence decisions taken by participating groups. An important objective of consultative processes, therefore, is better-informed decision making at all levels.

Consultation can go further and seek to build consensus among parties. Consensus building requires a concerted attempt to agree on the nature of problems and on policy options available. Such a common understanding will usually require common analysis. It is not easy to accommodate divergent and often firmly held interpretations of issues important to participants. Forming consensus is no mean feat; maintaining consensus is equally demanding.

Elaborate consultation can ultimately involve formal co-operative decision making. Representatives of government and of major private interests can negotiate among themselves to establish a compromise position which becomes the basis of public policy and of compliance by other parties. This form of consultation, which is often described as "corporatist", clearly requires highly centralized interest groups and close integration of those interest groups and government. It is a characteristic element in countries with a tripartite incomes policy and a broad social contract among business, labour and government. Corporatist or tripartite arrangements can extend to joint management of administrative agencies responsible for implementing accepted policies.

In Canada, the scope for consultative bodies with decision-making power is generally quite limited. Fragmentation and dispersal of authority in public and private sectors and the complexities of our federal system reduce the applicability of the tripartite model. Moreover, tripartite decision making would circumvent our parliamentary institutions in ways that most Canadians would reject. Corporatism also involves the potential danger that the interests of non-participating groups would be ignored.

Nevertheless, we Canadians need more effective consultation and consensus building in economic and social policy. As Commissioners have argued throughout this Report, Canada faces crucial new challenges, and responding to them will require sometimes painful adjustments. Many groups possess considerable capacity to block or impede these changes; they cannot and should not be imposed coercively. There is a crucial need for agreement on the manner in which the burdens and benefits of the necessary changes will be shared. All these factors demand that maximum efforts be made to reassure all groups that they will be treated fairly, and that they will participate in the collective choices which must be made.

Consultation can help to create shared perceptions of our nation's economic and social problems. Without such contact, disagreements over basic data on economic trends can deepen conflicts unnecessarily; public policy may fail to incorporate information and expertise from the private sector; and the sort of

broad consensus that would stabilize policies beyond the term of a single minister or government will not be formed. Government commitment to consultative procedures can reassure the private sector that the basic ground rules of public policy will not change suddenly and without warning. In this way, consultation can help to reduce uncertainty and co-ordinate expectations about economic prospects. Broadened participation by all sectors, including groups directly concerned with social aspects of economic policies, will help to balance economic benefits and social costs.

Formal consultative mechanisms seem especially important in a large regionalized country such as ours. Informal communication networks do not always extend across territorial, linguistic and cultural boundaries. Moreover, distances between the national capital and the major centres of commerce and industry prevent members of the public and private sectors from interacting easily. As the Task Force on Business/Government Interface observed:

> *In London, Paris, Rome or Tokyo, cross-fertilization takes place naturally. In Ottawa, the number of flights from Toronto and Montreal is only one tangible reflection of how much has to be done to create a structure where exchange can occur more readily and to leaven the 'company town' atmosphere of our national capital.*[1]

Recent developments appear promising. For example, special investigatory committees, sub-committees and parliamentary task forces have travelled across Canada to hold hearings. This mobility has given government access to a much broader range of public information and opinion. Teleconferencing offers further opportunities for communication and consultation among representatives of government and private sector interests.

Consultation aimed at consensus building is not without dangers. In industrial policy, for example, some critics insist that elaborate consultative mechanisms would impede adjustment. They would over-represent older troubled industries, tying government even more firmly to those seeking protection from change. Existing industries are often well organized politically; almost by definition, there is no political organization for "emerging" industries. Consultation, therefore, can become a protective barrier to the process of adjustment that furthers economic development. Perhaps competition or conflict would achieve greater economic flexibility than would consensus. Such warnings do stand as a caution against the construction of overly powerful bodies, especially those with quasi-decisional powers over specific areas of public policy.

Despite such concerns, however, the economic case for more-structured, continuing consultation among business, labour and government seems sound. There is no doubt that during the last decade, much of the acrimony of public debate over the economy has been the result, rather than a primary cause, of Canada's economic difficulties. If national consultation can ensure greater understanding of the social and economic problems confronting us, it will be well worth the effort it involves.

Consultation would also affect the quality of political life. The arrangements we use to conduct consultation must enhance, not undermine,

democratic processes. A powerful, institutionalized, tripartite system would constitute an alternative method of representing and accommodating the claims of one particular set of social interests, but this system would be in continuous tension with the principles of responsible government. Even if the sovereignty of elected bodies were not undermined by such corporatist practices, the centralization of authority required to operate tripartite institutions encourages élitist politics, accentuating the dominance of the executive over the legislature in the political realm and the power of central leaders over members in private economic institutions. While some democratic societies have long traditions of reliance on such élite accommodation, in other societies, including Canada, the image of powerful groups striking deals with government in private sessions evokes an uneasy response.

More modest consultative mechanisms can channel the inevitable and continuous interaction between public and private sectors and contribute to informed public debate. They can balance the pressures that groups put on government. A common criticism of pluralist democracy is that not all interests are equal. Some interests have far greater resources to devote to consultation with government, and informal *ad hoc* consultation favours the well organized and well funded at the expense of the poorly organized. Because formal structures of consultation require decisions about which groups should be heard, a more equitable balance of voices is likely to result.

Public consultative processes can contribute to more broadly informed debate over economic issues. If consultation takes place exclusively through private contacts between interest groups and senior officials and ministers, essential information and judgements remain hidden from the public, and the quality of parliamentary debate and media scrutiny is thereby impoverished. Public exchanges over economic issues can enhance the quality of debate, raising public awareness and improving media commentary, sharpening the critical perspectives of legislators, and exposing recommendations of interest groups to public scrutiny. Moreover, the opening of these debates to public scrutiny reinforces the ultimate control of the citizen over policy decisions and government operations. Private consultations would continue, of course, since they are clearly essential if certain aspects of relations among business, labour and government are to develop; but the consequences of modern economic policy are too far-reaching to be shaped exclusively in private. Effective consultation can assist in the economic and political affairs of a modern nation. Canada, however, has some distance to go in this direction.

Consultation in Canada: The Case of Business and Labour

In comparison with the elaborate, centralized, consultative structures in some Western countries, Canadian consultation has two striking characteristics. First, our consultative practices have tended to be fragmented, informal and episodic. There have been few attempts to sustain a structured, comprehensive dialogue between the public and private sectors. Secondly, we have, until recently, encouraged separate representation for each interest, with business and labour associations operating through different channels. We have placed little emphasis on bringing the representatives of different perspectives into

touch with government so that they can develop a common understanding of important economic issues. Indeed, the very term "three social partners", so common in Europe, is relatively unfamiliar to Canadians.

The fragmented competitive nature of consultation is obvious in relations between Canadian business and government. There is much contact between the public and private sectors. Managing the relationship has become a sizeable industry: it involves some 480 business associations and a growing army of professional consultants and specialized legal personnel; it requires officials responsible for government relations in major corporations; and it demands an increasing portion of the time of most chief executive officers. Many of these people are in almost daily contact with public officials. Figures 21-1 and 21-2 illustrate the growth of linkages between the public and private sectors.

The decentralized approach to consultation at the national level has strengths and weaknesses. It is a sufficiently diverse and flexible process to accommodate an endless series of specific issues created by the growing interdependence of business and government. Most contacts concern the administration of existing policies and regulations, and relate to fairly specific problems facing particular sub-sectors of the economy or even individual firms. In these instances, the consultative process works reasonably well.

FIGURE 21-1 Distribution by Sector of Associations Representing Business

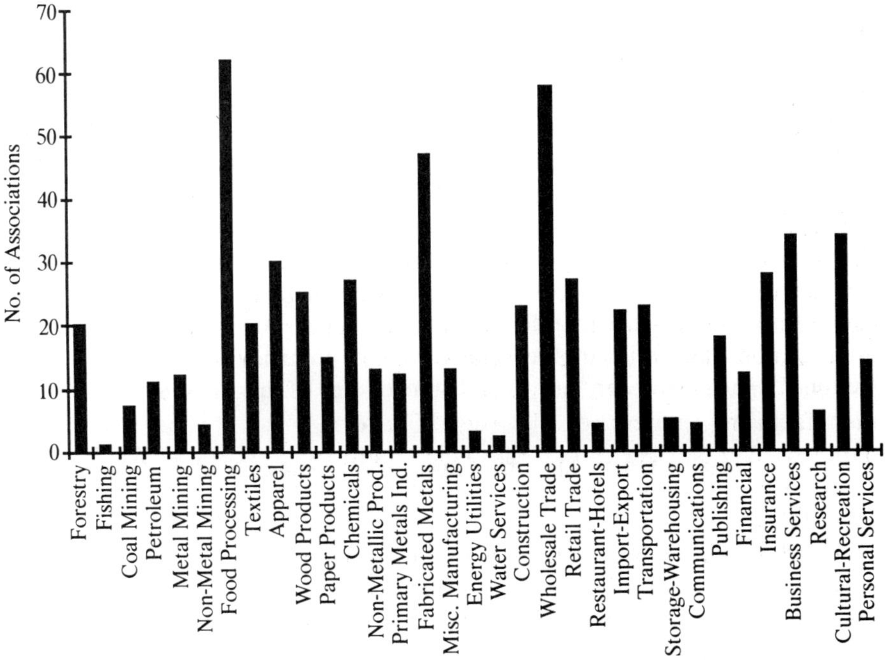

Source: William D. Coleman, "Canadian Business and the State", in *The State and Economic Interests,* vol. 32, prepared for the Royal Commission on the Economic Union and Development Prospects for Canada (Toronto: University of Toronto Press, 1985).

FIGURE 21-2 Period of Founding of Existing Associations Representing Business

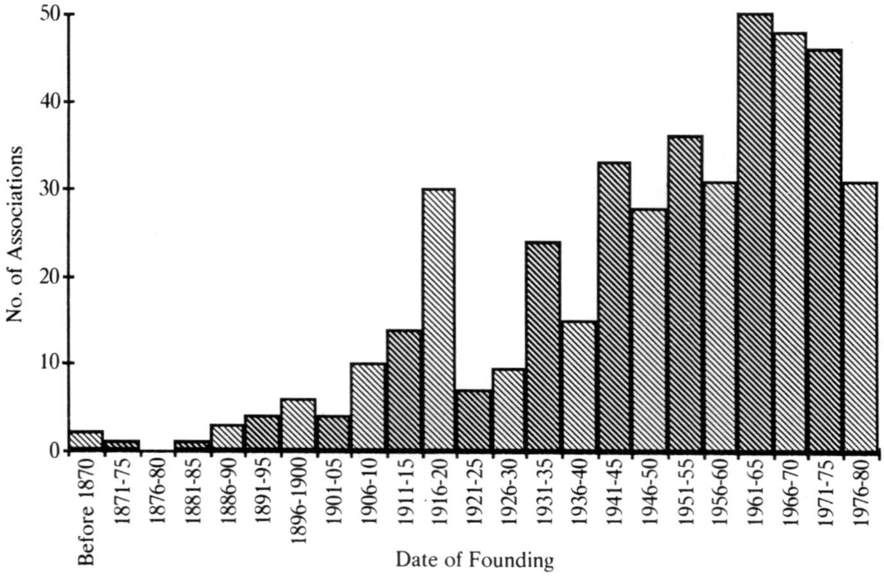

Source: William D. Coleman, "Canadian Business and the State", in The State and Economic Interests, vol. 32, prepared for the Royal Commission on the Economic Union and Development Prospects for Canada (Toronto: University of Toronto Press, 1985).

Disagreements abound, but communication networks are in place to maintain the relationships.

Most business associations represent special-product interests. There is no umbrella association to speak authoritatively for business as a whole. The Canadian Chamber of Commerce, the Canadian Manufacturers' Association, the Business Council on National Issues, the Canadian Export Association, the Canadian Federation of Independent Business, and the Canadian Organization of Small Business represent different constituencies or compete to represent some element of the business community. National business organizations do not yet present a broadly based position on major economic issues. Differences are inevitable between small businesses and major manufacturing enterprises, between Canadian-owned firms and multinationals, and between those firms which profit from exports helped by a low value for the dollar and those which are supported by subsidies and tariff protection.

An additional reason for poor consultation on broad economic issues is the continued reliance on informal, unstructured relations between government and business. During the Second World War and the immediate post-war period, contact between these two sectors was often based on personal relations which "worked" the more readily because leaders of both groups had relatively similar backgrounds and social views. Such relations, however, appear less prevalent today. Greater government activity in economic affairs

has generated many more points of friction. Changing social values have subjected all institutions to closer scrutiny. Consumer groups, environmentalists, nationalist organizations and organized labour all actively challenge the views of the business community. Changes in the federal bureaucracy, especially the growth of strong central agencies, have disrupted traditional contacts between businesspeople and line departments close to their immediate concerns. The growing importance of Cabinet committees and central agencies has reduced the autonomy of individual ministers and their departments, and made the task of all interest groups more difficult. According to one former participant in the process, the chief executive officer "who believes that a trip to see the minister or the deputy will solve his problem is operating on a false premise."[2]

Since traditional links have been eroded, the lack of formal consultation over broad economic policy becomes more important. Flurries of consultation – dialogue in crisis – occasionally fill the gap. For example, waves of private consultations initiated by the federal government preceded and followed the 1982 federal budget and the "Six and Five" program that it launched. *Ad hoc* discussions in the middle of a crisis, however, are not as effective as a sustained predictable relationship. Moreover, to rely on private contacts alone is to ignore the importance of consultative mechanisms in enhancing public debate.

Other groups, too, experience the same difficulties, in terms of internal structure and mechanisms for consultation. The Canadian union movement is characteristically decentralized, regionally diverse and occasionally subject to differences of view between public sector and private sector union leaders. The voluntary community, involved in social issues related to economic policy, is also diverse in outlook. It has strong traditions of local autonomy and participation, and the provinces have responsibility for many of the programs in which it participates.

Until recently, there has been little interest in building consensus among "social partners". Organized labour has traditionally participated through separate channels from those of business. Labour representatives have never liked the procedures. In their view, labour has never had close relations with national policy makers and has never participated fully in the formulation of national economic policy. Various advisory bodies were established after the Second World War, but labour has seen the results as mixed, at best. In protest against the Anti-Inflation Program of 1975, the Canadian Labour Congress severed formal consultative links with government, leaving the Economic Council of Canada and the short-lived Canada Labour Relations Council. A decade later, it has not re-established those links, and significant parts of the labour movement remain sceptical about the value of collaborative bodies.

In the past decade, however, there has been greater emphasis on consensus building among business, labour and government. Canadian governments have experimented with mechanisms involving all three groups or just business and labour. The Economic Council of Canada, founded in 1963, had a wide membership. In 1977, the federal government established 23 task forces to investigate the major sectors of Canadian manufacturing and the

Second Tier Committee to consolidate their work. The next year saw the setting up of the Consultative Task Force on Industrial and Regional Benefits from Major Canadian Projects; the purpose of this Task Force, co-chaired by a business leader and a labour leader, was to examine benefits from large-scale resource projects. In 1984, the Canadian Labour Market and Productivity Centre was founded to advise on labour resources and productivity. Several provinces have created consultative committees on economic policy or industrial relations. Quebec has been particularly active, holding sectoral conferences and *grands sommets* on its provincial economic problems.[3] Not all of these mechanisms have been successful or equally well regarded, and none has fundamentally altered Canadian economic policy. Nevertheless, they have all sought to involve business and labour in a search for common understanding on important economic issues, and they have provided experience that may help Canadians to develop more elaborate mechanisms for building consensus. Overall, Commissioners strongly urge that dialogue continue within sectors and industries on how to improve Canada's economic prospects. Discussions should bring together both business and labour representatives with representatives and officials from the federal, provincial and municipal levels of government, as well as with representatives from other groups as necessary. We Commissioners believe that prolonged discussions of this nature on a relatively narrow agenda are vital.

In developing an overall strategy for consultation between the public and private sectors on major issues, it is essential to build on Canadian experience in ways which are compatible with the institutional framework of business and labour, and with our parliamentary traditions. More effective consultation requires adjustments both in the private sector and in government. Intensive consultation would place severe demands on the national organizations that represent business and labour. To shape national consensus on major economic issues would require participating groups to develop clear positions and priorities. They could not leave the hard choices and decisions about trade-offs to government as has happened in some earlier advisory exercises. As a study of consensus mechanisms in Europe made very clear, the role of organizations representing business and labour is critical. Conflicts among employers and among employees are inevitable, but "their internalization and management by peak organizations makes the task of building national consensus that much easier for governments."[4] This concern led the Science Council of Canada to recommend that "the private sector seriously consider the need to build much stronger organizations" to participate in the formation of economic policy.[5]

To strengthen representation of the private sector forms only one side of the equation, however. More formal and continuous dialogue would also require establishment of new consultative mechanisms through which business and labour could communicate with government. The preceding review and recent Canadian experiments suggest possible directions. The new trend to establish business/labour and business/labour/government advisory bodies deserves support and encouragement. Such bodies can moderate conflicts and build common awareness in critical areas. In many fields, the interests of business and labour overlap significantly, although in some, their

interests are directly opposed, and this limits prospects for government to act on the basis of consensus. Moreover, lasting consensus on economic and social policy or economic management is unlikely, since transitional costs may be high for some sectors, and the international situation may change.

Recent Canadian experience suggests that it would be useful to develop guidelines to shape such initiatives. Commissioners are mindful of the caution expressed by a representative of the Canada West Foundation:

> *I am not convinced that it is possible to legislate meaningful consultation. I think it has to be a state of mind, a sense of confidence in [each] other that you are both trying to achieve the same goal.*
>
> (Canada West Foundation, Transcript, Calgary, November 8, 1983 [vol. 42], p. 8618.)

Acknowledging the validity of that caution, Commissioners believe the following considerations can enhance the success and usefulness of consultative arrangements:

- Consultative mechanisms are more likely to be successful when they focus on clear, specific objectives.
- Consultation should be a continuing process facilitated by reasonably predictable arrangements.
- Governments must make a firm commitment to maintain any consultative processes they undertake. Everyone's time is valuable. Effective consultative arrangements require that non-governmental participants be accorded some influence over the agenda and the decision-making schedule. Responsibility for the overall policy-making process, however, must rest with the government of the day.
- Consultative processes aimed at consensus building require fair representation among many groups in society and, usually, parity between business and labour.
- Effective consultation requires general awareness of appropriate information and governing assumptions. Sharing and co-operative refining of information are prerequisites to the consultative processes which we seek to encourage.

The matter of funding also arises in connection with consultation. The claim is sometimes made that public support is needed for the research, communications and travel associated with participation in various forms of consultation. This Commission itself received inquiries from prospective participants (including major national associations) in its hearings and consultations about the availability of financial assistance. We sympathize with the needs of individuals and small groups anxious to be involved in ongoing consultation, and we are aware that the tax treatment of expenses differs among groups. But we have no guidelines to offer on the weighting of competing claims for limited resources. Those responsible for consultation should respond to financial needs in accordance with their own general operations and the principle that diverse participation should be encouraged.

Commissioners believe that a network of special-purpose bodies would offer greater advantages to Canada than would a single, broad, advisory council. As one intervenor remarked in our hearings:

Public administration involves a collective decision process whose essential feature is the resolution of conflicting interests. This process rests on acceptance of a wide variety of institutions for mediation, negotiation and reconciliation.

(Rod Dobell, Brief, September 21, 1983, p. 35.)

For the purpose of consultation centred on specific industries or economic sectors, the guidelines we have suggested for business/labour/government involvement are appropriate. Where representatives of particular industries and economic sectors are to be consulted, relations between public and private representatives will largely involve contacts with the executive branch of government, will frequently be ongoing, and will emphasize specific and relatively short-term actions. Where consultation is intended to serve other functions, however, different institutional arrangements must be considered.

Parliament and Consultation

Canadians need a national consultative forum or process for determining general economic directions. The arrangement should permit representatives of business, labour, the voluntary sector, and government to exchange information and views about the state of the economy, to survey forecasts of medium-term prospects, to examine difficulties in various sectors, and to consider policy options. Any such forum should also help to inform public and parliamentary debate on the economy.

Commissioners have considered several approaches. One possibility would be to arrange a national economic summit like the one which was held in Australia in April 1983, or like the National Economic Conference held here in Canada in March 1985. A summit offers a number of advantages, including flexibility of agenda and membership. In a Canadian summit, provincial government participation should be encouraged. We suspect that on the grounds of tradition, provinces would regard their participation here as more appropriate than in a parliamentary forum, although this did not prove to be their attitude in the National Economic Conference. It is important to form realistic expectations of such meetings. The Australian conference ratified a detailed incomes policy and agreed to a fiscal framework for the government. Such consensus is unlikely in Canada. A Canadian summit is more likely to serve as a forum for debate than an instrument of consensus.

While a national summit seems to provide an ideal means of initiating intensive consultation, it has its limitations. Annual summits might prove cumbersome and, indeed, inadequate: a continuing dialogue requires a permanent forum. Furthermore, summits, like mechanisms for sectoral consultation, emphasize government involvement at the executive level. A possibility that this Commission finds more attractive is the formation of a permanent Economic Policy Committee of the House of Commons. The Committee would hold annual pre-budget hearings; take testimony about the nation's economic prospects from the Department of Finance, the Bank of Canada and the Treasury Board, and from related agencies such as the Economic Council of Canada and the Science Council; and gather the views of major groups, including business and labour associations. In addition, the

committee could hold hearings on other important economic issues throughout the year. Its hearings should be televised and should become part of the annual cycle of economic policy formation.

Such a committee could inform public and parliamentary debate, and become an instrument for collective debate about the economy. One brief to this Commission addressed this point:

> *Ultimately the skill of the Federal Government to give and share leadership in goal setting* with *Canadians and not* for *Canadians will determine its effectiveness in carrying out its mandate.*
>
> (National Council of YMCAs of Canada, Brief, November 30, 1983, p. 17.)

A permanent Committee would integrate economic interests into the policy-making processes of the House of Commons, the central representative body of Canadian life. In moving from specific problems to the more general issues of economic policy making, it becomes increasingly appropriate to link consultative mechanisms to Parliament, through which the government is ultimately responsible for its decisions.

This Commission's concerns about participation in consultative arrangements are also closely related to the subject matter or issues under consideration. Where discussions focus on sectoral issues with relatively clear objectives and defined scope, it is desirable to involve representatives of business and labour who are familiar with the detailed circumstances. When the object of consultation is broader and less constrained, taking into account the general directions of economic policy, representatives of other groups and constituencies should also be involved.

Commissioners believe that consultation through Parliamentary or legislative forums is most likely to further the ongoing process of public education about the nature of the issues involved in economic policy making and the need for negotiating difficult trade-offs. The greater visibility of legislative forums is an important advantage in this respect.

Reform of the Budget Process and Parliamentary Consultation

The participation of interest groups in the consultative process has particularly important implications for the preparation of the federal budget. Since interest groups both benefit from and bear some of the costs of the various components of the budget, it is desirable to make their demands more visible. Reform of the budgetary process should be viewed in a broader context than it has been in recent years.[6]

Canadians elect the members of the House of Commons and the provincial legislatures, making these the most legitimate political institutions in our constitutional system. Private interests make a different democratic claim on society, and it is less easy to define their legitimacy, which has always been in tension with parliamentary democracy. Today, established and emerging interests, now coming to the fore in a more rights-oriented society, make many claims on government. Yet while Parliament exists to hold the executive to account, there are no formal institutional arrangements or

governing principles to hold accountable the private interests, which are major beneficiaries of the national tax and expenditure system.

National bodies representing big and small business, labour, consumers, agriculture and other sectors present views on fiscal, monetary and social policy, privately and in ritualistic consultation before the Budget Speech. They often present views in such a way as to convey what they would do if they were the government; that is, they present their own views in the guise of the national or public interest. At the same time, they are unhampered by the responsibility for governing or the need to relate their own claims to those of others.

The democratic right of interest groups to express their views is undeniable. Indeed, the quality of the state's economic decisions depends on the continuing exchange of information with private sector interests. However, although the views of interest groups have considerable significance for all Canadians, they are not examined on a sustained basis. The contrast between our treatment of the government's positions and those of opposition political parties is clear: whereas we hold the government responsible for its actions, we do not hold private interests responsible for their actions in the public realm. Commissioners believe that this distinction requires some reconsideration, notably in the context of preparing the budget, where more extensive advance discussion with interests throughout society would be advantageous.

This Commission's research and hearings suggest that there have been changes in the part the budget has in setting national goals.[7] First, because the aims of elected politicians, both federal and provincial, have broadened greatly, budgets now reflect a wide range of social, as well as economic, goals. They permit governments to communicate priorities and to indicate that they share the values of various segments of the electorate; they also reflect the open and hidden claims on the tax and expenditure components of the public purse, which are made by interests in the political system. Secondly, the capacity of federal budgets to indicate major national goals clearly has been reduced by the breadth of objectives inherent in the budgets and the increased frequency of their presentation. Thus, their release has often represented tactical occasions, rather than presentations of coherent signals about the state of the economy. Bombarded by specific demands from interest groups and by persistent detailed criticism from opposition parties, governments have often wished to be seen as "doing something" in response.

Thirdly, the contribution which the national budget can make to goal setting is affected by the legacy of successive approaches to budget reform. Often-conflicting norms and principles, which are linked, in turn, to political ideologies, are the remnants of these approaches, which have included balanced budgeting, Keynesianism, monetarism and various versions of managerial rationality. Indeed, experts who have a specialized knowledge and perception of budgetary matters are increasingly involved in the process of preparing the budget. Their involvement has, to an extent, given the process a life of its own, independent of governmental direction.

Commissioners regret that federal budgets are being introduced with increased frequency, since their capacity to provide economic direction to the country has consequently been reduced. One could ask, for example, whether

the process of setting national goals has been improved: budgets now reflect a wide range of social and economic policy objectives, yet more goals imply more trade-offs and, accordingly, less clarity. From a democratic perspective, however, this proliferation of goals is not inherently undesirable. Indeed, Commissioners welcome the incorporation of micro-economic realities into the budgetary agenda. Nevertheless, we believe discussions of the budget must be restructured to permit scrutiny and debate in this more complex context.

Commissioners are convinced, too, that inadequacies in current practices of scrutinizing taxation and spending should be addressed through reform. Both taxation and expenditure are scrutinized to some extent: by Parliament, as it debates legislation; and by private interests, as they watch over their stakes in the fiscal process. However, whereas the Auditor General's Office monitors government spending at the federal level on a continuing basis, there is no similar agency to monitor taxation. This institutional imbalance needs to be addressed, a point which the 1984 annual report of the Auditor General's Office stresses.

Aside from this imbalance, there are other problems to be addressed in the monitoring process. The adoption of certain auditing practices by recent Auditors General indicates distortion in our system of financial accountability. In a comparatively short period of time, for example, the Auditor General's Office has received a vast increase in its resources to scrutinize spending. An Auditor General may not, however, direct his office to scrutinize policy *per se*, since the position is not an elected one. The office has therefore used "value-for-money" auditing to focus instead on "systems" of information and decision making. Meanwhile, elected members of Parliament lack adequate resources to scrutinize policy as their job demands. The practice of "comprehensive" auditing indicates another aspect of the problem; Commissioners believe that it is incorrect to equate the duties of the Auditor General's Office with those of Parliament itself. Recent statements to the effect that only the Auditor General can hold the government accountable indicate a need for change.

Commissioners would prefer to see the Office of the Auditor General focus on the more traditional auditing functions, that is, checking honesty, probity and efficiency in government finances. Broader aspects of policy and program should be the concern of elected members of Parliament. These politicians should emphasize social and political values, as well as fiscal values, while looking at the political goals which underlie spending and taxation, and while maintaining financial efficiency as a primary criterion.

In this way, while the Auditor General's Office examines financial efficiency as such, Parliamentarians, equally backed by analytical resources, would complement this analysis and other analyses. Both the Auditor General's Office and the Economic Council of Canada would provide analysis and research support for the House of Commons Economic Policy Committee as it scrutinized policy on taxes and expenditures. Elected politicians, backed by analytical support, would then be able to scrutinize proposed tax decisions before the introduction of the budget and throughout the year. Parliament could speak about programs plainly and directly, rather than keeping to the

indirect and convoluted language of "comprehensive" auditing employed by the Auditor General.

The broad contours of a reformed budget process would be along these lines: a standing House of Commons Committee on Economic Policy would hold an annual series of pre-budget meetings timed to allow its work to influence budget preparation. During televised hearings, it would analyse the government's performance. Although ten million Canadians will not suddenly become avid fans of fiscal-policy television, the complex issues involved in preparing the national budget will become more directly accessible to the citizens affected by the outcome. In addition, interest groups will have a better opportunity to learn the positions others are taking on questions of general concern. We believe that similar procedures to increase public involvement in, and understanding of, budget making would also be appropriate at the provincial level.

Other aspects of the budget process should also be changed in order to permit broader discussion and debate of the issues. Commissioners advocate departing once and for all from the rigid practice of budget secrecy. Such secrecy limits full internal discussion of the budget within the Cabinet; thus it not only reduces collective Cabinet responsibility for what is arguably the government's most important set of decisions, but also increases the probability of major errors, such as occurred in the 1981 Budget. Moreover, budget secrecy is out of step with current practice: such extreme secrecy does not accompany other decisions, despite comparable possibilities for private gain. Finally, tradition requires that the Minister of Finance resign when a breach of budget secrecy occurs. Although this step is no longer taken automatically in all instances, there remains an expectation fostered by the competitive political process that perhaps it should be. Confusion between evolving practice and historic expectation has thus produced a situation in which the practice of a basic convention of Parliament lacks clarity.

Commissioners are not arguing for the elimination of secrecy as such; Cabinet secrecy, for example, encourages frank debate within the executive. Secrecy also has important implications for financial issues. It prevents untimely disclosures of possible government decisions which could seriously affect financial markets, and it limits situations where "insiders" could use advance knowledge of economic decisions, or even of the possibility of such decisions, to their own financial gain. In addition, secrecy ensures that any major government decision is announced in an orderly way, rather than revealed unintentionally in bits and pieces. Nevertheless, these considerations certainly do not require the comprehensive budget secrecy that governments have attempted to secure in the past.

We believe that the convention of comprehensive budget secrecy must be reformed in order to begin a movement towards more effective advance discussion and consultative arrangements. Since the principal obstacle to a less comprehensive practice of budget secrecy is Parliamentary convention, we urge the House of Commons to initiate such a change.[8] This reform will have to include a more precise understanding of the circumstances in which strict budget secrecy must continue to apply and of those when its relaxation is appropriate.

Another issue to consider in the matter of reforming the budget process is the timing of budget presentations at both federal and provincial government levels. Commissioners believe that a reasonable case can be made for the two levels to agree to co-ordinate the presentation of revenue and expenditure budgets in all legislatures, adopting an arrangement whereby the federal budget would either precede or follow most provincial budgets by two or three months. Since provincial governments generally present their budgets in the spring, the federal government should attempt to align its practice with theirs; this would require some adjustments to its internal budget and planning cycle. Concurrent debate in all legislatures would serve to focus pre-budget consultation between federal and provincial governments and between the public and the private sectors. An obvious difficulty with this type of synchronization is that finance ministers do not readily give up the tactical flexibility that an uncertain budget date permits; and even an agreed date can always be circumvented by an "economic statement". However, by co-ordinating the presentation of the eleven budgets, a kind of nation-wide discussion of federal and provincial economic goals and priorities could be created. In our view, such an opportunity to discuss these priorities is much needed.

Overall, consultation among governments and between public and private sectors should complement parliamentary scrutiny of the federal budget. Commissioners are not proposing that any single institution can fulfil the need for wide-ranging budgetary consultations and debate which we believe Canada needs. Federalism, parliamentary government and the right of interest groups to associate freely and to lobby are central to our political life. Discussions about the economic goals and priorities of governments will therefore continue to take place: in intergovernmental settings, in discussions with ministers of finance and their officials, and in the proceedings of parliamentary and legislative bodies. Nevertheless, we believe that a parliamentary forum would provide the best means of address to right the two imbalances in our current budget process: the relative lack of scrutiny of taxation as compared with spending; and the failure to examine openly and thoroughly the fiscal, tax and spending proposals of major private interests. The changes we propose would strengthen the role of the House of Commons, Canada's primary democratic, representative institution, in making economic policies.

Notes

1. Canada, Task Force on Business/Government Interface, *Report*, prepared for the Department of Industry, Trade and Commerce (Ottawa: Minister of Supply and Services Canada, 1976), p. 25.
2. James Gillies, *Where Business Fails: Business Government Relations at the Federal Level in Canada* (Montreal: Institute for Research on Public Policy, 1981), p. 109.
3. Pierre Fournier, "Consultation in Canada: Case Studies and Perspectives", in *The State and Economic Interests*, vol. 32, and Ken G. Waldie, "The Evolution of Labour-Government Consultation on Economic Policy", in *Labour-Management*

Co-operation in Canada, vol. 15, prepared for the Royal Commission on the Economic Union and Development Prospects for Canada (Toronto: University of Toronto Press, 1985).

4. M. Cooper, *The Search for Consensus* (Paris: OECD, 1982).
5. Science Council of Canada, *Canadian Industrial Development: Some Policy Directions* (Ottawa: Minister of Supply and Services Canada, 1984), p. 52.
6. See G. Bruce Doern, "The Politics of Economic Policy: An Overview", in *The Politics of Economic Policy*, vol. 40, prepared for the Royal Commission on the Economic Union and Development Prospects for Canada (Toronto: University of Toronto Press, 1985).
7. Allan M. Maslove, Michael Prince, and G. Bruce Doern, *Federal and Provincial Budgeting*, vol. 41, prepared for the Royal Commission on the Economic Union and Development Prospects for Canada (Toronto: University of Toronto Press, 1985).
8. A number of recent studies review specific possibilities. See Conference Board of Canada, *Consultation and Budget Secrecy: Reforming the Process of Creating Revenue Budgets in the Canadian Federal Government* (Ottawa: The Board, 1985).

Parliamentary Government and Federalism: The Reconciliation of National and Regional Interests

National Institutions and the Representation of Regional Interests

Democratic government requires that all citizens be fairly represented in the governing councils where decisions are made on their behalf and where divergent interests must be reconciled. Representation takes many forms. At its heart is the equal representation of individuals, expressed in the term "one person, one vote", but it also covers the social and regional groupings into which any complex society is divided. Effective means of representation are not only requisites of democracy; they are also the foundation of effective government. As a practical matter, policy making will fail if the views of all relevant groups are not considered. If large sections of the population believe government to be unrepresentative, then its capacity to promote compromise, to provide dynamic leadership, and to secure the consensus necessary for voluntary compliance will be eroded.

History, culture, economics and the design of our political institutions have all ensured that within the national framework, Canadians think of representation in regional or provincial terms, in conjunction with, but in partial tension with, the equal representation of individuals. Thus representation in national institutions must be thought of not only as the representation of individuals, but also as the representation of regional or provincial interests. The creation of an appropriate system of representation, therefore, is not a straightforward issue to be determined by a simple formula.

Federalism is one primary means through which we Canadians structure our institutions to represent regional interests. Federalism responds to regional interests through its premise that for some purposes, provincial communities have the right to make their own decisions and to enact their own preferences or priorities, without being blocked by national majorities and without the need to secure national consent. For other purposes, federalism assumes that the relevant community is the whole country, and that the will of the national majority represented by the national government should prevail.

The growth of government and its changing roles have seriously blurred the distinction between provincial and national. Today the national government acts in a multitude of areas of local import and concern; provinces do much that is vital to national purposes.

The practice of contemporary federalism also suggests that one means – but not the only one – of reconciling national and regional interests is through the processes of intergovernmental relations. Indeed, that reconciliation is an essential purpose of what we know as "executive federalism". Commissioners do not, however, accept a model which sees the provincial governments as the sole representatives of matters of regional or provincial interest, and the federal government as the sole articulator for all matters of national interest. Rather, the logic of federalism assigns to provincial governments responsibility for representing the interests of their residents

within areas of provincial jurisdiction; and to the national government it assigns the responsibility for articulating the interests of Canadians in areas of federal jurisdiction.

The federal government, therefore, has a national role that requires sensitivity to provincial and regional interests. However well the institutions of federal-provincial relations work, they can be no substitute for a regionally representative federal government. As the one set of political institutions in which all Canadians are represented, the federal Parliament has a fundamental responsibility to serve as the arena in which we reconcile, accommodate, balance and compromise the interests of each and every region in national policy.

The national economy includes important regional variations in natural resources, size of local markets, access to international markets, and infrastructure for economic development. These variations are as significant now as they were at the time of Confederation. Recent experience with energy, industrial restructuring or reform of the Crow's Nest Pass Freight Rates confirms the persistence of regional dimensions in national policy. Commissioners' assessment of future policy issues arising from Canada's deepening involvement in the international environment and from pressures for continuing industrial adjustment suggest that Canada will require ongoing reconciliation of diverse regional perspectives. Equally, the federal government must be able to define and promote a national interest which is more than the sum of these regional parts, a national interest which transcends our provincial and regional selves.

Both these roles – responding to regional needs, and defining the national interest – require that the national government have the confidence of citizens throughout the country. Without a nation-wide base, the federal government's claim to be a national government is weakened. Its ability to act in the name of all Canadians will be seriously flawed. In a country as regionally divided as ours, the national government must be "regionally representative".

Regional representation has a number of possible meanings which need to be distinguished. First, in a formal sense, Canadians do enjoy equal representation as individuals, regardless of area of residence. A vote cast in British Columbia, for instance, carries approximately the same weight as one cast in Newfoundland. In the House of Commons, each province's number of seats is, with limited exceptions, proportional to its population. However, Canada's parliamentary system concentrates political power in the governing party and in the Cabinet. It is these institutions, therefore, which must be representative.

At one level, we can think of regional representation in a proportional sense: that is, a province or region will be fairly represented if its weight in the governing councils is proportional to its weight in the country as a whole. A province with 5 per cent of the population should carry 5 per cent of the weight in Cabinet and the caucus of the governing party. In a federal system, however, this proportion may be considered insufficient. We may wish to think of provinces as collectivities which, themselves, deserve equal representation or a weight of influence close to it. This view argues for a

departure from the proportional representation of Canadians as individuals; it suggests, instead, that a province with 5 per cent of the population might require more than 5 per cent of the influence in the national government. In the extreme, it can lead to arguments for equality of representation for provinces as provinces. The striking variations in the populations of Canada's provinces mean that in a system of representation based on majority rule and the equality of individual voters, the electoral power of the citizens of a few larger provinces will swamp that of the smaller provinces. If, therefore, our national institutions are to reflect the federal dimension of Canadian society, the dominance of majority rule based on the equal representation of individuals must be tempered.

There is an inherent tension between the concept of equal representation of individuals and those criteria of representation which suggest that the provinces with the smaller populations should have representation in excess of their proper percentage of the Canadian population. Moves to accommodate the latter notion inevitably encroach on the integrity of equal representation of Canadians as individuals. To give extra representation to smaller provinces is to deny equal representation to the individual citizens of the larger provinces. This dilemma of representation is inherent in federal systems where the provinces or states have unequal populations.

The questions raised by these issues are complex and difficult. The fact remains, however, that in recent years, by any measure of regional representation, our national institutions have been seriously flawed. It is not an exaggeration to speak of an institutional failure which has had profound consequences for the governance of Canada.

What are the dimensions of this failure? Despite the importance of regional differences in Canada, the present design of our national institutions gives remarkably little attention to regional interests. Federal systems around the world typically represent regional interests, not only through the division of powers between central and state or provincial governments, but also through the representation of provinces or states within the national government. In the original U.S. constitution, for example, states had equal representation in the Senate, and Senators were named by state legislatures. In West Germany, the second Chamber, the *Bundesrat*, is made up of ministers of state governments.

In Canada, where we draw on the British tradition of parliamentary government, we have built our federalism primarily on the division of powers. Our nation is, perhaps, unique among federal systems in our relative exclusion of the representation of regional interests from the centre.

Canadians have not, however, entirely ignored the need to represent regional interests in national institutions. One of the major issues in the debates leading to Confederation was the design and role of the Senate. Unlike the House of Commons, which was constituted on the basis of representation by population, the Senate reflected the new Dominion's regional composition by giving equal representation to Ontario, Quebec and the Maritimes. This arrangement was later extended to include the West. The Senate initially enjoyed legislative powers virtually equivalent to those of the House of Commons, but its potential to act as the regional body within the

national government and to temper the effect of majority rule in the House of Commons, was fundamentally compromised by the method of appointment to its ranks, and by the logic of responsible government. The federal Cabinet's power to appoint Senators deprived the appointees of effective links with provincial and regional communities and thus undermined their capacity to represent those communities and to be seen to do so. Responsible government meant that the Cabinet would be responsible to the elected House of Commons, rather than to the appointed Senate. Despite its broad formal powers, the Senate would therefore become a residual body – valuable in providing "sober second thought", in studying policy problems which had not attracted the attention of the Commons, or in dealing with certain technical non-partisan matters; but it would not become an effective forum for the articulation of regional interests.

The task of accommodating regional interests within the operation of national government would fall, instead, to the political parties, to the Cabinet in particular, and to the House of Commons. In many respects, these arrangements worked well. The model of party government developed in Canada has sometimes been called the "brokerage" model. Each national party would win support across the country: it would represent a coalition of regional interests, wielding considerable strength in party councils through politicians with strong bases of local and provincial support. The parties themselves, therefore, would serve as the arenas within which regional interests would be articulated and compromised. This model carried through into the structure of the Cabinet. From the first days of Confederation, federal Cabinets have been carefully built to ensure representation of all regions and of other interests as well. Our national government also developed the tradition of "regional ministers": powerful regional leaders within Cabinet, who would both press the interests of their own region and also serve as the government's primary regional spokespersons and dispensers of patronage.

Such a system is predicated on the ability of national parties to win support across the country, and to act as forums for balancing interests. Canadians can no longer have confidence in this process. The capacity of parties – the basic instruments of responsible government in a parliamentary system – to perform their intended role, has been called into question, and with it, the capacity of the central government to act as a national government.

The Institutional Failure of the Centre

The results of the federal election of 1980 tell the story in stark terms. Tables 21-1A and 21-1B illustrate that story. By 1980, our federal parties had become regionally polarized; no party had effective representation from across the country. The victorious Liberal Party won 52 per cent of all the seats in Canada, but they won only two seats in the West, both of them in Manitoba. By contrast, the Liberals won all but one of Quebec's 75 seats. They were thus required to govern with almost no representation from Western Canada. The reverse was true for the Progressive Conservatives in

TABLE 21-1A 1980 General Election Results: Seats and Popular Vote by Province

Province	Total Seats	Progressive Conservative		Liberal		NDP	
		% Vote	# of Seats	% Vote	# of Seats	% Vote	# of Seats
Newfoundland	7	36.0	2	47.0	5	16.7	0
Nova Scotia	11	38.7	6	39.9	5	20.9	0
New Brunswick	10	32.5	3	50.1	7	16.2	0
P.E.I.	4	46.3	2	46.8	2	6.6	0
Quebec	75	12.6	1	68.2	74	9.1	0
Ontario	95	35.5	38	41.9	52	21.9	5
Manitoba	14	37.7	5	28.0	2	33.5	7
Saskatchewan	14	38.9	7	24.2	0	36.3	7
Alberta	21	64.9	21	22.2	0	10.3	0
British Columbia	28	41.5	16	22.2	0	35.3	12
Yukon/Northwest Territories	3	30.6	2	37.2	0	31.5	1
Total	282	32.5	103	44.3	147	19.8	32

TABLE 21-1B 1984 General Election Results: Seats and Popular Vote by Province

Province	Total Seats	Progressive Conservative % Vote	Progressive Conservative # of Seats	Liberal % Vote	Liberal # of Seats	NDP % Vote	NDP # of Seats
Newfoundland	7	57.6	4	36.4	3	5.8	—
Nova Scotia	11	50.8	9	33.6	2	15.2	—
New Brunswick	10	53.5	9	31.9	1	14.1	—
P.E.I.	4	52.0	3	41.0	1	6.5	—
Quebec	75	50.2	58	35.4	17	8.8	—
Ontario	95	47.6	67	29.9	14	20.8	13
Manitoba	14	43.2	9	21.8	1	27.2	4
Saskatchewan	14	41.7	9	18.2	—	38.4	5
Alberta	21	68.8	21	12.7	—	14.1	—
British Columbia	28	46.7	19	16.4	1	35.0	8
Yukon/Northwest Territories	3	49.1	3	24.3	—	22.2	—
Total	282	50.0	211	28.0	40	18.8	30

Source: Canada, Office of the Chief Electoral Officer, *Thirty-Second General Election 1980: Report of the Chief Electoral Officer* (Ottawa: Minister of Supply and Services Canada, 1980), and *Thirty-Third General Election 1984: Report of the Chief Electoral Officer* (Ottawa: Minister of Supply and Services Canada, 1985).

their minority victory of 1979: they won three-quarters of the seats in the West, and only two in Quebec. In each election, one region considered itself excluded *de facto* from the governing councils of the nation. The sharp differences in regional party representation are misleading as an indication of party support. This becomes clear if we look at the proportions of the vote, rather than at seats won: the Liberals were able to gain significant support in the Western provinces; the Conservatives won some support in Quebec. But even at this level, the claim of any party to be truly "national" was not entirely persuasive.

The 1980 election result provided an extreme example of representational anomalies, but by no means a unique one. Region has long been a prime determinant of voting patterns. The Progressive Conservatives had been weak in Quebec since the conscription crisis of the First World War. The Liberals had been relatively weak in the West since the historic realignment of the vote engineered by John Diefenbaker in 1958. Only in Ontario and Atlantic Canada has there been roughly equal competition among the major parties. Governments with truly national mandates – those of 1958, 1968, or 1984, for instance – seemed to be the exception rather than the rule. This regional polarization was especially marked in each of the federal elections that took place between 1972 and 1980. The Progressive Conservative electoral success of 1984 dramatically demonstrates that it is still possible for a party to secure nationwide representation in the House of Commons. It is by no means clear, however, that prolonged periods of regionally imbalanced representation will not recur.

What accounts for the regional polarization of the party system so evident before 1984? Undoubtedly, the chief reason is to be found in the nature of the issues which divided Canadians. It is not so much that the ability of national institutions to bridge divisions declined, but that the river the bridges had to span grew so much wider. Thus, beginning in the 1960s, linguistic divisions revived conflicts deeply rooted in Canadian history. The national government's need to devote significant effort to language issues and to respond to Quebec's search for a larger role found relatively little sympathy in the West, where voters believed that federal concentration on Quebec led to the neglect of matters of more direct concern to Westerners. The later emergence of conflicts over energy pricing and development also divided the country regionally: any national government would have extreme difficulty, for example, in reconciling the interests of Ontario and Alberta in the matter of oil pricing and revenues in a period of world energy-price and -supply upheaval. The recent abatement of interest in such issues leaves Commissioners more optimistic about reconstituting a more integrated national politics. Even if this hope can be realized, however, the future will continue to present Canadians with renewed and unforeseen challenges which will pose fundamental regional dilemmas for those seeking national reconciliation.

The growth of governmental responsibility for all forms of well-being increases the difficulty of accommodating divergent regional interests, simply because national governments are held more responsible for economic conditions than they were previously. Again, in a highly regionalized economy, the challenge of successful balancing and integration becomes more

difficult for national institutions to meet. Expanded government also means that Ministers are more deeply involved in their administrative and policy-making roles, and so have less time and energy to devote to their more "representative" duties, including that of regional representation.

Recent change in the "technology" of politics has perhaps reduced incentives for parties to reorganize and thereby to integrate local, regional and national concerns. For example, television has contributed to a concentration of power in the Prime Minister's hands and seems to have detracted from the role of regional party leaders in shaping party policy. Television allows party leaders to communicate directly with voters on a country-wide basis. Similarly, sophisticated public opinion polling reduces the role of party rank and file, Members of Parliament and local leaders in communicating regional opinion to the national leadership. Recent reforms, such as public funding of elections, have also tended to weaken the relationships between national and provincial parties.

The electoral process also contributes to regional polarization of the party system. In 1980, the Liberal party won 22 per cent of the vote in British Columbia, 22 per cent of the vote in Alberta, and 24 per cent in Saskatchewan, yet it did not secure a single seat in the House of Commons. In the same election, the Progressive Conservatives won 13 per cent of the vote in Quebec, but achieved almost equally meagre returns in seats. Our electoral system of awarding the seat to the candidate with the largest number of votes provides no pay-off in terms of representation for votes cast for other candidates. In any given region, one party could have a very slim overall lead in votes, yet win every one of the seats. Unless a party thinks that an effective campaign will secure a significant number of seats, it has little incentive to try to win electoral support in regions where it is weak. Hence weakness is likely to reinforce weakness.

The interaction of our electoral system and voting patterns has resulted in regions being seriously over- or under-represented in governing parties. In the Liberal governments that held office between 1963 and 1984, the Western provinces had an average of only 8.3 per cent of the seats in the governing party. In the same period, Quebec was significantly over-represented in the Liberal caucus. In 1979, when the Progressive Conservatives came into power, the situation was reversed. Details are found in Table 21-2.

Another indication of the regional character of our party system is the sharp distinction between party adherence at the provincial and national levels: few provincial legislatures reproduce the party balances found in the federal government. In 1983, the Liberals, though in power in Ottawa, did not form the government in any province. As Table 21-3 shows, of a total of 698 seats in provincial legislatures, only 130 were Liberal. Moreover, irrespective of whether federal and provincial parties of the same name are simultaneously strong in both arenas, they have become increasingly autonomous: they are often supported by different organizations, are financed by different sources and aim at different goals. In recent years there has been relatively little movement of politicians from the provincial level to the national, or vice versa. Thus, in strong contrast to other federal countries such as Australia, Germany and the United States, and despite extensive

TABLE 21-2 Regional Composition of Government Caucus and House of Commons, Canadian General Elections, 1945 – 1984

		Regional Composition of Government Caucus				Regional Composition of House of Commons			
Election	Governing Party	West	Ont.	Que.	Alta.	West	Ont.	Que.	Alta.
1945	Liberal	15.2	27.2	43.2	14.4	29.4	33.5	26.5	10.6
1949	Liberal	22.6	29.5	34.7	13.1	27.5	31.7	27.9	13.0
1953	Liberal	15.9	29.4	38.8	15.9	27.2	32.1	28.3	12.5
1957	Prog. Conservative	18.8	54.5	8.0	18.8	27.2	32.1	28.3	12.5
1958	Prog. Conservative	31.7	32.2	24.0	12.0	27.2	32.1	28.3	12.5
1962	Prog. Conservative	42.2	30.2	12.1	15.5	27.2	32.1	28.3	12.5
1963	Liberal	7.8	40.3	36.4	15.5	27.2	32.1	28.3	12.5
1965	Liberal	6.9	38.9	42.7	11.5	27.2	32.1	28.3	12.5
1968	Liberal	18.1	41.3	36.1	4.5	26.5	33.3	28.0	12.1
1972	Liberal	6.4	33.0	51.4	9.2	26.5	33.3	28.0	12.1
1974	Liberal	9.2	39.0	42.6	9.2	26.5	33.3	28.0	12.1
1979	Prog. Conservative	43.4	41.9	1.5	13.2	28.4	33.7	26.6	11.3
1980	Liberal	1.4	35.4	50.3	12.9	28.4	33.7	26.6	11.3
1984	Prog. Conservative	28.9	31.8	27.5	11.8	28.4	33.7	26.6	11.3

Source: Canada, Special Joint Committee of the Senate and of the House of Commons on Senate Reform, *Minutes of Proceedings*, June 28, 1983, p. 10A:3, and information supplied to the Commission.

Note: Rows may not add up to 100% because of rounding.

TABLE 21-3 Party Membership in Provincial Legislatures, 1983

Province	Governing Party	Progressive Conservative	Liberal	Other	Total Seats
Newfoundland	Prog. Conservative	43	9	0	52
Nova Scotia	Prog. Conservative	38	12	2	52
P.E.I.	Prog. Conservative	21	11	0	32
New Brunswick	Prog. Conservative	39	18	1	58
Quebec	Parti québécois	0	46	76	122
Ontario	Prog. Conservative	70	33	22	125
Manitoba	New Democrat	23	0	34	57
Saskatchewan	Prog. Conservative	56	0	8	64
Alberta	Prog. Conservative	75	0	4	79
B.C.	Social Credit	0	0	57	57
		359	130	209	698

Source: Parliamentary Guide, 1984 (Ottawa, 1984).

interdependence of federal and provincial governments, the Canadian party system does not provide an effective means of bridging and integrating politics at the two levels. This is one reason why executive federalism, sometimes reminiscent of international negotiations, has become the dominant mode of intergovernmental relations.

Canadians have focused their attention on the regional polarization of political parties because it is parties which energize the whole political system. There are additional ways, however, in which the capacities of the institutions of the federal government to represent and accommodate regional interests have been attenuated or less than fully developed.

The first is party discipline. United disciplined parties are essential to the effective operation of party government. However, the ability of individual Members of Parliament to act as spokespersons for their province's interests is sharply limited. As a consequence of party discipline, the MPs regular advocacy of regional interests largely takes the form of participation in party caucuses and in private representations to ministers. It is equally difficult for MPs from the same region, but different parties, to form cross-party alliances to push their regions' interest. This difficulty contrasts with the situation in the United States, where, in a congressional system, weak party discipline gives Representatives and Senators wide scope to act as local representatives and encourages state politicians to build coalitions within national institutions for state interests, rather than to resort to negotiations at the executive level.

Another impediment to regional representation at the national level is the structure of the federal bureaucracy. Most ministries are organized around functions, such as Health and Welfare or Transport, or, like Veterans Affairs or Labour, around clienteles which are not primarily "regional". Of course, there are exceptions. The Department of Regional Economic Expansion (DREE) had a specific regional mandate, and its merger with Industry, Trade and Commerce to form the Department of Regional Industrial Expansion (DRIE) is an attempt to inject a more regional cast into the formation of

economic policy. The Federal Provincial Relations Office, reporting to the Prime Minister, is equally an attempt to ensure that regional and federal-provincial sensitivities are reflected at the highest levels of policy making. Nevertheless, administration in the central bureaucracy has not systematically given attention to the regional dimension of policy.

The prominence of federal Crown corporations and regulatory agencies has increased with the rise of the administrative state. These, too, have been criticized for insufficient sensitivity to regional considerations. These bodies vary significantly in their "independence" of policy direction and management control exercised by the political executive and the central agencies. In general, however, this component of the administrative state is furthest removed from the institutions intended to reconcile regional and national interests in national policy. Although the governing boards of these corporations and agencies are appointed by Cabinet, and although some attention is given to their regional composition, they are largely insulated from the political and policy environment of national government. Many Canadians believe that this autonomy fosters an insensitivity to regional concerns.

Some regulatory agencies, such as the Canadian Transport Commission (CTC), the Canadian Radio-television and Telecommunications Commission (CRTC), and the National Energy Board (NEB), have major regional concerns at the heart of their mandate. However, there are no explicit regional considerations either in the terms of reference of several such agencies or in the selection of the members of regulatory tribunals. While some of these bodies have made extensive efforts to take into account regional interests and to work with their counterpart provincial agencies, this has not been a consistent pattern.

Finally, as Commissioners have noted, the Senate has not been able to provide effective regional representation. The fact that its members are appointed has simply prevented it from playing such a role.

Commissioners conclude, therefore, that Canada's national institutions of government are not well designed to provide regional representation or to encompass the regional diversities of Canadian life within the process of national decision making. The principles and practices of representation by population, Cabinet government, party discipline, and majority rule have not encouraged an adequate response to the regionalism of a federal society. In addition, the limitations of regional representation in national institutions have been accentuated, in recent years, by the regional polarization of the party system.

The consequences of this institutional failure have been severe. They have significantly undermined the ability of the central government to act as the national government in either of the senses presented above: the federal government has become less able to articulate and defend a concept that the national interest transcends regional interests; it has become less able to promote reconciliation of competing regional interests in a fair and balanced manner. It has lost some of its legitimacy, thus experiencing reduction of its capacity to act decisively and effectively.

Public opinion data show that Canadians identify strongly and positively with both national and provincial communities. Indeed, in all provinces except Quebec and Newfoundland, the national community is valued slightly more highly than the provincial. Assessments of the national government are much less positive, however. Many Canadians, when asked about major areas of policy, state their belief that the federal government has the responsibility to act in the national interest. They see that government as having an ever greater effect on their lives.[1] Their views about the level of government which should be responsible for particular functions accord closely with the existing division of powers. Clearly, Canadians value a strong, effective, central government.

At the same time, many Canadians believe that provincial governments affect citizens' lives more significantly than does the federal government. Strong majorities feel themselves "closer" to the provincial governments and consider them more responsive. In the West and, to a lesser extent in the East, large numbers of Canadians believe that their regions have been unfairly treated by national authorities, and that they have been ignored and under-represented in national politics.[2] There is thus a wide gap between what citizens want and expect of their national government and their confidence in its ability to perform its roles fairly and effectively. The challenge inherent in the process of national institutional reform is to close this gap.

If we Canadians do not meet this challenge, the sense of exclusion from the governing councils which was evident in the 1970s and early 1980s will undoubtedly recur. Without strong regional representation in the caucus of each party—especially the party in power—governments' ability to be sensitive to each region is undermined. Correspondingly, their ability to communicate party policy to voters is reduced. In the absence of balanced regional representation, parties and governments run the risk of appearing, not as advocates of the national interest, but of the ill-disguised interests of particular regions. The power of governments to act will be inhibited, not by lack of constitutional authority, but by lack of political authority. Their ability to be fair redistributors of resources will be weakened by the belief held in under-represented regions that their concerns receive inadequate attention. Persistent regional imbalances in national institutions can ultimately strain the very fabric of Confederation.

Moreover, the less able national institutions are in providing forums for regional reconciliation, the more that role will fall to federal-provincial relations. The less credibly the national government can claim to speak for a region, the more credible become the assertions of provincial premiers that they are the appropriate advocates, not only for matters under provincial jurisdiction, but for matters of federal responsibility, too, and the more citizens will turn to their provincial governments. Indeed, the regional polarization of national politics, is related in complex ways to the growth of provincial government assertiveness and federal-provincial conflict.

For all these reasons, Commissioners believe that to reform national institutions so that they better represent the whole country in its regional dimensions is a fundamental requirement. The 1984 election of a new

government with nation-wide support is encouraging: it shows that even with unchanged political institutions, regional polarization is not inevitable, and that through their own internal processes, political parties can overcome the institutional hurdles. Canadians must recognize, however, that these results were not facilitated by our institutions themselves; indeed, they occurred in spite of our institutional arrangements. It is therefore essential to address the larger institutional issues.

Directions for the Reform of our National Institutions of Government

With this analysis in mind, let us set out our goals and explore the ways to achieve them. We wish to ensure that Canada's national institutions of government will, and will be seen to be, representative of, and responsive to, the interests and concerns of all regions and provinces in Canada. We wish to ensure that Canadians in all regions can be confident that through their representatives, they are present in the forums that make critical decisions, the most important of which are the Cabinet and our two Houses of Parliament. These are the most visible sites for representation. While the principles of representation of individuals and the majority rule it produces are the fundamental underpinnings of responsible government, Commissioners believe that in a federal system—and especially in one where the populations of provinces vary so greatly—Canadians must temper the practice of majority rule to accord relatively greater weight to smaller provinces and regions.

In the matter of representation in Parliament, Commissioners wish to emphasize two essential considerations. In terms of the House of Commons, representation as such is not at issue, for all regions and provinces are now represented in that body. The first issue is the representation of regions and provinces within particular parties to a degree more closely related to their electoral support. The second issue is better balanced provincial representation. Here Commissioners view the Senate, our second chamber and the body which, in federal systems, typically bears the responsibility for representing state and provincial communities, as the appropriate site for reform. We do not wish to modify the basic principle of representation by population, on which the House of Commons is properly constituted. On the other hand, we do seek to make the parliamentary caucus of our parties more representative of Canada's regions. Our proposed solution attempts to meet both these concerns by moving to an elected Senate where membership is weighted towards the smaller provinces, and where election is based on proportional representation. This change will simultaneously strengthen the position of the less populous provinces in the joint Senate-House of Commons caucus of the parties, and also contribute, through proportional representation, to a distribution of those caucus members in each party which is closer than the present arrangement to their actual electoral support in the regions.

These modifications must be made in ways consistent with the tenets of responsible government. This means that the Cabinet must remain

responsible to the House of Commons which, itself, must continue to be chosen on the basis of population. It also means that reforms must be consistent with the concept of cohesive, disciplined, political parties. Finally, Commissioners believe that the achievement of a regionally representative central government, or the building into national institutions of the concept of representation by region, must not and need not undermine the ideal of a national government which is responsive to national constituencies and which pursues comprehensive national goals. Regional representation is a precondition of national government, not a substitute for it.

Four possible areas for reform are present. All have been extensively canvassed in recent years, as many groups have sought to strengthen the regional responsiveness of the national government.

Reform of Political Parties

The most visible of the institutional failures described above are the regional polarization of political parties and, with occasional exceptions such as that provided by the election of 1984, the recurring inability of any party to achieve a nation-wide constituency. The first advice, then, to political parties must be to "heal themselves". The onus should be on party leaders and party members to ensure that their parties develop a comprehensive vision of Canada and put forward programs and policies which can command broad support across the country. Electoral strategies which cultivate the interests of some regions over others, or which "write off" whole sections of the country, must be recognized as inimical to the long-term interests of both country and party, even if they should offer short-term electoral advantage. Macdonald, Laurier, King were able to make their parties the "governing party" for extended periods precisely because of their ability to build sustainable national coalitions.

Internal party reform – including, Commissioners believe, the desirable strengthening of links between national and provincial parties – is primarily a matter for the parties themselves to undertake. We have seen in recent years worthwhile and important, though not always successful, efforts by all parties to overcome their regional biases in support and representation. Beyond approving continuing efforts in this direction, however, we do not presume to suggest how parties should order their internal affairs.

The view that national parties are the principal cause of the failure to reconcile national and regional interests ignores the basic fact that even with a nationally representative governing party in power, our parliamentary system does not provide any mechanism by means of which the regional interests of the less populous provinces are able to temper those of more populous provinces. A nationally representative governing party, such as that elected in 1984, is still subject to domination by the elected representatives of the more populous provinces. There are good reasons to doubt, therefore, that even nationally representative governing parties can reconcile national and regional interests to the degree Commissioners consider necessary.

The Electoral System

Party strategies, however, are more than a product of the aspirations of leaders and tactical advisers. They are also shaped by the powerful framework of rules within which the electoral game is carried out. The most important of these is the electoral system.

As we have seen, Canada's "first-past-the-post" electoral system has the effect of dramatically reinforcing the regional disparities in party support at the level of representation. The party caucus is far less regionally representative than is the party's electoral base. Moreover, this situation creates incentives for parties to strengthen their regional bastions, and not to "waste" time and money on a region where they are in a minority.

As a result, there have been a number of recent proposals to reform the electoral system to counter these effects. Most such proposals aim to introduce a greater element of "proportionality" into the system so as to bring a party's percentage of seats more into line with the percentage of votes it is able to win in each province or region. Full proportionality ("PR") on a provincial basis, employing what is known as the "list system", would constitute each province as a single constituency. Voters would cast ballots for a party rather than for an individual candidate. Each party would be allocated a number of seats proportional to the votes it won, and MPs would be drawn from party-compiled lists. There are myriad variations on this fundamental theme, but they need not concern us here.[3]

Proposals for such a comprehensive list system have never achieved wide support in Canada. They would constitute a major departure from our existing system. The direct link between citizen and member, achieved by casting votes for an individual candidate in a single constituency, would be broken. Party organization, which would select candidate lists, would be given more power than most Canadians would wish. Moreover, complete PR would render minority – or perhaps coalition – governments the norm in Canada. In the 25 elections that have been held since 1900, the victorious party has won a majority of the votes cast only seven times. That has happened only twice since 1945: in 1958 and 1984. Full proportional representation would also almost certainly make it easier for new parties to enter the political fray: indeed, there would be considerable possibility of creating a fragmented multi-party system, one which would strongly encourage the emergence of narrowly focused parties, including regional parties. Pure PR would thus ensure a match between seats and votes, but at the cost of denying ourselves the benefits of stable majority governments and of forgoing our traditional relationships with our elected representatives.

Another standard method of proportional representation, which involves multi-member constituencies, could also, if comprehensively applied, produce almost complete proportionality between seats and votes on both a national and a provincial basis. Such a system would preserve the link between voters and candidates, since Canadians would still vote for individual candidates and thus would not contribute to the same enhancement of power of the party organization as does a list system. It would, therefore, be less destructive of our traditions. On the other hand, if comprehensively applied, it, too, would

result in the election of minority governments, an outcome which Commissioners consider undesirable. Accordingly, we do not recommend such a wholesale change of electoral arrangements for the House of Commons. We are attracted, however, to such a system for the Senate, where its effect would not undermine stable majority government, for government would continue to be determined by party majority in the House of Commons.

Such considerations have led most proponents of electoral reform applicable to the House of Commons to suggest that we introduce some elements of proportionality, without going the full distance. The most common suggestion is for some form of "topping-up" mechanism to operate in the House of Commons. The present electoral system would continue to determine the allotment of most of the seats, but after a certain point, the "topping-up" arrangements would come into effect. Each province or region would have a pool of party candidates: if party members, elected directly under the present system, fell short of the number needed to supply representation proportional to the popular vote, additional MPs would be selected from the pool in accordance with clearly formulated rules to supply more proportional representation. West Germany uses such a system, effectively combining single-member districts with full proportional representation in the *Bundestag*.

In Canada, the Pépin-Robarts Task Force on Canadian Unity suggested increasing membership in the House of Commons by "about 60". The additional seats would be awarded to candidates selected from party lists announced before the election and would be distributed on the basis of percentages of the popular vote.[4] In 1980, a report for the Canada West Foundation[5] suggested reducing the number of single constituencies in the Commons from 282 to 255 and adding 75 new MPs, who would be chosen from party lists. Each voter would cast two ballots, one for a constituency candidate and one for a party. On the basis of the latter votes, seats would be allocated proportionally among the parties.

These "partial" PR systems have the virtue of keeping most of the current system intact. Most are also designed to minimize the risk of producing minority governments. By the same token, of course, they can go only part of the way to matching seats and votes. An important cost of such proposals is the addition of considerable complexity to our electoral system. Two types of members would sit in the House of Commons, selected in different ways; and it is not clear what the effects of the change would be on the internal dynamics of the parties and on citizens' expectations.

Commissioners conclude that reform of the electoral system for the House of Commons is not practicable at the present time. Such proposals have received little evident public support. A movement to full PR, whatever the PR system employed, would introduce unpredictable, but potentially far-reaching, changes into our party system and the functioning of responsible government. While it would solve the immediate problem of balancing seats with votes, the cost might be large. "Add-on" systems would have fewer possible consequences for majority government, but they would only partially solve the problem of improving regional representation within the parties in Parliament. In our view, then, electoral reform is a second-best solution.

Commissioners do think, however, that it is time for Canada to explore the potential effects and benefits of proportional representation in Parliament. We shall present our position in the context of Senate reform.

The House of Commons and Regional Representation

A third area for change, and one closely linked to parties and the electoral system, is the House of Commons. It may be possible, by modifying this element of our system of government, to give greater freedom to individual MPs to act as "regional" spokespersons. Considerable progress has recently been made within all parties to develop a more extensive system of regional groupings within the party caucus, and Commissioners endorse these developments. There are, however, two limitations to the expression of regional interests within the caucus: first, it presumes that the caucus as a whole is regionally representative, a condition which we have seen all too frequently does not obtain. Secondly, this expression takes place in the privacy of the caucus room; when the Members emerge, party discipline imposes itself. This custom means that however vigorous the expressions of regional opinion in caucus, it is not easy for voters to see the process in action.

The proposal most often discussed as a possible resolution of this problem is to lift the strictures imposed by party discipline and allow MPs full rein to act publicly as regional spokespersons. Commissioners' proposal to provide a more important role for parliamentary committees, especially before party positions become fixed, is a step in this direction. We do not wish, however, to go further. Party discipline, we have observed, is deeply entrenched in our parliamentary tradition. Moreover, it is a vital device for ensuring policy coherence and for achieving responsible government. We do not wish to tamper with such a fundamental element of the present system. Again, if MPs came to define themselves primarily as regional advocates, they might indeed express regional interests, but they might not be able to reconcile and accommodate differences. Party leaders, with an eye to national success, are more likely to balance regional interests than are individual MPs with an eye to success in their own constituencies.

The possible reforms Commissioners have reviewed so far are designed to deal with the way in which Canadian voters select members of the House of Commons and, by extension, the Cabinet. Such reforms could ensure that each region has at least some voice in the governing councils, and that each party and the Cabinet have an elective base in every part of the country. We believe, however, that it is essential to address another dimension of the problem: the need to temper majority rule by giving greater weight to smaller areas.

The Senate and Regional Representation

In most federal systems, the second chamber of the national parliament reflects the federal character of the country. Typically, second chambers allot more influence to smaller regions than their population would warrant: in the United States, for example, each state has two Senators, despite huge variations in population.

What is the potential for Senate reform in Canada? As we have seen, the composition of the Canadian Senate reflects the regional character of our nation. The way in which Senators are selected, however, decisively undercuts the Senate's role as a regional counterweight to a House of Commons where seats are based on population. There are many functions a second chamber can perform and many issues in Senate reform. Commissioners wish, however, to emphasize the potential of Senate reform to bring greater regional responsiveness to central institutions. Commissioners are not alone in this view. Beginning in the mid-1970s, as regional conflict intensified, as the regional polarization of political parties increased, and as provincial governments responded with proposals for decentralization and requests for a greater voice in federal policy making, attention turned more and more to the alternative response of reform at the centre. The Senate was the most frequently chosen vehicle.

In assessing the possibilities and objectives for reform of the Senate, Commissioners have been mindful of a more extreme option which some critics have put forward from time to time: abolition of the second chamber. In our consultations, one of the provincial premiers proposed abolition. In the winter of 1984–85, when the Senate took, some thought, undue time to consider a money bill, there were new and serious cries for abolition. Commissioners understand this view and believe it to be based on two quite valid criticisms: that the present appointed Senate is illegitimate in the modern sense of "representation", and that it is ineffective in its duties of regional representation. For these reasons, we do not favour retaining the *status quo* for the Senate.

This Commission proposes radical reform of the Senate, but not its abolition. We take this position for three reasons. First, our priority is to promote Parliament as the principal forum for public debate in Canada; to abolish the Senate would be a move in the wrong direction. Secondly, we wish to see the reconciliation of national and regional interests in Parliament, and we believe that the Senate can make a major contribution to that end. Thirdly, although there have been endless suggestions for reform of the Senate and a good deal of public support for reform, political and institutional self-interest has prevented the public will from being done. We think that this situation may be changing. We are of the opinion that there is renewed interest on the part of all the institutions concerned. Thus we are persuaded that, practically speaking, serious Senate reform is no longer a "non-starter", and we are convinced that for a more effective Parliament, it is essential.

Issues in Senate Reform

The design of a reformed Senate depends on the purposes that we wish it to serve. To determine those purposes, we must answer several questions. What should be the basis of representation? How should we select members? What powers should the Senate have? What should be its relation to political parties and the House of Commons?

Commissioners wish to incorporate the concept and practice of regional representation more clearly within the structure of national institutions. The Senate is the institution that should embody the federalist principle at the centre. The House of Commons will continue to represent individuals on the basis of population. Should each province, then, have equal representation in the Senate? We do not go so far: our objective is simply to establish a greater weight of influence for less populous regions relative to the more populous. In intergovernmental relations, provincial governments are, and should be, equal, a state which reflects their juridical equality and their responsibility for governing their respective provinces. Yet our institutional arrangements also recognize differences among the provinces to serve certain purposes. For some constitutional amendments, for example, size and numbers of provinces are combined to establish a voting formula. In our national government, where representation by region takes place within a single jurisdiction, a comparable adjustment is also appropriate. We wish to temper, not overrule, representation by population.

The Senate is part of Parliament, and Parliament is pre-eminently a representative body. For that reason, and because a reformed Senate must build on Canada's practice of party government, we join those who have argued that the Senate should be an elected body. Appointment of members by the national executive is inappropriate in our democracy. Numerous proposals for reform or replacement of the Senate have suggested an alternative method of appointment, by provincial governments or legislatures. The Senate would become a House of the Provinces or a Council of the Federation. According to some proposals, Senators would be direct delegates of provinces, casting their votes as a bloc under instruction from provincial governments. Provincial ministers might head delegations. The model for such proposals is the West German second chamber, the *Bundesrat*. Under this model, the Senate might become the chief arena for the conduct of intergovernmental relations.

Commissioners reject this model on the ground that it is inconsistent with the democratic principle mentioned above. It would mix oil and water in that it would inject into our representative parliamentary process members of provincial governments with executive responsibilities. We must keep separate the executive function and the representative function of the legislature. Moreover, such a model represents an erroneous view of Canadian federalism. It supposes that provincial governments are appropriate spokespersons for regional interests in the national arena. On the contrary, federalism implies that provincial governments are the instruments of their populations for provincial purposes, and that federal MPs and Senators are equally provincial representatives for national purposes. Senators, therefore, should certainly represent provinces, but not provincial governments. We should not convert Parliament into an instrument for managing the interdependence of different orders of government.

If Senators are to represent the citizens of their various regions, those citizens must choose Senators directly. The only legitimate way to do this in a democracy is by means of the franchise. But how is this to be done? One possibility is to apply the first-past-the-post system used for House of

Commons elections. There would be many fewer constituencies, as the Senate would be smaller than the House of Commons. The constituencies, of course, would be correspondingly larger. In this way, election of Senators could achieve Commissioners' objective of giving greater influence to small regions, but it would not guarantee more regionally representative caucuses. The distortions of the current electoral system would reappear in the Senate. Indeed, the larger the constituency, the more potential there is for distortion. Thus representation in the Senate would likely be even more unbalanced than it is in the House of Commons. A Senate whose members were elected by simple pluralities in single-member constituencies would not represent a useful change; such a reform might even be a counterproductive move.

For these reasons Commissioners suggest election of Senators by proportional representation. This method is likely to supply the governing party with elected representatives (MPs or Senators) from all regions for its parliamentary caucus. The governing party would have to be more responsive to representatives of the less populous provinces because these would be given extra weighting in a reformed Senate to enable them to secure passage of legislation. Regional interests would not override party interests, but they would most certainly temper them. A Senate elected by proportional representation would usually permit the governing party to constitute a Cabinet that included representatives from all regions because it would contain men and women from all regions capable of assuming Cabinet positions.

Commissioners recommend that Senators be elected in six-member constituencies. This number is large enough to realize the intended effects of proportional representation, yet allows for some recognition of the regions within provinces. On this basis, given a Senate composed of 144 members, Prince Edward Island would have one six-member constituency, Quebec and Ontario would have four such constituencies, and all other provinces would have two six-member constituencies. Yukon and the Northwest Territories together would share six Senators. The design of these constituencies, whether single or multi-member, would have to await division of the Northwest Territories.

Commissioners believe that a Senate reformed along the lines we have proposed would implement the federalist principle in our national institutions. It would improve regional representation in Parliament, and thus in the Cabinet and in the caucuses of all parties. To elect the Senate as we have recommended can strengthen democratic processes and enhance the position of Parliament in relation to the executive. (See Table 21-4.)

Adoption of proportional representation for the Senate would also provide a useful test of that system more generally. It could have some important consequences. In the long run, citizens might come to see Senators elected by proportional representation as more legitimate than MPs elected by the first-past-the-post method, and this view might have interesting implications for relations between the two Houses. Under proportional representation, the governing party would rarely have a majority of Senate seats, though it is highly unlikely, either, that a non-governing party would have a majority in the Senate. Simultaneous elections of both Houses and party organization of

TABLE 21-4 Projected Distribution of Senate Seats (144) under Proportional Representation as Determined by 1984 Election Results

Province	Progressive Conservative		Liberal		NDP	
	% Vote	No. of Seats	% Vote	No. of Seats	% Vote	No. of Seats
Newfoundland	57.6	7	36.4	4	5.8	1
Nova Scotia	50.8	6	33.6	4	15.2	2
New Brunswick	53.5	6	31.9	4	14.1	2
Prince Edward Island	52.0	3	41.0	3	6.5	0
Quebec	50.2	13	35.4	9	8.8	2
Ontario	47.6	12	29.9	7	20.8	5
Manitoba	43.2	6	21.8	3	27.2	3
Saskatchewan	41.7	5	18.2	2	38.4	5
Alberta	68.8	9	12.7	1	14.1	2
British Columbia	46.7	6	16.4	2	35.0	4
N.W.T. and Yukon[a]						
Totals	50.0	73	28.0	39	18.8	26

Source: Canada, Office of the Chief Electoral Officer, *Thirty-Third General Election 1984: Report of the Chief Electoral Officer* (Ottawa: Minister of Supply and Services Canada, 1985).

Note: Table 21-4 shows the provincial distribution of the 144 Senate seats in the 1984 election, assuming the use of proportional representation on a province-wide basis, if voters had expressed the same party preferences for Senate candidates as for House of Commons candidates.

a. The distribution of the six seats allocated to the Northwest Territories and Yukon has not been projected because the issues of choosing an electoral system and dividing the Northwest Territories remain to be resolved.

elections should reduce the danger of such an impasse and of the paralysis that might follow.

Party organization represents an important principle. A number of proposals have sought to insulate Senate elections from party politics, and from the allegedly short-run electoral considerations that dominate the House of Commons. They would do so by eliminating party labels and having candidates run as individuals, by separating Commons and Senate elections, by instituting lengthy terms for Senators, or by holding elections for the Upper House on fixed dates. The Joint Committee on Senate Reform,[6] for example, called for nine-year, non-renewable terms, in order to give Senators credibility as regional representatives and "a significant degree of independence of party". Commissioners believe, on the contrary, that it is undesirable to attempt to compartmentalize and separate the Senate and the House of Commons in this way. Party is the organizing device for political representation in Canada, and Canadians should not deny that fact. Moreover, it is our aim to ensure, through the Senate, regional representation in the caucuses of

all national parties. A reformed Senate must strengthen party government, not undermine it.

Except in the passage of money bills, the powers of the present Senate are formally co-equal with those of the House of Commons. Restraints on the Senate's exercise of its powers are political and conventional: the House of Commons is the democratic body, and the Cabinet is responsible to it. Giving the Senate an electoral base necessitates rethinking its powers. How much authority does the Senate need to achieve the goals we have set? Our aim is to ensure regional sensitivity and to temper majority rule. It is not to override the vital principle of responsible government.

An elected Senate which actually used the powers of the present Senate to initiate, veto and amend legislation could indeed complicate responsible government. Moreover, a government with a majority in the Commons might seldom have a Senate majority. Commissioners believe, accordingly, that with the exception noted below, the Senate should have a suspensive veto of six months on all ordinary legislation. This period should prove ample for it to consider fully the regional viewpoint and give pause to unrestrained majorities in the House of Commons. Yet it would be clear that ultimately, the will of the majority in the House of Commons would prevail.

Other supporters of a suspensive veto power for the Senate have explored variations in the procedures for its application. It has been suggested, for example, that a bill passed by the House of Commons and subsequently rejected by the Senate should require a second adoption by the House of Commons before it could be presented to the Governor General.[7] Detailed procedures relating to timing, to the use of special majorities and to different classes of legislation will require careful attention. The objective must be to structure a balance between the principles of regional representation in a reformed Senate and of majority power in the House of Commons, without producing deadlock or otherwise rendering the parliamentary process too unwieldy.

To this point, Commissioners have emphasized the Senate's role as a regional or provincial body. We also believe that a reformed Senate can contribute to representing and reconciling the interests of French- and English-speaking Canadians. The Senate can be both a regionalist and a dualist chamber. Thus, we propose that on matters of special linguistic significance, passage of a law would require the support of both a majority of the Senate and a majority of francophone members. The Senate veto in such matters would be absolute, not simply suspensive.

Commissioners believe that an elected Senate such as we have described would enhance the representative element of the national government by ensuring strong representation from all regions in the caucus of each party and in the Cabinet. We believe that it would strengthen the voice of the smaller provinces and give their people greater confidence that national majorities in government would pay special attention to their interests. Moreover, it would do so by strengthening, rather than weakening, responsible party government.

In analysing the potential role of a reformed Senate, Commissioners have emphasized the regional dimension of Canadian life, and the capacity of

national institutions to represent that dimension and blend it with other concerns in the making of policy. With that perspective in mind, we have concentrated on regional concerns because, as our recent experience eloquently testifies, national institutions have had great weaknesses in that respect. We now wish, however, to pause and remind Canadians that we take for granted that the more regionally elected Senate we propose is to do more than bring a regional focus to its appraisal of policy. The Senate should continue to perform its useful role of applying basic "sober second thought" to all legislation and of generally improving legislation. There is an indispensable role for a second chamber in the national parliament, independent of regional representation. The conduct of inquiries, the control of the modern administrative state, the public airing of issues and other functions will continue to be responsibilities of a reformed Senate. Commissioners do not wish these responsibilities to be forgotten in the concentration on regional concerns, where a reformed Senate has much to offer.

Regional Representation and Responsiveness in the Executive Branch of Government

Commissioners believe that we Canadians must also consider additional measures to strengthen the political legitimacy of the central government. A final critical area for improvement is the sensitivity of the executive branch to regional concerns.

Commissioners wish to look first at the Cabinet and, specifically, at the function of regional ministers. The influence of certain powerful regional ministers has been evident in relation to such highly visible government activities as grants, contracts, projects and subsidies awarded on a regional basis. But government secrecy and the complexity of the administrative state have limited clear understanding of the regional minister's role.

The status of regional ministers has varied, depending on a number of factors, including the leadership style and political strengths of the Prime Minister. In recent years, moreover, regional ministers have had to cope not only with increasingly complex Cabinet decision-making processes, but also with a cumbersome administrative system. In addition, the functions of the regional minister have extended into federal-provincial relations. Regional ministers have often found themselves constrained both by the general environment of federal-provincial relations and by the elaborate machinery that manages and controls those relations.

The implications of these changes for regional representation in Cabinet decision making have been two-fold. First, regional ministers, who in addition to discharging their portfolio responsibilities articulate the interests of their region in Cabinet deliberations, have a more difficult task because of the increased complexity of these structures and processes. They cannot intervene as easily as they used to do, to press the case for their regions or to operate their portfolios in the service of their regions. Secondly, the composition of the Cabinet's committee structure has generally taken into account the requirement of regional representation that applies to the Cabinet itself. Recently, too, the Cabinet Committee for Economic Development Policy

became the Cabinet Committee for Economic and Regional Development. From 1982 to 1984, a central agency, the Ministry of State for Economic and Regional Development (MSERD), served this committee; the Ministry was unique among the central agencies in that it had a series of regional offices in each province, headed by a senior official. These institutional features enhanced regional responsiveness in Cabinet decision making.

It is surprising that the Cabinet has not done more to strengthen administrative support for regional ministers. As the demise of the short-lived MSERD suggests, regional representation is an essentially political function which ministers perform primarily through administrative inputs and policy analysis. Representation of regional interests in the Cabinet decision-making process is part of Canadian politics, but the institutional design of our decision-making systems has not actively promoted this element. We wish to strengthen this dimension of our institutional arrangements.

In a few notable instances, ministers have used their departmental authority to promote regional interests, despite departmental organizations that largely ignore regional policy development and exclude policy planning and development from their regional offices. With few exceptions, policy planning and development take place at departmental headquarters, while regional offices focus on program delivery and line operations. When Ministers promote regional interests, the result is often partisan. This political intervention seldom takes place within well-designed national policies promoting regional development. This situation will remain the norm until line departments stress regional policy planning and development at both central and regional offices.

Organizational arrangements to facilitate representation of regional interests have emerged only slowly within the executive branch and have met with opposition from a number of quarters. Not surprisingly, those hesitant about, or even opposed to, the promotion of regional interests in the development of national policies become more numerous as one moves closer to the heart of central Canada and the national capital. Yet most areas of public policy affect regional interests directly or indirectly. The appointment of the Cabinet Committee on Economic and Regional Development in 1982 constituted the most explicit acknowledgement of this reality to date. This committee is one of the most important within the Cabinet. It represents the culmination of a quarter-century of evolution that has seen the executive give increased organizational attention to the regional dimension of national policy. For the first time, the Cabinet officially acknowledged that all ministers, departments and agencies of economic development were responsible for regional development.

The record of the last three decades is one of slow but steady progress, as the executive branch has made changes in the administrative structures and processes of the national government. Three conclusions arising from this experience stand out as critical.

First, to be regionally responsible a national organization must establish a unit that focuses on the regional dimension of its policies and programs. Without this focus, the organization will respond to regional concerns only at the insistence of its minister, the Prime Minister, the Cabinet or interest

groups. In those cases, moreover, the outside pressure will limit its capacity to react as required. Secondly, to be regionally responsive, most organizations must carry out some decentralized policy planning in regional offices. Notwithstanding the ease with which we can transport information and personnel, planning based on regional views, needs and opportunities requires personnel who are active in the field full time. Thirdly, the Cabinet must decentralize the central agency that supports its decision making on regional development, in order to facilitate co-ordination in the regions among departmental and agency officials involved in policy planning.

Lessons learned over the past quarter-century include appreciation of the degree to which organizations will resist restructuring for purposes that their personnel consider external to their central mission. Only rarely have departments and agencies of economic development responded to the objectives of regional development by way of the organizational changes noted above. Too often they regard regional development as nothing more than a political imperative to which they must give lip-service to the degree on which Ministers insist. Many considered the Department of Regional Economic Expansion (DREE) a nuisance and the Ministry of State for Economic and Regional Development (MSERD) a threat to the sectorally oriented missions of other departments.

Resistance to regional responsibilities has lessened the capacity of the executive branch to be as regionally responsive as it should be and has thus undermined the effectiveness of political representation of regional interests in the Cabinet. The policy effectiveness of the national government has suffered because ministers must rely primarily on their political officials and their political contacts, who possess neither the expertise nor the experience of administrative officials. Accordingly, it is essential to overcome this resistance to regional responsibility.

Reform of the Senate along the lines Commissioners recommend should affect the priority attached to regional representation and responsiveness within the executive branch of the national government. The ways in which the Prime Minister and the Cabinet organize the executive branch will, of course, depend on other factors as well. Nonetheless, we have concluded that the Cabinet should give more attention to the organizational capacity of the executive branch to respond to regional interests.

First, Commissioners recommend that the central agencies be so structured as to secure more accurate information on regional dimensions for the Cabinet to use in making policy decisions. This requires regional offices like those established in 1982, with the reorganization of the central agency that served the Cabinet Committee on Economic and Regional Development. These offices still exist, but outside the central administrative apparatus that serves the Prime Minister and the Cabinet. We think it desirable to re-establish such offices within the Cabinet secretariat.

Secondly, Commissioners recommend increased decentralization of departments and agencies for the purposes of policy planning and development. Ministers with sectorally organized departments must incorporate the regional dimension fully in departmental planning and policy development.

This step, in turn, requires the inclusion of regional officials in departmental decision making.

These two recommendations are mutually supportive. Only decentralized policy planning and development can produce regional information adequate to support Cabinet decision making. At the same time, regional officials in line departments and agencies must be aware of the Cabinet's priorities and decisions, and this requires continual interaction with other departments and agencies in a region, as well as with the region's central agency officials.

Thirdly, Commissioners recommend that a reformed elected Senate establish a committee to approve all appointments of the heads of major Crown corporations and all the members of major regulatory agencies. Some significance must be attached to appointees' region of origin. Those nominated by the Prime Minister and the Cabinet should be subject to parliamentary scrutiny because these boards exercise powers delegated by Parliament. In our view, a reformed Senate with strengthened regional representation is the appropriate chamber of Parliament to undertake this scrutiny.

Although some Canadians would argue that Senate approval would do little to improve our present practice, Commissioners believe that it would help to achieve better regional representation on these bodies. It would promote greater public confidence that the appointments meet the regional criterion. Such a public process would force the Cabinet to give greater attention to the merits of those whom they nominate because nominees would be subject to public scrutiny. This open process should make Crown corporations and regulatory agencies more sensitive to regional considerations in conducting their operations and coming to their decisions.

Notes

1. Richard Johnston, *Public Opinion and Public Policy in Canada*, vol. 35, prepared for the Royal Commission on the Economic Union and Development Prospects for Canada (Toronto: University of Toronto Press, 1985).
2. *Ibid.*
3. For more detail, see William Irvine, "A Review and Evaluation of Electoral System Reform Proposals", in *Institutional Reforms for Representative Government*, vol. 38, prepared for the Royal Commission on the Economic Union and Development Prospects for Canada (Toronto: University of Toronto Press, 1985).
4. Donald V. Smiley and Ronald L. Watts, *The Reform of Federal Institutions*, vol. 39, prepared for the Royal Commission on the Economic Union and Development Prospects for Canada (Toronto: University of Toronto Press, 1985).
5. David Elton and Roger Gibbons, *Electoral Reform: The Need Is Pressing, the Time Is Now* (Calgary: Canada West Foundation, 1980).
6. Canada, Special Joint Committee of the Senate and of the House of Commons on Senate Reform, *Report* (Ottawa: Queen's Printer, 1984).
7. *Ibid.*, p. 30.

CHAPTER 22

Federalism and the Canadian Economic Union

CHAPTER 22

Federalism and the Economic Union

Introduction

Two themes dominated the preceding review of national institutions: the need to strengthen responsible representative government in the face of the growth of the administrative state and the need to reform the institutions of national government to reflect provincial and regional diversities more fully. These themes are central to Commissioners' analysis of the institutions of federalism and to our assessment of the Canadian economic union. We must ensure that federalism – the institutional framework that assigns authority to two orders of government – works democratically and promotes reconciliation of national and regional interests.

"Government" in Canada is the result of the activities of both federal and provincial orders, and of their interactions. Canadians thus continue to ask how well federalism serves our economic and social needs. The functional approach taken by Commissioners to the reform of federalism and to the concept of the economic union reflects our mandate: "To respond to the challenges of rapid national and international change ... and to secure sustained economic and social progress, it will be of importance to achieve ... greater support for the Canadian economic union". We are to consider "the integrity of the Canadian economic union as it relates to the unity of Canada and the ability of all Canadians to participate in increased economic prosperity". We are asked to suggest institutional changes to "encourage the further development of the Canadian economic union."

These instructions emphasize the breadth of the concept of economic union. At its narrowest, that concept implies a concern to reduce or eliminate barriers or impediments to the ability of Canadians to live, work, trade and invest anywhere in the country. Indeed, a major reason for appointing this Commission was a concern that policies of both levels of government were eroding this aspect of the economic union and reducing the efficiency of the

national economy. In a federal country, however, "economic union" has other meanings as well. The expression implies active policies to foster and facilitate trade and exchange among Canadians. It implies common economic and social policies, and the building of institutions to develop them. It also implies the need for institutional mechanisms to ensure that the benefits that flow from the economic union are distributed throughout the country. Moreover, it requires that governments co-ordinate their use of public revenues and the performance of their responsibilities so as to meet the needs of Canadians. The concept of the economic union includes all these dimensions: all the relationships relevant to the economic well-being of Canadians and to the maintenance of a strong, competitive economy.

The economic union is also a political concept that captures something vital about Canadian citizenship and the existence of our country. If we were to calculate the benefits in terms only of efficiency and incomes, we would have less concern with distribution and sharing, and little desire to ensure the use of some common standards across the country. We would be content with free movement of goods and worry little about the rights of citizens to live and work in locations of their choice. Economic union within Canada would be like economic union with any other country. Somewhere, sometime, a purely economic calculus would no doubt lead some Canadians to choose to "go it alone". The objective of building a Canadian economic union has meaning because we are first a national political community. Threats to the economic union are threats to the national community because they erode the ties of affinity and interest that bind Canadians together.

Commissioners have organized this examination of federalism and the economic union around four key concerns:

- Has federalism balkanized or fragmented the Canadian economic union? Have internal barriers to trade reduced efficiency or lowered incomes? As many critics have suggested, are the costs of existing barriers to the Canadian economic union too high?
- Does federalism frustrate or enhance our ability to manage the economy? Do the complexities of federalism account for some of the weaknesses in current policies? Is federalism likely to inhibit achievement of some of the economic goals that this Commission has set out?
- Has the practice of Canadian federalism resulted in an unfair sharing of the benefits and costs of participation in Confederation? Sharing has always been fundamental to our sense of Canadianism and to the success of the Confederation arrangements. The federation could not long survive if citizens in different regions felt the rules were systematically stacked against them, and that policy was systematically biased. Yet perceptions of unfairness among regions run through Canadian history, and these perceptions persist.
- Do joint use of the common financial base and the system of transfers between governments respond to the needs of taxpayers and the need for flexibility?

Federalism has proved a flexible, adaptable instrument in the past and is likely to do so again. We require, not dramatic transformation, but ordered

change rooted in specific needs and objectives, and sensitive to the underlying principles of Canadian federalism.

How best, then, are we to reconcile intergovernmental co-ordination and management of intergovernmental conflict with the norms of democracy and accountability? Institutions – the division of powers, the amending process, the mechanisms of intergovernmental relations – are vital. If they can respond to citizens' needs, manage conflicting interests and facilitate decisive action, we Canadians can have confidence in our ability to face the future.

In this chapter Commissioners look at the instruments through which Canadians can balance often-conflicting values and concerns: federalism, parliamentary government and the Charter of Rights; national versus provincial majorities; aggregate national income versus regional development; freedom of movement versus community preservation; uniformity and diversity; and others. Such balancing is the essential task of all our institutions, national and federal.

Numerous forces at work today make a reconsideration of federalism especially desirable. Increased international competition necessitates reassessment of our domestic institutions to make sure that they facilitate rather than frustrate successful adaptation. The emergence of new demands and new social groups, and the call for more effective mechanisms for consultation between governments and citizens pose additional challenges. We should take stock of the cumulative effects of incremental changes in federal institutions since the end of the Second World War, and make sure that these institutions can serve us in future.

Maintaining the Economic Union: The Problem of Internal Barriers

The sections which follow assess the Canadian economic union. Commissioners look first at some statistical evidence concerning the patterns of trade within Canada in order to provide an overview of the country as an economic union. This is an essential preliminary to describing and analysing the character and effects of internal barriers. Next we identify policies which might distort trade and the flow of labour and capital. We then examine the cost of these distortions and speculate on some of the economic and political consequences. And finally, we draw conclusions about the significance of internal barriers for Canada's economic union and propose a number of institutional reforms to reduce the costs and promote greater internal integration.

Trade and Factor Flows

Table 22-1 provides an overview of Canadian production and trade. Total traded output in 1979, the most recent year for which detailed information is available on interprovincial[1] trade, exports and sales within the provinces, was nearly $444 billion. Slightly more than half of this production consisted of services. Manufactured products made up another third, with primary goods

TABLE 22-1 Destination of Goods and Services, Canada, 1979

	('000 $ and per cent)							
	Total		Within Province		Rest of Canada		Exports	
	Value	Per Cent of Total Ouput	Value	Per Cent	Value	Per Cent	Value	Per Cent
Primary	44 036 860	10	19 950 220	45	10 069 840	23	14 016 800	32
Manufacturing	158 804 590	36	69 652 570	44	43 796 010	28	45 356 010	28
Total goods	202 841 450	46	89 602 790	44	53 865 850	27	59 372 810	29
Services	241 029 450	54	198 478 140	82	33 598 080	14	895 230	4
Total	443 870 900	100	288 080 930	65	87 463 930	20	68 326 040	15

Source: Statistics Canada, Input-Output Division, Interprovincial Trade Flow Data, 1979.

constituting only 10 per cent. The first lesson to be learned from these data is the striking importance of the local provincial market. Nearly two-thirds of everything produced in Canada in 1979 was first sold in the province in which it was produced. One-fifth of total output moved across provincial boundaries within Canada, while 15 per cent was marketed abroad.

When we exclude trade in services, the picture changes. Since many services can only be traded or provided locally, the elimination of the service category from the statistical picture reveals more clearly the significance of trade, within Canada and abroad, for provincially produced goods and resources. Only 44 per cent of total output of goods was initially marketed within the province of origin. More than one-quarter of goods – nearly $54 billion-worth in 1979 – was shipped interprovincially. This figure is only slightly less than the $59 billion-worth of exports recorded in that year. For the Canadian economy as a whole, therefore, interprovincial trade is about as important as foreign trade. In comparing broad commodity groups, we note that primary products tend to be aimed more for the export market than for other provinces (32% as compared to 23%), while producers of manufactures rely equally (28%) on sales to other provinces and to the export market.

These are general observations. There are many primary products, mineral fuels among them, for which markets outside the province dominate, and others, such as dairy products, that are produced almost exclusively for local markets. Similarly, there are some manufactured products that find their main markets outside Canada, and some services that trade extensively across regions.

Patterns of trade among provinces, which are summarized, for 1979, in Table 22-2, are especially important to understanding the economic union and the policy issues associated with it. As might be expected, the two central provinces dominated trade. Ontario accounted for nearly 40 per cent of all interregional shipments in Canada, and Quebec for another 25 per cent. Most of the total for each province consisted of shipments to the other, a factor which made their trade dominance even more significant. Alberta contributed 17 per cent of interprovincial Canadian trade in goods, largely in the form of energy. No other province recorded more than 6 per cent of the interprovincial total. Given existing trade patterns, barriers to interprovincial trade within Canada could therefore most significantly affect interprovincial trade between Ontario and Quebec. In comparison, if almost any other bilateral trade between provinces – except for oil and gas – were to be halted altogether, the cessation would not noticeably affect national totals.

Aggregate trade flows do not tell the entire story, however. It is equally necessary to assess the importance of participation in the economic union to the economic well-being of each province. If, for example, a small province is highly dependent on sales to other regions, and if these transactions are threatened by internal barriers to trade, that province has every reason to be concerned even if, in total, the economic impact will appear to be small. We must therefore look at the economic union from the viewpoint of each member.

The significance of provincial, national, and international markets varies for each province. Table 22-2 shows the destination of goods by province and

TABLE 22-2 Destination of Goods by Province 1979

	('000 $ and per cent)							
	Total		Within Province		Rest of Canada		Exports	
	Value	Per Cent	Value	Per Cent	Value	Per Cent	Value	Per Cent
Newfoundland	2 312 630	100	638 090	28	495 260	21	1 179 280	51
P.E.I.	367 170	100	147 800	40	143 120	39	76 250	21
Nova Scotia	4 114 910	100	1 650 180	40	1 400 920	34	1 063 810	26
New Brunswick	3 923 590	100	1 148 770	29	1 116 090	29	1 658 720	42
Quebec	45 969 900	100	21 922 850	48	13 115 810	28	10 931 230	24
Ontario	84 700 930	100	40 001 260	47	20 920 730	25	23 778 930	28
Manitoba	6 149 200	100	2 142 550	35	2 503 720	41	1 502 930	24
Saskatchewan	6 644 170	100	1 681 270	25	1 900 400	29	3 062 500	46
Alberta	26 259 410	100	10 186 630	39	9 056 800	34	7 015 990	27
British Columbia	21 742 550	100	9 882 080	45	3 158 520	15	8 701 950	40
Yukon & N.W.T.	656 990	100	201 310	31	54 480	8	401 200	61
Canada	202 841 450	100	89 602 780	44	53 865 860	27	59 372 790	29

Source: Statistics Canada, Input-Output Division, Interprovincial Trade Flow Data, 1979.

Note: Totals may not add to a hundred because of rounding.

territory. For six of the provinces, the provincial market is more important than interprovincial sales or exports: Quebec (48%), Ontario (47%), B.C. (45%), P.E.I. (40%), Nova Scotia (40%), and Alberta (39%). Three provinces, Newfoundland, New Brunswick and Saskatchewan, as well as the northern territories, find their largest markets outside Canada. The export market is the destination for 51 per cent of Newfoundlands's output of goods. For New Brunswick and Saskatchewan, exports account for 42 and 46 per cent respectively of goods sold. Only Manitoba's sales to other provinces (41%) are greater than sales within the province (35%) and sales abroad (24%). The importance of secondary markets varies significantly for each province.

For the purpose of considering the secondary markets, we turn first to those provinces for which the internal provincial market is the largest of the three destinations for goods. In Ontario and Quebec, where about half of the output is first sold within the province, the remainder is evenly divided between shipments to other provinces and exports (25% and 28%, and 28% and 24% respectively). British Columbia's exports (40%) are nearly as important as its intraprovincial sales (45%), and its shipments to other Canadian provinces and the northern territories (15%) are relatively small. For the three other provinces in this group, Prince Edward Island, Nova Scotia and Alberta, British Columbia's pattern for secondary markets is reversed: the interprovincial Canadian market is the destination for more provincially produced goods than the export market.

For the three provinces for which the largest markets are outside Canada, again, the relative importance of the secondary markets is varied. For New Brunswick and Saskatchewan, intraprovincial markets and shipments to other Canadian regions are approximately equal in importance. Newfoundland's intraprovincial markets (absorbing 28% of production) are more significant than markets in the rest of Canada (21%). This pattern is even stronger for the northern territories, where internal sales (31%) are significantly more important than shipments to the rest of Canada (8%).

Only for Manitoba and Saskatchewan do sales to other provinces exceed sales within the province, although Saskatchewan is significantly more export oriented than Manitoba. In this one sense then, Manitoba's economy seems to be the most directly bound up with the future of the Canadian economic union. Yet intraprovincial sales (29%) and interprovincial trade (29%) are of equal significance for New Brunswick. Prince Edward Island, Alberta and Nova Scotia depend almost as much, relatively speaking, on sales to other provinces as they do on their internal provincial markets, so one should probably group these provinces with Manitoba as well.

An alternative view of the Canadian economic union may be formed by examining a province's sources of supply of goods and services. Table 22-3, which details the source of goods by province for 1979, distinguishes among internal supply, purchases from other provinces, and imports from abroad. With some interesting differences from production of goods, similar patterns are apparent. Ontario and Quebec dominate in an absolute sense as they did in relation to the destination analysis shown in Table 22-2, although not by as wide a margin. Together these two provinces receive half of all goods shipped

TABLE 22-3 Source of Goods by Province, 1979

	('000 $ and per cent)							
	Total		Within Province		Rest of Canada		Imports	
	Value	Per Cent	Value	Per Cent	Value	Per Cent	Value	Per Cent
Newfoundland	2 576 130	100	638 090	25	1 526 240	59	411 800	16
P.E.I.	601 020	100	147 810	25	391 900	65	61 340	10
Nova Scotia	5 786 830	100	1 650 170	29	2 156 050	37	1 890 620	33
New Brunswick	5 109 040	100	1 148 780	22	2 197 990	43	1 762 880	34
Quebec	50 593 240	100	21 922 860	43	12 564 480	25	16 105 890	32
Ontario	87 302 180	100	40 001 260	46	14 797 690	17	32 503 300	37
Manitoba	7 092 600	100	2 142 540	30	3 214 940	45	1 735 110	24
Saskatchewan	6 400 660	100	1 681 270	26	3 339 230	52	1 380 170	22
Alberta	21 555 330	100	10 186 620	47	7 047 430	33	4 321 280	20
British Columbia	22 085 430	100	9 882 070	45	6 238 300	28	5 965 050	27
Yukon & N.W.T.	664 730	100	201 310	30	391 640	59	71 780	11
Canada	209 767 190	100	89 602 780	43	53 865 850	26	66 298 620	32

Source: Statistics Canada, Input-Output Division, Interprovincial Trade Flow Data, 1979.

Note: Totals may not add to a hundred because of rounding.

interprovincially, as compared to the 63 per cent of goods they ship out. Alberta and British Columbia account for another one-quarter of such sales. The rest is distributed among the remaining, smaller economies.

While nationally, 32 per cent of goods were imported, international suppliers are not the principal source of goods for any province. Ontario, Quebec, British Columbia and Alberta supplied the largest portion of their goods locally. The other six provinces and the northern territories purchased more goods from other parts of Canada than from abroad or from suppliers in other provinces.

The preceding information can be combined to calculate interprovincial and international trade balances for each province. The results of the calculations for 1979 are reported for goods alone in Table 22-4, and for goods and services combined in Table 22-5. In these tables we can more clearly see the implications of what the Canadian economic union means for each province. The tables also provide some insight into the debates over how "fair" Confederation is to individual regions.

A trade deficit, denoted in the tables by means of a minus sign, indicates that a province is consuming more than it is producing: that is, its consumption exceeds its output. In the long-run, this deficit must be off-set by transfers of funds from other parts of the country. Conversely, an overall trade surplus means that the region must either be accumulating financial claims on non-residents, or there must be a policy-induced transfer of funds out of the region. Thus the trade aspects of the Canadian economic union are directly related to the fiscal transfers reviewed in a later section of this chapter.

As Table 22-4 indicates, only Alberta and Saskatchewan show a surplus on overall trade in goods. Alberta shows a positive balance on both internal and external transactions, while Saskatchewan's success in international markets offsets a deficit in trade with other provinces. In 1979, all other provinces in Canada consumed more in the way of primary and secondary products than they produced. For three of these, Nova Scotia, New Brunswick and Manitoba, this was true for both interprovincial and international trade. In Newfoundland, Prince Edward Island, Saskatchewan, British Columbia and the northern territories, a positive balance with foreign nations partially offset a deficit with other Canadian regions. For central Canada, the situation was exactly the reverse. Large external deficits were covered, in part, by a surplus of sales over purchases from other provinces.

In Table 22-5, which adds trade in services, the picture alters somewhat. Now all four Western provinces show a surplus, selling more than they import. Alberta does so both nationally and internationally. British Columbia and Saskatchewan sell more in export markets than they import from abroad, but buy more from other provinces than they sell to them. Manitoba reverses the record of British Columbia and Saskatchewan. Nova Scotia shows a deficit both internationally and interprovincially.

As to trade within Canada, four provinces, Quebec, Ontario, Manitoba and Alberta, were net sellers of goods and services to the other six. In international trade, Newfoundland, Prince Edward Island, New Brunswick, Saskatchewan, Alberta and British Columbia produced surplus trade

TABLE 22-4 Trade Balances on Goods by Province, 1979

	('000 $)		
	Balance with Other Provinces	Balance on External Trade	Overall Balance
Newfoundland	−1 030 980	767 480	−263 500
P.E.I.	−248 780	14 910	−233 870
Nova Scotia	−755 130	−826 810	−1 581 940
New Brunswick	−1 081 900	−103 560	−1 185 460
Quebec	551 330	−5 174 660	−4 623 330
Ontario	6 123 040	−8 724 370	−2 601 330
Manitoba	−711 220	−232 180	−943 400
Saskatchewan	−1 438 830	1 682 330	243 500
Alberta	2 009 370	2 694 710	4 704 080
British Columbia	−3 079 780	2 736 900	−342 280
Yukon and N.W.T.	−337 160	329 420	−7 440

Source: Calculated from Statistics Canada, Input-Output Division, Interprovincial Trade Flow Data, 1979.

TABLE 22-5 Trade Balances on Goods and Services by Province, 1979

	('000 $)		
	Balance with Other Provinces	Balance on External Trade	Overall Balance
Newfoundland	−1 174 790	878 400	−296 390
P.E.I.	−275 790	24 140	−251 650
Nova Scotia	−850 880	−871 870	−1 722 750
New Brunswick	−1 264 960	173 380	−1 091 580
Quebec	218 660	−4 294 840	−4 076 180
Ontario	7 463 330	−7 357 420	−105 910
Manitoba	108 350	−55 790	52 560
Saskatchewan	−1 862 010	2 087 500	225 490
Alberta	1 710 800	2 984 310	4 695 110
British Columbia	−3 683 430	4 114 790	431 360
Yukon and N.W.T.	−389 280	343 790	−45 490

Source: Calculated from Statistics Canada, Input-Output Division, Interprovincial Trade Flow Data, 1979.

balances, as did the northern territories. The other four provinces produced deficits.

This pattern of overall trade imbalances has changed since 1974.[2] Ontario moved from a large surplus to a small deficit in 1979. This shift reflects the dramatic change in energy prices and the consequent large outflow of funds to the oil-producing provinces. The only other notable changes are shifts in Manitoba and British Columbia from deficit to surplus. While British Columbia's surplus reflects energy developments, the shift in Manitoba's trade pattern is more difficult to explain, although it, too, probably reflects spin-offs of Western energy development.

Two general conclusions from this brief overview of the pattern of production and trade within the Canadian economic union help inform subsequent sections of this chapter. First, interprovincial movements of goods and services are a small portion – about one-fifth – of the total activity of the Canadian economy. As Commissioners explain subsequently, we do not believe that these movements are restrained significantly by existing barriers. Secondly, the position of individual provinces within the economic union varies significantly, most notably in the discrepancies between sales to other provinces and purchases from them.

Market Integration and the Concept of the Economic Union

An economic union represents an advanced stage of economic integration. It involves the removal of customs duties among participating jurisdictions, the creation of a common external tariff, the elimination of barriers to the free movement of goods and the factors of production (labour and capital), and the harmonization of economic policies. In addition, in an economic union, certain policies which were previously the responsibility of the participating jurisdictions are transferred to, or co-ordinated through, a central authority.

Canada was intended to be, and has clearly become, much more than an economic union. It is useful, nevertheless, to employ the concepts and principles associated with the theory of economic unions to analyse interprovincial economic and political linkages within the Canadian federation. Accordingly, we must be concerned with the internal flows of goods, services, labour and capital, as well as with government policies in the form of distortions and barriers that affect those flows, and with the purposes or justifications for those policies.

The concept of distortion is very broad, including any policy which interferes with the resource-allocation functions of the market, thereby preventing the free flow of capital, labour or goods and reducing the advantages that can be gained from specialization and exchange. We shall concern ourselves here with those government interventions that distort interprovincial trade or factor flows in the sense that observed exchanges are different from what they would be in a totally unfettered environment. We shall not examine intraprovincial distortions which may affect the nature of economic activity within provinces.

Some policies, appropriately termed "barriers", restrict transactions among provinces; when this happens, the economic costs can be identified as

unexploited gains from trade. These gains constitute the traditional concerns of economic unions. Other types of policies may have the effect of augmenting interprovincial trade. Sometimes this outcome is intentional, as, for example, the decision in 1973 to divert Western oil supplies from U.S. markets to Eastern Canada. Sometimes it is only an incidental effect of a policy directed to other ends. Tariffs, for instance, are used to promote industrial development, but in a country of specialized regional economies, external tariffs increase the volume of internal trade. In these instances, it is much more difficult to identify the economic costs, as these costs are a complex mixture of diverted trade, extra transportation charges and the like. Typically, there is also an interregional distribution effect which, politically at least, often dominates efficiency concerns.

The concern about "maintaining", "protecting", "preserving" or "ensuring" the Canadian economic union is not new. As early as the 1930s, the concern about an emerging Canadian "tax jungle" was paralleled by concerns about "obstacles" to trade within Canada. The *Report* of the Royal Commission on Dominion-Provincial Relations (the Rowell-Sirois Commission) addressed the issue directly:

> *The member states of a federation at the outset are likely to be states which have imposed tariff barriers and, perhaps, other obstacles as well, to their trade with one another. These states or provinces after federation are apt to reach a stage of development at which there is bound to be political pressure in favour of some form of local protectionism. The desire to maintain and to augment the provincial revenue, to develop new industries, to ensure employment during a period of depression, to protect wage levels and working conditions against "unfair competition" or "social dumping", may all, at one time or another, contribute to this demand for local protectionism, which may appear even in municipal politics.*[3]

As the range of governmental concerns has broadened, and as the resources and policy instruments available to governments have increased in the post-Second World War period, the potential for such protectionist policies has grown dramatically.

The current interest in the integrity of the economic union emerged prominently during the constitutional discussions of 1979 and 1980. Debate was fuelled by a number of dramatic examples of provincial protectionism and by reaction to more aggressive provincial economic development strategies. The focus on internal barriers to trade united two developments: the political concerns of the federal government and some provinces about the implications of provincial protectionism, and the renewed interest among policy makers in the importance of the free market as the engine of growth. The latter concern was as much related to federal intervention in the economy as to that of the provinces.

The anticipated benefits of forming an economic union are the potential gains from specialization and trade, based on the theory of comparative advantage. In the Canadian context, the varying economic bases in the different regions of the country create different comparative advantages and hence the opportunity for mutually profitable interregional trade. Where

economies of scale in production are important, and the individual regions are small, the gains from trade can be that much greater. The greater the harmony in such policy areas as product standards, labelling requirements and consumer-protection laws, the larger will be the gains. Further gains are possible if the participants in the economic union, by exploiting some bargaining power that no member alone possesses, can shift the international terms of trade in their favour.

By preventing trade flows that would otherwise occur, internal barriers preclude the gains from specialization and exchange. The region that imposes them will have to produce products or services itself, thereby using more resources than necessary because of its comparative disadvantage. The costs of the barrier, then, are equal to the difference between what could be produced or supplied if resources were allocated optimally and what actually is produced. This represents an economic loss in the sense that it involves real output forgone which can never be recouped. The greater the volume of trade suppressed by these barriers, the more the potential benefits of an economic union will be dissipated.

Trade liberalization within Canada does not mean that every possible combination of interregional exchange will generate a surplus. Nor does it imply that even where a surplus results, it will be the largest possible for any given member. Benefits are critically dependent on the nature of the economies of members of the economic union, relative to the economies of non-participating jurisdictions, and on the most likely option to the existing or proposed arrangement. Economic gains, or "trade creation", occur when the opening of trade results in production being shifted from high-cost local suppliers to lower-cost sources elsewhere within the economic union. The larger market also allows producers to take advantage of the economies of scale associated with larger production runs. However, if imports switch from lower-cost external sources to higher-cost sources within the economic union, trade is said to be "diverted". The fact that some members may be internationally cost competitive in their main outputs, while others are not, suggests the possibility that an internal market with a common external tariff can produce unequal regional advantages for its members.

The second facet of common-market economic integration deals with factor markets: labour and capital. Interregional factor mobility can also add to national output. At any given moment, a nation has a fixed supply or endowment of capital and labour, distributed among its various regions. Total output will be at a maximum when the values of the contributions of the last units of capital and labour employed are identical across regions. Under certain conditions, free mobility will generate this optimal interregional distribution of factors. If capital and labour are paid the value of their contribution to output, any differences in productivity across regions will be reflected in wages or rates of return. Assuming that at least some workers or owners of capital perceive the potential gain and react to it, the reallocation will be made. As migrants leave a region, the contribution of those remaining rises, since there is a greater supply of capital and resources per worker. For the corresponding reason, the relative contribution of workers falls in the destination area. Since these changes will be reflected in factor rewards, the

theory is that migration should continue until all wage differences, and hence all real productivity differences, are removed. If there are real costs to migration, a gap will remain, but the result will still represent an optimal factor distribution, provided that prices and wages are flexible.

The potential cost of barriers is also evident in relation to the integration of factor markets. Barriers which stop migration short of the point where factor prices are equalized prevent some economically efficient movements. Total national output will be lower than it might be, since factors which could be more productive in another region are prevented from relocating. The difference between actual gross national product (GNP) and its potential in a free factor-flow situation represents the economic cost of the impediments. Whether these costs are justified in terms of overall well-being depends on the values attached to the maintenance of local communities and their preferences for a distinctive pattern of life, including distinctive public services.

An additional, though indirect, contribution of free factor mobility to aggregate output comes about through the role that mobility plays in the interregional adjustment process. Regional economies will grow at different rates because of the uneven effects of such developments as technological change or shifts in the terms of trade. Individually, each region would have to adjust to such dislocations internally, generally through some combination of changes in prices, incomes and employment. Adjustments through the exchange rate are impossible because of the absence of regional currencies. Since wages and prices are typically "sticky" downwards, the brunt of the adjustment in declining areas will be in the form of unemployment.

If factors are free to relocate between regions, however, there is a further avenue of adjustment to external shocks which reduces the extent of internal adjustment required. Migration provides the opportunity for residents of regions adversely affected to benefit directly from some of the gains of those more favourably situated. If it is possible for people to relocate, there is less need to worry about diversifying employment possibilities in each region. Free factor mobility provides a type of employment insurance, permitting the fullest possible gains from interregional specialization and trade. Those unlucky enough to be caught in a declining industry in one region can move to expanding industries located in another. This insurance feature is even more pronounced if the economic union provides, as most do, for regional adjustment assistance. Thus interregional mobility, like freedom of trade, is an integral feature of any economic union, permitting optimal allocation of resources within the national economy and easing the costs of adjustment to economic shocks.

These, then, are the basic concepts to be derived from the theory of economic integration. They illustrate the conditions under which integrating product and factor markets across regions can increase aggregate output and thus, by inference, how interprovincial barriers can obviate such gains.

This economic perspective is reason enough for Canadians to be concerned about the state of the economic union. To the desire to maximize economic well-being, however, must be added the political objectives of an economic union. Barriers to mobility and trade may weaken our sense of national identity. From this perspective, Canadians would oppose fragmentation of the

economic union, even if we were assured that the direct economic costs were negligible.

Political opposition to fragmentation has several dimensions. It is derived, in part, from a sense of common citizenship, which involves both individual and commercial expectations of a broad stage on which to pursue economic opportunity and personal development:

> *Just as all Canadians should be free to seek work and operate freely anywhere in the country, Canadian businesses should be allowed to compete on an open and fair basis anywhere in the country.*
>
> (Maclean Hunter Limited, Brief, November 14, 1983, p. 6.)

The political arguments for economic union also involve a sense of national community, perhaps a sense of place in a complex international environment, and an appreciation of the necessity for sharing risks and opportunities amongst its members:

> *The Economic Council of New Brunswick retains the vision of an independent Canada and of a society with a distinct identity. For us, to be Canadians is to recognize and support free trade across the whole of Canada, unimpeded by barriers imposed by the law or by big business; but it is also to recognize the necessity for a fairer sharing of the rewards of this efficiency which we expect to attain.*
>
> (*Conseil économique du Nouveau Brunswick Inc.*, Brief, September 13, 1983, p. 6.)

Political criteria lead Canadians to think somewhat differently about the economic union than pure market criteria would suggest. The only market justification for a barrier is its correction of an already existing one. Moreover, economic theory does not distinguish between Canadian economic union and any other kind. Indeed, its logic asserts that the larger the market, the better. It argues, too, that multilateral free trade would make our worry about the domestic market less pressing. In contrast, the political view of the market is explicitly concerned with the Canadian economy and its health. It was a political view of the Canadian economic union which produced the national policy and which justified the decision to build a railway across a continent. An economic view of the economic union asserts that integration within Canada is merely a "second-best" alternative to involvement in a multi-national market. A political view argues that building economic linkages among Canadians is of value in itself, and that it increases personal contacts and relationships among Canadians which contribute to a sense of shared identity and common citizenship. It also adds a great many other considerations, such as equality, social justice, a clean environment and other social goals, to the assessment of well-being. Thus, it potentially justifies a much wider variety of what economists call "distortions" including, most notably, policies such as equalization that are intended to ensure a fair regional distribution of benefits and regional economic development policies designed to enhance the contribution of regional economies to the national welfare.

The previous reference to a political concern for provincial/regional economies and communities makes it clear that the political criteria

applicable to the evaluation of barriers and distortions differ from economic criteria in supporting two distinct perspectives. These perspectives reflect the values that Canadians place on the national community, on the one hand, and on provincial communities, on the other. From the perspective of the national community, barriers which may be trivial in economic terms may be politically significant if they offend against our sense of Canadian citizenship. From the provincial perspective, barriers which many would oppose for economic reasons because they generate significant economic costs for Canadians, may be considered politically desirable by others because they strengthen provincial communities. These alternative political criteria not only differ from economic criteria in the policies to which they lead, but also differ from each other. This tension between national and provincial political criteria with respect to evaluating the economic union is inherent in federalism.

With these considerations in mind, Commissioners turn to the legal dimensions of the economic union.

Constitutional Protections

The basic elements of the Canadian economic union are found in the Constitution Act, 1867. Section 121 eliminated customs duties and other similar duties among the provinces: "All Articles of the Growth, Produce, or Manufacture of any one of the Provinces shall, from and after the Union, be admitted free into each of the other Provinces."

The Courts have interpreted this section as a general principle applicable to both orders of government, forbidding the erection of tariff barriers to the free circulation of goods among the provinces. The actions of the central government have tended to be less rigorously examined, since that government is presumed to act in the national interest. Furthermore, section 121 applies only to trade in goods; it does not apply to factors such as capital and labour, and it is uncertain whether it would apply to services and non-tariff barriers.

In spite of the existence of section 121, it has been more common for the Courts to use section 91(2) – the regulation of trade and commerce – to invalidate provincial legislation restricting interprovincial trade of goods. To maintain the appropriate balance between Parliament and the legislatures, however, the Supreme Court has recognized the provincial power to regulate some aspects of trade within the province, even in cases where the interprovincial flow of goods was affected by provincial production controls, marketing schemes, the creation of monopolies, and the like. The efficacy of sections 121 and 91(2) has been further limited because these sections can more easily be employed to focus on legislative and regulatory interventions of governments, rather than on administrative aspects such as purchasing policies and grant giving. On the other hand, the exclusive jurisdiction of Parliament over interprovincial and international transport systems greatly reduces the likelihood that policies would be formed in the field of transportation which could be detrimental to the free movement of goods within Canada.

The provisions for the free flow of goods in the economic union have recently been augmented by provisions with respect to the mobility of labour. Section 6 of the Canadian Charter of Rights and Freedoms assures the individual of the right to settle and earn a living anywhere in Canada. This provision of the Charter which deals with the mobility of labour automatically deals in part with the issue of constitutional protection for interprovincial trade in services. However, there are qualifications on the constitutional protection of personal mobility. Moreover, section 6 of the Charter does not clearly address the issue of services that may be provided across provincial borders without the need for personal mobility. Technology makes it possible for such services as information processing, counselling and professional advice of a legal or financial nature to be provided almost anywhere in Canada from a fixed location. This component of the service economy within the Canadian economic union does not now enjoy a secure constitutional safeguard.

The possibility that section 121 may be interpreted as applying to services and to non-tariff barriers is suggested by the opinion of Justice Rand of the Supreme Court of Canada in *Murphy* v. *CPR*.[4] Justice Rand used the words "fetters" and "impediments" rather than the traditional language of customs duties or taxes. He emphasized the importance of the free flow of "commerce" within Canada, rather than the narrower concept of articles, goods or products:

> *I take section 121, apart from custom duties, to be aimed against trade regulation which is designed to place fetters upon or raise impediments to or otherwise restrict or limit the free flow of commerce across the Dominion as if provincial boundaries did not exist.*

Commissioners would favour a broad reading of section 121 that includes protection from tariff barriers for the free flow of services within the Canadian economic union. Present uncertainty regarding the interpretation of section 121, however, inclines us to support in principle a constitutional amendment to clarify the situation. As an interim measure, guidelines developed through intergovernmental discussion and negotiation are desirable to preclude the development of tariff barriers to internal trade in services. We examine shortly procedures for responding to the problems of non-tariff barriers applicable to both goods and services within the Canadian economic union.

The Constitution deals with the free flow of capital through the division of powers; it gives the federal government primary jurisdiction, including responsibility for currency and exclusive power to regulate the banks, comprehensive power in the field of taxation, and other general powers applicable to capital flows. Provinces have regulatory authority over "near-banks": institutions such as trust companies and credit unions. Provinces also have some power to control capital inflows, derived from their jurisdiction over resources, local enterprises, land use, and their extensive regulatory and other authority pertaining to property and civil rights; this last includes control over securities markets, pension funds and insurance.

Internal Barriers to Trade

As the preceding section has shown, the constitutional framework, while providing the essential guarantees of an economic union, has some important gaps and ambiguities which have permitted a wide variety of impediments to grow up. Here Commissioners identify a few distortions that significantly affect the free flow of goods and factors in Canada.[5] A survey of the policies involved may give the impression that any and all deviations from pure free movement of goods and factors of production are inherently bad. If that were so, our job would be simple: we would write a cast-iron constitutional provision which would rule out all such deviations. If we were to do that, however, we would probably also be recommending an end to federalism or to any federal regional policies. In fact, of course, a great many barriers, federal and provincial, are justified on political or economic grounds.

Federal Government Policies and Interprovincial Trade

It is a common assumption that impediments to the free flow of trade are primarily, if not solely, a result of provincial government activity. Substantial distortions also result, however, from federal government actions. Historically, the most controversial federal distortion – one which "artificially" inflates trade among provinces and distorts the interregional terms of trade – is the tariff. The tariff has allowed manufacturers to sell greater volumes of domestically produced goods to consumers at higher prices than would otherwise be possible. Since production of manufactured goods has been concentrated in central Canada, while consumption is dispersed throughout the national market, the tariff results in an interregional redistribution of income.

Although these traditional concerns have been attenuated by the general drop in tariffs, they remain important. The recent voluntary restrictions on automobile imports and the continuation of import quotas on clothing give a further advantage to the manufacturing economies to the detriment of consumers. Such measures have stimulated strong misgivings in some regions.

Federal transportation policies, particularly the structure of rates, can also create economic distortions in the volume of interregional trade; nevertheless, there have been strong reasons to favour such policies in order to develop outlying regions. The subsidization of freight rates for the movement of statutory grains, which was in effect more or less continuously from 1897 to 1983, meant that Prairie farmers received a greater return per acre for growing those grains than they would otherwise have done.[6] Less grain was produced in other parts of Canada because of this statutory advantage, and as a side-effect, development of the livestock and food processing sectors in the West was discouraged.

The Western Grain Transportation Act, passed in 1983, allowed Canadian National and Canadian Pacific Railways to charge more for moving grain and to receive an annual subsidy. However, because the subsidy is still paid to the railways rather than to farmers, freight rates remain below the actual costs of moving grain; therefore there continues to be a disincentive to

diversify. Freight rates in Eastern and Atlantic Canada have also been subsidized, in an effort to promote interregional trade, although in recent years, this subsidy has been progressively reduced.

Certain features of Canadian energy policy in the last decade – price and export controls, and subsidies to energy exploration – are also relevant to the present review. Price controls have kept energy prices below world-market prices, thereby encouraging excessive consumption and hence interprovincial shipments of oil and natural gas. Export restrictions have diverted output from destinations in adjacent areas of the United States to locations in Eastern Canada. Subsidies for exploration have favoured frontier areas over established ones, thereby distorting the sequence and location of resource development. Recent energy-policy announcements are likely to attenuate such distortions.

Another source of federally induced distortions is government purchasing policy. In contrast to the examples cited above, purchasing policies have had the effect of restricting interprovincial trade. For this reason, the efficiency costs are more easily identified with the operation of the economic union. Federal government procurement is decentralized through the Regional Supply Centres of the Department of Supply and Services (DSS). These regional offices solicit bids from suppliers within specific "geographic bidding areas", subject to such considerations as cost and availability of competent suppliers. Bidding practices are intended to ensure " . . . equity of opportunity to compete for government business by all competent suppliers in the area or region." In addition, when the purchase is made by DSS headquarters, but the product is to be used in the Western or Atlantic provinces, purchases are to be made from suppliers in those regions, subject to cost factors.[7]

Other federal policies could be discussed in light of their significance for the operation of the economic union. As federal governments have increasingly used tax laws, grants and other provisions to stimulate particular sectors or activities such as research and development, the possibility of regional distortions has grown, since these activities are often regionally concentrated. The granting of industrial subsidies to promote regional development has been an explicit attempt to influence the locational decisions relating to projects.

Federal-Provincial Policies

On occasion, both orders of government act together to create policies that impede interprovincial trade. National agricultural marketing boards, for example, create barriers by introducing rigidity into patterns of production or imposing restrictive regulations.

National supply-management boards are of particular interest. Such boards are established pursuant to the Farm Products Marketing Agencies Act. Products come under the scheme if there is substantial agreement among producers, and the Minister of Agriculture acts. Once a product is brought within the scope of legislation, the relevant federal agency can delegate authority to designated provincial bodies. Overall quotas are allocated to each

provincial body, which then sets out quotas for specific producers. Currently, the production of eggs, chickens, turkeys and tobacco is regulated under these arrangements.

Such market sharing contributes to rigidity in production patterns. Low-cost producers are effectively prohibited from selling into neighbouring areas. Regional quotas are allocated in proportion to total Canadian production over the previous five years. Quotas are not altered, even if the costs of production change, unless the governing bodies decide to vary them. The Act requires that the agency consider the principle of comparative advantage in allocating quotas, but for the production of chickens, eggs and turkeys, the emphasis is on provincial self-sufficiency rather than economic efficiency. In effect, producers cannot produce more than their assigned quotas, and the market is closed to new producers.

Provincial Policies

One of our intervenors described a general concern about provincial policies:

> *Each province, in an effort to enhance the position of its own producers, engages in practices which tend to limit the free movement of goods within Canada. Examples are product promotions, tendering preferences, marketing legislation. Each of these and similar instances may be quite laudable in themselves. But the number and the frequency is growing. The result will be a fragmenting of the Canadian marketplace — a marketplace that is greater than the sum of its provincial parts.* (Canadian Meat Council, Brief, October 27, 1983, p. 14.)

Provincial governments create distortions by imposing provincial trade barriers. By examining major provincial barriers, Commissioners can try to distinguish deliberately discriminatory policies from those incidental to the pursuit of legitimate provincial social or economic objectives.

Provincial governments, as buyers of goods and services, have shown a tendency to favour local producers of those goods and services. In 1981, purchases of goods and services by provincial and local governments, and hospitals, amounted to the equivalent of 15.2 per cent of gross national product. A preferential purchasing policy may be implicit or explicit, a matter of practice or of law. The usual methods of preferential procurement involve selective or single tender instead of public tender; inadequate publicity or information on bidding, through the use of local source lists; short time limits for the submission of bids; performance requirements tailored to what local businesses can provide; residence requirements for vendors; and preferential margins for local suppliers.

These policies may reach beyond purchases made by governmental agencies and departments to include purchases made by hydro companies, municipal public transit, school systems, railways, airlines, telephone companies, and resource industries characterized by provincial ownership or involvement. A recent study by the Canadian Manufacturers' Association (CMA) indicates the kinds of problems that can emerge. The four Canadian firms manufacturing wire and cable for use in telecommunications, for

example, operate 16 plants, located in every province except Prince Edward Island and Newfoundland. They must establish a regional presence to qualify as suppliers to provincial telephone companies. In the CMA's view, three or four plants would be more efficient and better able to compete internationally.

All provinces have a public monopoly in the sale of liquor. Three types of liquor policies create barriers to interprovincial trade. Provinces may discriminate against out-of-province producers by supporting local products. This discrimination may include preferences in advertising support, in shelf-positioning at retail liquor outlets, in listing requirements, and in pricing policies. Preferential pricing, for instance, has the same function as an internally applied tariff. Furthermore, governments may limit private purchases from other provinces by imposing a quota system or by levying taxes on purchases. Finally, a province may have special packaging requirements that make it too costly for out-of-province products to enter the market. One surprising consequence of provincial regulation of alcoholic beverages, for example, is that consumers in the state of Washington can buy Old Fort beer from Prince George, B.C., and New Englanders can buy New Brunswick's Moosehead, but many Canadian provinces sell neither.

Provincial industrial policies designed to promote economic development often include subsidies and incentives that can harm out-of-province producers. Incentives to direct investment have included financial assistance through grants, loans, tax holidays and loan guarantees; direct equity participation; and provision of infrastructure at public expense. A host of federal programs of industrial assistance have similar, but much broader, effects, though they are often implemented jointly with provinces.

Provincial governments have established a vast range of regulations that also affect interprovincial trade. They have done so, primarily through their jurisdiction over "property and civil rights" and trade within the province. Among these regulations are standards for building or construction, for products and for the environment, and of commercial contract law. This Commission heard of the following case:

> *[An example of problems in interprovincial trade] is the situation that arose when the local tomato crop in Essex County was ready for harvesting and packed in litre baskets according to the new federal legislation for shipment to the Quebec market, which takes a rather substantial amount of the Essex County crop, only to have it refused there on the grounds that the province of Quebec still insisted on the old measurement methods and insisted on bushel baskets rather than litres.*
>
> (Windsor-Essex County Development Commission, Transcript, Windsor, October 18, 1983 [vol. 27], p. 5258.)

In addition, some professional licensing practices affect trade in services. All these measures can impose additional costs on buyers and sellers operating across provincial boundaries, and they may well inhibit the development of markets across Canada that would otherwise occur.

In all the above ways, federal and provincial policies, amounting to the imposition of non-tariff barriers (NTBs), can operate detrimentally to affect

the operation of the Canadian economic union. When the volume of interregional trade is reduced by NTBs to a level below what it would otherwise be, the costs to the economic union equal the extra resource costs of failure to exploit fully the gains from trade and specialization.

The Costs of Interprovincial Barriers to Trade

Economic analysis typically shows that distortions of the sort we have described have a small effect on output costs. Various calculations estimate that welfare losses for 1974 fell between a low of $130 million, or 0.11 per cent of gross national product (GNP) and a high of $1750 million, or 1.54 per cent of GNP, depending on the assumptions made.[8] More recent work for this Commission reinforces the conclusion that the economic costs are small.[9] This is a field, however, where estimates are imprecise and controversial. In the foreign-trade field, for example, some recent estimates suggest that the gains from international trade liberalization may be much greater than earlier models suggested. The newer models attempt to take into account the significance of economies of scale. They might have equally dramatic effects if applied to the domestic market. Moreover, the question arises: How small is small? As one participant in our hearings observed, 1 per cent of GNP is "equivalent to the GDP of Newfoundland, not a trivial sum." (Anthony Scott, Brief, December 12, 1983, Appendix, p. 1.)

The explanation for the apparently low costs of barriers is straightforward. Table 22-2 shows that just slightly more than one-quarter of Canadian goods (27%) moves interprovincially. Barriers directly affect little of that portion; most products move quite freely. For those subject to restrictions, distortions in the form of preferences are typically quite small. The combination of generally small distortions applying to a subset of products that in turn make up only a quarter of the total national output, together with the economic methodology underlying the calculations, explain the low numbers.

As presentations made to this Commission have argued, however, measurable economic costs are not the whole story:

> *Discrimination based upon province of origin is not a basis upon which to make commercial awards of business when provincial governments or their agencies are involved . . . we would like to be able to compete freely and equally from St. John's to Vancouver with no impediments. We are quite happy with an open market competitive bid system. What we are not happy with is what we consider discriminatory and artificial constraints to [our] doing business within Canada . . . The bottom line is that it is easier to do business in the United States than it is in some of our provinces within Canada.*
>
> (J.D. Smart, Transcript, Toronto, December 7, 1983 [vol. 63], pp. 13173–74.)

This quotation suggests that the costs of barriers to trade may be extremely significant for individual firms, even if aggregate costs for the national economy do not appear to be large. Do these barriers seriously frustrate some individual firms as they buy and sell in the Canadian market? The presence of "economic union" in this Commission's mandate clearly invited private-sector groups to comment on barriers. Participants who did so in our hearings

were primarily engaged in the manufacturing sector, and principally from central Canada.

A survey of 651 manufacturing industries, conducted by the Canadian Manufacturers' Association, found that one-fifth had encountered difficulties in selling goods as a result of provincial restrictions. Larger firms seeking to serve the whole national market complained most. Restrictive policies may, in theory, help small firms, but the same survey showed that only 7 per cent of all firms and only 6 per cent of small ones reported any benefit from procurement rules. The CMA itself believes that proliferation of barriers slows growth in interprovincial trade. A CMA *Position Statement* declares that "we urge all governments to reverse the protectionist trend". Internal barriers, it argues, "cause firms to become increasingly dependent on government". Smaller firms can "fall into a vicious circle where they cannot compete outside the local market". In the CMA view, "our small, fragmented domestic market must be strengthened if Canadian industry is to optimize its efficiency to maximize its competitiveness".[10] If internal barriers scatter production over many small plants, how can we create the large, efficient firms which will succeed internationally? If sellers find that they cannot even count on access to the Canadian market, how can we expect them to be aggressive competitors on world markets?

Mobility of Capital

Although numerous controls pertaining to the transfer of assets or of corporate property have been established through the years, including regulations on certain public utilities and financial institutions, there have been few barriers to the free flow of capital in Canada. However, a number of incidents in the 1970s focused attention on the issue. In one case, the government of British Columbia blocked the take-over of MacMillan-Bloedel, a major forest-products firm, by Canadian Pacific Ltd. In another, the Quebec government moved to prevent acquisition of a trust company by extra-provincial interests. Both cases seemed to imply a concept of "provincial" capital versus "outside" capital, and both suggested that provincial governments wanted to protect strategic provincial interests just as the federal government acted towards foreign investment.

Could a province prevent capital from moving into its territory? In a legal direct sense the answer is probably no. But the provinces, like other governments, possess many levers which could be used to manipulate such movement. For example, provincial governments control access to provincial forest resources, and British Columbia could have used this leverage. Comparable issues have arisen with respect to land ownership. For example, Prince Edward Island wished to prevent properties along its shoreline from falling into the hands of non-residents and to keep prices from passing out of reach of provincial residents. Accordingly, it passed the Prince Edward Island Lands Protection Act to require non-residents purchasing such land in excess of 10 acres to gain prior approval of its Cabinet. Similarly, in order to preserve family farms, the Saskatchewan Farm Ownership Act limits the amount of farmland that can be held by non-residents or by "non-agricultural corporations".

Government attempts to restrict capital inflows have attracted a good deal of attention, though they are rarely a major concern. Far more important than these high-profile take-over bids are provincial measures to encourage capital either to enter or to remain in the province; these are designed to stimulate local growth. The chief concern is that provinces will embark on a bidding war for a limited supply of capital investment. It is not at all clear, however, whether any of the inducements provinces might use would lead to a misallocation of capital and thus to investments in activities less productive than other possible uses. As long as Canada remains open to international capital markets, provincial government inducements will rarely stand in the way of potentially productive projects in other regions. They might, nonetheless, lead to investment in projects that would not otherwise be financially possible.[11] From the perspective of the economic union, restrictions on capital mobility appear to be of comparatively limited significance, even though efficiency costs within a region might be substantial. In general, there are few restrictions on the mobility of privately held investment funds across provinces, and in an open economy such controls are unlikely to be imposed.

More important, perhaps, are the pools of investment capital that provinces can control more directly. These include the pools of capital created by the Alberta Heritage Savings Trust Fund, and by a similar, smaller, trust fund in Saskatchewan. Other provinces could create such institutions, depending on, for example, the success of oil and gas development off the shores of Newfoundland and Nova Scotia. In addition, provinces control the use of the money in their public pension funds. The most important such instance is Quebec's *Caisse de dépôt et de placement*, which manages both the money generated by the Quebec Pension Plan and that generated by the pension fund of Quebec public employees. Outside Quebec, funds associated with the Canada Pension Plan are allocated provincially.

Provincially-owned Crown corporations create additional pools of capital. In varying degrees, all of these promote development within the province. However, there are conflicts between advocates of a policy of investing accruing funds at market rates and thus allowing the Crown corporation to achieve a "good track record" and advocates of investing at lower rates in pursuit of specific policy goals, and a related conflict between viewing the agencies as autonomous bodies and considering them as instruments of government policy. If these agencies acquire control of major corporations, they could induce these corporations to locate facilities within the province or otherwise act to prejudice their other shareholders – in effect to "beggar their neighbour". Such concerns underlay the proposed federal Bill S-31, the Corporate Shareholding Limitation Act, which would have limited shareholding of provincial agencies in federally regulated transportation companies. Such dangers, however, seem more potential than actual. Provinces using their holdings in private corporations to "divert" activities to themselves might face not only the discipline of the market-place, but also retaliatory action by the federal or other provincial governments.

Why should provinces not use revenues generated by their own resources, such as Heritage Funds, to promote development? They may provide infrastructure or invest in activities not otherwise able to attract funds. The

investment policies of the Alberta Fund though much criticized, have husbanded revenue for the future and stimulated economic activity. Similarly, the *Caisse*, together with a network of other Quebec investment institutions, has helped to develop a strong, self-confident, francophone, business community which is now playing a larger role in Canada. Such developments, it can be argued, tend to strengthen Confederation, not weaken it. However, as Commissioners have noted earlier, if such funds are used to provide subsidies for local firms, they can harm out-of-province producers.

Another provincial activity that can impede mobility of capital and might contribute to a misallocation of funds is provision of inducements to private investors, through tax concessions, loan guarantees, grants and the like. All provinces use a wide variety of such incentives; all seek to encourage investment through provision of infrastructure and various services. Complementing such provincial programs is a similarly wide range of federal programs. Alberta claims that it withdrew from the Tax Collection Agreements to collect its own corporation income tax so that it could offer tax inducements to capital. Other provinces have considered such a move. Among the measures introduced or contemplated by various provinces are several that distort allocation of capital and the operation of the common market. In 1979, for example, Quebec introduced a program that allows its residents a tax deduction equivalent to the cost of purchasing new share issues in Quebec-based companies.[12] Provincial governments also have programs to stimulate small business. For most such programs, the amounts involved are limited; therefore, assuming open capital markets, their effect is likely to be over-investment in subsidized activities, rather than insufficient investment in productive uses elsewhere.

This last point suggests that our chief concern should be not with barriers to capital mobility, but with managing our capital markets to ensure an effective national market. Those seeking funds should be fully informed about potential capital sources, and those with capital should have the means to know about investment opportunities across the whole country.

Personal Mobility

Canada is a nation of immigrants, from the first aboriginals who crossed the Bering Strait, to the first French settlers of the St. Lawrence Valley, to the United Empire Loyalists, to the eastern Europeans and others who settled the West at the turn of the century, to the immigrants who have entered the country since the Second World War. We Canadians have also been mobile within our borders: eastern Canadians helped to populate the West; after the Second World War, prairie farmers moved to urban areas; more recently, Newfoundlanders have found jobs on western oil rigs. We have also been mobile across national borders: until the United States introduced strict immigration quotas in the 1960s, it often proved more of a lure to mobile Canadians than did other parts of Canada.

The 1981 Census, as Table 22-6 shows, indicated that just over six in ten Canadians more than five years old lived in the province in which they were born; one in eight Canadians were immigrants; the remaining quarter had

moved from another province. There are huge variations among provinces. Newfoundland, with 83 per cent of its residents born there, and Quebec with 88 per cent of provincially born residents, had the most stable populations. In the Maritime provinces, in Manitoba and in Saskatchewan, from 56 to 66 per cent of residents live in the province of their birth. In British Columbia and Alberta only about one-third of residents are native to the province, in the Northwest Territories, one-quarter and in Yukon, one-tenth.

TABLE 22-6 Proportion of Population 5 Years and Over Living in the Same Province as at Birth, 1981

	At Birth (%)	Born Abroad (%)
Canada	61.1	13.3
Newfoundland	83.0	2.4
P.E.I.	56.0	5.5
Nova Scotia	59.7	6.8
New Brunswick	63.0	5.0
Quebec	87.9	6.4
Ontario	62.8	19.5
Manitoba	60.2	8.4
Saskatchewan	66.4	6.2
Alberta	35.0	11.8
British Columbia	37.9	18.6
Yukon	10.6	11.4
N.W.T.	23.1	8.6

Source: Calculations made using data from Statistics Canada, *Mobility Status*, Cat. No. 92-907 (Ottawa), vol. 1, table 6, pp. 6-1 to 6-6.

Between 1972 and 1984, an average of 380 000 persons a year moved across provincial boundaries: that is, about 15 for every 1000 Canadians.[13] Such figures conceal large variations in population flows in the past few years. As Table 22-7 shows, between 1971 and 1983, five provinces – Newfoundland, Quebec, Ontario, Manitoba and Saskatchewan – and the northern territories experienced net out-migration. During this period, the overall statistical record contradicts the traditional image of the Maritime provinces as a source of population for other regions. Conversely, Ontario, traditionally a magnet for mobile people, was a net loser of population through internal migration for most of the period 1971–81. Quebec experienced net population decline on the balance of internal migration in every year. On balance, Manitoba lost population to other provinces every year but one. Saskatchewan had a similar record for most years, though it gained more people from other provinces in the mid-1970s than it lost through out-migration.

Throughout the 1970s and early 1980s, Alberta and British Columbia experienced rapid population growth from internal migration, gaining 278 153 and 227 247 residents, respectively. These two provinces, as Table 22-8 records, were the destination for 40 per cent of all migrants from 1971–

TABLE 22-7 Balance of Internal Migration for Provinces and Territories, 1971–72 to 1982–83

Year	Nfld.	P.E.I.	N.S.	N.B.	Que.	Ont.	Man.	Sask.	Alta.	B.C.	Yukon and N.W.T.
1971–72	910	290	−371	612	−20 461	14 080	−8 311	−19 207	3 575	27 044	1 840
1972–73	−537	923	4 276	2 077	−20 072	960	−5 770	−16 164	5 564	27 333	1 410
1973–74	−3 316	502	1 274	1 448	−15 135	−2 886	−1 596	−11 604	2 235	30 496	−1 418
1974–75	495	1 390	2 233	6 103	−9 299	−29 535	−6 912	378	22 576	11 831	739
1975–76	591	649	3 895	6 561	−12 643	−21 179	−4 238	5 845	24 621	−4 419	317
1976–77	−4 149	154	−799	−82	−26 366	−6 402	−3 531	3 182	34 710	5 016	−1 733
1977–78	−4 311	700	−416	−1 348	−46 429	8 510	−4 674	−1 719	32 543	17 576	−432
1978–79	−3 374	−74	−357	−1 171	−30 884	−4 325	−10 746	−2 878	33 426	22 005	−1 622
1979–80	−3 597	−358	−2 732	−2 761	−29 976	−22 362	−13 864	−4 493	41 435	40 164	−1 456
1980–81	−3 552	−1 251	−2 836	−4 989	−22 841	−33 247	−9 403	−3 808	44 250	37 864	−187
1981–82	−5 693	−856	−1 936	−2 842	−25 790	−5 665	−2 625	−323	36 562	8 705	463
1982–83	1 665	209	1 428	2 491	−22 568	15 112	389	2 660	−3 344	3 632	−1 664
Total	-24 814	2 278	3 668	6 099	-280 464	-86 939	-71 281	-47 951	278 153	227 247	-3 743

Source: Statistics Canada based on data from *International and Interprovincial Migration in Canada*, Cat. No. 91-208 and Cat. No. 91-210 (Ottawa, various years).

TABLE 22-8 Percentage Distribution of Interprovincial Migration by Province of Origin and Destination, Average for 1971–72 to 1982–83

Province	Origin	Destination
Newfoundland	3.3	2.7
Prince Edward Island	1.0	1.0
Nova Scotia	5.6	5.7
New Brunswick	4.5	4.6
Quebec	13.9	7.6
Ontario	25.8	23.4
Manitoba	7.8	6.3
Saskatchewan	6.9	6.2
Alberta	15.8	22.5
British Columbia	13.6	18.3
Yukon and N.W.T.	1.8	1.7
Total	100	100

Source: Statistics Canada, based on data from *International and Interprovincial Migration in Canada*, Cat. No. 91-208 and Cat. No. 91-210 (Ottawa: various years).

72 to 1982–83. These patterns of internal migration reflected larger economic trends in the period. In 1970–71, for example, only 12.4 per cent of migrants leaving Ontario went to Alberta; but for the period 1970–71 to 1981–82, an average of 24.9 per cent entered that province. In 1971–72, fewer than 3000 Atlantic Canadians moved to Alberta; in 1981–82, over 14 000 did so. Following the slow-down in western resource development in 1982, these patterns reversed. In 1983 and 1984, Alberta was a net loser in interprovincial population movements. A return flow was evident, and Ontario and the Maritimes were once again recording net gains in in-migration.

Thus while we Canadians are a nation of regions and of settled communities, we are quite mobile. This mobility facilitates economic adjustment as individuals move from areas of lower to higher economic opportunity. It also spreads ideas, thus contributing to mutual awareness and understanding, and to a sense of citizenship. In addition, it allows citizens to respond to intergovernmental competition in policy by "voting with their feet", thus taking advantage of one of the virtues of federalism.

The British North America Act of 1867 did not formally enshrine the principle of the free circulation of persons within the Canadian economic union, although on occasion, the courts have found support for this principle in the common law. For example, in a decision[14] handed down in 1951, in the case of *Winner* v. *S.M.T. (Eastern) Ltd.*, Mr. Justice Ivan Rand of the Supreme Court stated that:

> *A province cannot, by depriving a Canadian of the means of working, force him to leave it: it cannot divest him of his right or capacity to remain and to engage in work there: that capacity inhering as a constituent element of his citizenship status is beyond nullification by provincial action.*

Section 6 of the Charter of Rights and Freedoms recognizes the right of all Canadian citizens and all permanent residents of Canada to move freely throughout the country and to earn a living in any province. This clause binds both Parliament and the Canadian government, as well as the provincial legislatures and governments. Yet there are limits to these rights of mobility, which we shall consider in Chapter 23 in the context of a more extended discussion of the Charter.

Economic incentives are the main forces shaping migration flows, particularly for Canadians in the labour force. Not surprisingly, there are more moves over relatively short distances than there are journeys across the entire country. People also tend to move from lower- to higher-income areas, and to be influenced by prospects for higher wages and better job opportunities.

Other factors or personal characteristics are also important. Better-educated citizens, for example, are more mobile. Language differences exercise a major influence over decisions to move: French-speaking Canadians now seldom move to English-speaking areas; and there is little movement of English-speakers into Quebec. Data indicate that on balance, French-speaking Quebec is gaining francophones as a result of interprovincial migration. Between 1971 and 1976, for example, net in-migration to Quebec was 4.5 per cent for francophones and 0.4 per cent for anglophones. Knowledge of English seems to be an important determinant in the contemporary decision either to stay in Quebec or to move to another province. A unilingual anglophone is much more likely to make such a move than a unilingual francophone. This is one reason why Quebec is gradually becoming a more French-speaking society. These data suggest that mobility depends largely on personal decisions, based on the expectations of individuals and families, and on their own cultural and linguistic characteristics.

Government policies, too, may influence the decision to migrate. For example, high levels of taxation at the provincial and municipal levels may encourage some people to move or deter them from doing so. Variations in "net fiscal benefits", a combination of levels of taxation and levels of services, appear to have encouraged migration to Alberta during the resource boom, independent of the relative decline in the Ontario economy and rapid development in the West. This type of influence may well become more decisive if provincial variation in taxation rates and government services continues to grow, especially in such highly visible areas as taxes on income and retail sales. To the extent that equalization and other transfers restrain divergence in tax rates, personal mobility will more likely respond to other economic signals and individual preferences.

As Commissioners have concluded earlier in this Report, there is also evidence that Unemployment Insurance benefits reduce the incentive for citizens to move in search of new job opportunities. The effect of other differences between provinces – licensing requirements for professionals, different school systems, and the like – is not easy to assess.

Finally, cultural factors themselves may be influenced by policy. The size and distribution of the population of francophone Canadians outside Quebec reflects, to a considerable extent, the relative absence throughout much of

Canadian history of sympathetic approaches to French-language minorities by the other provincial governments and their electorates. More recently, the federal government has sought to ensure rights of minority-language education and to provide its services in minority languages across Canada, partly in order to make it possible for French-speaking Canadians to be mobile outside Quebec without giving up their language.

To evaluate fully the effect of barriers to personal mobility in Canada, it would be necessary to know both the proportion of the labour force affected by those restrictions and the degree of their severity. The costs of such barriers would include the costs to individuals of relocating, despite restrictions, as well as the reduction in overall economic performance resulting from any labour shortages that can be attributed to the barriers. The complexity of the process of analysing certain types of mobility barriers accounts for the lack of data on the costs of existing restrictions on labour-force mobility. We can, however, provide illustrations of barriers to interprovincial mobility, and speculate generally on their implications for the economic union.[15]

A number of provinces have introduced guidelines or restrictions giving preference in employment to local residents. Some of these rules apply to private employers; others operate in the public sector. For example, regulations introduced in 1978, under Newfoundland's Petroleum and Natural Gas Act, provide that: "It is deemed to be a term of every permit or lease that a permittee or lessee shall give preference in his hiring practices to qualified persons normally resident in the province." The 1985 offshore-resources agreement between Canada and Newfoundland calls for "first consideration" to be given to goods and services provided in Newfoundland, where these are competitive in price, quality and delivery. Newfoundland residents are to receive "first consideration" for training and employment opportunities, "consistent with the Canadian Charter of Rights and Freedoms."

Other jurisdictions, too, have imposed restrictions. Mobility restrictions in the Quebec construction industry became the subject of interprovincial controversy a few years ago, even though the government had introduced them in response to problems within the provincial industry. Quebec and Nova Scotia extend preferences to provincial residents in hiring for the public service. The federal government has set down comparable requirements to promote employment opportunities for Northern residents in resource development. By extending procurement policies from goods to services, governments have created further restraints on labour mobility.

Some Canadians see licensing and certification requirements for certain trades and professions as threats to labour mobility:

> *Two closely inter-related problems pervade the area: lack of uniformity of standards between the provinces and lack of reciprocity (i.e. recognition of out-of-province training or experience).*[16]

Provincial governments confer licensing authority on professional associations in order that they may safeguard the public from injury or abuse. In turn, these associations may create barriers to exclude other professionals from

encroaching on their jurisdiction. It is not always easy, however, to distinguish requirements which ensure competence from those which discriminate against non-residents seeking entry. In trades, licensing and certification requirements are often simply voluntary; provisional certification is frequently available, and the provinces may soon agree to recognize trade qualifications obtained under an Interprovincial Standards Examination.

Lack of portability of private pension plans deters labour mobility and thus may affect interprovincial mobility and transfers of workers among employers. As the loss of accumulated pension benefits has already attracted attention in other studies, Commissioners do not pursue this issue. Loss of entitlement to social services during a period of requalification and provincial income-support schemes may also inhibit interprovincial mobility. In provinces where municipalities administer such programs, local practices may limit eligibility for benefits in ways that deter mobility. The conditions established for the shared-cost Canada Assistance Plan, however, ensure a high degree of protection against such discriminatory measures as residence requirements.

Differences in educational systems across Canada may also deter potential migrants concerned about disruption of their children's education. Limited studies of this difficulty suggest that incompatibilities among educational systems are not a major deterrent to interprovincial mobility. Indeed, differences in educational criteria and standards can occur within a province, as well as among provinces.

Established social, cultural and community ties inhibit interprovincial labour mobility in Canada. Of the cultural ties, language appears to be the most significant. Quebec's Charter of the French Language may well deter the relocation to Quebec of Canadians who do not speak French, or of those who, because of the combined effects of the Quebec Charter and the Canadian Charter of Rights and Freedoms must forgo the right to have their children educated in English if that is their preference. In addition, the tendency of francophone Quebecers to become increasingly unilingual restricts their mobility outside the province, where there are few jobs for unilingual francophones:

> *However painful it may be, workers from the Maritimes have only to change their location if they move to Toronto. Such mobility does not endanger the survival of the English Canadian community in general. For Quebec, however, [such] a move virtually corresponds to expatriation.*
>
> (*Conseil Exécutif National du Parti Québécois*, Brief, December 7, 1983, p. 30.)

Official bilingualism in other provinces, generous minority-language education and a network of French-language/communication services across Canada would facilitate mobility for French-speaking Canadians. Commissioners have no illusions that it is possible to establish throughout Canada, fully bilingual cultural milieux in which francophones would find permanent cultural and linguistic security. Nevertheless, both ongoing adjustment to economic change and the securing of social justice require provision of official-language services and related institutional support across Canada.

This development is needed to facilitate at least temporary movement by francophone Canadians to employment opportunities in various regions of the country if they so wish. Similarly, corresponding language facilities in English and better training in French will facilitate movement of anglophones into Quebec.

Migration can ease interregional adjustment and smooth out disparities in employment and wages. The persistence of such disparities might suggest that the mechanism is not working well. Some of these differences, however, reflect location preferences and migration costs, and thus do not represent disparities in the true sense of that term. Moreover, we must qualify the view that movement should tend to equalize wages. Migration rates are higher among the young, the best-educated and the most productive workers. To the extent that these phenomena occur, movement out of a province might reduce, rather than increase, the average per capita incomes of the smaller population which remains. As tax receipts drop, tax rates might increase, or public services might decline. Thus, while interprovincial migration might not completely eliminate persisting disparities, given these and other qualifications, it can probably still be concluded that the levels of mobility we do experience have made regional disparities smaller than they might otherwise have been.

Just as important as the economic consequences of interprovincial barriers to personal mobility are the effect of barriers on citizens' ability to relocate for personal advancement and satisfaction. The existence and maintenance of a national Canadian community requires that such ability be as great as possible. In this context, Commissioners conclude that the onus for justifying barriers to personal mobility should fall on the governments introducing them.

Competition Policy

One of the fundamental reasons for setting up an economic union is to enhance economic competition among member states. It stands to reason, therefore, that competition policy would be an integral part of the debate on the barriers to trade. Indeed, this is the approach adopted in the Treaty of Rome,[17] which reflects a clear intention to link the development of the European Economic Community not only to the conduct of the member states, but also to that of private business. Article 85 prohibits agreements between firms that affect trade among the member states and restrict competition among firms. Article 86 prohibits abuse by one or more firms of a dominant position. In practice, these provisions prevent private companies from imposing restrictions on trade analogous to those imposed by public authorities, such as import duties, quantitative restrictions and comparable trade barriers.

Thus competition policy in the European Community is, first and foremost, a tool of economic integration. Viewed from that perspective, it appears to have been fairly successful, as indicated by the large number of decisions of the European Commission and the European Court of Justice which strike down reciprocal exclusive-dealing agreements, agreements on market-sharing,

the fixing of production or sales quotas and of prices, and various practices that amount to "an abuse of a dominant position". Canadians have not approached competition policy as a tool of economic integration: in the context of the economic union, we have not focused on the possibility that the private sector might erect barriers to trade.

Nevertheless, as one study of Canadian federalism and the theory of economic integration has concluded, an effective competition policy is necessary to realize gains from the common market.[18] Because economic activity ignores provincial boundaries, and labour, capital and technology are mobile, it is difficult for provincial governments to regulate anti-competitive practices successfully: such regulation must be federal if it is to be effective. Mr. Justice Brian Dickson of the Supreme Court of Canada stressed in his concurring judgement, handed down in *Attorney General of Canada* v. *Canadian National Transportation Ltd.*, that

> *[A] scheme aimed at the regulation of competition is . . . an example of the genre of legislation that could not practically or constitutionally be enacted by a provincial government . . . If competition is to be regulated at all it must be regulated federally.*[19]

Justifications for Barriers

So far Commissioners have treated barriers and distortions primarily as if they were inherently undesirable: mechanisms incompatible with a sense of Canadian citizenship, inconveniencing citizens, misallocating resources and lowering economic efficiency. Does this definition always fit? Would Canadians, even in principle, wish to do away with every policy that might operate as a barrier? The answer is clearly no! There are many justifications for barriers and distortions.

Some of these justifications are themselves related to the economy. Some barriers may, in fact, correct for or counteract other barriers. A great many industrial policies are aimed at altering incentives and directing investment into areas that the market itself would not select. Other distortions are justified by a wide variety of social and cultural goals, all considered as contributing to our well-being. Thus social policies redirect resources on grounds of equity, and Canadian-content rules are aimed at protecting our sovereignty or cultural distinctiveness. Within a federal system, the goal of interregional sharing expressed by means of equalization payments and regional development implies non-market allocations essential to the Confederation bargain. Therefore, to determine which barriers are or are not justified involves a complex economic and political calculus, in which different interests will contend.

In principle, distortions imposed by the federal government may be more defensible politically than those imposed by provinces. If the federal government has the interests of the whole country in view, presumably provinces concern themselves with the interests of their own residents. In theory, at least, the Government of Canada, drawing members from across the whole country, makes the trade-offs and balances the concerns of winners

and losers. The national electorate can hold that government accountable, and it cannot pass off the costs of its actions to another jurisdiction. In contrast, if a discriminatory action by one province has harmful or costly consequences for residents of another province, residents of the latter have no means of holding the government of the other province to account, although they may demand that their own province retaliate. A final reason to take a more sympathetic view of federal distortions is that the stronger richer provinces may use distortions to increase their advantages over the smaller and poorer. Federal actions may be able to restore the balance.

The obvious rejoinder to such an analysis is that it depends critically on the degree to which the federal government is nationally representative; electoral politics may make it otherwise. It is, in part, such concerns that led Commissioners to recommend when we considered national institutions, that regional balance be strengthened at the centre.

Should we take a different stand in the matter of provincially imposed barriers? Many such barriers are implicit in the nature of Canadian federalism, with its multiple governments. In many instances, creation of impediments to trade or mobility is a by-product of legislation designed to meet appropriate provincial goals and to respond to the varying legitimate demands or preferences of provincial electorates. For example, provinces may formulate legislation on product standards to protect consumers. These standards may well vary from province to province, taking into account regionally significant factors from climate to culture. It remains difficult, of course, to judge whether a provincial regulation serves local needs or constitutes disguised discrimination against producers in other provinces. For example, stricter consumer-protection laws in one province may inhibit trade; they are not discriminatory, however, as long as the same rules apply to domestic and out-of-province producers. The situation requires examination on a case-by-case basis, and Commissioners will propose a mechanism to undertake this activity. Such examination must take into account and balance such factors as the comparative value of uniformity and diversity, and the object of the regulation as compared with its effect.

More generally, provincial variations in requirements touching education, health care or product standards can impede interprovincial movement of goods, capital and labour. For businesses that operate in several provinces or whose operations include both provincially- and federally-regulated activities, the very existence of numerous sets of regulations, even if there were no substantive variations, would have some costs. For example:

> *C-I-L is a typical national employer . . . Employment relationships within C-I-L thus are subject to twelve of the thirteen [including territorial] jurisdictions which legislate labor law. The transfer of an employee from one Province to another, or from one segment of our business to another even without a geographic relocation, can significantly change the rules. In C-I-L's view, this adds unnecessary cost and complexity to running our business with no advantage to employees and much disadvantage to productivity.*
>
> (C-I-L Inc., Brief, October 27, 1983, pp. 6–7.)

Most provincial barriers represent efforts to promote provincial economic development. The Constitution envisions such activity, and the provinces have been involved in it since the first days of Confederation. Voters expect provincial governments to promote economic development within the province: to encourage new industries, support diversification and maintain employment. This is the sense in which we speak of provincial economies, as well as a national economy.

Much more problematic are policies designed to overcome or counteract federal policies, or those designed to discriminate against residents of other provinces. Provinces with greater resources may be in a far better position to compete for capital and investment than those less well endowed. To the extent that investors can play off one government against another, they may obtain uneconomic subsidies or bid wages and protection of the environment down to the lowest common denominator, an international, as well as a domestic, phenomenon.

The result may be the classic "prisoner's dilemma": all provinces have an interest in co-operative effort, in this instance to harmonize policies, but each has an incentive to "cheat" to its own short-run advantage. Provinces may obtain mutually beneficial arrangements when each abstains from actions that might be individually advantageous if others do not retaliate, but mutually destructive if they do. Such arrangements, however, are notoriously unstable. There is always the lure of the short-run advantage and the illusion that other parties might not notice one's actions.

Commissioners' recommendations are intended to reduce the likelihood that governments will form such patterns of behaviour. Federalism justifies variation among provinces in response to local preferences; it does not justify outright discrimination against other provinces. The need to accommodate diversity of preferences, which argues for decentralization, must be balanced against the objective of gains from trade, which calls for greater centralization or uniformity of policies. As almost all of the above examples suggest, conflicts arise between interpersonal and interregional considerations. Commissioners recommend a political process to enable Canadians to distinguish between legitimate preferences and outright discrimination, and to help weigh the benefits of legitimate practices against the costs they may impose on the economic union.

Assessing the Effect of Barriers

> *We do not ignore the political realities behind these barriers but if they are instituted as solutions to certain problems, they must also be recognized as the problems they are for others and as trends in the wrong direction.*
>
> (J.K.C. Mulherin, Brief, August 2, 1983, pp. 4–5.)

Commissioners agree with this statement, but in doing so we do not accept the view that Canada has already become hopelessly balkanized. The direct costs of existing interprovincial trade barriers appear to be small. There are many barriers to interprovincial trade and factor mobility, but their

quantitative effect on the level of economic activity in Canada is not sufficient to justify a call for major reform. There is also — at least at present — substantial harmonization across provinces in areas such as taxation, insurance and securities regulation, where economic efficiency strongly suggests the importance of such co-ordination. Nevertheless, there has been recurrent concern about the state of the Canadian economic union from at least the era of the Royal Commission on Dominion-Provincial Relations (the Rowell-Sirois Commission) in the 1930s. We must address the nature of such concern and consider institutional responses to it.

There are at least two possible explanations for apprehension about the effect of internal barriers to trade. First, costs are small because barriers are limited, and interregional co-operation and co-ordination are still substantial. Economic costs could easily and quickly become much larger. The unravelling process, once begun, could proceed a considerable distance. The validity of this concern is not easy to assess. Certainly, economic losses would multiply as barriers proliferated, and the losses could become quite significant. The important question is whether Canadian governments would ever allow themselves to be caught up in such a process of mutual destruction. The small open nature of most provincial economies constrains this type of behaviour because the costs of most barriers are ultimately borne by the residents of the province imposing them. Nevertheless, this kind of behaviour is certainly possible, even when participants have certain knowledge that in the long term, everyone will suffer as a result.

Secondly, some observers may suspect that economic studies have failed to measure all the costs of market fragmentation. No one, for example, has measured the extra compliance costs associated with the existence of many labour or building codes rather than one. Similarly, we have little detailed knowledge about the extent to which such factors as the non-portability of pension plans inhibit, or even prevent, personal mobility, with resulting costs to the economic union. On the surface, these items seem small. In fact, they may well be quite large, particularly for producers who market goods and services across the country. Most affected are producers who principally supply or service provincial governments, their agencies or institutions under provincial regulation.

This pattern is consistent with the evidence obtained in this Commission's hearings. Though relatively few intervenors raised the issue of barriers, those who did regarded that issue as crucial, describing the great difficulty of overcoming hurdles that inhibit sales across the country. Some intervenors claimed that it sometimes seemed easier to develop foreign markets than those in Canada. We do not know how many others have made no attempt to overcome the barriers or have been reluctant to develop an active presence in other Canadian provinces because they lacked assurance that they would have continued access to those markets. Research to date does not tell us whether existing barriers have kept firms smaller and less efficient than they would otherwise have been, although logic suggests that to some extent this must indeed be so.

Commissioners hope that effective operation of the Canadian economic union can improve Canada's position in a competitive international economy.

If this is to occur, further analysis will be necessary. It may be, as analysts of the "experience curve" in relation to manufacturing have suggested, that firms able to expand quickly their output of new products will achieve significant advantages, on the assumption that some unit-production costs will decline as output increases. A research paper prepared for this Commission, describes some of the considerations involved:

> *The speed with which [a firm] can keep doubling its output depends upon how far ahead of the competition it is, the size of the market and how easy to serve it might be. A small market limits the speed with which output can be increased, and places a severe limit on the ultimate size of output that can be achieved. If the firm is competing against foreign firms that have access to a much larger market and are able to accumulate output much faster, it may find that the small market represents an impossible hurdle to international competitiveness.*[20]

Thus gains forgone or to be forgone in the future also justify continuing vigilance over interprovincial barriers to trade. Finally, not all the costs of such barriers are economic. For a Canadian producer to find it easier to sell in the United States or in other foreign markets than in another province is inconsistent with the full development of our national community.

Responding to Barriers: Towards a Code of Economic Conduct

Through preceding considerations, Commissioners have come to some important conclusions about the state of internal barriers and Canada's economic union. First, despite recent expressions of concern that the economy is becoming increasingly balkanized and fragmented, the Canadian economic union generally functions effectively. Goods, capital, services and people move relatively freely within the Canadian common market.

There are, however, a large number of impediments to free movement, and many distortions affect the common market. While, in aggregate, the lost economic output from these distortions appears quite small, we Commissioners do not believe that this lost output represents the full measure of the problem, and many Canadian companies and individuals indicate that in fact, the policies in question create considerable difficulties for them. Above the economic rationale, the political rationale for the national right to free movement has a powerful attraction for most Canadians. For a producer to find it easier to sell in another country than in another province offends our sense of Canadianism.

Commissioners consider, too, that the effect of these distortions – and the need for effective co-ordination of economic policy – are likely to increase as Canadians face greater competition from the outside world. Under these circumstances, we Canadians should make internal arrangements that stimulate international competitiveness and facilitate adjustment.

The barriers that exist are often justified in the name of important values. Federalism and the response of governments to local preferences necessarily imply that policies will often differ among jurisdictions. Some lack of harmonization will result, particularly when innovative solutions are introduced by different Canadian governments in response to emerging

problems. Important economic, social and cultural goals may justify government interventions that directly or indirectly affect the free movement of factors. Commitment to redistribution of income and equality of opportunity — both emphasized in this Report — justify some federal barriers. Thus, in particular cases, the challenge is not to eliminate a barrier, but rather to balance the economic benefits of free movement against other goals which Canadians hold. The trade-offs are not exclusively between economic efficiency and political diversity or provincial autonomy within the federation, for Canadian federalism also involves a Canada-wide community that has its own requirements. Moreover, as the Canadian Charter of Rights and Freedoms makes evident, the rights held by individuals have implications for the economic union.

The existence of our Canadian economic union implies not only that the free market should be allowed to operate, but also that governments should take positive measures to facilitate the operation of that market, to overcome market imperfections, and to pursue stabilization and effective industrial and social policies; it also calls for a broad regional sharing of the benefits of economic integration. This factor, in turn, suggests the need for positive measures of co-operation and co-ordination as much as for effective policing of barriers to movement. All these considerations govern this Commission's suggestions for the future.

Section 121

Section 121 of the Constitution Act, 1867 provides important basic support for internal freedom of trade in goods. It can be regarded as a customs-union clause rather than as a common-market provision. Remarkably few cases have cited this section, and its applicability to interprovincial non-tariff barriers (NTBs) and to trade in services is uncertain. Stronger wording of the section would emphasize the fact that formal, legally enforceable, constitutional provisions are the bed-rock on which more political and administrative arrangements are built. In recent years, this rationale has led others to make several specific proposals along these lines.

Commissioners believe, also, that constitutional protection of the economic union should eventually be strengthened; this should be done by amendment of the Constitution if future judicial interpretation does not confirm a broad reading of section 121. In particular, constitutional protection against tariff barriers should encompass trade in services as well as in goods. In recommending this modernization, we support several other previous commissions and task forces that have sought to enhance the effectiveness of the economic union. However, we are sensitive to the need to balance efficiency in the Canadian economic union with other interests in the federation. We are conscious also of the limitations facing courts in their deliberations on economic matters. The difficulties or limitations are particularly significant in relation to non-tariff barriers where complex economic and political considerations arise simultaneously. In the light of these considerations and of the current uncertainty about the scope and significance of NTBs, we suggest that this aspect of formal constitutional amendment should be preceded by

the development of guidelines in the form of a Code of Economic Conduct. This amendment itself might also take the form of an addition to section 121 to cover non-tariff barriers to goods or to services.

A Code of Economic Conduct

To respond to the challenge of making productive trade-offs between competing values, the governments of Canada should take steps to develop a "Code of Economic Conduct" which will begin to identify the policies and practices that are, and are not, acceptable in the Canadian economic union. For several reasons, however, Commissioners do not propose that this code be incorporated into the Constitution Act. For one, we have reservations about placing further responsibilities on the courts in an area where complex economic and political trade-offs often seem to be required. Many practices that have attracted attention in relation to the economic union fall into grey areas that even a strengthened section 121 cannot easily reach. Allegedly discriminatory government actions often take place at the administrative level or in informal practices not covered by law. These are hard to identify and to monitor through judicial mechanisms. We believe a Code of Economic Conduct could cover these areas more effectively.

Commissioners have emphasized the need for complex and sensitive trade-offs: "barriers" are not black and white. Countries like Australia, with very strong constitutional rules governing the common market, have found governments at both levels frustrated. However wise, judges are ill-equipped to make these trade-offs. They must decide whether a given act is right or wrong: they cannot easily suggest compromises or alterations in the policy. Judges have no mandate to make policy proposals to promote the positive development of the economic union that we believe to be necessary. Nor can courts initiate cases: they can only respond to cases brought before them. In addition, our legal traditions have not emphasized the kind of evidence and analysis that would be relevant to the decision making we foresee.

A Code of Economic Conduct is a relatively new concept. There are many important questions to be explored, and we would need considerable experience to "get it right". This argues for a cautious and incremental process. In Commissioners' judgement, it would not only be undesirable to try to write and constitutionalize a code now, but the exercise would almost certainly founder in the constitutional amendment process. A constitutionalized code formulated today would probably include so many opting-out, *non obstante* and exemption clauses that it would perhaps only legitimize what it was designed to prevent. Nor would it be easy to modify and adapt a constitutional code in the light of changing circumstances. Thus we recommend a more informal, negotiated Code of Economic Conduct. The governments of Canada should develop a Code that would spell out the principles of the economic union, begin to identify and describe practices that are and are not acceptable, and provide mechanisms of enforcement. We believe that it would eventually be appropriate to entrench the principles of the Code in the Constitution, although we have concluded that the enforce-

ment of the details of the Code would be carried out most effectively with the assistance of an expert Commission on the Economic Union.

It would not be appropriate for Commissioners to put forward a detailed proposal for a Code of Economic Conduct. Nevertheless, on the basis of our consultations and research, and in the context of our conclusions about development prospects for Canada, we suggest general guidelines for consideration:

- The starting point should be that the "burden of proof" lie with the authority imposing the barrier. Our assumption is in favour of the economic union. Deviations from that model ought to be publicly justified.
- The code should confirm general principles of the economic union applicable to both the federal and provincial governments. These principles should encompass:
  - Reduction of barriers to the movement of capital, labour, goods and services throughout Canada
  - Non-discrimination against persons (individuals and organizations) based on province of residence
  - Commitment to minimizing the costs of provincial programs that might fall on residents of other jurisdictions and to prior consultation for this purpose
  - Recognition of the need for an effective transportation, communications and information infrastructure to provide positive support for national economic development that would confer significant regional benefits.
- The code should also begin to identify the major policy areas where reduction of barriers to internal trade can best be effected. Attention should focus not only on the form of the barriers (procurement, subsidies and so on), but also on the anticipated effects or consequences. Commissioners base this conclusion on our observation that the possibilities for substitution between types of barriers are extensive, and on the great disparities in the size and economic development of the provinces and in their potential to inflict injury on other provinces or their residents. For immediate consideration, we suggest looking at barriers that inhibit the capacity of Canadian enterprises to achieve international competitiveness.

Initially, governments should negotiate the Code, and public and governmental pressure should enforce it. The intergovernmental process (involving, ultimately, the reformed national institutions Commissioners recommend) would provide the appropriate forum for dealing with the politically sensitive issue of internal barriers to trade. After Canadians have gained experience with the operation of the code, we should entrench its principles in the Constitution, and enforce the details of the code itself through some form of binding intergovernmental agreement which an expert commission appointed by federal and provincial governments would enforce.

The principal vehicle both for initiating the development of a Code of Economic Conduct and for implementing it should be a federal-provincial Council of Ministers for Economic Development, established under the umbrella of the First Ministers' Conference. This ministerial council would be assisted by a Federal-Provincial Commission on the Canadian Economic

Union consisting of a group of experts appointed by the Council. The commission would have responsibility for preparing materials for the Council as directed; initiating research to explore the state of the economic union and methods for improving it; receiving complaints from private actors, including groups, individuals and corporations affected by government actions which threaten the economic union; investigating and reporting on such alleged actions, and making recommendations to the public and the ministerial council.

As a start to the process of developing the Code, Commissioners propose the following procedure. The Council would ask the federal and provincial governments to list any barriers imposed by other governments that it believes harm individuals, a provincial economy, or the national economy. Each government would then defend those of its policies so identified. The expert Commission on the Canadian Economic Union would analyse barriers and their justifications, identify violations of the principles of the economic union, and recommend specific contents of the proposed code. The Council of Ministers of Economic Development would proceed to act on this report. Such a process would parallel working methods of the General Agreement on Tariffs and Trade (GATT).

There are several advantages to this procedure. To develop the Code should show governments the character of one anothers' policies and the mutually destructive effects of barriers that create a situation in which no one actually gains. Practical experience with the Code should lead to further sensitivity in its application. Continual discussion of the issues involved should help to convince governments of the potential advantages of co-operation. Incentives to "cheat", or to introduce new discriminatory policies, should prove less attractive when parties realize that they would be returning to the table time and again to deal with infringements on the Code. Moreover, the Council would provide a forum where the two goals of policing barriers and co-ordinating positive policies would be integrated.

Balancing the economic union against other goals is an essentially political process that should take place in a political forum. Because the policies at issue are those of both orders of government, the appropriate vehicle is an intergovernmental body. For several reasons, however, this body should receive advice from the expert Commission on the Economic Union that Commissioners have proposed. First, much research and investigation remains to be done. This would be best accomplished by a group with particular expertise who are nevertheless closely tied to the political process. The Federal-Provincial Commission on the Economic Union would be made up of independent experts, appointed by the Council of Ministers. Members would not be officials of federal or provincial governments; nor would they act as delegates or representatives. Secondly, the involvement of those whose primary commitment was to explore ways to improve the economic union would introduce to the process participants without vested interests as governments. Their freedom from involvement in government responsibilities should enhance their capacity to "blow the whistle". More important, they would be a group with a strong incentive to search for creative alternatives

and new solutions which governments, sometimes tied to their own bureaucratic interests and client groups, might find it difficult to do.

The commission's role in receiving complaints and conducting enquiries would be fundamental. It would open the process to individuals and groups outside government, and bring their concerns directly to bear on a matter of intergovernmental relations. In this way, impediments to the union could be fully explored. The fact that the commission would report its findings publicly would enhance its accountability. Governments which practice discriminatory policies would be much more regularly subject to the glare of publicity. At a minimum, the arrangement would force governments to justify their activities. Commissioners believe that this circumstance in itself would provide more effective policing than do existing arrangements. If, after a probationary period, the principles were eventually entrenched, the proposed commission could take on a more formal adjudicative role. It could, for example, become a regulatory agency, but one which regulates governments. This would constitute an experiment in administrative law with few precedents in Canada. For that reason, it might be viewed as more appropriate and more consistent with our traditions to have the Supreme Court enforce a formalized code. Commissioners believe, however, that a specialized body is to be preferred, and that such a body would avoid some of the problems with judicial decision making identified earlier.

Finally, Commissioners note that the federal government has a distinctive role to play in safeguarding the economic union. Its role as the national government means that its primary focus must be on the health of the whole, and that it must continually foster the development of positive linkages of all kinds among Canadians. In other sections of this part of our Report, we discuss in more detail how this can be accomplished. Here we simply note some of the instruments available. Conditions in shared-cost programs such as the Canada Assistance Plan or Canada Health Act can ensure portability, accessibility and non-discrimination against residents of other provinces. Such provisions could also be used in other shared-cost programs more directly related to employment, such as training, job creation, and Economic and Regional Development Agreements (ERDAs). Federal assistance to bilingual education and enhancement of its own capabilities to provide French-language services are important means of facilitating mobility. Federal administration of provincial income taxes under the Tax Collection Agreements is also an effective tool. More generally, development of the federal power over interprovincial trade and commerce could help to ensure the effective operation of the economic union. Commissioners turn to these and related economic policy concerns in subsequent sections of this Report.

Notes

1. For the purposes of our discussion, we refer to trade between provinces and trade within Canada involving Yukon and the Northwest Territories as 'interprovincial'.
2. John Whalley, "Induced Distortions of Interprovincial Activity: An Overview of Issues", in *Federalism and the Canadian Economic Union*, edited by Michael J. Trebilcock *et al.* (Toronto: University of Toronto Press for Ontario Economic Council, 1983), p. 175.

3. Canada, Royal Commission on Dominion-Provincial Relations, *Report*, Book II, *Recommendations* (Ottawa: King's Printer, 1937), p. 62.
4. *Murphy* v. *C.P.R.* [1958] S.C.R. 626, 15 D.L.R. (2d) 145.
5. For a more extensive survey, see John Whalley, *Regional Aspects of Confederation*, vol. 68, prepared for the Royal Commission on the Economic Union and Development Prospects for Canada (Toronto: University of Toronto Press, 1985).
6. John Whalley, "The Impact of Federal Policies on Interprovincial Activity", in *Federalism and the Canadian Economic Union*, edited by Michael J. Trebilcock *et al.* (Toronto: University of Toronto Press for Ontario Economic Council, 1983), pp. 211–13.
7. Canada, Supply and Services Canada, *Supply Policy Manual*, Directive #3052, December 30, 1983, pp. 7, 9.
8. See Whalley, "Induced Distortions of Interprovincial Activity".
9. Wayne R. Thirsk, "Interprovincial Trade and the Welfare Effects of Marketing Boards", in *Perspectives on the Canadian Economic Union*, vol. 60 (Toronto: University of Toronto Press, 1985).
10. Canadian Manufacturers' Association, "Interprovincial Trade Restrictions", a CMA Position Statement (Toronto, 1984).
11. See Philip Mathias, *Forced Growth* (Toronto: James Lorimer, 1971), for case studies of unproductive projects induced by special incentives.
12. An Act respecting stock saving plans and to amend again the Taxation Act and to amend the Securities Act, S.Q. 1979, chapter 14, as amended.
13. These and the following figures are drawn from Statistics Canada, *Current Demograhic Analysis: Report on the Demographic Situation in Canada, 1983*, by Jean Dumas (Ottawa: Minister of Supply and Services Canada, 1984), pp. 46 ff.
14. See *Winner* v. *S.M.T. (Eastern) Ltd.* [1951] S.C.R. 887, 919 (S.C.C.)
15. A fuller treatment of these questions is provided in Michael J. Trebilcock, John Whalley, Carol Rogerson, and Ian Ness, "Provincially Induced Barriers to Trade in Canada: A Survey", in *Federalism and the Canadian Economic Union*, edited by Michael J. Trebilcock *et al.* (Toronto: University of Toronto Press for Ontario Economic Council, 1983), pp. 243–351.
16. *Ibid.*, p. 273.
17. The treaty establishing the European Economic Community, executed in Rome, March 25, 1957.
18. A.E. Safarian, *Canadian Federalism and Economic Integration* (Ottawa, Information Canada, 1974), pp. 58–73.
19. *Attorney General of Canada* v. *Canadian National Transportation Ltd.* (1983), 3 D.L.R. (4th) 16 (S.C.C.)
20. F.J. Chambers, "Internal Constraints in the Evolution of International Economic Policy for Canada", in *Selected Problems in Formulating Foreign Economic Policy*, vol. 30 (Toronto: University of Toronto Press, 1985).

Economic Management and Federalism

The Canadian economic union consists of far more than the essentially negative role of government presented in Commissioners' discussion of internal trade barriers. Governments discharge a variety of functions in managing the economy. The regional character of the Canadian economy and the distribution of powers in the Constitution decide which governments exercise these functions and the values and goals which they pursue. How have the federal dimensions of our society and our institutions affected the ability of the Canadian state to manage the economy and to promote sustained economic performance? How do we reconcile the realities of divided and shared authority with the economic and social needs of the country and its regions? Do we foresee economic challenges that will require us to modify the institutions and practices of federalism?

This Commission has concluded that the international environment will press ever closer on Canadians, increasing competition and creating major issues of adjustment for workers, firms, sectors, and regions. The emergence of an ever-wider range of claims for rights, many of them for economic entitlements, may introduce new constraints on the formation of economic policy.

Commissioners have also identified some basic policy directions which we believe essential to Canadian success in an interdependent world. We wish to secure Canada access to the world economy and to project Canadian interests more vigorously. We emphasize the overwhelming imperative of continuing adjustment, which will require flexibility, innovation and adaptability throughout the economy. Canadians, we believe, must rely on the incentives and disciplines of the market more fully than in the past, placing less weight on some forms of government intervention, especially in the allocation of scarce resources to productive tasks. Commissioners emphasize also the necessity for effective social policies to cushion the costs of adjustment for individuals and to equip Canadians better to take advantage of new opportunities.

Macro-economic policies are essential for providing a more stable framework within which individual enterprises can grow. Industrial policy must facilitate adjustment and adaptation, through responsive systems of education and training, financial and labour markets, and technological innovation. Canadians must moderate and contain the inevitable political pressures that have too often made industrial policy a process that obstructs, rather than facilitates, change. Thus the long-standing governmental roles of allocation and stabilization remain. So, too, does the traditional concern with distribution, not only among groups identified by class, age or sex, but also among those bounded by region and province. In a period of rapid change and uncertainty, the ways that Canadians share the burdens and benefits of adjustment are a fundamental political issue.

Newer responsibilities are likely to add to the importance of Canadian governments. International forces will require more effective articulation of Canadian national interests abroad. Meanwhile, we shall have to work harder to manage the domestic effects of international developments. Governments

will also face greater pressures to accommodate the social divisions attendant on the increased complexity of industrial society. In the face of a society at once more fragmented internally and more open internationally, Commissioners believe that governments ought to try to reinforce Canadians' sense of national community and of the mutual obligations that are the counterpart of the rights of citizenship.

Canadians can pursue these political, social and economic ends through our federal and provincial governments as they work individually in their own areas of jurisdiction and co-operatively in areas of co-ordinated action. Policy debates within federalism are simultaneously debates about what should be done and who should do it. Increasingly, too, they have become debates about how both orders of government can exercise their formal power in such a way as to increase policy coherence and reduce the costs of duplication of services.

Federalism and the Economy: The Record

How well equipped are we Canadians to adapt federalism to present and future challenges? We can find part of the answer in the record of the past. During the Depression and into the post-Second World War period, many observers considered that federalism was perhaps an obsolete institution, and that it was certainly an impediment to the ability of the state to respond to major new concerns in the modern industrial economy. The failure to cope with the massive dislocations of the Depression era seemed proof enough of the validity of their view.

First, critics argued, federalism emphasized territorially based communities and cultural differences; it seemed at odds with the modernizing trends then eroding the significance of such differences, stressing national values and cultures over local ones, and focusing political divisions on economic, rather than territorial, distinctions. Secondly, changes in economic organization, notably the development of large corporations operating nationally — and, to an ever greater extent, internationally — exceeded the capacity of small political units to ensure that they served the public interest. Thirdly, and most important, the new functions of government both in managing the economy and in building the welfare state seemed to require centralization. The new emphasis on stabilization policy, for example, implied to some analysts that fiscal powers should rest in the hands of one political authority, rather than be dispersed among many. The welfare state, with its ideal of national standards, seemed to imply a similar need for concentration; only the federal government could mobilize sufficient resources to overcome the disparities in the capacities of provincial governments to assume responsibilities in the welfare field. Only the federal government, many concluded, could act as an effective redistributor among persons and regions.

The experience of the 1930s convinced many Canadians that the rigidities of our federal system made government incapable of undertaking these new tasks. Much of the criticism was directed at the courts, which struck down innovative government efforts — such as Prime Minister R.B. Bennett's 1935 New Deal — to respond to the new needs. Others accused the provinces of

using federalism as a screen for the parochialism of leaders and the defence of vested interests. There were calls for fundamental constitutional revision to reform federalism.

And reform it we did, but in ways which were essentially faithful to the spirit of federalism and to the retention of regional identities and interests. The 1945 White Paper on Employment and Income[1] enunciated Ottawa's fundamental commitment to stabilization and demand management, and to an open international economic order; it established the federal government's dominant position in economic management. The relative centralization of post-war fiscal arrangements underlined this position. Through constitutional amendment – as with Unemployment Insurance in 1940 and Old Age Pensions in 1951, or through use of the spending power, as with Family Allowances, as well as through the development of shared-cost programs in health, social welfare and other fields, the federal government established its predominant role in the Canadian social security system. Through equalization and, later, through regional development programs, the federal government extended its responsibility for interregional redistribution.

Despite the growth of federal responsibilities, the provinces have also been principal actors in many areas of vital importance for economic management, such as education, health, social services, occupational health and safety, and labour/management relations. Provincial governments often acted imaginatively and effectively to meet new needs. They developed schools, universities and hospitals, and the infrastructure necessary to support the huge growth of cities and suburbs. Throughout much of the post-war period provincial revenues and expenditures grew at a much faster rate than those of the federal government. Thus governments grew at both levels.

Much of what we did involved a creative blending of federal initiative and financial support with provincial administration. This development allowed provincial governments considerable freedom to respond within the framework of broad conditions established by the federal government to maintain national standards. The shared-cost program was the hallmark of this co-operative federalism.

Economic management and administration of welfare affected the character of Canadian federalism. At the same time, the federal dimensions of the Canadian state powerfully influenced the ways in which we undertook these new tasks. We proved that with minimal formal change we could adapt the practice of federalism and achieve great flexibility in the use of the institutions we inherited.

In the 1960s, federal-provincial collaboration became more complex. We saw a continuation of federal initiatives – in regional development, in the Canada Pension Plan, enacted in 1965, and in medicare, initiated in 1968; all of these steps required provincial co-operation. Provinces, having acquired greater strength and self-confidence, bargained for bigger shares of fiscal resources and became more active in economic and social development. This was especially true of Quebec, where the reforms of the Quiet Revolution led the provincial government to organize many of the major social and economic functions of government around the provincial state. Quebec opted out of a number of shared-cost programs by means of the Established Programs

(Interim Arrangements) Act and established its own contributory pension plan.

By the 1970s, several developments had strained federal-provincial collaboration in economic and social management. The economic difficulties of those years called into question the effectiveness of post-Second World War techniques of economic management. The widespread consensus among citizens and governments about the policies began to erode. Much of this growing dissension expressed itself through rival economic policies; effective co-ordination became at once more important and more difficult to achieve. Provincial and federal governments began to search for new approaches, developing more comprehensive industrial policies and making more aggressive use of subsidies, procurement policies, public enterprise and other instruments.

These developments exacerbated regional divisions, muted during the Second World War and the early post-war period, which re-emerged forcefully in Quebec after 1960, and in the West after 1970. In the 1970s, there was renewed concern with the persistence of regional disparities, which had not disappeared with aggregate national growth in the late 1950s. Regional differences in economic matters reached their apex in the interregional and federal-provincial battles over energy. These shaped the pattern of conflict in the federation and foreshadowed much of the subsequent constitutional crisis.

Increased provincial activity in economic management, dubbed "province-building", was not a new phenomenon. Dynamic provincialism had emerged in the late nineteenth century, especially in the recessions of 1874–79 and 1886–96, when the promised benefits of Confederation were slow to materialize. As central Canada industrialized in the early twentieth century, many of the essential underpinnings of development – roads and urban services, for example – were provincial responsibilities. Provincial ownership of resources (extended to Alberta, Saskatchewan and Manitoba only in 1930) acted as a further basis for provincial activism: hydro-electric power developed under provincial ownership, and the provinces promoted the processing of resources. In the 1930s, as Canadians sought answers to the crisis of the Depression, several provinces experimented with new forms of economic policy and political organization. Social Credit in Alberta and the Co-operative Commonwealth Federation (CCF) in Saskatchewan were prime examples. These experiments produced conflicting programs and federal-provincial tensions, many of which ended up in the courts. In all of them, federal and provincial governments tended to advocate the interests of different groups and industries. All had involved both conflict over federal and provincial jurisdiction, and regional grievances about the exercise of federal powers.

The province building of the 1960s and 1970s had similar sources. Provincial governments sought to diversify their economies to mitigate the "boom-and-bust" cycles associated with economies based on world trade in natural resources, and to provide a wider range of economic opportunities for their inhabitants. During the Quiet Revolution, Québécois sought to use an activist provincial state to redress the historic under-representation of

francophones in the ownership and management of the provincial economy. The instruments that they used included *Hydro-Québec*, the *Caisse de dépôts et placements*, the *Société générale de financement*, and sweeping reforms to the education system. In many respects these efforts proved successful. The growth of the private sector which they encouraged later helped to create and sustain a more self-confident, aggressive, francophone private sector, which has become an innovative force in the Canadian economy.

In the West, notably in Alberta and Saskatchewan, shifting international terms of trade propelled the province-building drive. The new situation opened the possibility of bringing about a permanent shift in economic power, which would reduce the historic dependence of the West on external economic and political forces. Resource development complemented the historic sense of grievance. As in Quebec, province building in the West presupposed a high degree of confidence in the ability of citizens, through their governments, to alter their economic circumstances.

Province building, in both its political and economic dimensions, has been one of the most striking recent features of Canadian federalism. The reverse side of the coin has been a high level of federal-provincial conflict. Yet we should not exaggerate the significance of province building. Federal fiscal, monetary and tariff policies remained critical determinants of regional, as well as national, economic development. The federal government continued to be responsible for the great proportion of industrial development expenditures. Moreover, while all provinces became more active in economic development, only a few had either the inclination or the capacity to pursue ambitious development "strategies". For many provinces, regional development could be achieved only with extensive federal participation.

As a result of expansion of activity by both levels of government, interdependence among governments increased significantly. As each level responded to new concerns, using whatever constitutional levers were available, policies were intermingled. The situation became less compatible with the classic "watertight compartments" model of the division of powers. The contemporary categories within which we thought of economic and social policy were rarely congruent with the categories set out in the British North America Act.

Each order of government found that to achieve its goals it needed to take account of resources and instruments belonging to the other. The process of "intrusion" worked both ways. Policies at one level often spilled over to affect policies at the other. In addition, the expansion of government responsibilities for economic well-being sharpened the concern with "fairness" in the federal system because Canadians increasingly perceived distributional outcomes as the products of government policies, for which governments should be held accountable, rather than as the products of impersonal and uncontrollable market forces.

Federalism and Economic Management

The challenges that federalism produces for economic management arise at two levels. The first focuses on the regionalized nature of our economy and

society. Virtually every national economic problem is simultaneously a regional problem. Regional needs and interests will differ; policies well suited to the needs of one region may well be unsuitable for others. This would be true even if Canada were a unitary state. The regional constraints on federal economic policy making come not only from provincial governments, but also from the interests of regions as articulated by their representatives in the federal caucuses and the Cabinet.

Federal institutions themselves are also the source of economic management concerns: the interests and policies of the two orders of government, the division of powers between them, and the means through which they interact. Each government responds to a different set of constituencies, and thus is likely to articulate different economic concerns and different responses to them. The existence of ten provincial governments probably accentuates natural regional differences. This division tends to shape discussion of economic policy into a "regional" mould, minimizing or blurring issues defined in alternative ways.

Further complicating economic management is the fact that the two orders of government divide or share the levers or instruments for policy making. The Constitution Act, 1867 created this overlap, but the change in our views of economic management has accentuated the complexity of the situation. Both orders can claim a wide range of powers to justify policy initiatives. The federal government has the broadest range of economic powers: the power to levy both direct and indirect taxes; control over currency and banking, interprovincial and international trade and commerce, and interprovincial transportation; and the general powers under "Peace, Order, and good Government". But the courts have consistently refused to grant plenary economic powers to the federal government, and have instead sought to ensure the integrity of the provincial powers. The courts have ruled that broad interpretation of such ideas as "inherent national concern" and "general trade" would potentially embrace such broad scope that "provincial jurisdiction based on property and civil rights, regulation of the local social environment, and the administration of justice would not survive except in radically diminished form". The courts have been wary of permitting any "unbalancing extensions" to federal constitutional powers related to the economy.[2]

There are many alleged consequences of this state of affairs. Some say that federalism unduly complicates the process of policy making. Decision-making costs increase, as 11 sets of political authorities must co-ordinate their activities. The result in shared fields often seems to be immobility and indecisiveness; substantial policy change often seems to require a high degree of consensus or a massive exertion of political will. Citizens who seek responses and decisions from governments face a complex process and must put up with the duplication, uncertainties and delays of divided jurisdiction. Governments must devote considerable effort to working with one another, and may have greater difficulty responding to demands for consultation with interest groups whose interests are expressed in non-territorial terms. Federalism seems to be the enemy of policy that is planned, comprehensive, coherent, uniform and consistent.

This list of the costs of the federal system might lead to a prescription for sweeping centralization under the unifying hand of a strong central government. But Commissioners disagree that such a prescription is required. First, as the Rowell-Sirois Royal Commission on Dominion-Provincial Relations emphasized when it confronted the same question, it is contrary to the respect for provincial diversity that is inherent in federalism. Secondly, it is not only the existence of two orders of government that makes economic management complex; it is also the existence of underlying economic and social differences among regions, which would confront a unitary government as much as a federal one. Indeed, the centrifugal pressures associated with federalism are only one aspect of the larger centrifugalism in our political institutions. Even within the federal government, economic policy makers have different viewpoints, represented by different departments and agencies, each oriented to its own set of policy objectives. Hence there is little reason to assume that coherent planning would result from centralization alone.

Modern governments face an almost impossible range of demands. The "reach" of the state has in many ways outrun both our administrative and technical capacities, and our capacity to ensure democratic accountability. One approach to minimizing this problem is to try to limit the range of state interventions: to encourage the state to do less, but to do it better. Another is to recognize the advantages of sharing power and responsibilities among governments. No one government has to try to do everything, or to be responsible for everything. No one set of institutions has to be the focus for all the demands and expectations of citizens, or to try to resolve all the divisions and conflicts of society. In a country as diverse as Canada, centralization would be a recipe for paralysis.

Federalism, then, offers some major advantages for economic management: it is not simply a problem to be overcome as best we may; it is a strength. It provides greater stability by diffusing conflict and expectations throughout the system. It offers the opportunity to tailor economic policies to the specific needs and concerns of citizens and groups in different parts of the country. It minimizes the ever-present danger of the spectacular failure that can result when all the eggs are put in one basket. In a world of uncertainty and rapidly shifting economic challenges, where there is little understanding of what is likely to work best, it provides the opportunity for experiment and learning, for flexibility and inventiveness. It enhances sensitivity to different viewpoints and permits canvassing of multiple sources of information and intelligence in different settings. We can try different models for improving labour relations, for integrating education and training, for stimulating the flow of investment, and for diffusing technology. Indeed, economic development in federations is likely to exceed that in centralized states as a result of the beneficial effects of competition in the public sector.

Federal and Provincial Roles

These considerations shape Commissioners' views about improving on Canada's record of economic management in the federal system. The challenge is to get the greatest benefit from the diversity that federalism

encourages, while at the same time seeking to overcome or reduce the effect of the inevitable tensions and complexities that federalism engenders.

We must all recognize that both federal and provincial governments have legitimate and important functions in managing the economy, and that these functions are not identical: there is a real division of labour between the two orders of government, partly as a result of our constitutional tradition and partly as a result of our needs. The federal government must concern itself first and foremost with the needs of the whole national economy. This responsibility derives both from its political mandate as the only government elected by all Canadians and also from its powers and resources. The provincial governments, in turn, will focus on the needs of their own economies.

First, the federal government is, and must be, primarily responsible for Canada's presence in the international world, and for mediating between that world and domestic economic and political life. This requires a predominant federal role in the negotiation and ratification of treaties, in co-ordinating federal and provincial activities abroad, and in managing the domestic adjustments that follow from international activities. Secondly, the federal government must be the advocate and catalyst for the effective functioning of the economic union. It must minimize the effects of federal and provincial barriers to interprovincial trade, and maximize the benefits of the economic union. Thirdly, the federal government is primarily responsible for stabilization policy. Fourthly, the federal government is primarily responsible for redistribution between regions and provinces, between social and economic interests, and among individual citizens.

Thus the federal task is to provide a unified national framework for private economic activity and provincial initiatives to encourage economic development. The federal government also has an immediate and direct role in the lives of citizens. In its various functions, the federal government must be sensitive to the effects of its policies on various regions, and to the necessity of balancing and reconciling regional preferences. The forces demanding change may be national in character, or even global, but individual citizens, living in particular places and conscious of their own needs and concerns, must cope with the effects of change, and the federal government must help them to do so.

Commissioners' view does not imply that in all these areas the federal government need have a monopoly. We use advisedly such words as "predominant". In most of these areas, provinces, too, have a role. To the extent that international obligations require implementation within areas of provincial jurisdiction, provinces must concern themselves with the international domain. The very scale of provincial taxing and spending, along with the interdependence of federal and provincial fiscal systems, means that they must be involved in stabilization policy. Provincial preferences with respect to social policy supplement and modify federal activity in redistribution. And since legitimate provincial activities in response to local preferences account for many of the provincially induced barriers to trade, the provinces must participate in negotiating and implementing codes of conduct concerning the economic union.

Similarly, the provinces in their own right have important functions relating to economic development. Their political base requires them to concern themselves with the economic well-being of their region, as do the powers allocated to them under section 92 and other parts of the Constitution Act, 1867. Many of these powers and responsibilities appear vital to satisfactory economic performance in the future.

Just as federal activity in management of the economy does not preclude provincial involvement, so there is, and must be, an awareness of the national interest in the conduct of many of these provincial responsibilities. The federal government can provide this element in a variety of ways. The courts could broaden the general economic powers already allocated to the federal government, notably trade and commerce, "Peace, Order, and good Government", and the power to enact criminal law. Canadian courts have not followed the American example and defined these powers as plenary ones, which would confine provincial legislation to those areas in which the federal government has chosen not to act. In Canada the courts have conditioned, restricted or frustrated sweeping assertions of federal economic powers. Constitutional amendment is an alternative means to extend the federal role, as occurred with unemployment insurance in 1940. But, as we have seen, we have used this device rarely, especially in the field of economic powers.

The federal government can use co-operative action for the same purpose, especially through its spending power. It can set up various contractual arrangements, such as purchase of specific "places" for training purposes in provincial technical colleges. The network of such arrangements is now immense.

Finally, the federal government, through its own activities within its own jurisdiction, can set a tone, establish priorities and promote new ideas or approaches. Thus highly visible consultation, the conduct of research and publicity on an issue such as forest management, and use of the public forum provided by a parliamentary committee can provide economic leadership that alters the climate of ideas within which both orders of government act. The federal government can act as catalyst and innovator without designing and delivering programs.

Transcending all these considerations of powers and mechanisms is the need for a common sense among all Canadians about what we want governments to do. If, through the recommendations that Commissioners have made in previous chapters, we have been able to clarify that point, the requisite adaptations of the institutions of federalism should follow. The words of Samuel Beer, a leading student of American federalism, apply also to Canada: "The lesson of the future is that role follows purpose. If we are to design a new federalism, we must first restore our sense of national direction."[3]

Within this broad conception of a division of responsibilities among governments, Commissioners approach specific issues from a functional problem-oriented perspective. We believe that effective economic management is, in general, much more than a matter of making the appropriate division of constitutional authority. Contemporary decision making requires the co-operation of numerous actors, both public and private. No one can

force that co-operation except within very narrow limits. Hence we must have institutions that reflect diverse viewpoints, give them access to the decision-making process, and work out accommodations among them.

Commissioners do not mimimize the realities of federal-provincial conflict over economic management. We believe, however, that it is essential to qualify interpretations of federalism and economic management that emphasize conflicts. While some governments have been more interventionist and others less so, all are part of, and responsive to, the same broad domestic and international climate. There are a great many areas of common interest. The performance of the national economy is essential to the performance of each provincial economy. Each province, therefore, has a positive interest in co-operating with the federal government in order to manage overall growth successfully. At the same time, overall national development depends on the economic performance of the provinces, for the provinces are essential participants in the process of national economic growth.

We can also learn from experience. By the early 1980s, it had become clear to all participants that the hostility and confrontation over energy and other issues had gone too far. The resulting climate of uncertainty and confusion was harming investment and confidence. Governments have reacted, and now appear willing to seek more co-operative relationships in economic management.

Economic Management for the Future

In previous chapters, this Commission has spelled out its goals for economic and social policy. It is time to recapitulate these objectives and to show how we propose to achieve them within the context of the Canadian federal system. How will federalism affect our ability to achieve these goals? How, in turn, might their achievement affect our practice of federalism in the future? In some areas we shall suggest changes in the operation of the federal system so as better to achieve the objectives we seek; in a few others we shall temper and modify the objectives in the light of values and concerns intrinsic to Canada's federal and regional character.

Federalism and Canada's International Stance

There is no alternative to making our way in the open and competitive international environment, but the necessity of doing so also presents us with unparalleled opportunities. Specifically, Commissioners have urged Canadians to seek freer trade with the United States and to continue to extend multilateral free trade. More generally, we have urged Canadians to accept a more activist international stance on a wide range of issues.

Does the structure of powers within Canadian federalism inhibit or impede our ability to achieve these objectives? Does it affect our ability to make the necessary adaptations and adjustments at home? To answer these questions we must explore some features of the division of powers with respect to foreign affairs, especially within the economic sphere. We do indeed have

some serious lacks in our institutional armoury which, if not supplied, may seriously weaken our effectiveness.

Section 132 of the Constitution Act, 1867 dealt with the management of Canada's external relations at Confederation:

> *The Parliament and Government of Canada shall have all Powers necessary or proper for performing the Obligations of Canada or of any Province thereof, as Part of the British Empire, towards Foreign Countries, arising under Treaties between the Empire and such Foreign Countries.*

The treaty-making power itself remained with the British Parliament at Westminster. This arrangement reflected the way that most Canadians saw themselves at the time: as citizens of the wider British Empire, rather than as possessors of a distinctive Canadian nationality. As a result, our Constitution included no clearly considered treaty power compatible with the existence of a federal state.

As Canada matured as an independent country, it became increasingly plain that diplomatic representation by another country, however friendly or experienced, could not secure Canadian interests. Our participation in the First World War showed us and our Allies that Canada was a distinct political community, and that we Canadians should be able to conduct external relations for ourselves. The aspiration for independence became a legal reality with passage of the Statute of Westminster in 1931.

From that point on, Canada was a sovereign state for purposes of international law, and the Government of Canada had the right to represent the nation on the international stage. Federal leaders believed that this authority extended to the negotiation and implementation of treaties. In the Labour Conventions Case (1937), however, the Judicial Committee of the Privy Council, then Canada's highest court, held that the federal power to implement treaties referred only to those matters that fell within federal jurisdiction under section 91 of the Constitution Act, 1867. The federal mandate did not extend to the acceptance or enforcement of obligations within provincial jurisdiction under section 92. Thus the division of powers prevented the Parliament of Canada from enacting a law to carry out an international treaty on a matter within provincial competence.

In the intervening half-century, Canada has adopted an increasingly active role in the international scene, entering into a large number of treaties covering a wide range of subjects. Nonetheless, recognizing the limitations on its ability to implement at home some aspects of undertakings to which it might commit itself abroad, the Government of Canada has been hesitant to assume international obligations that require provincial legislative action.

As long as international trade relations focused primarily on the tariff, a matter clearly under federal jurisdiction, the Labour Conventions Case did not prove a major constraint on Canadian participation in forums such as the General Agreement on Tariffs and Trade (GATT). However, as these international discussions have come to focus more and more on non-tariff barriers such as subsidies, discriminatory purchasing policies, and product standards designed to exclude competition, the constraint has become a great

deal more serious. Many of the practices addressed in these discussions fall within provincial jurisdiction.

International law largely assumes the existence of unitary sovereign states; it has little sympathy with, or understanding of, the sharing of power within those states. A number of international agreements contain "federal state" clauses, in which the federal state commits itself to its best efforts to secure compliance from sub-national governments, while the other states involved acknowledge the limits imposed by federal constitutions. Still, such clauses clearly do not solve the problem. Unless the negotiating parties in international negotiations can fully commit their own countries to abide by the agreements signed, they will have only limited ability to secure concessions. Informal undertakings made by provinces or states to comply with negotiated international agreements will not solve the problem. The Tokyo Round of the GATT negotiations saw discussion of the pricing policies of Canadian provinces on imported wine and spirits. Ontario signed a "statement of intent" committing itself to a change in policies, but under pressure from domestic producers, it soon found ways to circumvent the agreement, claiming that the statement of intent was not legally enforceable.

This constitutional gap in the treaty-making power promises to cause increasing problems for Canada in the future, significantly hampering our ability to work out effective agreements and constraining our full participation in the international community. In Commissioners' view, the federal government is, and must remain, the principal representative of Canada abroad. It is the Government of Canada that must negotiate treaties. Nevertheless, this broad federal power must recognize the reality of the federal division of powers within the Constitution. This is why Commissioners reject the notion of granting unrestricted authority to the federal government to conclude and enforce implementation of any treaties that contain provisions lying outside federal jurisdiction.

We must seek a procedure whereby treaties, once concluded, are binding and enforceable on both federal and provincial authorities within Canada. That necessity, in turn, requires the involvement of provincial governments. We must distinguish two stages in this process: negotiation and implementation. Again, Commissioners turn to trade for an example. During the Tokyo Round negotiations, there emerged a very successful procedure to involve provinces in the adoption of Canada's negotiating position. This procedure permitted formulation of trade-offs among the complex interests of different regions. The federal negotiators became fully aware of provincial concerns, and provincial governments became more familiar with the larger issues. Canadian negotiators could then carry on discussions with representatives of other countries without fear of provoking conflict at home.

Commissioners believe, as we said in Part II, that a consultation procedure of this type should become a regular feature of Canadian international negotiations, especially those pertaining to free trade with the United States. If provincial consultation at the negotiating stage works successfully, it should ensure that any resulting treaty will receive provincial support. Federal-provincial consultation should also extend to co-ordination of treaty implementation.

Provincial representatives may appropriately be members of the Canadian bargaining team itself in some instances, especially when the main issues fall under provincial jurisdiction. It is vital, however, that Canada be able to speak with a single voice in any discussions, and therefore that domestic disagreements be resolved early. Commissioners believe that informal consultation will be sufficient for the process that we have set out for movement toward freer trade with the United States. It is unnecessary to complicate this process with a simultaneous debate about the Constitution and the division of powers with respect to treaty-making, ratification and implementation.

For the longer run, however, Commissioners believe it essential to give serious consideration to resolving the constitutional situation. International forces will press even harder against our institutional capacities and will challenge our constitutional values. In Commissioners' discussion of national institutions, we noted the necessity of helping Parliament to hold the executive accountable for its conduct of international affairs and, accordingly, recommended that the practice of parliamentary ratification of international treaties be securely established.

Commissioners now extend this principle to encompass federalism. In situations where a proposed treaty imposes obligations on provinces that lie within areas of provincial jurisdiction, provincial legislatures should approve the relevant sections. Two possible mechanisms suggest themselves; a general constitutional amendment concerning treaty ratification could embody either one. On the one hand, provinces could accede to treaty provisions individually. The relevant provisions would come into effect in a particular province only when ratified by its legislature. This method has a serious flaw: an international agreement made by Canadian negotiators might have effect in some provinces but not in others. The result would almost certainly prove confusing and unacceptable, and it could mean that a small number of provinces could vitiate the benefits of a particular arrangement for the whole country.

On the other hand, as Commissioners set out in Part II, the constitutional amendment formula could come into play. Sections of a treaty imposing obligations on provinces would come into effect on the passage of resolutions in the legislatures of two-thirds of the provinces, representing at least half the Canadian population. Some observers might object that this solution might involve an undesirable restriction on the federal government's ability to negotiate for Canada abroad. Commissioners would reply, however, that the federal government does not now have the power to implement provisions of treaties within provincial jurisdiction, and that provincial agreement to an amendment giving unrestricted authority in this field to the Government of Canada is virtually inconceivable. We note, also, that this formal recognition of the provincial role in ratification carries with it the benefit that it can facilitate the enforcement of a treaty. Once implemented in this way, commitments made by the central government would be the law of Canada. The provinces would be under obligation to adhere to the terms of such agreements and could be challenged at law if they did not. We believe that

the procedure represents the best compromise between the imperative of effective participation in international discussions and the imperative of respecting the federal Constitution.

There is further uncertainty surrounding the treaty-making power. Can provinces themselves conduct international activities? At least one province has argued that provinces have the same legal power to conclude treaties under section 92 of the Constitution Act, 1867 as the federal government has under section 91. The argument is far from conclusive. Nevertheless, in the past 25 years, provincial activities outside Canada have proliferated, ranging from formal and informal agreements, to representation abroad, to membership in international organizations. For a number of years Quebec has had a Department of External Trade, and it recently split its Ministry of Intergovernmental Affairs into a Canadian section and a Ministry of International Relations. In February 1985, British Columbia created a Ministry of International Trade and Development, and international trade matters are an important focus of ministries of industry, development and trade in several other provinces.

Provincial international activities take many forms. Perhaps the most contentious have involved Quebec's desire to establish an international presence in accordance with its perception of itself as a distinct national community and the primary representative of francophones in Canada. In the 1960s and 1970s, a large number of well-publicized disputes took place in which Quebec sought agreements with countries such as France and Belgium and representation on organizations related to *la francophonie*. The federal government took the position that all such activities must operate under the federal umbrella; Quebec took the position that it had its own independent authority to conclude agreements.

Commissioners believe that it is possible to reconcile these competing positions. One model that might produce reconciliation takes the form of successive agreements between the government of Quebec and the federal government about immigration. Through these agreements, Quebec has received a direct voice in the selection of immigrants, in recognition of its special concern with the linguistic make-up of its population. Under this arrangement, Quebec immigration officials have joined Canadian immigration offices abroad. At the same time, the federal government has retained ultimate authority for selection of immigrants, for establishing levels, and for undertaking similar responsibilities. It should be possible to work out agreements in other fields, whereby, on matters affecting the French language, francophone culture and education, and civil law, Quebec would have the right to conduct discussions with other countries, to acquire direct representation in some international organizations, and to supply members to Canadian delegations.

Other provincial activities abroad pose less difficult political problems. Most fall into two categories: trade promotion and the management of relations with contiguous American states. The tradition of provincial offices abroad dates back to 1868, when Ontario and New Brunswick set up offices in London. Today, provincial governments maintain about 40 offices abroad,

most created since the 1960s. About half of these offices are in the United States, though no province has yet opened an office in Washington. They primarily promote trade and seek investment, though on occasion, they have had more political responsibilities, as when they participated in lobbying in London concerning the federal constitutional initiative of 1980. In addition, provincial governments frequently conduct trade missions abroad.

Such promotional activities have some potential for damaging Canadian interests. They can carry provincial competition for markets and investment into the international arena, although the regional specialization of the Canadian economy is likely to limit this result. They also permit Canada to project a discordant voice abroad, thus undermining our bargaining power. In this Commission's view, however, trade promotion abroad is a natural extension of provincial economic responsibilities at home. As long as the provinces are merely promoting themselves, they are little threat to the integrity of Canada's national interest. Indeed, there is much room for greater federal-provincial and interprovincial co-operation here; the regional expertise of provincial governments can support federal government efforts, and provinces can use the international skills and resources of Canadian trade officials. Interprovincial co-operation is also possible. At this point, then, Commissioners recommend that the federal government monitor and keep informed of provincial activity, without exercising direct control. Responsibility for international trade gives the federal government a clear mandate to regulate and, if necessary, to override external economic activities, undertaken by the provinces, which involve formal agreements with other states or the creation of state-to-state trading relationships.

Finally, the long border between Canada and the United States creates a host of relationships between American states and Canadian provinces. A 1974 study[4] by the State Department of the United States found 766 existing state-provincial agreements or understandings. A study published in 1978[5] found that British Columbia was involved in 649 different interactions with both federal and state governments in the United States. Meetings between Premiers and state Governors have become regular events, among them such gatherings as the annual Conference of Eastern Premiers and New England State Governors. Recently, states bordering on the Great Lakes agreed with Quebec and Ontario concerning water diversion from the Great Lakes Basin. Most such interactions involve limited co-operation on mutual problems and pose few questions about Canadian sovereignty. Commissioners are of the opinion, however, that it should be the responsibility of provinces to inform the federal Department of External Affairs about any such agreements, and that the Department should establish procedures for monitoring such undertakings.

Domestic Economic Management

Earlier in this Report Commissioners emphasized the greatly expanded role that government has performed since the end of the Second World War, a development common to all major industrialized countries in the Western world. While many taxpayers appear to consider that government has

overextended itself, few hark back to the 19th century as the "good old days". Today we have a mixed economy in which the invisible hand of the market is still very powerful; but it is not the only hand. Governments do help to manage or give direction to economic activity although the free-enterprise system is self-regulating to a considerable extent.

Continued specialization in economic activity, with its counterpart of increasing interdependence on both a national and a global scale, has meant that decision making has become an intricate and complex process in the private and public sectors. Entanglement and overlapping activities are inevitable; there can be no turning back of the clock.

A central theme of this Report is that relative to current practice, governments should rely more on market forces and less on intervention designed either to frustrate or to anticipate those forces. Commissioners' recommendation for extending the process of international trade liberalization reflects this theme. So, too, does our proposed industrial policy, concerning which we indicate that a targeted approach is unlikely to be more effective than a market-oriented set of broad framework policies. This theme of market competition does not, however, offer a panacea for management of the economy. Governments must still set the rules of the game, both domestically and internationally. Specialization and interdependence will no doubt intensify with technological change, "networking" all economic players, both private and public, into a tighter and tighter web.

This development need not be at all ominous, as long as well-developed lines of communication are in use, and as long as the competition for Canada's human, capital and natural resources results in their employment in highly valued activities. Nevertheless, governments face some very difficult trade-offs. Regional diversity in Canada, for example, makes consensus building an extremely protracted process. Sectors of the economy have regional dimensions which appear to pull in opposite directions, towards protectionism, on the one hand, and freer trade on the other. The federal government, in forging national policies, must recognize these divergent regional interests. At the same time, it must give consistent policy signals to the larger international community, on which 30 per cent of Canada's gross national product depends.

Through their tax, expenditure and regulatory policies and programs, governments in Canada influence the growth in productivity of the whole economy. Various policy and program combinations can affect in different ways productivity growth and, hence, the standard of living of all Canadians. Furthermore, the actions of government influence the competitiveness of domestic industry to a considerable degree.

These observations about the role of government apply in all countries; our particular task is to ensure that Canadian governments function at least as effectively as governments in other countries. It is vital that public administration in Canada be conducted in a highly competent fashion. We Canadians should therefore pursue our broad societal goals in ways that, consistent with those goals, maximize the returns from our human, capital and natural resources.

In this context, our federal form of government poses both advantages and disadvantages for managing the domestic economy. The allocation of constitutional responsibilities between two distinct orders of government lets Canadians match publicly provided goods and services with the preferences of constituent groups across the country. Federalism itself is testimony to the fact that in many instances, we do not need national consensus in order to provide public goods and services. Our educational systems need not, and should not, be uniform, for community views vary greatly across Canada. By contrast, however, there are occasions when national consensus is necessary. National defence provides one obvious example, but some dimensions of managing our domestic economy also require national consensus. Clearly, our position on trade cannot be split in such a way as to respect the protectionist leanings of some Canadians and the free-trade leanings of others. If we are to move toward free-trade on a multilateral or a bilateral basis, a common purpose must prevail.

The advocates of federalism, among whom we Commissioners count ourselves, champion federalism as the optimal form of government: a system that provides more checks and balances against monolithic government than unitary states. Dividing constitutional responsibilities between two orders of government highlights the excesses or inadequacies of any one government. Federalism, in short, is a competitive system of government, which defies tight compartmentalization of constitutional responsibilities.

It is this very competition, however, that many see as being carried to unproductive extremes. Bidding between governments to direct private investment in favour of selected constituents can locate industry where the need is greatest, thereby realizing the broad social benefits associated with private investment. Such competition, however, can go to the point where, through skilful demands of private investors, a firm or group of firms appropriates the entire benefit. Moreover, bidding and competition between federal and provincial governments can fragment an industry, leading to smaller scales of operation and higher costs. Of more general concern, such competition can fracture the Canadian common market through creating barriers to the free movement of goods, people and capital.

These advantages and disadvantages of our federal form of government call for institutional mechanisms tailored to the policy issue at hand. There is no panacea, such as some standard model of co-ordination and co-operation between 11 governments. Co-ordination and co-operation carry their own costs, and it is not obvious that the anticipated benefits always outweigh these costs. This Commission suggests a case-by-case policy approach, beginning with macro-economic demand management and progressing through the micro-level decisions of resource allocation.

Stabilization Policies and High Employment

To counter the vagaries of the business cycle, governments employ demand-management policies designed either to stimulate or to moderate overall aggregate demand for goods and services. The first blush of enthusiasm for Keynes-inspired demand-management policies, however, has gradually faded.

There is now a much greater appreciation than there was during the immediate post-Second World War period of the difficulty of forecasting events and the lags involved in realizing the expected results from policy changes. In addition, economists now recognize public expectations as integral to the economic system, thus challenging the old notion of a trade-off between employment and inflation. Further, the interdependence of national economies and the rapidity of capital movements seriously constrain the latitude available to a small economy like Canada's to counter external "shocks". Independence in domestic policy making is a more modest privilege than most such states/economies appear willing to accept.

In Part III of this Report, Commissioners indicated that the makers of demand-management policies ought to consider the medium to the long term, using discretionary changes in policy only in periods of serious and prolonged recession or "overheating" of the economy. We indicated, too, that structural and institutional features of our economy meant that high levels of unemployment (in the 6.5 to 8 per cent range) were an inevitable adjunct of avoiding inflationary pressures. Until we redress these structural and institutional features by such means as reforming the Unemployment Insurance system and the functioning of labour markets, we should not use demand-management policies to push unemployment below rates of 6.5 to 8 per cent. Control of inflation, we pointed out, is an essential part of good economic management.

In Part III, we outlined several measures for cushioning the employment consequences of the business cycle in order to contribute to the goal of higher employment while maintaining price stability. Wage and price controls and other forms of wage contracts, including "gain sharing", were among the measures we suggested. In some senses these measures are possible substitutes for traditional demand-management policies, but they are also complements. Indeed, wage and price controls are likely to be effective only if demand-management policies are acting in tandem to restrain the economy. Discretionary demand-management policies are less important if gain sharing is widespread, for it is easier to maintain production and employment in periods of depressed markets.

What are the implications of these findings for the constitutional division of powers? And what is the significance of the institutional mechanisms for co-ordination and co-operation between federal and provincial governments? The response depends on the particular instrument employed to obtain stabilization and higher employment.

Fiscal Policy

Its critics often view federalism as fracturing the decision-making system, with the result that governments move in different directions. For many years the exercise of fiscal policy seemed to serve as an illustration of this premise. The provinces, by increasing taxes or cutting expenditures, could frustrate any attempts of the federal government to create more spending, either by increasing federal spending or by reducing taxes. Alternatively, provincial tax cuts or expenditure increases could frustrate attempts by the federal

government to restrain an overheated economy. The potential for this counter-productive behaviour has clearly increased since 1945, with the growth of provincial governments relative to the federal government. Whereas the federal government accounted for 58 per cent of total government spending in 1950, it accounted for only 49 per cent in 1980. The change in the percentage shares is even greater if we express them net of intergovernmental transfers paid to other levels of government.

Paralleling the faster growth of provincial expenditures, provincial tax revenues have also grown more rapidly in recent decades. Retail sales tax is important to most provinces, and some have, on occasion, lowered rates to increase consumer demand in periods of recession. Ontario and Quebec have both used variations in sales-tax rates to help particular sectors of their economies. In 1978, the federal government, in an effort to provide some short-term stimulus, promised to reimburse provincial governments if they undertook to cut their retail sales taxes. In response, Quebec cut its sales tax more heavily than requested, but only for selective products prominent in Quebec's industrial output, initiating federal-provincial conflict which limited the effectiveness of the project.

Despite the potential for divergent fiscal policies, and instances, as in 1978, of poorly co-ordinated fiscal policy, it is not at all clear that our federal form of government hampers effective management of demand. The two orders of government have generally harmonized their tax bases, and federal influence over private-sector spending remains strong through the structure and level of taxation.

Federal and provincial governments do not formally co-ordinate expenditure levels, but this has not proved to be a major problem for federal fiscal policy. Ministers of Finance from the eleven governments usually meet at least once a year to consult on their budget plans, and the Continuing Committee of Officials on Fiscal and Economic Matters, established in 1955, has further facilitated communication. The federal government, in formulating its own fiscal policy, is thus able to give some consideration to the activities of the provincial governments. The size of federal expenditures, although diminishing as a share of total public outlays, has not declined in relation to the gross national product, and its potential for affecting the level of total demand in the economy has not significantly eroded.

Thus Commissioners do not see federalism as a major impediment to the continued effectiveness of federal fiscal policy. Accordingly, our recommendations are relatively small in scale. We believe that consultation among Finance Ministers has proved useful, and we recommend formal recognition of this process, entailing designated times and specified procedures. There should be closer co-ordination of the timing of federal and provincial budgets, in order to reduce uncertainty during the period when federal and provincial governments are formulating their budgets. These more closely co-ordinated budgets should affect the frequency and timing of the formal meetings of the Ministers of Finance. Finally, we recommend ways to help maintain the current level of harmony in the tax base.

Monetary Policy

Monetary policy seeks to regulate the supply of money and credit in the economy as a whole. It must be co-ordinated with fiscal policy in such a way that the two complement each other in stabilizing the economy. As with fiscal policy, there is no question that the federal government possesses the constitutional authority to pursue these goals. The federal government has authority, under section 91 of the Constitution Act, 1867, over currency and coinage, banking, the incorporation of banks, and the issue of paper money and legal tender. With these instruments, it is able to influence, at least to some degree, interest rates and the exchange rate. The growing activity of the so-called "near-banks" (that is, the provincially chartered trust and loan companies and credit unions) affects the ability of the central bank to influence the supply of money. Parliament concluded, however, when it revised the Bank Act in 1980, that this situation did not pose a significant problem for monetary policy. Similarly, as major borrowers of funds in international markets, provinces can influence the exchange rate; yet again, the main instruments of control lie in federal hands. The issues for federalism, then, are economic and political rather than constitutional.

An important political issue related to monetary policy has been the demand by some provinces for a regionally differentiated policy. The fact is, however, that the mobility of capital within the economic union does not permit interregional variation in interest rates. Moreover, as Commissioners have already noted, we do not believe that macro-economic policy is an appropriate instrument for pursuing regional development. In any event, recent experience has shown that a small open economy such as Canada's cannot follow a monetary policy which is isolated from the world financial system. The constraint is international, not domestic.

Incomes Policies

Incomes policies are intended to moderate the rate of inflation by controlling price increases and increases in wages and salaries. In Chapter 3, Commissioners argued against the adoption of a permanent incomes policy in Canada. We do not believe that such a policy is consistent with the flexibility and adaptability required in a rapidly changing world. Moreover, since the regulation of labour, property and civil rights – all of which are affected by incomes policy – lies largely within provincial jurisdiction, a permanent incomes policy would redistribute the powers and responsibilities of both orders of government. If temporary controls become necessary on an emergency basis, however, the federal power has the authority to impose them under the "Peace, Order, and good Government" clause. This authority was clearly affirmed in the 1975 Inflation Reference Case.

While Commissioners do not advocate a permanent incomes policy, there are two approaches to the issue that would not suffer from the constitutional objections that face permanent wage and price controls: a tax-based incomes policy (TIP), or a policy, like the recent "Six-and-Five" program, that applies only to federal employees and employers falling within federal labour

jurisdiction. A TIP would certainly require federal-provincial consultation, since it would involve important changes in federal tax law with major implications for the provinces. Indeed, it would require provincial acquiescence, if not full-fledged support, since the provincial governments could issue regulations or modify their taxes in such a way as to neutralize the federal tax incentives that are supposed to make the program work. The use of a Six-and-Five type approach to incomes policy, whether on a permanent or temporary basis, avoids the thorny question of the division of powers by confining federal regulations to those employers and employees over which it has jurisdiction. This group does not constitute a majority of employers and employees, but it is large enough so that an incomes policy that applied to it could have a significant affect on the economy and serve as a demonstration for the provinces and for the private actors whom they regulate. The federal government could further extend the range of a policy of this type by making conformity to these restraints a condition of some or all of its procurement contracts.

Finally, provincial governments have also promoted restraint. As with the federal Six-and-Five program, they have recently concentrated on restraining public sector wage increases and on controlling provincially regulated prices. The provincial programs have varied considerably in response to local conditions and the political and economic objectives of each government. In several provinces, such as British Columbia, Quebec and Newfoundland, they have produced vigorous internal conflict. This variation is again consistent with Commissioners' emphasis on the advantages of federalism in allowing for variety and experiment, and on diffusing conflict widely. These differences in approach, however, took place within a broad common framework which was the product of the common conditions within which provinces and the federal government found themselves.

Labour Market Restructuring: Gain Sharing

Commissioners view change in the structure of labour markets as perhaps the best way of reducing the high levels of structural unemployment that fiscal and monetary policies appear incapable of altering. Many factors affect the functioning of labour markets. Effective information channels can link workers to changing employment opportunities. Mobility grants can facilitate this matching process. Education and training can ensure the right mix of skills in the work-force.

Intervention in the wage-setting process is another factor that can affect labour markets. It can take the form of minimum wage policies, tax and other incentives designed to influence labour and management in bargaining, and regulations covering labour relations, such as those relating to union certification and the right to strike. Most of these factors fall primarily within provincial jurisdiction. Does this fact limit the capacity of the federal government to act and, more generally, impede effective policy?

Commissioners' chief recommendation with respect to labour markets in Part III was the use of federal tax incentives to encourage the private sector to determine wage levels, to some extent, by the employer's market gains. We

believe that the federal government, operating in its own jurisdiction, can pursue such an objective through the tax system. We do not expect such action to generate serious inter-regional or intergovernmental tensions.

Finally, as Canada tries out new approaches to finding answers for these questions, the variety and experimentation that federalism allows again offers an important advantage. Provincial labour laws have a great deal in common: common origins in federal wartime labour-relations legislation: and similarities in the economic and political forces at work. There are also significant variations from province to province. British Columbia, Saskatchewan, Ontario and Quebec have made important innovations, many of them the subject of controversy. In recent years, in several jurisdictions, policies favourable to organized labour have given way to a more restrictive approach, particularly with respect to the public sector. The point here is not whether individuals approve or disapprove of such changes, but the possibility for variety and experiment. Labour/management relations are indeed a national concern, but it does not follow that provincial regulation is inappropriate as a means to deal with it.

Infrastructural Development

Transportation and communication networks link the citizens spread out across our vast nation, facilitating the exchange of goods, services and ideas among them. Financial institutions discharge an important function in matching investment funds with Canadian needs and opportunities. These sorts of material and symbolic ties have helped to build the Canadian nation as witness the vital contribution of the Canadian Pacific Railway. All these networks are essential, not only to the economic health of Confederation, but also to the maintenance of the political unity that is the ultimate rationale for the existence of the economic union. Economically and politically, they are essential to making a living reality of the concept of economic union.

Transportation

Canada must develop a coherent regulatory regime encompassing all the major forms of transportation that knit the country together: railways, highways and trucking, Great Lakes and ocean shipping, and aeronautics. Canada's Constitution does not expressly confer jurisdiction over a general category of transportation. However, section 92(10) of the Constitution Act, 1867 placed navigation and shipping, railways, canals and telegraphs in federal jurisdiction, and gave the federal government power to declare other works and undertakings running beyond provincial boundaries within its purview.

The courts have interpreted the "Peace, Order, and good Government" clause of section 91 as granting constitutional authority for federal regulation of the aeronautics industry. The federal government now has clear jurisdiction over the whole of that sector. Clearly established jurisdiction is not always enough, however, as the authors of one research study made for this Commission have suggested.[6] They concluded that provincial ownership or

share holding in important regional airlines has frustrated federal attempts to use airline regulation as an instrument of national economic development. This is at least part of the reason, they argue, for recent federal moves toward deregulation of airlines.

The constitutional problem associated with federal regulation of railways and trucking is rather different. Judicial interpretation of subsections (*a*) and (*b*) of section 92(10) has resulted in the assigning of federal jurisdiction over the regulation of interprovincial undertakings of these kinds and of provincial jurisdiction over intra-provincial undertakings. The federal share of this split jurisdiction has gradually widened as the courts have held that transportation units which perform both interprovincial and intra-provincial functions fall under exclusive federal jurisdiction. The federal government also has jurisdiction over undertakings connected to, or forming part of, a broader interprovincial undertaking.

This approach has granted the federal government sufficient jurisdictional latitude to implement national transportation policies in these sectors, and in the railway sector it appears to have used this authority appropriately. The same cannot be said, however, with respect to the trucking sector, where, under Part III of the National Transportation Act, the federal government has delegated its powers to license and regulate to provincial regulatory agencies. This delegation has resulted in ten different sets of trucking-industry regulations, each formulated by two orders of government. The consequent arrangement is expensive to administer and confusing in its effects. At the time of writing, the governments of Canada are engaged in discussions with the intent of harmonizing these regulations, and agreement seems within reach. If that does not happen, serious consideration should be given to consolidating responsibility for interprovincial trucking under federal jurisdiction.

Communications

Electronic communication links are as vital to the Canadian economic union as were railways in the past. The aims of federal policy with respect to communications parallel those already identified for transportation. So does the constitutional status of federal regulation, which the courts have interpreted as giving the federal government exclusive jurisdiction over radio communication in its various forms, including radio, television, cable television, microwave and satellite.

The jurisdictional situation with respect to telephones and related forms of telecommunications is, however, unique. The courts have recognized neither the type of split jurisdiction that applies to trucking nor the exclusive jurisdiction of one order of government. Instead, a patchwork of jurisdictions has gradually evolved. Canada's two largest telephone companies and two specialized domestic common carriers fall within federal jurisdiction. Seven major provincial carriers and a host of smaller companies come under provincial regulation. To cap it all, no one regulates Telecom Canada, an association of the ten principal carriers that co-ordinates the operation of Canada's only national, public, switched-telephone network.

This jurisdictional patchwork has made it difficult to develop a national telecommunications policy, and this failure, in turn, has hindered the creation of alternative national networks and services. By international standards, Canada has an advanced and effective telecommunications system. As befits a country where the conquering of distance is a fundamental challenge, Canada has pioneered a number of important technological advances in telecommunications. We are in danger, however, of failing to keep up with the adoption of new facilities, and of falling behind the United States. Hence it is important that we clarify jurisdiction and roles.

Federal attempts to develop and pursue a comprehensive national policy on telephones and telecommunications began in 1968. At the same time, provinces were also exploring the part played by communications in economic development and culture. By the 1970s, they were seeking greater constitutional authority in the field. These conflicting objectives gave rise to bitter federal-provincial conflicts and very little effective action, as distinctions between content and hardware or between inter- and intra-provincial communications broke down under the impact of rapid technological change. Canadians must change this situation.

Three possible directions for change exist. First, the federal government might assert jurisdiction over the entire telecommunications sector. This action would bring the provincially regulated telephone companies, along with Telecom Canada, under federal regulation, but it would be very difficult. Several provinces actually own their telephone companies, and there are many aspects of services within a province that are the legitimate concern of provincial governments; these include, for example, services to remote areas and integration of cable and telephone services.

A second possible solution would be to formalize concurrent jurisdiction, with federal paramountcy. This arrangement would allow the federal government to regulate those aspects of telecommunications that are essential to interprovincial and international services and to maintenance of an effective nation-wide, telecommunications system. Provinces would retain the authority to regulate with respect to local dimensions. Such concurrency would provide a high degree of flexibility in responding to technological changes. Shared jurisdiction of this sort, however, does have dangers as American experience has shown: intrastate and interstate services use the same facilities so that separate state and federal regulation of local and interstate rates is both difficult and expensive to manage.

The third option would be joint regulation. Under this arrangement, both federal and provincial governments would delegate their regulatory authority to a common federal-provincial regulatory agency. This adjustment would involve a major change in the role and composition of the existing Canadian Radio-Television and Telecommunications Commission, either by shifting some of its responsibilities to a new body or by involving provinces in CRTC appointments and procedures. While such an arrangement might overcome some of the problems of two-tier regulation, it would lessen flexibility and reduce the responsibility and accountability of both orders of government.

On balance, concurrent jurisdiction with federal paramountcy is Commissioners' preferred option, since it meets the key objectives of ensuring

a nation-wide network for communication flows of all kinds and of showing sensitivity to provincial interests.

Financial Institutions

Just as our transportation and communications systems create a vital link between buyers and sellers, and between producers and consumers, so financial institutions form a critical component of the economic infrastructure, providing the key links between Canadian savers and investors. Historically, four distinct types of financial institution have been the basis of our financial system: banks, trust companies, insurance companies and securities brokers. Each of these four could tap only some sources of savings and would make only certain types of investment. At present, this system is undergoing fundamental transformation. The four types of financial institutions are becoming less and less distinct as each takes on functions previously performed exclusively by one of the other types.

Rapid technological change, spurred by international competition, is one of the driving forces behind this transformation. These changes have made it possible for financial institutions to offer consumers "one-stop shopping" for financial services. Quebec is deregulating its financial institutions, and this action, in turn, has put pressure on other provincial governments to follow suit. Constitutionally, the federal government holds exclusive jurisdiction over the banks, while provincial governments regulate the securities markets and the brokers that operate within them. The constitutional regime governing the trust and insurance companies is more complex.

The current constitutional arrangements have proved adequate to the effective regulation of the four types of financial institution, but the convergence described above raises new constitutional issues. If the four types are disappearing, the distinct regulatory regimes organized around them automatically become obsolete. The Economic Council of Canada has argued that in their place, we should adopt a "functional" approach to regulation, applying uniform rules to the performance of specific financial services such as stock broking, regardless of the institution performing them.[7] For example, the federal Bank Act would regulate the "banking" functions of trust companies. In this respect, technological developments in the financial sector seem to require the same sort of regulatory change already mentioned above as relating to telephones and telecommunications. The issue, for our purposes here, is whether the existing division of powers can permit effective regulation based on function.[8]

This issue has several facets. Does development of an effective, functional system of regulation require federal leadership? If it does, has the federal government constitutional authority to provide such leadership? If it has, would exercise of such leadership provoke substantial provincial opposition? And, most significant, what are the most important directions to pursue?

These questions are much easier to ask than they are to answer. With respect to the first, the record is mixed. Despite the regulatory fragmentation, we have developed a highly efficient, nationally integrated financial system. For a very long period, the banks have served as nation-wide institutions.

Recent developments in other branches of the financial industry are also moving in the same direction. Indeed, it has been one of the historic regional grievances in Canada that the financial industry has been too concentrated and therefore insensitive to the financial needs and opportunities of specific areas.

Provincial regulation of the stock markets constitutes a particularly interesting example. In principle, there seems to be a strong argument for federal regulation. In practice, we have achieved much the same result with provincial jurisdiction because of the leading role that Ontario, the centre of the Canadian financial industry, has been able to play, often in partnership with Quebec. One research study prepared for this Commission[9] argues that there is no pressing reason to tamper with this arrangement: provincial regulation has satisfied national purposes. Other research[10] is less sanguine about the future. Technological change, the increasing international integration of capital markets, and the desire of provinces, especially Quebec, to regulate markets in pursuit of provincial development goals are all likely to place greater strains on the existing system in the near future.

In light of the importance of our financial institutions for effective economic development and adaptation to a more competitive world, it is essential that we find answers to these questions with all possible speed. The investigative committee which recently produced a report on the regulation of Canadian financial institutions,[11] a federal joint committee comprised of representatives of the federal government and the industry, investigated some of these problems. This process did not fully involve the provinces, which is unfortunate, given that much of the expertise in this area is provincial, and in view of the divided jurisdiction noted above. This is an area in which the Council of Ministers Responsible for Economic Development could monitor developments.

Adjustment and Social Policies

Within a framework of freer trade and effective policies of stabilization and infrastructural development, Canadian workers and employers must adapt creatively to changing economic circumstances, moving out of activities with declining prospects and seizing new opportunities. We shall review three groups of policies, all designed to facilitate this process. In all these areas, both federal and provincial governments play important roles.

Reducing Obstacles to Market Allocations

In Part III of this Report, Commissioners spelled out some major recommendations to reduce barriers to market allocation of resources. We emphasized the importance of restraining the natural political impulse to "bail out" specific industries. Obviously, this issue involves no question of the division of powers in the federal system: our call is simply for restraint. Yet Canadians should recognize that federalism probably increases the tendency to pursue "rescue" policies. Industries in trouble, whether large or small in economic terms, are important in the lives of individual provinces and communities.

Provincial governments may therefore have a comparatively large stake in those industries. Therefore, if the federal government resists the impulse to bail them out, there will be much greater pressures on the provincial governments to intervene, and for them to add their voices to increase the pressure on the federal government.

In one respect, a less-interventionist federal industrial policy will tend to mitigate intergovernmental and interregional conflict. One common source of regional grievance is the perception that political considerations motivate highly visible discretionary federal bail-outs which favour particular regions. A common reaction is, "Why did you not do the same for us?" In the long run, greater restraint by the federal government in taking such decisions should strengthen general perceptions of its fairness and even-handedness.

Competition policy and product standards are vital to effective market allocation. Effective competition policy is essential to developing the full benefits that can accrue from an economic union. Canada has not been very aggressive in encouraging competition, and one reason for this may be our constitutional situation. Canadian legislation relating to competition has found its constitutional justification almost exclusively in the federal power to make criminal law. This arrangement has resulted in limiting the policy tools and the range of remedies available, and in creating some ambiguity about the location, federal or provincial, of the power to launch prosecutions. It provides an excellent example of the tendency for the exigencies of federalism to constrain the tools and instruments through which policy is pursued.

The recent Canadian National Transportation case[12] decided by the Supreme Court cleared up some of these questions. In his concurring judgment, Mr. Justice Brian Dickson argued that the regulation of competition is one of those activities which provincial governments could not practically or constitutionally enact, for "If competition is to be regulated at all, it must be regulated federally." Mr. Justice Dickson raised the question of whether this situation implied that the federal government could justify legislation on competition under the general trade and commerce power set forth in section 91(2), rather than under the criminal law power. In Commissioners' view, it is essential to resolve this ambiguity. Clearly, regulating competition is an aspect of overall regulation of trade and commerce throughout Canada. We propose, accordingly, that section 91(2) be amended explicitly to include federal regulatory power over "competition".

Closely related to competition policy is the regulation of labelling and product standards. The recent cases involving Labatt's and Dominion Stores appear to have thrown the federal powers in this area into considerable confusion. These decisions invalidated important sections of the federal Food and Drug Act on the grounds that they purported to impose standards on products that were made and traded intra-provincially. In the Labatt's case,[13] however, the product in question was beer, a standardized product, advertised and sold across Canada by national companies, which simply happened to be made in breweries in each province. To see brewing and a host of analogous kinds of production as a local activity is, as one economist commented, "dangerously out of touch with the modern economy's seamless web of production, promotion and sale of consumer goods."[14] In the Dominion Stores

case,[15] the issue was federally defined grading standards for apples, where much the same analysis applies. Taken together, these decisions appear significantly to narrow the interpretation of the federal power under section 91(2) to regulate trade and commerce throughout the country. Widely varying standards and definitions in commonly used products can impose high costs on producers and consumers. Thus Commissioners recommend a further addition to the general trade and commerce power: the regulation of product standards.

Neither of these cases involves important regional issues. In both, effective remedies seem beyond reasonable provincial capacities. Few provinces have shown interest in legislating in these fields. Indeed, in earlier rounds of constitutional discussion, a majority of provinces signified their willingness to contemplate a constitutional amendment with respect to product standards.

A final element favouring elimination of obstacles to market allocation is a view that Canadian governments should move toward reducing, or at least rationalizing, the burdens of regulation in as many fields as possible. Again, this is a general recommendation that Commissioners urge on both orders of government. In a number of fields, such as environmental standards, consumer protection and occupational health and safety, economic actors find themselves subject to regulation from two or more sources, either in the form of ten different provincial regulatory regimes, or in the form of federal and provincial regimes. This plethora of systems can be costly. On the other hand, in the field of the environment, we recommend a strengthened regulatory framework. In many instances, these are relatively new areas of government activity into which both orders moved, and in which stable relations have yet to be worked out.

Commissioners wish to emphasize two points. First, where there are divergent provincial regulatory regimes, the most appropriate model is harmonization of provincial laws through interprovincial mechanisms. Secondly, where the problem arises out of a division of regulatory regimes between federal and provincial orders, we believe, as with telecommunications and finance, that the appropriate principle is functional regulation: the regulation of specific activities rather than of specific institutions.

Encouraging and Facilitating Adaptation

Throughout our Report, we Commissioners have emphasized the need to encourage mobility of workers from areas of low to high employment opportunity. We have recommended a Transitional Adjustment Assistance Program (TAAP) to increase incentives for relocation and training. We have urged removal of existing incentives, found especially in the Unemployment Insurance system, that support certain types of inefficient industries. We have also called for more effective collection and dissemination of information about job opportunities across the country. The federal government has authority to address all these issues. We do realize, however, that the emphasis on adjustment through mobility does seem to push against the emphasis on "place prosperity", that is, on sustaining existing communities, which often underlies federal regional policy and much provincial industrial

development policy. In our view, Canadians must continually balance place prosperity against national efficiency and individual mobility against the preservation of communities. Government action can certainly increase the prosperity of some places in some circumstances. Where this is not possible, TAAP offers an ideal form of adjustment assistance.

Training. Commissioners argued in Part V that the development of a skilled and adaptable Canadian work-force is essential for effective adaptation to new possibilities. We argued, too, for shifting the balance between institutional and on-the-job training in the direction of the former approach and claimed that the TAAP would help to achieve this end. Training activities are a field of long-standing and complex federal-provincial relationships. On the one hand, training is an essential element of national economic management, closely linked to many other federal programs, such as Unemployment Insurance, and to the successful meeting of the needs of a national labour market. On the other hand, training is part of the educational process, which is a matter of provincial jurisdiction.

Through shared-cost programs, the federal government has helped to develop vocational training schools and community colleges in the various provinces. Under the federal Adult Occupational Training Act, the emphasis shifted to the federal purchase of student places in training courses for individuals selected for training. Under the National Training Act of 1982, somewhat greater emphasis was placed on funding training through the private sector, a thrust with which Commissioners sympathize. There is much room here for experimentation and innovation. We do not believe, however, that it is necessary to shift powers or responsibilities. Since "training" is such a multi-faceted process which can extend through a whole lifetime, federal and provincial governments, and the public and private sectors, must all participate. The need here is for effective co-ordination. We believe that within a broad national framework, the government of Canada and of each province should work out a specific mix of programs for that province; the duty of the federal government should be to contribute its perspective of the needs of the national labour market, and that of the province to contribute the prespective of its market.

Education. Almost every one of our values, from national identity, to social and cultural values, to economic effectiveness, affects education. In Part V, Commissioners noted the special concern of many intervenors for the character and quality of Canadian education. We concluded that Canada's educational institutions, particularly those of the post-secondary sector, are not always fully ready to facilitate adaptation or to emphasize excellence. Significant changes must be made, and we argued that there is a strong case for reorientation of federal activity in this field to assist in making them.

The federal government already acts extensively in education, for the most part in post-secondary education and research. In 1983–84, the federal government spent more than $3 billion on education-related matters; more than half of this amount consisted of cash payments for post-secondary education under the Established Programs Financing (EPF) arrangements.

There are no conditions attached to the EPF transfers, and the amounts allocated no longer bear any direct relationship to actual spending in the field.

Commissioners make few recommendations with respect to primary and secondary education. There is little scope for federal activity here. The interprovincial Council of Ministers of Education (CMEC) has done extensive work co-ordinating curricula and facilitating exchanges and the like, and it could extend its work. We believe that more needs to be done to monitor quality and standards in primary and secondary education, and to conduct related research. Ideally, changes in these directions would be the result of a private-sector initiative, and the work done would influence both orders of government. Finally, we note that in the Constitution Act, 1982, Canadians did commit themselves to one crucial "national standard" in education: the right to education in the local minority official language in every province, subject only to the condition "where numbers warrant".

Commissioners believe that post-secondary education is so much part of a national and indeed even an international, system, and is so necessary to innovation, both because of its training of skilled personnel and because of research, that reorientation of the federal role is essential, even though we believe that the provinces can and must retain jurisdictional responsibility in this sector. In Part V, we developed two broad options. The first is to channel federal support for post-secondary education directly to students. A move in this direction would require careful consultation with provinces. Since, under present arrangements, the federal government's share of funding of post-secondary education varies considerably from province to province, it would be essential that the transition not introduce regional inequities.

Such a scheme of unconditional direct grants to students would, Commissioners believe, be a constitutional exercise of the spending power. However, if the federal government were to use the grants as a more active instrument of federal intervention – for example, by using them to determine admission standards to universities, or by providing differential grants scaled to particular fields and disciplines – the situation would become more complex. Such use might be challenged successfully as federal legislation in an area of provincial jurisdiction and therefore an invalid use of the spending power. On a more practical basis, it could produce havoc in the system if provinces and universities were continually scrambling to adapt to changing federal definitions of needs. Such a situation could arise if the provinces exercised little influence over these definitions, and if the federal government had no responsibility for the financial or administrative difficulties that their decisions produced. For these reasons, we do not believe that student grants or loans should be used differentially in this way.

If Ottawa and the provinces decide that the federal government should concern itself more with the content of educational policy, a second option would be to restore some conditionality to federal transfers in support of post-secondary education. The federal government would relate the transfers to actual spending and tie them to some clear national objectives. If we were to move in this direction, it would be essential, first, to spell out such objectives precisely.

More generally, Commissioners believe that considerable federal-provincial consultation is essential to determine realistically and productively overall levels of funding and of national educational goals in the post-secondary field. We note with sadness that concern with fiscal arrangements, rather than with the aims and purposes of post-secondary education, has dominated federal-provincial relations in this field.

Sharing the Benefits and Burdens of Adjustment

In Part V of this Report, Commissioners argued that an essential element of adjustment is shielding or protecting those who find themselves harmed by the process. Effective social policy – a well-designed social safety net – is a prerequisite for successful adjustment. Failure to manage fairly the disruptive effects of change will accentuate political resistance to such changes. This is true for individuals, communities, provinces and regions.

Adjustment policy and social policy are thus inextricably linked. As in adjustment policy, so in social policy, shared jurisdiction is central. The growth of the welfare state accounted for much of the post-Second World War change in the federal system and became a central aspect of co-operative federalism. The Constitution Act, 1867 assigned to the provinces responsibility for most aspects of social welfare. By the 1930s, economic, demographic and social change, combined with changing conceptions of social justice, had demonstrated that the provinces alone could not construct a modern "social service" state. Some shared-cost programs in pensions, health and other fields were undertaken as early as the 1920s; during the Great Depression in the 1930s, the federal government assumed more responsibility for assisting provinces to provide welfare and relief to their residents. During and after the Second World War, federal jurisdictional authority in the social policy field expanded as constitutional amendments gave the federal government authority over unemployment insurance and pensions. Through use of its spending power, that government introduced the Family Allowance program. The spending power also made possible the development of shared-cost programs in health, post-secondary education, and welfare, programs which incorporated innovations originally undertaken by provinces.

Today, with the sole exception of social assistance, the federal government is responsible for operating all the major income-security programs in the country, and is the source of most of the funds involved. It is also a central participant in hospital and medical care, and in funding social services, as well as social assistance, through the shared-cost Canada Assistance Plan (CAP). The provinces are responsible for the organization and delivery of social welfare, social services such as family counselling, and health care.

There is considerable flexibility in social policy. Provinces vary in their administration and funding of health care, though the Canada Health Act has narrowed provincial differences. Provinces retain considerable discretion in setting rates for welfare payments and in the organization and delivery of services. Through tax credits and direct payments, provinces supplement federal Old Age Security. The federal Family Allowance program permits

provinces to vary payment methods in accordance with their own social priorities.

The social policy system has also been able to accommodate Quebec's distinctiveness. In 1964, new federal-provincial arrangements permitted Quebec (and any other province) to opt out of a large number of programs, and to receive the equivalent federal funds in the form of increased tax shares. Quebec was able to enact its own contributory pension plan, the Quebec Pension Plan, which remains closely co-ordinated with the Canada Pension Plan, which operates for the rest of the country.

The centre-piece for Commissioners' proposals in this area is establishment of a Universal Income Security Program (UISP), which would entail a universally available income supplement, subject to reduction at a relatively low "tax-back" rate. Such a scheme, delivered either through the federal tax system or by means of direct transfers, appears to fall within federal jurisdiction. The present federal responsibility for Family Allowances, Unemployment Insurance and Old Age Security clearly establishes a broad federal mandate for income security, of which the UISP is a logical development. Moreover, we believe that individual provinces acting alone would not be capable of bringing such a program into operation.

To create the UISP, however, would involve a major change in federal-provincial relations, a change which Commissioners think would be healthy for the federal system. The 50/50 sharing of responsibility for welfare payments under CAP would end, and the provinces would become solely responsible for the provision of any supplement above the established guaranteed income level. Changes in the tax system would help to finance the UISP. Under one recommended approach, provinces would cede some tax room back to the federal government, which would then deliver the entire program. Under a less desirable arrangement, provincial governments would superimpose a provincial layer of payments on the federal transfer. Particularly under the first option, the UISP proposal would involve a major disentanglement of federal and provincial responsibilities: the federal government would have authority over basic income support, which would be set at a national minimum; the provinces would be free to increase the level of these benefits by supplementing the federal payments. Our proposal would therefore increase federal and provincial flexibility, and significantly improve accountability at both levels.

Provincial opposition to the UISP is likely, however, if the effect of this proposed program were to increase provincial responsibilities while diminishing the funds available to the provinces. The federal government should develop the program in close consultation with provincial governments. The disentanglement that the UISP calls for would not eliminate federal-provincial interdependence because any future changes in the program's levels would have immediate consequences for provincial burdens.

If it is not possible to proceed immediately with the UISP proposal, Commissioners advocate a number of smaller interim changes in social policy. First, family benefits should be rationalized by replacing current programs with a single demogrant or tax credit, to be progressively "taxed back" for

families with incomes of over $26 000 a year. This change would not raise major federal-provincial issues. A second immediate reform, which we advocated in Part V, is the revision of the Canada Assistance Plan to reduce the features that lead to a "poverty trap", creating disincentives for recipients to re-enter the work-force. This step would require considerable federal-provincial co-operation and co-ordination. The appropriate vehicle for achieving this is the Council of Ministers Responsible for Social Policy which we shall shortly propose.

Commissioners have also proposed making a number of changes in the Unemployment Insurance (UI) system. We have suggested making it more of a risk-related insurance scheme, extending the qualifying period for UI benefits, and removing regionally related subsidies built into the program. These changes will have important regional and federal-provincial ramifications. Regionally related Unemployment Insurance benefits, combined with a short qualifying period, have become a major part of the social fabric of many communities in the Atlantic provinces. Moreover, unilateral federal changes in Unemployment Insurance inevitably have major repercussions for provincial welfare costs.

The changes Commissioners have proposed would have the greatest effect on the poorer provinces with high rates of unemployment. Under current arrangements, provincial governments receive some protection from federal reductions in the level of UI transfers: under CAP, the federal government picks up half of any additional welfare costs. If CAP disappears, however, this mechanism will not be available, and the more expensive UISP will replace it. The effect of these UI changes on provincial budgetary requirements must therefore be weighed carefully, and the government must ensure that compensation is available for provinces especially hard hit by them. The main purpose of this change, after all, would be to increase the incentives for individual mobility, and not to shift burdens onto the provinces.

Single-industry resource-based towns raise a special adjustment problem. A mine closure or some similar event can devastate such communities almost overnight. The costs of such events extend far beyond the workers actually employed in the particular resource sector affected: to ease the burden of such economic shocks will require co-ordination of the activities of all three orders of government. Commissioners therefore propose a mechanism analogous to that used in other kinds of emergencies: an *ad hoc* federal-provincial-municipal task force that would include representatives of the community to co-ordinate these efforts. In Part V, Commissioners suggested that the TAAP, which would be funded by the savings accruing from the Unemployment Insurance reforms noted above, should compensate for losses of assets, such as the value of housing, caused by the sudden undermining of the community's economic base.

Conclusions

Federalism is inevitably a complex system of government, and one that provides little comfort to those with tidy minds. Nonetheless, we Canadians have adapted it successfully to the requirements of our post-Second World

War Canadian society, and it remains a means of permitting policy that is sensitive to the wide diversity of needs and interests across the country. Canadian federalism has also been a source of dynamism.

This Commission has now canvassed goals and objectives, asking whether their attainment will require major changes in the structure and operation of the federal system. Some readers will infer that our answer is yes. We have, after all, made a number of suggestions for significant change: for strengthening the federal power over trade and commerce by adding competition and product standards, for redefining federal responsibilities in post-secondary education, to mention two. Yet as we have examined each area, Commissioners have found a great deal of potential for flexibility. Our vision is not of a central government hamstrung by federalism in the face of oncoming challenges; rather, we have seen the wide scope for action within federal jurisdiction. Moreover, we have directed a number of our recommendations to the provinces, rather than the federal government, and we have concluded in most instances that the provinces have the ability to respond. Finally, we have recognized that in many policy fields, shared jurisdiction is not a constitutional accident, but a faithful reflection of the co-existence of legitimate provincial and national concerns. To call for complete centralization of powers, or for extensive decentralization, in such areas would almost certainly lead policy makers to neglect important dimensions and to be less sensitive to vital interests. Thus we think that shared jurisdiction in a field such as training is both necessary and desirable. Moreover, we believe that it is possible to design effective mechanisms through which to achieve the required co-ordination.

In addition, Commissioners believe that federal jurisdiction over trade and commerce and over "Peace, Order, and good Government" can evolve in the light of emerging economic needs. The courts have constrained the trade and commerce power, and the federal government has used "Peace, Order, and good Government" largely as an emergency power; but both powers have sustained legislation of inherent national importance. We expect that this will happen again. The need, as before, will be to balance the vitality of federalism against national needs. Any legislative extension of these two forms of federal power should clearly address a widely experienced need which existing legislation, whether federal or provincial, cannot deal with adequately, and which, to be effective, must apply uniformly across the country. Furthermore, such legislation, to be acceptable, would have to respect existing provincial economic patterns; these patterns could not be set aside without a compelling, demonstrated, national need, and even then, only to the extent necessary to meet the defined national purposes. Thus, we believe it essential to protect valid provincial objectives against open-ended federal intervention in the pursuit of national goals; but there might well be cases in which judges might incrementally adapt the general federal trade powers, applying a concept of "compelling national interest" that is broader than an "emergency power", but narrower than a simple undefined national interest. We hope for further judicial creativity in developing such constitutional mediating principles.

The virtues of federalism remain important from the perspective of democracy and effective policy making. Not only does the existence of

provinces with wide powers accord with the political sense that we Canadians have of ourselves but, in addition, the provinces offer other channels of access, forums for accommodation of conflicting interests, and arenas for adaptation, experimentation and gathering of information. The very complexity of federalism provides a resilience and capacity to absorb shocks not always found in highly centralized systems.

Nevertheless, with both orders of government deploying so many instruments in the pursuit of economic growth in a competitive international environment, Commissioners recognize the need for a high degree of co-ordination. There has been much searching for the "right" mechanism to achieve this co-ordination, along with virtually continuous change in the political structures through which the federal government integrates national and regional perspectives in its own policy-making process. Commissioners believe that the recently developed mechanism of the Economic and Regional Development Agreement (ERDA) provides a promising model. ERDAs provide for bilateral co-ordination on basic goals, together with a division of labour based on agreement as to which government will take responsibility for which areas. They become the umbrellas under which the governments work out more detailed agreements between particular departments. Within this framework, we think it desirable, on grounds of accountability, that each government seek to take responsibility for final design and implementation of the relevant components of the larger agreement. In discussions, the federal government should emphasize the perspective of the whole national economy and of the integration of each region within it, and maximize linkages between regions. In accordance with our consistent emphasis on adjustment, we also believe that federal efforts should assist Canada's provinces and citizens to adjust to the new competitive environment.

The constraints that federalism imposes on economic management are not primarily constitutional. Rather, they arise out of the regional structure of our country. It is not lack of authority, for example, that will limit federal efforts to place less emphasis on place prosperity and more on individual mobility. It is political opposition — and the need to balance conflicting signals from different parts of the country — that will prove the real difficulty. For this reason we must rely on political institutions, both at the national and the intergovernmental level. To reorient the focus of Canadian economic policy will not be easy, because it will require construction of new consensus on our strategy of instruments of development and distribution. To form this strategy is a task for democratic political leadership, guided by much talk among citizens in a multitude of forums.

Notes

1. Canada, Department of Reconstruction and Supply, *Employment and Income* (Ottawa: King's Printer, 1945).
2. John D. Whyte, "Constitutional Aspects of Economic Development Policy", in *Division of Powers and Public Policy*, vol. 61, prepared for the Royal Commission on the Economic Union and Development Prospects for Canada (Toronto: University of Toronto Press, 1985).

3. Samuel H. Beer "Federalism: Lessons of the Past; Choices for the Future", in Center for National Policy, *Federalism: Making the System Work* (Washington, D.C.: The Center, 1982), p. 20.
4. This study has been summarized in Roger F. Swanson, *International Perspectives on the Canada-U.S. Relationship* (New York: New York University Press, 1978), pp. 221–65.
5. See P.R. Johannson, "British Columbia's Relation with the United States", *Canadian Public Administration* 21 (Summer 1978): 212–33.
6. See Richard Schultz and Alan Alexandroff, *Economic Regulation and the Federal System*, vol. 42 (Toronto: University of Toronto Press, 1985).
7. See Economic Council of Canada, *Efficiency and Population: A Study of Deposit Institutions* (Ottawa: Minister of Supply and Services Canada, 1976).
8. Nicolas Roy, *Mobility of Capital in the Canadian Economic Union*, vol. 66, prepared for the Royal Commission on the Economic Union and Development Prospects for Canada (Toronto: University of Toronto Press, 1985).
9. See Thomas J. Courchene, *Economic Management and the Division of Powers*, vol. 67 (Toronto: University of Toronto Press, 1985).
10. Schultz and Alexandroff, *Economic Regulation and the Federal System.*
11. Canada, Finance Canada, *The Regulation of Financial Institutions* (Ottawa: The Department, 1985).
12. *Attorney General of Canada* v. *Canadian National Transportation Ltd.* (1983), 3 D.L.R. (4th) 16 (S.C.C.)
13. *Labatt Breweries of Canada Ltd.* v. *Attorney General of Canada* (1979) 110 D.L.R. (3d) 594.
14. David McQueen, "Commentary on James C. MacPherson, 'Economic Regulation and the British North America Act' ", *Canadian Business Law Journal* 5 (1980 – 81), pp. 225 and 227.
15. *Dominion Stores Ltd.* v. *The Queen* (1979), 106 D.L.R. (3d) 581.

Sharing the Benefits of the Economic Union

Canadian politics, it often seems, is the politics of regional interests and of regional grievance. Subjects which other countries more often discuss in terms of relations between capital and labour, Canadians discuss primarily in terms of regions and provinces. The question "Who gets what?" is expressed in terms of territory and geography. This is a constant of Canadian history, one grounded both in our varied social and economic structure, and in our political institutions as well. Canadians have recently emerged from a period in which this regional perception of advantage and disadvantage has been particularly evident. Throughout the 1970s, the issues which most divided Canadians seem to have pitted region against region. These perceptions frequently emerged in this Commission's hearings.

Across the country, we found a considerable sense of grievance: a sense that decisions made by the federal government do not reflect the needs of the regions affected by them, and less frequently, but still not insignificantly, that decisions are made which discriminate against certain regions. Survey results indicate that Canadians were divided in their responses to the question of whether their province had been treated fairly by the federal government. In a 1977 survey of five provinces, a slight overall majority believed that their province was treated fairly all of the time or most of the time. Only Ontario residents, however, were strongly positive in this view, while majorities in P.E.I., Quebec, Saskatchewan and B.C. considered that their province was treated fairly only some of the time, or, an infrequent response, none of the time. In a 1979 survey, more Canadians (31.5%) responded that their region paid more than its fair share of the costs of governing Canada than replied (5.4%) that their province paid less than its fair share. The most frequent response, however, (63.2%), with majorities in every province except Alberta (50.0%) believed that their region paid its fair share.[1] The picture, therefore, is mixed. The fact remains, however, that many Canadians sense that the "Confederation bargain" has somehow not worked out fairly, and that the federal government has at times been less the "national government" than the instrument of the most populous parts of the country.

Such beliefs stem from many sources. In part, they are the result of a sense of provincial identity in which the economic health of a particular province remains a vital reference point. The actions of provincial governments often reinforce these perceptions. They are, to some extent, a political, rather than an economic, phenomenon: a sense of exclusion from power in the national capital can powerfully reinforce regional grievances.

Regional grievance is not a new element in Canadian politics. Indeed, it has been a constant theme since the first days of Confederation. Regional protests have fuelled a succession of movements of political protest in the West: the Progressives, the United Farmers, Social Credit, the Co-operative Commonwealth Federation. Regional issues have also been a significant element of successive expressions of Quebec nationalism. While regional parties have been less successful in Atlantic Canada, groups such as the Maritime Rights movement of the 1920s have often expressed regional grievances in frequent calls for "better terms". Throughout Canada's history, regional grievances

have been expressed both as demands for more provincial autonomy that would allow provinces to shape their own future, and as demands for federal policies that would be more responsive to regional interests. Regional protests are simultaneously requests for a greater influence in national decision making, and insistence on the assertion of greater autonomy and freedom to make one's own decisions.

The sense of unfairness that has sometimes surfaced in Canadian experience has had different sources at different times and in different places. In the West, grievances were originally rooted in the perception that the National Policy treated the region as an economic hinterland to central Canada, as a source of raw materials and export earnings, and as a protected market for central Canadian manufacturing, transportation and financial interests. Historic conflict thus centred on issues such as the tariff and, to a lesser extent, on transportation policy. In the 1970s, it hinged on the provinces' sense that they were being denied the full benefits of the rising value of their natural resources, which they regarded as the means by which they could diversify their economies and shift economic and political power away from central Canada.

In the Maritimes, grievances were fuelled by the long decline of the Maritime economy in the nineteenth century, by the declining importance of the region to the country as a whole, and by the persistence of regional disparities. In the 1970s, resentment increased about continued dependence on transfer payments, at the same time that Nova Scotia and Newfoundland, in particular, realized the possibility of transforming their economies by developing off-shore resources. In Quebec, grievances stemmed from the perception that national policy favoured Ontario's economic development, and that the constraints of federalism limited Quebec's ability to take charge of its own economic development. Ontario also tended to react to the events of the 1970s in a "regional" fashion as it became aware that its dominant position in the Canadian economy was being threatened both by the increase in resource revenues in the West and by the assertions of nationalism in Quebec.

Provincial governments tended to express these regional grievances through complaints about the role and actions of the central government; they took the view that the pattern of economic development in Canada was not the product of natural economic forces, but rather of the exercise of political power by major interests acting through the central government. They also called on the federal government to redress the forces of the market by using its authority to compensate those regions which the market tended to leave behind.

Thus growing expectations of the role of government reinforced Canadians' tendency to see politics in regional terms. Moreover, the increasing importance of international forces on domestic life further supported a regionalist view. The diversity of provincial economic bases meant that international forces were likely to have different domestic effects. Consequently, regional strains of the 1970s pitted resource producers against resource consumers and manufacturers, or set areas with an interest in higher

resource prices against those with an interest in lower ones; they, however, were not primarily the product of domestically generated pressures, but rather of international forces which dramatically altered the terms of trade among Canada's regions.

All of these perspectives were reflected in the "battle of the balance sheets" that occurred in the late 1970s. This controversy involved elaborate and often polemical efforts to assess which parts of the country were or were not "losers", and to identify the regional distribution of the costs and benefits of federal government activities. There were few, if any, conclusive answers. It was easy enough to identify the sources of federal tax revenues, or show where Old Age Security, Family Allowances or regional development grants went; but it was much more difficult to assess the regional effect of broad structural policies. And indeed, to many Canadians, the entire attempt to identify regional winners and losers was misguided: was it not, after all, the national economy and the welfare of individuals which were important? These questions highlight the disjunction between our tendency to view Canada as a collection of regional economies with historic grievances, and our sense of Canada as a national economy in which each of the parts contributes distinctively to the well-being of the whole.

This approach also missed many of the more subtle dimensions of our sense of fairness with respect to the distribution of costs and benefits. Virtually all policies and programs distribute their benefits and costs differentially, and we assess such distributions in terms of many categories, including income classes, age and sex. Differences in regional benefits may be explicit and intentional, or they may be the result of redistributive policies defined in terms of other categories. For example, policies to assist the elderly will confer greater benefits in those provinces where the highest proportions of elderly Canadians reside. Moreover, where policies do deliberately discriminate, we tend to view them in different ways: discrimination in favour of the disadvantaged or the poor provokes different reactions from that in favour of the rich and powerful. Finally, we judge fairness not in terms of a single policy or program, but in terms of the cumulative effects of many policies; it is a systematic, repeated lack of response, or discrimination, which leads to alienation.

We Commissioners do not attempt to present our own balance sheet of Confederation. Rather, we focus on two specific policies: equalization and regional development. Both of these are aimed at alleviating the persistent regional disparities in the Canadian economy. Equalization and regional development are complementary policies. Equalization is intended to reduce the fiscal consequences of relative underdevelopment. Regional economic policy is intended to reverse underlying economic disadvantages. The more successful the latter, the less need there is for equalization.

Commissioners believe that the question of real and perceived fairness is very much a political issue. To the extent that Canadians focus their allegations on the "unfairness" and unresponsiveness of the central government and its agencies, reform must focus there. Fairness also has a federal dimension. It implies that provinces have a legitimate concern with the economic development of their own regions. It also suggests that provinces

must feel reasonably secure in the exercise of their constitutional powers and in the ownership of the resources within their borders. These last are essential to the exercise of an effective provincial role in economic development.

Equalization

Of all the issues discussed during successive rounds of constitutional debate, there was almost unanimous agreement to entrench in section 36 of the Constitution the commitment to equalization. In so doing, Canadians gave formal recognition to an essential component of the Confederation bargain: the idea that all citizens have a right to "reasonably comparable levels of public services" from their provincial governments at "reasonably comparable levels of taxation". Variations in policy to reflect local preferences were desirable; variation in the nature and quality of services because of inequalities in the ability to provide them was not.

The equalization program represents the most long-standing and explicit commitment to interregional sharing in Canada. It consists of unconditional payments from the federal government to the less well-off provinces. In 1985–86, these payments are estimated at $5 billion, payable to all provinces except British Columbia, Ontario, Alberta and Saskatchewan.

The apparent provincial-federal harmony suggested by agreement to entrench section 36 exists in spite of widespread misunderstanding about the actual nature of Canada's equalization arrangements. Equalization is often confused with regional development programs or income-maintenance and security measures for individuals. In the acrimony that followed the adoption of the National Energy Policy, Western separatist leaders sometimes portrayed equalization as a device for making direct transfers from energy-rich western provinces to energy-poor eastern ones. Various quarters have criticized equalization as too generous or as not generous enough; as necessary to an efficient allocation of capital and labour, or as a prime cause of distortions in these patterns; as too mechanical and routine, or as too *ad hoc*.

In Commissioners' view, equalization is a vital feature of the Canadian federation. While there are many reasons to be proud of what Canadians have achieved in this area, there is room for improvement. In view of the confusion surrounding the topic, Commissioners wish first to review the bases of our equalization arrangements.

Principles of Equalization

Equalization schemes would be unnecessary in a unitary state, where all taxes are paid to one government, and all public sector benefits flow from it. The government need not, and almost certainly would not, treat all individuals identically: higher-income groups would pay a larger portion of their income as tax; large families would receive more substantial basic deductions from gross income than would small families; those without earnings would receive more in the way of transfers than they would pay as tax. Such imbalances in

the tax-expenditure system would be deliberate; they would reflect, however imperfectly, a judgement about the fair distribution of benefits and burdens.

In a federal state, however, citizens are faced by two tax systems, and two sources of public goods and services. Their treatment by provincial governments would almost certainly vary. Some provinces would decide to provide relatively more goods and services through the public sector and to finance them through higher taxation. Others opt for more or less redistribution among income classes. Indeed, if there were not these differences among provinces, reflecting different local values or preferences, one of the main reasons for federalism would disappear.

Such provincial variations are not, in themselves, a problem. If governments faithfully implement the wishes of the local majority, the system is working as it should. Canadian diversity is reflected in variations in policy at the provincial level. With free interprovincial migration, the arrangement is even more likely to conform to citizens' preferences. In theory, by voting with their feet, citizens "sort" themselves into relatively homogeneous subgroups: those who prefer an active public sector go to provinces offering this feature, while others move to areas where the provincial government takes a different approach.

There is, however, another, less acceptable, reason for variation among provinces. Not all provinces were "created equal" in an economic sense. Per capita incomes vary owing to such factors as resource endowments, occupational and industrial mixes, degrees of urbanization, or ease of access to major markets. A lower average income, which reflects lower wages, smaller returns to investments, and less remunerative land and resource rents, means a lower fiscal capacity for the government of the region; that government will raise less revenue from a given taxation effort than will a wealthier neighbour. Consequently, a poorer province will either have to provide a lower level of government goods and services at tax rates comparable to those of other provinces, or it will have to impose higher tax rates to finance a comparable level of services, or it will "package" some combination of higher taxes and lower services. Whatever situation prevails, citizens in a poorer region will be treated differently by government from their counterparts in other provinces. This follows inevitably from the fact of unequal regional economic endowments.

Some might argue that such differences are simply the price of a federal system: provinces can only be truly free to design their own taxation and expenditure policies if they have full fiscal authority. If the result is a variation in interprovincial fiscal capacities, such variation is inherent in federalism. Federal income-maintenance and security programs will apply to those individual Canadians in genuine need of support.

Commissioners reject this argument for two reasons. First, and most important, this reasoning compromises our understanding of what it means to be Canadian. An essential element of citizenship in this country must be relatively equal access to basic government services, irrespective of place of residence. While Commissioners are content to see the provision of these services decentralized, we are loath to accept too much variation in individual

access to them across jurisdictions. This commitment to regional equality arises from the same foundations as our commitment to social welfare policies.

Equalization reflects Canadians' sense of a common obligation, of our interconnection and of well-being and satisfaction with the national community. These last convictions depend on our assurance that all of us are fairly sharing the benefits, and bearing the burdens, of maintaining our society. Equalization adds an important regional dimension to this sense of shared belonging: it implies that a strong Canadian community encompasses the existence of strong, healthy provincial communities. Individual equity alone does not capture our commitment as Canadians to these provincial communities. It is ultimately because of shared membership in the whole Canadian community that we understand the necessity for ensuring the vitality of each of its constituent parts.

If the first justification for equalization is one of equity and social justice, a second is efficiency. Recent research has shown that variations in the fiscal capacities of provincial governments can themselves constitute distortions which reduce aggregate national output. This result can be corrected by a properly designed equalization scheme. Since the efficiency argument is a recent one, and since it underlies so much of recent debate, as well as this Commission's recommendations, it is worth sketching briefly.[2]

National output is maximized when capital and labour are allocated across regions so that the contributions to gross national product (GNP) of the last unit of capital employed and the last unit of labour employed are identical. Under normal circumstances, free internal migration of capital and labour will automatically produce this optimal allocation of capital and labour. As long as productivity differences are reflected in wages or rates of return, and as long as at least a fraction of the labour force or of investors is sensitive to the earnings possibilities associated with such differences, migration will flow from low- to high-productivity regions.

But what if significant differences exist in the fiscal capacities of provinces? An employee who is contemplating migration is likely to compare not just private earnings across regions, but also the treatment to be expected from the public sector. If one jurisdiction promises greater government services relative to taxes than does another, and if expected earnings are similar, the migrant has an incentive to choose the location offering more generous treatment. The result could be an influx to this province, driving down wages and salaries to the point where the expected tax-expenditure benefits just offset the lower private earnings. The opposite is true of the fiscally poor region; private earnings must be higher to offset the relative paucity of tax-financed goods and services. This "fiscally induced migration" responds to policy signals rather than to market signals based on the most productive allocation. The result may be lower output, since there will be too many workers in fiscally generous regions and too few in the others.

Equalization payments provide a means of responding to both equity and efficiency problems in a federation. Provincial governments that have a fiscal capacity below an acceptable standard receive unconditional revenue

transfers, reducing the fiscal discrepancy among provinces. The transfers compensate, in effect, for the province's lack of a natural tax base. When fiscal differences are narrowed or removed, Canadians, wherever resident, achieve a more similar status in their overall relations to government, and the incentive for socially inefficient migration is reduced.

The transfers are intended only to make it possible for any province to provide basic public services at a prescribed standard without imposing undue taxation. Whether a province actually chooses to provide particular services, or how it allocates the funds, is entirely its own responsibility. As the Royal Commission on Dominion-Provincial Relations (the Rowell-Sirois Commission) stated, when discussing its National Adjustment Grants (the forerunner of equalization):

> *If a province chooses to provide inferior services and impose lower taxation it is free to do so, or it may provide better services than the national average if its people are willing to be taxed accordingly, or it may, for example, starve its roads and improve its education, or starve its education and improve its roads . . .*[3]

Thus, equalization payments are a means to ensure that all governments can adequately carry out whatever responsibilities they were assigned. Equalization involves no diminution of provincial freedom or authority, and no federal control over provinces. Indeed, to make equalization payments conditional in any way would obviate the very essence of federalism.

Equalization is an essential feature of Canadian federalism. It effectively reconciles the principle of provincial autonomy with the principle of equal access of all Canadians to basic government services. Without it, Canadians would require a more highly centralized federation or would need to be willing to tolerate greater differences in standards of living and less efficient migration of labour and capital. The Rowell-Sirois Commission was the first to make this point when explaining its proposal for National Adjustment Grants:

> *They are designed to make it possible for every province to provide for its people services of average Canadian standards and they will thus alleviate distress and shameful conditions which now weaken national unity and handicap many Canadians. They are the concrete expression of the Commission's conception of a federal system which will both preserve a healthy local autonomy and build a stronger and more united nation.*[4]

While circumstances have obviously changed from the post-Depression years of Rowell-Sirois, the sentiment is still valid.

To suggest that an equalization scheme is desirable raises two questions. First, should fiscal differences among provinces be fully, or only partially, equalized? There is a host of subsidiary technical issues associated with this question. Secondly, should the central government, the provinces, or the two orders of government combined operate and fund the program?

There is no right answer to the question, "How complete should equalization be?" The traditional response in Canada has been, in the words of the Rowell-Sirois Commission, that equalization is necessary to achieve "average

standards of services in every province." A former federal Finance Minister stated that the goal of equalization was to enable "each province to provide an adequate level of public services without having to resort to rates of taxation substantially higher than those of other provinces."[5] Significantly, nearly the same words appear in section 36 of the Constitution Act, 1982:

> *Parliament and the government of Canada are committed to the principle of making equalization payments to ensure that provincial governments have sufficient revenues to provide reasonably comparable levels of public services at reasonably comparable levels of taxation.*

Theoretically, it is relatively easy to design an equalization scheme that embodies the principle of reasonably comparable standards. In the approach that has evolved in Canada during four decades, the formula provides an equalization payment for any province in which average or representative provincial tax rates (not its own tax rate) would yield less revenue per capita than the yield in Canada generally. In the method used, an average or representative provincial tax base is first specified by listing all main revenue categories open to the provinces. Next, a representative provincial taxation effort is calculated. Here a taxation rate judged to be representative of the provinces overall is set for each of the revenue categories in the base. Applying those taxation rates to the base and standardizing for population, yields the revenue a province would collect if it had an average or representative fiscal capacity and levied average taxation rates. This figure represents the minimum amount of revenue that it is deemed a province of this size should be guaranteed.

The next step in the procedure is to calculate the actual tax base of each province. This calculation is done for each of the revenue categories contained in the representative base. Applying the representative or average provincial taxation effort (*not* the province's own tax rates) to this base produces the total revenue the province could raise if it taxed each of its revenue sources at national average or representative rates. If this figure exceeds the revenue floor as calculated above, it creates no problem.

Equalization entitlements are necessary, however, when a province's revenues from taxing its own base at representative or average rates fall short of the revenue floor. Since equalization is guaranteed to cover this shortfall, the province can duplicate the public sector performance of the representative or average Canadian province.

The important point to note is that the revenues which the province actually collects do not enter directly into the calculation. The comparison is not between what could be and what is; rather, it is between what could be if the province were the representative or average Canadian province, in terms of both tax base and taxation effort, with what could be if the province chose to tax its actual base at national average or representative rates. How the province actually taxes does not directly affect its equalization entitlements. If it taxes at greater than representative rates, its total revenue will be that much greater; equalization entitlements will not fall. Conversely, if it chooses to tax less, its equalization entitlement does not rise. This is the practical counterpart of the Rowell-Sirois principle of unconditionality.

To implement these general guidelines involves a large number of technical problems. What exactly would constitute a representative provincial tax base? Should all revenue categories potentially open to provinces be included, or only those they actually use? How should the situation be affected if not all provinces use all revenue sources open to them? Should it change if they do use all revenue sources available, but sometimes treat them quite differently? What is the proper basis for taxing each revenue category? Should the representative taxation level be hypothetical, or should it be linked to what Canadian provinces do in practice? Should profits of Crown corporations be considered government revenue? These are just a few of the possible questions to be considered in designing an equalization scheme. Sometimes, as we shall see below, the wrong design can create more general problems for equalization.

Canadian Experience

The first specific proposal for a formal equalization scheme was the National Adjustment Grants proposed by the Rowell-Sirois Commission. Previous attempts to even out discrepancies in provincial fiscal capacities were either implicit or *ad hoc*. The transfers to the provinces agreed to by the federal government in 1867 were, by their nature, equalizing in that they were per capita grants. There was no connection between the amount the federal government collected from residents of any province and the transfers made to that province. In addition, special payments were given to individual provinces or even to entire regions. New Brunswick received these special payments from the outset; Nova Scotia began to receive them a short time later. In 1926, the Royal Commission on Maritime Claims (Duncan Commission) investigated the financial claims of the Maritimes, and the Royal Commission on Banking and Currency in Canada (White Commission) did so, in 1933, for both the Maritimes and the Prairies. It took the depression of the 1930s and the imminent bankruptcy of several provinces to demonstrate that these *ad hoc* arrangements were not enough.

National Adjustment Grants, together with most of the Rowell-Sirois Commission's recommendations, were casualties of wartime emergency. The federal government assumed exclusive control of personal and corporate income tax and succession duties, paying "rents" to each province according to a predetermined formula which, like its forerunners, was implicitly equalizing. Equalization, as Canadians know it today, was formally implemented in 1957. The tax-sharing arrangement introduced in that year linked the amount that the federal government transferred directly to each province to the revenue collected from that province. Each province received 10 per cent of the personal income taxes collected in the province, 9 per cent of the corporate profits, and 50 per cent of federal succession duties. Clearly, 10 per cent of the personal income tax collected in a richer province represented more revenue per taxpayer than it did in a poorer one. To compensate for these differences, the federal government unconditionally transferred to each of the poorer provinces an amount that would bring its per

capita yield from these three standard taxes up to the average yield of the two wealthiest provinces (Ontario and British Columbia). By this calculation, every province but Ontario qualified for equalization transfers, and a total of $139.1 million was paid out to nine provinces in the 1957–58 fiscal year.

From the outset, the equalization system has become progressively more comprehensive. In 1962, provincial natural resource revenues were added to the tax-base calculation. The standard was also lowered to the national average yield of the taxes in the base. These two changes made Alberta and British Columbia ineligible for equalization payments. In 1967, 16 provincial revenue sources, including those not shared with the federal government, were added to the tax base. The number of taxes in the base was increased to 19 in 1972 and to 29 in 1977, thus bringing equalization more and more into line with real taxation practices.

During the 1970s, the equalization scheme was severely tested as a result of the dramatic increase in natural resource revenues concentrated in Alberta, British Columbia and Saskatchewan. Since the scheme involves federal payments, compensation was owed to all other jurisdictions, including populous Ontario and Quebec, for their lack of such revenues, even though the federal government, in a practical sense, did not have direct access to these revenues. Moreover, Ontario soon became a "have-not" province and would have qualified for payments. All of this was taking place in a period of rising concern about the size of the federal deficit in general. A series of *ad hoc* adjustments to the formula followed, mostly redefining the way energy revenues were treated. The rules were changed to exclude provinces with per capita incomes above the national average from eligibility for such compensation. Rising energy revenues required that the concept of "full equalization" be abandoned.

More than just technical or design issues were at stake during this period. The large energy revenues accruing to the Western provinces, Alberta in particular, raised anew the more basic question of determining appropriate equalization . Specifically, were other provinces entitled to larger equalization payments simply because Alberta's fiscal capacity was suddenly and dramatically increased? (In 1980, Alberta's "own-source" revenues had risen to 232 per cent of the national average.) Questions arose concerning, for instance, the way Alberta's windfall affected the demands a Nova Scotian placed on provincial public services. Past Canadian practice of reasonably comparable levels of services at reasonably comparable tax rates provided little guidance. Was the comparison to be made to the wealthiest provinces, as in the 1957 formula? If so, essentially full equalization of energy revenues was required. Or was it to be made only with national average tax yields, as in the system then in place, recognizing that this meant that slightly less than half of the energy revenues would be equalized? Were "adequate" standards more or less demanding than "comparable" ones? If so, this would imply the applicability of a relative rather than an absolute criterion. The federal government was finding even this more limited commitment increasingly difficult to finance. Without the energy-related changes to the formula, 1981–82 equalization payments would have been nearly $3 billion above the

level of the $4.61 billion otherwise estimated. Each additional dollar of resource revenue accruing to provinces would have required Ottawa to increase its outlay on equalization by 75 cents.[6]

Some analysts argued that there was no need to equalize any of this windfall gain. Because one province is suddenly wealthier, the ability of others to supply an acceptable level of public goods at an acceptable tax level has not been eroded. In other words, greater government revenues in one province do not create greater needs in another. Others argued for the alternative view that such dramatic differences as existed between the fiscal position of Alberta and the rest of the country were untenable. The fact that the largest province had experienced the greatest relative decline, and a smaller one had experienced the boom, gave political weight to this argument, since the residents of the more populous provinces could use their political influence on the national government to bring about greater sharing, either in the form of transfers or in lower prices.

For the first time, efficiency considerations also played a significant role in equalization debates. Some observers alleged that since Western energy revenues were only imperfectly equalized, an imbalance was created in the migration of capital and labour from one province to another. This imbalance, it was argued, was detrimental to Canada as a whole, since it was induced by government revenues rather than by enhanced economic opportunities. Research studies did indeed demonstrate some sensitivity of migration flows to net fiscal differences among provinces.[7] One contribution to the debate alleged that without a proper equalization scheme in place, the costs to Canada of moving to world energy prices would likely exceed those associated with keeping oil prices at an artificially low level.[8] The point was that efficiency dictated some equalization of resource revenues even if one were not convinced that it was required to achieve greater equality among Canadians.

The best-known exponent of this "new" view of equalization was the Economic Council of Canada (ECC) in its report *Financing Confederation: Today and Tomorrow*.[9] There, the concepts of provincial equity and economic efficiency were proposed as formal pillars of an equalization scheme, to replace the much less precise "comparable standards" criterion. This led the Council to propose full equalization of all provincial revenue sources, except those associated with resources. Only partial equalization of this last category was recommended. The Council argued that since resources are constitutionally the property of provincial residents, they should be treated as if they were private income and taxed at the prevailing personal or business-tax rate. Only the expected yield from applying this rate would count for equalization purposes. The ECC made a number of other proposals, most notably that the forgone revenue from low-priced hydro-electricity in Ontario and Quebec be counted as resource revenue.

The Council's views appeared too late to influence the negotiations leading to the current equalization measures. As part of the 1982 Fiscal Arrangements Act, these measures incorporated several changes from the previous formula. Equalization to the national average was replaced by equalization to a "five-province standard". Provinces were to be paid the difference between

their hypothetical revenue at national average tax rates and a representative level of funds obtained by applying national average tax rates to the weighted average per capita tax base of Ontario, Quebec, Manitoba, Saskatchewan, and British Columbia. Leaving Alberta out of the standard effectively did away with the energy-revenue problem; the formula simply ignores any revenue that province now receives. The exclusion of Alberta lowered entitlements stemming from resource revenues, but excluding the four Atlantic provinces raised entitlements based on most other revenue sources.

The 1982 Fiscal Arrangements Act also included other changes in equalization arrangements. Coverage was extended to include municipal revenues and 100 per cent of resource revenues; however, the exclusion of Alberta meant that the resource revenues included were a small fraction of those previously counted. A cap was placed on payments, limiting their growth to no more than the increase in the gross national product (GNP) since 1982. A minimum level of payment guarantee and transitional payments were included to offset the effect of particular changes in individual provinces. Quebec and Manitoba were the main losers from the changes; the position of the Atlantic provinces remained virtually unchanged. The effect of moving to the new system was to reduce equalization entitlements (including transitional payments) by 11 per cent or $560 million in 1982–83, although the payments were still some 13 per cent above those made the previous year under the formula then in effect.[10]

The Success of Equalization

Has equalization been effective in smoothing out differences in fiscal capacities across provinces? Have Canadians met the standards set by the Rowell-Sirois Commission 45 years ago? Since there is no precise measure of fiscal capacity, there are no definitive answers to these questions. Indirect measures, however, can be used to gain an idea of the influence of equalization.

The obvious first step in assessing relative fiscal capacities is to compare actual revenues per capita across provinces. These data are presented in Table 22-9. The first row indicates "own-source" revenue, that is, funds the provinces raised in 1981–82 by applying their own tax rates to their own taxation base. The variation among provinces is striking, ranging from per capita revenues of $1026 for Nova Scotia to $3900 for Alberta. The latter province, with its huge energy revenues, is admittedly an extreme example. By excluding Alberta and Saskatchewan, the range is considerably reduced: from $1026 to $1765. Nevertheless, there is a large disparity in the revenue available to the provinces; the four Atlantic provinces and Manitoba are the poorest, and Quebec, Ontario and British Columbia rank between them and Alberta and Saskatchewan.

The second row of Table 22-9 adds federal transfers other than equalization to own-source revenue. Since some transfers, are implicitly equalizing, the disparity among provinces is reduced to some degree, but it remains significant. Equalization transfers are added in the third row. This addition reduces significantly the disparity and the provinces' ranking changes.

TABLE 22-9 **Equalization and Provincial Finances, 1980–81**

Row	Nfld.	P.E.I.	N.S.	N.B.	Que.	Ont.	Man.	Sask.	Alta.	B.C.	Total
1. Own-source revenues ($ per capita)[a]	1 228	1 090	1 026	1 092	1 648	1 455	1 276	2 121	3 900	1 765	1 749
2. Own-source revenues plus federal transfers other than equalization ($ per capita)[b]	1 871	1 745	1 653	1 692	2 272	1 973	1 836	2 631	4 422	2 335	2 308
3. Gross provincial revenues (row 2 plus equalization) ($ per capita)	2 514	2 445	2 176	2 224	2 543	1 973	2 169	2 672	4 422	2 335	2 449
4. Equalization as a percentage of own-source revenues[c]	52.4	65.1	51.0	48.7	16.5	0.0	26.1	1.9	0.0	0.0	8.1

Source: Thomas J. Courchene, *Equalization Payments: Past, Present and Future* (Toronto: Ontario Economic Council, 1984), p. 153.

a. Population figures from Department of Finance (1982a, 15).
b. Same tables as in a above.
c. Equalization data adapted from MacEachen (1981, Table V-I). Own-source revenues calculated from Table II-4 of the same document.

Alberta is still the wealthiest province, but Ontario goes to the bottom of the list. Without resource revenues and decreed ineligible for equalization, Canada's most highly industrialized province apparently has the lowest fiscal capacity. The importance of equalization to some provinces is evident from the fourth row of Table 22-9. The payments amount to nearly two-thirds of the revenue Prince Edward Island is able to raise for itself and to about half the corresponding revenues for the other three Atlantic provinces.

The figures in Table 22-9, however, do not give an entirely accurate measure of relative fiscal capacities. They show the provinces' actual revenue, and therefore are a result both of revenue potential and of revenue-raising efforts. Since the purpose of equalization is to even out the ability of provinces to generate funds, a better test of the effects of the arrangement is to look at the results that would occur if each province were to apply the same rates.

Table 22-10 shows indices of tax base per capita for three periods since 1972. The first three rows demonstrate the considerable variation that exists for own-source revenue. While Alberta's own-source revenue is currently 217 per cent of the national average, Prince Edward Island's is only 55 per cent. The other Atlantic provinces do not fare much better. It is these figures, more than any others, which demonstrate the great need for equalization in the Canadian federation. Without compensation, the differences in the abilities of provinces to provide for their residents' welfare would be unacceptably high.

The variation among provinces has increased significantly since 1972, as a result of the sizeable Western energy revenues. The fourth to sixth rows of Table 22-10 demonstrate this point clearly. Note, however, that even without resource revenues, Alberta and Saskatchewan have still benefited the most from increased funds. This is because personal and business incomes are higher, retail sales are greater, and so on as a spin-off from energy activity. Finally Commissioners wish to point out the difference in Quebec's position in the two tables. Its relatively high figure in Table 22-9 compared to its relatively low position in Table 22-10 is a result of higher-than-average tax rates and demonstrates the importance of standardizing for actual taxation efforts when comparing relative fiscal capacities.

The seventh to ninth rows of Table 22-10 show the effect of equalization payments. These payments greatly reduce the variation among provinces. Prince Edward Island's revenues are now 83 per cent of a national average that is still highly inflated by Alberta's revenues. The position of the seven easternmost provinces varies only from 83 to 88 per cent of the national average. The addition of other federal transfers, as is shown in the final three rows of the table, reduces disparities further. The Atlantic provinces now have potential revenues of about 90 per cent of the national average. Ironically, Ontario now has the lowest potential revenues: 87 per cent of the national average. This is not because of low tax rates, as Ontario's tax effort is the average for the country; it does, however, explain why Ontario qualified for, but did not receive, equalization payments during the 1977–82 period. British Columbia and Saskatchewan stand fractionally above the national average; Alberta remains far out in front.

TABLE 22-10 Indices of Tax Base per Capita, Selected Fiscal Years

	(national average = 100)									
Measure of revenue base	**Nfld.**	**P.E.I.**	**N.S.**	**N.B.**	**Que.**	**Ont.**	**Man.**	**Sask.**	**Alta.**	**B.C.**
Own-source revenues[a]										
1972–73	62	59	72	71	85	110	90	85	134	120
1976–77	60	57	66	67	82	99	85	106	201	112
1981–82	59	55	66	66	78	94	79	112	217	111
Own-source revenues less natural resources										
1972–73	61	62	75	72	87	115	93	82	111	114
1976–77	62	62	72	73	89	108	92	101	128	112
1981–82	62	62	73	73	87	104	87	103	139	114
Own-source revenues plus equalization										
1972–73	85	84	87	87	90	104	93	94	125	113
1976–77	85	85	86	86	88	93	90	100	188	105
1981–82	83	83	84	84	86	88	88	105	203	104
Own-source revenues plus all transfer payments										
1972–73	95	102	91	92	95	101	95	93	121	106
1976–77	92	104	91	93	93	91	93	100	171	103
1981–82	90	96	89	92	90	87	90	106	186	102

Source: Thomas J. Courchene, *Equalization Payments: Past, Present and Future* (Toronto: Ontario Economic Council, 1984), p. 158.

a. Own-source revenues and equalization payments are determined on the basis of the *new* equalization formula as far as tax bases are concerned. What this means is that all renewable energy resource revenues and all property taxes enter the equalization formula. The equalization standard, however, is the national average level and not the five-province average that characterizes the present formula.

These figures demonstrate that equalization and other federal transfer payments are indeed producing an effect. They do a great deal to even out the access of provincial treasuries to public revenues. Commissioners would conclude that equalization has certainly contributed very significantly to reducing interprovincial differences in fiscal capacity.

The trend toward greater equalization appears to have stopped, however, and even perhaps to have been reversed, owing to the effect of energy revenues and, to a lesser extent, to that of the need for restraint: "Over time the level to which provincial revenues are equalized is falling relative to the national average level of fiscal capacity."[11] Thus, in 1972–73, after all transfers, no provincial government fell below 90 per cent of national average fiscal capacity. In 1981–82, however, two provinces did fall below this level. In 1972–73, the richest province had a capacity of 121 per cent of the national average; in 1981–82, it had 186 per cent of that average. More recent changes will also somewhat reduce the equalization commitment. It has been calculated[12] that for 1982–83, the new "five-province standard" reduces the total equalization payment by $732 million from what it would have been under the old formula, to $4.557 billion; but this reduction has been tempered by transitional payments to Quebec and Manitoba, the provinces hardest hit by the change. The capping of equalization payments by the rate of increase in GNP also signals that growth in equalization will not be open-ended.

Through equalization, Canada has dramatically reduced differences in the capacity of provinces to provide services for their citizens. Nevertheless, the disparities among provinces remain substantial, and the system has had great difficulty coping with the uneven effect produced by oil and gas revenues. Recent changes have reduced the overall level of equalization somewhat. We Commissioners also wish to emphasize our view that the concept of sharing, embodied in equalization, remains strongly supported by Canadians across the country. While specific aspects of the program are controversial, it is clear that the constitutional commitment of section 36 reflects national consensus.

Issues and Proposals

Canadians must first decide on the interpretation of the principle underlying equalization in Canada. Is a conservative interpretation of the words in section 36 of the Constitution Act, 1982, "reasonably comparable levels of public services at reasonably comparable levels of taxation", to prevail? Or is equalization to be a way for the less-prosperous jurisdictions in the country to share equally and automatically in the fortunes of their wealthier neighbours?

There is no correct answer to this query; the decision ultimately represents a judgement about the goals of Canada's federation. Commissioners are inclined to support a rather more generous interpretation of the nation's commitment to equalization than that inherent in the current equalization program. It is time, we believe, to go beyond a simple, minimum-standards criterion towards a fuller measure of revenue equalization. We base our recommendation for this move on one important reason: the provinces have clearly assumed a much greater role in the federation than they played in

1940, when Rowell-Sirois reported, or even in 1957, when the first equalization scheme was established. Individual Canadians are now much more dependent for a wide range of services on their provincial government. Given general acceptance that this is the direction which Canadians favour, the ability of provincial governments to provide these services becomes that much more important. Correspondingly, disparities among provinces become less tolerable.

The next question, to which, again, there is no correct answer, is: Who should operate the program? The answer depends on Canadians' view of the federation. Three models might be followed. First, equalization might remain the sole responsibility of the federal government. That government would almost certainly wish to consult with the provinces and with other interested groups, but it would not necessarily be bound by any representations. A variant of this model would give the provincial governments a somewhat more formal opportunity to contribute to program design, perhaps in exchange for granting the federal government access to tax sources such as resource revenues, which are now mainly a provincial responsibility.

The logic of the first model is that redistribution within the federation is, and should be, a responsibility of the national government. The problem is that the federal government's financial commitment is, in large part, a function of provincial taxation policies, yet Parliament is required to equalize revenue sources in which it does not share.

In recent years, a second, more confederal model, has attracted some attention. Some observers have suggested making equalization an interprovincial matter in which provinces would share among themselves. Each province's fiscal capacity would be calculated separately. Jurisdictions with a surplus would then contribute to a fund out of which payments would be made to financially disadvantaged regions. The calculations would include all revenue sources, even forgone revenue. The arrangement would be run exclusively by the provinces themselves; they would have to decide what percentage of fiscal surpluses would be taxed or what fiscal deficits compensated.

A third option is a "two-tier" scheme which would split equalization responsibilities between the two orders of government. While there are a number of proposals of this type, they all start by distinguishing resource revenues from all others, since resource revenues are fully within the provincial domain. The central government would continue to operate an equalization scheme similar to the pre-1982 arrangement, but without resource-revenue categories. Revenues to be paid out under this first tier would come from tax bases, many of which are shared with the provinces. Thus, if disbursements rose because of additional income-tax revenues in a rich province, the federal government would have access to the revenues, as well as responsibility for the payments.

Equalization of resource revenues would be the responsibility of the provinces as a group. Provincial governments would define the country's average resource-revenue capacity. As in the second model, provinces with revenues above this average would contribute some portion of their surplus to a fund from which payments would be made to provinces falling below the

average. Overall, the payments would balance exactly: total payments by resource-rich provinces would equal disbursements to the others.

Commissioners recommend that the federal government retain primary responsibility for operating the equalization program. The other two options are certainly attractive, but they suffer from two defects. There is no evidence, first of all, that the provinces would be willing to play the more prominent redistributive role required by the two other models. Trial proposals along these lines were met with great hostility a few years ago, and there is little reason to think they would fare any better today. Resource-rich provinces considered that such a scheme would deprive them of their rightful revenues; resource-poor provinces did not wish to be dependent on the good will of the more advantaged. More important, both schemes would deny the federal government some or all of its traditional redistributive role in the federation.

As we have seen, to translate the general principles of equalization into a workable scheme is an extremely complex task, especially in a volatile fiscal environment. With even minor alterations, an almost infinite number of possible "wrinkles" and statistical quirks can have important consequences for a particular province. Commissioners, therefore, can outline only some general recommendations which are consistent with our positions on sharing and with our view that the federal government is primarily responsible for equalization arrangements.

Canada should return to an equalization formula that includes all ten provinces in the base. The present system, which arbitrarily excludes five provinces from the calculation, allows too much room for distortion, strategy and unintended effects. For example, if a firm were to leave one of the excluded provinces, say Alberta, for one of the five included in the formula, say Ontario, then the equalization entitlements of recipient provinces would rise commensurate with the increase in the formula tax base. If the same firm were to move to Nova Scotia, the equalization scheme would be unaffected, since neither Alberta nor Nova Scotia is included in the five provinces used in the calculation. As one provincial finance minister stated (only half in jest), it may be to the advantage of the have-not provinces to push development expenditures Ontario's way. Equalization should be based on the broadest possible assessment of provincial fiscal capacities. To tinker with the number of provinces on which it is based in order to solve financial problems is undesirable and blurs the basic principles.

A portion of resource revenues—greater than zero but significantly less than 100 per cent—must be included in equalization. There is no magic figure, but the 20 to 30 per cent range seems an appropriate compromise between the extremes of theoretical purity and political reality. This sort of proposal has been endorsed by the Task Force on Fiscal Arrangements of 1981, the Saskatchewan government of the same year, and the Economic Council of Canada in its 1982 report.

The Task Force endorsed this proposal because, if natural resources were in private hands, 20 per cent of the sector's revenues could be expected to accrue to provincial budgets as taxes. This 20 per cent, therefore, should be the amount equalized. The Task Force also argued that only those resource

revenues used for budgetary purposes, and not those revenues being deposited in heritage funds, should enter equalization. In addition, resource revenues used to provide special or unusual benefits to citizens should be excluded. Commissioners believe that this is a reasonable approach to the thorny problem of which resource revenues to include. We also believe that the federal equalization payments arising from resource revenues should not exceed the revenues which the federal government can be said to obtain from taxation of resource activity.

The focus on rents from oil and gas resources ignores the implicit rents from other resource endowments. These, too, should be incorporated into sources of provincial revenue used in the equalization formula. Commissioners refer here mainly to the practice of underpricing electricity generated by provincial Crown corporations. The details of a proposal on this matter are included in the Economic Council's report.[13] We are content to endorse their view and to recommend that more work be done to make estimates of these forgone revenues more certain.

Finally, Commissioners believe that the idea of considering fiscal needs or the cost of providing services should receive careful consideration. The criterion of "reasonably comparable levels of public services" at comparable levels of taxation, set out in the Constitution, includes both sides of the equation. Most equalization schemes, however, focus only on the revenue side. They implicitly assume that the cost of providing services is the same across the country. This is obviously not so. Roads are more expensive to build in British Columbia than in Manitoba because of the terrain. A province such as Newfoundland, where services must be provided to a small, scattered, rural population, may incur greater costs than one where the population is more concentrated. Demographic profiles, which differ because of varying proportions of old people or of the unemployed, will lead to different levels of demand for services. "Reasonably comparable levels of public services" may therefore embody cost differentials, and there seems to be a strong case for building this component into the equalization system. The Australian equalization system, for instance, does so with considerable success.

There are, however, formidable obstacles to including expenditure needs in the equalization formula. To do so would require a "Representative Expenditure System"[14] to parallel the existing representative tax system. Canadians would have to agree on which provincial expenditures to include, and on how to assess differences in costs. Presumably, this assessment should reflect differences in per capita need (for example, the proportion of citizens of school age) and in unit costs (for instance, in building one kilometre of road). The formula would have to devise an "average" level of service, while leaving provinces free to make their own choices about whether to provide more or less of a given service. These are all formidable problems, both in concept and in the complexity of measurement and data collection that they entail. Their solution would require much more complete and standardized statistical bases. To delineate representative expenditures across the range of provincial services would entail more difficult political judgements than would agreement on representative taxes, and might also generate undesirable pressures for provincial uniformity. Nevertheless, over a long period,

Canadians have been successful in coping with the complexities inherent in an equity-based system of public finance. Commissioners believe that through the Council of Ministers of Finance, governments should begin to prepare the ground for an eventual incorporation of expenditure needs as a natural evolution of the equalization program.

Notes

1. R. Johnston, *Public Opinion and Public Policy in Canada*, vol. 35 (Toronto: University of Toronto Press, 1985).
2. See papers prepared for this Commission: Robin W. Boadway, "Federal-Provincial Transfers in Canada: A Critical Review of the Existing Arrangements", in *Fiscal Federalism*, vol. 65, and John Vanderkamp, "The Efficiency of the Interregional Adjustment Process", in *Disparities and Interregional Adjustment*, vol. 64 (Toronto: University of Toronto Press, 1985).
3. Royal Commission on Dominion-Provincial Relations, *Report*, Book II: *Recommendations* (Ottawa: King's Printer, 1939), p. 84.
4. *Ibid.*, p. 125.
5. "Statement by the Honorable Mitchell Sharp, Minister of Finance, to the Federal-Provincial Tax Structure Committee", in *Proceedings of the Federal-Provincial Conference, Ottawa, October 24–28, 1966* (Ottawa: Privy Council Office, 1966). Quoted in Thomas J. Courchene, *Equalization Payments: Past, Present and Future* (Toronto: Ontario Economic Council, 1984), p. 47.
6. Courchene, *Equalization Payments*, p. 190.
7. For a review of these studies, see Vanderkamp, "The Efficiency of the Interregional Adjustment Process".
8. Frank R. Flatters and Douglas D. Purvis, "Ontario: Between Alberta and the Deep Blue Sea?", Discussion Paper No. 402 (Kingston: Queen's University, Department of Economics, 1980).
9. Economic Council of Canada, *Financing Confederation: Today and Tomorrow* (Ottawa: Minister of Supply and Services Canada, 1982).
10. Courchene, *Equalization Payments*, pp. 350 –55.
11. *Ibid.*, p. 161.
12. *Ibid.*, Chapter 12.
13. Economic Council, *Financing Confederation*, p. 122.
14. Douglas H. Clark, "Canadian experience with the representative tax system as a means of measuring the relative fiscal capacities of provincial and local governments"; Testimony before the United States Senate Committee on Government Affairs, Subcommittee on Intergovernmental Relations, April 6, 1983.

Regional Economic Development

For a number of reasons, few of the issues in this Commission's mandate have proved more perplexing than regional development. Our canvass of the research community revealed that relatively little is known about how and why regional economies grow. Many theories abound, but none has gained wide acceptance.

Canada's success in spurring economic growth and industrialization in poorer areas is difficult to evaluate. We have experimented with many types of programs, policies and strategies, but as Premier Hatfield of New Brunswick stated in a submission to this Commission:

> *...despite the claims that significant funds have been spent, nothing which has been started has made an appreciable difference in the disparity between New Brunswick and the rest of Canada, in so far as benefits from establishing a viable industrial base are concerned.*
>
> (Government of New Brunswick, Brief, December 31, 1984, p. 1.)

The best that can be said is that we may have prevented the less-developed regions from falling further behind.

Perhaps partly because of this limited success, regional policy has defied our best efforts to devise an appropriate management framework. There has been constant debate about the level of government that should design and implement programs, the criteria for judging need, and the appropriate link between regional policies and more general national economic initiatives, such as stabilization or transportation policy. We appear to have spent nearly as much time arguing about how to implement measures that were doomed to failure as we have in searching for new solutions.

In a federal system, regional economic disparity is an inherently contentious issue; Canada is no exception to this rule. Inequalities across regions are at least as unsettling as those among individuals within a community. Sometimes economic adjustment requires migration, which places an extra burden on the individual. In these respects, unitary states are no different from federal systems. In a federal system, however, migration can weaken the provincial communities which federalism is designed to protect. In these situations, community survival is at stake. When attachments to regional communities are as strong as they are in Canada, or when migration involves the loss of language and culture as it can for French-speaking Québécois, the costs of adjustment are that much higher. We must think of development, therefore, not only in terms of Canada as a whole, but also in terms of regional economies and the provincial communities associated with them.

This view does not stand without challenge. Criticism takes several forms. One view states that we should think about the economic development of individuals, not of regions, for individuals are the essential focus of policy initiatives. From this perspective, preservation or development of communities should not be an objective of public policy. Moreover, to focus on inequities among regions diverts needed attention from inequities that have nothing at all to do with regions or territory. So, too, the pursuit of economic efficiency may play down regional policies. To try to diversify provincial economies in

order to transform them into self-sufficient entities is to deny all Canadians the fundamental advantages of economic specialization and complementarity. Almost by definition, from this viewpoint, regional development policies divert resources from the places of their greatest productivity to places where they will produce less and thus reduce the output of the economy as a whole. There is, therefore, a direct trade-off between aggregate national wealth and the wealth of each region.

One reply to this criticism is that while there may be a short-term trade-off between regional development and national income, there need not be in the long run. To the extent that regions underemploy resources, those resources are not contributing their full potential to national output. The national economy will be stronger to the extent that each region develops its potential. The opponent of regional development policy would probably reply that granting the objective, regional policies have so far not transformed the economic bases of provinces to make them more productive. On this reading, we have been able to compensate for inequities through interpersonal and regional transfers, but we have done little to alter the conditions that hold back development.

This debate about regional policies is especially important today. Some participants have argued that in the present economic context and in the face of increasing international competition, regional development may be a luxury that we can no longer afford, at least at the levels and in the forms that we have known. The critics argue that we should submit to the discipline of the market and thus allocate resources to their most productive use, however well justified other goals might be in social or cultural terms. The argument is not that we should abandon regional policy, but that we should de-emphasize it, "tilting" policy more toward national efficiency and less toward regional development. Moreover, just as Commissioners have done in our earlier discussion of industrial and social policy, we should try to make clearer distinctions between "welfare-compensation" dimensions of policy and developmental dimensions.

If regional economic development were simply about national efficiency, Commissioners would tend to support the critics. However, as we have argued throughout this Report, well-being is a larger, more inclusive concept; and well-being in Canada has an essential regional component. Regional development policies remain vital, and they must include both the reduction of disparities inherent in the concept of interregional transfers and the development aspect inherent in the notion of making the best use of Canadian resources in all regions. Thus, while Commissioners are anxious to minimize distortions and to ensure that considerations of efficiency discipline the provision of regional development funds, we believe that regional development must remain an essential component of Canadian policy and, indeed, of the Confederation bargain.

Regional development can be as much a hornet's nest for a Royal Commission as for governments. The stakes are large, emotions are charged, Canadians have a history of handling the process badly, and they know little about how it actually works. Nevertheless, for the reasons we have given and

because of the constitutional commitment of the Government of Canada and of the provincial governments to "promoting equal opportunities for the well-being of Canadians" and to "furthering economic development to reduce disparity in opportunities",[1] regional policy cannot be ignored.

Economic Growth, Income Distribution, Adjustment and Federalism

To this point in our Report, we Commissioners have concentrated on three aspects of economic life: economic growth, income distribution, and adjustment. We have considered these aspects from the perspective of the national economy as a whole and in light of its effect on individuals. Our discussion has proceeded as if all economic activity took place at one geographic point. Economic growth referred to increases in real per capita gross national product. Research has classified income distribution according to age, sex, occupation, and language or ethnic group. Adjustment referred to the problems of reallocating capital and labour from sectors in relative decline to those in ascendancy.

The first step in making this analysis more realistic is to recognize that economic activity is spread across Canada and that workers and businesses have a geographic location as well as an industrial or occupational classification. We must now identify the factors that make particular regions grow, and determine how regional economies affect, and are affected by, national patterns. We must also compare incomes across regions. Do workers or investors in one part of the country earn the same rewards as their otherwise identical counterparts in another part? Even adjustment takes on added complexity, for migration now provides an alternative to a fall in an individual's real earnings.

Provinces have formal constitutional status and possess real economic and social powers which make them important centres of economic activity. They are also communities to which residents have political commitments and emotional ties. Thus it makes sense to consider them as economic regions and to talk about their welfare in the same way that we speak of Canadian interests and aspirations.

To add this federal dimension to our analysis makes that analysis more complex. The aggregate growth rate of a province is not merely a part of a broader economic process. We must consider the ability of a political unit to provide for the continuing economic future of its residents. The locations of jobs or investments are important. It therefore becomes important to ask whether individuals can secure their livelihood in the provincial communities to which they are attached. We must do more than simply compare incomes of otherwise identical individuals across Canada. We must compare the per capita real incomes of entire regions, taking into account the different mix of occupations, demographics and circumstances.

To add federalism to the analysis introduces a host of political and social concerns to the consideration of interregional adjustment. Out-migration, for example, is not simply another adjustment mechanism. If movement is large

enough, it threatens regional communities. Thus population movements that seem justified on grounds of economic efficiency may be unacceptable because of these broader political and social values. We judge policy makers not just by their ability to provide jobs for those seeking employment, but also in terms of the availability of employment opportunities in the parts of the country where the unemployed live.

We have moved out of the economic domain and into the political realm. In doing so, we must ask: How much weight should our nation put on the maintenance of regional communities? How much are Canadians willing to sacrifice, in terms of national efficiency, to guarantee this end? Should the level of resources we commit to regional development be related to the performance of the national economy, falling as national economic growth slows? Does a fair distribution of income imply that per capita incomes be equal across provinces? Has an individual a right to expect a job in his or her chosen region, with wages comparable to those obtainable for the same job in more prosperous regions? Before attempting to answer these questions, we must understand the pattern of regional disparities in Canada.

Regional Disparities

What do we know about regional economic disparities in Canada? For a start, per capita earned or market income (excluding transfer payments) varies significantly among provinces. In 1981, for example, as Table 22-11 shows, Newfoundland's per capita market income was only 53.8 per cent of the national average, while Alberta's was 114.1 per cent. In that year, only three provinces, Alberta, Ontario and British Columbia, were above the national average, although Saskatchewan was close, at 98.7 per cent. Manitoba and Quebec form the next group, at slightly over 90 per cent, followed by Nova Scotia at about 70 per cent, while the other three Atlantic provinces stood below two-thirds of the mean income. This general pattern has changed little over the 60 years for which data are available, although individual rankings of provinces have occasionally altered.[2]

Earned income is generally the initial measure of economic disparity, since it most accurately reflects the relative strength and productivity of the various economies. Other measures represent more fully the relative economic well-being of individuals. If we add transfers to individuals to their earned income, we can form a better picture of total personal income. By this standard, the poorest province is now at 65.1 per cent of the national average, and the richest is at 110 per cent; these figures still represent a difference of slightly more than three to two. If we add the effect of the progressive income tax by assessing after-tax income rather than gross income, discrepancies narrow further. Calculating income per household rather than per person has an additional dramatic effect. On these terms, Newfoundland's disposable income per household rises to 87.6 per cent of the national average, and Prince Edward Island and New Brunswick become the poorest provinces, with per capita incomes 79 per cent of the national average. The shortfalls in per capita income have now become less than half of what they were on the

TABLE 22-11 Alternative Measures of Regional Income Disparities, 1971 and 1981

Index	Year	Nfld.	P.E.I.	N.S.	N.B.	Que.	Ont.	Man.	Sask.	Alta.	B.C.	Vuw[a] (%)
		(Canada = 100)										
Market income	1971	55.1	53.6	69.3	66.5	88.5	119.6	93.2	79.1	98.3	109.6	0.285
per capita[b]	1981	53.8	57.5	69.6	63.2	90.7	110.5	92.7	98.7	114.1	110.3	0.274
Personal income	1971	63.7	63.4	77.5	72.2	88.7	117.0	94.0	80.3	99.0	109.0	0.232
per capita[c]	1981	65.1	67.4	76.8	70.4	93.6	107.4	93.1	99.7	110.3	108.7	0.211
Personal disposable	1971	68.1	68.0	79.8	75.0	89.6	114.8	95.5	85.5	99.6	108.6	0.203
income per capita[d]	1981	67.3	71.6	78.7	72.3	90.8	108.3	97.9	104.4	109.0	109.4	0.195
Personal disposable	1971	90.1	76.2	84.9	84.4	94.1	111.1	91.6	82.8	97.6	99.4	0.136
income per household	1981	87.6	79.2	83.0	79.7	91.5	107.0	95.5	103.4	109.4	101.5	0.130
Real personal												
disposable income	1971	89.9	N.A.	82.7	89.3	96.2	106.3	96.4	88.3	97.2	89.8	0.102[f]
per household[e]	1981	81.5	N.A.	82.5	83.7	94.9	103.2	101.1	111.4	109.3	90.9	0.125[f]

Source: Based on data from Statistics Canada, *Cansim* (Matrices 555–562; 7002–7031) and *Census of Canada* (1971, 1981) as presented in Robert L. Mansell and Lawrence Copithorne, "Canadian Regional Economic Disparities: A Survey", in *Disparities and Interregional Adjustment*, vol. 64, prepared for the Royal Commission on the Economic Union and Development Prospects for Canada (Toronto: University of Toronto Press, 1985).

a. Unweighted Coefficient of Variation.
b. Defined as wages and supplementary income, net unincorporated business income, net farm incomes, and interest, dividend and miscellaneous investment income, all calculated on a per capita basis for the region as a percentage of that for Canada.
c. Personal income is market income plus transfers to individuals.
d. Personal disposable income is personal income less personal income taxes and contributions to social security.
e. Regional price indexes calculated from inter-city partial consumer price index (Winnipeg = 100, May 1971) and city consumer price indexes.
f. The values for this measure exclude P.E.I. and hence cannot be compared to those for the other income measures.

basis of earned per capita income. Adjusting for prices, in order to capture real purchasing power, produces another slight reduction in variations among provinces.

Why do earned incomes per person differ so markedly among regions? Two explanations tend to be offered, the first, perhaps, a little more frequently then the second: differentials in wage rates and differentials in employment rates. In other words, if Canadians actually employed in the poorer regions were to earn, on average, what their counterparts in wealthier areas earn, about one-half of the observed income disparity would disappear. The remainder would reflect the smaller proportion of people actually working. Thus the question becomes: Why do earnings and employment rates vary by region?

The most obvious answer to varying wages is that occupational and industrial structures vary. Fishermen do not make as much as corporate vice-presidents. If there are relatively more fishermen in Nova Scotia and relatively more executives in Ontario, earnings per capita will reflect the different occupational mix. Regional disparities in this circumstance, however, would reflect the usual spread of earnings across occupations or persons that characterizes all industrial societies.

Relatively little of the observed disparity appears to be grounded in occupational differences, however. Earnings for any given job, rather than differences in the types of job available, account for most of the income gap. The explanation for differential earnings lies in worker productivity. A number of factors might explain difference in output per employee. The "quality" and the amount of capital employed appear to account for some part of the gap: poorer regions have lower capital-to-labour ratios. Lower-income regions also have relatively fewer workers in the prime age groups and a work-force characterized by fewer years of education. Slower adoption of new technology, poorer management, fewer and smaller urban centres, and greater distance from important markets explain the remainder of the productivity gap.

To note these associations, however, is not to explain them. In fact, it is extremely difficult to sort out cause and effect. Education of the work-force appears to be lower in poorer regions because individuals with training are generally in a better position to migrate in search of better employment opportunities elsewhere. Lower capital expenditures per worker could simply reflect a poorer investment climate. The decision to adopt new technology as it becomes available depends primarily on the economic circumstances: the speed of adoption tends to reflect the buoyancy of the regional economy. Good managers tend to be promoted to head offices, irrespective of where they start out.

The other half of differentials in per capita earnings reflects lower employment rates in poorer regions. Typically, there are fewer people of working age in the poorer provinces; members of that age group, especially women, are less likely to seek work, and those in the labour force are more likely to experience unemployment. As with earnings, however, these patterns do not explain differences in employment rates. Lower participation reflects, but does not explain, a depressed economy.

On the basis of this analysis, three theoretical approaches to the problems of regional economic development may be distinguished. The first approach stresses interregional adjustment within the national economy. It focuses on the question: What adjustments must occur to equalize the rewards of similarly situated workers in different provinces, given the present underlying forces in the economy? The primary issue is removal of impediments to movement of labour and capital to the areas of their most productive use, that is, interregional adjustment. Theoretically, such adjustment would reward both labour and capital. It would not, however, equalize per capita incomes in each province. If skill levels, management quality, available technology and endowment of natural resources differ, then, even with perfect adjustment, average incomes will differ. Moreover, adjustment occurs largely through mobility of capital and labour: accordingly, this approach offers no guarantee of any particular level of economic activity in any province.

The second approach is compensatory. It emphasizes measures, not to facilitate adjustment, but rather to compensate individuals in a given region for the situation in which the market leaves them. Equalization transfers, considered above, are the Canadian archetype of this solution.

The third approach is developmental. Its policies are intended to stimulate economic development by addressing the underlying factors that cause relative underdevelopment. The market imperfections and the characteristics that each region brings to the national economy become the subject of government policy. Some of these characteristics – distance from markets or natural resources, for example – are relatively fixed, though transportation policies can alleviate the disadvantages of distance. Other aspects of economic structure, however, are more amenable, in principle, to policy efforts, and these are the object of regional development policy more strictly defined.

Canadians have experience with all three approaches: people have moved; incomes have declined; transfer payments have been made, and economic development programs established. In spite of all this, there has been remarkably little change in the level of measured disparities, although the differences do vary somewhat over economic cycles, widening in hard times, converging in good ones.

Interregional Market Adjustment

To ascertain how the pure theory of interregional market adjustment contributes to understanding regional disparities, we must address two questions. What pattern of income distribution should one expect to observe in a regionally diverse nation, such as Canada, in the ideal situation where all interregional trade and factor flows are complete? How does such an economy adjust to shocks to this equilibrium, and what are the implications of the adjustment for regional income distribution?

If there are no barriers to the interregional movement of goods and services, producers anywhere in the country can ship products wherever it is profitable for them to do so. If labour, capital and technology are also free to locate in any region, there is nothing to stop a construction worker in Ontario from taking a job in Quebec, or a dentist in Prince Edward Island from

setting up a practice in Alberta. How would these circumstances affect the distribution of income across provinces?

Under a number of highly restrictive assumptions, free trade in goods and services will equalize factor rewards across regions: wages, returns to capital, and product prices (excluding transportation costs) should be identical, regardless of province of residence. Factor mobility should operate in the same way. Thus, capital and labour will migrate in search of higher earnings to the extent that expected gains in real income to migrant or investor equal or exceed the costs of relocation. As individuals leave areas with lower wages, or capital moves from areas with lower rates of return, supply falls in relation to demand, pushing prices upward. The reverse happens in the region of destination, where prices decline as a result of greater supply.

If migration is responsive to expected differences in real income, theory is able to predict migration from high- to low-unemployment areas, taking into account wage differences. In fact, there are many kinds of labour in a complex modern economy; the variety reflects different types and levels of training, skill and experience, and hence different levels of wages and salaries. Migration can thus equalize earnings within skill groups, but not within the work-force as a whole. The same observation holds true for capital. In the short run, at least, firms typically commit plant and equipment to designated uses and cannot readily reassign them for other purposes. In addition, different investment prospects bear different risks to the investors and are thus likely to be undertaken only at appropriate rates of return. Capital mobility will equalize returns only within a given class of risk.

The theory of interregional market adjustment holds that migration will equalize wages (within skill groups) and "risk-adjusted" returns to capital, but not per capita incomes. This last equalization would occur only if each region had an identical endowment of resources, capital, technology and skilled labour. As long as economic bases differ, so will work-force characteristics and investment patterns. Land and resources are fixed elements in the economic base, and adjustment through trade and migration will not alter them. Regions with relatively large pools of skilled labour, or valuable resources, will have higher per capita incomes than regions with smaller pools of skilled labour or fewer resources. Adjustment, then, consists of the changes that occur within a given set of human and natural resources under internal free trade.

There are two important questions relating to market adjustment. How do trade and factor markets respond to those changes in relative prices and earnings potentials that result from economic shocks? How quickly does adjustment correct any disequilibrium? What happens, for example, when the value of one region's output falls over the long term perhaps as the result of a shift in the terms of trade against its exports, or the exhaustion of an important resource? Clearly, the region can no longer produce the same per capita income for the same number of residents as it did before. Two types of market response, or some combination of them, are logically possible. First, and most obviously, some residents could leave the region. As long as this population outflow is not destabilizing – that is, as long as it does not reduce the ability of the regional economy to produce goods and services

efficiently – fewer people will share a proportionately lower aggregate output, thereby restoring the previous level of per capita income. Alternatively, the region might support the same population, but at lower per capita incomes. Falling aggregate demand for the region's output will put downward pressure on output and factor prices. If these are flexible, full employment will result, but incomes will be lower. If prices are not sufficiently responsive, unemployment will result. It will also reduce aggregate income and restore equilibrium in the short run. Over time, the unemployed, if they are unassisted, will either have to migrate in search of employment, or will put downward pressure on local factor prices. Either way, the total income of the region will eventually adjust to the reduced value of its output that is the result of changed circumstances.

What does the same theory hold for the pattern of regional incomes and the efficiency of interregional adjustment? Differences in factor prices cannot exist for long if there is interregional mobility of products and factors, for market adjustments will eventually remove them. If markets are relatively efficient in recognizing and acting upon differences, factor prices will become similar across regions. If natural "frictions" or policy-induced distortions impede adjustment, however, the correspondence will not be as close. A number of public policies in Canada have been designed to facilitate this form of market adjustment.

Indeed, we Canadians have relied primarily on the individual decisions of private economic actors to facilitate adjustment through mobility of factors in response to changing economic incentives. Adjustment of this type has been quite effective in the past. For example, as the terms of trade shifted in favour of Western resource producers in the 1970s, not only labour but also capital and financial institutions responded. The subsequent shift away from resources has brought a corresponding flow of these factors to Ontario. The process of adjustment through the migration of labour and capital has been facilitated by a wide range of policies, including Employment Canada's efforts to match workers and opportunities, and grants or tax deductions against moving expenses to assist relocation. More generally, federal support for post-secondary education, health care and other public services help to overcome the barriers to mobility inherent in variations of provincial policy in these areas. Language policies also help to reduce some of the cultural barriers to personal mobility. We have already seen that equalization payments contribute to efficient reallocations of labour and capital.

Compensatory Policies

The second policy option is compensatory. Equalization payments provide the obvious example. Provinces qualify for these payments by virtue of an unacceptably low taxation base. Payments flow, by design, to some provinces and not to others. They are intended to offset natural economic disadvantages, not to change the underlying forces of the economy. Another example is the regional differentiation of Unemployment Insurance (UI) terms and benefits. The variability within the UI system acknowledges that unemployment is more likely to occur in some parts of Canada than in others and to

last longer when it does occur. More generous terms and benefits make up for these differences. It is, in general, these policies that produce the reduction of disparities in personal income treated earlier. The transfers applied can render market adjustments less necessary: they allow recipient regions to maintain consumption levels; they prevent real per capita incomes from falling; and they obviate the necessity for individuals to migrate who might otherwise have to do so. Hence the population base can remain intact, reducing downward pressure on wages. While these results may seem entirely positive in terms of individuals or families, from the market point of view, compensatory policies can hinder adjustment. Where there is a high level of transfers, wages and unemployment remain too high.

Developmental Policies

The third policy option, while still explicitly regional in focus, is developmental in intent. It has been defined as follows:

> *Economic development ... refers to the structural transformation of an economy such that, over time, it becomes increasingly capable of sustaining its capacity for further expansion out of its own, internal resources. Since the prerequisites for such sustained expansion include an increasingly differentiated and integrated economic structure, combined with incentives for its key actors to accumulate capital, to innovate, and to be efficient, the goal of development policy is to ensure that such prerequisites are created.*[3]

Developmental policies are not designed to adapt to, or to compensate for, economic circumstances; rather they address the means of changing those circumstances or of supporting specific regions in their attempts to alter their own capacities in order to overcome their disadvantages.

These developmental approaches often emphasize a broader range of historical, political and even cultural factors than do market-based theories. Some, in particular, see a pattern of cumulative forces, in which the dynamics of the market lead to even greater concentration of productive forces at the centre. Availability of large markets, of economies of scale, of sophisticated specialized services, of a highly skilled labour pool, and like circumstances all attract capital and labour from peripheral regions. Consequently, these regions lose many of their most dynamic citizens and are able to offer fewer advantages to new investors. Cumulative growth at the centre, in this view, can thus lead to cumulative decline elsewhere. Regional policies seek to counter these forces.

Canada has employed some form of regional development policy throughout its history. Much of development policy aimed at sectors has had a strong regional basis where sectors have been concentrated in one or a few regions. In the oil and gas, auto, fisheries and timber sectors, for examples, a substantial portion of activity has been concentrated in a few regions. At the turn of this century, the federal government imposed export duties on uprocessed logs to increase the extent of processing in central Canada and British Columbia. During the Great Depression, relief measures were targeted regionally; the Prairie Farm Rehabilitation Act is a well-known

example. Moreover, national development policies, such as those to enable or promote the movement of goods and services across the country have proved beneficial to the regions. The building and extending of our great national railways and highways fall in this category. Indeed, these implicitly regional policies have undoubtedly been more vital to regional development, broadly defined, than have the explicitly regional development programs of the Department of Regional Economic Expansion (DREE) and other comparable agencies.

Explicit regional efforts, however, had little part in federal economic policy immediately after the Second World War. Instead, emphasis was placed on promoting aggregate economic growth and stability, and on creating the outlines of the modern welfare state. The federal government expected that poorer regions, to the extent that they entered the calculations at all, would benefit from the general economic prosperity: "Regional development was seen as natural adjunct of national development."[4] By contrast, from the close of the Second World War, Britain used regional policy as a pillar of its post-war full-employment policy.

In Canada, the first explicit policies to be aimed at decreasing regional economic disparities were developed in the wake of the 1957 report of the Royal Commission on Canada's Economic Prospects (the Gordon Commission). Sustained national economic growth, the Commission and supporting research studies found, had not eliminated regional disparities. Political action soon followed in the form of Prime Minister Diefenbaker's announcement of the "Roads to Resources" program. In addition, the federal government introduced winter-works bonuses to support construction activity undertaken in times and areas of relatively high unemployment.

The Agricultural Rehabilitation and Development Act (ARDA) of 1961 introduced a long succession of boards, agencies, committees and departments. The target was rural poverty. The goal was to find ways to keep marginal farmers on the land through better techniques of land use. A more explicitly regional (as compared with sectoral) focus for development efforts came in 1962 with the creation of the Atlantic Development Board (ADB), although at the time, the new board was assigned only a research and advisory role.

Regional development took on added importance with the change in government that took place in 1963. In that year, the new government of Lester Pearson gave the ADB a program orientation and funds to disburse, most of which subsequently went toward social infrastructure projects. In 1964, ARDA became the Agricultural and Rural Development Act, and a new department, Forestry and Rural Development, assumed responsibility for its application. ARDA's focus changed from purely agricultural assistance to more general rural economic development. The new department designated Special Rural Development Areas for attention. The Fund for Rural Economic Development (FRED), established in 1966, had an even broader mandate: it was to implement comprehensive rural development strategies in locations judged to be "promising". Areas which did not meet the criteria were to receive adjustment aid; out-migration was deemed inevitable, and the only task was to make this process as painless as possible.

Not only rural areas received government attention. The federal government introduced the Area Development Agency (ADA) in 1963, to promote industrial development in poorer regions. Firms locating in designated areas could qualify for tax exemptions, for accelerated depreciation allowances and, with the introduction of the Area Development Incentives Act in 1965, for cash grants.

These early regional development efforts were scattered throughout the federal bureaucracy, each with different and sometimes tenuous links to the provincial governments concerned. In 1969, with the establishment of the Department of Regional Economic Expansion, consolidation of regional programs took place. Regional economic development was now to have a departmental focus; the new portfolio:

> *. . . was not to be just another line department but rather was to initiate and facilitate cooperative efforts between the line departments, when so authorized to coordinate the implementation of programs and, when necessary, to proceed on its own.*[5]

The appointment of a senior minister to the portfolio emphasized the importance to be attached to the task.

DREE continued to use many of the same policy instruments as its predecessors and also introduced new approaches partly because industrial assistance was added to its responsibilities. It designated certain urban centres in poorer provinces as "Special Areas", thereby making them eligible to receive funds that would support the provision of social infrastructure. These towns and cities were to be the "nodes" or "growth poles" around which economic development would centre and spin off throughout the region. Under the Regional Development Incentives Act (RDIA) the practice continued of designating certain areas as eligible to receive loan guarantees and subsidies for firms choosing to locate in them.

The initial enthusiasm that greeted DREE soon disappeared. Observers criticized the department on two grounds. First, its very policies became suspect. It soon gained the reputation of dispensing large sums of money with negligible results. The industrial incentives grants, in particular, attracted severe criticism. Some critics charged that these grants did not noticeably affect firms' locational decisions; that even when they did, such decisions involved only reallocation of economic activity from one underdeveloped region to another; and that the incentives DREE offered created significant and costly distortions. Even the infrastructure grants under the Special Areas program became targets, as "growth pole" theory fell into disfavour among planners.

The second major concern with DREE lay in its administrative approach. The department appeared to be too centralized and too inflexible, especially with respect to the economic development objectives of provincial governments. There was also considerable tension within the federal bureaucracy between DREE, with its explicit regional development mandate, and line departments, with their more sectoral approach. Often the latter – Transportation, Energy and Fisheries, for example – could affect a region's economy much more significantly than could any policy that DREE was able to mount with its limited funding.

As a result of these pressures, the federal government reorganized DREE in 1973, and instituted the system of General Development Agreements (GDAs). It negotiated with each province a separate agreement wherein the general developmental goals to be pursued were outlined. Committees of officials drawn from both orders of government devised specific projects that were to be run on a shared-cost basis by the province. DREE staff, including a senior Assistant Deputy Minister, were relocated to each of the regions, in order to provide more local expertise. In Newfoundland, the federal government paid for up to 90 per cent of project costs; it paid for 80 per cent of such costs in Nova Scotia and New Brunswick, 60 per cent in Quebec, Manitoba, and Saskatchewan, and 50 per cent in the three wealthiest provinces. Prince Edward Island continued to be covered by an existing federal-provincial development agreement. This DREE procedure was a radical departure from earlier forms of federal-provincial consultation on economic development.

The federal government's approach to regional economic development also changed. The emphasis on growth centres was abandoned. Projects were organized on a smaller scale, but were to encompass a wider range of sectors and to be distributed thoughout any given province. The province, more than a particular region, became the relevant planning unit, and "the focus on provinces meant that regional development policy was really provincial development policy".[6] It was during this period, too, that regionally differentiated investment- and employment-tax credits and Unemployment Insurance benefits were introduced.

Members of both the federal and the provincial governments soon began to criticize the GDA approach. Some provincial governments wanted even more control over program implementation, although most viewed the GDA period favourably, especially as compared to the arrangements that had preceded it and that were to follow. During the course of this Commission's hearings, we Commissioners heard a number of expressions of provincial support for the GDA approach. The real difficulties with GDAs were on the federal side. Ministers of line departments wanted more influence over DREE programs. They saw DREE as tied too closely to provincial priorities. As a result of these bureaucratic tensions, the intended provincial and federal co-ordination and integration of regionally sensitive policies encountered difficulties. Another ground for criticism was found: federal politicians considered that they were not receiving enough political credit for programs that were federally funded, sometimes to the level of 90 per cent. Provinces, however, were in a better position than the national government to represent themselves as the source of the largesse, and often took advantage of this opportunity.

A sometimes-bewildering succession of administrative reorganizations followed. In 1982, responsibility for regional economic development shifted from a particular department to economic ministries as a whole: "The regional perspective [was to] be brought to bear on the work of all economic development departments and in all economic decision making by the Cabinet."[7]

As part of the necessary reorganization, DREE's regional programs were combined with the industry and small-business interests of the Department of Industry, Trade and Commerce (ITC) to form a new Department of Regional

Industrial Expansion (DRIE). Both DREE and ITC were disbanded as separate departments. The Cabinet Committee on Economic Development became the Cabinet Committee on Economic and Regional Development, and the Ministry of State for Economic Development became the Ministry of State for Economic and Regional Development (MSERD). A number of other changes were made, including the appointment of senior Federal Economic Development Co-ordinators (FEDCs) for each province. The merging of regional development considerations with those of more general economic development policies was now complete, at least for administrative purposes. In the process, concern shifted from "regional development" in the sense, primarily, of development of slow growth areas, to "regional development" as the need to focus on economic development in each province.

The basic instrument of economic planning under this system was the Economic and Regional Development Agreement (ERDA), which the federal government was to sign with each province. As with the GDAs of an earlier period, these agreements were to be the overall planning documents within which specific policies and projects would be developed. Within this accepted framework, however, the emphasis would be focused on each government's direct delivery of its own programs, to allow the federal government its proper political due. Federal economic effort in a province and its links with provincial economic interests would be more fully co-ordinated through the FEDCs. Little in the ERDAs was original, and its projects turned out to be very similar to those of the GDAs.

Still further changes were in store. In June 1984, MSERD was disbanded. Responsibility for regional economic development was assigned to a single Minister of State for Regional Development operating under DRIE. In September 1985, even this position was abolished. Regional development policy is now the direct responsibility of the Minister of Regional Industrial Expansion.

Evaluation

How successful have been our regional development policies? To answer this question definitively would require an ability to compare the present state of economic development in those regions receiving assistance to its imagined state in the absence of such policies; unfortunately, such a task is impossible. Some research, however, has shed light on the effect of certain regional development policies.

Researchers have devoted most of their attention to RDIA grants, chiefly because they are the most visible and most contentious, even though industrial subsidies have represented only a small portion of total government spending on regional development. Initially, researchers tried to determine whether grants actually influenced the locational decisions of firms. A 1971 survey by the Atlantic Provinces Economic Council[8] (APEC) found that only 20 per cent of firms polled said that even without the grants, they would have located in the designated area. The other 80 per cent were presumably influenced by the grant to some degree, although the survey gives no indication as to whether the actual grants proved merely adequate or were

unnecessarily generous. A DREE study completed in 1973 produced results similar to the APEC's.

In 1977, the Economic Council of Canada published a comprehensive study of regional economic development in which it attempted to evaluate the effectiveness of DREE grants. It compared unemployment, income and migration rates in the recipient regions before and after the inception of the grant program. It concluded that "job opportunities in the Atlantic region have improved over the last few years, although nothing much seems to have changed elsewhere."[9] Nevertheless, it is impossible to establish that DREE policies necessarily had anything to do with this outcome.

To meet this uncertainty, the Economic Council undertook its own study of the success of grants in influencing firms' location in the Atlantic provinces. It found that 25 per cent of DREE-supported establishments were definitely influenced by the grant program, and that another 34 per cent were possibly so influenced. Little evidence was found that the subsidies "crowded out" other economic activity in the region, and so the net gain remained at 25 per cent to 59 per cent. As a final step, the Council compared the increment to national output from DREE-created jobs with the cost of providing those jobs. Even with conservative estimates of the grant's effectiveness in determining plant location, the program appeared to be successful. The additional contribution to national output from workers who would otherwise have been unemployed, more than covered the cost of the funds used.

The Economic Council's overall evaluation of the industrial subsidy program was cautiously optimistic:

> *Our own assessment of previous evidence, together with our analysis of data on the births and deaths of establishments in one region only (the Atlantic), has led us to the view that the subsidy program is far less successful than published estimates of job creation would imply. To that extent, the critics are right. But the subsidies, nevertheless, seem successful enough to be a paying proposition. The value of the jobs created appears to outweigh the inefficiency involved in locating production inappropriately.*[10]

The Council was unable to come to any definite conclusion on the other components of regional development policy, such as the infrastructure grants.

Other writers have been more critical of the DREE programs. One, for instance, concluded that:

> *In the current situation, the publicly-recognized RDIA goal is employment in certain depressed regions . . . DREE fails to achieve the greatest number of new jobs, and incurs a higher cost per new job created, by continuing with the subsidies which are inconsistent with their goals.*[11]

The specific complaint, based on rigorous statistical analyses of the program and its effects, was its bias towards capital-intensive production techniques. Another analyst was even more sweeping in the criticisms put foward:

> *In view of all the uncertainties inherent in the subsidization of firms – the absence of solid evidence that investment in the designated regions is really increased, the even greater doubt about employment, the effects on distribution*

of income among persons, the possibility of inequity in the government's dealings with firms, the probable reduction in national income in Canada as a whole, and the lack of any real assurance that modernization and progress are fostered in the designated regions — I wonder if it might not be best for the federal government to restrict its subsidy program to the support of poor people . . . and to such transfers to provinces as are agreed upon in federal-provincial negotiations, and to keep its distance from firms' decisions about the location of investment.[12]

A research paper prepared for this Commission, summarized the available evidence on regional development initiatives:

Despite widely varying policy thrusts and economic circumstances, there has been little improvement in the relative position of most of the poorer provinces as measured by income net of transfers . . . It seems reasonable to conclude that there has been no discernible progress with regard to regional development. This finding alone would appear to be a serious indictment of the many policy efforts, and very large public sector outlays that, it was argued, could achieve that goal.[13]

Nevertheless, as Commissioners have noted, it may be that the policies have prevented regional imbalances from getting worse. Nor has it been shown conclusively that if Canada had devoted greater resources to regional development, more progress would have been made.

Criticisms of regional development efforts have gone well beyond arguing that they are simply ineffective. A much discussed and controversial view partially attributes continuing regional economic disparities to the design of these transfers.[14] Economic circumstances create excess aggregate supply in a region. Wages and prices fail to adjust properly, with the result that unemployment triggers transfer payments of various kinds into the region, including individual compensation to the unemployed and additional equalization entitlements to the host provincial government. The receipt of these transfers blocks further adjustment in the form of out-migration or falling real wages. Without such adjustment the region is forever unable to regain its former economic standing, for its wage rates remain out of line relative to its labour productivity.

Transfers have been associated with some of the least suitable of the provincial economic policies.[15] The argument rests, essentially, on what is known as moral hazard. If provincial governments are not forced to bear the full costs of their actions, they will implement policies, highly attractive on some grounds, perhaps, which they would otherwise avoid. Unrealistic minimum-wage laws, language policies and restrictions on non-resident land ownership are three examples cited. These popular programs can be implemented because the distortions they cause are paid for, at least in part, by others. For example, Unemployment Insurance covers those persons who are displaced by minimum-wage legislation, while equalization payments offset some of the adverse economic consequences resulting from the other two examples cited.

This system results in a state that observers refer to as "transfer dependency". It creates a vicious circle in which economic misfortune begets

transfers which, in turn, father poor economic policies which beget further economic misfortune. All private, as well as government, economic agents in the recipient regions are acting rationally within the existing system of incentives, yet the outcome is continued economic stagnation. This situation causes increasing expense to the economic union as a whole.

Whatever the merits of this argument in principle, it is still subject to empirical assessment. Some evidence exists to support certain aspects of the thesis, but to date, no complete assessment has been made. Work on unemployment-insurance and labour-market adjustments[16] tends to support the notion that transfers do affect interprovincial migration. More than one analysis has concluded that the 1971 changes to the unemployment insurance scheme, which made it significantly more generous, acted to retard out-migration from the Atlantic provinces.[17] These studies suggested that this migration, given the relative income and unemployment levels of the source and probable destination areas, would be socially beneficial. Attention has also been drawn to research suggesting that:

> *The UI program reinforces the concentration of unstable and short term jobs in the regions with high unemployment and a high concentration of seasonal industries.*[18]

Commissioners note that such criticisms are directed at impediments to effective adjustment processes. They do not address the effectiveness of policies to improve the economic base of disadvantaged regions.

These debates centre on the uncertainties involved in developing regional development policies. The uncertainties operate at a number of levels. One policy choice must take into consideration aggregate national income growth and the growth of each particular province or region. The central concern here is whether measures to promote the latter reduce the former by diverting resources to areas of lower reward; or, conversely, whether in the long run, regional development programs contribute to the growth of the national economy. Commissioners' recommendations seek to minimize this dilemma by emphasizing that regional development policy should focus as much as possible on improving the productive capacity of poorer regions.

A choice must also be made between "compensatory" policies designed to minimize the gap between earned and total incomes, and those policies which are developmental, or which promote adjustment. "Compensation" is designed to soften the effect of market forces on individuals. In Part V of this Report, however, Commissioners have recommended redesigning Canada's social policies to enhance Canadians' concept of social justice while reducing the barriers to adjustment. These recommendations, if put into practice, will have important regional effects. We have shown, too in this chapter, that equalization, a compensation program, also has important positive implications for efficiency.

In addition, tension exists between interregional market-adjustment policies, which are aimed primarily at facilitating the mobility of labour and capital to areas of their greatest productivity, and developmental policies, which are aimed at improving the productive capacity of individual regions. We Canadians, Commissioners believe, have decided that policies must be

blended in order to make it possible for those who wish to move to do so; but the economic and social viability of all our regions must be promoted as well.

These policy decisions have been reflected in administrative tensions. As our analysis suggests, Canadians have never settled on a stable blending of policies in this area. We have moved from a sectoral orientation, under ARDA, to a more generally directed economic development approach, including adjustment out of the region, FRED, to a strategy of creating growth poles, under ADA and DREE. Specific policies have ranged from adjustment assistance to infrastructure grants, to tax breaks, to direct subsidies, to regionally differentiated investment and employment credits.

Nor have we Canadians settled on the proper relation between federal and provincial responsibilities for encouraging and supporting regional economic development. Early federal efforts were highly centralized and tended to ignore provincial wishes. During the GDA period, however, the reverse was true: the federal government financially supported province building. The pendulum then swung briefly in the opposite direction.

The federal government has been unable to form a satisfactory link between its regional development responsibilities and its broader role in managing our national economy. The most obvious manifestation of this failure is apparent in the constant rearrangment of the federal bureaucracy, first, to bring regional interests into a separate department, then to encourage all departments to consider regional implications, and finally, to drift back to the single-ministry concept. We are thus faced with three questions: What is the appropriate division of labour between the federal and provincial governments? How should the Government of Canada balance its regional economic with its national responsibilities? What policies and programs should be pursued?

Conclusions

We Commissioners would not go so far as to label Canada's continuing regional economic disparity a crisis. We do, however, view it as a serious problem. The nature of individual Canadians' future economic prospects should not depend so significantly on their province or place of birth. Regional development must therefore remain one of Canada's primary policy goals. Commissioners are equally convinced, however, of Canadians' need to reconsider our view of regional economic disparity, our notions of what we should do to overcome it, and our ideas about the institutional mechanisms we should bring to the task. Some of the propositions Commissioners advance are principles we are urging Canadians to accept, some are statements of economic constraints that Canadians have no choice but to accept, and some are conclusions drawn from our research and hearings. Together they form a package that we hope will serve to guide regional policy formation in the years to come. The proposals are designed to be consistent with this Report's broad themes concerning principles both of economic adjustment and of federalism.

Our first proposal concerns the concept of regional disparity. In our opinion it is time to stop viewing inequalities simply in terms of per capita income

differences. Transfers, both to individuals and governments, have rendered this focus unnecessary. Individual Canadians now have a variety of support mechanisms to fall back on in the event of personal hardship, and our proposals in Part V, especially those concerning the new Universal Income Support Program (UISP) and the Transitional Adjustment Assistance Program (TAAP), if adopted, will further improve this situation. Our equalization scheme, imperfect as it is in some respects, would allow each provincial government the means to provide its residents with a comparable level of public goods and services, without imposing the burden of unduly high taxation rates. There is, in fact, less variation in per capita incomes across regions now than there is among individuals within provinces. To the extent that Canadians are truly concerned with income inequality, our first priority should be the vertical dimension of the problem, that is, its application to individuals.

The core factors of regional inequality are wage differences for given types of employment, and variations in employment rates. A job is important, first and most obviously, because it provides a source of income. But it offers more than that. In a society such as ours, a steady job also provides a sense of self-worth and dignity that the most generous transfer scheme could never duplicate. In a federal state, there is even more at stake. The availability of jobs in a region also provides the population base necessary for the survival of that community.

Commissioners conclude that Canada's past policies have compensated quite adequately for regional economic disparities, but that they have been markedly unsuccessful in promoting self-sustaining economic development. The complex mix of transfer programs has substantially evened out per capita incomes across regions, but it has not provided the foundation for robust future economic development.

Commissioners also find some merit in the thesis that Canadians' difficulty in establishing acceptable employment rates in some parts of the country lies partly in the distortions created by a variety of well-intentioned, but misguided, economic policies. Canadians' concern with compensating regions for their economic shortcomings has been partially responsible for those regions' maintaining this status. We have neglected to structure policies and programs to provide the proper incentives to firms, workers and governments. A cycle of transfer dependency has been created whereby economic disparity begets compensation which, in turn, induces behaviour that sustains economic disparity. To make this point perfectly clear, Commissioners are not suggesting that transfer dependency explains all regional economic disparity. There were, after all, significant disparities of this sort in the decades before the 1950s, when few such transfer programs existed. We are simply suggesting that inappropriate incentives are part of the explanation of some of the present problems in this field.

Commissioners believe that regional economic well-being is the responsibility of all levels of government, including municipal government. The role of provinces and municipalities is clear. The justification for including the federal government lies in Canadians' concept of what it means to be a citizen

of this country and the practical need to integrate regional development with national development.

We come now to an important economic constraint which relates directly to the institutional design issue. There is typically, but not always, a fundamental conflict between the goals of regional economic development and those of national efficiency. The location of economic activity is normally not neutral. For a variety of complex reasons, some regions of Canada are simply better situated than others to support internationally competitive enterprises. Furthermore, as this analysis of our economic union has shown, the fewer the barriers to interprovincial trade flows, the more efficient is our national economy and the greater the ease with which capital and labour can be reallocated interregionally. Yet distortions in these markets are often the product of otherwise defensible efforts by both federal and provincial governments to encourage economic development in Canada's poorer regions.

A political constraint accompanies this economic one. The clashing of goals often means that regional economic development produces political tension which operates at two separate levels. The federal public service itself is torn between departments with a national and a sectoral focus, and those with a more explicit regional mandate. Added to this tension is the unavoidable federal-provincial conflict. Whenever the national government undertakes economic policies that are designed for a specific place, as regional development measures are by definition, it impinges on provincial government plans.

In the recommendations set forth in this Report, Commissioners focus both on the federal government's regional development policy, and on that government's implementation of its policy. As we noted above, the federal government has a legitimate role to play in regional development, but its involvement in this policy sphere has typically conflicted with its overall national responsibilities. Thus a further requirement emerges: whatever the federal government does in this field should not be inconsistent with provincial plans. This position is consistent with the basic principles of federalism, but it does not imply that the federal government must blindly support whatever development strategies the provinces put forward.

Does this complex of constraints leave any scope for federal initiative? We Commissioners believe that it does. We return to the two areas of disparity that we find important, wages and employment rates to define the proper federal role. Wage gaps are created because labour productivity for given types of employment is not equal across regions. If output per worker in poorer regions could be brought up to the level that exists in wealthier ones, one important source of regional differences would be removed. The same statement holds true for employment-rate differences: if any Canadian, irrespective of region, had an equal chance of obtaining permanent employment, the other main source of regional disparity would disappear.

The form that the Government of Canada's involvement in regional economic development should take follows logically from these observations. Our national government's responsibility should be to work to remove differences in labour productivity across regions and any factors that impair

the efficient operation of regional labour markets. If poorer regions adopt technology more slowly, the federal government might help to accelerate this process. If labour skills are deficient, it could help to provide retraining. If there are structural problems in matching labour skills with employment demands, it could establish information centres.

This proposal is an extension of the argument advanced in Part III of this Report. There the object in seeking government action was to correct for market failures of whatever origin. Intervention was seen as economically efficient or socially beneficial if Canadian firms were experiencing problems in adopting the latest technology or in reallocating capital and labour from "sunset" to "sunrise" industries or in improving the competitive position of groups in the labour force that historically have been unable to compete on equal terms. The private market-place fails in these instances when it does not generate the socially most desirable outcome.

Commissioners have simply added to this analysis another dimension that is inherent in regional disparities. Specifically, we would assert that the market has failed if it has not provided comparable firms in all regions of the country with equal access to capital, technology, and labour and management skills. In Part III, we asked whether private actors would bring the latest technology to Canadian industry at rates that would allow Canada to compete in the international market-place. If the answer was no, then an industrial strategy of some sort seemed justified. Here we ask whether these same agents will also diffuse this same technology adequately to all regions of the country. If not, then regional policies seem warranted.

These policies would not attempt to bring the same industrial or occupational structure to each regional economy. The object would simply be to ensure that industries that do locate naturally in poorer regions can produce as efficiently as their counterparts elsewhere. A brewery or government office in Atlantic Canada, for example, should be no less productive than its counterpart in Ontario. Almost certainly, however, there would continue to be a greater concentration of high-technology industries in the latter province.

A similar analogy applies to employment differentials. Commissioners are concerned about unemployment at the national level and seek policies to reduce it because we do not believe that the labour market is sufficiently responsive to effect this on its own. In Canada, however, as we noted above, unemployment has a marked regional dimension as well. The national unemployment figure is an average of consistently higher jobless rates in some provinces and consistently lower rates in others. Moreover, these differences tend to widen as aggregate unemployment rises and to narrow as it falls.

The inference to be drawn from the first observation is that all regional labour markets are not equally efficient at matching jobs and workers to meet given levels of aggregate demand. That the gap widens as national economic activity slows is evidence that changes in aggregate demand do not spread evenly to all regions. In both instances, markets fail in the sense that they do not operate equally effectively across the country. As with differences in productivity, then, this failure establishes the rationale for the federal government's regional policy.

It is considerably easier to establish that something should be done about differences in employment rates than it is to recommend exactly what to do. In part, the differences will disappear naturally, with elimination of productivity gaps and equalization of wage levels for given types of employment. As long-term equilibrium is established, there will be less out-migration of younger and more highly educated workers. Participation rates will also rise as the economic outlook improves. These two effects together will raise to the national average, the ratio of those seeking work to total provincial population eliminating part of the difference in employment rates.

The difficulty for policy purposes is compounded by the third component of differences in employment rates: unemployment rates that are much higher in poorer regions. It is important to be realistic on this point. There is absolutely no guarantee that as productivity levels, and hence wage rates, rise toward the national level, there will be enough jobs generated in the poorer regions to employ fully the existing labour force. Let us examine what underlies these possibilities. Suppose that federal and provincial governments raise labour productivity in poorer regions. Their action will have two distinct effects. First, a region will need less labour to produce any given level of output. Secondly, costs may fall for those products that the region produces in competition with suppliers elsewhere, suggesting that total output could increase. The net effect is uncertain. If the labour-saving bias in productivity improvement is strong and the scope for capturing new markets weak, net job destruction will result. The converse will occur under reverse conditions. To date, there is simply no firm evidence about the balance of these alternative outcomes in the different regions of Canada.[19]

It is at this point that Commissioners introduce a sharp distinction between federal and provincial functions in regional economic development. The federal government, we wish to suggest, should not involve itself directly in regional job creation. Its responsibilities end with its commitment to overcome regional productivity gaps and labour-market imperfections. It has served regional equality if identical employments fetch roughly similar compensations, and if adjustment to change in labour markets proceeds equally efficiently in all regions. In addition, the federal government should bring to discussions of regional development a direct concern with building complementary and mutually beneficial links among provincial economies. In other words, it should set regional policy in a national framework.

Provincial governments and their electorates typically want more than this from economic policies. Specifically, they have absolute employment targets as well. They wish generally that all current and future residents will be able to find suitable employment locally. This emphasis on place prosperity is both understandable and defensible when it comes from a provincial government. It should not, however, unduly concern the federal government. Commissioners believe that community preservation, to the extent that people want it, is ultimately the responsibility of citizens and of their local and provincial governments. The federal government must not stand in the way of achieving that goal, in the sense that its economic and social policies must not consistently discriminate against particular groups, but neither need it devote resources directly to meet that goal. Provinces, however, must have access to

such funds and be free to use them in this manner if they so desire. The following conclusions form the basis of our recommendations:

- In the interests of the efficiency of the national economy and of promoting interregional adjustment, the federal government should modify certain regionally distorting programs, in directions consistent with the analysis presented in Part III of this Report.
- The federal government should direct regional development programs toward improving regional productivity and the efficiency of the labour market.
- Provinces should take full responsibility for place-specific employment measures as part of their own regional development policies. In order to increase their capacity to address local needs, provinces receiving equalization payments should also receive Regional Economic Development Grants from the federal government.
- Co-ordination of these federal and provincial activities should take place through continuation of the mechanism of Economic and Regional Development Agreements.
- A sustained federal commitment to regional development requires that a single central agency be responsible for injecting regional concerns into the programs of individual federal departments and for co-ordinating federal efforts.
- Commissioners believe that the total federal financial commitment to regional development, which would combine the Regional Economic Development Grants with funds spent through ERDAs, should increase significantly over the next few years.

Notes

1. Constitution Act, 1982, s. 36.
2. This review is based on a research study for the Commission: Robert L. Mansell and Lawrence Copithorne, "Canadian Regional Economic Disparities: A Survey", in *Disparities and Interregional Adjustment*, vol. 64, prepared for the Royal Commission on the Economic Union and Development Prospects for Canada (Toronto: University of Toronto Press, 1985).
3. N. Harvey Lithwick, "Federal Government Regional Economic Development Policies: An Evaluative Survey", in *Disparities and Interregional Adjustment,* vol. 64, prepared for the Royal Commission on the Economic Union and Development Prospects for Canada (Toronto: University of Toronto Press, 1985).
4. *Ibid.*
5. Peter Aucoin and Herman Bakvis, "Regional Responsiveness and Government Organization: The Case of Regional Economic Development Policy in Canada", in *Regional Responsiveness and the National Administrative State*, vol. 37, prepared for the Royal Commission on the Economic Union and Development Prospects for Canada (Toronto: University of Toronto Press, 1985).
6. Lithwick, "Federal Government Regional Economic Development Policies".
7. Office of the Prime Minister, Press Release, January 12, 1982.
8. Atlantic Provinces Economic Council, *The Atlantic Economy: Fifth Annual Review* (Halifax: The Council, 1971).

9. Economic Council of Canada, *Living Together: A Study of Regional Disparities* (Ottawa: Minister of Supply and Services Canada, 1977), p. 158.
10. *Ibid.*, p. 125.
11. Robert S. Woodward, "The Effectiveness of DREE's New Location Subsidies", *Canadian Public Policy* (Spring 1975), pp. 228–29.
12. Dan Usher, "Some Questions about the Regional Development Incentives Act", *Canadian Public Policy* (Autumn 1975), p. 575.
13. Lithwick, "Federal Government Regional Economic Development Policies".
14. Thomas J. Courchene, "Avenues of Adjustment: The Transfer System and Regional Disparities", in *Canadian Confederation at the Crossroads: The Search for a Federal-Provincial Balance*, edited by Michael Walker (Vancouver: Fraser Institute, 1978).
15. *Ibid.*
16. Jean-Michel Cousineau, "Unemployment Insurance and Labour Market Adjustments", in *Income Distribution and Economic Security in Canada*, vol. 1, prepared for the Royal Commission on the Economic Union and Development Prospects for Canada (Toronto: University of Toronto Press, 1985).
17. Jean-Michel Cousineau, "La mobilité interprovinciale au Canada: le cas de l'Ontario, du Nouveau-Brunswick et de la Nouvelle-Écosse", *L'Actualité Économique* 55 (1979): 501–15; and Stanley L. Winer and Denis Gauthier, *Internal Migration and Fiscal Structure* (Ottawa: Economic Council of Canada, 1982).
18. Cousineau, "Unemployment Insurance and Labour Market Adjustments".
19. See the Economic Council of Canada's Newfoundland reference for an extensive discussion of these effects: *Newfoundland: From Dependency to Self-Reliance* (Ottawa: Economic Council of Canada, 1980).

Federal-Provincial Fiscal Arrangements

Fiscal arrangements are at least as important an institution of the federation as the machinery of intergovernmental relations. Like other countries with federal systems of government, Canada has departed a long way from the fiscal equivalent of watertight compartments, where each government carries out its taxing and spending decisions independently. In Canada, both orders of government exploit the major sources of taxation; tax changes by one order will therefore have immediate consequences for the other. Moreover, revenues flow between governments in massive amounts; attempts by the federal government to constrain expenditures are difficult when a quarter of its spending is in the form of transfers to the provinces; the same is true of provinces with respect to municipalities.

Taxation has a long and complex history in Canada, and fiscal arrangements have been a constant preoccupation of federal-provincial relations since 1867. The British North America Act gave the federal government unlimited taxing authority, while it restricted the provinces to direct levies. Since this meant that the lucrative customs duties and excise taxes of the day were removed from the provinces, the federal government agreed to make specified annual payments in "full and final settlement" of all claims on it. Under these arrangements, the provinces collected only 27 per cent of their total revenues in the first years of Confederation. Their taxation effort, including initial forays into direct taxation of income, increased gradually in the late nineteenth century and again after the First World War as their expenditure responsibilities grew. The federal government also began to levy income taxes during the First World War. Nevertheless, by the time of the onset of the Great Depression, provincial and local authorities were collecting over 70 per cent of Canadian public revenues.

The scramble for revenues in the 1930s led to a "tax jungle" of double-taxation and conflicting regulations. The overall structure of federal-provincial finance was extensively examined in the historic work of the Royal Commission on Dominion-Provincial Relations, the Rowell-Sirois Commission. The Commission recommended that the federal government collect all personal and corporate income tax and death duties, and remit funds to the provinces, but this recommendation met stiff resistance from the provinces. However, the Second World War brought about what a Royal Commission's recommendations could not. The federal government took over these tax sources for the duration of the war and, in exchange, made specified grants to the provinces under the Tax Rental Agreements. By most accounts, this was the high point of centralization in the Canadian tax system, just as the half decade leading up to the Depression had been the high point of decentralization.

The Tax Rental Agreements continued after the war, although with significant modifications in scope and structure, including the withdrawal of Quebec and the partial withdrawal of Ontario in 1947. Renewed in 1952, the first major change in the agreements came in 1957, when provinces were given a choice: they could continue to "rent out" the direct taxation field to the federal government; or they could levy their own income taxes and

succession duties, and have the government in Ottawa provide an offsetting "abatement" of federal tax payable. At the same time, fiscal equalization payments were explicitly introduced for provinces where income tax and succession duties yielded less than an Ontario-B.C. average. In a subsequent series of federal-provincial negotiations, the abatement of federal taxes was steadily increased to provide more "tax room" to the provinces. The federal personal income-tax abatement, originally set at 10 per cent of the federal tax payable, rose to 28 per cent by 1967. In 1962, in a further legal change, provinces were required to impose their own corporate and personal income taxes. However, the federal government would continue to collect provincial taxes free of charge as long as they conformed with federal rules under provisions of tax collection agreements. Otherwise, the provinces were free to establish and administer their own systems, which Quebec did for both corporate and personal income taxes, and which Ontario did for corporate income taxes.

Through these successive arrangements, wartime fiscal centralization was dramatically changed. If we look only at revenues raised by each level of government from its sources, the federal share declined from 73.9 per cent of the total in 1945, to 67.1 per cent in 1955, and to 43.3 per cent by 1983. The provincial and local share rose in the same years from 26.1 per cent to 32.9 per cent, to 56.7 per cent. At the same time, intergovernmental grants increased, making the shift even more dramatic. After transfers are accounted for, federal revenues dropped from 69.2 per cent of the total in 1945, to 32.6 per cent in 1983, and the provincial and local share rose from 30.8 per cent to 67.4 per cent.[1] The broader historical pattern, expressed in terms of gross national product (GNP), is shown in Table 22-12.

There are other indicators of relative decentralization and increasing flexibility. From the inception of the Tax Collection Agreements, provinces were free to fix their tax rates above or below the amount of the federal abatements. Their flexibility was enhanced later, when abatements ceased for personal income taxes. The provinces were to introduce various tax credits against provincial tax payable, thus increasing their autonomy and flexibility. These changes also led, especially in the 1970s, to increased diversification in provincial tax rates. In 1985, provincial personal income-tax rates as a percentage of the federal tax ranged from a high of 60 per cent in Newfoundland to a low of 43.3 per cent in Alberta and 43 per cent in the Northwest Territories. Provinces also gained more flexibility with respect to the grants they received from the federal government. A larger proportion of federal grants took the form of either unconditional payments (equalization) or block grants with few and broad conditions.

Intergovernmental transfers also increased: as a proportion of federal expenditure, they rose between 1945 and 1983 from less than 4 per cent to more than 18 per cent. Each government levies its own taxes, but only the federal government raises its entire revenue, excluding borrowing, of course, through taxation. The others – provinces, local authorities, and hospital boards – rely, to varying degrees, on transfers from other governments. In 1983, for example, the federal government received slightly more than $70 billion in revenue and transferred nearly $17.5 billion. In other words, for

TABLE 22-12 Total Government Revenue Expressed as a Percentage of Gross National Product, Before and After Exclusion of Intergovernmental Grants from Revenue of Recipient Government, Selected Calendar Years, 1926–1982

		Provincial[a]		Local		
Year	Federal	Including Grants	Excluding Grants	Including Grants	Excluding Grants	Total,[b] Excluding Grants
1926	7.6	3.4	3.0	6.7	6.3	16.8
1939	8.6	7.1	5.5	7.2	6.6	20.7
1946	22.1	6.1	4.6	4.4	3.7	30.4
1955	17.6	6.5	4.8	4.9	3.8	26.1
1965	16.4	11.4	8.9	7.5	4.8	30.3
1975	19.2	18.0	13.5	8.5	4.4	38.9
1982	18.4	20.8	16.5	8.8	4.7	42.0

Source: Canadian Tax Foundation, *The National Finances 1983–84* (Toronto: The Foundation, 1984), Table 3.7.

Note: Since figures are rounded, there may be some disparity in the totals.

a. Includes Newfoundland for years subsequent to 1947.
b. These totals also include revenues of hospitals and of the Canada and Quebec Pension Plans.

every three dollars the federal government collected in taxes for its own use that year, it collected an additional one for the sole purpose of turning it over to another political authority, most of these funds went to provincial treasurers.[2]

By far the largest category of transfers are federal contributions to health, education and welfare programs. In 1983–84, over $11 billion, or just over 60 per cent of the cash transfers, are accounted for in this manner: $7.6 billion under Established Programs Financing, $3.1 billion for the federal share of Canada Assistance Plan payments, $70 million for other health and welfare, and $182 million for bilingualism in education. The other large category is general purpose transfers of unconditional – principally equalization – entitlements, which total nearly $5.5 billion or about one-third of the total cash transfers. Miscellaneous transfers such as payments to municipalities and territories account for the remainder.[3] These payments are summarized in Table 22-13. Table 22-14 summarizes payments for previous years.

The more than $17 billion the provinces received as cash transfers in 1983 represented a fifth of the total funds at their disposal that year, a drop from just over a quarter in 1975.[4] The provinces, in turn, remitted one-third of their total revenue – $27.8 billion – to local governments and school and hospital boards. On a net basis, the provinces paid out over $10 billion more than they received. In effect, they financed their entire expenditure on goods and services from their own revenues or, in some instances, by borrowing. Local governments, by contrast, raised only about half of their total revenues

TABLE 22-13 Estimated Federal Transfers to the Provinces, Territories, and Municipalities, Fiscal Year 1983–84

	Nfld.	P.E.I.	N.S.	N.B.	Que.	Ont.	Man.	Sask.	Alta.	B.C.	Terri-tories	Total
						($ millions)						
Statutory subsidies[a]	9.7	0.7	2.3	1.8	4.7	6.0	2.2	2.2	3.6	2.5	—	35.7
Equalization												
Current year	536.0	114.8	536.0	488.5	2 475.5	—	290.5	—	—	—	—	4 440.6
Transitional payments	—	10.5	66.6	28.4	473.5	—	177.3	—	—	—	—	756.4
Prior years	–14.3	2.1	0.2	0.6	142.0	—	12.5	–22.9	—	—	—	120.1
Reciprocal taxation	10.5	4.1	23.9	12.5	47.0	64.5	na	—	—	na	—	210.5
Public utilities income tax transfer[a]	15.7	1.0	—	—	1.7	–9.7	0.3	—	116.6	3.3	–0.4	128.5
Youth allowance recovery	—	—	—	—	–252.8	—	—	—	—	—	—	–252.8
Total general purpose transfers	557.0	133.2	629.0	531.8	2 891.6	60.8	482.8	–20.7	120.2	5.8	–0.4	5 439.8
Established Programs Financing												
Cash payment												
Hospital insurance	92.5	19.9	137.8	113.1	751.8	1 307.9	159.5	172.0	254.7	421.7	8.9	3 439.9
Medicare	31.9	6.8	47.4	38.9	258.9	450.3	54.9	59.2	87.7	145.2	3.1	1 184.3
Post-secondary education	56.1	12.1	83.6	68.6	447.3	790.2	95.7	104.1	150.9	254.8	5.5	2 068.8
Extended health care	21.8	4.7	32.4	26.6	246.5	333.3	38.7	37.4	88.7	106.8	2.7	939.5
Total cash	202.3	43.5	301.3	247.2	1 704.5	2 881.7	348.8	372.6	582.0	928.5	20.1	7 632.5
Canada Assistance Plan[a]	71.4	19.7	93.2	119.2	909.4	848.1	99.3	125.5	343.6	496.8	14.0	3 140.2
Other health and welfare[a]	1.0	0.2	3.0	3.1	—	37.4	4.5	3.4	9.3	6.8	1.4	70.1
Bilingualism in education[a]	2.0	1.1	3.4	18.8	92.6	44.6	5.2	2.4	5.5	6.3	0.3	182.2
Group insurance	—	1.2	0.2	0.5	5.8	22.3	14.2	59.3	38.8	2.7	—	145.0
Territorial financial arrangements[a]	—	—	—	—	—	—	—	—	—	—	445.6	445.6
Municipal grants[a]	1.9	0.7	12.2	10.4	51.3	102.1	11.6	5.5	13.2	19.6	2.5	231.0
Other[b]												364.0

TABLE 22-13 (cont'd.)

	Nfld.	P.E.I.	N.S.	N.B.	Que.	Ont.	Man.	Sask.	Alta.	B.C.	Territories	Total
	($ millions)											
Subtotal	76.3	22.9	112.0	152.0	1 059.1	1 054.5	134.8	196.1	410.4	532.2	463.8	4 578.1
Total cash transfers	835.6	199.6	1 042.3	931.0	5 655.2	3 997.0	966.4	548.0	1 112.6	1 466.5	483.5	17 650.4
EPF tax transfer												
13.5 personal income tax points	63.2	13.3	120.2	89.0	1 095.4	1 922.8	173.0	181.8	624.0	654.8	16.9	4 954.5
1.0 corporate income tax points	2.3	0.6	4.2	3.0	46.9	96.1	7.6	9.9	79.6	24.8	0.8	275.8
Contracting-out tax transfer												
16.5 personal income tax points to Quebec	—	—	—	—	1 338.9	—	—	—	—	—	—	1 338.9
Total tax transfers	65.5	13.9	124.4	92.0	2 481.2	2 018.9	180.6	191.6	703.6	679.6	17.7	6 569.2

Sources: Canada, Treasury Board of Canada, Press Release, 83/10, February 22, 1983; Finance Canada, mimeographed data; Canadian Tax Foundation, *The National Finances 1983–84* (Toronto: The Foundation, 1984).

a. As from Treasury Board of Canada, Press Release, 83/10, February 22, 1983.

b. Includes adjustment for Manitoba, British Columbia, and prior years not allocated by province.

TABLE 22-14 Summary of Federal Contributions to the Provinces, Municipalities, and Territories, Fiscal Years Ending March 31, 1974 and 1981

	1974[a]	1981[a]
	($ millions)	
Payments to provinces		
General purpose transfers		
Equalization	1 517.0	3 590.4
Share of federal estate tax	0.1	—
Adjustments for prior years	—	—
Share of income tax on certain public utilities	25.9	134.8
Grants in lieu of provincial property tax	2.8	6.5
Income tax guarantee	42.6	—
Share of tax on undist. income	—	45.6
Reciprocal taxation	—	145.3
Statutory subsidies	33.8	34.1
Sales-tax/reduction program	—	—
Recovery of youth allowances	−53.1	−163.4
Other	0.2	—
Total general purpose transfers	1 569.3	3 793.2
Specific purpose transfers		
Hospital insurance	1 073.2	2 474.3
Medicare	676.2	857.1
Other health services	39.1	641.8
Social services	721.3	2 052.3
Education		
Post-secondary	485.1	1 600.3
Other	99.0	178.9
Transportation and communications	47.1	71.4
Other	248.4	642.8
Total specific purpose transfers	3 389.1	8 518.9
Total payments to provinces	4 958.4	12 312.2
Payments to local governments		
General purpose transfers	64.0	157.7
Specific purpose transfers	101.0	151.9
Total payments to local governments	164.9	309.5
Payments to territories		
General purpose transfers	85.3	273.0
Specific purpose transfers	10.8	48.7
Total payments to territories	96.1	321.7
Total federal payments	5 219.4	12 943.4

Source: Canadian Tax Foundation, *The National Finances 1983–84* (Toronto: The Foundation, 1984).

a. As from Statistics Canada, Federal Government Finance, Catalogue No. 68-211, various years.

themselves, and hospital boards only about 5 per cent. These latter jurisdictions are the main net recipients in the intergovernmental transfer system which is in place today.[5]

Table 22-15 shows the historical evolution of these intergovernmental transfers. The proportion of the federal budget committed to such transfers has generally increased, and provincial dependence on them has been fairly constant. There has been a decline in both of these dimensions, however, in the last few years.

As Table 22-16 illustrates, provinces vary greatly in their dependence on federal transfers. In 1980–81, all four Atlantic provinces met almost half their revenue needs from federal sources, though this proportion dropped somewhat by 1984–85. Similarly, Manitoba's proportion declined, from 38 to 30 per cent. Quebec received almost a quarter of its revenues from the Government of Canada. Ontario, Saskatchewan and British Columbia each received about 17 per cent from federal sources. Alberta, with its large resource revenues, was least dependent on federal sources.

The pattern, then, is one of extensive interdependence between the federal and provincial fiscal systems, marked by a relatively high degree of decentralization combined with an impressive degree of co-ordination. Why has it developed in this way?

At first glance, a tax system in which each level of government is fully responsible for raising and spending its own funds seems attractive. It is the arrangement most compatible with the tenets of classical federalism: in its designated sphere, each order of government is free to exercise its policy discretion. It is only logical that all levels be given the financial means to carry out their assigned responsibilities as they see fit.

Such a system encourages fiscal responsibility and thus accountability. Like individuals, governments are more careful about their actions if they

TABLE 22-15 Transfers as Proportion of Total Federal Expenditures and Total Provincial Revenues

	Federal Transfers to Other Government			Provincial Transfers From Other Governments		
Year	Total Transfers ('000 $)	Total Expenditures ('000 $)	Transfers as %	Total Transfers ('000 $)	Total Revenues ('000 $)	Transfers as %
1945	157	4 298	3.6	164	621	26.4
1955	450	4 806	9.4	465	1 842	25.2
1965	1 431	8 551	16.7	1 379	6 328	21.8
1975	7 670	35 508	21.6	7 577	29 830	25.4
1983	17 361	94 507	18.4	17 123	82 561	20.7

Source: Statistics Canada, *Historical Statistical Compendium*, prepared for the Royal Commission on the Economic Union and Development Prospects for Canada (Ottawa: Statistics Canada, 1985), Tables 5.4, 5.5.

TABLE 22-16 **Total Federal Transfers as a Percentage of Gross General Provincial Revenues**

	1980 – 81	1984 – 85
Newfoundland	47.7	47.2
Prince Edward Island	52.8	47.4
Nova Scotia	45.8	39.7
New Brunswick	43.9	42.4
Quebec	22.0	23.1
Ontario	17.3	16.1
Manitoba	37.6	30.3
Saskatchewan	16.9	14.9
Alberta	7.7	9.2
British Columbia	16.1	16.9
Canada	20.1	20.5[a]

Sources: Figures for 1980 –81 are based on data from Canadian Tax Foundation, *Provincial and Municipal Finances 1981* (Toronto: The Foundation, 1981), p. 46. Figures for 1984 –85 are based on data from Karin F. Treff, "Provincial Estimates fro 1984 –85", *Canadian Tax Journal* 32 (September-October 1984): 1003–12.

a. Includes the Territories.

know that they will be held directly responsible for them. This truism implies that the governments that do the spending should raise the taxes. It is too easy for governments to cater to narrow special-interest groups when they do not need to tax their constituents to finance the implementation of their promises.

Why, then, would a federation opt for any other system? There are a number of reasons. First, the provinces have an uneven fiscal capacity. For a given "tax effort", governments in poorer regions will raise less revenue than those in wealthier regions and, hence, will provide inferior services. Alternatively, they will have to tax at a higher rate to provide a comparable level of public sector goods and services. This poses problems of both equity and efficiency, and it is the primary justification for equalization.

A second problem is that separate income-tax systems are more costly to operate and are inconvenient for taxpayers. Two or more of the 11 different tax-collecting bureaucracies that such an arrangement would require, might stipulate that companies and individuals fill out each year potentially quite different tax-return forms. At a minimum, Canadians would want tax-collection efforts to be co-ordinated and governments to collaborate in the enterprise.

A third problem is that of matching revenues to expenditure responsibilities. Left to themselves, some levels of government would be unable to raise

sufficient revenue to carry out their constitutionally assigned expenditure responsibilities, while others would have more than adequate access to funds. The case has traditionally been made that the federal government has taxation capacity beyond its spending responsibilities, while the provinces, and especially the municipalities, are in the opposite situation. This circumstance is a result of the rapidly increasing demands on regional and local governments, coupled with inelastic tax sources. Recently the reverse has been considered more accurate; the federal government now faces the structural deficit problem, while the provinces – at least the resource-rich ones – have the capacity to run persistent surpluses. Whichever way the imbalance may run at any particular time, the implication of this position is that intergovernmental transfers are a necessary part of our fiscal arrangements.

An imbalance between revenue capabilities and expenditure responsibilities might arise because one order of government is excluded constitutionally from one or more of the important taxation sources. Another factor might be that while formal access exists, economic and political circumstances prevent authorities from making full use of some tax sources. Competition among the provinces or municipalities for investment or for skilled labour might lead those authorities to bidding down income and business taxes to, or even below, the costs of services provided. The central government faces less constraint in this respect. Thus it may be more efficient for the central government to levy the "correct" taxes on all income and redistribute the proceeds.

In the fourth place, regional governments operating in a completely decentralized tax and expenditure system might vary their tax and expenditure practices according to any local needs and aspirations they perceived. Such action is perfectly consistent with federalist principles, but it can pose problems for the nation more generally in the form of "spill-overs" and lack of tax harmonization. Both problems stem from the fact that individual jurisdictions tend to ignore the effects of their actions on residents of other regions.

It is inevitable in an economy where products and factors of production are traded between regions that taxation and expenditure decisions in one region will affect output, investment and migration decisions in another. Local authorities will have no reason to worry about these spill-overs, since they are not responsible for them; on the other hand they are not in a position to appropriate any of the political benefit from those spill-overs which are beneficial. Thus some governments may undersupply some services, such as higher education, the benefits of which they cannot fully capture because graduates may migrate to another jurisdiction. Under these circumstances, some citizens will be directly affected by the taxation decisions of a government over which they have no political control, and which they can neither reward nor punish; others, inside or outside local boundaries, will suffer from the undersupply of some forms of public services. One solution is to shift the taxation function and some aspects of expenditure to a more broadly based political authority, one that is responsible to all citizens affected by the policy it exercises.

Another problem stemming from spill-overs is that individual decision makers will not always make the correct decisions if they are not formally responsible for the outcomes. For example, jurisdictions that are able to "export" their tax burden – that is, shift it onto others – will tend to use this revenue source excessively. If citizens of other jurisdictions bear part of the cost, governments will tend to supply more services than residents might otherwise rationally choose. Tax exporting can therefore lead to government that is "too big". Similarly, if a jurisdiction cannot shift its tax burden outside its borders but fears the "leakage" of some of the benefits it provides, it might supply fewer government services than residents might rationally choose, thus producing a government that is "too small". Since a central government is by definition responsible to a more broadly based set of individuals, the spill-over effects of its taxing efforts are less serious, and it may, through shared-cost programs, be able to instigate more appropriate levels of expenditure on service programs under provincial jurisdiction.

A fifth problem is that Canada could eventually find itself with a completely disharmonized tax system in which taxation rates and even definitions of taxable income vary greatly across provinces. This state is the "tax jungle" which so concerned Canadians in the 1930s. Similarly, the nation could produce a completely disharmonized service-delivery system which lacked any portability of benefits and which made widely different services available from one jurisdiction to the next. In either situation, the principle of horizontal equity as applied to federalism would be eroded: that is, individual Canadians who are identical in every respect except in their province of residence and who should be treated equally by the government sector, would, in fact, be treated quite differently.

The obvious rejoinder to this concern is that the desire to implement different social and redistributive policies was the reason for establishing a federation in the first place. One can ask the central government to treat similarly situated Canadians in the same way, wherever they live, but the horizontal equity principle stops there: one cannot always expect provinces to do the same.

Another concern about the potential lack of tax harmony or national standards in service-delivery programs relates to economic efficiency. If labour or capital is treated differently enough by the various provincial tax-expenditure systems, location decisions can be affected; for example, when deciding upon whether and where to migrate, workers will take into account both their expected earnings and the package of government services they receive for taxes they pay. If this – rather than economic productivity – is what shapes decisions to move or to stay, then overall efficiency is sacrificed. However, if taxation can be arranged to remove all fiscal influences from the location decisions of capital and labour, and if governments can provide uniform services across Canada, economic output will again be at a maximum. How better is this uniformity to be achieved than by turning responsibility over to a central government and having it return part of the revenue to the provinces according to a pre-arranged formula?

Provinces can compete only for labour and capital, which are relatively mobile factors of production; but their treatment of less mobile factors, such

as land or equipment which is already in place, can vary. This situation may lead provincial governments to turn increasingly to just such sources to finance general expenditures. They bid down, perhaps to zero, some taxes, such as inheritance or succession duties, while they expect others, such as those on property, to bear a greater share of the burden.

In addition, if the processes of federalism engender harmony among provinces, their competition in the matter of tax and expenditure decisions may frustrate the achievement of provincial redistributive or economic-development goals. Generous redistributive schemes may drive out wealthy taxpayers and attract poor ones from neighbouring jurisdictions, undercutting the effectiveness of the scheme. Other provinces will quickly copy tax inducements to investment and in the end will achieve nothing. It may be that only a national government, which is able to exploit some monopoly taxing advantage, can implement a truly redistributive scheme or an effective development program. Distinct regional ventures in these areas, however attractive they may be in principle, may simply be infeasible.

A sixth problem with a decentralized tax and expenditure system is that it may impair the country's capacity to carry out meaningful counter-cyclical fiscal policy. Stabilization policy is traditionally held to be a logical function for the central government. Small regional governments will see most of their efforts dissipated because of the very open nature of their economies. Tax breaks will encourage spending on another province's output as often as they will promote expenditure on local production. Stabilization policy will therefore be less effective. Since the national economy is larger and more self-contained than any provincial economy, this problem is less severe for the federal government. For the Government of Canada to be able to carry out this role effectively, however, it must control a significant part of the total tax and expenditure base. Otherwise, provinces and municipalities might simply offset any federal measures by altering their own taxing and spending decisions in such ways as to reinforce, rather than counteract, the business cycle.

There are three common counter-arguments to this position. First, some economists now deny that any government, federal or other, can actually implement effective counter-cyclical stabilization policies. Secondly, even assuming that there can be a role for the federal government, it is not clear how large a share of total tax sources that government needs to carry it out. The share certainly does not amount to 100 per cent, as is sometimes implied, but it is difficult to know what would be a critical minimum. Finally, it is not necessarily true that provincial governments will act inappropriately.

As Commissioners noted in Part III of this Report, we do not agree that effective stabilization policies are impossible to implement, although we do suggest that several caveats should be observed in applying them. We also believe that the tax and expenditure base for the federal government is sufficient to allow it to conduct effective stabilization policies. We are further convinced that the harmonization of tax systems and the achievement of some national standards of service-program delivery are an important part of our Canadian nationhood; and we have noted instances, such as that relating to

post-secondary education, where the absence of conditions attached to federal funding arrangements may have resulted in a serious undersupply of services.

For these reasons we are convinced that the current interlinking of federal and provincial tax and expenditure arrangements is generally appropriate. This arrangement forms a solid basis for development and for program and institutional reforms.

Commissioners next address the mechanisms through which tax and program harmonization occurs. In what follows, we have not attempted to recommend specific proportions of overall revenues and expenditures appropriate for each level of government. In any event, these decisions might vary slightly from year to year, but more important, they can only be made pursuant to broader considerations of tax reform: before we can divide the pie, we must know its size, shape and flavour. That seems to us to require another investigation with a narrower mandate focused on the types of tax-reform issues raised earlier and the division of the resulting revenues.

Tax-Collection Agreements

The federal government presently administers and collects personal income taxes for all the provinces except Quebec. It defines what constitutes income, and what deductions are allowed the taxpayer, and it determines the amount of taxable income against which the provincial tax rate is levied. The provinces then apply a single percentage to the resulting "Basic Federal Tax", to calculate provincial tax payable before credits. At this point provinces are entitled to specify any tax credits of their own, such as those for property-tax allowances or political contributions. The federal government will administer these individual programs for a sliding-scale fee, provided that they meet certain criteria of simplicity and are not construed as altering the essential harmony of the overall tax system. This system is commonly referred to as "tax on tax". A taxpayer is taxed by the particular province in which he is resident on the last day of the calendar year.

The corporate income-tax arrangements are quite similar. The federal government defines the structure of the tax, and the participating provinces (all but Ontario, Quebec and Alberta) set their own rates against it. The provinces levy their rates, however, against corporate taxable income as defined for federal purposes, and not against federal tax payable. This means that the provinces are free to establish their own rate of tax or to vary rates, according to size of enterprise, for example. All provinces, even non-signatories, abide by a common formula for allocating the taxable income of corporations or businesses operating in more than one jurisdiction across provinces, a matter of great dispute in some other federal countries.

These principles suggest two questions concerning the current Tax Collection Agreements. First, do they provide an economical and convenient way of collecting tax revenues? That is to ask, do they minimize cost of administration and of taxpayer compliance? Secondly, do they provide the best possible trade-off between the wish to accommodate governmental autonomy and the need for fiscal harmonization?

There is little evidence to indicate how efficient the current Canadian arrangements are compared with those of a less centralized system. The Ontario Economic Council, however, attempted to estimate the costs to that province of establishing a separate personal income tax. It concluded that they would be "sizeable".[6] This suggests that co-ordinated administration and collection are valuable, and that a loss generated by the establishment of nine more agencies would be unfortunate.

The desirability of harmonization is a more powerful motive for tax collection agreements. The ideal federal tax system has been described as one in which:

> *One obtains the benefits of centralization in the form of tax harmonization and low collection costs while at the same time accommodating the desires of the provinces to pursue their own tax policies and structures in accordance with the desires of their limited constituencies in a manner which does not unduly fragment the economic union.*[7]

How well do the Tax Collection Agreements fare by this criterion?

The arrangements have served us well up to now. Canada has one of the most harmonized tax systems of any federation, notwithstanding its apparently decentralized features. Even non-signatories, for example, abide by the allocation formula for corporate tax. Yet the system still allows considerable regional diversity and offers much flexibility for provinces to decide how to raise their revenues.

The problem, however, is that this high degree of harmony and co-ordination shows signs of breaking down. Alberta has recently withdrawn from the corporate income tax agreements and established its own system. British Columbia has threatened to follow suit. Two provinces, Ontario and Alberta, have recently considered publicly withdrawing from the personal income-tax arrangements unless certain changes are introduced. In 1979, Quebec initiated a Stock Savings Plan which allowed a resident of that province to deduct up to $15 000 from provincial taxable income corresponding to purchases of new shares of Quebec companies. British Columbia recently introduced a Housing and Employment Bond Tax Credit which Ottawa has agreed to administer, and which will "erect barriers to interprovincial flows of enterprises and capital".[8]

A process which once was flexible enough to balance the need to accommodate regional diversity with the economic benefits of a nationally consistent tax environment has recently fallen somewhat short of meeting the challenge. In part, this is because the demands on it have increased significantly. Provinces now pursue a broader range of objectives in their economic and social policies, and are therefore much more insistent on indicating what tax policies they need.

When provincial and federal income-tax systems interlock, to change the federal revenue system can raise serious problems, for changes which increase or decrease taxable income necessarily affect the level of provincial revenues. For this reason, provinces have called for full consultation before such changes are made and have frequently criticized perceived federal failures to act on their request. Well-known examples of unilateral federal moves are the

introduction of indexing of personal income tax in 1974 and the significant structural changes of the federal budget of November 1981. (It was the latter move which prompted Ontario to consider the feasibility of withdrawing from the Tax Collection Agreements.) The tradition and practice of budget secrecy exacerbates the difficulty, since it effectively precludes advance consultations with, or advice to, provincial governments. The same is true with respect to federal understanding of proposed provincial budget initiatives.

There are two views about what should be done in the matter of the Tax Collection Agreements. One view holds that these arrangements should not be changed. Provinces have remained party to the Agreements to this point because they derive considerable benefit from them; a mass defection would be highly unlikely. Even if the process of fragmentation were to continue, however, it might not pose a serious problem. Canada's tax system is highly co-ordinated now, not because of the good will of politicians and public servants, but because the provinces, as small open economies, have little freedom to deviate from the practices of others without suffering economically. As locally sovereign jurisdictions, they are entitled to choose to do so anyway: poor decisions will be reflected in the results of the next election; good ones will be picked up and implemented by other provinces and eventually accepted by the federal government.

The alternative view does not deny the rationality of economic and political actors, but recognizes that some situations can lead them to behave in mutually destructive ways. Indeed, chains of action and reaction can leave everyone worse off than before. Rules which are commonly agreed to and clearly stated at the outset can do much, however, to prevent this type of mutually destructive behaviour.

Commissioners base a number of conclusions and recommendations on this analysis. The Tax Collection Agreements have served Canada well. They provide a considerable convenience to both citizens and governments. As a powerful inducement to maintain tax harmonization, they also strengthen the economic union. Therefore, they should be retained.

Nevertheless, the agreements are presently under considerable strain. The prominent role of provincial taxes in Canada's public finances, the often acrimonious nature of federal-provincial fiscal negotiations, and the tendency of provincial tax structures to diverge are all points that raise important issues. Canadians wish to maintain the agreements, but without diminishing either the accountability of legislatures or the flexibility of the system.

Provinces have two important concerns with the existing arrangements. First, the federal government is not required to notify provinces in advance of federal changes in the tax base or rate structure, although such changes will inevitably affect provincial revenues. However, the agreements provide a one-year revenue guarantee: where a federal change reduces provincial receipts by more than 1 per cent, provinces are compensated for the loss for one tax year, to give them time to adjust their rates in light of the change.

Unilateral federal changes are a greater problem for the personal income tax than for the corporate income tax, because of differences in the way the agreements are implemented. In the corporate case, provincial tax rates are applied to the federal tax base; this means that federal rate changes do not

affect provincial revenues; only changes in the base do so. In the matter of the personal income tax, provincial rates are applied after the federal rate has been set. This Commission recommends that the agreements be amended to place the personal income tax on the same footing as the corporate tax: that is, to apply the provincial rates to the common, federally-determined base. This measure would both reduce provincial vulnerability to federal tax changes and increase provincial autonomy, since provinces would be freer to make their own decisions about how progressive their tax structures should be. Earlier tax-collection agreements ensured uniformly progressive tax structures across the country; however, the permission given to provinces to include various tax-credit and -exemption programs in their tax administration has already modified this uniformity.

A second potential irritant is that while provinces and the federal government share the revenue base and have equal constitutional authority for taxation, it is the federal government which determines the tax base for provinces within the agreements. Some analysts argue that the tax bases should be determined jointly through negotiations among the participating governments and altered only by common consent.

This Commission does not recommend such a course. To require intergovernmental agreement on all changes to the tax base would unduly hamper flexibility and would reduce the federal government's accountability to Parliament for its financial activities. Under the present system, a province can opt out of the Tax Collection Agreements if it finds federal actions intolerable; the threat that it might do so is a reasonable guarantee of federal sensitivity to provincial interests. Moreover, under the agreements, provinces are permitted to request a variety of tax credits and exemptions which allow them considerable flexibility. The federal government will agree to administer such provincial programs if they meet three conditions: they must be administratively feasible; they must apply to income actually earned in the province involved; and they must not interfere, or have the potential to interfere, with the economic union. The great majority of provincial requests have been accepted, though some, such as British Columbia's proposals for a dividend tax credit for firms in the province, have been refused. Again, the incentives seem roughly right in this case: a province committed to a program can opt out of the agreements to implement it; the federal desire to avoid that occurrence should make it sympathetic to provincial proposals.

Although there is no need for fundamental change, two additional proposals would help to improve co-ordination of tax systems. First, as part of our larger concern to reduce the comprehensive budget secrecy Canadians have experienced and to ensure wide discussion of budget proposals in Parliament and provincial legislatures, Commissioners recommend that in developing any tax change which would significantly affect the federal-provincial relationship, the federal government consult with provinces in advance. Secondly, while we endorse the quinquennial review of federal-provincial fiscal arrangements, we suggest that the Council of Ministers of Finance should extend this consultation process to include a regular and broad review of current practices. To assist the Council, we recommend that a federal-provincial Tax Structure Committee of officials be formed to assess

definitions of taxable income, basic exemptions, marginal tax rates and related issues, and to monitor the division of tax room between the two orders of government in light of anticipated revenue and expenditure needs.

Commissioners emphasize that these proposals are meant to "fine-tune" a process which already works reasonably well. Co-ordination of fiscal arrangements and harmonization of the tax-collection system represent two of the achievements of our federal system.

Intergovernmental Transfers

As governments have extended their activities in the post-Second World War period, all federal systems have made increasing use of intergovernmental transfer arrangements. These arrangements permit one order of government to share in the funding of programs of another order by transferring funds or tax-collection authority. In Canada, the federal government transfers money and tax "room" to the provinces, and provincial governments transfer cash to municipal authorities and hospital boards.

In Canada, these transfers are massive. In 1983–84, the federal government transferred a total of $17.6 billion in cash payments to the provinces. Of this amount, about $5.5 billion took the form of "general purpose" or "unconditional" grants, mainly equalization payments. The remainder took the form of payments linked to specific programs. A total of $7.6 billion formed the cash portion of transfers under the Established Programs Financing arrangements, covering federal aid to health care and post-secondary education. Another $4.6 billion related to other shared programs. By far the most important of these is the Canada Assistance Plan, which received $3.1 billion. In addition, the Established Programs Financing arrangement, originally enacted in 1977, has divided the federal contribution to these programs into a cash portion and a transfer of equalized tax points. In 1983–84, the latter had the value of another $6.6 billion. The dollar value of all these transfers tripled between 1974 and 1984.[9]

The size of these figures suggests that management of intergovernmental transfers is a major issue for the federal system. Two sets of questions have loomed large in recent years and promise to pose difficulties for the future. The first set relates to whether there should be limits on the power of the federal government to spend funds in areas under provincial jurisdiction: To what extent should the federal government be able to use its spending power to project the national interest into areas not under direct federal authority?

The second set of questions arises from the serious strains created as governments struggle to restrain expenditure growth in order to reduce the size of public sector deficits: How will efforts to restrain spending at one level spill over to affect the programs of the other? Will cut-backs effected by one order of government increase the demand for services at the other? Alternatively, will they reduce the financial capacity of the other to pay for them? More specifically, should federal transfers to the provinces be protected or privileged in any way, given the high degree of provincial dependence on them?

While such concerns are never far from the surface in any federal country, both became particularly prominent in Canada after 1980. They were reflected, first, in the debates on federal-provincial fiscal arrangements and Established Programs Financing in 1982–83; later, they surfaced in the debate about health-care policy surrounding passage of the Canada Health Act in 1983.

Background

Intergovernmental transfers have been a key instrument in allowing the Canadian federal system to adapt to the new roles of government. While many of the new responsibilities of government clearly lay within areas of provincial jurisdiction, they were often beyond the financial means of provincial governments. Publicly financed health-insurance or greatly expanded post-secondary education systems, for example, were simply too costly for most provincial governments to support on their own. Moreover, in post-secondary education, where the mobility of graduates meant that spending by one province would spill over to benefit others, individual provincial governments, acting quite properly in their own interests, would provide a less extensive service than would be desirable from a national perspective. Federal assistance was required, therefore, to meet total national needs. Given the obstacles and objections to the constitutional transfer of all these responsibilities to the federal government and the broader desire to retain the advantages of federalism, a solution was found in the shared-cost program under which that government would pay part of the costs of meeting new needs. This program became the hallmark of post-war co-operative federalism, not only in social policy, but also in a wide range of economic development programs, such as construction of the Trans-Canada Highway. Today there are shared cost agreements, large and small, bilateral and multilateral, in almost every program category, and in virtually all government departments.

A wide variety of particular arrangements is possible under the shared-cost program. In general, these may be divided into two broad types: cost-matching arrangements and block-funding arrangements. In cost-matching arrangements, the federal government agrees to reimburse provincial treasuries for some fixed proportion (usually one-half) of provincial expenditures on programs covered by the agreements. The clearest current example is the Canada Assistance Plan, through which the federal government reimburses provincial governments 50 per cent of the costs of social assistance and social service programs, provided that the support goes to people "in need or likely to become in need". The post-secondary-education/financing arrangements in force from 1967 to 1977 comprised a slight variant under which the federal government transferred 50 per cent of institutional operating costs.

In block-funding arrangements, the federal transfer is less directly related to specific program costs and, instead, takes the form of an equal dollar-per capita transfer multiplied by the provincial population. The pre-1977

Medicare grant, for example, was based on the national average per capita costs of medical insurance programs in each year.

The major current block-funding arrangement is Established Programs Financing (EPF). Under that arrangement, transfers from the federal government to provinces are calculated in the following way. First, the per capita operating costs of health insurance and post-secondary education are established for 1975–76, the base year. Then one-half of this amount is compounded each year by an amount equal to the three-year moving average of nominal gross national product (GNP) increases. Finally, the result of these calculations is multiplied by the provincial population in the year for which payment is to be made. The subsequent transfer is made in the forms of cash and tax room. It is apparent, then, that block-funding transfers are not totally unrelated to program expenditures. EPF funding is related to 1975–76 program costs. However, the relationship deteriorates over time. There are also mixed transfer mechanisms: for example, the Hospital Insurance and Diagnostic Services transfers of 1957 to 1977 were based on 25 per cent of actual provincial expenditures and 25 per cent of national average per capita costs.

Cost-sharing arrangements may be more or less strongly conditional. In highly conditional programs, the federal government defines quite specifically the terms and conditions which provincial governments must meet in delivering programs if they are to qualify for the federal grant. Under less conditional arrangements, the provincial government receives funds almost regardless of the nature of its programs. The current funding arrangements for post-secondary education are highly unconditional: provinces receive transfers regardless of the support which they, in turn, provide for post-secondary education. By contrast, the current funding arrangements for health insurance under EPF and the Canada Health Act are highly conditional: provinces must deliver health-insurance programs which meet clearly defined criteria, and they are subject to clearly identified financial sanctions if they fail to do so.

Finally, as we have already mentioned, transfer arrangements may provide for the transfer to be in the form of either cash or tax-collection "room" which the federal government vacates in favour of provincial treasuries. The EPF arrangement, for example, provided for the federal government to withdraw from 13.5 percentage points of personal income tax and from 1.0 percentage point of corporate income tax, and allowed provinces to "occupy" that tax room and collect the revenues; this vacated tax room was intended to make up one-half of the total federal EPF transfer. Where funding is provided through tax transfers, federal control of provincial programs declines: tax points, unlike cash, cannot be cut or withdrawn; and provinces see tax points not as labelled for, or targeted to, specific programs, but rather as part of their general revenues. Responding to federal concerns that cash and tax transfers for post-secondary education were being diverted to other uses, provincial treasurers tended to reply that under EPF, there was no longer a direct link between the transfer and specific purposes; in their view, the transfer could be spent for any provincial purpose. While the federal

government considered the transfers to be "incentive grants", designed to influence provincial priorities, provinces tended to treat them as unconditional.

Taken together, all these elements of intergovernmental transfer arrangements make for a bewildering picture. However, the complexity provides at least one great service to Canadian governments: it makes the arrangements potentially very flexible. For example, if we Canadians wish to decentralize our fiscal system further and to provide more power and authority to provinces, we shall tend to choose arrangements which are block-funded, and which have few conditions and a significant tax-point transfer. On the other hand, clearly defined conditions can be imposed, among other purposes, to create a somewhat higher degree of centralization and national standards.

The federal and provincial governments have debated the character of transfer arrangements with the introduction of each major shared-cost program. In the 1950s and early 1960s, with the important exception of Quebec, there seemed to be broad consensus that these programs were an appropriate means to achieve desirable national standards, and to ensure that the full range of modern government services was available to all Canadians. Provinces themselves often called for greater federal financial involvement in the rapidly growing areas which were under provincial jurisdiction.

By the 1960s, consensus began to erode. Quebec governments had rejected shared programs even before the 1960s, on the grounds that they represented an unconstitutional use of federal spending power to invade provincial jurisdiction and to impose "national" values on a distinct Quebec society. This essentially negative reaction to federal programs was reinforced after 1960 as successive Quebec governments embraced the Quebec state and sought to use it to expand their own programs and to develop that province's society. The call, therefore, was not simply for federal restraint, but for increased provincial fiscal ability to pursue provincial priorities. One result was the Established Programs (Interim Arrangements) Act of 1964, which allowed any province to "opt out" of a large number of shared programs and to receive, through a combination of tax points and "topping-up" payments, funds equivalent to the funds that the federal government would have spent on the program if the province had chosen to participate.

Only Quebec took advantage of the arrangements to opt out, but as the welfare state matured, other provinces, growing more confident in their ability to manage their own affairs, increasingly resisted new federal initiatives. They also became more critical of federal "intrusions", arguing that they skewed provincial priorities, subjected provincial fiscal planning to the vagaries of federal decisions, and reduced provincial government flexibility, leading their legislatures to favour program areas where federal funding existed and to neglect those areas where it did not.

Further strains had developed by the 1970s. First, the federal government was concerned that Quebec's opting out and acceptance of tax points conferred a *de facto* special status; it therefore sought ways to restore the balance among provinces. Secondly, the federal government became more concerned about its ability to control its own expenditures; federal commit-

ment to supporting 50 per cent of program costs implied that the provinces' decisions determined a large part of federal spending. Moreover, the federal government worried that shared-cost programs generated few incentives to restrain spending: the arrangements implied that provinces could count on "fifty-cent dollars" for new expenditures; by the same token, if they did restrain spending, provincial treasuries retained only half of any savings.

All these forces pushed the federal government towards less centralized fiscal arrangements and underlay passage of the Established Programs Financing Act in 1977. The details of the arrangements were complex, but the principles were reasonably clear. Decentralization would be achieved by block-funding, by tax-point transfers and, for post-secondary education, by elimination of any direct link between either program expenditures or the terms and conditions under which programs were delivered. Overall costs would also be reduced by severing the links between payments and actual program costs; henceforth payments would be tied to increases in GNP, which, at the time, was rising more slowly than program expenditures. Federal contributions would be controlled and provincial incentives to restrain expenditure growth increased. Moreover, since the payments would be recast into a combination of cash and a transfer of tax points, all provinces would be brought more closely into line with Quebec.

The arrangements represented a major step towards greater provincial autonomy, towards "disentanglement" of federal and provincial responsibilities, and towards restraint. Once again, the flexibility of intergovernmental transfer arrangements had been demonstrated. However, the arrangements did not go the whole way to decentralization: the conditions attached to hospital insurance and Medicare remained unchanged; and provinces agreed to consult the federal government with respect to spending on post-secondary education.

By 1982, the situation had changed. First, rapid inflation in nominal GNP caused federal transfers to increase even faster than they would have done if they had remained tied to actual spending. Then, because of a guarantee built into the EPF formula (that the value of the tax points transferred to the provinces would always at least equal the value of the cash portion of the grant), as the recession hit, and as the yield of the transferred tax points declined, the proportion of federal transfers in the form of cash payments increased. Moreover, since transfers were no longer tied to program spending, the federal government believed that it had lost what little control it had once exercised over program content and standards. In a sense, the provinces had done with a vengeance just what EPF had invited them to do: they had restrained their expenditures in both health care and post-secondary education. In the health field, many provinces were experimenting with "user fees" and "extra billing" to limit the costs of health programs to provincial treasuries and thus reduce provincial, but not federal, spending. This led to federal concern that provinces were diverting funds to other purposes, with the result that, in post-secondary education especially, the federal share of total costs was rapidly increasing. Moreover, public opposition to perceived cut-backs and, particularly, to extra billing and user fees in health services translated into calls for federal action. Finally, in the wake of the Quebec

referendum and the constitutional debate, the federal government had become increasingly concerned about fiscal decentralization and the erosion of federal power. It believed that it had made too many concessions to the provinces, reducing its ability to affect vitally important programs, to account to Parliament for its expenditures, and to maintain direct links with citizens.

The federal government considered that the time had come to redress the balance; in 1982, it sought to regain some control over total expenditures and to restore a degree of influence for its programs. It capped, or established an upper limit on, transfers for post-secondary education and announced its intention to seek negotiations aimed at developing national standards and a defined federal role in that field. It also proceeded to develop the Canada Health Act. Its aim was to define clearly the original program conditions: universality, portability, accessibility, comprehensive coverage and public administration. In addition, it undertook to eliminate extra billing and user fees by applying dollar-for-dollar reductions in the federal transfers to provinces which used these devices. No federal-provincial agreement was reached on any of these issues, but since these were federal spending programs, the federal government was able to proceed on its own.

The intergovernmental debate focused on the complicated details of alternative formulae for transfer arrangements. The debate raised a larger question, however, about which alternative, in 1982, Canada should pursue. On the one hand, we could move farther along the path indicated by the EPF in 1977, and continue to decentralize transfer arrangements by making the transfers totally in terms of equalized tax points, by extending them to the Canada Assistance Plan, and by eliminating the conditions in the original Medicare and hospital-insurance programs. On the other hand, we could move back from the 1977 arrangements and return to more conditional funding arrangements by requiring provinces to be more accountable to the federal government for their use of federal transfers, and by developing a more direct policy-design role for the federal government. EPF might well have responded to the political requirements of the time, but it falls squarely between these two alternatives. And this, argues one observer, accounts for the instability of the arrangements. His conclusion with respect to post-secondary education applies to other areas as well:

> *The Government of Canada must decide whether it means the PSE [post-secondary education] fiscal transfers to be program-related or not. If it believes they* should *be, then the scale, and/or the rate of growth, of the federal payments (transfers) must be related to some measure of the scale, or [to] the rate of growth, of expenditures in the provinces on or for PSE . . . If, on the other hand, the Government of Canada means simply to make an unconditional per capita grant to the provinces . . . then all reference to post-secondary education should be removed from the Act. It is as simple as that.*[10]

The issues raised by EPF and by the Canada Health Act extend to larger questions about the federal spending power and its place in Canadian public policy.

The Federal Spending Power

Most shared-cost programs, as well as many programs (such as family allowances) which make payments to individuals, represent exercise of the federal spending power. The spending power is usually regarded as one of a number of general discretionary federal powers. Unlike the declaratory and disallowance powers, however, the federal spending power is nowhere explicitly defined. Rather, it is held to derive from more general principles. In part, it derives from the power of Crown prerogative, for all public revenues belong to the Crown, which is "a person capable of making gifts or contracts like any other person, to anyone it chooses to benefit." The Constitution requires that the Crown have the approval of Parliament or legislature; when this approval is obtained, the government may distribute revenues as it sees fit. This view implies that the donor of public revenues has the power to attach conditions to the grant, and the recipient has the power to refuse it.

The spending power has also been justified in the Constitution Act, 1867, under section 91(1A), "The Public Debt and Property", and under section 102, which authorizes a Consolidated Revenue Fund. Together these sections are said to confer on the federal government the right to spend for any purpose "provided the legislation does not amount to a regulatory scheme falling within provincial powers."[11]

Remarkably little constitutional assessment of the spending power has been attempted in the courts. Federal-provincial/shared-cost agreements have not been the subject of extensive legal challenges, and it does not appear that there are constitutional restrictions on the federal power to offer conditional grants to the provinces. The provinces are ultimately protected by their power to refuse to participate in these agreements; in political terms, however, this power may be more theoretical than real. The remaining constitutional uncertainty lies in grants awarded by the federal government to individuals and institutions, especially when such grants might be interpreted to constitute regulation within an area of provincial jurisdiction. Again, in this instance, the limited jurisprudence provides little guidance.

The question of limiting the federal spending power lies primarily in the political realm. This Commission believes there are a number of considerations which must be brought to bear. First, the federal government, in the name of national citizenship and the national political community, has the right and responsibility to respond to emergent needs and to changing conceptions of the national interest. The record of the past emphasizes the fact that the national interest is not static: rather it changes in response to changing international circumstances, changing issues, changing conceptions of citizenship, and changing aspirations. Matters once considered of purely local interest can, and do, become defined as national questions which demand national responses. There will often be emerging issues where provincial activity, even within provincial jurisdictions, is not a matter of indifference to the federal government. Where the federal government does not possess the constitutional authority, and where provinces are unable or unwilling to respond effectively to new needs, there is in the future, as there was in the past, a case to be made for wide federal freedom to put forward proposals for shared-cost programs.

The values of federalism, however, suggest that this ability should not be entirely unconstrained. The spending power introduces a necessary degree of flexibility into the federal system, but taken to its extreme, it can undermine the system by eroding the distinctions between federal and provincial responsibilities. On a more practical plane, federally imposed conditions in shared-cost programs — especially those which change frequently and without consultation with provincial governments — can hinder provincial attempts to plan and rationalize their activities and can admit possibly arbitrary and disruptive federal interventions into provincial administrative systems. To assess the federal spending power, we must therefore balance, on the one hand, the national interest and the associated concept of changing national objectives or values and, on the other hand, the preservation of the diversity of federalism and the administrative integrity of provincial systems.

Three other criteria must also be considered. Accountability must be a central aspect of our institutional reforms. One view of accountability argues strongly against the use of the spending power to promote shared-cost programs, for such programs can undermine the accountability of both orders of government. Provinces spend money which they are not responsible for having raised. The federal government transfers money to the provinces, but has little control over the manner of its spending. Citizens cannot hold the federal government accountable because they receive the services through the provincial government rather than directly. And Parliament cannot hold the federal government responsible because the federal government cannot specify precisely how the funds have been used. Under the Established Programs Financing arrangements, the severance of transfers from program costs and the lack of either effective program standards or enforcement mechanisms has accentuated this problem.

The principles of accountability push in the direction of disengagement. In principle, disengagement could be achieved either by transferring full responsibility for programs to the federal government or by transferring the full revenues required to the provinces. For health and education programs, the former strategy is not a real possibility in the Canadian federal system, although it might work for other, less contentious programs. The latter strategy would severely constrain the capacity of the federal government to act in the national interest on behalf of all Canadians. The development of clear conditions both for program delivery and for accounting provides an alternative approach to the accountability problem: with an appropriate legislative base, Parliament could hold the federal Cabinet responsible for its spending if the Cabinet, in turn, were able to hold the provinces accountable for their expenditure of the federal funds transferred to them.

Flexibility is another criterion which cuts two ways. In a larger historical sense, the spending power and shared-cost programs have made an essential element of flexibility available to the federal system. In a narrower sense, however, federally imposed conditions can reduce the flexibility of provinces in the operation of the programs. A classic example is the hospital-insurance program, where the focus on acute-care facilities inhibits experimentation with preventive medicine and chronic-care and after-care facilities. Some observers vigorously argue that the recent Canada Health Act, with its more

stringent federal sanctions against user fees and extra billing, its restatement and redefinition of the original program conditions, and its "suggestion" of how provinces might negotiate with physicians over fee schedules, has significantly reduced the capacity of provinces to experiment with more efficient delivery systems.

A final criterion is the desire to minimize administrative and decision-making costs. This consideration, too, argues for disentanglement. The more detailed the conditions of shared-cost programs, the more extensive are the bureaucratic resources that must be devoted to negotiation, monitoring and reporting, and the more room there is for bureaucratic wrangling. These considerations led the Royal Commission on Dominion-Provincial Relations (the Rowell-Sirois Commission) to warn against the "difficulties of divided jurisdiction" and to advocate retention, as far as possible, of the principle of "watertight" jurisdictional compartments. Hence it recommended that where federal initiative was essential, there should be a transfer of jurisdiction: shared-cost programs should be a last resort.

How can we balance these criteria and come to some conclusions about the appropriate uses of the federal spending power? Over the past two decades, advocates of change have made many proposals to clarify that power. There has been widespread agreement, even by federal governments, that the spending power should be subject to some constraints or limitations. Several possibilities have been examined.

One possibility is to abolish the spending power in areas of provincial jurisdiction. This proposal has received little support, for in the name of federalist purity, it would impose far too much rigidity. Indeed, since one impetus for many of the shared-cost programs was the desire of provinces for financial help in rapidly growing areas, it would likely be as unacceptable to many provincial governments as to the federal government. Commissioners therefore reject this option out of hand.

A second option would be to subject the federal spending power in areas of provincial jurisdiction to some form of consent mechanism. This is perhaps the most widely-canvassed approach: various mechanisms have been proposed by provincial governments, by the Quebec Liberal Party, by authors of the Pépin-Robarts Report, and by the Canadian Bar Association, among others. These groups would have used the device of a reformed Senate, made up of direct provincial delegates, to reach provincial consensus. Consent could also be registered by a First Ministers' Conference, or, as in our constitutional amending formula, by the supporting votes of an appropriate number of provincial legislatures.

In 1969, the federal government proposed that the federal spending power be explicitly laid down in the Constitution, that its power to make unconditional grants be unrestricted, and that conditional grants in relation to federal-provincial programs which are acknowledged to be within provincial jurisdiction require "broad national consensus" before Parliament exercises its power. The consensus would be determined jointly by Parliament and the provincial legislatures.[12] In later constitutional discussions that took place between 1979 and 1981, the federal government also expressed its willingness to embrace a substantial provincial consent mechanism.

Such proposals provide a strong guarantee of the federal principle: they provide a very strong incentive for the federal government to look first to its own jurisdiction and to consult before proceeding, in order to maximize its chances of winning the requisite provincial support. They also ensure the fullest possible debate: the federal government would be required to mobilize public support for its proposals, and provinces would have to justify any opposition before their own legislatures and electorates. It is probable that most of the major programs now in existence would still have been developed under such a scheme; the greater bargaining power this method gives to provinces, however, suggests that their legislatures might have been able to use the need for consent to win more favourable terms from the federal government or to gain leverage in other policy domains. Commissioners are not inclined to favour consent mechanisms which are too rigid, or which unduly hinder the Parliament of Canada from exercising its legitimate rights and performing its responsibilities.

A third option is provincial opting-out, an approach with which we have had considerable experience in the past. The concept is incorporated in the new constitutional amending process. In a sense, the right to opt out of a shared-cost program has always existed; no province is constitutionally obliged to participate. Most opting-out proposals, moreover, significantly reduce the provincial costs entailed by including compensation, or "fiscal equivalence" payments, to the non-participating provinces. Thus, the Canadian Bar Association recommended that any province should be able to opt out of a program and receive compensation equivalent to the amount of money it would have received from the federal government, provided that the province agreed to provisions respecting interprovincial portability. The 1969 federal proposal also included fiscal compensation, but in the form of grants to citizens, rather than to provincial governments.

Serious objections have been raised against opting-out. There is the fear of a chequer-board Canada, for of what validity are "national standards" if they exist in some provinces but not in others? Would federal MPs be permitted to vote on programs which do not operate in their home provinces? Why should federal revenues be turned over to provincial governments that are unwilling to participate in national programs which have broad public support and are constitutional? In spite of all these contrary arguments, however, opting-out has been defended on the grounds that it introduces a high degree of flexibility into the federal system. In particular, it allows a response to the distinctiveness of Quebec, while avoiding a situation in which Quebec might be able to block a program which is considered highly desirable in other parts of the country.

The spending power has been a vital instrument of flexibility and of response to changing definitions of the national interest. Commissioners believe it should be retained, subject to a number of guidelines. First, while we believe that this power is and should be a broad one, we are also convinced that it is not unlimited. We consider the judicial distinction between the federal legislation which makes grants or gifts and that which involves direct regulation in the fields of provincial jurisdiction, though it is not fully developed, to be the appropriate one. We believe, for example, that federal

loans, tax credits or grants to post-secondary students would be constitutionally justified, but that if they were to be used to require universities to establish entrance conditions, they could be challenged as an invasion of provincial jurisdiction. We hold the opinion that it is appropriate for the Supreme Court to spell out the constitutional limits more fully as it considers future cases.

Secondly, following the Rowell-Sirois Report, we believe that in principle, the federal government should look to a shared-cost program as a last resort, rather than as a first resort. Indeed, in many cases, it will be desirable to seek to mesh federal and provincial activities under a shared-cost program. In general, however, the democratic objectives of accountability and clarity of roles are more effectively secured if a government pursues programs under its own jurisdiction.

Thirdly, use of the spending power in an area of provincial jurisdiction requires broad national consensus. A reformed Senate with stronger regional representation would provide one device to secure this end. However, since such a Senate would represent individuals, and not governments, and since it is governments which are involved in the development and administration of shared-cost programs, even a reformed Senate would not provide a sufficient solution. Provincial governments must be directly and fully consulted.

Federal-Provincial Ministerial Councils should provide an effective vehicle for consultation. Commissioners would go beyond this proposal, however, and require the Prime Minister to make every effort to obtain broad consensus of First Ministers in advance of federal legislative action. Under present arrangements, consultation almost always occurs over new programs, since it is essential to their success that provinces agree to participate. Consultation is even more necessary, however, when the federal government proposes either to alter the terms and conditions of a program or to terminate it; since provinces are already participating, it is difficult for them to respond to such changes by leaving the program. We therefore believe that there should be considerable advance notice and opportunity for debate before conditions are changed or programs are terminated. It could be standard practice, for example, to design shared-cost programs so that they operate for five-year periods, as has been done with fiscal arrangements. At the end of each five-year period, the program would be renegotiated, but neither order of government would be able to alter the conditions unilaterally within the period.

Finally, we believe that flexibility and opportunities to innovate will be enhanced to the extent that the conditions of shared-cost programs are stated in terms of goals or ends, and the federal government does not dictate specific administrative means, but leaves their determination to provincial experience and initiative.

Federalism and Fiscal Restraint

A potential source of significant tension in federal-provincial fiscal relations in the present context concerns the cutting and trimming of programs for financial reasons. Again, the problem flows from interdependence and from

the likelihood that in the foreseeable future, all governments will be anxious to restrain expenditure and to manage their finances. The efforts of one order of government to do so will inevitably affect the budgetary situations of the others.

This development can come about in several ways, even when there are no fiscal transfers involved, and when each level of government is operating in its own jurisdiction. For example, a federal tightening of unemployment-insurance provisions might generate increased demand for provincial welfare services. In turn, provinces might try to reduce their welfare burden by instituting short-term/work programs which would last just long enough for the participants to qualify for Unemployment Insurance. More generally, one government's reductions in almost any area would be likely to generate political pressures on another order to step in to fill the gap. Commissioners make no recommendations here; the problem simply calls for sensitivity.

Of more direct interest are intergovernmental transfers. As fiscal conditions have become more volatile in recent years, numerous government actions have been taken which affect the level of transfers: these include a rapid series of changes in equalization as the system tried to respond to escalating oil and gas revenues in the 1970s; the capping of the escalators for post-secondary education and health-insurance transfers in the mid-1970s; or the more recent capping of post-secondary education transfers under the "Six-and-Five" anti-inflation program.

The question which arises is whether such transfers should be in some way insulated or protected from these kinds of budgetary changes. One perspective suggests that indeed they should be. This argument is based on the need for fairness and certainty, as well as on recognition of the high degree of provincial dependence on intergovernmental grants. Provinces, it is claimed, have been induced to participate in these programs on the understanding that the federal government would continue their support. They cannot effectively plan their own budgets if the amount of transfers remains uncertain. A particularly strong argument is sometimes made that equalization payments should be shielded from federal measures to control deficits, especially in light of the constitutional commitment to sharing now found in section 36 of the Constitution Act, 1982.

Those who view the situation from the contrary perspective ask: Why should the programs which happen to be delivered through intergovernmental mechanisms be privileged in any way over other kinds of federal expenditure? True, we justify these programs by reference to national objectives and national standards, but programs fully in federal jurisdiction presumably have similar justifications. True, budgetary uncertainty makes planning difficult, but tax revenues are also inherently uncertain; indeed, coping with uncertainty is part of the problem of governing. While the federal government may have induced provincial governments to enter particular program areas by offering cost-sharing arrangements, provincial governments have often initiated the requests for federal sharing. Moreover, if intergovernmental programs are protected, then any federal restraint measures will have to be concentrated disproportionately on a limited range of unprotected programs. Thus, in 1984, with about one-fifth of federal spending taking the form of

intergovernmental transfers and another fifth covering interest on the national debt, federal restraint measures would have to be concentrated on relatively few areas of discretionary spending. If transfers to individuals are also to be considered protected, then almost 70 per cent of federal spending would be locked in, and federal flexibility would be greatly reduced.

An interesting sidelight on these intergovernmental transactions is that it has fallen to the federal government to assume responsibility for most of Canada's public sector deficit. Without the tranfers, the federal deficit would be much smaller and the provincial deficits much larger. Thus, in 1982, the federal deficit, excluding intergovernmental grants, stood at $4.7 billion, but after the grants were included, it rose to $20.5 billion. The same thing happened at the provincial-municipal level. Before transfers were counted, provinces had a surplus of $7.4 billion; after grants to local authorities and hospitals were included, the provinces were in deficit by $1.6 billion. Local governments and hospitals are the massive recipients of transfers: collectively, they were in deficit by $25 billion in 1982, based on their own revenues; after transfers from other governments, they were roughly in balance.

In light of these considerations, how might Canada retain a desirable degree of federal flexibility and accountability to Parliament, while assuring provinces of some stability for their planning, and while protecting them against rapid unexpected variations in federal spending? The simplest option would be to require the federal government to give the provinces advance warning of proposals to cut federal transfers. One year's notice before the implementation of cuts, for example, would give provinces some time to adjust their revenues and expenditures to planned changes. This scheme, however, would provide only limited protection for provinces.

A second possibility is to review federal-provincial/transfer arrangements every five years and to limit the changes that the federal government can make, between reviews, without provincial approval. Such an arrangement could, for example, allow the federal government to adjust payments in any given year by up to 5 per cent; any greater changes would require provincial consent. An appropriate formula would have to be worked out. Alternatively, the federal changes in intergovernmental transfer programs could be linked to the average level of reductions in non-transfer programs.

A number of other proposals governing the application of federal restraint have also been made. For example, social programs could be insulated from any reductions. However, since these programs represent well over 80 per cent of all intergovernmental transfers, to exempt them would severely constrain the federal government. Another possibility is to vary the amount of reductions to take account of differences in provincial levels of need; we Commissioners discuss the difficulties of such a procedure in our analysis of equalization. Finally, provinces with higher revenues could bear the brunt of reductions, and poorer provinces could be protected. We believe, however, that the equalization program, and not individual shared-cost programs, is the appropriate mechanism for dealing with revenue disparities.

Again, to achieve balance is fundamental: the federal government must have enough fiscal flexibility to control its own budget, but it should not be able to cut with impunity transfers for shared-cost programs. We believe that

to give one year's notice of changes in these programs provides inadequate protection for the provinces. Rather, we consider it best to specify in advance the limits on permissible reductions. Furthermore, apart from conditions spelled out in the enabling legislation, the federal government should leave the provinces full freedom to decide for themselves how best to adjust their own programs and administrative systems to any reductions.

Finally, Commissioners believe that the managing of restraint is likely to cause major strains in the federation in the coming years. The temptation for each order of government to pass off its fiscal problems to the other will be acute, and the political pressure on the federal government to react to provincial measures will grow. To deal with such inevitable tensions will require a high degree of common trust, open exchange of information, and resilient institutions.

Notes

1. Calculated from Statistics Canada, *Historical Statistical Compendium*, prepared for the Royal Commission on the Economic Union and Development Prospects for Canada (Ottawa: Statistics Canada, 1985), Tables 5.1, 5.2, 5.3, 5.4.
2. *Ibid.*, Tables 5.4, 5.5.
3. Canadian Tax Foundation, *The National Finances 1983–84* (Toronto: The Foundation, 1984), Table 16.2.
4. Canada, Finance Canada, *Economic Review, April 1984* (Ottawa: Minister of Supply and Services Canada, 1984), Table 54.
5. *Ibid.*, Tables 55 and 56; and Canadian Tax Foundation, *The National Finances 1983–84*, Table 3.6 for hospitals (1982 data).
6. Ontario Economic Council, *A Separate Personal Income Tax for Ontario: An Ontario Economic Council Position Paper* (Toronto: The Council, 1983), p. 130.
7. Robin W. Boadway, "Federal Provincial Transfers in Canada: A Critical Review of the Existing Arrangements", in *Fiscal Federalism*, vol. 65, prepared for the Royal Commission on the Economic Union and Development Prospects for Canada (Toronto: University of Toronto Press, 1985).
8. Thomas J. Courchene, *Economic Management and the Division of Powers*, vol. 67, prepared for the Royal Commission on the Economic Union and Development Prospects for Canada (Toronto: University of Toronto Press, 1985).
9. Canadian Tax Foundation, *The National Finances 1983–84*, Table 16.2.
10. A.W. Johnson, *Giving Greater Point and Purpose to the Federal Financing of Post-Secondary Education and Research in Canada*, a report prepared for the Secretary of State of Canada (Ottawa, 1985), p. 23.
11. Canada, Government of Canada, *Federal-Provincial Grants and the Spending Power of Parliament* (Ottawa, 1969), p. 12.
12. *Ibid.*, pp. 36–42.

Intergovernmental Relations and the Institutions of the Federation

Commissioners have already reviewed the strengths and weaknesses of Canada's national institutions. Here we discuss more comprehensively the institutions of Canadian federalism: the division of powers, the amending formula, and the machinery of intergovernmental relations. Given the difficult policy choices with which we Canadians are confronted, how can we reform these institutions so as to facilitate effective policy making? How can these institutions better reflect the democratic values of openness, accountability and responsiveness that underlie the optimum approach to institutional change? This Commission's terms of reference asked that we respect "the spirit of the Constitution" and "assume a continuing Canadian federal structure not significantly different from its present form." Here we provide some thoughts about that spirit and suggest refinements to that structure, in light of Canada's current needs and values.

One of the most insistent messages which we Commissioners received in our hearings was that relations among federal and provincial governments appeared to be in disarray. There was simply too much conflict, too much bitterness and mistrust. Federal-provincial relations gave the impression of steady confrontations, with reporters and camera crews standing ready to dramatize the conflicts. The capacity of the country to deal with the concrete and pressing issues put forward seemed vitiated in a struggle — of more interest to the governments involved than to the citizens they represented — for position, for status, for "turf". Such conflict troubles Canadians because it diverts attention from the substance of policy and threatens to undermine confidence in our political institutions, perhaps even in the legitimacy of the constitutional order itself.

Canadians were concerned, too, about the actual or potential threats our practice of federalism holds for democratic values. As governments have more and more shared responsibility, it has become harder and harder for Canadians — and indeed for governments themselves — to determine which authorities are responsible for what areas of administration. Intergovernmental relations, a product of shared or overlapping responsibility, disproportionately involved the executive and bureaucratic levels of government. Intergovernmental consultation and agreement have removed important areas of policy from parliamentary control. Preoccupied with the intergovernmental dimension of their responsibilities, policy makers may be less inclined or less able to respond to groups whose concerns are not territorially defined. The intergovernmental process is often secretive, and issues disappear into the intergovernmental maze. As vital issues have been caught up in this process, interest groups have realized that their concerns are at stake. For this reason, they have insisted on broader access to the process, as demonstrated in the constitutional discussions of 1980–82 and in the debates on the Canada Health Act in 1983 and 1984.

The record demands, however, that these criticisms be tempered, for even in the periods of most bitter conflict, effective policy co-ordination was maintained in many areas. Moreover, the personalities of the chief partici-

pants and the weaknesses of the institutions are not the sole sources of conflict. Some features of the relationship do spur conflict: the primary cause has been genuine differences in interests, both regional and intergovernmental, differences which are, in effect, a natural outcome of regional diversity in the federation. In the consequent struggles, governments represented not only their own political interests, but also important visions of Canada and the material interests of their residents. It is unrealistic – indeed undesirable – to expect our institutions and intergovernmental arrangements to eliminate conflict. Nevertheless, we must try to ensure that they will not generate and perpetuate unnecessary conflicts based primarily on concerns for status.

Competition among governments, overlapping of functions, and duplication of services are inherent in federalism; indeed, they are one of its chief advantages. Policy is likely to be more responsive when citizens can turn to another level of authority if they find that the first does not listen to their concerns, and when governments compete for voters' allegiance. When issues are debated in intergovernmental forums, as well as in the legislatures, the full range of policy concerns and options is more likely to be canvassed. Thus, while we Canadians must seek to establish mechanisms that avoid the intensive conflicts of recent years, we must also recognize that federalism, like other elements of Canada's institutional framework, encourages competition and adversarial relationships which are seen as essential methods for enhancing the well-being of Canadians.

Finally, the very concept of accountability becomes complex in the federal context. The basis of accountability must remain the political responsibility of each government to its own residents, in 11 systems of government, rather than one. For our federal system, however, the Constitution provides an additional standard of accountability. Thus each legislature's majority, however large, will be subject to some restraints. The Canadian Charter of Rights and Freedoms limits the autonomy of governments. To the extent that governments make formal agreements, as in shared-cost programs, for instance, they have commitments to one another on the basis of contractual federalism. We should also realize that the problems that federalism poses for responsible government are only part of the challenge that the growth of the state poses for democracy. Thus we Canadians must seek to establish balance in our federal institutions. We must try to find middle ground between unregulated competition and implausible harmony, and between accountability of governments to citizens and collaboration among governments. These considerations suggest that it is important to define more clearly the "spirit of the Constitution".

Federalism and Constitutionalism

Constitutionalism in our federal system derives from several sources. First, there is constitutional law as interpreted by the Supreme Court of Canada. Secondly, there is convention: long-standing evolving principles, such as that of responsible government, and unwritten practices which, by tradition, by repeated precedents, and by the fundamental commitments of leaders, have become an accepted part of our constitutional order. The remedy for

violations of convention lies chiefly in the political process, although the courts may, on occasion, intervene. In the recent Constitutional Reference case, for instance, the Supreme Court of Canada recognized and defined the convention of substantial provincial consent to constitutional amendments as an integral part of our Canadian constitutional order, though not a judicially enforceable requirement. Thirdly, there is the concept of prudence, or self-restraint, on the part of decision makers. This quality is more than the simple desire to avoid antagonizing voters: politicians ought to have in mind – and often do – the effect their actions will have on the wider social fabric; of the extent of conflict these actions are likely to engender; of the consequences for national unity; and of the co-operation required of other jurisdictions. The chief elements of the spirit of our Constitution derive from these varied sources. They help Canadians to reconcile majority rule and minority rights, the interests of Canadian society and of provincial societies, and uniformity and diversity.

The spirit of our Constitution applies to the federal government and Parliament and to the provinces. One example of its workings is the evidence of the self-restraint of majorities in the House of Commons. In a country as diverse as ours, with provinces differing widely in population and with two major linguistic communities, respect for minority interests is critical. In some circumstances, insistence on the rights of a simple majority in Parliament and in the country is a recipe for disunity. To bridge diverse interests requires leadership of an especially high order, genuine respect for minority interests, and the search for policies and goals that will unite, rather than divide, Canadians.

The Constitution has given our federal government certain broad powers to act within areas of provincial jurisdiction and even, it may be, to bring about *de facto* changes in the division of powers. The powers of reservation and disallowance, now by convention virtually "dead letters", were once actively employed. Commissioners recommend that these powers be finally interred through an appropriate constitutional amendment.

Through the declaratory power, the federal government may declare that certain works and undertakings within a province are for the general advantage of Canada or for the advantage of two or more provinces. Though it remains available, the declaratory power has not been used in recent years. Through what is known as the "spending power", the federal government can attach conditions to financial grants to governments, institutions and individuals or can assign the expenditure of large amounts of federal revenue to the provinces. The "Peace, Order, and good Government" clause (Constitution Act, 1867, s. 91) permits sweeping, if only temporary, federal involvement in areas that are otherwise subject to provincial jurisdiction. Each of these powers has been the subject of important controversies, and there have been proposals that they be either abolished or limited, perhaps by the courts, perhaps by some kind of mechanism for reaching provincial consent before they are used.

Commissioners believe that the declaratory power, the spending power, and the "Peace, Order, and good Government" clause are important and flexible devices for use in an uncertain world, and that the national government

should retain them. Nonetheless, although we do not recommend formal limitations on their use, we consider these powers to have such potentially sweeping consequences for federalism that they must be exercised with special restraint, generally only after extensive discussion, and only when other federal powers provide no effective means through which government can act.

The spirit of the Constitution imposes equally important constraints on our provincial governments. Just as the federal government must tread cautiously when its activities affect provincial jurisdiction, so provinces must restrain their broad powers to spend, to engage in public ownership, or to tax, all of which can impinge on federal powers and on the interests of other governments. The provinces, too, must respect minorities. They must be sure that as they stimulate economic development, they do not impose excessive costs on the citizens and governments of other jurisdictions. This Commission has proposed some means to help ensure that this principle will be practised. Provincial adherence to such norms is all the more important as their functions have grown, and as they have claimed a right to help shape national policies. They, too, must take some responsibility for the whole institutional system of which they are a part.

The Division of Powers and Constitutional Flexibility

Commissioners' assessment of the institutions of federalism begins with the division of powers. Some critics have argued for a thorough rewriting of the division of powers set forth in the Constitution. Judicial interpretation and evolving practice have so shaped sections 91 and 92 of the Constitution Act, 1867 that they no longer provide a coherent guide to citizens or governments about the allocation of responsibility. The categories set out in those sections largely reflect mid-nineteenth-century attitudes towards government; they bear little relation to the functions of the state today or to the concepts and terminology of policy discussion. The areas of *de facto* concurrent federal-provincial jurisdiction have multiplied far beyond the formally designated fields of immigration, agriculture and pensions. This evolution of the division of powers, some would argue, has contributed to a Constitution that acts as a very weak disciplinarian of governments; in fact, say such critics, our Constitution has become highly permissive, offering a large number of "pegs" on which governments can hang almost any action they wish to justify.

Why not, then, modernize the division of powers to reflect more accurately the ways Canadians think about government today? There are several reasons why Commissioners do not make such a proposal. First, the Constitution, along with subsequent judicial interpretations, should serve not only as a guide to future action, but also as a record of our national past. It should force Canadians to rethink the lessons of former years. An evolving constitution reflects the movement of a complex society through time. It is not a continuous process of writing on blank slates. To rewrite *de novo* would be to erase the record of our collective experience and the lessons it contains.

Secondly, we see as a virtue the permissiveness and uncertainty of our Constitution. Our "living Constitution" gives us a great deal of flexibility in

adapting to new concerns and needs. The importance of this freedom is obvious when one considers how difficult it is to modernize and clarify the division of powers. Just to codify past judicial decisions into a statement representing the current situation would be a massive—and controversial—task. Moreover, none of the broad distinctions that one might think of to guide a fundamental revision appears easily applicable in an age of interwoven policy areas. Distinctions between social and economic policy or between national and local considerations often seem arbitrary. In everyday experience, changes in technology and communications and new patterns of thinking influence us constantly. It is not easy to make precise distinctions in our complex age.

Another reason for hesitation about comprehensive constitutional revision is that any reallocation of the full range of constitutional powers to accord with current concepts of government would probably become obsolete almost the day it was put in writing. Rather than gaining certainty and clarity, we might, instead, experience a long period of even greater uncertainty while we worked out the full meaning of new concepts and phrases. Indeed, we are now witnessing a process of this nature with respect to Canada's Charter of Rights.

The obvious increase in the number of areas of shared jurisdiction has not so blurred the division of responsibilities between governments as to make meaningless sections 91 and 92 of the Constitution Act, 1982. While "grey" areas abound, the headings of the Act do set out the different functions of each order of government. A broad set of powers, together with access to the national rostrum that Parliament provides, enables our federal government to speak for all Canadians as citizens of a national community, to express our national will, and to concern itself with relations among citizens and regions.

Our federal government lacks unlimited power to act wherever it sees fit, since it is disciplined by the Constitution. Potentially sweeping federal powers, such as "Peace, Order, and good Government" and the "Trade and Commerce" power might have curtailed much provincial activity if they had been broadly defined, but the judiciary sharply constrained them. Certainly, a much broader trade and commerce power in the U.S. Constitution has led to greater centralization. Because of the discipline imposed by the Canadian Constitution, federal representatives, in pursuing national goals, often need the co-operation of provinces, which undertake direct action in many of these domains. The division of powers, though introducing an element of complication, illustrates that the federal government has a responsibility and an orientation to the national interest quite different from the responsibilities of individual provinces.

The provinces, too, have many economic, social and cultural powers that impinge on national policy. Section 92 of the Constitution Act, 1867 gives them wide authority to provide local services and to regulate relations among individuals and groups. Moreover, the provinces possess important land and property rights. Thus provincial actions can have major effects on national policy.

As we have seen, there have been challenges to the current allocation of powers. Throughout the 1970s, various provincial governments called for an

extension of their jurisdiction in many areas; for limitations on a variety of federal discretionary powers; and for direct provincial participation in a number of fields of national policy making, especially those with major regional implications. These initiatives reflected the desire of many provinces to exercise greater control over their own economic and social development. In addition, some asserted that the voting power of central Canada and unbalanced representation in federal cabinets and governing parties led to federal policies unfair or unresponsive to the interests of the smaller provinces. These provinces therefore sought to counteract policies harmful to their interests, and demanded a voice in preventing them. Commissioners do not believe that the call for general decentralization of, or strong limitations on, federal powers is warranted. The present division of powers does not unduly hamper provinces in meeting the needs of their populations. Nevertheless, to the extent that the federal government has wielded its powers in ways unresponsive to the interests of some regions, Canadians must reform the processes and structures of the national institutions and improve intergovernmental institutional arrangements.

Representatives of the alternative view argue that the present constitutional arrangement unduly hampers the federal government's ability to pursue the national interest, and that our national government might require still greater powers. Again, this Commission does not believe that such a view is warranted: in most respects, the constitutional authority of our federal government is adequate. Provincial powers do not hamstring Ottawa's ability to respond to problems. Thus we Commissioners do not find, on the basis of our examination of the economic union and of policy management in the federal system, any compelling case either for significantly increasing centralization or for promoting decentralization. We see no merit in efforts to restore the classic model of "watertight compartments". In any event, such an enterprise would be doomed to failure. Certainly, disentanglement in specific areas might reduce confusion and the costs of decision making; generally speaking, however, overlapping of authority and *de facto* concurrence are not only inevitable, but also desirable. Shared responsibility opens up the possibility that the federal and provincial governments might compete to respond to citizens' problems. In this competition, the need to win popular support can temper the self-interest of governments. This assessment, however, does not deny the need for change and clarification of responsibility. It might well be to the advantage of Canadians to find ways to shift governmental powers back and forth in a more flexible fashion between provincial and federal governments. We recommend two possible methods of doing so.

The first method would be to amend our Constitution to permit legislative, as well as administrative, delegation of powers from one order of government to the other. Delegation of legislative powers has both critics and defenders. Its major advantage is flexibility. Responsibility for a particular matter might be transferred from one level of government to another without constitutional amendment. For any given issue, it is not necessary, however, to transfer responsibility to or from *all* provinces. This leeway makes our constitutional system even more flexible. Legislative delegation also permits *de facto*

consolidation of responsibilities for certain matters or activities which might otherwise have to be regulated under several constitutional powers by both levels of government. In addition, it offers some greater measure of certainty to private actors who, in some circumstances, might come under conflicting regulatory requirements.

Critics argue that legislative delegation would undermine the constitutional distribution of powers and promote governmental uncertainty, confusion and diminished accountability. They argue that such delegation might threaten federalism by opening the possibility of massive centralization or, alternatively, of drift towards highly decentralized confederalism. It is argued that powers, once delegated, would be impossible to recover.

Commissioners are sensitive to the existence of risks and benefits, but on balance, we consider that in practical terms, the federation would benefit from the possibility of legislative delegation. We do not, however, envisage such active resort to this procedure that the constitutional balance would be eroded. Under the present Constitution, governments may delegate administrative responsibilities to administrative bodies established by other levels of government. Commissioners propose expansion of the power of intergovernmental delegation to allow one jurisdiction to delegate law making authority over a particular matter to another jurisdiction. The legislatures of the jurisdictions concerned should consent to such delegations in advance. These transfers of authority might be for defined periods or for periods of indefinite duration; they might take place between the federal government and one, all or a few provinces.

The second method for transfer of responsibilities is the intergovernmental accord. The concept of an accord as an agreement with special status has only recently been made part of our federal practice, and at present it has no clear legal or constitutional status. Intergovernmental agreements, contractual or informal, have a long history; such arrangements include the Tax Collection Agreements, shared-cost programs, the General Development Agreements, and the Economic and Regional Development Agreements. There have been numerous interprovincial agreements as well. They have been a useful means of combining flexibility and a greater measure of certainty about intergovernmental matters.

The term "accord" appears to go beyond such agreements. An accord and the language associated with it seem to have some of the characteristics of a treaty and to imply some form of special standing. An accord is not a constitutional amendment, but it is more than a simple administrative agreement which any government could change unilaterally because of the doctrine of parliamentary sovereignty which prohibits one administration from binding its successors. An accord is more than an agreement backed by legislation, which a legislature could repudiate. The 1985 Atlantic Accord drawn up between the federal government and Newfoundland to provide for joint management of offshore resources and the sharing of revenues argues for clarifying both law-making delegation and accords between governments. It involves a significant shift of power and responsibility to the province and to a joint board. However, the new decision-making body is to apply existing federal resource-management legislation to the extent compatible with the

Accord. Because there is no constitutional power to delegate legislative authority, both the province and the federal government must pass "mutual and parallel" legislation to implement the scheme, and thereafter each must pass any amending legislation in identical form. The Accord provides that neither government will amend the legislation or regulations implementing the Accord without the consent of the other. This restriction on parliamentary and legislative freedom is not constitutionally valid. For this reason, the parties have provided for the possibility of entrenching the Accord in the Constitution itself if the Government of Newfoundland should obtain the requisite support from other provinces.

Accords raise a number of questions for the future. Have we here a new status for certain agreements between governments that might prove more flexible than formal constitutional amendment? Could governments use such agreements to set up temporary arrangements and procedures not capable of unilateral repudiation? Could terms be specified in a more detailed manner than would be suitable in the Constitution, but with comparable stability? Would such agreements be more easily modified in light of experience, but in the meantime provide greater certainty for all concerned? And if the answer to these questions is yes, should we give accords clearer legal status and enforceability? We conclude that we should, and we recommend an amendment to the constitution to permit such agreements and to give them legal standing. Intergovernmental agreements made pursuant to the amendment could not be terminated by any government or its legislature alone. The consent of all parties to the agreement would be required. In effect, for the term of the agreement (if specified), Parliament and the legislatures involved would be constitutionally permitted to bind their successors.

Constitutional Amendment

In the long term, amendment of the Constitution will remain an important device for adaptation of the federal system to new requirements. At the time of Confederation, Canada's Constitution contained no general procedure for amendment. In 1949, the federal government received the power to amend the Constitution in some areas that lay within federal jurisdiction, exclusive of changes affecting the division of powers, the Senate and other critical provisions. This gap in Canada's constitutional machinery has been politically embarrassing and had unfortunate practical consequences. Despite numerous attempts, however, Canadians did not acquire a general amending formula until 1982. Before that date, proposals for constitutional change always involved endless disagreement about methods of achieving them.

Now the rules are clear, if complex. Our new amending formula contains "provincialist" elements which represent the compromise required to forge constitutional agreement in 1981: it treats all provinces equally, and it denies the two largest provinces the veto that many earlier formulae had incorporated. There is no explicitly regional requirement applicable to building the requisite degree of consent. Most substantive amendments require the assent of the House of Commons, the Senate and two-thirds (that is, seven) of our

provinces, representing at least 50 per cent of the Canadian people. A few critical institutional matters, including changes to the amending formula, require unanimity. Amendments affecting some, but not all, provinces require the agreement of those involved. The most important form of protection for individual provinces is the opting-out provision: any province may decline to be bound by an amendment derogating from its powers or privileges. If an amendment affects education or other cultural matters, a province that chooses to opt out has the right to reasonable compensation.

A number of the new formula's features appear to make constitutional amendment easier to achieve: proposed amendments can now be initiated in any of 11 legislatures; amendment need no longer involve the complex "package deals" characteristic of past attempts. No province has a veto, and the Senate has only a suspensive veto. Despite these significant elements of flexibility, Commissioners do not expect frequent amendments. It remains relatively easy to construct a coalition large enough to block proposals. There is no provision for popular ratification to override the positions of governments. Most important, while opting-out may facilitate amendment even if some provinces object, we think that it will limit the frequency of change. Even if only one or two of the larger provinces opted out of any proposed amendment, the action could destroy the effect of any suggested change. More important, if provinces were to use the opting-out provision, the prospect of a "chequer-board Canada", where the operative Constitution varied from province to province, would loom large. We would expect any federal government to regard such a prospect with considerable misgiving and probably, indeed, to withhold consent if a pattern of opting out developed.

In practice, the new amending procedure may differ little from a requirement for unanimity. Constitutional amendment will probably occur only in non-controversial areas where a high degree of consensus has developed. However, Commissioners expect considerable reliance on the rich variety of other institutional devices available to Canadians; in particular, our governments are likely to use formal and informal agreements and delegation. Indeed, it is, in part, because we foresee this growing resort to these other instruments that we are led to recommend constitutional amendments to permit legislative delegation and binding intergovernmental accords. Such devices fill common substantive needs and "lower the stakes" of intergovernmental bargaining by allowing for renegotiation in light of experience.

A central element in any federal constitution is a final court of appeal to act as umpire of the system. Constitutional conflicts arise constantly. They may enter the judicial process through litigation initiated by citizens or private interests, or as a result of government actions, such as the reference procedure. Until 1949, Canada's umpire was the Judicial Committee of the Privy Council (JCPC) of the United Kingdom. Its interpretation of the British North America Act made Canada's Constitution far less centralized than the words of the Act seemed to imply. In 1949, however, the Supreme Court of Canada became our final court of appeal in constitutional matters. Its record since then demonstrates continuing sensitivity to the principles of federalism in the context of a changing society. In case after case, the Court has ensured the maintenance of a balanced federalism.

During the 1970s, heightened intergovernmental conflict greatly increased the volume and sensitivity of constitutional cases before the Supreme Court. On contentious matters such as energy, the Court's role was critical. Now, with the advent of our Charter of Rights, it may become even more so. There will be challenges to the actions of both orders of government, not only as to whether they have acted *ultra vires*, but as to whether they have violated the Charter. These considerations have led observers to suggest that the Court should be accorded a more explicit constitutional status, and that the procedures for the appointment of judges should be re-assessed in light of the court's enhanced constitutional role. We shall address these issues later in this Report.

Although judicial decisions may clarify the limits of constitutional jurisdiction within our federation, and although delegation of powers, accords and other arrangements may help to define governmental responsibilities, nevertheless federal-provincial and interprovincial relations will remain central to adaptation of the federal system. Accordingly, Commissioners turn to the structures and processes of intergovernmental relations in Canada.

The Machinery of Intergovernmental Relations

The machinery of intergovernmental relations helps to manage the complex linkages among the governments of Canada as each level of government operates across many policy areas and deploys a wide range of governing instruments, including spending, taxing and regulating. Subject to the limits of the division of powers, and given always the potential of the Supreme Court to act as final arbiter, the activities of federal and provincial governments are interwoven in many policy fields. Constant interaction is required as leaders at each level respond to the changing demands of citizens in an evolving economic and social context. The challenge, then, is for Canadians to design intergovernmental machinery for managing this interdependence and to do so without sacrificing our other political values.

It should be clear from the previous pages that Commissioners do not intend to suggest that the ideal or the primary goal that Canadians should seek in a reformed set of intergovernmental processes is continuous harmony and the avoidance of all conflict and controversy. We should expect—and we shall continue to have—a great deal of competition within the consultative forums of the federal system. The federal government, concerned with the whole country and serving a nation-wide electorate, will differ in policy matters from provinces serving more limited constituencies. Inevitably, governments will compete to gain the credit for distributing the pleasant policies and try to pass on the blame for the painful ones. Inevitably, different provincial governments will reflect the different needs arising from their particular economic structure and the social make-up of their jurisdictions. The democratic process in the federation involves competition for public support as governments try to produce the policies their constituents demand. The challenge is to ensure that competition does not impose excessive and disproportionate costs on other jurisdictions, that it is carried out in such a way that the interests of citizens play the foremost part in shaping its

outcome, and that the credibility of the institutions of federalism is not undermined. Indeed, while co-ordination is the desired result, the process of achieving it is often competitive and adversarial.

Commissioners do not desire governments within the federation to act jointly in every undertaking, binding one another to the lowest common denominator. Such a policy would deprive federalism of one of its major virtues: the opportunity to use diversity to advantage and to reap the rewards of flexibility and experiment. Total unanimity would be a recipe for paralysis and immobility. It would also clash with the principle of Cabinet responsibility, which makes each government answerable, through its legislature, to its own electorate.

Intergovernmental relations in the federal system involve several levels of interaction. At one end of the continuum, policy making is completely independent: governments take action without consulting others or considering their interests. Under this arrangement, other jurisdictions must adjust independently. A significant portion of federal and provincial policy making takes this form. Governments are, and should be, free to act autonomously within their own jurisdiction. When their policies have a major effect on other governments, however, interdependence requires explicit attention to the interests of others.

The second level of interaction is characterized by consultation. On this level, each government recognizes the effect of its actions on other jurisdictions and the fact that all are acting in the same areas and/or in closely related areas. Here it is important to provide the means for governments to keep one another informed and to provide opportunities for persuasion, pressure and influence. In an interdependent federation, areas of common action represent a large and recently growing category. Accordingly, the institutions which this Commission proposes are designed to encourage close and continuous consultation across a wide range of policy areas. Commissioners believe that governments in a federal system must strive for "a mutual comity which never overlooks advance notice and consultation [and] always strives for accommodation. This is just a necessity for a genuine working federal system in a developed country in the late twentieth century."[1]

The third level of intergovernmental relations involves efforts to achieve co-ordination. Here, governments will try to develop commonly acceptable policies and objectives which they will then implement within their own jurisdiction. The co-ordination of activities can take place in several ways. These ways can range from the general search for a common economic policy framework at a First Ministers' Conference, to detailed agreements on how federal and provincial policies will mesh in a particular province, as in the Economic and Regional Development Agreements.

Finally, there is joint decision making, which requires that federal and provincial governments act together, committing themselves to particular courses of action and standards of conduct. Shared-cost arrangements take this form. It is in this context that fears arise that the accountability of responsible governments will be sacrificed to the need for intergovernmenal consensus. We Commissioners share these fears, and we have taken them into account in making our suggestions for reform of intergovernmental relations.

Each one of these kinds of governmental interaction is exemplified in the vast network of relationships which have developed since the end of the Second World War, especially in the 1960s and 1970s. The "set-piece" First Ministers' Conference (FMC) provides the most obvious example. There are also many ministerial-level meetings on a wide range of subjects and even larger numbers of joint committees of officials. In addition to meetings of all 11 governments, there are hundreds, if not thousands, of bilateral meetings, or meetings between the federal government and groups of provinces. Interprovincial conferences have come to be of significant use, both in co-ordinating provincial responses to federal initiatives and – with less success – in harmonizing provincial policies. In addition to all these formal meetings, myriad informal contacts are made.

There has been considerable variation in the relations between the federal government and individual provinces. Canada has created an intricate network of intergovernmental relationships through which to manage interdependence, though these arrangements are nowhere mentioned in the Constitution and have almost no legislative base. This intergovernmental "industry" has been criticized on many grounds. To some observers, it constitutes a "third order of government", threatening to undermine the principles of parliamentary accountability. Other observers believe that the intergovernmental process introduces important biases into the consideration of public policy in Canada. They consider that the process focuses undue attention on the "second-order" questions of political status or on competition between levels of government rather than between parties, to gain credit among voters and to avoid blame. It is sometimes argued that in emphasizing the role of provincial governments, the intergovernmental process reinforces a tendency to define the regional dimensions of issues in terms of provinces, conveying the impression of homogeneity within provinces when, in fact, there are often as many differences within provincial jurisdictions as there are among them. The process also diverts attention from other problems, such as those relating to socio-economic status or gender, and reduces the opportunity for groups who represent such non-regional interests to mobilize and to secure a hearing. There is doubtless some truth in this view: the focus in intergovernmental discussions of economic policy differs from that chosen in discussions between the public and private sectors. This is an inevitable consequence of a federal system, but the difficulties should not be exaggerated. Intergovernmental discussions do take into account concerns expressed in the wider environment. When the public agenda emphasizes issues in which regional differences are slight, as in the construction of the post-war welfare state, the debates among governments can reflect that wider concern. Finally, federal or provincial Ministers and officials negotiating on specific matters frequently represent the interests of their client groups.

Another set of criticisms relates to the intergovernmental process itself. While there is considerable communication among governments, it is often sporadic and *ad hoc*. Governments naturally tend to call for consultations when it is to their political advantage; they are equally likely to ignore inconvenient calls. There has thus been no assurance that ongoing common problems will receive continuous attention. Even the issue of calling meetings,

especially First Ministers' meetings, has tended to be a matter of political debate which diverts efforts from the actual search for solutions to common problems. The public meetings, especially at the level of First Ministers, seem to put a premium on the strongest possible statements of position, rather than on a search for understanding and compromise. The process exposes differences more effectively than it contributes to their reconciliation.

In recent years, the intergovernmental process has been further hampered by the divergent expectations of participants. Provinces have tended to regard First Ministers' Conferences as opportunities to discuss the full range of federal policies and to assert an influence in national decision making. This tendency has been fostered by three developments. Provincial governments' growing strength and effectiveness permit them a claim to affect national policy and give many of them levels of expertise and knowledge equal, in certain fields, to that of the federal government. In the recent past, the weak representation in certain regions of the party in power has lent credibility to the provincial claim to represent these areas, even in national policy. Changes in the federal government's approach to managing our economy, have increased federal involvement in areas previously considered primarily provincial. Federal-provincial conflict tends to be more intense when governments are searching for new policy options in previously uncharted areas.

The federal government, on the other hand, has viewed First Ministers' Conferences on the economy as a mechanism for consultation on a wide range of issues. There have been occasional attempts at co-ordination, but it is probably fair to say that the federal government has resisted provincial suggestions to formalize a decision-making process on the basis of "executive federalism" primarily on the grounds that this would not fit well with the role of parliament in our system of responsible government. While the federal government acknowledges the helpfulness of provincial government views on national economic policy making, provinces have rarely welcomed the federal government's views on provincial policy or programs. Furthermore provincial governments have been reluctant to put forward views on how they might alter provincial policies to contribute to the resolution of fundamental country-wide problems. This imbalance in obligations at the First Ministers' table has led some observers to question what co-operative federalism really means.

Government growth has caused structural changes which have seriously affected intergovernmental relations. The role of "central agencies" and institutions, such as premiers' offices and Treasury Boards, has expanded as governments have sought means to achieve greater consistency and co-ordination in their operations. More centralized direction and attempts to establish greater fiscal and policy control over line ministries have been part of governments' efforts to identify and pursue more "global" or integrated visions of the public good. To some extent, these efforts have weakened an earlier pattern in which intergovernmental relations were mainly conducted among ministers and officials in operating departments with a specific policy mandate. Federal and provincial officials within such departments often shared common policy and professional goals, and responded to the same

groups in the population. Their common interests and activities fostered mutual trust and a sense of common purpose. At the First Ministers' level and within central agencies, the goals of political status are likely to be more prominent, and governments are likely to be less constrained by group pressure. The goal of co-ordinating policy across all fields within a single government often conflicts with management of intergovernmental co-ordination within a policy area.[2]

In such recent issues as that relating to the Constitution, the status of governments has also caused intergovernmental tension. Constitutional reform dominated the intergovernmental process for much of the period from 1968 to 1983; it was fuelled both by Quebec's wish for an enhanced status and by the West's desire for a new deal. Debate on the Constitution called directly into question the status and powers of government. The questions it raised were powerful and symbolic, not easily subject to the kind of "splitting-the-difference" compromises characteristic of more concrete and less emotionally charged issues. Since the purpose of the participating officials was to defend their government's vision of Confederation, there were fewer ties of common interest. The general absence from the process of well-informed interest groups meant that no one held the participants accountable or encouraged resolution of differences. In short, debate on the Constitution brought out the worst features of the intergovernmental process. While more co-operative relationships existed in many areas, battles over constitutional and energy issues tended to poison the whole range of intergovernmental relationships, turning the process into one of "good guys" versus "bad guys".

The foregoing assessment might suggest that the machinery of intergovernmental relations is so cumbersome and ineffective that it is beyond effective reform. Commissioners disagree. We must provide intergovernmental institutions to meet the need for co-ordination in several major fields where federal and provincial government actions and responsibilities overlap. Therefore the institutional arrangements which we propose are intended to consolidate the existing intergovernmental structure. Our aim is not to multiply intergovernmental bodies, but to make effective the machinery Canada already has in place. We hope to ensure that actions which may seriously affect other levels of government will be assessed in advance and will increase the openness of intergovernmental relationships, rather than introduce new constraints and limits. We also believe that it is vital to ensure reform of the overall process to make it more consistent with basic norms of political accountability and to improve public access to, and understanding of, intergovernmental relations.

Commissioners wish to encourage institutions and processes that will facilitate common trust, for without some general understanding of shared purpose, the best-designed institutions will fail. But shared purposes alone are not enough to establish positive relationships: they need to be supported by effective consultation and debate if co-ordinated results are to emerge. The constructive elements will arise from co-operation and recognition of the legitimacy of differences.

Proposals

Commissioners therefore propose that the First Ministers' Conference (FMC) be entrenched in the Constitution. First Ministers should meet annually on a fixed date, and other sessions should be called as necessary. The First Ministers' Conference is the capstone of the intergovernmental structure.

Throughout the recent constitutional debates there was discussion concerning a regular First Ministers' Conference. The FMC has been a major goal of most provinces, and at times, the federal government endorsed their aim. At the First Ministers' Conference held at Regina in February 1985, Prime Minister Mulroney committed his government to annual meetings on the economy for the next five years. Some might object to institutionalization of this most contentious federal-provincial body, where political differences predominate. Commissioners believe, however, that official status for the FMC would acknowledge the need to arrange a satisfactory forum of interdependence, and for federal and provincial governments to co-ordinate policies and activities. To ensure openness and accountability, some FMC sessions should be held in public, though private discussions should take place as necessary. To make the meetings fixed and regular would remove one of the more contentious aspects of recent FMCs: the arguments about when and whether one should be called. To a great extent, regular Conferences will avoid the build-up of hostilities and the artificial inflation of governmental and public expectations that result from such jousting.

The central purpose of FMCs should be to provide a forum where federal and provincial leaders can discuss policy needs and explore possibilities for action of national importance in both levels of jurisdiction. The FMC would not be a legislative body, and its decisions would not be binding on governments. Rather than legislate, it would seek a common policy framework. Formal voting rules, as such, would not be necessary. Legislative follow-up to discussions in the FMC and in the other bodies Commissioners suggest would be the responsibility of governments.

Nevertheless, the FMC would need to organize its own affairs. Commissioners envisage creation of additional Ministerial Councils, a step which we propose below. The FMC could restructure the Councils as necessary, define their mandates, assign them tasks, and receive their reports. It might wish to establish a voting rule to cover decisions about the structure, composition and mandates of Ministerial Councils.

Critical to the success of any intergovernmental institution is adequate preparation. This includes extensive prior discussion of the agenda, sharing of information, and private exploration of possible areas for agreement or compromise. The FMC could create an independent secretariat to support preparatory work, perhaps by upgrading the Canadian Intergovernmental Conference Secretariat, which now provides administrative services. This move would introduce into the system a group of officials whose objective would be the success of the system itself. Conversely, it would create some difficulties. An autonomous intergovernmental bureaucracy similar to the Commission of the European Community, for example, would be counter to

Canadian norms of responsible government. Commissioners therefore recommend the use of a better-established Canadian institution: a permanent committee of senior officials like the Continuing Committee of Officials on Economic Matters. Such a committee, with members designated by the First Ministers, should be appointed to support the FMC.

Although Commissioners have rejected the option of an independent secretariat to serve the FMC directly, third parties, not tied to the day-to-day interests of governments, can often help to facilitate agreements, by providing optional perspectives and new information, and by finding solutions that participants may be too involved to see. An Advisory Panel on Intergovernmental Relations might fulfil these functions and help the public to understand federal-provincial issues. We have looked at two models: the long-established Advisory Commission on Intergovernmental Relations (ACIR) in the United States, and Australia's Advisory Commission on Intergovernmental Relations. These commissions, established by legislation, consist of representatives of the federal and state governments (and, in the United States, of municipal governments), served by a small professional staff. In each country, the Commission studies various issues, conducts research and holds conferences. Their work has made notable contributions to good intergovernmental relations.

Members of such a commission or panel could act as informal mediators to help resolve conflict among governments. The techniques of mediation, developed in settings from labour/management relations to great-power negotiations, might help to resolve intergovernmental conflict in Canada. An advisory group could ease those relations behind the scenes, and provide information and analysis both to governments and to the public. First Ministers might eventually wish to consider the creation of such a body to assist in providing some or all of the possible contributions we have noted. Commissioners would suggest, however, that this additional element be considered only after some experience has been gained with the new structures and procedures we are recommending for the FMC and Councils.

Meetings at the ministerial level now cover many areas of government policy, but they, too, suffer to some degree from their sporadic nature. With some exceptions, notably the meetings of Finance Ministers, they do not provide continuous interaction and sharing of ideas and information. Commissioners recommend strengthening these relationships as part of our larger purpose of increasing the emphasis on concrete policy problems. This shift of focus is much more likely to occur in groups created to concentrate on specific problems. We therefore propose that the First Ministers' Conference appoint a number of Councils of Ministers to serve in major functional policy areas. Again, the meetings of Ministerial Councils should be held regularly, presumably more frequently than FMCs, to encourage development of common perspectives and exchange of information, and to establish trust among the participants. Like the FMC, Ministerial Councils would be served by continuing committees of officials. This Commission does not propose to list all the Councils that might be established or that already exist in some fashion. Our purpose is to suggest a core framework of federal-provincial mechanisms that would, in a more streamlined way, support First Ministers

in their collective and individual responsibilities. Commissioners propose that three central Ministerial Councils be established in the fields of Finance, Economic Development and Social Policy, areas related to major themes developed earlier in this Report.

The Council of Ministers of Finance

The Council of Ministers of Finance (or the Conference of Finance Ministers) stands as Commissioners' prototype for the other councils. Finance Ministers and Treasurers have met regularly for many years to monitor and negotiate fiscal arrangements, to discuss economic projections, to compare notes before budgets are prepared, and to discuss macro-economic policy. Our proposal simply formalizes the existence of the ministerial Council on Finance and requires, again, that it meet more frequently. Furthermore, its importance would be enhanced by our proposals for greater federal-provincial co-ordination in the budgetary process. This Council, as we discuss in the section on fiscal arrangements, would be supported by a new federal-provincial body of tax experts, the Tax Structure Committee, to conduct research and monitor developments in taxation.

The Council of Ministers Responsible for Economic Development

As Commissioners mentioned earlier, protection of the Canadian economic union is not simply a matter of preventing the erection of barriers or of finding the right enforcement officer. Rather, successful operation of the economic union requires that Canadian governments build a common set of purposes that will lead to co-ordinated effort in all the economic development activities in which governments engage. A Ministerial Council for Economic Development would provide the principal focus for discussion of such purposes and means to achieve them.

The successful operation of Canada's economic union also requires exchange of information among governments in order to prevent, especially at an early stage, the escalation of policies that are harmful to other jurisdictions. The Council of Ministers responsible for Economic Development would therefore monitor and assess the state of our Canadian economic union. Through the Council, governments might develop "a Code of Economic Conduct", as described above. The Council would seek agreement on common objectives in economic and trade policies and would encourage mutually beneficial linkages among regions.

A vital adjunct to the Council would be a Federal-Provincial Commission on the Economic Union whose members would be named by the Council. The Commission would monitor the state of the Canadian economic union, conduct research to identify barriers and possible areas for greater harmonization, and report publicly to the Ministerial Council on these matters. It would also provide for official hearings of individuals and groups who believe that existing barriers significantly frustrate their own activities. It would investigate their complaints, weigh them against other considerations,

and report both to the public and to the Council, offering recommendations for action.

Such a body would ensure public involvement in discussions of our economic union. It would also provide an independent source of advice aimed at strengthening the economic union. Moreover, by requiring governments to justify their actions publicly, it would increase their accountability. Commissioners anticipate that it would discover many areas in which differences in licensing standards and safety regulations neither serve distinct provincial or federal public purposes nor protect the public. Many, indeed, are simply the product of tradition, inertia and lack of awareness.

The Council of Ministers on Social Policy

The importance of social policy to many facets of Canadian life and the high degree of shared responsibility in the field of social policy strongly suggest the need for a Council of Ministers on Social Policy. Such a body could consider all facets of social policy, especially in the shared fields covered by the Established Programs Financing (EPF) and the Canada Assistance Plan (CAP). The recommendations on social policy set out earlier in this Report suggest a large number of reforms which will require intergovernmental consultation. Consultation with practising professionals and interested groups and individuals is particularly important in this area. Commissioners would encourage Parliamentary Committees to take a more active part in forming social policy, conducting research on the issues involved, and holding public hearings.

The FMC could establish other ministerial councils as necessary. It might, for example, appoint councils in such areas as employment training and the administration of justice. These structures would provide a framework for greater coherence in the federal-provincial system. Less structured forms of interaction would also occur automatically, in bilateral and interprovincial discussions of specific issues. Indeed, as we have noted, many such relationships already exist, and we see no reason why this process should not continue to evolve.

Throughout this Report, Commissioners have stressed the need to make governments more accountable to legislatures and voters. We have noted that the intergovernmental processes of executive federalism can sometimes undermine clear lines of accountability. We need continuous effort to minimize this tendency. Moreover, the intergovernmental process must be kept open to public view. Some of the proposals made above will assist this process. For example, the Federal-Provincial Commission on the Economic Union, in assessing complaints, will provide a public window. The proposals that the First Ministers' Conference be open, at least in part, will facilitate the same objective: governments will be accountable for their performance. If more functional and substantive discussion takes place between governments, participants should become more aware of the interests of affected groups.

This Commission, however, believes that even more could be done. Governments must be held accountable for their conduct of intergovernmental affairs. The best way to hold them accountable is through a parliamentary

or legislative committee. In recent years, the Task Force on Federal-Provincial Fiscal Arrangements (the Breau Task Force), parliamentary committees on the Constitution, and similar provincial bodies have demonstrated the value of parliamentary scrutiny of intergovernmental matters. All tempered the tendency of intergovernmental forums to focus on "who does what" with a healthy emphasis on what is to be done. Standing committees at both levels would be able to monitor these relationships more consistently. Commissioners therefore propose that Parliament and the legislatures establish permanent standing committees responsible for intergovernmental relations.

Interprovincial Harmonization

So far, Commissioners have concentrated on the federal-provincial dimension of intergovernmental relations. There are many interprovincial relationships and some important interprovincial institutions. Since the early 1960s, leaders of Canada's provincial governments have met annually in the Premiers' Conference. These meetings at first concentrated primarily on co-ordinating approaches to issues of provincial concern. More recently their aim has been to unite provinces in their response to federal initiatives, especially in relation to fiscal and constitutional matters. On a few occasions, provinces have forged compromises among themselves in order to take up a common position. The office of Conference chairperson rotates among the premiers; the incumbent often speaks for the provinces in dealings with the federal government. Provincial agreements are likely to affect federal-provincial relations, particularly on issues where provinces share common policy interests, mainly those, like the Constitution, that relate to their status as governments. On other economic and social questions, different regional needs and interests will often divide provinces as much as they do federal and provincial governments. Provinces will often wish to deal individually with the federal government, rather than as part of a group.

Within an economic union, harmonization of policies across jurisdictions is vital.[3] As we have seen, differences in product standards, licensing rules for occupations, and codes of commercial law can inhibit mobility and trade among member jurisdictions. It is necessary to seek a balance between the autonomy of member-states to enact policies to suit their own conditions and the uniformity that facilitates transactions among them.

In a federal system like Canada's, the federal government properly plays a central role in harmonization. This is why constitutional authority over interprovincial trade and commerce is federal, and why Commissioners believe that fields like competition, telecommunications and product standards should be primarily federal matters. The proposed Code of Economic Conduct is also a step toward harmonization. It is aimed at ensuring that federal and provincial economic-development activities do not erect barriers to the Canadian economic union.

There remains, however, a large domain of provincial regulatory activities derived mainly from provincial authority over property and civil rights. These activities can lead to variations in practice among provinces that inconven-

ience economic actors wishing to operate on a national plane. Where varying provincial laws create difficulties, transfer of responsibility to the centre is not the only possible response. An alternative device encourages provinces to harmonize their laws as much as possible, where this is necessary for the effective integration of the Canadian market. Much harmonization, of course, occurs spontaneously: all provinces are under similar pressures from constituents, and their policies are unlikely to vary much. As a government prepares to act in a field, it is natural for it to look first at the ways others have drafted their legislation. Innovations begun in one province can thus spread to others.

Canadians should also ask what mechanisms exist to promote more complete harmonization. The oldest such mechanism is the Uniform Law Conference of Canada, formerly the Conference of Commissioners on Uniform Law, founded in 1915. Its membership, which meets annually, includes representatives from the federal government, all the provinces and the territories. It has published more than sixty uniform acts in many fields. Twenty-four have been accepted in six or more jurisdictions, but only one has ever been adopted in all jurisdictions. There are many explanations for the modesty of this record. The Conference has a small secretariat and few research resources. Its members are all full-time officials employed elsewhere. The focus on drafting uniform laws has diverted attention from concentration on broad principles. The draft laws, developed in the common-law tradition, have met with little response in Quebec, with its Civil Code tradition. The Conference has done little to enlist outside groups in its work or to lobby for the adoption of its proposals.

A different mechanism for fostering harmonization is the formation of ministerial or official working groups. One such institution in Canada is the Council of Ministers of Education, which is intended to promote better exchange of information and development of common curricula. More narrowly focused committees have also had success. These include, for example, a federal-provincial group working on a central registry for security interests in aircraft, which was established in 1983.

Efforts at harmonization require strong pressure from outside, as when groups inconvenienced by provincial variations mobilize to promote unity. Federal and provincial law-reform commissions could exert such pressure. It would be relatively simple to extend their mandates to include responsibility for examining possibilities for interprovincial harmonization, although so far there has been little movement in this direction. Another important vehicle is professional groups with a nation-wide mandate, such as the Canadian Bar Association or the Canadian Institute of Chartered Accountants. In 1963, the Commercial Law Section of the Canadian Bar Association created a committee of experts to prepare a model Uniform Personal Property Security Act. The Committee has been influential in modernizing and harmonizing law in this area which is vital for interprovincial business transactions. At least seven provinces have passed, or are likely to pass, legislation embodying most of the features of the model law.

What are the lessons of this record of interprovincial harmonization? The evident lack of drive behind these efforts could have several meanings.

Perhaps there is already a significant degree of harmonization; perhaps existing gaps in harmonization pose relatively few costs; perhaps there is a great unfulfilled need for new institutions. Commissioners incline to the first two explanations. Overall, however, we believe that greater harmonization would maximize the advantages of the economic union. We do not recommend creation of additional institutional structures: the institutions we have described already should prove ample. Thus, the Council of Ministers for Economic Development will undoubtedly address interprovincial harmonization, as will the Federal-Provincial Commission on the Economic Union. The latter provides an opportunity for private actors to press for improved harmonization in particular areas. Similarly, the other ministerial councils can commission working groups to examine harmonization. The Premiers' Conference could look at the issue, delegating specific tasks to ministers or officials. Thus, mechanisms exist to respond to needs as they develop.

Conclusions

Commissioners have designed these proposals to rationalize the structure of intergovernmental relations. We wish to facilitate management of interdependence in the federal system, for Canadians cannot recreate the classic watertight compartments of federalism. We have made a number of suggestions for disentangling federal and provincial activities, such as a clearer division of labour in regional development policy and replacement of the Canada Assistance Plan by a federally operated income-supplementation scheme to which provinces would add their own programs. We believe that as the Councils of Ministers look at other programs, they can accomplish much more in terms of understanding and clarifying which government should implement which programs.

Commissioners have recommended some constitutional changes and have emphasized the need for more flexible procedures to promote delegation and intergovernmental agreements. There will remain many intergovernmental relationships arising from shared responsibilities and the need to adjust policy to changing needs. We Canadians can gain much by rationalizing the structure that already exists and by providing more effective forums for consultation and co-ordination. Commissioners' proposals should provide for more consultation and for mechanisms to ensure that this consultation is open to public scrutiny.

We Commissioners urge Canadians to consider our proposals for reform of intergovernmental arrangements in relation to our other recommendations for institutional change, especially those pertaining to the reform of national institutions. The federal government, in the conduct of its responsibilities, must possess the capacity to represent and accommodate the interests of all regions: intergovernmental relations are not a substitute for full regional representation at the centre. Similarly, enhanced regional representation in national institutions is not a substitute for intergovernmental relations. The existence of a formal division of powers and of two strong orders of government means that co-ordination is essential, no matter how regional representation in national institutions is achieved. Thus we see reform of the

centre and reform of the institutions of the federation not as alternatives, but as complementary: Canada needs not merely one or the other, but both, for different purposes.

Reform of national institutions along the lines Commissioners have proposed should change the character and dynamics of federal-provincial relations. Stronger representation from all provinces in national institutions will ensure that regional concerns will be represented in caucus and Cabinet. Moreover, through its Members of Parliament, a more regionally representative government should be able to communicate effectively with citizens in each province, in developing support for programs and initiatives and in responding to local needs. Such a government will be able to provide more effective leadership and to counter the claim that the provincial governments are Canadians' only legitimate representatives of local interests. One consequence of the present regionally imbalanced structure of representation in national institutions has been the almost impossible burden it placed on the intergovernmental process. A lesson of the recent past is that political integration comprises too large a task to be discharged by a single set of institutions. A healthy federal system is one in which there are multiple links binding together federal and provincial levels. These links exist, not just between governments, but in political parties, in bureaucracies, in the media, in associations of all kinds and, ultimately, in the minds of citizens.

Commissioners do not wish to conclude this discussion of intergovernmental relations without noting the profound importance of personal associations in social, commercial and family life that link Canadians in different parts of the country. In a federal society, the informal ties of citizens to one another, as well as to the state, are important means of moderating or restraining excesses. Communication across regions moderates tendencies to excessive differentiation; it also serves as the foundation for the tolerance of diversity which, in its turn, provides a healthy check on the unifying authority of the national government. Ultimately it is citizens who must discipline the conflicts among their governments.

Notes

1. J.A. Corry, "The Uses of a Constitution", in Law Society of Upper Canada, *Special Lectures 1978, The Constitution* (Toronto, 1978).
2. J. Stefan Dupré, "Reflections on the Workability of Executive Federalism", in *Intergovernmental Relations*, vol. 63, prepared for the Royal Commission on the Economic Union and Development Prospects for Canada (Toronto: University of Toronto Press, 1985).
3. Ronald C.C. Cuming, "Harmonization of Law in Canada: An Overview", in *Perspectives on the Harmonization of Law in Canada*, vol. 55, prepared for the Royal Commission on the Economic Union and Development Prospects for Canada (Toronto: University of Toronto Press, 1985).

CHAPTER 23

Citizens, Communities and the Federal State

CHAPTER 23

Citizens, Communities and the Federal State

Introduction: The Charter and Living Constitutionalism

The Canadian Charter of Rights and Freedoms and other provisions of the Constitution Act, 1982 involve the citizens and communities of Canada more fully in the constitutional order than they have previously been involved. Provisions of the Charter and the manner in which they are applied and interpreted by courts, legislatures and Canadians themselves will, in the years ahead, significantly alter relationships between our citizens and their governments. Canadians will take some time to adjust to the Charter. Commissioners' purpose in examining the Charter, therefore, is to make more widely known some of its possible implications. We wish to promote greater understanding and consideration of the problems and opportunities that arise from the Charter and in so doing, perhaps to assist in the process of adjustment. In this section of our Report, therefore, we Commissioners examine some of the ways in which we believe the Charter will affect Canadian politics and society in the future.

The Constitution Act, 1982 was the culmination of two years of intense negotiation and public discussion involving federal and provincial governments and many interested groups and persons across Canada. It was adopted after four years of almost continuous discussion, six years of prolonged crisis of national unity, fourteen years of sustained efforts to entrench the fundamental rights of citizens in the Constitution, and more than fifty years of search for an all-Canadian formula for constitutional amendment. When it emerged, the Constitution Act, 1982 was the product of this process: a compromise document reflecting both principle and pragmatism. It also signalled the beginning of a new era of Canadian constitutional history.

All the key actors in the constitutional reform process had a hand in shaping the Constitution Act, 1982. The signatures on the final accord were

those of the First Ministers or their delegate. Parliament played a significant role in formulating the resolution discussed by the First Ministers. The people of Canada participated both through the public hearings of the Special Joint Committee of Parliament and through intense lobbying efforts at various stages of the Constitution Act's genesis. The Supreme Court of Canada's important constitutional decision of September 1981 rekindled discussions between the federal and provincial governments.

The Constitution Act, 1982, represents a constitutional reform package. It is impossible to understand or explain each provision without reference to the Act as a whole. A comprehensive procedure for amending the Constitution of Canada effectively crowns the achievement of Canadian sovereignty over our domestic Constitution. In addition, the Constitution Act, 1982 has added a Charter of Rights and Freedoms to the basic constitutional law of Canada.

New institutions may be created and constitutions written or amended in relatively short periods of time. Once in place however, the institutional and constitutional framework profoundly affects the manner in which future public issues emerge, as well as the way in which they are resolved. The words of every constitution betray the era in which they were written, and the Charter of Rights and Freedoms provides no exception. Our Charter was enacted in 1982. It therefore reflects many of the concerns of the social movements of the 1970s, as well as that decade's intense concern with national unity. In the matter of equality rights, for example, the Charter differs markedly from the Canadian Bill of Rights legislated 22 years earlier. Moreover, we cannot understand the Charter's provisions on language and personal mobility rights without reference to political events of the 1970s.

Just as the approach to human rights has changed significantly over the past few decades, it will undoubtedly change in the future. Shifts in the balance between individual rights and the interests of the community as a whole, new understandings of the causes of discrimination and the ways in which it operates, and new concerns about equality will come to our attention. As societies evolve, their composition, needs and aspirations change. As a society grows and changes, so too does its understanding of the need to protect human rights and of what these rights may entail. The Charter will help to shape this evolutionary process.

How does an entrenched charter or bill of rights interact with this process? An entrenched charter provides at least a minimum guarantee and secure base of citizens' rights, but it should also adapt to meet new social conditions and challenges. The balance is not unlike that required in any constitution that aspires to survive periods of tumultuous change. A number of provisions in the Canadian Charter of Rights and Freedoms point to the need to develop a Charter jurisprudence that is sensitive to such a balance. The first section of the Charter states clearly that the rights and freedoms it guarantees are subject "only to such reasonable limits prescribed by law as can be demonstrably justified in a free and democratic society." How the courts balance the rights guaranteed by the Charter with the needs of society will help to determine how the Charter contributes to the development of our "living" Constitution. The Constitution Act, 1982 itself contains certain principles that are fundamental to this process of development.

The Charter and Parliamentary Supremacy

The Constitution Act, 1982 declared for the first time that the Constitution "is the supreme law of Canada and any law that is inconsistent with the provisions of the Constitution is, to the extent of the inconsistency, of no force or effect."[1] As part of the Act, the Charter of Rights and Freedoms is the supreme law of the land. This guaranteed constitutional protection of rights and freedoms supports Commissioners' view that the Charter is a new pillar of the Canadian constitutional order. Its arrival has especially important implications for the tradition of parliamentary supremacy in Canada. Legislation of Parliament and of the provincial legislative assemblies must conform with the Constitution, including the Charter.

The new supremacy of constitutional law has implications for Canada's institutional framework, as it has the potential to affect historic relationships between legislatures and the judiciary, as well as between citizens and their governments. Examination of the Charter as a pillar of the constitutional order must take into account the powers and authority of the courts in protecting the rights and freedoms guaranteed in the Charter because the courts must determine inconsistencies between the Constitution of Canada and legislation. The Charter reinforces the courts' general responsibility for this judicial review by assuring court access to anyone whose rights or freedoms guaranteed by the Charter have been infringed or denied. The courts also assume a vital role in determining the forms of compensation or redress that any such person may receive: the Charter provides that courts may order "such remedy as [they consider] appropriate and just in the circumstances."[2]

Two other significant provisions provide further insight into the role that may be expected of courts under the Charter and illustrate the subtleties which pervade the new supremacy of constitutional law in Canada. Section 1, the "reasonable limitations" clause, and section 33, the "general override" provision, contain limitations on the rights and freedoms guaranteed by the Charter. These two provisions indicate the sensitive constitutional balance between courts and legislatures.

The general override provision enables Parliament or the legislature of a province to pass laws that are inconsistent with some, but not all, of the Charter's guarantees. It was included in the Charter at the insistence of provinces concerned about changes in the relative power of legislatures and courts. The major concern was that the entrenchment of rights would detract from the principle of legislative supremacy. The override provision retains some aspects of that supremacy.

Designated pieces of legislation may operate despite the existence of Charter protection for the fundamental freedoms, including freedom of conscience, of opinion and expression, of peaceful assembly and association (s. 2), legal rights (ss. 7–14), and equality rights (s. 15). However, to give effect to a legislative override of any of the Charter's guarantees, Parliament or the legislative assembly must expressly declare that an Act will operate notwithstanding a constitutional guarantee included in section 2 or sections 7 to 15. Such an express declaration will have effect for a period of up to five

years, at which time it may be extended by the legislative body. This ensures that at least once every five years the legislating body will reconsider the specific use of the override. In such cases, parliamentary debate will provide the primary forum for scrutinizing the use of the general override power and for ensuring that its use is consistent with appropriate standards of responsible administration.

Commissioners are anxious that the Charter's general override provision should contribute to public awareness of legislation limiting the constitutional rights of citizens in Canada. In our view, overriding legislation should include a declaration of intent to legislate, notwithstanding a provision of the Charter, and should include not only reference to the specific rights being overridden, but also an explicit indication of the purpose of such legislative action. Such a statement of purpose would help to establish the scope of limitations and could also be referred to in discussions on whether to extend an override after the five-year period.

Shortly after Queen Elizabeth II proclaimed the Constitution Act in April 1982, Quebec's National Assembly passed legislation exempting Quebec laws passed prior to the Charter from sections 2 and 7 to 15 of the Charter. Quebec legislation that post-dates the Charter includes an express declaration of the non-applicability of these sections of the Charter. Although the National Assembly took these actions to reinforce the Quebec government's general repudiation of the Constitution Act, a legal challenge arising from the Quebec measure presents the Supreme Court of Canada with an opportunity to establish important rules about the use of the general override provision and the obligation of governments to adopt a specified form and content for invoking this clause.

In addition to its basic significance for parliamentary supremacy, the general override clause will have important consequences for the interaction of guarantees of rights and Canadian federalism. Since the national and provincial governments are able to enact the general override power in certain circumstances, wide variations among provincial governments' policies respecting fundamental, legal, and egalitarian rights in Canada are permitted. Variations in citizens' rights across the country are a possible consequence. The degree of variation which emerges will depend, in part, on the characterization of the right in jurisdictional terms. For example, if the courts decide that many of the fundamental freedoms, such as freedom of expression or legal rights, belong within federal jurisdiction, extensive variation is unlikely. In such instances a provincial override would obviously not apply, and courts could rule invalid provincial laws violating these rights, on the basis that the provincial government acted beyond the scope of its legislative authority under the Constitution Act. In areas within provincial jurisdiction, however, variation may be quite profound.

The use of the override by the national government would not result in rights variations among Canadians, but would of course take precedence over the specific right or rights with which the legislation is in conflict.

In Commissioners' view, the existence of the general override clause enables the courts to enforce more strictly the Charter guarantees of fundamental freedoms (s. 2), legal rights (ss. 7–14), and equality rights

(s. 15). Knowing that governments have recourse to a legislative override power if they believe the judicial tests are particularly inappropriate, courts should be able to establish very stringent tests for otherwise limiting fundamental, legal and egalitarian rights through the reasonable limitations provision of section 1 of the Charter.

In addition, the inclusion of the general override clause suggests to Commissioners that the drafters intended to provide few other opportunities for limiting the Charter's guarantees. This conclusion is supported by an examination of section 1, the second general authority for limiting the Charter's guarantees. Section 1 of the Charter has been called the "restrictive" clause, the "general limitations" clause or the "reasonable limits" clause. It applies to all the rights and freedoms guaranteed in the Charter. This provision makes explicit what in many constitutions is merely implicit: that no right is absolute. Circumstances may arise when some rights have to be balanced with other rights; there must be a balance, for example, between freedom of speech and protection of the reputation or privacy of individuals, and between the rights of individuals and the interests of the community. Nonetheless, conditions under which limitations on the rights guaranteed in the Charter can be imposed are stringent.

The section 1 provision makes clear that the rights and freedoms set out in the Charter are "subject only to such reasonable limits, prescribed by law, as can be demonstrably justified in a free and democratic society." It is for the courts to determine whether these conditions have been met in any particular circumstance. Early court judgements indicate that the onus of proof for meeting these conditions will fall on those who seek to limit rights and freedoms, rather than on those who claim that their rights and freedoms have been infringed or denied. Already the courts have indicated that they will not be satisfied by legislatures simply declaring that they deem an action to be reasonable and justified.

Changes to the wording of section 1 throughout the constitutional drafting process had the effect of making it more difficult to justify limitations on Charter rights. Initial drafts had provided that the Charter's guarantees were "subject only to such reasonable limits as are generally accepted in a free and democratic society with a parliamentary system of government." The accepted stronger wording that subsequently became the basis of the Constitution Act, 1982 required that limits be "prescribed by law" and be "demonstrably justified in a free and democratic society." These more stringent terms suggest standards of justification that will not be met through simple parliamentary consensus or executive decision.

Section 1 has the potential to affect profoundly the judicial process in Canada. In effect, this clause requires courts to determine whether legislative actions are justified and reasonable in a free and democratic society. Given the nature of the judicial process, courts can make such assessments only on a case-by-case basis. As noted above, however, the courts have already begun to establish their general approach. They appear to have adopted tests to ensure not only that the objective of proposed limitations is justified, but that the means of achieving it are also acceptable. In Commissioners' view, section 1 is meant to ensure that limits imposed on the rights and freedoms guaranteed in

the Charter are not only reasonable, prescribed by law, and demonstrably justified, but also constrain rights as little as possible in order for them to achieve their objectives. These criteria restrict legislatures and emphasize once again that legislative enactments and government practices must be consistent with the guaranteed rights and freedoms set out in the Charter.

Commissioners believe that the Charter marks a significant change in Canadian constitutional law and entails major consequences for the tradition of parliamentary supremacy. The Charter has enshrined the fundamental rights and freedoms of citizens in their relations with governments. Henceforth, provisions of the Charter interpreted by the courts will constrain government activities. The extent to which the Charter will directly affect Canadian society will be determined by the scope of the Charter's applicability, an issue also addressed in the Constitution Act, 1982.

The "applications section" of the Charter indicates that it applies:

> (a) *to the Parliament and government of Canada in respect of all matters within the authority of Parliament including all matters relating to the Yukon Territory and Northwest Territories; and*
> (b) *to the legislature and government of each province in respect of all matters within the authority of the legislature of each province.*[3]

The meaning of "Parliament" is relatively straightforward. The term "government" is much less precise and could be interpreted in a number of different ways. For example, government could encompass only the legislation, regulations and administration of Parliament and the legislative assemblies; more likely, it could also extend to Crown corporations, regulatory agencies and the judiciary. It could also be interpreted to include agencies and organizations that receive their funds from governments. It could even incorporate the contractual relationships of governments. While it seems clear that the drafters did not intend the Charter to apply to all aspects of private activity, there is a sizeable "grey area" where it is difficult to determine whether particular actions are "governmental", especially today, when governments act through a wide range of instruments and mechanisms.

The existence of a range of other plausible possibilities reflects the complex and pervasive interdependence of state, society and the economy noted throughout this Report. To define the extent of the term "government" is likely to be one of the most complex exercises in Charter interpretation. There is probably no one "correct" interpretation, but already there is a sizable literature offering various definitions and approaches.

The Supreme Court of Canada has attempted to come to terms with the meaning and scope of "government" in a number of past decisions. These approaches may usefully inform its definition of the term in reference to the Charter. No one seriously questions that the activities of a delegate of Parliament or of a legislative assembly will be covered by the Charter. With respect to the Charter, lower courts have upheld the general rule governing delegated authority: subordinates cannot do what their principals cannot do.[4] Similarly, the Supreme Court of Canada recently held that the term "government" includes regulation-making activities of various boards and

agencies, where these regulations are made subject to the approval of government.[5]

Other court decisions have distinguished between the public and private nature of an activity to determine whether that activity is rightfully considered a part of government.[6] By adopting such an approach, the court was able to conclude that a Crown corporation may be public in some aspects of its activities and private in others. This approach seems to Commissioners a flexible means of ensuring that the Charter has effect in the grey areas where public authority is exercised, as well as in the more visible legislative forums.

Commissioners believe that courts should take a flexible approach in determining whether an activity is governmental in nature, focusing in each case on the purpose of the specific actions in question. There are no firm rules to determine when private action becomes public action or vice versa. A "government-function test" would undoubtedly include within "government" such legislating bodies as municipal governments and school boards and such regulatory bodies as the Canadian Transport Commission and the Canadian Radio-television and Telecommunications Commission. It would not automatically cover the corporate and commercial activities of Crown corporations.

To determine when an actor is performing a public function is only part of the difficulty of defining the scope of government. There remains the matter of determining the amount of government involvement permissible in an activity before that activity becomes governmental — and thus subject to the Charter — rather than private. For example, if an organization of private interests receives funding from the government, should it be subject to the provisions of the Charter? Similarly, if an organization has a government contract to perform certain services, is that organization bound by the Charter, at least to the extent of its performance responsibilities under contract?

In Commissioners' opinion, infringement of rights may occur at the periphery of government involvement as easily and as often as in the more visible legislative process. A broad application would be a recognition that indirect governmental action may be as restrictive of individual rights as direct governmental action.[7]

Regardless of how courts interpret "government" in the context of section 32 of the Charter, Parliament and the legislative assemblies can use their authority as granting bodies and contractors to ensure that private organizations receiving public monies comply with the spirit of the Charter. Such compliance can be a component or condition of the funding or contract agreement. Using the approach known as "contract compliance", for example, a government can insist that firms doing business with it comply with specified hiring and personnel practices that conform to the spirit of the Charter. In such an instance, the firm would be complying with government regulations or policy and not with the Charter *per se*, and the government would have to establish appropriate enforcement mechanisms. The use of such compliance regulations could extend the spirit of the Charter and its guarantees to a wide range of activities.

Notes

1. Constitution Act, 1982, s. 52(1).
2. *Ibid*., s. 24(1).
3. *Ibid*., s. 32(1).
4. *McCutcheon* v. *City of Toronto* (1983), 147 D.L.R. (3d) 193, at 203.
5. *A.-G. Quebec* v. *Blaikie* (1981), 123 D.L.R. (3d) 15.
6. *Berardinelli* v. *Ontario Housing Corporation* (1978), 8 C.P.C. 100.
7. For further discussion see Mary Eberts, "The Equality Provisions of the Canadian Charter of Rights and Freedoms and Government Institutions", in *The Courts and the Charter*, vol. 58, prepared for the Royal Commission on the Economic Union and Development Prospects for Canada (Toronto: University of Toronto Press, 1985).

The Charter and Civil Liberties

The Charter enshrines in the Canadian Constitution several categories of rights and freedoms which can be divided into two broad groups: the traditional civil liberties of democracies and the rights concerned with problems of cohesion in the Canadian political community.

The first group includes four classes of rights enunciated in the Charter:

- Fundamental freedoms (s. 2) of conscience, religion, thought, belief, opinion, expression, association, peaceable assembly and freedom of the press
- Democratic rights (ss. 3–5) to vote and run for office and the guarantee of regular elections
- Legal rights (ss. 7–14) including, among others, the right to life, liberty and security of the person; the right to be secure against unreasonable search and seizure; the right not to be arbitrarily detained or imprisoned; the rights to be told promptly of reasons for arrest, to retain counsel, and not to be denied reasonable bail without just cause; the right to trial by jury, except in specified instances; and protection from double jeopardy
- Equality rights (s. 15) prohibiting discrimination, including discrimination based on race, national or ethnic origin, colour, religion, sex, age, or mental or physical disability.

In the traditional view, this group of rights is sometimes referred to as "negative freedoms": they protect and secure the freedom of individual citizens by limiting the power of government. There is, however, a major departure from this approach. The affirmative action provision accompanying equality rights permits governments to pursue programs to ameliorate the conditions of disadvantaged individuals or groups, even if these programs may violate the equality rights of others. We shall return to affirmative action below.

The "negative freedoms" approach was the dominant philosophy in Canadian thought on human rights before the 1970s. It gained particular prominence in the post-Second World War period and shaped the 1960 Bill of Rights. It was the main theme in most general and theoretical discussions of civil liberties. Attention focused above all on protecting the rights of citizens by seeking limitations on the use of discretionary power by the ever-expanding administrative state.

Since the 1920s, pockets of support for more stringent controls on government powers have developed across Canada. For example, the 1933 Regina Manifesto of the newly created Co-operative Commonwealth Federation (CCF) made a strong call for human rights protections against what it considered excessive police powers in specific sections of the Criminal Code and unjust procedures under the Immigration Act. The CCF called, also, for anti-discrimination legislation and affirmation of a Canadian commitment to the fundamental freedoms of speech, of association and of the press. In 1945, a CCF Member of Parliament introduced in the House of Commons the first motion proposing a constitutional bill of rights. It was the beginning of a long campaign to have a bill of rights included in the Constitution, with

guarantees for minority rights, equality rights, civil and religious liberty, freedom of speech, and freedom of assembly. In 1947, the provincial CCF government in Saskatchewan introduced the first comprehensive human rights legislation in Canada.

Parallel to this activity, during the Depression and the period of the Second World War, various bar associations across Canada expressed concern about violations of basic civil liberties. They were concerned primarily with violations of the so-called "economic rights": the right to choose the place and type of one's employment; to buy and sell available goods in the open market; to fix, or bargain for, prices; to import and export; to enter into or expand business; to be free of price control; and to lease and to terminate leases.[1] In 1943, the Canadian Bar Association established a Civil Liberties Section which prepared annual reports on various problems relating to civil liberties during the 1940s and began to consider a proposal for a Bill of Rights as the decade closed.

Public concern over the abuse of citizens' rights by government broadened with two events in the 1940s: the wartime treatment of Japanese Canadians and the secret conduct of spy trials. Japanese Canadians and other Orientals had experienced discrimination in Canada before the war, but after hostilities erupted with Japan in 1941, the Government of Canada, using authority under the War Measures Act, obliged Japanese Canadians living along the Pacific coast to surrender their lands, homes and property, and forced them to move to internment camps away from the coastal area. Later the federal government relocated many to other parts of Canada. Relocation programs lagged, and in 1945 the federal government announced that those who did not want to relocate could be voluntarily "repatriated" to Japan once such action became possible. As it became apparent that the decision to repatriate was not always "voluntary", and that it would apply to naturalized and Canadian-born citizens of Japanese ancestry, public support for the Japanese Canadians and outrage over the repatriation scheme led the federal government to rescind the order in 1947. The wartime treatment of Japanese Canadians has become a deep scar on Canada's civil rights record.

Secret orders-in-council and spy trials associated with the Igor Gouzenko affair in 1945 and 1946 also contributed to popular concern for the better protection of civil liberties and legal rights and provoked sharp criticism of the government's conduct. Using powers granted under the National Emergency Transitional Powers Act, the Minister of Justice was empowered to detain "in such place and under such conditions as he may from time to time determine" anyone whom he suspected of being likely to communicate secret information to a foreign agent. A number of arrests were made. The government did not lay charges at the time of arrest, held many of those arrested incommunicado, and did not advise them of their legal rights. Subsequently, a Royal Commission investigation, conducted *in camera* by two justices of the Supreme Court of Canada, led to charges against many of those arrested. When the public learned of the extraordinary nature of the procedures followed, the government was severely criticized. The Civil Liberties Section of the Canadian Bar Association argued that if Canadians tolerated such violations of basic civil liberties in peacetime, then "we [were]

. . . in grave danger of having substituted for the rule of law . . . the alien principles of the Totalitarian State."[2]

These two events contributed to growing concern about the protection of civil liberties in Canada, which culminated in the 1960 Bill of Rights. Although the War Measures Act authorized both events, the 1960 Bill did not curb the powers available to the Attorney General under that Act, except by requiring that Parliament debate any proclamation of the Act. The Charter of Rights and Freedoms makes no mention of the War Measures Act, though the courts are able to determine whether or not, in curtailing a guaranteed right or freedom, a proclamation of the Act meets the reasonable limitation test set out in section 1.

Support for more protection against the abuse of governmental authority grew during the 1950s also, as a consequence of events in Quebec. The courts determined that various pieces of Quebec legislation, directed primarily against activities of the Jehovah's Witnesses and the Communist Party of Canada interfered with such basic freedoms as freedom of religion, of assembly, and of speech. Moreover, in the much publicized case of *Roncarelli* v. *Duplessis*,[3] the Supreme Court of Canada determined that Premier Maurice Duplessis, acting in his capacity as Attorney General, had exceeded the authority of his office in violation of the fundamental constitutional principle of the rule of law.

Increasing awareness of the need to protect fundamental human rights was not unique to Canada during the post-Second World War period. The United Nations, formed at the end of the war, took steps to outline a model of human rights guarantees in the 1948 Universal Declaration of Human Rights and in a number of later conventions. Some of the momentum for a Canadian bill of rights and some of the ideas about what it should contain, were the product of a post-1945, world-wide, human rights movement and of Canada's desire to be an international leader in this field, as in other areas of international affairs. In 1950, the Special Committee of the Senate on Human Rights and Fundamental Freedoms (the Roebuck Committee) recommended that Canada adopt a bill of rights modelled closely on the United Nations Declaration.

After the Second World War, Canadians were redefining the basic symbols of the Canadian state in light of our continuing evolution from colony to nation. During debate on the Citizenship Act in 1946, for example, one MP noted that even if a bill of rights did no more than make explicit the traditions of liberty in parliamentary systems, it would be a symbol for all Canadians, and especially for new Canadians, of the norms and values of our country. An increasingly heterogeneous and ethnically diverse population no longer appeared able to rely on unwritten protections of civil liberties: a written code was needed.

Thus, when Parliament agreed to the Bill of Rights in 1960, the legislation reflected an idea whose time, in Canada, had come. The "negative freedoms" approach to civil liberties shaped the Bill, which guaranteed to citizens freedom from various forms of state action. The first two sections of this bill contained most of the guarantees of rights.

The first section established the continuity of its content with the existing practices and traditions in Canada:

> *It is hereby recognized and declared that in Canada there have existed and shall continue to exist . . . the following human rights and fundamental freedoms.*[4]

This section included equality guarantees prohibiting discrimination based on race, national origin, colour, religion or sex. The guarantees, limited to "equality before the law and the protection of the law",[5] were entirely consistent with the "negative freedoms" approach of this Bill, but they would seem inadequate to a later generation concerned as much with substantive equality as with procedural guarantees. Nonetheless, the Bill reflected the major equality concerns of its own day.

The second section of the Bill outlined guarantees of legal rights. An express declaration of Parliament could override these rights, but in the absence of such express declarations, the rights and freedoms outlined in the section would prevail. The protection of civil liberties under the Bill of Rights disappointed civil libertarians. With the major exception of the Drybones decision[6] in 1970, the Supreme Court of Canada was unwilling to elevate the Bill of Rights to a special constitutional status. As Supreme Court Justice Bora Laskin said in 1972:

> *. . . compelling reasons ought to be advanced to justify the Court . . . [employing] a statutory (as contrasted with a constitutional) jurisdiction to deny operative effect to a substantive measure duly enacted by a Parliament constitutionally competent to do so, and exercising its powers in accordance with the tenets of responsible government, which underlie the discharge of legislative authority under the British North America Act, 1867.*[7]

Even as the 1960 bill was being legislated, critics noted a number of weaknesses. The bill would apply only to matters of federal jurisdiction; even in the federal sphere, it had the status only of simple legislation and was not in any sense an entrenched or an overriding document. It explicitly permitted Parliament to legislate, notwithstanding its provisions. Some observers also foresaw major developments in human rights that would render the Bill of Rights inadequate almost immediately. In particular, some Canadians had begun to think that negative freedoms insufficiently guaranteed the rights of citizens. To limit the abuse of state power was necessary and desirable in a Bill of Rights; but it was necessary, also, to provide for means by which government could actively intervene on behalf of the rights of citizens and secure conditions which would allow all individuals to enjoy their rights. These views became increasingly popular, especially among members and activists in the civil rights movements of the 1960s.

The American civil rights movements of those years focused first on the rights of American Blacks, but as the movement developed, its message of equality was adapted to the interests of many other groups including women, the handicapped, young and old people, homosexuals, lesbians and others. Supporters of most of these movements wanted more than negative rights and freedoms. They demanded that government actively intervene to dismantle the obstacles to equality.

The Charter of Rights and Freedoms has moved Canada in this activist direction. While it continues to stress the traditional negative freedoms, it encourages governments to pursue greater equality for Canadians. For example, the guarantees of equality rights in the Charter enable governments to combat the underlying causes of discrimination more directly. The drafters of the Charter recognized that social and economic conditions can prevent enjoyment of equality rights; they believed that the freedom and rights of citizens require positive interventions of government, as well as the traditional negative freedoms.

The equality rights in the Charter (s. 15) expand on earlier equality provisions in two obvious ways. The provisions reflect a broad concern with the social and economic origins of inequality. The bases of discrimination specifically prohibited in the Charter – race, national or ethnic origin, colour, religion, sex, age or mental or physical disability – are not exhaustive; there is also a general guarantee of individual equality. Moreover, the guarantees of the Charter add "equality under the law" and "equal benefit of the law" to the equality categories previously found in the Bill of Rights. The equality rights guarantees are perhaps the most dramatic example of changed thinking on fundamental human rights since 1960, but similar patterns of change are also found in the other civil liberties of the Charter. This is true, for example, of the legal rights provisions, contained in sections 7 to 14.

Section 7 of the Charter, which begins with a general statement of legal rights, and which acts as an umbrella provision for the detailed sections that follow it, states that:

> *Everyone has the right to life, liberty and security of the person and the right not to be deprived thereof except in accordance with the principles of fundamental justice.*

Like other provisions of the Charter, this section deals, in constitutional terms, with relations between citizen and state. By setting out broad rights to "life, liberty and security of the person", the Charter underlines a fundamental value of Canadian society. The addition of "the right not to be deprived thereof except in accordance with the principles of fundamental justice" addresses vital issues of particular significance to criminal procedure. The phrase "principles of fundamental justice", which appears both in section 2 (*e*) of the Canadian Bill of Rights, and in the Charter, is designed to safeguard the right to a fair hearing, to notice of proposed charges, to present one's case before an impartial tribunal, and to cross examination. The drafters believed that a free and open court system based on adversarial testing of propositions and evidence designed to arrive at the truth is central to a free and democratic society. Such a system is an attempt to restrict possibilities for arbitrary action by the state.

In Canada, criminal law is the legislative responsibility of the federal government; criminal law is largely found in the federally-enacted Criminal Code of Canada. The provinces are responsible generally for the administration of justice, including criminal justice, within their own borders. The courts supervise the criminal-justice system to ensure its proper functioning, and impose rules for this purpose. The best known of these, the Judges' Rules,

contain conditions laid down by the British judiciary for procedures to be followed by police forces when taking statements from suspects.

The Canadian Bill of Rights continued the process of codifying both judge-made or "common" law and the principles implicit in the Criminal Code. Because of federal responsibility in this area, the fact that the Bill of Rights did not extend to provincial jurisdictions was not as important as it was for other guarantees of rights and freedoms. Thus the Charter's provisions concerning legal rights come from a long history of judicial interpretation and legislative enactment. The complex judicial evolution of the legal rights provisions in the Bill of Rights suggested the need for detailed provisions in the Charter.

The specific provisions contained in sections 8 to 14 of the Charter are designed to parallel the operation of the criminal process. Section 8 ("search or seizure") and section 9 ("detention or imprisonment") apply to citizens under investigation; section 10 relates to "arrest or detention"; and section 11 covers those "charged with an offence". Section 12 is a sentencing provision. Finally, two provisions applicable to witnesses round out the legal rights: section 13 provides that a witness, in giving evidence, cannot be incriminated in a subsequent proceeding, and section 14 provides interpretation facilities where a party or witness does not understand the language of the proceeding.

While the bulk of the legal rights provisions apply to the criminal-justice system, they are also important in other areas where citizens are subject to official control or regulation. For instance, while the definition of crime is a federal responsibility, provinces and municipalities impose sanctions in fields from securities law, where a penalty provision may include imprisonment, to parking offenses, where the $3 penalty is not yet extinct. The Charter now subjects proceedings related to these offences to the same legal rights that the Bill of Rights previously guaranteed for offences under the Criminal Code. Similarly, protection from "cruel and unusual treatment or punishment" is extended to the actions of a wide number of provincial institutions. Thus, for example, provincial mental health legislation, hospital acts, or procedures established for patients confined against their will may also be scrutinized by the courts in light of the Charter.

These legal rights provisions are designed as much to influence the administration of justice as to strike down or limit legislative initiatives. The administration of justice is the responsibility of the provincial Crown prosecutors as well as of the federal prosecutors, but legislative responsibility in criminal matters resides squarely with the federal government. To the extent that provincial behaviour in administering the law is governed by federal legislation which the provinces cannot amend, a province cannot alter its behaviour without the legislative support of the federal government. Thus, although the Charter's general override clause applies to the legal rights provisions, opportunities for provincial variations in criminal procedures are limited.

In the area of police powers, good administration and law enforcement necessitated a statement of direction to the criminal-justice community. Section 24(2) states:

Where, in proceedings under subsection (1), a court concludes that evidence was obtained in a manner that infringed or denied any rights or freedoms guaranteed by this Charter, the evidence shall be excluded if it is established that, having regard to all the circumstances, the admission of it in the proceedings would bring the administration of justice into disrepute.

In the course of an investigation, the police or the Crown may use inappropriate techniques and thereby obtain evidence that would not otherwise have been obtained. In what circumstances should evidence so obtained be admissible against an accused person? What is the appropriate sanction for activity that the court finds to be inappropriate?

The American "forbidden fruit" doctrine ruled that such evidence and all that flows from it are inadmissible in the courts. Thus juries do not hear a statement or confession that would otherwise be admissible or see physical evidence collected as a result of the statement. Suppose the police in Canada use a wiretap without appropriate authorization under the Criminal Code. In the conversations they record, they hear about the movement of drugs and thus effect an arrest. They have both oral evidence of a conspiracy and physical evidence at the time of the arrest. Fundamental policy choices arise in this situation. Should this evidence be admissible? If it is not, the suspects would be released; if it is, the courts appear to condone unlawful activity by agents of the state. Should a suspected felon be freed to compensate for the errors or wrongdoing of police personnel? The Charter gives judges considerable scope to control unacceptable police behaviour.

Legal rights will evolve within the general framework of the Charter, and it will be recalled that section 1 provides that both laws and actions that are demonstrably justified in some circumstances can be found valid despite apparent inconsistency with the Charter. However, the legal rights provisions themselves contain qualifications similar to those found in section 1. Phrases such as "principles of fundamental justice", "unreasonable search or seizure", "arbitrarily detained or imprisoned" or even "informed promptly" give the courts the responsibility to flesh out the evolving meaning of these standards.

The evidence rule outlined in section 24(2) and the internal qualifications in the legal rights guarantees require courts to consider the actions of the prosecution to ensure that in specific circumstances, an appropriate balance has been reached. These qualifications do not relate only to unreasonable laws, but to unreasonable activity. That is their principal thrust.

Notes

1. See Walter S. Tarnopolsky, *The Canadian Bill of Rights*, 2d ed. (Toronto: McClelland and Stewart, 1975), p. 5.
2. Canadian Bar Association, *1946 Proceedings* (Toronto, 1946), p. 144.
3. *Roncarelli* v. *Duplessis* [1959] S.C.R. 121.
4. Canada, Parliament, *Canadian Bill of Rights: An Act for the Recognition and Protection of Human Rights and Fundamental Freedoms* (Ottawa, 1960).
5. *Ibid.*
6. *R.* v. *Drybones* [1970] S.C.R. 282.
7. *Curr* v. *The Queen* [1972] S.C.R. 889, at 899.

The Charter, National Cohesion and the Canadian Community

The Charter contains some guarantees of rights best understood as efforts to promote social cohesion and national unity. The provisions in this group of rights are closely associated with the social role of the modern state as Commissioners have previously described it: that is, the task of representing and reconciling cultural, linguistic, territorial and other facets of our diversity. This broad group of rights in the Charter includes language rights, minority-language/education rights, mobility rights and the guarantee that the Charter is to be interpreted in a manner consistent with the preservation and enhancement of our multicultural heritage. These guarantees do not focus exclusively on individual rights. Though this remains a primary concern, these rights have profound implications for Canadian federalism and for relations between the national and provincial communities. This is particularly true of the minority-language/education and mobility rights.

Discussions during 1980–82 on these "national community" guarantees often seemed more a political tug-of-war between two levels of government than a discussion of the rights of citizens. The debate reflected that governments were quite naturally concerned with the consequences of the Charter's provisions for their jurisdictional authority, that the Charter was the centre-piece of the federal government's promise to the people of Quebec of "renewed federalism", following the Quebec referendum, and that inclusion of mobility rights was central to federal proposals for securing the economic union.

In the process of negotiation, the proposals were significantly altered. The provisions in the Charter reflect compromises and concessions. Federal-provincial relations and the issues of unity in the federation preoccupied Canadian politicians in the early 1980s and affected the Charter. Provisions of the Charter that relate to communities and national cohesion will illustrate the point. Commissioners will consider first the provisions respecting official languages and cultural groups and then turn to mobility rights.

Official Languages and Minority-Language Education

The Charter's guarantees for language rights and minority-language education are found in sections 16 to 23. In effect, sections 16 to 21 give constitutional status to parts of Canada's official languages legislation and to that of New Brunswick. Residents of Canada have the right to communicate in English or French with the federal government, to receive services in either official language where there is significant demand, or where it is reasonable for such services to be provided, and to use English or French in Parliament and in all courts of law under federal jurisdiction. Governments may expand, but not diminish, the rights guaranteed in the Charter.

Section 22 affirms that the language guarantees in the Charter do not abrogate or derogate "from any legal or customary right or privilege acquired or enjoyed before or after the coming into force of the Charter with respect to any language that is not English or French." However, the most significant

new language right created by the Charter appears in section 23. The Ontario Court of Appeal has suggested in a recent judgement that section 23 "creates a code which establishes minority language education rights for the nation."[1] Section 23 confers two rights:

- Parents who qualify under section 23 have the right to have their children receive publicly funded primary- and secondary-school instruction in the minority language of English or French wherever the number of children of such citizens warrants.
- Parents who qualify under section 23 have the right to have their children receive that instruction in English or French minority-language educational facilities provided out of public funds, again, where the numbers of children warrant.

Court judgements to date suggest that the number of parents required to make these provisions operational will vary from area to area within Canada.

There are three main criteria by which citizens can qualify for minority-language/education rights. Under section 23 (1)(*b*) the so-called "Canada clause", the children of Canadian parents whose primary-school instruction in Canada was in English or French have the right to receive their primary and secondary school instruction in the corresponding language if they live in a province where speakers of English or French form the linguistic minority. The brothers and sisters of children educated in English or French in Canada also have the right to primary and secondary instruction in the corresponding language. Canadian citizens also qualify for these rights for their children if their own mother tongue, the first language learned and still understood, is English or French. This last provision will not take effect in Quebec, however, until the National Assembly or the Government of Quebec authorizes it. This special provision for Quebec was part of an effort to accommodate the concerns of the provincial government on the future of French in Quebec, in return for the province's support for the package of reforms as a whole.

The rights expressed in section 23 pertain to individual citizens who live in a community with a significant number of others who have as their mother tongue the same minority official language. The courts must establish criteria for determining "where numbers warrant". Thus the continuing availability of this right will probably depend on the existence of appropriate concentrations of those speaking a minority official language. The number of children in any particular area may, in the future, fall below that needed to meet the "numbers" requirement. Courts may then conclude that public authorities in such areas no longer need to provide minority-language education and people who have become accustomed to these facilities may find them no longer available.

The section on minority-language education in the Charter confers positive rights. It requires governments to provide publicly funded facilities and/or instruction, where circumstances warrant, rather than merely permitting them to take action. Significant efforts to give expression to these rights in the federal arena date from the publication in 1967 of Book I of the Report of the Royal Commission on Bilingualism and Biculturalism. The Commission

recommended a number of steps, constitutional, legislative and policy-related, to enable the English- and French-language communities to co-exist and flourish in Canada.

Federal Official Language Legislation and Policies

Almost immediately after the tabling of the Report of the Royal Commission on Bilingualism and Biculturalism, the federal government adopted many of its recommendations. In 1969, Parliament passed the Official Languages Act, the first of a recent series of federal laws and programs to foster better relations between Canada's two major linguistic groups and promote linguistic equality in Canada. The Act improved on the British North America Act of 1867 by declaring English and French "offical languages", and by extending language rights to the activities of the Government of Canada generally and not just to those of Parliament. Henceforth the public had a right to communicate with, and to receive services from, federal departments, agencies, courts and Crown corporations in either official language.

To oversee implementation of the Official Languages Act, the government, in 1970, established the office of the Commissioner of Official Languages. The office has construed federal language policies broadly:

> *The whole purpose of the federal language effort is to resist the blandishments of a Canada split along language lines. The fundamental objective is to construct a society in which the minorities can expect to live much of their lives in their own language.*[2]

The federal government directs its language policies both at the federal public service and at Canadian society as a whole. In the federal public service, it has sought equitable participation of the two major linguistic groups, availability of government services in the two official languages, and establishment of both French and English as languages of work in the federal public service.

The proportion of francophones in the federal public service increased from 13 per cent in 1974 to 27.5 per cent in 1983, a figure roughly equivalent to the percentage of francophones in Canadian society. Areas of the country with a small francophone population, however, have very few bilingual public servants. In the four Western provinces, there were 50 000 federal public servants in 1983. Fewer than 800 of these were qualified bilinguals in designated bilingual positions serving approximately 185 000 francophones in the region.[3] The provision of federal services in French in those provinces suffers. Francophones are also underrepresented at different ranks and in different kinds of activities in the public service.

Failure to achieve an appropriate nation-wide distribution of bilingual public servants means that Canada remains a country divided along linguistic lines. Research suggests that the federal public service reflects a country divided into three groups: a Quebec group primarily French, but offering bilingual services; a narrow "bilingual belt" where services are provided in both official languages from Moncton, New Brunswick, to Sault Ste Marie,

Ontario, and anglophone Canada, where services are largely available in English only. The figures parallel the distribution of francophones in Canada: 80 per cent live in Quebec, and most of the remainder live in the Moncton-Sault Ste Marie bilingual belt.

Federal policies on language of work aim to allow official-language minorities a more natural, less restricted choice of working language in the federal administration. In practice, the goal remains elusive. Outside Quebec and the National Capital Region, French is rarely a language of work on a day-to-day basis. Setting up an infrastructure of "bilingual documentation" and "bilingual occupants of bilingual positions" has not made people feel free to work in whichever language comes most naturally. Data for 1981 released by the Treasury Board show that in internal communications in bilingual regions, anglophones use French 18 per cent of the time, while francophones use English 47 per cent of the time. In spite of the relatively low use of French by francophones, Treasury Board data show that francophones are relatively more satisfied than anglophones (72 per cent as compared to 49 per cent) with existing proportions of language use among public servants in bilingual positions. These data prompted the Commissioner of Official Languages to wonder whether "the question might reasonably arise whether we should leave well enough alone. In other words, is it not paternalistic to suggest that Francophones should want to use more French, despite apparent affirmations to the contrary?"[4]

The bilingualism program in the public service has had considerable success. In 15 years the participation rate of francophones has risen compared to their proportion of Canada's population, the number of bilingual anglophones has increased dramatically, and availability of bilingual public services has increased in some areas of our country. It is equally clear, however, that our bilingual goals for the federal public service remain elusive outside the limited bilingual-belt area; the language-of-work policy has had even more limited success.

The federal government also directs its language policies at the broader Canadian community. The objectives of these programs are to promote bilingualism among Canadians, to enhance and preserve minority official languages, and to foster an appreciation among all Canadians of the equal status of our two official languages. It is not Commissioners' purpose here to review these programs, but a brief comment on the program that the former Commissioner of Official Languages has called "a Canadian success story of the first order"[5] illustrates the rapid progress of bilingualism among anglophones.

According to one American authority on language acquisition:

> *Canadian immersion is not simply another successful language teaching programme – it may be the most successful programme ever recorded in the professional language-teaching literature.*[6]

Realization by anglophone Canadians of the economic and other benefits of bilingualism and widespread availability of the programs account for the popularity of French-immersion education in our country. Registration in these programs has grown phenomenally, and the number of schools offering

French immersion has increased by leaps and bounds. From 1977–78 to 1984–85, the number of schools offering French immersion programs increased by over 300 percent from 237 to 988. Total enrolment for 1984–85 is approaching 150 000.[7] Enrolment is still concentrated in the early grades, though there is a recent trend toward high-school immersion. Each year the size of the entering group grows.

Over the past decade, the federal government has encouraged several provinces to become officially bilingual. It expressed the hope that other provinces, particularly Ontario, would follow the example of New Brunswick, which declared a provincial Official Languages Act in 1969. Despite provincial support for immersion programs and minority-language education, as well as initiatives by provinces such as Ontario to increase bilingualism in the provision of public services and enhance French in other aspects of daily life, no province other than New Brunswick has so far passed, on its own initiative, legislation making French and English the official languages of the province.

While official bilingualism requires a supporting legal framework, bilingualism is not a matter simply of language laws. Recent public opposition to bilingualism in Manitoba and New Brunswick is a reminder that bilingualism policy in Canada can be set back by negative public reactions. It is therefore encouraging to note the public pressures for, and the positive responses of parents and children to, government-provided immersion facilities that will help to overcome language barriers. Yet much remains to be done. There must be further sustained effort to secure Canada's two official languages throughout the public service. Commissioners believe that it is important to consolidate the progress of the past and to continue to build on existing foundations. Our history, as well as more recent events, indicates that continued government leadership is essential.

Legislative and policy initiatives tell only part of the story of attempts to promote bilingualism and official language policy across Canada. The new constitutional rights to minority-language education and constitutional recognition of the two official languages, are central components of federal efforts to preserve and enhance official languages across our country.

Federal Constitutional Initiatives respecting Language since 1968

Since the Royal Commission on Bilingualism and Biculturalism recommended changes to the British North America Act, the federal government has advocated constitutional recognition of official languages and minority-language/education rights. That Commission recommended that section 93 of the British North America Act be amended to provide that:

Every province shall establish and maintain elementary and secondary schools in which English is the sole or main language of instruction, and elementary and secondary schools in which French is the sole or main language of instruction, in bilingual districts and other appropriate areas under conditions to be determined by provincial law; but nothing in this section shall be deemed to

prohibit schools in which English and French have equal importance as languages of instruction, or schools in which instruction may be given in some other language.[8]

Elsewhere in its Report, the Commission argued that parents should be free to choose the official language in which their children would be educated, and that this instruction be publicly funded where numbers warrant.

In a 1968 white paper, *A Canadian Charter of Human Rights*,[9] Justice Minister Pierre Trudeau proposed that the recommendations of the Commission be entrenched in a constitutional bill. A year later, as Prime Minister, he elaborated. Language rights, he said, were individual rights that should be guaranteed to all citizens no matter where they live in Canada. Language rights, like other human rights, were essential protections for individual citizens, both in their relations with governments and in their relations with one another.[10] Following publication of the Report of the Royal Commission on Bilingualism and Biculturalism, the Government of Canada proposed to entrench language rights and minority-language/education rights. Its position remained essentially unaltered throughout the 1970s.

There was a gradual movement away from the philosophy of universal free parental choice, caused by events in Quebec in the 1970s and the efforts of successive governments in that province to stem the declining use and status of French among Québécois. Acting on the recommendations of the provincial Commission of Inquiry on the Position of the French Language and on Language Rights in Quebec (Gendron Commission, 1972), in 1974 the provincial government of Robert Bourassa declared French the sole official language of the province. This declaration was not welcomed by the federal government, which was encouraging the provinces to move toward bilingualism. Moreover, in an attempt to steer immigrant children into French schools, the Quebec legislation restricted access to English-language education to those with demonstrated fluency in English.

With the election of the Parti québécois and the introduction of the French Language Charter (Bill 101) in 1977, Quebec's policy diverged even more decidedly from that of the federal government. In addition to declaring French the sole official language, the Quebec Charter declared that French would be the only language of official record in the National Assembly, that judgements rendered by Quebec courts would be in French, and that the French text of legislation would be the sole authentic version. Other parts of Quebec's French Language Charter dealt with matters affecting the use of French at work and in daily life.

Quebec's French Language Charter also stipulated that with certain limited and temporary exceptions, only children with at least one parent educated in English in Quebec would be admitted to English-language public schools, unless a reciprocal agreement was established with other provinces to guarantee access to French schools for students whose mother-tongue was French. In 1979, in St. Andrews, Nova Scotia, Canadian provincial premiers, at their annual meeting, agreed among themselves to establish such a reciprocity (the St. Andrews Accord). However, the "Canada clause" provision in the Charter of Rights superseded this Accord, establishing access

to minority-language instruction for the children of citizens qualifying under section 23 of the Canadian Charter.

These developments in Quebec during the 1970s, from the Gendron Commission Report to the Parti québécois's language legislation, had inescapable consequences for the federal government's language policy. Quebec's language legislation reinforced the federal government's resolve to protect French-language communities outside Quebec. The demands of Quebec's anglophone minority for the protection and security of its language demonstrated that English- as well as French-language minorities in Canada were seeking guarantees. It was clear, however, that the Quebec government would not accept universal free parental choice, which it believed, worked disproportionate hardships on the future of the French language in that province.

The provisions for minority-language/education rights in the 1982 Charter represented a compromise for the Government of Canada. That government had moved away from universal free parental choice, which was replaced by the "Canada clause"; in addition, the clause affecting new Canadians was not to be enforced in Quebec without that province's consent. Quebec's government would not accept the proposal: it was convinced that education, including language issues, remained, and should remain, under provincial jurisdiction and not be subject to external criteria. It has still not assented to the Constitution Act, 1982. Nonetheless, these provisions of the Canadian Charter are now the basic law of the land, and have as much effect in Quebec as elsewhere in Canada. Recent court proceedings have found parts of Quebec's French Language Charter inconsistent with the Charter of Rights and have ruled that in cases of conflict the Charter of Rights will prevail.[11]

Multiculturalism

Section 27 of the Charter states that the entire document is to be "interpreted in a manner consistent with the preservation and enhancement of the multicultural heritage of Canadians." This section will probably moderate and control laws that are offensive to the principles of a multi-ethnic society and cultural tolerance. By specifying multiculturalism as a distinctive aspect of the heritage of Canadians, the Charter recognizes the contribution and needs of the many cultural communities of Canada.

As a policy objective, multiculturalism is a new goal in Canada. The settling of the Prairies by European immigrants in the early twentieth century, the use of Chinese labourers before that to build the Canadian Pacific Railroad, and the even earlier migration of American Blacks to Nova Scotia are all part of the popular mythology of Canada as a culturally diverse "mosaic". Yet, at the end of the Second World War, Canadian national institutions only weakly reflected Canadian dualism, and there was little recognition of ethnic diversity. In the post-war period, the climate of opinion encouraged changes in our collective self-definition as a national community. Extensive immigration after the Second World War may have made the transformation inevitable. Changes within Canadian society have brought

with them pressures to change the symbols of government and society to reflect the multi-ethnic composition of our national community.

The Royal Commission on Bilingualism and Biculturalism inspired contemporary federal policies of multiculturalism, just as it did the current approach to language policies. That Commission had not intended to devote much attention to the "other ethnic" aspects of its mandate, but after receiving strong representations from a number of ethnic groups, it devoted an entire book of its six-volume report to a review of the "third force" in Canada.

The federal government's concern with bilingualism helps to explain the timing of the policy of multiculturalism. Indeed, multiculturalism, introduced on the heels of the 1969 Official Languages Act, was the federal government's attempt to defuse some of Western Canada's criticism of the bilingualism policies. Nevertheless, to interpret multiculturalism only as a means to secure broader support for bilingualism, as some Canadians have done, is to miss other important matters. In fact, the policy of multiculturalism corresponded to several interrelated developments. The changing character of Canadian society after the Second World War brought a partial informal redefinition of the nature of the Canadian community. Within that community, a reallocation of status among linguistic and ethno-cultural groups was under way.

The federal government intended its multiculturalism policy to form another element in that reshaping of society:

> *A policy of multiculturalism within a bilingual framework commends itself to the government as the most suitable means of assuring the cultural freedom of Canadians. Such a policy should help to break down discriminatory attitudes and cultural jealousies. National unity if it is to mean anything in the deeply personal sense, must be founded on confidence in one's own individual identity; out of this can grow respect for that of others and a willingness to share ideas, attitudes and assumptions. A vigorous policy of multiculturalism will help create this initial confidence. It can form the base of a society which is based on fair play for all.*[12]

The Royal Commission on Bilingualism and Biculturalism expressed the premise of the federal policy: "Man is a thinking and sensitive being; severing him from his roots could destroy an aspect of his personality and deprive society of some of the values he can bring to it."[13]

Within a few years of introduction of the new policy, however, it became clear that a gap had developed between stated objectives and results. Some critics saw public support to third-force cultural groups as no more than assistance to ethnic folklore, and they called multiculturalism a "song and dance" routine.[14]

To other critics, the policy appears to maintain cultural distinctiveness among Canadians who are, in fact, living together in one national community. Many members of ethnic groups in Canada fear being "locked in" by ethnic boundaries. As one multicultural group told this Commission, "Ethnic Canadians ... came here to be Canadians." (Council of National Ethnocul-

tural Organizations of Canada, Brief, October 31, 1983, p. 3.) Another group, however, told us:

> *As long as we have a society where the most appreciated values are those of the dominant group, whether it is the Anglo-Saxon group or the Anglo-Celtic group, to the detriment of values and traditions that other groups can offer, then these minority groups will always suffer discrimination even though it may not be legislated discrimination or overt discrimination.*
>
> (Thunder Bay Multicultural Association, Transcript, Thunder Bay, October 17, 1983 [vol. 26], p. 5191.)

Commissioners believe that multicultural policy should preserve ethnic diversity without isolating the very groups this policy seeks to assist. It should permit all Canadians to preserve and enhance the culture and traditions of their heritage, but it should also be consistent with Canadian aspirations for greater individual equality.

To adjust to a multicultural society requires more than mere recognition and accommodation of diversity at the symbolic level. When multiculturalism involves racial diversity – as has been increasingly true of Canada – a pressing need can exist to confront and combat racism. For visible minorities, racism can be a source of day-to-day anguish. Canadians do not think of themselves as racist, yet considerable evidence suggests that ethnic minorities, and particularly some "visible" minorities, are victims of systemic discrimination in Canada. A number of recent studies show that some visible minorities experience severely limited economic and social opportunities, and that the underlying cause is lingering racism.[15]

It is unlikely that transformation of the symbolic order, affirmative action programs, and even the Charter's prohibition of racial discrimination will root out systemic discrimination. *Equality Now*, the report of the Special Committee on Visible Minorities in Canadian Society, contains 80 recommendations to combat racial discrimination. These include proposals to improve language training for immigrants, introduce voluntary affirmative action in hiring and promotion policies, amend Criminal Code provisions respecting hate propaganda, extend support for multicultural arts, and promote respect for the observance of various national days and holy days of different cultures. We Commissioners have not, in our research, addressed the issue of racial discrimination in the same depth as has the Special Committee. We can observe, nonetheless, that racial discrimination in Canada results in an unjustified and indefensible denial of the rights of some individual Canadians and a tragic waste of human resources. Efforts must continue to increase individual equality throughout the Canadian community.

Mobility Rights

Commissioners wish also to consider mobility rights as they relate to Charter provisions concerning national cohesion. The Charter contains the first constitutional expression of mobility rights for Canadians.

Section 6 of the Charter guarantees the right to every citizen of Canada to enter, remain in and leave Canada. This right is in accordance with the

provisions of the United Nations International Covenant on Civil and Political Rights, ratified by Canada in 1976. The section guarantees, also, the right of citizens and permanent residents of Canada to live and seek employment anywhere in the country. The rationale for mobility rights within Canada is based on two assumptions: that barriers to personal mobility inhibit operation of the Canadian economic union, and that common citizenship implies freedom of movement within the country, unrestricted by provincially or federally created barriers.

Subsection 3 of section 6 restricts mobility rights in two ways. It permits limitations imposed by laws or practices of general application in a province (such as ordinary rules of employment concerning health, qualifications and union membership), where such laws or practices do not discriminate primarily on the basis of past or present province of residence. In addition, it permits provinces to impose reasonable residency requirements as a condition of eligibility for publicly provided social services. Subsection 4 enables provinces to pursue programs intended to ameliorate the conditions of socially and economically disadvantaged individuals when the provincial employment rate is below the national rate.

Quite apart from its potential to limit the mobility rights of Canadians, subsection 4 employs the terminology of "rate of employment", for which data are unavailable. The "rate of employment" is not the converse of the unemployment rate with which Canadians are familiar, the statistics of which are published monthly by Statistics Canada. One cannot infer that the rate of employment in a province is 90 per cent on the basis of knowledge that the provincial unemployment rate is 10 per cent.

Statistics Canada does publish statistics on the employment/population ratio which represents the number of persons employed, expressed as percentage of the population 15 years of age and over. However, officials of Statistics Canada and of several provincial Departments of Labour are not confident that these statistics would be accepted by the courts, for constitutional purposes, as appropriate indicators of the "rate of employment". So far the courts have not had occasion to pronounce on the issue. Thus, three years after the Charter came into affect, Canadians lack common understanding of the data base required to provide operational meaning to a key clause in the Charter which affects citizens' rights.

It is possible that when the "rate of employment" is defined by the courts, particular provinces with above-average rates of unemployment which represent the politically visible figure that evokes public reaction, may also have above average rates of employment and thus will be precluded from using subsection 4. It is also plausible that when a case finally reaches the Supreme Court, different governments will prefer different definitions and will employ competing statistical analyses to support their positions. The general assumption that all legislation is an experiment with the future applies with particular cogency to subsection 6(4) of the Charter.

This subsection, when judically interpreted, could affect the mobility of significant numbers of Canadians. The actual number of provinces entitled to implement measures intended to ameliorate the conditions of socially or

economically disadvantaged individuals in the province will depend on the distribution among the larger and smaller provinces of rates of employment.

In the light of this potential problem, it is well to remember that the provinces supported the right of personal mobility in the constitutional negotiations that preceded the adoption of the Charter. They sought amendments to the federal government's proposal on mobility rights, not in order to undermine the general purpose of the clause, but rather to ensure that provincial governments did not lose the authority to manage their societies effectively. As Allan Blakeney, then Premier of Saskatchewan, explained:

> *While remaining committed to the maintenance and improvement of the Canadian Economic Union, provincial governments must also accept their responsibility for providing economic opportunity to Canadians residing within their province.*[16]

A number of conditions limit the ability of provincial governments to override the mobility clause. Section 1 of the Charter, the "reasonable limitations" clause applies to provincial schemes for preferential employment. It stipulates that all restrictions on the rights and freedoms guaranteed by the Charter must be reasonable and demonstrably justified in a free and democratic society. Provincial laws, programs or activities must be directed at those who are "socially or economicaly disadvantaged." In provinces with below-average employment rates, programs may give certain preferences to residents meeting specific qualifications, but they must not impose blanket prohibitions of mobility. Perhaps most significant, from the perspective of the Canadian economic union, the provisions on mobility rights are likely to be most effective in the provinces where they are most needed: those where there is a greater chance of obtaining employment.

Commissioners believe that the courts will probably assume an important role in administering the mobility-rights guarantees. In so doing, they will become deeply involved in the task of reconciling national and provincial interests and citizens' rights. One observer has suggested that in determining the reasonableness of provincial actions limiting personal mobility, the courts will be obliged to balance the interests of the national community against the more particular interests of the local community:

> *There may then be no alternative to a balancing approach under which barriers to mobility will be unconstitutional unless the benefits created by their promotion of local interests demonstrably outweigh the burdens they impose on interprovincial mobility.*[17]

Commissioners also wish to note that even in circumstances where a province invokes its powers to limit the availability of mobility-rights guarantees, the federal government may still have considerable influence over the provision of mobility opportunities within that province. For example, the federal government might decide to prohibit mobility discrimination as a condition of provincial participation in programs that are jointly funded, or to attach comparable conditions to monies transferred to the provinces. However, the fact that limitations on mobility rights now have a constitutional status they

lacked before may make it politically more difficult for the federal government to secure contractual agreements overriding them. With respect to its own employees and employment practices, the federal government may, of course, establish its own practices, and possibly attach similar conditions to companies which work on federal contracts.

Notes

1. Reference Re Education Act of Ontario and Minority Language Education Rights, (1984) 10 D.L.R. (4th), pp. 491–547.
2. Canada, Commissioner of Official Languages, *Annual Report 1983* (Ottawa: Minister of Supply and Services Canada, 1984), p. *ii*.
3. Canada, Parliament, Standing Joint Committee of the Senate and of the House of Commons on Official Languages Policy and Programs, *Minutes of Proceedings and Evidence*, June 20, 1984 (Ottawa: Queen's Printer, 1984).
4. Commissioner of Official Languages, *Annual Report 1983*, p. 57.
5. Maxwell Yalden, "French Immersion . . . a Canadian Experience", *Language and Society*, No. 12 (Winter 1984), p. 3.
6. Stephen D. Krashen, "Immersion: Why It Works and What It Has Taught Us", *Language and Society*, No. 12 (Winter 1984), p. 61.
7. Canada, Commissioner of Official Languages, *Annual Report 1984* (Ottawa: Minister of Supply and Services Canada, 1985), p. 246.
8. Canada, Royal Commission on Bilingualism and Biculturalism, *Report*, Vol. 1 (Ottawa: Queen's Printer, 1967), p. 134.
9. Pierre Elliott Trudeau, *A Canadian Charter of Human Rights* (Ottawa: Queen's Printer, 1968).
10. Canada, *The Constitution and the People of Canada: An Approach to the Objectives of Confederation, the Rights of People and the Institutions of Government* (Ottawa: Queen's Printer, 1969).
11. For example, see *Attorney General of Quebec* v. *Quebec Association of Protestant School Boards* (1984), 54 N.R. 196 (S.C.C.).
12. Canada, House of Commons' *Debates*, Vol. VIII, 1971, p. 8545.
13. Canada, Royal Commission on Bilingualism and Biculturalism, *Report*, Vol. 4 (Ottawa: Queen's Printer, 1969), p. 5.
14. See Raymond Breton, "Multiculturalism and Canadian Nation-Building", in *The Politics of Gender, Ethnicity and Language in Canada*, vol. 34, prepared for the Royal Commission on the Economic Union and Development Prospects for Canada (Toronto: University of Toronto Press, 1985).
15. Canada, House of Commons, Special Committee on Visible Minorities in Canadian Society, *Equality Now* (Ottawa: Queen's Printer, 1984); Royal Commission on Equality in Employment, *Report* (Ottawa: Minister of Supply and Services Canada, 1984); and Urban Alliance on Race Relations and the Social Planning Council of Metro Toronto, *Report* (Toronto, 1985).
16. Powers over the Economy, Opening Statements, Saskatchewan position presented at the First Ministers' Conference, Ottawa, 1980, Doc. 800-14/025, p. 2.
17. John B. Laskin, "Mobility Rights under the Charter", *Supreme Court Law Review* 4 (1982), p. 104.

The Charter and the Politics of Rights

The Charter provides new opportunities for the involvement of Canadians in public decision making. Based on its provisions, members of the public can question the actions of governments as they affect fundamental rights and freedoms of citizens. This is a new feature in the Canadian political process. Formerly the main judicial protections against legislated interferences with civil liberties and human rights were found in the division of powers. This division between the spheres of federal and provincial constitutional authority was often invoked to prevent one level of government from acting, even if such actions would be permissible if undertaken by the other level of government. Limited resort to the Canadian Bill of Rights was also available to protect rights at the federal level, as were less reliable arguments about an "implied" bill of rights in our parliamentary tradition which was also relevant to matters in provincial jurisdiction. More often, questions of fundamental rights violations simply were not raised before the courts.

Citizens now have a wide range of grounds from which to argue the violation of basic rights and freedoms. While the Charter selectively recognizes the supremacy of Parliament or the legislatures, this supremacy must be explicitly invoked by the legislatures either under the general override clause or under provisions qualifying mobility rights or permitting affirmative action programs. Furthermore, a court must be satisfied that the legislated schemes are reasonable and demonstrably justified. Thus the Charter provides important new opportunities for determining the limits of legislative authority.

During the three years that the Charter has been in effect, most of the visible action in establishing these limits has occurred in the judicial arena. Nonetheless, governments are already guided by the Charter in their day-to-day deliberations about new legislation and amendments to existing statutes and regulations. While the Charter may not appear to be in the forefront of the legislative process, it can never be far from the minds of the lawmakers.

As lawyers and their clients seek new interpretations and applications of the Charter in the courts, Canada will undoubtedly become a more litigious society. The Charter will also contribute to a greater consciousness of fundamental rights in Canada, among citizens and governments alike. In addition, the Charter may contribute to improving the democratic parliamentary process by providing a new incentive to discuss legislation fully, in terms of its implications for the rights and freedoms of citizens.[1] Thus, Commissioners believe that the Charter will alter the conduct of politics, both directly by bringing to bear on political decision making the spectre of judicial constraint and less directly by furthering the development of a political culture predisposed to review government actions from the perspective of the rights of citizens.

The Charter offers incentives to Canadian interest groups possessing the resources and the will to sustain costly and lengthy court proceedings. In the past, these groups have not made extensive use of constitutional litigation as a tactic in seeking to bring about a policy change. While various interest groups have challenged government regulatory policies sporadically, on grounds of federalism, there has been no Canadian parallel to the American interest-

group practice of initiating "test cases" supported by "legal defense funds". This lack is no doubt explained by the previous absence of significant constitutional prohibitions other than the federal division of powers, and the Canadian legal community's widely-held perception that policy making was not the proper business of the courts.

Some groups, however, have already begun to organize for such litigation. The recently established Legal Education and Action Fund for women is a good example. Its supporters hope that this fund, inspired by the successful example of the American Legal Defense and Educational Fund, Inc. of the National Association for the Advancement of Colored People (NAACP) and other similar programs in the United States, will ensure that women derive maximum benefit from the equality rights set out in the new Charter. This hope is premised on the belief that collectively supported efforts on behalf of women will be more effective than the individual legal initiatives women have undertaken in the past.[2]

Some groups and individuals will use the Charter to introduce issues to the political agenda and to advance particular causes in public proceedings. Is there a possibility that claims for entitlements based on the Charter will be over-used? Some may consider that the broad and general language of the Charter's principles provides almost unlimited possibilities for constitutional arguments across virtually all of public policy. Judicial decisions will contribute to setting limits to these possibilities and procedures, and the courts' early judgements will be crucial. But what will the public's attitude be toward use of the Charter? Will the Charter's emphasis on rights-based citizenship become the foundation for rights-seeking political behaviour?

Commissioners believe that the Charter will affect the ways Canadians think about and discuss politics. Over the past few decades, a popular language of citizens' rights has begun to emerge in Canada, and it has already affected political behaviour across a wide range of issues. In what ways, then, will the Charter's guarantees of rights affect the day-to-day political behaviour of citizens? Some analysts have argued that a strong tradition of rights seeking can erode the moral basis of a community and undermine considerations of duty and obligation. They suggest that the language of rights can lessen the willingness of community members to view their own rights in a balanced relationship to the rights of others and to the consensus underlying the community as a whole. In the broader context of the so-called "inflation" of human rights, one political philosopher has recently argued that rights-seeking behaviour and the advancement of rights claims on the basis that human rights are justified by natural law can disrupt the normal process of political bargaining and discussion:

> *Those who advance political claims under the aegis of human rights, believing that their causes are sanctified by the most powerful of all moral considerations, are in no frame of mind to negotiate ... Confronted by such massively heavy artillery, opponents of causes whose advocates invoke human rights are virtually compelled to resort to unduly heavy weaponry themselves ... The human rights perspective tends to extend political controversies beyond their plausible limits and thereby inhibits reasonable political debate.*[3]

Such a perspective does not depend on the legal or constitutional recognition of such rights; rather it presents essentially political claims as human rights. However, Constitutional recognition of a wide range of citizens' rights, many expressed in very general terms, can provide extra ammunition for those advancing such claims.

A seasoned federal public servant recently speculated about the challenges, as he saw them, of governing in a rights-seeking society:

> *The exquisite refinement of the overall field of human rights into a multitude of rights-seekers and rights-protectors has been a major development over the past ten years, and as the principal growth industry in government, rights have become a major preoccupation of public administrators . . .*
>
> *Canada is in danger of becoming a rights-ridden country . . .*
>
> *There is very little that can be done to contain the growth of the rights movement, given the difficulty of justifying opposition to any kind of right.*[4]

Commissioners do not wish to overstate the consequences of these developments. The Charter also expresses traditions of community values, and its tests of reasonableness and demonstrable justification clearly indicate that rights will not be extended on an unlimited basis. In the last analysis, however, only the citizenry itself can restrain the potential excesses of rights-bearing citizenship. The success of any charter of rights in enhancing the quality of citizenship relies at least as much on the degree of sophistication and responsibility that citizens bring to their use of the document as on its interpretation and enforcement by the courts.

In educating the Canadian public concerning their rights and freedoms, the Charter emphasizes the need for constant balancing between the reasonable and justified needs of the community and respect for the rights of its individual members. However, the Charter has clearly and appropriately shifted the balance in favour of the constitutional protection of the rights of citizens in their relations with governments. Certainly the benefits of this shift derive from an alert, fair-minded, and responsible citizenry, acting both individually and collectively in its political and legal affairs. It is good to be aware of the consequences that can follow when that trust is violated. But Commissioners believe that such awareness will reinforce Canadians' commitment to ground our community's future in the protected rights of individual citizens, and that it will strengthen the community as a whole. Similarly, such awareness will strengthen Canadians' resolve to protect and respect the rights of others and the collective needs of the community as a whole. Commissioners wish to emphasize that the Charter has provided a new defence for the protection of rights in Canada. Although the federal-provincial division of powers will remain important in some alleged violations of rights and freedoms, it will no longer bear the same responsibility. The Charter has placed protection of citizens' rights on a more independent footing in the Constitution.

Notes

1. Peter H. Russell, "The First Two Years in Charter Land", paper prepared for Workshop of Canadian Government Area Group, Department of Political Science, University College, University of Toronto, March 19, 1984.
2. M. Elizabeth Atcheson, Mary Eberts, and Beth Symes, *Women and Legal Action: Precedents, Resources and Strategies for the Future* (Ottawa: Canadian Advisory Council on the Status of Women, 1984), pp. 41–42.
3. Thomas C. Pocklington, "Against Inflating Human Rights", *The Windsor Yearbook of Access to Justice* 2 (1982), p. 85.
4. H.L. Laframboise, "The Future of Public Administration in Canada", *Canadian Public Administration* 25 (Winter 1982), pp. 509–10.

Equality Rights and the Charter

One of the recurring themes put forward at this Commission's hearings and a central message from representatives of women's groups, aboriginals, visible minorities and the handicapped was that Canada must work harder to become a society marked by more equality. Many of these groups challenged traditional notions of equality and outlined an interventionist role for governments in creating circumstances that would help individuals and groups to share the opportunities, benefits and burdens of Canadian society more fairly.

We Commissioners discovered at our hearings what is confirmed in the massive literature on equality: the understanding of equality has changed substantially at the popular level over the past few decades. The guarantees of equality rights recently incorporated in the Canadian Charter of Rights and Freedoms reflect many of these changes. The Charter-making process itself benefited from some of the most sustained and highly focused debates on equality ever to occur in Canada during the public hearings before the Special Joint Committee of the Senate and of the House of Commons on the Constitution of Canada.

There has been a significant shift in emphasis from procedural equality, that is equality before the law, to more substantive notions of equality. Many advocates of procedural equality hoped that prohibition of overt discrimination would secure equal opportunity. However, more and more Canadians have come to adopt the view that while removing procedural barriers is a necessary step towards equality, it is not a sufficient one. Social, cultural and economic conditions are obstacles to equal opportunity. In fact, many groups and individuals argue that equality includes not merely equal opportunity, but equal enjoyment of the outcomes and benefits of those opportunities. Notions of substantive equality address these concerns. The increased efforts of governments to combat the causes and effects of discrimination, and to ensure a more nearly equal distribution of the opportunities and benefits of Canadian society relate directly to this new concern for substantive equality.

By challenging traditional notions of equality, recent debates have forced reconsideration of some long-standing justifications for setting limitations on equality. Canadians have had to examine more closely common assumptions about inequality. During our hearings, we Commissioners heard that widespread social values and attitudes are at the root of persistent inequality in Canadian society, and that changing these values and attitudes should be an integral part of efforts to promote equality.

Equality has always been a powerful idea in democratic societies. The basic nature of any political community is reflected in its treatment of the issues associated with rights to equality. We Canadians can learn a great deal about the nature of our community by examining closely the guarantees of equality found in section 15 of the Charter. As with other powerful social ideas, however, equality is controversial, and the Charter's guarantees of equality will continue to provoke political debate and legal and political activity.

Guarantees of equality are only one part of the Charter. Interpretations of other sections of that document will affect the interpretation and application

of the equality guarantees. Of particular importance are the "reasonable limitations clause" (s. 1) and the "general override provision" (s. 33) which allows federal and provincial governments to override guarantees of equality.

Although section 15 sets out the Charter's basic equality rights, other sections may be directly relevant to the interpretation of the equality guarantees. For example, the sexual-equality guarantee of section 28 provides that: "Notwithstanding anything in this Charter, the rights and freedoms referred to in it are guaranteed equally to male and female persons." Section 28 applies to all rights covered in the Charter. Section 27, reviewed above, refers to the preservation and enhancement of Canada's multicultural heritage, while section 25 states that the guarantees set out in the Charter do not abrogate or derogate from any treaty or aboriginal rights pertaining to Native peoples. Sections 16 to 23 provide for the use of official languages and for minority-language education – cornerstones of equality programs for official language groups – and protect certain rights respecting other languages in Canada. In the absence of judicial interpretations of the Charter's equality guarantees, Commissioners can only speculate on their ultimate effect. We believe, however, that all of these provisions contain some signposts of the Canadian commitment to equality.

Section 15: Equality Guarantees

The guarantees of equality contained in section 15 of the Canadian Charter of Rights and Freedoms came into effect on April 17, 1985. The section reads:

> ***Equality Rights***
>
> *15(1) Every individual is equal before and under the law and has the right to the equal protection and equal benefit of the law without discrimination and, in particular, without discrimination based on race, national or ethnic origin, colour, religion, sex, age or mental or physical disability.*
>
> *(2) Subsection (1) does not preclude any law, program or activity that has as its object the amelioration of conditions of disadvantaged individuals or groups including those that are disadvantaged because of race, national or ethnic origin, colour, religion, sex, age or mental or physical disability.*

In effect, four guarantees of equality are presented in section 15(1): equality before the law, equality under the law, equal protection of the law, and equal benefit of the law. These four guarantees and the relevant provisions previously mentioned indicate that the constitutional order now embodies a very broad definition and concept of equality.

The guarantee of equality before the law is similar to that set out in the Canadian Bill of Rights. Our courts have interpreted the Bill of Rights as requiring equality in enforcement and application of laws. This guarantee is fundamentally important to procedural equality, but critics view its restriction to matters of procedure as a basic weakness. By 1982, there was a strongly perceived need to supplement this guarantee of procedural equality with rights of a more substantive nature.

The guarantee of equality under the law as stated in the Charter made clear that the guarantees of equality applied to the substance of legislation. Earlier the courts had interpreted equality before the law to apply only to the administration of the law. They had concluded that inequality in legislation itself was beyond the reach of the Bill of Rights. That interpretation severely limited the effectiveness of earlier guarantees of equality: it permitted legislatures to make distinctions on the basis of sex or race, or on other grounds, as long as the law was administered equally.

The guarantee of equal benefit of the law in the Charter avoids situations in which individuals could be deprived of basic legislative benefits. The new guarantee is intended to overcome unfortunate precedents. The Bliss case concerned a woman who had worked enough weeks to qualify for regular Unemployment Insurance benefits, but not long enough to claim maternity benefits.[1] Because her inability to work was the result of pregnancy, she failed to qualify even for regular Unemployment Insurance benefits. The court held that there was no denial of sexual equality: the discrimination was not between women and men, but between pregnant women and everyone else, a form of discrimination that was not prohibited. The court said also that the case had to do with benefits and that, in its opinion, the Bill of Rights did not contain a guarantee of equal benefits. Women's groups and others rejected this interpretation and fought successfully for the stronger guarantee now explicitly found in the equal-benefits provision of the Charter.

The right to equal protection of the law again echoes the Bill of Rights, although the latter guaranteed only the right to "the protection of the law". There has been little jurisprudence on this provision. An aspect of discrimination that may be encompassed by the equal-protection clause, but that is not included under the other guarantees is discrimination resulting from laws that appear to be neutral, but that have discriminatory effects. We shall review shortly the systemic discrimination that can result from these seemingly neutral practices.

Section 15(1) further states that these equality guarantees apply without discrimination and, "in particular", without discrimination on the basis of race, national or ethnic origin, colour, religion, sex, age, or mental or physical disability. The enumeration of some specific characteristics raises several questions. Can individuals complain about a denial of equality based on other grounds? If so, will the test for the validity of the challenged actions differ from the one applied in cases where discrimination on one of the enumerated grounds is alleged? For example, will the courts act against discrimination on the basis of age, which is enumerated in section 15, more stringently than against discrimination on the basis of sexual preference, which is not specifically mentioned? If there is such a scale, what is the principle for ranking the grounds?

The use of the phrase "in particular" in section 15 suggests that the list of grounds on which discrimination is prohibited is open-ended: while section 15 lists specific grounds on which discrimination is prohibited, this list is not exhaustive. If the courts follow the jurisprudence under the Bill of Rights, they will probably give protection on enumerated grounds. Will they treat non-enumerated grounds differently?

An individual arguing denial of equality rights on some ground not specified in section 15 might have to show that the specific ground deserves constitutional protection; such a requirement places an additional burden on the individual. The courts may prove to require substantial evidence before finding that legislation discriminates on the basis of non-enumerated grounds.

The courts will obviously be the central actors in establishing the application of section 15(1) of the Charter. But governments themselves can bring their own laws into conformity with the spirit of the Charter's provisions, especially where they become aware of discriminatory practices. Attitudes to equality change: one generation's idea of equality may seem discriminatory to the next. Where attitudes and understanding change beyond the established requirements of the Charter, governments, perhaps better than courts, can ensure that laws conform to the broad spirit and objectives of the Charter's guarantees.

Like the other rights guaranteed by the Charter, equality rights are not absolute. Some limitations on equality have received general support in the past: limits on various age groups, for example, in matters such as the age of majority, voting age and mandatory retirement. The equality guarantees in the Charter are subject to the general override power of legislatures, which means that governments can legislate notwithstanding the general constitutional guarantee of equality. The active constraint on governments in such instances is public opinion; in fact, governments need defend their actions in this regard before no other court. Where governments have not explicitly overridden an equality guarantee, the judiciary may itself consider whether a limitation is demonstrably justified, given the norms and traditions of a free and democratic society.

Thus two processes will shape the evolving meaning and scope of the Charter's equality guarantees. First, public opinion expressed through the political process may support recognition of new groups in terms of the equality guarantees, and will also condition the authority of governments to place restrictions on established equality rights through use of the general override provision. Secondly, judicial interpretation of the equality guarantees and of the justified limitations on equality in the context of a free and democratic society will have important effects.

The possibility of a scale of protected interests or grounds on which discrimination by governments is constitutionally prohibited will require further careful consideration. Some analysts have suggested that an approach developed in the United States may be useful. The equal-protection clause in the American Constitution does not enumerate specific grounds of prohibited discrimination. Thus, U.S. courts have had to determine, with reference to American history, which grounds are the most invidious and to devise standards to apply in scrutinizing offending legislation. Strict judicial scrutiny is usually applied to legislative distinctions based on race and nationality, for example. This means that the courts will strike down a law that discriminates on such grounds unless the government can demonstrate that it is pursuing a compelling end, and that the discriminatory classification is necessary to promote that interest. Where sexual discrimination is alleged, the courts have applied an intermediate test of scrutiny. Here, the discrimina-

tion imposed by a law must be substantially related to an important government interest, or else the courts will hold it to be an unconstitutional violation of the equality clause. The courts have devised a minimal-scrutiny test for legislation that discriminates on other grounds. Under minimal scrutiny, the American courts require simply that the classification rationally be thought to bear a relationship to a constitutionally permitted objective of government.

In Canada, the constitutional framework for the protection of equality differs from that of the United States. Our Charter explicitly provides that race, national or ethnic origin, colour, religion, sex, age, or mental or physical disability are worthy of constitutional protection. However, a legislative distinction based on age may not require the same degree of justification as one based on other enumerated grounds. For instance, there may be demonstrably justifiable government objectives related to distinctions based on age that would not be acceptable on the basis of racial classifications. The protection of children is a possible example. It appears to be possible within the framework of section 15 of the Charter and the general limitations clause contained in section 1 to recognize different degrees of justification.

Other sections of the Charter may affect the degree of constitutional protection accorded to members of a particular group. They may enhance or detract from protection relating to the classifications set out in section 15. The separate requirement that all the rights in the Charter apply equally to men and women (s. 28), for example, will probably strengthen the prohibition of discrimination on the basis of sex. Similarly, the guarantees of religious equality in section 15 may be strengthened by the general guarantee of freedom of religion as a "fundamental freedom" elsewhere in the Charter. Nevertheless, the constitutional protection given to denominational schools may restrict or qualify those rights. In addition, while section 15 guarantees equality without discrimination on the basis of age, the Constitution Act, 1867 places upper age limits on members of the Senate and members of the superior courts.

Thus we Canadians may not need to adopt the three levels of scrutiny developed in the United States, but our courts may require different degrees of justification for protecting various types of equality.

Equality and Ethnicity

As with the Bill of Rights which preceded it, the Charter prohibits discrimination on the basis of race and national or ethnic origin. Unlike the Bill of Rights, however, the Charter also outlines circumstances in which such distinctions become relevant for the rights of Canadians. It does so in the matter of language guarantees. While "national origin" and "mother tongue" are certainly not synonymous, the guarantees of minority-language education make distinctions among new Canadians largely, if indirectly, on the basis of their national origin, just as the guarantees also distinguish between Canadians who claim neither English nor French as their mother tongue and those who do.

The protection of aboriginal and treaty rights in the Charter may be a better example of the conflict that can arise between the equality rights of individuals and rights recognized on the basis of ethnicity. Sections 35 and 37 of the Constitution Act, 1982 and section 25 of the Charter recognize aboriginal and treaty rights. Some comments will illustrate the collective nature of these rights, and their potential conflict with the spirit of other sections of the Charter and with equality rights in particular. The Constitution Act, 1982 contains no directly comparable provisions for other groups.

In addition to recognizing and affirming aboriginal and treaty rights, section 35 of the Constitution Act, for the first time in Canadian history, recognizes Métis people, together with Indians and Inuit, as the aboriginal peoples of Canada. As amended following the Constitutional Conference of First Ministers in March 1984, section 35 guarantees all aboriginal and treaty rights referred to in this section equally to men and women. Through this amendment, section 35 now conforms with the Charter's provision of sexual equality. The innovative section 37 of the Constitution Act, 1982 provided for aboriginal participation in future discussion of constitutional matters that directly affect the aboriginal people of Canada. The consequent meetings were "a first" in Canadian history: in addition to the First Ministers, the leaders of major aboriginal groups attended.

Section 25 of the Charter provides that the Charter shall not be interpreted in a manner that abrogates or derogates from aboriginal rights. This section does not attempt to create new rights. As with certain other provisions in the Charter – those pertaining to language (s. 21) or to other rights not specified in the Charter (s. 26) – the function of section 25 is to ensure that the Charter does not diminish any rights and freedoms existing independently of it. As amended in 1984, section 25 provides that:

> *The guarantee in this Charter of certain rights and freedoms shall not be construed so as to abrogate or derogate from any aboriginal, treaty or other rights or freedoms that pertain to the aboriginal peoples of Canada . . .*

Several questions arise from the provisions on aboriginal rights in the Charter. Can section 25 be used to challenge existing laws that have limited or taken away treaty or land-claim rights? The courts will have to answer this question. More generally, how can, and how should, we balance the individual rights of all Canadians with the collective rights of some groups within the broader national community? Canadians as a whole will have to answer this type of question.

The dominant political culture in North America places great emphasis on the protection of individual rights and freedoms. In Canada, we can see that emphasis embodied in the 1960 Bill of Rights, in provincial and federal human rights legislation and, since April 1982, in our Charter. The aboriginal cultures, however, have a quite different emphasis. The 1981 Report of the Métis and Non-Status Indian Constitutional Review Commission, entitled *Native People and the Constitution of Canada*, states:

> *. . . the dominant socio-cultural system in Canada is liberalism which places emphasis on the individual, individual rights and private property. This is in*

contrast to the value system of Native peoples which places a far higher value on the collectivity or upon the community. It is ironic that non-Native Canadians, with all their liberal ideological baggage, cannot understand the significance to the Native peoples, or for that matter to any self-conscious minority group of being recognized as a collectivity. They do not realize that a cultural minority faces certain death by assimilation if the political system forces it to deal with the majority culture as individuals.[2]

It is from these different and, to a degree, conflicting cultural premises that problems arise in the protection of individual rights within the context of aboriginal communities.

When individual and collective rights conflict, which value system will prevail? Will it be the non-aboriginal Canadian society or the aboriginal community? What would happen if a member of a self-governing aboriginal community challenged that community's collective decision on the basis of his or her individual rights as enshrined in the Charter of Rights and Freedoms? Some analysts have argued that the purpose of section 25 is to ensure that aboriginal rights prevail over other provisions in the Charter.[3]

Aboriginal self-government, intended to provide protection for collective rights, introduces complexities for the protection of individual rights within the jurisdictional domain of aboriginal governments. Aboriginal organizations are particularly sensitive to this issue and recognize the need to balance individual and collective rights.

Some would argue that all individuals within aboriginal communities should be entitled to the full protection of the Charter and of the Canadian courts, that the Charter should apply within the jurisdiction of aboriginal governments as it applies within the jurisdiction of the federal and provincial governments, and that individuals should have access to independent appeal procedures. As Commissioners have argued in our section on aboriginal self-government, members of aboriginal communities should retain their rights as Canadian citizens. We view the Charter as contributing to a definition of Canadian citizenship. To exempt aboriginal communities from the individual-rights guarantees of the Charter would be to diminish fundamentally the citizenship of aboriginal Canadians.

The longstanding controversy over section 12.1.b of the Indian Act, which penalized Indian women who married non-Indian men by requiring them to forfeit their Indian status, demonstrated that these concerns about individual and collective interests are not simply abstract issues. They do arise in practice. Conflicts between collective rights, aboriginal rights and individual rights will arise; individuals living within aboriginal communities will appeal to external forms of protection. The manner in which such conflicts are resolved is integrally related to our sense of Canada.[4]

The multiple purposes of the Charter are the source of potential conflict between individual and group rights. The Charter not only encompasses the individual rights of Canadians, but it also addresses contemporary concerns about national cohesion. Earlier, Commissioners examined how the accommodation of provincial communities, both through the specific provisions respecting personal mobility rights and the general override

provision, may interfere with the mobility of individual Canadians and with other rights guarantees. We noted that over-use of these legislative powers could introduce so much variation across the country that the concept of individual rights in a national community could be undermined. We accepted that provisions for variation reflect the historic reality of the Canadian community and argued that recourse to these provisions will be moderated by the spirit of the Charter. The Charter recognizes certain fundamental rights and freedoms of Canadians in constitutional terms. This new status for citizens' rights requires that departures from stated constitutional norms be justified by those who have the authority to introduce such departures.

Commissioners believe that the provisions underlying the special status of various cultural groups in Canada can be understood on the same basis. The multicultural design of Canada, the official status of two languages, and the more recent official affirmation of aboriginal rights reflect deliberate choices worked out by the political process. Canadians value the cultural distinctiveness of our various ethnic communities, and we have self-consciously styled ourselves a country of immigrants; at critical points in our national history, we chose to develop as a bilingual nation, where mother tongue would carry certain special rights. Yet this celebration of group differences is at best only half of our personality. We are also a society of individuals, nurtured by the traditions of democratic liberalism. In such a society, one does not interfere lightly with the equality of citizens. Neither is the celebration of our group differences a justification for denying opportunities for individuals to develop their abilities to the full. Appropriately, section 15(1) of the Canadian Charter of Rights and Freedoms makes a broad and general guarantee of the equality of every individual and prohibits discrimination based on such grounds as race and national or ethnic origin. This is Canada's fundamental commitment to equality.

The Affirmative Action Clause

Section 15(2), a counterpart of section 15(1), protects governments from constitutional challenges in instances where they have taken positive action to rectify situations where groups are at a disadvantage because of past discrimination. Section 15(2) represents an exemption from subsection (1) where the object of a law, program, or activity is to ameliorate conditions of disadvantaged individuals or groups. This provision was included in the Charter to avoid problems which occurred in the United States when affirmative action programs were introduced. In a number of decisions, the U.S. Supreme Court ruled these programs unconstitutional. They were deemed to constitute a form of reverse discrimination contrary to the equal-protection guarantees. To avoid these problems, the framers of the Canadian Charter made it clear that any affirmative action program with the appropriate objective would be exempt from section 15(1).

Section 15(2) does not require that governments take affirmative action, although it is conceivable that the courts, through the remedies section of the Charter, could require that an affirmative action program be initiated in

order to remedy past discrimination. While the courts could do this, section 15(2) provides a valuable mechanism for governments to take initiatives toward the attainment of equality in Canada.

In an earlier chapter of this Report, Commissioners concluded that affirmative action is useful for achieving greater equality of opportunity and wage parity for men and women in the labour force. Affirmative action can also be used to combat discriminatory attitudes and to provide role models for disadvantaged groups. In recent years, it has become more popular as an instrument for combatting what is now commonly referred to as "systemic discrimination". The recent Royal Commission on Equality in Employment (the Abella Commission)[5] recommended mandatory affirmative action programs, both federal and provincial, for improving equality of opportunity for employment for women, the handicapped, visible minorities and Native peoples. Similarly, the recent Special Committee of the House of Commons on Visible Minorities[6] recommended the establishment of voluntary affirmative action programs to assist visible minorities to overcome systemic discrimination. In 1981, the Special Committee on the Disabled and the Handicapped[7] recommended that federal government departments, agencies, and Crown corporations expand or implement affirmative action employment programs for the disabled. In the past, this technique has also been used to promote the participation of francophones and Native peoples in the public service, as well as the participation of the disabled and of women.[8]

In this Commission's hearings, many groups and individuals spoke about various forms of systemic discrimination. This form of discrimination is invisible and often unconscious, having grown up over time and become embedded in our culture. It is different from overt discrimination, which manifests itself in clearly expressed prejudice. Overt discrimination occurs, for example, when a property owner says "I will not rent my apartment to a family on welfare," or an employer says "I will not hire a woman." This kind of discrimination is prohibited by law, and a victim of such prejudice can seek redress with Human Rights Commissions and through other legal protections. Systemic discrimination is of a different kind; it can operate unconsciously so that individuals may not be aware that their attitudes and behaviour systematically exclude or discriminate against some people. For example, seemingly neutral job requirements such as standards of height and weight may constitute a barrier to whole sections of society.

Systemic discrimination cannot be easily eliminated. To alter discriminatory attitudes and traditions involves changes in our public and economic institutions and practices, as well as in our personal lives. For instance, some participants in our hearings argued that to equalize employment opportunities for women requires that we, as a society, collectively change practices and attitudes toward family responsibilities, child care and the division of domestic work. It requires, as well, that we change early socialization and educational patterns by which we encourage one set of values for boys and another for girls. The Canadian Advisory Council on the Status of Women told us that the time has come for a re-examination of our societal attitudes and practices in these areas:

Education, adult training, community facilities, working hours, and support services for families with children must be re-examined to see how they are influenced by the stereotype of the traditional family, in which the woman devotes all her time to ensuring the well-being of the other members. These biases must be corrected, and we must change our social organization so that a mother can find the independence and financial security she needs in the labour market just as easily as a father can. The cooperation of all levels of government and the participation of all economic agents will be needed to bring about this transformation.

(Canadian Advisory Council on the Status of Women, Brief, November 30, 1983, p. 44.)

To be sure, there has been much progress on these matters in recent years, within families, in school counselling, in university-enrolment patterns and elsewhere. Public awareness of these matters is an important first step in the direction of greater equality. And in recent years, a growing number of community services and support networks have sprung up across the country to assist people who experience systemic discrimination. In our hearings, testimony abounded about the useful services these voluntary organizations provide. But these same intervenors were adamant that to rely on voluntary agencies and individual self-help is not enough. Active government involvement is required to eliminate systemic discrimination. There are several reasons for this.

First, the process would occur more quickly with effective government leadership. Without concerted government action, individuals continue to suffer the effects of discrimination for longer than is tolerable or necessary. In October 1984, the Report of the Royal Commission on Equality in Employment called for a "massive policy response to systemic discrimination".[9]

Secondly, as the Saskatchewan Action Committee on the Status of Women reminded Commissioners, the issue of equality is one which the whole of society must address:

The women's question . . . is one that needs to be addressed by all of us, not just women . . .

Women's issues, which basically are concerned with how we can operate on a basis of equality and independence in all aspects of society, have to be taken seriously, and it is our belief that this calls for nothing less than the restructuring of society, so that women, as society's largest minority, will have a chance to participate.

(Saskatchewan Action Committee on the Status of Women, Regina, Transcript, November 24, 1983 [vol. 5], pp. 10770–71.)

Failure to intervene can be regarded as tacit confirmation by government, and therefore by society as a whole, that we accept the existing patterns of discrimination. As the Abella Report argues:

If we do not act positively to remove barriers, we wait indefinitely for them to be removed. This would mean that we are prepared in the interim to tolerate prejudice and discrimination. By not acting, we unfairly ignore how inherently

invalid the exclusionary distinctions are, and we signal our acceptance as a society that stereotypical attributes assigned to these... groups are appropriate justifications for their disproportionate disadvantages.[10]

Finally, if groups or individuals have been disadvantaged in the past, it is not possible to make them equal simply by removing obstacles. For example, when the "separate but equal" doctrine relating to race and education facilities was declared an infringement of equal-protection guarantees in the United States, it did not immediately put Blacks on an equal footing. Years of discrimination, resulting in inferior education, meant that Blacks, on average, could not meet many job standards which were based on "white" educational norms.

The Canadian constitutional guarantee of equal protection of the law, combined with the affirmative action provision, allows governments to intervene against systemic discrimination. Section 15(2) of the Charter can serve as a mechanism by which governments can promote equality. In the first instance, such programs would have effect in the public service and throughout "government", as provided in the Charter's application section.

Although affirmative action is an appropriate means to combat many forms of systemic discrimination, we Commissioners do not wish to imply that it is a panacea for all disadvantaged persons. Affirmative action, as our review in the context of social security (Part V) indicated, is also not without costs to society.

It remains essential to retain and improve measures to equalize opportunities within, as well as among groups. For this reason, affirmative action proposals in labour markets are often accompanied by proposals to improve access to training and employment for the most disadvantaged members of a given sub-group.

A related policy difficulty is defining the disadvantaged group. Statistical categories can be very misleading. "Visible minority" may be one such category. Recent research indicates that on many scores – education, income, mobility, standards of living – there is a great variation among groups defined as "visible minorities". For example, male Filipinos (60 per cent) and Koreans (57 per cent) are much more likely to have attended college or university than Blacks (26 per cent) or Natives (17 per cent). Similarly, in 1980, the salary range of "visible minorities" varied widely: Canadian-born male university graduates of Japanese origin were likely to earn an average salary of $28 202 and their Chinese counterparts a comparable $24 370, in contrast to Canadian-born male university graduates of Indo-Pakistani origin whose average salary was $13 186. These data suggest that programs which do not distinguish among "visible minority" groups may not be directing benefits towards those who need them most.[11]

A further serious drawback to affirmative action – one that must continuously be weighed in the minds of legislators who introduce such programs – is that in favouring one group, they discriminate against another. The Charter permits this discrimination, and Commissioners believe that when a community decides to rectify the situation of its disadvantaged members, it is appropriate that such actions not be barred by the Constitu-

tion. Constitutional permission does not, however, resolve the difficult moral issue that must be faced: Does the desire for group-based equality of results justify the inevitable interference with individual equality of opportunity?

In some situations, systemic discrimination warrants the use of techniques such as affirmative action. Above all, however, Canada is a society committed to individual equality of opportunity. Short-term programs that interfere with this principle are acceptable only because Canadians believe that in the longer run, they contribute to genuine equality of opportunity for all citizens.

This Commission agrees that circumstances exist where inequalities are directly related to membership in some identifiable group within Canadian society. In such circumstances, steps can and should be taken to ameliorate the general conditions of inequality. We wish to emphasize, however, that equality ultimately applies to individual Canadians. The main redress for inequalities and the major emphasis on ensuring equality of opportunities for all Canadians should therefore be through government action in support of the individual as such, and not because he or she is a member of some particular group.

Notes

1. *Bliss* v. *Attorney General of Canada* [1979] 1 S.C.R. 183.
2. Métis and Non-Status Indians Constitutional Review Commission, *Native People and the Constitution of Canada* (Ottawa: Mutual Press, 1981), p. 2.
3. For example, Douglas Sanders, "The Rights of the Aboriginal Peoples of Canada", *Canadian Bar Review* 61 (March 1983), pp. 326–27.
4. For a more complete discussion, see Roger Gibbins and J. Rick Ponting, "An Assessment of the Probable Impact of Aboriginal Self-Government in Canada", in *The Politics of Gender, Ethnicity and Language in Canada*, vol. 34, prepared for the Royal Commission on the Economic Union and Development Prospects for Canada (Toronto: University of Toronto Press, 1985).
5. Canada, Royal Commission on Equality in Employment, *Report* (Ottawa: Minister of Supply and Services Canada, 1984).
6. Canada, House of Commons, Special Committee on Visible Minorities in Canadian Society, *Equality Now* (Ottawa: Queen's Printer, 1980).
7. Canada, House of Commons, Special Committee on the Disabled and the Handicapped, *Obstacles* (Ottawa: The Committee, 1981).
8. Canada, Public Service Commission, *A Report on Equal Opportunity Initiatives – PSC and Departments* (Ottawa, no date), Annex I.
9. Royal Commission on Equality in Employment, *Report*, p. 254.
10. *Ibid.*, p. 5.
11. For more discussion, see the argument of Conrad Winn, "Affirmative Action and Visible Minorities: Eight Premises in Quest of Evidence", forthcoming in *Canadian Public Policy*, from which the data on visible minorities are taken.

The Supreme Court of Canada and the Constitution: Institutional Implications

The Supreme Court of Canada faces demands on its decision-making capacity because of the federal character of our country, differing views on the limits of public action, the evolution of private law, and the introduction of the Canadian Charter of Rights and Freedoms.[1] A number of analysts believe that under the Charter, more policy decisions will be made by Canadian courts. Some, indeed, speak of the "politicization" of the judicial process, and suggest that we should anticipate its continuation. This process partly reflects the gradual "legalization" of society, for since the Second World War, more and more issues which have been drawn into the arena of public debate and conflict find their way to the courts for judicial resolution.

The demands made on the Supreme Court have implications for the structure and design of the judiciary. Commissioners do not believe that the institutional issues of the judiciary are a major national priority for reform. They are important, however, particularly as the role of the Court is seen to be expanding. In our brief review of the major issues, Commissioners wish to underline the need to be sensitive to the character of the judicial process and to the particular responsibilities of courts in our overall institutional framework.

Federalism, the Charter and the Composition of the Supreme Court

Conflicting views about the nature of Canadian society have often focused on the judicial process. Canadian federalism, involving two orders of responsible parliamentary government with overlapping jurisdictions, imposes on the Supreme Court of Canada obligations to decide constitutional matters. The abolition of civil appeals to the Judicial Committee of the Privy Council (JCPC), in 1949, meant the replacement of an external umpire by a Canadian tribunal appointed in accordance with a statute of the Parliament of Canada. At that point the Supreme Court assumed final responsibility for Canadian constitutional interpretation.

In the 1950s and 1960s, little constitutional conflict arose over the division of powers. In the 1970s, however, heightened intergovernmental conflict and increased reliance on regulatory powers greatly increased the volume of constitutional cases before the Court. Governments sought final resolutions or enhanced bargaining power, and private litigants tried to use the distribution of powers to constrain state intervention. On contentious matters, such as energy and constitutional reform, the Court's decisions have been of the highest importance. Inevitably, some observers have expressed concern about the legitimacy of the Court as a federal-provincial umpire. Could a court nominated by one order of government, they demanded, function as an impartial tribunal in division-of-power cases? Though studies of the Court's judgments since 1949 suggest that it has performed this difficult role in a balanced and sensitive manner, concerns of legitimacy continue to arise.

The Court's function in the federal system has given rise to various reform proposals, usually centred on the appointment process, and on the size and composition of the Court from the perspective of representation.

Regional representation was at the heart of most recent recommendations until the Charter of Rights brought new representational claims. At any given time since 1949, the Court has had no justices from five of the provinces and none from either territory. Since 1949, the Court has never included a judge from Newfoundland or Prince Edward Island, and for several decades did not include a judge from British Columbia.

Commentators have put forward claims for extended or more secure regional representation on the Supreme Court. If judges are selected from across Canada, the Court is more likely to be responsive to conditions and developments throughout the country. This argument supposes that a judge's connection with the law of a province or with regional conditions endues him or her with special knowledge of that region or province. This argument is an extension of concerns expressed by Canadians before 1949, when the JCPC in London served as the final court of appeal for Canadian law, including constitutional law. Such a regional pattern of judicial selection might better reflect the federal character of the Canadian Constitution and, it is argued, enhance the acceptability of decisions. Advocacy of this nature has been particularly extensive in recent years as a number of constitutional decisions of great significance to Canadian federalism have been placed in the hands of judges.

The suggestion that regional variations among the judges are important often meets with the reply that this regional quality is difficult to discern and even more difficult to bring to bear on the Court's decision making. Some observers have also criticized the suggestion because it takes no account of the differences within regions. British Columbians may wonder why, for Supreme Court purposes, they have been consigned to the same region as Alberta, Manitoba and Saskatchewan. Newfoundland does not have the same legislative, political, social or legal history as any of the Maritime provinces, yet most regionally oriented proposals would cluster all four provinces together for the purpose of selecting a judge. If geography and knowledge of local conditions actually are important factors in judicial decision making, then perhaps the appointments of justices from Quebec and Ontario should be geographically distributed throughout those two vast and internally diverse provinces. Perhaps members of the bench and bar from outside Toronto and Ottawa or Montreal and Quebec City, should be allocated seats on the Supreme Court bench.

Besides discounting intra-provincial differences, the regionalist approach to judicial appointments also tends to ignore judicial independence. The late Chief Justice Bora Laskin once remarked:

> *It saddened me that there was so little understanding manifested either about the nature of the Court's work or about the significance of the fidelity of its members to their oaths of office, so little appreciation of the importance of cohesion and collegiality in the dispatch of the Court's work. That work has no regional and, certainly, no political tie-in.*[2]

The Supreme Court deals "with national issues, with matters of general public importance that have no special regional connotation." The Court is a national institution, yet in a different sense from the Senate or the federal executive, upon whose actions it may sometimes be required to pass judgment. Furthermore, the argument in favour of emphasizing regional considerations in appointments may be weakened if the Court's role in deciding division-of-powers cases declines relative to its other responsibilities.

This Commission supports a view recently advanced by a leading student of the judicial process:

> *When we consider both the issues which the Supreme Court is called upon to decide as well as the nature of the adjudicative process, it is difficult to accept that the representation of regional interests either could be or should be prominent in the work of the Supreme Court. It seems very doubtful that there is a Western, or Atlantic or Ontario or Quebec position which must be articulated in the Court's deliberations if it is to make sound decisions on the subjects that are coming to dominate the Court's docket – namely, review of the federal administrative process, the interpretation of the Criminal Code and other federal statutes and disputes arising under the Constitution, including the Charter of Rights and the division of powers.*[3]

As the Canadian Bar Association Committee on the Constitution has pointed out, "A court is not a board of arbitration. It is a judicial body."[4] The members of the Supreme Court of Canada do not perform representative functions in the Canadian institutional and constitutional system. Judicial merit alone is the criterion by which the Court's membership and performance should be assessed. Accordingly, Commissioners reject arguments that the composition of the Supreme Court should be regionally representative. Existing provision in the Supreme Court Act for the appointment of Quebec members is based on the distinctive legal traditions of that province, and should be maintained.

Until recently, the Supreme Court's constitutional cases largely consisted of disputes or references about federal and provincial legislative jurisdiction. It was primarily in this context that relations between citizens and the state were adjudicated, although the Court did consider individual cases in relation to the Canadian Bill of Rights. The rise of Charter litigation will probably increase the number of cases involving citizen/state relations. In terms of successful motions for leave to appeal, Charter cases are already outnumbering other constitutional cases. This situation may give rise to new types of representational claims based on the social and economic characteristics of judges. Commissioners also reject these criteria for the selection of Supreme Court judges.

The Supreme Court Appointment Process

The process of appointment to the Supreme Court is frequently confused with the representation issue. That is, those who regard the Supreme Court as a representative body – a view Commissioners reject – also expect the appointment process to be representational. As new representational claims

are made, the appointment process is likely to emerge again as a subject of public concern. We attribute the current relative lack of interest in this issue, which was observable in our hearings, to the high quality of appointments that have been made under existing procedures. Whatever new process may be adopted – and we see no urgent need to replace the current arrangements – the judicial merit of appointees should remain the central criterion.

The chief issue in the appointments process is the perception that it does not adequately involve the constituencies of our political system. Although the existing informal procedures which the Prime Minister follows before he makes appointments to the Supreme Court do involve extensive discussions, some Canadians consider that they take too little account of concerned interests or advice. Numerous options have been put forward.

The *Report* of the Royal Commission on Constitutional Problems[5] (the Tremblay Commission), published in 1956, suggested that provinces should participate in the nomination of Supreme Court judges. The Victoria Charter proposals of 1971 contained a complex formula for securing the agreement of federal and provincial authorities concerning any appointment to the Court. It was recommended that the Attorney-General of Canada consult the Attorney-General of the province with which a potential appointee has the closest connection. If the two failed to agree on an appointee, the Minister of Justice would propose establishment of a nominating council; the choice among possible forms of this council would rest with the provincial Attorney-General. The body would consist primarily of the chief federal and provincial law officers or their nominees. The federal Minister of Justice would submit at least three names to the Council, from which it would make a recommendation. The Special Joint Committee on the Constitution in 1972 endorsed the consultative method set forth in the Victoria Charter, but questioned its failure to allow the provinces to nominate candidates.

Some of Canada's legal scholars favour a form of consultation or collaboration, such as a permanent nominating commission to be used, not just for the Supreme Court of Canada, but for all superior court appointments. The commission could consist of Members of Parliament and of provincial legislatures, representating all political parties, and including non-lawyers. It would maintain a list of suitable prospective appointees from which the appointing authority would choose appointees.

The Constitutional Amendment Bill, proposed in 1978, embodied the proposals of the Victoria Charter and took them one step further. It provided that after the Attorney-General of Canada and the provincial Attorney-General had agreed, or after the nominating council had broken the deadlock over an appointment, the nomination would then be submitted for ratification to a new "House of the Federation" which would replace the existing Senate and would be more representative of our federal diversities. The House would be required to affirm or reject the nomination within a limited time.

Ratification of Supreme Court appointments by a reconstituted upper house gained adherents during the constitutional debate of the 1970s. The Government of British Columbia favoured nomination by the federal government, after consultation with the provinces, and ratification by a reformed Senate. The Canadian Bar Association Committee on the

Constitution, the Pépin-Robarts Task Force on Canadian Unity,[6] and the Beige Paper of the Quebec Liberal Party[7] have made similar proposals.

An Alberta proposal specified that only the provincial governments would suggest appointees to the special constitutional panel it proposed. The Pépin-Robarts Report recommended that the federal Cabinet be required to consult with Quebec's Attorney-General before filling a civil-law vacancy. Where a common-law vacancy occurs, the Cabinet would consult all other nine provincial Attorney-Generals about possible appointees. The variety of suggested reforms is large, but all assume consultation or negotiation with a provincial Attorney-General or provincial representation in a reformed national upper house.

As Charter cases come forward in greater numbers, Commissioners would expect proposals for appointment procedures based on social and economic grounds, just as earlier proposals advocated intergovernmental arrangements. Because the Supreme Court adjudicates cultural, economic and social issues, new methods of selection might assess all "relevant" qualities of a potential appointee. In a research paper prepared for this Commission,[8] the authors discuss the possibility of an Appointing Council that would survey likely candidates and decide who should be named to the Court. Ideally, the Council's members would be diverse in vocational background, age, economic and social status, ideological orientation and racial, ethnic and regional origin. Instead of choosing judges according to region or other sociological criteria, the Appointing Council itself could reflect a cross-section of Canada. Partisan and regional considerations would arise at the time of selecting the members of the Appointing Council, rather than at the stage of judicial appointment. Commissioners are unconvinced, however, that such drastic reform is needed.

The appointment process is inherently political in the broad institutional sense. Measures to shift responsibility from the Prime Minister to some designated group or institution necessarily involve replacing one political process with another. Consistent with our view of the role of Parliament, Commissioners believe that if revised arrangements are to supplement the existing political process of consultation through the Prime Minister, the modified process should involve Parliament and should be equally broad. The elected Senate we have recommended would be an appropriate body to perform the ratification function in a rearranged appointment process. An elected Senate would be both broadly representative and regionally sensitive and thus would largely meet the traditional concerns of the provinces and the socio-economic concerns emerging from the Charter of Rights and Freedoms.

Constitutional Status

While the Supreme Court has some degree of constitutional recognition, as set out in sections 41 and 42 of the Constitution Act, 1982, and in section 101 of the Constitution Act, 1867, it is a matter of controversy whether it is entrenched to the degree that changes in its fundamental features require action by both orders of government. There are several arguments supporting

its more definite constitutional entrenchment. Some Canadians consider it inappropriate that the Court which adjudicates on the division of powers in the federal system is a statutory creation of the federal government. However impartial the Court's record, critics insist, its image of neutrality should be strengthened. Moreover, with the Charter only recently in place, we Canadians should ensure that nothing can block or obstruct judicial power to protect citizens' rights against unconstitutional government action. Constitutional status for the Court would confirm and safeguard its symbolic importance as defender of essential values in Canadian society.

Commissioners recommend explicit entrenchment in the Constitution of the status of the Supreme Court of Canada and, in particular, of its independence, although we believe it inappropriate to remove responsibility for the administration of the Court from the federal government.

Notes

1. See A. Wayne MacKay and Richard W. Bauman, "The Supreme Court of Canada: Reform Implications for an Emerging National Institution", in *The Courts and the Charter*, vol. 58, prepared for the Royal Commission on the Economic Union and Development Prospects for Canada (Toronto: University of Toronto Press, 1985).
2. B. Laskin, "What Everyone Should Know About the Supreme Court of Canada", address to the Empire Club, Toronto, March 12, 1981.
3. Peter H. Russell, "Constitutional Reform of the Judicial Branch: Symbolic vs Operational Considerations", *Canadian Journal of Political Science* 17 (June 1984), pp. 237–38.
4. Canadian Bar Association, Committee on the Constitution, *Towards a New Canada* (Montreal: Canadian Bar Foundation, 1978), p. 60.
5. Quebec, Royal Commission on Constitutional Problems, *Report* (Quebec: Éditeur officiel du Québec, 1956).
6. Canada, Task Force on Canadian Unity, *Report* (Ottawa: Minister of Supply and Services Canada, 1979).
7. The Constitution Committee of the Quebec Liberal Party, *A New Canadian Federation* (Quebec, 1980).
8. MacKay and Bauman, "The Supreme Court of Canada".

CHAPTER 24

The Canadian Constitutional System and Unresolved Community Issues

Canada's Constitutional System and Unresolved Community Issues

Introduction

The political answer to the complex question of our identity as a people has never been static; nor have Canadians reached agreement in this matter. Yet governments, through institutional and legislative changes, must represent and respond to the pluralism of Canadian society even as the components of that pluralism shift in response to factors, often international, over which governments have little control. In 1985 there are pressing community issues on our agenda, several of which Commissioners consider below, together with proposed reforms.

Commissioners intend these reforms to produce a closer fit between the social dimensions of community and the institutional arrangements that express and incorporate them. The way we govern ourselves must reflect the national and provincial communities and the ever-emerging social cleavages within them. The reforms we propose reflect our understanding of the existence of a single Canadian people. A common citizenship brings together people divided by language, ethnicity, sex, province, life-style, income and other sources of diversity. We would like to help encompass these many groups in an institutional framework that does not smother distinctions or stifle conflict, but that does facilitate co-operation and the recognition that Canadians are one people.

The Constitution Act, 1982, with its Charter of Rights, its amending formula and its natural resources clause, was a compromise influenced, notably in the case of the Charter, by citizens' input. Although the Government of Quebec was not a signatory to the agreement that led to the Constitution Act, the Act's provisions are applicable to, and judicially enforceable in, that province. The Government of Quebec, the province that is home for over 80 per cent of French Canadians, does not view the Act as a legitimate part of the Constitution. Its concerns involve both the Charter and

the amending formula. Other political forces in Quebec share these concerns in modified ways. The ground of division, therefore, is not going to go away.

Patriation and the Constitution Act are, accordingly, incomplete achievements. Quebec's unwillingness to agree to the constitutional changes recently introduced is the major unresolved community issue in Canada today. Given the apparent decline in "nationalism" in Quebec, Commissioners suggest that a sympathetic and sensitive response to the province might lead to constitutional *rapprochement*, and we make proposals with the intent of achieving that objective.

In general, the harmonious co-existence of French- and English-speaking Canadians, which would include appropriate institutional and constitutional recognition, requires effort at three levels. First, there must be recognition of the essential role played by the Government of Quebec in cultivating a flourishing French-speaking majority population. Secondly, the national government must reflect Canada's linguistic duality in its overall operations. Thirdly, Canada as a whole, in both its national and its provincial dimensions, must be responsive to, and supportive of, the official-language minorities, francophone outside Quebec and anglophone within.

In addition to institutional questions relating to Quebec and to French-speaking Canadians, other institutional questions arise that relate to Canada's northern territories, to aboriginal self-government and to municipalities. Several significant proposals for change in the organization and structure of governments in Northern Canada have been under consideration for some time. It is appropriate, in Commissioners' view, to encourage the continuation of the processes that are presently under way, with the intent of bringing the governmental arrangements of the Northern territories more into line with practices across the rest of Canada; at the same time, Canadians should implement measures that are sensitive to the distinctive social, economic and cultural features of the region.

In the matter of aboriginal self-government, Commissioners support the introduction of measures to increase the influence and control exercised by Native peoples over their social and economic affairs. This objective is based on the distinctive place aboriginals hold in Canadian society as the first peoples of Canada, and on the constitutional recognition which they now enjoy. It is by no means clear, however, that the implications and consequences of aboriginal self-government as they might affect Canada's overall governing arrangements have been examined with sufficient care. Indeed, there are several areas where further reflection is required.

Canada's local government arrangements vary significantly across the land. This diversity corresponds to differences in size and financial resources and to the fact that local government is constitutionally the responsibility of the provinces. Commissioners note, nevertheless, significant developments in the size, complexity and responsibility of local governments, and we believe that there are a number of measures to consider that would strengthen the capacity of municipalities to make the fullest contribution possible to Canadian society and economic development.

The Place of Quebec in Confederation

Since the beginning of the 1960s, the debate about Quebec's place in Confederation has given rise to considerable discussion in Canada. It is not surprising, therefore, that following the 1980 referendum and set against a backdrop of economic crisis, some Canadians concluded that the dispute had monopolized too much time, and that it should be set aside in favour of the study of other important questions of interest to all Canadians. In fact, with the coming into force of the Constitution Act, 1982, the argument about Quebec faded so far into the background that some Canadians concluded that the problem could solve itself, given an active policy which guaranteed each and every citizen equal linguistic rights. Later attempts to revive the debate seemed not only futile, but also hazardous. Yet, in a matter of a few years, the issue of Quebec's place in Confederation was back on the constitutional agenda. Indeed, circumstances had seldom seemed more propitious for the issue's resolution. The Government of Quebec and the federal government have clearly stated that they wish to reach an agreement. In addition, some provincial premiers have indicated their support for such an initiative. Such demonstrations of good will, while they do not reduce the complexity of the problems involved, at least offer hope that in the near future, a decisive step in the right direction may be taken.

Quebec as a Distinct Society

In order to reach a lasting agreement between Quebec and Canada, one which ensures Quebec's place in Confederation and contributes both to the prosperity of the province and to that of the country as a whole, it is essential from the outset to go beyond the traditional clichés about the unique nature of Quebec. In this way, a realistic interpretation will emerge of the facts which apply to Quebec in 1985. However, two specific pitfalls must be avoided. The first mistake would be to seek a cultural homogeneity which embodies Quebec's distinctiveness: if such homogeneity ever existed, it is certainly no longer characteristic of the province. The second error would be to overlook the collective aspect of the Quebec issue and to view it as a straightforward question of individual rights which could be exercised everywhere in Canada. Since the matter concerns living, working and thriving in a mother tongue, the collective dimension is not to be underestimated.

The period between the beginning of the 1950s and the present has witnessed a fundamental transformation of Quebec society; indeed, a comparison of the report of the Quebec Royal Commission on Constitutional Problems (the 1956 Tremblay Report) and its description of Quebec society with the present reality creates the impression of two entirely different worlds. In 1956, the Tremblay Report described a Quebec which was culturally distinct and essentially rural, and which was characterized by its regard for religious values, its opposition to economic materialism, and its fundamental political conservatism, that is, its opposition to the development of the machinery of government. Behind this facade, however, ideas were

evolving which had not yet attracted a great deal of attention. Various groups and movements were questioning the traditional concept of authority, debating the secularization of the state, and, most notably, considering new economic, social and cultural trends. The end of the Duplessis era and the advent of the 1960s saw the introduction of a major change in Quebec, which took the rest of Canada by surprise: the old structure was crumbling; the traditional power of the clergy was rapidly becoming a thing of the past; and the state was emerging as an instrument of social and economic reform. Quebecers continued to develop and to refine this new instrument up to the beginning of the 1980s: the education system was overhauled; the social security system was thoroughly reviewed; and a pension regime was introduced. Several provincial Crown corporations were established, notably in the economic sector; and, finally, various measures were adopted which had been designed to open Quebec to external influences. The unprecedented defence and recognition of bureaucratic and political machinery as a significant element in the reinforcement of Quebec nationalism were also to give rise to repeated requests for greater provincial constitutional powers.

At the beginning of the 1980s, however, and after the referendum on Quebec's sovereignty, a new situation developed. In the public sector, on the one hand, escalation of the political debate between Quebec and the federal government was blocked. To the extent that Quebec's independence, hypothetical though it was, was set aside as an objective, the ongoing debate about Quebec came to centre on the province remaining in Confederation. Moreover, the apparatus of provincial government was being perceived in a new light: increasingly cumbersome and costly, it was no longer seen as the sole instrument of development for Quebec society. In these circumstances, the quest for expanded constitutional powers abated to some extent, especially since it was quite difficult to exercise fully powers which had already been recognized. On the other hand, and in tandem with these political changes, a new attitude developed concerning the role of the private sector in the economy. Spurred by the increasing number of francophone entrepreneurs making their mark in the traditionally anglophone business world, Quebecers discovered a new interest in business: the old demon of materialism had been exorcised. Indeed, in 1985, nearly 40 per cent of all students seeking Masters' degrees in Business Administration at Canadian universities are Quebecers.

Throughout this period, moreover, the self-image of Quebecers and the social reality of the province underwent substantial changes. Those who had previously described themselves as "French Canadians" took to defining themselves, with increasing frequency, as "Quebecers". A new nationalism appeared, which was less preoccupied with survival, increasingly forward looking, and fundamentally linked to the territory of Quebec. When the Parti québécois came to power, this new nationalism was hailed as the manifestation of the vitality of a society which had at last discovered its identity. Paradoxically, however, the more the provincial government sought the support of a majority of all Quebecers, the clearer it became that ethnic origin could not be the corner-stone of the new nationalism. Indeed, Quebec culture, deeply influenced by common historical experience, has been losing its homogeneity little by little as increasing numbers of immigrants settle in

the province. Moreover, it has been evolving along with Quebec political life, to which it is indissolubly linked. Thus, during the 1960s and 1970s, Quebec culture was oriented around the assertion of a new collective identity. With the arrival of the 1980s, not only has the province's culture become more open and pluralistic but, in the opinion of some observers, its very existence is threatened by the overwhelming influence of American culture. In fact, Quebec's culture has evolved and adapted. Formerly, Quebec defined itself in terms of its opposition to English Canadian culture; increasingly linked to language rather than to ethnic origin, however, the province now seeks a new identity in the North American and international settings.

Another significant change occurred when the position of Quebec's anglophone minority was eroded within a 20-year period by the Quebec government's increased involvement in the linguistic sphere. Quebec anglophones – economically powerful, politically influential and solidly entrenched on the basis of a network of well-developed institutions largely under their control – had traditionally identified themselves as part of the Canadian majority. However, they gradually came to recognize their minority status within the province of Quebec. Moreover, the exodus from Quebec of a considerable number of anglophones, because of the combined effects of Bill 101 and the economic recession, contributed to the further weakening of the position of this minority. Such a trend was not, in fact, new: Quebec's anglophone population, standing, in 1981, at approximately 11 to 12.5 per cent of its total residents, has been constantly decreasing for a hundred years. At the turn of the century, for example, the population of Quebec City, the Eastern Townships and certain rural districts had included substantial anglophone minorities; but the numbers of these minorities have decreased over the years. What is new is the acceleration of this trend: between 1971 and 1981, there was a decrease of 10 per cent in the anglophone population of the province, which is now largely concentrated in the city of Montreal.

At the beginning of the 1980s, the anglophone minority sensed that its survival in Quebec was threatened in much the same way that francophones had perceived that their survival was threatened 20 years before. Quite soon, however, a new consciousness of its affiliation to Quebec appeared. On the anglophone minority's conviction that it had contributed to the province's development in the past was superimposed the awareness of a new role to be played and of added responsibilities to be assumed. Increasingly bilingual and influenced by organizations such as Alliance Quebec, the anglophone minority defined its new identity in Quebec, thus contributing to the transformation of Quebec society as a whole. A new image of Montreal gradually emerged: that of a city with a majority francophone population, but also a multi-ethnic and bilingual city, rich in its diversity, vigorous in its culture and economy, and open to the world.

Nevertheless, some problems remain unsolved. Bill 101 in particular, to the extent that it projects the image of a unilingual Quebec, is the object of repeated attacks by the anglophone minority. The members of this group will not accept second-class status. Under the terms of the Constitution Act, 1867, the province is officially bilingual with respect to its legislative and judicial institutions. That stipulation does not make either Quebec's refusal to

recognize English as an official language in the province or the restrictions imposed on the use of English in the sphere of communications more acceptable to the anglophone minority. The very severity of some of their attacks on Bill 101 is worrying and, unfortunately, is sometimes perceived as an indication that what is sought is a return to the situation which existed prior to 1960. In the changing Quebec of the 1980s, reciprocal trust has perhaps begun to emerge between the francophone majority and the anglophone minority, but it must become more firmly established.

In view of all these changes, Canadians may well wonder what is left of Quebec's uniqueness. To answer this question, we must return to basics. At the outset, Quebec's chief characteristic is the presence within its boundaries of a majority francophone population which controls and determines the orientation of its political and social institutions. The fact of the majority status of francophones in Quebec as compared to their minority status outside that province is fundamental. As the editor of *Le Devoir* wrote recently, "If it is true that the Canadian duality transcends geographic boundaries, it is equally true that it would lose all its meaning if Quebec were to disappear tomorrow."[1] Behind this observation, however, lies a still more basic reality which defines the very essence of Quebec society. As the principal, though not the exclusive, centre of politically structured French life in Canada, Quebec society remains fundamentally and linguistically isolated, an island of French life in the anglophone mainstream. Once outside Quebec, living and working in French and, in more general terms, flourishing in French, becomes difficult, except in some parts of New Brunswick and Ontario which border Quebec. This difficulty continues, despite the significant progress in the provision of bilingual education and public service realized during recent years. A Statistics Canada study based on final census data for 1981 has recently confirmed some researchers' conclusions that the French language is losing ground everywhere in Canada with the exception of Quebec.[2]

Because of its isolation, Quebec is unavoidably committed to never-ending negotiations and accommodations with its external environment. For nearly two centuries, Quebec dealt with the world around it by turning inward and rejecting external values. More recently, following the Quiet Revolution, a new basis for accommodation was set out in the sovereignty-association proposal of the Parti québécois. Considered too radical by a majority of citizens, this proposal was rejected in favour of a kind of renewed federalism with the rest of Canada. This development, however, has not materialized. As a result, Quebec remains constitutionally isolated, in the sense that the provincial government has not yet accepted the 1982 constitutional accord. It is encouraging that the recent *rapprochement* between Quebec and the federal government indicates a mutual desire to end this isolation.

The arrangement which is likely to be worked out will be especially important from a symbolic point of view. As a response to Quebecers' clear expression of their wish to associate with the rest of Canada, as indicated in the 1980 referendum, the new compromise will be all the more meaningful if constitutional recognition is given to the counterpoint of Quebec's uniqueness and its right to retain its differences. Above and beyond this recognition of the distinctive nature of Quebec society, it is the existence of the whole

francophone community, in other words, of Canada's basic duality, which is at stake. Notwithstanding such recognition, the fundamental linguistic isolation of this community will endure. The essential question for Quebec and for francophones outside Quebec will remain unchanged: How can the French element of our populations retain its identity in North America? If a satisfactory answer is to be worked out, some important problems will have to be resolved in practice. If, for example, Quebec's economy does not provide the opportunities for employment which francophones need in order to thrive in their language, if the francophone intellectual contribution finds no outlet outside of Quebec, and if the efforts of Quebec to develop economic and cultural links with the outside world are discouraged, then Quebec society, confined as it is, will be in danger of stagnation. The recognition of Quebec's unique character and of Canada's dualistic nature, however, constitutes an affirmation that with the support of the rest of Canada, solutions to these problems can be found. Above all, both Quebecers and francophones outside of Quebec must themselves, individually and collectively, find these answers in the economic and cultural spheres. The new element will be that this search for answers will take place in a context of recognition and affirmation of the cultural complementarity which is, after all, at the heart of the Canadian experience.

There is, therefore, an unforeseen opportunity to conclude a new agreement between Quebec and the rest of Canada. At the outset, what is required in principle is a statement in the preamble of the Constitution which might be worded along the following lines:

> *Recognizing the distinctive character of Quebec society as the principal though not the exclusive centre for Canadian francophones and accepting as fundamental the duality of the Canadian federation . . .*

At the time of the 1980 constitutional negotiations, participants in intensive discussions on this subject came close to reaching consensus. Commissioners believe that in 1985, on the basis of a text such as the one we have just suggested, such an agreement could be reached quickly enough.

Thereafter, the problems arising from Quebec's distinctive character could be considered. Precisely because they are specific to Quebec and interest the rest of Canada only indirectly, their solution would not, for the most part, necessitate constitutional changes. Some problems could be adequately dealt with through intergovernmental agreements, others through delegation of power. The compilation of a complete list would be impossible, as new problems continue to arise. However, one issue which Canadians must address without delay and in some detail is that of fundamental guarantees, since it relates directly to the constitutional agreement of 1982.

Fundamental Guarantees

When the Constitution Act, 1982 came into force, Quebec once again found itself in the position of saying no to the rest of Canada. This resistance, however, unlike Quebec's earlier opposition to the Fulton-Favreau formula and to the Victoria Charter, did not result in an escalation of the debate with

the rest of Canada, for the ultimate threat, that of independence, had been dissipated two years earlier. From that time on, the issue of the recovery of the right of veto in Quebec, or rather of the concession of a right of veto (for the right which the province believed it had was denied by the Supreme Court several months later), became an essential condition for the resumption of the dialogue. For a minority group within the Canadian collectivity – as Quebecers were frequently told they were – the possibility of saying no and of exercising a veto inevitably assumes fundamental significance in the face of the firm will of the majority. It should not be surprising that this issue recurs. Deeply rooted in Quebec's political culture, the veto right effectively provides the guarantee that basic foundations will not be undermined.

Clearly, however, to revive discussion of the right of veto is not an easy matter. At the end of 1982 and the beginning of 1983, the possibility of guaranteeing a right of veto for Quebec had been considered, but it had to be set aside when some provinces expressed reservations about the resumption of negotiations on this subject. No doubt it was still too early to initiate such a discussion. With the perspective of several years, however, and with the benefit of a clearer appreciation of the necessity for resolving the issue of Quebec's adherence to the Constitution Act, 1982, to disentangle the elements of viable solutions certainly no longer appears to be an impossible undertaking.

The ultimate goal would be to act so that in the future, Quebec would not have a constitutional amendment imposed upon it which would, in its view, affect its essential interests as a distinct society. To accomplish this objective, two approaches are possible. The first is that of the right of veto as such, which permits a province to block the general adoption of a constitutional amendment. The second is the right to opt out, which does not preclude the adoption of an amendment; rather, it shelters those provinces which exercise the right to opt out from the effects of that amendment. It is widely believed, however, that in order for the opting out provision to be perceived as the equivalent of the right of veto, the former provision must entail full compensation for supplementary costs incurred. Such costs will differ according to circumstances and will often prove difficult to estimate. It cannot be claimed, for example, that a province which refuses to relinquish an element of its jurisdiction will assume new costs directly; rather, the penalty will result from the fact that citizens in the province will eventually find that they are being taxed for federal services which are not being provided there. On the other hand, where a straightforward regulatory power is relinquished, these costs may be insignificant as, for example, in the hypothetical case where an amendment grants the federal Parliament the exclusive right to incorporate companies or to establish safety standards applicable to consumer goods. The current amending formula recognizes the right to opt out with compensation when provincial legislative responsibilities in the fields of "education and other cultural matters" are transferred to Parliament. In effect, Quebec has the equivalent of a veto in these spheres. It remains to be seen whether the same formula can be extended to other jurisdictional sectors which devolve on the provinces from the Constitution. To respond adequately

to this question, however, we must first consider the advantages and disadvantages of adopting such a course.

The main advantage of a general right of opting out with full compensation is found in the formula's marked flexibility. Those provinces which favour a constitutional amendment, provided that there are enough of them, can achieve their goal without interference from those which disagree. The latter group can express its opposition without being penalized for doing so. Moreover, the formula respects the principle of the equality of provinces, each of which has the right to opt out. However, it also has disadvantages which are far from insignificant. In particular, it entails the very real risk of a proliferation of special status arrangements. This danger is inherent even in the current formula, which provides the right to opt out without compensation; extension of that formula to include an entitlement to generalized compensation obviously entails a greater risk. Having said this, we should not overestimate the risk. Constitutional amendments requiring a transfer of jurisdiction from provincial legislatures to Parliament are still quite rare, and, in the last resort, the federal government is always entitled to delay presentation of an amendment until it is certain of the support of the majority of provinces. Another difficulty arising from this formula is that it requires negotiation on the extent of compensation; in the case of disagreement, we might assume that for the time being, the federal government's offer would prevail unless the matter is eventually appealed to the courts. In other respects, it is possible that the exercise of the right to opt out would, in certain circumstances, have practically the same effect as a right of veto. This would apply especially where the objective was to find a uniform solution for the whole of Canada. Finally, it should be stressed that the formula of opting-out with full compensation would not apply to amendments affecting national institutions; the Constitution Act, 1982 explicitly precludes the right of opting out in such instances. Bearing in mind these factors, it may now be interesting to consider whether a right of veto as such meets Quebec's need for protection in a more satisfactory manner.

Like the possibility of opting-out, that of the right of veto presents both advantages and disadvantages. Since the right of veto leads directly to the rejection of a proposed amendment, it can in no sense result in a proliferation of special status. Moreover, if this right of veto were granted on a broader basis, as in the Victoria Charter formula, no exclusive advantage would accrue to Quebec. The Victoria formula required the agreement, not only of a majority of provinces, but also that of each province which had ever had a population constituting 25 per cent of the country's total population, a provision which applied to Quebec. This formula also required the assent of two of the Atlantic provinces and of two of the Western provinces, provided that the combined populations of the latter totalled at least 50 per cent of the entire population of the four Western provinces. On the negative side, the right of veto allows one or several provinces, depending on the formula used, to obstruct the course favoured by the majority. If this right is granted to Quebec, it might be perceived as placing an unwarranted restraint on constitutional change, in light of Quebec's traditional stance. Finally, the

right of veto, even granted on a regional basis in accordance with the Victoria formula, would create an imbalance between those provinces which can exercise it individually and those which can only do so by aligning themselves with others. The only solution to this problem would be to grant the right of veto to each one of the provinces, thereby risking a constitutional impasse.

Could the provision of a right of veto to the Province of Quebec alone be acceptable in certain circumstances? An interesting hypothesis, recently put forward,[3] would modify the current amending procedure so that when changes to national institutions or transfers of provincial legislative powers were proposed, but no compensation was offered, Quebecers would retain a collective right of veto, to be exercised by means of a referendum. In recognition of the importance of such a decision, a designated special majority might be required. The responsibility for deciding whether such public consultation was necessary would rest with the Government of Quebec, whose task it would be to choose between the opting-out formula, where applicable, and the right of veto subject to confirmation by referendum. This concept has the fundamental advantage of substantially retaining the present amending formula while still protecting the essential interests of Quebec. The referendum would also introduce an element of participatory democracy, which tends to make the use of a right of veto more acceptable. A variant of this formula might delegate to the Quebec National Assembly the responsibility for deciding whether or not to invoke the right of veto, provided that such a decision was supported by a majority of two-thirds or three-quarters of the members.

Another proposal, which was put forward by the Government of Ontario several years ago, would require, as a prerequisite for any constitutional amendment, the approval of two-thirds of the provinces, representing 85 per cent of Canada's population. In effect, such a formula would give Quebec a right of veto, since that province's population is scarcely likely to decline to less than 15 per cent of the total population of Canada. This proposal was rejected, however, because it meant, among other things, that the opposition of three of the four Atlantic provinces would not suffice to defeat an amendment.

Still other solutions could be considered. From whatever vantage point Canadians examine the problem, it must be acknowledged that the granting of a minimal guarantee to Quebec entails, in one sense or another, a political cost. If resolution of the situation requires, at all costs, the retention of the principle of provincial equality, there are concurrent risks: special status arrangements could multiply if the right of opting out with full compensation is generalized; or the Canadian Constitution could remain fixed in its present form if all the provinces are given an identical right of veto. Alternatively, to grant the right of veto either on a regional basis, in accordance with the Victoria Charter, or only to the province of Quebec would inevitably undermine the principle of provincial equality, a principle which was hard won by the Western and Atlantic provinces during recent constitutional negotiations.

In these circumstances, which solution should be chosen? For a number of people, the Victoria amending formula is still the one which seems to go

furthest towards reconciling the concerned parties' interests, including those of Quebec. It is unfortunate that at present, it seems hardly possible to return to the Victoria formula, given the unequivocal opposition of some provinces during the 1981 constitutional negotiations. Moreover, since the effect of the current amending formula will not be clear until after it has been tested, it seems unlikely that a return to the Victoria formula can receive serious consideration prior to the constitutional conference which must, by 1997 at the latest, re-examine the whole issue of constitutional amendment. In the meantime, the simplest way of providing Quebec with the guarantee it requires, without jeopardizing the principle of provincial equality, is to give each province the right to opt out with full compensation in every case. This solution, which had the support of eight of the ten provinces in 1981, still seems to be the most acceptable to all of them. Furthermore, most of the pitfalls inherent in this formula are also found in the current amending formula. Commissioners therefore recommend this second formula as the preferred solution with regard to jurisdictional transfers from the provincial legislatures to Parliament.

Where changes in national institutions are concerned, the opting-out formula is inapplicable by virtue of the Constitution Act, 1982. The only way to afford Quebec protection would be to grant it a right of veto. If we assume, once again, that a return to the Victoria formula is impossible in the short term, the only other possibilities would be to grant a right of veto either to all the provinces or exclusively to Quebec. Clearly, the easiest solution would be to grant a right of veto to all the provinces as now pertains, for example, in the matter of determining the composition of the Supreme Court of Canada. This solution might prove costly, however, since it could immobilize our institutions for a prolonged period. To grant a right of veto to Quebec alone would be more difficult politically, but at the same time, it would conform more closely to the desired objective insofar as we acknowledge and seek to protect the distinctive character of Quebec society. From this perspective, every constitutional change which reduces the constitutional guarantees granted to Quebec and related to its special nature could be the object of a right of veto. Thus, if a double-majority formula were introduced in the operation of the Senate for certain defined purposes, Quebec's right of veto would prevent a reduction of this protection without that province's consent. Indeed, the introduction of the double-majority formula in the Senate could itself serve as a right of veto. One possible way to accomplish this would be to change section 47 of the Constitution Act, 1982, to grant the Senate an effective right of veto in cases involving changes covered by the double-majority rule. Whatever solution is chosen, however, Commissioners believe that it is important for Quebec to have protection in the matter of any amendment to institutions described in section 42(1) of the Constitution Act, 1982, insofar as such amendments call into question the special character of Quebec and the duality of Canada.

Both the guarantees relating to the amending process and the recognition in the Constitution's preamble of Quebec's uniqueness should facilitate Quebec's approval of the 1982 constitutional accord. Nevertheless, in order for a lasting agreement to be concluded between Quebec and Ottawa, other

issues must be resolved, some relating to national institutions, others to the division of legislative powers. We do not intend to examine every one of these matters here: to do so would be to exceed the mandate of this Commission. It may be useful, however, to consider briefly the means for ensuring that the fundamental interests of Quebec are taken into consideration within federal parliamentary institutions.

We have mentioned the possibility that the Senate might be granted a veto in relation to language matters. Such an idea is not new. In 1978, Bill C-60 and, more recently, the Report of the Special Joint Committee on Senate Reform supported the proposal that any bill with linguistic implications should require the endorsement of a double majority in the Senate, that is, a majority of all Senators and a majority of francophone Senators. Such a measure would positively contribute to reassuring Quebec and francophones outside Quebec that the French language would be protected. In effect, apart from the right of veto granted, the mere fact of having to decide in certain cases whether legislation has linguistic significance would inevitably draw attention to this particular aspect of federal legislation. The new visibility thus accorded to the linguistic dimension of federal interventions would provide a supplementary means of protection for Quebec and for all francophones in the rest of Canada. As was pointed out in the Report of the Special Joint Committee, such a double-majority formula could not be adopted without creating certain problems, particularly with regard to the development of conflict-resolution procedures, the identification of francophone senators, and the criteria to be used for determining which bills should be subject to the double-majority rule. The advantages, however, seem clearly to outweigh the disadvantages. Commissioners are therefore prepared to recommend the adoption of a proposal that "legislation of linguistic significance", or, more precisely, every legislative Act concerning the French language and related cultural questions, should require the ratification of a double majority in the Senate.

As far as the House of Commons is concerned, Quebec's relatively large population has always assured it a significant influence in this elected Chamber. However, the birth rate in Quebec has now declined to such an alarming extent that there is talk of a day when the province might no longer represent 20 per cent of the population of Canada. It is only a single step from that point to considering a provision which would guarantee Quebec a given proportion of seats in the Commons. Such a step, however, must not be taken too hastily. In effect, such forecasts are long-term ones, and many circumstances can change in the short term. On the other hand, the remaining Canadian provinces, with the exception of Prince Edward Island, the smallest one, have always accepted the consequences of representation proportional to the size of their population, and it is unlikely that they would now agree to exempt Quebec from the principle. If the position of Quebec were to become truly critical in the future, there would always be an opportunity to reconsider the matter. For the moment, the protection accorded by the double-majority rule in the Senate, as suggested above, seems adequate, since it would operate regardless of the actual number of francophones in Canada.

Problems Related to the Division of Powers

The problems related to the division of powers, on the other hand, raise more immediate problems, which will require for their resolution not only considerable imagination but also a real willingess to compromise. The experience of the last 15 years has tended to show that where real compromise is sought in an essentially functional perspective, as with Family Allowances and immigration, solutions can be found: agreements may be defined in bilateral accords or in some form of delegation, two methods of co-operation be formally recognized which this Commission has recommended earlier for inclusion in the Constitution. Alternatively, agreements may be defined by the more complex process of constitutional amendment. In either event, the long-term results will more often than not reflect both parties' desire for co-operation. This does not mean, of course, that points of disagreement will not arise. The several problems cited below, insofar as can be determined, are of interest to other provinces as well as to Quebec. There is no doubt, however, that they are matters of special importance to Quebec.

Quebec will always regard certain sectors, such as education, as highly sensitive. Thus, with regard to the question of minority-language education, the Government of Quebec continues to believe that the coming into force of the Charter deprived it of an important part of its jurisdiction. Before Quebec endorses the Constitution Act, 1982, it may seek certain changes in section 23. Access to English-language education for the brothers and sisters of a child who has received part of his or her education in English in another province is stipulated in section 23(2). It seems to be feared that this arrangement could quite easily be used with the sole aim of side-stepping the linguistic regulations imposed by the province in the field of education. However, the Supreme Court has already ruled that the Quebec clause decreed by Bill 101 is unconstitutional with respect to section 23(1)(*b*) and section 23(2) of the Charter. It will undoubtedly prove difficult now to reopen discussion of the Canada clause, the more so because, as even the Government of Quebec admits, this clause does not threaten the linguistic balance in the province. Furthermore, under section 41 of the Charter and subject to section 43, which concerns amendment of provisions relating to some, but not all provinces, any amendment to the Constitution of Canada pertaining to the use of the English or the French language requires the unanimous consent of the provinces. One possible way to re-open the debate might be to broaden the issue so as to include the discussion of section 23(1)(*a*), which accords the right to minority-language education to Canadian citizens "whose first language learned and still understood is that of the English or French linguistic minority population of the province in which they reside." This section remains to be ratified by Quebec under the procedure of section 59. Whatever the approach used, however, it will be difficult to negotiate a satisfactory arrangement without at some point involving the linguistic minorities themselves.

If we proceed beyond this question to consider a much more far-reaching problem, such as the establishment of "national standards" in education, we can readily imagine Quebec's reaction: such a project will be viewed *a priori*

as a serious attack on its exclusive jurisdiction. This attitude, we must recognize, is not new. During the 1950s, Premier Duplessis refused to accept federal government subsidies for the province's universities. More recently, in 1984, the universities of Quebec took a similar stand concerning some subsidies provided by the federal government for the development of centres of excellence. In co-operation with the Government of Quebec, these institutions had submitted a list of proposals with an assigned order of priority. The federal government changed this order of priority. Because this change was considered an act of unwarranted interference, the universities agreed to accept the funding offered, but announced that they would place it in trust until an agreement was reached between Quebec and the federal government. The change of government in the autumn of 1984 resolved this problem, for the new federal government accepted the Quebec universities' original order of priority in its entirety. Canadians should not conclude from this disagreement, however, that Quebec is opposed to any co-operation with the federal government and the other provinces in the search for national standards in education. Nevertheless, education is clearly a field where Quebec believes that it has very special interests to protect, and where it will agree to consider itself bound only by formulae which do not threaten what it views as its own ultimate responsibility. Bearing in mind the serious concerns about the quality of education in Canada which many Canadians have expressed to this Commission, it seems highly desirable to seek without delay means of reaching agreement between Quebec and the federal government. In this manner, the excellence sought by all concerned Canadians may be achieved.

Similarly, it is foreseeable that in such fields as international affairs and communications, Quebec will continue to assert its traditional views in order to gain more room to manœuvre. Isolated on a predominantly anglophone continent, Quebec has no choice but to seek contact with the outside world and, in particular, with the international francophone community. However, efforts made in that direction during the last two decades have provoked some adverse reactions in the federal government: Quebec's aims have not always been considered compatible with federal responsibility in the field of external affairs. At present, a certain *modus vivendi* seems to have been reached. Sooner or later, however, the real question will have to be considered, that is, the issue of Quebec's role in this field in relation to that of the rest of Canada. Similarly, there is the matter of Quebec's role in communications, an especially critical field for the future of Quebec's culture. Major developments that have taken place in the last 15 years in the communications field, such as cable television, computer technology and video films, afford a glimpse of the increasingly important penetration into Quebec of the English language. Determined efforts must be made, in close co-operation with other francophone countries, to halt this process by further encouraging both the development of original French material and the translation into French of material in other languages. Otherwise, there may be serious consequences for the future of the French language and French culture in Quebec and Canada. In these two areas, working solutions can easily be developed by

recourse to the previously mentioned instruments of delegation or intergovernmental agreements.

Finally, in the economic realm, the major problem will be to provide employment for a population whose mobility is restricted because of language. The unrestricted movement of people which is now guaranteed by the Constitution may be a reality in the rest of Canada, but it remains theoretical where francophone Quebecers are concerned. Between 1976 and 1981, whether because they did not speak English or because they wished to avoid assimilation, fewer than 1 per cent of francophone Quebecers left the province temporarily or permanently to settle elsewhere in Canada.[4]

To recognize the problem is one thing; to find a solution is another. In the wake of *The Report of the Commission of Inquiry on the Position of the French Language and on Language Rights in Quebec* (the Gendron Report) and in direct application of the principles set out in the white paper entitled *La politique de la langue française*, published several years ago, the Government of Quebec launched an extensive campaign designed to enhance the position of French as the language of work. While it is undeniable that the status of the French language and of francophones in Quebec has improved considerably in recent years, it has not been conclusively shown that the recent language legislation is the principal source of such improvement. Nevertheless, it is certain that these measures have had an effect,[5] most notably in the form of initiatives taken by the business community whether indirectly, in anticipation of legislative changes, or directly, in response to the introduction of language legislation. However, other factors, too, have played a part. These include the growth of francophone-controlled businesses and the development of the private sector within the province. A complete picture should also reflect the loss of jobs resulting from the movement of head offices, a shift caused by the implementation of these provincial language policies, even though, in some instances, the real reasons for these relocations may have been quite different. Whatever the degree of effectiveness of these policies, it is doubtful that they could be entirely abandoned in the immediate future. In some respects, they can be viewed as affirmative-action programs designed to improve employment opportunities for Quebec's francophones. In the long run, however, the economic prospects of Quebec's francophones will depend much more on the vitality of Quebec's private sector. The new entrepreneurship which has developed in Quebec in recent years provides good reason to be hopeful on this point. Because of its outward-looking perspective, this new entrepreneurship could contribute not only to the development of Quebec's economy, but also to its greater involvement both in the Canadian economy and in the North American economy as a whole.

Francophone Communities outside Quebec

The problem becomes much more complex when we turn to the situation of francophone communities outside Quebec. Admittedly, the Canadian Charter of Rights and Freedoms has afforded these communities certain individual guarantees in the fields of education and government services. It must be

acknowledged, however, that the ability to flourish as communities remains inextricably linked to the development, in various provinces, of active and diversified institutions which contribute to the establishment and meet the underlying needs of a genuine francophone milieu for francophones. In this regard, the situation varies dramatically from one province to another. In New Brunswick, which is well equipped from this point of view, francophone communities enjoy a relatively favourable position with a very low assimilation rate. The farther one goes from Quebec, however, the more difficulty public and private institutions experience in consolidating scattered communities which offer progressively fewer opportunities to work in French. The latest report of the Commissioner of Official Languages and a recent study by Statistics Canada agree that the assimilation rate is so high in some provinces that the affected francophone communities are in danger of disappearing completely in the foreseeable future. Indeed, the situation can, in certain respects, be considered critical.

Can this trend be arrested? Or must we Canadians resign ourselves to the sight of francophone communities outside Quebec disappearing one after another? Such a result would document the defeat not only of a government policy, but also of a vision of Canada shared by a great many citizens: that of a country in which linguistic and cultural communities are valued to such a degree that they are accorded constitutional protection. Clearly, prompt action is required.

For a start, it is essential to reaffirm Canada's commitment to the principle of linguistic duality. In order to do so, it is necessary, on the one hand, to recognize the dual nature of Canada in the preamble of the Constitution as suggested above and, on the other hand, to promote the acceptance of French and English as official languages in the greatest possible number of provinces. In this regard, there is no doubt that if Ontario should decide to make such a move, the effects would be felt not only in that province, but throughout the rest of Canada, and that these effects would increase support for the principle of linguistic duality. Commissioners cannot stress sufficiently the importance we attach to the extension of the principle of bilingualism in Ontario, which has the largest francophone minority. If it is unrealistic in other respects to believe that all the provinces will someday demonstrate the level of commitment assumed constitutionally by Quebec and New Brunswick, it is certainly not unreasonable to hope that, given conditions appropriate to each of them, basic guarantees will be offered to their linguistic minority.

Beyond the principles and symbols, however, lies the reality. Whereas very real progress has been made in the last 15 years in affirming the bilingual character of Canada, these results nonetheless vary greatly, depending on the sector or region involved. In general, they clearly fall somewhat short of true equality. Another part of this Report, which deals with equality, provides an analysis of the situation of bilingualism in Canada. Generally speaking, however, it suffices to consult the reports of the Commissioner of Official Languages to determine how difficult and delicate a process the implementation of bilingualism in the federal public administration has proved to be. Similarly, at the provincial level, recent problems encountered in Manitoba

and New Brunswick attest to the complexity of any strategy designed to make linguistic equality a reality in Canada.

Must we then conclude that the introduction of official bilingualism in Canada proceeded too quickly, and that there is now a need to mark time in this area? Some Canadians, who object to the considerable costs entailed by such a policy, and who fear the emotional reactions to which it gives rise, would favour such delay. In our view, however, such a solution would call into question the gains already made. On the contrary, the need is to seek to do more for bilingualism and, especially, in a more effective way.

A first means by which this end may be accomplished is the judicial one. Under section 133 of the Constitution Act, 1867, section 23 of the Manitoba Act of 1870, or sections 16 to 23 of the Canadian Charter of Rights and Freedoms, individuals could go to the courts to seek a judgement upholding their fundamental linguistic rights. In fact, during the past ten years, several such judgements have reminded the various governments concerned of their duties in the matter of linguistic rights. But this solution requires a long and arduous journey, and, unfortunately, one that sometimes fails to achieve results. Moreover, in the Ontario Reference Case, based on section 23 of the Canadian Charter of Rights and Freedoms, the Ontario Court of Appeal held that the judicial authority is not the only custodian of Canadians' constitutional rights, and that Parliament and the legislatures also have responsibilities in the field of linguistic rights. The court added: "Minority linguistic rights should be established by general legislation assuring equal and just treatment to all, rather than by litigation."[6]

In view of this comment, we Commissioners believe that above all, it is up to Parliament and the federal government to set the example if only because of the experience they have gained in the application of the Official Languages Act. More specifically, the Commissioner of Official Languages should be encouraged to pursue vigorously the job of educating the public, as well as overseeing the implementation of the pertinent acts and regulations. In this connection, the recommendations put forward by the Special Joint Committee on Official Languages should be seen as evidence of the need to upgrade the Commissioner's position in terms of both mandate and resources. These various recommendations should, insofar as possible, receive government support.

The fact remains that despite all these efforts, the scattered nature and small populations of francophone communities outside Quebec make the survival of some of them as French-language environments very problematic. *La Fédération des francophones hors Québec*, especially sensitive to this aspect of the problem, published a report several years ago, entitled *Une espace économique à inventer*, in which it presented recommendations designed to strengthen the economic underpinnings of francophone communities outside Quebec. Shortly afterwards, in 1982, the Federation organized a national symposium on the economy. More recently still, another conference on the subject "From Linguistic Protection to Economic Development" was held at the University of Moncton. What emerged from the Federation's report, as well as from the symposia, was a clear sense of the

importance of establishing an economic "space" where it will be possible for Canadian francophones outside Quebec to live, work and develop their culture in French.

This orientation bears out the conclusions of some research undertaken on this Commission's behalf, which found that the survival of Canadian francophone communities outside Quebec depends on establishing centres of activity structured around public and private francophone institutions. Here again, it would be unrealistic to believe that all francophone communities outside Quebec could develop such centres of activity by using a single model. For some provinces, such centres would have a basically cultural orientation: they would develop to the greatest extent by successfully integrating the largest possible number of Canadians who now have a working knowledge of French and those who have attended French-immersion courses. In other provinces, notably Ontario and New Brunswick, the economic component, which enhances the cultural aspect, will necessarily be more important. Just as in Quebec, however, it is, above all, the individual initiative of francophones themselves which will bring about such a development. Government support, however useful it may be, will never take the place of individual initiative. Commissioners believe that there must be movement in this direction if the long-term survival of francophone communities outside Quebec is to be ensured.

Conclusions

Beyond all the problems to which Commissioners have alluded, and which are in some ways inherent parts of Canada's political development process, we must emphasize our country's inestimable richness embodied in the complementary relationship between its two chief linguistic groups. It is now time to turn the page which records the past history of Quebec's relations with the rest of Canada and to begin another to record the new era of co-operation. With the recognition of the duality of Canadian society and the distinctive character of Quebec society, it seems inevitable that problems will continue to arise in the future, but it also seems likely that these problems will be solved as a by-product of the search for the parties' common interest.

Notes

1. Jean-Louis Roy, *Le Devoir*, October 6, 1984, p. 11.
2. Jean Laponce, "The French Language in Canada: Tensions Between Geography and Politics", *Political Geography Quarterly* (1984): 91–104.
3. Jacques Frémont, *Le Devoir*, May 9, 1984, p. 11.
4. Mireille Baillargeon, "Évolution et caractéristiques linguistiques des échanges migratoires interprovinciaux et internationaux de Québec, 1971" (Quebec: Conseil de la langue française, 1983), Table 4.
5. See François Vaillancourt, "Statut du français et des francophones au Québec: 1960–1980" (Montreal, 1984).
6. Reference Re Education Act of Ontario and Minority Language Education Rights, (1984) 10 D.L.R. (4th): 491–547.

The Northern Territories

While this Commission has looked, in general, at the problems facing Canada from a national rather than a regional perspective, the situation of Canada's Northern territories merits special attention because it is unique within the federation and within the Canadian economic union, and because most Canadians lack a full appreciation of the challenges facing Northerners. The North is of inestimable significance to the future of the Canadian economy. Although the high cost of developing non-renewable resources will probably prevent dramatic growth over the medium term, the vast northern territories have untapped resources that will help to supply Canada's industrial raw materials and energy fuels long into the next century. They are also the homeland of Canadians of many origins and of a rich blend of cultural characteristics. The interests and aspirations of Northerners must be accommodated within any strategy for the development of Canada's economic wealth.

In some ways, the success with which political leaders integrate competing national and regional interests in the Northwest Territories (NWT) and Yukon will be one of the most important tests of our Canadian federation over the next two decades. The fundamental issues of collective rights versus individual rights and of national unity versus regional diversity are crystalized in the North today. The mistakes made elsewhere in the federation over many years can be avoided in the North because there the slate is almost clean. The opportunity remains to find solutions to many of the dilemmas that plague the politics of southern Canada and to make the northern jurisdictions a symbolic demonstration of the kinds of creative solutions possible within the context of Canada's institutional framework.

Before commenting on and making recommendations about the special issues and problems of the Northwest Territories and Yukon, Commissioners wish to review some general background about the North: its people, its economy, its politics and its special constitutional relationship to the rest of Canada.[1]

Background: Society, Economy and Culture

Northern Society

As we Commissioners learned from our hearings and discussions in several northern communities, to understand Northern issues requires an appreciation of the internal diversity of the North. The Northwest Territories and Yukon are dissimilar in many respects, and even within the Northwest Territories there are significant differences among the Mackenzie Valley, the Mackenzie Delta-Beaufort Sea, Kitikmeot, Keewatin, Baffin and high Arctic regions. Hence, while this Commission will make some generalizations, it recognizes the North as a vast and diverse area.

About 47 000 Canadians live in the Northwest Territories and approximately 23 000 in Yukon: a mere 70 000 souls scattered across an area comprising approximately 40 per cent of Canada's land mass. Not only is our

Northern population small, it is also extremely diverse culturally and linguistically. In the Northwest Territories, the Inuit comprise 35 per cent of the population; they live in the north and east, beyond the tree line. They share a common language, with several regional dialects, and have retained close cultural ties with the Inuit of Alaska and Greenland. The Indians of the Mackenzie Valley and the Great Slave Lake region, the Dene, comprise 17 per cent of the territory's population and speak several languages, all of which share the Athapaskan root. Most of the Métis live in the same regions as the Dene, sharing the same communities and lands. The Métis make up an estimated 6 per cent of our Northern population. The remaining 42 per cent are non-Natives, often temporary residents or transients who work for government departments, in schools or on resource-development projects. In the Great Slave-Mackenzie Valley region, growing numbers of non-Natives are permanent residents who view the Northwest Territories as their home.

In Yukon, the Indian people comprise approximately one-quarter of the total population. Most speak Athapaskan dialects; a few, in the south-west, speak a dialect of Tlingit-Haida. There are no Inuit in Yukon, and most non-status Indians identify with the status Indians and are counted as "Natives" in territorial statistics. Some non-Natives in Yukon are transients and temporary residents, but most are long-term or permanent Yukoners, many with family connections in the territory going back several generations. The long-term residence of non-Native Yukoners and the minority status of the Native population has produced conflict, but both sides desire a mutually acceptable accommodation of Native and non-Native interests, recognizing that political development of the territory depends on that compromise.

The Northern Economy

To understand the economy of the North, we must look at the Northwest Territories and Yukon in relation to the economies of Canada and the world, and examine them in terms of economic relations within the two territories. The Northern economy is based on the production of staples, and the most significant of these are non-renewable resources. The North exports these staples to the South in raw or relatively unprocessed form. Because the export price of non-renewable resources depends largely on world prices in markets over which our Northern economy has no control, the North suffers from virtually complete economic dependence, from economic instability, and from "boom-bust" cycles. Thus, while the future wealth of the North probably lies in developing its non-renewable resources, that sector is extremely volatile. For this reason, it may prove too fragile and too unstable to support long-term employment.

The large scale of most Northern development projects and their extraordinarily high production costs require the use of development capital from non-Northern sources. Accordingly, governments and multi-national corporations dominate the financing of most such projects. Moreover, while the North possesses a strong, if not stable, primary sector and a large and comparatively stable service sector (chiefly owing to governments' activities),

secondary manufacturing is virtually non-existent. Transportation, production and labour costs inhibit growth in labour-intensive manufacturing and make it, too, an unlikely source of long-term employment. (See Table 24-1.)

TABLE 24-1 Distribution of Labour Force by Industry, 1981

Industry	Yukon	NWT	Canada
Agriculture	0.64	0.13	3.92
Forestry	0.53	0.38	0.82
Fishing/Trapping	0.30	1.19	0.30
Mining (including oil and gas)	10.00	10.88	1.71
Manufacturing	2.26	2.08	18.09
Construction	6.88	4.98	6.13
TCU[a]	11.99	10.60	7.63
Trade	12.82	10.65	15.96
FIRE[b]	3.76	3.51	5.06
CBPS[c]	23.31	24.02	27.71
Public Administration	19.21	25.29	7.23
Undefined/N.A.	8.42	6.28	5.44

Source: Statistics Canada, 1981 Census of Canada.

a. TCU = Transportation, Communications and Utilities.
b. FIRE = Finance, Insurance and Real Estate.
c. CBPS = Community, Business and Personal Services.

The Northwest Territories and Yukon have three distinct economies. Only Native peoples participate in the traditional or subsistence economy. The pure subsistence economy, while based on staple production, does not depend on export of the product. Very few Natives are involved exclusively in the subsistence economy; most supplement their hunting and fishing activities with frequent, if temporary, forays into the wage economy. Generally speaking, the traditional economy is healthier in remote communities than in larger and more accessible centres, and many Inuit, because they live in remote areas, continue to subsist mainly on "country food".

The North's second economy is an extension of Canada's Southern wage economy. Many Northern non-Natives participate in this economy, and growing numbers of Natives, too, work for governments in resource-development projects, and in other enterprises in the private sector. Natives are not more fully involved in the wage economy of the North because of their lower skill levels, their place of residence, their unwillingness to relocate, and the importation of Southern non-Native workers. The most important reason, however, is that the wage economy undermines the traditional Native economy. Regular employment in the wage economy allows no time for hunting, and many Native people are unwilling to give up that way of life to earn a stable income.

In addition, the North has a social-assistance or "welfare" economy. Most of the beneficiaries are Native, though few exist entirely on this income. They

use the money primarily to buy food staples, rifles, ammunition, snowmobiles, outboard motors, and other equipment and supplies, thus buttressing the traditional economy.

The three economies interact, and many Native people occupy a place in each of them from time to time. For instance, seasonal employment clearing brush can be supplemented by trapping, hunting and fishing, and all these sources of income are ultimately supported by social assistance. Thus, while the greatest potential for job creation in the Northwest Territories and Yukon is in the non-renewable/resource sector, any analysis of our Northern economy must recognize and allow for the importance of subsistence hunting and fishing as a complement to the wage economy.

The Political Culture of the North

Political institutions, attitudes and debate in the Northwest Territories and Yukon are all rooted in the liberal democratic values of Southern Canada, but not exclusively so. The traditional values of the Native community interact with the basically liberal values of Northern non-Natives to produce a distinctive political culture. For instance, Natives place a far higher value than non-Natives on the collectivity: the community. This "collectivism" derives from the precarious nature of life in traditional hunting and gathering societies, where the survival of the tribe, the clan, the extended family or the community is more important than the fate of any one individual. Individualism is a luxury that traditional societies often cannot afford.

A corollary of this collectivist concept of society is the absence or weakness of the notion of private property in both the Indian and the Inuit cultures. The concept of individual possession, a cornerstone of liberal societies, is replaced by the principle of community sharing. Thus individuals are not perceived as owning things but, rather, as using them; and, when a particular item is not in use, it automatically reverts to a "common" status where it is free to be used by some other member of the group. Nowhere does this concept appear more clearly than in Native attitudes to the land.

Members of the Indian and Inuit cultures hold the land and its resources in reverence, for the community depends on the land for survival. The Native peoples feel a oneness with the land, for they believe that the people and the land are extensions of the same Being, and the traditional Native religions foster respect for the land and for the plants and animals that share it with humans. Native persons view the world around them as a homeland given to them, to which they must adapt in order to survive. This concept contrasts starkly with the "Southern" notion of the "frontier", which sees the environment as essentially alien and hostile. This view holds that humans must adapt the Northern environment to their own use: they must conquer or domesticate it and make it useful.

The Native concept of the land has led to conflict over development of non-renewable resources in the North. There is a very practical fear that such projects may do irreparable damage to the environment, and so destroy the renewable resources on which the Native economy and the traditional way of life depend. In addition, extraction of non-renewable resources is alien to the

Native culture. The Native economy uses the fruits of the land, extracting only renewable resources and never permanently alienating any of its wealth. Thus, while Natives are gradually coming to accept development of non-renewable resources, they continue to be concerned about the effect on their traditional economy and on their way of life.

Collectivism appears also in decision making by consensus. As a result, the entire community has a right and even an obligation to participate in such decisions. This collectivist concept of society enabled Northern peoples to govern themselves in an orderly and systematic fashion centuries before the arrival of the first European explorers.

Consensual decision making does not eliminate the need for leadership, but, unlike Southerners, the Dene and the Inuit do not see political power as monolithic. Liberal political theory links the concept of political authority to that of sovereignty. Patterns of authority in the modern liberal state are basically unitary and hierarchical. In contrast, Native society is characterized by more diffuse political authority: its communities follow different leaders for different kinds of activities. The form of decision making varies for hunting, spiritual matters, family matters, settlement of internal disputes or punishment of wrongdoers. Consensus determines who is most suited to lead in any given situation. Thus, there is a functional division of labour: the best hunters will dominate in one area, a shaman in another, and the tribal elders in still others. Institutional transplants from the South have ignored these basic political principles, and as a result, many have failed.

Political Economy and Political Culture

The wage economy too, does not mesh easily with Native values, and the incongruity makes it difficult to integrate Native workers into the Northern labour force. Indians or Inuit entering the wage economy must abandon collectivist values and set aside the sense of community so integral and so essential to their way of life, since their work in the wage economy is not for the collective good of the community, but for individual gain. The change of values represented in this experience contributes to aboriginals' alienation from their culture which, in turn, undermines traditional social structures and patterns of authority. Consequently, Native people come to see power and influence in terms of income or monetary wealth, rather than in terms of traditional skills. Elders who remain within the traditional economy may clash with younger people who have chosen non-traditional employment.

The wage economy forces Natives to uproot themselves and their families from their homes in order to find work. This disruption, coupled with the fact that most wage employment is found in relatively urbanized settings, can cause alienation, serious social disorientation, and a loss of the sense of community. While informing young Natives entering the wage economy about its pitfalls can moderate these negative effects, the basic dilemma lies in the incompatibility of the wage economy and traditional Native values.

The wage economy, particularly that tied to the extraction of non-renewable resources, alienates Native people from the land. All aspects of a traditional hunting and gathering society – its social values, political culture,

art, legends, religion, social structure—reflect its central purpose of survival through the use of renewable resources. To remove this central purpose and to replace it by either a wage or a welfare economy could destroy the core of Native culture and ultimately threaten its survival.

Northern Native peoples have recently begun to adapt to the development of non-renewable resources. They are balancing traditional priorities with the pressures of mega-projects and Southern encroachments on their communities, and they are setting up corporate mechanisms such as locally-controlled development corporations. These institutions, coupled with the older community-based co-operatives, permit Natives to participate in the wage economy through institutions which they themselves control, and which are therefore sensitive to the traditional economy and way of life. All Canadians hope that such "bridging" methods can be further developed.

The economic and cultural factors outlined above interact with one another and shape political and constitutional issues in the North. Economic development will affect the fate of the Native culture. It is a fragile culture under siege, not because of deliberate attack from non-Natives, but because of rapid development in the North. Thus, economic and cultural changes, as well as pressures from the South, set the agenda for political discourse.

Issues and Recommendations

Long-term economic growth in Northern Canada depends on the exploitation of non-renewable resources. The Northwest Territories and Yukon represent over one-third of Canada's land, and their petroleum and mineral resources have scarcely been touched. For these reasons and because of the continuing, though reduced, importance of resource development to our national economy, the futures of Canada and of the North are inextricably intertwined. However, while development of non-renewable resources may be essential for Northern development, it is not the only important issue in the region.

There are cultural, economic and political issues in the North that clearly distinguish it from the rest of our country. One of the North's most significant distinguishing features is its Native people. The plight of Native Canadians is of concern throughout Canada, but in the North, Native issues actually dominate political discourse. Ultimately, these and other controversial matters with institutional dimensions will affect the nature and pace of development in the region. Canadian decision makers must deal with all these issues quickly and sensitively, not only to ensure development, but also to arrange for the Native and non-Native people of the Northwest Territories and Yukon to enjoy the same rights and benefits as other Canadians.

Native Northerners and Political and Economic Change

Aboriginal Claims

Most Canadians now accept that Native people in the North have a legitimate claim to lands used traditionally in subsistence hunting and fishing,

as well as a right to financial compensation for past alienation of their lands and resources. Most support the concept of fair and prompt settlement of the aboriginal claims of Native Northerners, and the federal and territorial governments have committed themselves to negotiating such a settlement with representatives of the four main Native groups. Unfortunately, ten years of negotiations have settled only one of the four major claims, that of the Inuvialuit, the people of the Mackenzie Delta-Beaufort Sea region. Failure to settle the other three claims has retarded economic development, blocked constitutional change, and prevented creation of a separate territory in the Eastern Arctic. It is high time to conclude negotiations, ratify settlements, and proceed with economic and political development of the North for the benefit of all Northerners and of Canadians generally.

Negotiations on aboriginal claims hang on two issues: extinguishment of claims and political rights. The former has produced a stalemate between the governments and Native organizations. Natives have argued that the claims settlement should guarantee aboriginal rights in perpetuity, while the federal and territorial governments argue that statutory and constitutionally entrenched protections should replace traditional aboriginal rights. Since much of the dispute hinges on semantics, abandoning the term "extinguishment" in the deliberations would help to eliminate this obstacle. The settlement should "affirm" the specific aboriginal rights being recognized and acknowledge that the lands and moneys involved are being ceded in perpetuity.

Special political rights for aboriginal peoples have been a prominent issue in recent years in all parts of Canada. There is growing willingness to consider "special status", or "Native self-government" for Native Canadians: institutional arrangements that would allow Native people more control over their cultural affairs, education and social services, and that might even guarantee them representation in national institutions such as the Senate. While the liberal values of individualism and universality have so far dominated our Canadian political culture, we should certainly feel free to seek other means of accommodating the special interests of collectivities in our federal institutions. Land-claims negotiations, however, are an inappropriate forum for developing such mechanisms. Because these mechanisms would affect the rights of both Native and non-Native Canadians, Parliament, the legislatures of the Territories, and constitutional conferences would be ideal settings for discussion. In this Commission's view, Natives should participate on boards and commissions dealing with matters directly affecting their lands and renewable resources, but they should not attempt to use the claims process to entrench either legislative jurisdiction or special representation in legislative bodies pertaining to any order of government.

The federal government might wish to consider negotiating a deadline for settlement of Northern aboriginal land claims, after which funding of Native negotiating teams would cease. The federal government, Commissioners believe, should state unequivocally that legislative powers, sovereignty and special political status will not be part of any claims settlement, but that such settlements will not in any way restrict the power of Native peoples to take advantage of special political rights defined by other forums at some time in

the future. While the agreements, in our opinion, should be seen as affirmations of aboriginal rights rather than as extinguishments, they should also be final and binding on Native groups, the territorial governments, and the federal government. Certainly, further delay in reaching final settlements will serve no one well.

The Renewable Resources Sector

While all Northerners have a stake in the future of renewable resources in the two Territories, these resources constitute the economic base for Native people. The renewable resource economy contains commodity production and subsistence. The most important component of the renewable resource sector is the traditional economy of the Native people. The key problems in commodity production revolve around the fur industry. At the best of times, this industry faces severe market fluctuations, and the recent European boycott and the increasingly powerful lobby against leg-hold traps have left it in a state of virtual collapse. This decline has meant significant losses in revenues for Northern Natives and has put additional strain on Northern social services. While the fur trade is no longer a major component of the Canadian economy, it has, until recently, supplemented other sources of income, and it complements the subsistence activities of Native people, particularly in Northern Canada. While it is unlikely that the fur trade will ever again be a major part of the Northern economy, Commissioners suggest that the federal and territorial governments should continue to explore means of countering the anti-trapping lobby, of finding new markets, and of developing alternatives to the fur industry.

One possible alternative to the fur industry is Northern commercial fishing, for the northern seas offer potential for the commercial harvesting of fish and other seafood. This possibility requires further study. In the meantime, the federal government should ensure that regulatory agencies and marketing boards dealing with the fishing industry do not unintentionally retard or block development of a Northern fishery through exclusive concentration on the problems and interests of the Atlantic- and Pacific-coast or inland fisheries.

The subsistence portion of the traditional economy is quite healthy. Subsistence hunting and fishing, particularly in more remote communities, are not disappearing; indeed, they are a significant part of the Northern economy. A tendency among analysts to dismiss the traditional economy stems from the difficulty in measuring it and from the view that hunting and gathering are outmoded activities. In the North, however, approximately 30 per cent of the real income of Northern Natives comes from the harvesting of country food, and that harvest provides a significant percentage of the protein needs of Northerners.

Thus, in the North, the subsistence economy has a place analagous to that of agriculture in the South. Accordingly, the framers of policies and programs aimed at bringing Native people into the wage economy should recognize that like farming, subsistence hunting and fishing are an occupation. The territorial and federal governments should therefore explore the possibility of

developing means to upgrade and strengthen the subsistence component of the North's economy by, for instance, allowing tax breaks for full-time hunters comparable to those available to farmers in the South. They should also ensure that training and development do not focus on development of skills marketable only in the non-renewable sector. Such programs should take account of the cyclical participation of Native Northerners in the Northern wage economy and in production of country foods for personal and family consumption. Some funds earmarked for training might usefully be devoted to upgrading traditional skills, as well as to improving employment prospects in the wage economy.

Constitutional and Institutional Development in the Northwest Territories and Yukon

Three basic constitutional issues dominate the political agenda within and about the North. Two of these issues, responsible government and devolution of power from the federal to the territorial level, are of equal concern in both Territories. The third, the division of the Northwest Territories into two separate jurisdictions, is of direct concern only to the people of that Territory.

Commissioners believe that responsible government and continued devolution of federal responsibilities to the territorial government should occur with or without division of the Northwest Territories. Nevertheless, it is unlikely that such constitutional development will take place before the issue of division is settled. Creation of two new territories may require different rates of constitutional development in order to accommodate local priorities and different administrative and employment capacities. In this connection, Commissioners wish to emphasize several points: governments should not let the issue of division of the Northwest Territories frustrate the aspirations of the people of Yukon for full responsible government; our recommendation of responsible government should be taken to apply equally to an undivided Northwest Territories or to the two new territories that might emerge following division; our recommendations concerning devolution of authority to the territorial governments should apply equally to the territories that might emerge after division. In addition, the federal government timetable for devolution should not be imposed on the new territories, and the elected representatives of those territories must participate in setting the priorities for transfer of power. It must be recognized, however, that there is urgency to resolve the issue of division so that constitutional evolution in the Northwest Territories can proceed.

Responsible Government

In Canada responsible government has three main features. The Cabinet, or executive council, can be "the government" only if it has the support of a majority, that is, the "confidence", of the legislature; the Cabinet exercises the powers of the Crown; and the executive is responsible to the legislature for the "public purse", that is, for all matters of supply and "ways and means".

Yukon has achieved *de facto* the first two of these features of responsible government. Its Commissioner acts in a manner analogous to that of a Lieutenant-Governor in a province, and the Legislative Assembly has the power to vote non-confidence in the government. In this Commission's view, the federal government should amend the Yukon Act to reflect this reality.

The Commissioner of the Northwest Territories still exercises some policy-making power in the day-to-day operations of government, and it is not clear whether the Legislative Assembly can vote non-confidence in the Executive Council. The Northwest Territories is the last jurisdiction in Canada without responsible government, and we Commissioners believe that there is no justification for continued denial of this right. The federal government should, in our opinion, grant the Legislative Assembly powers commensurate with those of Yukon's Assembly.

Some Canadians will argue that responsible government cannot exist without a well-developed party system, and that the Northwest Territories, unlike Yukon, lacks political parties at the territorial level. The expectation of executive authority, however, will ultimately motivate the loose and shifting coalitions of non-party governments to transform themselves into disciplined parties. The federal government should therefore amend the Northwest Territories Act to give that area responsible government.

The third requisite for full responsible government is, of course, complete control of the public purse. With the current system of funding, the federal government must still agree on a basic set of spending targets for each of the Territories. If a Territory has had financial troubles, the federal government has usually provided additional support. The territorial governments desire a system of formula financing which would give them both greater fiscal autonomy and corresponding responsibility. Such a system would make federal transfers predictable over long periods and allow for long-range budgetary planning. Hence, the federal and territorial governments should negotiate financial arrangements to give the territorial governments full power over the public purse and to impose genuine responsibility and accountability for expenditure.

Devolution of Authority

Over the past two decades, the Northern Territories have evolved from virtual colonial status to the acquisition of responsibility for a wide range of "provincial" services. The logical end of this process is provincehood, although four barriers might delay progress towards provincial status for a decade or more. These are the Territories' small populations, their uncertain revenue base, their unresolved internal disputes, and the practical considerations of a national interest in the North. Our new constitutional amending formula specifies that creation of a new province requires the consent of at least two-thirds of the existing provinces, representing 50 per cent of our population, and of the federal parliament; to secure agreement might prove a formidable task. Existing provinces might oppose creation of new provinces simply because it would alter the balance of the amending formula. (For instance, if there were 13 provinces, two-thirds (9) of the provinces with more

than 50 per cent of Canada's population could amend the Constitution without the approval of any of the four Western provinces.) Nevertheless, though even territorial leaders who aspire to provincehood are not demanding it immediately, the people of the North are making a legitimate request for *de facto* status. Commissioners believe that the federal government should indicate its commitment to some form of provincehood for the Territories as an ultimate goal and should grant Northerners all the benefits of Canadian citizenship.

The North will probably overcome the first three barriers to provincehood mentioned above. Population, now growing largely through increase of the resident population, will expand through migration as economic development proceeds. Similarly, as the Northern economies evolve, the revenue base will expand, and the Territories will develop a more adequate tax base. The internal problems, settlement of land claims and division of the Northwest Territories, will probably be settled within the next few years.

The fourth barrier to provincehood will be the most difficult to surmount. It is represented in the question: Is it appropriate for 70 000 residents of the Northern Territories to assume control over approximately 40 per cent of Canada's land? The question implies its own answer, and that answer leads Commissioners to believe that there should be continuing national interest in the development of Northern Canada. Few, even of the most strident of Northern autonomists, would dispute this conclusion. As one Northerner stated in our hearings, "The North is the future of Canada." Because we accept the validity of that statement, we consider that the future of the North should be the concern of Northerners and of all Canadians. The federal and territorial governments must find a means of sharing responsibility for development. The people of the Territories must have some influence on decisions that affect them and their homeland, and so too must the federal government in its role of representative for all Canadians.

Where there is no demonstrable national interest, territorial governments should have powers like those of the provinces. Thus the federal government, in consultation with the territorial governments, should establish a timetable for the transfer of provincial-type responsibilities in areas such as health, the institution of criminal proceedings, labour relations, inland waters and renewable resources. Joint-management arrangements might prove to be valuable transitional tools. Timetables might vary from territory to territory and from one type of jurisdiction to another, but devolution to the Territories of most aspects of these matters should be completed within five years. Opponents of such a proposal may raise the issue of costs, but the federal government is presently bearing the costs of performing these functions, and the territorial governments could perform them just as efficiently. While there might be marginal additional costs because of negative economies of scale in such small jurisdictions, savings from the dismantling of parts of the Northern program of the Department of Indian Affairs and Northern Development will at least partially offset them.

There is a clear national interest in non-renewable resources and ownership, and control over land for their development. Various approaches could facilitate co-operative federal-territorial sharing of these responsibili-

ties: delegation of powers to the territory, but with a federal veto in matters of an overriding national interest, or concurrent jurisdiction with federal paramountcy. Joint management similar to that of the offshore resources agreement between the federal government and Nova Scotia or Newfoundland is also a possibility. It is important, however, for the federal and territorial governments to devise mechanisms to involve the territorial governments more fully in decisions affecting development of non-renewable resources. Moreover, any such arrangement should define the circumstances where there could be a federal override.

It probably would not be in the national interest to transfer all lands in the Territories to the territorial governments in a single action. However, once the mineral and petroleum potential of territorial lands becomes known, and once such issues as aboriginal land claims and national parks and park reserves have been settled, the federal Crown could begin to transfer large parcels of land to the Territories. Such transfers, if made gradually, would in no way compromise the national interest and would give the territorial governments both increased revenue potential and greater effectiveness in development of renewable resources, tourism, municipal affairs and territorial parks. The governments should begin negotiations to transfer to the Territories the surface rights to Crown lands that do not directly bear on the national interest and that have not been ceded to the Native people through the settlement of claims.

In the short term, at least, ownership and control over non-renewable resources will rest with the federal government. However, the people of the North should enjoy a fair share of the revenues and royalties generated by resource-development projects. The federal government should consider arrangements for sharing resource revenues with the Territories; these arrangements could be similar to those negotiated with Nova Scotia and Newfoundland. The Government of Canada would have to integrate such an arrangement within the formula for federal-territorial financial transfers so that windfalls from non-renewable resources would result in automatic prorated reduction of transfer payments. Moreover, there should be an overall ceiling on revenues accruing to the Territories from non-renewable resources.

Provincial status is normally a prerequisite for full participation in federal-provincial conferences. However, although provincehood is not in the immediate offing for the Territories, Commissioners are of the opinion that the federal government should provide for direct participation of their governments in such deliberations. This involvement is particularly important for discussions of matters directly concerning Northern residents. It does not require a constitutional amendment, and it could occur immediately.

Finally, one important symbolic step for the Territories would be to remove the provision in section 42(1)(*e*) of the Constitution Act, 1982 that allows for extension of existing provinces into the Territories without agreement of the people of the Northwest Territories and/or Yukon. The federal government should initiate an amendment requiring agreement of the legislative assembly of the territory concerned before existing provincial boundaries could be extended north of the sixtieth parallel.

Division of the Northwest Territories

In the period since 1979, the Legislative Assembly, a territorial plebiscite, and Liberal and Conservative federal governments all have supported in principle division of the Northwest Territories and creation of a new territory of Nunavut in the eastern Arctic. Unfortunately this goal still seems distant. Difficult issues remain: location of the boundary and of seats of government, the form of government, and the timing of the division. Of these, the boundary is the most difficult issue to resolve.

Members of the Constitutional Alliance of the Northwest Territories are still discussing the boundary. The Nunavut Constitutional Forum (NCF) has been arguing for a line that runs diagonally, southeast to northwest, roughly following the treeline. The Western Constitutional Forum (WCF) generally favours a north-south boundary from the sixtieth parallel to the Arctic Ocean, west of the community of Baker Lake and east of the Committee for Original Peoples' Entitlement (COPE) communities. The two forums have reached a tentative agreement, but have not yet ratified it.

Two sub-issues delay settlement of the boundary. First is the issue of community: Will the people of the Western Arctic (Inuvialuit) and those of the Central Arctic join Nunavut or the Western Territory? Geography and transportation and communication links suggest that they would choose to join the Western Territory, but cultural and linguistic ties with the Inuit of the eastern Arctic point to the likelihood of their joining Nunavut. Choice of a boundary involves human considerations, particularly the wishes of the people affected. The January 1985 agreement between the NCF and the WCF would have left the Inuvialuit communities in the Western Territory and allowed the Central Arctic communities to make their choice by referendum. However, the NCF withdrew its support for the boundary agreement at the end of February 1985, and the issue remains unsettled.

The second issue derives from the implication of the boundary for access to natural resources. To be economically viable, both Nunavut and the Western Territory must have a sound resource base. The dispute is centred on control of the western Keewatin – the unpopulated lands between Great Slave Lake and Baker Lake, with their potentially rich resources – and the Mackenzie Delta-Beaufort region, with its petroleum resources. The ideal boundary would leave each territory with sufficient renewable resources to maintain the subsistence economy and sufficient non-renewable resources to provide an adequate revenue base. Unfortunately, each side is reluctant to compromise.

Since all orders of government and most residents favour division, the federal government should press the Constitutional Alliance to act. Uncertainty about division colours all aspects of northern development, and doubts about the fate of the territory have slowed economic growth, hampered settlement of land claims, and retarded devolution. Hence, Commissioners recommend that the Government of Canada give the Constitutional Alliance an early deadline for establishing the boundary internally. Failing an internally-generated and ratified agreement, we believe that the federal government should establish an independent boundary

commission. This body would hear arguments from the two constitutional forums and make recommendations concerning a boundary. Although, ultimately, it would be the duty of federal and territorial governments to ratify any boundary chosen, no division should be forced on the people of the Northwest Territories.

Ownership and control of resources in western Keewatin and the Beaufort-Mackenzie Delta region would no doubt remain temporarily with the Crown in right of Canada. A long-term solution would probably involve agreement between Nunavut and the Western Territory to share resource revenues and/or to accept transfers of federal revenues in place of revenues from non-renewable resources. For renewable resources, such as wildlife and fish, the two territories should work out joint management and harvesting strategies. Such resources, particularly caribou, migrate annually over a wide area and exhibit a particularly irreverent attitude to political boundaries in the course of their wanderings.

After territorial division, the WCF and the NCF should decide the structure of government, respecting, of course, the Charter of Rights. Ideally, institutions should reflect the political values of all Northerners, protect aboriginal rights, and represent minority interests fairly. The federal government should encourage creativity and innovation in the development of new and uniquely northern institutions, although the Charter of Rights will necessarily set the broad guidelines for the range of legitimate options.

It appears reasonable to approve a longer residence requirement for voters to protect the fragile social structure of the Northwest Territories and Yukon from the harmful effects of massive immigration of temporary residents to work on development projects. Commissioners suggest, however, that the requirement should be two or three years of residence, not ten. Similarly, while special political status might protect ethnic and cultural minorities, such status should not compromise the basic democratic principle of representation by population. The federal government must ensure that the new institutional arrangements do not contradict the spirit of the Canadian constitutional tradition.

Creation of two new territories will make Canada's North "more governable"; will give considerable satisfaction to the region's inhabitants, particularly the Inuit of the eastern Arctic; and will better accommodate different rates of political and constitutional development in the various areas of the region. However, the new institutions that division will require will cost more than those of the present system, at least in the beginning. The Government of the Northwest Territories and the two constitutional forums must therefore accept federal involvement in institution-building where federal appropriations will be affected.

When division of the Northwest Territories would occur would depend on several factors: a boundary settlement, cost of the transition and the provision of federal funds to pay for it, and availability of public servants and infrastructure to support the new government of Nunavut. To staff the public service would take time, and the process might delay establishment of Nunavut. The predominantly-Inuit Eastern Arctic wants a government sensitive to the cultural needs of Native residents and able to conduct its

affairs in the Inuktitut language. Thus an imported bureaucracy, even one that would serve only for the first years of the new territory's existence, would defeat one of the main goals of the creation of Nunavut. The hard reality, however, is that few Inuit have the background or training to staff senior management and technical positions in the public service. The federal and territorial governments should therefore evaluate existing educational, training and development programs for Northerners with a view to creating a comprehensive program to prepare Native people to staff Nunavut's public service. The same type of program could also increase the number of Native Northerners in senior positions in the Western Territory.

National Issues and Northern Perspectives

Some issues of national concern have distinctive northern dimensions and special significance in the North. Commissioners review three of these in order to emphasize that all Canadians must be sensitive to the distinctive character of Northern aspects of national policy.

The Northern Ecology

The Canadian North constitutes one of the last unspoiled ecosystems in the world. It is not simply a Canadian treasure, but part of the world's natural heritage. Sections of this Report have noted the need for caution in developing non-renewable resources. Commissioners have warned against destroying the base for the traditional Native economy, emphasized preservation of renewable resources, despite the desire to develop gas, oil and mineral resources, and urged protection of endangered species, habitats and ecosystems. Over and above all these considerations, however, Canadians must recognize the intrinsic value of the northern ecosystem. We must all learn to value wilderness – the unspoiled aesthetic virtue of the North – in the way that Northerners do. There are convincing practical arguments for respecting the northern environment, and they supplement the awareness, particularly strong among Native peoples, that the environment is the very ground of our existence and instrinsically worthy of our respect and even of our awe. We Canadians must never allow short-term economic strategies, however attractive, to destroy our North, which we hold in trust for the future.

International Trade

Much of this Report has looked at Canada's international trade prospects. More specifically, it has concentrated on Canadian relations with our closest trading partner, the United States. Northerners have a common interest with all Canadians in trade with the rest of the world, but two issues may be of special concern to them: trade with Alaska, and trade with the entire circumpolar region.

The major flow of Canada-U.S. trade is between Canada and the continental United States, but trade between Alaska and Yukon is of great

importance to Northerners. The Yukon government and a number of interest groups have suggested freer economic relations with Alaska. Commissioners recommend research on a special bilateral trade agreement affecting the far northwest. Yukon's only access to ocean is through the Alaskan ports of Haines and Skagway. Some Canadians have suggested that Skagway, which has land links with the rest of Alaska only through highways in British Columbia and Yukon, could become a "free port".

Some Northerners would like to further relations with other parts of the circumpolar region. The Inuit of Canada share linguistic and cultural ties with Greenland, Alaska and the Soviet Union. They have formed the Inuit Circumpolar Conference to maintain cultural ties and to address problems of common Arctic concern. Spokespersons for the Canadian Inuit have indicated a desire to see these links sanctioned officially. They want to foster international efforts to protect the Arctic environment, and they wish to facilitate economic and cultural exchange among the circumpolar peoples.

Technological Innovation and Arctic Sovereignty

There are urgent reasons for Canadians to develop technology suitable for the Arctic. Given our oil and gas exploration in the Beaufort Sea and our permafrost studies relating to pipelines, we should be developing a comparative advantage in such fields. Even more important, Canada must affirm legal and technological sovereignty over the Northwest Passage and other Arctic waters. Indeed, it is essential to maintenance of Canadian sovereignty in the Arctic that federal and territorial governments support research and development in technologies appropriate to the region. As one participant pointed out in a seminar sponsored by this Commission, the former is meaningless without the latter:

> *If Canada is to exercise the necessary control to maintain the sovereignty it claims to have acquired over the waters of the Northwest Passage, it must develop a full range of sea- and land-based services to ensure that its control is factual and effective ... it should be able to provide the following services: marine navigational aids; icebreaking and escorting; marine search and rescue; marine emergencies/pollution control; marine mobile communications services; ports, harbours, and terminals; vessel inspection services; vessel traffic management; marine resupply administration and support; pilotage; and training.*[2]

Conclusions

There are many issues of concern to Northerners that Commissioners have not specifically addressed in this section. We consider these issues as among national priorities, and we address them elsewhere in this Report. We wish to emphasize here, however, that the distinctive interests of Northerners, both Native and non-Native, must receive the same consideration as those of Canadians in the provinces. Canada must integrate the Northern territories into the federation so that their people can enjoy the rights and privileges

enjoyed by other Canadians. The Northern territories must gradually be granted powers equivalent to those exercised by provinces in the South. In this way, we can foster the distinctiveness and diversity of the North, thus enriching the Canadian cultural fabric, while giving Northerners the opportunity to participate equally in the full benefits of the national community.

Notes

1. Background information on the North is contained in the volume *The North*, vol. 72, prepared for the Royal Commission on the Economic Union and Development Prospects for Canada (Toronto: University of Toronto Press, 1985). Commissioners are also grateful for the enthusiastic response of Northerners in the hearings process and for their informative submissions.
2. Donat Pharand, "Sovereignty and the Canadian North", in *The North*, vol. 72, prepared for the Royal Commission on the Economic Union and Development Prospects for Canada (Toronto: University of Toronto Press, 1985).

Aboriginal Self-Government

As Commissioners have noted, issues emerge from time to time concerning the status of particular groups within the Canadian community. At such times Canada has used institutional and constitutional mechanisms to help resolve these concerns. The experience of aboriginal peoples reveals how difficult it is to accommodate their aspirations for enhanced status and social and economic improvement within the existing constitutional and institutional framework.

Many actors in many forums have tried to improve the conditions of aboriginal peoples and to increase their influence on decisions that affect their lives. There have been federal-provincial discussions, land-claims negotiations, court cases, direct appeals to the Crown, and representations to international bodies such as the United Nations. Issues involved have included: recognition of aboriginal and treaty rights, the vote, provision of health and housing services, facilities for aboriginal people in urban Canada, compatibility of resource development and environmental protection, and, most recently, aboriginal self-government.

Self-government is the most prominent aboriginal issue today. Some aboriginals claim an inherent right of sovereignty, in which they include self-government. Others see self-government as a pre-condition to solving the social, cultural and economic problems facing aboriginals. The primary official forum for discussion of aboriginal self-government has been the series of constitutional meetings instituted as a result of section 37 of the Constitution Act, 1982.

Discussion of self-government has not fully taken into account the implications of various reform proposals for the Canadian constitutional order. Proposed models of aboriginal self-government vary in their compatibility with the overall structure of Canadian government and the rights and obligations of Canadian citizenship. Therefore, the outcome of the debate over aboriginal self-government will affect relations of aboriginal peoples, not only with the governments of Canada, at the federal, provincial and municipal levels, but also with other Canadians. Commissioners believe it important to ensure that the approach ultimately taken conforms broadly with the institutional and constitutional structure of Canada, particularly with Parliament, federalism and the Charter of Rights.

The position of aboriginal peoples in Canada also has international implications. Canadian aboriginals have established, and will undoubtedly further develop, contacts with aboriginal groups in other lands to exchange information and to improve their understanding of matters of common interest. Moreover, international organizations have demonstrated significant interest in aboriginal affairs, and this interest extends to the condition of aboriginal peoples in Canada. Since these matters will remain of interest to some members of the international community, this country's record will be subject to review and criticism. No transfer of decision-making authority in the form of self-government, however comprehensive, will relieve our national community from its ultimate responsibility for the well-being of aboriginal people, as for all Canadian citizens. The discussions under way, therefore, deeply affect each of us.

Commissioners' primary focus is the compatibility of aboriginal self-government with the Canadian constitutional system. We believe that it is important, however, to consider aboriginal goals and aspirations for self-government, and the social, economic and historical circumstances out of which they have developed.

Social and economic statistics gathered by Statistics Canada and other agencies are disturbing. Life expectancy for aboriginal Canadians – status Indians, non-status Indians, Métis and Inuit – is ten years less than for non-aboriginal citizens. The incidence of alcoholism among aboriginal people in 1982 was 13 times that for non-aboriginals. About 10 per cent of the prison population is Native, a proportion that represents about five times the ratio of Native people to Canada's overall population.

The 1981 Census of Canada reported that four in ten aboriginal people had never attended high school; for non-aboriginal Canadians the figure was two in ten. The proportion of aboriginal income made up of government-transfer payments was more than double that for non-aboriginals. The percentage of aboriginal families headed by single parents was almost double that of non-aboriginal families. More than 16 per cent of aboriginal homes were in need of major repairs, and one in six was overcrowded; the figures for non-aboriginal homes were 6.5 per cent and one in 43, respectively.

The 1984 Royal Commission Report on Equality in Employment[1] found aboriginal people concentrated in low-paid, low-skill jobs, with aboriginal men earning 60.2 per cent of the average income for non-aboriginal men, and aboriginal women earning 71.7 per cent of the average income for non-aboriginal women. In this Commission's hearings in Victoria, the United Native Nations, a B.C. provincial organization representing off-reserve, non-status Indians and Métis, told us that 60 per cent of Native people living in Victoria were unemployed, 82 per cent lived under the poverty line, and 95 per cent had not completed Grade 12.[2]

Many aboriginal groups argue that census and survey statistics such as these reflect the fact that Native peoples live in a culture not their own, where important decisions affecting their lives and their children's futures are beyond their control. Witness after witness appearing before the House of Commons Special Committee on Indian Self-Government in Canada (the Penner Committee) in 1983 spoke of a "legacy of injustice, exploitation, bureaucratic insensitivity and non-Indian self-interest".[3]

Although relations have evolved between status Indians living on reserves and the Government of Canada, they remain circumscribed by the Indian Act which was first enacted in 1876. The Indian Act is based on federal jurisdiction as laid out in the Constitution Act, 1867, section 91(24): "Indians, and Lands reserved for the Indians". Until the end of the Second World War, the Indian Affairs Branch took a custodial approach to its responsibilities for Indians. Indeed, benign neglect and indifference often characterized the administration of Indian affairs. However, several factors led to gradual changes in attitudes and policy toward Indians after the war: there was increased acceptance of a positive role for the state in promoting the economic and social well-being of its citizens; governments acquired greater administrative capacity; citizens became more conscious of their

rights; and the end of formal European colonialism in Africa and Asia helped to focus attention on the conditions of indigenous peoples elsewhere.

The federal government revised the Indian Act in 1951. Then, in 1960, it extended the vote in federal elections to all Indians; prior to that date, status Indians had usually been required to give up their status to obtain the right to vote in federal elections. The tempo of policy change quickened during the 1960s. The federal government made groping attempts, reflected in policy initiatives, policy reversals and new programs, to come to terms with the long history of neglect toward Indians under federal jurisdiction. It set up community-development programs and Indian advisory boards, increased its grants to Indian bands, and transferred some responsibilities to provincial governments. These steps met with mixed success.

In 1966, a thorough examination of the conduct of Indian affairs, *A Survey of the Contemporary Indians of Canada* (Hawthorn Report),[4] recommended rejection of assimilation or integration as a policy option in favour of retaining special status for Indians. The report suggested that Indians should be regarded as "citizens plus": they should possess general rights and duties of citizenship, and additional rights as charter members of the Canadian community. The report recommended that the Indian Affairs Branch ensure that the "plus" aspects of Indian citizenship be respected. In its 1969 *White Paper on Indian Policy*, however, the federal government adopted a different approach, recommending repeal of the Indian Act and the special status it afforded Canadian Indians. The Indian people resisted the 1969 proposals, and the federal government subsequently dropped them.

A policy of devolution, or the transfer to individual bands of responsibility for managing and delivering services, began in the late 1960s and continued through the 1970s. Funds from the budget of the Department of Indian Affairs and Northern Development, administered by bands, increased steadily from $34.9 million in 1971 to $526.6 million in 1982–83, a fifteen-fold increase. Although the federal government passed responsibility for delivery of services to the Indians, it kept control of programs and budgets.

During the 1970s, grants and contributions to bands and associations, as well as to provincial governments, more than doubled as a percentage of the Department's budget designated for Indian and Inuit affairs. This is testimony not only to the transfer of responsibility but also to increased federal funding of Native associations. Extensive government financial support for political organizations, channelled primarily through the Department of Indian Affairs and Northern Development and the Secretary of State, eventually allowed status and non-status Indians and Métis to articulate their demands for reform. This politicization has made both aboriginals and non-aboriginals much more aware of the needs of Canada's Native peoples.

Financial support for political organizations helped mobilize aboriginal peoples. Métis and non-status Indians became increasingly visible in political life in the 1970s as the concept of "aboriginal" evolved and grew to encompass a much larger population than just status Indians. This broadened understanding of aboriginal ethnicity led to the inclusion of Indian, Inuit and

Métis peoples in the constitutional definition of "aboriginal peoples" contained in section 35 of the Constitution Act, 1982.

The enlarged definition of aboriginal peoples has compounded the difficulties in thinking about their many problems and grievances. It is difficult, for example, even to define and assess the size of the component groups. The constitutionally recognized categories of Indian (status and non-status), Métis and Inuit are ambiguous. Status, or registered, Indians are persons accorded status by the Indian Act whose names are recorded on a register kept by the federal government. The 1981 Census reported approximately 290 000 status Indians. However, Department of Indian Affairs and Northern Development 1985 population projections place the number of status Indians at 366 000. The Inuit, approximately 25 000 in number, live beyond the tree line. They comprise a distinct cultural group, and a substantial majority of them speak Inuktitut.

The boundaries of the remaining two categories of aboriginal peoples overlap and are indistinct. Non-status Indians are formerly registered Indians who lost their status through enfranchisement, Indian women who lost their status through marrying non-Indians, or descendants of members of these two groups. The core Métis population are descendants of people of mixed aboriginal and European ancestry who lived in Western and Northern Canada and possessed a distinct socio-cultural identity in the nineteenth century. However, there is no universally accepted definition of "Métis". The term is sometimes used to refer to all people of mixed aboriginal and non-aboriginal ancestry who lack legal Indian status. As a result, non-status Indians sometimes identify themselves as Métis and vice versa. Using self-identification, the 1981 Census counted approximately 173 000 Métis and non-status Indians; but other estimates range as high as 300 000 to 435 000. Métis and non-status Indian organizations, in particular, dispute the 1981 Census figure. For instance, in Ontario alone, the political organization for Métis and non-status Indians claims to represent 185 000 people. In addition to the core population of Métis and non-status Indians, between 400 000 and 600 000 others identify themselves for certain purposes as part of this group.

If and when Parliament passes Bill C-31, a bill to amend the Indian Act, it will cast into a state of flux the categories of status and non-status Indians. The federal government estimates that the amendment would permit 68 000 non-status Indians to apply for registration under the Indian Act and for the rights and benefits associated with this status. This estimate includes 16 000 women who lost their status because they married non-Indian men and 6000 people who were enfranchised under a particular section of the Indian Act for reasons now deemed unfair, such as joining the armed forces or completing university. The other 46 000 people who could apply to have their status reinstated are first-generation descendants of these people. The enlarged category of aboriginal peoples, and the fluidity of their component groups, raise complicated and serious policy questions, in particular about self-government.

Aboriginal claims for self-government are an understandable response to social, economic and historical circumstances and are in accord with the

political awakening evident in aboriginal populations around the world. Commissioners recognize the need to enhance aboriginals' decision-making capacity and autonomy, based on the distinctive place of aboriginals in Canadian society as the first peoples of Canada, and on the broadened constitutional recognition they now enjoy.

According to a research study done for this Commission,[5] aboriginal peoples in Canada seek greater self-determination and social justice, economic and social development, and protection of aboriginal cultures through self-government. They want greater control over their own destiny and an end to their subordination to political and bureaucratic authorities outside their own ethnic group. They seek economic development to end their poverty and unemployment, and they expect self-government to contribute to that result. They also consider self-government to be an important prerequisite in addressing social problems.

Many Canadians, who deplore the historical and continuing injustices visited on Canada's aboriginal peoples, recognize and support aboriginal goals for self-government. But while the goals are clear, the way to realize them is not. Commissioners doubt that aboriginal self-government, which remains an ambiguous concept, is the surest means of achieving all aboriginal goals. Indeed, we are concerned that the single-minded pursuit of self-government might unwittingly delay the massive effort which is needed to solve the major social and economic problems of aboriginal communities. Nevertheless, the process of defining self-government has already begun within the framework of constitutional discussions; and Canadians must assess it in terms both of its capacity to meet aboriginal aspirations and of its compatibility with our system of government.

Models of Aboriginal Self-Government

The concept of aboriginal self-government does not imply any single model or form of institutional arrangements. It is therefore exceedingly difficult both to assess the capacity of self-government to satisfy aboriginal goals and to assess the compatibility of what is still an abstract concept with the Canadian system of government and the principles of Canadian citizenship.

We should think of a continuum of models, based on the origins or derivation of authority. Near one end of the continuum is the model contained in the federal government's 1969 *White Paper on Indian Policy:* bands would acquire municipal status under provincial jurisdiction. Nearby on the continuum is the proposed legislation for band government developed by the Government of Canada following abandonment of the *White Paper* policy: a band was to be a federal municipality operating under enabling legislation and exercising delegated authority. These and similar proposals have a legislative, rather than a constitutional, foundation: on this basis, aboriginal governments would exercise delegated authority.

In contrast are proposals which give aboriginal governments a constitutional basis, with guaranteed jurisdiction similar in principle, although not necessarily in scope, to that of provincial governments. The Penner

Committee made such a proposal, recommending the establishment of Indian First Nation governments. The committee recognized the symbolic importance of the term "First Nation" to Indian aspirations for self-government and used it in its report, in order to make it more familiar to the Canadian public.

> *In recent years indigenous peoples have given new expression to their distinctiveness and their origins. Names have assumed a special significance . . . Indian peoples in Canada have thus extracted from history an English term that had been used in the Royal Proclamation, in treaties and in major legal decisions in the United States – the word 'nation'. Together they refer to themselves as 'First Nations', a term with historical and political significance.*[6]

Although the terms of reference of the Special Committee had restricted its mandate to the study of band governments on Indian reserves, the form of self-government it recommended could be extended to any aboriginal community with a land base.

The Penner Committee recommended that "the right of Indian peoples to self-government be explicitly stated and entrenched in the Constitution of Canada." The Report stated emphatically:

> *The surest way to achieve permanent and fundamental change in the relationship between Indian peoples and the federal government is by means of a constitutional amendment. Indian First Nation governments would form a distinct order of government in Canada with their jurisdiction defined.*[7]

The extreme position at this "constitutional" end of the continuum views self-government as an aboriginal right based on the Royal Proclamation of 1763, which in organizing governments for Britain's newly acquired North American territory had recognized aboriginal rights to lands not formally surrendered. According to this concept, aboriginal sovereignty was never relinquished, and it is the basis of self-government; the right to self-government is therefore already present in the Constitution Act, 1982, as an integral part of the aboriginal rights protected under section 35. At the Constitutional Conference of First Ministers on Aboriginal Constitutional Matters, in March 1984, for example, Chief David Ahenakew of the Assembly of First Nations stated:

> *The federal government cannot* give *us self-government. It has never been yours to give. It has always been ours. You can recognize it, enhance it, facilitate it, but if you were to give it to us or devolve it to us or permit it to us it would not be self-government.*[8]

Aboriginal associations and councils participating in the current discussions have shared the position that true aboriginal self-government must have a constitutional, rather than a legislative, foundation. Prime Minister Trudeau's promise at the 1984 First Ministers' Conference to include in the Constitution the right of aboriginal peoples to self-governing institutions represented the federal government's acceptance of a constitutional basis for aboriginal self-government. However, seven provinces at the 1984 Conference did not support constitutional entrenchment.

At the April 1985 First Ministers' Conference on The Rights of Aboriginal Peoples, Prime Minister Mulroney sought support for a constitutional amendment from the required number of provinces and the participating aboriginal associations. Seven provinces seemed to be prepared to support a compromise constitutional amendment which would affirm, in principle, the right of aboriginal Canadians to self-government, within the context of the Canadian federation; it would, however, leave to a political accord any further commitment to negotiate terms of self-government. The support of a number of these provisionally supportive provinces was conditional on the acceptance of the amendment by the aboriginal associations, but this agreement was not immediately forthcoming. The Conference therefore adjourned without reaching agreement, and the question of how to implement self-government remains unresolved. A number of provinces expressed concern about how aboriginal government would be integrated into the existing institutional and constitutional structure. Nevertheless there is now a greater sense that the federal and provincial governments are prepared to accept the goal.

Implementing Aboriginal Self-Government

Everyone engaged in the debate about aboriginal self-government recognizes that if and when agreement is reached on the basis of authority for aboriginal governments, legislation will have to provide for the recognition and implementation of this new status. Such legislation must state how membership in self-governing aboriginal communities will be determined, stipulate the means of recognition, and define the powers to be exercised.

There have been discussions between the federal government and Indian representatives on legislation to establish the framework of Indian Nation governments. Bill C-52, which dealt with self-government for Indian Nations, died on Parliament's order paper in June 1984; it was a first attempt to formulate such a framework. Although this draft legislation pertained only to Indians and not to the wider aboriginal community, it did not settle the form and substance of self-government for even this one component group. Proponents of self-government recognize, moreover, that since the varying aspirations and diverse circumstances of different Indian and other aboriginal nations throughout Canada may require different types of arrangements, each aboriginal government could possibly exercise a unique set of powers. The Penner Report, Bill C-52 and Prime Minister Mulroney, in his call to proceed on a case-by-case basis, have each recognized this possibility.

Most discussion of self-government assumes the existence of a land base or a territorially defined jurisdiction. However, aboriginal self-government which requires a land base would exclude a large heterogeneous segment of the aboriginal population: most non-status Indians, those Métis living outside communities where they form a majority, and the approximately one-in-four status Indians who do not live on Indian reserves or Crown-land settlements. Their interests might be overlooked by an approach to self-government which concentrates on a land-based model.

The size and wealth of existing status-Indian and Métis communities (which differ greatly in population, extent of land base and natural resources, level of community and personal wealth, and geographic remoteness) impose additional constraints on land-based self-government. Seventy-two per cent of the status-Indian population, approximately 216 000 individuals, lives on more than 2000 reserves. There are 579 bands, which are generally recognized as the principal units for self-government; their average population is 516 members, but 48 per cent of the bands have fewer than 300 members. The large number of relatively small communities poses many problems for self-government, including serious diseconomies of scale. Nevertheless, administrative complexities, distance between communities, cultural diversities and distinctive histories reduce the prospect of amalgamating bands.

Many of the existing communities have only weak fledgling economies. Even after receiving land-claim settlements, resource revenues and any additional land grants from governments, many communities will need ongoing financial assistance. Most of the local communities that might receive powers of self-government are, in effect, small villages with limited resources.

It is difficult to conceive of a form of self-government that is not territorially based. However, if our goal is to provide greater autonomy for all the aboriginal people of Canada, we cannot ignore the fact that many of them (perhaps 75 or 80 per cent, according to one estimate)[9] lack a land base or live outside communities where aboriginals represent a majority. Indeed, aboriginal leaders, especially some Métis, have tentatively begun to explore possible forms of self-government which are not territorially based. Self-government premised on jurisdiction over individual dispersed citizens could, for example, grant taxing powers or make unconditional transfers to one or more pan-Canadian aboriginal authorities which, in turn, could deliver services or make transfer payments to individual aboriginal Canadians. Once constitutional discussions have more clearly defined the aboriginal and treaty rights which are recognized by section 35 of the Constitution Act, 1982, pan-Canadian aboriginal authorities could assume some form of responsibility based on any, or all, of these rights. Commissioners remain sceptical, however, that Canadians can develop workable models which would be both acceptable to the Canadian aboriginal community and reasonably efficient, and which would respect Canada's constitutional order. Accordingly, while we do not entirely reject the idea of limited self-government without a land base, we believe that other solutions will have to be found to solve the problems and satisfy the aspirations of the large majority of the aboriginal population who cannot look forward to a territorial jurisdiction.

How would self-governing, land-based aboriginal communities relate to federal and provincial governments and to the intergovernmental system? Aboriginal governments might exercise either constitutionally based authority or delegated authority. Such governments would almost certainly differ from one another in the extent of their jurisdictions and might also differ in their respective mixes of national and provincial jurisdictional powers: under

section 91(24) of the Constitution Act, 1867, Parliament could delegate jurisdiction that was otherwise provincial to such self-governing communities. Moreover, it could do so in varying degrees for different communities and in combination with varying amounts of delegated federal jurisdiction which would continue to apply to other Canadians. In its report, the Penner Committee proposed that "Parliament should move to occupy the field of legislation in relation to 'Indians, and Lands reserved for the Indians' and then vacate these areas of jurisdiction to recognized Indian governments." The report recommended that this be done "in all areas in which Indian First Nations wished to exercise jurisdiction."[10]

Although the legal and constitutional situation is complex, the federal and provincial governments might be able also to delegate special mixes of powers to those aboriginal communities which are not covered under section 91(24) of the Constitution Act, 1867. The complexities would be further compounded if particular self-governing aboriginal communities were to bridge the gap between their jurisdictional authority and their actual administrative and fiscal capacities by arranging for either level of government to provide programs.

There are complex practical issues relating to the manner in which such governments, with their potentially distinct mixes of powers, could fit into the structure of Canadian federalism. Self-governing communities that exercise powers delegated by the federal government pose fewer problems; presumably, the federal government could act on behalf of such aboriginal governments in the intergovernmental arena. The matter might not be so simple, however, in the case of aboriginal governments which possess constitutionally recognized authority. There could develop a very large number of sovereign self-governments representing a distinct order of government. The intergovernmental complexities of federalism could not successfully accommodate even a small proportion of these governments, either at the federal-provincial bargaining table or in more focused arenas where the governments of the federal system meet.

This problem cannot easily be overcome by accepting aboriginal associations as substitutes for the leaders of self-governing communities because participants in intergovernmental arenas must possess executive authority, and must be capable of delivering on their commitments. In order for aboriginal associations to be able to negotiate and accept agreements without worrying that individual community governments might repudiate them, they would themselves have to possess the status and authority of governments. If this were so, however, the widespread premise that the local community is the essential unit of self-government would be invalidated. Accordingly, Commissioners recommend that future discussions of aboriginal self-government clearly address the issue of how to fit such governments into the intergovernmental arena.

Several problems immediately become apparent. Given that aboriginal self-governments possessed sovereign authority, the legitimacy of their members' exercising the federal and provincial franchises would be questionable if the jurisdiction of self-governing communities overlapped significantly with that of either or both orders of government. It would not be easy to resolve this

dilemma by having representatives of aboriginal constituents vote only on those matters where aboriginal governments did not wield jurisdiction; in virtually all instances, aboriginal voters are intermingled in particular constituencies with non-aboriginal voters. While all functioning political systems contain anomalies, their multiplication should not be an unthinking consequence of policy directed to other objectives. Commissioners recommend, therefore, that discussions of aboriginal self-government address its compatibility with the possession of the federal and provincial franchise.

Self-government entails recognition of the collective rights of particular aboriginal communities. This raises difficult questions about the individual rights of members of those communities. Some observers have suggested that if self-government is given a constitutional basis, then section 25 of the Constitution Act, 1982, dealing with aboriginal rights and the Charter, is relevant, and it follows, therefore, that the Canadian Charter of Rights and Freedoms does not apply. However, the federal government's draft legislation enabling the establishment of Indian Nation governments through the delegation of authority explicitly provided for Indian Nation constitutions to be consistent with the Charter. Further, it stipulated that an Indian Nation government could not pass legislation in conflict with the Charter, and that the Governor in Council would hold powers of disallowance over laws of Indian Nations.

Commissioners believe that aboriginal Canadians, even as residents of self-governing communities, must retain the rights of Canadian citizenship. This entails the full application and protection of the Charter.

In conclusion, Commissioners sympathize with the aspirations of aboriginal peoples to achieve self-government. The existing situation is clearly unacceptable, and aboriginal peoples must have a larger say in determining their own priorities and governing their own affairs. The fact remains, however, that proposals for aboriginal self-government raise issues of great complexity. A solution involving land-based self-government is inapplicable to most aboriginals. Where it could be instituted, local resources and fiscal capacity are minimal, and extensive intergovernmental transfers would be necessary.

The complexities of integrating self-governing communities into the larger Canadian federal and parliamentary systems are intimidating. We understand the revived ethnic identity that stresses differences rather than a full application of the benefits and obligations of Canadian citizenship. Nevertheless, Canada must not reverse a policy which makes available to aboriginals full citizenship rights, of which status Indians in particular were long deprived. We must respect the Charter and avoid forms of self-government which would weaken the legitimacy of aboriginal Canadians' continued participation in the wider Canadian political process. Enhancement of aboriginal autonomy must not jeopardize aboriginals' continued enjoyment of the rights of Canadian citizenship.

Commissioners do not view realism as comprising a disservice to aboriginal peoples. The complexities and difficulties of self-government warrant a more detailed consideration than they have so far received.

Notes

1. Canada, Royal Commission on Equality in Employment, *Report* (Ottawa: Minister of Supply and Services Canada, 1984).
2. United Native Nations, Brief, September 20, 1983, p. 1.
3. Canada, House of Commons, Special Committee on Indian Self-Government, *Indian Self-Government in Canada: Report of the Special Committee* (Ottawa: Queen's Printer, 1983), p. 40.
4. Harry B. Hawthorn, ed., *A Survey of the Contemporary Indians of Canada: A Report on Economic, Political, Educational Needs and Policies* (Ottawa: Information Canada, 1966).
5. Roger Gibbins and J. Rick Ponting, "An Assessment of the Probable Impact of Aboriginal Self-Government in Canada", in *The Politics of Gender, Ethnicity and Language in Canada*, vol. 34 (Toronto: University of Toronto Press, 1985).
6. Special Committee on Self-Government, *Indian Self-Government in Canada*, p. 11.
7. *Ibid.*, p. 44.
8. Federal-Provincial Conference of First Ministers on Aboriginal Constitutional Matters, March 8–9, 1984, Transcript (Document 800-18/004), p. 32.
9. Gibbins and Ponting, "An Assessment of the Probable Impact of Aboriginal Self-Government in Canada".
10. Special Committee on Self-Government, *Indian Self-Government in Canada*, p. 59.

Municipalities

Local governments in Canada are, to use a well-worn phrase, the "creatures of provincial governments". Section 92(8) of the Constitution Act, 1867 gives the provinces authority over "municipal institutions in the province". Under this constitutional head, provincial legislatures have exclusive authority to legislate on municipal matters; they cannot delegate this authority to local government or to the national government. They can, however, legislate the establishment of municipal institutions and assign to them responsibilities. Legislatures can also eliminate municipal institutions, combine them, separate them, give them added or reduced responsibilities, and increase or decrease their financial support. Strictly speaking, then, there is no constitutionally distinct municipal level of government.

But Canadian local governments are very robust "creatures" indeed. Despite their lack of constitutional status and the fragile legal basis on which they rest, they have proved an enduring feature of Canada's governing system. Many cities existed – albeit as much smaller settlements – before the provinces or, indeed, Canada existed as governmental bodies and the provinces grew around these settlements. The most obvious example is St. John's, Newfoundland, North America's oldest city and the capital of Canada's youngest province.

Local government, as this Commission was told repeatedly during our hearings, is big government. Canada's two largest cities, Toronto and Montreal, constitute almost half the populations of Canada's two largest provinces, Ontario and Quebec. Toronto has more people than eight of the ten provinces, Montreal more than seven. Montreal has the fourth-largest government budget in Canada, Toronto the fifth largest. Some 21 Canadian cities have more people than the smallest province, Prince Edward Island. Half of Canada's population is now concentrated in ten cities. In terms of procurement – buying goods and services – local governments, collectively, now spend more than the federal government.

In terms of the lives that Canadians lead and the concerns they have, local government is a third order of government. To many, it is the most important order, dealing with matters of the most direct and immediate concern, and providing the most accessible and effective way to take advantage of many federal and provincial programs. Indeed, a fourth order of government has emerged: regional and metropolitan governments and authorities provide common services to citizens residing in a number of neighbouring local jurisdictions. This order, too, is a creature of provincial governments.

There is immense variety in the way in which local government is carried out in Canada. No standard rule applies. Each province has authority to make laws for municipal institutions. Each legislature is supreme in the way it uses or does not use that authority. Each province has chosen its own approach to local government, producing great diversity of approaches, both among provinces and within them. Nevertheless, the provinces have tended to be very sensitive to the successes and failures of approaches taken elsewhere. Amid variety, there is a broadly shared approach to local government from province to province. The details vary, but the general direction has been

similar. In different ways, for example, provinces have assumed the once-local responsibility for health, education and welfare.

If this system has not proved tidy, it has proved creative: each province effectively serves as a laboratory for every other province. The system has permitted a sensitive and flexible approach to local conditions. Relations between cities and provinces have been dynamic. There are, however, problems within this system. The obverse of flexibility is uncertainty. Provincial legislation affecting municipalities can, and often does, change unexpectedly. The instruments available to local governments, such as zoning, have been primarily negative or preventive rather than positive. Positive policy-making instruments rest with the provinces. Moreover, local government has become increasingly complex, because of both civic expansion and more sophisticated provincial legislation.

The federal government affects – on occasion decisively – the capacity of civic governments to carry out their tasks. Federal policy on interest rates is a critical factor in local finance. The federal government is a major landholder, landlord and developer in many cities. Moreover, local decisions can enhance or diminish the effectiveness of federal policies such as those relating to housing. Thus local-federal relations are critical both for municipalities and for the federal government.

To a significant degree, municipal governments depend on federal understanding of local needs and conditions; at the same time, the national economy is becoming more dependent on cities. Relations between local and federal governments are difficult to develop, however, because of the provinces' exclusive jurisdiction over local government. There are political and constitutional limits on the way federal and local governments can accommodate to their interdependence.

Canadian cities do face problems. Nevertheless, the vigour and dynamism of local governments and the communities they serve have created tremendous opportunities. Commissioners will deal with these problems and these opportunities in light of what we heard from representatives of local government and other concerned parties, and what we have learned from our own research.[1]

Canada has developed some of the most liveable cities in the world. They are clean, safe and well-equipped. Since the Great Depression, when a number of cities, as well as provinces, fell into financial difficulty, our municipalities have been well administered and financed, under provincial control and guidance.

There were many obstacles and challenges to such a happy outcome: the massive shift of people from rural to urban areas, expanded use of the automobile and resulting growth of suburban areas, a general increase in population, and the need for infrastructure to support large, complex urban societies. In addition, post-Second World War development of the welfare state complicated the picture by shifting to senior governments responsibility for matters once considered local: relief for the unemployed, welfare, health and education.

Commissioners are conscious that Canadians have been doing something right at the level of the local community, be it village, town, city or

metropolis. We make suggestions and recommendations below with this fact very much in mind. We shall look at issues that we find are of general concern throughout Canada: the constitutional status of local government; intergovernmental relations, at both local-provincial and local-federal levels; revenues and responsibilities; urban policy; and the local role in economic development. These issues are closely interconnected. Indeed, many of the possibilities in the final four areas of concern turn on the approach taken to the issue of constitutional status. We shall therefore start there.

The Constitutional Status of Local Government

The fact that local governments are the "creatures" of provincial governments has far-reaching effects. The most important of these are uncertainty and legislative and institutional complexity of municipal government. Simple acts of the provincial legislature can change local government, and frequently do. Because of judicial interpretation which has prevented delegation of power to local governments, municipal acts must set out specifically what local governments may and may not do in administering policies approved by provincial legislatures. The resulting highly detailed legislation has added great complexity to local administration. "This circumstance", Marion Dewar, the Mayor of Ottawa, told us, "is a far cry from the brief division of responsibilities between the federal and provincial governments as set out in the Canadian Constitution." (City of Ottawa, Brief, November 31, 1983, p. 10).

One immediate consequence is that municipal councils must approve every administrative action that implements a policy and often are bogged down in administrative detail that might be better delegated. While this makes decision making more open than it is at the federal and provincial levels, it also diverts time and attention from broader questions that may affect far more of a community's citizens.

The provinces have used their authority to create not only local governments, but also a whole range of special-purpose commissions, boards and authorities. The City of Toronto, for example, has within its borders some 101 provincially created authorities. Some of the provincially created boards provide means for local citizens to appeal decisions made by local councils or other administrative boards, but such appeals are complex and expensive.

The very confined nature of municipal planning powers sharply constrains the capacity of local governments to plan in a positive way, that is, to set out development goals and standards. In effect, provincial law and judicial interpretation have confined local governments to negative approaches to the control, rather than the stimulation, of urban development. Zoning, approving subdivisions, and making land-use plans are activities typical of this approach. Such devices allow a city to prevent certain uses of property by private owners. They prevent some of the worst abuses in development, but they are very cumbersome; in fact, they may discourage and occasionally prevent some of the best types of development.

Discretionary forms of control such as spot zoning, holding zones, development reviews, and "minor" adjustments approved by committees of

adjustment have circumvented this limitation. However, as our research indicates, this tendency has transformed zoning from a system based on clearly defined rules to one based on political bargaining. Municipal councils find themselves squeezed by provincially established limits on their powers to direct development toward approved goals, private developers' plans for the use of their property, the need to expand the main basis of municipal revenue, the property tax, and the resistance of property owners adversely affected by development.

In our hearings, we Commissioners heard proposals to resolve some of these problems by giving local governments explicit constitutional status as a distinct order of government, with clearly defined powers and responsibilities. For instance, Mayor Elizabeth Kishkon of Windsor put to this Commission the City's recommendation that:

> *In light of the importance of local government to the majority of Canadian citizens, both in terms of direct provision of service and as a major force in the economy, municipalities be formally recognized in the Canadian Constitution as the third level of government with a guaranteed right of existence.*
>
> (City of Windsor, Transcript, Windsor, October 13, 1983 [vol. 25], p. 4721.)

Mayor Dewar of Ottawa went even further, suggesting that a number of Canada's major cities should become "provinces".

Commissioners did not detect, or expect, great enthusiasm from the provinces for providing the cities with clear and constitutionally based powers. We observed no enthusiasm whatsoever for transforming any major city into a province in its own right. While we agree that constitutional status could resolve a number of concerns of local governments and might simplify provincial administration by placing urban policy in the hands of the governments most sensitive to cities' needs – that is, local governments – we heard a number of cautionary voices. Dr. John Graham told us in Halifax: "We don't want another layer of jurisdiction with certain sovereign powers unto itself. Surely we have a complicated enough system." (John Graham, Transcript, Halifax, June 6, 1984 [vol. 6], p. 1275.)

Although constitutional status for municipalities might rather simplify Canada's governmental system than complicate it, Commissioners heard others question the proposal, not so much for cautionary reasons as for practical ones. Paul Godfrey, representing the Municipality of Metropolitan Toronto, put the practicalities to us this way: "We have gone through that process before . . . I do not want . . . to come out and call for a role in the Constitution because I do not believe that will happen." (Municipality of Metropolitan Toronto, Transcript, Toronto, December 1, 1983 [vol. 55], pp. 11525, 27.)

Others focused their attention and energies on matters they considered of higher priority. Michael Harcourt, Mayor of Vancouver, argued that Canada is changing from an Atlantic-based economy to a Pacific-based and more urban economy. These trends, he said, are important "whatever our Constitution says – and the Constitution is almost irrelevant in that context." (Michael Harcourt, Transcript, Vancouver, June 11, 1984 [vol. 9], p. 2123.)

Commissioners deduce from these comments and others made by representatives of other cities and by intervenors at our hearings that some local leaders favour a secure status in the Constitution. Even these leaders, however, do not expect to obtain what they wish and are inclined to seek other, more attainable objectives. Because we concur in this general assessment, we do not recommend explicit constitutional status for municipal governments. We do, however, suggest that each provincial government systematically examine relations between itself and its local governments. Together with municipal leaders, provincial governments should address the growing complexity of those governments, the insecurity of financing, and the mismatch of revenues and responsibility. Together they should look for ways to harness the undoubted capacities of municipal administrations. Such constructive discussions may well indicate that in some provinces, both municipal and provincial governments would benefit from an enhanced or a constitutional status for major cities. Should that prove so, Commissioners see no impediment to a single province seeking an amendment to the Constitution Act that would specify the constitutional status of one or more cities within its boundaries. Alternatively, a province could enter into a binding arrangement under the intergovernmental agreement clause we have proposed for the Constitution. In any case, such examination and discussion seem essential in order to improve relations between local governments and both provincial and federal governments.

To deal with the uncertainty which local governments feel about possible alterations to their powers, Commissioners recommend that provinces consider adopting special procedures for changing local responsibilities. The most straightforward mechanism would be a regulation that changes to municipal acts or city charters require approval of two-thirds of the members of a provincial legislature. In most provinces at most times, this would necessitate that the government and the opposition agree on proposed changes. An alternative, affording even stronger protection, would be a referendum either on a province-wide basis or in the municipalities affected by a major change.

Intergovernmental Relations

For much of the last quarter-century, intergovernmental concern has focused on the state of federal-provincial relations. There are two other intergovernmental relationships, however, that are of increasing importance. The first is the relationship between provincial governments and local governments, and the second is the relationship between the national government and local governments, in particular the governments of Canada's largest cities.

As we have remarked, one of the social changes of the post-war years has been the urbanization of Canada. Three-quarters of Canada's citizens live in urban areas, with most concentrated in a few cities. The non-urban economic sectors, agriculture and resources, have declined in relation to the urban sectors of manufacturing and services. This trend appears likely to continue for a time.

All of these factors suggest to Commissioners that interdependence among governments will increasingly involve issues of concern to local governments. The fact that local governments have no status under the Constitution, however, impedes improvement of relations among the three orders of government. To promote the best delivery of government programs, many of them related to job creation, the federal government has preferred to deal directly with local governments. The potential advantages of a direct federal-local relationship are significant: the shorter the lines of communication between national and local leaders, the better their understanding of one another is likely to be and the greater the probability of joint success. The provinces, however, have insisted that in accordance with the Constitution, federal relations with local governments be conducted through provincial offices. They argue that even where local governments are administering federal programs or spending federal money, direct federal relations with those governments constitute an intrusion into an area of provincial responsibility. Constitutionally, this contention is correct, even if the activity in question is clearly in the federal jurisdiction. Thus conflict arises between what is practical and what is constitutional.

Since it is unlikely that the Constitution will be amended to change this situation, governments of all orders must find an alternative means to improve their relationships with one another. In fact, they have already tried a number of means. One was the tri-level conference, attended by federal, provincial and local representatives. Such conferences took place in the 1970s, but none has been held recently. Various representatives of municipalities suggested to this Commission the possibility that such conferences might be held in the future. Commissioners endorse this approach as a useful way for each level of government to appreciate the situations faced by the others. It might be advantageous on occasion, to schedule tri-level meetings in conjunction with federal-provincial First Ministers' meetings.

Another attempt to improve intergovernmental relations was the creation of a federal Ministry of State for Urban Affairs. This ministry, created in 1971, was disbanded in 1979. A number of spokespersons for local governments suggested that the federal government re-establish such a department to provide a forum for direct dealings between municipal authorities and the federal Cabinet and senior bureaucracy. While Commissioners believe that this idea has some merit, there are grounds for hesitation. The proliferation of advisory ministries within the federal administration has contributed to the growth of government, increased its complexity, and reduced the capacity of any particular advisory ministry to be either fully aware of, or to represent the interests of, those whom it was intended to represent. In addition, most matters affecting local government also affect provincial interests. The creation of a federal ministry of urban affairs, therefore, might simply improve federal-municipal communication at the cost of making federal-provincial communication more difficult. Commissioners conclude that the municipal interest lies in better communication with those ministers whose responsibilities directly affect local interests: for example, the Ministers of Finance, Transport, Public Works, Regional Industrial Expansion, and the minister responsible for housing policies.

An alternative to the creation of a new ministry might be the use of parliamentary processes to anticipate and to monitor the effect of federal measures on local administration. This means could provide a forum for the expression of local concerns and needs. It has the significant advantages that it is more open to public participation and scrutiny, including the scrutiny of provincial governments, and that it could serve to heighten ministerial sensitivity to local problems. Commissioners recommend that this task be assigned to the parliamentary committee on intergovernmental relations that we considered in Chapter 22.

Commissioners believe that local administration of a number of federal responsibilities would prove more responsive to local needs and conditions. Given Canada's Constitution, such responsibilities cannot be delegated directly to local governments, but must be routed through provincial governments. Since, however, the latter may be just as far removed from local concerns as the federal authorities, Commissioners do not believe that to delegate administration to provincial governments would always produce the beneficial effects desired. Decentralization of federal administration to federally-appointed bodies operating in the local areas is a preferable approach. Such a step has already been taken, for instance, in the management of harbours. Federal Port Authorities, established under federal legislation, are providing local administration in a manner that appears to be considerably more sensitive than that of the previous centralized administration.

Commissioners believe that similar approaches should be considered in two areas of considerable concern to municipalities. One of these areas is that of land management, where federal powers to expropriate, hold or develop land often produce development that is at variance with local priorities. In our hearings, some intervenors suggested that local authorities should have some responsibility for the management of federal properties in urban areas. We agree that local authorities, appointed by the federal government, could manage properties in a manner more sensitive both to local preferences and to local market opportunities.

A second area of concern is airport management, where the federal responsibility for air transportation has a direct effect on, and is directly affected by, local government development. Commissioners believe that in some instances, the establishment of local airport authorities might considerably improve sensitivity to local conditions, provide a more effective and integrated air-transport system, and improve service to air travellers. In Chapter 22, Commissioners recommended a Constitutional amendment to allow the delegation of constitutional authority among governments. This change would enable the federal government, through agreement with the relevant province, to delegate to local governments the responsibility for siting, developing and administering some designated airports. This arrangement differs somewhat from the federally established local authority model we considered for the management of federal lands in urban communities, but it offers a means to achieve a similar objective: greater responsiveness to local needs and conditions through decentralized administration of federal responsibilities.

Provincial-local relationships are also an issue of intergovernmental affairs. Because provincial governments must provide a legislative basis for all local government action, the provincial-local relationship involves considerable difficulty and requires considerable sensitivity. In the absence of constitutional amendments, which would allocate responsibilities to local governments, provinces should give high priority to examining, clarifying and simplifying the relationships each has with local governments. This action would serve to lighten the burden of both local and provincial administration. Most important, in Commissioners' opinion, it would be of significant benefit to taxpayers who find local concerns complicated by a maze of provincially created boards, agencies and public authorities dealing with poorly defined and shifting responsibilities.

Revenues and Responsibilities

In 1982, municipal government expenditures rose to $33 billion, representing, as Table 24-2 shows, over 9 per cent of the nation's gross national expenditure. Nevertheless, municipal leaders throughout the country are concerned that the anticipated expenditures they must make are vastly greater than their available resources. Municipalities have repeatedly sought sufficient fiscal autonomy, through access to sources of revenue other than the property tax, to finance the responsibilities of local government. Provincial governments, however, have steadfastly withheld that power, and so municipalities remain dependent on transfers or subsidies from the two other levels of government. Commissioners are concerned with the ways in which local governments are funded. They spend more than twice as much as they raise from taxes. This expenditure results in a dependence on revenue sources beyond their control and, consequently, uncertainty about the amount of funding provided in any given year. Long-term financial planning and budgeting is therefore extremely difficult. Moreover, municipal residents are uncertain of their ability to hold government accountable for taxing and spending.

TABLE 24-2 Sources of Local Government Revenue, 1982

	Billion $	%
Property tax	10 840.9	32.1
Corporate tax	1 237.4	3.7
Other tax	282.2	.8
Total taxes	12 361.4	33.6
Grants in lieu of taxes	945.0	2.8
Self-generated revenues	4 832.5	14.3
Government subsidies	15 608.1	46.3
Grand Total	33 747.0	100

Source: Jacques L'Heureux, "The Division of Powers and Municipalities", in *Intergovernmental Relations*, vol. 63, prepared for the Royal Commission on the Economic Union and Development Prospects for Canada (Toronto: University of Toronto Press, 1985).

For a variety of reasons, Canada's tri-level transfer system makes accountability very difficult, because of the size of the expenditures by one order of government that are funded from taxes raised by another. This problem of accountability is compounded for local governments by the way in which provincial subsidies are provided. In all provinces, in recent years, more and more provincial grants to municipalities have been conditional: that is, they have been provided on the express condition that they be spent in particular ways. In effect, these conditions reduce the choice available to local governments in the matter of expenditures, which means that municipal authorities cannot be held accountable for the allocation of a large portion of their budgets.

Local governments have expressed concern about the detrimental effects of the conditional grant system on the accountability and, consequently, on the discipline of Canada's public financing system. Their more immediate concern, however, is the rigidity of the system. In Charlottetown, Alderman George MacDonald told this Commission:

> *Very often, the federal [grant] programs are such that we have to start saying, "Here is the money. Start reading all the guidelines and try making up a story to get it" rather than [the Federal government] saying "What are your needs? Can we help you?"*
> (City of Charlottetown, Transcript, Charlottetown, September 19, 1983 [vol. 10], pp. 2468–69.)

While Mr. MacDonald's comments point to the problems of federal-provincial-local relations and to the need for improved communication among all three orders of government, they also indicate the inflexibility that conditional grants, whatever their source, impose on local governments, particularly given the degree of municipal dependency.

There are a number of ways to balance local revenues with local responsibilities and, consequently, to provide more flexibility to local governments and to reduce the need for, and thus the rigidities of, conditional grants. One method transfers certain responsibilities from local to provincial governments. This shift has already been made, in large part, however. In 1913, for example, net expenditures by local governments amounted to almost $14 per capita, while those made by the provinces amounted to $7 per capita. In 1980, by contrast, local expenditures had reached the sum of $696 per capita, while provincial expenditures had multiplied to $2219 per capita.[2] These figures reflect increased provincial responsibility for health, education and welfare, and increased local spending, after the Second World War, for infrastructure and local schools. Provincial governments have also begun to assume responsibility for local school costs. Four provinces now accept virtually complete responsibility for school financing. Because many local responsibilities have already effectively become provincial, however, the possibility of further major transfers of responsibility from local to provincial governments is limited.

To change the structure of local revenues offers more possibilities for correcting the imbalance. The largest portion of local revenues, aside from grants from other levels of government, comes from property taxes. Despite

the significant advantages of these taxes, their regressive and relatively inelastic character presents considerable difficulties to local government. For this reason, sales taxes and income taxes are often suggested as means to increase local revenues; but these taxes raise other problems: administration, the taxation of non-residents, inter-urban equity, and great variations in the tax bases among communities.

This Commission believes that it would be preferable for the provinces to dedicate a specific portion of income- or sales-tax revenues for local government financing. We recommend that each province look for appropriate ways to carry out this action. While this arrangement would subject municipalities to some of the vagaries of economic conditions that beset federal and provincial revenues, a designated percentage share of these tax revenues would, in our opinion, enable municipalities to make their own economic assessments of their likely revenues as a basis for long-term planning and budgeting. Local governments would still depend to some extent on provincial grants. Commissioners also recommend that, to the extent possible, provincial governments shift their municipal financing arrangements to provide increased unconditional funding rather than conditional grants.

We believe this arrangement would enable greater flexibility and greater effectiveness in terms of local expenditures, in that local governments are better placed for, and by and large, have greater expertise in, judging what types of expenditures will best meet the community's needs and best take advantage of the unique opportunities it has. This approach is at variance with the one we take to federal-provincial transfers. However, unlike the federal-provincial relationship, in which basic responsibilities are allocated by the Constitution, the provincial-local relationship is determined by a province. That is, provinces have already established the "conditions" for municipal spending of provincial grants by establishing the responsibilities local governments must meet. To add conditions to conditions, we believe, merely increases complexity.

Urban Policy

Although municipal governments are often seen to exercise the power to plan and establish urban policy, their control of planning is, in reality, constitutionally limited and their role primarily reactive. Private property owners and developers initiate development, often working along with senior governments; provincial governments control, review and generally dominate the planning process. Municipal governments can, however, determine the course of development through their decisions on services and infrastructure, such as streets and transit systems. Nevertheless, their dependence on the provinces for financial assistance limits their capacity to initiate and promote development. Municipal capital spending is scrutinized by provincial governments; and most municipal planning and urban-policy decisions are subject to provincial review.

This Commission believes that effective urban planning or policy recognizes that local governments, more than federal or provincial governments, are aware of urban issues and better able to deal with them. We

believe that in general, local governments can most effectively establish and carry out urban policy. Therefore, while acknowledging that the provinces have different systems for dealing with urban issues, we recommend that they grant greater and more general authority to local government. Commissioners also believe that a considerable reduction is desirable in the number of special purpose bodies, such as planning boards that are created by the provinces to act independently of local governments. These bodies should consolidate their functions as far as possible so that elected politicians are accountable locally rather than provincially. An increase in local authority depends, of course, on establishing greater, more secure and unconditional sources of financing, and on developing greater federal and provincial sensitivity to local needs and to the local effect of senior-government policies.

The Local Role in Economic Development

This Commission believes that local government, particularly the major cities, will play a significant role in Canada's economic evolution. When deciding whether to move to a particular city or country, companies often look at more than the traditional bases of development, such as location relative to markets, available rail or air transportation, land availability and tax structure. They look also at the safety and cleanliness of a city, the quality of its restaurants and shopping facilities, and the presence of amenities such as parks, art galleries, symphony, opera, theatres, and major league-sports facilities. Canada has many advantages to attract business and investors, and the reputation of our cities is growing. At the same time, however, the attractiveness of a city—its capacity to act as a magnet for able people, particularly those with the scarce skills around which companies, industries and local employment are built—is relative and changing. Canadian urban communities must compete to remain relatively more attractive than other cities throughout the world.

Since we expect economic development to become still more urban, it is vital for provincial and federal governments to recognize that the quality of urban life in Canada is an economic asset of prime importance. The hearings and research of this Commission, however, reveal a build-up of entanglements, irritants, unnecessary restrictions and complications, and undesirable complexities, all of which may dampen the remarkable dynamism that has marked Canadian urban development in the post-war years.

This Commission recommends that each province examine and modify its own municipal government system to provide greater discretion to local governments, to simplify legal, institutional, and constitutional arrangements, and to develop clear and direct lines of communication between local and provincial decision makers. We believe that these changes would allow city governments to exploit fully their capacity to improve economic and social conditions for their citizens, for the provinces, and for Canada as a whole.

Notes

1. For Commission research studies on municipal issues see: Stanley M. Makuch, "Urban Law and Policy Development in Canada: The Myth and the Reality", in *Labour Law and Urban Law in Canada*, vol. 51; Harry M. Kitchen and Melville L. McMillan, "Local Government and Canadian Federalism", and Jacques L'Heureux, "The Division of Powers and Municipalities", in *Intergovernmental Relations*, vol. 63 (Toronto: University of Toronto Press, 1985).
2. Kitchen and McMillan, "Local Government and Canadian Federalism".

Conclusions and Recommendations

The more government Canadians have, the more democratic we must become. The institutions of responsible parliamentary government remain the key to keeping government our servant rather than seeing it become our master. Commissioners regard Parliament as the principal forum for public debate and intend our recommendations to contribute, in general, to the strengthening of this institution.

To restore Parliament as the principal forum for national debate, we must not only bolster its democratic processes, but we must also improve its capacity to reconcile national and regional interests. We wish neither to reassert the dominance of the national government in line with the prevailing opinion at the time of Confederation, nor to establish the provincial order of government as an integral part of national government.

With regard to federalism and intergovernmental relations, two basic needs influence Commissioners' general objectives. First, it is desirable to clarify where possible, by constitutional amendment, by delegation or intergovernmental agreement, or by more clearly defined policy directions, the responsibilities distributed between federal and provincial governments. Secondly, recognizing the complexity of modern government and the interdependence within our federation, it is desirable to introduce greater certainty and stability into existing intergovernmental processes. We seek neither to eliminate intergovernmental conflict nor to further the development of non-accountable institutions. Rather we seek to secure and give greater public recognition to minimal processes and structures that will moderate the excesses and costs of unresolved conflict and channel creative solutions to common problems.

Commissioners view the Charter of Rights and Freedoms both as a guarantee of specific rights and freedoms of citizens and as an important element of the framework within which Canadian society can evolve. This is consistent with our view that constitutional law should be responsive to social change and evolving values and attitudes, and that it should stabilize the pace and direction of such change.

Responsible Government and Public Accountability

■ The Canadian practice of party government has restricted the opportunities for Members of Parliament to participate in the development of public policy outside the confines of party caucuses. Organized special interest groups now challenge MPs as representatives and frequently bypass them.

- MPs could gain more influence over public policy if members in committee could investigate and debate matters of public interest on which party positions have not yet been established or fully determined. The separation of legislative committees from investigative committees would help to achieve this end by serving to provide Parliament and the government with policy

analysis and guidance distinct from that which is received from administrative officials or extra-parliamentary sources.

- Parliament need not diminish the activities of interest groups, but it should provide the principal public forum for these interests to define their concerns. Parliament should encourage these groups to present their positions and demands for an open examination in relation to general interests. There should be a small number of parliamentary committees focusing on comprehensive policy matters – the budget, regulatory policy, Crown corporations, and federal-provincial relations, for example – and these would be ideal forums for such scrutiny.
- Agencies such as the Public Service Commission, the Office of the Commissioner of Official Languages, the Privacy and Information Commissioners and the Office of the Auditor General have important functions, but receive insufficient direction and control from our elected representatives in Parliament. In order to ensure accountability of these agencies, Parliament must define their procedures and basic strategies. Commissioners suggest that the Public Service Commission, the Office of the Commissioner of Official Languages, and the Privacy and Information Commissioners review their work before a Parliamentary Committee on the Public Service. This committee would study the success of these agencies in meeting the various criteria set by Parliament. The same committee, since it would be familiar with the performance of these agencies, should review their financial estimates. The Public Accounts Committee would perform this role in relation to the Office of the Auditor General.
- The federal government has formalized Cabinet structures, processes and support services in recent years, in order to restore ministerial and parliamentary control over an expanded and complex administrative structure. Although central agencies have partially checked the dispersal and diffusion of power to public servants, they can do so effectively only when under the close direction of ministers; otherwise, central agencies themselves become yet another layer of bureaucracy to be controlled.
- We have given too much autonomy and discretion to non-departmental forms of government organization such as Crown corporations and regulatory agencies. Such autonomy has undermined the principles of responsible government. To correct this situation, Commissioners recommend that greater "control" of Crown corporations be defined in the context of a reformed competition and regulatory environment, and not just in the framework of administrative accountability, in accordance with the current trend. Especially for commercial Crown corporations, governments need greater strategic control, not day-to-day interference in management decisions. Moreover, Cabinet

should strengthen its review of regulations formulated by regulatory agencies.

- Although some prominent political appointments have violated the ideal of a neutral public service, it is not true that the senior bureaucracy has become politicized. The system of appointments by Order-in-Council based on professional merit on the recommendation of the Clerk of the Privy Council has worked well. However, political advice to the Prime Minister has traditionally been the basis of appointments to a large number of boards and agencies. This category may be too large; the public might be better served if more of these appointments were based exclusively on merit. An all-party group designated by the proposed Parliamentary Committee on the Public Service should review the current use of Governor-in-Council appointments to boards and agencies, the foreign service, high levels in departments, and Ministers' staffs, in order to help distinguish between two categories of positions: those where partisan sensitivity justifies political appointments, and those where partisan sensitivity is not at issue and where professional merit should prevail. Commissioners' opinion is that this general review process should be continuous, and that appointments of no clear partisan value should be made on a basis of "merit".
- In light of the accelerating challenge to democratic controls presented by the increasing international responsibilities of the state, Commissioners believe it is desirable to provide secure foundations for parliamentary ratification of international treaties and for other measures to ensure parliamentary review of executive action in the international domain. □

Representative Government and National Socio-Economic Interests in Economic Policy Formation

It is important to facilitate more direct and continuous involvement of representatives of Canadian interest groups in public decision making, especially in economic policy. Those interests need to interact more with one another and to take greater account of the broader concerns and conflicts within Canadian society for the resolution of which Parliament itself is ultimately responsible.

In comparison with the formal structures that have developed in some Western nations, Canadian consultative practices tend to be fragmented, informal and episodic. Current practices may be inadequate in light of recent Canadian experience and anticipated needs, such as the continuing pressures of economic adjustment. However, we do not recommend a corporatist or tripartite style of government/private sector relations.

■ Although substantial secrecy is necessary in relation to the preparation and release of the budget, Commissioners recommend that guidelines are needed to allow less comprehensive budget

secrecy than now exists. We urge the House of Commons to initiate a change in the convention of comprehensive budget secrecy in order to set in motion steps towards more effective advance discussion and consultation arrangements.

It would be desirable to seek federal-provincial agreement on the timing of budgets, so that their presentation could be co-ordinated, with the federal budget either preceding or following most provincial budgets by two or three months. Pre-budget consultation should occur in several forums, but particularly in the House of Commons.

A continuing national dialogue on general directions for economic policy requires a permanent national forum. This Commission favours establishment of a permanent Economic Policy Committee of the House of Commons. The Committee would hold an annual series of pre-budget hearings timed to allow its work to influence budget preparation. It would take testimony about the nation's economic prospects from the Department of Finance, the Bank of Canada, and the Treasury Board, as well as from agencies such as the Economic Council of Canada; it would also gather the views of major groups, including national representatives of business, labour and other associations.

- The Committee would scrutinize the government's performance and the revenue and expenditure implications of the positions of key interests. It should schedule its budget review to co-ordinate with its other responsibilities and with the timing of the annual First Ministers' Conference. Moreover, it would be necessary to adjust the internal priorities and planning cycle of the federal government in light of the accepted federal-provincial cycle.

■ Continuation of sectoral and industry-by-industry dialogue on improving Canada's economy is essential. Discussions should bring together representatives of business and labour, and federal, provincial and municipal governments and other groups, as necessary. Government participation may not always be required. In light of these conclusions, Commissioners recommend that such sectoral discussions be developed within the following guidelines:

- Consultative mechanisms should focus on clear, specific objectives. This approach will make them more likely to be successful.
- Consultation should be a continuing process with reasonably predictable arrangements. Permanent or standing groups may be required in some cases.
- Governments must make a firm commitment to any consultative process they undertake. Effective consultative arrangements require that non-government participants have some influence on the agenda and decision-making schedule. Responsibility for the overall policy-making process, however, rests with the government of the day.

- Consultative processes aimed at consensus building must be supported by fair representation from many groups in society and, normally, by parity between business and labour.
- Sharing and refining of information are prerequisites to these consultative processes. □

National Institutions and the Representation of Regional Interests

Commissioners believe that the federal principle requires that the House of Commons, chosen on the basis of representation by population, be balanced by a second chamber based on representation by region. Our institutions should recognize the federal principle, provide greater regional representation, and respond to regional interests in national policy making and administration.

■ Commissioners recommend that the Senate embody the federalist principle and provide the regional representation lacking in the House of Commons.

- A reformed Senate must build on our practice of party government in its elections, caucuses and discipline. The Senate must be elected, and election to the two Houses should take place at the same time.
- In the Senate, representation should be weighted in favour of the less populous regions. All regions need not be considered equal, for the Senate should only temper, not obstruct, representation by population.
- The Senate should be elected by a system of proportional representation. The governing party is more likely to have elected representatives from all regions within its parliamentary caucus, even if, for one or some regions, they secure places only in the Senate. A Senate elected on this basis should ensure that the governing party will usually be able to constitute a Cabinet that includes members from all regions.
- We recommend that Senators be elected in six-member constituencies. This number is large enough to effect the intended proportional representation and yet to allow for some recognition of the regions within provinces. Yukon and the Northwest Territories could elect their Senators on simple plurality. Existing numbers of Senators would be modified and distributed as follows:

	Existing	**Proposed**
British Columbia	6	12
Alberta	6	12
Saskatchewan	6	12
Manitoba	6	12
Ontario	24	24

Quebec	24	24
New Brunswick	10	12
Nova Scotia	10	12
Prince Edward Island	4	6
Newfoundland	6	12
Yukon	1	2
Northwest Territories	1	4
	104	144

- The Senate does not require a veto to temper, on regional grounds, the legislative majority of the House of Commons. Commissioners believe that the Senate should have a six-month suspensive veto, except in relation to legislation with linguistic significance; such legislation would require approval of a majority of francophone Senators, as well as of the Senate as a whole.
- If Senate reform along the lines proposed here is not adopted within a reasonable time, efforts should be made to reform the electoral system of the House of Commons to enhance regional representation. In that event, Commissioners favour the proposal of the Task Force on National Unity to add 60 members to the Commons, distributed to parties on the basis of their share of the national popular vote and allocated to provinces on the basis of the degree to which the parties were "underrepresented" in seats won, or not won, in relation to their share of the popular vote in each province. □

Many federal departments and agencies have not assumed responsibility for regional development within their mandates. This failure has lessened the executive branch's capacity to be regionally responsive and has undermined the effectiveness of regional representation in Cabinet.

- This Commission therefore recommends that:
  - The central administrative agencies should be structured so as to provide more regional information upon which the Cabinet can base policy decisions. This requires that regional offices be part of the central agency apparatus supporting the Cabinet and the Prime Minister.
  - The Cabinet should decentralize departments and agencies for purposes of policy planning and development. Sectorally organized departments should incorporate the regional dimension fully in departmental planning and policy development. There should be regional officials in the central administrative decision-making of departments.
  - Regional representation should receive consideration in nominations to the boards of Crown corporations and regulatory agencies. If the Senate becomes an elected body, appointments of the heads of major Crown corporations and

all members of the governing boards of major regulatory agencies should be subject to the approval of a Senate committee to be established for this purpose. □

Barriers within the Canadian Economic Union

Despite recent expressions of concern that the Canadian economic union is becoming increasingly balkanized and fragmented, goods, capital, services and people now move relatively freely within the Canadian common market.

While lost economic output from impediments to free movement and distortions of the common market appears small, private economic actors have indicated that the policies in question create considerable difficulties for them. Even more than the economic rationale, the political rationale for the national right to free movement is a powerful idea for most Canadians.

The effect of these distortions – and the need for effective co-ordination of economic policy – are likely to increase as Canadians face greater competition from the outside world. We should create incentives to international competitiveness, and we should facilitate appropriate adjustments.

The economic union implies elimination of internal barriers and positive measures to facilitate operation of the market, to overcome market imperfections and to pursue effective stabilization, industrial and social policies. All regions must share in the benefits of economic integration.

Internal barriers may be the response of governments to local preferences, and often reflect our commitment to redistribution of income and opportunity. Thus, the challenge, in particular cases, is not simply to eliminate the barriers through constitutional prohibition or other means, but rather, how to balance the economic benefits of free movement against other goals to which Canadians aspire. The trade-offs to be made are not exclusively between economic efficiency and political diversity or provincial autonomy within the federation: Canadian federalism also involves a national community with its own requirements. Moreover, as the Canadian Charter of Rights and Freedoms makes clear, individual rights have implications for the economic union.

The goal of regional development requires that Canadian economic policy must seek not only to maximize aggregate national income, but also to encourage the economic development of individual regions.

■ Commissioners urge that a broad view be taken of the scope of section 121 of the Constitution Act, 1867, consistent with an interpretation that section 121 covers services as well as goods and non-tariff barriers as well as tariffs. However, in light of existing controversy and uncertainty, it may be prudent to seek eventual clarification by constitutional amendment.

- We would recommend a limited amendment to include services to reflect current conceptions of the nature of interprovincial trade. On the issue of non-tariff barriers to trade in goods and services, we recommend as an interim step that governments agree to a Code of Economic Conduct.

- The governments of Canada should develop a Code of Economic Conduct to spell out acceptable practices, set out the principles of the economic union, and provide for enforcement. We advance a series of general guidelines for consideration:
  - The code should confirm general principles of the economic union applicable to both the federal and provincial governments:
    - Reduction of barriers to the allocation of capital, labour, goods and services throughout Canada
    - Non-discrimination against persons (individuals and organizations) based on province of residence
    - Commitment to minimizing the costs of provincial programs that might fall on the residents of other jurisdictions, and to prior consultation for this purpose
  - Recognition of the need for a transportation, communications and information infrastructure to support national economic development with significant regional benefits.
- The burden of demonstrating that a barrier did not violate the principles of the Code should lie with the authority imposing the barrier.
- The Code should identify major areas where reduction of barriers to internal trade should begin. Attention should focus not only on the form of the barriers, but also on the anticipated effects. The possibilities of substitution between types of barriers are extensive, and provinces vary in economic development and in their potential to inflict injury on other jurisdictions or the residents of those jurisdictions. Those drafting the Code might first consider barriers that prevent Canadian enterprises from being internationally competitive.
- Initially governments should set up the Code, and public and governmental pressure should enforce it. The intergovernmental process would provide the appropriate forum for dealing with the politically sensitive issue of internal barriers to trade. After experience with the operation of the Code, we should move to entrench its principles in the Constitution and to enforce the Code through some other form of binding intergovernmental agreement.
- To develop the Code of Economic Conduct, monitor the state of the economic union, and explore methods for co-ordinating policies, the First Ministers' Conference should create a Council of Economic Development Ministers.
- To initiate the process of identifying and controlling internal trade barriers, Commissioners propose the following procedure. The Council will ask each government to list barriers imposed by other governments that they believe harm its provincial economy or its residents. Next, each government would be required to explain and defend those of its policies identified at the first stage. A Federal-Provincial Commission on the

Economic Union would receive this material, and would analyse the barriers, their probable consequences, and the justifications declared. The Commission would identify violations of the principles of the economic union and make recommendations concerning specific terms for the proposed Code. It would send this report to the Council for action.

- A Federal-Provincial Commission on the Economic Union which would serve the Council of Economic Development Ministers would have responsibility for preparing materials for the Council as directed:
  - Analysing the first round of barriers identified by the Council's initial inquiry
  - Initiating research on the state of the economic union and methods for improving it
  - Receiving complaints from groups, individuals and corporations affected by government actions threatening the economic union, investigating them, and reporting on them, with recommendations, to the public and the Council.

If a Code is eventually made legally enforceable, the Commission could become a regulatory agency, but one that regulates governments. □

Economic Management

In several specific areas related to our concern with the international environment, the Canadian economic union, and economic adjustment, Commissioners believe that constitutional changes are desirable for more effective economic management; Canada requires a procedure which would allow treaties, once concluded, to be binding and enforceable on both federal and provincial authorities within Canada.

■ We recommend a constitutional amendment to provide that where a proposed treaty contains provisions that require implementation by provincial legislatures or affect rights within areas of provincial jurisdiction, the relevant sections should be ratified by provincial legislatures. We propose the application of the amendment formula for this purpose so that sections of a treaty imposing obligations on provinces would come into effect on the passage of resolutions in the legislatures of two-thirds of the provinces, representing at least half of Canada's population. We do not see this recommendation as having immediate application to negotiations with the United States on a free-trade agreement. We would recommend, however, that a constitutional solution be in place before the proposed trade agreement would come up for review in the 1990s.

■ To clarify jurisdiction and roles in the field of telecommunications, we recommend concurrent jurisdiction with federal paramountcy.

■ To clarify responsibility regarding certain aspects of overall regulation of trade and commerce, we propose that section 91(2) be amended to provide explicitly for federal regulatory power over competition and product standards.

■ If intergovermental agreement is not reached soon on the harmonization of regulations respecting interprovincial trucking, we recommend that serious consideration should be given to bringing this matter under federal jurisdiction. □

Equalization

The principle of equalization, an essential element of Canadian federalism, represents a commitment to all provinces that economic misfortune will not undercut their constitutional role. It contributes to a true decentralization of government functions, in spite of the differing economic capacities among provinces.

Commissioners stress the distinction between equalization payments and regional development programs. The former are intended to offset economic disadvantages, while the latter are intended to reverse this disadvantage. Equalization payments are necessary only because of our lack of success in combatting regional economic disparities. In practice, this means that regional development financing must be added to equalization disbursements; the federal government should not cut one in favour of the other.

■ The federal government's responsibility for interregional redistribution gives it a leading role in designing and operating the equalization scheme. Commissioners recommend that the following changes to the equalization system be discussed with the provinces:

- Canada should return to a representative tax system that includes all 10 provinces in the base. The present five-province calculation base allows too much room for distortion, strategic behaviour and unintended side-effects.
- Equalization payments should include some portion of resource revenues. There is no magic figure here, but the 20 to 30 per cent range seems an appropriate compromise, since it approximates the amounts that would accrue to provincial treasuries in the form of tax revenues if natural resources were in private hands.
- The concept of including needs as part of the entitlements calculation is attractive. Commissioners recognize, however, that this can develop only slowly, given the amount of data required and the serious practical difficulties involved. The inclusion of needs in the calculation will be especially important if the Northern territories enter the scheme. □

Regional Development

This Commission believes that regional development must remain an essential component of Canadian policy and, indeed, of the Confederation bargain as now reflected in section 36 of the Constitution Act, 1982. It must be recognized, however, that policies intended to promote regional development have often hindered the overall efficiency of the national economy in that they impeded inter-regional adjustment and distorted regional development. Canadians need to reconsider the way in which we look at regional economic disparity, what we do to overcome it, and the institutional mechanisms we bring to the task.

■ We recommend a new federal-provincial system of sharing regional development expenditures and responsibilities.

- The federal government should direct regional development programs toward improving regional productivity and the efficiency of the labour market. To these ends, such programs should include measures to improve worker and management skills, enhance research and development efforts, ensure a high level of infrastructural support, and supply assistance for intra- and inter-regional mobility. The federal government should not only provide such programs on a national basis, but should also make a special effort in the less developed provinces. While it might make sense, too, for the federal government to provide assistance for plant modernization as a means to enhance regional productivity, we believe that it should provide this type of assistance on a national basis, if at all, or that the provincial governments should take on this responsibility on a regional basis.
- Under this arrangement, the federal government would end all explicit and direct regional employment-creation programs. While national schemes would continue, federal subsidies, tax breaks, and so on, intended only to generate jobs in, or attract firms to, a particular locale, would be eliminated. Similarly, the federal government would terminate regionally differentiated unemployment-insurance programs, tax credits, and other measures that tend to distort regional labour markets. Funds formerly allocated to these types of programs would instead become the source of Regional Economic Development Grants.
- Provinces that qualify for equalization payments would be eligible for Regional Economic Development Grants. The amounts of the grants would be determined by a formula on a per capita basis, and they would be proportionate to the degree of fiscal disparity identified by the equalization formula. As noted earlier, equalization payments are necessary to offset economic disparities, while the purpose of these new grants would be to reduce future disparities. They would be re-negotiated every five years.

- Provinces would assume full responsibility for local or place-specific employment measures as part of their own approach to regional development. They would be free to use the Regional Economic Development Grants for this purpose, subject only to two conditions:
  - Each recipient province would sign an Economic and Regional Development Agreement (ERDA) with the federal government, which would set out a broad economic development plan for the province (and for each other province) and would indicate the measures to be carried out by both orders of government. Some elements of these packages might take the form of shared-cost programs or federal contributions to provincial activities; in general, however, Commissioners recommend that under the ERDA umbrella, each government remain responsible for the implementation and delivery of its own programs, in order to enhance accountability.
  - The recipient province would be required to sign the proposed Code of Economic Conduct to improve the functioning of the Canadian economic union.
- While recognizing the immediate need for financial prudence at the federal level, Commissioners believe that the total federal financial commitment to regional development – combining the Regional Economic Development Grants and other funds spent through ERDAs – should increase significantly over the next few years.
- The federal government would continue to play an important role in other development efforts which have significant regional impacts such as:
  - A reformed equalization system
  - The proposed Universal Income Security Program and the Transitional Adjustment Assistance Program
  - Sectoral policies, such as those pertaining to fisheries, agriculture, and forestry. These should be designed according to criteria for good sectoral policy (see Parts III and IV of this Report) but they ought to also be developed in close consultation with provincial governments where these are affected to an important degree.
- A sustained federal commitment to regional development requires that a single central agency be responsible for injecting regional concerns into the programs of individual federal departments, and for co-ordinating federal efforts. It would appear to Commissioners that the Federal-Provincial Relations Office (FPRO) reporting to the Prime Minister, would be the appropriate existing body. We believe also that the Federal Economic Development Co-ordinator (FEDC) or other senior officials resident in each province could help to co-ordinate federal activities within each province, interacting with the provincial government and establishing links with local

economic interests. The federal government should enlarge the responsibilities of such federal regional officials, who should report directly to FPRO. □

Fiscal Arrangements

Tax Collection Agreements

The Tax Collection Agreements have served Canada well. They are convenient for both citizens and governments, and they help to maintain harmony and contribute to the strength of the economic union. They should be retained. Nevertheless, the agreements are presently under considerable strain, and are in some danger of disintegrating. This Commission's proposed reforms are based on the desire to maintain the agreements, but not at an excessive cost either in terms of the accountability of legislatures or in terms of the flexibility which exists in the system.

■ Commissioners therefore recommend that:

- The agreements be amended to place the personal income tax on the same footing as the corporate tax, applying the provincial rates to the common, federally determined base. This measure would not only reduce provincial vulnerability to federal tax changes, but would also enhance provincial autonomy, since it would become easier for provinces to decide how progressive their own tax rates should be.
- The federal government consult with provinces before introducing any tax change which would have a significant effect on the federal-provincial relationship. This recommendation is consistent with Commissioners' larger concern to reduce budget secrecy for federal and provincial governments and to ensure that federal budget proposals receive wide discussion in Parliament.
- To provide greater consultation on taxation matters of a more fundamental nature, Commissioners recommend that a new federal-provincial Tax Structure Committee be given the following mandate:
  - As part of the regular process of the quinquennial review of federal-provincial fiscal arrangements, the Tax Structure Committee would re-examine the definitions of taxable income, basic exemptions, marginal tax rates, and the like. This is really an endorsement and extension of a consultation process which is already in effect. The Tax Structure Committee would also monitor the division of tax room between the two orders of government, in light of anticipated revenue and expenditure needs, and of the difficulties of managing restraint.

– As part of the overall concern for the economic union, the Tax Structure Committee could also discuss the implications of federal or provincial tax credits and subsidies. It would thus assist the Council of Economic Development Ministers which, we propose, be responsible for the development of an overall intergovernmental Code of Economic Conduct. This Committee would be composed of representatives of all governments, including those now outside the agreements. □

The Spending Power and the Impact of Fiscal Restraint on Intergovernmental Transfers

Although Commissioners do not recommend formal limitations on the spending power, we consider that this power has important consequences for federalism and therefore should be exercised with special restraint and subject to certain guidelines concerning its use.

■ Commissioners thus recommend that the spending power be retained as a vital instrument for flexible responses to changing definitions of the national interest, subject to the conditions that:

- The judicial distinction between federal legislation providing grants or gifts and federal legislation involving direct regulation in fields of provincial jurisdiction is appropriate and should be further refined.
- As a matter of principle within the federation and for purposes of accountability and clarity of roles, the federal government regard new shared-cost programs as a last resort in pursuing its objectives.
- The use of the federal spending power in areas of provincial jurisdiction be supported by broad national consensus. In addition to the contribution to consensus which an elected Senate with stronger regional representation will make, consultation through the Federal-Provincial Ministerial Councils and, ultimately, the First Ministers' Conference is essential, not only in relation to new programs, where it will occur in any case, but also in relation to the proposed alteration or termination of a program by the federal government. Designated periods of operation of, say, five years, could be considered for program renegotiation.
- In order to retain a desirable degree of federal flexibility and accountability to Parliament while assuring provinces some stability for planning and protection against rapid unexpected variations in federal spending, we recommend that:
  – Federal-provincial transfers be subject to a review on a five-year basis.
  – During that period, the federal power to make adjustments be limited to, say, 5 per cent in any given year, without provincial approval. □

Intergovernmental Relations and the Institutions of the Federation

The intense intergovernmental conflict Canada experienced in the 1970s may be partly attributed to institutional limitations. Interdependence in modern federalism is inescapable and needs to be managed, as do the excesses of intergovernmental competition.

This Commission's goal is to encourage a more functional approach to federalism, one not oriented towards centralization/decentralization, but one which emphasizes the potential contribution of Canada's federal arrangements to the well-being of Canadians. Canadians should create political institutions to co-ordinate activities involving both orders of government.

While greater co-ordination of federal-provincial affairs would be desirable, Commissioners believe that the diversity of government action inherent in a federal state is also a positive contribution to society. Thus we have tried to strike a balance between encouraging institutional diversity or competition and proposing new measures of federal-provincial co-ordination.

■ Commissioners do not recommend comprehensive constitutional amendment as a means to modernize the division of powers. Instead, we urge the use of more flexible instruments to clarify or transfer the location of responsibility. To this end, we recommend that:

- The power of intergovernmental delegation be expanded so that, on a particular matter, law-making authority could be delegated to another jurisdiction. Such delegations should be approved by the legislatures of all jurisdictions involved
- Constitutional amendment be used to establish a procedure that would permit the Parliament of Canada and provincial legislatures to enter into intergovernmental agreements that would be binding on their successors
- The powers of reservation and disallowance, now by convention virtually "dead letters", be formally interred by means of an appropriate constitutional amendment.

■ To provide essential recognition of the need to manage intergovernmental interdependence, and the need to co-ordinate policies and activities, the First Ministers Conference should be established in the Constitution with the requirement that it meet at least once each year. Such an institution must in no way encroach on the principles of responsible government.

■ First Ministers may eventually wish to consider the creation of a body comparable to the Advisory Commissions on Intergovernmental Relations in the United States and in Australia. "Third parties" of this nature may facilitate behind-the-scenes resolution of intergovernmental conflicts and contribute to improving the context of information, analysis and public opinion to which the intergovernmental process will need to respond.

■ Despite a plethora of federal-provincial bodies, current intergovernmental discussions are sporadic and lack co-ordination. Our purpose is to suggest a core framework of federal-provincial mechanisms which, in a more streamlined way, would support the First Ministers in their collective and individual responsibilities. Commissioners propose that the First Ministers' Conference appoint a network of Councils of Ministers to serve in major functional policy areas and to be supported by continuing committees of officials. We believe that three central Ministerial Councils should be established in the fields of Finance, Economic Development, and Social Policy. We therefore recommend that:

- The *Council of Finance and Treasury Ministers* which now exists and meets from time to time regarding fiscal arrangements, economic projections, and macro-economic policy be formalized to encourage greater regularity of assembly, better co-ordination of budgetary preparations, and to receive the findings of the new Tax Structure Committee, which would monitor tax developments
- The *Council for Economic Development* seek agreement on common objectives in economic development and trade policies and identify opportunities for mutually beneficial links among regions. The Council would be responsible for monitoring and assessing the state of the economic union and would serve as the vehicle through which to develop a "Code of Economic Conduct".
- The Ministerial *Council on Social Policy* consider all facets of social policy, especially in the fields covered by Established Programs Financing and the Canada Assistance Plan. Consultation with practicing professionals and interested groups and individuals is particularly important in this area. We would encourage Parliamentary Committees to play a stronger role in this activity.
- To ensure that governments are held accountable for their conduct of intergovernmental affairs, Commissioners recommend that Parliament and the provincial legislatures should establish permanent standing committees responsible for Intergovernmental Relations. □

Differing provincial regulations create inconvenience for those who wish to operate nationally. The impetus for interprovincial efforts towards harmonization must arise through the pressure of groups adversely affected by interjurisdictional variations. Commissioners therefore propose no specific institutional changes designed to enhance harmonization of provincial laws.

The Charter of Rights and Freedoms

The Charter and Constitutional Government in Canada

The Charter of Rights and Freedoms signals a significant transformation of the relationship between citizens and the state in Canada. Most noteworthy are the important limitations imposed on the constitutional authority of legislatures and the elevated role of the judiciary as guardians of the constitutional rights and freedoms of individuals. The Charter will also further the rights of citizens to review and assess government actions, and it will contribute to a fuller and more regular discussion of citizen rights in Parliament. Its guarantees will probably become the basis for individuals and groups to introduce issues to the national and provincial political agendas.

The scope and application of the Charter will be tested constantly through both the legal and political processes. The Charter is not, however, a springboard for unlimited claims of citizen rights, for there are reasonable limits to its guarantees. Ultimately, its effectiveness in protecting the rights and freedoms of citizens and in enhancing democracy will be determined by the way in which citizens use this document.

■ This Commission believes that the changes recorded and introduced by the Charter should be given a broad scope in interpretation and application. Departures from its guarantees should meet stringent tests and conditions, justifying the circumstances of exception.

■ The Charter's general override provision should contribute to public awareness of legislation limiting the constitutional rights of citizens in Canada. Overriding legislation should include a declaration of intent to legislate, notwithstanding a provision of the Charter, and should include not only reference to the specific rights being overridden, but also an indication of the purpose of such legislative action. Such a statement of purpose would help the courts to ensure that limitations do not exceed what is necessary to achieve their objective; it could also be a useful reference point in discussions on whether to extend the override after the five-year period.

■ Commissioners do not suggest constitutional amendments to change and improve upon the Charter's words. Rather we consider various interpretations of the Charter which we think will serve to maximize the desirable impact it can have on Canadian society. Two examples illustrate our approach:

- We favour a broad and flexible application of the Charter at the periphery of government activity, as well as in its more visible legislative forms.
- Similarly, in the matter of the Charter's guarantees of personal mobility rights, we conclude that preferential provincial employment schemes permissible under the Charter should be

strictly limited to the socially and economically disadvantaged within a province. Such programs should not preclude the federal government from simultaneously pursuing employment-opportunities programs in that province. □

Inherent in the Charter of Rights and Freedoms is an attempt to overcome some of the problems of national unity that have pre-occupied Canadians since the mid-1960s. This is especially evident in the Charter's provisions respecting mobility rights, official languages and minority official-language education, as well as multiculturalism.

With regard to ethnic diversity in Canada, Commissioners believe that multiculturalism policy should seek to create circumstances that permit all Canadians to preserve and enhance their cultural heritage within the broader Canadian tradition of individual equality. Multiculturalism is not a justification for cultural or racial discrimination. For visible minorities, in particular, racism must be addressed through more than multicultural policy. There is a systemic aspect to racial discrimination in Canada. As with other pattterns of systemic discrimination affecting groups such as women, the handicapped and other identifiable groups, the Charter plays an important role as both an educative and legal instrument in enhancing equality.

The Charter's equality-rights guarantees embody a broad definition and understanding of equality. These guarantees reflect contemporary notions of substantive equality in giving assurance of equal benefit of the law and equality under the law. By enabling affirmative action programs, the Charter responds to contemporary concerns about discrimination against various groups in society.

■ Commissioners believe that governments have a leadership role to play in breaking down these patterns of discrimination and we believe, too, that affirmative action is a valuable tool for this purpose. Accordingly, we view the provision in the Charter enabling governments to pursue affirmative action programs as a valuable reinforcement of government's role. Equality, however, must ultimately relate to individuals, and affirmative action must be supplemented with other programs designed with individual equality as the ultimate goal.

■ The Charter both contains guarantees of individual equality and elsewhere recognizes special rights of various groups, such as official-language minorities and Canadian aboriginals. We believe that when group rights are inconsistent with rights of individual equality, the latter, as a general rule, should prevail. □

The Supreme Court of Canada

The members of the Supreme Court of Canada do not perform representative functions in the Canadian institutional and constitutional system. Judicial merit alone is the criterion by which the Court's membership and performance should be assessed. Accordingly, Commissioners reject arguments that the composition of the Supreme Court should be regionally representative.

Existing provision in the Supreme Court Act for the appointment of Quebec members is based on the distinctive legal traditions of that province. We also reject socio-economic representational claims about Supreme Court of Canada membership, which we anticipate may emerge as the Court addresses complex Charter litigation involving citizen-state relations.

The central issue in the appointments process is the perception that it does not adequately involve the constituencies ultimately affected by Supreme Court decisions. Although the existing informal procedures followed by the Prime Minister before making appointments to the Supreme Court do involve extensive discussions, they are sometimes perceived as not taking sufficient account of concerned interests or advice. Measures to shift responsibility from the Prime Minister to some designated group or institution necessarily involve replacing one political process with another. If a broadly based political process of consultation is to be replaced by alternative arrangements, an elected Senate has much to commend it.

■ The constitutional status of the Supreme Court and, in particular, the independence of the Court, should be clarified by entrenchment, although there is no reason to remove responsibility for the administration of the Court from the federal government.□

Quebec

The Distinctive Character of Quebec Society

Quebec is characterized by the presence within its borders of a largely francophone population which controls and gives direction to its own political and social institutions. The existence of this institutional framework which re-enforces the distinction between the majority status of francophones within Quebec and the position of francophones elsewhere in Canada is central to *la spécificité du Québec*. The very essence of Quebec society lies in the fact that it is the principal, though not the exclusive, focus for the political dimensions of French life in Canada. To a large extent, Quebec remains a linguistically isolated society, an island of French in an overwhelmingly anglophone sea. For Quebec and for francophones outside the province, the central challenge will always be how to remain French in North America.

This challenge entails practical problems in the cultural and economic domains for whose resolution Quebecers and francophones outside Quebec, individually and collectively, are, themselves, ultimately responsible. But constitutional recognition of Quebec's distinctiveness and of Canada's duality would provide an affirmation that answers to the practical economic and cultural problems of French life can be pursued within the Canadian context and with the support of the rest of Canada. The necessary compromises could thus be worked out in a clearly understood context of recognition and affirmation of a cultural complementarity which is at the very heart of the Canadian experience.

■ The initial requirement at the level of principle to secure a renewed understanding between Quebec and the rest of Canada is

a statement in the preamble to the Constitution along the following lines:

Recognizing the distinctive character of Quebec as the principal, though not the exclusive, centre for Canadian francophones and accepting as fundamental the duality of the Canadian federation . . .

Fundamental Guarantees

As a consequence of Quebec's uniqueness, steps should be taken to ensure that no future constitutional amendment as noted below be imposed on Quebec which that province might consider to affect its fundamental interests as a distinct society:

- Concerning transfers of legislative powers from the provinces to Parliament, the simplest means to provide Quebec with the necessary protection, without putting the principle of equality of the provinces in question is to grant each province the right to opt out of any general arrangement with full compensation in all cases.
- In relation to reforms of national institutions which are not covered in the present opting-out formula, the only means to protect the interests of Quebec is through the right of veto. An obvious solution would be to grant all provinces such right in conformity with the equality principle. In the long run, this move could, however, freeze the natural development of our national institutions. Although granting Quebec the right of veto is an arrangement politically more difficult to obtain, it is closer to the intended objective, for it is the distinctive character of Quebec society for which protection is sought. It is important that Quebec have a right of veto on any amendment to the institutions described in section 42(1) of the Constitution Act, 1982, if such an amendment touches on the special character of Quebec and the duality of Canada. One method of implementing such veto would be to amend immediately section 47 of the Constitution Act, 1982, in order to grant French-speaking Senators the right to block proposed amendments affecting Quebec under the double-majority formula described below.

The Senate and Quebec

- With regard to federal legislation, any proposed bill with linguistic implications, before becoming law, should require a double majority of the Senate: that is, the approval of a majority of all Senators and of a majority of francophone Senators. Such veto would be a full rather than a suspensive veto. In light of the protection offered by this double-majority proposal, Commissioners see no need for specific guarantees to Quebec of a certain proportion of seats in the House of Commons.

Division of Powers

- Because of Quebec's distinctiveness, the most obvious fields where conflicts may arise between that province and the federal government are education, external relations, immigration, communications and culture. There are ways in which Quebec could participate in dealing with these areas. While we make no recommendations, we do suggest that legal mechanisms such as delegation and inter-governmental agreements may provide a better means of accommodating the specific interests of Quebec than would constitutional amendment.

Francophones Outside Quebec

- The diverse communities of Francophones in Canada outside Quebec are currently in a state of crisis. If they are to survive and flourish, prompt action is required. Commissioners suggest that beyond recognizing the principle of duality in the Preamble, governments should make efforts to extend the recognition of French and English as the official languages of individual provinces. Ontario in particular, with its large French-speaking population, should proceed promptly to implement official bilingualism. Such a step would set an example for other provinces.
- Scattered French-language communities outside of Quebec face difficulties in developing a French-language working environment. Efforts to solve this problem should be geared towards the development of French-language centres of activity. These centres would vary from province to province, depending on the population and geographic concentration of francophone Canadians. In some areas, the centres would be of an essentially cultural or educational nature, and in other areas, such as in New Brunswick, they could include a strong economic component.
- Furthermore, this Commission wishes to point out that implementation of language rights has not kept up with the intended policy of bilingualism. We believe that litigation, while generally useful, is not the proper tool for making improvements in this direction, since it is a lengthy and costly method of dealing with these problems.
- Instead, we recommend that stronger support be given to the role of the Commissioner of Official Languages. □

Aboriginal Self-Government

Measures to increase the influence and control exercised by aboriginal people over their social and economic affairs are desirable. Our commitment to this objective is based on the distinctive place of aboriginals in Canadian society

as the first peoples of Canada and on the constitutional recognition they now enjoy.

Institutional reforms to enhance the autonomy of aboriginal peoples focus on the idea of self-government. Implications of aboriginal self-government for Canada's overall institutional framework and, in particular, for the three pillars of the Canadian constitutional order, Parliament, federalism and the Charter, have not yet been clarified. Indeed, many important issues have been avoided and should be addressed more squarely. The fundamental changes to our national and provincial institutions that are now being contemplated need broad Canadian understanding if they are to be acceptable in the long run. The pace of discussions, as well as the comprehensiveness of debates in Parliament and the legislatures should reflect this concern.

The Northern Territories

The economic, social and environmental challenges of development in Northern Canada will remain of continuing concern to Canadians. From an institutional perspective, significant questions must be addressed – some of these in the near future.

- No Canadians – Natives and non-Natives, Northerners and Southerners – can be well served by further delays in the settlement of aboriginal land claims. Final agreements affirming and delimiting aboriginal rights should be actively encouraged. If necessary, deadlines should be established by the parties, and discussions could proceed without reference to the issues of legislative powers, sovereignty and special political status, which could be dealt with subsequently in other settings.

- The Yukon Act and the Northwest Territories Act should be amended to reflect the current practices of responsible government in Yukon and to encourage comparable evolution in the Northwest Territories. In both territories, new formula-based financial arrangements should be negotiated, to increase the predictability of transfers and to promote genuine responsibility and accountability for expenditures.
- On the basis of federal commitment to the ultimate goal of some form of provincehood in the Northern territories, the governments involved should establish a timetable for the transfer of provincial-type responsibilities in areas such as health, labour relations, inland waters, renewable resources and the institution of criminal proceedings. Additional measures should be taken to:
  - Advance the process of transferring to territorial governments responsibilities for Crown lands that do not bear directly on the national interest and that have not been ceded to the Native people through claims settlements

- Institute resource-revenue/sharing arrangements comparable to the types of agreements worked out with Nova Scotia and Newfoundland
- Confirm participation of the territorial governments in federal-provincial forums where matters of direct concern to Northern residents are being discussed. Joint-management arrangements may be valuable transitional procedures.

■ Failing an internally generated and ratified agreement on division of the Northwest Territories, the federal government should establish an independent boundary commission to recommend a boundary on the basis of arguments from the two constitutional forums. Subject to the spirit of the Canadian constitutional tradition and the need to recognize the essential quality of Canadian citizenship, the structure of post-division government should be left to the discretion of the respective constitutional forums. □

Municipalities

Local governments are an enduring and important feature of government in Canada, despite their lack of constitutional status. Variations in approaches to local government in different provinces have permitted sensitivity, dynamism and creativity in the city-province relationship. Existing arrangements have contributed to the development of some of the most liveable cities in the world. Local governments have experienced uncertainty and frustration because of limited policy-making instruments and their relations with provincial and federal governments, but responses to current concerns must begin from the premise that we have been doing something right. Canada's major cities should be provided with the legal, financial and institutional means to fulfill their economic development role. By and large, this involves removing constraints that prevent their involvement in development.

■ Although Commissioners do not recommend changing the constitutional status of local governments, the federal and provincial governments should increase the involvement and responsibility of local authorities. The federal government should review with the provinces the possibility of occasional tri-level conferences; improve communications between municipalities and ministers whose responsibilities affect local interests; assign responsibility to investigate the significance of local concerns in national policy to the proposed Standing Committee for Intergovernmental Relations; and explore opportunities for the decentralization of specific responsibilities, including airports and federal urban properties to federally-appointed local agencies. The use of the delegation amendment, as Commissioners have earlier proposed, may become a means to delegate directly to local

governments responsibility for such questions as siting, development and administration of some airports through agreement with the relevant province.

■ The provincial governments should continue to assess possibilities for assuming financial responsibility for requirements greatly exceeding local revenue sources. Commissioners also recommend that the provinces examine ways to designate a specific portion of income or sales-tax revenues for local government financing. Commissioners believe that revenues to local governments should be increasingly unconditional. □

Compendium of Conclusions and Recommendations

For the convenience of the reader, the "Conclusions and Recommendations" from each part of this Report are collected here.

Part I

Global Outlook

Conclusions and Recommendations

As we peer into the future, there is only one central fact about which we can be reasonably certain: there are powerful forces loose around the globe that will profoundly affect the lives of all of us here in Canada. The global outlook is full of danger signals; a majority of the world's citizens are facing very troubled prospects.

Commissioners have noted two very distinct trends in world affairs which are disturbing when viewed together. The world today has become more interdependent in economic, social and technological matters. We all share problems and opportunities as global citizens. However, the political will and international institutional machinery have not kept pace with this growing interdependence. While Commissioners are not alarmed by this divergence, we are concerned that it be recognized, and that steps be taken to rebalance altruism and self-interest on the international stage.

In entering what may well be a very turbulent period, Canadians occupy a privileged position that may make the prospective problems of the global community appear quite remote. We enjoy a comparatively high standard of living; we possess abundant natural and human resources; and we have in place a political fabric and institutions that up to now have proved themselves reasonably capable of providing the framework of laws and regulations, policies and programs required to serve our national interest best.

But "no man is an island, entire of itself", as John Donne astutely observed more than three and a half centuries ago. As Commissioners noted at the outset, Canada is more exposed than most nations to developments taking place in the world, because of far-reaching links of trade, aid and diplomacy. Canadians are highly vulnerable to adverse impacts, both direct and indirect, but we are also in a favoured position, in many ways, to seize opportunities as they arise.

In addition, however, the very breadth and depth of Canada's involvement in affairs around the world appear to impose upon Canadians a special responsibility to take up the important role that may be available to us: to contribute to a resolution of some of the more critical global problems that will arise in the years ahead. This view is based on Commissioners' deep belief that the major problems facing the global community are rooted in social, political and institutional structures, values and norms. In part, Canada's contribution might be made in material forms and by way of education, training and technology. Conceivably, however, we could play an even more important role as a catalyst, in bringing other nations together to work in concert for the resolution of global challenges and problems.

As Commissioners stressed at the beginning of this section, and as we reiterate now, we can at best perceive only dimly how the future will unfold. Undoubtedly, many current projections of prospective developments and their likely consequences will prove wrong in degree or in kind. It is crucially important, however, that Canadians should carefully search out the primary forces in play around the world, constantly monitor their action and interaction, and stand ready to respond, as circumstances require, either alone or in combination with other nations. While many future developments abroad will certainly have a direct impact on our nation, in many instances we may well have greater cause for concern about the indirect consequences for us of global impacts on other countries.

This Commission underlines the importance of recognizing five critical features of the global system:

- The degree of interdependence will continue to increase in the foreseeable future, causing the domestic policies of any one country to be significantly affected and, in some instances, dominated by global forces and the policies of larger countries.
- While the eradication of poverty and famine is within the grasp of most developed nations and certainly of Canada, it is not even on the horizon for most of the world's peoples.
- The dangers and challenges identified in the physical, economic and political global environment are so significant that the general increase in well-being of all dwellers on the planet is at risk.
- The principal limits to growth are not physical, but political, social and institutional. The major challenge thus lies in the fruit of technological and institutional ingenuity.
- Global interdependence demands that decisions be based on long-term goals and be made in the broadest possible context.

■ In view of this assessment of the global environment, Commissioners urge that the fundamental global priority within the context of peaceful co-existence become the general increase of the well-being of all nations and peoples, and the urgent eradication of malnutrition and starvation.

- Given the high degree of global uncertainty that this Commission has identified, it is important that Canadians understand both the privileged position we occupy on this planet and the

human imperative this places on Canada to provide leadership in those areas of critical concern to the world, where our nation has a capacity to provide that leadership. Commissioners recommend that as a matter of high priority, Canada pursue a more activist foreign policy based on the concept that Canada now occupies a more responsible position as one of the principal powers. Combining humanitarian and pragmatic interests, Canada should:

- Seek to broaden Canadian and world understanding of the meaning of interdependence and the threats and opportunities which confront civilization. This approach includes giving higher priority to issues relating to the natural environment and especially to the implications for global well-being of the continuing population explosion.
- Vigorously support reform of the multilateral system represented by the United Nations and its specialized agencies to bring the institutional machinery into line with the substantive problems and opportunities of the future.
- Pursue bilateral and regional initiatives where these are appropriate and essentially outward-looking in a multilateral context.

■ This Commission has reviewed the broad sweep of global interdependence in an effort to identify those areas where Canadians will be offered both challenges and opportunities over the next quarter century. We Canadians must take account of this interdependence in designing our own national policies. In particular, Commissioners recommend that:

- In the decades ahead, Canada's policy makers integrate environmental decisions with those on economic development. This policy will be essential, for there is, in this Commission's view, no ultimate trade-off between economic development and the preservation and enhancement of a healthy environment and a sustainable resource base.
- Canadian economic policies be developed increasingly in a global context. This process requires a fuller recognition of the long-term and structural changes evolving, particularly in the areas of trade, technology and the role of governments, in the struggle for competitiveness. The incentives for work effort and productive contribution should be enhanced in a more flexible market environment.
- Canadian social support mechanisms and programs be designed more efficiently to accomplish the feasible task of removing the blight of poverty within Canada and to establish our national economy on a flexible, but secure, social infrastructure
- Parliament be reinforced as the principal forum for national debate and reconciliation of international, national and regional interests. □

PART II

Canadian Opportunities in an Open World

Conclusions and Recommendations

The global environment presents Canada with enormous challenges and opportunities. Rapid growth of imports from the developing countries, a changing trade-policy environment and domestic pressures on our trading partners for new protection imperil Canadian jobs. By contrast, growth and technical progress abroad offer us new export opportunities and chances to benefit from access to cheaper and higher-quality products than we can produce. As Commissioners noted at the beginning of this Part, the challenge is one of change, adaptation and adjustment; the opportunities may be unlimited. In light of these developments, however, the choices Canadians must make are difficult.

We Commissioners have been frequently reminded, in the course of our task, that Canada's domestic economy is largely defined by its relationship to the wider global economic system. Canada's last Royal Commission on our economic prospects captured this point:

> *Something of Canada's essence is defined by its external relations. Much of its economic structure can be explained only in terms of its external trade . . .*
>
> *The ships loading lumber on Vancouver Island or aluminum ingots on the Saguenay are reminders of how deeply our material well-being is involved in the prosperity of other countries, even outside the boundaries of North America.*[1]

Canada's economic development, then, as well as our government's economic development policies, are significantly affected by conditions beyond our borders. As a relatively small, "open" economy, Canada is particularly vulnerable to outside influences on its trade and economic performance. In order to foster stability and predictability in some of these external forces, successive Canadian governments have sought to develop formal rules for conducting relationships with our trading partners. The pursuit of this

objective has always involved an essential problem: How are we to reconcile conflicting priorities among national objectives and the requirements of a stable international economic system? To resolve inherent conflicts has required a continual process of negotiation and compromise at both the domestic and the international level. Governments have often had to adjust and put to positive use the constant tension between the forces of economic protection and trade liberalization.

For almost forty years, Canada has pursued a largely multilateral approach to its foreign economic policy; indeed we have been one of the strongest supporters of the multilateral system centred on the GATT and the International Monetary Fund. This approach was the most effective way to improve and secure access for our products and to instil order, stability and predictability into that process. Even on the import side, we have found that we must negotiate multilaterally to open our own market, in exchange for access to foreign markets. This action has proved a useful tool of industrial policy and has allowed for orderly adjustment of the economy through foreign competition.

To a great extent, Canadian trade policy has been, and will continue to be, developed as a trade-off between the business objective of securing improved access to foreign markets, the economic need to promote efficiency and competitiveness in the domestic economy, and the political need to maintain our sovereignty and freedom of action. The international trade and payments system largely determines the design and use of particular policy instruments. For Canadian producers and investors, there are several tests of this international system. Can our government successfully improve market access for those sectors where Canadian production is, or can be, competitive in world markets? Will it maintain current access available to Canadian producers? Will it protect producers from unfair or injurious foreign competition? Because private sector investment is necessary for growth and job creation, Canadian producers need to be confident that their access is secure, and that foreign governments will not move to frustrate the efforts to market Canadian goods abroad.

The multilateral system of rules is intended to facilitate decisions favouring adjustment and to penalize decisions favouring protection, but it needs political will to make it work. Between 1973 and 1979, the Tokyo Round of trade negotiations provided a framework for organizing political will. The negotiators sought to reduce trade barriers and to move the ongoing management of trade relations in the direction of freer trade. For the past six years, however, there has been no such framework.

A new round of GATT negotiations may be initiated, to concentrate on elaborating world trade law and removing remaining barriers to world trade, and to provide a basis for organizing political will to resist protection. The results of a future GATT negotiation are not certain, however, nor are they just around the corner. A new round of negotiations requires complex co-ordination and revolves largely around the interests of three or four players: the United States, the European Community, the less-developed countries (LDCs) as a group, and, perhaps Japan. Canada can make an important contribution, but we cannot control either the agenda or the outcome. Even to

influence the outcome requires adroit negotiators. The Community is reluctant to come to the table. The United States is eager, but as yet has no negotiating authority. The LDCs are willing, but insist on some problematic pre-conditions and do not agree on the agenda. Japan is willing, but largely because a new round would facilitate management of its trade relations with the United States and the European Community.

Canada's economic growth is critically dependent on secure access to foreign markets. Our most important market is the United States, which now takes up to three-quarters of our exports. More, better and more secure access to the U.S. market represents a basic requirement, while denial of that access is an ever-present threat. We are extremely vulnerable to any strengthening of U.S. protectionism. Early bilateral negotiations with the United States could provide opportunities for the two countries to negotiate reduction or elimination of tariff and other barriers to cross-border trade, at a pace and on a scale not likely to be achieved multilaterally in a further GATT round. Such negotiations could also be used to win agreement on rules designed to deal with special or unique problems affecting cross-border trade; they would provide a more secure shield against a U.S. policy of protection.

The pursuit of Canada-U.S. free trade is not at odds with efforts to strengthen and improve the existing multilateral framework. Rather, Commissioners see it as a complementary approach, involving concentration of our efforts and scarce resources on our most important market. We see multilateral negotiations proceeding in parallel. In our view, such a two-tiered approach is the best way to ensure that Canadian industry will win sufficient access to foreign markets to invest and grow with confidence. At the same time, it will allow us to open our market in an orderly fashion and thus ensure that trade policy dœs its part in encouraging the development of a more competitive and more productive economy.

Commissioners see negotiations with the United States as neither panacea nor disaster, but as a prudent course which will help to make us richer and, by making us richer, strengthen the fabric of our country and increase our self-confidence. While this course may initially make Canada more dependent on the U.S. market, it will offer our nation a more secure relationship and thus make us less vulnerable. Ultimately, it should strengthen and diversify our economy, achieving for us goals that we have long sought, but which have eluded us, largely because our domestic manufacturing sector has been too weak to attain them.

Negotiations leading to freer trade, whether pursued bilaterally or multilaterally, will be of little use if they are not supported by the right domestic policies. Our support for freer trade, therefore, depends in no small way on the recommendations Commissioners develop later in this Report. These recommendations should contribute to strengthening the competitiveness and productivity of Canada's domestic economy. Trade policy alone will not be enough.

Commissioners, like others who have enquired into Canada's relations with developing countries, see a need for Canada to take more positive action to help these countries through aid and trade measures. We have reached this conclusion, not only on humanitarian grounds, but also on the basis of our

perception of Canada's own interest. Development of stronger links with these countries through aid and trade will pay dividends to future generations of Canadians, by contributing to a more stable world environment and by nurturing future trading partners.

We believe that the approaches we recommend below will help to strengthen our country. They will allow Canadians to pursue the gradual transition from a staple economy to a fully-industrialized modern economy, living in harmony with, but distinct from, our friends and allies.

Recommendations

■ Having carefully considered the analyses presented above, Commissioners make the following general recommendations:

- Canadians have benefited from and contributed to the multilateral system of trade and payments developed primarily in the last 40 years, and we should continue to support that system as the mainstay of our foreign economic policy. Canada is sufficiently strong and independent, however, to pursue bilateral intitiatives, including better economic relations with the United States, within the framework of multilateral relations.
- Canadian import policy in general should be based on a recognition of its costs to consumers and the costs of delaying adjustment. Canada should minimize any new protection, reduce protection gradually as part of bilateral or multilateral negotiations, and accelerate adjustment processes.
- Export promotion should be pursued aggressively and with greater reliance on private sector mechanisms, but the degree of subsidization this may involve should be within internationally accepted rules and practices.

International Trade

International trade is the life-blood of the Canadian economy. It is a major contributor to Canadian growth, jobs and real incomes. In view of the changing nature and patterns of international trade, Canadians are now confronted with several options in formulating trade policy. This Commission has identified three major approaches, each of which has several variations. Canada might:

- Maintain its present policy. It might keep to the level and type of protection currently in place, but make selective efforts both to improve access abroad and to protect Canadian industry on a limited case-by-case basis.
- Participate actively in a new round of multilateral trade negotiations under the auspices of the GATT, in order to improve and secure our country's access to foreign markets, to open up our own market, and to strengthen the legal framework for international trade.

- In addition to taking the initiative for the elimination of trade barriers at the multilateral level, open negotiations with the Government of the United States to reach an agreement on a substantial reduction of barriers, tariff and non-tariff, between Canada and the United States.

This Commission rejects any generalized move toward greater protection or toward import substitution as a general policy to insulate Canadian producers from the international economy. This approach, while perhaps the most comfortable in the short term, would lead, in the longer term, to major inefficiencies in the national economy, a loss of jobs and lower incomes, and would contribute to an erosion of the multilateral system. In our view, a policy of maintaining the *status quo* would carry the serious risk of taking Canada backwards to a more protectionist position.

■ Commissioners recommend that multilateral trade negotiations under the GATT remain a central theme of Canadian trade policy; thus Canada should move quickly to define its objectives for the forthcoming round. The GATT has served Canada well, and our nation's participation in further strengthening this international system of co-operation is a general insurance policy for the future. Broadly stated, Canada's objectives should include:

- A more ordered world trading environment: that is, sufficiently stable, predictable and transparent international trade relations to instil a degree of business confidence that will lead to job-creating investment
- More secure access to our major markets, particularly the U.S. market
- Improved opportunity for the further processing of our natural resources before export, by reducing foreign barriers to manufactured goods
- Improved access and trading conditions for agricultural and fishery products
- An improved framework of international rules which will encourage orderly adjustment in the Canadian economy.

■ Commissioners recommend that the Government of Canada, at the same time it undertakes an initiative at the multilateral level to eliminate trade barriers, open negotiations with the Government of the United States to reach agreement on a substantial reduction of barriers, tariff and non-tariff, between Canada and the United States. Such an agreement would have to stand within the terms of Article XXIV of the GATT, and it would provide for a reduction of barriers between the two countries, but would leave each country with freedom of action to maintain separate trading policies with other economic partners. We do not recommend a more intensive arrangement such as a common market or an economic union, where even closer integration would take place between these two economies.

- Commissioners recommend that Canada negotiate a legal arrangement with the United States which incorporates strong safeguards to limit spill-over from the arrangement and thus to protect substantive policies, such as those pertaining to culture and defence, which are functionally unrelated to trade in goods and services. Indeed, a policy that creates no linkage should be explicitly confirmed in order to avoid surprises if the Government of Canada, as we recommend, were to pursue a more aggressive policy of support for indigenous cultural expression as a concomitant of a bilateral trade initiative.
- Commissioners recommend that this legal arrangement attempt to regulate three general types of barriers that currently restrict trade between the two countries. We recommend that:
  - Tariffs be phased down to zero over a period of perhaps ten years. Effective rules of origin must be developed.
  - An approach should be developed to use measures of contingent protection as follows:
    - For measures governing "fair" trade (such as safeguard action) and "unfair" trading practices (such as anti-dumping and countervailing-duty proceedings), enforcement would be shifted from national administrative tribunals to a new Canada-U.S. intergovernmental body established under the arrangement; this body would be known as the "Canada-U.S. Trade Commission" (CUSTC).
  - Detailed codes of national conduct would be required to govern resort to other non-tariff measures such as discriminatory federal and state-government/procurement practices, product standards and federal customs, classification rules and administrative procedures. Again, these matters should be subject to review of the CUSTC.
- This Commission holds that a free-trade arrangement should incorporate explicit provisions which reflect the proportionately greater costs of adjustment that Canadians will face. The Canadian economy needs more time for adjustment than does the U.S. economy. We therefore recommend a two-track approach to phasing in the tariff cuts to allow U.S. rates of duty generally to be reduced either at a faster rate or earlier than Canadian tariffs. The Canadian government should quickly develop strategies for adjustment which are compatible with the framework of adjustment assistance proposed in Part V of this Report, that is, the new Transitional Adjustment Assistance Program. The emphasis of government programs should be on assisting workers to adjust to new employment opportunities. In addition, a reoriented industrial policy, as set out in Part III, will encourage the flexibility and growth orientation required by a freer-trade environment.
- This Commission recommends that the Government of Canada urge the Government of the United States to implement the

free-trade arrangement by amending U.S. federal and, if necessary, state legislation to conform to the arrangement, and that they do so under a "fast track" procedure which would require Congress to pass implementing legislation within 90 days of the President's formal declaration that he intends to sign an international agreement binding the United States. We also recommend, however, that a formal treaty eventually be struck once both governments have had sufficient experience with the arrangement.

- This Commission recommends that negotiations in Canada proceed on the basis of a broadly based, federal-provincial consensus, and that provinces be prepared to give legislative assent to the provisions of the arrangement, in keeping with the high degree of consultation that will be required to achieve federal-provincial consensus. We also recommend that in the longer term, Canadian governments establish a federal-provincial constitutional procedure: sections of the treaty that impose obligations on provinces would come into effect across Canada when two-thirds of provincial legislatures, representing at least half of Canada's population, passed resolutions in support of the treaty.
- This Commission recommends the formation of a three-tiered Canada-U.S. intergovernmental institution to provide basic executive and administrative decisions; technical staff services; adjudication of complaints and appeals under the agreement. We further recommend the following mechanisms:
  - A committee of national officials at the ministerial level to be responsible for the enforcement of the agreement's obligations
  - A supporting body of officials known as the "Canada-U.S. Trade Commission" (CUSTC) to manage non-tariff barriers, but subject to appellate review by the Ministerial Committee
  - A standing arbitral panel with binding powers as a board of last resort, to resolve disputes arising from conflicting interpretations of the agreement. Such a panel would consist of two Canadians, two Americans and one neutral member to be chosen by the members of the panel.
- International trade and industrial policy are inextricably linked. In Canada, there is the added dimension of cultural and social implications. To undertake successful negotiations on freer trade with the United States will require an extraordinary management effort by the Government of Canada. The Commissioners, while making no specific recommendation on how best to prepare the way for the negotiations, wish to express concern that the current federal departmental structure dœs not appear to provide the degree of integration required to carry out a major negotiation of this kind. It may be that an Office of the Special Trade Negotiator should be established, and that the incumbent should report directly to the Prime Minister.

Development Assistance

■ The motives of altruism and long-term national interest coincide in this Commission's recommendations for Canadian objectives pertaining to Canada's relations with developing countries. In pursuing these objectives, Canadians should be aware that the primary responsibility for development rests with the nations in question, and that although greater international efforts are required, difficult intranational, social and institutional issues are often the fundamental impediments to progress, just as they are in all nations. Commissioners recommend:

- An improvement in both the quantity and the quality of Canada's aid performance. Canada should advance to the Lima target of 0.7 per cent of GNP, not by 1995, but by 1990, and aim to achieve 1 per cent of GNP by the year 2000. The Canadian government should reduce the fraction of our aid which is tied, and to facilitate this reduction, we should rely more on multilateral than on bilateral aid.
- That Canada work within global institutions to improve the receptivity of these bodies to proposals helpful to developing countries. Canada should, for instance, systematically seek ways to involve developing countries more fully in a future round of GATT negotiations.
- That the Canadian government be ready to consider proposals for mitigating some of the more harmful effects of the international debt crisis on developing countries. Canadians should resist pressures for economic protection that would apply to exports from these countries. A more constructive and conciliatory approach to developing countries and their problems will not only help these countries, but also yield longer-term dividends for all countries. □

Note

1. Canada, Royal Commission on Canada's Economic Prospects, *Final Report* (Ottawa: Queen's Printer, 1957), p. 17.

PART III

Growth and Employment

Conclusions and Recommendations

General

Canada's growth and employment prospects depend heavily on developments in trade and in the use of our human and natural resources. Regional development policy and the institutional framework of our federal form of government also affect our growth and employment prospects. Part III of this Report addresses other components that affect these prospects: the role of capital, technology and management; the choice of industrial policy; the demand management or setting of monetary and fiscal policies; and the flexibility of wages and prices in responding to the vagaries of the business cycle. While the following recommendations are addressed separately, their strength depends significantly on their integration with the recommendations in the rest of this Report.

Governments must be prepared to vary their role in the allocation of human, capital and natural resources in response to changes in external and domestic pressures. In general, however, governments should endeavour to facilitate the operation of the market mechanisms of our economy, rather than to seek occasions for further intervention.

■ In the management of the economy, governments must acknowledge the considerable international and domestic constraints on policy. They cannot provide quick solutions to every economic difficulty. Rather, they should set the medium- and long-term framework within which solutions can be worked out.

Although economic growth is a key means of increasing the welfare of all members of society, Commissioners do not advocate the pursuit of maximum growth at all costs. The claims of growth must be balanced against those of equitable income distribution, employment security and environmental quality. □

Recent Performance and Prospects

Canada's post-Second World War performance was strong until 1973; after that date, inflation began to climb rapidly, and productivity growth declined. Since the 1981–82 recession, unemployment has been our most serious policy concern.

This Commission has examined four independent projections of Canada's likely economic performance in the absence of major policy changes. These forecasts suggest that Canada's growth rate in real gross national product over the next two decades will closely parallel the U.S. rate. Annual real growth in Canada should average 3 per cent during the late 1980s, and decline to about 2.5 per cent during the 1990s, in keeping with a decline in the rate of labour-force growth. The growth prospects for natural resource-based production seem weak, especially in mining and forestry.

■ Most analysts predict that unemployment will remain at relatively high levels in Canada throughout the 1980s. Current high rates of unemployment are associated with insufficient total real demand relative to total supply. In addition to this critical problem, there are major structural problems which, unless addressed, will not allow unemployment to drop below 6.5 to 8 per cent over the long term. This level is unacceptable by this Commission's standards, and the problem of reducing the structural unemployment rate must be addressed. □

Employment growth and productivity growth are essentially independent. Growth in the labour force is the principal cause of employment growth. Productivity growth increases both the supply of output and real demand to roughly equivalent degrees. Thus, growth and employment goals are not in substantial conflict over the longer run. We can improve productivity without harming long-run employment growth; more generally, technological unemployment is unlikely to become a major problem. Rather, increased productivity and technological change are the key to longer-term growth in real income and economic welfare.

Some fields have experienced an increase in the rate of technological innovation over the past two decades, but the overall rate is difficult to estimate. The decline in productivity growth since 1973 might suggest a decline in the pace of technological innovation. However, the recent increase in the share of gross national expenditure spent on research and development (R&D) in the United States and Canada will raise the pace of technical change and contribute to a recovery in productivity growth.

Industrial Policy

Canada's industrial policy has shifted since 1945, emphasizing, in turn, nationalistic goals or trade liberalization, development of the manufacturing sector or development based on natural-resource wealth.

Industrial policy in Canada incorporates a wide range of policy instruments, some of which have purposes related to trade or to general economic

policy. Neither the federal government nor the provinces have blueprints for industrial policy. This omission reflects a fundamental reliance on market forces and private-sector enterprise as the engine of growth.

Commissioners' review of foreign industrial policy indicates that policies that work in some countries may not work in others. Despite Japan's low expenditure on R&D, that country has been successful in the knowledge-intensive industries. France and Germany have very different industrial policies, despite being members of the European Community. France has a highly targeted interventionist approach, while Germany's approach is more market oriented. There would seem to be no particular mix of industrial policy instruments that ensures success.

Canadians differ on the proper role of government in promoting economic growth and employment. The polar extremes of a strictly hands-off approach and a highly interventionist, targeted, industrial policy appear to overlook the complexities of policy formation and practice.

■ Relative to current practice, Commissioners favour a more market-oriented industrial policy. More particularly, we favour letting the market work and placing less emphasis on government intervention to protect declining industries. We have reviewed the possibility of a more specifically targeted approach – the strategy of "picking winners" – but we believe it unlikely that such a highly interventionist approach would meet with greater success overall than would a more neutral policy.

For several reasons, some modes of intervention make sense; hence Commissioners do not favour a strictly hands-off approach. Furthermore, while there is little evidence in Canada or abroad that a targeted industrial policy is more effective than a market-oriented approach, other countries will continue to experiment. Canada should monitor these experiments carefully and consider strategic ways of strengthening its areas of comparative advantage. In our judgement, however, Canada has relied on intervention too often, too extensively and in too *ad hoc* a fashion.

Canada's industrial policy should emphasize broad-based support programs that work in tandem with basic market forces. To the extent that government involvement is required as, for example, in R&D support, benefit/cost criteria should guide it.

This Commission dœs not propose a blueprint for industrial development; indeed, to attempt a detailed formulation would be counter-productive. We believe, however, that consistent with our emphasis on market mechanisms, there should be a clearly stated framework for industrial policy. Such a framework would facilitate both private-sector decision making in Canada and the co-ordination of government policies and programs. This stated framework should express the strategic objective for industrial policy. Commissioners believe that the productivity of Canadian industry should predominate over other concerns, and that we should concentrate on improving our competitive position.

Commissioners believe that industrial policy should fortify incentives for excellence, for the efficient allocation of resources, and for adjustment to new economic realities. Such a policy would produce increases in real income, fuller employment and the means to address income distribution.

To improve the productivity of Canada's human, capital, and natural resources, and the competitive position of Canadian industry, industrial policy should include the following elements:

- A supportive macro-economic framework that while controlling inflation, promotes growth of output and employment at a reasonably even pace, in accordance with the economy's capacity
- A commitment to freer trade and the freer flow of investment. We favour both multilateral freer trade and bilateral free-trade negotiations with the United States.
- A commitment to strengthening Canada's labour, capital, technology and management resources.

Capital, Technology and Management

Recommendations respecting education and training are addressed in Part V of this Report.

■ With respect to capital, technology and management, this Commission makes the following recommendations.

Capital Formation

- International comparisons suggest that Canada has not suffered from any serious lack of investment over the last two decades. However, some recent economic analyses indicate that the tax treatment of savings and investment may result in a capital stock (that is, national wealth) that is too small.
- While this Commission has not reviewed the tax system in detail, it does appear to us that government should examine the effect of this system on savings and capital formation. This examination should consider the adequacy of the current allowances for inflation in the tax treatment of savings and investment. It should also consider the desirability of altering the current personal tax system by substituting an expenditure base for the income base.

Domestic R&D

The effectiveness of R&D expenditure is more important than setting a target level in relation to GNP.

- To increase the effectiveness of domestic R&D, governments should consider the following measures:
  - Ensure the availability of existing incentives to all business through some type of refundability of tax losses.
  - Broaden the definition of R&D while lowering the rate of tax subsidy, even though we recognize that such a broadening could give rise to administrative problems.
  - Ensure that adequate resources are devoted to obtaining information about foreign technological developments and to disseminating information on technological developments to domestic industry.
  - Encourage excellence by concentrating Canadian effort on projects, research and development of world-scale value through "networking" between experts within Canada, as well as internationally.
  - Reduce protection of domestic industry and encourage it to be more competitive internationally.

Technological Acquisition

New technologies are increasingly shared on a global basis, and the originating country has little lead time over others to exploit its advantage. Canada draws extensively from the world pool of new technologies, in part through investment in Canada by multi-nationals. New manufacturing technologies spread more slowly in Canada than they do in other countries.

- A potential solution is to liberalize trade and to reduce the existing barriers to the flow of equity capital.
- Public policy in education and the gathering and dissemination of information could improve technological adaptation in Canada. Post-secondary institutes should place more emphasis on science, engineering and business courses. Universities should be more active in the commercialization of inventions. The National Research Council's initiatives on information gathering and dissemination could be a model for other agencies. Technology brokers, contract-research organizations and think-tanks have assisted technology acquisition in other countries. Both the private and public sectors in Canada should consider more activity of this nature.

Management and Entrepreneurship

- Increased international competition demands that Canada draw on world-class management. We should have greater exposure to competition, a reorientation of small-business/assistance programs, and strengthened business schools. Closer bonds between business and the arts community would improve product design.

- Entrepreneurship is another key component of national economic development. While small business is a vital source of entrepreneurship, other sources also require encouragement. Governments should consider changing regulations to stimulate equity investment by financial intermediaries in small and medium-sized firms, and change the tax system to make equity ownership more attractive.

Framework Policies

Another element that is needed to improve Canada's economic position is a commitment to framework policies that encourage the private sector to adapt to change and the efficient allocation of Canada's human, capital and natural resources. Framework policies include tax policy, competition policy, general regulatory policy, foreign investment and adjustment policy.

■ Our recommendations in each of these areas are as follows.

Tax Policy

- While Commissioners have not undertaken a comprehensive review of tax policy, they have investigated the issue in general terms and looked at some specific problems. Tax policy has a fundamental influence on economic and social choices.
- We recommend a thorough review of the influence of the tax system on decisions that distinguish work and leisure, and consumption, savings and investment. Policy makers must become more aware of the efficiency costs of the tax system. In addition, Canadian tax policy must recognize the fluidity of capital flows.
- There appears to be merit to building on recent changes that moved personal income tax in the direction of a personal consumption tax.
- Governments should review non-neutralities in the corporate tax structure and consider indexing of capital assets for inflation. Alternative accounting methods of defining the corporate tax base, such as the cash-flow approach and the refundability of negative taxes, are also worthy of review. Such provisions could replace fast write-offs of exploration and development expenses in the resource sectors, and accelerated capital-cost allowances in the manufacturing sector.

Competition Policy

Canadian industry appears to have become more concentrated at the producer level over the past decade. However, trade liberalization and deregulation have reduced concentration at the seller level. Mergers and conglomerates can result in undue concentrations of economic power; they can also improve efficiency and competiveness internationally.

- Canada's competition policy should better reflect both of these realities. Commissioners recommend that Parliament empower the Director of Investigation of the Combines Investigation Act to report on all developments that impede competition in Canada, including trade protection and regulatory provisions. We recommend further that governments exercise greater discretion respecting mergers and conglomerates, directing restraining provisions to those cases where a clear threat to competitive practices is evident. With increased trade liberalization, the primary area of concern could be the non-internationally trading sectors of the economy. Canadian firms should retain the right to co-operate with one another in export markets, provided that they do not reduce domestic competition, and clarification should be offered through advance rulings. All large corporations, public and private, Canadian owned and foreign owned, should be required to file annual reports with the government.

The Regulatory Framework

Commissioners do not accept the simplistic notion that regulation should always be kept to a minimum. Some current problems, such as those associated with the environment, can probably be addressed only through an increase in regulatory activity. In many other areas, however, a reduction in regulation, and a concomitant increase in competition, would substantially increase economic efficiency. Even where regulation is necessary, it could in many cases be made simpler and more responsive to changing conditions.

- We recommend that government undertake to review and reform the regulatory framework as a whole. Regulatory agencies should be subject to closer Parliamentary scrutiny than they are at present, and their mandates should be more clearly and closely defined. Whenever possible, regulatory activity should be subject to a "sunset clause": that is, it should be limited in advance to a specific term.

Crown Corporations and Privatization

- The sale of some Crown corporations to the private sector would be a logical adjunct of deregulation, since it would enhance competition. By the same token, the federal government and the provinces should arrest the tendency toward nationalization or mixed enterprises, particularly insofar as this tendency is associated with industry bail-outs. Both levels of government should reassess the functions of these Crown corporations and mixed enterprises. If the functions or objectives of a given Crown corporation could be met more effectively by other means, the enterprise in question should be either phased out or

sold to the private sector. If a Crown corporation is to be privatized, foreign buyers should not normally be excluded from bidding for the assets. Exceptions to this rule include cases where purchase by a foreign buyer would result in barriers to entry by other competitors, or where the industry in question should be reserved for Canadians.

Foreign Investment

Over the past 15 years or so, Canadian ownership of our industries has increased substantially. It is now appropriate to re-examine mechanisms for monitoring foreign investment in Canada. Bill C-15 provides some useful guidelines, but further innovations are required to balance the need for international equity funds and the need to foster good corporate citizenship.

- The review of foreign investment proposals should be conducted by a quasi-judicial tribunal to ensure full public disclosure and political accountability. Fast-track procedures and practices for the handling of commercial confidences would need to be developed. Commissioners believe that new foreign investments need no longer be reviewed; the tribunal should review acquisitions only. The threshold for review should be raised from $5 million in gross assets to at least $50 million in order to focus resources on the larger and more critical take-overs. The review process should emphasize the competitive and technological conditions surrounding the proposed foreign take-over. The government should clarify the standards governing the post-entry behaviour of foreign investors by promulgating a general code of conduct applicable to all major firms, domestic and foreign, operating in Canada. To promote compliance with the code of conduct and to improve our understanding of the consequences of foreign control, the government should legislate an annual reporting requirement for all major firms or for corporate groups operating in Canada with assets in excess of $50 million. Firms should be required to disclose specified types of information relevant to their observance of these guidelines. Canadian directors should be required to file an annual statement detailing their firm's efforts to achieve the objectives of enterprise performance set out in the proposed code of conduct.

Adjustment Policy

- Whenever possible, adjustment assistance should be provided to workers rather than to firms. Commissioners recommend the institution both of tougher international agreements and of mandatory reference to a neutral agency, such as the Tariff Board, in order to make it more difficult for governments to

resort to protection of declining industries. By the same token, we also recommend that it be made more difficult for governments to resort to the use of firm-specific subsidies; this could be done by attaching conditions to the recipients, and by requiring the costing of off-budget subsidies. If firm-specific subsidies are given in declining sectors, the assistance should go to the most viable, and not the weakest, firms. Part V deals at length with our recommendations regarding labour adjustment policies. Declining single-industry communities require special labour-adjustment assistance.

If the economy is flexible and adaptable, adjustment will probably be much easier, and involve less unemployment. In addition, real income levels will be improved. Flexibility in prices and wages – or, more generally, the development of successful incentives – is the key to achieving a flexible and adaptable economic structure.

Infrastructure Support Services

This Commission views policies regarding transportation, communications and infrastructure generally as vital components of an industrial policy designed to enhance Canada's productivity growth and overall competitiveness. Commissioners note with concern the shrinking share of government expenditure devoted to such infrastructure.

■ We urge both the public and the private sector to view investment in the transportation and communications field as a priority. While Commissioners recognize that a strong public role in this field is both inevitable and desirable, we conclude that deregulation and a more market-oriented approach is desirable.

The private sector should be encouraged, through the tax system and government programs, to adopt the technological and other measures necessary to establish a first-rate transportation and communications network across the country. Canada needs better mechanisms for accommodating divergent regional-investment policies and regulatory policies that have national implications.

Government Intervention

■ Government should provide itself with a clear set of guidelines to determine the nature of its intervention at the sectoral or firm level. Given the difficulty of measuring the costs and benefits of intervention, Commissioners recommend that selective intervention be used sparingly. Few cases warrant special attention, and the burden of proof should be on those that propose intervention at the sectoral or firm level. A strict limit on the funds budgeted for intervention is essential. Intervention should be undertaken only where there is clear evidence of market failure, or in industries that exhibit substantial economies of scale, or where high risk and

large size make it difficult for market forces to operate adequately. Where these considerations prevail, the following guides should apply:

- The benefits of intervention must demonstrably exceed its costs.
- If efficiency is not the overriding objective, the objective should be achieved at the least cost.
- There must be sufficient consultation with business and labour to ensure that the chosen means of intervention are appropriate.
- International obligations must not be jeopardized.

The Economic Union

■ A commitment to a strengthened economic union is a vital element of a healthy Canadian economy. Barriers to the free flow of labour, capital goods and services should be minimized, and integration of policies should be harmonized. □

Stabilization and High Employment

For structural and institutional reasons, the rate of unemployment consistent with stable inflation in Canada is in the range of 6.5 to 8 per cent. Expansionary monetary and fiscal policies cannot sustain levels of unemployment below this range over the longer term. A permanent reduction in such "structural" unemployment would require structural changes, by which we mean such policies as freer trade, labour-market adjustments, and new mechanisms for labour-management relations.

The current rate of unemployment (about 11 per cent) is well above the rate consistent with stable inflation. This unacceptably high rate is the result of an insufficiency of total demand relative to total supply. Impediments to reducing unemployment by even 3 to 4.5 percentage points are the large federal government deficit, the high real current rates of interest and the extraordinarily complex role played by expectations.

Limitations in forecasting and lags in the effect of policy action argue against moderating short-run fluctuations in economic activity through discretionary action. The federal government should use stabilization policy to achieve non-inflationary growth in demand in the medium term, while preserving automatic fiscal stabilizers. However, economists disagree about the strength of the self-righting forces in the economy, that is, the forces that will drive unemployment toward its "natural" or full-employment level. Commissioners believe that discretionary stimulus or restraint can help in periods of major extended divergence in demand from a non-inflationary growth path.

Global interdependence, especially in capital markets, limits the degree to which policy can insulate an open economy such as Canada's from foreign developments. Given our flexible exchange rate, we can choose our inflation rate in the long run, and to that extent, we can have a made-in-Canada macro-economic policy. But the influence that we can hope to have on real

demand in our own economy is likely to be short term in nature and rather limited in scope.

■ To preserve independence in domestic policy for Canadian authorities, this Commission recommends a flexible exchange rate. We do not recommend exchange controls or an interest equalization tax to control capital outflows.

Commissioners share the widespread concern about the size of the federal government's deficit. We recognize that if the government dœs not reduce the current structural deficit, it will have to increase taxes just to pay interest costs and will find its flexibility seriously constrained.

■ Commissioners recommend a strategy of gradual deficit reduction, given the current outlook of slow recovery. To stabilize or decrease the debt/GNP ratio, the government will need to reduce the deficit by about 1.5 per cent of GNP, which would be equivalent to $10 billion by 1990–91. The practice of laying out an explicit medium-term fiscal plan, introduced in the December 1979 budget and continued since, is useful. We favour using a combination of tax increases and rather broad expenditure reductions to reduce the deficit. The precise means of achieving this reduction are a matter for shorter-term government policy, but Commissioners offer one possible means for consideration. This would be to set the indexing factor for the personal income tax and for some transfer-payment programs at *x* percentage points below the rate of inflation and to hold the price factor for all other expenditure programs – except foreign aid and national defence – at *x* percentage points below the rate of inflation. Setting these annual indexing factors three percentage points below inflation for a period of three years would generate a reduction in the deficit of about 1.5 per cent of GNP, thereby reducing the deficit and by that amount the deficit/GNP ratio from the 6 to 7 per cent range projected for the late 1980s.

■ Under present circumstances of high unemployment, a shift to a less expansionary fiscal stance, so as to reduce the deficit, should be more than matched by a temporary shift to a less restrictive monetary stance. A moderate increase in the projected growth of demand, which might significantly reduce unemployment and strengthen investment, should still be consistent with a further reduction in inflation.

While Commissioners recognize that adherence to a steady monetary-growth guideline can help to ensure that a stable, non-inflationary environment will be maintained, shifts in the demand for money during the past few years have made this approach difficult to apply. Furthermore, such an approach might lessen governments' ability to adjust the mix of monetary and fiscal policy in order to balance consumption and investment, and to balance the sectors of the economy that are strongly influenced by the exchange rate and the sectors that are not.

■ As a compromise solution, the government could relate demand-management/policy targets to the growth of nominal GNP. This policy would require a willingness to adjust both monetary-growth targets to nominal GNP, in the event of significant shifts in relation of the money supply, and monetary and/or fiscal policy in the event of severe prolonged departures of nominal GNP from a steady growth path. Commissioners recommend that the joint setting of monetary and fiscal policy be consistent with non-inflationary growth of nominal demand.

Commissioners have also considered potential adjustments to lessen the distortions and damage that any continuing inflation imposes. We share what seems to be a general preference that has emerged over the last few years, to emphasize low and stable inflation rather than structural adjustments that would make it easier to live with inflation.

■ Despite the preceding conclusion, Commissioners believe that serious consideration should be given to indexation of financial assets, accounting systems and tax systems. To adjust the tax system to take inflation into account would improve its neutrality in general and lessen the incentive to rely on debt financing in particular.

In Commissioners' judgement, permanent wage and price controls or even a permanent tax-based incomes policy would probably not prove acceptable to Canadians and would not be consistent with our general approach of promoting a flexible, adaptable and growth-oriented economy.

■ We do, however, recommend the temporary use of controls or incentive-based incomes policies if the country needs to reduce inflation again. Furthermore, the use of temporary controls could bring about a more rapid reduction of unemployment than presently seems to be in prospect. Such temporary controls should be the subject of negotiation with business and labour groups.

Commissioners believe that a formal voluntary incomes policy, which would involve commitments to respect common guidelines for wage increases and for price or profit patterns, will be difficult to achieve, given the structure of labour and product markets in Canada.

■ We recommend, however, continued informal and formal consultation on a broad range of economic issues, and increased openness about the bases of economic policy formation. Such an approach might assist public understanding and encourage realistic attitudes about wages and prices. It might also contribute to lower unemployment.

■ Commissioners believe that gain sharing—that is, making compensation more dependent on the current performance of the firm or industry—offers the most promising approach to achieving greater cyclical stability in employment and productivity growth.

Gain-sharing would be viable only in an environment of greater trust and openness, and thus we tie our recommendation for its use to our position on consultation noted above.

Commissioners recommend to labour, business and governments that they consider some form of incomes policy, coupled with supportive monetary and fiscal action, to increase employment. Without such a comprehensive approach, reduction of unemployment to the level of 6.5 to 8 per cent may be a lengthy and difficult process. Furthermore, without such a demonstration of political will by all major groups in society, and by individuals as well, the prospects for undertaking major structural changes to reduce unemployment below 5 per cent would appear to be less bright. This basic challenge of political will is the central determinant of improved economic performance. □

PART IV

Natural Resources and Environment

Conclusions and Recommendations

The natural resource sector's contribution to Canada's economic well-being, cultural life, and political traditions and institutions has been immense. Because natural resources have been so important to Canada's past, however, we tend to exaggerate their importance to our future. In fact, the resource sector has not grown at a rate commensurate with the economic expectations we have developed in the years since the Second World War; nor does its projected growth match our hopes for the decades to come.

It has become clear in recent years – if it was not clear before – that Canada's natural resource endowment is not unlimited. We are losing our agricultural land to suburbs and shopping centres. Our stands of readily accessible, high-quality timber are largely gone, and our richest and most accessible deposits of ore and fossil fuels are already in production. Our mismanagement of the fishery has meant that we have not been able to reap the potential benefits of the designation of the 200-mile offshore zone in 1977. These problems of supply are compounded by prospects of lower demand in world markets for forest products and most non-fuel minerals. Moreover, our forestry and minerals industries can expect increasingly stiff competition from countries with lower production costs, and this competition will be made all the more difficult by the rapid advances in products and process technology.

These problems do not mean that our basic resource industries will disappear. Relative to other nations, Canada remains well endowed with natural resources. The outlook for oil and gas, a few minerals, hydro-electricity, and Western grains is favourable. The dollar value of production in the resource sector will continue to grow. Nevertheless, the share of output in this sector will decline, relative to the share of output in other sectors of our economy, although the decline will not be as rapid as it was in the first two post-war decades. Total exports of resource products will continue to

expand, and the terms of trade are unlikely to turn against us in any dramatic fashion. Increasingly, however, we shall have to supplement resource exports with exports of more highly processed products if we are to maintain our capacity to buy the goods and services of other nations. The pattern of relative decline will mean that we can generally expect no net gain in resource-sector employment in the future: a growing proportion of Canadians will find their jobs in factories or offices. Indeed, the decline in the resource sector's share of total employment is the clearest indication that the sector will not be the engine of economic growth that it was in the past.

The prospect of a decline in the relative importance of the resource sector in relation to our national economy is no reason to neglect that sector's problems or its claims. Resource industries are still essential to the economic life of many regions of Canada. Moreover, we have an obligation to pass on to future generations a variety of viable resource industries founded on a natural endowment that is as secure and as healthy as we can make it. Canada's success in resource production owes as much to human ingenuity as it dœs to the resource endowment itself, and many of the problems of the sector can be overcome, or at least diminished, by appropriate applications of that ingenuity. We must apply new methods, new processes, new public policies, and new thinking to the problems of maintaining both the competitiveness of the resource industries and the integrity of the natural environment that is their base.

■ Chapter 12 set out this Commission's detailed recommendations for the individual resource sectors. The thrust of our recommendations for dealing with the challenges ahead in each resource sector is as follows:

- For agriculture, we recommend a range of measures, from expansion of foreign markets, to increased R&D, to reform of national supply-management marketing boards, planned to enhance the efficiency of a sector which has great potential over the long term.
- For forestry, we recognize a legacy of mismanagement and recommend significant changes in the way the forest sector operates, as well as a major infusion of public and private investment.
- For the fishery, what has been lacking is political will, and we recommend measures to build on the fundamental reforms of the Kirby and Pearse Reports to shift the balance in public policy toward building a viable economic base in Canada's coastal regions.
- For minerals, we recognize generally the more limited possibilities. We recommend a more realistic approach to adjustment and a movement towards a profit-based tax system.
- For energy, we recommend a new framework based on the principles of efficiency, fairness and predictability, and a complete overhaul of the fiscal regime for oil and gas.

- For the environment, we recognize the growing challenge and the need to integrate decisions related to environment and economic development. We recommend a series of measures to correct the incentives which are aimed at protecting the environment; and, in general, we propose strengthening the regulatory framework.

Commissioners believe that it is important, however difficult, to assess the problems and opportunities of the resource sector in a more comprehensive way, just as, for example, governments focus from time to time on the general issues of the manufacturing sector.

■ The following general principles briefly relate Commissioners' detailed recommendations to the management of the resource sector as a whole:

- We conclude that in Canada, with all its rich resource heritage, there is no conflict, in the long term, between the stewardship, preservation and enhancement of the natural resource base and growth prospects for the traditional resource industries. Consequently, we perceive a vital need to integrate environmental decisions and decisions related to economic development, and our proposals for action in each of the particular resource sectors reflect this perception. Thus we recommend a study of the loss of prime farm land to non-agricultural uses and emphasize our concern about the problem of soil deterioration and soil salinity. We support the infusion of large sums of both public and private monies into reforestation and silviculture, and we recommend that the duration of leasing agreements between governments and forest companies be increased in order to provide an incentive for long-term management of forest tracts. Finally, in recognition of the fact that natural resources belong to the Canadian people and must be passed on to future generations, we believe that private developers should continue to pay governments a royalty based on production for oil and gas and minerals.
- In many other places in this Report, we call for less government intervention; in the area of environmental regulation, however, we are obliged to call for more. Over the long term, the task of environmental regulation promises to be immense. We shall have to deal with growth in the number and size of projects that may adversely affect the environment, with an increasing number of pollutants and hazards, with the irreversible, and sometimes unquantifiable, effects of a growing range of industrial substances and processes, and with the emerging international aspects of our environmental responsibility. Consequently, we recommend that governments increase their spending to provide the analytical resources needed to support

the long-term regulatory task. We further recommend that federal environmental processes be put on a statutory basis, and that federal and provincial review processes be brought into greater harmony.

- Changes in the pattern of world trade have offered new opportunities and new challenges to the Canadian resource sector. Our ability to realize the opportunities – and to survive the challenges – will depend on our ability to design resource strategies suited to a global context. This consideration has led us to recommend that the grains sector and the fishery sector pursue marketing and production strategies that will give them access to the new and rapidly growing markets in the developing countries. Whether it is a question of expanding our markets or of beating the competition, we believe that it is within Canada's interest to work for free trade, both at the multilateral level and at the bilateral level, with the largest purchaser of Canadian resource products, the United States. The adjustment problems that would derive from freer trade and the bargaining tactics that would be necessary to bring it about would vary with each resource.
- We believe that in many instances a stricter adherence to market principles and an increase in the incentives to the private sector would brighten the prospects of Canada's resource industries. Thus we consider that a commitment to market pricing for both oil and gas would provide the incentive essential to increased exploration and development. For oil and gas and minerals, we believe that the establishment of a taxation scheme based largely on profits rather than on output volumes would both promote the development of marginal supplies and allow the industry to make more rational resource-allocation decisions. Although we do not advocate transferring ownership of forest tracts to private industry, we do suggest that such modifications to the land-tenure system as increasing the duration of leasing agreements would promote more responsible forest management. Finally, we recommend a phasing-out of national agricultural-supply/management marketing boards and their replacement by an income-stabilization scheme designed to moderate large fluctuations in farmers' incomes.
- We believe that there is room for significant improvement in the efficiency of both the regulatory framework and the handling, licensing and transportation infrastructure that supports the resource sector. We underline the important effect of the Crow Rate on the transportation of all bulk commodities, especially Western grains. We support further movement in the direction of market-rate principles when the Western Grains Transportation Act comes up for review, but we leave it to the Committee of Inquiry on Crow Benefit Payment (Hall Committee) to advise on specific adjustments to the payment of the Crow

Benefit. In the minerals area, we recognize that the regulatory structure is cumbersome and slow, and we recommend that governments undertake a systematic review of their regulatory processes with a view to streamlining them. We would also draw attention to the fact that fisheries management has all too often led to overcapacity, unnecessary tensions, uneven product quality and, thus, lost opportunity. For oil and gas, we recommend a simpler taxation regime and a simpler pricing formula, both of which would decrease medium- and long-term uncertainty.

- The resource sector has undergone far-reaching adjustments since the Second World War. Further adjustment will be both essential and unavoidable, although perhaps less dramatic than it has been in the past. We believe that if a given operation has failed to realize a profit over a sustained period, adjustment is inevitable and should be allowed to take its course; governments should not intervene to support uneconomic activity. Mines that can no longer produce an ore competitively should be phased out, and we believe that in general, the same principle holds for the fishery. As we pointed out above, however, government action is necessary in some areas to guard against deterioration in the quality of our renewable resource base. In particular, we recommend a substantial increase in both public and private expenditures for the renewal of the Canadian forest.

  There must be and can be a balance in the adjustment process between efficiency and fairness to people whose livelihoods or communities have long depended on traditional resource industries. In the case of the family farm, we recognize the special problems created by farmers' limited access to equity capital, by the volatility of farm prices, and by the principle that the land is to be passed to future generations. We therefore support the retention of special credit schemes for agriculture and, as mentioned above, we urge consideration of an income-stabilization scheme to replace national supply-management boards. By the same token, we support replacement of Unemployment Insurance for fishermen by a new production-bonus and income-stabilization program, a scheme that would promote more efficient behaviour without reducing total benefits. Fishermen would also be eligible for income supplementation under the Universal Income Security Program (UISP) proposed in our recommendations on social security. In the minerals sector, we recommend the provision of adjustment assistance for communities and individuals affected by mine closures.

- Research has a large pay-off, but often the benefits seem too distant to the producer of the resource to justify the expenditure. We recognize that there must be renewed Canadian effort in fundamental research, especially in the traditional resource

industries, if Canada is to match progress in competitor countries. Research into soil deterioration and new crop varieties warrants long-term funding by government. So dœs research related to aquaculture and to maintenance and improvement of the forest base. We have also called for an increase in expenditure on training in forestry. Finally, we support a stepped-up research effort in the field of environmental management, where we believe that the institutional capacity to provide scientific advice on a systematic basis is essential.

- In view of the importance of resources to Canada's future economic prospects and of the need to take a more integrated view of the problems and opportunities in the resource area as a whole, we recommend the establishment of a Council of Resources Ministers to provide leadership for increased federal-provincial co-operation. We recognize that various ministerial groups (for example, on agriculture and mines) now exist, but we believe that it is important for a co-ordinated strategy across the range of resources to be developed, based on the principles we have outlined above. We also recommend the development within the federal government of a greater capacity to analyse the contributions and problems of the resource sector as a whole. □

PART V

Human Resources and Social Support

Conclusions and Recommendations

This Commission wishes to make a number of general observations concerning some of the issues we have reviewed in this part of our Report. Several of the major recommendations proferred in this section are best considered as a package. Thus the reforms Commissioners propose for Unemployment Insurance (UI), the new Universal Income Security Program (UISP) and the new Transitional Adjustment Assistance Program (TAAP) would have maximum efficacy if they were implemented together. The savings generated by the UI changes would finance the TAAP, and the UISP would provide financial assistance if some incomes were lowered by the adjustments. The TAAP would support the effect of changes in the UI system that would promote economic adjustment, while the UISP and some elements of TAAP would cushion any resulting difficulties experienced by individual Canadians.

Since the overall level of social policy expenditures in Canada is low by OECD standards, there is no strong general case for attacking the deficit by reducing social expenditures. However, reallocation and restructuring could greatly improve the system and would be valuable in providing help to those who most need it, while containing overall costs.

Looking forward, Commissioners can see no trends that will inevitably undermine the fundamental viability of social programs. Such factors as the aging of the Canadian population or the demands imposed by technological and economic change require careful planning, but none is likely to prove so large as to make our programs unsustainable, particularly if the reforms suggested in this part of our report are carried out.

We Commissioners are of the opinion that tax and transfer systems cannot be given valid consideration in isolation from each other. Thus, major reform of our income-security programs also requires reform of some aspects of personal taxation.

Labour Markets and Unemployment Insurance

After considering Canadian labour markets, Commissioners are of the view that Canada's most important goals are to create more jobs and to improve the situation of individual Canadians by eliminating any inappropriate incentives in current programs. We undertook our analysis on the assumption that current trends in participation rates will continue, bringing a steadily increasing proportion of women into the labour force. While these trends are basically manageable, particularly given our assumption, detailed in Part III, that labour supply itself creates demand for labour, they do portend continuing high levels of unemployment – and continuing preoccupation of policy makers with that problem – for the next five to eight years, and they do add significantly to the training requirements Canadians must face.

We note in our analysis of labour markets that the highest proportion of current unemployment is either created by deficiency of aggregate demand or by structural factors such as mismatches between available job requirements and skills. A significant amount of unemployment is also created by "frictional" effects, that is the inevitable lags and delays as workers move from one job to another. We have dealt in Part III with aggregate demand deficiency. Here we recommend several measures to facilitate adjustment and training, thus reducing structural unemployment. We also recommend changes in unemployment-insurance and income-security programs which will lower frictional unemployment. Without undertaking changes such as those we are recommending, it will be almost impossible, even in the long run, to reduce unemployment below 6.5 to 8 per cent of the work-force, the current non-accelerating inflation rate of unemployment (NAIRU). Since we consider even those levels to be unacceptably high, we lay great emphasis on these types of reform.

Some increase in unemployment is also engendered by our existing UI programs. First, by making unemployment relatively "cheaper" for individuals, it has, in some cases, a negative effect on job search. Secondly, by providing, through its benefit structure, that individuals in some areas may qualify for 40 weeks of benefits by 12 weeks of work, it encourages regular cyclical unemployment; a feature taken advantage of by both employers and employees. Again, by providing extended benefits in some areas but not others, it discourages labour-force adjustment, while providing no extended benefits to large numbers of unemployed Canadians. Moreover, because its premium structure is unrelated to the risk of unemployment, it penalizes steady employers and employees and shifts benefits towards firms and employees with unstable employment patterns.

■ With respect to Unemployment Insurance, Commissioners recommend that the federal government consider a package of changes such as the following:

- Experience rating which establishes premium rates that are proportional to the risk of unemployment. These rates should generally be calculated on a firm-by-firm basis.
- A reduction of the benefit rate to 50 per cent of insurable earnings

- An increase of the entrance requirement to 15-20 weeks of insured work over the preceding year
- Tightening of the link between the maximum benefit period and the minimum employment period; for example, establishing a ratio of two or three weeks of work as qualification for one week of benefits
- Elimination of the extended benefit period based on regional unemployment rates.

These changes would reduce UI benefit costs by at least one-sixth in respect of the reduction in benefit rates and approximately one-sixth in respect of the elimination of regional extended benefits. The cost reductions that could be achieved by the other changes are too sensitive to behavioural change even to be estimated by methods available to this Commission. However, total savings of at least $4 billion at April 1985 rates of unemployment are probable.

- Commissioners therefore recommend that:
  - The savings in respect of the first three UI reforms be passed along as reductions in overall premium levels. (The regional extended benefits are financed from consolidated revenues.)
  - Personal and corporate taxes be raised by an amount equivalent to premium reductions to create a Transitional Adjustment Assistance Fund. The government savings from termination of extended benefits should be added to the fund.

■ This Commission recommends that the Transitional Adjustment Assistance Fund be used to finance a Transitional Adjustment Assistance Program. This program would provide adjustment assistance for Canadians who have exhausted their UI benefits, or whose lay-offs appear permanent, provided that they were willing to move or to undertake retraining to improve their employment prospects. The program would provide greatly expanded support for:
- Portable wage-subsidy programs
- Mobility grants
- Training programs
- Early retirement.

In addition, the TAAP could be used to provide compensation for losses in assets, such as housing, which occur as a result of the decline of communities. It should also be possible for TAAP funds to be used on a pooled basis to assist workers to purchase equity in plants which would otherwise shut down or in other forms of local economic development projects. In general, the extent of entitlement of workers to TAAP funds should be proportional to their length of attachment to the labour force, since older workers will typically experience greater transitional difficulties than younger workers.

■ Commissioners recommend that existing policies promoting equal pay for work of equal value should be maintained. However,

these may involve some negative consequences. If they are used apart from affirmative action programs, for instance, they may actually result in reductions of employment opportunities for disadvantaged groups. Moreover, they can serve to move Canadians too far away from a market-determined to an administered wage system. Commissioners therefore recommend that legislation emphasize creation of equal employment opportunities through affirmative action, rather than the principle of equal value. Commissioners generally approve the approach put forward by Judge Rosalie Abella. This would involve:

- Legislated requirements for affirmative action by all employers covered by the Canada Labour Code
- Encouragement of all provincial jurisdictions to follow suit
- Contract compliance action by the federal government and Crown corporations.

We are not convinced, however, that sufficient attention has been paid to the costs of equal employment-opportunities programs or, particularly, to the issues of equity among the various disadvantaged groups in Canadian society.

- We therefore recommend that the program be phased in following:
  - A three year experimental program of affirmative action in Crown corporations
  - Extensive consultations with the private sector to ensure effective but least expensive implementation to begin in three years' time.

This Commission believes that the programs are more likely to be effective if they are supported by legislation and backed by an adequate enforcement agency.

- We therefore recommend:
  - Legislated equal employment-opportunities provisions, rather than guidelines
  - Establishment of fully adequate levels of funding for the federal Human Rights Commission and equivalent provincial institutions.

■ Work schedules are necessarily established on the basis of understandings between employer and employees that will express a balance between the requirements of the work process and the desires of the employee. This Commission has found, however, that some factors exist which may interfere artificially with the achievement of this understanding. Any such factors should be eliminated in order to achieve fuller flexibility of labour-market arrangements, thus enhancing both employee satisfaction and productivity.

- Commissioners therefore recommend such changes as:
  - Basing Unemployment Insurance, Worker's Compensation and CPP premiums on hourly earnings, with a ceiling on contributions that applies to hourly rates rather than to weekly or annual compensation
  - Eliminating the bias against some categories of reduced hours in creating eligibility for paid holidays or termination notice
  - Encouragement of pro-rating of fringe benefits. □

Immigration

In the past decade, Canadian immigration policy has become more restrictive than our historical norm, both with respect to numbers of immigrants and with respect to the criteria for admission. We Commissioners do not believe that this narrowing is necessary or appropriate, given the long-term projections for Canada's population growth. We are concerned, however, about the overall implications of a more open immigration policy.

■ We therefore recommend:

- A major examination of Canadian demographic trends and their implications for our government's future immigration policies
- That the same study examine, by means of open debate and other methods, the cultural, linguistic and racial implications of other forms of immigration policy
- Establishment of a long-term plan for immigration that, depending on the results of the study described above, will move to higher numbers of immigrants over a number of years. This new plan should place less emphasis on narrow occupational requirements and more emphasis on broadly skilled and generally capable immigrants. □

Labour/Management Relations

■ This Commission notes the very great importance of the labour movement in Canada and throughout the developed world in improving the pay and working conditions of workers. To this end, we wish to recommend generally that all Canadian governments provide a supportive legislative environment for the labour movement and for collective bargaining.

The adversarial system of union-management relations needs to be re-examined. Management must respond to employee concerns about job security and job satisfaction, and to the often-untapped capability of all employees to contribute to improved productivity and product quality. Unions must find new ways to facilitate and to participate in this process; they should have and take the opportunity to do so, not by relinquishing their representation of

employee interests, but by adding to it a responsibility for helping to achieve the levels of competitiveness essential to the survival of the enterprise.

Since reductions in strikes and lock-outs could be achieved by the following measures, Commissioners recommend that:

- Labour-relations boards be permitted to create multi-employer and multi-union bargaining units when this is likely to facilitate the bargaining process. Such units should not be imposed but, rather, could be permitted on the application of one or both sides.
- More information be shared by the parties to industrial disputes.

Commissioners are not persuaded that shorter contracts or forced centralization of bargaining structures are likely to improve labour-management relations significantly. Changes in these areas should therefore proceed on a voluntary basis. The right to strike or lock out must be rationally limited by the need to maintain the health and safety of the public.

Employer-employee relations in Canada seem likely to be most responsive to improvement at the level of individual firms, plants and union locals. Overall solutions proposed at the provincial or national level seem unlikely to be as effective as local solutions.

- Commissioners therefore recommend that governments support, on a local and voluntary basis, such features as:
  - Preventive mediation programs
  - Quality-of-working-life programs
  - Gains-sharing/compensation arrangements.

■ Occupational Health and Safety is an area of important and growing concern. Since great improvements can still be made, this Commission recommends:

- Greater emphasis on these issues at higher levels of corporate management. Management failure in this area is bound to result in higher levels of government intervention.
- More complete experience rating of worker's compensation premiums in order to provide direct financial incentives for firms to minimize health and safety problems, in order to ensure that the full social costs of hazardous work environments are reflected in prices.
- Continued and increased reliance on the internal responsibility system rather than increased government intervention. This requires:
  - Mandatory, joint health-and-safety/labour-management committees in all eleven jurisdictions, such as currently exist in nine
  - Vesting real responsibility in those committees rather than leaving them with only an advisory role

- Continual revision of standards by governments as new information about hazards becomes available. This is most important in dealing with occupational health problems. At a national level, these standards could most appropriately be developed by the Canada Centre for Occupational Health and Safety. The appropriate jurisdictions would then apply the standards.

Commissioners are particularly concerned with occupational health issues. Because occupational diseases typically have long incubation periods, it is often difficult to evaluate the effects of industrial processes on workers. That same factor makes it difficult to establish a direct link between occupational factors and specific diseases, and therefore current worker's compensation programs are not well adapted to handling occupational disease.

- In addition to our recommendation of continual development of standards and monitoring of processes, Commissioners also urge that:
  - The federal and provincial governments consider the immediate implementation of a comprehensive social insurance disability plan to deal with the longer-term effects of occupational health problems, as well as with other forms of disability in the working-age population. This plan could be implemented either by expanding worker's compensation into a comprehensive disability scheme or by extending the present disability provisions of the Canada and Quebec Pension Plans. A federal-provincial working party is currently considering this measure, but progress in developing this idea has been slow. □

Education and Training

In Canada education and training programs discharge multiple functions. They constitute an important way in which young Canadians learn to live together in our community, and they are the most important means by which labour-force skills and knowledge are adjusted to labour-market demands. They also provide a major means of upward mobility. Our post-secondary educational institutions are also the major source of basic research and of much applied research, and they are important repositories of our culture.

Commissioners anticipate no diminution in the general importance of post-secondary education and training. Indeed, PSE is likely to increase in importance as the demand grows for high levels of knowledge and research. Training programs, particularly those relating to industrial training, are likely to become more important as Canadians adjust to the shifting realities of the labour market. The Transitional Adjustment Assistance Program, by providing greatly increased support for training, may be a particularly important factor in this adjustment.

Commissioners are concerned about several features of our educational and training system. In particular we are convinced that:

- Higher levels of excellence are desirable and achievable.
- More flexibility is desirable.
- Use of the PSE system by low-income Canadians is insufficient.
- The current federal-provincial transfer arrangements are inappropriate.
- The current balance between industrial and institutional training is still tilted too far towards the latter.
- There is inadequate provision for retraining and re-education in adult years.

With respect to post-secondary education, Commissioners believe that it is desirable to consider substantial changes in financing mechanisms in order to create a more competitive, dynamic and diversified system. The current EPF transfer arrangements are quite inappropriate for achieving those objectives. They should be changed to encourage reform of the system, but in a way that will minimize direct federal intervention in this area of provincial jurisdiction, while still allowing for the achievement of national objectives.

There has been very considerable informal discussion of the intergovernmental transfer arrangements for post-secondary education over the last five years, but there have been no formal federal-provincial negotiations. Commissioners believe that it is important for federal and provincial governments to enter immediately into serious discussion of other methods of funding than the current mechanism both because the present arrangements are less than satisfactory, and because the uncertainty about possible future arrangements may be impeding necessary reforms to the sector. Several broad options are available. Our federal government could:

- Withdraw completely from this sector and cede enough tax points to the provinces to cover its current contributions
- Return to the pre-EPF funding formula
- Provide an amount equal to provincial "own source" funding, exclusive of the tax points transferred under EPF
- Freeze its basic contributions at current or slightly lower-than-current levels while matching on a 50/50 basis incremental provincial spending on education. Alternatively, incremental funding could be earmarked to support high-level university-based research.
- Undertake a form of direct-to-student financing, allowing for variable PSE fee schedules.

This Commission dœs not recommend federal withdrawal from PSE involvement. Many of the benefits of post-secondary education are national in scope, and provincial governments might tend to undersupply this sector unless there were some federal presence, particularly if they believe that graduates are likely to leave the province. Many representations and briefs emphasized the importance of involvement of the Government of Canada in this field.

Among the cost-sharing options are:

- A return to pre-EPF arrangements. This would be a step back to a basically unsatisfactory system.
- Provision by the federal government of amounts equal to provincial "own source" funding. This move would constitute a massive cut-back by the federal government, part of which would probably be passed on by provincial governments to already hard-pressed institutions.
- Freezing of basic federal contributions with cost-matching of increments. This stance would exert relatively little "leverage" on provincial government expenditures in this sector and would mean starting from a basically unsatisfactory base point. However it is probably the most desirable of the cost-sharing options, particularly if some of the incremental funds are used to support research.

With the possible exception of the final choice, none of the cost-sharing options seems likely to be satisfactory. None is likely to improve the incentives for institutions to achieve the flexiblity and excellence which Commissioners think desirable. We believe that the complex institutional arrangements for PSE have created very considerable inertia in the system, to the detriment of the student and society as a whole. We therefore believe that the direct-to-student/funding option, although it is the most radical and thus difficult for PSE institutions and governments to accept, may be a preferable approach. In order to institute that approach, the following changes would be required:

- The federal government should terminate the PSE cash portion of its EPF grants to the provinces, ceding the EPF tax points plus further equalized tax points in an amount equivalent to the Quebec abatement. All of the cash portion of EPF, including transitional adjustment payments, should be replaced with an education-expense tax credit or grant, to be increased annually at a rate equal to nominal GNP increase.
- Provincial governments should be encouraged to deregulate the fee structure of post-secondary institutions.
- Provincial transfers to institutions might appropriately be based on an equal per-student figure, without differentiation for particular programs, and be related directly to enrolment.
- Students should be responsible for a portion of education costs. Beyond that point, the federal credit should vary with the amount of expenses and tuition fees, up to a limit. The amount of the grant should vary only with fees and expenses directly related to education, and no attempt should be made to direct students into "demand" programs by means of a variable grant structure.
- A portion of the current EPF transfer (and some additional funding) should be reallocated to granting councils, which should begin to cover overhead costs of funded research.

A variant of this approach would provide much higher grants to graduate students than to undergraduates. This approach would greatly increase the "value" of graduate education for institutions and thus encourage specialization and excellence.

■ Commissioners strongly recommend that federal-provincial discussions aimed at rectifying an unsatisfactory situation should begin immediately, that they should consider a range of options such as we have suggested here, and that they should proceed with all urgency toward a conclusion. We believe that close further attention is merited for the options which:

- Replace intergovernmental transfers with direct-to-student transfers. Careful consideration should be given to the variant which makes much larger transfers to graduate students.
- Freeze current federal cash contributions. The federal government would match provincial expenditure increases on a 50/50 basis.
- Freeze current federal cash contributions while redirecting considerable amounts (perhaps one-half) of what would have been the incremental amounts into funding of university-based research. The rest of the funds should be used to match, on a 25/75 federal-provincial basis, larger provincial government contributions to universities.

■ With respect particularly to primary and secondary education, this Commission recommends the formation of an independent national commission to monitor quality and standards in primary and secondary education and to conduct and record research in related areas. We urge that the private sector take the lead in establishing and financing this commission. With respect to occupational training programs, Commissioners believe that the direction of reform presently being followed by the federal government is generally appropriate. Increased attention to on-the-job and job-related training is to be encouraged.

■ This Commission also recommends that the federal government:

- Provide a special wage subsidy for labour-force entrants who have not had other forms of vocational training or post-secondary education. The subsidy would normally be provided to persons 15 to 18 years of age and to women entering the labour force after discharging family responsibilities. The subsidy could be financed by eliminating other job-creation programs for young people.
- Provide, under the Income Tax Act, for a Registered Educational Leave Savings Plan which workers could use to help finance the cost of training. Careful consideration must be given to the type of program eligible for RELSP financing and to the possibility of requiring completion of any training or education undertaken in order to qualify for the advantage.

Commissioners wish to point out that the TAAP described earlier might significantly increase training requirements in Canada.

Access to higher education by low-income students should be an important avenue of upward mobility in Canada. However, for a variety of reasons, low-income students make far less use of higher education than do middle-income students, thus impeding both their own upward mobility and Canada's labour-force efficiency. Several of the barriers faced by low-income students are not susceptible to immediate government reduction. Family-socialization patterns and peer pressures can be influenced only very indirectly. But governments can and should ensure that undue financial barriers are not blocking the educational prospects of low-income students.

■ This Commission therefore recommends strongly that further attention be paid to improving access for low-income students. At the least, therefore, we recommend continued support for the Canada Student Loans Program and its provincial equivalents, and we recommend that loan limits be changed in consonance with other policy changes proposed in this Report, to remove any financial barriers that might exclude otherwise-qualified low-income students. We also wish to emphasize the importance of continuing to grant scholarships for students who excel, no matter what their income level, and of offering bursaries for low- or moderate-income students with above-average grades who might otherwise be reluctant or unable to continue their education.

Commissioners are concerned, however that the CSLP is increasingly unable to deal with the issue of student independence of parental support. Therefore we do not reject the concept of contingent-repayment loan schemes, and we recommend that governments continue to consider that possibility. □

Income-Security Programs

While this Commission dœs not view Canada's problems over the next quarter-century as unmanageable, Commissioners do believe that many – perhaps most – Canadians will have to face the need to make adjustments that will maximize their own opportunities in the face of the effects of economic change. For most Canadians, these adjustments will not be severe, but for some they will be very difficult. This is particularly true for low-income Canadians, families with children that lack income adequate to meet family needs, and workers in peripheral regions or peripheral jobs. Economic change has always caused these Canadians more difficulty than middle-income Canadians, and it will continue to do so. Moreover, even without the impact of change, there are over one million Canadian families whose incomes are inadequate to cover any but the barest necessities, and many of these can be considered the "working poor": families where one or more breadwinners are employed all or most of the year, but where incomes are still inadequate to meet their needs.

Middle- and upper-income Canadians get a great deal of public and private support as they adjust to economic change. They receive tax-supported

education and training, and their employers often foot a substantial portion of their adjustment costs. Low-income Canadians receive relatively little such support. In general, it often seems true that the poorer one is, the more one is left to one's own devices to cope with the forces of change or destiny.

For these reasons, among others, Commissioners believe that all Canadians have a duty and a right to share the costs of adjustment and to provide help to those who need it. That has always been the basic rationale for many of Canada's income-security programs, and it should remain so.

We Commissioners are also persuaded that there is enough money in our current personal tax-expenditure and transfer-payment programs to provide a comprehensive program of support for all deserving Canadians, but that current programs are often fundamentally flawed so that the current safety net is inappropriate. We believe that Canada can do much better than it has done in providing income support for our working poor and for those undertaking adjustments in their own lives in order to build a better future for themselves and their children.

■ The Transitional Adjustment Assistance Program would go some way towards providing assistance, but other reforms, too, are required. Thus Commissioners believe that the provision of a Universal Income Security Program with a universally available income guarantee, subject to reduction at a relatively low "tax-back" rate, constitutes the most appropriate foundation for Canada's income security programs.

- We therefore recommend that the UISP replace existing federal tax and transfer programs including:
  - GIS
  - Family Allowances
  - Child Tax Credits
  - Married Exemptions
  - Child Exemptions
  - The Federal Share of CAP Social Assistance Programs
  - Federal Social Housing Programs
- The replacement of these programs would make possible a universally available guarantee, in 1985, of approximately $2750 per adult (and for the first child in a single-parent family) and $750 per child with benefits reduced at a 20-per cent rate as other income was available. The elderly should receive an enriched option. A substantially larger guarantee of $3825 per adult could be provided if the personal income-tax exemption were also included.
- The UISP should be put in place at the same time as the broad Unemployment Insurance reforms described above. The entire package should be in place in 1988. The package should be phased in, however, with a two-stage approach. In the first stage, which should begin immediately, the Family Allowance, Child Tax Credit, and Child Tax Exemptions should be eliminated and replaced with a single demogrant or tax credit of

approximately $1000 per year in 1985, payable monthly. The total amount should be available to families with a total annual income of up to $26 000. Beyond that level, benefits might be reduced at a 25 per cent rate. Experience rating for UI should also begin immediately, and social assistance payments under the CAP should be restructured to replace the present pre-emptive reduction of benefits above the current work-related/expenses level with a 50 per cent reduction rate. At the second stage of implementation, to be completed by the beginning of 1988, the full range of UI, UISP and TAAP changes outlined above should be in place.

Commissioners wish to emphasize that recommended benefit levels and structures are indicative only. While we believe them to be correct and appropriate levels in mid-1985, they will change with time. Moreover, the interrelationship among such features as basic guarantees and tax-back levels can be varied to achieve a number of effects.

We also wish to emphasize that while the federal government could implement most parts of this proposal unilaterally, these reforms are likely to be far more effective if they are carried out in co-operation with provincial government changes. The major reason for this is that provincial governments automatically receive larger tax revenues whenever the federal government eliminates tax exemptions and deductions. If the full value of these programs is to be maintained for the social policy sector, it will be necessary for the provincial governments either to provide harmonized transfers or to cede some tax points back to the federal government in return for delivery of the income-transfer arrangements.

- Commissioners recommend therefore, that these proposals be the subject of urgent and serious federal-provincial discussion. We urge the Government of Canada to introduce them to the federal-provincial agenda at an early federal-provincial ministers' meeting and to move forward quickly towards implementation.

The UISP is not intended to provide fully adequate benefits for all Canadians who have no other earnings or income; it is primarily a supplementation program intended to compensate for the fact that there is often a considerable mismatch between earnings and needs. Commissioners therefore recommend that provincial governments continue to provide needs-tested social assistance as a top-up to UI and UISP benefits where these do not fully meet pertinent needs. The equivalent of the current provincial share of social assistance payments should be adequate for this purpose. In addition, provincial governments could reap a substantial increase in tax revenues from some of the tax changes which would accompany the inception of the UISP. It is desirable that these funds should also be used to support income-security programs; that arrangement would make provision of topping-up arrangements financially easy.

The UISP seems to Commissioners to be the essential building block for social security programs in the twenty-first century. Should governments not

be able to implement it, a series of less complete reforms would at least ameliorate some of the worst features of the existing systems.

- Thus, failing the implementation of the UISP, Commissioners recommend:
  - Reform of the family-benefits program to reduce or eliminate the child tax exemption and the family-allowance program and to increase the child tax credit, which should also be made payable on a monthly basis
  - Reform of social assistance provisions of the Canada Assistance Plan to eliminate pre-emptive taxation of social assistance benefits as other income from employment, training allowances or similar sources is received. ☐

We wish to emphasize that these are partial reforms only, and that the more comprehensive UISP is a preferable choice.

Social Services

This Commission did not undertake an extensive review of Canada's social service programs. We did, however, receive many representations about them, and we did develop several recommendations.

■ Commissioners support the continuing devolution of responsibility for delivering social services to the community level and to non-profit associations. We strongly recommend, however, that this devolution not be handicapped by a reduction in funding, and that governments retain sufficient staff to exercise their monitoring responsibilities. The maintenance of funding is particularly important, since we could see no evidence whatsoever that social services, which include support for children, the elderly, the disabled and those with shorter-term social problems, are overfunded. Indeed, considerable evidence of underfunding was presented to us in our hearings.

- The major social services will also benefit from:
  - Further forms of assistance which will help users to become more self-reliant
  - Better integration of various forms of social and medical services at the community level

Access to many social services in Canada is now impeded by the "needs-based" approach of the Canada Assistance Plan. Only those "in [financial] need or likely to become in need" have free access to services, so that many Canadians just above the poverty level are effectively precluded from receiving such important support as family, marital and financial counselling or child-support services.

■ This Commission recommends that the current federal-provincial financing arrangements be severed from social

assistance financing and renegotiated to provide Canadians with broader access to these services.

■ This Commission is not persuaded that extensive delegation of responsibility for social services to the profit-seeking part of the private sector is likely to improve significantly the services provided to Canadians. Where such privatization is practiced, we recommend that it be done in the context of very careful government regulation of the provision of services. Profit maximization, in our view, is not always the best motive whereby to govern human transactions.

There are currently two major task forces working at the national level to review day care in Canada; therefore this Commission has not conducted research in this area. Commissioners do, however, wish to note that the current CAP day-care guidelines actually serve to make access to publicly supported day care quite difficult for middle-income Canadians, and that the current $2000 tax exemption for child-care expenses is much more valuable to upper-middle/class Canadians than to the majority of Canadian families. Both these provisions require reform.

■ Finally, Commissioners wish to pay tribute to the hundreds of thousands of Canadians who work through the voluntary sector to help their fellow citizens. We recommend that all levels of government should continue to support and nurture such activity by providing fully adequate support and supervision for the programs dispensed through the voluntary sector. □

PART VI

The Institutional Context

Conclusions and Recommendations

The more government Canadians have, the more democratic we must become. The institutions of responsible parliamentary government remain the key to keeping government our servant rather than seeing it become our master. Commissioners regard Parliament as the principal forum for public debate and intend our recommendations to contribute, in general, to the strengthening of this institution.

To restore Parliament as the principal forum for national debate, we must not only bolster its democratic processes, but we must also improve its capacity to reconcile national and regional interests. We wish neither to reassert the dominance of the national government in line with the prevailing opinion at the time of Confederation, nor to establish the provincial order of government as an integral part of national government.

With regard to federalism and intergovernmental relations, two basic needs influence Commissioners' general objectives. First, it is desirable to clarify where possible, by constitutional amendment, by delegation or intergovernmental agreement, or by more clearly defined policy directions, the responsibilities distributed between federal and provincial governments. Secondly, recognizing the complexity of modern government and the interdependence within our federation, it is desirable to introduce greater certainty and stability into existing intergovernmental processes. We seek neither to eliminate intergovernmental conflict nor to further the development of non-accountable institutions. Rather we seek to secure and give greater public recognition to minimal processes and structures that will moderate the excesses and costs of unresolved conflict and channel creative solutions to common problems.

Commissioners view the Charter of Rights and Freedoms both as a guarantee of specific rights and freedoms of citizens and as an important

element of the framework within which Canadian society can evolve. This is consistent with our view that constitutional law should be responsive to social change and evolving values and attitudes, and that it should stabilize the pace and direction of such change.

Responsible Government and Public Accountability

■ The Canadian practice of party government has restricted the opportunities for Members of Parliament to participate in the development of public policy outside the confines of party caucuses. Organized special interest groups now challenge MPs as representatives and frequently bypass them.

- MPs could gain more influence over public policy if members in committee could investigate and debate matters of public interest on which party positions have not yet been established or fully determined. The separation of legislative committees from investigative committees would help to achieve this end by serving to provide Parliament and the government with policy analysis and guidance distinct from that which is received from administrative officials or extra-parliamentary sources.
- Parliament need not diminish the activities of interest groups, but it should provide the principal public forum for these interests to define their concerns. Parliament should encourage these groups to present their positions and demands for an open examination in relation to general interests. There should be a small number of parliamentary committees focusing on comprehensive policy matters – the budget, regulatory policy, Crown corporations, and federal-provincial relations, for example – and these would be ideal forums for such scrutiny.
- Agencies such as the Public Service Commission, the Office of the Commissioner of Official Languages, the Privacy and Information Commissioners and the Office of the Auditor General have important functions, but receive insufficient direction and control from our elected representatives in Parliament. In order to ensure accountability of these agencies, Parliament must define their procedures and basic strategies. Commissioners suggest that the Public Service Commission, the Office of the Commissioner of Official Languages, and the Privacy and Information Commissioners review their work before a Parliamentary Committee on the Public Service. This committee would study the success of these agencies in meeting the various criteria set by Parliament. The same committee, since it would be familiar with the performance of these agencies, should review their financial estimates. The Public Accounts Committee would perform this role in relation to the Office of the Auditor General.

- The federal government has formalized Cabinet structures, processes and support services in recent years, in order to restore ministerial and parliamentary control over an expanded and complex administrative structure. Although central agencies have partially checked the dispersal and diffusion of power to public servants, they can do so effectively only when under the close direction of ministers; otherwise, central agencies themselves become yet another layer of bureaucracy to be controlled.
- We have given too much autonomy and discretion to non-departmental forms of government organization such as Crown corporations and regulatory agencies. Such autonomy has undermined the principles of responsible government. To correct this situation, Commissioners recommend that greater "control" of Crown corporations be defined in the context of a reformed competition and regulatory environment, and not just in the framework of administrative accountability, in accordance with the current trend. Especially for commercial Crown corporations, governments need greater strategic control, not day-to-day interference in management decisions. Moreover, Cabinet should strengthen its review of regulations formulated by regulatory agencies.
- Although some prominent political appointments have violated the ideal of a neutral public service, it is not true that the senior bureaucracy has become politicized. The system of appointments by Order-in-Council based on professional merit on the recommendation of the Clerk of the Privy Council has worked well. However, political advice to the Prime Minister has traditionally been the basis of appointments to a large number of boards and agencies. This category may be too large; the public might be better served if more of these appointments were based exclusively on merit. An all-party group designated by the proposed Parliamentary Committee on the Public Service should review the current use of Governor-in-Council appointments to boards and agencies, the foreign service, high levels in departments, and Ministers' staffs, in order to help distinguish between two categories of positions: those where partisan sensitivity justifies political appointments, and those where partisan sensitivity is not at issue and where professional merit should prevail. Commissioners' opinion is that this general review process should be continuous, and that appointments of no clear partisan value should be made on a basis of "merit".
- In light of the accelerating challenge to democratic controls presented by the increasing international responsibilities of the state, Commissioners believe it is desirable to provide secure foundations for parliamentary ratification of international treaties and for other measures to ensure parliamentary review of executive action in the international domain. □

Representative Government and National Socio-Economic Interests in Economic Policy Formation

It is important to facilitate more direct and continuous involvement of representatives of Canadian interest groups in public decision making, especially in economic policy. Those interests need to interact more with one another and to take greater account of the broader concerns and conflicts within Canadian society for the resolution of which Parliament itself is ultimately responsible.

In comparison with the formal structures that have developed in some Western nations, Canadian consultative practices tend to be fragmented, informal and episodic. Current practices may be inadequate in light of recent Canadian experience and anticipated needs, such as the continuing pressures of economic adjustment. However, we do not recommend a corporatist or tripartite style of government/private sector relations.

■ Although substantial secrecy is necessary in relation to the preparation and release of the budget, Commissioners recommend that guidelines are needed to allow less comprehensive budget secrecy than now exists. We urge the House of Commons to initiate a change in the convention of comprehensive budget secrecy in order to set in motion steps towards more effective advance discussion and consultation arrangements.

It would be desirable to seek federal-provincial agreement on the timing of budgets, so that their presentation could be co-ordinated, with the federal budget either preceding or following most provincial budgets by two or three months. Pre-budget consultation should occur in several forums, but particularly in the House of Commons.

A continuing national dialogue on general directions for economic policy requires a permanent national forum. This Commission favours establishment of a permanent Economic Policy Committee of the House of Commons. The Committee would hold an annual series of pre-budget hearings timed to allow its work to influence budget preparation. It would take testimony about the nation's economic prospects from the Department of Finance, the Bank of Canada, and the Treasury Board, as well as from agencies such as the Economic Council of Canada; it would also gather the views of major groups, including national representatives of business, labour and other associations.

The Committee would scrutinize the government's performance and the revenue and expenditure implications of the positions of key interests. It should schedule its budget review to co-ordinate with its other responsibilities and with the timing of the annual First Ministers' Conference. Moreover, it would be necessary to adjust the internal priorities and planning cycle of the federal government in light of the accepted federal-provincial cycle.

Continuation of sectoral and industry-by-industry dialogue on improving Canada's economy is essential. Discussions should bring

together representatives of business and labour, and federal, provincial and municipal governments and other groups, as necessary. Government participation may not always be required. In light of these conclusions, Commissioners recommend that such sectoral discussions be developed within the following guidelines:

- Consultative mechanisms should focus on clear, specific objectives. This approach will make them more likely to be successful.
- Consultation should be a continuing process with reasonably predictable arrangements. Permanent or standing groups may be required in some cases.
- Governments must make a firm commitment to any consultative process they undertake. Effective consultative arrangements require that non-government participants have some influence on the agenda and decision-making schedule. Responsibility for the overall policy-making process, however, rests with the government of the day.
- Consultative processes aimed at consensus building must be supported by fair representation from many groups in society and, normally, by parity between business and labour.
- Sharing and refining of information are prerequisites to these consultative processes. □

National Institutions and the Representation of Regional Interests

Commissioners believe that the federal principle requires that the House of Commons, chosen on the basis of representation by population, be balanced by a second chamber based on representation by region. Our institutions should recognize the federal principle, provide greater regional representation, and respond to regional interests in national policy making and administration.

■ Commissioners recommend that the Senate embody the federalist principle and provide the regional representation lacking in the House of Commons.

- A reformed Senate must build on our practice of party government in its elections, caucuses and discipline. The Senate must be elected, and election to the two Houses should take place at the same time.
- In the Senate, representation should be weighted in favour of the less populous regions. All regions need not be considered equal, for the Senate should only temper, not obstruct, representation by population.
- The Senate should be elected by a system of proportional representation. The governing party is more likely to have elected representatives from all regions within its parliamentary

caucus, even if, for one or some regions, they secure places only in the Senate. A Senate elected on this basis should ensure that the governing party will usually be able to constitute a Cabinet that includes members from all regions.

- We recommend that Senators be elected in six-member constituencies. This number is large enough to effect the intended proportional representation and yet to allow for some recognition of the regions within provinces. Yukon and the Northwest Territories could elect their Senators on simple plurality. Existing numbers of Senators would be modified and distributed as follows:

	Existing	Proposed
British Columbia	6	12
Alberta	6	12
Saskatchewan	6	12
Manitoba	6	12
Ontario	24	24
Quebec	24	24
New Brunswick	10	12
Nova Scotia	10	12
Prince Edward Island	4	6
Newfoundland	6	12
Yukon	1	2
Northwest Territories	1	4
	104	144

- The Senate does not require a veto to temper, on regional grounds, the legislative majority of the House of Commons. Commissioners believe that the Senate should have a six-month suspensive veto, except in relation to legislation with linguistic significance; such legislation would require approval of a majority of francophone Senators, as well as of the Senate as a whole.
- If Senate reform along the lines proposed here is not adopted within a reasonable time, efforts should be made to reform the electoral system of the House of Commons to enhance regional representation. In that event, Commissioners favour the proposal of the Task Force on National Unity to add 60 members to the Commons, distributed to parties on the basis of their share of the national popular vote and allocated to provinces on the basis of the degree to which the parties were "underrepresented" in seats won, or not won, in relation to their share of the popular vote in each province.

Many federal departments and agencies have not assumed responsibility for regional development within their mandates. This failure has lessened the executive branch's capacity to be regionally responsive and has undermined the effectiveness of regional representation in Cabinet.

- This Commission therefore recommends that:
  - The central administrative agencies should be structured so as to provide more regional information upon which the Cabinet

can base policy decisions. This requires that regional offices be part of the central agency apparatus supporting the Cabinet and the Prime Minister.

- The Cabinet should decentralize departments and agencies for purposes of policy planning and development. Sectorally organized departments should incorporate the regional dimension fully in departmental planning and policy development. There should be regional officials in the central administrative decision-making of departments.
- Regional representation should receive consideration in nominations to the boards of Crown corporations and regulatory agencies. If the Senate becomes an elected body, appointments of the heads of major Crown corporations and all members of the governing boards of major regulatory agencies should be subject to the approval of a Senate committee to be established for this purpose. □

Barriers within the Canadian Economic Union

Despite recent expressions of concern that the Canadian economic union is becoming increasingly balkanized and fragmented, goods, capital, services and people now move relatively freely within the Canadian common market.

While lost economic output from impediments to free movement and distortions of the common market appears small, private economic actors have indicated that the policies in question create considerable difficulties for them. Even more than the economic rationale, the political rationale for the national right to free movement is a powerful idea for most Canadians.

The effect of these distortions – and the need for effective co-ordination of economic policy – are likely to increase as Canadians face greater competition from the outside world. We should create incentives to international competitiveness, and we should facilitate appropriate adjustments.

The economic union implies elimination of internal barriers and positive measures to facilitate operation of the market, to overcome market imperfections and to pursue effective stabilization, industrial and social policies. All regions must share in the benefits of economic integration.

Internal barriers may be the response of governments to local preferences, and often reflect our commitment to redistribution of income and opportunity. Thus, the challenge, in particular cases, is not simply to eliminate the barriers through constitutional prohibition or other means, but rather, how to balance the economic benefits of free movement against other goals to which Canadians aspire. The trade-offs to be made are not exclusively between economic efficiency and political diversity or provincial autonomy within the federation: Canadian federalism also involves a national community with its own requirements. Moreover, as the Canadian Charter of Rights and Freedoms makes clear, individual rights have implications for the economic union.

The goal of regional development requires that Canadian economic policy must seek not only to maximize aggregate national income, but also to encourage the economic development of individual regions.

■ Commissioners urge that a broad view be taken of the scope of section 121 of the Constitution Act, 1867, consistent with an interpretation that section 121 covers services as well as goods, and non-tariff barriers as well as tariffs. However, in light of existing controversy and uncertainty, it may be prudent to seek eventual clarification by constitutional amendment.

- We would recommend a limited amendment to include services to reflect current conceptions of the nature of interprovincial trade. On the issue of non-tariff barriers to trade in goods and services, we recommend as an interim step that governments agree to a Code of Economic Conduct.
- The governments of Canada should develop a Code of Economic Conduct to spell out acceptable practices, set out the principles of the economic union, and provide for enforcement. We advance a series of general guidelines for consideration:
  - The code should confirm general principles of the economic union applicable to both the federal and provincial governments:
    - Reduction of barriers to the allocation of capital, labour, goods and services throughout Canada
    - Non-discrimination against persons (individuals and organizations) based on province of residence
    - Commitment to minimizing the costs of provincial programs that might fall on the residents of other jurisdictions, and to prior consultation for this purpose
    - Recognition of the need for a transportation, communications and information infrastructure to support national economic development with significant regional benefits.
- The burden of demonstrating that a barrier did not violate the principles of the Code should lie with the authority imposing the barrier.
- The Code should identify major areas where reduction of barriers to internal trade should begin. Attention should focus not only on the form of the barriers, but also on the anticipated effects. The possibilities of substitution between types of barriers are extensive, and provinces vary in economic development and in their potential to inflict injury on other jurisdictions or the residents of those jurisdictions. Those drafting the Code might first consider barriers that prevent Canadian enterprises from being internationally competitive.
- Initially governments should set up the Code, and public and governmental pressure should enforce it. The intergovernmental process would provide the appropriate forum for dealing with the politically sensitive issue of internal barriers to trade. After

experience with the operation of the Code, we should move to entrench its principles in the Constitution and to enforce the Code through some other form of binding intergovernmental agreement.

- To develop the Code of Economic Conduct, monitor the state of the economic union, and explore methods for co-ordinating policies, the First Ministers' Conference should create a Council of Economic Development Ministers.
- To initiate the process of identifying and controlling internal trade barriers, Commissioners propose the following procedure. The Council will ask each government to list barriers imposed by other governments that they believe harm its provincial economy or its residents. Next, each government would be required to explain and defend those of its policies identified at the first stage. A Federal-Provincial Commission on the Economic Union would receive this material and would analyse the barriers, their probable consequences, and the justifications declared. The Commission would identify violations of the principles of the economic union and make recommendations concerning specific terms for the proposed Code. It would send this report to the Council for action.
- A Federal-Provincial Commission on the Economic Union which would serve the Council of Economic Development Ministers would have responsibility for preparing materials for the Council as directed:
  - Analysing the first round of barriers identified by the Council's initial inquiry
  - Initiating research on the state of the economic union and methods for improving it
  - Receiving complaints from groups, individuals and corporations affected by government actions threatening the economic union, investigating them, and reporting on them, with recommendations, to the public and the Council.

If a Code is eventually made legally enforceable, the Commission could become a regulatory agency, but one that regulates governments. □

Economic Management

In several specific areas related to our concern with the international environment, the Canadian economic union, and economic adjustment, Commissioners believe that constitutional changes are desirable for more effective economic management; Canada requires a procedure which would allow treaties, once concluded, to be binding and enforceable on both federal and provincial authorities within Canada.

■ We recommend a constitutional amendment to provide that where a proposed treaty contains provisions that require

implementation by provincial legislatures or affect rights within areas of provincial jurisdiction, the relevant sections should be ratified by provincial legislatures. We propose the application of the amendment formula for this purpose so that sections of a treaty imposing obligations on provinces would come into effect on the passage of resolutions in the legislatures of two-thirds of the provinces, representing at least half of Canada's population. We do not see this recommendation as having immediate application to negotiations with the United States on a free-trade agreement. We would recommend, however, that a constitutional solution be in place before the proposed trade agreement would come up for review in the 1990s.

■ To clarify jurisdiction and roles in the field of telecommunications, we recommend concurrent jurisdiction with federal paramountcy.

■ To clarify responsibility regarding certain aspects of overall regulation of trade and commerce, we propose that section 91(2) be amended to provide explicitly for federal regulatory power over competition and product standards.

■ If intergovermental agreement is not reached soon on the harmonization of regulations respecting interprovincial trucking, we recommend that serious consideration should be given to bringing this matter under federal jurisdiction. □

Equalization

The principle of equalization, an essential element of Canadian federalism, represents a commitment to all provinces that economic misfortune will not undercut their constitutional role. It contributes to a true decentralization of government functions, in spite of the differing economic capacities among provinces.

Commissioners stress the distinction between equalization payments and regional development programs. The former are intended to offset economic disadvantages, while the latter are intended to reverse this disadvantage. Equalization payments are necessary only because of our lack of success in combatting regional economic disparities. In practice, this means that regional development financing must be added to equalization disbursements; the federal government should not cut one in favour of the other.

■ The federal government's responsibility for interregional redistribution gives it a leading role in designing and operating the equalization scheme. Commissioners recommend that the following changes to the equalization system be discussed with the provinces:

- Canada should return to a representative tax system that includes all 10 provinces in the base. The present five-province

calculation base allows too much room for distortion, strategic behaviour and unintended side-effects.

- Equalization payments should include some portion of resource revenues. There is no magic figure here, but the 20 to 30 per cent range seems an appropriate compromise, since it approximates the amounts that would accrue to provincial treasuries in the form of tax revenues if natural resources were in private hands.
- The concept of including needs as part of the entitlements calculation is attractive. Commissioners recognize, however, that this can develop only slowly, given the amount of data required and the serious practical difficulties involved. The inclusion of needs in the calculation will be especially important if the Northern territories enter the scheme. □

Regional Development

This Commission believes that regional development must remain an essential component of Canadian policy and, indeed, of the Confederation bargain as now reflected in section 36 of the Constitution Act, 1982. It must be recognized, however, that policies intended to promote regional development have often hindered the overall efficiency of the national economy in that they impeded inter-regional adjustment and distorted regional development. Canadians need to reconsider the way in which we look at regional economic disparity, what we do to overcome it, and the institutional mechanisms we bring to the task.

■ We recommend a new federal-provincial system of sharing regional development expenditures and responsibilities.

- The federal government should direct regional development programs toward improving regional productivity and the efficiency of the labour market. To these ends, such programs should include measures to improve worker and management skills, enhance research and development efforts, ensure a high level of infrastructural support, and supply assistance for intra- and inter-regional mobility. The federal government should not only provide such programs on a national basis, but should also make a special effort in the less developed provinces. While it might make sense, too, for the federal government to provide assistance for plant modernization as a means to enhance regional productivity, we believe that it should provide this type of assistance on a national basis, if at all, or that the provincial governments should take on this responsibility on a regional basis.
- Under this arrangement, the federal government would end all explicit and direct regional employment-creation programs. While national schemes would continue, federal subsidies, tax

breaks, and so on, intended only to generate jobs in, or attract firms to, a particular locale, would be eliminated. Similarly, the federal government would terminate regionally differentiated unemployment-insurance programs, tax credits, and other measures that tend to distort regional labour markets. Funds formerly allocated to these types of programs would instead become the source of Regional Economic Development Grants.

- Provinces that qualify for equalization payments would be eligible for Regional Economic Development Grants. The amounts of the grants would be determined by a formula on a per capita basis, and they would be proportionate to the degree of fiscal disparity identified by the equalization formula. As noted earlier, equalization payments are necessary to offset economic disparities, while the purpose of these new grants would be to reduce future disparities. They would be renegotiated every five years.
- Provinces would assume full responsibility for local or place-specific employment measures as part of their own approach to regional development. They would be free to use the Regional Economic Development Grants for this purpose, subject only to two conditions:
  - Each recipient province would sign an Economic and Regional Development Agreement (ERDA) with the federal government, which would set out a broad economic development plan for the province (and for each other province) and would indicate the measures to be carried out by both orders of government. Some elements of these packages might take the form of shared-cost programs or federal contributions to provincial activities; in general, however, Commissioners recommend that under the ERDA umbrella, each government remain responsible for the implementation and delivery of its own programs, in order to enhance accountability.
  - The recipient province would be required to sign the proposed Code of Economic Conduct to improve the functioning of the Canadian economic union.
- While recognizing the immediate need for financial prudence at the federal level, Commissioners believe that the total federal financial commitment to regional development – combining the Regional Economic Development Grants and other funds spent through ERDAs – should increase significantly over the next few years.
- The federal government would continue to play an important role in other development efforts which have significant regional impacts such as:
  - A reformed equalization system
  - The proposed Universal Income Security Program and the Transitional Adjustment Assistance Program

– Sectoral policies, such as those pertaining to fisheries, agriculture, and forestry. These should be designed according to criteria for good sectoral policy (see Parts III and IV of this Report), but they ought to also be developed in close consultation with provincial governments where these are affected to an important degree.

- A sustained federal commitment to regional development requires that a single central agency be responsible for injecting regional concerns into the programs of individual federal departments, and for co-ordinating federal efforts. It would appear to Commissioners that the Federal-Provincial Relations Office (FPRO) reporting to the Prime Minister, would be the appropriate existing body. We believe also that the Federal Economic Development Co-ordinator (FEDC) or other senior officials resident in each province could help to co-ordinate federal activities within each province, interacting with the provincial government and establishing links with local economic interests. The federal government should enlarge the responsibilities of such federal regional officials, who should report directly to FPRO. □

Fiscal Arrangements

Tax Collection Agreements

The Tax Collection Agreements have served Canada well. They are convenient for both citizens and governments, and they help to maintain harmony and contribute to the strength of the economic union. They should be retained. Nevertheless, the agreements are presently under considerable strain, and are in some danger of disintegrating. This Commission's proposed reforms are based on the desire to maintain the agreements, but not at an excessive cost either in terms of the accountability of legislatures or in terms of the flexibility which exists in the system.

■ Commissioners therefore recommend that:

- The agreements be amended to place the personal income tax on the same footing as the corporate tax, applying the provincial rates to the common, federally determined base. This measure would not only reduce provincial vulnerability to federal tax changes, but would also enhance provincial autonomy, since it would become easier for provinces to decide how progressive their own tax rates should be.
- The federal government consult with provinces before introducing any tax change which would have a significant effect on the federal-provincial relationship. This recommendation is consistent with Commissioners' larger concern to reduce budget secrecy for federal and provincial governments and to ensure that federal budget proposals receive wide discussion in Parliament.

- To provide greater consultation on taxation matters of a more fundamental nature, Commissioners recommend that a new federal-provincial Tax Structure Committee be given the following mandate:
  - As part of the regular process of the quinquennial review of federal-provincial fiscal arrangements, the Tax Structure Committee would re-examine the definitions of taxable income, basic exemptions, marginal tax rates, and the like. This is really an endorsement and extension of a consultation process which is already in effect. The Tax Structure Committee would also monitor the division of tax room between the two orders of government, in light of anticipated revenue and expenditure needs, and of the difficulties of managing restraint.
  - As part of the overall concern for the economic union, the Tax Structure Committee could also discuss the implications of federal or provincial tax credits and subsidies. It would thus assist the Council of Economic Development Ministers which, we propose, be responsible for the development of an overall intergovernmental Code of Economic Conduct. This Committee would be composed of representatives of all governments, including those now outside the agreements. □

The Spending Power and the Impact of Fiscal Restraint on Intergovernmental Transfers

Although Commissioners do not recommend formal limitations on the spending power, we consider that this power has important consequences for federalism and therefore should be exercised with special restraint and subject to certain guidelines concerning its use.

■ Commissioners thus recommend that the spending power be retained as a vital instrument for flexible responses to changing definitions of the national interest, subject to the conditions that:

- The judicial distinction between federal legislation providing grants or gifts and federal legislation involving direct regulation in fields of provincial jurisdiction is appropriate and should be further refined.
- As a matter of principle within the federation and for purposes of accountability and clarity of roles, the federal government regard new shared-cost programs as a last resort in pursuing its objectives.
- The use of the federal spending power in areas of provincial jurisdiction be supported by broad national consensus. In addition to the contribution to consensus which an elected Senate with stronger regional representation will make, consultation through the Federal-Provincial Ministerial

Councils and, ultimately, the First Ministers' Conference is essential, not only in relation to new programs, where it will occur in any case, but also in relation to the proposed alteration or termination of a program by the federal government. Designated periods of operation of, say, five years, could be considered for program renegotiation.

- In order to retain a desirable degree of federal flexibility and accountability to Parliament while assuring provinces some stability for planning and protection against rapid unexpected variations in federal spending, we recommend that:
  - Federal-provincial transfers be subject to a review on a five-year basis.
  - During that period, the federal power to make adjustments be limited to, say, 5 per cent in any given year, without provincial approval. □

Intergovernmental Relations and the Institutions of the Federation

The intense intergovernmental conflict Canada experienced in the 1970s may be partly attributed to institutional limitations. Interdependence in modern federalism is inescapable and needs to be managed, as do the excesses of intergovernmental competition.

This Commission's goal is to encourage a more functional approach to federalism, one not oriented towards centralization/decentralization, but one which emphasizes the potential contribution of Canada's federal arrangements to the well-being of Canadians. Canadians should create political institutions to co-ordinate activities involving both orders of government.

While greater co-ordination of federal-provincial affairs would be desirable, Commissioners believe that the diversity of government action inherent in a federal state is also a positive contribution to society. Thus we have tried to strike a balance between encouraging institutional diversity or competition and proposing new measures of federal-provincial co-ordination.

■ Commissioners do not recommend comprehensive constitutional amendment as a means to modernize the division of powers. Instead, we urge the use of more flexible instruments to clarify or transfer the location of responsibility. To this end, we recommend that:

- The power of intergovernmental delegation be expanded so that on a particular matter, law-making authority could be delegated to another jurisdiction. Such delegations should be approved by the legislatures of all jurisdictions involved
- Constitutional amendment be used to establish a procedure that would permit the Parliament of Canada and provincial legislatures to enter into intergovernmental agreements that would be binding on their successors

- The powers of reservation and disallowance, now by convention virtually "dead letters", be formally interred by means of an appropriate constitutional amendment.

■ To provide essential recognition of the need to manage intergovernmental interdependence, and the need to co-ordinate policies and activities, the First Ministers' Conference should be established in the Constitution with the requirement that it meet at least once each year. Such an institution must in no way encroach on the principles of responsible government.

■ First Ministers may eventually wish to consider the creation of a body comparable to the Advisory Commissions on Intergovernmental Relations in the United States and in Australia. "Third parties" of this nature may facilitate behind-the-scenes resolution of intergovernmental conflicts and contribute to improving the context of information, analysis and public opinion to which the intergovernmental process will need to respond.

■ Despite a plethora of federal-provincial bodies, current intergovernmental discussions are sporadic and lack co-ordination. Our purpose is to suggest a core framework of federal-provincial mechanisms which, in a more streamlined way, would support the First Ministers in their collective and individual responsibilities. Commissioners propose that the First Ministers' Conference appoint a network of Councils of Ministers to serve in major functional policy areas and to be supported by continuing committees of officials. We believe that three central Ministerial Councils should be established in the fields of Finance, Economic Development, and Social Policy. We therefore recommend that:

- The *Council of Finance and Treasury Ministers* which now exists and meets from time to time regarding fiscal arrangements, economic projections, and macro-economic policy be formalized to encourage greater regularity of assembly, better co-ordination of budgetary preparations, and to receive the findings of the new Tax Structure Committee, which would monitor tax developments
- The *Council for Economic Development* seek agreement on common objectives in economic development and trade policies and identify opportunities for mutually beneficial links among regions. The Council would be responsible for monitoring and assessing the state of the economic union and would serve as the vehicle through which to develop a "Code of Economic Conduct".
- The Ministerial *Council on Social Policy* consider all facets of social policy, especially in the fields covered by Established Programs Financing and the Canada Assistance Plan. Consultation with practicing professionals and interested groups and individuals is particularly important in this area. We would

encourage Parliamentary Committees to play a stronger role in this activity.

- To ensure that governments are held accountable for their conduct of intergovernmental affairs, Commissioners recommend that Parliament and the provincial legislatures should establish permanent standing committees responsible for Intergovernmental Relations. □

Differing provincial regulations create inconvenience for those who wish to operate nationally. The impetus for interprovincial efforts towards harmonization must arise through the pressure of groups adversely affected by interjurisdictional variations. Commissioners therefore propose no specific institutional changes designed to enhance harmonization of provincial laws.

The Charter of Rights and Freedoms

The Charter and Constitutional Government in Canada

The Charter of Rights and Freedoms signals a significant transformation of the relationship between citizens and the state in Canada. Most noteworthy are the important limitations imposed on the constitutional authority of legislatures and the elevated role of the judiciary as guardians of the constitutional rights and freedoms of individuals. The Charter will also further the rights of citizens to review and assess government actions, and it will contribute to a fuller and more regular discussion of citizen rights in Parliament. Its guarantees will probably become the basis for individuals and groups to introduce issues to the national and provincial political agendas.

The scope and application of the Charter will be tested constantly through both the legal and political processes. The Charter is not, however, a springboard for unlimited claims of citizen rights, for there are reasonable limits to its guarantees. Ultimately, its effectiveness in protecting the rights and freedoms of citizens and in enhancing democracy will be determined by the way in which citizens use this document.

■ This Commission believes that the changes recorded and introduced by the Charter should be given a broad scope in interpretation and application. Departures from its guarantees should meet stringent tests and conditions, justifying the circumstances of exception.

■ The Charter's general override provision should contribute to public awareness of legislation limiting the constitutional rights of citizens in Canada. Overriding legislation should include a declaration of intent to legislate, notwithstanding a provision of the Charter, and should include not only reference to the specific rights being overridden, but also an indication of the purpose of such legislative action. Such a statement of purpose would help the courts to ensure that limitations do not exceed what is necessary to achieve their objective; it could also be a useful reference point in discussions on whether to extend the override after the five-year period.

■ Commissioners do not suggest constitutional amendments to change and improve upon the Charter's words. Rather we consider various interpretations of the Charter which we think will serve to maximize the desirable impact it can have on Canadian society. Two examples illustrate our approach:

- We favour a broad and flexible application of the Charter at the periphery of government activity, as well as in its more visible legislative forms.
- Similarly, in the matter of the Charter's guarantees of personal mobility rights, we conclude that preferential provincial employment schemes permissible under the Charter should be strictly limited to the socially and economically disadvantaged within a province. Such programs should not preclude the federal government from simultaneously pursuing employment-opportunities programs in that province.

Inherent in the Charter of Rights and Freedoms is an attempt to overcome some of the problems of national unity that have pre-occupied Canadians since the mid-1960s. This is especially evident in the Charter's provisions respecting mobility rights, official languages and minority official-language education, as well as multiculturalism.

With regard to ethnic diversity in Canada, Commissioners believe that multiculturalism policy should seek to create circumstances that permit all Canadians to preserve and enhance their cultural heritage within the broader Canadian tradition of individual equality. Multiculturalism is not a justification for cultural or racial discrimination. For visible minorities, in particular, racism must be addressed through more than multicultural policy. There is a systemic aspect to racial discrimination in Canada. As with other pattterns of systemic discrimination affecting groups such as women, the handicapped and other identifiable groups, the Charter plays an important role as both an educative and legal instrument in enhancing equality.

The Charter's equality-rights guarantees embody a broad definition and understanding of equality. These guarantees reflect contemporary notions of substantive equality in giving assurance of equal benefit of the law and equality under the law. By enabling affirmative action programs, the Charter responds to contemporary concerns about discrimination against various groups in society.

■ Commissioners believe that governments have a leadership role to play in breaking down these patterns of discrimination and we believe, too, that affirmative action is a valuable tool for this purpose. Accordingly, we view the provision in the Charter enabling governments to pursue affirmative action programs as a valuable reinforcement of government's role. Equality, however, must ultimately relate to individuals, and affirmative action must be supplemented with other programs designed with individual equality as the ultimate goal.

■ The Charter both contains guarantees of individual equality and elsewhere recognizes special rights of various groups, such as official-language minorities and Canadian aboriginals. We believe that when group rights are inconsistent with rights of individual equality, the latter, as a general rule, should prevail. □

The Supreme Court of Canada

The members of the Supreme Court of Canada do not perform representative functions in the Canadian institutional and constitutional system. Judicial merit alone is the criterion by which the Court's membership and performance should be assessed. Accordingly, Commissioners reject arguments that the composition of the Supreme Court should be regionally representative. Existing provision in the Supreme Court Act for the appointment of Quebec members is based on the distinctive legal traditions of that province. We also reject socio-economic representational claims about Supreme Court of Canada membership, which we anticipate may emerge as the Court addresses complex Charter litigation involving citizen-state relations.

The central issue in the appointments process is the perception that it does not adequately involve the constituencies ultimately affected by Supreme Court decisions. Although the existing informal procedures followed by the Prime Minister before making appointments to the Supreme Court do involve extensive discussions, they are sometimes perceived as not taking sufficient account of concerned interests or advice. Measures to shift responsibility from the Prime Minister to some designated group or institution necessarily involve replacing one political process with another. If a broadly based political process of consultation is to be replaced by alternative arrangements, an elected Senate has much to commend it.

■ The constitutional status of the Supreme Court and, in particular, the independence of the Court, should be clarified by entrenchment, although there is no reason to remove responsibility for the administration of the Court from the federal government. □

Quebec

The Distinctive Character of Quebec Society

Quebec is characterized by the presence within its borders of a largely francophone population which controls and gives direction to its own political and social institutions. The existence of this institutional framework which reenforces the distinction between the majority status of francophones within Quebec and the position of francophones elsewhere in Canada is central to *la spécificité du Québec*. The very essence of Quebec society lies in the fact that it is the principal, though not the exclusive, focus for the political dimensions of French life in Canada. To a large extent, Quebec remains a linguistically isolated society, an island of French in an overwhelmingly anglophone sea.

For Quebec and for francophones outside the province, the central challenge will always be how to remain French in North America.

This challenge entails practical problems in the cultural and economic domains for whose resolution Quebecers and francophones outside Quebec, individually and collectively, are, themselves, ultimately responsible. But constitutional recognition of Quebec's distinctiveness and of Canada's duality would provide an affirmation that answers to the practical economic and cultural problems of French life can be pursued within the Canadian context and with the support of the rest of Canada. The necessary compromises could thus be worked out in a clearly understood context of recognition and affirmation of a cultural complementarity which is at the very heart of the Canadian experience.

■ The initial requirement at the level of principle to secure a renewed understanding between Quebec and the rest of Canada is a statement in the preamble to the Constitution along the following lines:

Recognizing the distinctive character of Quebec as the principal, though not the exclusive, centre for Canadian francophones and accepting as fundamental the duality of the Canadian federation . . .

Fundamental Guarantees

As a consequence of Quebec's uniqueness, steps should be taken to ensure that no future constitutional amendment as noted below be imposed on Quebec which that province might consider to affect its fundamental interests as a distinct society:

- Concerning transfers of legislative powers from the provinces to Parliament, the simplest means to provide Quebec with the necessary protection, without putting the principle of equality of the provinces in question is to grant each province the right to opt out of any general arrangement with full compensation in all cases.
- In relation to reforms of national institutions which are not covered in the present opting-out formula, the only means to protect the interests of Quebec is through the right of veto. An obvious solution would be to grant all provinces such right in conformity with the equality principle. In the long run, this move could, however, freeze the natural development of our national institutions. Although granting Quebec the right of veto is an arrangement politically more difficult to obtain, it is closer to the intended objective, for it is the distinctive character of Quebec society for which protection is sought. It is important that Quebec have a right of veto on any amendment to the institutions described in section 42(1) of the Constitution Act, 1982, if such an amendment touches on the special character of Quebec and the duality of Canada. One method of implementing such veto would be to amend immediately section 47 of the

Constitution Act, 1982, in order to grant French-speaking Senators the right to block proposed amendments affecting Quebec under the double-majority formula described below.

The Senate and Quebec

- With regard to federal legislation, any proposed bill with linguistic implications, before becoming law, should require a double majority of the Senate: that is, the approval of a majority of all Senators and of a majority of francophone Senators. Such veto would be a full rather than a suspensive veto. In light of the protection offered by this double-majority proposal, Commissioners see no need for specific guarantees to Quebec of a certain proportion of seats in the House of Commons.

Division of Powers

- Because of Quebec's distinctiveness, the most obvious fields where conflicts may arise between that province and the federal government are education, external relations, immigration, communications and culture. There are ways in which Quebec could participate in dealing with these areas. While we make no recommendations, we do suggest that legal mechanisms such as delegation and inter-governmental agreements may provide a better means of accommodating the specific interests of Quebec than would constitutional amendment.

Francophones Outside Quebec

- The diverse communities of Francophones in Canada outside Quebec are currently in a state of crisis. If they are to survive and flourish, prompt action is required. Commissioners suggest that beyond recognizing the principle of duality in the Preamble, governments should make efforts to extend the recognition of French and English as the official languages of individual provinces. Ontario in particular, with its large French-speaking population, should proceed promptly to implement official bilingualism. Such a step would set an example for other provinces.

- Scattered French-language communities outside of Quebec face difficulties in developing a French-language working environment. Efforts to solve this problem should be geared towards the development of French-language centres of activity. These centres would vary from province to province, depending on the population and geographic concentration of francophone Canadians. In some areas, the centres would be of an essentially cultural or educational nature, and in other areas, such as in

New Brunswick, they could include a strong economic component.

- Furthermore, this Commission wishes to point out that implementation of language rights has not kept up with the intended policy of bilingualism. We believe that litigation, while generally useful, is not the proper tool for making improvements in this direction, since it is a lengthy and costly method of dealing with these problems.
- Instead, we recommend that stronger support be given to the role of the Commissioner of Official Languages. □

Aboriginal Self-Government

Measures to increase the influence and control exercised by aboriginal people over their social and economic affairs are desirable. Our commitment to this objective is based on the distinctive place of aboriginals in Canadian society as the first peoples of Canada and on the constitutional recognition they now enjoy.

Institutional reforms to enhance the autonomy of aboriginal peoples focus on the idea of self-government. Implications of aboriginal self-government for Canada's overall institutional framework and, in particular, for the three pillars of the Canadian constitutional order, Parliament, federalism and the Charter, have not yet been clarified. Indeed, many important issues have been avoided and should be addressed more squarely. The fundamental changes to our national and provincial institutions that are now being contemplated need broad Canadian understanding if they are to be acceptable in the long run. The pace of discussions, as well as the comprehensiveness of debates in Parliament and the legislatures should reflect this concern.

The Northern Territories

The economic, social and environmental challenges of development in Northern Canada will remain of continuing concern to Canadians. From an institutional perspective, significant questions must be addressed – some of these in the near future.

- No Canadians – Natives and non-Natives, Northerners and Southerners – can be well served by further delays in the settlement of aboriginal land claims. Final agreements affirming and delimiting aboriginal rights should be actively encouraged. If necessary, deadlines should be established by the parties, and discussions could proceed without reference to the issues of legislative powers, sovereignty and special political status, which could be dealt with subsequently in other settings.

- The Yukon Act and the Northwest Territories Act should be amended to reflect the current practices of responsible government in Yukon and to encourage comparable evolution in the Northwest Territories. In both territories, new formula-

based financial arrangements should be negotiated, to increase the predictability of transfers and to promote genuine responsibility and accountability for expenditures.

- On the basis of federal commitment to the ultimate goal of some form of provincehood in the Northern territories, the governments involved should establish a timetable for the transfer of provincial-type responsibilities in areas such as health, labour relations, inland waters, renewable resources and the institution of criminal proceedings. Additional measures should be taken to:
  - Advance the process of transferring to territorial governments responsibilities for Crown lands that do not bear directly on the national interest and that have not been ceded to the Native people through claims settlements
  - Institute resource-revenue/sharing arrangements comparable to the types of agreements worked out with Nova Scotia and Newfoundland
  - Confirm participation of the territorial governments in federal-provincial forums where matters of direct concern to Northern residents are being discussed. Joint-management arrangements may be valuable transitional procedures.
- Failing an internally generated and ratified agreement on division of the Northwest Territories, the federal government should establish an independent boundary commission to recommend a boundary on the basis of arguments from the two constitutional forums. Subject to the spirit of the Canadian constitutional tradition and the need to recognize the essential quality of Canadian citizenship, the structure of post-division government should be left to the discretion of the respective constitutional forums. □

Municipalities

Local governments are an enduring and important feature of government in Canada, despite their lack of constitutional status. Variations in approaches to local government in different provinces have permitted sensitivity, dynamism and creativity in the city-province relationship. Existing arrangements have contributed to the development of some of the most liveable cities in the world. Local governments have experienced uncertainty and frustration because of limited policy-making instruments and their relations with provincial and federal governments, but responses to current concerns must begin from the premise that we have been doing something right. Canada's major cities should be provided with the legal, financial and institutional means to fulfill their economic development role. By and large, this involves removing constraints that prevent their involvement in development.

■ Although Commissioners do not recommend changing the constitutional status of local governments, the federal and provincial governments should increase the involvement and responsibility of local authorities. The federal government should review with the provinces the possibility of occasional tri-level conferences; improve communications between municipalities and ministers whose responsibilities affect local interests; assign responsibility to investigate the significance of local concerns in national policy to the proposed Standing Committee for Intergovernmental Relations; and explore opportunities for the decentralization of specific responsibilities, including airports and federal urban properties to federally-appointed local agencies. The use of the delegation amendment, as Commissioners have earlier proposed, may become a means to delegate directly to local governments responsibility for such questions as siting, development and administration of some airports through agreement with the relevant province.

The provincial governments should continue to assess possibilities for assuming financial responsibility for requirements greatly exceeding local revenue sources. Commissioners also recommend that the provinces examine ways to designate a specific portion of income or sales-tax revenues for local government financing. Commissioners believe that revenues to local governments should be increasingly unconditional. □

Clarence L. Barber

The Commission's Final Report is a long and complex document and I support many of its recommendations. However, in certain areas I do not agree with the tone and thrust of the Report and I outline here my differences in viewpoint and conclusions.

My major concerns arise in connection with the Report's treatment of unemployment and inflation, monetary, fiscal and exchange rate policy and related topics. This is an area economists call macro-economics. The views expressed in the Report in this area may well reflect the views expressed in the Commission's research program. However, the profession is deeply divided on many of these topics and my own views differ substantially from those expressed in the Report.

1. There can be no doubt that the developed world today is suffering severely from the legacy of the extremely tight monetary policies pursued over the period from 1980 to 1982. These policies were based on a belief that the first step towards achieving good economic performance is to bring and keep inflation under control. What the world's central bankers may have failed to understand is that in breaking inflationary expectations they may also have destroyed the world's *real growth expectations*. It may be that far from setting the stage for good economic performance, they have ushered in an era of slow growth and semi-stagnation.

   In capitalist enterprise economies, real growth is largely dependent on the strength of private investment spending. Because capital equipment is typically long-lasting, business firms will only carry out these expenditures when they are confident that a growing economy will bring about their utilization. Thus, it is anticipated real growth that is one of the keys to a prosperous high-employment economy. As Keynes so strongly emphasized, the volume of capital spending required to sustain high employment

growth is related to the savings level. In countries where the savings rate is high, such as in West Germany and Japan, a high rate of investment is required if this savings is to be realized in new capital equipment. In its absence, a high rate of savings simply results in a depressed economy and high government deficits, such as we have in Canada today. One of the primary causes of the high level of unemployment that exists in much of the developed world today may well be an excessive level of saving, that is, saving in excess of the amount private business firms are willing to invest. By the same token, the relative prosperity of the U.S. economy may reflect the comparatively low-saving level of the American people.

Private capital spending is weak in many countries today and this undoubtedly reflects uncertainty about future growth. As long as the world economy was growing steadily, as it was throughout the period 1948 to 1973, capital spending was strong. Since then, with much slower growth and more restrictive government policies, capital spending has been weak. In a sense the world economy has lost its growth momentum. It may not be easily restored.

2. The Report stresses the view that there is no long run trade-off between unemployment and inflation. If we attempt to reduce unemployment below a range of 6.5 to 8.0 per cent, it is argued, inflation will gradually accelerate. When unemployment rises above this level, the inflation rate will decline. I find it hard to reconcile this view with the exceptionally low unemployment levels achieved by many countries over the period from 1948 to 1973 with relatively moderate, if gradually increasing, inflation. For example, over this period unemployment rates averaged 1.5 per cent in the Netherlands, 1.6 per cent in Australia and 2.0 per cent in France and West Germany. I doubt that the "no trade-off" conclusion can be held with any certainty.

   During the Commission's hearings, at least two economists argued that government policy should give priority to employment over inflation. We should aim, they argued, to reduce unemployment to some relatively low level, say 5 per cent, and if inflation developed along the way, deal with it directly. I think there is considerable merit in this point of view. I don't think we know with any certainty at what unemployment level inflation may become a problem, particularly in the context of stable commodity and energy prices, such as we experienced in the fifties and sixties.

3. The Commission's Report takes the view that some form of incomes policy may be useful on a temporary basis, but argues against any role for incomes policy on a longer-term basis. I disagree. I believe that it would be possible to work out on a co-operative basis between representatives of labour, business and government, a form of incomes policy which could contribute substantially to moderating the inflationary impact of future commodity price shocks.

4. I do not agree with the view that says we should take almost immediate steps to deal with our structural deficit problem. The federal deficit is primarily the result of a major private sector failure, the failure of the private sector to spend on new capital goods as much as it is saving. The

deficit, in turn, has represented a kind of *massive bail-out* to private sector savers, many of them in the higher income brackets. In the absence of the federal government's willingness to incur a deficit, these excess savings would have caused incomes to fall and unemployment to increase, perhaps to unprecedented levels. Canada would soon grow out of its deficit problem if we could stimulate a revival in capital spending and a reduction in saving rates. When we get back to 6 or 7 per cent unemployment, it may be time to adopt tax measures to reduce the deficit. The sooner we get there, the smaller our national debt will be at that time.

5. I view the suggestion that Canada should consider shifting from an income tax system to an expenditure tax system with a great deal of scepticism. If its effect would be to increase Canada's already high savings rate, the result might well be a disaster. I also have grave doubts about its effects on our income distribution.

6. If Canada should negotiate a free trade area agreement with the United States, one of the keys to a successful outcome will be a well-managed exchange rate. Canada's exchange rate policy should be oriented to the country's need for foreign investment as reflected by the difference between private sector capital spending and saving at a high level of employment. When capital spending exceeds saving at high employment levels, the difference can be made up either by means of a government surplus or through a current account deficit. When savings exceed capital spending, a current account surplus may be appropriate. The exchange rate is an appropriate method of adjusting our current account position. To achieve this will require the proper mix of monetary and fiscal policy.

   The Bank of Canada could be of substantial assistance to private operators in the exchange market if it published on a regular basis a purchasing power parity value for the Canadian dollar, both as against the U.S. dollar and on a trade weighted basis. The appropriate price for use in such a measure is the implicit price of GNP.

7. Our experience in the early eighties has shown the enormous power that can be exercised by central bankers. In view of this, I believe that some steps should be taken to make the Governor of the Bank of Canada more accountable for his actions.

8. Finally, I must record the view that the Commission's macro-economics research program failed to deal with a number of important economic issues. Thus, there was no serious examination of why the sustained prosperity of the sixties suddenly gave way to stagflation in the early seventies. Nor was there an examination of the basis of the commodity price explosion between 1972 and 1974. Again, the whole question of capital investment which is so essential to the functioning of our economy, received very little attention, even though there has been very little growth in volume of capital spending in the developed world since 1973. Perhaps most important of all, demographers are now predicting that Canada may have a stationary or declining population within 35 years. We know little about how well a private-enterprise economy would perform in such a context. The subject is in need of serious examination as the Commission's Report recommends.

Albert Breton

I. Introduction

I hold with considerable conviction to the notion that the mechanisms which discipline and constrain democratic politics, especially democratic politics in federal states, operate with as much force as those which discipline and constrain economic life. That is not a widely shared view, though it is one that is gaining ground. The traditional and more conventional view is that economic mechanisms are so constraining as to be essentially deterministic, while politics, being the exercise of power, can be set in motion or stopped, as it were, at will. In that view, politics is always capricious and beyond rational explanation.

To my knowledge, Commissioners never held to the traditional view of politics, but it is fair to say, I believe, that neither did most of us accept the notion that political mechanisms are as constraining as economic ones. Over the last two and a half years, our views of politics, and especially of democratic politics in federal systems, have moved quite far away from the traditional concept, as readers of the Commission's Report will have been able to witness for themselves. However, in my opinion, the movement has not been sufficiently great. In a way, that is understandable because breaking away from traditional modes of thought, even in the face of dire necessity, is never easy.

The discussion that follows, submitted as a supplementary view to the Commission's Report, is therefore a clarification and an extension of the theory of democratic politics in federal states, a theory which I call the theory of competitive federalism. To put it differently, in what follows, I provide a brief but more extensive analysis of the mechanisms of competitive federalism, indicate some reforms that are necessary if we wish these mechanisms to be more efficient, and draw a few implications of the theory for certain key issues. I insist that there is still much research to be done in this area and many problems to be resolved. However, I believe that what can be defended seriously at this moment should be present in the debates which the Commission's Report will no doubt engender. Hence this document.

The following discussion is divided into four sections. After this Introduction, Section II examines the nature and properties of competitive politics in a federal state. In Section III, I derive implications of that analysis for a number of questions such as those of the economic union, intergovernmental grants, and municipal governments. Section IV concludes my statement.

II. Theory

It has been and, to a large extent, remains conventional wisdom that the two pillars which define Canada's political institutions — parliamentary government and federalism — lack congruence.[1] That view springs from an *a priori* abstract and formal definition of what constitutes parliamentarism to which is added a no less abstract and formal notion of federalism. The presumed lack of congruence has had enormous influence, not only on the way Canadians think about politics, but also on the way they have condi-

tioned the evolution of their political institutions. It is true that for almost a century and a quarter Canadian parliamentarism and federalism have coexisted in more or less harmonious fashion, but the general tendency – still present in the Commission's Report – to set parliamentary institutions and federalism in opposition or, if not, to view them as separate and unrelated to one another, is at the root of many of our difficulties.

From the beginning of their history as a country to the present, Canadians have reflected on their political institutions with one eye on the United Kingdom and the other on the United States. England was and remains a unitary-parliamentary system, while the U.S. was and is a federal-congressional structure. Hence the following questions: Could a federal-parliamentary system work? Should priority be given to parliamentarism or to federalism? With which one of these two pillars is democracy more closely associated?

I wish to argue that parliamentarism and federalism are congruent; that the issue of having to give priority to either in opting for democracy is a false one; and that it is possible to reform our national and federal institutions in ways that increase their effectiveness, while remaining true to their fundamental genius. A clarification of these issues is necessarily an intellectual exercise, one which requires the selection of a particular language. Being an economist by training and by preference, I feel more at ease formulating and discussing issues, even those outside the traditional frontiers of economics (problems of politics and of society, the traditional domains of political science and of the other social sciences), in the language of that discipline. At the same time, such a strategy makes it easier to draw on the powerful methodology of economics. There is, finally, a third bonus that comes from stating the issues of politics in the language of economics: it makes it easier to go from political to economic real life questions and issues and it makes it easier to formulate a theory of politics that is "compatible" with economic theory. I know from having worked with sociologists and political scientists over many years that the translation from one language to another is a relatively easy matter and that nothing substantive is altered in the process.

Parliamentary (that is, responsible or party) government was not designed. It evolved in response to pressures and influences applied first to monarchs by powerful interests and then, throughout history, to those in office by new emerging centres of power. The dynamics of parliamentarism are appropriately, if somewhat summarily, encapsulated by the expression "elite accommodation".

There is not much competition (or not many "checks and balances": the kinds of behaviours associated with political competition within governments, as distinguished from competition between governments) in such a system. There are, of course, the checks and balances that come from powerful interests, whether economic (like business and labour, though these are not usually of equal strength), religious (churches), intellectual (academics and research organizations), and so on. There are also the checks and balances that come from the Question Period in the House of Commons, from the log-rolling that takes place in caucus and from public opinion. Finally, and very

importantly, there is the competition that originates in the requirement of popular support elicited in contested elections at more or less regular intervals.

All in all, however, competition is quite weak, especially when Cabinet is supported by a good parliamentary majority. The weakness of the checks and balances that come from the lack of separation between the executive and legislative branches is aggravated by the "independence" of the judiciary, an independence which is reflected in the doctrine of "parliamentary supremacy", as contrasted to the doctrine of "judicial review". (I return to this question below (Section III.4), when I discuss the place of the Charter of Rights and Freedoms in Canadian politics.)

A necessary implication of the foregoing is that the preferences, aspirations and opinions of the public, unless they are adopted by the power elites, are not likely to be represented as vividly as they would be in a system in which competition was more vibrant. This overly schematic description of parliamentarism would be even more incomplete if I did not immediately add that the system is susceptible to improvements. The system is capable, as history documents, of absorbing further checks and balances, while at the same time remaining faithful to its own virtues and genius.

The Report contains recommendations which go in the direction of improving competition, such as those aimed at removing budget secrecy and at reforming the Senate, recommendations that I support, although I will have more to say on Senate reform below. But one could go further. I would suggest that in addition *serious consideration should be given to finding ways of reducing party discipline in the House of Commons and, to the extent that it exists, in Parliamentary Committees as well, for all matters, except budgetary ones.* If that was done – slowly, but deliberately – the power of elected representatives would be increased, their ability to voice the opinions of their constituents would be enhanced, and the capacity of constituents to influence governments would be augmented.

Responsible or party government in unitary states, however fine-tuned to better reflect the preferences of citizens, remains a weak mechanism in the performance of the task I have just noted. But when responsible government is married to federalism, that job is done much more effectively. I must hasten to add that some marriages are more successful than others and that some federal structures are better designed than others. I will explore these issues in the pages that follow and indicate what I believe are the ingredients of a good federalism and of a good marriage of federalism with party government. However, the central proposition holds: parliamentary government combined with federalism give the citizens of a country a more effective set of institutions for reflecting their will, preferences and aspirations. Responsible government is democratic government; but responsible government plus federalism is extended democracy, simply because there is more competition.

I must, therefore, address two preliminary questions: How does federalism introduce more competition in any system of government, more particularly, in a system of responsible government? Is competition a "good" thing, that is, something we should want in our political institutions? I will seek to answer

these two questions in Sections II.2 and II.4 below. As an introduction to that discussion – and in recognition of the fact that competition is so central to my view of politics and of democracy – I must devote some space to clarification of the meaning I give to the word competition.

1. Competition

The development of mainline economic thought in the Anglo-American tradition – by any measure the overwhelming tradition – has systematically restricted the notion of competition to price competition. This tradition has come to focus on the conditions under which this kind of competition leads to (Pareto) efficiency, that is, to that state in which no one individual can be made better off without someone else being made worse off. Significantly, this neo-classical tradition has not associated any particular behaviours or activities with its definition of competition.

Since the conditions under which competition is optimal in one sense or another will be examined later on for the case of competitive federalism, it may be worth noting that it is only in the case of price competition that the conditions are known under which competition is Pareto optimal. In other words, under certain conditions, Adam Smith's "invisible hand" allocates resources efficiently for the case of price competition. Although there has been much discussion in the literature on advertising and quality competition, and less, though still a respectable amount, on competition involving research and development expenditures, innovation and technology, it is not known if these various forms of competition are socially efficient. Until recently, the weight of opinion in the profession would have been, I believe, that they were not. Things have been changing in recent years, but no consensus, not even a minimal one, has emerged.

I mention this to underscore that even if it is not possible to specify all the conditions – those that are necessary as well as those that are sufficient – under which political competition in a federal state is optimal, that does not constitute a basis for rejecting such competition, any more than our inability to specify necessary and sufficient conditions for economic competition to be efficient is a satisfactory ground for rejecting market organization.

Price competition must be contrasted to other kinds of competition, which have from time to time retained the attention of economists and others. There are a number of strands in the literature associated with such labels as "working competition" and "countervailing power". One of the more important of these is the notion of *entrepreneurial competition*, sometimes also called Austrian or Schumpeterian competition. In the early 1900's an important number of (to become distinguished) Austrian economists (notably Joseph Schumpeter, Ludwig Mises and Frederick Hayek), seeking to come to grips with the crucial Marxian question of the dynamics of capitalism, proposed theories of economic development in which that particular notion of competition played a central role.

In the words of Schumpeter, one of the ablest analysts of this kind of competition:

In capitalist reality as distinguished from its textbook picture, it is not that kind of competition (price competition) which counts but the competition from the new commodity, the new technology, the new source of supply, the new type of organization . . . competition which commands a decisive cost or quality advantage and which strikes not at the margins of the profits and the outputs of the existing firms but at their foundations and their very lives. This kind of competition is as much more effective than the other as a bombardment is in comparison with forcing a door, so much more important that it becomes a matter of comparative indifference whether competition in the ordinary sense functions more or less promptly; the powerful lever that in the long run expands output and brings down prices is in any case made of other stuff.[2]

Notwithstanding the fact that barriers are sometimes erected to soften the impact of entrepreneurial competition, one must acknowledge that in seeking to understand the economic factors that determine how resources are allocated, as well as the forces that have shaped the broad development of capitalism, the Austrians' notion of competition is more useful than that of mainline neo-classical theory.[3]

It is not an accident that the extension of the analytical tools of economics to politics was initiated by Schumpeter (although Niccolo Machiavelli and John Stuart Mill, among others, had anticipated the possibility): it was a natural outgrowth of his work on entrepreneurial competition. Politicians, in that view, are entrepreneurs who compete for resources by introducing new politics, by developing new forms of organization, by heralding new unifying symbols, by structuring a new social consensus, etcetera. Recent writers have characterized entrepreneurial competition as "alertness to opportunities".[4] If that is a good definition of entrepreneurship, it cannot be limited to the realm of economics, but extends naturally to politics and to other areas of life. To be sure, the "*modus operandi* of competition" (to use a Schumpeterian expression) will vary between business and political entrepreneurs, but their behaviour will have enough in common to be called competitive.

Having said that, it must be recognized that not much is known about competitive processes. Earlier, in referring to intra-governmental competition – the competition between political parties, between the executive, legislative and judicial branches of government (when such competition exists), between the various departments and bureaus that constitute the bureaucracy of a particular governmental unit, such as that of Quebec or Saskatchewan – I used the American expression "checks and balances". These words correspond to more or less specific and precise behaviour and are useful in characterizing that kind of competition. In his study of *American Capitalism*,[5] Galbraith used the evocative term "countervailing power" in an effort to describe a particular process of competition. Recently, Nelson and Winter[6] have sought to model entrepreneurial competition in terms of two activities: "do research" or "do imitation". A friend of mine, having read an earlier draft of this statement, suggested that the behaviour associated with federal-provincial competition was "complement and countervail". To illustrate, if the federal government chose to subsidize post-secondary education by giving money directly to students instead of giving it to provincial governments, these latter could "complement" by targeting their

spending on education more closely to their own priorities, or "countervail" by taking the money away from students.

This area of study is in its infancy. I cannot therefore associate particular competitive processes with the various kinds of entrepreneurial competition that I will discuss below. Because it is appropriate, I use the words "checks and balances" for intra-governmental competition; otherwise, for politics as for economics, I use the word competition, having in mind entrepreneurial competition, but no particular behavioural process.

2. *Federalism*

At its simplest, that is, before introducing real world complications into the picture – a task to be undertaken later – a federal state can be formally defined as a type of political organization in which there are at least two levels of jurisdiction – in Canada, national and provincial – between which the entire set of constitutional powers is divided. The assignment of these powers between the governmental levels is not made by one level alone. That distinguishes federalism from confederalism, a system in which the assignment of powers is made by the provinces alone, and from unitary states, structures in which powers are assigned by senior governments acting in isolation. According to that definition, Canada is and has been a federation and never a confederation. The Canadian provinces, on the other hand, in their relationship with their municipalities, are unitary states.

The division of powers and the mode through which it is effected define federalism well, albeit in a way that is too formal to be very useful in understanding how such a system actually works. From that point of view, what is much more important are the implications of any division of powers for the operations of, and relationships between, the governments of the federation, all of which are responsible governments. The central and most important implication is that in the search for popular support – something that is as needed for the effectiveness of governing parties as revenue is essential for the effectiveness of business firms – the governments of a federation will find themselves competing with each other. Federalism thus adds more competition to that already present in responsible or party government.

One point needs emphasis. Political competition is not something that politicians choose or want, whatever their commitment to federalism and, more broadly, to liberty and to democracy. In that respect, they are exactly like business entrepreneurs who do not want competition either. Competition arises from the necessity to respond to the actions of others; it is "forced" on people by the environment. One does not even have to be aware that one is competing to be competitive. A business firm that adopts a new technology to reduce its costs is acting competitively; one that advertises and places some of its output on sale is acting in a competitive fashion; someone who supports a particular social movement or a particular lobby is competing; as is the politician who seeks harmony with provincial governments by removing the contentious questions from the agenda of federal-provincial encounters.

There is so much mystification about this that I must dwell on two corollary points, at the risk of seeming to insist on the obvious for those who

have seen their way clear on the subject. First, there is the whole bag of issues that are best summarized by the words "co-operative federalism". What is co-operative federalism and how is it to be distinguished from other types of federalisms? To my knowledge, the expression has never been formally defined. That may not be a lacuna because we all have, from practical experience and observation, a good intuitive idea of what is meant by these two words. Two or more persons working together to lift a heavy object; two or more persons engaged in a search for something lost; two or more persons removing snow from a road; these are examples of the kind of behaviour we have in mind when we think of co-operation. In other words, someone helping someone else achieve a certain goal or objective.

Co-operative federalism by analogy would exist if all the politicians of a federation worked together to achieve some collective end. Instead of working on their own for their citizens, governments would work together for the betterment of all "the people". Before examining what is meant by co-operative federalism in more detail, I would like the reader to ask him or herself why it is that we do not, as societies, organize the search for justice on a co-operative basis, but instead set defence against prosecuting attorneys in courts of law? Why do we not organize the working of party politics on a co-operative basis, but instead pit political parties against each other in grand electoral contests? Why do we not organize the search for truth on a co-operative basis, but instead require scholars and scientists to compete for research funds and for limited space in research publications? And, finally – though the list could go on – why do we not organize the production of goods and services on a co-operative basis, but instead implement laws that make co-operation an offence?

These examples underline the fact that in some areas, co-operation is *not* an efficient principle of social organization and that it is less efficient than competition, essentially because co-operation can easily degenerate into collusion, conspiracy and connivance and that this is not necessarily good! In the case of federalism, would co-operation be a better principle of social organization than competition? I will only begin to answer this question here; the answer will be completed in Section II.5. To answer the question, it must be recognized that co-operative federalism is aimed at removing the competition which is a natural by-product of federal organization. Consequently, to be able to answer the question, it is necessary to know whether competition is a "good" feature of political organizations. I do not address this issue before Section II.4.

I have posed the question here, however, because I wish to stress that the notion of co-operative federalism is part and parcel of the politics of "élite accommodation" which plays such an important role in the dynamics of party governments. Indeed, in practice, co-operative federalism is nothing but executive federalism. This has been defined by Smiley "as the relations between elected and appointed officials of the two orders of government in federal-provincial interactions and among the executives of the provinces in interprovincial interactions".[7] I will argue later that there is a place for a limited executive federalism. The executive federalism contemplated by co-operative federalists, however, effectively extends to all the areas of federal-

provincial contact. It transfers to executive and bureaucratic bargaining and negotiation what properly belongs to the realm of the political.

Co-operative federalism does not necessarily eliminate federalist competition, but by moving it into executive and bureaucratic offices and corridors, it mutes its public manifestations and its effectiveness. The heart of co-operative federalism is secret deals, not the stuff on which a lively democracy thrives! There are other implications of the doctrine of co-operative federalism; I mention two.

A first is a by-product of drumming into the psyche of Canadians the belief that federalism is or should be co-operative. Once that is achieved, it provides a fruitful background for the arguments of those, sometimes in one province, sometimes in another, who wish to promote and foster separatism. Indeed, a process that is inherently competitive, even if it is called co-operative, is bound to throw up incidents which separatists – themselves competitive individuals – will use to argue that "the system does not work", because on a particular matter the politicians of a province have been rebuffed or have simply lost in the competitive game. It would be relatively easy to document that the rhetoric of Canadian separatists is often based on the notion that federalism is not as co-operative as one had been led to believe it should be. I cannot undertake that documentation task here. I simply note that if Canadians had been helped to understand that federalist politics, like all politics, is inherently competitive, the propaganda of separatism would have fallen on more barren ground.

A second implication of the doctrine of co-operative federalism relates to the condemnation, by those who adhere to it, of unilateralism, that is, of independent action by any one government of the federation. Unilateral action by one government is, of course, a derogation from co-operation, since when one is acting alone one is not co-operating. Consequently, those who espouse co-operative federalism decry unilateral action on the part of any government in the federation. Although in principle, the condemnation applies to all, in practice it strikes much harder at the federal government, simply because the provinces, if they want to act in unison, have to come to an agreement – something that is not easy to do for essentially competitive entities. To put it differently, in the normal course of affairs, the central government is likely to act unilaterally more often than the provinces, to the extent that these wish to act as one, because the costs of co-ordination are positive. A condemnation of unilateralism, if enforced, would therefore affect the central government more than the provinces.

Co-operative federalism, because it proscribes unilateral action, is therefore a disguised ploy to shackle the federal government, to prevent it from addressing the problems it alone can resolve and is constitutionally responsible for resolving. Indeed, condemning federal unilateralism is condemning the federal government for acting constitutionally! This is so true that if one takes the trouble to go behind the language of co-operative federalism, to the reality of the arguments which it seeks to convey, one discovers either confederalism or a conservative view which seeks to reduce the role of the federal government and, indeed, of all governments in society.

In concluding this argument, I note that the condemnation of unilateralism is also a denial that the division of powers between orders of government is essential to federalism. That indeed is the crux of the matter. Co-operative federalism, if it came to pass, would deny federalism itself. Those who seek co-operative federalism and labour for its realization, seek and labour for a unitary state, disguised in the trappings of federalism, but from which competition would have been reduced to a minimum or even eliminated.

The second corollary point related to the mystification surrounding the notion of political competition pertains to the language of competition and of federalism. Competition in the marketplace, in courtrooms, in parliaments, on hustings, in university seminars, and wherever it takes place is sometimes smooth, so smooth that one could be led into believing that it is not there. But at other times, it is rough, so rough that outsiders are often at a loss in trying to understand why so much energy and effort are displayed, why opponents are characterized in such vile fashion, why the parties become uncouth and impolite in the process of competing. In describing this second circumstance, it is not uncommon for the outsiders, who would have no problem with "well-behaved" competition, to describe the situation in terms of conflict, rancour, combat, suspicion, disharmony, and so on, and to attach to these expressions a negative connotation. The stage is then set for appeals to co-operation and for a rhetoric that praises the virtues of co-operative federalism.

Words have emotional content. For that reason, debates and disagreements are sometimes resolved by using a different language. It is important, however, that the change in vocabulary be only that, not the occasion for unnecessary changes in institutions. When competition is acrimonious one may wish to reduce its acrimoniousness; that can be a legitimate objective. But it is not because we choose to relabel a competitive process by some other name, such as conflict, disharmony, or rivalry, that we will have improved things. Indeed, if relabelling leads to the search for unwarranted institutional changes, we may have worsened the situation. Prosecuting and defence attorneys may be uncouth and antagonistic to each other; things could possibly be better if such behaviour did not exist, but surely justice would not be well served, if, to remove such behaviour, courtroom procedures were transformed from competitive into co-operative ones!

Many a time I have been struck by the fact that those who resist the notion of competition and its reality in fact take offence at the language of competition. The question of how a language can be made more genteel and gracious is an interesting and difficult one. It may be possible to have a genteel and graceful competitive federalism, but whether it is or not has little bearing on whether competitive federalism is desirable or not.

Before moving on to a discussion of the costs and benefits of political competition and to an overall evaluation of its worth, I must deal with two subjects that are likely to be of most interest to specialists of co-operative federalism, but which must be cleared up if what I call competitive federalism is to be understood. For that reason, I encourage even those who are not co-operative federalists to stay with me through the next section.

3. Not Co-operation and Not Anarchy

The "proof" that co-operation in federations is beneficial has traditionally been based on sentimentalism and romanticism. Many people do not mind this, but scholars have generally sought to extract themselves from such clutches; consequently they have searched for a rigorous theory of federalism that would provide them with the desired proof. One of the theories used by these scholars derives from an application to federalism of the theory of games, specifically an application of the theory of the non-co-operative game known as "prisoner's dilemma".[8]

That theory is a representation of a situation in which non-co-operative behaviour on the part of individuals leads to an outcome that is inefficient, in that if the individuals could enter into a pre-game binding agreement to co-operate, they would choose another outcome than the one that obtains in the absence of co-operation. In the words of Luce and Raiffa, the prisoner's dilemma game can be characterized as follows:

> *Two suspects are taken into custody* and separated. *This district attorney is certain that they are guilty of a specific crime, but he does not have adequate evidence to convict them at a trial. He points out to each prisoner that each has two alternatives: to confess to the crime the police are sure they have done, or not to confess. If they both do not confess, then the district attorney states he will book them on some very minor trumped-up charge such as petty larceny and illegal possession of a weapon, and they will both receive minor punishment; if they both confess they will be prosecuted, but he will recommend less than the most severe sentence; but if one confesses and the other does not, then the confessor will receive lenient treatment for turning state's evidence whereas the latter will get "the book" slapped at him.*[9]

If they could co-operate, the two suspects would decide not to confess. But being separated and held incommunicado, they will both confess, each to "receive lenient treatment", but both will get "the book". This serves to show that non-co-operative behaviour is inefficient.

The question is whether the prisoner's dilemma game is an appropriate model to think about and to analyse federalism. In other words, will the co-operative behaviour which would lead to efficient results in the prisoner's dilemma game also lead to efficient results in the case of federalism? The answer must be a resounding no. The prisoner's dilemma game is simply not an appropriate model for federalism. Why? For two reasons.

The first and the most obvious is that the governments of federal states are not kept incommunicado. In Canada, with close to one thousand federal-provincial meetings per year, it is hard to assume that the parties are separated.

The second reason for the inapplicability of the prisoner's dilemma model to federalism is more basic. As the Luce and Raiffa narration makes clear, there are no gains from competition in a prisoner's dilemma model: there are only gains from co-operation. To understand the full burden of this point, assume that the parties in the game are not criminal suspects, but ordinary

oligopolists. Would we also conclude that they should co-operate (collude?) to improve their position? The logic of the prisoner's dilemma model would seem to push us in that direction. In this "oligopolist's dilemma" game, it is our instinct as economists – for those of us who are – which keeps us in check; we know that the logic of co-operation appears correct only because consumers are left out of the game. Once their presence is acknowledged, it is easy to understand that competition is for their benefit. We must conclude that co-operation benefits the oligopolists, while competition serves consumers. That is why the prisoner's dilemma model cannot be used to analyse oligopolies.

It is essentially for the same reason that the prisoner's dilemma game cannot be used to analyse federalism. In this case, citizens are left out of the picture. They are the ones who benefit from competition. If that is the case, how are thoughtful scholars led to adopt a completely inappropriate model to analyse federalism? The answer must be that underlying the use of the prisoner's dilemma model is the (tacit) assumption that provincial governments perfectly embody the interests of the people of their respective provinces. There is no role for competition because each provincial government is assumed to be serving its people perfectly! All models of co-operative federalism in fact make the same assumption.

We are therefore back to competition and to competitive federalism. But competitive behaviour is not unconstrained or anarchical behaviour; indeed competition would not survive, still less be efficient, if such behaviour was the rule. In fact competitive behaviour is restrained and disciplined behaviour.

One thing that can discipline competition is legally enforced property rights. One of the best definitions of these is that provided by Dales. I quote:

> *In everyday conversation we usually speak of "property" rather than "property rights", but the contraction is misleading if it tends to make us think of property as* things *rather than as* rights, *or of ownership as outright rather than circumscribed . . . When you own a car, you own a set of legally defined rights to use the vehicle in certain ways and not in others; you may not use it as a personal weapon, for example, nor may you leave it unattended beside a fire hydrant. Among the most important rights you do have are the right to prevent others from using the vehicle, except with your permission and on your terms, and the right to divest yourself of your ownership rights in the vehicle by selling them to someone else. We may say, then, that ownership always consists of (1) a set of rights to use property in certain ways (and a set of negative rights or prohibitions, that prevent its use in other ways); (2) a right to prevent others from exercising those rights, or to set the terms on which others may exercise them; and (3) a right to sell your property rights.*[10]

Property rights extend beyond physical objects like cars, to things such as bonds, shares of stock and money. They extend to one's time (which can be sold as labour or consumed as leisure); it is important that they extend to roads, canals, air waves, and, as the Law of the Sea Conference made abundantly clear, especially during the last four or five years of negotiations, to the oceans and the seabeds.

It is important to stress that property rights may or may not be related to private property. Indeed, property rights can be vested in individuals, in groups (such as corporations) and in governments or other public bodies. That is, property rights can be private or collective. On August 8, 1983, *The Globe and Mail* reported on a debate in the Department of External Affairs in Ottawa on whether the Antarctic should be considered the "common heritage of mankind" or be assigned to "a select group of nations that already have scientific and commercial interests in Antarctica" (p. 9); that is a debate about property rights.

But sometimes legally-enforced property rights do not exist. That may result from failures in legislation or in law enforcement, but it may also derive from intrinsic problems as in the case of public goods, intellectual property, common property, and so on. In such instances, substitutes have to be found if they do not "spontaneously" arise; otherwise competition will be inefficient. I cannot here analyse all the – sometimes nearly perfect, sometimes much less than perfect – substitutes for legally-enforced property rights. I suggest two which I believe have a special role in disciplining competition in federal states. The first is trust, which, even if it is important, cannot be legislated and is less susceptible to improvement through institutional reform. I will, consequently, just mention it. The second is "monitoring",[11] which I introduce here, but will discuss at length below, in Sections II.8 and II.9.

Trust can be a substitute for property rights. It need not, obviously, be a perfect substitute for them, in the sense that both trust and legally-enforced property rights can co-exist. Trust is a substitute for property rights if the competing parties are confident (i.e. trust, believe) that each will abide by the rules of the game. The parties compete, but there are certain behaviours and activities which are proscribed – possibly only through tacit understanding – and to which neither party will resort.

Another substitute for property rights (and for trust) is "monitoring". The function of property rights is to define penalty-reward structures which, if they are efficient, ensure that one party does not, through his or her actions, impose costs on others that are out of proportion to the benefits he or she derives for these actions. A "monitor" can obviously do this. A "monitor" can be a person, but it can also be an institution. I distinguish below between horizontal and vertical competition. The first refers to interprovincial competition, while the second relates to federal-provincial competition. I will argue that the federal government and a number of "self-regulating" federal institutions are natural "monitors" of horizontal competition. I will also argue that the natural "monitor" of vertical competition is a reformed Senate. Before I can do justice to that problem, there are a number of issues that must be cleared up.

One point needs to be emphasized immediately, however. Property rights are never perfect, trust is never absolute, and "monitors" as well as "monitoring" devices are all of human fabrication. Because of this, competition is never absolutely efficient. It will sometimes attain its maximum efficiency, which may be far from the ideal; at other times it will even attain less than that maximum. That is true in politics, as it is in economics.

There is no doubt that at times competition in the Canadian federation has been less than efficient, possibly even destructive. The problems of economic union, which are at the centre of the Royal Commission's mandate, raise this question with urgency. Are certain policies adopted by governments in the pursuit of local objectives, but which impede the free flow of resources, inefficient competitive policies? I address this and other like questions below.

It is important, however, when faced with a situation of inefficient competition not to conclude that competition is always inefficent. When such situations arise, we must turn our attention to the property rights, the trust and the "monitoring" which are supposed to guarantee the efficiency of competition, and seek ways to strengthen all of them or any one of them. I try to do this in the pages that follow.

4. Checks and Balances

The remainder of Section II deals with the benefits and the costs of competition: this subsection with intra-governmental competition and the next five with intergovernmental competition. In this section I ask and seek to answer the following question: Are checks and balances a "good" thing? There are at least two different ways of answering this question. One which is more formal, in that it focuses on structural features of political institutions, and a second one which is more behavioural in that it concentrates on the mechanisms and responses which characterize institutions marked by checks and balances, compared to those which are not. Because there is an element of truth in both lines of inquiry — although it will soon transpire that I accord more importance to the second — I will look at each in turn.

As the words checks and balances indicate, a system in which they play an important role is one in which more barriers have to be opened, more hoops jumped, more obstacles circumvented and more impediments negotiated in an effort to obtain the passage and implementation of a piece of legislation, than would be the case in a system in which they played a lesser role. From a static short-run point of view, checks and balances reduce the legislative and executive efficiency — defined as the ratio of laws passed and implemented to the time and effort put in passing them — of political institutions.

Looked at from another point of view, the reduced efficiency of law-making bodies is nothing but the greater popular control over the exercise of political power which is automatically achieved by the fact that checks and balances exist. In terms of this formal way of looking at the problem, one's view about the costs and benefits of checks and balances — and about whether they are "good" — centres one's conception of the role and importance of political power for the conduct of public affairs on the one hand, and on the extent to which that power should be controlled for the greater blossoming of individual and collective liberty on the other.

The virtues of efficiency versus control are not as easily described as the above formulation may inadvertently signal. Indeed, in some instances, liberty is guaranteed by a swift and unequivocal exercise of political power. For this reason, constitutions which recognize that there is a genuine trade-off between political power and liberty nonetheless acknowledge that that trade-

off is not always "well-behaved" – that, in other words, it is sometimes subject to exceptions – by vesting in constitutions clauses which permit the rapid employment of power in emergency situations, such as that pertaining to "peace, order and good Government" in the Canadian Constitution.

From a structural point of view, parliamentary systems, such as the Canadian system, are characterized by far fewer checks and balances than are congressional systems such as the American. Thus from a short-run static or formal point of view, the Canadian political system, if we disregard its federal dimension, would seem to be more efficient at "making laws" than the American system, again neglecting the federal dimension. Or to put the point differently, political power is more controlled in the American political system than in the Canadian system.

However, the effective differences in the law-making efficiency of the two systems are not as great as one would have to conclude from an analysis of their structural characteristics. Should one impute the similarities in the two systems to characteristics of federalism or should one look elsewhere? There is little doubt that federalism has an important role to play in explaining the *de facto* similarity in the law-making performance of the two systems, but the second aspect of checks and balances that I noted at the beginning of the section is also of great importance.

This second aspect pertains to the dynamics of checks and balances. A system which places barriers and other impediments to the passage of legislation at the same time and in the very fact of forcing people to deal with the barriers and with the other impediments, stimulates discussion and debate on the matters to be legislated. It is as if the items remained longer on the agenda and consequently attracted the interest – voiced approval or disapproval – of a larger number of persons.

The people who develop an interest in discussing and debating matters kept on the agenda by the checks and balances are not only those who have a professional or para-professional concern for the matter – politicians, bureaucrats, lobbyists and others like them – but members of the general public, including academics, free-lance intellectuals, writers, social critics, organized groups and others. The greater involvement in public affairs which checks and balances generate will, in general, not be limited to haphazard intervention, but will stimulate the publication of magazines and other periodicals intensely concerned with the evolution of policy. It will, in other words, stimulate organized interest in public affairs.

Strong checks and balances will also mean that those citizens who get involved in public discussions and debates will want to engage in meaningful participation and consequently will seek to acquire more information on public affairs than professionals would of themselves freely choose to make available. The pressures for more information imply that over the longer term, the presence of more checks and balances leads to less secretive political institutions.

As a consequence, checks and balances, by raising the level of political involvement on the part of citizens, increase the legitimacy of the political process. Checks and balances still act to control the exercise of political power, but because, from a dynamic point of view, they raise the legitimacy

of that political power, they make its exercise more efficient. The dynamic longer-term effects of checks and balances partially or even completely reverse the static shorter-term effects.

I wish to emphasize that the foregoing argument about dynamic effects reversing the static ones does *not* mean that law-making will be more rapid in systems with more checks and balances compared to those with fewer. The efficiency of checks and balances must be sought elesewhere. I mention two possible areas.

In a system with more checks and balances there should be fewer policy reversals over time. That is, changes in governments as a result of elections should produce fewer returns to the *status quo ante*. It is possible to argue, for example, that the cycle of nationalization and de-nationalization of certain industries which has taken place in Britain would not have happened if the British parliamentary system had had more checks and balances. This is a blatant case; the reader can surely provide some possibly less blatant but still spectacular cases in Canada.

A second area of increased efficiency of checks and balances due to the long-term effects over-turning the short-term one pertains to social consensus. More social consensus means that the difference between majorities and minorities have less saliency. As a consequence, other things being equal, it is easier to enforce laws. (The "other things being equal" relates to the desire or will of the population to have laws enforced, as revealed, among other things, in the amount of resources they choose to allocate to that task.)

The dominance of long-term over short-term effects is important. It provides part of the basis for the recommendation I made earlier for a reduction of party discipline in the House of Commons and in Parliamentary Committees for all non-budgetary matters. The reduction of party discipline would slow down the passage of legislation but, in the longer run, the benefits of this slow-down will be a more politically involved citizenry and policies and programs that are more broadly accepted by citizens. It is for this reason that I support the recommendations of the Commission's Report that are aimed at reducing and even eliminating the secrecy surrounding the budgetary process. I also support, for the same reason, the establishment of a permanent Economic Policy Committee of the House of Commons, which would hold annual pre-budget hearings and whose proceedings would be televised. In short, I support both recommendations because they increase checks and balances.

I deal with Senate reform later. I simply note here that any reform which increased the legitimacy of the Senate would automatically increase its ability to check and balance. Again, that would sometimes slow down the passage of legislation, but in the long run, through the process described above, it would increase the involvement and the participation of Canadians in public affairs. That must be deemed a net benefit. Checks and balances within our national institutions, as long as they are designed with care and prudence, are therefore of overall benefit.

What about the competition that is introduced in the political system through the medium of federalism? Is it also of overall benefit? That is the question to which I now turn. To proceed with the analysis, I distinguish

between the competition which organizes the relationship of federal and provincial governments and that which structures the relationships of the provinces with each other. I call the first vertical competition and the second horizontal competition. I examine each of these under different aspects in the next five sections.

5. *Division of Powers*

Competition plays no role in the conventional approaches to federalism, whether these approaches derive from political science, law or economics. Competition is (unwittingly) removed by two assumptions which are both, in my view, unacceptable. The first of these, which will occupy my attention in this section, rests on a confusion between what could be called the *de jure* and the *de facto* division of powers. The second assumption, which I will analyse in Section II.7, relates to what may be called the territorial basis of interests and, hence, of community: the idea that federal states rest or are based on territorially more or less well-defined communities.

There can be little doubt that from a *legal-constitutional* point of view, an optimal assignment of powers is one in which the degree of concurrency, of overlap or of joint occupation of any one power has been reduced to a minimum. Constitutions that embody such an assignment are sometimes said to be the hallmark of "classical federalism". The need for the smallest possible degree of *de jure* concurrency does not originate in a desire for neatness, nor is it a relic inherited from the long-dying nineteeth century conception of political sovereignty enshrined in early definitions of federal countries as states constituted of two "sovereign and independent orders of government".

Instead, a minimal degree of *de jure* concurrency is required by the necessity of "judicial accountability". Ultimately, when things come to a crunch, a court must be able to decide whether a government has the authority to implement a particular policy or not; whether it is acting *intra vires* or *ultra vires*. If there is no "compartmentalization" within which legal authority can be exercised, there will be no basis on which a court can make decisions and, in fact, no meaning to a juridical division of powers. I will insist below that courts, and in particular the Supreme Court, are often called upon to act as "monitors" of federalist competition and to insure that competition is efficient. They cannot play that role unless the degree of *de jure* concurrency is small, for if it is significant, the courts would find it harder to impute responsibility to one or the other governments involved.[12] The fundamental democratic principle that parliament must be accountable becomes meaningless.

That much seems incontrovertible. But at the political or *de facto* level things are different: there, concurrency is the rule. We have to be clear about what that means if we do not want to become victims of the confusion between *de jure* and *de facto* concurrency which pervades the literature and which is used to argue against competitive federalism.

Before examining why an air-tight *de facto* division of powers is not possible in principle, let me illustrate the nature of the problem with a few

examples. Consider the (welfare) economist's standard classification of powers into allocation, redistribution and stabilization, to which may or may not be added a revenue power, depending on how the first three have been defined. Now assume that for whatever reason, the redistribution and stabilization powers *de jure* are assigned to the federal jurisdictional level while allocation is somehow, again *de jure*, divided between the federal and provincial levels. If the division of the allocation powers is air-tight, we have a "classical" assignment of powers.

Now suppose that some provincial governments decide to use some of their allocation powers – those in areas such as education, transportation, or urban land use – in ways that fully respect the Constitution, but which change the distribution of income in a direction that the federal government does not like, so that that government feels obliged to implement policies of its own to "re-establish" the distribution of income it desires. Would not the air-tight separation of powers have *de facto* been broken? I believe so, since the federal government's actions are now governed by decisions taken at the provincial level.

Consider a second case. Suppose that to stabilize the economy the federal government increases or reduces some or all of the expenditures resulting from policies implemented under the allocation powers juridically assigned to it in a way that is respectful of classical federalism's dictum regarding concurrency. But, from a behavioural point of view, will it still be respectful of that division? Not if there is any relationship between federal and provincial policies, because if there is, decisions by the federal government will impact on the provinces, and, what is even worse, not equally.

We can now turn to general principles. As I hope the examples have made clear, the various day-to-day policies which can be implemented by the governments of a federation under the powers which have juridically been assigned to them, stand in all sorts of relationships to each other. In the way citizens look at these policies (formally, in the utility functions of citizens), some will be independent, while many others will be either substitutes or complements to each other. On the other side of decision making, in the way politicians and bureaucrats look at policies (formally at the technical level of "production" and implementation), policies will be independent, substitutes or complements, but not necessarily in the same way as they are for citizens.

That is the reason why *de facto* all powers tend to be concurrent. It is important to be clear about what that means and what it does not mean. It does not mean that both orders of government will, at the same time, legislate in the same policy area. It simply means that governments at the two jurisdictional levels will, in general, be legislating in policy areas that are closely related to each other. As noted, that "closeness" has two possible sources: the preferences of citizens and the technical properties of production and implementation technologies. In other words, policies can be related to each other in one fashion or another because of the way citizens value them; or they can be related, because their production and implementation connects them to each other. These connections create the *de facto* concurrency.

Once this is acknowledged, it is impossible not to recognize at the same time that governments at different jurisdictional levels will be in competition

with each other. The competition originates in the desire of governments to obtain the support of citizens by providing them with the policies they want. Since these policies will not have the same relationships in the preferences of citizens and in the technical structure of the implementation techologies that they have in constitutional documents, governments at one level will be implementing policies which are substitutes or complements to policies that are the responsibility of governments at another level, hence the competition.

Does this *de facto* concurrency – the outcome of characteristics of policies and of the political process – imply that constitutions do not matter? That the juridical division of powers is meaningless? That any *de jure* division of powers would be equivalent to any other? The answer to these questions must be an emphatic no. There are better and there are worse *de jure* divisions of powers. There is a view – the outcome of the confusion between *de jure* and *de facto* concurrency – which holds that the best constitutional assignment of powers is the one which leads to the smallest degree of competition possible. The bookshelves of Canada's libraries are littered with constitutional blueprints aimed at working out a division of powers that would eliminate *de facto* concurrency, so as to eliminate federalist competition.

Such constitutional blueprints are impossible to design for the only reason that people and the environment change. A blueprint that succeeded in assigning powers so as to suppress competition today would be obsolete, in that respect, tomorrow. What then is the optimal constitutional division of powers? To answer that question would take me too far afield. In addition, it is not, for the issues that concern me here, of prime importance; consequently I skip over the question.[13]

6. Executive Federalism

The discussion of the last section clearly acknowledges the existence of interdependence. Indeed, it associates interdependence with two prime sources: the preferences of citizens and the characteristics of "production and implementation" processes. The question I address here is whether that interdependence calls for federal-provincial co-operation and co-ordination.

The question is easy to answer. To the extent that interdependence originates in the properties of the preferences (utility functions) of citizens, there is no need for formal institutionalized co-ordination. Indeed, one should rely on vertical competition between governments at different levels to deal with the co-ordination problem. The rule is the same as for market co-ordination. That is one reason why in its day-to-day operations federalism tends to be "messy", but one should keep in mind that it is this messiness which is the secret of its efficiency!

When we turn to the interdependence on the production and implementation side, there is a strong case for formal federal-provincial co-ordination. That is the limited case for Executive Federalism. The co-ordination activities are embodied in federal-provincial committees which involve various levels and various departments of governments, all of which seek to find better ways to "produce" and implement the policies which have been decided upon and designed by the political arm of governments.

There is a real temptation, reinforced by the internal logic of parliamentary government, to extend executive federalism beyond production and implementation questions to the elaboration, formulation and design of policies. If the temptation is not resisted – and it must be acknowledged that many times in the past it has not been – Executive Federalism serves to reduce the beneficial effects of competition.

For this reason, I believe it is important that *federal-provincial consultation on virtually all matters follows, not precedes, debates in the House of Commons and in provincial parliaments. Parliamentary debates should extend to a specification of the areas that could be reasonably co-ordinated and those which should not be.* This kind of sorting is currently undertaken at the Cabinet level. Bringing these matters before Parliament would increase checks and balances and hence democracy. It should be favoured on that ground. Furthermore, *it is essential that such matters be debated publicly if a reformed Senate is to perform its "monitoring" role efficiently.* To those who argue that this will slow down the decision-making process, I reply with the argument developed earlier, that such a procedure will increase public involvement in public affairs and, over the longer term, will make for a more politically mature citizenry.

But a more intense involvement of parliament in the policy design of federal-provincial matters and a restriction of executive federalism to "production" and implementation of policies are not sufficient for efficient competition. *Efficient competition also requires that more information be available to the public,* not only on the federal-provincial and provincial-provincial policies that are co-ordinated, but on the nature and form of the co-ordination. At present, in the *Access to Information Act*, federal-provincial communications are accorded a status equal to that of national security. That is ludicrous and should be changed.

7. The Territorial Basis of Interest

The search for a basis that would make it possible to define a community has absorbed much time and effort in the last two or three centuries. Such a search has had many motivations, some more noble than others. One of these has been the belief that some notion of community was a necessary adjunct to the definition of the still dominant, and not receding, idea of the nation-state. Community was therefore sought along cleavages or lines of demarcation between people such as race (colour, blood and cranial measurements having been the most important indexes of race), language, ethnicity, religion, and in more recent times, culture and "society", these defined in purely socio-institutional terms.

Much of the reflection on federalism developed in juxtaposition to that on the nation-state. In addition, federalism appeared to some as a way of salvaging the idea of community, based on whichever cleavage was cherished at that moment, together with the notion of some minimum efficient size of country. It is not an accident, therefore, that in much of the literature on federalism – even fairly sophisticated literature – federalism as a "community of communities" or as a compact, a confederation or an alliance of communities based on particular cleavages, keeps coming up.

In Canadian thought, this intellectual atavism has nourished two dominant views of what may be called communitarian federalism and a number of minor derivatives which it would serve no purpose to even acknowledge. The first of these dominant traditions, and by far the one with the highest profile, asserts — in language that has changed as times and circumstances have changed — that Canada is made up of two "peoples", "two races", "two cultures", or "two societies". According to that view, the fact that there are ten provinces in Canada is seen either as an illusion — a way of shifting attention away from the cherished dichotomy — or as a sinister ploy to deprive one of the peoples-races-cultures-societies of its identity (one that is re-defined as the terms of the dichotomy are re-defined).

The second major tradition of Canadian communitarian federalism acknowledges the fact that there are ten provinces in the country, and goes on the assert that they constitute ten communities. History has played havoc with the first or "dichotomy" tradition as the constant change in language indicates. But things are worse for the "ten-provincial-communities" tradition, if only because any definition of society and culture that has the barest elements of operational significance will not be applicable at the same time to the provinces and to the nation. In other words, if one adopts a definition of culture or society that makes Alberta, Ontario, Quebec and Newfoundland — the provinces most often mentioned — into distinct communities based on cultural or societal dimensions, then on that definition Canada will not be a community.

Before indicating why we must divest ourselves of these atavistic intellectual notions, let me note one implication of the doctrine of communitarian federalism. Since the communities are based on race, language, culture, or whatever, there is no place for horizontal competition between the various provincial governments, because a provincial government, which is assumed to be catering to a community of individuals whose preferences are assumed to be defined by communal characteristics, will be able to do very little, if anything, of interest for individuals of another community whose preferences are defined on an altogether different set of communal characteristics. And, may I add, as a matter of logic, the federal government is superfluous, in that system. It is true that it has a role to play in the "dichotomy" tradition where it is seen as the government of one people-race-culture-society, replacing the nine other superfluous provincial governments!

Horizontal competition has no role to play in a model of communitarian federalism because that notion of federalism is always used as a device to collectivize interests. To put it differently, the notion of community is used as an instrument to make the interests of Manitoba dominate those of Manitobans and the interests of Prince Edward Island those of individual Islanders. Consequently, only the government of the community can know the interests, preferences and aspirations of the community. Other governments, not being of the "proper" race, blood, language, religion or culture, are by definition strangers to these interests. It is a neat assumption to use to remove competition.[14]

It is essential to acknowledge that provinces are made up of people, some of whom have traits that are similar to those of other people in the same

province and in other provinces, but also of some who have dissimilar traits. There is no province in Canada that is made up of a homogeneous mass of people and there is no province in Canada in which the interests, preferences and aspirations of all the people are the same. And it is to be hoped there never will be.

But even if there were, even if the people of Canada were sub-dividable into *x* or *y* homogeneous globs of humankind, that would not furnish us with a rationale for a federal state. That rationale, as the *Federalist*[15] in the great debates that preceded the Philadelphia Convention of 1787 recognized, is to provide the political system with more (additional to those in each government) competition to insure that over the long run, political power is exercised both efficiently and legitimately in the interests of citizens. In a political system based on parliamentary rules of the game, the importance of additional competition cannot be over-emphasized.

The foregoing is *not* a denial of the existence of communities. I recognize that these exist and that they play an irreplaceable role in the life of people. Without the communities provided by families, professions, workplaces, churches, associations and groups of various sorts, anomie, disintegration, and even a Hobbesian "war of all against all" would be the norm. I am only saying that there is no independent definition of community that can serve as a guide to the design of federal structures and to their governance. *The task of governments is to meet the preferences of citizens who happen to be in the provinces or in the country they have been elected to govern.* Meaningful provincial communities do not exist, except as provinces.

8. Nation Building and Province Building

Earlier, in Section II.3, I noted that unless property rights are well-defined, unless trust is sufficient or unless "monitoring" is efficient, competition will not produce the beneficial results which it can be expected to produce. I repeat that it is possible to have property rights that are so inappropriately specified and/or so poorly enforced, to have such a lack of trust, or to have "monitoring" that is so inefficient, that the effects of competition will be perverse. This is therefore a central issue. In this subsection, I look at some of the factors that govern or at least should govern horizontal competition. In Section II.9 I turn my attention to the same question for the case of vertical competition. I must insist immediately on two points: first, as I have already noted, it is not possible, given the present state of knowledge and research, to describe all the conditions – those necessary and those sufficient – that make for efficient horizontal political competition in a federation; second, in the discussion on the division of powers (Section II.5), on executive federalism (Section II.6), and on the territorial basis of interest (Section II.7), I have already indicated some of the conditions that are necessary for efficient competition. Those that follow are additional.

The first of these conditions pertains to a notion of "competitive equality". To be sure, efficient horizontal competition does not require that all competing units be of equal size any more than efficient competition in markets requires that firms be of equal size. But it must be that the large

units are not in a position to continually dominate, coerce, and in other ways prevent the smaller units from making independent autonomous decisions; nor are they in a position to inflict "disproportionate" damage on them. The smaller units must be able to compete with the strong on an equal footing. This problem is more acute in some federations than in others, and is certainly an important one in the Canadian federation in which the disparity in the size of provinces is large and possibly growing.

The responsibility for insuring that the smaller units are able to compete against the larger ones cannot lie elsewhere than with the federal government. That is a first reason why the central government is different from provincial governments. How does the central government play this role or fulfill this responsibility? Before answering this question, let me note that it cannot be an easy role to play, because, as I have already indicated, the federal government, also competes with the provinces. We are faced with the situation in which a government, competing with those at another level, must act to insure that the competition between the latter is "fair" and "productive". That is necessarily a difficult task, one that cannot be left exclusively to the day-to-day push and pull of politics, but must be institutionally entrenched. I discuss the problem in Section II.9.

Conventional wisdom about public policy in Canada is overlaid with the words "nation-building" and "province-building". When the view is not made explicitly, it is implicit that nation-building is the business of the central government, while province-building is that of the provinces. I would like to suggest that a look at the record would indicate that that attribution is largely wrong: the central government in Canada (and I would submit in other federal countries also) has been and continues to be engaged in province-building as much, if not more in certain instances, than the provinces themselves. That is one of the ways it acts as a "monitor" of horizontal competition.

How does the federal government foster province-building? It is not possible in this brief statement to indicate all the ways this is done. It will do if I give examples taken from various modes of interventions to illustrate what I mean; the reader will then be able to provide more examples for him or herself.

One notorious example of federal province-building was the creation of the Borden Line, the line which forced a differential price in oil and oil products, such that the prices east of the Ontario-Quebec border were lower than those west of that line. The policy permitted the development of an oil industry in Western Canada at a time when the pure economics of the case would not have permitted that to happen. Although it was not called province-building, nor labelled regional policy either, there can be no doubt that the policy played that role, and quite effectively so.

A second example of province-building is the entire set of policies which have come to be labelled regional policies and over which there is still so much uncertainty and controversy. An analysis would indicate that the federal government has always pursued regional policies: it has always tailored or adjusted relevant policies to regional or provincial realities. However, the modern development of regional policies begins in the post-war

period, more exactly in the 1950s, and continues to expand and grow until the present. This is not an accident. If one of the roles of regional policy is to insure that the smaller and least favoured provincial governments are able to compete with the larger and more favoured ones, it must be that regional policies will grow and acquire more significance as the intensity of competition increases. The most casual observation confirms that the extent and the degree of horizontal competition in the Canadian federation have grown enormously in the post-World War II period as the provinces have "come of age". This coming of age has manifested itself in a number of ways, not the least of which is the increase in the size of provincial budgets – relative to the total of public expenditures – and the development of competent, mature provincial bureaucracies.

A third example of province-building policies by the central government – that is, of policies which make all provincial governments, if not equal, at least capable of horizontal competition that is efficient and productive – is equalization payments. These grants, to which I devote some discussion in Section III, are primarily an instrument aimed at improving the competitive position of the weaker *governments* of the federation and ameliorating the productive features of the competition in which they are engaged *vis-à-vis* other provincial governments. They are not instruments aimed at achieving "horizontal equity" between the inhabitants of the provinces. This does not mean that considerations of equity and of narrow (neo-classical) economic efficiency do not enter their design. But these grants would be of minor importance if their primary role of acting as province-builders was set aside. That is why it was appropriate for the federal government, after the increase in the price of crude oil that made the Ontario government a "have-not" government, to change the equalization formula so that government remained a "have" government: in the competitive game, it is hard to imagine that the Ontario government is not a "have" government.

One could continue giving examples, (for example, transportation policy, procurement policy, etc.), but the point, I hope, is made. Before moving on, I stress two subsidiary points. First, the fact that the various programs I have listed to illustrate the nature of province-building by the federal authorities exist, does not mean that they cannot be improved. Therefore, the fact that the federal government engages in province-building activities does not tell us whether it does too much or too little of it. The second point, which I mention only to remove all ambiguity, is that even if the federal government pursues province-building policies, this does not mean that the provincial governments do not also pursue policies aimed at the same end. Furthermore, province-building policies, whether federal or provincial in origin, contribute to nation-building. These obvious points have to be made only because the conventional dichotomy between nation-building and province-building tends to obscure them.

Besides competitive equality, another condition, this one pertaining to the appropriability of costs and benefits of public policies, must be satisfied. (A not dissimilar condition must also rule in markets if competition there is to be efficient.) The condition requires that the benefits and costs of decisions made by the government of a province be borne by the people living in that

province, and, therefore, by the government of the province. This condition is particularly relevant for costs, so let me re-state it with respect to that variable. In competing to attract businesses to its jurisdiction, either by supplying particularly attractive local public goods, such as theatre, concerts, or dance, by offering tax advantages, or by buying part of the ouput of the sought-after enterprises, the government of a province should not be able to shift the burden of the offered amenities to the citizens of other jurisdictions. It is clear that otherwise the competition would be inefficient. There is already considerable machinery in place in Canada to ensure that benefits and costs are appropriated by decision makers themselves. This is particularly the case in the field of taxation. But there is room for improvement. I will return to this question when I address the issue of "economic union" in Section III – a matter that is important enough in our terms of reference to have given the Commission part of its name.

Were I engaged in writing a formal treatise instead of presenting a broad framework that can help decide on appropriate policies, I would devote considerable space to another condition for efficient competition which could be called "entry". For competition to be efficient, those who can elicit more suppport should be able to enter the competitive arena and those less effective at doing that should have to leave it. Although there is some evidence – mostly American – that the life expectancy of political incumbents has been increasing, it is not known whether that phenomenon is "natural" or contrived.[16] Should future research indicate that anywhere in the Canadian federation, entry by existing or new political parties to the apparatus of state is reduced by artificial contrivances, that would be a matter for serious concern, because that would greatly reduce the competitive nature of Canadian politics, not only between parties, but overall.

The matter is particularly important in respect of electoral rules, because these may, under certain circumstances, prevent the representation of groups of citizens in political institutions. There is some weak evidence that the operation of electoral rules in Canada, both nationally and provincially, may be artificially lengthening the tenure of incumbents. If that is ever seriously documented, these rules should be altered.

9. Who Monitors the Monitor?

"Who monitors the monitor?" is the most fundamental question of economic, social and political organization. It was raised in the first century of our era by Juvenal (nam quis custodiet ipsos Custodes?) and continues to be asked to this day.[17] It is a fundamental question, but, ironically, it is one that possesses no satisfactory logical answer. For, indeed, if one finds a monitor (guard) who will guarantee that an appointed monitor (guard) will do an assigned job well, how are we to know that the first monitor will do his or her job the way it should be done? Economists have been somewhat cavalier with the question, and, given how hard it is to answer, they are somewhat justified. They have usually assumed that the state should monitor property rights, competition and market behaviour, but have seldom asked who should or would monitor the state. Economics, indeed, has no worthwhile theory of politics.

I suspect that it is this fundamental question, lurking in the back of people's minds, which is the biggest impediment to an acceptance of the obvious fact that democratic politics is competitive. The idea of competition is, of course, intimately related to the notion that individuals pursue their own interest. If politics is competitive and driven by self-interest, who will monitor politics? To assume that politics is not competitive, or should not be, has been the classical way out of the problem. The assumption will not do and, indeed, has never done.

Historians report that when the Fathers of the Canadian federation met in Quebec City and in Charlottetown in 1864 and 1867, as well as when the Constitutional Convention met in Philadelphia in 1787, the debates on the division of powers in both cases took very little time. Agreement was reached almost immediately on the conviction that the proposals envisaged were reasonable, and that in any case, marginal changes in the division of powers could be achieved subsequently either formally, informally, or by judicial interpretation. The wisdom of both groups of Fathers has been vindicated by history.

What required much time and debate and was the source of intense bargaining in both cases was the Senate. To my knowledge, why things happened that way has not been considered, nor has an explanation been provided of why the structure of the Senate mattered so much to these wise men. The explanation, I wish to suggest, rests on the fact that senates play an absolutely central role in "monitoring" the vertical competition that exists in federations – the competition between the federal and provincial (state) governments. Because of that central role, it is desirable that senates be designed so as to guarantee that competition is as fair and as unbiased as possible. In my view, the Americans understood this,[18] whereas the Canadians did not; they were too British in their outlook to understand federalism and the role of a senate in that form of political organization.

The Senate acts as a "monitor" of vertical competition by injecting a provincial dimension in the central government. In a well-functioning federation, although it would always be an integral part of the central government, a senate would in some important sense be related to both orders of government. The Supreme Court was therefore right, and revealed a profound understanding of federalism, when it recently argued that the federal government could not alone, that is, without the provinces, change the basic structure of the Canadian Senate.

It is interesting to note, in passing, that the New Democratic Party as well as its predecessor, the Canadian Commonwealth Federation, have consistently favoured, not the reform of the Canadian Senate, but its abolition. One must also acknowledge that these parties – less so in recent years than in the past – have often been luke-warm *vis-à-vis* federalism as a way of organizing politics.[19] I find great logic in that position, and, to me at least, it confirms that in a federation, a senate has an important "monitoring" role to play. To the extent that federalism becomes absorbed in the interstices of NDP thought, I would expect that party to move from abolition to reform of the Senate.

A senate can only play a "monitoring" role if it has legitimacy, and, in our time, *that can be achieved only if it is popularly elected.* Comparisons with the House of Lords in the United Kingdom are beside the point. The United Kingdom is not a federation and therefore whether the House of Lords has legitimacy or not cannot be an impediment to a role of "monitor" of vertical competition.

However, legitimacy is not enough. If a senate is to inject a provincial dimension in the federal government and thus become capable of "monitoring" vertical competition efficiently, *the basis of representation must be provincial*, not regional, as is current practice. The persistent confusion between provinces and regions that one encounters in the literature and in public debates is a close cousin, I believe, to the notion that interests are communal. The size of provinces and the location of their frontiers are not "rational" in any real sense of that term, but they are there and they determine the jurisdictions of provincial governments.

There is a growing recognition in Canada that the basis of representation in the Senate should be provincial, but there seems to be no rationale underlying this developing awareness. Because the notion of provincial representation is not derived from a well-structured theory of federalism, but appears to be no more than a component of the current Zeitgeist, it could be as fleeting as all Zeitgeists. It is therefore important to know why provincial representation is better than regional representation.

The House of Commons is elected on the principle of popular representation: that is as it should be. But if the Senate is to "monitor" vertical competition efficiently, it must be elected on a different basis. *The best rule would be, as is the most common practice in other federations, to make all provinces equal.* Thus, each province could elect ten or twelve senators. The current practice is not only inefficient, it is perverse, since it gives more, considerably more, senators to the large regions (provinces), thus adding to the "competitive inequality" that is inherent in size differences, however measured. It is hard to imagine that the larger and more powerful provincial governments – Ontario and Quebec – would accept changes in the rules of the game that would oblige them to compete more fairly with Manitoba and Prince Edward Island; but without being an incurable dreamer, one can hope that the genuine sense of fairness that characterizes Canadians may, one day, induce these governments to adopt such a change.

The primary role of the Senate should *not*, therefore, be that of a "chamber of sober second thought", although it would continue to play that role. *Its primary role should be to give saliency to the provincial dimensions of public policies.* I stress that this is not essentially a representation role; it is a "monitoring" function. In other words, in the competition over resources and policies that takes place in the national government, it is imperative, if the competition is to be efficient, that provincial interests be competing with each other on an equal footing. It is not sufficient, to put it still differently, that provincial interests be represented appropriately in national debates. They must be able to vie with each other on a basis of "competitive equality"; otherwise the checks and balances that characterize national politics will be

biased against the weaker provinces, even if their points of view are represented. A capacity to compete is more than a capacity to talk; it is also, and radically, a capacity to exert a real influence on decisions. That is the real meaning underlying the notion of "monitored" competition.

To fulfill its "monitoring" role, the Senate should keep some distance from the House. This would be achieved *if the Senate was not elected on the same basis as the House.* I have already noted that the basis should be provincial and that equal representation of the provinces should be the objective. In addition, *it would be best if the Senate was elected on the basis of proportional representation, at fixed intervals and for fixed periods.* If these were the rules, the distance between the House and the Senate would be great enough to insure that the Senate could "monitor" vertical competition effectively. If the distance was any less, it would be too much a creature of the House of Commons to do effective "monitoring".

It has often been suggested that the Senate be given a six-month suspensive veto. That raises a difficult problem. A suspensive veto, it would seem, is not consistent with legitimacy acquired at the ballot box. Elected Senators are unlikely to be satisfied with a temporary delay, especially if the matter is a pressing one. At the same time, it is important to leave the matter of confidence in the Cabinet with the House. What should be done? I think that it would be best if the Senate was not given a suspensive veto. *Instead, a bill that was amended or defeated in the Senate should be passed anew by the House of Commons.* That would leave the ultimate power with the House, and would be conducive to bargaining between MPs and Senators. A suspensive veto does not encourage compromise.

The Senate is not the only national body that serves to "monitor" vertical competition. That is also done by the Supreme Court. It is that body which interprets the division of powers and determines the competitive behaviours which, from a legal point of view, are constitutional and those which are not. In the absence of an efficient Senate, the burden which must be carried by the Supreme Court, in its role of "monitor" of vertical competition, tends to be too heavy. However, the remedy for the problem is *not* to reform the Supreme Court, as some have proposed, but to reform the Senate.

III. Applications

A theory of competitive federalism, such as the one adumbrated in the foregoing pages, has great power not only in providing an integrative and unifying framework to matters which otherwise appear not to have any meaning and consequence, but also in making it possible, as I hope I have already shown, to address matters of institutional reform in other than a purely *ad hoc* fashion. That is true in respect of Senate reform, a matter that has provoked countless suggestions, not many of which, however, are anchored in a strong rationale related to the purpose or role of that body. That is also true for the institutions of Executive Federalism and for regional development policy, a subject to which I return below.

In the discussion that follows, I wish to demonstrate the power of the theory by applying it to sundry issues that have been raised in one locality or

another during the Royal Commission's hearings. These are usually matters on which there is considerable debate, that is, matters which are difficult to discuss because of the lack of a consistent framework of analysis. Applying the theory of competitive federalism to these questions and deriving the recommendations for reform which seem to follow from it will shed more light on the approach.

I will look at five questions which are "natural" questions for a theory of competitive federalism. Because neither time nor space allow an extensive and detailed treatment, I will only sketch the problems and point to the solutions. The reader will have to supplement the development with his or her own insights. I will examine the following five questions in the order indicated, although that order is not an index of significance or of saliency: 1) economic union; 2) intergovernmental grants, that is, equalization payments and established program financing; 3) Tax Collection Agreements; 4) the Charter of Rights and Freedoms; and 5) municipal governments.

1. Economic Union

Economic development policies, of which industrial and regional policies are a sub-set, now play an important role in the policy arsenal of every jurisdiction. Many times, of course, they are not called by that name; they may even be implemented as a part of other policies. For example, it has been said that industrial and regional considerations play a significant role in the defence and military expenditures of the United States government;[20] it is, in any case, a fact that the Pentagon publishes yearly a map which displays defence expenditures by congressional districts!

These economic development policies are, as I have already argued, the product of federalist competition, but in two different senses. First, some of these policies are responses by federal and provincial governments to opportunities created either by the demands of citizens or by comparative public entrepreneurial capacity. For simplicity, I will call these demand-supply development policies. Secondly, some policies are implemented, mostly by the federal government, but not inappropriately also by both orders of government acting together, to ameliorate the degree of "competitive equality" between the provinces of the federation in order that competition between them be more efficient and productive.

It is absolutely essential to keep the above distinction in mind in analysing industrial and regional policies, and, more generally, economic development policies. The distinction is a feature of federations which is absent from unitary states. In the latter, indeed, the only source of economic development policies is demand and supply considerations; the establishment of property rights aimed at making federalist competition efficient is, by definition, absent in these political structures.

Though it is important to distinguish between the two identified "sources" of development policies, it is also indispensable to keep in mind that they are not independent of each other. The relationship between them can be put in the following way: the more efficiently designed the economic development policies that serve to promote "competitive equality" and thus to "monitor"

federalist competition, the higher the benefit-cost ratio of development policies implemented in response to demand-supply considerations.

To see why that must be so, we must first identify the benefits and the costs of the development policies I have called demand-supply policies. The benefits are easily ascertained, at least for those who assume that when governments respond to what people want, they raise the well-being of these citizens.

The costs arise because economic development policies almost invariably create impediments or barriers to the free movement of goods, services (for example, the services of lawyers, nurses, etc.), labour, capital and entrepreneurship. These barriers – in the present discussion solely a by-product of responses to the demands of citizens – reduce the specialization that would otherwise be achieved in the use of scarce resources. It is these barriers that constitute the "economic union problem".

The affirmation made above that if the economic development policies designed to "monitor" federalist competition are efficient, the ratio of the benefits and costs just defined would be maximized, rests on the notion that federalist competition is a self-corrective mechanism. To put it differently, federalist competition, like all competition, if it is well "monitored", is efficient in the sense that it will economize on scarce resources in achieving the objectives willed by people. Indeed, efficient "monitoring" means, among other things, that costs imposed on others in the competitive pursuit of a target must be proportionate to the benefits obtained. In addition, self-correction or restraint is brought about by the fact that under efficiently "monitored" federalist competition, the benefits of economic development policies are closely related to their own costs.

If the above analysis is correct, it has one empirically testable implication: there should be more inefficient barriers to the free flow of resources in unitary than in federal states. In unitary states, indeed, the discipline of competition is much weaker, and the obligation to meet the preferences of citizens less constraining. I should insist that to test the proposition, one must focus on demand-supply development policies, and exclude from the analysis those policies implemented to make federalist competition efficient. It is not an easy proposition to test, but my own casual observation of both unitary and federal states supports the proposition.

In the Canadian context, "monitoring" is not as efficient as it could be, not only because the Senate does not interject the "proper" provincial dimension in federal institutions, but because Executive Federalism is too "encompassing", and because of other reasons, some of which have been noted above. Consequently, the economic development policies that should serve to improve "competitive equality" and to make federalist competition more productive are less than optimal; and the benefit-cost ratio associated with demand-supply policies is lower than it could be.

What should we do to correct that situation? The best solution is to reform the Senate and the institution of Executive Federalism along the lines recommended earlier, as well as implement other measures, such as those suggested in this supplementary view, that would make federalist competition more efficient. If this was done, the only other things that would be needed would be to implement the recommendations of the Commission's Report

pertaining to section 121 of the Constitution Act and those relating to interprovincial trade.

If significant institutional reforms cannot be achieved, then *as a second-best solution*, I support the Report's recommendation that a Federal-Provincial Commission on the Economic Union be established to implement a "Code of Economic Conduct" that would be a "monitor" of the economic union. My own version of the code, would, however, require that the distinction made above between what are in effect "framework" policies and demand-supply policies be entrenched and respected. The code would then be aimed at restricting the implementation of demand-supply development policies that have an "obviously low" benefit-cost ratio. The code should seek to achieve through administrative and bureaucratic means what, in a more ideal situation, would be the "automatic" outcome of the operations of Parliament, federal-provincial machinery, and federalist competition.

2. *Intergovernmental Grants*

All theories of intergovernmental grants reflect or are derived from some theory of federalism. That thought may seem obvious, but it bears repeating, because there are many theories of government grants which present themselves as independent of any conception of federalism. I do not have the time nor the space to demonstrate that point here; that will have to wait. It will be clear, however, that the theory of grants that follows is an integral part of the theory of competitive federalism. It does not rest on such intractable and pious notions as "Canadians are a sharing people" or "Canadians are compassionate"; it does not, in other words, derive firstly from notions of equity, because if equity was the basis for governmental grants, one would be led immediately to the view that transfers should be made to persons, not to governments.

I have already indicated that the role of government grants is the promotion of "competitive equality" between the provincial governments of the Canadian federation. The purpose of this section is to amplify this point. I consider equalization payments first, and then turn my attention to the financing of established programs.

I must repeat that in a federation, the competition that I have called horizontal takes place between the *governments of the federation*. Equalization payments are aimed at making that horizontal competition work more efficiently. That rationale is not inconsistent with section 36(2) of The Constitution Act, 1982 which says that equalization payments are made "to ensure that provincial governments have sufficient revenues to provide reasonably comparable levels of public services at reasonably comparable levels of taxation".

An efficient equalization formula redistributes tax revenues between provincial governments but, importantly, it does so according to certain (temporarily fixed) rules and thus acts as an "automatic monitor" of horizontal competition. Equalization payments, therefore, allow weaker provincial governments to "hold their own" *vis-à-vis* stronger ones in federalist competition; but also, they serve to deter any provincial government

from engaging in competitive actions that would be privately beneficial to itself, but socially inefficient and destructive.

Let me give an illustration of this last point. Suppose that a provincial government sought, through predatory behaviour, to attract the head offices of corporations to its province, so as to increase corporate profits in the province and hence revenues from that source. In the absence of an equalization formula (or of other "monitoring" devices), such action, even if destructive, could be profitable to the province. But an efficient equalization formula would produce a reduction in equalization payments to the province and would thus deter such predatory behaviour. It is clear that the deterrent should not be absolute; indeed, it should be incremental. It is also clear that an efficient equalization formula need not subject all provinces to the same marginal deterrence. The current formula, based on a five-province standard, is different in that respect from the older formula which was based on a ten-province standard, but it is not necessarily inferior to it. To come to a decision on the matter requires a judgement about the relative competitive ability of provincial governments.

Equalization payments do redistribute income but their primary rationale and their prime function is allocational. It is because of this allocational role that equalization receives the support of all provincial governments, those of the "have" and those of the "have-not" provinces. It is also because of the allocational function that equalization payments have to be unconditional; if they were not, they would suppress federalist competition.

In this regard, it is important to stress that an efficient equalization formula should "monitor" competition, not seek to eliminate it. Suppose, for example, that a provincial government, as a result of some fortuitous or deliberately sought event, benefits from a windfall revenue which would permit it to compete more effectively with other provinces for resources and people; should the equalization formula redistribute all of this windfall between the provincial governments and thus impede federalist competition? Certainly not. Such a provincial government is indeed in the same position as a firm which, following a favorable event, is able to expand its clientele at the expense of other firms.

Those who would suppress federalist competition in that way usually embrace a Benthamite notion of government, according to which governments act in the public interest because the public interest is their business, and because to be in public life is to be motivated by the public interest. When governments are assumed to always maximize social welfare functions, why have competition, indeed, why have governments in the first place?

I note in passing that the view of equalization grants advanced here is, broadly speaking, the one to be found in the *Report* of the Royal Commission on Dominion-Provincial Relations, commonly known as the Rowell-Sirois Report. It is true that that Commission's conception of federalist competition appears to be different from mine, at least on a first reading: it seems to be arguing that federalist competition is essentially destabilizing and destructive. That Commission's views reflect the analysis of the realities of interprovincial fiscal competition during the 1930s, as well as the prevalent idea of the period which viewed competition as generally inefficient even in markets.

The "monitoring" role of the federal government in the 1930s was by any reckoning quite limited. It is intriguing that Rowell-Sirois recommended the introduction of National Adjustment Grants (NAG), admittedly different from, but close in spirit to the present equalization grants which I argue make competition more productive. The Commission also recommended that the NAG be unconditional. The rationale for its recommendation, though shunning the language of competition, is so suffused with its spirit that it is worth quoting at length:

> *It should be made clear that while the adjustment grant proposed is designed to enable a province to provide adequate services (at the average Canadian standard) without excessive taxation (on the average Canadian basis) the freedom of action of a province is in no way impaired. If a province chooses to provide inferior services and impose lower taxation it is free to do so, or it may provide better services than the average if its people are willing to be taxed accordingly, or it may, for example, starve its roads and improve its education, or starve its education and improve its roads – exactly as it may do today. But no provincial government will be free from the pressure of the opinion of its own people and if, when it applies for an increased adjustment grant on the basis of need, it has to produce figures which indicate that although it might, without specially heavy taxation, have provided better education but did not do so, it has, of course, to justify this to its own voters.*[21]

But, given the *Zeitgeist* of the period, the Rowell-Sirois Report could not imagine that, even after the implementation of the NAG, the federal government would become a true "monitor" of horizontal federalist competition. For that reason, it proposed dealing with competition by re-assigning taxation and significant expenditure powers to the federal government. That was the solution adopted everywhere at that time. It rested on a confusion between competition and the mechanisms that insure its efficiency: property rights, trust, "monitoring", and so on – a confusion which still today is far from fully exorcised.

That notwithstanding, there is still something that we can learn from the Rowell-Sirois Report and from section 36(2) of the Constitution Act which reflects that Commission's view of NAG. To put it as simply as possible, the current equalization formula reflects only the revenue needs of provincial budgets. *Competitive equality would require a formula designed to reflect expenditure needs as well*, but only if the costs of incorporating the expenditure side in the equalization formula do not exceed the benefits.

Equalization grants are negotiated grants; the negotiating parties are the federal and provincial governments. Because these grants are aimed at improving "competitive equality" between the provinces, the role of the federal government cannot be symmetrical to that of the provinces, for if it was, the outcome of the negotiations could easily be more competitive inequality instead of more competitive equality. Indeed, a neutral role on the part of the federal government would eliminate the "monitoring" function that must be played by the central government. In some circumstances, it may even be necessary for the federal government to act unilaterally as it did a few years ago, that is, to forego all negotiations with the provinces.

The Established Program Financing agreements, as they currently exist, are of a class and kind that is altogether different from the equalization payments. Their intent and purpose is to limit and even to eliminate interprovincial competition in certain areas. Whether that is good or bad is not at issue here. (In fact, I support the recommendation of the Commission's Report that the mode of financing of education be changed with the aim of increasing interprovincial competition at the level of post-secondary education.)

But if, for any reason, the federal and provincial governments choose to restrict horizontal competition in certain domains, such as is presently done in health and education, *then the grants used for that purpose must be conditional grants*. The situation in which we currently find ourselves regarding this matter derives from the fact that the grants are unconditional. Unconditionality, in turn, is the product of a reliance on a theory of intergovernmental grants in which the decision makers are neither real governments, nor competitive.

The problem which unconditionality creates is analogous to a "free rider" problem. By agreement and by choice of financial instruments, federalist competition is suppressed in, let us say, post-secondary education. The device used to suppress competition is "national standards" or "minimum standards". Since competition is eliminated, unconditional money will not be spent in that area, but will tend toward areas where competition is greater. Consequently, "national standards" are not achieved, federalist competition is distorted, and federal-provincial relations soured.

3. Tax Collection Agreements

There are substantial real economies of scale in tax collection. It is not clear and certainly not known whether these economies persist over all the taxable units in the country. But it is not impossible that they do. There are therefore advantages, possibly large, to the Tax Collection Agreements whereby the federal government collects personal income taxes for all provincial governments (except that of Quebec), and also collects the corporation income tax (except for the governments of Alberta, Ontario and Quebec).

The economies of scale derive from many sources. Not unimportant among them are the following: the tax bases used by all parties must be defined in the same way and, secondly, though tax rates can differ, they cannot differ by much. The Tax Collection Agreements therefore serve as a way of reducing tax competition between the provinces and possibly between the provinces and the federal government. The economies of scale in tax collection are not, therefore, dissimilar to the economies of scale that would result if dress manufacturers were to sign a Fashion Standardization Agreement whereby dress styles and designs would be restricted and differences in them greatly limited.

The analogy is appropriate not only in illustrating how the Tax Collection Agreements restrict competition, but in indicating why so many tax experts think they are a good thing! It is, indeed, only recently – some thirty to forty years after the introduction of "monopolistic competition" as a model of

markets in which businesses compete with each other through the medium of fashion and product characteristics – that economists openly acknowledge that product differentiation may raise economic welfare instead of always reducing it.

The point can be put differently. There are often costs, in addition to advantages, in exploiting economies of scale. In the case under consideration – the Tax Collection Agreements – the benefits of standardized tax bases and (to some extent) rates are readily appreciated. The costs resulting from restriction of competition and over-standardized bases and rates are, however, no less real even if less direct and palpable.

The foregoing does not mean that tax collection agreements should not exist. But the advantages must be balanced against the costs. After study, it may be decided that collection agreements should bring together the provinces in three or four sub-sets in which the federal government would not be involved. The bulk of the economies of scale could thus be exploited and the benefits of tax competition reaped.

Whatever is done, it is well to stress that tax competition would not necessarily produce large differences in tax bases and rates. Indeed, to the extent that there are no differences in preferences of citizens and in technologies of production, competition would operate to eliminate differences in tax rates. However, if there are real differences, especially in the preferences of citizens, competition would guarantee that these are not forgotten. Since differences in preferences between provinces are not absolute (see Section II.8), there is a "natural" limit to the extent to which competition would lead to differences in tax bases and rates.

4. The Charter of Rights and Freedoms

Everybody who has made it into the twentieth century and who pronounces on the matter supports rights and freedoms. The issue, if there is one, is not there; it is instead with the notion of a charter that has constitutional strength. The argument is sometimes made that a charter of rights and freedoms encroaches on parliamentary supremacy by allowing the judicial branch of the Government to pass judgement on and to review matters that have been decided by Parliament (as well, of course, as on other matters).

The flavour of the argument that a charter of rights and freedoms is not congruent with parliamentarism resembles, in many ways, the one to the effect that federalism and parliamentarism are not congruent. In fact there is enough resemblance between the two lines of reasoning that one can venture the hypothesis that those who in 1981–82 opposed a charter for Canada, would in 1864–67 have opposed the formation of the Canadian federation.

However that may be, let me ask if a charter and parliamentary institutions really lack congruence. The answer suggested by the theory of competitive federalism is that a charter and parliamentarism are congruent, because a charter makes the whole political system more competitive. It does this by bringing the courts, more especially the Supreme Court, more effectively into the competition that characterizes the political process. First, it sharply increases the competition between the judiciary and the two other branches of

government — the executive and the legislative. That, by itself, is a major contribution of the Canadian Charter, for inevitably, over the longer term, the competition will tighten the democratic link between governments and citizens, by giving more importance to citizens, as citizens, in the political process. One implication of this is that the Charter will heighten the degree of competition between the public and the private sectors and to the extent that the latter responds, will truly raise the well-being of Canadians *by increasing market competition.*

It is important to note that the closer government-citizen link that the introduction of the courts in the political process will foster is not limited to the federal government, but will affect all the governments of the federation. To put it differently, the interests of citizens will, henceforth, not be met and served by eleven parliaments only, but also by the courts since citizens will be able to use the courts to be better served by parliaments. Through this second channel, the Charter of Rights and Freedoms will stimulate horizontal competition in the federation. This has already begun: through the courts, interests in one province are challenging rulings and laws in another. That can only serve the public good.

There is a third channel through which the Charter will affect the working of the political process, namely, by strengthening the ability of the Supreme Court to "monitor" vertical competition between the central and the provincial governments. This is achieved through the ability of governments at each level to appeal to the courts if they believe that decisions of governments at one level bias the workings of competition in an unfair and inefficient way. As I have already noted, that role of the courts, and again especially of the Supreme Court, is likely to be considerably larger than it should be unless the Senate is reformed in a way that introduces an effective provincial dimension in the federal Parliament.

The Supreme Court, of course, already "monitors" vertical competition. The reason why that role is likely to grow in the future derives from the fact that with the Charter, the pressure of citizens on their governments will increase and, consequently, governments will vie with each other more aggressively.

To the question of whether the Charter of Rights and Freedoms is a real third pillar of political institutions in Canada, congruent with parliamentarism and federalism, the answer must therefore be a resounding yes. The Charter, by bringing citizens more directly into the political process, increases the degree of competition in the system and, by making "elite accommodation" more difficult, will force the system to be more attentive to the preferences of all citizens.

5. Municipal Governments

Municipalities, as the saying goes, are creatures of provincial governments. This means that the government of a province can unilaterally alter the boundaries of municipal jurisdictions, alter the division of powers between itself and municipalities and overrule decisions made locally in all areas of policy. As time has passed, there has been a tendency for the provinces to

consider and to treat municipal governments in many important areas, as *de facto* administrative bodies. It is noteworthy that this has been going on at the same time that provincial politicians, in their dealings with the federal government, were arguing in favour of more decentralization.

Should municipalities be creatures of the provinces, or would Canadians be better off if municipalities were more autonomous decision-making bodies, thus more capable of reflecting the preferences of their citizens and of adjusting to local circumstances? In other words, would the allocation and distribution of resources be more efficient if the municipalities stood *vis-à-vis* the provinces more or less as the latter stand *vis-à-vis* the federal government?

The standard case against an entrenched division of powers between the provinces and the municipalities is that it would lead to a recapitulation at a lower level of the problems encountered at a higher level: on the one hand conflict, rancour and disharmony, and on the other, overlap and duplication. At this point, the reader will not be surprised if, in relation to the first point, I simply say that in my language that means competition, something which, if well "monitored", I hold to be beneficial. With respect to the second point, I simply note that duplication and overlap are, in practice, what competition implies, whether we have market or political competition in mind. The point is readily grasped in the context of competitive markets: how could they be competitive if only one firm supplied a particular product?

The above objection to an entrenched division of powers between provincial and municipal governments is based on a misconception of federalism. Another objection is more simple-minded: it is that provincial governments will be opposed to the idea and consequently that it has no chance of being implemented. The objection is simple-minded because it is obvious that the provinces will be opposed to the notion; no one likes competition when that competition is directed at him or her; no elite with power readily gives it up! One should therefore expect provincial officials to marshal all available arguments— including ridicule—against the idea that if municipal officials were given entrenched powers, the country would be better governed.

Canadians would be better served if municipalities had entrenched powers. Such entrenchments would be provincial-municipal matters. They would be different from province to province. In some cases, a provincial entrenchment law might state that (say) the division of powers between the two orders of government would require some direct participation of municipalities. In other cases, the entrenchment might be more limited, so that changes in the division of powers (say) would be legislated in the provincial legislature, but require a two-thirds majority to pass. Other forms are possible.

No entrenchment can be meaningful unless municipalities are provided with tax bases that can generate revenues capable of matching expenditures. There would, of course, still be "equalization grants" to help "monitor" horizontal intermunicipal competition, but the present total mismatch of revenues and expenditures would have to be corrected.

If one province chose to promote the well-being of its citizens by giving entrenched powers to its municipal governments, it should be aware that the problems that it would face would be no different from those that have to be

resolved in federalism as we now know it. In acting as "monitor" of the horizontal competition that would exist between the municipalities, it would have to face the issues of competitive equality, of the appropriability of benefits and costs of local decisions, and others like them. These are not trivial problems, nor are they problems that the highly competent officials now employed at each of the two levels of government – provincial and municipal – could not resolve, if they chose to.

When we come to the matter of "monitoring" vertical competition – that between the provinces and the municipalities – I would suggest that this could be more economically and more effectively done by the federal government than by any other body. That role could be fulfilled by a department, such as the now defunct Department of Urban Affairs, which would develop "municipality-building" policies. The reason for placing the responsibility with respect to vertical competition with the federal government is simply that municipal governments will compete not only with municipalities located in the same province, but with municipalities everywhere in the country. In view of that, it appears difficult to avoid the conclusion that however difficult such a role would be for the central government, no one else can substitute for it.

IV. Conclusion

In the Introduction to this document, I stated my conviction that the mechanisms that discipline democratic politics, especially in federations, are as constraining as the mechanisms that discipline economic behaviour. I trust that the discussion in the two preceding sections, which has outlined a theory of competitive federalism, has gone part of the way in showing that this conviction can be held rationally. I also believe that further developments of the theory of competitive federalism will reinforce the rational basis for such a conviction.

To conclude this already long document, I ask the following question: what does it mean to say that the mechanisms of democratic politics and those of economics are equally constraining? At its most simple, it means that there are, not one, but two broad arenas in which people seek to obtain the things which increase their well-being: markets and governments. Markets, when they are well-structured and competitive, do a good job over the longer term in allocating resources in ways that maximize the well-being of the population. That is a generally accepted proposition and one in which I strongly believe. What is less accepted, but an idea in which I nonetheless believe just as strongly, is that governments, when they are well-structured and competitive, do as good a job as markets, and like them over the longer term, allocate resources in ways that maximize the well-being of people.

I must therefore reject the *a priori* notion that markets are more efficient, more flexible, and more responsive to change than governments. In some circumstances and in the performance of certain tasks, that is certainly the case. However, unless one specifies the circumstances and the tasks – an undertaking which requires the use of comparable theories of politics and of economics as well as solid empirical comparative research – affirmations to

the effect that governments are less efficient, less flexible and less capable of responding to change than markets, add up to little less than propaganda.

If comparable[22] markets and governments do equally well, why not suppress one and give all the responsibilities and the kudos to the other? The reason is that they do not weigh the preferences of people in the same way and do not perform the same tasks equally well. There are some jobs which markets do better and others which governments are best at performing, although it is difficult, *a priori*, to sort them out. There is an enormous literature[23] devoted to that question, but it is not, on the whole, a very helpful one.

It is known,[24] however, that to solve this assignment problem on the basis of principles, one must contrast the relative efficiency of governments and markets in the performance of the tasks to be assigned. That is more easily said than done, because as just noted, comparisons must, at the very least, start with two theories, one of politics and one of economics. Furthermore, the two theories must have enough in common to make the comparisons possible and meaningful.

Conventional welfare economics – the most common theory used by economists to address the assignment problem – lacks a theory of politics; instead, it uses the assumption that governments seek the "common good".[25] It therefore "solves" the assignment problem by assumption. Indeed, if governments pursue the common good and if one can demonstrate "market failure", one must conclude that the tasks which markets fail to do perfectly should be assigned to the state. In recent years, a "reverse logic" has been used to generate the opposite conclusion. In that case, the assumption is made that markets always allocate resources efficiently. It then suffices to demonstrate "government failure" to argue that those tasks which governments fail to do perfectly should be assigned to markets.

That reverse logic model also solves the assignment problem by assumption. Why? First, because the work on market "imperfections" – on the increasing returns to scale of many technological processes, on the declining marginal revenue of many business enterprises, on the often less than arm's length relationship in transfer pricing, on the incidence of tie-in sales, on the presence of entry deterring strategies by oligopolists, on the downward stickiness of many prices (including, of course, the price of labour), on price fixing arrangements, on racial, gender and other forms of discrimination, and on other market imperfections – is not usually brought to bear on the matter. Second, because that model also lacks a theory of politics; it demonstrates "government failure" by reference to market mechanisms alone.

The search for a solution to the assignment problem based on first principles is probably beneficial, although that is not certain. My own view of how modern societies work is that the assignment question is "resolved" through competition between governmental and market institutions and that that competition, in turn, is shaped and conditioned by the demands of the public and by the supply of entrepreneurial talent to each sector. Consequently, a growing government sector reflects first the fact that people want not only the things governments supply better, but also those things which governments provide differently than markets, and second, the fact that more

aggressive and talented entrepreneurs have found their way in that sector. A declining government sector reflects opposite tendencies. If I am allowed a conjecture, I would suggest that a number of things which are done by governments in Canada could have been done privately, if private sector entrepreneurs had been more imaginative and more aggressive. In that sense, the success of business lobbies in preventing the implementation of an effective competition policy has contributed to the growth of the public sector in Canada.

However that may be, if markets and governments are two competing arenas for meeting the preferences, objectives and desires of people, it is no longer possible to hold to the view, so dear to those who adhere to a Benthamite notion of politics, that all taxes, regulations, subsidies and other forms of intervention by public bodies always cause "distortions".

The notion of distortion is not an easy one to work with. Consider the simplest possible case, that is the case of an economy made up of perfectly competitive neo-classical markets in which the cost of a unit of resources allocated to any use – producing goods and services, moving them around, informing people of their quality, etc. – is exactly equal to the social value of that unit of resources. In such an economy, there are no distortions by construction. The presence of monopolies, pollution, sticky prices, and of taxes, quotas, subsidies, regulations and other public interventions *may*, by introducing a wedge between private and social valuations of resources, create distortions. But they may not. If we acknowledge that governments can influence monopolies, pollution, regulations and taxes, it is essential to know why interventions take place before calling them distortions. It would indeed be a perversion of language to put the name distortion on a deliberately sought policy objective.

An illustration may help. Suppose that the population of a jurisdiction unanimously agrees to ask its government to levy a tax on alcoholic beverages, because, assuming that these are harmful to health, it believes that people could not resist the temptation of drinking more if prices were lower. If the government levies the demanded tax, it would simply be wrong to say that the tax is a distortion; it is an efficient instrument used in the pursuit of a particular objective, which it is hardly the business of analysts or observers to approve or condemn.

The situation would be different if the demand for the tax was not unanimous. Those who found themselves in the minority, unlike the others, would face a distortive tax. It is, therefore, impossible to know if public intervention is distortive or not without a theory of politics. Given that fact, declarations to the effect that the tax system should be neutral, that industrial policy should mimic the market, or that Crown corporations should be privatized, unless they are grounded both in economics and politics, may cause serious distortions, if ever implemented, by preventing the political system from doing its job effectively.

I have run out of time and space and so rest my case. I hope that the theory of competitive federalism which I have suggested above, both as a model of what actually goes on in the Canadian political arena and as a guide to institutional reform, serves as a useful clarification and extension of the

discussion of these matters in the Commission's Report and that it helps nourish the public debates which that Report will stimulate.

Notes

1. To these two pillars, a third, in the form of a Charter of Rights and Freedoms, has been added in 1982. I will consider its implications in Section III.
2. J.A. Schumpeter, *Capitalism, Socialism and Democracy* (New York: Harper and Row, 1942, 1975) pp. 84–85.
3. Mainline neo-classical theory is a very large building. There are consequently almost always some more or less obscure rooms in it in which little-talked-about subjects are being worked at. Work on research and development, on innovation and invention, on technical change, and even on the economics of entrepreneurship has been carried out by someone or other at all times. Much of this will surely be re-interpreted and given new life in the light of the recent re-discovery of entrepreneurial competition.
4. I. Kirzner, *Competition and Entrepreneurship* (Chicago: University of Chicago Press, 1973).
5. J.K. Galbraith, *American Capitalism, The Concept of Countervailing Power* (Boston: Houghton Mifflin, Sentry edition, 1962).
6. R.R. Nelson and S.G. Winter, "Simulation of Schumpeterian Competition", *American Economic Review* (February, 1977).
7. D.V. Smiley, *Canada in Question: Federalism in the Eighties*, (Third Edition, Toronto: McGraw-Hill, Ryerson, 1980) p. 91.
8. A research paper done for the Commission also uses that model. See J.A. Brander, "Economic Policy Formation in a Federal State: A Game Theoretic Approach" (1984). Brander rationalizes the use of the prisoner's dilemma model on the basis of what he calls the "public interest" approach to politics. But it is essentially a "collectivist" or "organicist" assumption. See below.
9. R.D. Luce and H. Raiffa, *Games and Decisions* (New York: John Wiley and Sons, 1957), pp. 95. Italics added.
10. J.H. Dales, *Pollution, Property, and Prices* (Toronto: University of Toronto Press, 1968) pp. 58-59. Italics in the original.
11. There is no good word to identify that activity or the role of "monitor". I use this word because it seems to me to be the most neutral. I would take any acceptable synonym as a substitute.
12. *De jure* concurrency is often inevitable. Such cases have led to the development of doctrines such as that of "paramountcy" that help settle the accountability issue.
13. The reader, if he or she desires, can form an impression (but no more) of how I would address the question by referring to A. Breton and A. Scott, *The Economic Constitution of Federal States* (Toronto: University of Toronto Press, 1978) which is largely concerned with that matter, but in a different framework of analysis.
14. Earlier, in condemning the use of the prisoner's dilemma model as a model of federalism, I noted that it was this very same assumption which had led to its adoption. From the point of view of classical political science doctrine, the assumption derives from "organicist", as contrasted to "non-organicist" or "personalist" approaches to behaviour. The lure of organicist assumptions, even on the best minds, is always somewhat of a puzzle to me.
15. A. Hamilton, J. Jay and J. Madison, *The Federalist* (New York: The Modern Library, 1787, 1937).

16. It is possible that the life expectancy of "incumbents" is also increasing in the marketplace.

17. Juvenal's question is: "For who will guard the guards themselves?". Among the more important contemporary students of the question are J. Rawls, *A Theory of Justice*, (Cambridge: Belknap Press, 1971), R. Nozick, *Anarchy, State, and Utopia*, (New York: Basic Books, 1974), and J.M. Buchanan, *The Limits of Liberty: Between Anarchy and Leviathan* (Chicago: University of Chicago Press, 1975).

18. The Americans did not understand that role for the Senate perfectly. They designed a Senate to which Senators were appointed by the States. That proved to be a disaster. Their present elected Senate, giving equal weight to all the states, is as close to the ideal as one can hope to come in designing an efficient "monitor" of vertical competition.

19. A classic exposition of that view is F.R. Scott, "Social Planning and Canadian Federalism" in M. Oliver, ed., *Social Purpose for Canada* (Toronto: University of Toronto Press, 1961). The resistance to federalism is, in effect, a traditional feature of democratic socialism. That case is nowhere better put than in H.J. Laski, "The Obsolescence of Federalism" in A.N. Christensen and E.M. Kirkpatrick, ed., *The People, Politics and Politicians* (New York: Holt, 1941).

20. R.B. Reich, "An Industrial Policy of the Right" *The Public Interest* (fall, 1983).

21. Canada, *Report of the Royal Commission on Dominion-Provincial Relations* (Ottawa: King's Printer, 1940) Book II, p. 84.

22. The kind of problems raised by Mancur Olson in his *The Rise and Decline of Nations* (New Haven: Yale University Press, 1982) can affect markets and governments equally. For that reason, they are neglected in the following discussion. It would be easy to incorporate them in the analysis.

23. I have in mind the literature of welfare economics. At one time, that literature even served as a basis for the formulation of a theory of government. See W.J. Baumol, *Welfare Economics and the Theory of the State* (Cambridge: Harvard University Press, 2nd Edition, 1969).

24. See, for example, G.S. Becker, "Competition and Democracy", *The Journal of Law and Economics* (October 1958).

25. In modern welfare economics, governments are assumed to be maximizing a social welfare function. The "common good" is then defined by choosing a particular degree for the elasticity of substitution among the utilities of persons in society.

E. Gérard Docquier

Preamble

With a view towards contributing to the debate over the economic future of Canada, I wish to submit for the public record a statement on the parts of the Final Report of the Royal Commission on the Economic Union and Development Prospects for Canada with which I dissent.

There are at least four areas with which I cannot agree – some in total and some in part. These are: the lack of a serious effort to eliminate unemployment; the advocacy of U.S.-Canada bilateral free trade; proposals to roll back the Unemployment Insurance Program; and some recommendations on labour-managment relations.

My most fundamental disagreement with the Final Report is over unemployment. Unemployment is the single most important question facing Canadians today. It affects not only how much wealth there is to be distributed amongst society's members, it also reflects itself in the tragic unravelling of our social fabric. The unemployed are not statistics to be manipulated on charts and graphs – they are human beings with faces and personalities with a right to live in dignity, a right they are deprived of today. In this way the Commission has failed the people of Canada.

A Commissioner's Personal Account

In 1982, I was asked to serve on the Royal Commission on the Economic Union and Development Prospects for Canada. Canadians were living through the worst recession since the 1930s. My union, the United Steelworkers of America, the largest private sector union in this country, had 205 000 members in 1979. By mid-1982, that number had dropped to 128 000. I could put names and faces to many of those numbers. The devastation of the recession led me into homes where I found fear, pleas for help, and often-times hunger. I felt at first hand, as an immigrant, as a worker, and as a Quebecer, the personal costs associated with the destruction of our social fabric. Thousands of miners lost their jobs. Permanently. Dozens upon dozens of plants locked their doors. Permanently. Hundreds of thousands were thrown into the streets, losing their jobs and often-times their homes. Families were torn apart. By mid-1982, thousands had exhausted their unemployment insurance benefits. Many of the people I knew and represented were thrown onto the welfare roles. Many lost the means to feed and to house their children.

Canadians have experienced dramatic changes in technological, economic, political and social conditions that have recognizably altered the world in which we live. These changes have been no less fundamental than the Industrial Revolution of the last century. When the Commission was established, there was a need to devote time and resources to finding out what Canadians thought of these changes and how we should respond to achieve the future we wanted.

Canadians have been victimized by a recession over which we have had no control and to which we can see no end. We have undergone a progression of

emotions that have ranged from fear and insecurity to anger, and from loss of dignity and humiliation to despair. Our fears have been heightened by watching the rest of the world go through the same agony. We are not alone. We are all helpless. Soup kitchens, food lines, and unions of the unemployed have become daily reminders of the vulnerability of Canadians to severe structural change. And still, permanent jobs are disappearing. Our country, one of the richest in the world, seems incapable of stabilizing the economic and social environment. The human hemorrhage continues.

I was haunted by these concerns because I knew that the changes we were experiencing were more than just the result of a short-term recession. I felt a great deal of uneasiness about participating in such a process. The Canadian Labour Congress and the Government of Canada were at odds on almost every issue that faced the working people of Canada. There was virtually no dialogue on the major issues that confronted the main participants in our society. Nevertheless, I felt that the Commission's mandate was broad enough to encompass the views of those Canadians who are never asked what they think of our economic problems. Their voice needed to be heard in shaping the solutions to our problems. I came to the conclusion that it would be unthinkable not to have the labour movement represented on the Commission. I talked to many people whose advice I respect, first, within my union and, second, within the labour movement. Having received the full support of my membership, and the endorsement of the Canadian Labour Congress, I agreed to sit as a Commissioner.

In many ways, the experiences that have shaped me differ from those that have shaped the rest of the Commissioners with whom I have travelled across this vast country during two complete rounds of hearings. The majority of us, however, did have one thing in common – our concern was for the future, for what the country might become in the 21st century. We may have had differences of opinion, but we all had a sincere and deeply-held respect for the Canadian people.

Statement on the Final Report

Not long after the start of our mandate, it became clear that the work of the Commission would be separated into two tracks. While the Commissioners concerned themselves with the day-to-day experiences of Canadians, the staff of the Commission embarked upon a research program that was noticeably divorced from the realities expressed by those who appeared before us. For the most part, this theoretical research was based on assumptions which I do not support.

The research has exposed for me two views that have been treated as a new orthodoxy: "self-reliance" and "market forces" became the constant litany. I resist the casual adoption of this language because it does not match our reality. This new economic orthodoxy assumes that: we are overly dependent; most unemployment is voluntary; we lack initiative; and that government spending is out of control. Yet, we are the people who work in Faro, on Little Cornwallis Island, in Hibernia and in James Bay. We are the people who

have developed the Canadarm. We are the people who gained the attention and respect of the world for the odyssey of one-legged runners.

The Final Report of the Commission states: "We have not come up with a single, simple, compelling message." I clearly heard a single, simple, compelling message: "*Canadians want to work.*" While the Report includes rhetoric about the priority of jobs, its research program and recommendations do not reflect a commitment to a full employment economy – a job for everyone who wants one. *Our number one objective is jobs.*

The mandate of the Royal Commission on the Economic Union and Development Prospects for Canada was to report and to recommend to Canadians on their economic future. Instead, it has produced a Report more preoccupied with our past. In many fundamental ways, the Commission's Report has done a great disservice to those Canadians who have shaped our nation. The economic philosophy of the Report is expressed in its Introduction:

> *We seek a new relationship between the political system and the economy and society within which incentives will induce the making of choices compatible with social goals.*

I disagree fundamentally with this principle. Our social goals are clear. They have not changed. Indeed they should not change. Canadians want to work. *Our goal is to create jobs for those that have been deprived of employment.* At the same time, we want to take care of those amongst us who are incapable of caring for themselves. We have long accepted the moral and ethical responsibility to protect those least able to fend for themselves. This is the legacy of the Canadian experience. Our commitment is to full employment and to social justice.

The major concern in the current political environment should be to allocate our financial resources for the attainment of these social goals. *The task of economic management should serve social development.* The biggest single problem which threatens to retard both our economic and our social development is unemployment.

The continuous stream of lay-offs, plant closures and production cutbacks have caused unemployment to increase dramatically. From August 1981 to December 1982, total official unemployment reached 12.9 per cent. The official unemployment rate has been above 10 per cent since May of 1982, and by March of 1985 it remained at 11.2 per cent. When hidden unemployment and underemployment are added, the real level of unemployment is much higher. In March of 1985, Statistics Canada's *Supplementary Survey* showed that at least 270 000 men and women have given up looking for work. They are no longer counted as officially unemployed. Since 1982, approximately 700 000 full-time, permanent jobs have disappeared. Our younger workers, those under the age of 25, are particularly hard hit. By March of 1985, the official jobless rate for our sons and daughters had soared to 17.5 per cent. More than 300 000 jobs have disappeared for this age group alone.

We cannot speak of growth or recovery in an economy where so many of those for whom we have responsibility continue to be jobless. In this society,

our self-worth is still largely defined by a job. What will happen to a society where 35-year olds will hold a job for the first time? What will happen to their work habits? What will happen to our work ethic? What will happen to an economy whose spending habits are not driven by the formation of new family units, of productive employees and consumers? How many of we older Canadians will continue to stay in the job market to support our 30-year-old children? Can the word "growth" ever become a positive word to a generation that has no work? How many of us have looked into the eyes of our sons and daughters, our nieces and nephews, our grandchildren, and asked, "What will become of this lost generation?" How can we have a future if we waste it now in joblessness and despair?

For those of us who live in daily contact with the unemployed, the pressures of not being able to affect change have become intolerable. The growth that has been generated by our economy during the last three years is *jobless growth*.

From 1981 to 1983, unemployment has added one million more "new poor" to the ranks of poverty. Poverty is not a rural, regional or "those too lazy to work" problem. Poverty exists from one end of this country to the other. There were 967 000 poor families in 1983 and the majority of those, 557 000, lived in large cities. In poor families, more than one million of our children are being denied a decent upbringing.

Families headed by women have a far higher likelihood of being poor than families headed by men, and the numbers are growing. Of the total number of families headed by women under 65 years of age in 1983, more than 50 per cent were living in poverty, compared to 11 per cent for families headed by men. Close to one-third of all poor families are headed by single-parent women.

To be elderly, a woman and living alone also means to be poor in Canada. Almost 60 per cent of unattached women over 65 years of age are in that desperate situation. It's not much better for men – poverty has claimed 48 per cent of all elderly unattached males. There are 2 500 000 recipients of Old Age Security in Canada. In 1983, 1 500 000 had incomes below $9000.

Poverty includes men and women of all ages, farmers and fishermen, the sick and the disabled, and the unemployed. Contrary to popular belief – large numbers of the "working poor" are men and women with jobs who don't earn enough to escape poverty.

In 1982, well over one-half of the heads of poor families worked, and nearly two-thirds of all poor families had at least one wage-earner. The problem was that they could not get full-time jobs with a decent salary. I am convinced that the only protection these men and women have is the minimum wage law. I fundamentally disagree with the view of the Commission's Report that such laws are simply "rigidities" and insignificant to improving the lot for the working poor.

By February of this year, total employment was back to slightly above the August 1981 level. However, the number of full-time jobs was still 150 000 below the August 1981 level. Permanent full-time jobs have been replaced by part-time jobs of unknown duration and low pay.

In the goods producing industries, close to 500 000 jobs were lost and only 200 000 have been regained. There are still 300 000 fewer jobs in goods producing industries than there were in August 1981.

For youth, there has been no recovery of the jobs lost. By March 1985, employment for workers under 25 years of age was still 300 000 lower than in August of 1981. The youth unemployment rate is 17.5 per cent.

The growth in joblessness of the last two years has occurred despite the strong growth in exports – which grew in volume by nearly 9 per cent in 1983 and by a dramatic 22 per cent in 1984. However, the domestic economy continues to be weak. *Greatly increased trade has not increased our levels of employment.*

I can speak personally of this failure by referring to the changes in composition of the Steelworkers' membership. The changes over the last half decade reveal fundamental structural upheavals. The mining sector, particularly base metals and coal, were among the hardest hit. There has been no recovery. (See Table 1.)

TABLE 1 Mining Membership 1980–84

Sector	Percentage Change
Iron mining	– 47.7
Copper	– 42.8
Silver	– 39.5
Nickel	– 44.7
Coal	– 33.1

The Canadian steel industry has also undergone significant work force loss. (See Table 2.)

TABLE 2 Steel Industry Membership 1980–84

Sector	Percentage Change
Basic steel and rolling mills	– 22.9
Steel wire and nails	– 23.6
Pipe and tube	– 19.2
Structural fabricators	– 31.2

There have also been important membership losses in the metal fabricating sector which consumes the production of the steel industry. (See Table 3.)

Several factors have led to these changes. The recession, new sources of foreign competition for traditional industries, and technological change are all moving us toward a more service-oriented economy. These changes are

TABLE 3 Metal Fabricating Membership 1980–84

Sector	Percentage Change
Iron foundries	– 42.0
Steel foundries	– 48.0
Hand tools	– 40.0
Farm equipment	– 53.7

eroding the traditional wage and job structure upon which our patterns of consumption, social opportunity and support have been built. The "middle class", as we have known it, is in danger of disappearing. Incomes are becoming more polarized. We will have even more poor, and more rich, with less and less in between.

In absolute numbers, our Union's membership has gradually returned to 160 000 individuals – the level of the late 1960s. But our new members have come largely from the lower wage service sector. New groups we have organized include security guards, restaurant and rest home workers.

How does the Commission see these problems being resolved? It has adopted a simplistic belief in "free trade" with the United States and with the rest of our trading partners. *This will not solve our unemployment problems.* The last few years have proven it. Nor will we be lifted out of our current and future problems by "getting the incentives right" and relying on the invisible hand of the market.

Real business investment in plant and equipment fell 9 per cent in 1982 and declined by a further 12 per cent in 1983, levelling off in 1984. By the end of last year it was over 20 per cent below the peak reached during the second quarter of 1981. At the same time, tax incentives to corporations, which by 1980 had reduced the federal corporate tax rate to 15 per cent of profits from 36 per cent, have had little effect on stimulating investment and creating growth over the last three years. In the 1950s, corporations paid 58 per cent of federal income taxes while individuals paid 42 per cent. In the 1970s and 1980s, *corporations had their share of federal taxes reduced to under 30 per cent. The share paid by individual taxpayers rose to over 70 per cent. Businesses need customers, not tax incentives.* As long as our industries can satisfy demand for products by operating at three-quarters of capacity, there is no need to expand, to invest or to create jobs.

Tax incentives have not encouraged or resulted in more jobs. For some, tax incentives may have become good politics, but they are not good economics. Indeed, it is this tax structure that is the underlying reason for the problem of underfunding experienced by governments today. Manipulating Canadians' behaviour through the tax system has not been successful. Many of the social objectives that the tax system was designed to achieve have not materialized and the revenue-raising capacity of the tax system has been seriously eroded. I see two reasons for this: slow economic growth and the unfairness of the tax system. The well-advised or the wealthy pay far less than their fair share. Major changes to the tax system are a necessity. Tax reform should begin

with the introduction of a minimum tax on high income earners. It is unacceptable to think that in order to have more economic growth we have to create more inequality.

I do not believe that we are over-governed and that the key to renewed growth and prosperity lies in a federal administration that will abandon Canadians to the whims of the market. Among the most forward-looking sections of the Report are those covering social support and human services.

The Report recognizes that:

> *Since the overall level of social policy expenditures in Canada is low by OECD standards, there is no strong general case for attacking the deficit by reducing social expenditures.*

The recommendations propose a package of changes to our income security programs. The Report endorses a guaranteed annual income in the form of a Universal Income Security Program (UISP) as the most appropriate foundation for Canada's income security programs. I welcome this initiative as both a step in the direction of social justice, and a recognition of the importance of social support to our economic vitality.

The Transitional Adjustment Assistance Program (TAAP) would provide adjustment assistance for Canadians who have exhausted their unemployment insurance benefits. Through this program it would also be possible to assist workers to purchase equity in plants, or invest in other forms of community economic development projects. I do not agree with the proposal that funding for the program should be drawn from "savings" from the Unemployment Insurance program.

The proposed Unemployment Insurance "reforms" represent a reduction of benefit levels, and an increase in the qualifying period. This amounts to an outright attack on the unemployed. The victims should not be punished for their plight. The way to reduce the costs of unemployment insurance is to create jobs.

Furthermore, the packaging of the above proposals does not distinguish between income support programs and insurance programs.

Further, the Report identifies occupational health and safety as an area of importance and growing concern. The recommendation calls for:

> *The federal and provincial governments to immediately consider the development of a comprehensive social insurance disability plan to deal with the longer-term effects of occupational health problems, as well as with other forms of disability in the working age population. This plan could be implemented either by expanding worker's compensation into a comprehensive disability scheme or by extending the present disability provision of the Canada and Quebec Pension Plans.*

This too is welcomed as it has long since passed that the needs of the disabled in Canada, regardless of cause of disability, have been met.

With respect to occupational training, increased attention is paid to encouraging on-the-job and job-related training. The recommendations call for a special wage subsidy for labour-force entrants who have not had other forms of vocational training or post-secondary education. In addition, the

recommendation is made to provide for a Registered Educational Leave Savings Plan. I disagree with this proposal and would opt instead for a levy-grant system on employers.

Recognizing that our children are the ones who must shape our future, access to higher education for low-income students becomes an area of special concern. The educational system is being starved through lack of funding. Deregulation of the fees structure is no solution.

I agree with the general recommendations on labour-management relations; however, I do so for different reasons and without endorsing all of the findings and comments. Collective bargaining plays a critical role in the distribution of income in this country. It determines, both directly and indirectly, the income of the vast majority of Canadians. I must express reservations about some of the Quality of Working Life experiments that have taken place. Furthermore, I reject the proposal of gain-sharing as a substitute for negotiated wage increases.

The Commission recommends that:

Labour relations boards be permitted to create multi-employer and multi-union bargaining units when this is likely to facilitate the bargaining process.

Our voice was heard in shaping these solutions.

The Report is obsessed with Canada's "competitiveness". There is no doubt that we should strive for economic efficiency. If competitiveness were our only goal, corporations would probably pay no taxes, we would ignore the environmental impact of economic activity and we would abolish social security. None of these objectives are acceptable to Canadians.

The drive for "competitiveness" almost always is an attack on wage levels. The competitive game is a game we cannot win. Someone, somewhere in the world, with enough starvation or repression, will underbid us. It is neither necessary nor desirable to encourage mindless wage-bashing.

The Report describes, sometimes eloquently, the growing phenomenon of global economic interdependence. Interdependence has the potential for developing international solidarity, co-operation and peace. I support the general description of the global environment in the Report, including its human, environmental, economic and political aspects. The danger of workers being pitted against other workers has been dramatically increased as a result of recent monetary and fiscal policies. Canadians have been placed in the position of destructive competition for shares of low-growth markets, made worse by global attacks on current wage levels. These conditions now threaten to destroy the international system of trade and finance established after the Second World War. This system is badly in need of reform. It is especially true, if it is to continue to encourage and assist the development of the countries of the Third World. The collapse of this system would be disastrous. Some of these sentiments are expressed in the Report and I wish to affirm them.

I disagree with the Report on the Third World debt problem. The Third World debt problem has not been resolved. Furthermore, it places insurmountable pressures on fragile economies when they are expected to repay

their debts both in the time periods and on the terms being dictated to them. The debt issue is not resolved and the problem will not go away. It also makes other problems worse. Third World producers are dumping goods on the world market as they desperately try to earn foreign currency to pay off interest and debt re-scheduling payments which have continued to mount. This undermines prices and intensifies the global wage squeeze, which in turn generates more and more protectionist pressures, so that the system is brought to the verge of collapse.

The Report makes much of the recent developments in U.S.-Canadian trade. Our increasing dependence on U.S. trade, however, should be seen as a sign of weakness and trouble in our economy, not as a major opportunity for growth. Trade with the Americans must continue. Furthermore, Canada can indeed be seriously harmed by some of the protectionist proposals being put forth in the United States Congress. *An even greater reliance on that imbalanced relationship in the form of a comprehensive Free Trade Agreement is, however, dangerous.* First of all, the current situation is highly artificial. The acceleration of exports to the U.S. in recent years is the combined outcome of a highly over-valued U.S. dollar and continued high real rates of interest in Canada. The spread in interest rates today is as high as it was in August of 1981 when the rate was 23 per cent. As the Americans turn to correct their huge trade deficit, Canada will not escape Congressional notice. Canada is second only to Japan in terms of a trade surplus, and even higher by total volume. The Report recommends addressing this by negotiation of a free trade agreement with the United States. I believe that free trade does not represent a solution to our economic problems. I believe in negotiated trade between nations, within the framework of multilateral agreements. *Unrestricted free trade with the Americans is a blind and imprudent act*, described by some as a necessary leap of faith. Negotiated, secure access to U.S. markets is something I support. However, the terms for access to Canadian markets must include production and employment guarantees, such as were secured in the Auto Pact, and since then embodied in Canadian-content regulations. These are included in the option of "managed trade" which I favour, but which the Report explicitly rejects.

There is an alternative to the free trade option and that is promotion of import substitution and a direct role for government in an industrial strategy. This does not have to mean that a bureaucrat in Ottawa picks the country's economic winners and losers. The Commission recommends free trade as a solution to unemployment and growth. The research work extensively and repeatedly claims that there will be an increase in income and employment as the result of free trade. What all the studies and computer simulations cannot tell us is when these presumed benefits are to flow and to whom:

> *[. . .] in the long run, Canada would benefit substantially from bilateral free trade with the United States, particularly from access to the expanded, unrestricted market and from economies of scale.*

The surge in exports in the last two years has not solved our unemployment problem. Whatever gains may result will be diffuse and longer term, while the

pain is immediate and specific. A Camco Steelworker laid off in London asks: what is my future, where is my next job, and what support systems are available to my family?

On stabilization policy and unemployment, the fundamental problem identified by the Report is a highly abstract academic construct called the "NAIRU" (non-accelerating inflation rate of unemployment). This in plain English, is to say that there is a new "natural" rate of unemployent of 6.5–8.0 per cent. *Anything below 6.5 per cent is regarded as voluntary unemployment.* Canadians do not accept this. The unemployment rate of a society is a social and political choice; there is nothing natural about it. The current rate of unemployment of 11.2 per cent is unacceptable to all Canadians. Suggesting that approximately 1 000 000 men and women, 8 per cent of the work force, are "voluntarily" unemployed is ridiculous. Recommending that 1 000 000 Canadians should resign themselves to an unemployed existence is criminal. Endorsement of the NAIRU concept in the Report relegates Canadians to a twenty-first century of underdevelopment.

Finally, as for the Commission's discussions of constitutional matters and its recommendations in this area, I cannot associate myself with its views, nor will I comment on them. Matters in the constitutional arena are in too much of a state of flux in Quebec at this moment in our history to enable me to make any reflections that are of lasting value. Until the Quebec debate over the Constitution is more clearly defined I shall withhold comment.

Lament for a Lost Opportunity

The research work of the Commission and the Final Report have provided the people of Canada and the Government of Canada with no better understanding of the problem or its solutions. Original research on the causes of our unemployment was not undertaken. As a result of its argumentation, the Report leads its uncritical readers to the conclusion that unemployment is not the major problem facing Canadians today, or even if it was, that there is nothing that government can do to resolve it.

Unemployment *is* the major problem facing Canadians today. The gap between the "haves" and the "have-nots" has continued to widen. The recession and the joblessness of many of us has accelerated the process of adding to the ranks of the poor.

The work of the Commission has fallen short of fulfilling its mandate. Many of the serious problems facing the next generation of Canadians remain unanswered or inadequately addressed. The "single, simple, compelling message" expressed by Canadians is reflected in the Papal Encyclical *Laborem Exercens*:

> *Human work is* a key, *probably* the essential key, *to the whole social question. . . .*

The Report has endorsed market based fantasies as a solution to our nearly two million unemployed. Instead, I advocate the continued responsibility of government to manage the economic environment and to encourage new forms of popular participation in public institutions.

John R. Messer

Economic man is an imperfect fiction created by economists. He does not exist as a whole person in real life.

Nor are nations born, nurtured and built as strictly economic entities. Left to economic determinism, it is not likely that Canada would exist today as a relatively independent, sovereign state. The north-south economic advantage would have prevailed, the tenuous east-west ties would have collapsed, and the history of Canada would have been much shorter. That this did not happen was the result of the exercise of political will – of the competition between political and social objectives on the one hand, with economic objectives on the other.

We live very much in a *political* economy; and I, for one, would have it no other way. It is in this context that I record a supplemental view to the Commission's Report. While there are appropriate references to the political role, the Report embraces the currently fashionable economic nostrum which judges market determinations as "good" and government interventions as "bad". In some cases I support the particular judgement. But I do not accept the general proposition that "the best government is the least government".

On this point, I find the arguments of my fellow Commissioner, Dr. Albert Breton, persuasive. I quote from his statement:

> *. . . what does it mean to say that the mechanisms of democratic politics and those of economics are equally constraining? At its most simple, it means that there are, not one, but two broad arenas in which people seek to obtain the things which increase their well-being: markets and governments. Markets, when they are well-structured and competitive, do a good job over the longer term in allocating resources in ways that maximize the well-being of the population. That is a generally accepted proposition and one in which I strongly believe. What is less accepted, but an idea in which I nonetheless believe just as strongly, is that governments, when they are well structured and competitive, do as good a job as markets, and like them over the longer term, allocate resources in ways that maximize the well-being of people.*

With respect to the relationship between the two sectors and the division of roles, Dr. Breton says this:

> *My own view of how modern societies work is that the assignment question is "resolved" through competition between governmental and market institutions and that that competition, in turn, is shaped and conditioned by the demands of the public and by the supply of entrepreneurial talent to each sector. Consequently, a growing government sector reflects first the fact that people want not only the things governments supply better, but also those things which governments provide differently than markets, and second, the fact that more aggressive and talented entrepreneurs have found their way in that sector. A declining government sector reflects opposite tendencies.*

On the whole, Canada has been an economy of markets and governments. Governments have actively intervened in the transportation, resource development, energy and agriculture sectors over time. While every

intervention has not always had positive results, we are, in my view, the better economy and the better country on balance.

I would go further. Whatever may be said for the market as the determinant of economic efficiencies, it is a singularly insensitive instrument in measuring social consequences. Not only is it appropriate for government to arbitrate those consequences; to do so is a prime political responsibility. And if, in exercising this responsibility, a government deems it advisable to curb the "freedom" of the market, that too is appropriate. Thus, I find myself at odds with some of the basic underpinnings of the Commission's Report. In no section do I feel more strongly about this than the one which discusses agriculture.

The Family Farm

I find the most logical focus for discussing the agricultural sector to be the primary unit of agricultural production – the family farm. Certainly one must examine markets and marketing, transportation and grain handling, research and development, land use, import replacement and other economic components. But the agricultural sector is more than simply the production, distribution and marketing of food products. As a society, we have a substantial investment in a particular mode of agricultural production: the individually-owned and operated family farm. Unless we are prepared to sacrifice that investment, it behooves us to examine our agricultural and economic policies as they affect the family farm.

There are those that imply that this focus is pure sentimentality. Not true. All that space between Canada's major population centres is not a vacuum. Much of it is filled with farm families and small communities which serve farmers and farm production. When we talk about preserving the family farm, we're talking about preserving jobs, communities, and all the infrastructure of schools, hospitals, power, roads and other services. We are talking about the Wheat Pools, of course, which have served Prairie farmers with such distinction over the past half century. But we are also talking about community co-operatives and credit unions, and small business people, such as farm machinery dealers and other entrepreneurs, who are important participants in the small farming communities across Canada. This is the family farm economy.

It is true that agriculture, in the national context, has shrunk in importance over time relative to other industries. But to say this overlooks its regional importance. In Saskatchewan, which I know best, agriculture is not only the king-pin of the economy, its family-farm base is the core of our way of life for urban as well as rural people. Of course, the family farm is no more a static entity than any other part of our economy. It has changed, and it will change, in response to economic and technological forces. But through all the changes of the past, and with all the changes in farm size, the basic nature of the production unit remains.

For these reasons, I find the discussion of the family farm in the Commission's Report both confused and out of touch with reality. Although

many of the economic problems farmers face are the subject of comment, most are dismissed as cyclical problems which farmers have faced before. The question of growing farm size and an accelerated reduction in the number of farmers is disposed of as an economic necessity. I disagree with this view.

To take the Saskatchewan example, a myriad of public programs, federal and provincial, were put in place between 1946 and the present to assist family farmers to be more productive and to reduce costs. They have included the rapid extension of rural power, an improved road network, improved access to credit, farm machinery testing, tax relief, and the Land Bank, to cite only a few. These and other actions, of course, did not halt the process of farm consolidation and the reduction of the farm labour force. But they were public policy responses which improved farm viability and made the adjustment process less damaging to individuals and the community. I would argue, they also slowed the pace and severity of farm consolidation.

If the market is allowed to take its course in current circumstances, the wrong farmers will be lost. The most vulnerable farmers today are not the inefficient, the marginal, the bad managers. They are the young farmers who acquired their land and machinery at high prices, but who are among the most innovative and productive farm managers to be found. If the Report has its way, we would say, "Hands off, market forces are the best arbiter." Then we would lose some of our most productive farmers. True, efficiency will not be served.

The Commission's Report also fails to consider the alternative costs to society of moving, resettling, retraining and finding productive employment for the displaced farmer. Or, alternatively, the social and economic costs of swelling the ranks of the unemployed. Particularly in times like the present, these costs are high indeed.

The Commission's Report also appears to endorse accelerated urbanization. The costs of rural depopulation are not addressed, except to reject the idea that there are any special attributes associated with rural life. But surely these costs are real: in lost employment, lost investment, underutilized infrastructure, and resettlement costs. I would have a difficult time in my native province in dismissing these costs as unsubstantial.

The family farm is in greater jeopardy today than many believe it to be. The recession, present economic trends, high interest rates, the rising cost of inputs and lower product prices have all depressed the farm economy. The natural hazards, regional drought, flooding and pests, have added an additional squeeze. The resulting decline in farm land values has brought many farmers – particularly young and able farmers who entered the industry at the wrong time – close to insolvency.

That many of these events are cyclical, as the Report points out, makes them no less real for the farmers concerned. That the generic family farm has survived down-cycles in the past is also true, but irrelevant. I reject the conclusion that these are persuasive reasons to suggest that governments should simply permit survival to be determined by market forces. Public policy responses to assist with interest rates, loan restructuring and working capital requirements for many of these farmers are both appropriate and necessary.

With respect to the longer term development of the agricultural sector and the family farm, I find myself in full agreement with the Commission's recommendation for greatly expanded research and development. I will comment later on some specific areas which hold promise for the family farm of the future.

I would like now to turn to the Commission Report's discussion of some key areas of agricultural policy which will help shape agricultural production in the future: marketing arrangements, transportation and grain handling, and prices and input costs.

Marketing

The individual farmer and the individual consumer fit well into the classic model of the free market. They each have minimal market power, compete freely with other producers/consumers in selling/buying food products. Unfortunately, other participants in the market fit less well. In transportation, processing and retailing, for example, those standing between the producer and consumer tend to dominate the market.

The historical fact is that the individual agricultural producer in Canada has had virtually no power in the market place. Left exposed, his cash receipts have been the residual sum remaining after processors, commission agents and retailers have taken their share of the end price. It was only through intervention, either through collective action of producers or through public action, that farmers have been able to gain even modest market power. The modesty of that power is clearly demonstrated by the fact that domestic food consumers in Canada enjoy the second lowest food costs, as a percentage of income, in the world. Only in the United States, blessed with a more favourable climate and a much more competitive food processing and retailing environment, do consumers fare better.

Producer marketing boards are a target of the Commission's Report. My argument with the Report is with both what is said and what is not said (or not said clearly enough). The Report correctly distinguishes between institutions which simply provide marketing muscle and expertise for producers of a particular product (for example, the Canadian Wheat Board) and those which, in addition, manage the supply of the product through quotas and other means. Yet, having done so, the Report by implication damns all marketing boards.

What troubles me in the discussions of supply-management marketing boards is the assumption that the other actors in food marketing – processors, wholesalers and retailers – do not engage in practices which affect supply and price. Let me cite two contrary examples in my home province of Saskatchewan.

Saskatoon and Regina are very similar food markets, in both size and location. Yet for several years, the price of a basket of groceries in Regina has consistently cost 10 to 12 per cent more than an identical basket in Saskatoon. The reason: the Regina market is dominated by a single large retailer, while two are battling to dominate Saskatoon. This no doubt benefits Saskatoon consumers in the short run, but when the chains sort out their

market share in Saskatoon – as they will – one can be sure that retail margins will rise to or above the Regina level. And because they will have eliminated some of their independent competitors, their market shares will be larger.

In another example, Weston and McGavin recently engaged in a price war in Saskatchewan which saw the price of bread drop below the cost of production. It is doubtful that Weston and McGavin were fighting each other, but rather were attempting to gain market share by forcing independent bakers out of the market.

The point is that these exercises in market power are designed to reduce, not enhance, competition. Furthermore, they demonstrate the power which the independent producer of, say, eggs, milk or poultry faces in marketing his product.

If it is supply management *per se* which the Report finds objectionable, why is there no criticism of supply management which is exercised, not through government intervention but through market domination? The drive to control supply, and therefore maximize prices and profits, is ever-present in our economy. One needs only look at the big three auto manufacturers. If there are too many cars, prices do not fall appreciably; production is cut back.

Similar examples in the food industry are not unknown. One can manage supply in two ways: create a government marketing board which can act on behalf of a number of small firms producing to quota, or reduce the number of firms so that in concert or by tacit agreement they can accomplish the same thing. The latter can happen and does happen. And one device which makes it easier to accomplish is vertical integration.

Having said that, I agree that there are some problems with supply management by boards as currently practiced. Among these, the capitalization of quotas is a major problem. Nevertheless, I cannot agree that all these marketing boards should be scrapped. I support the maintenance of Canadian production, both nationally and regionally. I support the equal opportunity of producers to access markets. I reject the idea that any insurance scheme could provide a satisfactory alternative.

In the larger sense, I find wholly unacceptable the implicit assumption in the Report that managing price and/or supply through economic power in the market place is entirely acceptable (whatever the effect on the consumer), whereas public intervention to provide some balance of market power for the farmer is not.

Grain Handling and Transportation

In its discussion of the Canadian response to export opportunities for grains (essentially, wheat), the Commission's Report deals with three main issues:

- The development and production of varieties other than hard, red spring wheat which will make Canada more competitive in changing world markets
- Inefficiencies in the country elevator system and the associated grain transportation system
- The resolution of the compensation issue pursuant to the abandonment of the Crow rate.

I support the Commission's view with respect to the first; I have reservations and disagreement about the apparent conclusions with respect to the second and the third.

The country elevator system as it has evolved is certainly not above criticism. I share the view that the technology exists which could reduce the historical shrinkage charge to farmers. It should be applied. There may well be changes in the grading system which could improve the efficiency of grain storage and movement.

But the Commission's Report stops there, without comment on the efficiency of railways in serving the country elevator system and the grain producers. The assumption appears to be that the *movement* of grain from shipping point to export position – now that the railways are to receive compensatory rates – will be highly efficient. How is that assumption to be tested? Grain producers and the elevator system have no transport options in Western Canada. There are no inter-modal alternatives. They are captive to a single transportation mode and to two giant, non-competitive rail companies.

Furthermore, one important thrust of these companies in improving their corporate efficiency in grain transport is to *shift* some of their costs onto others. Clearly, their *corporate* efficiency – and the visible costs of the rail transport of grain – will be improved if they move grain from larger, mainline terminals instead of dispersed country elevators.

But, surely, any useful analysis of the system must include *all* the costs, whether borne by the railways directly, or by governments, communities and producers in the form of larger farm trucks, road building and maintenance, fuel, employment, rural community decline, etc.

The Report's broad conclusion that "there is much room for reorganization of the entire system" may be true. But the sketchy and selective evidence considered, combined with the absence of a comprehensive analysis of benefits and costs, robs it of significance.

The failure to consider the key monopoly role of the railways in the system carries over to the Report's consideration of the Crow rate compensation issue. The elimination of the Crow Rate in its present form represents an abrogation of a fundamental historical concession, which farmers had received in return for the costs imposed on them by the other features of the National Policy. If this circumstance is not to be reversed, then the problem is to manage the decision so that the grain producers, and not others, reap the benefits to which they are entitled. That was the deal. And how those benefits are paid is crucial to fulfilling the deal.

The Commisson's view is that freight rates should be fully compensatory. The economic argument as it relates to the primary producer is that this is the only way to remove market distortions which are disadvantageous to livestock production and processing in the Prairies. I will deal with that argument in a moment. First let me deal with one potential result of the Commission's proposal which is totally ignored in the Report: the imposition of grain freight rates which vary on a cost-per-mile basis, or variable freight rates.

If we turn over to the railways the determination of rates, there will be no brake on the railways' ability to reshape the country elevator system and the system of rural communities of which it is a vital part. By offering lower per-

mile rates from mainline points – as the CNR is already proposing – the process will be underway, and the shifting of costs will begin. If this reshaping of Western society is to occur, it should be a conscious decision by the people most directly concerned on the farms and in the communities of Western Canada – based on an assessment of *all* the costs – and not left to "market" determination managed by the railways. One great advantage of the statutory Crow rate was that it was neutral in its impact on shipping points except as to distance from export position. This equity cannot be preserved except through performance guarantees attached to compensatory payments by government to the railways, leaving the basic rate structure in position.

The main argument advanced in the Report for full compensatory freight rates – the distortion in location of livestock processing – I find unpersuasive. To give this argument credence, one must assume that:

- There are economic advantages to the producer to be derived from a major shift in the structure of prairie agriculture from grain into livestock.
- There is a market in North America and the world capable of absorbing a substantial increase in red-meat production.

The Report presents no evidence to support either of these assumptions. A study prepared for The Prairie Pools by Arcus Consulting Ltd., however, casts serious doubt on both. Arcus was asked to project, among other things, the impact on the livestock industry of the adoption of a "pay the producers" formula. Among Arcus' key conclusions were the following:

> *Increased livestock output (in Western Canada) is projected under the inelastic domestic grain demand scenario. . . The effect of this increase is a small net gain in livestock gross revenues in Western Canada. . . primarily from changes in the chicken and pork sectors. . . offset in part by a decline in gross revenues of beef producers in the prairie area.*
>
> *Livestock producers in the rest of Canada would suffer a decline in gross revenues in this situation.*

The Prairie Pools conclude that, because of the structure of the North American meat packing industry, it is doubtful there would be greatly increased slaughtering in Western Canada or, indeed, anywhere in Canada.

Citing Agriculture Canada figures, Roy Atkinson pointed out in his submission to the Commission that "beef consumption – on a per capita basis – on the North American continent is now some 20 per cent lower than it was only six or seven years ago." (Roy Atkinson, Brief, November 28, 1983, p.11.)

It is my own conclusion that substantial shifts to greater production and slaughtering of livestock in Western Canada simply would not occur in the short or medium term, and they would not occur at all unless totally unforeseen new markets were found.

Farm Prices and Input Costs

The relationship between farm prices and input costs, currently central to the survival of many family farms, has not received adequate treatment in my

view. The facts are, of course, that over time farm prices have been much more cyclical than input costs; that the rising trend lines in input costs has been much steeper than has the trend line in farm prices. When farmers feel and say the problem is getting worse, they are right. The problem is *both* cyclical and secular.

There are perhaps three appropriate responses, one of which is identified in the Commission's Report. Farmers must become even more efficient, changing farm practices, continuing to adopt new technologies, all underpinned by substantial increases in research and development.

A second necessary response, particularly in the short run, is government intervention to reduce current input costs. The costs of fuel, fertilizers, herbicides and operating capital are the most critical. On the Prairies, at least, reductions in the price of farm fuels and lower interest rates for operating loans would seem to be the most practical measures for governments to adopt.

A third possible, if less desirable, response would be government action to support prices. For export commodities like grain, there are many attendant problems in addition to the required expenditure of public funds. But, while I do not recommend this course of action at this time, I would point out that the United States has been heavily involved in support payments to grain farmers for many years, and the European Economic Community even more so. These are our competitors in grain export.

The Commission's Report considers stabilization programs only as a possible substitute for marketing boards, which they are not. A number of stabilization programs are in place in Canada, for example, federally for grain farmers, and in some provinces for pork producers. They are important in the context of dealing with the volatility of prices and production in agriculture, not because they add significant new resources, but because they help even out cash flow. They should be improved and extended to producers of other agricultural products on a federal or federally-approved basis for provinces to administer.

Access to Capital and Intergenerational Land Transfer

The Commission's Report is correct in its conclusion that farmers are disadvantaged in their access to capital under terms appropriate to the risks and variability of cash flow typical of the farm enterprise. It recommends, without being specific, the retention of special credit schemes for agriculture. Presumably this means the Farm Credit Corporation, since the Report suggests that programs such as the Saskatchewan Farm Purchase Program and Ontario's Beginning Farmer Assistance Program have not been effective. No evidence to support the latter judgement is presented.

What is missing here, in light of the current pressures on farmers, is any reference to the need for the restructuring of debt, particularly for those young farmers who entered the industry or expanded at the height of land prices. No special credit programs currently in place fill this need. Nor can

we expect it to be filled by commercial credit institutions. Again, I would argue, this is a role for government which is both appropriate and necessary. Action is urgently needed.

On the question of intergenerational land transfer, the Report recognizes the problem, but again, is non-specific in its recommendations. I would place much greater emphasis on the problem than the Report appears to do, particularly because it compounds the already severe capital accumulation problems of a highly capital-intensive industry. To recapitalize the land resource every generation is a very costly and increasingly unworkable way to provide for the retirement of the older generation.

Yet the impetus for farmers to look to land accumulation as the way to provide for retirement is very strong. Existing alternatives are few. The Canada Pension Plan is inadequate, both because of its level and because many farmers would fail to qualify for maximum contributions every year. Retirement Savings Plans look less attractive than land to most farmers because, historically, the appreciation in land values has provided a more attractive return. Nevertheless, better solutions should be sought. The Land Bank alternative, despite the controversy surrounding it, has much to commend it. Perhaps in time it will become more acceptable to the farm community.

I would like to see other, more innovative approaches explored. For example, why not a government-sponsored contributory retirement plan for farmers similar to that available to many employees in the private and public sectors? It would need to be flexible to relate contributions to the variability of farm income. It would need to be locked in to ensure its application to retirement. It would require some measure of matching contributions from government to make it attractive. But, if successful, it could lessen appreciably the farmer's felt need to accumulate land as his only retirement security. This would lessen the pressure on land prices when farm incomes are high. It would permit more flexible arrangements for land transfer on retirement, which could improve the chances of the son or daughter or other young farmer taking over. It would make a direct contribution to maintaining the viability of the family farm.

On these two issues – access to capital and intergenerational land transfer – I agree with most of what the Report says. It simply does not say enough.

The Family Farm of the Future

I have attempted to make a two-part case: first, that any analysis of the Canadian agriculture sector must be sensitive to the continuity of its family-farm base on both economic and social grounds; and, second, that the continuity of the family farm and its rural community base will require much stronger government participation and presence than the Report calls for.

This participation and presence is crucial, whether one looks at maintaining and improving the resource base, developing the needed research and development capability, increasing export opportunities, making marketing

agencies more effective (with or without supply management), providing more and better income stabilization programs, or dealing with other cyclical problems which create periodic crises in agriculture.

Given the needed public policy responses, the family farm of the future can make an even greater contribution to higher productivity in agriculture and to rural social and economic development than it has in the past.

In the process, the family farm will assuredly change, and the transition will not always be easy or simple. But those changes will include:

- greater emphasis on the management of the farm enterprise, inluding widespread adoption of management technology
- higher capitalization (although not necessarily in land)
- a more intensified use of the land base
- greater diversification (although not necessarily on individual farm units).

There will be no single model for the family farm in the future, any more than there has been in the past. The nature of the land resource, changing demand, marketing opportunities and other factors will continue to shape individual enterprises. Increasingly, however, entrepeneurship will determine who prospers and who does not. Management skills, informed risk-taking, the adoption of new technology, and adaptation to changing conditions will be key factors.

As more intense cropping practices are adopted (for example, continuous cropping), and as a greater variety of product options becomes feasible through research and market development, the push toward ever greater land accumulation will diminish in many farming areas. Already a number of farmers in the grain belt have concluded that their present land base is sufficient. This trend will become stronger. New techniques and more intensified land use will, however, increase capital requirements, and the availability of debt capital on terms appropriate to the nature of the farm enterprise will continue to be a central need.

Diversification will become much more sophisticated than the traditional mixed-farm model. It is likely to involve greater variety in crops on the one hand, and greater diversity among specialized enterprises on the other. Livestock production in the form of the traditional cow-calf enterprise is likely to give way to more specialized activities geared closely to markets.

There will be fewer farm units, but the pace of consolidation will slow. Rural communities will continue to change, but many will survive and some will grow. And the basic rural social system will continue to serve the farmers and their families in an evolving fashion.

This vision, and all it implies, can be reality if policy-makers in Canada frame their agricultural policies, not on a narrow economic analysis and a commitment to "free market" solution, but on a holistic analysis of social and economic benefits and costs. If they do, the agricultural sector will continue to lead the others in productivity. If they do, the Canadian economy will perform better. If they do, Canada will be a better place for all of us.

Laurent Picard

Acknowledgements

Readers will note that I have borrowed heavily from Bruce Scott's chapter in *U.S. Competitiveness in the World Economy*, edited by Bruce Scott and George C. Lodge. The same is true of *The Japanese Industrial System* by Charles I. Macmillan, by far the best and most comprehensive treatment of the Japanese industrial system that I have read. Victor C. Clarke, former Vice-President, Corporate Planning and Development, Canadian General Electric, and Professor Morty Yalovsky of McGill's Faculty of Management will recognize their substantial contribution. I was also very impressed by the paper written for this Commission by Professor Richard Harris of Queen's University, Department of Economics. The errors and misrepresentations are obviously mine.

* * *

Mr. Tomès. Sir, we have reasoned upon your daughter's distemper; and my opinion, as for my part, is that it proceeds from a great heat of blood: so I'd have you bleed her as soon as you can.

Mr. Des Fonandrès. And I say that her distemper is a putrefaction of humours, occasioned by too great a repletion, therefore I'd have you give her an emetic.

Mr. Tomès. I maintain that an emetic will kill her.

Mr. Des Fonandrès. And I, that bleeding will be the death of her.

Mr. Tomès. It belongs to you indeed to set up for a skilful man!

Mr. Des Fonandrès. Yes it does belong to me; and I'll cope with you in all kinds of learning.

Mr. Tomès. Do you remember the man you killed a few days ago?

Mr. Des Fonandrès. Do you remember the lady you sent into the other world three days since.

Mr. Tomès. (To Sganarelle) I have told you my opinion.

Mr. Des Fonandrès. (To Sganarelle) I have told you my thoughts.

Mr. Tomès. If you don't bleed* your daughter out of hand, she is a dead woman.

Mr. Des Fonandrès. If you do bleed her, she'll not be alive a quarter of an hour hence.

Excerpts from *Love's the Best Doctor*, a comedy by Molière. Act II, Scene IV. *Molière's Comedies*, vol. 2 (J.M. Dent & Sons Ltd., London, 1929) pp.63-64.

* * *

*Read: Cut the deficit.

This is not a minority report, but a supplementary note. With the give and take usually common in trying to develop a consensual position, I totally

support the recommendations of this Report. But given the very broad mandate of this Commission, it was impossible in the main text to express or review some processes of analysis that were too specific. I have decided to write these brief notes on the process of strategy formulation because I was somewhat disturbed by the way the problem of an industrial policy is generally stated and debated publicly.

I believe that the way the debate on that question has developed in the past four years is often futile and dysfunctional. It is too often stated in terms of extreme positions, one being taken by the non-interventionists and the other one by the "picking winners and losers" theorist. This debate, which started in the U.S. a few years ago, has really created an almost irrelevant and misleading forum. I think this has some implications for the interpretation of the recommendations of this Commission concerning an industrial policy for Canada, recommendations which I have already said that I support wholeheartedly. Hence, I should like to comment on the process of that public debate and to initiate what appears to me a necessary review of the structure of the debate itself.

I have divided my notes into four main parts: first, a review of the polarization of the debate on industrial strategy and its misleading consequences; secondly, an overview of the concept of strategy, particularly related to some misconceptions concerning what a strategy is all about; thirdly, a review of the Japanese, the NIC and the near-NIC national strategies; and finally what all this means for Canada.

It all started with a feeling of *déjà vu*. At the very beginning of the public audience-symposium-colloquium process of this Commission and right through to the end, the problem of the Canadian industrial policy has been described in an extremely polarized fashion. One side, which could be described as a Keynesian perspective of what the role of the state should be, was opposed to the Adam Smith view. One can look at it in terms of intervention versus non-intervention or in different terms: that is, in terms of the market as a regulating mechanism as opposed to the government as a regulating mechanism. These positions have been described as if they were opposed, conflictual, contradictory and totally polarized.

The crunch really came for me when, at a symposium in a Canadian university, an economist described his view that the redistribution of income was an inefficient way of managing an economy, and that basically, for every dollar raised through taxation and redistributed, the efficiency was somewhere between 65 per cent and maybe 35 per cent. (I don't remember the exact figure.) This means that of every dollar raised and redistributed, only 35 cents to 65 cents were really efficient; the rest was lost in the cost of distribution.

If that was the case, and given the fact that Western industrialized countries, and specifically Canada, have long since made the decision for redistribution of income so as to attain some degree of equity and fairness, then, I thought, the question became not a question of distribution or no distribution, but more specifically, of studying the process and the mechanics of redistribution of income so as to improve their efficiency.

If the real cost of redistribution is 45 cents or 55 cents or 65 cents per dollar, I thought, maybe there is a way of improving that by 10 per cent, 15 per cent, or 40 per cent. And, I naïvely asked the economist who made the point: "Could you elaborate on that and explain to me how you measure the efficiency of redistribution, and on what basis you come up with figures of that level?" The answer came very fast: "Adam Smith has said all of that 200 years ago." Surely the question was naïve, but the answer was obviously brutally simplistic and ideological.

Despite my obvious lack of training in economics, or maybe thanks to it, it struck me very early in the process of the debate that these were not useful ways of analysing and developing a national strategy. It appeared to me that no more than you can critically evaluate the validity of Euclid, Lobachevsky or Riemann geometries, by staying inside the structure of any of these geometries, you cannot resolve the problem of developing a strategy by staying inside an interventionist or non-interventionist, Keynesian or Smithian theory. These might be useful abstractions to help clarify decision, but one would need something like a metaeconomics science to critically evaluate their usefulness in a given context in the same way that we have to work at the level of a metageometry to review critically and use each geometry in a useful fashion. The debate about the validity of the different geometries raged fifty or sixty years ago, and one philosophy professor told me very simply and very candidly that his unassailable position was that the Euclidian geometry was more perfect than the others because geometry deals with the continuum, and the Euclidian continuum is more homogenous than the Riemann or the Lobachevsky continuum. If Einstein had agreed with that philosopher's view, the theory of relativity would be a museum piece, or maybe it would not exist at all.

All through that debate, as I said, I had that feeling of *déjà vu*. I was wondering "Why? What is the origin of that feeling?" when I suddenly remembered a time long ago, when I was very much interested in the history of Europe and France at the end of the nineteenth century. After the Napoleonic wars, the students and military academics in France debated for thirty years the different merits of the offensive and defensive approach in war, based on the Napoleonic campaigns, and the debate raged with one school of thought claiming that the defensive was the best approach, and another school of thought replying that the offensive was the best defensive.

During that time, the Prussian generals were also laboriously studying the Napoleonic campaigns and were developing a strategy similar to the 1805 strategy of Ulm in the Austerlitz campaign, when Napoleon, scarcely firing a gun, defeated the Austrian army of General Mack. The Prussians developed the Moltke strategy, which they used to encircle and defeat the French army at Sedan in 1870, giving the *coup de grâce* to the Second Empire, without a major battle. I understand that some people still consider this particular debate in the French military academies to be of an extremely high and stimulating intellectual quality. *But what is the bottom line*?

That was the feeling of *déjà vu* that I had when I was hearing the ideological debate raging about the role of the market or the role of the state

in developing national strategies. Let me say that ideology or theory are bad advisors in a strategic situation.

There was a parallel debate on the question of whether economics was dependent on political science, as a superseding doctrine, or sociology, or the other way around, but I have always found these discussions fruitless and futile. To develop a national strategy, one has to keep in mind the economic, social, technological, and political dimensions, not one of them superseding the other, but all throwing different lights at different angles on a unique object.

The game, then, is competitiveness, and so let me say a few words about strategy. First of all – and it should be so well known that I wonder why it should be repeated, but it obviously has not been integrated into the thinking of many people who talked to us about strategy – a strategy has a global purpose; *in any implementation of a strategy there are bound to be tactical mistakes.*[1] I have heard it said about the Japanese that they have made a number of mistakes. Their investment in steel twenty years ago is considered a mistake, and that mistake "obviously" disqualified any attempt to develop a national strategy. Even if that was the case, and I pretend that it is not, this would not in any way weaken the role of a strategy in the economic development of Japan.[2]

As I have said, the strategy of Japan, what we could call the "targeting strategy" of Japan, has been an incredible success. To say that some part of it has been a "flop" is not an indication that the strategy itself is not good. One has to look only at the result of the development of the Japanese economy in the last twenty years to see that surely something was done right.

What was the strategy of Japan, broadly defined?

First of all, after the war, Japan became involved in soft industry sectors like textiles and in a lot of cheap imitations. As this approach succeeded, in a second phase the Japanese moved into the heavy-industry sector, investing in shipbuilding, steel, aluminum, cars, etc. As this strategy became very successful also, they moved to a third sector which is the high-technology, high-income/sensitive, high-value/added sector viewed in a global context of international trade. Up to now, therefore, there have been three phases in that strategy.[3]

I need not give details on the results: it is obvious to anybody who reads the newspapers or the economic magazines that this strategy was an incredible success and even one threatening to the Western world. In the development of its strategy, as Japan moved from one phase to the other, it tended to decentralize to other countries, by subcontracting and by making external investments, some elements of the previous phase of its strategy. For instance, as the Japanese were moving into the heavy-industry sector, they started to decentralize towards the NICs part of their light-manufacturing industry. Now, as they move towards high technology, they have been investing in and supporting shipbuilding in Korea, Hong Kong, Singapore, and other areas. Moreover, as these nations are moving into heavy industry, they have started the process of investment and decentralization towards the near-NICs to export the first phase of their industrial development.

This strategy of targeting has been highly successful for Japan, and though it is too early to say, it seems that it is showing substantial success for the Group of Four. Why? Let me use a metaphor to explain. A corporation organized along a divisional structure can have and manage an integrated strategy across its organization, despite the heavy competition among divisions that usually exists in a successful corporation.[4] On the contrary, in a conglomerate, the basic strategy needs to be developed by each of its parts. The divisions or the parts of the conglomerate are so different and so autonomous that each one needs to develop its own strategy, and the strategy of the whole is, in part, derived from the strategies of the parts. To apply that metaphor, Japan is like a divisional organization. It has a homogeneous population, a highly homogeneous and cohesive system of values, an authoritarian political structure, and on top of these, a language and an insular mentality which protects it from the Western world's marketing invasions. It has also developed a deep dedication to the export markets, based on the fear generated by its lack of natural resources, and it enjoys a very large domestic market; these are also elements in its success. This gives the Japanese the chance, despite, or thanks to, the very tough competition existing among industries and among companies, to develop an integrated strategy, managed through a complex structure of consensus development, and to use targeting most successfully.

To define the last phase of their strategy, that is the high-technology, high-income sensitive development that they started 15 years ago, the Japanese did exactly what any firm does: they carried out global market research to find what the growth areas were.[5] The Japanese did this in terms of the global system, that is, in terms of the interdependence and the internationalization of markets; and they chose as a domain to target the income-sensitive product or, in other words, the product for which demand increases strongly with the increase in the global standard of living. That has been their strategy and in that they have been very successful. It is also the strategy that most successful firms follow if the environment permits.

What does this means for Canada and its industrial policy?

I have indicated why it was possible to develop a very coherent strategy of targeting in Japan. That is not possible in the same way in the United States and Canada because of the social, political and legal contexts. The different institutions and the different governments are too autonomous to hope to use a divisional model for developing a strategy. The metaphor applying to Canada and the United States is much more that of the "conglomerate". And a strategy which is possible for Japan or somewhat similar nations like Korea, Singapore or Hong Kong is not a strategy available *in the same way* to Canadians or Americans. Moreover, Canada lacks a very large market to start with.

Consequently, the strategy of choosing "winners" or "losers" or, to express it more accurately, the strategy of targeting, which is available as a strategy for Japan, is not available in the same way for a Canadian or an American political system. We have to find something else.

Because the strategies available to countries like Japan are not applicable *in the same way* in a Canadian or North American context, the temptation

has been for many to deny that one of the reasons for Japanese success is their implementation of explicit strategies. That is, again, a futile and possibly a destructive approach. The Americans denied for a long time the possibility of success of guerilla warfare in Vietnam because they were confident in their resource-driven strategy and were not in a position to develop a guerilla strategy. The result is history.

With each increase in international trade – it increased by about 10 per cent last year – the stakes in the export market get higher, the number of players increases, and the competition becomes even fiercer. But most important, Japan and some Asian countries, by questioning the validity of the conventional interpretation of the Ricardian theory of comparative advantage, have shaped a new form of competition and have somewhat reshaped the nature of international trade.

The many recommendations of this Report on free trade, education, the incentive system, macro-economic policy, resource management, and the social support system describe the essentials and form the basis of a strong national strategy for Canada.

Conclusions

Many years ago, Canadian General Electric started a process to study the possibility of moving from a broad product-line base confined to the Canadian market, to a world mandate and a rationalization strategy. I understand that from the time Canadian General Electric decided to look at the possible new strategies and the time they were in a position to start to implement them in the corporation, it took four years. It should not be expected, then, that this Royal Commission could, in a year and a half to two years, define a complete strategy for the country.

Targeting is not an available strategy for Canada today. Too much has still to be understood before we can properly evaluate that option. As indicated in this Report, we should have a tilt towards high technology and export, but stop there for the moment. However, we should remain attentive to any recommendations which could help to reinforce our industrial base. We should constantly remind ourselves that the "targeting" debate is far from being closed at this time, and that strategy formulation and implementation are fundamentally search processes which are in perpetual evolution.

Notes

1. I always remind my students during my course on strategy that to win the Stanley Cup in the National Hockey League, a team has to win four games out of seven, not four out of four. If one were to follow the way that strategy is often evaluated and decide that a strategy is not good because something was lost, because one of the products involved (e.g. the IBM PC Junior computer) has not been a success, it would be tantamount to saying that to really win the championship of the Hockey League, you should not lose one game during the whole season. The IBM PC Junior might have been a bad tactical mistake or might have been mismanaged or might have been a very good decision involving risk, hence the possibility of losing, which is what business and good strategy are all about. It is much too early to say.

2. The English have a very good way of describing that when they talk about someone "who won all the battles but lost the war". Surely if someone "won all the battles but lost the war", the guy on the other side "lost all the battles but won the war".
3. Let me say clearly here that I am not suggesting that the Japanese defined at the start a three-phase strategy. Their strategy did evolve – as does any strategy – as their successes and defeats indicated, and as the world environment changed. Developing a strategy and implementing it are continuous "search processes". Despite the fact that some Japanese policy makers or policy analysts deny that they have looked for high-value/added but concentrated on high-income/sensitive, high-technology products, it is clear that in the long term these products will also be the high-value/added products.
4. See Waterman and Peters *In Search of Excellence*. A highly successful company usually enjoys a fierce internal competition, which is one reason for its success. Again, the debate to try to resolve the conflict between consensus and competition in the Japanese decision-making process is a futile exercise. Consensus and competition are not conflicting, but complementary, elements in a successful system.
5. Again, let me say that I am not pretending that the Japanese "hired a management consultant" and asked for world marketing research. I am really talking about a very large process, not necessarily co-ordinated, involving thousands of people and organizations, which developed into a relatively explicit and precise set of strategies. (see Henry Mintzberg and Alexander McHugh: "Strategy Formation in an Adhocracy", in *Administrative Science Quarlerly*, June 1985. Another reference would be Bourgeois III and Brodwin: "Strategic Implementation: Five Approaches to an Elusive Phenomenon", *Strategic Management Journal*, Vol. 5, 1984, pp. 241–264.)

Jean Casselman-Wadds

It seems to be unanimous that reform of the Senate is desirable. I agree entirely. However, I do not agree that the solution is election of Senators. On the contrary, I fear that this recommendation has only the advantage of being dramatic. Although election of Senators has supporters, in my opinion, not enough thought has been given to their responsibilities after election.

Very little concern has been expressed for the vast increase in election costs. These are already horrendous and, I believe, part of the cause of public disillusionment with governments generally. This disillusionment would increase if election costs doubled and another layer of promises and possible contradictions were presented to voters. If senatorial electioneering were not aggressive and purposeful, it would be disappointing and voters could well be confused as to the purpose.

If elections occurred – either by choice of the Prime Minister or lack of confidence in the government – in close succession, as has happened in the past, senatorial electioneering would either be repetitive or extremely partisan. A Senate overwhelmingly supportive of the party in power would very likely be the result, the very situation which has existed. Political patronage might well increase, leading to still further discontent with government.

Unless the responsibilities were increased and clarified, the behaviour of the Senate might remain the same, unless the desire for re-election created a demand for more responsibility and power. In this case, governments would be involved in time-consuming reforms of the Constitution. This would distract from concentration on governing and attention to the immediate economic and social problems. Again, this is the very situation we wish to correct.

Election of the Senate would require such planning and negotiating that even its most enthusiastic supporters admit that it is a solution for the distant future. We have examples from other countries that going through the election process in itself does not guarantee high calibre of participation.

I would prefer laying this recommendation aside and concentrating on what would seem to me to have more immediate prospects of results. Since better co-ordination in the workings of provincial and federal governments seems to be another unanimous goal, I would prefer a broader-based system of appointments to the Senate which would include recommendations from a variety of sources, including provincial governments. Coupled with this, I would recommend mandatory attendance, with replacement automatic after a stated period. In the past, Senate Committees have done very worthwhile work, not always fully recognized and appreciated. These should be given more responsibility and more prominence.

I believe our system of appointment still has merit, and itself could be reformed quickly! I believe the Prime Minister should be supported by a Senate Appointment Advisory Council. The Council would draw up lists of meritorious candidates by province and pay particular attention to a variety of socio-economic considerations to ensure a broadly representative set of candidates. Appointments based on recommendations from a broader process

would likely be of more local origin and could overcome some of the isolation felt by certain regions and socio-economic interests. The Prime Minister would appoint the Council, in consultation with the Official Leader of the Opposition, at the outset of the government's mandate. The Prime Minister would not be restricted to the nominations list but would be guided by it.

It is quite clear that the Senate should be reformed. I believe that the incremental steps I am proposing are in the right direction and have the benefit of being practical. Other reforms would likely evolve once a real determination is shown to recognize the Senate's potential contribution to Canadian society. If it is important, let us do it now.

APPENDICES

APPENDIX A

Orders in Council and Exchange of Letters with the Prime Minister

P.C. 1982-3438

CANADA

PRIVY COUNCIL

Certified to be a true copy of a Minute of a Meeting of the Committee of the Privy Council, approved by Her Excellency the Governor General on the 5 November, 1982

The Committee of the Privy Council have before them a report from the Prime Minister, the Right Honourable Pierre Elliott Trudeau, submitting:

That Canada is a country of tremendous opportunity, committed to the sustained economic and social progress of its people, to the reduction of economic and fiscal disparities between regions, and to a fair distribution of the advantages and burdens of national development;

That significant changes are occurring in the world economy, particularly in the sphere of industrial activity, the utilization of natural resources and movement of capital within and among countries, changes which will have important consequences for Canada;

That existing economic relationships among countries and among individuals and groups within countries are characterized on the one hand by increasing interdependence and at the same time by intensified competition;

That to respond to the challenges of rapid national and international change in order to realize Canada's potential and to secure sustained economic and social progress, it will be of importance to achieve greater understanding of the aspirations of the regions of Canada, greater co-ordination between actions of governments in Canada and greater support for the Canadian economic union.

Therefore, the Committee of the Privy Council, on the recommendation of the Prime Minister, advise that the Honourable Donald Stovel Macdonald together with such other persons as may be named from time to time be appointed Commissioners under Part I of the Inquiries

Act to inquire into and report upon the long-term economic potential, prospects and challenges facing the Canadian federation and its respective regions, as well as the implications that such prospects and challenges have for Canada's economic and governmental institutions and for the management of Canada's economic affairs.

The Committee further advise that the study include an examination of and a report on:

(a) the appropriate national goals and policies for economic development, including consideration of the following:

- trends in labour market requirements and conditions;
- developments in the supply of raw materials, including energy sources;
- capital requirements and the cost structure in a highly competitive, technologically-sophisticated and interdependent world environment;
- trends in productivity, standards of living and social progress;
- industrial adjustment and growth;
- regional economic development opportunities and constraints in a national economic framework;
- the integrity of the Canadian economic union as it relates to the unity of Canada and the ability of all Canadians to participate in increased economic prosperity;

(b) the appropriate institutional and constitutional arrangements to promote the liberty and well-being of individual Canadians and the maintenance of a strong and competitive economy including consideration of the following:

- means for improving relations between governments, business, labour and other groups in Canadians society;

...3

- the appropriate allocation of fiscal and economic powers, instruments and resources as between the different levels of governments and administrations;

- changes in the institutions of national government so as to take better account of the views and needs of all Canadians and regions, and to encourage the further development of the Canadian economic union.

The Committee also advise that in pursuing such inquiry and preparing the report, the Commissioners proceed by reference to the following principles:

(a) the Canadian economy is founded on the enterprise and productivity of individual Canadians supported by a unique mixture of public and private sector activity that reflects the traditional values of Canadian society;

(b) Canadian economic policy must be assessed in the context of its relationships to Canadian political and economic independence and to the broader aspirations of Canadians as must be reflected in the responsibilities of governments;

(c) the Government of Canada has the primary responsibility for managing the national economy, for encouraging reasonably balanced economic growth among the various regions of the country and for ensuring that fiscal disparities among provinces are reduced, while at the same time the provincial governments also have important responsibilities in the development and carrying out of economic and social policy;

(d) the report should take account of, and respect, the spirit of the Constitution of Canada and assume a continuing Canadian federal structure not significantly different from its present form.

The Committee also advise that the Commissioners:

...4

1. be directed, within the ambit of their work, to seek the views of all provincial and territorial governments as well as interested Canadians from all walks of life and all regions of the country;

2. be authorized to establish such advisory bodies of prominent Canadians as they deem desirable to assist them in the examination of any aspect of their terms of reference;

3. be authorized to adopt such procedure and methods as they deem appropriate for the proper conduct of the inquiry;

4. be assisted by the officers and employees of the departments and agencies of the Government of Canada as may be required for the conduct of the inquiry, particularly in having access to written material;

5. be authorized to sit at such times and in such places in Canada as may be required;

6. be authorized to exercise all of the powers conferred upon them by section 11 of the Inquiries Act;

7. be authorized to engage the services of such staff and technical advisers, including counsel, as they consider necessary or advisable to aid them in the conduct of the inquiry at rates of remuneration and reimbursement as may be approved by Treasury Board;

8. be authorized to rent office space and facilities for public hearings in co-operation with the federal Department of Public Works as they may deem necessary at such rental rates as are consistent with the policies of the Department of Public Works;

9. be authorized to publish special studies as may be appropriate from time to time;

10. be directed to submit their report to the Governor in Council with all reasonable dispatch but no more than three years from now;

...5

P.C. 1982-3438

- 5 -

11. be directed to file with the Dominion Archivist the records of the inquiry as soon as reasonably may be after the conclusion of the inquiry.

The Committee further advise that the Honourable Donald Stovel Macdonald be the Chairman of the Commission.

CERTIFIED TO BE A TRUE COPY – COPIE CERTIFIÉE CONFORME

P. J. Pitfield

CLERK OF THE PRIVY COUNCIL – LE GREFFIER DU CONSEIL PRIVÉ

P.C. 1982-3582

CANADA

PRIVY COUNCIL

Certified to be a true copy of a Minute of a Meeting of the Committee of the Privy Council, approved by Her Excellency the Governor General on the 25 November, 1982

The Committee of the Privy Council, on the recommendation of the Prime Minister, advise that the following persons be appointed Commissioners under Part I of the Inquiries Act, of the Royal Commission on the Economic Union and Development Prospects for Canada, established by Order in Council P.C. 1982-3438 of 5th November, 1982:

The Honourable William M. Hamilton
Vancouver, British Columbia

Mr. Daryl Kenneth Seaman
Calgary, Alberta

Mrs. Mary Angela Cantwell Peters
St. John's, Newfoundland

Mr. E. Gérard Docquier
Toronto, Ontario

Mr. Clarence Lyle Barber
Winnipeg, Manitoba

Her Excellency Mrs. Jean Casselman-Wadds

Mr. Michel Robert
Montreal, Quebec

Mr. Albert A. Breton
Toronto, Ontario

Dr. Catherine T. Wallace
Fredericton, New Brunswick

The Committee further advise that Mr. Gerald Godsoe of Halifax, in the Province of Nova Scotia, be appointed Executive Director of the Commission.

CERTIFIED TO BE A TRUE COPY - COPIE CERTIFIÉE CONFORME

CLERK OF THE PRIVY COUNCIL - LE GREFFIER DU CONSEIL PRIVÉ

P.C. 1983-158

CANADA

PRIVY COUNCIL

Certified to be a true copy of a Minute of a Meeting of the Committee of the Privy Council, approved by Her Excellency the Governor General on the 25 January, 1983

The Committee of the Privy Council, on the recommendation of the Prime Minister, advise that the following persons be appointed Commissioners under Part I of the Inquiries Act, of the Royal Commission on the Economic Union and Development Prospects for Canada, established by Order in Council P.C. 1982-3438 of 5th November, 1982:

The Honourable John R. Messer
Tisdale, Saskatchewan

Mr. Laurent A. Picard
Outremont, Quebec

Mr. Thomas K. Shoyama
Ottawa, Ontario

CERTIFIED TO BE A TRUE COPY – COPIE CERTIFIÉE CONFORME

Gordon F. Osbaldeston

CLERK OF THE PRIVY COUNCIL – LE GREFFIER DU CONSEIL PRIVÉ

Office of the Prime Minister — Cabinet du Premier ministre

Release

Date: November 5, 1982

For release: Immediate

The Prime Minister announced today that the government has appointed The Honourable Donald S. Macdonald chairman of a Royal Commission on the Economic Union and Development Prospects for Canada.

The terms of reference are "perhaps the most important and far-reaching that have ever been assigned to any Commission in our history," he said.

The Prime Minister said that while short-term action is necessary to counter the adverse effects of the recession and lay the groundwork for the return to prosperity,"we must look further ahead to see in what ways the country and its institutions might change to take full advantage of future opportunities for development.

"We now live in a much more competitive, technologically-sophisticated and interdependent world environment," the Prime Minister said. "It is time we stood back to look at all these changes and, in the light of what has happened, to look ahead at what the next generation of development can bring -- if we do things right."

Moreover, the Prime Minister emphasized the need for Canadian institutions to keep up with a rapidly changing environment.

.../2

Canada

"If we are to prosper," he said, "we must find ways to lessen the clamour of federal-provincial argument, and to reach consensus with far less pain. But if this is to be achieved, we must ensure that national policies are designed so that all parts of Canada can benefit from them, and that national institutions are truly reflective of regional needs."

The Royal Commission is being asked to:

- assess Canada's economic potential over the longer-term;
- recommend national economic goals, and national policies for the attainment of those goals;
- recommend ways in which the institutions of the national government -- particularly those institutions which are vital to economic development -- can better reflect the views of all Canadians and regions;
- recommend institutional arrangements to handle more effectively relations between governments, business and labour, and the fiscal and economic aspects of federal-provincial relations.

The Prime Minister stressed the wide scope of the work assigned to the Royal Commission, the broadly representative and diverse nature of its membership, and the likelihood that its recommendations will contribute significantly to a brighter economic future for Canada. He expressed the hope that support for its establishment and cooperation with its work as it proceeds, will come from the House of Commons, all government and legislative organizations in Canada and from Canadians everywhere.

Royal Commission on the Economic Union and Development Prospects for Canada

CANADA

Commission royale sur l'union économique et les perspectives de développement du Canada

September 7, 1984

Dear Mr. Mulroney:

My first words are those of congratulations on an historic electoral success. I know that in taking on these heavy responsibilities of forming a new government you will be reviewing a number of ongoing activities and assessing options and I felt that it would be appropriate to offer to you and to the Clerk of the Privy Council a current report on the work of the Royal Commission.

My fellow Commissioners and I are at the stage where we are drawing together almost two years of preparatory work involving the largest consultative and research effort in Canadian history. While our mandate requires us to report by November 5, 1985, I have prepared a course which would complete a final report well before that date.

The Commission budget is $21.7 million. We have completed the bulk of our work at a cost of $16.3 million in actual and committed funds. I would hope that we can conclude our task at a total cost of under $20 million overall.

I have provided the Clerk of the Privy Council with a status report on our activities which I have enclosed. Should you or your officials wish further information or to meet with Commissioners or senior staff we would be very pleased to do so.

Yours sincerely,

Donald S. Macdonald

Hon. Donald S. Macdonald
Chairman

The Honourable Brian Mulroney
Prime Minister Elect
Room 627, Wellington Building
House of Commons
Ottawa, Ontario
K1A OA6

P.O. Box/CP 1268
Ottawa, Canada
K1P 5R3

Canada

CANADA

PRIME MINISTER • PREMIER MINISTRE

Ottawa, K1A 0A2
November 2, 1984

Dear Mr. Macdonald:

I was pleased to learn that you and the Minister of Finance, the Honourable Michael Wilson, have had the opportunity of reviewing together the work of the Royal Commission on the Economic Union and Development Prospects for Canada.

Pursuant to that meeting, I wish to confirm the Government's views on how the Commission should complete its mandate.

You are no doubt aware that the effective resolution of the economic problems currently besetting Canada constitutes the priority for the Government: how to reduce deficits while remaining sensitive to the needs of Canadians, how to stimulate the entrepreneurial capabilities of Canadians, how to expand our markets abroad, how to attain optimum levels of employment in all regions of the country, and how to ensure that the talents of young Canadians are put to effective and productive use. The Government, therefore, will be particularly interested in the Commission's proposals respecting these matters.

The Honourable Donald S. Macdonald,
Chairman,
Royal Commission on the Economic Union
and Development Prospects for Canada,
151 Sparks Street,
Ottawa, Ontario.
K1P 5R3

I understand that it is the Commission's intention to present its final report in June of 1985 or soon thereafter, and it is the Government's hope that this goal will be met. The Government likewise hopes the Commission will complete the publication of pertinent research papers no later than November 5, 1985. I was also informed that you plan to hold the Commission's total expenditures at about $20,000,000 and wish to convey the Government's hope that you will be able to achieve this target, and thus stay well within the three-year budget of $21,790,000 initially proposed.

It is my intention to make this letter public so that Canadians may be informed of the Government's views on the work of the Commission.

Please accept my best wishes as you endeavour to complete your work in a timely fashion, within budget and with a focus on Canada's pressing economic problems.

Yours sincerely,

APPENDIX B

Schedule of Written Submissions

Aalborg, Anders O.
Abbott, Donald P.
Abbott, Mark
Acadian Federation of Nova Scotia
Action travail des femmes du Québec inc.
Activités-Jeunesse
Adair, D. Brent
Adair, John E.
Adams, William G.
Agricultural Institute of Canada
Agrinove, Coopérative agro-alimentaire
Aird, Paul L.
Ajax-Pickering Board of Trade
Alberta College, Institute Faculties Association
Alberta Committee of Consumer Groups of Disabled Persons
Alberta Historical Resources Foundation
Alberta New Democratic Party
Alberta Oil Sands Technology and Research Authority
Alberta Teachers' Association
Alberta Wheat Pool
Alberta Wilderness Association
Alcan Aluminium Limited
Alert (Charlottetown Branch)
Alexander, Donald A.
Allan, Robyn
Alliance of Canadian Cinema, Television and Radio Artists
Alston, John M.
Amoco Canada Petroleum Company Limited
Amonson, David L.
Andrade, M.L.R.
Anderson, D.M.
Andrew, Caroline and Jean-Pierre Gaboury
Angus, Iain
Aquin, Creighton
Aram International

Archer, S.S.
Armstrong, John L.
Armstrong, Pat and Hugh
Arundel-Evans, Rick
Ashton, Ernie
Ashton, Steve, MLA
Asia Pacific Foundation of Canada
Assembly of B.C. Arts Councils and The Community Arts Council of Vancouver
Assembly of First Nations
Association canadienne-française de l'Alberta
Association coopérative d'économie familiale de Québec
Association des femmes collaboratrices
Association des mines de métaux du Québec inc.
Association des propriétaires de Québec inc.
Association féminine d'éducation et d'action sociale
Association for the Protection of Fur-Bearing Animals
Association of British Columbia Professional Foresters
Association of Canadian Advertisers Inc.
Association of Canadian Community Colleges
Association of Canadian Distillers
Association of Canadian Financial Corporations
Association of Consulting Engineers of Canada
Association of Deans of Pharmacy of Canada
Association of Professional Engineers of British Columbia
Association of Professional Engineers of Saskatchewan
Association of Universities and Colleges of Canada
Association of University of New Brunswick Teachers
Association of Women Electors of Metropolitan Toronto
Association of Yukon Communities
Association québécoise de la qualité
Associés R.C.P. Associates Inc.
Atkinson, Roy
Atlantic Conference on Learning Disabilities
Atlantic Provinces Chamber of Commerce
Atlantic Provinces Economic Council
Atlantic Provinces Transportation Commission
Atomic Energy of Canada Limited
Attawapiskat Band
Audain, Tunya
Audley, Paul
Auf der Maur, Frank
Austin, The Honourable Senator Jack
Axworthy, The Honourable Lloyd
Baffin Tourism Association
Baird, D.C.
BAKAVI, Design for Living Inc.
Bank of Montreal
Barber, Alan
Barnett, Enid
Barron, M.I.
Barron, R.E.
Beck, Gerry K.J.
Beckton, Clare
Beer, R.J.
Bégin, The Honourable Monique
Bell, A.J.
Bell Canada
Bell Canada Enterprises Inc.

Benesh, John B.
Benson, C.A.
Benton, S.B.
Bertrand, Guy
Beutel, Austin C.
Beynon, Peter K.
Biddell, John L.
Biggin-Pound, W.J.
Biggs, William M.
Bishop, J.W.
Blakeney, The Honourable Allan, Leader of the Opposition, Saskatchewan
Board of Trade of Metropolitan Toronto
Boddy, Dale
Boigon, Irving D.
Boily, Robert
Bombardier Inc.
Bonyun, Denis
Boros, Stephen D.
Boyd, John B.
Boyd, Michael
BP Selco Inc.
Brace, Bruce R.
Bradley, William
Bradshaw, Nancy
Breiland, Haakon Johan
Brett, Peter
Brewis, T.N.
Brian Hull and Associates
BRITEX
British Columbia and Yukon Territory Building and Construction Trades Council
British Columbia Association of Social Workers
British Columbia Central Credit Union
British Columbia Federation of Women
British Columbia Health Association
British Columbia Institute of Technology
British Columbia Law Union
British Columbia Resources Investment Corporation
British Columbia Wildlife Federation
British Columbians for Mentally Handicapped People
Britten, Patrick
Brown, Denis
Brown, George
Brown, Rupert D.
Brown, Walter F.M.
Bruneau, Angus
Brunelle, Dorval
Bruton, Len T.
Buckley, F.W.
Bujold, Bernard
Bulpin, Donald
Burke, Roger J.
Burns Foods Limited
Burns Fry Limited
Business Council on National Issues
Busque, Paul-André
Byrne, Gerald
Cadeddu, Salvatore
Cadillac Fairview Corporation Limited

Cairns, W.L.
Calgary Association of Voluntary Agencies
Calgary Chamber of Commerce
Calgary Council for Advanced Technology
Calgary Research and Development Authority
Camco
Cameron, Douglas
Cameron, Sandy, Leader of the Opposition, Nova Scotia
Cameron, W.J.
Campbell, A.J.
Campbell, Duncan D.
Campbell, J.G.
Campeau Corporation
Canada Jaycees
Canada Oil and Gas Lands Administration (Nova Scotia Office)
Canada West Foundation
Canadian Advisory Council on the Status of Women
Canadian Agricultural Chemicals Association
Canadian Air Line Employees' Association
Canadian Air Line Pilots Association
Canadian Art Museums Directors' Organization
Canadian Artists' Representation
Canadian Association for Adult Education
Canadian Association for the Club of Rome
Canadian Association of Housing and Renewal Officials
Canadian Association of School Administrators
Canadian Association of Social Workers
Canadian Association of University Teachers
Canadian Association of Women Executives
Canadian Association on Gerontology
Canadian Bankers' Association
Canadian Bankers' Association/Investment Dealers Association of Canada
Canadian Bar Association
Canadian Business and Industry International Advisory Council
Canadian Business Equipment Manufacturers Association
Canadian Cattlemen's Association
Canadian Centre for a Changing Society
Canadian Centre for Philanthropy
Canadian Chamber of Commerce (Montreal)
Canadian Chamber of Commerce (Ottawa)
Canadian Chemical Producers' Association
Canadian Co-operative Wheat Producers Limited
Canadian Conference of Catholic Bishops
Canadian Conference of the Arts
Canadian Congress for Learning Opportunities for Women
Canadian Construction Association
Canadian Council for International Co-operation
Canadian Council of Furniture Manufacturers
Canadian Council of Professional Engineers
Canadian Council on Social Development
Canadian Crafts Council
Canadian Day Care Advocacy Association
Canadian Direct Marketing Association
Canadian Electrical Association
Canadian Electrical Distributors Association
Canadian Environmental Advisory Council
Canadian Environmental Law Research Foundation
Canadian Export Association

Canadian Federation of Agriculture
Canadian Federation of Communications Workers
Canadian Federation of Deans of Management and Administrative Studies
Canadian Federation of Humane Societies
Canadian Federation of Independent Business
Canadian Federation of Independent Petroleum Marketers
Canadian Federation of Labour
Canadian Federation of Professional Foresters' Associations
Canadian Federation of Students
Canadian Food Processors Association
C.F.B. Chatham Steering Committee
Canadian Forestry Association
Canadian Forestry Service
Canadian Foundation for Economic Education
Canadian Friends of Schizophrenics
Canadian Gas Association
Canadian General Electric Company Limited
Canadian Hardware and Housewares Manufacturers Association
Canadian Health Coalition
Canadian Hospital Association
Canadian Importers Association Inc.
Canadian Industrial Renewal Board
Canadian Institute for Advanced Research
Canadian Institute for Economic Policy
Canadian Institute of Chartered Accountants
Canadian Institute of Forestry
Canadian Institute of Mining and Metallurgy
Canadian Institute of Planners
Canadian Labour Congress
Canadian Life and Health Insurance Association Inc.
Canadian Machine Builders' Association
Canadian Manufacturers' Association
Canadian Manufacturers' Association (PEI Branch)
Canadian Meat Council
Canadian Medical and Biological Engineering Society Inc.
Canadian Mental Health Association
Canadian Museums Association
Canadian National Railways
Canadian Nurses' Association
Canadian Organic Producers Marketing Cooperative Limited
Canadian Pacific
Canadian Pension Conference
Canadian Pensioners Concerned Inc.
Canadian Petroleum Association
Canadian Pulp and Paper Association
Canadian Real Estate Association
Canadian Red Cross Society
Canadian Rehabilitation Council for the Disabled
Canadian Research Institute for the Advancement of Women
Canadian School Trustees' Association
Canadian Shipbuilding and Ship Repairing Association
Canadian Society for Chemical Engineering
Canadian Society for Professional Engineers
Canadian Society for the Study of Higher Education
Canadian Soft Drink Association
Canadian Teachers' Federation
Canadian Textiles Institute
Canadian Trucking Association

Canadian Union of Public Employees
Canadian Urban Transit Association
Canadian-Arab Cultural Centre
Canola Crushers of Western Canada
Canterra Engineering Limited
Cape Breton Co-operative Council
Cape Breton Development Corporation
Cape Breton Joint Expenditure Board
Capeling, Ralph R.
Capital Families
Capital Region Development Commission Inc.
Cappell, Joel
Carlson, Gary
Caro, Denis H.J.
Carpenters and Joiners Union, Local 494
Carrefour québécois des travailleurs de la famille
Carrier-Sekani Tribal Council
Carrothers, A.W.R.
Carson, John W.
Carter, Larry Ernest
Cartier Circle
Carver, Horace B., MLA
Cassidy, Michael, MPP
Cassivi, Yvon
Catholic Family Services of Saskatoon
Catholic Social Services
Catholic Women's League of Canada
Cauchon, Dona
Cawkell, David M.
Caya, Martin
Celanese Canada Inc.
Central Interior Tribal Councils
Centrale de l'enseignement du Québec
Centrale des syndicats démocratiques (Montréal)
Centrale des syndicats démocratiques (ville de Québec)
Centre-femmes de Beauce
Chalifoux, John
Chamber of Commerce Northwest Inc.
Chambre de commerce de Chicoutimi
Chambre de commerce de la province de Québec
Chambre de commerce et d'industrie du Québec métropolitain
Charron, Edgar B.
Chartrand, Harry
Chase, Lloma Jane
Checkland, Edward and Russell Pendergast
Chemical Institute of Canada
Chilliwack Community Arts Council
Chorney, Paul
Chouinard, Faustin
Christian Farmers Federation of Ontario
Christian Labour Association of Canada
Chumir, Sheldon M.
Church, R.B.
Churches of Edmonton
Ciera Technology Limited
C.I.L. Inc.
Citizens for Public Justice
City of Calgary

City of Charlottetown
City of Chicoutimi
City of Edmonton
City of Fredericton
City of Halifax
City of Hull
City of Lethbridge
City of Moncton
City of Ottawa
City of Vancouver
City of Windsor
City of Windsor, Mayor's Committee on Services for the Unemployed
City of Winnipeg, Department of Environmental Planning
City of Yellowknife
A.R. Clarke & Co. Limited
Clément, Michèle
Clements, Bryan
Cliche, Nicolas
Cloutier, L.
CNCP Telecommunications
Co-op Union of Canada and the Canadian Co-op Credit Society
Co-operative Housing Foundation of Canada
Co-operative Trust Company of Canada
Coalition for National Voluntary Organizations
Coalition for the Protection of Human Life
Coalition of Social Organizations in Cape Breton
Coffin, Garth
Coldwell, Susan
College of New Caledonia
Collenette, The Honourable David M.
Comact Inc.
Cominco Limited
Common Ownership Development Association
Communauté urbaine de Montréal
Communications Workers of Canada
Communist Party of Canada
Communist Party of Canada (British Columbia)
Community Council of Greater Victoria
Community Forum on Shared Responsibility
Community Nursing Registry of Windsor Inc.
Community Services Council (Newfoundland and Labrador)
Community-Based Health Services Coalition
Compu-Guard
Confédération de l'Union des producteurs agricoles
Confédération des caisses populaires et d'économie Desjardins du Québec
Confédération des syndicats nationaux (Chicoutimi)
Confédération des syndicats nationaux (Montréal)
Confédération des syndicats nationaux (Saint-Georges-de-Beauce)
Confédération des syndicats nationaux (ville de Québec)
Confederation of Alberta Faculty Associations
Confederation of Regions Party of Alberta
Conférence des associations de créateurs et créatrices du Québec
Conseil canadien de la coopération
Conseil de la coopération du Québec
Conseil de la sculpture du Québec
Conseil du patronat du Québec
Conseil économique d'Alma et de Lac-St-Jean inc.
Conseil économique de Beauce

Conseil économique du Nouveau-Brunswick inc.
Conseil exécutif national du Parti québécois
Conseil jeunesse provincial inc.
Conseil régional de développement de la région administrative de Québec
Conseil régional de développement Saguenay-Lac-Saint-Jean-Chibougamau
Conseil régional de la Pastorale La Chaudière
Conservation Council of New Brunswick
Conserver Action Research and Education Inc.
Consolidated-Bathurst Inc.
Construction Industry Development Council
Consulting Engineers of Alberta
Consumer and Corporate Affairs (Combines Investigation Act)
Consumers' Association of Canada
Consumers' Association of Canada (Manitoba)
Consumers' Association of Canada (Ontario)
Consumers' Association of Canada (Yukon)
Control Data Canada Limited
Conzelmann, B.
Cooper, Lawrence O.
Corner Brook Chamber of Commerce
Corporation des artisans de Québec
Corporation of the Borough of East York
Couchman, Robert
Council of Forest Industries of British Columbia
Council of National Ethnocultural Organizations of Canada
Council of Nova Scotia Association of Social Workers
Council of the City of Winnipeg
Counterpoint Waterfront Community Development Corporation
Courtright, J.M.
Cowan, D.G.
Cowan, Keith
Cowie, Wilbur Elliott
Cox, Daniel Jack
Cran, Emily Elizabeth
Crédit Suisse
Credit Union Central
Creelman Hill, Cynthia
Crispo, John
Croft, John G.
Crossroads Resource Group
Crysler, John
Cunningham, Ruth
Curtis, B.E.
Dakota Ojibway Tribal Council
Dalrymple, D.G.
Daly, Donald J.
Daly Gordon Securities
Dansereau, Pierre
Darcel, Colin
Dartmouth Chamber of Commerce
Davidson, Jim
Davis, Edgar H.
Davis, The Honourable Jack, MLA
Daybreak Non-Profit Shelter Corporation
De Boer, John
de Fayer, T.L.
de Lasala, Jennifer
Decima Research Limited

Decore, Laurence, Mayor of Edmonton
Demers, Télesphore
Dennison, W.J.
DeYoe, Donald A.
Dhensaw, Robert
Diament Knitting Mills Limited
DiCastri, Daphne
Dicks, Dennis J.
Didier, René
Diplômés de l'Université de Montréal
District of Chilliwack
District of Lynn Lake
District of Mackenzie
Dixon, Gordon F.
Dixon, Robert J.
Dobell, A.R.
Doerr, John A.
Dolling, G.
Dome Petroleum Limited
Dominion Marine Association and the Canadian Shipowners Association
Dominion Textile Inc.
Doré, Charles
Dow Chemical Canada Inc.
Doyle, J. Donald
Dragon, Jean-Jacques
Du Pont Canada Inc.
Dubé, Francine
Dwornik, Andrew S.
Dyer, John
Dysart, Shirley, MLA
Dyson, William
Ecology Action Centre
Economic Council of Canada
Economic Development Advocacy Committee, County of Strathcona No. 20
Economic Development Commission of the Cariboo Regional District
Elce, Ivan
Electrical and Electronic Manufacturers Association of Canada
Elliott, Jim
Emberley, Kenneth
Empey, William F.
Employers' Council of British Columbia
Engineer, Homi M.
Enright, John A.
Environment Canada
Equipment Lessors Association of Canada
Erola, The Honourable Judy
Faculty Association of St. Thomas University
Fair, John E.
Fairweather, Gordon
Falconbridge Limited
Family Farm Foundation of Canada
Family Service Association of Metropolitan Toronto
Family Service Bureau of Regina
Federal Superannuates National Association
Federated Anti-Poverty Groups of British Columbia
Federated Co-operatives Limited
Federated Women's Institutes of Canada
Fédération de l'Union des producteurs agricoles de la Beauce

Fédération de l'Union des producteurs agricoles du Saguenay-Lac-Saint-Jean
Fédération des associations de professeurs des universités du Québec
Fédération des caisses populaires Desjardins du Saguenay-Lac-Saint-Jean
Fédération des femmes canadiennes-françaises
Fédération des femmes du Québec
Fédération des franco-colombiens
Fédération des francophones hors Québec inc.
Fédération des syndicats du secteur aluminium inc.
Federation of Canadian Municipalities
Federation of Community Development Corporations of Canada
Federation of New Brunswick Faculty Associations
Federation of Nova Scotian Heritage
Federation of Saskatchewan Indian Nations
Federation of Sikh Societies of Canada
Fédération québécoise anti-pauvreté inc.
Fedorick, Joy
Fell, R. Bruce
Fenech, V.
Fernie Womens' Resource Centre
Fetherstonhaugh, John
Film Factory Limited
Fiorino, Albert F.
First United Church
Firth, C.B.
Fisheries Council of Canada
Fishermen's Survival Coalition
Fleck Bros. Limited
Fleming, Blake C.
Flewwelling, Herb
Ford, J. W.
Formula Growth Limited
Fors, P.B.
Fortune, John
Foster, W.E.
Fox, The Honourable Francis
Frank, Andre Gunder
Franklin, John N.
Fraser Institute
Fredericton Chamber of Commerce
Friends of the Earth
Frobisher Inn
Gagnon, Jean
Gallagher, Jack P.
Galley, Ann
Garde-Hansen, H.
Garneau, Raymond
Garner, Peter H.
Gatenby, R.
Gayfer, E.R.
Gaz Inter-Cité Québec inc.
General Synod of the Anglican Church of Canada
Genstar Corporation
Gibson, Gordon and Peter McCormick
Gillen, Ralph L.
Girard, Georgette
Goering, J.W.L.
Goldberg, Michael A.
Goldie, D.M.M.

Goldsack, Douglas
Gomero, Orlando
Gomes, Mary Jane and Emil Kolompar
Gonick, Cy
Gorling, G.
Gorman, Ryan M. and Peter R.
Government of Alberta
Government of New Brunswick
Government of Newfoundland and Labrador
Government of Nova Scotia
Government of Ontario
Government of Prince Edward Island
Government of Saskatchewan
Government of the Northwest Territories
Government of Yukon
Grace, Norman
Grand Council of the Crees (of Quebec)
Gray McKinlay Associates
Gray, James K.
Great Lakes Forest Products Limited
Great Lakes Waterways Development Association
Greater Charlottetown Area Chamber of Commerce
Greater Summerside Chamber of Commerce
Greater Victoria Chamber of Commerce
Green Party of Ontario
Grocery Products Manufacturers of Canada
Grolle, E. Hendrik
Groupe d'action pour l'avenir technologique et industriel de la région de Québec
Gue, Frank S.
Gulf Canada Limited
Habitation populaire de Québec inc.
Haji, G.
Halifax Board of Trade
Halifax County Municipality
Halina, J.W.
Hall, The Honourable Emmett M.
Halo, Julius
H.N. Halvorson Consultants Limited
Hamill, Louis
Hamilton and District Labour Council
Hancock, Alma
Hancox, Kenrick G.
Harper, Paul
Hattersley, J. Martin
Hawker Siddeley Canada Inc.
Hay Associates Canada Limited
Haydu, Stephen C.
Hayos, Vera M.
H.C.A. Development Consultants
Heading, Roddy
Health Coalition of Nova Scotia
Heap, Dan, MP
Hearn, Edward M.
Help the Aged
Hemming, Timothy C.S.
Henderson, Ian
Henry, Lawrence D.
Heritage Canada Foundation

Heritage Ottawa
Heritage Winnipeg
Herzstein, Robert
Higgins, Brian
Hildebrand, John L.
Hill, Stuart B.
Hills, Keith
Hitchins, D.H.
Hoinkes, Robert H.
Holman, Lucy
Honeywell Limited
Hope-Simpson, Peggy
Hopkins, Leonard D., MP
Hopperton, Hugh E.
Housing and Urban Development Association of Canada
Houston, Charles W.
C.D. Howe Institute
Hudson, Elizabeth R.
Hughes, C.D.
Hum, Derek
Human Resources Development Association
Hunaus, F.
Hunsley, Terrance M.
Hutcheon, A.D.
Ilett, James
Immigrant and Multicultural Services Society
Imperial Oil Limited
INCO Limited (Sudbury)
INCO Limited (Thompson)
Income Maintenance for the Handicapped Coordinating Group
Indian and Northern Affairs Canada
Industrial Cape Breton Board of Trade
Infonorth Computing Inc.
Inniss, Scott
Innuit Group
Institute for Environmental Studies
Institute of Association Executives
Institute of Donations and Public Affairs Research
International Association of Machinists and Aerospace Workers
International Business Council of Canada
International Union of Operating Engineers, Local 115
International Union, United Automobile, Aerospace and Agricultural Implement Workers of America
International Woodworkers of America
Interprovincial Steel and Pipe Corp. Limited
Inuit Circumpolar Conference
Inuit Tapirisat of Canada
Jacob, Joseph W.
James Bay Crees
James Bay Tribal Council of the Nishnawbe-Aski Nation
Janssen, W.P.
Jean, Michèle
Jewett, G.A.
Johnson, Brian A.
Johnson, Eunadie
Johnson, Martine, Mayor of Frobisher Bay
Johnston, The Honourable Donald
Jorgenson, Dianne E.

Julian, Henry
Jull, Peter B.
Jurdant, Michel and Barbara Tessier
Kagawa, Dean
Kaiser, K.
Kantor, Mark G.
Kastner, Arnold
Katimavik (Group #24)
Katimavik (Group #152)
Katimavik (Group #4448)
Kavana, James
Keewatin Inuit Association
Keewatin Regional Council
Kekuli Audio Visual Society
Kendal, Peter
Kennedy, Terrence
Kent, William
Khachatourians, George G.
Kierans, Thomas W.
Kingfisher Management Limited
Kirkman, Fred
Kitchener Chamber of Commerce
Klasen, Olaf
Korey, George
Kristjanson, Leo F.
Kurland Development Corporation
L'Université du troisième age
Labour Council of Metropolitan Toronto
Ladell, B.W.
Lakehead Social Planning Council
Lalonde, Claude
Lambton County Board of Education
Lamontagne, Lorne and Alex Murchie
Langelier, Denis
Larson, L.A.
Laubach Literacy of Canada
Laubach Literacy of Canada (Ontario)
Laurentian Group
Lavoie, Jean-Claude, Mayor of Shipshaw
Le Beau, Pierre
LeBlanc, Ronald C.
Le Groupe Desgagnés inc.
Lehner, Joseph V.
LeMay, M. Martial
Lemire, Jean-Marc
Lemprière, J.V.
Lethbridge Chamber of Commerce
Lethbridge Interagency Committee
Lethbridge Research Station
Lewis, L.A.
Liberal Party of Manitoba
Life Underwriters Association of Canada
Lindseth, Roy O.
Lingman, Bob
Lister, Rota Herzberg
Little, Thomas B.
Local Exchange Trading System
Lockett, Wilfred G.

London Life Insurance Company
London Status of Women Action Group
Lone Rock Resources Limited
Long, Gus
Loomis, Reg. D.
Jim Lotz Associates
Low, Ken
Lowry, Peter J.
Lubbock, Michael R.
Luttervelt, Douglas H.
Maass, G.
Macaree, David
MacBain, Al, MP
MacDonald, R.A.
Machinery and Equipment Manufacturers' Association of Canada
Macintosh, Norman B. and John Coleman
MacIsaac, Ronald F.
Mackie, James F.
MacKinnon, Frank
MacLaren, G.W.
Maclean Hunter Limited
MacLean, Vincent J., MLA
MacMillan, Bruce
MacMillan, George S.
Maine, Frank
Mainland Dairymen's Association
Maire, André
Makivik Corporation
Malcolmson, Kim
Management Council for Responsible Employee Relations
Mangalam, Mr. and Mrs.
Manitoba Action Committee on the Status of Women
Manitoba Advisory Council on the Status of Women
Manitoba Anti-Poverty Organization Inc.
Manitoba Association for Children and Adults with Learning Disabilities
Manitoba Association of Urban Municipalities
Manitoba Federation of Labour
Manitoba Keewatinowi Okimakanak Inc.
Mardon, J. and G.N. Ionides
Marine Workers' Federation
Maritide Co. Limited
Maritime Electric Company Limited
Maritime Lumber Bureau
Maritime Telegraph and Telephone Company Limited
Marquis, Benoit
Masters, Wayne
Matejko, Alexander J.
Mathes, A.F.
Maund, Jacqueline K.
Maynard, Murray R.
McAllister, Ian
McAllister, Kenneth
McClusky, John B.
McDonald, Neil
McElcheran, William
McGill University
McLoughlin, Peter F.M.
McMaster University

McRuer, John D.
McWilliam, Shirlie
Meincke, Peter
Memorial University of Newfoundland, Faculty of Business Administration
Mennonite Central Committee Canada
Mensah, Spero
Mental Health Association in Saskatchewan
Métallurgie Frontenac Limitée
Métivier, Gilles
Meyer, Jack L.
Michael Doyle and Associates Limited
Michael Jarvis Consultants Limited
Michael, Cliff, MLA
MIDAS Reform Organization of Alberta
Miller, Bernard F.
Miller, J.L.
Mining Association of British Columbia
Mining Association of Canada
Minto Family Life Education Centre Inc.
Miramichi Region Development Corporation Inc.
Mitchell, Ian H.
Mobilisation contre la misère
Moncton Volunteer Centre
Monenco Limited
Montgomery, James L.M.
Montreal Economic Promotion Committee
Moore, Samuel A.
Morison, George
Morley, Joseph A.
Moss, Lawson Co. Limited
Motor Vehicle Manufacturers' Association
Mount Saint Vincent University
Mowers, Cleo W.
Municipality of Metropolitan Toronto
Municipality of the District of Lunenburg
Munro, The Honourable John C.
Murgaski, Victor
Murphy, Rod, MP
Murray, G. Betty
Murray, R.V.
Nance, Phillip and Krista
Narbey, Greg
Nashwaak Consulting
Nasogaluak, William and Doug Billingsley
National Action Committee on the Status of Women
National Council of Welfare
National Council of Women of Canada
National Council of YMCAs of Canada
National Farmers Union
National Farmers Union (PEI)
National Pensioners and Senior Citizens Federation
National Research Council of Canada
National Spiritual Assembly of the Baha'is of Canada
National Union of Provincial Government Employees
Native Canadian Petroleum Association and Canada Geothermal Oil Limited
Native Communications Inc.
Natural Sciences and Engineering Research Council of Canada
Nazaire, Lionel

Neary, Stephen A., MLA
Neufeld, John W.
Nevison, Myrne
New Brunswick Advisory Council on the Status of Women
New Brunswick Association of Métis and Non-Status Indians
New Brunswick Federation of Labour
New Brunswick Liberal Party
New Brunswick New Democratic Party
New Brunswick Premier's Council on the Status of Disabled Persons
New Brunswick Public Employees Association
New Brunswick Telephone Company Limited
New Brunswick Young Liberal Association
New Dawn Enterprises Limited
Newfoundland and Labrador Arts Council
Newfoundland and Labrador Federation of Labour
Newfoundland and Labrador Federation of Municipalities
Newfoundland and Labrador Human Rights Association
Newfoundland and Labrador Youth Advisory Council
Newfoundland Association of Social Workers
Newfoundland Light and Power Co. Limited
Nicholls, A.L.
Nicholson, G. Paul
Nicolaou, Anthony D.
Niemi, Fo
Nishnawbe-Aski Nation
Non-Organized Workers of Thunder Bay
Nordair
Nordicity Group Limited
Norman Regional Development Inc.
Norrie, G.C.
North Shore Citizens Committee for Responsible Forest Management
North-South Institute
Northeastern Ontario Energy Conservation Association
Northern Canada Power Commission
Northern Development Council of British Columbia
Northern Flood Committee
Northern Ontario District Council of Lumber and Sawmill Workers Union
Northern Telecom Limited
Northwest Territories Association of Municipalities
Northwest Territories Chamber of Mines
Northwest Territories Public Service Association
Northwest Territories Registered Nurses Association
Northwestern Ontario Municipal Association
Northwestern Ontario Women's Centre
Nova Scotia Advisory Council on the Status of Women
Nova Scotia Farmers' Union
Nova Scotia Federation of Labour
Nova Scotia New Democratic Party
Nova Scotia Nurses' Union
Nova Scotia Teachers' Union
NOVATRON
Nunavut Constitutional Forum
Nuu-Chah-Nulth Tribal Council
Oberlander, H. Peter
Oberle, Frank, MP
Oberti, Oberto
O'Brien, Chris
O'Brien, Terry

Ocean Harvesters Limited
Office de la pastorale sociale du diocèse de Québec
Ogden, Michael
Oliver, J.W.
Olshanoski, Stan
Ontario Association of Family Service Agencies
Ontario Business Improvement Area Association
Ontario Committee on the Status of Women
Ontario Confederation of University Faculty Associations
Ontario Federation of Agriculture
Ontario Federation of Students
Ontario Institute of Agrologists
Ontario Public Service Employees Union
Ontario Secondary School Teachers' Federation
Ontario Teachers' Federation
Operation Solidarity
Ophek, Eli
Ordre des comptables agréés du Québec
Ordre des ingénieurs du Québec
Osborne, John E.
Ottawa Symphony Orchestra
Ottawa-Carleton Board of Trade
Otto, Carl H.
Ouellet, The Honourable André
Overs, John E.
Oxley, F.O.
Pacific Group for Policy Alternatives
Palliser Wheat Growers Association
Palmer, James S.
Panarctic Oils Limited
Paradigm Health
Parliament, H.E.
Parti libéral du Québec
Partington, R.J.
Paterson, Ross H.
Paul, Ross H.
Paus-Jenssen, A.
Payne, Fern G.
Payne, G.
Peeters, Martin
Peitchinis, Stephen G.
People United for a Non-Exploitive Society
People, Words and Change
Percival, Alan Hardy
Perel, Motty
Perley, Daniel R.
Perrault, Charles
Peters, Abe
Peters, H.
Petro-Canada
Pétromont Inc.
Pettick, Joseph
Pfeifer, Conrad
Pictou County Research and Development Commission
Piper, T.C.
Pitfield, The Honourable Senator P. Michael
Placer Development Limited
Planetary Initiative for the World We Choose

Podhy, Pauline
Policy Analysis and Research Management
Pollution Probe
Polysar Limited
Polyvalente "Le Boisé", Atelier de culture
Pomerleau, Hervé
Ponderosa Park Development Company Limited
Porter, Stephen
Pousette, John
Prairie Implement Manufacturers Association
Pratt & Whitney Canada Inc.
Precision Engraving Co. Limited
Presber, T.C.
Prince Edward Island Advisory Council on the Status of Women
Prince Edward Island Egg Commodity Marketing Board
Prince Edward Island Federation of Agriculture
Prince Edward Island Potato Marketing Board
Prince George and District Labour Council
Prince George and District Senior Citizens Activity Centre
Prince George and District United Way
Prince George Chamber of Commerce
Prince George Community Arts Council
Prince George Region Development Corporation
Procycle Inc.
Professional Institute of the Public Service of Canada
Prospectors and Developers Association
Pross, A. Paul
Provincial Advisory Council on the Status of Women (Newfoundland and Labrador)
Public Interest Advocacy Centre
Pugsley, William H.
Pulsifer Sr., Orville B.
Puziak, M.D.
Quebec Federation of Senior Citizens
Quittner, J.K.
Rawson Academy of Aquatic Science
Ray, A.K.
Raycroft, J.G.
Raynauld, André
Récupération Bois-Francs Inc.
Reese, Peter J.
Regional Municipality of Sudbury
Regional Municipality of York
Registered Nurses' Association of British Columbia
Reid, James F.
Rémillard, Gil
Rental Housing Council of British Columbia
Réseau d'action et d'information pour les femmes
Retail Council of Canada
Retail Council of Canada (Winnipeg)
Richard, J.G.
Ricks, James, and Frances A.
Riddell, C.H.
Roberts, Richard
Roberts, Stan C.
Robertson, Alec
Robertson, Gordon
Robson, C.A.
Roussel, Claude

Rowan, William O.
Roy, Fabien
Roy, Réal
Royal Bank of Canada
Rudnyckyj, J.B.
Rumball, Donald A.
Rupert, Gary B.
Rural Learning Association
Russell, D.P.
Ryan, R. Lloyd
St. Clair College
St. Francis Xavier University
Saint John Board of Trade
St. John's Board of Trade
St. Patrick's Social Justice Committee
Salonius, P.O.
Saltsman, Max
Sarasin, André C.
Sarnia/Lambton Economic Development Commission
Saskatchewan Action Committee on the Status of Women
Saskatchewan Chamber of Commerce
Saskatchewan Co-ordinating Council on Social Planning
Saskatchewan Council for International Co-operation
Saskatchewan Environmental Society
Saskatchewan Federation of Agriculture
Saskatchewan Federation of Labour
Saskatchewan Mining Association Inc.
Saskatchewan Teachers' Federation
Saskatchewan Urban Municipalities Association
Saskatchewan Working Women
Saskatoon Board of Trade
Saskatoon Union of Unemployed Workers
Schey, John A.
School of Economic Science
Science Council of Canada
Scott, Anthony
Scott, Christopher
Scott, Donald P.
Scott, James A.
Scott, Paul
Scott, Stephen
Seaboard Lumber Sales Company Limited
Seafarers' International Union of Canada
Sebella, Carol John
Seeley, Larry E.
Semotiuk, Andriy J.
Settle, Winston
Sévigny, Roseline and Noëlla Porter
Shargool, Peter D.
Shashka, Gus
Shaw, N.
Shelford, Cyril M.
Shell Canada Limited
Shepard, Merrill W.
Sheps, Lillian
Shields, R. and W. Sheridan
Shields, William S.
Shiell, Maisie

Shoe Manufacturers' Association of Canada
Shumuk, Ivan
Sierra Club of Western Canada
Simek, Stefan
Simmons, Helen
Simpson, C.H.
Singh, Hira
Singhal, Raj K.
SLACAN
Sloan, A.
Smith International Canada Limited
Smith, Donald S.
Smits, Nel
Smyth, Steven
SNC Group
Snow, Kathleen M.
Snyder, Harold L.
Sobolewski, André
Social Action Commission, Roman Catholic Diocese of Charlottetown
Social Planning and Research Council of Hamilton and District
Social Planning and Review Council of British Columbia
Social Planning Council of Metropolitan Toronto
Social Planning Council of Ottawa-Carleton
Social Planning Council of Winnipeg
Société de développement de Jonquière inc.
Société inter-port de Québec
Société Saint-Thomas d'Aquin
Society of Atomic Energy of Canada Limited Professional Employees (Pinawa)
Society of Atomic Energy of Canada Limited Professional Employees, Executive (Chalk River)
Society of Management Accountants of Canada
Software Industry Development Association
Sommet Québécois de la jeunesse
Sorensen, Lynda, MLA
Sorrenti, Adam M.
South Grenville District High School, Students of Grade 13 Geography
Southern Kings and Queens Community Advisory Board
Spangehl, Ed
J.H. Stacey Professional Research and Information Services
Standards Council of Canada
Staples, Richard
Startin, Don
Status of Women Action Group (Victoria)
Status of Women Council (Yukon)
Steering Committee for Implementing the Ecosystem Approach
Stein, Carol
Stewart, Ross and Evaleen Jaager
Steyaert, Octaaf
STOP Inc.
Storefront for Voluntary Agencies
Students' Union of Nova Scotia
Sub Committee on Youth Unemployment
Sudbury 2001
Sudbury Federal New Democratic Party
Sun Life Assurance Co. of Canada
Sutherland, R.E.
Swanson, M.L.
Sydney Steel Corporation

Syed, Javed
Symes, Beth and Marilou McPhedran
Syms, J.C.
Syndicat des producteurs de bois de la Beauce
Syndicat des travailleurs de la société asbestos limitée inc.
Tallman, F.R.J.
Task Force on Micro-Electronics and Employment
Taylor, A.
Taylor, D. Angus
Technical University of Nova Scotia
Teconomics Limited
Telephone Pioneers of America (Canada - Region 1)
Thakur, Hari K.
Therriault, Clément Guy
3rd Dimensions and Associates Limited
Thomas, F.R.
Thomas, Morley
Thomas, Roy
Thompson Chamber of Commerce
Thompson Industrial Commission
Thompson, Brian
Thompson, Dixon
Thompson, Fred G.
Thompson, Kirk
Thunder Bay and District Council of Clergy
Thunder Bay and District Labour Council
Thunder Bay Economic Development Corporation
Thunder Bay Indian Youth Friendship Society
Thunder Bay Multicultural Association
Toolsie, Rampersand
Toppin, Don
Toronto Board of Education
Toronto Jewish Congress
Tourism Industry Association of Canada (Montreal)
Tourism Industry Association of Canada (Ottawa)
Town of Oromocto
Town of Prescott
Town of Swan River
Transalta Utilities Corporation
Travel Industry Association of the Northwest Territories
Trent University
B.A. Tripp and Associates Limited
Trust Companies Association of Canada
Trzecieski, Mike A.
TVOntario
Twigg, John
Ubriaco, Rita
Ultramar Canada Inc.
Unemployment Committee of Regina
Union des municipalités du Québec
Union of Ontario Indians
United Church of Canada, Working Unit on Social Issues and Justice
United Grain Growers Limited
United Mine Workers of America, District 18
United Mine Workers of America, District 26
United Native Nations
United Steelworkers of America
United Steelworkers of America, Hamilton Steelworkers Area Council

United Steelworkers of America, Local 6500
United Steelworkers of America, Local 6166
United Steelworkers of America, Local 1064
United Steelworkers of America (Whitehorse)
United Way Canada
United Way of Central Quebec
United Way of Fredericton
United Way of Greater Toronto
United Way of Montreal
United Way of Ottawa-Carleton
United Way of Quebec
United Way of the Lower Mainland
United Way of Thompson
United Way of Winnipeg
University College of Cape Breton
University of Alberta Association of Academic Staff
University of British Columbia, Centre for Continuing Education
University of Calgary Faculty Association
University of Calgary Students' Union
University of Lethbridge
University of Manitoba, Faculty of Agriculture
University of Regina
University of Regina Faculty Association
University of Saskatchewan, MBA Students, College of Graduate Studies
University of Toronto, Students Administrative Council
University of Waterloo
University of Windsor
University of Windsor, International Business Studies Research Unit
University of Winnipeg Working Group
Urban Development Institute Canada
Urban Transportation Development Corporation Limited
Ursel, Norman H.
Valcin, Yvon
Van Leeuwen, Bert
Van Roggen, The Honourable Senator George
Vancouver Board of Trade
Vancouver Island Building and Construction Trades Council
Vancouver Unemployed Action Centre
Vancouver Women in Trades Association
Vanier Institute of the Family
Via Rail Canada Inc.
Victoria Labour Council
Vincent, Kimbell R.
Vogler, Kersten H.O.
Voluntary Planning Board
Volunteer Centre of Calgary
Vosper, Velma
Wahn, J.D.
Wallace, James
Wallace, Scott A.
Walsh, E.D.
Ward, Neil
Wardair International Limited
Warner, G.B.
Warner, I.D.
Watson, John R.
Wayman, Morris
Weaver, Bill W.

Webb, Geoff
Webb, J. Tom
Weeren, Donald J.
Weppler, Reuben
Weser, Ernest J.
Western Constitutional Forum
Western Energy Investments Limited
Western Stock Growers' Association
Western Transportation Advisory Council
George Weston Limited
Whelan, The Honourable Eugene F.
White, Walter E.
Whitehorse Chamber of Commerce
Whitney, Joanne
Whyte, John Donaldson
Wiggett, Edward G.
Wilkinson, Ken
Willey, Gerald A.
Williams, Merlyn M.
Williamson, Ian B.
Wills, Charles E.
Willson, Bruce F.
Willson, W.H.
Wilson, L.R.
Windsor and District Labour Council
Windsor Chamber of Commerce
Windsor Coalition for Development
Windsor Women's Incentive Centre
Windsor-Essex County Development Commission
Winnipeg Chamber of Commerce
Winnipeg Co-ordinating Committee for Disarmament
Winnipeg Commodity Exchange
Winnipeg Labour Council
Wise, Dorothy
Women Against the Budget
Women and Economic Development Committee of the Northwestern Ontario Women's Decade Council
Women United for a Non-Exploitive New Age
Women Unlimited
Women's Information and Referral Centre
Women's Involvement Committee of Upper Trinity South
Women's Network Inc.
Woodbridge, Reed and Associates Limited
Woods, Elizabeth
World Federalists of Canada
Wyeth Limited
Yorston, Wilfred
Young Women's Christian Association of Calgary
Young Women's Christian Association of Canada
Young Women's Christian Association of Metropolitan Toronto
Young Women's Christian Association of Thompson
Young, David R.
Yukon Chamber of Mines
Yukon Territorial Public Service Association
Yukon Visitors Association
Zimmermann, Hans G.

Written Submissions to the Commission

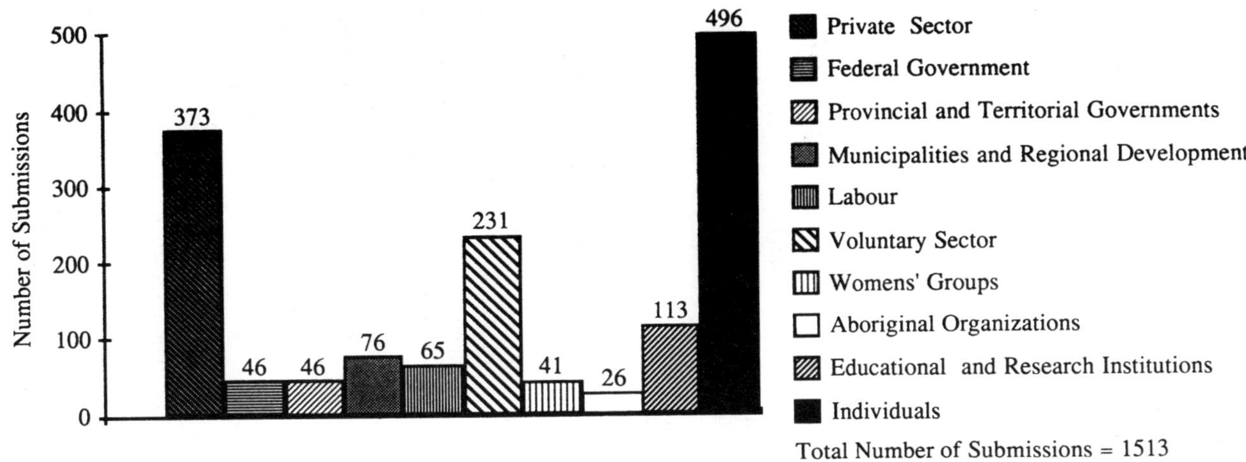

APPENDIX C-1

Schedule of Provincial and Territorial Government Participation

	Date of Hearing
British Columbia[3]	20 June 1983[1]
Alberta	18 June 1983[1] 15 November 1983[1]
Saskatchewan	28 March 1983[1] 23 November 1983[2]
Manitoba[3]	29 March 1983[1] 28 November 1983[1]
Ontario	21 February 1983[1] 5 December 1983[2]
Quebec[3]	28 February 1983[1] 27 October 1983[1]
New Brunswick	2 June 1983[1] 23 September 1983[2]
Nova Scotia	18 January 1983[1] 13 October 1983[1]
Prince Edward Island	3 June 1983[1] 9 December 1983[1]
Newfoundland and Labrador	24 February 1983[1] 20 September 1983[2]
Yukon	31 March 1983[1] 9 September 1983[2]
Northwest Territories	30 March 1983[1] 12 September 1983[2] 27 November 1984[1]

[1] private meeting
[2] public hearing
[3] no written submission received

APPENDIX C-2

Schedule of Federal Government Participation

	Location and date of hearing
Atomic Energy of Canada Ltd.	Hull, December 14, 1983
Canadian Forestry Service (Environment Canada)	Not heard
Canadian Saltfish Corporation	St. John's, September 21, 1983
Economic Council of Canada	Toronto, December 8, 1983
Environment Canada	Not heard
Heritage Canada Foundation	Hull, December 12, 1983
Minister of Agriculture	Regina, November 24, 1983
Minister of Communications	Montreal, November 3, 1983
Minister of Consumer and Corporate Affairs	Not heard
Minister of Health and Welfare	Not heard
Minister of Indian Affairs and Northern Development	Not heard
Minister of Labour	Ottawa, December 16, 1983
Minister of State for Economic and Regional Development and Minister Responsible for Science and Technology	St. John's, December 21, 1983
Minister of State for Social Development	Vancouver, September 8, 1983
Minister of State for Multiculturalism	Not heard
Minister of Transport	Winnipeg, November 28, 1983
Minister Responsible for the Status of Women	Ottawa, December 15, 1983
National Research Council of Canada	Hull, December 14, 1983
Natural Sciences and Engineering Research Council of Canada	Hull, December 14, 1983
Northern Canada Power Commission	Whitehorse, September 10, 1983
Petro-Canada	Toronto, December 2, 1983
Science Council of Canada	Hull, December 14, 1983
Standards Council of Canada	Ottawa, December 16, 1983
Via Rail Canada Inc.	Ottawa, December 16, 1983

APPENDIX C-3

Schedule of Local and Regional Government Participation

City of Vancouver	September 6, 1983
District of Chilliwack	September 6, 1983
City of Whitehorse	September 9, 1983
City of Prince George	September 12, 1983
District of Mackenzie	September 12, 1983
Village of Pouce Coupe	September 12, 1983
Peace River-Liard Regional District	September 12, 1983
City of Yellowknife	September 13, 1983
City of Charlottetown	September 19, 1983
City of Sydney	September 22, 1983
City of Moncton	September 22, 1983
Town of Oromocto	Not Heard
City of Fredericton	September 23, 1983
Town of Frobisher Bay	September 26, 1983
Town of Inuvik	September 29, 1983
Community of Rankin Inlet	October 1, 1983
Municipality of Halifax County	October 11, 1983
Municipality of the District of Lunenberg	Not Heard
City of Halifax	October 13, 1983
City of Windsor	October 17, 1983
City of Thompson	October 19, 1983
District of Lynn Lake	October 19, 1983
Regional Municipality of Sudbury	October 19, 1983
Municipality of Shipshaw	October 27, 1983
City of St. George-de-Beauce	Not Heard
City of Chicoutimi	October 27, 1983
City of Jonquière	October 27, 1983
Town of Anjou	October 31, 1983
City of Calgary	November 7, 1983
City of Lethbridge	November 10, 1983
City of Edmonton	November 14, 1983
Town of Swan River	Not Heard
City of Winnipeg	November 28, 1983

Municipality of Metropolitan Toronto	December 1, 1983
Corporation of the Borough of East York	Not Heard
Regional Municipality of York	December 9, 1983
Town of Prescott	Not Heard
Town of Carlyle	December 12, 1983
City of Ottawa	December 16, 1983
City of Hull	December 16, 1983

APPENDIX C-4

Schedule of Participants in Public Hearings Fall 1983

Vancouver, British Columbia
September 6, 1983

Canadian Manufacturers' Association
Vern C. German, Chairman
William B. Boggs, Immediate Past Chairman; Chairman, Canada Systems Group
Doreen Braverman, Director; President, Fleming Decal and Sign Limited
Peter O'Dell, Director; General Manager, Borden Chemical, Western Division
Graeme C. Hughes, Executive Vice-President and Secretary
J. Laurent Thibault, Executive Vice-President
Charles Garneau, Assistant Secretary to the Board

Canadian Council on Social Development
Michael Clague, President and Chairman
Terrance Hunsley, Executive Director

City of Vancouver
Michael Harcourt, Mayor of Vancouver
Brian Carter, Consulting Economist, Vancouver Economic Advisory Commission (VEAC)
Thomas Hutton, VEAC Secretariat; Assistant Manager, Economic Development Office, City of Vancouver
Stuart Backerman, Social Planner (Cultural Affairs), Social Planning Department, City of Vancouver
Shirley Chan, Executive Assistant

Operation Solidarity
Art Kube, President, B.C. Federation of Labour
Larry Kuehn, President, B.C. Teachers' Federation
Pam Chapple, Health Sciences Association
Nora Paton, Chief Executive Officer, B.C. Nurses' Union
Clay Perry, B.C. Federation of Labour

District of Chilliwack
G.B. Clark, Mayor of Chilliwack
Jerry Pirie, Alderman

Pacific Group for Policy Alternatives
David D. Schreck, Pacific Group Steering Committee
David Rice, Pacific Group Steering Committee

B.C. Central Credit Union
Harry A. Down, Chief Executive Officer, First Pacific Credit Union
P.P. Podovinikoff, Chief Executive Officer, B.C. Central Credit Union
Richard J. Thomas, Director, Government Affairs

Mining Association of British Columbia
Tex C. Enemark, President and Chief Executive Officer
A.J. Petrina, Senior Vice-President and Chief Operating Officer, Placer Development Limited
Ralph W. Huenemann, Director of Research, Mining Association of British Columbia

Vancouver, British Columbia
September 7, 1983

Theme Panel: The Global Economy
The Honourable Senator George Van Roggen
Bernard Wood, Director, North-South Institute
Philip C. Barter, Chairman, Vancouver Board of Trade
Jim Matkin, President, Employers' Council of British Columbia
Michael Goldberg, Associate Dean of Commerce and Business, University of British Columbia
Jack Munro, President, International Woodworkers of America, Regional Council No. 1
Philip Legg, Assistant Research Director, International Woodworkers of America, Regional Council No. 1

British Columbia and Yukon Territory Building and Construction Trades Council
Roy Gautier, President
Clive Little, Director, Communications and Education

Mainland Dairymen's Association
Albert Van Esch

The Roberts Group
Stan C. Roberts, President, Fraser Resources Inc.; Chairman, Swinwood and Associates Inc.

Registered Nurses' Association of British Columbia
Bernadet Ratsoy, President
Gloria Parker, Vice-President
Pat Cutshall, Executive Director
Elizabeth Kirkwood, Director

British Columbia Health Association
Charles W. Grierson, President
Patricia Wadsworth, Executive Director
E.M. Tomasky, Assistant Executive Director, Administrative Services

Vancouver, British Columbia
September 8, 1983

Association of British Columbia Professional Foresters
Peter Ackhurst, President; Forestry Manager, Vancouver Region,
B.C. Ministry of Forestry
William Dumont, Vice-President
R. Jones, Consulting Forester

Council of Forest Industries of British Columbia
Ron Longstaffe, Chairman; Executive Vice-President,
Canadian Forest Products Limited
David McInnes, First Vice-Chairman; President and Chief Executive Officer,
Weyerhaueser Canada Limited
Tom Rust, Former Chairman; President and Chief Executive Officer,
Crown Zellerbach Canada Limited
Don Lanskail, President and Chief Executive Officer

Peter McCormick and Gordon Gibson

The Honourable Senator Jack Austin, Minister of State for Social Development

Fédération des franco-colombiens
Marc Roy, President
Claude Roberge, Political and Economic Officer
Pierre Lapointe, President, Chambre de commerce franco-colombienne

Assembly of British Columbia Arts Councils
Donna V. Yates, President
Bruce Hunter, Director; Honorary Treasurer, Community Arts Council of Vancouver
Anne Macdonald, Executive Director, Community Arts Council of Vancouver

Placer Development Limited
C. Allen Born, President, Chairman and Chief Executive Officer

H.N. Halvorson Consultants Limited
H.N. Halvorson

University of British Columbia Centre for Continuing Education
Ann Ironside, Program Director of Public Affairs; President, Canadian Association
for Adult Education
Vince Battistelli, Associate Director

David R. Young

Vancouver, British Columbia
September 9, 1983

British Columbia Law Union
Judi Gedye, Barrister and Solicitor
Craig Paterson, Barrister and Solicitor
Doug Sanders, Professor of Law, University of British Columbia
Paisley Woodward, Researcher

Asia Pacific Foundation of Canada
John Bruk, Chairman

British Columbia Association of Social Workers
Stuart Alcock, Vice-President
Christopher J. Walmsley, Executive Director

Social Planning and Review Council of British Columbia
Tim Beachy, President
Richard B. Splane, Immediate Past President
Virginia Langdon, Executive Director

Federated Anti-Poverty Groups of B.C.
Gus Long, Editor
Barbara Davies, Co-ordinator, Co-Pro
Mary Billick, Co-ordinator, Community Housing Registry

First United Church
Leslie Black, Community Worker
Linda Ervin, Commissioned Minister and Community Worker

British Columbians for Mentally Handicapped People
Val Fish, Moderator; Employment Presenter
Janice Balfour, Housing Presenter
Jim Balfour, Assistant to Moderator
Peter Russell, People First, North Shore

André Sobolewski

Women Against the Budget
Diane Ellis, Women's Research Centre
Megan Ellis, Women Against the Budget

Bill W. Weaver

Vancouver Women in Trades Association
Kate Braid
Allison Stewart
J. Blair

British Columbia Institute of Technology
Gordon Thom, President
Drug Svetic, Vice-President of Education
Craig Greenhill, Director, Planning
Duncan MacPherson, Vice-President, Administration; Bursar
David Hume, Provincial Consultant

Whitehorse, Yukon
September 9, 1983

Government of Yukon
The Honourable C.W. Pearson, Commissioner
J. Ferbey, Deputy Minister of Economic Development and Intergovernmental Affairs
F. Fingland, Deputy Minister of Finance

City of Whitehorse
Florence Whyard, Mayor of Whitehorse
John Pearce, Alderman

Whitehorse, Yukon
September 10, 1983

Yukon Visitors' Association
Barry Redfern, Executive Director
June Hampton, President
William Braden, Government-Industry Relations Committee

Northern Canada Power Commission
J. Smith, Chairman and Chief Executive Officer
Harold Kaldor, Regional Administrator
Mel Foster, Financial Consultant

Association of Yukon Communities
André Carrell, Executive Director

Council for Yukon Indians
Joe Willie, Vice-Chairman, Economic Development

Whitehorse Chamber of Commerce
Patrick Dixon, President

Yukon Chamber of Mines
G. MacDonald, President

Yukon Teachers' Association
G. Johnston

Yukon Territorial Public Service Association
Jim McCullough, Business Agent

United Steelworkers' Union
B. Rudychuk
S. Frei, President, Local 8243 (Faro)
J. Kline, President, Local 953 (Tungsten)
D. Rody

Status of Women Council
Audrey Lougheed

Yellowknife, Northwest Territories
September 12, 1983

Government of the Northwest Territories
The Honourable Arnold James McCallum, Minister of Economic Development and Tourism

Métis Association of the Northwest Territories
Wally Firth, President
Harold Cook, Vice-President
Larry Tourangeau, Vice-President

Northwest Territories Chamber of Mines
Terrence Daniels, General Manager

Consumers' Association of Canada (Yukon Branch)
Sandra Ketchum, President
Chris Tricoteux, Vice-President
Anna-Marie Dawe, Northwest Territories National Board
Joan Halpenny, Former President

Northwest Territories Registered Nurses' Association
Patricia Felhaver, President

Northwest Territories Motor Transport Association
Mr. Ladorbruk

Northwest Territories Teachers' Federation
Blake Lyons

Yellowknife, Northwest Territories
September 13, 1983

Northwest Territories Association of Municipalities
Anita Perry, Executive Director

Inuvik Chamber of Commerce
D. Hill, Executive Director

Dene Nation of the Northwest Territories
Steven Kakfwi

Nunavut Constitutional Forum
The Honourable Dennis Patterson, Chairman

Lynda Sorenson, MLA

City of Yellowknife
Michael Ballantyne, Mayor of Yellowknife

Travel Industry Association of the Northwest Territories
Patricia McMahon
Andrew Goussaert
Albert Eggenberger

Storefront for Voluntary Agencies
Elizabeth Seaton, Executive Director
Gary Lathan, Executive Director, YWCA
Michèle Boon, President, YWCA
Eya Lewycky, Executive Director, Mental Health N.W.T.
Chris Allerston, Supervisor, Yellowknife Day Care Association

Northwest Territories Public Service Association
Andrew T. Lamb

Stefan Simek

Northwest Territories Friendship Centres
Tom Eagle, President

Prince George, British Columbia
September 12, 1983

Mr. O'Connor

Northern Development Council of British Columbia
E. Mercier, Chairman; Mayor of Prince George
J. Hannam, Deputy-Chairman; Chairman, Peace River-Liard Regional District
M. Laloge, Mayor of Pouce Coupe
V. Ciccone, Administrator, District of Mackenzie

College of New Caledonia
Charles J. McCaffray, Principal

Carrier Sekani Tribal Council
Archie Patrick, President
Edward John, President, Tunnisal Timber

Prince George and District Senior Citizens Activity Centre Society
A. Holdner, President
K. Matthews, Director
Z. Taylor, Secretary

Immigrant and Multicultural Services Society
Dietrich Elias, Vice-Chairman
R. Yip, Finance Chairman
G. Baldwin, Legal Advisor

Prince George and District United Way
Murry Krause, Executive Director
Maureen Pfliger, Executive Director, Prince George Crises Intervention Society
Susan Cook, Regional Director, Northern B.C. and Yukon Canadian Red Cross Society
Mike Millard, Executive Director, YM/YWCA
Brian Gardiner, Executive Director, Big Brothers/Big Sisters
Lorna Dittmar, Executive Director, Prince George Association for Individuals with Mental Handicaps

Community Seminar
Charles J. McCaffray, Principal, College of New Caledonia
M. Hill, Aim High: Association for the Mentally Handicapped
Monica Becott, Town Centre Business Association
John Backhouse, Alderman; Regional Librarian, College of New Caledonia
L. Dino, Head Librarian, Prince George Public Library

Paul McCallum

Prince George, British Columbia
September 13, 1983

Council on Forest Industries, Northern Interior Lumber Sector
John F. Whitmer, President, Balfour Forest Products Inc.
Russ J. Clinton, Vice-President, Woodlands, West Fraser Mills Limited
Don H. Gould, General Manager, The Pas Lumber Company Limited

Mark H. Gunther, Group Vice-President, Pulp and Paper,
Canadian Forest Products Limited

Prince George and District Labour Council
Donna Sacuta, Secretary-Treasurer
C. Hatherly, Executive Board
Ernie Myers, Executive Board
Bev Robinson, Co-ordinator, Prince George Unemployed Action Centre

Prince George Chamber of Commerce
Richard Ingram, President

Robert Dhensaw

Prince George Region Development Corporation
B. Philips, President
D. McMann, Manager

Economic Development Commission, Cariboo Regional District
Mary Ellen Glover, Economic Development Commissioner
R. Fossum
L. Urquhart

Victoria, British Columbia
September 14, 1983

Software Industry Development Association
D. H. Keen, Chairman
R. Fast, Vice-Chairman; President, Canadian Information Processing Society
Raymond G. Ginnever, Director, KG Consulting Limited
Len Bruton, Dean of Engineering, University of Victoria
Donald A. Alexander, Intercontinental Computer Technology Limited

The Honourable Jack Davis, MLA

Rod Dobell, Professor of Public Administration, University of Victoria

Greater Victoria Chamber of Commerce
W. T. Anderson, Immediate Past President
A. Lane, Past President
J. Currie, Vice-President
C. Steele, Past President

Sierra Club of Western Canada
Jim Bonfonti, Chairman
Michael Doherty, Regional Conservation Representative

Capital Families
Bernice Levitz Packford, Executive Director
David Nordstrom, Co-ordinator, Links Program for Parents of Teens

Victoria, British Columbia
September 15, 1983

Vancouver Island Building and Construction Trades Council
Jack Zettler, Trustee

Christopher Jones, Secretary-Treasurer

Keith Cowan

G. W. MacLaren

District of Shuswap-Revelstoke
Cliff Michael, MLA
Marlene Floss
George Gybo

Victoria Labour Council
J. W. Groves, Secretary-Treasurer

Status of Women Action Group
Stella Lord, Co-ordinating Committee
Diana Butler, Treasurer

Frances A. Ricks, School of Child Care, University of Victoria and
Jim Ricks, Director, Integrated Services, Child and Family Development

United Native Nations, Zone Five
Vic Wells, Chairperson
M. Crossley

Nuu-chah-nulth Tribal Council
George Watts, Chairman

Local Exchange Trading System
Michael Linton, Trustee
Lori Milne, Advisor

Women United for a Non-Exploitive New Age
Mary Christodoulou, Co-ordinator

Community Council of Greater Victoria
James Anglin, Vice-President
Derek Dashwood

Charlottetown, Prince Edward Island
September 19, 1983

Charlottetown Chamber of Commerce
David W. Hooley, President
Keith Mullins, General Manager

Atlantic Provinces Chamber of Commerce
William Wedlock, Chairman, Summerside, P.E.I.
Stuart Peters, Chairman-Elect and Vice-Chairman, Halifax, N.S.
J. Kenneth Langdon, President, Moncton, N.B.

Greater Summerside Chamber of Commerce
Derek D. Key, President-Elect
Earl G. Cannon, General Manager

Canadian Manufacturers' Association (P.E.I. Branch)
Wendell MacDonald, Chairman-Elect

John Morrisson, Vice-Chairman
C. M. Hickey, Secretary-Manager

City of Charlottetown
Frank Moran, Mayor of Charlottetown
George MacDonald, Alderman; Chairman, Town Planning Board
Harry Gaudet, Development Officer

Maritime Electric Company Limited
R. W. Smith, President
W. G. Lea, Counsel and Director

Horace B. Carver, MLA

National Farmers Union
Marie Hendricken, Women's Advisory Committee
Alan Ling

Prince Edward Island Federation of Agriculture
Eldred Simmons, President
Eric Hammill, Secretary-Manager

Prince Edward Island Egg Commodity Marketing Board
Bert Haneveld, Chairman
A. Macdonald, Manager

Donald Glendenning, President, Holland College

Social Action Committee of the Roman Catholic Diocese of Charlottetown
Mary Boyd, Director
Michael Leclair
J. P. Hendriken

Prince Edward Island Advisory Council on the Status of Women
D. M. Crane
H. Orford
H. Macdonald

St. John's, Newfoundland
September 20, 1983

Newfoundland and Labrador Federation of Municipalities
Ron Fagan, President
Doug Smith, Executive Director

Ocean Harvesters Limited
Alec Moores, General Manager

Government of Newfoundland and Labrador
The Honourable Brian Peckford, Premier
Cyril Abery, Deputy Minister, Intergovernmental Affairs Secretariat
B. E. Knight, Director, Economic and Social Programs,
Intergovernmental Affairs Secretariat
David Vardy, Clerk of the Executive Council

Newfoundland Light and Power Co. Limited
D. Templeton, President
A. Ryan, Vice-President, General Manager
D. Black, Legal Counsel
J. Landrigan, Staff Analyst

Newfoundland and Labrador Federation of Labour
William A. Parsons, President
Frank Taylor, Secretary-Treasurer
Nancy Riche, Eastern Vice-President
D. McGrath, Newfoundland Fish Food and Allied Workers Union

Women's Involvement Committee of Upper Trinity South
Wendy Murdoch, President
Florence Cranford
Evelyn Cranford

Harold L. Snyder, Director, Centre for Cold Ocean Resources Engineering, Memorial University of Newfoundland

Abe Peters, President, ACTRA (Newfoundland and Labrador Branch)

P. Dunn

Newfoundland and Labrador Human Rights Association
B. Riggs, President

St. John's, Newfoundland
September 21, 1983

St. John's Board of Trade
Bernie Beckett, Vice-President, Government Affairs
Greg Canning, Director of Legislation
Doug May, Royal Commission Committee
Brian Greene, Assistant General Manager

William Wells, President, Canadian Saltfish Corporation

The Honourable Donald Johnston, Minister of State for Economic and Regional Development and Minister of State for Science and Technology
Harry Swain, Departmental Secretary, MSERD
Gordon Slade, Federal Economic Coordinator, Newfoundland

Liberal Party of Newfoundland
Steven A. Neary, Leader of the Opposition
Melvin Baker, Researcher

Provincial Advisory Council on the Status of Women (Newfoundland and Labrador)
Ann Bell, President
Nancy Riche, Eastern Vice-President, Newfoundland and Labrador Federation of Labour
D. Robbins, Administrator

Memorial University of Newfoundland, Faculty of Business Administration
James Barnes, Dean of Business Administration
Robert Sexty, Professor

Newfoundland and Labrador Arts Council
Ken Pittman, Executive Director

Newfoundland Association of Social Workers
Wanda Lundrigan, President
Maureen Browne, Chairperson, Social Policy and Planning Council

Community Services Council of Newfoundland and Labrador
Karen McGrath, President
John O'Brien, Treasurer; Chairman, Research Advisory Committee
Frank Hawkins, Past President
Penelope Rowe, Executive Director

Newfoundland and Labrador Youth Advisory Council
Sean Daley, Chairman
Alanna M. Hanrahan, Executive Secretary
Douglas Riche, Provincial Coordinator

Sydney, Nova Scotia
September 22, 1983

Cape Breton Joint Expenditure Board
Jim Cunningham, Executive Director
J. Wadden, Warden, County of Cape Breton
M. Macdonald, Mayor of Sydney
J. MacCormack, Administrator, Community and Social Development, City of Sydney

Cape Breton Development Corporation
A. Roy Maclean, Vice-President, Corporate Planning
John Dodge, Vice-President, Industrial Development
A. Verschuren, Director, Long-Range Planning

Sydney Steel Corporation
J. D. Coffin, Manager, Traffic
H. S. MacLeod, Executive Assistant to the President
L. A. Hicks, Manager, Commercial Services
J. W. Macdonald, Manager, Marketing

United Steelworkers of America, Local 1064
Paul Grezel, President
Benny O'Neill, Financial Secretary
Winston S. Ruck, Staff Representative

United Mine Workers of America, District 26
Bob Burchell, International Teller, Canada

University College of Cape Breton
W. M. Reid, President

Industrial Cape Breton Board of Trade
Hector Dipersio, President
Wayne Lorway, Chairman, Government Affairs Committee
W. MacIntyre

Coalition of Social Organizations in Cape Breton
Reverend J. Capstick, President

Sister P. Butts, Political Scientist, University College of Cape Breton
Richard Sevigny, Director, Family Services of Eastern Nova Scotia
J. Currie, Manager, Steelmaking, Sydney Steel Corporation
Mary Kay MacLeod, Beaton Institute, University College of Cape Breton

The Honourable Vincent J. MacLean, MLA

Women Unlimited
Elizabeth Cusack Walsh
Cheryl AuCoin
Fran Manson

Federation of Community Development Corporations of Canada
Greg MacLeod, President
Tom O'Leary, Executive Director

New Dawn Enterprises Limited
R. MacSween, Chairman
Marcel Leroy, Board of Directors
John Hanratty, Research Officer

Reverend A. Maroun, President, Cape Breton Alternate Energy Society

Moncton, New Brunswick
September 22, 1983

City of Moncton
George S. Rideout, Mayor of Moncton
Murray MacLean, City Manager

Conseil économique du Nouveau-Brunswick inc.
Jean Chiasson, President
Ronald Leblanc, Professor of Economics, University of Moncton
Rino Volpé, Vice-President, Marketing, Compagnie Assomption Mutuelle-Vie
Valmond Chiasson, President, Association des empaqueteurs de poisson du Nouveau-Brunswick
Georges Wybouw, Director, Administration Research Centre, University of Moncton

Activités-Jeunesse
Marie-France LeFort, President
Joseph LaBelle, Executive Director

René Didier, Dean of Administration, University of Moncton

Federation of New Brunswick Faculty Associations
C.W.J. Eliot, President
Catherine Dagg-Murphy, Executive Director
Donald Poirier
Arsène Richard

Fisheries Council of Canada
Ronald W. Bulmer, President
Ian Langlands, Past Chairman; Vice-President, National Sea Products Limited
F.J. Frontain, National Vice-Chairman; Marketing Manager, United Maritime Fishermen

New Brunswick Federation of Labour
Timothy McCarthy, President
J. Albert Richardson, Secretary-Treasurer
John Murphy, Executive Secretary

New Brunswick Association of Métis and Non-Status Indians
Philip D. Fraser, Vice-President

Moncton Volunteer Centre
Steven Campbell, Chairman, Advisory Board

New Brunswick Advisory Council on the Status of Women
Madeleine LeBlanc, Chairperson
Elspeth Tullock, Researcher

Bernard Bujold

Fredericton, New Brunswick
September 23, 1983

City of Fredericton
Elbridge Wilkins, Mayor of Fredericton
George Robinson, Councillor
Richard Danziger, Director of Planning
John Robison, City Administrator

Capital Region Development Commission Inc.

John S. MacGillivray, President
Stanley R. Price, General Manager
Linda M. Furlought, Assistant to the General Manager
G. Robinson

Maritime Lumber Bureau
Anthony E. Rumbold, Executive Director

New Brunswick Telephone Company Limited
James A. Coombs, Vice-President, Operations

Government of New Brunswick
The Honourable Richard Hatfield, Premier

Liberal Party of New Brunswick
J. Raymond Frenette, Leader of the Opposition
Ronald LeBlanc, Economic Advisor
William Connell, Researcher, Opposition Office

New Brunswick New Democratic Party
Robert Hall, MLA
Tom Good, MLA, Finance and Energy Critic
David Brown, MLA, Social Services Critic
Allayne Armstrong, MLA, Critic on Women's Issues
Jules Halé, Council of Beresford

Saint John Board of Trade
Mary E. Travis, President

Lynda A. Heffernan, General Manager
Paul Hansen, Assistant Manager, Saint John-Fundy Region
Development Commission

Fredericton Chamber of Commerce
Bryan Ferguson, Consultant
David McClure, Computer Sales
Josh Shea, Managing Director, Modern Building Cleaning (NB) Limited

United Way of Fredericton
J. Andrew Cook, President
Kenneth Bartlett, Executive Committee
Sharon Cupples, Director

Association of University of New Brunswick Teachers
Gerald M. Clarke, President
Allan Sharp, Vice-President
Jon Thompson, Past President

Faculty Association of St. Thomas University
Howard Cody, Assistant Professor of Political Science
Claudia Whalen, Associate Professor of Psychology
Joan McFarland, Associate Professor of Economics
John Patterson, Assistant Professor of Romance Languages, French
Roger Moore, Professor of Romance Languages, Spanish

Peter Salonius

Frobisher Bay, Northwest Territories
September 26, 1983

John Amagoalik

Martine Johnson, Mayor of Frobisher Bay

Cynthia Mallin, Baffin Tourist Association

William Kungl, President, Chamber of Commerce

Des Micklos, Frobisher Inn

Brian Pearson

Cambridge Bay, Northwest Territories
September 28, 1983

Pearl Benijk, Communications Officer, Kitikmeot Inuit Association

Don McGillivery, Teacher

Stephen Bedingfield, Cambridge Bay Housing Association

Peter Scott, Superintendent, Economic Development and Tourism,
Government of the Northwest Territories

Keith Peterson, Commerce Officer, Government of the Northwest Territories

Cambridge Bay, Northwest Territories
September 29, 1983

George Hargrave, Trainer, Inuit Broadcasting Corporation

Students from Ilihakuik School

Howard Jones

John Komack, Ikaluktutiak Eskimo Co-operative

Harold Greary, Manager, Fred H. Ross and Associates

Residents of Cambridge Bay

Inuvik, Northwest Territories
September 29, 1983

John Hill, Deputy Mayor of Inuvik

Doug Billingsley

William Nasogaluak

Gary Morrison, Northwest Territories Teachers' Association

Chief MacCaulley, Inuvik Dene Band

Cynthia Creelman Hill

Tuktoyaktuk, Northwest Territories
September 30, 1983

Father Lemeur

Rankin Inlet, Northwest Territories
October 1, 1983

Henry Kablalik, Deputy Mayor of Rankin Inlet

Peter Ernerk, Keewatin Inuit Association

George Wesko

Cathy Towtongie, Executive Officer, Keewatin Regional Council

John Todd, President, Keewatin Chamber of Commerce

Jack Anawak, Vice-President, Keewatin Inuit Association

David Mellany, Environmental Consultant

Gordon Ray, Legislative Assembly, Keewatin North

Caroline Anawak, Rankin Inlet Community Education Committee

Halifax, Nova Scotia
October 11, 1983

Mount St. Vincent University
Margaret Fulton, President
Christine Ball, Co-ordinator, Women's Studies Programme
Susan Clark, Dean of Professional and Human Resource Development
Wendy MacLean, Assistant Professor of Economics

Britex Limited
Sandy Archibald, President

Municipality of Halifax County
Arthur MacKenzie, Warden
Murdock MacKay, Chairman, Halifax County Industrial Commission
Kenneth Meech, Chief Administrative Officer
Jack MacLeod, Consultant, Halifax County Industrial Commission

Technical University of Nova Scotia
J. Clair Callaghan, President
Les Jaeger, Special Assistant to the President
Donald A. Roy, Dean of Engineering
E. Banniassad, Dean of Architecture
William Smith, Special Program Co-ordinator

Novatron Information Corporation
Daniel F. Potter, President and Chief Executive Officer

Nova Scotia Federation of Labour
J.K. Bell, Secretary-Treasurer
Leo F. Mackay, Executive Secretary

Voluntary Planning Board
Allan C. Shaw, Chairman
Lance R. Hale, Executive Director

Dartmouth Chamber of Commerce
Robert Adams, President
Robert A. Guildford, Immediate Past President
Peter J. Meltam, Past President
Philip Raymond, Chairman, Burnside Industrial Park Committee
John Ross, Chairman, Civic Affairs Committee
Robert Yorston, Chairman, Retail Committee
Roger Perry, Chairman, Taxation Committee
Peter F. Dorrington, Chairman, Royal Commission Task Force

Atlantic Provinces Transportation Commission
E.S. Bailey, Chairman
Craig Dickson, General Manager
Austin S. Durant, Senior Traffic Analyst

Ecology Action Centre
Susan Holtz, Senior Researcher

Nova Scotia New Democratic Party
Alexa McDonough, MLA, Leader, Nova Scotia NDP
Michael Bradfield, MLA, Resource Critic

Halifax, Nova Scotia
October 12, 1983

Theme Panel: Regional Development
Fred MacKinnon, Director, Senior Citizens' Secretariat
David M. Mann, Chairman, Atlantic Provinces Economic Council; Vice-Chairman, Petro-Canada
David A. Ganong, First Vice-Chairman, Atlantic Provinces Economic Council; President, Ganong Brothers
William Belliveau, Vice-Chairman, Atlantic Provinces Economic Council; President, Info Marketing Limited
Angus A. Bruneau, President, Bruneau Resources Management Limited
Paul LePage, Sub-district Director, Atlantic Region, United Steelworkers of America

National Anti-Poverty Organization
Patrick Johnston, Executive Director
Marie Hamilton, President, Halifax-Dartmouth Anti-Poverty Organization
Linda Gregory, President, Alert, Prince Edward Island

Human Resources Development Association
Harold D. Crowell, Chairman; Director of Social Planning, City of Halifax
Daniel Hunter, General Manager

Halifax Board of Trade
Robert P. Radchuck, President
Ross Haynes, Director
William Moore, Chairman, Economic Development Committee

Nova Scotia Teachers' Union
Harold P. Doucette, President
Norman Fergusson, Executive Secretary
W. Ron MacPherson, Executive Assistant

Maritime Telegraph and Telephone Company Limited
E.J. Hicks, Vice-President, Finance and Administration
Joseph Morley

Halifax, Nova Scotia
October 13, 1983

City of Halifax
Peter Connell, Director, Engineering and Works; Acting City Manager
Bernard Smith, Director, Finance

Health Coalition of Nova Scotia
Ian Johnson, Chairperson
Leo McKay, Vice-Chairperson
Mary Morison, Nova Scotia Women's Action Committee

Canadian Pensioners Concerned Incorporated
Doreen Fraser, President
Edith Harvie, Director

Nova Scotia Nurses' Union
Lois Hall, President
Thomas Patterson, Executive Director
John Yates, Labour Relations Officer

Pictou County Research and Development Commission
B. MacCulloch, Executive Director

Sandy Cameron, Leader of the Opposition, Province of Nova Scotia

Acadian Federation of Nova Scotia
Gilles LeBlanc, President
Marie-Germaine d'Entremont, Economic Portfolio
Denise Samson, Executive Director

Marine Workers' Federation of Nova Scotia
Rick Clarke, President
James Bell, Secretary-Treasurer

Jim Lotz, Owner-Manager, Jim Lotz Associates

Canada Oil and Gas Lands Administration (Nova Scotia)
Win Potter, Director-General
Maurice Taschereau, Administrator

Thunder Bay, Ontario
October 17, 1983

Thunder Bay Economic Development Corporation
James Johnson, Chairman
Richard Charbonneau, General Manager

C.A. Benson, Associate Professor of Forest Management, Lakehead University

Canadian Pulp and Paper Association
John Fisher, Chairman and Chief Executive Officer
Charles Carter, Past Chairman of the Board; Chairman and President, Great Lakes Forest Products
Howard Hart, President
Gordon Minnes, Secretary
David Wilson, Director, Economic and Statistical Services
David Barron, Assistant Manager, Forest Management

Northern Ontario District Council of Lumber and Sawmill Workers Union
Tulio Mior, President, Northern Ontario District Council
Fred Miron, President, Lumber and Sawmill Workers Union, Local 2693
Erik J. Hautala, Vice-President, Lumber and Sawmill Workers Union, Local 2693

Thunder Bay and District Labour Council
Wayne Doherty, President
Frank Mazur, Vice-President

Iain Angus

Ruth Cunningham, Director, Women's Program, Confederation College

Northwestern Ontario Women's Centre
Fiona Karlstedt, Adminstrator
Margot Blight

Non-Organized Workers of Thunder Bay
Glen Chochla, President
Guy Guinter

Denis Langelier, Co-ordinator, Performing Arts Program, Confederation College

Chamber of Commerce Northwest Inc.
W.G. Brayshaw, Program Co-ordinator

Canadian Federation of Humane Societies
Nancy Erickson, President

Rita Ubriaco

Thunder Bay Multicultural Association
Frank Obljubek, President
Peter Michailishin, Vice-President
John Potestio, Vice-President

Joy Fedorick

Richard Staples

Thunder Bay, Ontario
October 18, 1983

Thunder Bay and District Council of Clergy
Reverend Richard Darling, Baptist Church
Reverend Ralph Fluit, Christian Reformed Church
Reverend Bernard Lee, United Church
Bishop John O'Mara, Roman Catholic Church

Bert Curtis, President, Confederation College

Norman Grace, Development Consultant

Hawker Siddeley Canada Inc.
D.T. Nelligan, Director, Finance, Canadian Car Division

Canadian Forestry Association
K.A. Armson, President

Northwestern Ontario Municipal Association
John Parry, President; Mayor of Sioux Lookout

Lakehead Social Planning Council
Don Smith, Executive Director
Prue Morton, Past President

Women and Economic Development Committee,
Northwestern Women's Decade Council
Liz Poulin, Chairperson, Decade Council
L. Wall, Economic Development Committee

Thunder Bay Indian Youth Friendship Society
Xavier Michon, Executive Director
Leslie Nawagesic, Program Director

Nishnawbe-Aski Nation
Frank Beardy, Grand Chief
Dennis Cromartie, Commissioner

Windsor, Ontario
October 17, 1983

City of Windsor
Elizabeth Kishkon, Mayor of Windsor
Michael Brode, Executive Assistant

Subcommittee on Youth Unemployment,
Mayor's Committee on Services for the Unemployed
Carol Libby, Chairperson; Director, Youth Unemployment Counselling, St. Clair College

Windsor Coalition for Development
Reverend Robert Warden, Executive Director

Third World Resource Centre
George Crowell

Wyeth Limited
Peter Van Den Eynde, President and General Manager

University of Windsor, International Business Studies Research Institute
Jay Michael Hoffman, Graduate Research Assistant
Neil Martin Zworth, Graduate Research Assistant

St. Clair College of Applied Arts and Technology
Bruce McAusland, President
T.V. McCarthy, Executive Director, Educational Planning and Development

Windsor Women's Incentive Centre
Joan Jolin, Executive Director
Sheelagh Conway, Past Executive Director
Cathy Rohler, Workshop Co-ordinator
Eilleen Forshaw, Board of Directors

Lucy Holman

Ontario Business Improvement Area Association
David Novick, President

United Brotherhood of Carpenters and Joiners of America, Local 494
Frank Hutnik, Financial Secretary
Steven Lough, Receiving Secretary

Community Nursing Registry of Windsor Inc.
Elsie Sweet Darel, Manager Director
Dolores Wikinanish, Social Worker/Liaison

Sam S. Archer

Windsor, Ontario
October 18, 1983

Mayor's Committee on Services for the Unemployed
George Macdonald, Chairman
Dan Spinner, Interim Executive Director

Windsor-Essex County Development Commission
Clare Winterbottom, Chairman
Bert Weeks, Board of Directors
J. Edwards, Past Chairman
Guy DiPonio, Development Commissioner

Windsor Chamber of Commerce
Raymond Fletcher, Vice-President
Art Belanger, Chairman, Taxation Committee

Windsor and District Labour Council
Gary L. Parent, President

Thompson, Manitoba
October 19, 1983

Thompson Industrial Commission
Adrian DeGroot, Chairman; Deputy Mayor of Thompson
Blake Maxfield, Vice-Chairman
Al Topham
Douglas Kearn
Kenneth Biberdorf, Director, Thompson Chamber of Commerce

Norman Regional Development Incorporated
Walter Perepeluk, President; Mayor of Lynn Lake
Charles S.M. Mortimer, General Manager

United Steelworkers of America, Local 6166
Morgan Svendsen, President
Buster Gurney, Vice-President

Inco Limited
Walter Curlook, Executive Vice-President
William P. Clement, President, Manitoba Division
Dennis Nagata, Corporate Media Relations

Mennonite Central Committee of Canada
Menno Wiebe, Director, Native Concerns
Reverend V. Redecop, United Mennonite Church

District of Lynn Lake
Walter Perepeluk, Mayor of Lynn Lake

Manitoba Keewatinowi Okimakanak Incorporated
Philip Michel, Chief, Barren Lands Band

Northern Flood Committee
J.I. Keeper, Executive Director

Thompson Chamber of Commerce
Harvey R. Hanson, President
D. Turpie, Director
Kenneth Biberdorf, Past President, Director

United Way of Thompson
Douglas McEwen, President
Charles S.M. Mortimer, Secretary
Kenneth Biberdorf, Director, Thompson Chamber of Commerce

Thompson Crisis Centre Incorporated
Eunadie Johnson, Executive Director

Native Communications Incorporated
Ron Nadeau

Alexander Murchie and Lorne Lamontagne

Bryan Clements

Federal Riding of Churchill
Timothy Drew

Sudbury, Ontario
October 19, 1983

Sudbury 2001
Narasim Katary

L.E. Seeley

Inco Limited
Charles F. Baird, Chairman and Chief Executive Officer
Winton Newman, President, Ontario Division

Canadian School Trustees' Association
Ernie Checkeris, President

Infonorth Computing Incorporated
Richard Danielson, President
Karen Danielson, General Manager
W. Skinner, Director

Max L. Swanson

Federal Association of the Sudbury New Democratic Party
Rosemary Blenkinsop
Philip Brown

Northeastern Ontario Energy Conservation Association
Mike Zudel, Director
S. Hunniset

William Bradley

Ken Noble

Regional Municipality of Sudbury
Tom Davies, Chairman
Peter Wong, Mayor of Sudbury; Chairman, Economic Development Committee
Herbert Akehurst, Chief Administrative Officer
Robert Bateman, Chairman, Sudbury and District Chamber of Commerce
Ron MacDonald, President, Local 6500, United Steelworkers of America

James Bay Tribal Council
Paul Martin, Manager and Director, Nishnawbe-Aski Resource Development Project

Attawapiskat Band Council
John B. Nakogee, Chief
Reg Loutit

Sudbury, Ontario
October 20, 1983

Falconbridge Limited
William James, Chairman, President and Chief Executive Officer
Gordon Slade, Vice-President, Canadian Nickel and Copper Operations

Douglas Goldsack, Dean of Science and Engineering, Laurentian University

James Grassby, Lecturer, Financial Planning, Cambrian College

United Steelworkers of America, Local 6500
Ron MacDonald, President
Dan Sweezey, Chairman, Safety and Health Committee
Keith Lovely, Local Union Officer
Gary Ransom
Alan Lamirande

Enid Barnett, Economics Department, Laurentian University

Quebec, Quebec
October 24, 1983

Conseil régional de développement de la région administrative de Québec
François Hubert, Professor of Geography, Laval University
Gilbert Hamel, Executive Director

Habitation populaire de Québec inc.
Jean-Charles Paradis, President
Gaston Rhainds, Executive Director
Louis-Marie Asselin, Mathematician and Statistician
Jean Fréchette, Consultant, Co-operative and Community Development

Office de la pastorale sociale du diocèse de Québec
François Thibodeau, Director
Yvan Tremblay, Associate Director
Annine Parent-Fortin
Camille Albert

Sommet Québécois de la jeunesse
Pierre Noreau, President
Sylvain Fortier, Treasurer
Johanne Fortin, Board of Directors

Gaz Inter-Cité Québec
Gilles Barbeau, President
Guy Bertrand

Conseil de la coopération du Québec inc.
Paul Dolan, President
Jean-Eudes Bergeron, Vice-President
Louis-Georges Gervais, Executive Director
Paul-Émile St-Pierre

Quebec, Quebec
October 25, 1983

Theme Panel: Adjustment and Uncertainty
Paul Labbé, President, Office canadien pour un renouveau industriel
Jean-Paul Hétu, President, Centrale des syndicats démocratiques
Ernest Drew, President and Chief Executive Officer, Celanese Canada
Charles Perrault, President, Perconsult Limited

L'Association des mines de métaux du Québec
Michel Lefebvre, President
Réjean Labonté, Director

Métallurgie Frontenac Limitée
Denis Rousseau, President
Réjean Labonté, Director

Centre Étape Inc.
Noëlla Porter, Executive Director
Roseline Sévigny, Recreation, Tourism and Communications Consultant

André C. Sarasin

Barbara Tessier

Association des Femmes Collaboratrices
Marie-Reine Laberge, President
Denise Blanchette, Co-ordinator
Jeannine Robichaud, Researcher

Quebec, Quebec
October 26, 1983

Société inter-port de Québec
Jacques Bourassa, President
Gérald Brassard, Executive Director
Gilles Drolet, Director, Administration
Jean-Pierre Bordua, Director, Marketing
Bernard Dupont, Director, Operations

Corporation des artisans de Québec
Pierre Bélanger, President
Jean-Pierre Tremblay, Executive Director

Chambre de commerce et d'industrie du Québec métropolitain
Yvon Dolbec, President
Gérald St-Pierre, Director
Pierre Talbot, Executive Director and Vice-President
Jean-Luc Dutil, Vice-President
Michel Létourneau
Robert Girard

Association des propriétaires de Québec
Marcel Tremblay, President
Lucien Gauvin, Press Secretary

Groupe d'action pour l'avenir technologique et industriel de la région de Québec
Jean-Guy Paquet, Chancellor, Laval University
André Lemay, Executive Director
Yves Giroux, Deputy Vice-Chancellor, Laval University

Yvon Valcin and Laurence Valcin

Confédération des syndicats nationaux
Sylvio Gagnon, Executive Secretary
Clément Bélanger, President, Société Asbestos Limitée
Peter Baknis

Réseau d'action et d'information pour les femmes
Marcelle Dolment, Co-ordinator
Cécile Ugueux
Monique Beaulieu
Claudette Beaulieu

Chicoutimi, Quebec
October 27, 1983

Société d'expansion économique du Saguenay inc.
Ulric Blackburn, President; Mayor of Chicoutimi
Clément Vaillancourt, Executive Director

Société de recherche sur la faillite Sagamie
Claude Lalonde, President
Carol Boudreault, Vice-President
Michel Lechasseur, Vice-President

Société de développement de Jonquière inc.
Francis Dufour, Mayor of Jonquière

Conseil régional de développement Saguenay-Lac-Saint-Jean-Chibougamau inc.
J. Fernand Tremblay, President
Jacques Desbiens, Consultant
Mariette Martel, Vice-President, Economic Affairs
Louis-Gaétan Fortin, Executive Director
Gérard Claveau, Executive Vice-President

Fédération des syndicats du secteur inc. aluminium
Lévis Desgagné, President
Jean-Marc Dubois, Secretary
Antoine Potvin, Technical Adviser
Jacques Hubert, Union Representative
Gilles Harvey, Union Representative

Municipality of Shipshaw
Jean-Claude Lavoie, Mayor of Shipshaw

Fédération de l'Union des producteurs agricoles du Saguenay-Lac-Saint-Jean
Germain Simard, President
Bertrand Tremblay, President, Chaîne coopérative du Saguenay
Hubert Doré, President, Nutrinor
Jean-Paul Poirier, Associate Secretary, Syndicat des travailleurs forestiers
Jean-Marie Couët, Secretary

Confédération des syndicats nationaux
Pierre Mercille, Vice-President
Serge Lemelin, President, conseil central Saguenay-Lac-Saint-Jean
Claude Rioux, Economist, Research Service of the CSN

Chicoutimi Chamber of Commerce
François Tremblay, President
Guy Mineault, Director

Fédération des caisses populaires Desjardins du Saguenay-Lac-Saint-Jean
Jean-Claude Hudon, President
Jean-Eudes Bergeron, Executive Director
François Gilbert, Administrator
Joseph Fleury, Executive Secretary

Conseil économique d'Alma et du Lac-Saint-Jean inc.
Rénald Martin

Lionel Pelletier

Guy Mineault

Fédération de l'Union des producteurs agricoles de la Beauce
Gérard Lehoux, President
Clément Nadeau, President, Syndicat des aériculteurs de la Beauce
Roch Poulin, Secretary, Syndicat des producteurs en serres de la région 03
Pierre Giguère, Development Technician
Lucien Gagné, Information Technician

Comact Inc.
Robert Gilbert, Associate Director

Saint-Georges-de-Beauce, Quebec
October 27, 1983

Conseil économique de Beauce
Jean-Denis Poulin, President
Serge Roy, Executive Director

Hervé Pomerleau, President, Hervé Pomerleau Inc.

Fabien Roy

Confédération des syndicats nationaux (Saint-Georges-de-Beauce)
Gérald Larose, President
Normand Piché, President, Conseil central de Québec

Centre-femmes de Beauce
Lise Paquet, Co-ordinator

Paul-André Busque

Conseil régional de la Pastorale La Chaudière
Sylvain Chartier, Recording Secretary

Procycle Inc.
Raymond Dutil, Vice-President, Executive Director

Agrinove, Co-opérative agro-alimentaire
Rosaire Lapierre, President
Jean-Louis Lavoie, Executive Secretary
Jacques Légaré, Treasurer

Montreal, Quebec
October 31, 1983

Communauté urbaine de Montréal
Pierre Des Marais II, President
Daniel Wermenlinger, Executive Director
Stephen A. Bigsby, Director, Economic Expansion
Guy Gravel, Director, Planning Service

Montreal Economic Development Commission
Pierre Goyette, President, Montreal Chamber of Commerce
James Cadieux, Chairman, Economic Policy and Information Committee, Montreal Board of Trade
André Vallerand, Executive Vice-President; Executive Director, Montreal Chamber of Commerce
Gordon J. Fehr, President, Montreal Board of Trade
Alex Harper, Executive Director, Montreal Board of Trade

Union des municipalités du Québec
Jean Corbeil, Vice-President; Mayor of Anjou
Jean Bélanger, Director, Research

Pétromont Inc.
Barry P. Welford, Vice-President, Marketing and Commercial Expansion
Serge Guérin, Vice-President, Administration and Human Resources

Jean-Yves Gravel, Planning Officer

Dorval Brunelle, Professor of Sociology, Université du Québec à Montréal

Pierre Dansereau, Professor Emeritus, Université du Québec à Montréal

Canadian Textiles Institute
Eric Barry, President
J. White, Chairman
Frank Brady, Co-Chairman, Advisory Panel on Textiles and Clothing
Ray Chevrier, Chairman, Trade Policy Committee
Jim Robertson, Vice-President, Human Resources

Dominion Textile Inc.
Thomas R. Bell, President and Chief Executive Officer
Alex R. McAslan, Executive Vice-President, Operations
Charles A. McCrae, Executive Vice-President, Administration and Resources
Francis P. Brady, Senior Vice-President
Paul E. Boudreault, President, Sales Yarn Company

Shoe Manufacturers' Association of Canada
Jean-Guy Maheu, President

Centrale des syndicats démocratiques
Jean-Paul Hétu, President
Pierre-Yvon Ouellet, Research Centre

Confédération des syndicats nationaux
Gérald Larose, President
Sylvio Gagnon, Executive Secretary
Pierre Mercille, Vice-President
Monique Simard, Vice-President
Peter Bakvis, Researcher
Claude Rioux, Researcher

Montreal, Quebec
November 1, 1983

Theme Panel: The Role of Government
Raymond Garneau, Chairman and Chief Executive Officer, Montreal City and District Savings Bank and Crédit Foncier
Louis Laberge, President, Fédération des travailleurs du Québec
Fernand Daoust, Executive Secretary, Fédération des travailleurs du Québec
Wendy Dobson, Executive Director, C.D. Howe Institute
Richard Lipsey, Research Consultant, C.D. Howe Institute
Jean-Maurice LeClair, President and Chief Executive Officer, Canadian National Railways
Linton R. Wilson, President and Chief Executive Officer, Redpath Industries

Seafarers' International Union
Andrew C. Boyle, Executive Vice-President
Paul Martin Jr., President and Chief Executive Officer, Canada Steamship Lines Inc.

Bell Canada
James C. Thackray, Chairman
Dale Orr, Chief Economist

Ordre des comptables agréés du Québec
Robert Gobeil, President
Guy d'Orsonnens, Treasurer
André Desrochers, Director, Administration
André Dupras, Director, Communications

Fédération de l'âge d'or du Québec
Maurice Fortin, Administrator, Conseil régional du Québec
Charles Douville, Resource Person, Conseil des Aînés
Simone Daigneault, Secretary, Conseil régional
Rita Cambron, Research Officer

Women's Information and Referral Centre of Montreal
Maureen Lofthouse, Vice-President
Sandy Mielitz, Treasurer
Mona Forrest, Director

United Way of Montreal
Jean Lessard, President, Executive Director
Michel Giroux, Special Assistant to the Executive Director

Quebec Chamber of Commerce
Charles Langlois, President
Arthur Earle, First Vice-President
François Paradis, Vice-President, Economic Affairs
Jean-Paul Létourneau, Executive Vice-President
Marcel Tardif, General Manager, Public Affairs
Pierre Lemieux, Economic Advisor

Montreal, Quebec
November 2, 1983

Makivik Corporation
Mary Simon, President
Robbie Tookalook, Mayor of Great Whale River, Kuujjuarapik
Lazarusie Epoo, Mayor of Inukjuak
Charlie Arngak, Mayor of Kangirsujuaq, Welcome Bay
Adamie Tumassi, Major of Kangirsuk, Payne Bay
Kitty Annanack, Mayor of Kangiqsualujjuag, George River
Tikkili Kleist, representing the Mayor of Kujjuaq
Willie Angnatuk, representing the Mayor of Tasiujaq
Josepe Agma, representing the Mayor of Aupaluk
Maggie Tukkiapik, representing the Mayor of Quaqtaq
Matthewsie Luuku, representing the Mayor of Ivujivik
Peter Matte, representing the Mayor of Akulivik

Laurentian Group
Claude Castonguay, President and Chief Executive Officer
Jean-Marie Poitras, Chairman
Jacques A. Drouin, Executive Vice-President

La Confédération des caisses populaires et d'économie Desjardins du Québec
Raymond Blais, President
Yvon Daneau, Assistant to the President and Executive Secretary
Yves Morency, Economist
Hervé Hébert, Director

François Richard, Director
René Croteau, Assistant to the President

Conseil du patronat du Québec
Sébastien Allard, President
Ghislain Dufour, Executive Vice-President
Denis Beauregard, Research Director
Jean-Claude Murray, Director
Raymond Larocque, Director

Ex-Commission d'étude sur la formation professionnelle et socio-culturelle des adultes
Michèle Jean, President
Michel Blondin, Responsible for Education, Metal Workers' Union
Claude Desmarais, Director, Adult Education Services, Chambly Regional School Board

Action travail des femmes du Québec
Dominique Leclercq
Simone Bernier

Diplômés de l'Université de Montréal
Jean-Pierre Roy, President
Jean-Claude Lauzon, Vice-President
Yves Desjardins-Siciliano, Vice-President

McGill University
David L. Johnston, Principal and Vice-Chancellor
Stanley Frost, Director, History of McGill Project

Union des producteurs agricoles
Jacques Proulx, Chairman
François Coté, Director, Studies and Research Service

STOP inc.
Charles Mallory, President
Roger de Ladurantaye
Derek Morton, Editor, STOP Press

Stuart Hill, Associate Professor of Entomology and Ecological Agriculture Projects, McGill University

Association féminine d'éducation et d'action sociale
Louise Joly, Vice-President
Lise Houle, Public Relations Officer

Ian B. Williamson

Montreal, Quebec
November 3, 1983

Canadian Chamber of Commerce
Samuel F. Hughes, President
Robert Paquin, Past Vice-Chairman, Association of Canadian Advertisers Incorporated
Anna L. Guthrie, Chairman, Economic Policy Committee

Bruce R. McPherson, President, Canadian Council of Furniture Manufacturers
Frank C. Ferguson, President, Canadian Direct Marketing Association
Stanley G. Wild, President, Canadian Electrical Distributors Association
Normand St-Jean, President, Canadian Hardware and Housewares Manufacturers' Association
David E.P. Armour, President, Electrical and Electronic Manufacturers' Association of Canada
George A. Peapples, Motor Vehicle Manufacturers' Association
Bill Pattison, Chairman, Tourism Industry Association of Canada
Peter Huffman, Vice-President, Administration, Winnipeg Commodity Exchange

The Honourable Francis Fox, Minister of Communications

Consolidated Bathurst Inc.
William I.M. Turner Jr., Chairman and Chief Executive Officer
A.K. Narang, Senior Vice-President, Planning and Administrative Services
T.J. Wagg, Vice-President, Finance

Formula Growth Limited
John W. Dobson, President
Ian Soutar, Vice-President

Bombardier Inc.
Laurent Beaudoin, Chairman and Chief Executive Officer
Raymond Royer, President, Public Transport Division
Yvon Turcot, Public Affairs Consultant

Fédération des femmes du Québec
Denyse Bélanger-Rochon, President
Marie-Françoise Marchis-Mouren, Vice-President, Finance
Ginette Busque, Vice-President, Statutes and Regulations
Ruth Rose Lizée

Ultramar Canada Inc.
William J. Berry, Manager, Government Affairs
Graham Cooper, Government Liaison
François Marcil, Manager, Commercial Marketing

Ordre des ingénieurs du Québec
Pierre Bournival, President
R. Rémi Arsenault, Service Manager, Planning and Development, Gaz Metropolitain inc.
Roger Blais, Director, Centre d'innovation industrielle, École polytechnique de Montréal
John H. Dinsmore, Chairman and Chief Executive Officer, Pétromont inc.
Roland Doré, Director, École Polytechnique de Montréal
Alice Savage, Equipment Planning, Hydro-Québec
Claude Comtois, President, Lalonde, Girouard, Letendre et Associés
Gilles Perron, Secretary

United Steelworkers of America
Clément Godbout, Director, District 5
Émile Vallée, Research Assistant
Raymond Sliger, Area Supervisor
Vince Chapin

Calgary, Alberta
November 7, 1983

City of Calgary
Ralph Klein, Mayor of Calgary

Canadian Petroleum Association/Independent Petroleum Association of Canada
Edward W. Best, Chairman, Canadian Petroleum Association; President, B.P. Exploration Canada Limited
J.R. Dundas, President, Independent Petroleum Association of Canada; President and Chief Executive Officer, Roxy Petroleum Limited
John D. Porter, Managing Director, Independent Petroleum Association of Canada
William A. Elser, Executive Vice-President, Atcor Resources Limited
R.H. Carlyle, Senior Vice-President, Gulf Canada Resources Inc.
Hans Maciej, Technical Director, Canadian Petroleum Association

J.P. Gallagher, Chairman and Chief Executive Officer, Dome Canada Limited

Gordon F. Dixon

Ralph R. Capeling, Manager, Oil Sands, B.P. Exploration Canada Limited

Calgary Research and Development Authority
William D. Croft, President

Dome Petroleum Limited
John M. Beddome, President and Chief Operating Officer
Donald R. Gilley, Vice-President, Corporate Planning

TransAlta Utilities Corporation
M.M. Williams, President and Chief Executive Officer
H.G. Schaefer, Senior Vice-President, Financial and Corporate Planning

Brian Thompson

Carol Stein

Calgary, Alberta
November 8, 1983

Social Issues Committee, Young Women's Christian Association, Calgary
Elizabeth J. Galatiuk, Chairperson
Patricia J. Cooper, President, Calgary Association of Voluntary Agencies
Paula MacLeod, YWCA Social Issues Committee

Canadian Association of Social Workers
Glenn Drover, President
Gayle Gilchrist James, Past President
Richard Ramsay, Secretary

Calgary Association of Voluntary Agencies
Don Karst, Executive Director, Calgary Family Service Bureau
Lillian Tyler, Past President, Immigrant Aid Society
Maureen Crane, Chief Executive Officer, Calgary YWCA

University of Calgary Faculty Association
John Woods, Vice-President
R.G. Weyant, Dean, General Studies
Michael A. Ward, Chairman, Civil Engineering Department

Canada West Foundation
David K. Elton, President
R.A.D. Beck, Economic Consultant
Arthur J.E. Child, President, Burns Foods Limited
A.W. Howard, Chairman, TransAlta Utilities Corporation
Michael Mears, Vice-President, Mancal Limited

Alberta Wheat Pool
Allan J. Macpherson, President
Allan W. Beattie, Director, Public Relations
Bruno A. Friesen, Manager, Member Services

Western Stock Growers' Association
Ian Watt, President
Pat Rutledge, Second Vice-President

Calgary, Alberta
November 9, 1983

British Columbia Resources Investment Corporation
Walter J. Riva, Director
William S. Cameron, Vice-President, Corporate Planning

Canadian Hunter Exploration Limited
James K. Gray, Executive Vice-President

John Dyer, Assistant Superintendent, South West Area, Calgary Board of Education

Westmills Carpets Limited
J. William Ford, President and Chief Executive Officer

Chambers of Commerce
Donald Stanley, President, Alberta Chamber of Commerce
Donald Cross, President, Calgary Chamber of Commerce
Edward George, President, Edmonton Chamber of Commerce
Fred A. Stewart, Chairman, Government and Economic Affairs Comittee, Calgary Chamber of Commerce
Douglas McArthur, Vice-Chairman, Government and Economic Affairs Committee, Calgary Chamber of Commerce

James S. Palmer and Murray Edwards

Calgary Council for Advanced Technology
Bruce G. Hartwick, Chairman; Vice-President, NOVA Corporation
Roy Lindseth, President, Teknica Resource Development Limited
Keith E. Cooper, Vice-President, Research, University of Calgary
Steven Slipp, Partner, Clarkson Gordon
Conrad Kockerbeck, President, Global Office Automation Systems Limited

Action Studies Institute
Ken Low, President

Louis Hamill, Associate Professor of Geography, University of Calgary

Ernie Ashton

Dianne E. Jorgenson

Carol John Sebella

Lethbridge, Alberta
November 10, 1983

City of Lethbridge
Edward Martin, Alderman
Dennis S. O'Connell, Director, Economic Development

University of Lethbridge
John Woods, President and Vice-Chancellor

Lethbridge Research Station
D. Gordon Dorrell, Director
D.B. Wilson, Acting Assistant Director
Donald C. Mackay, Head, Soil Science Section
Ernest E. Swierstra, Head, Animal Science Section

Lethbridge Interagency Committee
Robert Richards, Executive Director, Southern Alberta Community Living Association
Mary C. Walker, Chief Operating Officer, Young Women's Christian Association of Lethbridge and District
Lorita Ichikawa, Executive Director, Lethbridge Family Services

Canadian Cattlemen's Association
Gary Jones, President
Stan Wilson, Second Vice-President
Brian Heidecker, Ex-officio
Charles Gracey, Executive Vice-President

Canadian Meat Council
David Adams, General Manager
A. Tolton, Director, Field Services, Western Canada

Confederation of Alberta Faculty Associations
Al Hunter, President
Michael Kubara, Professor of Philosophy, University of Lethbridge
Luke Stebbins, President, University of Lethbridge Faculty Association

St. Patrick's Social Justice Committee
Thomas L. Cain, Chairman
Sister Pat MacDonald, Social Justice Committee
Bosco Baptista, Social Justice Committee
Sister Ann McClelland, Social Worker, St. Michael's Hospital

Lethbridge Chamber of Commerce
David Irving, Chairman
George Lermer, Chairman, Governmental Affairs Committee

Bert Hargrave, MP

Edmonton, Alberta
November 14, 1983

City of Edmonton
Laurence Decore, Mayor of Edmonton

Canadian Institute of Planners
K.B. Clark, President

J. Martin Hattersley

Consulting Engineers of Alberta
R. W. Bowes, Vice-President
Harold V. Page, Managing Director

Principal Group
Donald M. Cormie, President, Chairman and Chief Executive Officer

Smith International Canada Limited
Denis G. Gaulin, Host Division Manager
Lawrence P. Howorth, Controller and Chief Financial Officer

Association canadienne-française de l'Alberta
Guy Goyette, President
Roger Lalonde, Past President

Lakeland College
Roy V. Murray, President

Athabaska University
Ross H. Paul, Vice-President, Learning Services

Father Russell Pendergast and Reverend Edward M. Checkland

Catholic Social Services
Father William Irwin, President and Chief Executive Officer
Andrew Michalski, Vice-President, Family Services
Paul Nahirney, Consultant, Planning and Development

Andriy J. Semotiuk

Alberta Committee of Consumer Groups of Disabled Persons
Nancie Krushelnicki, Executive Director
Len Seaby

Native Canadian Petroleum Association and Canada Geothermal Oil Limited
R.E. Wolf

MIDAS Reform Organization of Alberta
A.J. Hooke

Western Energy Investments Limited
L.D. McIlroy, President

Gordon King

David M. Cawkell

Edmonton, Alberta
November 15, 1983

Theme Panel: Technology, Productivity and Work
Stephen G. Peitchinis, Professor of Economics, University of Calgary
C.W. Bowman, Chairman, Alberta Oil Sands Technology and Research Authority
Fred W. Pomeroy, President, Communications Workers of Canada
William Dyson, William Dyson Associates
Walter F. Light, Chairman and Chief Executive Officer, Northern Telecom Limited

Fraser Institute
Michael A. Walker, Director

Inter-Church Ad Hoc Committee of Edmonton
Sheranne Johnson, Social Justice Commission, Roman Catholic Church
Reverend Martin Garber Conrad, Lutheran Church of America
Reverend Roy Darcus, Church in Society Committee, Anglican Church
Betty Marlin, Conference Staff, Social Action Ministry, United Church
Reverend David Summers, Church in Society, United Church
Desmond Berghoffer, Anglican Church

Alberta New Democratic Party
Grant Notley, Leader of the Official Opposition
Davis Swan, Energy Critic
Jim Russell, Chairman, Economic Development Committee

Edmonton, Alberta
November 16, 1983

Economic Development Advocacy Committee, County of Strathcona No. 20
Robert A. McAlpine, Chairman
I. F. Markson, Chief Commissioner
G.W. Lavold, Economic Advisor
Warren Thomas, Reeve

Confederation of Regions Party of Alberta
Elmer Knutson, Leader of the Party
Alma E. Hancock, Chairperson, Monetary Advisory Committee
Shirley Bassani, Executive Director
Nora Galenzoski, Financial and Monetary Committee

Reginald D. Loomis, Stuart R. Loomis and William G. Brese

R.B. Church, Associate Dean of Medicine, University of Calgary

Association of Deans of Pharmacy of Canada
John A. Bachynsky, President

Alberta Teachers' Association
Norval Horner, District Representative
N.P. Hrynyk, Associate Executive Secretary

H. Peter Oberlander, Director, Centre for Human Settlements, University of British Columbia

Woodbridge, Reed and Associates Limited
Peter Woodbridge, President
Richard Dempster, Manager, Alberta Office

Atco Limited
Ronald D. Southern, President

George Shaw MacMillan, President, George Shaw MacMillan and Associates Limited and **Edward James Thompson,** Project Manager, PCL-Braun-Simons Limited

Saskatoon, Saskatchewan
November 21, 1983

Saskatchewan Urban Municipalities Association
H.E. Taylor, President; Alderman
M.K. Clary, Vice-President, Towns
G.A. Bristow, Vice-President, Villages
R.A. Wankling, Executive Director

Saskatoon Board of Trade
James T. Lyon, Chairman, Policy Committee
Phil Walker, President-Elect
Bert Salloum, Secretary-Manager

Saskatchewan Mining Association
Ralph Cheesman, Manager
Ken Haapanen, Chairman, Uranium Section; Vice-President, Mining, Eldorado Nuclear
Jim Bonny, Vice-President, Marketing
M. Henningson, General Manager, Operations, Cominco Potash

Saskatchewan Environmental Society
Ann Coxworth, President
Bertram Weichel

MBA Students, University of Saskatchewan, College of Graduate Studies
Edmond Price, Professor of Commerce, University of Saskatchewan
John David Spriggs, Associate Professor of Agricultural Economics, University of Saskatchewan
Neil Larsen
Rick Horocholyn
Noreen Hetherington
Greg Posehn
Wes Mills
Justin Li
Larry Saloff
Anisar Rahman

Saskatchewan Teachers' Federation
Frank Garritty, President; Vice-President, Canadian Teachers' Federation
Mel Lofstrom, General Secretary
Gary Genge, Assistant General Secretary
Fred Herron, Executive Assistant

Lloyd Kristjanson, President, University of Saskatchewan

George Khachatourians, Professor, University of Saskatchewan

Association of Professional Engineers of Saskatchewan
Oscar W. Hanson, President
William A. Bullee, Vice-President
William H. Eatock, Past President

Federated Co-operatives Limited
Vernon Leland, President
Dennis Thomas, Manager, Public Relations Division

Co-operative Trust Company of Canada
Ed Gerbert, Chief Executive Officer
John Wall, Vice-President, Corporate Services

John Benesh

Federation of Saskatchewan Indian Nations
Sol Sanderson, Chief, Federation of Saskatchewan Indian Nations
J.P. Woods, Director, Corporate Development, SINCO Developments Limited
Andrew Michael, Chief

Saskatoon Union of Unemployed Workers
Brian Krempien, President
Stuart Goldie, Vice-President
Mike Dunn

Saskatoon, Saskatchewan
November 22, 1983

Theme Panel: Resource Management
Graham Walker, Deputy Chairman, Pemberton, Houston, Willoughby
Michael Percy, Associate Professor of Economics, University of Alberta
A. Paus-Jenssen, Professor of Economics and Political Science, University of Saskatchewan
M. Norman Anderson, Chairman and Chief Executive Officer, Cominco Limited

The Canadian Baha'i Community
Douglas Martin, Secretary
Ed Muttart, Treasurer and Assistant Secretary
Huguette Matte-Vaillancourt, Co-ordinator of National Education and Information
Allison Healy, Committee for the Development of Baha'i Spiritual Assemblies
Husayn Banani, National Spiritual Assembly of the Baha'is of Canada

United Church of Canada - Working Unit on Social Issues and Justice
Reverend Robert G. Lindsey, Senior Staff Officer, Church in Society Committee
Mervin Harrison, Chairperson, Working Unit on Social Issues and Justice
John Jacquemain, National Officer for French-English Relations

Canadian Day Care Advocacy Association
Judith Martin, Chairperson
Larry Stewart

Saskatchewan Working Women
Susan Gilmer, Provincial President
Lorraine Moulding, Saskatoon Co-ordinator
Christine Smillie, Provincial Treasurer

Canadian Airline Employees Association
Tom Saunders, President
Jane Armstrong, Research Analyst

Regina, Saskatchewan
November 23, 1983

Saskatchewan Federation of Agriculture
Robert McGillivray, President
Garf Stevenson, Vice-President
Linda Boxall, Executive Member
Clarence Hookenson, Director
Gary Carlson, Executive Secretary

Canadian Co-operative Wheat Producers Limited
E. Ted Turner, Chairman
Greg S. Arason, Corporate Secretary
Ron Weik, Manager, Research

Family Farm Foundation of Canada
Gordon MacMurchy, President
Harry-Jae Elder
Donette Elder
Hartley Furtan, Head, Department of Agricultural Economics, University of Saskatchewan
Ken Jenson
Brian Kramer
Eric Kramer

National Farmers Union
Wayne Easter, President
Stuart A. Thiesson, Executive Secretary

Credit Union Central of Saskatchewan
Leslie R. Tendler, President; General Manager, Sherwood Credit Union
Norman A. Bromberger, Chief Executive Officer
Keith Sproule, First Vice-President
Robert Cowan, Executive Committee
Terry MacDonald, Manager, Research

Canadian Organic Producers Marketing Co-operative Limited
Alfred Moore, President
Allan Dietrich, Vice-President
Doreen Reitenbach, Treasurer
Elmer Laird, Director
Ray Demong, Director

Prairie Implement Manufacturers Association
Donald Ego, Chairman
W.C. "Bill" Spiers, President
Hubert Lux, First Vice-President
Ken McKenzie, Second Vice-President
Ivan Thue, General Manager

Western Transportation Advisory Council
Martin Crilly, President
The Honourable J.W. "Jim" Garner, Chairman; Minister of Highways and Transportation, Government of Saskatchewan
Douglas Fletcher, Vice-President, Prairie Region, CN Rail
Don Garcia, Director; President, Canadian Area, International Longshoremen's and Warehousemen's Union
Colonel Robert Houston, Honorary Director

Government of Saskatchewan
The Honourable Robert Andrew, Minister of Finance
The Honourable Eric Berntson, Deputy Premier; Minister of Economic Development and Trade

Regina, Saskatchewan
November 24, 1983

The Honourable Allan Blakeney, Leader of the Opposition, Saskatchewan New Democratic Party

Saskatchewan Council for International Co-operation
Bryan Tudor, President
Jack Risk, Secretary
William Harding, former Board Member
Christine Meissner, South Saskatchewan Committee for World Development
Mardele Harland, Executive Secretary

Robyn Allan

The Honourable Eugene F. Whelan, Minister of Agriculture

Saskatchewan Chamber of Commerce
Marcel de la Gorgendière, President
Robert Finlay, Executive Director

Saskatchewan Federation of Labour
Nadine Hunt, President
Barbara Makeechak, Executive Assistant

Unemployment Committee of Regina
Catherine McCann, Chairperson
Myrna Nerbas, Treasurer

Canadian Nurses' Association
Helen Preston Glass, President
Ginette Rodger, Executive Director

United Mine Workers of America, District 18
Mike Tamtom, President
William Stuart, Secretary-Treasurer
Lynn Abraham, Sub-District Board Member

Prospectors and Developers' Association of Canada
H. Douglas Hume, President
Edward Shiller, Director, Public Affairs, Falconbridge Limited

Saskatchewan Action Committee on the Status of Women
Palma Anderson, President
Arlene Franko, Co-ordinator

University of Regina
Donald Shaw, Vice-President
Cam Blachford, Dean of Graduate Studies and Research
David Bamford, Director, Budgets
Judy Alexander, Head, Department of Economics, University of Regina

Thomas Kierans

Winnipeg, Manitoba
November 28, 1983

Manitoba Association of Urban Municipalities
Jae Eadie, Vice-President; Councillor, City of Winnipeg
Rochelle I. Zimberg, Executive Director

Winnipeg Chamber of Commerce
James Wright, President
Charles M. Winograd, Member
William Draper, General Manager

The Honourable Lloyd Axworthy, Minister of Transport

Canadian Real Estate Association
Allan Poapst, Past President
Pierre Beauchamp, Executive Vice-President
Mack Parliament, Director, Research and Publications
David Humphreys, Ottawa Representative

Manitoba Advisory Council on the Status of Women
Roberta Ellis, Chairperson
Ruth Vogt, Council Member
Pauline Russell, Council Member
Lilian McIlwain, Council Member

Catholic Women's League of Canada
Bernadette Russell, Chairperson, Ad Hoc Committee on the Economy
Mary Bennett, Provincial Community Life Convener
Stella Carson, Provincial Resolutions Convener
Shirley Scaletta, Ad Hoc Committee on the Economy
Evelyn Wryzykowski, Ad Hoc Committee on the Economy

Manitoba Anti-Poverty Organization Inc.
Lori Bell, Vice-President
Olga Foltz, Executive Director
Tim Herkert, Advocacy Worker
Laura Steiman, Secretary
Willy Carleton

Conseil jeunesse provincial inc.
Michel Roy, President
Robert Mousseau
André Dufresne

Canadian Agricultural Chemicals Association
J.S. King, Chairman; President, Chipman Inc.
J.D. Nattress, Vice-Chairman; Vice-President, Monsanto Canada Inc.
John Oliver, Treasurer; Vice-President, Eli Lilly Canada Inc.
I.D. Raynor, Chairman, Government Relations, Manitoba Council, Canadian Agricultural Chemicals Association

Social Planning Council of Winnipeg
Lenore Good, President
Isabel Auld, Vice-Chairman, Social Policy Formation Committee
Robert Fenton, Associate Professor of Economics, University of Winnipeg
E. Tim Sale, Executive Director

United Way of Winnipeg
Roy Essery, President
Kris Kristjansson

Winnipeg Co-ordinating Committee for Disarmament
Lynne Gibbons, Past Co-Chairperson
J. Allan Mossbarter, Curate, St. George's Anglican Church
Derek Wilson

City of Winnipeg, Department of Environmental Planning
Steven Barber, Historic Projects Co-ordinator
George Siamandas, Executive Director, Heritage Winnipeg Inc.

Crossroads Resource Group
William Goddard, Co-ordinator
Kenneth Emberley

J.D. Wahn, Professor of Administrative Studies, University of Manitoba

University of Manitoba, Political Economy Group
Cy Gonick, Head, Department of Economics, University of Manitoba
Robert Chernomas, Assistant Professor of Economics, University of Manitoba
Fletcher Barager
Stephen Gelb
Michael Janzen

Dakota Ojibway Tribal Council
Carl Roberts, Chairman; Chief, Roseau River Band
Lawrence Henry
Roy McKinney, Chief, Swan Lake Band
Morris Bear, Birdtail Sioux Band
Rufus Prince, Tribal Government Advisor
Andrew Beaulieu, Band Manager, Sandy Bay
Alfred Everett, Tribal Administrator
Don Graveson, Director, Economic Development
Larry Clark, Advisor
Ray Mason, Economic Development Councillor, Swan Lake Band

Winnipeg, Manitoba
November 29, 1983

Theme Panel: Labour-Management Relations
Alfred Carrothers, Dean of Common Law, University of Ottawa

Bernard Miller, Vice-President, Atlantic Canada Region, Air Canada
Richard Martin, President, Manitoba Federation of Labour
Gary Doer, President, Manitoba Government Employees' Association
Rodrigue Bilodeau, Chairman and Chief Executive Officer, Honeywell Limited

Association of Canadian Community Colleges
W.G. Forbes, President; President, Red Deer College
Gérard Raymond, First Vice-President; Principal and Chief Executive Officer, Campus de Bathurst, Collège communautaire du Nouveau-Brunswick
C.H. Howard, Second Vice-President; Director and Chief Executive Officer, Red River Community College

National Union of Provincial Government Employees
John Fryer, President; Vice-President, Canadian Labour Congress
J. Richard Proctor, Assistant to the President
Gary Doer, President, Manitoba Government Employees' Association

Manitoba Federation of Labour
Richard Martin, President
Gary Russell, Director of Research

Winnipeg Labour Council
Paul Moist, First Vice-President
Howard Matthews, Delegate

Derek Hum, Professor, St. John's College, University of Manitoba

Liberal Party of Manitoba
Diana Ryback, President
David Matas

Winnipeg, Manitoba
November 30, 1983

Canadian Federation of Agriculture
Glenn Flaten, President
David Kirk, Executive Secretary

University of Manitoba, Faculty of Agriculture
Robert C. McGinnis, Dean of Agriculture
J.C. Gilson, Professor of Agricultural Economics
E.W. Tyrchniewicz, Head, Department of Agricultural Economics and Farm Management
L.E. Evans, Head, Department of Plant Science
G.E. Laliberté, Head, Department of Agricultural Engineering
M.E. Seale, Associate Dean of Agriculture
S.C. Jay, Head, Department of Entomology

Grocery Products Manufacturers of Canada
George Fleischmann, President and Chief Executive Officer
Thomas D. Smyth, Vice-Chairman; President and Chief Executive Officer, H.J. Heinz Company of Canada Limited
John D. Herrick, Director; Chairman, General Mills Canada, Inc.
A. Jan d'Ailly, Director; President, Natalik Inc.

Canadian Food Processors' Association
Michael Teeter, Vice-President
Elmer Banting, President
Taketo Murata, Chairman
Clare Proctor, Vice-Chairman
Arthur W. Walker, President, Hardee Farms International Limited

Canola Crushers of Western Canada
Robert Broeska, Executive Director
John Smythe, Vice-Chairman

Retail Council of Canada
Alasdair J. McKichan, President
Gerald Doucet, Senior Vice-President, Policy
J.P. Carter, Vice-President; General Manager, Food Division
Mervin Booty, President, Westfair Foods Limited
James Waters, Vice-President, Canada Safeway
Raymond Bertrand, President, Canada Grocery Distributors Institute

Consumers' Association of Canada (Manitoba Branch)
Ruth Titheridge, Chairperson, National Food Committee
Margaret Soper, Vice-President, National Consumers' Association; Chairperson, Manitoba Food Committee
Joan Friesen, National Food Committee

Kenneth Emberley, Crossroads Resource Group

Toronto, Ontario
December 1, 1983

Municipality of Metropolitan Toronto
Paul Godfrey, Chairman
Douglas P. Floyd, Executive Director, Economic Development
Richard O'Brien, Chairman, Economic Development and Planning Committee of Metropolitan Toronto
Donald R. Richmond, Deputy Commissioner, Community Services; General Manager, Metro Housing Co. Limited

Canadian Federation of Independent Business
John Bulloch, President
Patricia Johnston, Senior Vice-President
Brien Gray, Vice President
Richard Wietfeldt, Chief Economist; Director, Research
Pierre Clément, Chargé d'affaires, Québec

Vanier Institute of the Family
Johann W. Mohr, President
Doris Badir, Chairperson, Executive Committee
Robert Glossop, Co-ordinator, Programs; Director, Research
David Ross, Consultant

Canadian Institute for Economic Policy
Walter Gordon, Chairman
Abraham Rotstein, Vice-Chairman; Professor of Economics, University of Toronto

York University, Faculty of Administrative Studies, Economic and Corporate Development, Research Unit
Donald J. Daly, Professor of Economics

Data Resources of Canada
William F. Empey, Vice-President and General Manager

Canadian Business and Industry International Advisory Council
J. Hugh Stevens, Chairman; Chairman, Canada Wire and Cable Limited
William George Deeks, Chairman, MNE Committee; Executive Vice-President, Noranda Sales Corporation Limited
Graeme Clive Hughes, Executive Vice-President and Secretary, Canadian Manufacturers' Association
Deane D. Sherman, Trade Policy Committee; Manager, Government Relations, C.I.L. Inc.
J.E. Toten, Vice-Chairman, Business and Industry Advisory Committee to the OECD; Special Advisor, Bank of Montreal

Canadian Importers Association Inc.
Keith Dixon, President
Bryan Martin, Chairman; President, Sony Canada Limited
Robert F. Gulliford, Vice-Chairman; Vice-President, Royal Bank of Canada
Tim Chisholm, Vice-Chairman; President, Ronald A. Chisholm Limited
Tom S. Nease, Past Director; President, Adidas Canada
Richard S. Gottlieb, Director; Legal Counsel, Association Footwear Import Committee

United Auto Workers
Robert White, Director for Canada, International Vice-President
Sam Gindin, Director, Research
Buzz Hargrove, Assistant to the Director

Toronto, Ontario - Panel A
December 2, 1983

Social Planning Council of Metropolitan Toronto
Reverend Eilert Frerichs, President
David Wolfe, Board of Directors; Assistant Professor of Political Science, University of Toronto
Jeffrey Patterson, Senior Project Director
Leon Muszynski, Program Director

Labour Council of Metropolitan Toronto
Wally Majesky, President
Michael Lyons, Executive Secretary
Irene Harris, Director, Projects

Toronto Board of Education
Penny Moss, Chairman
Bob Spencer, Trustee
Charles Taylor, Superintendent of Curriculum

Petro-Canada
W.H. Hopper, Chairman and Chief Executive Officer
John McNicholas, Director, Economics, Public Policy and Regulatory Affairs

Urban Transportation Development Corporation Limited
Kirk W. Foley, President and Chief Executive Officer
P.H. Stevenson, Vice-President, Corporate Affairs

Canadian Bankers' Association
Robert M. MacIntosh, President
Robert W. Korthals, President, Toronto-Dominion Bank
A. Warren Moysey, Senior Executive Vice-President, Canadian Imperial Bank of Commerce
Hugh S. Hardy, Senior Vice-President, Public Affairs, Royal Bank of Canada

Camco Incorporated
Colin M. Harper, President and Chief Executive Officer
Raymond Thompson, Vice-President, Corporate Planning and Development

Board of Trade of Metropolitan Toronto
John Clarry, President
Stanley Edwards, Chairman, Economic Policy Committee
Fred Hamilton, Vice-President
W.S. Campbell, Treasurer
Bengt V. Gestrin, Economic Policy Committee

Cartier Circle
Peter Detmold, President
Kevin Charlebois, Vice-President
W.H. Pope, Professor of Economics, Ryerson Polytechnical Institute
George Mowbray, President, MPI
D.G. Hull, Manager, Canadian Business Opportunities, DSS

Toronto, Ontario - Panel B
December 2, 1983

G.A. Jewett

Peter Lowry

Burns Fry Limited
Peter Andersen, Chief Economist
Carl Wostenholme, Director, Government Finance
Ben Joyce, Senior Economist

Association of Canadian Financial Corporations
Malcolm Stewart, Chairman; Executive Vice-President, Commercial Credit Corporation Limited
Andrew Salmon, First Vice-Chairman; Vice-President, Ford Credit Canada Limited
Donald Bennett, Second Vice-Chairman; President, Household Finance Corporation
Robert McClure, Director; President and General Manager, Genelcan Limited
Carne Bray, President

Executive Committee, Foreign Bank Section of the Canadian Bankers' Association
Roy Hall, President, National Westminster Bank
Terry Upson, President, Chemical Bank of Canada
N. Choi, President, Korea Exchange Bank of Canada
Giacono Morandi, President, Banca Commerciale Italiana of Canada

Canadian Life and Health Insurance Association Inc.
Ian Mair, Past-Chairman; President for Canada, Prudential Insurance Company Limited
John Panabaker, Chairman; Chairman and Chief Executive Officer, Mutual Life Insurance Company
Jean-Denis Vincent, President, Alliance Compagnie Mutuelle d'Assurance-Vie
Gerald M. Devlin, Executive Vice-President

National Pensioners and Senior Citizens' Federation
John Van Waggoner, First Vice-President
Jack Lerette, Office Manager
Joyce King, Secretary
Reg Screen, General Board

London Life Insurance Company
Earl H. Orser, President and Chief Executive Officer
Tom Allan, Vice-President, Investments
Norm Epp, Vice-President, Finance
Bob Lackey, Vice-President, Corporate Planning
Jim Etherington, Director, Corporate Affairs

Toronto, Ontario - Panel A
December 5, 1983

Canadian Association of University Teachers
Sarah J. Shorten, President
Donald C. Savage, Executive Secretary

Ontario Secondary School Teachers' Federation
Malcolm Buchanan, President
Jim Head, Executive Officer
Vince Greco, Research Committee
Wendell Fulton, Legislative Researcher
Shelagh Luka, Status of Women Committee

Government of Ontario
The Honourable Larry Grossman, Treasurer of Ontario
Bryan Davies, Assistant Deputy Minister, Office of Economic Policy
Brock A. Smith, Assistant to the Deputy Minister, Office of Budget and Intergovernmental Finance, Ministry of Treasury and Economics
Gregor Robinson, Senior Policy Advisor

Canadian Foundation for Economic Education
Gary Rabbior, Executive Director

Canadian Association of Women Executives
Elizabeth Stewart, President; Director of Planning, TransAmerica Life Insurance
Barbara Eastman, Chair, Legislative Committee; Policy Advisor, Royal Bank of Canada
Patricia O'Malley, Vice-President, External Relations; National Director, Accounting Resources, Thorne Riddell
Lucy Greene, Chair, Affirmative Action Subcommittee; Assistant Director, Individual Insurance Marketing, Sun Life
Nuala Beck, Legislative Committee; Vice-President, Director, Pitfield, MacKay, Ross Limited

Society of Management Accountants of Canada
William Richardson, President
D. Teal Lowery, Vice-President
Reginald Dugré, Vice-President
William E. Langdon, Executive Vice-President

Trent University
Donald Theall, President and Vice-Chancellor
Erica Cherney, Chairman
Susan Wheeler, Director, Communications

Canadian Machine Builders' Association
J.J. Havlik, President
H.B. Iron, Secretary-Treasurer
John Kershaw, Director

Canadian Association of School Administrators
Larry Moss, President
Wayne Kyle, President-Elect
Louise Lapalme, Executive Secretary
Freeman Witty, Past President

C.I.L. Incorporated
C.H. Hantho, President and Chief Executive Officer
D.I.W. Braide, Senior Vice-President
R.J. Gallivan, Senior Consultant, Human Resources

Toronto, Ontario - Panel B
December 5, 1983

Ontario Federation of Students
Ian Nelmes, Chairperson
Terry Fallis, Chairperson, Economic Policy Committee
Richard Balnis, Researcher
Tony Palmer, Economic Policy Committee

Management Council for Responsible Employee Relations
R.J. Gallivan, Senior Consultant, Human Resources, C.I.L. Inc.
A.Y. Fortier, Director, Corporate Relations, Noranda Mines
V. Harris, Manager, General Industrial Relations, Stelco Inc.
S.J. Surma, Vice-President, Industrial Relations, Ford Motor Company
E.A. Taylor, Vice-President, Human Resources, Westinghouse (Canada) Limited

Canadian Society for Professional Engineers
Greg McNeice, President
Peter De Vita, President-Elect
Murray McInroy, Secretary
Aziz Akhtar, Director
Walter Bilanski

Ontario Confederation of University Faculty Associations
Bill Jones, President
Patrick Wesley, Executive Director
Helen Breslauer, Senior Research Officer

Canadian Congress for Learning Opportunities for Women
Susan McCrae Vander Voet, Executive Director
Dorothy MacKeracher, Advisory Committee
Audrey Swail, Ontario Director

Toronto, Ontario - Panel A
December 6, 1983

CNCP Telecommunications
J.G. Sutherland, President
Carl Beigie, Advisor
Ruth Corbin, Director, Policy Development
Joe Schmidt, Vice-President, Regulatory and Government Matters

Canadian Business Equipment Manufacturers' Association
Charles H. Rust, President; President, STC Canada Inc.
Peter Brophey, Vice-President; Vice-President, Corporate Affairs, Xerox Canada Inc.
Grant Murray, Director; Vice-President, Law and Corporate Relations, IBM Canada Limited
John Neufeld, Director; President, Arconas Corporation

Canadian Electrical Association
Milan Nastich, President; President and Chairman, Ontario Hydro
Donald Priestman, Chairman, Economic Section; Corporate Economist, B.C. Hydro
Mitchell R. Rothman, Vice-Chairman, Economic Section; Chief Economist, Ontario Hydro

University of Waterloo Faculty of Engineering
W.C. Lennox, Dean
E.L. Holmes, Director, Research
J.A. Buzacott, Professor of Management Science
John Schey, Professor of Mechanical Engineering

Frank Maine, President, Frank Maine Consulting Limited

Toronto, Ontario - Panel B
December 6, 1983

Dow Chemical Canada Inc.
James M. Hay, Chairman

Christian Farmers' Federation of Ontario
Tom Oegema, President
Elbert van Donkersgoed, Research and Policy Director
Martin Oldengarm, General Manager

Ontario Institute of Agrologists
Donald McArthur, Executive Director
Bert Christie, President-Elect
Murray MacGregor, Professor of Agricultural Economics, University of Guelph

Ontario Federation of Agriculture
Harry Pelissero, First Vice-President
Brigid Pyke, Second Vice-President
Harry Zwerver, Executive Director

S. Veeraraghavan, Manager, Research Department
Susan Johnston, Assistant Manager, Research Department

Canadian Urban Transit Association
A. Ross, President
A. Cormier, Executive Director
Don Kershaw, Associate Members' Committee

Bank of Montreal
William D. Mulholland, Chairman and Chief Executive Officer
Lloyd Atkinson, Senior Vice-President, Chief Economist

Bell Canada Enterprises
A. Jean de Grandpré, Chairman and President
Orland Tropea, Deputy Chairman
F. Dale Orr, Chief Economist

Canadian General Electric Company Limited
Alton S. Cartwright, Chairman and Chief Executive Officer
David F. Abel, Vice-President, Corporate Strategic Planning

BP Selco Inc.
Patrick C. MacCulloch, President and Chief Executive Officer

Toronto, Ontario - Panel A
December 7, 1983

Crowntek Incorporated
Joseph Zelikovitz, Vice-President, Technology Planning

Nordair Limited
Kurt P. Peiffer, Executive Vice-President
André Bourque, Vice-President, General Counsel and Secretary
Moira Hudgin, Senior Manager, Tariffs and Regulatory Affairs

Canadian Airline Pilots' Association
Donna Burgess, Research Analyst
Major-General R.F. Herbert, Chairman, Headquarters Special Projects

Slacan Division of Slater Steel Industries Limited
J. David Smart, General Sales Manager

Canadian Mental Health Association
Léandre Desjardins, Chairperson, Human Impact of Unemployment Committee
Sharon Kirsh, Project Coordinator, Human Impact of Unemployment Project
Peter Penz, Human Impact of Unemployment Committee

United Way of Metropolitan Toronto
John E. Richardson, Chairman, United Way Board of Trustees
James MacKay, Chairman, Government Relations Committee
Anne Golden, Director, Planning, Allocations and Government Relations
Ted Garrard, Associate, Planning, Allocations and Government Relations

Canadian Red Cross Society
David Balfour, President
George Weber, Secretary General
Dwight Mihalicz, Executive Assistant to the Secretary General

Canadian Centre for Philanthropy
Edward Waitzer, President, Agora Foundation
Gerald Wright, Vice-President, Donner Canadian Foundation
Harry Beatty, Legal Counsel, Ontario Association for the Mentally Retarded
John O'Leary, Director, Development, Frontier College

Institute of Donations and Public Affairs Research
Richard A. Hopkinson, President
Mary Louise Clements, Ontario Representative
Peter R. MacGibbon, Director
Charles Perrault, Director

Social Planning and Research Council of Hamilton and District
Anthony Butler, President
Jody Orr, Senior Research Associate

Hamilton and District Labour Council
William C. Thompson, Secretary; Chairman, Political Action Committee
Lynn Spencer, Executive Officer; Chairperson, Full Employment Committee

Toronto, Ontario - Panel B
December 7, 1983

Genstar Corporation
Angus MacNaughton, Chairman
Ross Turner, President
Malcolm Carden, Manager, Corporate Planning

Ontario Public Service Employees Union
Sean O'Flynn, President

TVOntario
David Walker, Executive Director

National Action Committee on The Status of Women
Doris Anderson, President
Chaviva Hosek, Vice-President; Chairperson, Federal-Provincial Relations Funding Committee
Jennifer Keck, Member-at-Large
Laurell Ritchie, Employment Committee

Paradigm Health
Neville Chenoy, Health Care Planning Consultant, Sisters of St. Joseph
Suzanne Jackson, Health Policy Analyst, Ontario Council of Health
Robert James, General Practitioner; Chairman, OMA Committee on Psychosomatic Medicine
Christine Daly, Health Care Planning Assistant, Sisters of St. Joseph

Canadian Rehabilitation Council for the Disabled
Jean Caine, First Vice-President
Bruce Savage, Regional Vice-President, Ontario
J.R. Sarney, National Executive Director

Marilou McPhedran and Elizabeth Symes

Family Service Association of Metropolitan Toronto
Irene Fink, President
Robert Couchman, Executive Director
Judy Sutcliffe, Chairperson, Social Action Committee
William Oaker, Public Relations Committee

YWCA of Metropolitan Toronto
Ellen Campbell, Executive Director
Anne Wood, Chairperson, Social Justice Committee
Jean Emond, Chairperson, Employment Subcommittee
Jennifer Robertson-Decker, Chairperson, Social Action Committee
Judy Campbell, Social Action Co-ordinator

Toronto, Ontario
December 8, 1983

Theme Panel: Growth and Development
David Slater, Chairman, Economic Council of Canada
Arthur Smith, Past Chairman, Economic Council of Canada
Robert A. Mundell, Professor of Economics, Columbia University
André Raynauld, Past Chairman, Economic Council of Canada

Gunnar Tannis

Peter R. Gorman III and **Ryan M. Gorman**

Canadian Association on Gerontology
R. Bayne, President
Norman Blackie, Executive Director
Sheila Neysmith, Chairperson, Social Welfare Division

Don Toppin, Chairman, Committee on Toronto/2000

Austin Beutel

A.R. Clarke and Co. Limited
David Goldberg, President
Gary Goldberg, Executive Vice-President
Martin O'Connell, Consultant

Toronto, Ontario - Panel A
December 9, 1983

Maclean-Hunter Limited
Donald G. Campbell, Chairman and Chief Executive Officer

Housing and Urban Development Association of Canada
John Sandusky, President-Elect
Kenneth Kyle, Chief Operating Officer

Regional Municipality of York
Robert Forhan, Chairman
Michael McDonald, Executive Assistant

University of Toronto, Institute of Environmental Studies
Henry A. Regier, Associate Director; Professor of Zoology
R.E. Munn, Professor of Physics and Environmental Studies
D. MacKay, Professor of Chemical Engineering and Environmental Studies
A.P. Grima, Associate Professor of Geography and Environmental Studies

Green Party of Ontario
Susan Berlin
Joell Vanderwagen
Ron Pate

Canadian Environmental Law Research Foundation
Doug Macdonald, Executive Director
Marcia Valiante, Research Director

Community Forum on Shared Responsibility
Kenise Murphy Kilbride, Steering Committee
David Walsh, Steering Committee

Dan Heap, MP

Toronto, Ontario - Panel B
December 9, 1983

Anglican Church of Canada
Right Reverend John Bothwell, Bishop of Niagara
Venerable Archdeacon Harry Hilchey, General Secretary, General Synod
Reverend Peter Hamel, Consultant, National Affairs
Reverend Don Brown, Consultant, Social Ministries

Council of National Ethnocultural Organizations of Canada
Laureano Leone, President
Andrew Cardozo, Consultant

Alliance of Canadian Cinema, Television and Radio Artists
Bruce MacLeod, National President
Paul Siren, General Secretary
Jane Craig, Director, Communications

Paul Audley and Associates Limited
Paul Audley, President

Campeau Corporation
Robert Campeau, Chairman and Chief Executive Officer
David King, President and Chief Operating Officer
Andrew Jacob, Senior Director, Commercial Development and Special Projects
Jack Carr, Professor of Economics, Director of Graduate Studies,
Associate Chairman, University of Toronto

Communist Party of Canada
William Kashtan, General Secretary, Leader of the Party
William Stewart, Labour Secretary
John Maclennan, Ontario Organizer
Gerry van Houten, Director, Research

Public Interest Advocacy Centre
Andrew Roman, Executive Director and General Counsel
Kathy McLeod

Hull, Quebec - Panel A
December 12, 1983

Canadian Labour Congress
Dennis McDermott, President
Shirley Carr, Executive Vice-President
Richard Mercier, Executive Vice-President
Ronald Lang, Director, Research
D. O'Hagan, Chief Economist

Business Council on National Issues
Rowland Frazee, Chairman; Chairman and Chief Executive Officer, Royal Bank of Canada
Thomas d'Aquino, President
Gordon Fisher, Vice-Chairman
Peter Vivian, Senior Associate
Dwayne Wright, Senior Associate
Jock Finlayson, Director, Policy Analysis and Research
Todd Rutley, Research Associate

Mining Association of Canada
Harold Fargey, President
William James, First Vice-President
Walter Curlook, Second Vice-President
John Bonus, Managing Director
Roy Woodbridge, Director, Mineral Economics

Canadian Federation of Labour
James McCambly, President
Ken Rose, Vice-President, International Brotherhood of Electrical Workers
Warner Baxter, Vice-President, International Union of Elevator Constructors

International Association of Machinists and Aerospace Workers
Val Bourgeois, Administrative Assistant
Louis Erlichman, Director, Canadian Research
Joseph Hanafin, Director, Canadian Public Relations

Machinery and Equipment Manufacturers' Association of Canada
Joseph Romanow, President
Kirk Tambling, Chairman; Vice-President and General Manager, WEEM United
William Mallory, Past Chairman; President, Ingersoll-Rand Canada
Lorne Varcoe, Vice-Chairman; President, Dorr-Oliver Canada Limited
James Hepburn, Vice-Chairman; Vice-President, John T. Hepburn Company

Alcan Aluminium Limited
David Culver, President and Chief Executive Officer
Harold Corrigan, Vice-President, Corporate Relations
Neil Matheson, Public Affairs Analyst

Pratt and Whitney Canada Incorporated
Elvie L. Smith, President

Canadian Federation of Deans of Management and Administrative Studies
Bud Johnston, Director; Dean of Business Administration, University of Western Ontario
Claude LeBon, Dean of Administrative Sciences, Laval University
Michael Maher, Chairman; Dean of Management, University of Calgary
John Carson, Immediate Past-Dean of Administration, University of Ottawa

Canadian Council of Professional Engineers
John Evans, President
Alex Hemstock, President-Elect
Claude Lajeunesse, Executive Director
John R. McDougall, Chairman, Canadian Engineering Manpower Council
Norm Johnson, Executive Committee; President, Johnson Industries

Federation of Canadian Municipalities
Edward Brady, President; Mayor of Carlyle
Doreen Lawson, First Vice-President; Alderman of Burnaby
Marion Dewar, Second Vice-President; Mayor of Ottawa
Frank Moran, Third Vice-President; Mayor of Charlottetown
Beryl Gaffney, Alderman
James Knight, Executive Director
Penina Coopersmith

Hull, Quebec - Panel B
December 12, 1983

Canadian Construction Association
Robert Nuth, President
Donald P. Giffin, Chairman
Robert B. Schuett, Vice-Chairman
John C. Halliwell, Director, Labour Relations
William Nevins, Chief Economist
Russell Scrim, Vice-President, Beaver Construction

Cadillac Fairview Corporation Limited
Bernard Ghert, President and Chief Operating Officer
Miles McMenemy, Senior Vice-President, Corporate Affairs

Urban Development Institute of Canada
Edward Sorbara, President
Rick Bertrand, Executive Secretary

Heritage Canada Foundation
John Mackenzie, Chairman
Douglas Franklin, Director, Public, Corporate and Government Relations

Canadian Shipbuilding and Ship Repairing Association
Henry M. Walsh, President

Dominion Marine Association and Canadian Shipowners' Association
Rear Admiral Robert W. Timbrell, President

Association of Consulting Engineers of Canada
Malcolm Williams, President; Vice-President, C.B.C.L. Limited
Collin Smallridge, Vice-President; Vice-President, Lavalin Inc.
Roger Pinault, Managing Director
Royal Galipeau, Director, Communications

SNC Group
Jean-Paul Gourdeau, President and Chief Executive Officer
Camille Dagenais, Chairman
Jacques Lefebvre, Vice-President, Public Affairs

Hull, Quebec
December 13, 1983

Theme Panel: National Institutional Reform
Pierre Tremblay, Editor-in-Chief, *Le Droit*
Clare Beckton, Associate Professor of Law, Dalhousie University
Allan R. Gregg, President, Decima Research Limited
Gordon Fairweather, Chief Commissioner, Canadian Human Rights Commission
The Honourable Senator P. Michael Pitfield

Canadian Advisory Council on the Status of Women
Lucie Pépin, President
Diane Bellemare, Economist, Université du Québec à Montréal
Magrit Eichler, Ontario Institute for Studies in Education
Jennifer Stoddart, Director, Research Services
Mary-Lee Stevenson, Senior Research Officer

Canadian Conference of Catholic Bishops
The Most Reverend Rémi de Roo, Bishop of Victoria; Chairman, Episcopal Commission for Social Affairs
Mgr. Gérard Drainville, Bishop of Amos; Episcopal Commission for Social Affairs
Tony Clarke, Co-Director, Social Affairs Department

Exécutif national du Parti québécois
Bernard Landry, National Executive
Nadia Assimopoulos, National Executive
Jules-Pascal Venne, Adviser

Retail Council of Canada
Alasdair J. McKichan, President
Gérard Doucet, Senior Vice-President
George Eaton, Chairman; Deputy Chairman, T. Eaton Company
F. Hennig, Executive Vice-President, Corporate Operations
W.M. Crossin, President, Merle Norman Cosmetics

Task Force on Microelectronics and Employment
Margaret Fulton, Chairperson; President, Mount St. Vincent University
Ratna Ray, Director, Women's Bureau, Labour Canada

Hull, Quebec - Panel A
December 14, 1983

Fédération des francophones hors Québec inc.
Léo LeTourneau, President
Jean-Bernard Lafontaine, Director General
Richard Chevrier, Researcher

Jean-Pierre Gaboury

Canadian Chamber of Commerce
Samuel Hughes, President
C.M. "Red" Williams, Chairman, Agriculture Committee
Lorne Seitz, Senior Vice-President, International Affairs
John Lang, Chairman, Natural Resources Committee
John Bonus, Natural Resources Committee
Marsha Gordon, Policy Co-ordinator
Ken Page, Chairman, Education Committee

Tourism Industry Association of Canada
Garth Campbell, President and Chief Executive Officer
John Lawson, Vice-President

Coalition of National Voluntary Organizations
Ian Morrison, Chairman
Beatrice Olivastri

Association of Universities and Colleges of Canada
W. Andrew MacKay, President
Ronald Watts, Principal, Queen's University
Robert Patry, Director, Government Relations

Canadian Federation of Students
Graham Dowdell, Chairperson
Eileen Dooley, Accessibility Researcher
Bruce Tate, Economic Policy Researcher
Diane Flaherty, Executive Officer

Rural Learning Association
Ted Jackson, President
Alex Sim, Past-President
Susan Wismer, Community Economic Development Project

Canadian Association For Adult Education
Ian Morrison, Executive Director
Paul Bélanger, Director

Canadian Teachers' Federation
Brian Shortall, President
Stirling McDowell, Secretary-General
Wilfred Brown, Director, Economic Services

Centrale de l'enseignement du Québec
Ginette Dion, Vice-President
Pierre Beaulne, Economist

Canadian Union of Public Employees
Jeff Rose, National President
John Calvert, Senior Officer, Research Department
Gil Levine, Director, Research Department
Tony Wohlfarth, Officer
Randy Sykes, Assistant Director

Prince Edward Island Potato Marketing Board
Kees Visser, President
Don Anderson, Manager
Norman Clarey, Past Chairman

Garth Wilkie, Vice-Chairman
Donald MacKenzie, Grower-Exporter

Hull, Quebec - Panel B
December 14, 1983

Science Council of Canada
Stuart Smith, Chairman
James Gilmour, Director, Research
Guy Steed, Associate Director, Research

National Research Council of Canada
Larkin Kerwin, President
William A. Cumming, Executive Vice-President
Robert de Coster

Agricultural Institute of Canada
Clay Switzer, President
A. Terauds, General Manager
J. Dumanski

Natural Sciences and Engineering Research Council of Canada
Gordon MacNabb, President
Arthur Bourns, Visiting Research Officer

Professional Institute of the Public Service of Canada
Jack Donegani, President
Ken Gibson, Acting Manager, Employment Relations
Ida Irwin, Assistant Information Officer

Canadian Chemical Producers' Association
Jean Bélanger, President
Graham C. Gibb, Director, Economic Affairs
Wilburt Canniff, Assistant to the President; Director, Special Projects

Canadian Gas Association
D. Earl Alderson, President and Chief Administrative Officer; President and Chief Operating Officer, Canadian Gas Research Institute

Canadian Federation of Professional Foresters' Associations
Allen Hopwood, Past President, Association of B.C. Professional Foresters
William Hall, Ontario Professional Foresters' Association
Claude Turmel, Ordre des ingénieurs forestiers du Québec

Canadian Institute of Forestry
Gilbert Paillé, President
R.J. Bourchier, Executive Director
P.J.B. Duffy, Chairman, Working Group, Forest Policy

Canadian Export Association
Paul Soubry, Chairman
Reg Barclay, Vice-Chairman
Tom M. Burns, President

Atomic Energy of Canada Limited
James Donnelly, President and Chief Executive Officer
Ara Mooradian, Senior Vice-President
Paul O'Neill, Corporate Executive Vice-President
Fred Belaire, Director, Economic Planning

Conseil canadien de la coopération
Henri-Paul Trudel, President
Denis Rochon, Vice-President
Richard Savoie, Executive Committee
Yvan Forest, Director-General

Canadian Soft Drink Association
Tibor P. Gregor, Executive Director

Ottawa, Ontario - Panel A
December 15, 1983

Theme Panel: Federal-Provincial Relations
Gordon Robertson, President, Institute for Research on Public Policy
Gil Rémillard, Professor of Law, Laval University
Anthony Scott, Professor of Economics, University of British Columbia; MacKenzie King Professor, Canadian Studies, Harvard University
John Whyte, Professor of Law, Queen's University
Rad Latimer, President and Chief Executive Officer, TransCanada PipeLines

YWCA of Canada
Dana Stehr, Executive Director
Lynne Tyler, National Board

Pat and **Hugh Armstrong**

The Honourable Judy Erola, Minister Responsible for the Status of Women
Maureen O'Neil, Co-ordinator, Status of Women
Susan Sheehan, Senior Analyst, Economic Policy
Monique Charlebois, Senior Analyst, Legal Policy

The National Council of the YMCA's of Canada
Charles Greb, Chairperson
Rix Rogers, Chief Executive Officer
Anthony Patterson, Government Relations Advisory Committee
Jane Côté, Director, Ottawa YM-YWCA
Rick Patten, Director, Ottawa Office

Canadian Hospital Association
Claire Labrèche, Chairman
Jean-Claude Martin, President
Daniel LeTouzé, Vice-President, Research

Canadian Health Coalition
Richard Haughian, Chairperson
Carol Richardson, Executive Co-ordinator
Margaret Vowles, National Senior Citizens and Pensioners' Organization
Joseph Hanafin, International Association of Machinists

Ottawa, Ontario - Panel B
December 15, 1983

Tom de Fayer

Roger Voyer, Principal, Nordicity Group Limited

Tom Atkinson, Senior Project Director, Research for Management, Hay Associates Canada Limited

Kimon Valaskakis, Director, GAMMA Group

Ottawa, Ontario - Panel A
December 16, 1983

The Honourable André Ouellet, Minister of Labour
Mark R. Daniels, Deputy Minister
William P. Kelly, Senior Assistant Deputy Minister

Canadian Institute of Chartered Accountants
William D. Grace, First Vice-President; Chief Financial Officer and Director, Canadian Utilities Limited
N. Glenn Ross, Partner, Coopers and Lybrand
James R. Brown, Senior Partner, Peat, Marwick, Mitchell and Co.

Grand Council of the Crees of Quebec
Billy Diamond, Grand Chief and Chairman
James O'Reilly, Legal Advisor

Inuit Circumpolar Conference
Mark Gordon, Vice-President for Canada; First Vice-President, Makivik Corporation
Rhoda Innuksuk, Executive Council Member for Canada
Peter Jull, Special Assistant

City of Ottawa
Marion Dewar, Mayor of Ottawa

South Grenville District High School - Grade 13 Geography Class
Donna Burns
Terry Byrd
Clint Cameron
Heather Creamer
Sherry Marshall
Gary Heuvel

Social Planning Council of Ottawa-Carleton
Frank Martin, Executive Director
Joseph Verbruggen, Chairman, Income and Employment Committee
Jim Davidson, Co-ordinator, Income and Employment Committee
Catherine Casserly, Income and Employment Committee

City of Hull
Michel Légère, Mayor of Hull

Co-operative Union of Canada and Canadian Co-operative Credit Society
Ray Siemens, President, Co-operative Union of Canada
John Nicholson, Chairman, Canadian Co-operative Credit Society
Jonathan Guss, Corporate Counsel; Vice-President, Government Affairs, Canadian Co-operative Credit Society
Bruce Thordarson, Executive Director, Co-operative Union of Canada

Michael Boyd

Ottawa-Carleton Board of Trade
John Ferguson, Treasurer; President, JRF Financial Consultants Limited
Kevin Charlebois, Chairman, Finance and Taxation Committee; Vice-President, JRF Financial Consultants Limited

Co-operative Housing Foundation of Canada
Glenn Haddrell, Executive Director
Tom Webb, Government Relations Consultant
Robert Dowler, Research Program Co-ordinator

Ottawa, Ontario - Panel B
December 16, 1983

Canadian Conference of the Arts and Canadian Crafts Council
Micheline Tessier, President, Canadian Conference of the Arts
Brian Anthony, Acting National Director, Canadian Conference of the Arts
Patricia McClelland, President, Canadian Crafts Council
Peter Weinrich, Executive Director, Canadian Crafts Council

United Way of Canada
André Mailhot, President
Robert Myers, Executive Director

National Council of Women of Canada
May Nickson, Vice-President
Amy Williams, Past President

Canadian Research Institute for the Advancement of Women
Jill McCalla Vickers, Chairperson, Social Policy
Mary Lynn Stewart-McDougall, Associate Professor of History, Simon Fraser University

Michael Cassidy, MPP

Via Rail Canada Inc.
Harold Renouf, Chairman

Standards Council of Canada
Jean Roy, President
John Woods, Executive Director
Hugh Adam, Director, National Standardization
Albert Tunis, Director, Education and Information

Canadian Federation of Communications Workers
Boris Mather, Federal Chairman
James Kinkaid, Researcher

APPENDIX C-5

Schedule of Participants In Public Debates May, June 1984

Montreal
May 30, 31, and June 1, 1984

Agenda

Day 1:	a.m.	Jobs and Costs; Education and Training; Social Support
	p.m.	High Quality Basic Education
		Youth and Unemployment: A Special Case?
Day 2:	a.m.	Trade and Industrial Development; Productivity; Resources and the Environment
	p.m.	Industrial Restructuring: Adjustments
Day 3:	a.m.	Intergovernmental Relations and the Economic Union; National Institutions
	p.m.	The Role of the Supreme Court
		The Unfinished Constitutional Agenda

Moderator

Marc Laurendeau, Columnist for *La Presse* and Commentator for Radio Cité FM.

Participants	**Attended**
Warren Allmand, MP, Chairman, Standing Committee on Labour Employment and Immigration	Day 3
Gérald Beaudoin, Law Faculty, University of Ottawa	Day 3
Denyse Bélanger-Rochon, President, Fédération des femmes du Québec	Day 1
Diane Bellemare, Economist, Université du Québec à Montréal	Days 1, 2 and 3
Roger Blais, Centre d'innovation industrielle de Montréal, École polytéchnique de Montréal	Day 2
Michel Blondin, Officer responsible for education and training, United Steelworkers of America	Day 1
Michael Boyd, Michael Boyd Investments Ltd.	Day 2
James Cadieux, Chairman, Economic Policy and Information Committee, Montreal Board of Trade	Day 2
Gretta Chambers, Columnist, *The Gazette*	Day 1

David Culver, President and Chief Executive Officer, Alcan Aluminium Limited	Day 2
Jean de Grandpré, Chairman, President and Chief Executive Officer, Bell Canada Enterprises	Days 1 and 2
Louis P. de Grandpré, Lafleur, Brown, de Grandpré	Day 3
Robert Després, Chairman, Atomic Energy of Canada	Day 2
René Didier, Dean of Administration, University of Moncton	Day 1
Vaughan Dowie, Executive Director, Alliance Quebec	Day 1
Ernest Drew, President and Chief Executive Officer, Celanese Canada	Day 2
Claude Ducharme, Desjardins, Ducharme	Day 3
Ghislain Dufour, Executive Vice-President, Conseil du patronat du Québec	Days 1 and 2
Anne Dutil, President, Procycle	Day 2
Martin Franklin, Economic Policy and Information Committee, Montreal Board of Trade	Day 3
Gérard Gras, 1st Vice-President, Confédération de l'union des producteurs agricoles	Day 2
Howard Hart, President, Canadian Pulp and Paper Association	Day 2
David Johnston, Principal and Vice-Chancellor, McGill University	Day 1
Richard Lande, Economic Policy and Information Committee, Montreal Board of Trade	Day 3
Gonzague Langlois, Director General, Association des mines de métaux du Québec	Day 2
M.A. (Mun) Lavigne, Chairman, Business-Education Committee, Montreal Board of Trade	Day 1
Jean-Claude Lavoie, Mayor of Shipshaw	Day 1
Louis LeBel, bâtonnier du Québec	Day 3
J. Maurice LeClair, President and Chief Executive Officer, Canadian National	Day 3
Jacques Lefebvre, Vice-President, Public Affairs, SNC Group	Days 2 and 3
Pierre Lortie, President, Montreal Stock Exchange	Day 2
André Mailhot, President, United Way Canada	Day 1
Yves Morency, Confédération des Caisses populaires et d'économie Desjardins du Québec	Day 2
Michel Nadeau, First Vice-President, Caisse de dépot et de placement du Québec	Day 2
Alex K. Paterson, Chairman, Alliance Research and Education Institute	Day 3
Gil Rémillard, Law Faculty, Université Laval	Day 3
Michel Rhéaume, President, Association québécoise de la qualité	Day 2
Raymond Royer, Executive Vice-President, Bombardier Inc.	Day 2
Claude Ryan, MLA, Argenteuil	Day 3
Guy St-Pierre, President and Chief Executive Officer, Ogilvie Mills Ltd.	Day 2
David Schulman, Economic Policy and Information Committee, Montreal Board of Trade	Day 2
Louise Séguin-Dulude, Hautes études commerciales	Days 1 and 2
Thérèse Sévigny, Vice-President, Audience Relations, Radio-Canada	Day 3
Monique Simard, First Vice-President, Confédération des syndicats nationaux	Days 1, 2 and 3
Rodrigue Tremblay, Professor of Economics, Université de Montréal	Days 2 and 3

Participant	Attended
Ann Usher, Canadian Association for Adult Education	Day 1
Louise Vaillancourt, Board member, Bell Canada Enterprises	Day 3
John Weldon, Professor of Economics, McGill University	Day 1

Halifax
June 4, 5 and 6, 1984

Agenda

Day 1:	a.m.	Jobs and Costs; Education and Training; Social Support
	p.m.	Job Creation Through Self-Reliance
Day 2:	a.m.	Trade and Industrial Development; Productivity; Resources and the Environment
	p.m.	Regional Economic Development The Future of Traditional Resource Sectors in the Atlantic Region
Day 3:	a.m.	Intergovernmental Relations and the Economic Union; National Institutions
	p.m.	Intergovernmental Relations and the Economic Union

Moderator
Rod Dobell, President, Institute for Research on Public Policy

Participants	**Attended**
Sandy Archibald, President, Britex Ltd.	Day 1
Frederic Arsenault, Deputy Minister, New Brunswick Office of Government Reform	Day 2
Elizabeth Beale, Chief Economist, Atlantic Provinces Economic Council	Days 1, 2 and 3
Ann Bell, President, Newfoundland Advisory Council on the Status of Women	Day 1
Ron W. Bulmer, President, Fisheries Council of Canada	Day 2
J. Clair Callaghan, President, Technical University of Nova Scotia	Day 3
Rev. John Capstick, Coalition of Social Organizations in Cape Breton	Days 1 and 2
George Cooper, McInnes, Cooper & Robertson	Day 3
Harold D. Crowell, Chairman of the Board, Human Resources Development Association	Day 1
Peter Dorrington, Chairman, Dartmouth Chamber of Commerce	Day 3
D.A. Eisenhauer, President, Atlantic Bridge Co. Ltd.	Day 2
Christine Fagan, Chalker, Green, & Rowe	Days 2 and 3
Emery Fanjoy, Secretary, Council of Maritime Premiers	Days 2 and 3
Brian Flemming, Stewart, Mackeen & Covert	Day 3
Phil Fraser, Vice President, New Brunswick Association of Métis and Non-Status Indians	Day 1
Margaret Fulton, President, Mount Saint Vincent University	Day 1
John Godfrey, President, University of King's College	Days 1 and 3
John Graham, Economist, Dalhousie University	Day 3
Brian Greene, Assistant General Manager, St. John's Board of Trade	Day 2
Lance Hale, Executive Director, Voluntary Planning Board of Nova Scotia	Days 1 and 3
Eric Hammill, Secretary-Manager, P.E.I. Federation of Agriculture	Day 2

Alanna Hanrahan, Executive Secretary, Newfoundland and Labrador Youth Advisory Council	Day 1
Susan Holtz, Ecology Action Centre	Day 2
Tom Kent, Editor, *Policy Options*	Day 2
Eric Kierans, Economist, Dalhousie University	Days 2 and 3
A. Marino Kristjanson, Director of Research and Analysis, Association of Universities and Colleges of Canada	Day 1
Gilles LeBlanc, President, Fédération acadienne de la Nouvelle-Écosse	Day 1
David Leckie, President, Stokely-Van Camp of Canada Inc.	Day 2
B. MacCulloch, Executive Director, Pictou County Research and Development Commission	Day 1
Marilyn MacDonald, Former Editor, *Atlantic Insight*	Days 1 and 2
Wendell MacDonald, Chairman, Canadian Manufacturers' Association, P.E.I. Branch	Day 2
Robert McKay, Manager, Regional Affairs, Petro Canada Exploration	Days 2 and 3
Fred MacKinnon, Director, Nova Scotia Senior Citizens Secretariat	Day 1
Greg MacLeod, Director, Federation of Community Development Corporations	Day 1
Sylvestre McLaughlin, Director General, Conseil économique du Nouveau-Brunswick inc.	Days 1, 2 and 3
Peter J. Nicholson, Executive Assistant, Bank of Nova Scotia	Day 2
Dan F. Potter, President, Novatron Information Corp.	Day 1
Paul Pross, Acting Director, Public Administration, Dalhousie University	Day 3
W.S. Robertson, President and Chief Executive Officer, Maritime Tel and Tel	Day 2
Penelope Rowe, Executive Director, Community Services Council	Days 1 and 3
A.M. Sinclair, Economist, Dalhousie University	Day 2
David Slater, Chairman, Economic Council of Canada	Day 2
Harold Snyder, Faculty of Engineering, Memorial University	Day 2
Elizabeth Walsh, Women Unlimited	Days 1 and 3
Lyndon Watkins, Editor, *Daily News*	Day 1
R.F. Weary, President, Bowater, Mersey Paper Co. Ltd.	Day 2
Bill Wells, President, Canadian Saltfish Corporation	Day 2
Fred Wien, Director, Maritime School of Social Work	Day 1
Gerald Yetman, President, Nova Scotia Federation of Labour	Day 2

Vancouver
June 11, 12 and 13, 1984

Agenda

Day 1:	a.m.	Jobs and Costs; Education and Training; Social Support
	p.m.	Improving the Delivery of Services; Systematic Lifelong Learning
Day 2:	a.m.	Trade and Industrial Development; Productivity; Resources and the Environment
	p.m.	Secure and Growing Markets

Day 3: a.m. Intergovernmental Relations and the Economic Union; National Institutions
p.m. Consultation in the Decision and Policy-Making Process

Moderator
Rod Dobell, President, Institute for Research on Public Policy

Participants	**Attended**
Judith Alexander, Professor of Economics, Simon Fraser University	Day 1
Robert Allen, Professor of Economics, University of British Columbia	Day 2
David Anderson, Professor of Law, School of Public Administration, University of Victoria	Days 2 and 3
Larry Bell, Chief Executive Officer and General Manager, Vancouver City Credit Union	Day 3
Judith Bezeredi, Director, Health Department, City of Vancouver	Days 1 and 2
Joan Blair, Women in Trades	Day 1
Doreen Braverman, Director, Canadian Manufacturers' Association; President, The Flagshop	Day 3
John Bruk, Chairman, Asia Pacific Foundation of Canada	Day 2
Len Bruton, Dean of Engineering, University of Victoria	Day 1
Diana Butler, Victoria Status of Women Action Group	Day 1
Marilyn Callaghan, Professor of Social Work, University of Victoria	Days 1 and 2
William S. Cameron, Vice-President, Corporate Planning, British Columbia Resources Investment Corporation	Day 2
J.V. Clyne, Former Chairman, MacMillan-Bloedel; Visiting Professor, Simon Fraser University	Day 3
Charles Connaghan, Connaghan & Associates	Day 2
Nancy Cooley, Director, Intermediate Technology Development Group	Day 2
W.L. Day, President, Douglas College	Day 3
Glenn Drover, President, Canadian Association of Social Workers; Director of Social Work, University of British Columbia	Days 1 and 3
Tex Enemark, President, Mining Association of British Columbia	Days 1, 2 and 3
J.E. (Ted) Fletcher, Vice-President, B.C. Group, Cominco Ltd.	Day 2
Pat Fulton, Former Regional Director, New Horizons	Day 1
Michael Goldie, Russell & DuMoulin	Day 3
Ian Gray, Former Chairman, CP Air; Visiting Professor of Business Administration, Simon Fraser University	Day 1
Craig Greenhill, Director of Institute Planning, British Columbia Institute of Technology	Day 3
Jack Hannam, Vice-Chairman, Northern Development Council	Days 2 and 3
Michael Harcourt, Mayor, City of Vancouver	Day 3
George Hogham, Professor of Social Work, University of British Columbia	Day 3
Art Kube, President, British Columbia Federation of Labour	Day 2
Larry Kuehn, President, British Columbia Teachers' Federation	Day 1
Joy Leach, Past President, British Columbia Trustees Association	Days 1 and 3
Martin Levin, Alderman, Victoria	Day 3
Bernice Levitz Packford, Executive Director, Capital Families	Day 3

Gus Long, Editor, Federated Anti-Poverty Groups of British Columbia	Days 1 and 3
J. Ronald Longstaffe, Executive Vice-President and Director, Canadian Forest Products Ltd.	Day 1
John S. MacDonald, President, MacDonald Dettwiler & Associates Ltd.	Day 2
Darlene Marzari, Former Alderman, Greater Vancouver Regional District	Day 3
James G. Matkin, President, Employers' Council of British Columbia	Days 1, 2 and 3
Richard McAlary, Chief Economist, B.C. Central Credit Union	Day 2
Charles McCaffray, Principal, College of New Caledonia	Days 1, 2 and 3
Edward McWhinney, Professor of International Law and Relations, Simon Fraser University	Day 3
Audrey Moore, Mayor of Castlegar; President, Union of British Columbia Municipalities	Day 3
Ian Morrison, Executive Director, Canadian Association for Adult Education	Day 1
William A.W. Neilson, Professor of Law, University of Victoria	Day 3
David Nordstrom, Co-ordinator, Capital Families	Day 1
Peter Pearse, Professor of Forestry-Economics, University of British Columbia	Day 1
George Pederson, President, University of British Columbia	Day 1
Bruce Pepper, President, Vancouver Board of Trade	Day 2
Clay Perry, International Woodworkers of America	Day 2
Art Phillips, Former Mayor of Vancouver	Day 2
John Poole, President, Daon Development Corporation	Day 2
Gideon Rosenbluth, Professor of Economics, University of British Columbia	Day 1
W. Saywell, President, Simon Fraser University	Day 2
W. Joseph Scott, Chairman, Prince Rupert Port Corporation	Day 3
Colin Smith, Owner and Manager, The Dolphins Fishing Resort, Campbell River	Days 1 and 2
Douglas Spray, Deputy Minister and Chairman, Steering Committee on Macdonald Commission, Executive Council, Yukon Government	Days 1, 2 and 3
Michael Walker, Director, Fraser Institute	Day 2
Alan Williams, Lawyer and Former Attorney General, British Columbia	Day 3
Jacob S. Ziegel, Professor of Law, University of Toronto	Day 3

Calgary
June 18, 19 and 20, 1984

Agenda

Day 1:	a.m.	Jobs and Costs; Education and Training; Social Support
	p.m.	Jobs and Equity
Day 2:	a.m.	Trade and Industrial Development; Productivity; Resources and the Environment
	p.m.	The Development and Husbanding of Natural Resources; The Agri-Food Industry

Day 3: a.m. Intergovernmental Relations and the Economic Union; National Institutions
p.m. National Institutional Reform: The Senate and the House of Commons

Moderator
Rod Dobell, President, Institute for Research on Public Policy

Participants	**Attended**
Palma Anderson, President, Saskatchewan Action Committee on the Status of Women	Days 1 and 3
Ted Azevedo, President, Saskatchewan Seniors Association Inc.	Day 1
Lloyd Barber, President, University of Regina	Days 1 and 2
David Brooks, Marbek Resource Consultants Ltd.	Day 2
Bob Church, Faculty of Medicine, University of Calgary	Day 2
Patricia C. Cooper, Canadian Advisory Council on the Status of Women	Days 1 and 3
Lawrence Copithorne, Professor of Economics, University of Calgary	Day 2
William D. Croft, President, Calgary Research and Development Authority	Day 1
Laurence G. Decore, Mayor, City of Edmonton	Day 3
Gordon Dorrell, Director, Lethbridge Research Institute, Agriculture Canada	Day 2
David K. Elton, President, Canada West Foundation	Day 3
Glenn Flaten, President, Canadian Federation of Agriculture	Day 2
J.P. Gallagher, Former Chairman and Chief Executive Officer, Dome Canada	Day 3
William A. Gatenby, President and Chief Executive Officer, Texaco Canada Resources Ltd.	Day 2
Roger Gibbins, Professor of Political Science, University of Calgary	Day 3
Gordon S. Gibson, Gibson & McCormick	Day 3
Bill Gold, Associate Editor, *Calgary Herald*	Days 1, 2 and 3
John Hagg, Chairman, Northstar Resources Ltd.	Day 1
John Harapiak, Manager of Agronomy, Western Co-operative Fertilizers	Day 2
J. Martin Hattersley, Hattersley, Mitchell & Follett	Day 3
Brian Heidecker, Canadian Cattlemen's Association	Day 2
Charles Hetherington, President and Chief Executive Officer, Panarctic Oils Ltd.	Day 2
The Honourable William Jarvis, MP	Day 3
Donald L. Karst, Executive Director, Calgary Family Service Bureau	Day 1
The Honourable Otto Lang, Executive Vice-President, Pioneer Grain Company Ltd.	Days 2 and 3
Léo Létourneau, President, Fédération des francophones hors Québec	Day 3
Gordon MacMurchy, President, Family Farm Foundation of Canada	Day 2
Allan J. Macpherson, President, Alberta Wheat Pool	Day 2
Thomas Maxwell, Vice-President and Senior Economist, Conference Board of Canada	Days 1 and 2
Peter McCormick, Professor of Political Science, University of Lethbridge; Canada West Foundation	Day 3
Donald K. McIvor, Chairman and Chief Executive Officer, Imperial Oil Limited	Day 2

Robert McKeon, Churches of Edmonton	Day 1
Alasdair J. McKichan, President, Retail Council of Canada	Day 2
Gwyn Morgan, President, Independent Petroleum Association of Canada	Day 2
A.R. Nielsen, Chairman, Canadian Petroleum Association	Days 1 and 2
James S. Palmer, Burnet, Duckworth & Palmer	Day 3
Richard Plain, Consumers' Association of Canada (Alberta)	Days 1 and 3
Chief Sol Sanderson, President, Saskatchewan Federation of Indian Nations	Days 1, 2 and 3
Brian L. Scarfe, Professor of Economics, University of Alberta	Day 1
Ian Smyth, Executive Director, Canadian Petroleum Association	Days 1, 2 and 3
Harvey Stalwick, Faculty of Social Work, University of Regina	Day 1
Don Stanley, President, Alberta Chamber of Commerce	Day 1
Stuart A. Thiesson, Executive Secretary, National Farmers Union	Days 1 and 2
Tim Tyler, Faculty of Social Welfare, University of Calgary	Day 1
Norman E. Wagner, President and Vice-Chancellor, University of Calgary	Day 1

Toronto
June 26, 27 and 28, 1984

Agenda

Day 1:	a.m.	Jobs and Costs; Education and Training; Social Support
	p.m.	The Implications of a Changing Demographic Profile
Day 2:	a.m.	Trade and Industrial Development; Productivity; Resources and the Environment
	p.m.	What are the Criteria for Determining the Openness of the Economy?
Day 3:	a.m.	Intergovernmental Relations and the Economic Union; National Institutions
	p.m.	Assuring Freedom of Trade Within Canada; Reconciling Conflicting Interests

Moderator
Rod Dobell, President, Institute for Research on Public Policy

Participants	**Attended**
Lou Applebaum	Day 1
Ken Armson, Past President, Canadian Forestry Association	Day 2
Charles Black, Vice-President, Health Insurance, Canadian Life and Health Insurance Association	Day 1
James Black, President, Molson Companies Ltd. and Chairman, Canadian Manufacturers' Association	Day 3
John Bossons, Professor of Economics, University of Toronto	Day 2
Garth Campbell, President, Tourism Industry Association of Canada	Day 2
Stephen Clarkson, Professor of Political Science, University of Toronto	Day 2
Gail Cook, Executive Vice-President, Bennecon Ltd.	Day 2
Robert Couchman, Vanier Institute of the Family	Day 1
Gordon Cressy, President, United Way of Greater Toronto	Day 1
C. William Daniel, Chairman, Shell Canada	Day 2
Richard Danielson, Infonorth Computing Inc.	Day 2

Tom d'Aquino, President, Business Council on National Issues	Day 2
Marion Dewar, Mayor of Ottawa; Second Vice-President, Federation of Canadian Municipalities	Day 3
Anne Fawcett, Senior Partner, The Caldwell Partners	Day 2
Jan K. Fedorowicz, Manager, International Policy, Canadian Chamber of Commerce	Day 2
Ivan Feltham, Vice-President and General Counsel, Canadian General Electric	Day 3
Paul Fox, Principal, Erindale College, University of Toronto	Day 3
Ralph Garber, Dean, School of Social Work, University of Toronto	Day 3
Robert Gordon, Principal, Humber College	Day 1
Alexander Gray, President and Chief Executive Officer, Gray Tool Company of Canada Ltd.	Day 1
Hugh Hardy, Senior Vice-President, Royal Bank	Day 1
Douglas Hartle, University of Toronto	Day 3
Chaviva Hosek, National Action Committee on the Status of Women	Days 1, 2 and 3
Graeme Hughes, Senior Vice-President, Policy, Canadian Manufacturers' Association	Days 1, 2 and 3
Sam Hughes, President, Canadian Chamber of Commerce	Day 3
William James, Chairman, President and Chief Executive Officer, Falconbridge Limited	Day 2
Patrick Johnston, Executive Director, National Anti-Poverty Organization	Days 1 and 2
Andrew G. Kniewasser, President, Investment Dealers Association of Canada	Day 2
Hal R. Kroeker, Director, Public Policy Planning, Massey-Ferguson Limited	Day 2
Ken Kyle, Chief Operating Officer, Canadian Homebuilders Association	Day 2
Laureano Leone, President, Council of National Ethnocultural Organizations	Day 1
Peter M. Leslie, Director, Institute of Intergovernmental Relations, Queen's University	Day 3
Boris Mather, Federal Chair, Canadian Federation of Communications Workers	Day 3
Judith Maxwell, Consulting Economist, Currie, Coopers & Lybrand Ltd.	Day 2
Jim McCambly, President, Canadian Federation of Labour	Days 1, 2 and 3
Ian Morrison, National Voluntary Organizations	Day 3
Penny Moss, Chairman, Toronto Board of Education	Day 1
Donald A. Noble, Executive Vice-President, Finance and Administration, Northern Telecom Limited	Day 2
Dale Orr, Chief Economist, Bell Canada	Days 1 and 2
Jeffrey Patterson, Director of Research, Social Planning Council of Metro Toronto	Days 1, 2 and 3
Marilyn Pilkington, Osgoode Hall Law School	Day 3
Beryl Plumptre	Day 1

Elizabeth Poulin, President, Northwestern Ontario Women's Decade Council	Day 1
Gordon R. Robertson, Institute for Research on Public Policy	Day 3
Ken Rose, International Vice-President, International Brotherhood of Electrical Workers	Day 3
Anthony Scott, MacKenzie King Professor, Canadian Studies, Harvard University	Day 3
Leonard Shifrin, freelance columnist	Day 1
Byron Spencer, Professor of Economics, McMaster University	Day 1
The Honourable Robert Stanbury, Chairman and Chief Executive Officer, Firestone Canada Inc.	Day 1
Jennifer Stoddart, Director of Research, Canadian Advisory Council on the Status of Women	Days 1, 2 and 3
Jill Vickers, Director, Institute of Canadian Studies, Carleton University; Board Member, Canadian Research Institute for the Advancement of Women	Day 3
Peter E. Vivian, Business Council on National Issues	Day 3
F. Dwayne Wright, Business Council on National Issues	Day 1
Jean Wright, Economic Policy Researcher, Canadian Federation of Students	Day 1

The Collected Research Studies

The studies listed below were prepared as background papers for the Royal Commission on the Economic Union and Development Prospects for Canada. Although written under the auspices of the Commission, the views expressed and the conclusions and recommendations contained in the studies are solely those of the authors and do not imply endorsement by the Chairman and Commissioners. At the time of writing, a few of the studies listed have not yet been completed or approved.

The studies have been grouped in volumes (also identified below) and, in co-operation with the Royal Commission, are being published in English by the University of Toronto Press, and in French by the Canadian Government Publishing Centre (Supply and Services).

The research program of the Commission was carried out under the direction of Ivan Bernier (Law and Constitutional Issues); Alan Cairns (Politics and Institutions of Government); and David C. Smith (Economics). Kenneth Norrie and John Sargent acted as co-directors of research for the concluding phase of the Economics program.

Economics

François Vaillancourt
Research Co-ordinator, Income Distribution and Economic Security, Volume 1

VOLUME 1: INCOME DISTRIBUTION AND ECONOMIC SECURITY IN CANADA

François Vaillancourt	Income Distribution and Economic Security in Canada: An Overview
Mireille Ethier	The Underground Economy: A Review of the Economic Literature and New Estimates for Canada
B.G. Dahlby	The Incidence of Government Expenditures and Taxes in Canada: A Survey
Bernard Fortin	Income Security in Canada
Jean-Michel Cousineau	Unemployment Insurance and Labour Market Adjustments
Mireille Ethier	Survey of Pension Issues
Gilles Grenier	Health Care Costs in Canada: Past and Future Trends
Jonathan R. Kesselman	Comprehensive Income Security for Canadian Workers

Donald G. McFetridge
Research Co-ordinator, Industrial Structure, Volumes 2-8

VOLUME 2: CANADIAN INDUSTRY IN TRANSITION

Donald D. McFetridge	The Economics of Industrial Structure: An Overview
Michael Charette, Robert R. Henry and Barry Kaufman	The Evolution of the Canadian Industrial Structure: An International Perspective
R.S. Khemani	Extent and Evolution of Competition in the Canadian Economy
E. Craig Elford and William T. Stanbury	Mixed Enterprises in Canada
John R. Baldwin and Paul K. Gorecki, with J. McVey	Canada-U.S. Productivity Differences in the Manufacturing Sector: 1970–1979
Donald J. Daly	Rationalization and Specialization in Canadian Manufacturing
Paul M. Bishop and Harold Crookell	Specialization and Foreign Investment in Canada

VOLUME 3: TECHNOLOGICAL CHANGE IN CANADIAN INDUSTRY

Jeffrey J. Bernstein	Research and Development, Patents, and Grant and Tax Policies in Canada
Ned Ellis and David Waite	Canadian Technological Output in a World Context
Edwin Mansfield	Technological Change and the International Diffusion of Technology: A Survey
Donald J. Lecraw	Corporate Operation and Strategy in a Changing World Environment
Donald G. McFetridge and R. J. Corvari	Technology Diffusion: A Survey of Canadian Evidence and the Public Policy Issues
Isaiah A. Litvak and Christopher J. Maule	The Canadian Aluminum and Steel Industries

VOLUME 4: CANADIAN INDUSTRIAL POLICY IN ACTION

Donald G. McFetridge	The Economics of Industrial Policy: An Overview
Harold Crookell	The Impact of Government Intervention on the Major Appliance Industry in Canada
Sandford F. Borins and B. Boothman	Crown Corporations and Economic Efficiency
John Chant	An Agenda for Research on Financial Markets

Keith Acheson	Economic Regulation in Canada: A Survey
Donald G. McFetridge	Commercial and Political Efficiency: A Comparison of Government, Mixed and Private Enterprises

VOLUME 5: ECONOMICS OF INDUSTRIAL POLICY AND STRATEGY

Donald J. Lecraw	Industrial Policy in the United States: A Survey
Reuven Brenner and Léon Courville	Industrial Strategy: Inferring What It Really Is
Marsha Chandler and Michael J. Trebilcock	A Comparative Survey of Industrial Policies in Selected OECD Countries

VOLUME 6: THE ROLE OF SCALE IN CANADA-U.S. PRODUCTIVITY DIFFERENCES

John R. Baldwin and Paul K. Gorecki	Canada-U.S. Productivity Differences in the Manufacturing Sector 1970-1979

VOLUME 7: COMPETITION POLICY AND VERTICAL EXCHANGE

F. Mathewson and R. Winter	Competition Policy and the Nature of Vertical Exchange

VOLUME 8: THE POLITICAL ECONOMY OF ECONOMIC ADJUSTMENT

Michael J. Trebilcock	The Political Economy of Economic Adjustment: The Case of Declining Sectors

John Whalley
Research Co-ordinator, International Trade, Volumes 9-14

VOLUME 9: CANADIAN TRADE POLICIES AND THE WORLD ECONOMY

John Whalley (in collaboration with Colleen Hamilton and Roderick Hill)	Canadian Trade Policies and the World Economy

VOLUME 10: CANADA AND THE MULTILATERAL TRADING SYSTEM

John Whalley	Canada and the Multilateral Trading System: An Introduction
Colleen Hamilton and John Whalley	The GATT and Canadian Interests: Summary of the Proceedings of a Research Symposium
Rodney de C. Grey	The Service Industries: A Note of Caution about the Proposal to Negotiate Rules About Traded Services
Colleen Hamilton and John Whalley	Non-Tariff Barriers and Canadian Trade Policy: Summary of the Proceedings of a Research Symposium
William Diebold	Cartelization and Managed Trade: The Problem of Quantitative Restrictions
Margaret Biggs	The Developing Countries in the International Trading System
Gerald K. Helleiner	Underutilized Potential: Canada's Economic Relations with Developing Countries
Colleen Hamilton and John Whalley	Canada and the Future of the Global Trading System: Summary of the Proceedings of a Research Symposium
C. Michael Aho	What Changes Are Needed at the International Level for Improving Trade Relations
John M. Curtis	Which Way: Canadian Trade Policy in a Changing World Economy
Ronald J. Wonnacott	Notes from an Address on the Proposal for a Canada-Japan Free Trade Area

VOLUME 11: CANADA-UNITED STATES FREE TRADE

Roderick Hill and John Whalley	Introduction: Canada-U.S. Free Trade

Roderick Hill and John Whalley	A Possible Canada-U.S. Free Trade Arrangement: Summary of the Proceedings of a Research Symposium
Ronald J. Wonnacott	Potential Economic Effects of a Canada-U.S. Free Trade Agreement
Mel Watkins	Reservations Concerning a Free Trade Area
Bruce W. Wilkinson	Some Comments on Canada-U.S. Free Trade
William Diebold	U.S.-Canada Free Trade: An American View
James R. Markusen	Canadian Gains from Trade in the Presence of Scale Economies and Imperfect Competition
Richard G. Harris	Summary of a Project on the General Equilibrium Evaluation of Canadian Trade Policy
John R. Baldwin and Paul K. Gorecki	The Relationship between Trade and Tariff Patterns and the Efficiency of the Canadian Manufacturing Sector in the 1970s: A Summary
David F. Burgess	The Impact of Trade Liberalization on Foreign Direct Investment Flows
Colleen Hamilton and John Whalley	U.S. Trade Policies and Canadian Interests: Summary of the Proceedings of a Research Symposium
Raymond J. Ahearn and Alfred Reifman	The Future of U.S. Trade Policy
Peter Morici	Trends in U.S. Trade Policy and Non-Tariff Barriers
Andrew R. Moroz	Some Observations on Non-Tariff Barriers and their Use in Canada
Thorald K. Warley	Issues in Canadian Agricultural Trade Policy
Colleen Hamilton and John Whalley	Regional Considerations and Canadian Trade Policies: Summary of the Proceedings of a Research Symposium
James R. Melvin	The Regional Impact of Tariffs
Ronald A. Shearer	Regionalism and International Trade Policy
John F. Earl	U.S.-Canada Free Trade: A View from the East

VOLUME 12: DOMESTIC POLICIES AND THE INTERNATIONAL ECONOMIC ENVIRONMENT

Roderick Hill and John Whalley	Domestic Policies and the International Economic Environment: An Introduction
A.E. Safarian	Government Control of Foreign Business Investment
W.L. Marr and M.B. Percy	Immigration Policy and Canadian Economic Growth
André Raynauld	Export Insurance and Financing in Canada
Roderick Hill	Domestic Adjustment to Trade Policy Changes and External Shocks: Summary of the Proceedings of a Research Symposium
J. David Richardson	Factor Market Adjustment Policies in Response to External Shocks
Matthew Robertson and Alex Grey	Trade-Related Worker Adjustment Policies: The Canadian Experience
Michael J. Trebilcock	The Political Economy of Business Bail-outs in Canada
Department of Regional Industrial Expansion	Canada's Industrial Adjustment: Federal Government Policies and Programs
Roderick Hill	Exchange Rates, Financial Markets and Trade Liberalization: Summary of the Proceedings of a Research Symposium
John Williamson	Exchange Rate Misalignments, Trade and Canadian Policy
J. David Richardson	Some Links between Exchange Rates and Trade Policy

David Longworth	Some Exchange Rate Policy Considerations When Trade is Liberalized

VOLUME 13: TRADE, INDUSTRIAL POLICY AND INTERNATIONAL COMPETITION

Richard G. Harris	Trade, Industrial Policy and International Competition

VOLUME 14: CANADA'S RESOURCE INDUSTRIES AND WATER EXPORT POLICY

Bruce W. Wilkinson	Canada's Resource Industries: A Survey
Anthony Scott	The Design of Water Export Policy

Craig Riddell
Research Co-ordinator, Labour Markets and Labour Relations, Volumes 15-18

VOLUME 15: LABOUR-MANAGEMENT CO-OPERATION IN CANADA

Craig Riddell	Labour-Management Co-operation in Canada: Introduction
Ontario Department of Labour	Ontario Initiatives with Respect to Preventive Mediation and Quality of Working Life
Keith Newton	The Quality of Working Life in Canada: A Survey
R.J. Adams	Two Policy Approaches to Labour-Management Decision Making at the Level of the Enterprise
Joseph M. Weiler	The Japanese Labour Relations System: Lessons for Canada
Ken G. Waldie	The Evolution of Labour-Government Consultation on Economic Policy

VOLUME 16: CANADIAN LABOUR RELATIONS

Craig Riddell	Canadian Labour Relations: An Overview
Pradeep Kumar	Union Growth in Canada: Retrospect and Prospect
Robert Lacroix	Strike Activity in Canada
Robert J. Davies	The Structure of Collective Bargaining in Canada
David A. Wilton	Public Sector Wage Compensation

VOLUME 17: WORK AND PAY: THE CANADIAN LABOUR MARKET

Craig Riddell	Work and Pay: The Canadian Labour Market
S.F. Kaliski	Trends, Changes, and Imbalances: A Survey of the Canadian Labour Market
Frank Reid	Reductions in Work Time: An Assessment of Employment Sharing to Reduce Unemployment
Alice Nakamura and Masao Nakamura	A Survey of Research on the Work Behaviour of Canadian Women
Morley Gunderson	Discrimination, Equal Pay and Equal Opportunities in the Labour Market

VOLUME 18: ADAPTING TO CHANGE: LABOUR MARKET ADJUSTMENT IN CANADA

Craig Riddell	Adapting to Change: Labour Market Adjustment in Canada – An Overview
Steven Globerman	Formal Education and the Adaptability of Workers and Managers to Technological Change
Robert C. Allen	The Impact of Technical Change on Employment, Wages, and the Distribution of Skills: A Historical Perspective
Morley Gunderson	Alternative Mechanisms for Dealing with Permanent Layoffs, Dismissals and Plant Closings
James B. Davies	Training and Skill Development

John Sargent
Research Co-ordinator, Macroeconomics, Volumes 19-25

VOLUME 19: MACROECONOMIC PERFORMANCE AND POLICY ISSUES: AN OVERVIEW

John Sargent	Macroeconomics Retrospective

John Sargent	Prospects and Long-Term Policy Issues
John Sargent	Selected Macro-Institutional Issues

VOLUME 20: POST-WAR MACROECONOMIC DEVELOPMENTS

Ian Drummond	Economic History and Canadian Economic Performance Since the Second World War
Brian O'Reilly	Prices in the post-War Period
Brian O'Reilly, W.R. White and Robert Ford	Price Flexibility and Business Cycle Fluctuations in Canada: A Survey
Peter Howitt	Indexation and the Adjustment to Inflation in Canada
David Laidler	International Monetary Economics in Theory and Practice
Paul Boothe, Kevin Clinton, Agathe Côté and David Longworth	International Asset Substitutability
John Chant and Steve Easton	Developments in Canadian Financial Markets, 1962 to 1982

VOLUME 21: FISCAL AND MONETARY POLICY

Douglas D. Purvis and Constance Smith	Fiscal Policy in Canada: 1963–1984
Neil Bruce and Douglas D. Purvis	Consequences of Government Budget Deficits
Gordon R. Sparks	The Theory and Practice of Monetary Policy in Canada, 1945 to 1983
Yves Rabeau	Regional Stabilization in Canada
Jean-Marie Dufour and Daniel Racette	Monetary Control in Canada
Robin W. Boadway and W. Steven Clark	The Government Budget, the Accumulation of Capital, and Long-run Welfare
A. Asimakopulos	Keynesian Theories of Accumulation and their Policy Implications: A Critical Review

VOLUME 22: ECONOMIC GROWTH: PROSPECTS AND DETERMINANTS

Michael Denny	The Prospects for Productivity
John Helliwell, Mary E. MacGregor and Tim Padmore	Economic Growth and Productivity in Canada: 1955 to 1990
A.R. Dobell and B.R. Kennedy	Global Futures and Canadian Prospects: A Review of the Global Modelling Literature
Gregory V. Jump and Thomas A. Wilson	Savings in Canada: Retrospective and Prospective
Judith Gold Douglas S. Green and John Sargent	A Note on Demographic Projections for Canada – Review and Implications

VOLUME 23: LONG-TERM ECONOMIC PROSPECTS FOR CANADA: A SYMPOSIUM

John Sargent	Long-term Economic Prospects for Canada: A Symposium

VOLUME 24: FOREIGN MACROECONOMIC EXPERIENCE

John Sargent	Foreign Macroeconomic Experience: A Symposium

VOLUME 25: DEALING WITH INFLATION AND UNEMPLOYMENT IN CANADA

Craig Riddell	Dealing with Inflation and Unemployment in Canada: Options and their Consequences
Craig Riddell	Incentive-Based Income Policies: Survey and Assessment
Craig Riddell	Wage Inflation in Canada

David Laidler
Research Co-ordinator, Economic Ideas and Social Issues, Volumes 26, 27

VOLUME 26: APPROACHES TO ECONOMIC WELL-BEING

David Laidler	Economic Ideas and Social Issues: An Overview
Lars Osberg	The Measurement of Economic Well-Being
A.G. Blomqvist	Political Economy of the Canadian Welfare State
Robin W. Boadway and Neil Bruce	Theoretical Issues in Tax Reform
France St-Hilaire and John Whalley	Reforming Taxes: Some Problems of Implementation
William Schworm	Public Policies for Controlling Environmental Use

VOLUME 27: RESPONSES TO ECONOMIC CHANGE

C. Knick Harley	Resources and Economic Development in Historical Perspective
David W. Conklin	Entrepreneurship, Innovation and Economic Change
Charles K. Rowley	Rules versus Discretion in Constitutional Design
Dan Usher	The Growth of the Public Sector in Canada
Claude Montmarquette	Economic Rationality and Political Behaviour in Canada
John McCallum and André Blais	Government, Special Interest Groups and Economic Growth
Robert Bish	Improving Productivity in the Government Sector: The Role of Contracting Out

Politics and Institutions of Government

Denis Stairs and Gilbert R. Winham
Research Co-ordinators, Canada and the International Political/Economic Environment, Volumes 28-30

VOLUME 28: CANADA AND THE INTERNATIONAL POLITICAL/ECONOMIC ENVIRONMENT

Denis Stairs and Gilbert R. Winham	Canada and the International Political/ Economic Environment: An Introduction
Jock A. Finlayson	Canadian International Economic Policy: Context, Issues and a Review of Some Recent Literature
Michael C. Webb and Mark W. Zacher	Canadian Export Trade in a Changing International Environment

VOLUME 29: THE POLITICS OF CANADA'S ECONOMIC RELATIONSHIP WITH THE UNITED STATES

Denis Stairs and Gilbert R. Winham	The Politics of Canada's Economic Relationship with the United States: An Introduction
J.L. Granatstein	The Issue That Will Not Go Away: Free Trade Between Canada and the United States
Kim R. Nossal	Economic Nationalism and Continental Integration: Assumptions, Arguments and Advocacies
Charles Pentland	North American Integration and the Canadian Political System
Jock A. Finlayson	Canada, Congress and U.S. Foreign Economic Policy
Gary C. Hufbauer and Andrew J. Samet	U.S. Response to Canadian Initiatives for Sectoral Trade Liberalization, 1983 to 1984

VOLUME 30: SELECTED PROBLEMS IN FORMULATING FOREIGN ECONOMIC POLICY

Denis Stairs and Gilbert R. Winham	Selected Problems in Formulating Foreign Economic Policy: An Introduction
Gerald Wright	Bureaucratic Politics and Canada's Foreign Economic Policy

Robert Boardman	The Foreign Service and the Organization of the Foreign Policy Community: Views from Canada and Abroad
F.J. Chambers	The Emerging Cost Structure of Canadian Firms: Some Implications for International Economic Policy
R.B. Byers	Canadian Defence and Defence Procurement: Implications for Economic Policy

Keith Banting
Research Co-ordinator, State and Society in the Modern Era, Volumes 31, 32

VOLUME 31: STATE AND SOCIETY: CANADA IN COMPARATIVE PERSPECTIVE

Keith Banting	Images of the Modern State: An Introduction
David R. Cameron	The Growth of Government Spending: The Canadian Experience in Comparative Perspective
Alan Cairns	The Embedded State: State-Society Relations in Canada
Anthony H. Birch	Political Authority and Crisis in Comparative Perspective

VOLUME 32: THE STATE AND ECONOMIC INTERESTS

Keith Banting	The State and Economic Interests: An Overview
Leo Panitch	The Tripartite Experience
Ken McRae	Linguistic Diversity and Economic Decision-Making: Three European Case Studies
William D. Coleman	Canadian Business and the State
Pierre Fournier	Consultation in Canada: Case Studies and Perspectives
Andrew Martin	The Politics of Employment and Welfare: National Policies and International Interdependence

Alan Cairns and Cynthia Williams
Research Co-ordinators, Constitutionalism, Citizenship and Society, Volumes 33-35

VOLUME 33: CONSTITUTIONALISM, CITIZENSHIP AND SOCIETY IN CANADA

Alan Cairns and Cynthia Williams	Constitutionalism, Citizenship and Society in Canada: An Overview
J.R. Mallory	Evolving Canadian Constitutionalism
Cynthia Williams	The Changing Nature of Citizen Rights
R. Rainer Knopff and F. L. Morton	Nation-Building and the Charter
Charles Taylor	Alternative Futures: Legitimacy, Identity and Alienation in Late 20th Century Canada

VOLUME 34: THE POLITICS OF GENDER, ETHNICITY AND LANGUAGE IN CANADA

Bernard Blishen	Continuity and Change in Canadian Values
Raymond Breton	Multiculturalism and Canadian Nation-Building
Eric Waddell	State, Language and Society: The Vicissitudes of French in Quebec and Canada
Sandra Burt	Women's Issues and the Women's Movement in Canada Since 1970
Roger Gibbins and J. Rick Ponting	An Assessment of the Probable Impact of Aboriginal Self-Government in Canada

VOLUME 35: PUBLIC OPINION AND PUBLIC POLICY IN CANADA

Richard Johnston	Public Opinion and Public Policy in Canada: Questions of Confidence

Peter Aucoin
Research Co-ordinator, Representative Institutions, Volumes 36-39

VOLUME 36: PARTY GOVERNMENT AND REGIONAL REPRESENTATION IN CANADA

David E. Smith	Party Government, Representation and National Integration in Canada
Paul G. Thomas	The Role of National Party Caucuses
Peter Aucoin	Regionalism, Party and National Government

VOLUME 37: REGIONAL RESPONSIVENESS AND THE NATIONAL ADMINISTRATIVE STATE

Kenneth Kernaghan	Representative and Responsive Bureaucracy: Implications for Canadian Regionalism
Peter Aucoin and Herman Bakvis	Regional Responsiveness and Government Organization: The Case of Regional Economic Development Policy in Canada

VOLUME 38: INSTITUTIONAL REFORMS FOR REPRESENTATIVE GOVERNMENT

John C. Courtney	The Size of Canada's Parliament: An Assessment of the Implications of a Larger House of Commons
Peter C. Dobell	Some Comments on Parliamentary Reform
William P. Irvine	A Review and Evaluation of Electoral System Reform Proposals
V. Lemieux	The Referendum and Canadian Democracy

VOLUME 39: INTRASTATE FEDERALISM IN CANADA

Donald V. Smiley and Ronald L. Watts	The Reform of Federal Institutions: Intrastate Federalism in Canada

G. Bruce Doern
Research Co-ordinator, The Politics of Economic Policy, Volumes 40-43

VOLUME 40: THE POLITICS OF ECONOMIC POLICY

G. Bruce Doern	The Politics of Economic Policy: An Overview
David A. Wolfe	The Politics of the Deficit
John N. McDougall	Natural Resources and National Politics: A Look at Three Canadian Resource Industries
James R. Rice	Politics of Income Security: Historical Developments and Limits to Future Change
Leon Muszynski	The Politics of Labour Market Policy

VOLUME 41: FEDERAL AND PROVINCIAL BUDGETING

Allan M. Maslove, Michael J. Prince and G. Bruce Doern	Federal and Provincial Budgeting: Goal-Setting, Coordination, Restraint and Reform

VOLUME 42: ECONOMIC REGULATION AND THE FEDERAL SYSTEM

Richard Schultz and Alan Alexandroff	Economic Regulation and the Federal System

VOLUME 43: BUREAUCRACY IN CANADA: CONTROL AND REFORM

Sharon L. Sutherland and G. Bruce Doern	Bureaucracy in Canada: Control and Reform

André Blais
Research Co-ordinator, Industrial Policy, Volumes 44, 45

VOLUME 44: INDUSTRIAL POLICY

André Blais	Industrial Policy in Advanced Capitalist Democracies: An Overview
André Blais	The Debate on Canadian Industrial Policy
David Marsh	The Politics of Private Investment

Marsha A. Chandler	The State and Industrial Decline: A Survey
Lynn K. Mytelka	The State and Foreign Capital in the Advanced Industrial Capitalist Countries
Conrad Winn	Ministerial Roles in Policy Making: Vote Seeker, Shaman, and Other Incarnations
Michael M. Atkinson	The Bureaucracy and Industrial Policy
Andrew B. Gollner	Industrial Policy and Business-Government Relations
Steven B. Wolinetz	The Role of Trade Unions in Industrial Policies, 1945–1984
Allan Tupper	Federalism and the Politics of Industrial Policy

VOLUME 45: THE POLITICAL SOCIOLOGY OF INDUSTRIAL POLICY

André Blais	The Political Sociology of Industrial Policy

Law and Constitutional Issues

Ivan Bernier and Andrée Lajoie
Research Co-ordinators, Law, Society and the Economy, Volumes 46-51

VOLUME 46: LAW, SOCIETY AND THE ECONOMY

Ivan Bernier and Andrée Lajoie	Law, Society and the Economy: An Overview
H.W. Arthurs	Law as an Instrument of State Invervention: A Framework for Enquiry
Guy Rocher	Canadian Law from a Sociological Perspective
Liora Salter	Law and Values

VOLUME 47: THE SUPREME COURT OF CANADA AS AN INSTRUMENT OF POLITICAL CHANGE

Andrée Lajoie, Pierrette Mulazzi and Michèle Gamache	Political Ideas in Quebec and the Evolution of Canadian Constitutional Law, 1945 to 1985
Patrick J. Monahan	The Supreme Court and the Economy
Guy Tremblay	The Supreme Court of Canada: Final Arbiter of Political Conflicts

VOLUME 48: REGULATIONS, CROWN CORPORATIONS AND ADMINISTRATIVE TRIBUNALS

Patrice Garant	Crown Corporations as Instruments of Economic Intervention: Legal Aspects
Roderick A. Macdonald	Understanding Regulation by Regulations
David J. Mullan	Administrative Tribunals: Their Evolution in Canada from 1945 to 1984

VOLUME 49: FAMILY LAW AND SOCIAL WELFARE LEGISLATION IN CANADA

Julien D. Payne	The Impact of Family Law in Canada on the Financial Consequences of Marriage Breakdown and Divorce
Mary Jane Mossman	Family Law and Social Welfare in Canada
Robert D. Bureau, Katherine Lippel and Lucie Lamarche	The Evolution and Trends of Social Welfare Legislation in Canada, 1940 to 1984

VOLUME 50: CONSUMER PROTECTION, ENVIRONMENTAL LAW AND CORPORATE POWER

Edward P. Belobaba	The Development of Consumer Protection Legislation in Canada: 1945 to 1984
D. Paul Emond	Environmental Law and Policy: A Retrospective Examination of the Canadian Experience
Stanley M. Beck	Corporate Power and Public Policy

VOLUME 51: LABOUR LAW AND URBAN LAW IN CANADA

Joseph M. Weiler	The Role of Law in Labour Relations
Fernand Morin	The Use of Legislation to Control Labour Relations: The Quebec Experience
Stanley M. Makuch	Urban Law and Policy Development in Canada: The Myth and the Reality

John J. Quinn
Research Co-ordinator, The International Legal Environment, Volumes 52-54

VOLUME 52: THE INTERNATIONAL LEGAL ENVIRONMENT

John J. Quinn	The International Legal Environment: An Overview
P. Soldatos	Continentalism in Canada-U.S. Relations: The Free-Trade Approach
Frank Stone and Carol Osmond	Institutional Arrangements for Managing Canada-U.S. Bilateral Economic and Trade Relations
John P. Palmer and Robert James Aiello	International Technology Exchange: An Economic Analysis of Legal Proposals

VOLUME 53: CANADIAN ECONOMIC DEVELOPMENT AND THE INTERNATIONAL TRADING SYSTEM

M.M. Hart	Canadian Economic Development and the International Trading System: Constraints and Opportunities

VOLUME 54: CANADA AND THE NEW INTERNATIONAL LAW OF THE SEA

Douglas M. Johnston	Canada and the New International Law of the Sea

Ronald C.C. Cuming
Research Co-ordinator, Harmonization of Law in Canada, Volumes 55, 56

VOLUME 55: PERSPECTIVES ON THE HARMONIZATION OF LAW IN CANADA

Ronald C.C. Cuming	Harmonization of Law in Canada: An Overview
William A.W. Neilson	Interjurisdictional Harmonization of Consumer Protection Laws and Administration in Canada
Terry J. Wuester	The Harmonization of School Legislation in Canada: Elementary and Secondary Levels

VOLUME 56: HARMONIZATION OF BUSINESS LAW IN CANADA

Jacob S. Ziegel	Harmonization of Provincial Laws, with Particular Reference to Commercial, Consumer and Corporate Law
Philip Anisman	The Regulation of the Securities Market and the Harmonization of Provincial Laws
Ronald C.C. Cuming	Harmonization of Personal Property Security Law
Marvin G. Baer	Harmonization of Canadian Insurance Law

Clare F. Beckton and A. Wayne MacKay
Research Co-ordinators, Institutional and Constitutional Arrangements, Volumes 57, 58

VOLUME 57: RECURRING ISSUES IN CANADIAN FEDERALISM

Clare F. Beckton and A. Wayne MacKay	Institutional and Constitutional Arrangements: An Overview
Stephen A. Scott	The Canadian Constitutional Amendment Process: Mechanisms, Directions and Prospects
Peter M. Leslie	Canada as a Bicommunal Polity
George J. Szablowski	Treaty-Making Power in the Context of Canadian Politics: An Exploratory and Innovative Approach

VOLUME 58: THE COURTS AND THE CHARTER

Henri Brun	The Canadian Charter of Rights and Freedoms as an Instrument of Social Development
A. Wayne MacKay and Richard W. Bauman	The Supreme Court of Canada: Reform Implications for an Emerging National Institution
Mary Eberts	The Equality Provisions of the Canadian Charter of Rights and Freedoms and Government Institutions
Gilles Pépin	The Problem of Section 96 of the Constitution Act, 1867.

Federalism and the Economic Union

Mark Krasnick (Law and Constitutional Issues); Kenneth Norrie (Economics); and Richard Simeon (Politics and Institutions of Government)
Research Co-ordinators, Federalism and the Economic Union, Volumes 59-72

VOLUME 59: FEDERALISM AND ECONOMIC UNION IN CANADA

Kenneth Norrie, Richard Simeon and Mark Krasnick	Federalism and the Economic Union in Canada

VOLUME 60: PERSPECTIVES ON THE CANADIAN ECONOMIC UNION

Wayne R. Thirsk	Interprovincial Trade and the Welfare Effects of Marketing Boards
Ivan Bernier and Nicolas Roy	The Concept of Economic Union in International and Constitutional Law
Nola Silzer and Mark Krasnick	The Free Flow of Goods in the Canadian Economic Union
Sanda Rodgers-Magnet and Joseph E. Magnet	Mobility Rights: Personal Mobility and the Canadian Economic Union

VOLUME 61: DIVISION OF POWERS AND PUBLIC POLICY

Gérard Bélanger	The Division of Powers in a Federal System: A Review of the Economic Literature, with Applications to Canada
John D. Whyte	Constitutional Aspects of Economic Development Policy
Garth Stevenson	The Division of Powers
Frederick J. Fletcher and Donald C. Wallace	Federal-Provincial Relations and the Making of Public Policy in Canada: A Review of Case Studies

VOLUME 62: CASE STUDIES IN THE DIVISION OF POWERS

H. Scott Fairley	Constitutional Aspects of External Trade Policy
Nigel D. Bankes, Constance D. Hunt and J. Owen Saunders	Energy and Natural Resources: The Canadian Constitutional Framework
Charles M. Dalfen and Lawrence J.E. Dunbar	Transportation, Communications: The Constitution and the "Canadian Economic Union"
Bruce H. Wildsmith	Fisheries, Harmonization and the Economic Union

VOLUME 63: INTERGOVERNMENTAL RELATIONS

J. Stefan Dupré	Reflections on the Workability of Executive Federalism
James A. Brander	Economic Policy Formation in a Federal State: A Game Theoretic Approach
Kenneth McRoberts	Unilateralism, Bilateralism and Multilateralism: Approaches to Canadian Federalism
K.J. Huffman, J.W. Langford and William A.W. Neilson	Public Enterprise and Federalism in Canada

Jacques L'Heureux	Municipalities and the Division of Powers
Harry M. Kitchen and Melville L. McMillan	Local Government and Canadian Federalism

VOLUME 64: DISPARITIES AND INTERREGIONAL ADJUSTMENT

Robert L. Mansell and Lawrence Copithorne	Canadian Regional Economic Disparities: A Survey
John Vanderkamp	The Efficiency of the Interregional Adjustment Process
N. Harvey Lithwick	Federal Government Regional Economic Development Policies: An Evaluative Survey
Mireille Ethier	Regional Grievances: The Quebec Case
Francis J. Anderson and Norman Bonsor	Regional Economic Alienation: Atlantic Canada and the West

VOLUME 65: FISCAL FEDERALISM

Robin W. Boadway	Federal-Provincial Transfers in Canada: A Critical Review of the Existing Arrangements
Peter A. Cumming	Equitable Fiscal Federalism: The Problems in Respect of Resources Revenue-Sharing
Claude Forget	The Harmonization of Social Policies
Anthony F. Sheppard	Taxation Policy and the Canadian Economic Union

VOLUME 66: MOBILITY OF CAPITAL IN THE CANADIAN ECONOMIC UNION

Nicolas Roy	The Free Movement of Capital in the Canadian Economic Union

VOLUME 67: ECONOMIC MANAGEMENT AND THE DIVISION OF POWERS

Thomas J. Courchene	Economic Management and the Division of Powers

VOLUME 68: REGIONAL ASPECTS OF CONFEDERATION

John Whalley	Regional Aspects of Confederation

VOLUME 69: INTEREST GROUPS IN THE CANADIAN FEDERAL SYSTEM

Hugh G. Thorburn	Interest Groups in the Canadian Federal System

VOLUME 70: CANADA AND QUEBEC, PAST AND FUTURE: AN ESSAY

Daniel Latouche	Canada and Quebec, Past and Future: An Essay

VOLUME 71: THE POLITICAL ECONOMY OF CANADIAN FEDERALISM: 1940 TO 1984

Richard Simeon	The Political Economy of Canadian Federalism: 1940 to 1984

The North

VOLUME 72: THE NORTH

Michael S. Whittington	Introduction: Northern Studies
Jack C. Stabler	Developing Planning North of 60: Requirements and Prospects
Michael S. Whittington	Political and Constitutional Development in the N.W.T. and Yukon: The Issues and the Interests
George Braden	Indicators of Southern Attitudes Toward the N.W.T., 1979 to 1983
Gordon Robertson	Northern Political Development Within Canadian Federalism
Peter Burnet	Environmental Perspectives in the 1980s
Donat Pharand	Sovereignty and the Canadian North
William G. Watson	A Southern Perspective on Northern Economic Development

Staff of the Commission

Senior Officers

Executive Director
J. Gerald Godsoe

Director of Policy
Alan B. Nymark

Secretary
Michel Rochon

Senior Advisers
David Ablett
Victor Clarke
Carl Goldenberg
Harry Stewart

Directors of Research
Ivan Bernier
Alan Cairns
David C. Smith

Co-Directors of Research
Kenneth Norrie
John Sargent

Director of Administration
Sheila-Marie Cook

Policy Co-ordinators

Jamie Benidickson*
Michael Hart**
David Husband
Anne Martin
Richard Van Loon

Research Co-ordinators and Executive Assistants

Peter Aucoin
Keith Banting
Clare Beckton
André Blais
Lilla Connidis
Ron Cuming
Bruce Doern
Karen Jackson
Mark Krasnick
David Laidler
Andrée Lajoie
A. Wayne MacKay
Don McFetridge
Kenneth Norrie
John Quinn
Craig Riddell
John Sargent
Jacques Shore
Richard Simeon
Denis Stairs
François Vaillancourt
John Whalley
Cynthia Williams
Gilbert Winham

Secretariat Officers

Jacques Bérard
Michelle d'Auray
Tom Eisenhauer
Robert Gale
Maurice Ginzer
Murray Hardie
Mary Hegan
Michel Lamontagne
Denise Ommanney
Line Robillard Heyniger
Judith Wolfe

Chief Editors for Final Report

Jo File
Christiane Kaisin

Communications

Robert Pattillo – Director
Angèle Garceau – Assistant Director

Director of Publishing

Ed Matheson

Chief of Information Services

Leslie Wake

Special Adviser

Michel Vastel

* Also served as Special Assistant to the Chairman
** A voluntary consultant

Alphabetical Listing of Staff

Ablett, David
Allain, Lise
Aucoin, Peter
Banting, Keith
Baron, Jane
Beauchamp, Jean-Marie
Beckton, Clare
Bednarek, Helen
Benidickson, Jamie
Bérard, Jacques
Bernier, Ivan
Black, David
Blais, André
Bonin, Paul
Boucher, Catherine
Bruneau, Theresa
Burrows, Diane
Cairns, Alan
Calverley, Collett
Cardinal, Ainslea
Cardinal, Lynne
Carpentier, Monique
Chagnon, Pierre
Charbonneau, Nicole
Charland, Pierre
Chase, Vicky
Clarke, Victor
Cleinge, Marguerite
Connell, Susan
Connidis, Lilla
Cook, Sheila-Marie
Cornwall, Kay
Cowtan, Barbara
Crow, Ruth
Cuming, Ron
D'Aoust, Louise
D'Auray, Michelle
David, Debra
D'Avignon, Denyse
Desranleau, Claude
Deluca, Tina
Dibgy, Caroline
Doern, Bruce
Doncheff, Gina
Ediger, Beth
Eisenhauer, Tom
Éthier, Mireille
File, Jo
Gale, Robert
Garceau, Angèle
Gervais, Jacqueline
Ginzer, Maurice
Glyde, Jan
Glynn, Douglas
Godsoe, J. Gerald
Gold, Judith
Goldenberg, Carl
Goneau, Sylvie
Goudge, Stephen
Grady, Patrick
Grandjean-Joyeux, Virginie
Green, Douglas
Guilbault, Françoise
Halliday, Patricia
Hamm, Cynthia
Hardie, Murray
Harris, David
Hart, Michael
Hawkins, Robert
Hegan, Mary
Herold, Richard
Higgins, Robert
Hill, Roderick
Hooper, Anne
Huffman, Kenneth
Husband, David
Innes, Katie
Jackson, Karen
James, Marian
Julian, Matthew
Justinich, David
Kaisin, Christiane
Krasnick, Mark
Kymlicka, William
Laframboise, Marc
Laidler, David
Lajoie, Andrée
Lalonde, Michel
Lamb, Brenda
Lamontagne, Michel
Lavalley, Raymond
Lavictoire, Denis
Laviolette, Suzanne
Leduc, Pierre
Leduc, Yves
Lee, Nancy
Leishman, Tim
Liebman, Dan
Lyle, Bob
MacDonald, Bruce
MacKay, Wayne
Manti, Orlando
Marchand, Hélène
Martin, Anne
Martin, Bernice
Martin, Joyce
Matheson, Ed
McCoomb, Ann
McCracken, Wendy
McCullagh, Trish
McFarlane, Kenneth
McFetridge, Don
McInnes, David
McLean, Sandra
McQueen, Rod
Menard, Yvon
Mercier, Sylvie
Merritt, Anne
Mitchell, Ilene
Montpetit, Yvon
Morgulis, Samuel
Morel, Anne
Nakay, Emmy
Norrie, Kenneth
Nymark, Alan
O'Heron, Herbert
Ommanney, Denise
Ossent, Verena
Ouimet, Pierre
Paquette-Gagné, Brenda
Paquette, Diane
Parry, John
Pattillo, Robert
Pawlowicz, Jean
Pirozynska, Julita
Poisson, Gisèle
Pootmans, Diana
Potvin, Dan
Potvin-Chartrand, Josée
Prichard, Robert
Quinn, John
Reid, Mado
Renaud, Marcel
Riddell, Craig
Robillard Heyniger, Line
Robinson, Ian
Rochon, Michel
Roy, Nicolas
St-Denis, Robert
Sarazin, Bernadette
Sargent, John
Saucier, Carole
Scala, Alex
Scott, Ann
Scott, Ursula
Sheldon, Marilyn
Shore, Jacques
Silzer, Nola
Simeon, Richard
Smith, David
Sojonky, Sheila
Stairs, Denis
Stebbing, Donna
Stewart, Harry
Storozuk, Laureen
Testa, Assunta
Thorne, Eunice
Toner, Glen

Urquhart, Ian
Vaillancourt, François
Vanier, Yves
Van Loon, Rick
Vastel, Michel
Wake, Leslie
Wall, Peggy Ann
Whalley, John
Williams, Cynthia
Wilson, Mark
Winham, Gilbert
Wolfe, Judith
Woollcombe, Ann

Summer Students
Abelson, Donald
Connell, Elaine
Daneau, Pierre
D'Avignon, Lyse
Groulx, Julie
Lawrence, Rosalyn
McPhadden, Bryan
Roach, Kent
Sinclair, Ian

NOTE: Staff listed were employed for varying periods of time.

ACRONYMS

AAC	Annual Allowable Cut
ACIR	Advisory Commission on Intergovernmental Relations (U.S.)
ADA	Area Development Agency
ADB	Atlantic Development Board
AIB	Anti-Inflation Board
AIP	Anti-Inflation Program
AOTA	Adult Occupational Training Act
APEC	Atlantic Provinces Economic Council
ARDA	Atlantic Regional Development Agency
ASEAN	Association of South East Asian Nations
BEDM	Board of Economic Development Ministers
BILD	Board of Industrial Leadership and Development (Ontario)
BIS	Bank for International Settlements
BTSD	Basic Training for Skill Development
CAP	Common Agricultural Policy (European Community)
CAP	Canada Assistance Plan
CARICOM	Caribbean Common Market
CASE	Counselling Assistance to Small Enterprise
CBC	Canadian Broadcasting Corporation
CCC	Canadian Commercial Corporation
CCF	Co-operative Commonwealth Federation
CCSD	Canada Council on Social Development
CDC	Canada Development Corporation
CEGEP	Collège d'enseignement général et professionnel
CEIC	Canada Employment and Immigration Commission
CEO	chief executive officer
CERI	Canadian Energy Research Institute
CIDA	Canadian International Development Agency

CIO	Congress of Industrial Organizations
CLC	Canadian Labour Congress
CLMPC	Canadian Labour Market and Productivity Centre
CMA	Canadian Manufacturers' Association
CMEC	Council of Ministers of Education of Canada
CMITP	Canada Manpower Industrial Training Program
CMTP	Canada Manpower Training Program
CNTU	Confederation of National Trade Unions
COFACE	Compagnie Française d'Assurance pour le Commerce Extérieur
COLA	cost-of-living adjustment
COMECON	Council of Mutual Economic Assistance
COPE	Committee for Original Peoples' Entitlement
COPS	Canadian Occupational Projection System
CPI	Consumer Price Index
CPP	Canada Pension Plan
CRTC	Canadian Radio-Television and Telecommunications Commission
CSLP	Canada Student Loans Program
CTST	Critical Trades Skill Training
CUPE	Canadian Union of Public Employees
CUPW	Canadian Union of Postal Workers
DAs	Development Areas
DISC	Domestic International Sales Corporation (U.S.)
DREE	Department of Regional Economic Expansion
DRI	Data Resources Incorporated
DRIE	Department of Regional Industrial Expansion
DSS	Department of Supply and Services
EARP	Environmental Assessment and Review Process
EC	European Community
ECC	Economic Council of Canada
ECSC	European Coal and Steel Community
EDC	Export Development Corporation
EEC	European Economic Community
EEO	Equal Employment Opportunity
EFTA	European Free Trade Association
EMS	European Monetary System
EPA	Environmental Protection Agency (U.S.)
EPF	Established Programs Financing
EPU	European Payments Union
ERDA	Economic and Regional Development Agreement
ESOP	Employee Stock Ownership Plan
EURATOM	European Atomic Energy Community
FAO	Food and Agriculture Organization (U.N.)
FCC	Farm Credit Corporation
FEARO	Federal Environmental Assessment and Review Office
FEDC	Federal Economic Development Co-ordinator
FIRA	Foreign Investment Review Agency

FIRB	Foreign Investment Review Board
FISP	Family Income Security Plan
FMC	First Ministers' Conference
FPP	Farm Purchase Program
FPRO	Federal Provincial Relations Office
FRED	Fund for Rural Economic Development
FSCs	Foreign Sales Corporations
GAI	guaranteed annual income
GATT	General Agreement on Tariffs and Trade
GDA	General Development Agreement
GERD	Gross Expenditures on Research and Development
GDP	gross domestic product
GERD/GNP	gross expenditure on research & development in proportion to gross national product
GIS	Guaranteed Income Supplement
GNE	gross national expenditure
GNP	gross national product
GPP	gross provincial product
GSP	Generalized System of Preferences
IAEA	International Atomic Energy Agency
IBRD	International Bank for Reconstruction and Development (World Bank)
ICAO	International Civil Aviation Organization
IDA	International Development Assistance
IEA	International Energy Agency
IFC	International Finance Corporation
IIASA	International Institute for Applied Systems Analysis
ILO	International Labour Organisation
IMCO	Inter-Governmental Maritime Consultative Organization
IMF	International Monetary Fund
IPHC	International Pacific Halibut Commission
IPSFC	International Pacific Salmon Fisheries Commission
IRAP	Industrial Research Assistance Program
IRDP	Industrial and Regional Development Program
ITC	Department of Industry, Trade and Commerce
ITO	International Trade Organization
ITU	International Telecommunications Union
JCPC	Judicial Committee of the Privy Council
JPC	Japan Productivity Centre
LDCs	less-developed countries
MFA	Multi-fibre Agreement
MFN	most-favoured nation
M1	a limited definition of the money supply
MITI	Ministry of International Trade and Industry (Japan)
MNE	multi-national enterprise
MRC	Medical Research Council
MSED	Ministry of State for Economic Development
MSERD	Ministry of State for Economic and Regional Development

MSSD	Ministry of State for Social Development
MW	megawatts
NAIRU	non-accelerating inflation rate of unemployment
NASA	National Aeronautics and Space Agency (U.S.)
NATO	North Atlantic Treaty Organization
NCCU	National Council of Canadian Universities
NEB	National Energy Board
NEP	National Energy Program
NGGLT	Natural Gas and Gas Liquids Tax
NIC	newly industrialized country
NIEO	New International Economic Order
NOP	National Oil Policy
NORAD	North American Aerospace Defense
NRC	National Research Council
NSERC	National Science and Engineering Research Council
NTA	National Training Act
NTBs	non-tariff barriers
NTP	National Training Program
OAS	Old Age Security
OCAP	Ontario Career Action Program
ODA	Official Development Assistance
OECD	Organisation for Economic Co-operation and Development
OEEC	Organization for European Economic Co-operation
OISE	Ontario Institute for Studies in Education
OPEC	Organization of Petroleum Exporting Countries
OPIC	Overseas Private Investment Corporation
OTIP	Ontario Training Incentive Program
PCC	Petroleum Compensation Charge
PCO	Privy Council Office
PGRT	Petroleum and Gas Revenue Tax
PIPs	Petroleum Incentive Payments
PMO	Prime Minister's Office
PR	proportional representation
PSE	post-secondary education
PSSRA	Public Service Staff Relations Act
QPP	Quebec Pension Plan
QWL	quality of working life
QWLC	Quality of Working Life Centre
RDIA	Regional Development Incentives Act
R&D	research and development
RELSP	Registered Educational Leave Savings Plan
RETSP	Registered Education and Training Savings Plan
RHOSP	Registered Home Ownership Savings Plan
RPP	Registered Pension Plan
RRSP	Registered Retirement Savings Plan
SBDC	Small Business Development Corporation
SDAs	Special Development Areas
SDRs	Special Drawing Rights (on International Monetary Fund)

SFFAP	Special Farm Financial Assistance Program
SRTC	Scientific Research Tax Credit
SSHRC	Social Sciences and Humanities Research Council
STAA	Surface Transportation Assistance Act
TAAP	Transitional Adjustment Assistance Plan
TDIP	Trade Disruption Insurance Program
TIP	tax-based incomes policy
UI	Unemployment Insurance
UISP	Universal Income Security Program
UNAEC	United Nations Atomic Energy Commission
UNCLOS	United Nations Convention on the Law of the Sea
UNCTAD	United Nations Conference on Trade and Development
UNDP	United Nations Development Program
UNEP	United Nations Environment Program
UNIDO	United Nations Industrial Development Organisation
UPU	Universal Postal Union
UTDC	Urban Transportation Development Corporation (Ontario)
WCB	Workers' Compensation Board
WFP	World Food Program
World Bank	The International Bank for Reconstruction and Development
WPM	world product mandate
WIPO	World Intellectual Property Organisation